Jimmy Swaggart Bible Commentary

II Corinthians

JIMMY SWAGGART BIBLE COMMENTARY

- Genesis [656 pages 11-201]
- Exodus [656 pages 11-202]
- Leviticus [448 pages 11-203]
- Numbers
  Deuteronomy [512 pages 11-204]
- Joshua
  Judges
  Ruth [336 pages 11-205]
- I Samuel
  II Samuel [528 pages 11-206]
- I Kings
  II Kings [560 pages 11-207]
- I Chronicles
  II Chronicles [528 pages 11-226]
- Ezra
  Nehemiah
  Esther [288 pages 11-208]
- Job [320 pages 11-225]
- Psalms [688 pages 11-216]
- Proverbs [320 pages 11-227]
- Ecclesiastes
  Song Of Solomon [288 pages 11-228]
- Isaiah [688 pages 11-220]
- Jeremiah
  Lamentations [688 pages 11-070]
- Ezekiel [528 pages 11-223]
- Daniel [416 pages 11-224]
- Hosea
  Joel
  Amos [496 Pages 11-229]
- Obadiah
  Jonah
  Micah
  Nahum
  Habakkuk
  Zephaniah [544 pages 11-230]
- Haggai
  Zechariah
  Malachi [448 pages 11-231]
- Matthew [888 pages 11-073]
- Mark [624 pages 11-074]
- Luke [736 pages 11-075]
- John [736 pages 11-076]
- Acts [832 pages 11-077]
- Romans [704 pages 11-078]
- I Corinthians [656 pages 11-079]
- II Corinthians [608 pages 11-080]
- Galatians [496 pages 11-081]
- Ephesians [576 pages 11-082]
- Philippians [496 pages 11-083]
- Colossians [384 pages 11-084]
- I Thessalonians
  II Thessalonians [512 pages 11-085]
- I Timothy
  II Timothy
  Titus
  Philemon [704 pages 11-086]
- Hebrews [848 pages 11-087]
- James
  I Peter
  II Peter [736 pages 11-088]
- I John
  II John
  III John
  Jude [384 pages 11-089]
- Revelation [592 pages 11-090]

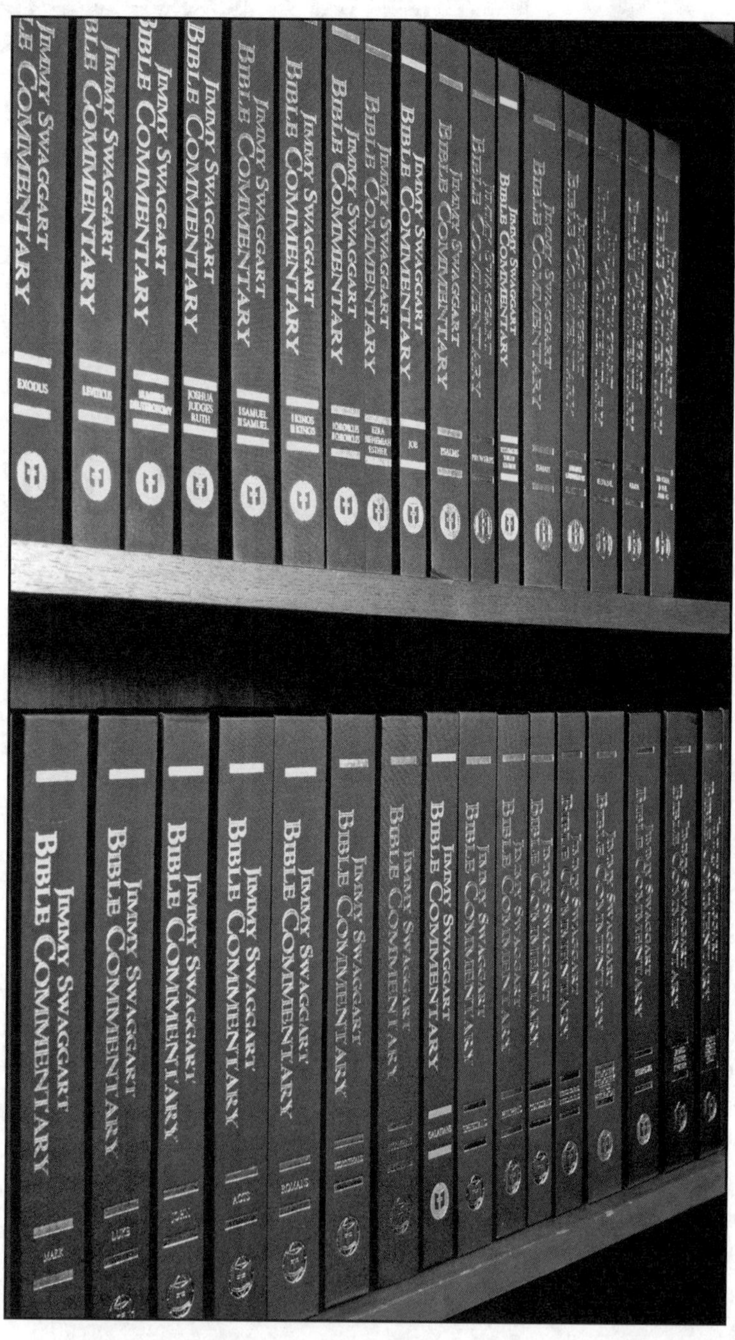

For prices and information please call: 1-800-288-8350
Baton Rouge residents please call: (225) 768-7000
Website: www.jsm.org • E-mail: info@jsm.org

Jimmy Swaggart Bible Commentary

II Corinthians

World Evangelism Press

ISBN 978-1-934655-11-5

www.jsm.org • email: info@jsm.org

20 21 22 23 24 25 26 27 28 29 / Sheridan / 13 12 11 10 9 8 7 6 5 4

TABLE OF CONTENTS

INTRODUCTION

THREE DIVISIONS

As will be obvious I think, II Corinthians is presented in three sections regarding subject matter; the first being Chapters 1-7, the second, Chapters 8 and 9, with the third incorporating Chapters 10-13.

Titus, it seems, had been sent to Corinth with the First Epistle to the Corinthians and directed to return to Troas where Paul planned to meet him. His nonarrival at Troas made the Apostle so anxious about the condition of the Corinthians that he crossed over to Macedonia where he met Titus, who gladdened him with the news that his Letter had produced the happiest results.

The Apostle then wrote this Second Epistle, which like the first, deals with a departure from the moral teaching that was given in the Epistle to the Romans.

To those who were faithful to the Truth, he addressed words of the deepest affection; and to those who were unfaithful, words of restrained severity. Both these features appear in this Epistle.

The simplicity, the grandeur, the affection, the severity, the humility, the intelligence, and the authority of the Epistle, form a literature that is supernatural, and which has never been, and can never be, equalled by the ablest writers (Williams).

THE PERSONALITY OF PAUL

It is inconceivable that anyone would oppose Paul, but yet some did, and sadder still, even some who had been brought to Christ as a result of this man's Ministry, which entailed at times great hardship. Consequently, the Apostle in II Corinthians defends his character and Apostleship in a powerful manner. And yet, he does it, or at least the Holy Spirit through him, in a manner that is totally different from arguments and apologies made by most others. Of course, it is different because he was inspired by the Holy Spirit.

Having addressed that briefly, Paul I think, more so than any other writer in the New Testament exposes his own feelings. We learn more as to what type of man he was from that which he wrote, especially in II Corinthians, than we do from any other of his Epistles. As a result of that, this Letter carries a very human touch as well as the supernatural — and yet, the Holy Spirit Authored it all, with Paul merely being the instrument.

THE PURPOSE OF THIS EPISTLE

The object of this Epistle, therefore, and subjects discussed, are various. They are to show Paul's deep interest in the spiritual welfare of the Corinthians, and all others, even down to this moment for that matter. He expresses his gratitude that his former letter had been so well received, and had so effectually accomplished what he wished to accomplish.

Every intent is to carry forward the work of reformation among them which had been so wondrously commenced. Consequently, the Epistle is substantially of the same character as the first. It was written to a Church where great dissensions and other evils prevailed; it was designed to promote a reformation, and is a model of the manner in which evils are to be corrected in all Churches.

In connection with the First Epistle, it shows the manner in which offenders in the Church are to be dealt with, and the spirit and design with which the work of discipline should be entered on and pursued.

Though these were local evils, yet great principles are involved of use to the Church in all ages: and to these Epistles the Church must refer at all times, as an illustration of the proper manner of administering discipline, of carrying on the Work of God, and of silencing the attacks of enemies.

TIME AND PLACE

It is believed that II Corinthians was written from Macedonia, probably Philippi after the events of Acts 19:23; 20:3. It was probably written in A.D. 59 or 60, about a year after the writing of I Corinthians.

It is said that Romans contains the philosophy of Christianity, while I Corinthians contains the problems of Christian Churches, but II Corinthians deals with the practice of personal Christianity. As someone has also said, it is biographical rather than theological. It is largely the record of Paul's personal Christianity. In this sense, Paul stands as an example for Christians of all ages. If we could forget that he was an Apostle and think of him only as a Disciple, his experience would stand out as a cross-section — and a composite — of all Christian experience.

As we will see, this Epistle is in no sense systematized and given in an orderly manner as was Romans, or even I Corinthians. It was not conceived in the study but forged on the anvil of trial and suffering. It will, therefore, as stated, be found to be a record of actual life experiences rather than philosophical ideals. Here will be found a philosophy of life not so much in expressions as in experiences. The great Truths that appear here are presented quite incidentally as a part of one man's life. Here is a Christian realism that is brutally frank and meticulously honest. It is fearless to face any life situation. It is unafraid, unabashed, and unashamed.

THE GREAT TEST

Scarcely any Doctrine of the Christian Faith escapes the grueling test of life's problems, nor is it meant to escape such. Practical Christianity is designed by the Holy Spirit to meet these problems head-on. Here, indeed, is life in the crucible of human experience.

Consequently, I think that the predominate word of this Book is *"tribulation,"* incidentally a word that is not too well accepted in modern Gospel circles. It traffics in the facts that have to do with the serious business of living. It can be truly said to set forth life at its worst in the world, in order to show forth life at its best in the Christian.

To receive its contents, we should read it and receive it as if it had been written both to us and for us, as in a sense it was.

LIFE

Here we shall find that life endures. It is not endurance as dogged patience, nor is it merely the will to endure. Instead, it is a way to endure. Life endures because it has within itself the enduring life. This enduring life is the life that begins in Faith and the New Birth and matures under the Blessings of Grace, and yes, of adversity as well! It is that phase of life which fearlessly and frankly faces current personal problems, which is what makes this Book so vitally interesting.

THE CHRISTIAN

The Christian must be prepared for the emergencies and difficulties of life, just as any other individual. To deny that, is to deny the Gospel. As well, we are not miraculously protected from common troubles. Even in our most cherished position as a Child of God, life has its problems. As someone has said, even the privilege of prayer must be considered in this light for *"when we pray for rain we must be willing to put up with some mud."* We must be ready to suffer inconveniences in our own plans in order to reach the highest places in life.

Difficulties are not all pure liability. They are often necessary and beneficial even as the winnowing process is beneficial to grain and the smelting process is to precious metal. *"There are defects in many characters which apparently can be removed only by some terrible experience."* It is unfortunate that this is necessary, but it would be more unfortunate if it were not accomplished.

THE MAN, PAUL

Paul's authority as an Apostle can be best confirmed, I think, by the genuineness of his life. This is what is set forth in this Epistle which is without doubt, as stated, the most biographical of all his writings.

That the Holy Spirit allowed the Apostle to present himself in this manner, for that I will ever be grateful. Even as I dictate the notes to this Introduction to this Great Epistle, I sense the Presence of God. Perhaps, it is because I see in Paul, his hurts, disappointments, frustrations, and yet great victories, a little bit of Jimmy Swaggart, and hopefully you will see yourself as well.

To say that I am grateful that the Holy Spirit allowed this man to present himself in this manner would be an understatement. To know that one so great, used so mightily of God, actually the Master Builder under Christ of the Church, yet faced the same fears and disappointments that I face, is a great encouragement to me. I know that it will be to you as well.

And yet, this is what makes Christianity, this Christ-centered experience, so vitally different than anything else in the world. First of all, Bible Christianity had its origin in Heaven, and is centered in Christ, but yet is so very practical, and that's what makes it great.

APPRECIATION

Once again I want to thank a host of people for their help respecting our efforts to put on paper that which we feel within our heart concerning commentary on this Great Epistle. To name them all would be impossible, and yet to attempt to do so would of necessity omit some that definitely should be included, and because of human frailty on my part.

To the Scholars of which I am not, and who have gone before me, no doubt spending untold hours, even lifetimes, providing material which has made my efforts somewhat easier, I am indebted to their labor, their consecration, their love for the Word of God, as well as their Scholarship. I have gleaned heavily from untold sources, for the most part names which once shown brightly, but whose voices are now silent, with their souls and spirits now with the Christ they wrote about with such devotion. I am indebted to them.

As usual, Frances and Donnie handle untold duties regarding Family Worship Center, as well as this particular Ministry of World Evangelism, in order that I may devote much time to this effort. For me to properly express my enjoyment at attempting to open up the Word of God in this manner regarding these Commentaries, of that words fail me. Time and time again, the Spirit of God will move upon my feeble efforts, sometimes to the extent that I cannot continue to dictate, as for a few moments I sense the Grace and the Glory of that which the Holy Spirit is giving. If somehow the Lord has helped me to transfer this to the pages on which you now look, then perhaps it will be the blessing to you that we intend. If it is, all the glory belongs to the Lord, as should be obvious.

It is June 12, 1998, as I begin Commentary on the Second Epistle of Paul the Apostle to the Corinthians. I will end this Introduction and in a sense begin the Commentary with a short poem I learned many years ago. I have quoted it elsewhere in another Volume, but I think it would be again, appropriate here.

"I can see far down the mountain, where I have wandered many years.
"Often hindered on my journey, by the ghosts of doubts and fears.
"Broken vows and disappointments, thickly strewn along the way,
"But the Spirit has led unerring, to the land I hold today."

Jimmy Swaggart

THE BOOK OF II CORINTHIANS

NOTES

(1) "PAUL, AN APOSTLE OF JESUS CHRIST BY THE WILL OF GOD, AND TIMOTHY OUR BROTHER, UNTO THE CHURCH OF GOD WHICH IS AT CORINTH, WITH ALL THE SAINTS WHICH ARE IN ALL ACHAIA:"

The phrase, *"Paul, an Apostle of Jesus Christ by the Will of God,"* immediately legitimizes that which is to be said. Paul's relation to the Churches addressed is far more than mere personal concern as will appear throughout the Letter. It is Apostolic. His high and holy office is involved directly and completely in all that is contained in this Letter.

THE ROLE OF THE APOSTLE

As Prophets were given the spiritual leadership under Jehovah in Old Testament times, Apostles assume that role under Christ under the New Covenant. Paul also wrote, *"And are built upon the foundation of the Apostles and Prophets, Jesus Christ Himself being the Chief Corner stone"* (Eph. 2:20).

"Apostle" in the Greek is *"Apostolos,"* and means *"he that is sent,"* in effect, sent with a special message. It has nothing to do with one being a Missionary, as many think. It pertains to the *"Message"* and not geography.

Unfortunately, religious man has never been satisfied to carry out the Work of God in the manner allotted or directed by the Holy Spirit, but rather desires to chart his own course. Consequently, it has been Satan's business from the very beginning to force the Church into a position of ignoring the Message of the Apostle, whatever that Message might be, and rather be led by man-appointed potentates, etc. That is what ultimately destroyed the Early Church, ultimately bringing on the Catholic scourge, and continues to plague the Church no less at this present hour.

At this time, men elected by popular ballot to man-devised offices in religious Denominations, exert authority and control over most of the Church, which is not God's way and, in fact, has never been His way. When the voice of the Apostle appears, it is by most either ignored, ridiculed, or efforts made to destroy the messenger. Nevertheless, this in no way sets aside God's correct order, for He is still setting Apostles in the Church, thereby giving them the Message He wants the Church to have.

THE WILL OF GOD

An Apostle is *"one sent from"* a superior on a commission; he thus represents his superior, is his ambassador. This is *"the Will of God,"* and Apostles in actuality answer only to *"Jesus Christ."* Consequently, the Corinthians should know that Christ's own representative is writing to them.

The appellative *"Christ Jesus"* is more than *"belonging to Christ Jesus"*; it indicates origin and agency: *"Called and sent by Him."* It is *"through God's Will,"* not accidentally by a set of circumstances, or temporarily, or growing into this position. God's Will is His volitional act which placed Paul, and all other such Apostles from then until now into their respective office.

AUTHORITY

It is often thought that Paul places his authority upon the scales, and that *"Apostle"* intends to stress authority. However, this view is not borne out by this Epistle. At times, Preachers thus expect their mere authority to produce submission. *"Apostle of Christ Jesus"* is, first of all, written with regard to Paul himself and expresses his own consciousness of bearing a most heavy responsibility with regard to this Office. He writes as one who feels this weight. It is his first concern to discharge his own Apostolic obligation. He is accountable to Christ Jesus, and Christ Jesus Alone.

Moreover, this Epistle shows that his whole soul is in his Office. We see his deep emotions throughout the Epistle, this fervent reaching out to the Corinthians, etc. It is this that is truly Apostolic.

Place authority in this light and it will appear more truly how Paul expected it to affect the Corinthians, and all others for that matter. They were to respond, not by compulsion, but by a satisfied, even by an enthusiastic following, not to say submission.

Modern Denominations too often take the exact opposite tact. They speak, and expect others to humbly submit, even though what is demanded may in fact be unscriptural. Such automatically proclaims that such is not of God.

True spiritual authority deals in love, and expects response, not by compulsion as stated, but by desire. Such is the way of Christ. He never threatens, coerces, forces, or demands. It is only pseudoreligious authority which does such, not that given by the Lord Jesus, and which truly graces the Office of the Apostle.

The phrase, *"And Timothy our Brother,"* proclaims a high honor for this young man.

He is associated with Paul in the address of the Epistles to Philippians and Colossians, and with Paul and Silas in the two Epistles to the Thessalonians.

At times Paul did this in the writing of his Epistles, even as he added Sosthenes in his first Epistle to the Church at Corinth (I Cor. 1:1).

WHY DID AT TIMES PAUL DO THIS?

First of all, the Holy Spirit told him to do such, because it is inconceivable that he would have done such considering that he is writing the Word of God, without the Lord directing him. However, that the Lord informed him as to the reason, we are not told.

I personally think it was a matter of training for these particular individuals, but at the same time, the fact that Timothy is not called by an official name lets the Corinthians feel that not mere authority is dictating to them. His

NOTES

making this *"Brother"* in a sense the joint-writer of this Letter brings out the full appeal of brotherhood that is intended in the Work of God. The Apostolic and the Brotherly word blend into one.

As mentioned, in I Corinthians 1:1 we read, *"Sosthenes, the brother,"* exactly as here, such makes it a title of honor. Brethren will heed a brother. Consequently, and as stated as well, we see that it is not the weight of authority that Paul urges but one that is even heavier and harder to resist, that of community, brotherhood, and love. How so much this is needed in the modern Church, which far too often addresses itself from its leadership in a dictatorial fashion, which is the spirit of the world and never of Christ.

The phrase, *"Unto the Church of God which is at Corinth,"* presents in the midst of this deep and wide corruption, a flourishing little colony of heaven. *"Church"* means *"Assembly,"* and more particularly, *"called out ones."* They were called out of darkness unto light, from Satan to God, from the natural to the spiritual.

CHURCH

If it is to be noticed, Paul generalizes his use of *"Church"* to indicate, not an ecumenical Church, but the Spiritual and Heavenly significance of each and every local *"Body"* which has Christ as its *"Head,"* and by which God demonstrates His manifold wisdom through the creation of *"one new man"* out of all races and classes.

In God's purpose there is only one Church, one gathering of all under the Headship of Christ. But on earth it is a plurality, seen wherever two or three gather in His Name. There is no need to explain the relation between the one and the many. Like the Believer, the Church is both local and *"in heaven."* Paul likens the Local Church to a body whose members are mutually dependent (I Cor. 12:12), and to a building being erected, especially a Temple for God's Spirit (I Cor. 3:10).

GROWTH

Metaphors of growth are used, and also the image of a flock being fed (Acts 20:28; I Pet. 5:2). In fact, *"Church"* is not a synonym for *"people of God"*; it is rather an activity of the *"people of God."*

NOTES

THE FIRST CHURCH AT JERUSALEM

The Church in the Christian sense appeared first in Jerusalem after the Ascension of Jesus. At the beginning, it was made up of the predominantly Galilean band of Jesus' Disciples together with those who responded to the preaching of the Apostles in Jerusalem, which thousands did.

At first, it seems as if though its members saw themselves as the elect remnant of Israel destined to find Salvation in Zion (Joel 2:32; Acts 2:17) and as the restored Tabernacle of David which Jesus Himself had promised to build (Acts 15:16; Mat. 16:18). Jerusalem was thus the Divinely-appointed locale for those who awaited the final fulfillment of all God's Promises (Acts 3:21). Consequently, it did not see itself, at least at the beginning, as going into all the world to preach the Gospel, but rather that Jesus would come back at any time to restore Israel.

JEWISH CHARACTER

The essentially Jewish character of the Jerusalem Church should be noted. Its members accepted the obligations of the Law and the Worship of the Temple. In fact, this was the cause of many problems when Paul began to reach out to the Gentiles.

Their distinctive belief was that Jesus of Nazareth was Israel's Messiah, that God Himself had vindicated this by raising Him from the dead after He had suffered for Israel's Redemption, and that *"the great and manifest day"* of the Lord was even now upon them and would culminate in a final appearance of the Messiah in Judgment and Glory.

At the first, it was called *"the Sect of the Nazarenes"* by a professional Orator (Acts 24:5; 28:22), while its own adherents called their distinctive Faith, *"the Way."*

It was more or less tolerated by Judaism throughout the thirty-odd years of its life in Judaea, except when the Jewish authorities were disturbed by its acceptance of Gentile Churches abroad.

THE FIRST LEADERSHIP

The first leadership of the Church was by the twelve Apostles, especially Peter and John, but this soon gave way to that of Elders in the regular Jewish manner, with James the Brother of Jesus as the Senior Pastor with many others under him (Acts 15:6; Gal. 2:9). In fact, the leadership of James extended through most of the life of the Jerusalem Church, possibly from as early as the thirties (Acts 12:17; Gal. 1:19) until his execution in A.D. 62.

In fact, the *"Throne of David"* was a much more literal hope among believing Jews than we commonly realize, and James was also *"of the house and lineage of David,"* being probably the second born after Jesus.

(Joseph, the foster father of Jesus and the father of James as well as the other brothers, was in the direct lineage of David through Solomon. In other words, had the Davidic lineage continued, Joseph would have been King of Israel, and then Jesus. As well, Mary went back to David through another son, Nathan. So, their lineage to the kingly throne was impeccable, fulfilling, at least to this point, the Promise given to David by the Lord [II Sam. Chpt. 7].)

Eusebius reports that a cousin of Jesus, Simeon son of Clopas, succeeded James as Pastor of the Church in Jerusalem, and that Vespasian, after the capture of Jerusalem in A.D. 70, is said to have ordered a search to be made for all who were of the family of David, that there might be left among the Jews no one of the royal family.

THE CHURCH AND ITS DISPERSION

Of course as we now know, and Paul graphically knew, the ideas of the Church in Jerusalem were not according to the Word of God. In other words, they were still clinging to the thought and idea that the Lord would soon *"restore again the Kingdom to Israel"* (Acts 1:6-7). That's at least one of the reasons they were slow to embrace Gentiles. So, it was the task of the Holy Spirit to circumvent this thinking and push the Church beyond its Jerusalem borders.

This was done first of all by the Greek-speaking Jews of the Dispersion who came as pilgrims to Feasts, or for various reasons were staying in Jerusalem. Such Jews were often more wealthy than those of Jerusalem, and displayed piety by bringing *"alms to their nation"* (Acts 24:17). These Jews, as stated, were called *"Hellenists,"* which means they spoke the Greek language and otherwise adopted the Greek way of life.

At the outset, there were some problems in the Church in Jerusalem due to persecution, and a committee was needed to administer the relief for those in need, and it seems that the Seven appointed were, to judge by their names, Hellenists (Acts 6:5). It was apparently through this Hellenist element that the Gospel overflowed the narrow stream of Judaistic Christianity and created fresh streams in alien territories.

Stephen, one of the Seven, came into debate in a Hellenist Synagogue in Jerusalem (of which Saul of Tarsus was possibly a member) and was charged before the Sanhedrin with blaspheming the Temple and the Mosaic Law. His defense portrays great Scriptural knowledge on his part, in that he understood that the Law and Temple had all been fulfilled in Jesus, which means that he may have thought somewhat differently than some of the leadership of the Church in Jerusalem (Acts Chpt. 7).

In fact, the persecution which followed his death may have been directed against this sort of tendency among the Hellenist Believers rather than against the Law-abiding Apostles who remained in Jerusalem when others were *"scattered."* Consequently, the Gospel was *"scattered,"* i.e. taken to other places as well.

Next we have Philip, another of the Seven, taking the Gospel to Samaria, with Peter himself soon ministering to the Gentiles at Caesarea (Acts Chpts. 8, 10).

ANTIOCH

It was more than likely the Hellenists who went from Jerusalem to Antioch and there preached to the Gentiles without any stipulation about the Mosaic Law. In fact, after Stephen, the Hellenistic element in the Jerusalem Church seemed to disappear, as stated, possibly forced to leave, with its strictly Jewish character then prevailing. Some of its members seemed to disapprove of the Gospel being offered to Gentiles without obligation to keep the Law and even tried to press their point of view in the new Churches among the Gentiles (Acts 15:1; Gal. 2:12; 6:12). Actually, this was at least one of Paul's greatest problems.

Officially, it seems that the Jerusalem Church gave its approval not only to Philip's mission in Samaria and the Baptism of Cornelius at Caesarea but, as well, to the policy of the new Church at Antioch and its Missionaries. But yet there were some in Jerusalem, as stated, who seemed to desire to cling to the old Law.

NOTES

THE COUNCIL AT JERUSALEM

In A.D. 49, a Council of the Jerusalem Church was formally asked what should be demanded of *"those of the Gentiles who turn to God."* It was determined that, while Jewish Believers would continue to circumcise their children and keep the whole Law, these requirements should not be laid on Gentile Believers. But yet, the Church in Jerusalem, seemingly never did rid itself of the Mosaic Law. It continued to try to keep the Law, despite the fact that Jesus had already fulfilled the Law.

James was murdered at the instigation of the High Priest in A.D. 62. When the war with Rome broke out in A.D. 66, the Church came to an end. Its members took themselves, says Eusebius, to Pella in Transjordan. Wondrously enough, not a one of its members died in that holocaust by Titus when the city was totally destroyed in A.D. 70, and because they remembered the Words of Jesus and thereby left (Lk. 21:20-24).

Thereafter, they divided into two groups: the Nazarenes, who keeping the Law of Moses themselves, had a tolerant attitude toward their Gentile fellow-Believers, and the Ebionites, who inherited the Judaizing view of obligation to the Law. Later Christians listed the Ebionites among the heretics.

This should be a lesson to all modern Believers, that irrespective as to the grandness of its beginnings, if a Church leaves the True Gospel of Jesus Christ, it will ultimately be destroyed.

THE CHURCH AT ANTIOCH

In fact, Antioch, not Jerusalem, became the model of the *"new Church"* which was to appear all over the world. It was evidently founded by Hellenistic Jews. Here Believers were first called *"Christians"* by their Gentile neighbors (Acts 11:26). Antioch became the springboard for the expansion of the Gospel throughout that part of the world.

The key figure at first was Barnabas, himself perhaps a Hellenist but enjoying the full confidence it seems, of the Jerusalem leaders who sent him to investigate the move of God in Antioch.

In fact, it was Barnabas who brought Paul, the converted Pharisee, from Tarsus, and who went with Paul on his first Missionary journey.

There were important links between Antioch and Jerusalem. Prophets from Jerusalem came up and ministered (Acts 11:27), as did Peter himself and delegates from James (Gal. 2:11-12).

But the greatest fame of the Church at Antioch was that it *"commended"* Barnabas and Paul *"to the Grace of God for the work which they fulfilled"* (Acts 14:26).

PAUL AND THE CHURCH

While Paul and Barnabas were clearly not the only Missionaries of the first generation, still, we know next to nothing about the labors of others, including the Twelve Apostles themselves. It is Paul, as no other man, who was used by the Holy Spirit to found the Church. He even referred to himself as the *"Masterbuilder"* (I Cor. 3:10).

His method was to found Churches in great cities such as Ephesus, and then reach out to other cities in that particular province (Acts 19:10; Col. 1:7).

During those times, with the New Testament in the process of being written, the Old Testament in Greek was the Sacred Scripture of all these Churches, and the key to its interpretation was indicated by Jesus being its fulfillment.

Even though there were no denominational or organizational links between Paul's Churches, there definitely were natural affinities of fellowship between Churches in the same Province, and possibly all over (Col. 4:15-16; I Thess. 4:10). Even as we are now studying, all were led and guided by Paul in matters of the Faith — hence, the role of Paul's Epistles and the visits of Timothy — but the authority held by Paul, even as we have already stated, was spiritual and not coercive (II Cor. 10:8; 13:10). Local administration and discipline were autonomous (II Cor. 2:5-10). No Church had superiority over any other, each being a spiritual authority in a sense within itself.

OTHER CHURCHES

We do know there were other Churches other than those founded by Paul, but of those Churches knowledge is scanty.

For instance, there was a Church at Rome, which instigated Paul's great Epistle to the

NOTES

Romans, which was not founded by him. In fact, *"Brethren"* came to meet Paul and his party when they went to Rome, but our knowledge of the Church there is limited to what Paul said.

The address of I Peter shows that there was a group of Churches scattered along the Coast of the Black Sea and its hinterlands (Pontus, Galatia, Cappadocia, Asia, and Bithynia).

These are the parts which Paul was prevented from entering (Acts 16:6-7), at least at that time, which may, among other things, imply that they were the scene of another man's foundation, perhaps the work of Peter himself. But we learn nothing distinctive of these Churches from Peter's Epistles.

This exhausts our knowledge of the founding of particular Churches in New Testament times. A little more about the Asian Churches emerges from the statements given in Revelation Chapters 2 and 3. As well, it is thought that Churches must surely have been founded at least in Alexandria and in Mesopotamia, if not farther East, but of this there is no certain evidence.

LIFE AND ORGANIZATION

Of the life and organization of the Churches generally, we have only the information given by Paul. Yet what we know makes us confident that their unity lay in the Gospel itself, acceptance of the Old Testament Scriptures and acknowledgement of Jesus as *"Lord and Christ."*

In fact, no one New Testament Church, nor all the Churches together of that time, exercises any ceremonial authority over our Faith today. This Divine Authority belongs only to the Apostolic Gospel as contained in the whole of the Scriptures.

(Bibliography: F.J.A. Hort, *"The Christian Church"*; R. Newton Flew, *"Jesus and His Church"*; Lietzmann, *"The Beginnings of the Christian Church"*; F.F. Bruce, *"The Spreading Flame."*)

The phrase, *"With all the Saints which are in all Achaia,"* refers to all of Greece. Directly, Paul may have been referring to the District or Province of which Corinth was the Capital, but indirectly, he was referring definitely to the whole of that area, and actually to all Believers for all time.

SAINTS

"Saints" is in Acts 9:13 used already by Ananias of Damascus as a designation for

Christians, and this designation was current in the early days of the Church.

It means *"separated unto God by Faith in Christ."* It is the Sainthood of true Faith that indicates the cleansing of pardon through Christ's Blood, the beginning of a new life in Christ, the putting away of sin more and more.

This term never indicates total Sanctification in the sense of perfectionism so that these *"Saints"* never sin after becoming Saints (Phil. 3:12; I Jn. 1:8-10), which all Believers do at conversion.

In the first Eleven Verses of this Epistle, the Apostle's heart expresses the joy felt in the midst of fierce persecutions by the report that Titus brought him of the spiritual condition of his beloved children at Corinth — who themselves also were suffering persecution for the Name of Jesus.

And yet, regrettably, in the midst of those persecutions, they could applaud the teacher who advocated incest — a sin even guarded against among the heathen — and that brought such dishonor to the Name, which it seems was at least part of the cause of which they were suffering affliction! Such is man's natural heart!

Paul, hearing of their repentance, assured himself that they also would enjoy the same comfort from God that he himself did. So, Grace in the heart of the Apostle laid hold of what there was of good among the Corinthians in the expectation that evil would surely be judged — for Grace does not discredit because of the presence of evil.

Consequently, those who would throw out all the good because fault is found would have to throw out all good everywhere, which of course is facetious. Living for Jesus is a growth process. As such, the Lord uses Believers, and in fact, continues to use Believers in the midst of this growth process. If He didn't, there would not be anyone to use. So, those who would discredit all good because some fault is found are at the same time discrediting themselves.

(2) "GRACE BE TO YOU AND PEACE FROM GOD OUR FATHER, AND FROM THE LORD JESUS CHRIST."

The phrase, *"Grace be to you and peace from God our Father,"* presents *"Grace"* as the cause and *"Peace"* as the effect. Grace is what God gives, and Peace is what we receive. Peace will be in proportion to the Grace we appropriate.

NOTES

GRACE

It is hardly too much to say that the Mind of God has in no word uttered itself and all that was in His Heart more distinctly than in this word *"Grace."*

The word in the Greek is *"Charis."* Consequently, we will look first at the way the word was used in pagan Greece, Greece with its philosophy, its athletics, its poetry and drama, its wonderful architecture and statuary, its blue skies and rugged mountains, its love of the beautiful.

The word itself is a beautiful word, *"Charis."* It is pronounced *"ca-reese."*

The song writer wrote:

"Grace! 'Tis a charming sound,
Harmonious to the ear;
"Heav'n with the echo shall resound,
And all the earth shall hear.
"Saved by Grace alone! This is all
my plea:
"Jesus died for all mankind and Jesus
died for me."

But sadly, the Greeks of the pre-Christian Era knew nothing of the fact that Jesus had died for them, even though *"Grace"* was their word.

JOY TO THE HEARERS AND BEHOLDERS OF IT

First of all, Grace is *"that property in a thing which causes it to give joy to the hearers or beholders of it."*

After awhile it came to signify not necessarily the Grace or beauty of a thing, as a quality appertaining to it, but the gracious or beautiful thing, act, thought, speech, or person it might be.

In the Greek schools, the terminology came to imply ever a favor freely done, without claim or expectation of return. Thus Aristotle, defining Grace, lays the whole stress on this very point, that it is conferred freely, with no expectation of return, and finding its only motive in the bounty and free-heartedness of the giver. Consequently, the Greeks did not use it too very much, and because few people fell into this category.

CLASSICAL MEANING

This beautiful Greek word was taken over by the Holy Spirit, Who inspired the writers to use it in the New Testament. In a few instances, it has its distinctively classical meaning, but in the other places where it is used, it takes an infinite step forward to a deeper, richer, more wonderful content of meaning.

Luke uses it in its purely classical meaning when he says, *"And all bear Him witness, and wondered at the gracious words which proceeded out of His mouth"* (Lk. 4:22).

Here the word has its classical meaning of that property in our Lord's Words which caused them to give joy to the hearers. How wonderful it must have been to hear the Lord Jesus speak in human speech and human tones. Not only was the content of His Words gracious and beautiful, but the tones of His Voice must have reflected all the depth of His Personality, the intensity of His convictions (Jn. 2:17), the fervor of His desire to serve (Mat. 20:28), the pathos and tenderness of His sorrow (Mat. 23:37-39). It was the infinite God speaking with human lips and in human tones.

AN ACTION BEYOND

Both Luke (17:9) and Paul (Rom. 6:17; II Cor. 8:16) use *"Charis"* in its classical meaning of *"thankfulness."* Peter uses the word in its meaning of *"that which is beyond the ordinary course of what might be expected, and is therefor commendable,"* in his first Epistle (I Pet. 2:19-20), where the words *"thankworthy"* and *"acceptable"* are the translations of *"Charis"* which appears in the Greek text.

Surely, for a slave to manifest a spirit of patient submission toward a master who mistreats him, is an action beyond the ordinary course of what might be expected and is, therefore, commendable. The usual reaction on the part of a slave who has been mistreated is to rebel against his master. Consequently, this is a beautiful example of what one means by *"Grace."*

A FAVOR CONFERRED FREELY, WITH NO EXPECTATION OF RETURN

How this purely classical meaning of the word describes what took place at Calvary is that which we desire to observe and understand.

All the human race could expect in view of its sin was the Righteous wrath of a Holy God, which culminated in an eternal banishment from His Glorious Presence. But instead, that Holy God stepped down from His Judgment Seat and took upon Himself at Calvary's Cross the guilt and penalty of human sin, thus satisfying His Justice and making possible the bestowal of His Mercy. And this He did, not for those who were His friends, but His bitter enemies, unlovely creatures saturated with sin.

NOTES

Charis in classical Greek referred to a favor conferred freely, with no expectation of return, and finding its only motive in the bounty and free-heartedness of the giver. This favor was always done to a friend, however, never to an enemy.

Right here *"Charis"* leaps forward an infinite distance, for the Lord Jesus died for His enemies (Rom. 5:8-10), a thing unheard of in the human race. Consequently, this took *"Grace"* to its ultimate conclusion. Surely, this was beyond the ordinary course of what might be expected and is, therefore, commendable to say the least!

THE LOVE OF GOD

This is what John is speaking of in his First Epistle (I Jn. 3:1) when he says, *"Behold, what manner of love the Father has bestowed on us, that we should be called the Children of God."* Yes, what manner of love?

The words *"what manner of"* are from a Greek word which means *"what foreign kind of."* That is, the love shown by God at the Cross is foreign to the human race. Man simply does not act that way, and to be frank, man, at least within himself, is powerless to conduct himself that way (Rom. 5:7-8, 10).

That is why God's action at the Cross in dying for lost humanity is action beyond the ordinary course of what might be expected and is, therefore, commendable beyond words. Here is one of the strongest proofs of the Divine Source of the Bible. The substitutionary Atonement never came from the philosophies of man, because such was and is impossible, but from the Heart of God.

NO ROOM FOR GOOD WORKS IN ORDER TO MERIT SALVATION

This, the word *"Charis"* comes to its highest and most exalted content of meaning in the New Testament. It refers to God's offer of Salvation with all that it implies. That Salvation was procured at Calvary's Cross with all its personal sacrifice included and is now offered to one who is His bitter enemy and who not only is undeserving of that Salvation, but instead deserves punishment for his sins. Consequently, such that is offered without any expectation of return, but given out of the bounty and free-heartedness of the giver, proclaims Grace.

This means that there is no room for good works on the part of the sinner as a means whereby he could earn his Salvation, or after Salvation whereby he might retain that Salvation. And that is very important, a fact which Romans Chapter 6 proclaims. (Please see commentary on that great Chapter.)

Paul sets Grace over against works as things directly in opposition to one another so far as the means of Salvation is concerned (Rom. 4:4-5; 11:6). But Paul is very careful to make plain that good works naturally issue from and are required by Grace, but yet, and as stated, can never be the cause of Grace (Titus 2:11-12).

UNLIMITED

Furthermore, he shows that this Grace is unlimited in its resources. In Romans 5:20 he says, *"Where sin abounded, Grace did much more abound."* The word *"abound"* is from a different Greek word than that which is translated *"abounded."* It is a compound word which means *"to exist in superabundance."* The translation could read *"Grace existed in superabundance, and then more Grace added to this superabundance."*

Thus, Salvation is a Gift, to be received by the open hand of Faith, not something to be earned.

Dear Reader, if you have been attempting to find acceptance with God by your good works, if you have been depending in the least upon any personal merit, will you not now cast aside all this, and accept the free Grace of God by Faith in Jesus Christ as your Personal Saviour, the One Who died on the Cross for you, pouring out His Precious Blood as the God-appointed Sacrifice for sins?

"For God so loved the world that He gave His Son, the Only Begotten One, that whosoever believeth in Him might not perish but have everlasting life" (Jn. 3:16).

(I am indebted to Kenneth Wuest for the material on Grace.)

PEACE

The *"Peace"* here stipulated by the Apostle concerns Justifying Peace. By that, we mean the Peace that automatically comes to the believing sinner when he avails himself of the Grace of God, i.e. *"gives his heart to Christ."* The unbeliever has no Peace with God, and in fact, such is impossible for two reasons:

1. God is unalterably opposed to sin, and the unbeliever is loaded down with sin, in fact, *"dead in trespasses and sins"* (Eph. 2:1). Inasmuch as sin is the cause of all the problems in the universe, which proclaims the terrible condition of man as a depraved sinner after the Fall, God is at war with this condition even as His Righteousness demands. It is referred to as *"enmity"* (Eph. 2:15-16).

2. Most of the world refuses to accept the Great Atonement for sin carried out by Jesus Christ and at such great price; consequently, considering that price, and its refusal by most of humanity, *"God is angry with the wicked every day"* (Ps. 7:11). That is the reason He said, *"Kiss the Son, lest He be angry, and ye perish from the way, when His Wrath is kindled but a little. Blessed are all they that put their trust in Him"* (Ps. 2:12).

So, when the unbeliever comes to Christ, in effect, becoming a Believer, this enmity is removed because of Repentance and Faith, and then Peace is bestowed. As stated, it is *"Justifying Peace."*

THE CAUSE OF THE DEEP SEARCHING BY MANKIND

Because of being cut off from God, the unbeliever is unaware that his real problem, which he never seems to solve irrespective of what direction he takes, is this lack of Peace.

A lack of Peace spells guilt, which is at least one of the reasons that man attempts to perform good works in his effort to merit Salvation or to assuage this guilt feeling. Of course, it is impossible to be removed in that manner.

Man is a spiritual being, and as such is not whole until he once again comes into communion with his Creator, which can only be done through Jesus Christ. Consequently, outside of Jesus Christ, he searches for something to fill this void, but finds that he is never successful.

GOD OUR FATHER

"Father" in the Greek is *"Pater,"* and signifies a *"nourisher, protector, upholder."* One can call God *"Father"* only by accepting His Free

Grace, as extended through Jesus Christ, and the price He paid at Calvary. Consequently, this destroys the Fatherhood of God, and the brotherhood of man. While God is the Creator of all, He is not the Father of all, that coming about through the born-again experience. And then again the Believer is adopted into this Family, which makes Believers somewhat different in relation to God than Jesus.

Christ never associated Himself with others by using the personal pronoun *"our,"* as referring to His Father. He always used the singular, *"My Father,"* His relationship being unoriginated and essential, whereas ours is by Grace and Regeneration (Mat. 11:27; 25:34; Jn. 20:17; Rev. 2:27; 3:5, 21).

Whereas the Everlasting Power and Divinity of God are manifest in creation, His Fatherhood in Spiritual Relationship through Faith is the subject of New Testament Revelation, which of necessity waited for the presence on earth of the Son (Mat. 11:27; Jn. 17:25). Consequently, this Spiritual Relationship is not universal, but only for those who accept Christ Jesus as their own personal Saviour (Jn. 1:12; 8:42; Gal. 3:26).

The phrase, *"And from the Lord Jesus Christ,"* means that Grace and Peace come equally from God the Father and from the Lord Jesus Christ. The Two are made a unit Source of Grace and Peace and are placed on an equality. The Greek is so plain that no Scholar will deny these facts.

Both Names express the Revelation which these Persons have made of Themselves in connection with the Work of saving us. *"Our Father"*— we, His Children through Faith in Christ Jesus; *"the Lord Jesus Christ"* — He Who redeemed, purchased, and won us so that by Faith we are now His Own, live under Him in His Kingdom, and serve Him in everlasting Righteousness, Innocence, and Blessedness (Luther). Both terms express Deity, but Deity in the blessed and gracious sense, the sense in which Grace and Peace, too, are meant.

The greeting as given by Paul is brief, but the terms employed are in their combination so weighty that they constitute the basis of the entire Biblical and Christian theology (Lenski).

(3) "BLESSED BE GOD, EVEN THE FATHER OF OUR LORD JESUS CHRIST, THE FATHER OF MERCIES, AND THE GOD OF ALL COMFORT;"

NOTES

The phrase, *"Blessed be God,"* is the commencement proper of the Epistle; it is the language that is full of joy, and that bursts forth with gratitude in view of Mercy.

BLESSED BE GOD

If it is to be noticed, eleven out of the fourteen Epistles of Paul (if Paul wrote Hebrews) begin with exclamations of Praise, Joy, and Thanksgiving.

This entire Passage is one that is exceedingly valuable, as showing that there may be elevated joy in the midst of deep affliction, and as showing what is the reason why God visits His servants with trials. The phrase *"Blessed be God"* is equivalent to *"Praised be God,"* and is an expression of Thanksgiving. It is the usual formula of Praise and shows entire confidence in God.

It is one of innumerable instances which show that it is possible and proper to bless God in view of the trials with which He visits His people, and of the consolations which He causes to abound.

The phrase, *"Even the Father of our Lord Jesus Christ,"* presents Jesus as Deity, and God as His Own Unique Father in a way which cannot be said of anyone else, even as we have explained.

THE ETERNAL SONSHIP OF CHRIST?

Even though the orthodox view is that Jesus has always been the Son of God, after studying this for some years, it is my belief that whereas Jesus has always been God, is God presently and ever shall be God, He has not always been the Son of God. Sonship with Christ refers to humanity, not to Deity. As God, He had no beginning (Micah 5:2; Jn. 1:1-2); was not begotten or He would have had a beginning as God; and as a consequence was not always God's Son.

As man, He had a beginning, was begotten, and was God's Son (Ps. 2:7, 12; Mat. 1:18-25; Lk. 1:35; Heb. 1:5-6).

In these Passages it is clear that there was a certain day when God was to have a Son and the Son have a Father. It was to be in the future from the time that the Prophets spoke. If Sonship refers to Deity, then this Deity had a beginning on a certain day and He was not eternal, which we know is incorrect. But if it refers to humanity, then all Scriptures are clear and we have no man-made mystery of the so-called eternal Sonship of Jesus Christ.

If it refers to both Deity and humanity, then when did He become God, when was He begotten, how could He have been eternal?

If He had a beginning and was begotten then He was not, nor is He an Eternal God. If He was a Son of God by creation, then He is no greater than Angels and other beings who had beginnings.

Multiplied problems increase and become unanswerable with Scripture if we hold to the theory of Eternal Sonship, but all questions are clear when we accept the plain statements of Scripture that Sonship refers to humanity (the Incarnation) and not to Deity, even though Jesus never ceased to be God even while He was Man.

The phrase, *"The Father of Mercies,"* presents a Hebrew form of expression, which actually means *"Merciful Father."* God the Father is the Source of all Mercies, and, in fact, His Mercy endureth forever (Ps. 136).

MERCY

Mercy is an automatic derivative of Grace. In other words, once God chose Grace as the vehicle through which He would deal with humanity, and Grace by its very nature had to be a choice, Mercy was then inevitable. In other words, once Grace was freely chosen, God has no choice but to extend Mercy, that quality being a natural outflow of Grace.

It can be called *"The Father of the Compassions"* (or *"pities"*) which recalls Psalms 103:13: *"Like as a father pitieth his children, so the Lord pitieth them that fear Him."* It is the tender feeling of pity for those in distress.

The idea is, of God's Faithfulness to an individual, despite human unworthiness and even defection. It is portrayed readily in the Old Testament by the persistent refusal of God to wash His hands of wayward Israel, despite their rebellion.

Mercy is the gracious favor of the superior, in this case God, to the inferior, in this case human beings, all undeserved. It is because of His Mercy that we are saved (Eph. 2:4; Titus 3:5).

The phrase, *"And the God of all comfort,"* presents God as the Source.

COMFORT

"Comfort" in the Greek is *"paraklesis,"* and means *"to call near, to invite, to give solace and consolation."*

NOTES

"Come" means *"together with,"* and *"fort"* refers to strength. It carries the idea of *"braving together,"* in other words, we do not brave the storms of life alone.

Along with God the Father, God the Holy Spirit is another Comforter (Jn. 14:16, 26). The beautiful title for Him, *"Paraclete,"* comes from the same Greek word translated *"comfort."* John also used it of Jesus Himself, the One Who is our Heavenly Advocate (I Jn. 2:1). Consequently, that means that all Three Members of the Godhead, serves as the Source of all Comfort.

Here the two greatest human needs are met by the two greatest Divine Provisions. Man is born a sinner and a sorrower. He needs Mercy for his sins and comfort for his sorrow.

For man's sins God provides Mercy. We who deserve justice are rather shown Mercy. As David said: *"He hath not dealt with us after our sins; nor rewarded us according to our iniquities. For as the heaven is high above the earth, so great is His Mercy toward them that fear Him"* (Ps. 103:10-11).

(4) "WHO COMFORTETH US IN ALL OUR TRIBULATION, THAT WE MAY BE ABLE TO COMFORT THEM WHICH ARE IN ANY TROUBLE, BY THE COMFORT WHEREWITH WE OURSELVES ARE COMFORTED BY GOD."

The phrase, *"Who comforteth us in all our Tribulation,"* as should be obvious, does not deny the presence of Tribulation, but does guarantee comfort in the midst of Tribulation.

THE MANNER OF GOD'S COMFORT

God ministers Mercy for our sins through His Son. This is done historically by the Cross where *"He is the propitiation for our sins"* and experimentally, by Regeneration.

For man's sorrow God provides comfort. There is no exemption from sorrow, and there is no exception in God's comfort. He is the God of *"all comfort."*

Comfort is more than condolence and consolation. It is more than sympathy that soothes our torn and bleeding hearts. This help is of the nature of inner Peace. It is more than pious assistance. God, the One called alongside to help, bolsters the soul and strengthens the foundations. He rock-ribs the footings of life. He provides the Balm of Gilead. And in the midst at times of falling tears and a broken heart, we can say: *"I will magnify the Lord."*

The Comfort of God is not only a variety of Blessing, it is also by various means.

In one case it is the comfort of God's Word: *"Wherefore comfort one another with these words."* In another case it is the comfort of God's Love. Then it may be the comfort of Christ's Presence, for He said: *"I will never leave thee, nor forsake thee."*

Again it is the comfort of Christ's Resurrection. Together with all these it is also the comfort of Christ's Coming. These combine to be the Ministry of God's comfort for our sorrow.

A POINT OF CONTACT

The remedy for sin and sorrow is found in Christ's Redemption. Sin was met by Crucifixion. Sorrow was met by Resurrection. Both remedies remain as historical provisions until our faith lays hold of them in a personal acceptance and experience of Christ.

There must be a point of contact between our sin and sorrow and God's Mercy and Comfort. The meeting place is Faith and the New Birth. Mercy is not the consequence of our good intentions anymore than comfort is the consequence of our yearnings. We must establish a point of contact with God.

It must be Life on a new basis. When our Faith reaches out to embrace God's Son the place of contact is reached and the flow of Mercy and Comfort begins like the water that gushes from an artesian well.

TRIBULATION

"Tribulation" in the Greek is *"thlipsis,"* and means *"burdened, anguish, affliction, persecution, trouble."*

The great bulk of the Biblical references to Tribulation are to sufferings endured by the people of God. The central and dominating factor in the Biblical understanding of such suffering, however, is the mystery of the Tribulation of the Messiah (Isa. 63:9; Col. 1:24; Rev. 1:9). The Scripture says, *"Though He were a Son, yet learned He obedience by the things which He suffered"* (Heb. 5:8).

This does not mean that He learned to be obedient, for that would have inferred that He had been disobedient, which never was the case.

NOTES

The thought is that Jesus established His integrity by living a normal human life in which obedience was demanded. By actually living out obedience he was *"perfected"* in the sense of being demonstrably qualified to become *"The Source of Eternal Salvation for all who obey, i.e., believe in Him"* (Heb. 5:9). All the Tribulations of Believers stand in this light. It can be summed up as follows:

CHRIST

Inasmuch as Christ is opposed in one way or the other by most of the world, the very fact of one making Him one's Savior, entails Tribulation. It is the norm for the experience of the Christian community. Thus, Tribulation is inevitable and to be anticipated (Mat. 13:21; Jn. 16:33; Acts 14:22; Rom. 8:35; 12:12; I Thess. 3:3; II Thess. 1:4; Rev. 1:9).

The Tribulation of Israel under the Old Testament finds its counterpart in the Tribulation of the Church under the New (Heb. 11:37; 12:1). Tribulation is particularly the lot of the Apostles who exemplify in a special manner the path of suffering Discipleship (Acts 20:23; II Cor. 1:4; 4:8, 17; 6:4; Eph. 3:13).

THE AFFLICTIONS OF THE MESSIAH

The Tribulation of the people of Christ is in some sense a participation in the sufferings of Christ (II Cor. 1:5; 4:10; Phil. 3:10; Col. 1:24; I Pet. 4:13).

Underlying the New Testament teaching here possibly is the notion of the so-called *"afflictions of the Messiah,"* a tally of suffering to be endured by the Righteous before the consummation of the Redemptive purpose of God.

LIKENESS OF CHRIST

The tribulations of the people of Christ are instrumental in promoting our moral transformation into the likeness of Christ (Rom. 5:3; II Cor. 3:18; 4:8-12, 16).

In particular the experience of tribulation promotes the upbuilding of the community through enabling the comforting of others in similar experiences (II Cor. 1:4; 4:10; Col. 1:24; I Thess. 1:6).

THE LAST DAYS

The tribulations of the people of Christ are eschatological as well, i.e., they belong to the last age, meaning they will increase at this time.

As such, they are a witness to the in-breaking and presence of the Kingdom, and its soon to be expansion (Mat. 24:9-14; Rev. 1:9; 7:14).

The idea is, that Tribulation during these last days, is going to increase rather than decrease, as taught by some. Some claim that a proper confession can eliminate all Tribulation; however, such thinking only portrays a lack of knowledge of the Word of God. Tribulation for the followers of Christ is inevitable, and in these last days, the time of Apostasy, which is a falling away from the Truth, it is more inevitable than ever.

The phrase, *"That we may be able to comfort them which are in any trouble, by the comfort wherewith we ourselves are comforted by God,"* proclaims the purpose of God. By the means which we have been comforted, by those same means we will offer comfort.

It may not be all the truth to say that we cannot comfort unless we ourselves have known sorrow, but it is certainly true that we cannot feel another's sorrow until we have felt the sting of pain. Neither can we ever know the sweetness of comfort until we have felt the soothing touch of God's love upon a broken heart.

The Psalms of David are the sweetest words of comfort because his pen had been dipped in the ink of affliction.

Whoever will feel the keenest and serve the best must have his feelings hurt the most.

TOO MUCH CUTTING AND HURTING

There is altogether too little of the Ministry of comfort. Too many Christians are busy these days in the disgraceful orgy of criticizing instead of the blessed Ministry of comforting. Instead of calming troubled waters, they are stirring them up. Instead of going about in the Master's Name soothing and comforting they are cutting and hurting.

It is so easy to seek comfort and so difficult to give it. Most of us want sympathy and kindness for our own troubles and are gravely offended if we are neglected. So few seek out the broken hearts of men that they might reproduce in these the comfort God has produced in them.

Have you ever been comforted? It is an obligation for you then to be a comforter. Has God come alongside to help you in an hour of calamity? It is required of you then to be a companion to another in his hour of calamity.

NOTES

Begin today to do what you have neglected for so long.

THE EXPERIENCE OF GOD'S COMFORT

This kind of Ministry does not require wealth or education. All it requires is the experience of God's comfort. All it takes is the understanding of a broken heart and the wealth of Divine Love. If you have these things, you have all you need to perform a great service (Laurin).

(5) "FOR AS THE SUFFERINGS OF CHRIST ABOUND IN US, SO OUR CONSOLATION ALSO ABOUNDETH BY CHRIST."

The phrase, *"For as the Sufferings of Christ abound in us,"* relates to our identification with Christ (I Pet. 4:13).

Jesus' identification with humans meant He would suffer for their sins (Isa. Chpt. 53). The Lord does not mislead His followers with a false illusion that they will never suffer (Col. 1:24). In fact, He cautioned James and John, as well as the other Disciples who were listening, that they would indeed drink from the cup of suffering which He drank (Mat. 20:22-23). They would even be baptized, or immersed, in it (Mk. 10:38-39).

A WARNING

Jesus also warned His Disciples that they would experience the same hate the world's system hurled at Him (Jn. 15:18-25). When people who claim to be Christians manifest hate toward fellow Believers, they are really siding with the world.

The world's system will allow them to display such emotion, but this action will not exempt them from also facing the world's hatred. The world only uses those people until its purposes are satisfied. It will afterward turn on them (Rossier).

THE SUFFERINGS OF CHRIST

The sufferings of Christ are the sufferings which He endured in the days of His flesh, and they were not exhausted by Him, but overflow to us who have to suffer as He suffered, bearing about with us His dying, that we may share His Life. Consequently, all our tribulation is also connected with Christ in such a manner that

Paul calls it *"the sufferings of Christ."* In what sense this is to be understood Jesus Himself explains in John 15:18-21, especially in the statement: *"All these things will they do unto you for My Name's sake."*

The thought is not that in Glory Christ continues to suffer these sufferings, but that His original sufferings which as far as His suffering is concerned, were completed at the time of His death, continue after a fashion in those who are connected with Him. The very same hatred that killed Him on the Cross now hurts His Believers who are one with Him by Faith in His Name. This thought explains such passages as Matthew 20:22-23; Romans 8:17; Galatians 6:17; Philippians 3:10; Colossians 1:24; Hebrews 13:13; I Peter 4:13.

The *"sufferings of Christ"* are not to be construed by a continuation of His Atoning Work on the Cross. He plainly said that was finished. The sufferings of the Cross were once for all. They cannot be repeated. Neither Paul nor we can reproduce Christ's suffering for any atoning purpose, but since Christ suffered for us we are to bear the sufferings of others.

So, the idea of suffering is not to atone for sin, for that has already been done, but rather for His Cause, and because we name His Name.

The phrase, *"So our consolation also aboundeth by Christ,"* means that the more we suffer for Christ, the more Grace and Comfort abound by Christ (I Cor. 10:13). Consequently, it may be observed as a universal Truth, that if we suffer in the Cause of Christ, if we are persecuted, oppressed, and pressed on His account, He will take care that our hearts shall be filled with consolation.

All of this may sound quite negative, actually quite morbid, and it would be indeed if the Verse did not promise us the *"abounding,"* or *"overflowing"* Comfort of God and all that refers. This more than compensates for any suffering that comes because we have chosen to identify with Christ. In other words, He returns far more Blessing, than we originally give of ourselves respecting us suffering for His Cause.

(6) "AND WHETHER WE BE AFFLICTED, IT IS FOR YOUR CONSOLATION AND SALVATION, WHICH IS EFFECTUAL IN THE ENDURING OF THE SAME SUFFERINGS WHICH WE ALSO SUFFER: OR WHETHER WE BE COMFORTED, IT IS FOR YOUR CONSOLATION AND SALVATION."

NOTES

The phrase, *"And whether we be afflicted,"* doesn't mean as it seems in the English translation, that one may or may not be afflicted, but that affliction is inevitable. The idea is, that Christ paid a tremendous price to provide Eternal Salvation for mankind (I Pet. 2:23-25). We enter into these sufferings of Christ as Believers, even as we have already mentioned, not that we may add to the price already paid for man's Redemption, for that is not needed, but rather to take the Gospel to the world. Paul and Timothy paid dearly to take the Gospel to the Corinthians, and especially Paul. It is the same with all who would do the Work of the Lord. Consequently, what the readers see in Paul and in Timothy, is how much they must bear in their work of spreading the Gospel.

The Holy Spirit wanted the Brethren at Corinth to know that Paul had been in great peril. He was the object of Satanic hatred. His life was a constant battle against adverse forces and circumstances. So will all who truly enter this race respecting Holiness and the Work of the Lord.

The phrase, *"It is for your Consolation and Salvation,"* in essence refers to two things:

1. Paul had to suffer greatly, even as we have said, in order that Salvation be brought to those who were outside the Ark of Safety.
2. The afflictions and victory he experienced through the comfort of the Lord, served as encouragement for every Believer who had to likewise face the Powers of Darkness.

PERSONAL EXPERIENCE

Inasmuch as the Holy Spirit allowed the great Apostle to say these things and for purpose and reason, I think He would not be adverse to me making mention of the following.

I too, even as all who truly take the Gospel to a lost world, have been the subject of Satanic hatred. In no way do I mean to make that an excuse for wrongdoing or failure, because such is always the fault of the individual; however, if anyone thinks that such happenings are brought about for little reason at all, but that they just happen, such thinking shows that they have little understanding of the situation at hand. It is a case of intensive spiritual warfare, and for the sole purpose and reason that the

Gospel of Jesus Christ is being taken to lost souls. Satan will use anything at his disposal to stop that, as should be obvious.

Consequently, any Believers who would speak lightly of such a thing, or judge it wrongly, simply have no idea of what is actually happening. As well, and fearfully so, they can open themselves up to the Powers of Darkness for such attitudes (Gal. 6:1-2).

WAS THIS AFFLICTION GREATER IN PAUL THAN OTHERS?

I think so.

First of all, Satan will direct his efforts the greatest extent toward those who are causing him the most damage. That should go without saying. However, the Lord has given each Believer sufficient strength as to the need of the time, irrespective as to what that may be. While Satan would definitely be allowed more latitude against someone like Paul, at the same time, the Lord furnishes greater defensive measures for that particular individual. However, that is the ideal and not necessarily the way things always turn out.

There is no man or woman, irrespective as to how much they are being used by the Lord, but that there is great room for spiritual growth. Consequently, the Lord uses these things, even as He did with Paul, to draw us closer to Him, while at the same time pointing out spiritual deficiencies in our own lives. Everything with the Child of God is a learning process, and its a process that never ends, even for someone as Paul.

The phrase, *"Which is effectual in the enduring of the same sufferings which we also suffer,"* in essence says that if Paul and Timothy were able to overcome, and they definitely were, then such should proclaim itself as an example for the Corinthians and all others that we may overcome as well.

EXAMPLES

We see in this, or else we should, that the experiences of Believers and we speak in the realm of victory, should serve as examples for others. Should there be failure, the Lord certainly derives no glory from that, but He definitely does derive glory from victory over failure in any capacity. In fact, Paul gives us that example from his own experience in Romans Chapter 7.

NOTES

However, the modern Church is in such a state, that it hardly will receive admonishing from one who has gained the victory in a certain area, but will mostly take council only from those who have never had any battles. Consequently, the counsel and direction received from that source is of little consequence. In fact, much of the modern Church would throw out the Psalms written by David if he lived now, especially considering the terrible problems he had. However, the Lord did not throw them out; furthermore, He allowed His Only Begotten Son to be named after David (Mat. 1:1).

Believers must understand, that the loss of a battle is not the loss of a war. As well, the individual who has won the war, irrespective that he may have lost a battle or two along the way, can give direction that will be of tremendous value to all who would be sensible enough to hear and receive.

The phrase, *"Or whether we be comforted, it is for your Consolation and Salvation,"* now turns from the affliction to the *"comfort."*

The danger in studying these Verses lies in getting our minds fixated on the affliction and loosing sight of the comfort. In fact, the passage emphasizes the latter as primary and only alludes to the former (afflictions) as necessary to explain the *"comfort."*

Affliction is inevitable. The way we face it may vary considerably from one person to another; however, the *"comfort"* received by Paul and Timothy was meant to serve as an example for others. In other words, even though afflictions will come, *"comfort"* definitely will come as well, and will be much greater than the afflictions.

IN ENDURANCE

Paul does not say that the comforting works endurance but rather works *"in endurance."* That point is worth noting, for the phrase implies that the readers are already *"in"* this endurance, and that the Divine Comforting operates in it by strengthening and increasing it.

The sufferings must, of course, be such as can be called *"the sufferings of Christ,"* and note that being buffeted for our faults is a quite different matter (I Pet. 2:19-23).

As well, and strangely enough, some of the griefs caused Paul were caused by the Corinthians.

We may remember how much Jesus had to endure from the Twelve. Think of the pain which Philip caused Him (Jn. 14:8-9), of Peter's frequent rashness which was so trying to Jesus, of Peter's denial, and especially of Judas. Many a rebuke had to be spoken by Jesus' lips. These things are in a way constantly repeated.

The injuries inflicted by those who are outside are far less painful than the injuries inflicted by those who are inside.

The entirety of the idea of this Sixth Verse is that whatever we do, we must not make our Brother's load heavier, but above all do what we can to make it lighter. Far too many Believers do not function in the realm of *"comfort and consolation,"* but rather the opposite, of criticism and hurt. God help us that we make our Brother's journey a little easier instead of adding burdens to his already considerable load.

(7) "AND OUR HOPE OF YOU IS STEDFAST, KNOWING, THAT AS YE ARE PARTAKERS OF THE SUFFERINGS, SO SHALL YE BE ALSO OF THE CONSOLATION."

The phrase, *"And our hope of you is stedfast,"* presents Faith in God that despite all the problems of the Corinthians, victory would ultimately be assured. There is a tremendous lesson here as should be obvious.

LOVE HOPETH ALL THINGS

How can Paul be so stedfast regarding the Corinthians, especially considering all the problems which were evident in this particular Church?

"This hope of ours for you," Paul is saying, *"is as firm as it has ever been."*

Why so firm?

Because back of it is *"the Father of Compassions and God of all Comforting."* It thus rests on the knowledge *"that as you are partakers of the Sufferings, so also of the Comforting."*

Some think that this knowledge is the information that was brought from Corinth by Titus, consequently encouraging Paul. While it no doubt did encourage him, still, *"this hope of ours"* has a more solid basis.

It was in the heart of Paul and of Timothy before Titus arrived; it was only confirmed by his good report. If Titus had brought bad news, he who wrote: *"Love hopeth all things"* (I Cor. 13:7), would still have hoped on and in this hope Paul's Faith would have worked for Corinth (Lenski).

NOTES

One can either see the bad in a situation, or one can see the good. The bad speaks of a lack of Faith, a lack of Trust, while the good speaks of that which one can see by the eye of Faith, but which may not be readily observant. But as stated, *"Love hopeth all things."*

The phrase, *"Knowing, that as ye are partakers of the Sufferings, so shall ye be also of the consolation,"* places the two in unity. No *"sufferings,"* no *"consolation."* And always, the *"consolation"* is far greater than the *"suffering."*

It is the nature of Christianity to thrive on adversity. Christianity was born and grew up in the midst of persecution. Let none of us entertain the notion that we are to be free from it.

At the same time, we have the consolation that the Comfort of Christ will be ours, which as stated, is always greater than the problem or difficulty.

HOW HAVE YOU STOOD IT, MANY HAVE ASKED?

Many have asked Frances and I that very question, concerning what we have gone through.

The answer is that of which Paul here speaks, the great and glorious *"Comfort"* given by Christ. The beautiful thing is this:

Of course, and as we have already stated, if any of us do something wrong, there will always be suffering for that; however, if we properly take it to Christ, which is the only thing which can be done, even then, in other words, even though we have failed, His comfort will be immediate. The key is in taking the situation to Him, and doing so properly with Trust and Faith that He will make matters right.

Yes, I have had many to make the statement, *"He must be living in a dream world,"* or *"He doesn't know how bad it really is,"* or words to that effect. Oh yes, I know in fact more than anyone else exactly what people think, and no, I'm not living in a dream world. I face reality every day. However, I face it in Christ. This one thing I know:

What a person is, is what they are in Christ, not what other people may say or think. As well, no person can take that away from any Believer.

However, much of the suffering we have endured, in fact the far greater portion, has not been because of failure on our part, even though that was real enough, but rather from fellow Believers who should have been of help, but were rather the opposite. In other words, instead of making the load lighter, they did all they could to make it heavier.

But yet, all of this was a part of the test. How would we react toward these people? We had to do, and was very glad to do exactly what Jesus said, *"Love your enemies, bless those who curse you . . . and pray for those who despitefully use you"* (Mat. 5:44).

THE COMFORT HE PROVIDES

Countless times, Frances and I have gone to the prayer meetings which we conduct every day, very heavy of heart. The Spirit of God would move greatly, functioning in the exact capacity as Paul here speaks, and we would leave greatly encouraged. In fact, it happened as late as last night (6-15-98). The Spirit of the Lord washed through that room, where about 15 or 20 of us had gathered to seek the Lord. It was a beautiful display of the Power of God. The *"comfort"* and *"consolation"* at least in my heart, was of such magnitude, that when I left that prayer meeting, I was not the same person who walked through the door about an hour earlier. That's how we've been able to endure.

(8) "FOR WE WOULD NOT, BRETHREN, HAVE YOU IGNORANT OF OUR TROUBLE WHICH CAME TO US IN ASIA, THAT WE WERE PRESSED OUT OF MEASURE, ABOVE STRENGTH, INSOMUCH THAT WE DESPAIRED EVEN OF LIFE:"

The phrase, *"For we would not, Brethren, have you ignorant of our trouble which came to us in Asia,"* tells us where it was, but not necessarily when, though it was probably recent, nor exactly what it was.

Because there is no reference to this incident in I Corinthians, this affliction must have occurred in the short span of time between the writing of the two Epistles. Since it happened in Asia, it must have taken place before Paul left for Macedonia.

Some people think it was some kind of physical illness, but this is not very plausible because there is no evidence to justify such a conclusion.

Others believe it is a reference to the riot in Ephesus (Acts 19:23-41), but there is little evidence of that either, for the simple reason that Paul did not really appear before this unruly crowd (Acts 19:30-31).

NOTES

Some have said that Paul's adversaries actually laid in wait and tried to kill him (I Cor. 16:9). There has even been a suggestion that he was thrown to the wild beasts while in Ephesus (I Cor. 15:32). Some suggest that his suffering was precipitated by the refusal of some in Corinth to repent, even after he wrote to them several times.

Dr. Bernard Rossier ventured this thought and I concur, *"I frankly doubt that he was referring to any physical suffering, although he certainly experienced more than his share of it. I honestly believe the extreme anguish was caused by 'religious' people who violently opposed his efforts because of jealousy, etc. This could well have been caused by Judaizers who came into Corinth, nearly causing the loss of that Church.*

"They permitted the Devil to use them to the extent that Paul despaired of his very life. While we cannot be positive about what happened, this interpretation seems more consistent with what we see in Paul's lengthy defense of his Apostolic Call (II Cor. Chpts. 10-12). Very little can affect a person more than opposition from fellow 'Christians.'"

The phrase, *"That we were pressed out of measure, above strength, insomuch that we despaired even of life,"* proclaims, I think, oppression by the Powers of Darkness to such an extent, that Paul thought that it would kill him.

Even though Paul is using the pronoun *"we,"* indicating plurality, still, I think that he is specifically speaking of himself here and not others.

Several statements should be made, and questions asked and hopefully answered, concerning this very eventful time in Paul's life and ministry. To be sure, the Holy Spirit allowed the Apostle to reveal this, and for a purpose and reason. It is up to us to glean that which the Holy Spirit desires.

NOTHING HAPPENS TO A BELIEVER BUT THAT GOD CAUSES OR ALLOWS IT

I realize the heading just given comes as a surprise to some Believers; however, even though a Believer can increase or lessen certain things by a variety of situations, still, Satan does not have free latitude with any Believer (Job Chpts. 1-2).

Believers belong to the Lord, whether the least or the greatest, and as such, and especially considering the tremendous price paid for our

Redemption, we should know and understand that the Lord exerts within certain parameters total independence of action. He does not violate the free moral agency of the Believer, or anyone for that matter, but at the same time He jealousy guards the Believer against the Evil One. He allows Satan certain latitude, but only under strict guidelines, which Satan must not cross. Of course, Satan means it for our harm, while the Lord allows such for our good.

WERE THESE STATEMENTS AS GIVEN BY PAUL A BAD CONFESSION AS SOME SUGGEST?

Only those who have an improper understanding of the Word of God would even remotely suggest such a thing. Those who believe such, think that all is ruled by the Believer's confession, which to a great extent rules God out, with the Believer charting the course.

While our confession is certainly important, the mere refusal to state such things in no way stops such action, nor does the stating of such bring about such action.

Confession had absolutely nothing to do with this situation, neither does it have much to do with what happens to others as well. Merely confessing something whether good or bad, does not set into motion certain negative or positive influences as some teach. According to these people Mark 11:24, can bring about any desired effect in ones life. Not so!

Some attempt to use the Word of God against God, and by that I mean this.

In other words, if certain things are said in the Scripture, they teach, the Believer can have it irrespective as to what it might be, which completely negates the Will of God in the matter. Every Promise in the Word of God, however, is always predicated on the Will of God. It is not left up to mere confession, as important as that might be.

WAS PAUL LACKING IN FAITH?

No! But I do think his Faith was somewhat misplaced as we will later see.

Of course, he would be lacking in Faith if Faith was determined as some of the modern Teachers determine such. In other words, Faith, according to these Teachers, solely has to do with *"things,"* and by that I speak of money, absence of all difficulties, etc.

NOTES

The Truth is, Biblical Faith incorporates every single thing that we are *in* the Lord, or do *for* the Lord. The basic Faith foundation is our Salvation and then our Sanctification.

In fact, every single attack engineered by Satan against the Child of God, and irrespective as to its direction, is but for one purpose and that is to weaken and hopefully destroy our Faith in God. In other words, he wants the Believer to simply quit and give up. To be sure, such Faith has absolutely nothing to do with money or things of that nature. As we've already stated, the Lord allows Satan only certain latitude in such situations. He does it for our good.

SPIRITUAL WARFARE!

There have probably been more books written on Spiritual Warfare in the last few years than all the other centuries put together. The sadness is, that most of the people writing these books have absolutely no knowledge of what they are writing about. In other words, they have had very little, if any, spiritual warfare themselves, and yet they conclude themselves to be experts in battles which have not been fought and victories which have not been won.

Spiritual Warfare is very real, and has absolutely nothing to do with some of the foolishness that passes for such presently.

Sometime ago I ministered in a particular Church. On the night before my Service of the next evening, a young man preached on this very subject, *"Spiritual Warfare."* During the Altar Service he called the Saints around, and they engaged in *"Spiritual Warfare."* Their idea of such, was them becoming *"militant,"* which called for them to stomp their feet and scream loudly at the Devil, demanding that he do certain things, etc.

Such is hardly worth the breath to expose it, and yet it seems plausible to some Christians.

Others, if it is to be remembered, dressed up in combat fatigues and wore a dog tag around their neck, which was supposed to denote some type of Spiritual Warfare.

The list is almost endless, but to be sure, Satan must laugh at such foolishness and foolishness it is.

What Paul was experiencing here, whatever direction it took, was Spiritual Warfare at its highest. The oppression by the Powers of Darkness was so severe, that even as the text suggests, Paul despaired of his life.

It evidently lasted for some days, and affected him spiritually and mentally, which probably had an effect upon him physically as well. This type of Spiritual Warfare incorporates demon powers which attack the Child of God, and in such a way that it's not easy thrown off. It is only those who have never experienced such that would be so foolish as to minimize this of which Paul speaks.

To be sure, warfare of this nature is little enjoined against those who are of little threat to Satan's kingdom of darkness. By that I mean the following:

I speak of souls being saved, Believers being Baptized with the Holy Spirit, sick bodies being truly healed (not mere hype), and people delivered from bondages of darkness by the Power of Jesus Christ. If those things are truly happening, Satan is going to do everything within Hell's power to hinder and even stop such if possible. This is what Paul was facing. Those who are little seeing such results, are little hindered by the Powers of Darkness.

WHY DOES THE LORD ALLOW SUCH?

The Lord allows such happenings, even at times to the degree of this mentioned by Paul, for our good. Faith must always be tested, and great Faith must be tested greatly.

It is not that God desires to know, for He already knows all things. It's for us to know. To be sure, during these times we generally learn that we are not nearly as strong as we thought we were, not nearly as spiritual as we thought we were. We learn that our Faith is not what it ought to be, and neither is our Trust. Unfortunately (or fortunately) such can only be learned in the crucible of affliction.

So, those who claim to have all the answers, if the truth be known, probably do not even know the questions. Those who have never lost a battle, simply haven't fought any. Those who have never failed in actuality, have never really entered the conflict.

Justification is an instant process, which means that the Lord fights *for* us. Sanctification is a lengthy process, actually one which never ends, and in this process the Lord is fighting in us. Even though it is the Lord doing the fighting, at least that's the way it ought to be, still, the spillover can be difficult at times.

NOTES

There's an old African adage that says, *"When elephants fight, ants get trampled."*

(9) "BUT WE HAD THE SENTENCE OF DEATH IN OURSELVES, THAT WE SHOULD NOT TRUST IN OURSELVES, BUT IN GOD WHICH RAISETH THE DEAD:"

The phrase, *"But we had the sentence of death in ourselves,"* refers to the fact that Paul actually believed that he was going to die.

The words, *"in ourselves,"* mean *"against ourselves"*; or, *"We expected certainly to die."*

Some claim that the Greek text is such that he still carried the same sentence when he wrote this statement; however, according to other Scholars, and which I think is correct, the problem was not still present but had been conquered, but its aftereffects were still very much present to the mind. This is what, I think, the Greek Text portrays. In other words, *"We, ourselves, have had the verdict of death within our own selves, and still feel this dire experience."*

THE SENTENCE OF DEATH

Paul had been brought to the point *"beyond ability,"* to the point of despair, where all struggle, even mental struggle, was useless, where he waited only for the deathblow to fall. Not even the least confidence in himself or in his resources was left to him.

If he had such confidence in anything which he might do, it had utterly deserted him. He was absolutely naked and stripped. But yet, this was the very purpose of God.

The phrase, *"That we should not trust in ourselves, but in God which raiseth the dead,"* tells us the reason for this great trial. It was meant to teach not only submission, but absolute trust in God (Jer. 17:5).

ONLY GOD!

The Lord took the Children of Israel into the howling wilderness after their deliverance from Egypt, even though another way, one much more hospitable was available. He did it for a purpose.

He wanted them to learn Trust in Him, that He could meet their needs in this howling wilderness, in effect, that they had no alternative but to trust God. This is what happened with Paul.

He had reached a point where only trusting God was left to Him, but even God was able to save him by nothing less than a miracle, yea, the greatest miracle, His Power to raise the dead.

So close was he to death, that his deliverance was identical with raising him from the dead, or at least this is the manner in which he presents the situation.

This Divine Purpose is the high point of Paul's narration.

Trusting in God Who raises up the dead, Who so recently demonstrated in the case of Paul that He is, indeed, such a God. Paul was to trust Him more fully regarding all future difficulties at Corinth or elsewhere.

When hope has left us and death is the only prospect, then God stands forth, the God Who raises up the dead. Such situations are His opportunity, for He, and He Alone, is able to meet them.

One reason that distress must reach the extreme point where all human help is utterly gone and we, ourselves, realize that and give up completely, is *"that we get to placing confidence, not on our own selves, but* (with finality) *on the God Who raises up the dead."* When that experience is needed, God provides it. Paul really confesses that He needed it, needed it at this time. That is comfort, and great comfort at that, for us lesser men.

NOTES

NOT WITH PAUL ONLY

Few would probably be placed in the same straits as Paul, but yet, I think all of us, at least all who truly love and believe the Lord, must undergo some similar experience. It can come in many shapes, forms, and directions.

Since late 1991, we have had to trust God to meet the financial needs of this Ministry, with every single door shut, and our ability to raise funds not just crippled, but totally taken away.

For a Ministry such as ours, a tremendous cash flow is needed, which must have the confidence of the people. When that confidence has been totally eroded, and through our own fault, then one begins to get the picture as to how difficult the situation actually is.

God has called me for Television, as well as for citywide Crusades, and that is the reason we see so many people saved. But yet, despite the fact that we see tremendous results, with great numbers of people hearing the Gospel, still, and as is obvious, the expenses are great due to Television air time costs, etc.

Consequently, since late 1991, we have had to trust God implicitly for all of our income. He promised during that time, that He would meet the needs of the Ministry. He has done that by performing miracle after miracle.

PRAYER

Sometime in January (1998) at one of our nightly prayer meetings, when things looked extremely difficult regarding the finances, the Lord beautifully and wondrously spoke to my heart that night.

He said to me, *"Several years ago, the Ministry owed $30 million dollars, and, today, it doesn't owe anyone anything, at least as far as money is concerned."*

And then He said, *"Satan had tried to destroy you, but I have delivered you totally and completely."*

I was seated on the floor during this time of prayer. There must have been about ten or fifteen people present. The Power of God covered me to such an extent at that particular time, that it's very difficult for me to even properly explain how I felt. I think I can say without fear of exaggeration, that the Presence of God from that particular Prayer Meeting that night, regarding what the Lord spoke to my heart, lingered with me, in fact, not leaving at all, for nearly two months. I've never had quite anything to happen like that all of my life. I literally walked in the Presence of the Lord for that length of time, as the Lord reminded me that He had performed miracle after miracle, doing exactly what He told me in late 1991 He would do.

So, I have at least some knowledge and in more ways than one, as to what it means to have no alternative but to trust God. In fact, this Ministry, at least as far as Satan was concerned, was dead. So, the Lord had to literally raise the dead, which He has done, and for which we give Him all the Glory.

When one has no other recourse and no other resource, when one must trust God for there is no other alternative, to be frank, at times it is a fearful place. But yet, at the same time, I can honestly say that since late 1991, this period of time has been the most wonderful, the most rewarding, and the most fulfilling I have ever known.

No, that doesn't mean the absence of all problems or difficulties. Sometimes I think these do nothing but increase. But what it does mean is that in the midst of all of this, there is a Peace that passeth all understanding. To be placed in a circumstance where God must act or else there is no hope, presents the greatest teaching tool there is.

(10) "WHO DELIVERED US FROM SO GREAT A DEATH, AND DOTH DELIVER: IN WHOM WE TRUST THAT HE WILL YET DELIVER US;"

Three things are said here in this one passage, things so great, wonderful, and glorious that we must not allow them to be lost on us. They are as follows:

DELIVERANCE

1. *"Who delivered us from so great a death"*: Paul is speaking of his experience just mentioned, and how the Lord so wondrously performed a miracle for him. Again, what it actually was we do not know.

I think the Holy Spirit desired that Paul be vague regarding the actual happening. He wanted us to know that God is our answer in any and all circumstances, not just those as they related to Paul. This we do know, the way and manner in which the Holy Spirit gave the Word, is all done by design and purpose, and for a reason.

So, He wants us to know and understand, that irrespective as to what the problem is, that He will deliver us.

2. *"And doth deliver"*: speaks of the present tense. In other words, He is delivering us right now.

If one could look into the spirit world, especially into the realm of darkness, one would see Satan no doubt fomenting many evil devices against us, while at the same time, the Lord is delivering us. Much of the time this goes on without our having firsthand knowledge, but the idea is this:

He is delivering us at this very moment. Not so much has, as wonderful as that was, and not so much shall, as grand as that will be, but is doing so at this very moment. One can only shout, *"Hallelujah!"*

This is a delivering process that never stops.

"Deliver" in the Greek is *"rhuomai,"* and means *"to rush to the rescue and to do so currently, i.e., now."*

NOTES

3. *"In Whom we trust that He will yet deliver us"*: The idea is, that the Lord has done so in the past, He is doing so presently, and because of the past and the present, He will do so in the future. We have His Word!

SATAN CANNOT

I have told many congregations that they should remember that when Satan tells them that he is going to do thus to them, that in fact, he is not going to do anything. If he could have done so, he would have done so a long time ago. The reason he hasn't done so is because he cannot do so. It's just that simple!

He tells you he is gong to kill you! Have no fear, he would have done it a long time ago if he could have done so. The simple fact is he cannot kill you, he simply does not have that power.

He tells you that he is going to drive you into bankruptcy. If he could do such, he would have already carried it out a long time ago. As stated, he hasn't done so because he doesn't have the power to do so.

To be frank, Satan would have loved to have killed Paul. The Apostle was causing him more problems than anyone else in the world at that time. To be sure, he tried his best, but the Lord said, *"So far and no further."* Once again, one must shout, *"Hallelujah!"*

The idea of all of this is found in the one word, *"trust,"* but yet, even as the Ninth Verse says, *"not . . . in ourselves, but in God."*

TRUST

To be sure, men do not give up trust in themselves easily, especially someone with the personality and demeanor of Paul. He was a man with tremendous zeal, talent, ability, fortitude, and courage. As well, he was a man of great Faith. Perhaps few, if anyone in the world of his day had his Faith. That certainly is not bad, but good; however, sometimes such can be turned against us as we turn Faith into works, which then ceases to be trust in God, but rather in ourselves. It is a fine line.

What does it mean to really trust God?

If this experience as given by Paul is to be any example, and it certainly is meant to be, total trust in the Lord is when we no longer trust in anything else, and especially ourselves.

He has delivered, He is delivering, and He shall yet deliver!

NOTES

I want us to carefully look for a moment at the idea of Paul frankly admitting his fear. He told how depressed he was and how he gave up hope of surviving. His reactions were as normal as ours, and his experiences were as common as ours, though undoubtedly greatly increased and intensified. My point is this:

When a person is this frank and open, which most will never be, this shows that Paul places no more trust in himself, but all in God. Men are afraid to admit fear, or failure, or to be open such as this. Most would automatically claim that those who do so have no faith; however, such an attitude which Paul had, shows the very opposite. It shows he really had great Faith, and it was Faith which was anchored in the right Source, the Lord Jesus Christ, and not himself.

When one's trust is in themselves (and I speak of all, Preachers and laypersons alike), every word must be one of greatness and grandeur, and for the simple reason that it is *"self"* which is being promoted, and where we have placed our trust. However, to be frank and open even as Paul, requires Trust to be totally in the Lord and none in ourselves.

FAITH BORN OF FAILURE

When Paul surveyed his situation and asked himself what the end would be, he had to sentence himself to death. It was futile to trust in himself. It was impossible to find adequate human resources wherever he looked.

Paul was beyond help from man. But he still had God and he found a new Trust in God. It taught him to rely no more on his own strength, but in God Who can even raise the dead.

Here was faith born of failure, which is a statement almost never heard nowadays. Here was a new confidence in God. Out of a bitter experience that was so perilous that it almost took his life, Paul found a new Faith.

These experiences either leave us better or worse. We either have more faith when it's all over, or we are more fearful. Either we are mellowed or we are embittered.

To be sure, there is no bitterness here in Paul, but rather the very opposite.

I realize that most have never thought of Faith coming out of failure; however, to be sure, it is quite possible that this is where most Faith originates. In that failure, everything else is stripped away, and one must anchor solely on the Word of God. Faith is then born anew, which is what the Holy Spirit intended all along.

Some would claim that Paul did not fail here. I beg to disagree.

The direction of Faith that Paul had (too much in himself) was not equal to the task. One can tell by his terminology that his Faith failed. He, himself, had recently written, *"Whatsoever is not of Faith is sin"* (Rom. 14:23). Nevertheless, the failure of his Faith, would only insure the birth of a newer and higher Faith, a Faith, to be sure, which had no dependence at all in self, but totally in God.

(11) "YE ALSO HELPING TOGETHER BY PRAYER FOR US, THAT FOR THE GIFT BESTOWED UPON US BY THE MEANS OF MANY PERSONS THANKS MAY BE GIVEN BY MANY ON OUR BEHALF."

The phrase, *"Ye also helping together by prayer for us,"* proclaims Paul's deep conviction of the efficacy of intercessory prayer (Rom. 15:30-31; Phil. 1:19; Phile. vs. 22).

HELPING TOGETHER BY PRAYER

The words rendered, *"helping together,"* means cooperating, aiding, assisting; and the idea is that Paul felt that his trials might be turned to good account, and give occasion for thanksgiving and that this was to be accomplished by the aid of the prayers of his fellow Christians. He felt that the Church was one, and that Christians should sympathize with one another. By this statement, Paul established the connection which one Christian's prayers have to another Christian's need. It is the vital connection of aid and assistance. Called here *"helping together by prayer,"* it is an effectual and necessary means of assistance that we render to each other.

THE EFFECT OF PRAYER

The idea also is that the effect of prayer accrues not only to the benefit of the one for whom we pray, but results in blessing to the one who prays.

In the Bible, Prayer is worship that includes all the attitudes of the human spirit in its approach to God. The Christian worships God when he adores, confesses, praises, and supplicates Him in Prayer. The highest activity of which the human spirit is capable may also be thought of as communion with God, so long as due emphasis is laid upon Divine initiative.

A man prays because God has already touched his spirit. However, Prayer in the Bible is not a *"natural response"* (Jn. 4:24). *"That which is born of the flesh is flesh"* (Jn. 3:6), consequently, the Lord does not *"hear"* every Prayer (Isa. 1:15; 29:13).

The Biblical Doctrine of Prayer emphasizes the Character of God, the necessity of a man's being in Saving or Covenant Relationship with Him, and his entering fully into all the privileges and obligations of that relation with God.

THE PROPHETS

Prayer was an indispensable part of the Ministry of the Prophets of old. The very reception of the Revelatory Word of God involved the Prophet in a prayerful relation with the Lord. Actually, prayer was absolutely essential to the Prophet receiving the Word (Isa. 6:5; 37:1-4; Jer. 11:20-23; 12:1-6; 42:1).

The Prophetic Vision came to Daniel while he was at Prayer (Dan. 9:20).

We know from Jeremiah's writings that while Prayer was the essential condition of, and reality in, the Prophet's experience and Ministry, it was often a tempestuous exercise of the spirit (Jer. 18:19-23; 20:7-18), as well as a sweet fellowship with the Lord (Jer. 1:4; 4:10; 10:23-25; 12:1-4; 14:7-9, 19-22; 15:15-18; 16:19; 17:12).

THAT WHICH JESUS SAID ABOUT PRAYER

As to Jesus' Doctrine of Prayer, this is set principally in certain of His Parables. In the Parable of the friend who borrowed three loaves (Lk. 11:5-8), the Lord inculcates importunity in Prayer; and the ground on which the confidence in importunate Prayer is built is the Father's Generosity (Mat. 7:7-11). The goodness and generosity of God are very important, and should always be understood accordingly. The Lord delights in doing good things for His Children.

The Parable of the Unjust Judge (Lk. 18:1-8) calls for tenacity in prayer, which includes persistence as well as continuity. God's delays in answering prayer are due not to indifference, but to love that desires to develop and deepen faith which is finally vindicated.

In the Parable of the Tax Collector and the Pharisee (Lk. 18:10-14), Christ insists on humility and penitence in prayer and warns against a sense of self-superiority.

NOTES

HUMILITY AND PRAYER

Self-humiliation in prayer means acceptance with God, self-exaltation in Prayer hides God's face. Christ calls for charity in Prayer in the Parable of the Unjust Servant (Mat. 18:21-35). It is Prayer offered by a forgiving spirit that God answers.

Simplicity in prayer is taught in Matthew 6:5; 23:14; Mark 12:38-40; Luke 20:47. Prayer must be purged of all pretence. It should spring from simplicity of heart and motive, and express itself in simplicity of speech and petition.

The Lord also urged intensity in Prayer (Mat. 26:41; Mk. 13:33; 14:38). Here watchfulness and faith combined in sleepless vigilance. Again in Matthew 18:19, unity in Prayer is emphasized.

If a group of Christians who have the mind of Christ pray in the Spirit, their Prayers will be effectual. But prayer must also be expectant (Mk. 11:24). Prayer that is an experiment achieves little, in other words, I will try it and see if it works. Prayer which is the sphere where Faith operates in surrender to God's Will achieves much (Mk. 9:23).

OBJECTIVES

On objectives in Prayer, Jesus had little to say. Doubtless He was content to let the Holy Spirit prompt His Disciples in Prayer. What aims He actually referred to in Prayer are to be found in Mark 9:28; Matthew 5:44; 6:11, 13; 9:36; and, Luke 11:13.

As to method in Prayer, the Lord had two important things to teach. First, Prayer is now to be offered to the Father in Jesus' Name (Jn. 16:23). As He insisted on Faith then (Mk. 9:23), and tested sincerity (Mat. 9:27-31), and uncovered ignorance (Mat. 20:20-22), and opposition to sinful presumption (Mat. 14:27-31), in those who petitioned Him, so He does today in the experience of those who offer Prayer to the Father in His Name.

IN HIS NAME

As we have already stated, Prayer is now to be offered in the Name of Christ (Jn. 14:13; 15:16; 16:23), through Whom we have access to the Father. To pray in the Name of Christ is to pray as Christ, Himself, prayed, and to pray to the

NOTES

Father, as the Son has made Him known to us: and for Jesus, the true focus in Prayer was the Father's Will. Here is the basic characteristic of Christian Prayer: A new access to the Father which Christ secures for the Christian, and prayer in harmony with the Father's Will because offered in Christ's Name.

As to the Lord's practice of Prayer, it is well known that He prayed in secret (Lk. 5:15; 6:12), in times of spiritual conflict (Lk. 22:39-46; Jn. 12:20-28), and on the Cross (Mat. 26:46; Lk. 23:46).

In His Prayers He offered Thanksgiving (Mat. 26:27; Lk. 10:21; Jn. 6:11; 11:41), sought guidance (Lk. 6:12), interceded (Mk. 10:16; Lk. 22:31-34; 23:34; Jn. 17:6-19, 20-26), and communed with the Father (Lk. 9:28). In fact, the burden of His High-Priestly Prayer in John Chapter 17 is the unity of the Church.

THE LORD'S PRAYER

Regarding the Lord's Prayer, it will suffice to say that after invocation (Mat. 6:9) there follow six petitions, of which the first three have reference to God's Name, Kingdom, and Will, and the last three to man's need of bread, forgiveness, and victory:

The Prayer then closes with a doxology which contains a threefold declaration concerning God's Kingdom, Power, and Glory. It is *"like this"* that Christians are bidden to pray.

THE ACTS OF THE APOSTLES

The Book of Acts is an excellent link between the Gospels and the Epistles because in Acts, the Apostolic Church puts into effect our Lord's teaching on Prayer.

The Church was born in the atmosphere of Prayer (Acts 1:4). In answer to Prayer, the Spirit was poured out (Acts 1:4; 2:4). Prayer continued to be the Church's native air (Acts 2:42; 6:4, 6). There remained in the Church's thinking a close connection between Prayer and the Spirit's Presence and Power (Acts 4:31). In times of crisis, the Church had recourse to Prayer (Acts 4:23; 12:5, 12). Throughout the Acts, the Church Leaders emerge as men of Prayer (Acts 9:40; 10:9; 16:25; 28:8) who urge Believers to pray with them (Acts 20:28, 36; 21:5).

THE PAULINE EPISTLES

It is significant that immediately after Christ revealed Himself to Paul on the Damascus road, it is said of Paul, *"Behold, he is praying"* (Acts 9:11). Probably for the first time Paul discovered what Prayer really was, so profound was the change in his heart which conversion had effected. From that moment, he was a man of Prayer.

In Prayer, the Lord spoke to him (Acts 22:17). Prayer was Thanksgiving, intercession, the realization of God's Presence (Eph. 1:16; I Thess. 1:2). He found that the Holy Spirit assisted him in Prayer as he sought to know and to do God's Will (Rom. 8:14, 16).

In his experience there was a close connection between Prayer and the Christian's intelligence (I Cor. 14:14-19). Prayer was absolutely essential for the Christian (Rom. 12:12). The Christian's armor (Eph. 6:13-17) included Prayer which Paul describes as *"all Prayer"* to be offered at *"all seasons,"* with *"all perseverance,"* for *"all Saints"* (Eph. 6:18).

And Paul practiced what he preached (Rom. 1:9; Eph. 1:16; I Thess. 1:2); hence, his insistence upon Prayer when writing to his Fellow-Believers (Phil. 4:6; Col. 4:2).

THE MANNER IN WHICH PAUL PRAYED

In his Epistles, Paul is constantly breaking out into Prayer, and it is instructive to glance at some of his prayers because of their content:

1. In Romans 1:8-12, he pours out his heart to God in Thanksgiving, insists upon serving Christ with his spirit, intercedes for his friends in Rome, expresses his desire to impart to them a spiritual gift, and declares that he, too, is depending upon them for spiritual uplift.

2. In Ephesians 1:15-19, Paul again thanks God for his converts, and prays that they may receive the Spirit through Whom comes knowledge of God and illumination of heart, in order that they may know the hope of God's calling, the wealth of God's inheritance, and the Greatness of God's Power which had been demonstrated in Christ's Resurrection.

3. Again, in Ephesians 3:14-18, the Apostle pleads with the Father for his fellow-Christians that they might be increasingly conscious of God's Power, to the end that Christ might indwell them, and they might be rooted in love, that each together, being perfected, might be filled with the fullness of God.

Both of these *"Ephesian"* Prayers are well summed up in Paul's threefold desire that

Christians should receive knowledge and power issuing in the love of Christ, through which as individuals and as a group they should achieve maturity.

4. In Colossians 1:9, Paul again prays that the Believers should know God's will through spiritual wisdom and understanding, that practice might agree with profession, and that they might have power for their practice, and be thankful for their immense privilege and position in the Lord Jesus.

PRAYER AND THE HOLY SPIRIT

But perhaps Paul's greatest contribution to our understanding of Christian Prayer is in establishing its connection with the Holy Spirit.

In fact, Prayer could probably be called a Gift of the Spirit (I Cor. 14:14-16). The Believer prays *"in the Spirit"* whether in his native language or in Tongues (Eph. 6:18; Jude vs. 20); hence, Prayer is a cooperative operation between God and the Believer in that it is presented to the Father, in the Name of the Son, through the inspiration of the indwelling Holy Spirit.

In fact, considering the Light that has been poured out on the world in this century regarding the *"Latter Rain"* respecting the Holy Spirit, I think without this experience that Prayer cannot really be an effective medium in the heart and life of the Believer. While any Christian certainly can pray, still, I think the Baptism with the Holy Spirit, with the evidence of speaking with other Tongues, is such a boon to Prayer, that to attempt Prayer without this Great Gift presents an exercise which is not very productive. That is at least one of the reasons that the Lord commanded His followers to be Baptized with the Holy Spirit before they attempted anything in the Work of the Lord (Acts 1:4).

HEBREWS

The Epistle to the Hebrews makes a significant contribution to an understanding of Prayer. Hebrews 4:14-16 shows why Prayer is possible: It is possible because we have a Great High Priest Who is both Human and Divine, because He is now in the heavenly place, and because of what He is now doing there.

When we pray, it is to receive Mercy and find Grace. The reference to the Lord's Prayer Life in Hebrews 5:7-10 really teaches what Prayer is: Christ's *"prayers"* and *"supplications"* were *"offered up"* to God and in this spiritual service He *"learned obedience"* and, therefore, *"was heard."* In Hebrews 10:19-25 the emphasis is upon corporate Prayer and the demands and motives which it involves.

The place of prayer is described in Hebrews 6:19.

JAMES

The Epistle of James has three significant passages on prayer.

Prayer in perplexity is dealt with in James 1:5-8; correct motives in prayer are underlined in James 4:1-3; and the significance of prayer in time of sickness is made clear in James 5:16-18.

JOHN

In his First Epistle, John points the way to boldness and efficacy in Prayer (I Jn. 3:21), while in I John 5:14-16, he establishes the relation between prayer and the Will of God, which is so very, very important, and shows that efficacy in Prayer (power to produce an effect) is especially relevant to Intercession.

THE WILL OF GOD

The heart of the Biblical Doctrine of prayer is well expressed by B. F. Westcott: "True prayer — the prayer that must be answered — is the personal recognition and acceptance of the Divine Will (Mk. 11:24; Jn. 14:7)."

"It follows that the hearing of Prayer which teaches obedience is not so much the granting of a specific petition, which is assumed by the petitioner to be the way to the end desired, but the assurance that what is granted does most effectively lead to the desired end. Thus we are taught that Christ learned that every detail of His Life and Passion contributed to the accomplishment of the work which He came to fulfill, and so He was most perfectly 'heard.' In this sense He was 'heard for His Godly fear.'"

The phrase, *"That for the gift bestowed upon us by the means of many persons thanks may be given by many on our behalf,"* refers evidently to his deliverance from so imminent a peril, whatever it may have been. He felt this was owing to the prayers of many persons on his behalf. He believed that he had been remembered in the petitions of his friends and fellow

NOTES

Christians, and that his deliverance was owing, at least in part, to their supplications.

THE ATTITUDE OF PAUL

First of all, Paul was anxious that God be praised for this deliverance, not only by him, but all of the Corinthians as well. The Lord had mercifully interposed, in answer to the prayers of His people, and it was proper that His Mercy should be extensively acknowledged.

Paul was desirous, and rightly so, that God should not be forgotten.

He is perhaps intimating here, that those who had obtained Mercies by prayer, were prone to forget their obligation to return thanks to God for His gracious and merciful interposition.

As well, we must not forget that the Church at Corinth had many problems, which Paul addresses specifically in his First Epistle, and as well in his Second. Nevertheless, despite these difficulties, some very intense, Paul still sought the prayers of these individuals.

What does that tell us?

It tells us many things. First of all, Paul was showing that he had confidence in them, despite the correction he had been forced to impose. At a time like this, such goes a long way. Even though the Apostle had to set the record straight, still, he lets them know by what he says regarding their prayer for him, how much confidence he actually has in them despite the difficulties and problems. How that must have encouraged many of the Corinthians.

Second, he no doubt knew that there were at least some of these Corinthians who really knew how to touch God, and in fact, walk close to Him. What few there are of that kind, and please believe me they are scarce, proverbially speaking, they are worth their weight in gold. As Paul, there are people who I personally know who I strongly desire to pray for me, because I know their lives and I know their touch with God. In other words, the Lord answers their prayers.

And last, such portrays the humility of this Apostle, that despite the fact he is Paul, under Christ, the founder of the Church, still, he needs the prayers of God's people. Over and over again he expressed that.

(12) "FOR OUR REJOICING IS THIS, THE TESTIMONY OF OUR CONSCIENCE, THAT IN SIMPLICITY AND GODLY SINCERITY,

NOTES

NOT WITH FLESHLY WISDOM, BUT BY THE GRACE OF GOD, WE HAVE HAD OUR CONVERSATION IN THE WORLD, AND MORE ABUNDANTLY TO YOU-WARD."

The phrase, *"For our rejoicing is this,"* one could say refers to *"boasting."*

BOASTING?

There is a certain type of pietism (false humility) which tells the Christian never to boast, at least not about anything in himself, Paul is free from this inhibition. He boasts of his good conscience and his good Christian conduct; in fact, in Verse 14 he makes the readers of this letter his boast and himself and his assistants the boast of his readers. It is one way of glorifying God for what He has produced in us and through us.

Some people consider themselves to be so humble that their humility fails to acknowledge with joy what God has done. The boasting that is reprehensible glories in what we are and what we achieve of ourselves (Lk. 18:11-12). However, we shall find a great deal of genuine boasting in this Epistle, which the Holy Spirit allowed, and which is proper and right.

The phrase, *"The testimony of our conscience,"* presents this to which Paul frequently appeals (Acts 23:1; 24:16; Rom. 9:1; I Cor. 4:4).

CONSCIENCE

Paul had an approving conscience. It did not condemn him on the subject, though others might accuse him. Though his name might be vilified, yet he had comfort in the approval which his own conscience gave to his course.

Paul's conscience was enlightened by the Gospel, and, thus, its decisions were correct. Whatever others might charge him with, he knew what was the aim and purpose of his life. As we have previously stated, what a person is in Christ is what that person actually is irrespective of what others may say. Paul is not actually rejoicing or boasting in his testimony per se, but in the reason for the testimony.

Paul had been charged with insincerity by certain enemies at Corinth. They wrote letters that impugned his character. Against these unjust accusations Paul defended himself, but only for the sake of the Kingdom of God, and not for himself personally.

Sometimes a servant of Christ can defend himself and should, not for his own carnal satisfaction, but for the sake of his Ministry. However, many times he can only suffer in silence awaiting the vindication God will bring.

CONSCIENCE AS USED IN THE BIBLE

The Old Testament has no word for *"conscience."* Consequently, its origin must, therefore, be sought in a world of Greek, rather than Hebrew, ideas.

In the Old Testament it is said, *"David's heart smote him,"* which plays the part of conscience (I Sam. 24:5).

The New Testament use of *"conscience"* must be considered against the background of *"the idea of God, Holy and Righteous, Creator and Judge, as well as Redeemer and Quickener."* The Truth of this remark is evident from the fact that the New Testament writers see man's conscience negatively as the instrument of judgment, and positively as the means of guidance.

We know that it is possible for the conscience to grow seared and ultimately insensible (I Tim. 4:2). Thus, it is essential for the conscience to be properly educated, and indeed informed by the Holy Spirit. That is why *"conscience"* and *"Faith"* cannot be separated.

CONSCIENCE AND FAITH

By Repentance and Faith man is delivered from conscience as *"pain"*; but Faith is also the means whereby his conscience is quickened and instructed. To walk in *"newness of life"* (Rom. 6:4) implies a living, growing Faith through which the Christian is open to the influence of the Spirit (Rom. 8:14); and this in turn is the guarantee of a *"good"* or *"clear"* conscience (Acts 23:1; I Pet. 3:16).

WHAT A GOOD CONSCIENCE DEMANDS

An important and developed use of conscience as outlined by Paul occurs in Romans 2:14. The implication of this passage is that God's general Revelation of Himself as good, and demanding goodness, faces all men with moral responsibility.

For the Jews the Divine demands were made explicit in the Law of Moses, while the Gentiles, as Paul put it, performed *"by nature"* what the Law requires. But the recognition of holy obligations, whether by Jew or Gentile, is something individually apprehended (the Law is *"written on their hearts"* [Rom. 2:15] and, according to personal response, morally judged [for *"their conscience also bears witness"* with the understanding of their heart]). Thus, *"conscience"* belongs to all men, and through it God's Character and Will are actively appreciated.

At the same time, it may be regarded as a power *"apart"* from man himself (Rom. 9:1).

NOTES

THE BENEFITS OF CALVARY

Paul continues in Hebrews with both the negative and positive reference of conscience. Under the terms of the Old Covenant, man's guilty conscience in relation to God could not be perfected (Heb. 9:9); but deliverance has been made possible by the Work of Christ under the terms of the New Covenant (Heb. 9:14), and by the appropriation of the benefits of the death of Jesus on the Cross.

In terms of spiritual growth, therefore, a worshipper's conscience may be described as *"good"* (Heb. 13:18).

To summarize, the New Testament's significance of *"conscience"* is twofold: It is the means of moral judgment, painful and absolute because the judgment is Divine, upon the actions of an individual completed or begun; and it also acts as a witness and guide in all aspects of the Believer's Sanctification.

(Bibliography: J. Dupont, *"Gnosis"*; O. Hallesby, *"Conscience"*; C. A. Pierce, *"Conscience In The New Testament"*; W. D. Stacey, *"The Pauline View Of Man."*)

The phrase, *"That in simplicity and Godly sincerity, not with fleshly wisdom, but by the Grace of God, we have had our conversation in the world,"* proclaims the manner in which the Apostle describes himself, and as well, that the Holy Spirit allowed him to do such. So it is not mere boasting, but rather a necessary defense. Let's look at what the Apostle said:

SIMPLICITY

"Simplicity" in the Greek is *"haplotes,"* and means *"singleness, liberality, and bountifulness."* However, Farrar says the actual word is *"Holiness,"* translated from *"hagiotes,"* which should have been used rather than the former.

He says that *"Holiness"* seems to have been altered to *"simplicity,"* both on dogmatic grounds and because it is a rare word, at least the word used here for holiness, only occurring in Hebrews 12:10.

Either way, it stands opposed to double-dealings and purposes; to deceitful appearances, and crafty plans; to mere policy and craftiness in accomplishing an object.

A man under the influence of this, is straightforward, candid, open, frank; and he expects to accomplish his purpose by integrity and fair dealing, and not by stratagem and cunning.

Policy, craft, artful plans, and deep-laid schemes of deceit belong to the world; simplicity of aim and purpose are the true characteristics of a real Christian.

AND GODLY SINCERITY

This actually says *"the sincerity of God."* It is the sincerity that God produces and approves; and the sentiment is, that a pure relationship with the Lord, produces entire sincerity in the heart. Its purposes and aims are open and manifest, as if seen in the sunshine. The plans of the world are obscure, deceitful, and dark, as if in the night.

Conscience testified that Paul, and no doubt Timothy as well, had confined their conduct within this sphere drawn by these qualities. Holiness is a broad term which covers the whole relation to God and the devotion to Him. Sincerity signifies honesty and uprightness, without duplicity, and refers to the relation toward men.

NOT WITH FLESHLY WISDOM

This speaks of the wisdom which is manifested by the men of this world, by cunning, policy, expediency, in other words crafted to deceive.

This phrase stands opposed to simplicity and sincerity, to openness and straightforwardness. Paul here means to disclaim himself, and his fellow-laborers, all such carnal policy which distinguishes the mere men of the world. And if Paul deems such policy improper for him, we should deem it improper for us.

If he would not use such to advance himself, we should not either. If he would not employ it in the promotion of good plans, neither should we.

NOTES

Fleshly or worldly wisdom has been the curse of the Church and the bane of True Salvation. In fact, it is to this day exerting a withering and blighting influence on the Church.

The moment that such plans are resorted to, is proof that the vitality of Trust in God is gone. In fact, any man who feels that his purposes cannot be accomplished but by such carnal policy, should set it down as full demonstration that his plans are wrong, and that his purpose should be abandoned.

James said, *"This wisdom descendeth not from above, but is earthly, sensual, devilish"* (James 3:15).

BUT BY THE GRACE OF GOD

Consequently, we have *"fleshly wisdom"* and *"God's Grace"* as the sources, the former making holiness and sincerity in us impossible, the latter producing both.

Such debased wisdom is the evil source in us, God's Grace is the Divine Power from above. Fleshly wisdom fits means to an end and thus looks wise, looks attractive because it looks wise, and thus, deceives us. It is the Devil's invention which deceived Eve.

To the contrary, God's Grace, which is itself the pure favor of undeserved love, draws us upward into a life that is holy and sincere. The Grace of God was the atmosphere which the Apostle breathed, this sphere in which he worked.

The idea is, that God had shown favor to Paul, as he will anyone who will humble themselves to Him. As a result, God had directed him, and had kept him from the crooked and devious ways of mere worldly policy.

The idea seems to be not merely that he had pursued a correct and upright course of life, but that he was indebted for this to the Grace and favor of God — an idea which Paul omitted no opportunity of acknowledging.

In other words, he is saying that despite the will to conduct himself in an upright manner, that within itself would not have been sufficient for him to have carried out these desires. God's Grace which translates into God's Power, i.e., *"enabling Grace,"* is the direction alone in which such can be accomplished.

Men are forever attempting to gain the high plateau within the means of their own ability, but none ever have, and in this fashion none ever shall. Only the Lord can enable one to do so, and He does so by His Grace, i.e., unmerited favor, which benefit is given on the premise of a broken and contrite spirit on the part of man.

WE HAVE HAD OUR CONVERSATION IN THE WORLD

The word, *"conversation"* presently refers to oral discourse; however, in Scripture it means *"conduct."* In the sense of this Passage, it means that Paul had conducted himself in accordance with the principles of the Grace of God, and had been influenced by that and that alone.

Paul uses the word *"world"* in the sense, that he practiced such conduct not only in the Church, but everywhere, i.e., *"the world."* It means everywhere, wherever I have been. It had been and continued to be his common and universal practice.

The phrase, *"And more abundantly to youward,"* actually says *"especially towards you."*

This was added, doubtless, because there had been charges against him in Corinth, that he had been crafty, cunning, deceitful, and especially that he had deceived them, in not visiting them as he had promised. He affirms, therefore, that in all things he had acted in the manner to which the Grace of God prompted, and that his conduct, in all respects, had been that of entire simplicity and sincerity (Barnes).

(13) "FOR WE WRITE NONE OTHER THINGS UNTO YOU, THAN WHAT YE READ OR ACKNOWLEDGE; AND I TRUST YE SHALL ACKNOWLEDGE EVEN TO THE END;"

The phrase, *"For we write none other things unto you, than what ye read or acknowledge,"* answers his critics who apparently accused him of being deceitful in writing, in other words, different than he was in person.

SHAME

It is a melancholy thought that even such a one as Paul was reduced to the sad necessity of defending himself against such charges as that he intrigued with individual members of his Churches, wrote private letters or sent secret messages which differed in tone than those which were read in the public Assembly.

Some may wonder at the necessity of such action by Paul; however, if Satan could succeed in turning these Believers against Paul, exactly as he was trying to do, the great Ministry of the Apostle, all designed by the Lord, could not then be any benefit to these particular individuals, whomever they may have been. This is one of Satan's greatest tactics. He seeks to undermine, to demean, to debase, the God-called Preacher in the eyes of the Church, in order that they will not hear his Message. Unlike Paul, too often we foolishly do things which give Satan latitude in this capacity, which makes his task easier.

Unfortunately, even though Satan will use anything at his disposal to carry out this evil design, those with whom he is the most successful are those who claim Christ.

The phrase, *"And I trust ye shall acknowledge even to the end,"* simply refers to the fact that Paul's honesty and integrity had been simple and straightforward from the day they had first met him, and it would continue to be that way until he died or Jesus came. They should understand that they could count on that.

These people had received at least four letters from Paul, as thought by some, so they should have been aware of his honesty, whether he was present in person or communicating in written form. The manner in which he says this in the Greek presents a purposeful play on words to show that he said what he meant and meant what he said. His letters could be taken at face value; they contained no hidden innuendos or undertones.

I wonder if these people who were accusing Paul of deceit actually understood that they were in reality accusing the Holy Spirit? They were finding fault with what Paul had written, little realizing it seems, that it was the Holy Spirit Who was in fact the Author, with Paul only being the instrument. To lay one's hands negatively upon that which is of God, is a very serious thing indeed. Whenever that which belongs to God is opposed, even as did Paul, one in fact, is opposing God. Even though the Lord is merciful and gracious, still, this is a position that no one in their right mind wants to find themselves.

(14) "AS ALSO YE HAVE ACKNOWLEDGED US IN PART, THAT WE ARE YOUR REJOICING, EVEN AS YE ALSO ARE OURS IN THE DAY OF THE LORD JESUS."

The phrase, *"As also ye have acknowledged us in part,"* refers to the fact that some did honor

NOTES

him; he hopes that all will do so; but he can only express this as a hope, for he is aware that there are calumnies abroad respecting him, so that he cannot feel sure of his unbroken allegiance.

In fact, some, if not most, of the Corinthians had been faithful to his teaching and to himself, but some had not (Rom. 11:25; 15:15, 24; I Cor. 11:18; 12:27; 13:9).

The phrase, *"That we are your rejoicing,"* expresses the idea that some of the Corinthians, possibly even most, knew and understood how privileged they had been to have heard the Gospel from Paul. They realized that after a fashion, they owed their very souls to this man who had heard from the Lord, had obeyed, and brought the Gospel to this pagan city. Some had understanding respecting the price that had been paid by this Apostle, at least as far as was possible for Laypersons to understand. At any rate, Paul was their rejoicing and rightly so.

In effect, Paul had addressed this very thing by saying to them in his First Epistle, *"For though ye have ten thousand instructors in Christ, yet have ye not many fathers: for in Christ Jesus I have begotten you through the Gospel."*

He then said, *"Wherefore I beseech you, be ye followers of me"* (I Cor. 4:15-16).

INTERRELATIONSHIP

The phrase, *"Even as ye also are ours,"* presents an interrelation of Christians which reveals the importance of confidence in each other and steadfastness to each other.

Paul could not get along without them and they could not get along without him. There is a sense in which we do not need the approval of our Brethren for, *"If God be for us, who can be against us?"* But if the pattern of unity and the harmony of the body is to be preserved and kept intact, the confident and ultimate relation which one Believer has to another must be preserved (Laurin).

The phrase, *"In the day of the Lord Jesus,"* actually refers to the *"Judgment Seat of Christ."*

The idea is, that the evil work of those who were attempting to undermine Paul, if not before, would definitely come to light at that time of judgment, and those who had lent themselves to the petty things of gossip and talebearing which divided Brethren, would be exposed.

Laurin said, *"Let us be big and noble and Christlike so that the review of our lives by the scrutiny of Christ will cause rejoicing instead of regret at that coming Day."*

NOTES

To be sure, The Judgment Seat of Christ will reveal all, every motive, every intent, even as Jesus at that time judges all!

(15) "AND IN THIS CONFIDENCE I WAS MINDED TO COME UNTO YOU BEFORE, THAT YE MIGHT HAVE A SECOND BENEFIT;"

The phrase, *"And in this confidence I was minded to come unto you before,"* refers to the previous Verse and the conviction held by Paul, that they rejoiced in he and Timothy as Ministers of Christ. In this Paul shows, that however some of them might regard him, yet he had no doubt that the majority of the Church there would receive him kindly.

PREVIOUS PLANS

His purpose had been at first to pass through Corinth on his way to Macedonia, and to remain some time with them (I Cor. 16:5-6). This purpose he had now changed; and instead of passing through Corinth on his way to Macedonia, he had gone to Macedonia by the way of Troas.

Some of the Corinthians having, as it would seem, become acquainted with this fact, had charged him with insincerity in the promise, or fickleness in regard to his plans. Probably it had been said by some of his enemies that he had never intended to come to them.

This may seem like a small thing, and one may wonder as to why the Holy Spirit thought it necessary to be included in the Sacred Text, especially when we consider that it was merely the prattle of a few disgruntled people in the Church at Corinth. However, it is much deeper than appears on the surface.

SATAN'S INTENTIONS

Behind the charges by some at Corinth against Paul, was the idea that Paul was really not an Apostle. He will address that a little later in this Epistle. Of course, the idea is, that if Paul actually is not an Apostle then the Gospel he preached which brought these Corinthians to Christ is bogus as well. In effect, and as we shall see later, the very fact of their Salvation proclaims that Paul is exactly what he says he is. So, if Satan cannot be successful in that, he will try to make people believe that while Paul might have preached the Gospel correctly which brought about their Salvation, other than that, his Ministry is of little consequence. In other words, these false teachers at Corinth, whomever they may have been, were trying to make the Believers at Corinth believe that they had outgrown Paul. So they will accuse him now of being a lightweight, fickle, lacking in integrity, etc.

FLIMSY

We at once see how flimsy such ground there was for challenging his veracity and his reliability; how only ill-will or something worse could prefer such a charge against any man on such grounds, to say nothing about one who was so proved as was Paul among the Corinthians.

He had even informed them about his change of plans. He had not assigned reasons for the change, had not thought it necessary, he had expected enough goodwill on the part of the Corinthians to suppose that he was acting on the basis of good reasons. But no; from the report of Titus he now learned that he was still being attacked on this score.

He takes up this point first. It is so easy to settle. Yet the charge is an odious one, especially when it is brought against an Apostle. It belongs to that type which opponents love to make against Ministers: he is not a man of his word, in fact, when it suits him he lies. We now see why Paul writes as he does in Verses 12-14 regarding the testimony of his conscience, regarding his conducting himself in Holiness and sincerity and not in fleshly wisdom.

The phrase, *"That ye might have a second benefit,"* refers to Grace or favor.

A SECOND BENEFIT

"Benefit" in the Greek is *"Charis,"* which of course means *"Grace."* It refers to the benefits of Grace which Paul's Ministry would naturally bring to them on his second visit.

The phrase, *"Second benefit,"* does not have some mysterious meaning as some claim, thinking that Paul could pass out Gifts of the Spirit at random, etc. It merely referred to the second time of his being there, the first time being when he founded the Church. Inasmuch as his knowledge of the Word of God was so great, they would learn new Truths, consequently anchored more firmly in the Word of God and their Salvation, constituting a *"second benefit,"* the first being when they had gotten saved.

NOTES

It was not idle boasting on Paul's part. It was a fact.

In Truth, any God-Called Preacher who ministers to people, especially someone who is totally consecrated to the Lord, always provides a *"benefit,"* i.e., *"Grace and Favor,"* to their listeners or followers. In fact, I think one could say without fear of exaggeration, that men and women who are truly God-Called, therefore, truly Anointed, are God's greatest gifts to the human race. Those who shine the light and point out the way are of more value than one could ever begin to realize.

It is said that had it not been for the Ministry of John and Charles Wesley, that England would have suffered the same bloody revolution as experienced by France. But it was the Gospel of Jesus Christ, preached by these men and others like them, who turned England away from bloody doom, to become the mightiest influence in the world at that time.

Paul graphically speaks of this in Hebrews Chapter 11, concluding by saying of these men and women, *"Of whom the world was not worthy"* (Heb. 11:38).

(16) "AND TO PASS BY YOU INTO MACEDONIA, AND TO COME AGAIN OUT OF MACEDONIA UNTO YOU, AND OF YOU TO BE BROUGHT ON MY WAY TOWARD JUDAEA."

The phrase, *"And to pass by you into Macedonia,"* proclaims that which had been his original intention. If one looks at the map, it is obvious that this was not the direct way, but as stated, rather by Troas.

The phrase, *"And to come again out of Macedonia unto you,"* refers to a second visit to them he had hoped to make, but with neither plan coming to fruition, at least at this time. So, he had planned to visit them on the way to Macedonia, and then when that mission was complete to come by them a second time. All of this would have taken several months. In fact, he had originally planned to spend the winter with them (I Cor. 16:6).

The plan to go by Sea from Ephesus to Corinth on the way to Macedonia, was given up by the time I Corinthians was written. It seems that this original plan had been made known to the Corinthians, in all probability in a letter which preceded I Corinthians, a letter which is lost but is mentioned by Paul in I Corinthians 5:9. The new plan, regarding which I Corinthians Chapter 16 informed the Corinthians, was in process of execution as Paul writes II Corinthians.

The phrase, *"And of you to be brought on my way toward Judaea,"* presents that which he had previously planned to do, but with plans now altered.

It seems that the new plan is not now to divide his visit at Corinth as previously intended, but now to make just one stay in that city. I Corinthians 16:6 presents the new plan.

His object in going to Judaea was to convey the collection for those in need in Jerusalem, which he had been in so much pains to collect throughout the Churches of the Gentiles.

(17) "WHEN I THEREFORE WAS THUS MINDED, DID I USE LIGHTNESS? OR THE THINGS THAT I PURPOSE, DO I PURPOSE ACCORDING TO THE FLESH, THAT WITH ME THERE SHOULD BE YEA YEA, AND NAY NAY?"

The question, *"When I therefore was thus minded, did I use lightness?"*, refers to him changing his mind concerning the proposed visit to Corinth, at least concerning the date he would go, but that it was not done lightly. The insinuation is that he earnestly sought the Lord about the matter, and felt moved upon by the Holy Spirit to change his plans. Consequently, it was not fickleness on his part, as some were claiming at Corinth.

The beginning of the question, *"Or the things that I purpose, do I purpose according to the flesh . . .?"*, once again refutes another charge that he was not led by the Spirit, but rather by his own selfish desires, i.e., *"the flesh."* Probably no man ever lived who formed his plans of life less for the gratification of the flesh than Paul.

The conclusion of the question, *"That with me there should be yea yea, and nay nay?"*, addresses itself to another accusation against the Apostle, that his *"yes"* meant nothing, and neither did his *"no!"*

The idea is, according to his detractors, that he was inconsistent, readily making promises and then breaking them, which Paul of course, denies. It is even thought that some were using this as a title or insult for him in public, *"old yea yea, and nay nay!"* At any rate he is answering their insults.

NOTES

Who would be so foolish as to insult the great Apostle in this fashion?

This one thing is certain, the Holy Spirit was so indignant over this situation, that he recorded it that the entire world and for all time may be aware of this fickleness, but not on the part of Paul, but rather his detractors.

(18) "BUT AS GOD IS TRUE, OUR WORD TOWARD YOU WAS NOT YEA AND NAY."

The phrase, *"But as God is true,"* presents the Apostle appealing to the highest order. He, in effect, is saying that as God does not speak out of both sides of His mouth at the same time, neither did he. Now Paul's irony begins to surface. It is as if he were saying, *"Would it not be the height of incongruity for a reliable God to use an unreliable vessel through which to save you Corinthians?"* Paul did not claim to be perfect, but he did claim that the Faithfulness of God was a part of his demeanor, which was the very opposite of what these opponents were saying (Rossier).

The phrase, *"Our word toward you was not yea and nay,"* merely refutes the charge without giving any personal explanation. In fact, even as we shall see, he would place the entire scenario on an entirely higher level than his own personal feelings.

The idea is, *"God is faithful and true."* He never deceives; never promises that which He does not perform. So true is it, that the idea of the faithfulness of God is the argument which Paul urges why he felt himself bound to be faithful also. That faithful God he regarded as a witness, and to that God he could appeal on this occasion.

Even though the particular subject under discussion concerned the promise which he had made to visit them, still, he seems to make his affirmation general, respecting everything he did, whether preaching, or communication, whether orally or in writing. In all of this there was not any inconsistency or changeableness. In essence he is saying that it was not his character to be fickle, unsettled, or vacillating.

If there is anything in the world that is true, this certainly is. Paul was one of the most steadfast, straightforward individuals who ever lived. In fact, his detractors had actually chosen his strongest point in order to criticize him, which was not wise to say the least, on their part. Actually, that's the reason he answers in the manner in which he did. To charge Paul with an unstable attitude and lifestyle, is somewhat like saying that water is not wet.

(19) "FOR THE SON OF GOD, JESUS CHRIST, WHO WAS PREACHED AMONG YOU BY US, EVEN BY ME AND SILVANUS AND TIMOTHEUS, WAS NOT YEA AND NAY, BUT IN HIM WAS YEA."

The phrase, *"For the Son of God, Jesus Christ, who was preached among you by us,"* places the argument over Paul's integrity squarely on the Gospel he preached. The idea is this:

THE WORD OF GOD THAT IS PREACHED IS THE CRITERIA

The Holy Spirit had the Apostle to deal with this question in this manner. If a person truly preaches the Gospel, which will result in people being saved, lives being changed, Believers being Baptized with the Holy Spirit, sick bodies healed and people delivered, at the same time his character and trustworthiness will follow suit. A bad character does not preach a true Gospel. That doesn't mean the person is perfect, for such does not exist; however, it does mean that God will not anoint an individual to preach such a Message, which results in life changing effects, if that person is not living for God as one should. The preaching of the *"Son of God, Jesus Christ,"* as the Redeemer of lost mankind, with signs following, is the criteria. Unfortunately, the greatest criteria of all, this absolute proof, is seldom given any credence at all, but rather the fanciful tales of men!

To bring it down to plain street talk, if a man or woman is preaching the True Gospel of Jesus Christ, and it is anointed by the Power of God which results in life changing experiences, that is the proof of the character of the Preacher. The Lord does not anoint crooks, thieves, the immoral, or the ungodly. Neither is it true that the Lord merely anoints His Word irrespective as to who is preaching it. If that is the case, why aren't all Preachers Anointed?

The Holy Spirit is very particular, He does not easily lay His hand of approval or help on just anyone.

The phrase, *"Even by me and Silvanus* (Silas) *and Timotheus* (Timothy), *was not yea and nay,"* means that what they preached was not a vacillating Gospel. In other words, it was an unchanging Gospel, which proved itself in the lives of these very Corinthians. It brought them out of sin and darkness.

These readers knew God's Son, Jesus Christ, Him *"Who was preached among them."* Because of their soul's contact with Him they knew that He was never yea and nay but had always been and thus now is yea only. Nothing in Him or in His Word was ever or is now questionable.

PAUL'S ANSWER

We preached Him, says Paul, preached Him *"among you,"* and you believed, trusted Him as what He is, absolute and blessed yea. We were the instruments, Paul says, and you received our Message. He even specifies: *"By means of me and Silas and Timothy."*

The point is that the Corinthians had trusted these instruments of God, had trusted their Message and their character, for the two went together. No mighty yea-Christ could have been transmitted by yea-and-nay heralds.

A great Church was built at Corinth, with the Great Yea and Amen put into the hearts of the Corinthians by these instruments of God. Does that say anything about these instruments, the God Who employed them, the Son of God, Jesus Christ, for Whom they were employed?

Does the Salvation of great numbers of souls, with great numbers of lives being wondrously and gloriously changed, say anything about the instrument who delivers that Message, or the Son of God, Jesus Christ, Who employs the instrument, i.e., the Preacher?

It certainly should say something. In fact, it speaks volumes!

The phrase, *"But in Him was yea,"* carries the idea of One Who changes not (I Sam. 15:29; Mal. 3:6).

THE FAITHFULNESS OF GOD

First of all, God has kept His Promise about His Son, the Lord Jesus Christ. Down through the centuries, multitudes have depended on the Faithfulness of God to send the Messiah (Gen. 3:15). In fact, if Christ had not come, the entire Old Testament Revelation would have proven false. But He did come, and He gave Himself for the sins of mankind (I Jn. 4:10).

NOTES

Paul and his Evangelistic Team were not proclaiming a hoax; they were proclaiming with certainty that Jesus Christ is the great *"Yes."* That means He does not say *"Yes"* to one person and *"No"* to another at least regarding the same Promise, nor does He cast out anyone who comes to Him in humble repentance (Jn. 6:35-37).

Considering such Faithfulness, God will not use anyone who does not fit the same mode, as certainly did Paul and his Associates, as well as untold others who have followed down through the centuries (Rossier).

(20) "FOR ALL THE PROMISES OF GOD IN HIM ARE YEA, AND IN HIM AMEN, UNTO THE GLORY OF GOD BY US."

The phrase, *"For all the Promises of God in Him are yea,"* means that not one Promise of God is *"no"* to the one who will believe and meet His conditions.

IN JESUS

All the Promises of God which fill the Old Testament are wrapped up in Jesus. In other words, the Tabernacle and Temple were both types of Jesus. As well, all of the Sacred Vessels were types of Christ.

The Feast Days proclaimed what His work would be, and the Sabbath represented His Salvation, which would bring *"rest."*

The Sacrifices, which were offered in the hundreds of millions down through the centuries, were all types of His vicarious, Atoning Work at Calvary. So, truly, all the Promises of God are *"in Him."*

Not only are they *"in Him,"* but, as well, they have everyone come to pass, at least the Promises which were due. Regarding past performance, one can guarantee oneself of future performance.

TRUTH

"Truth" is thus Christ's very Name (Jn. 14:6).

All the Promises center *"in Him"* as their *"yea"*; wherefore they are fulfilled *"through Him"* as their *"Amen." "Amen"* is the transliterated Hebrew word for *"truth."*

Christianity is not just a religious system replete with honorable ideas and ethics. It centers around a Person, Jesus Christ, the One Who faithfully fulfilled the Will of God (Heb. 10:7).

NOTES

The phrase, *"And in Him Amen,"* means, that's the way it is, and it will not change. In other words, you can take it to the Bank.

In Revelation 3:14, the Lord Jesus is called the *"Amen."* As stated, the word means true, faithful, certain; and the expression here means that all the Promises which are made to men through the Redeemer shall be certainly fulfilled. They are Promises which are confirmed and established, and which shall by no means fail.

The phrase, *"Unto the Glory of God by us,"* in effect says that the fulfillment of all the Promises which God has made to His people shall result in His Glory and Praise as a God Who is Trustworthy.

The fact that He has made such Promises is an act that tends to His Own Glory — since it was of His Mere Grace that they were made; and the fulfillment of these Promises in and through the Church, shall also tend to produce elevated views of His fidelity and goodness (Barnes).

THE PROMISES OF GOD

A promise is a word that goes forth into unfilled time. It reaches ahead of its speaker and its recipient, to mark an appointment between them and the future.

A promise may be an assurance of continuing or future action on behalf of someone: *"I will be with you," "They that mourn shall be comforted," "If we confess our sins, God will forgive us our sins."*

It may be a solemn agreement of lasting, mutual (if unequal) relationship: as in the Covenants. It may be the announcement of a future event:

"When you have brought the people from Egypt, you will serve God on this mountain." The study of Biblical Promises must, therefore, take in far more than the actual occurrences of the word. In fact, an oath often accompanied the Word of Promise (Ex. 6:8; Deut. 9:5; Heb. 6:13).

GOD'S WORD DOES NOT RETURN VOID

That what He has spoken with His Mouth He can and will perform with His Hand is the Biblical signed manual of God, for His Word does not return void. Unlike men and heathen gods, He knows and commands the future (I Kings 8:15, 24; Isa. 41:4, 26; 43:12, 19; Rom. 4:21).

Through the Historical Books of the Bible, a pattern of Divine Promise and historical fulfillment is traced, expressive of this Truth.

JESUS CHRIST

The point of convergence of the Old Testament Promises (to Abraham, Moses, David, and the Fathers through the Prophets) as stated, is Jesus Christ. All the Promises of God are confirmed in Him, and through Him affirmed by the Church in the *"Amen"* of its worship (II Cor. 1:20).

The Old Testament quotations and illusions in the Gospel narratives indicate the fulfillment. God has kept His Word. The Promised Word has become flesh. The New Covenant has been inaugurated — upon the *"Better Promises"* prophesied by Jeremiah (Jer. Chpt. 31; Heb. 8:6-13). Jesus is its guarantee (Heb. 7:22), and the Holy Spirit of Promise its first installment (Eph. 1:13-14).

THE CHURCH

Awaiting the Promise of Christ's coming again and of the new heavens and a new earth (II Pet. 3:4, 9, 13), the Church sets forth on her Missionary task with the assurance of His Presence (Mat. 28:20) and with the news that *"the Promise of the Father"* — the Holy Spirit (after Joel 2:28) — is given to Jew and Pagan in Jesus Christ, fulfilling the Promise to Abraham of universal blessing through his posterity.

The Promise is correlated to Faith and open to all who, by imitating Abraham's Faith, become *"Children of the Promise"* (Rom. 4:9; Gal. Chpt. 3).

(Bibliography: G. K. Chesterson, *"A Defense of Rash Vows"*; J. Bright, *"Covenant and Promise"*; J. Jeremias, *"Jesus' Promise to The Nations."*)

What a Mighty God we serve!

GOD

Inasmuch as we are looking at the Promises of God, on which I have penned all my hopes, past, present, and future, along with untold millions of others, perhaps this would be a good time to investigate a little further this One we have come to know, through His Son, and our Saviour, the Lord Jesus Christ.

God is and He may be known. These two affirmations form the foundation and inspiration of all that is Christian.

NOTES

The first is an affirmation of Faith, the second of experience. Since the existence of God is not subject to Scientific proof, although I personally think it can definitely be proved from a scientific basis, it must of necessity, be a postulate of Faith; and since God transcends all His Creation, He can be known only in His Self-Revelation.

Biblical Christianity, i.e., Salvation in Christ, is distinctive in that it claims that God can be known as a Personal God only in His Self-Revelation in the Scriptures. The Bible is written not to prove that God is, but to reveal Him in His activities. For that reason, the Biblical Revelation of God is, in its nature, progressive, reaching its fullness in Jesus Christ His Son.

In the light of His Self-Revelation in the Scriptures, there are several affirmations that can be made about God.

HIS BEING

In His Being, God is Self-existing. While His creation is dependent on Him, He is utterly independent of the creation. He not only has life, but He is life to His universe, and has the Source of that life within Himself.

Very early in Biblical History this mystery of God's Being was revealed to Moses when, in the wilderness of Horeb, He met with God as fire in a bush (Ex. 3:2).

The distinctive thing about that phenomenon was that *"the bush was burning, yet it was not consumed."* To Moses this must have meant that the fire was independent of its environment: it was self-fed. Such is God in His Essential Being: He is utterly independent of every environment in which He wills to make Himself known.

This quality of God's Being probably finds expression in His Personal Name *"Yahweh,"* and in His Self-affirmation; *"I am Who I am"* that is, *"I am the One Who has Being within Himself"* (Ex. 3:14).

THE FOUNTAINHEAD OF ALL THERE IS

This perception was implied in Isaiah's Vision of God: *"The Lord is the Everlasting God, the Creator of the ends of the earth. He does not faint or grow weary . . . He gives power to the faint, and to Him Who has no might He increases strength"* (Isa. 40:28-29). He is the Giver, and all His creatures are receivers.

Christ gave this mystery its clearest expression when He said, *"For as the Father has life in Himself, so He has granted the Son also to have life in Himself"* (Jn. 5:26).

This makes independence of life a distinctive quality of Deity. Throughout the whole of Scripture God is revealed as the Fountainhead of all there is, animate and inanimate, the Creator and Life-Giver, Who Alone has life within Himself.

HIS NATURE

In His Nature God is Pure Spirit. Very early in His self-disclosure as the Author of the created universe, God is represented as the Spirit Who brought light out of darkness, and order out of chaos (Gen. 1:2-3).

Christ made this disclosure of God as the Object of our Worship to the woman of Samaria: *"God is a Spirit, and those who worship Him must worship Him in spirit and in truth"* (Jn. 4:24). Between these two affirmations there are frequent references to the Nature of God as Pure Spirit and as Divine Spirit. He is called the *"Father of Spirits"* (Heb. 12:9), and the combination *"the Spirit of the Living God"* is frequently used.

PURE SPIRIT

In this respect we must distinguish between God and His creatures that are spiritual. When we say that God is Pure Spirit, it is to emphasize that He is not part spirit and part body as man is. He is simple Spirit and for that reason He has no physical presence.

When the Bible speaks of God as having eyes, ears, hands and feet, it is an attempt to convey to us the senses that these physical parts convey, for if we do not speak of God in physical terms we could not speak of Him at all. This, of course, does not imply any imperfection in God.

Spirit is not a limited or restricted form of existence, it is the perfect unit of Being. In fact, it may not be an improper exegesis of Scripture, or do violence in any way to the Person of God, to say that God has a Spirit Body. The Word of God certainly lends credence to such, and that alone matters. We must be careful that we do not explain away God as One Who cannot be understood, etc., as I am concerned some actually do.

NOTES

And yet, when we say that God is infinite spirit, we pass completely out of the reach of our experience. We as humans are limited as to time and place, as to knowledge and power. God is essentially unlimited, and every element of His Nature is unlimited. His infinity as to time we call His *"Eternity,"* as to space His *"Omni-presence,"* as to knowledge His *"Omniscience,"* as to power His *"Omnipotence."*

TRANSCENDENT

His infinity likewise means that God is transcendent over His universe, which means to be beyond the limits of all possible experience and knowledge. It emphasizes His detachment as Self-existing Spirit from all His creatures. He is not shut in by what we call nature, but infinitely exalted above it.

Even those Passages of Scripture which stress His local and temporal manifestation lay emphasis also on His Exaltation and Omnipotence as a Being external to the world, its Sovereign Creator and Judge (Isa. 40:12-17).

At the same time God's infinity implies His *"Immanence."* By this we mean His all-pervading Presence and Power within His creation. He does not stand apart from the world, a mere spectator of the work of His Hands. He pervades and fills everything, organic and inorganic, acting from within outwards, from the center of every atom, and from the innermost springs of thought and light and feeling, a continuous sequence of cause and effect.

IN HIM WE LIVE AND MOVE AND HAVE OUR BEING

In such Passages as Isaiah Chapter 57 and Acts Chapter 17 we have an expression of both God's Transcendence and His Immanence. In the first of these Passages His Transcendence finds expression as *"the High and Lofty One Who inhabits eternity, Whose Name is Holy,"* and His Immanence as the One Who dwells *"with Him also Who is of a contrite and humble spirit"* (Isa. 57:15).

In the second Passage, Paul, in addressing the men of Athens, affirmed of the Transcendent God that *"the God Who made the world and everything in it, being Lord of heaven and earth, does not live in shrines made by man, nor is He served by human hands, as though He needed anything, since He Himself gives to all men life and breath and everything,"* and then affirms His Immanence as the One Who *"is not far from each one of us,"* for *"in Him we live and move and have our being"* (Acts 17:24, 28).

HIS CHARACTER

God is personal. When we say this we assert that God is rational, Self-conscious and Self-determining, an intelligent Moral Agent. As Supreme Mind, He is the Source of all rationality in the universe. Since God's rational creatures possess independent character, God must be in possession of character that is Divine both in its transcendence (over all) and immanence (Presence and Power everywhere).

The Old Testament reveals a personal God, both in terms of His Own Self-disclosure and of His people's relations with Him, and the New Testament clearly shows that Christ spoke to God in terms that were meaningful only in Person to Person relationship. For that reason, we can predicate certain mental and moral qualities of God, such as we do of human character.

Attempts have been made to classify the Divine attributes under such headings as Mental and Moral, or Communicable and Incommunicable, or Related and Unrelated. Scripture would seem to give no support to any of these classifications, and in any case God is infinitely greater than the sum of all His attributes.

HIS NAMES

God's Names are to us the designation of His attributes, and it is significant that God's Names are given in the context of His people's needs. It would seem, therefore, more true to the Biblical Revelation to treat each attribute as a manifestation of God in the human situation that called it forth, compassion in the presence of misery, long-suffering in the presence of ill-treatment, Grace in the presence of guilt, Mercy in the presence of penitence, suggesting that the attributes of God designate a relation into which He enters to those who feel their need of Him.

That bears with it the undoubted Truth that God, in the full plenitude of His Nature, is in each of His attributes, so that there is never more of one attribute than of another, never more love than justice, or more Mercy than Righteousness. If there is one attribute of God that can be recognized as all-comprehensive and all-pervading, it is His Holiness, which must be predicated of all His attributes, Holy Love, Holy Compassion, Holy Wisdom.

NOTES

HIS WILL

God is Sovereign. That means that He makes His Own plans and carries them out in His Own time and way. That is simply an expression of His Supreme intelligence, power, and wisdom. It means that God's Will is not arbitrary, but acts in complete harmony with His character. It is the forth-putting one might say of His power and goodness, and is thus the final goal of all existence.

DECREE AND PRESCRIBE

There is, however, a distinction between God's Will which prescribes what we shall do, and His Will which determines what He will do. To define this, we might say that God has a *"Decretive Will"* (that which He Decrees) which will always come to pass, and a *"Preceptive Will"* (that which He Prescribes), which He enjoins upon His creatures the duties that belong to them. The *"Decretive Will"* of God is thus always accomplished, while His *"Preceptive Will"* is most of the time disobeyed.

PERMISSIVE WILL?

When we conceive of the Sovereign sway of the Divine Will as the final ground of all that happens, either actively bringing it to pass, or passively permitting it to come to pass, we recognize the distinction between the active Will of God and His Permissive Will. Thus, the entrance of sin into the world must be attributed to the Permissive Will of God, since sin is a contradiction of His Holiness and Goodness.

There is thus a realm in which God's Will to act is dominant and a realm in which man's liberty is given permission to act. The Bible presents both in operation. The note which rings through the Old Testament is that struck by Nebuchadnezzar of old: *"He does according to His Will in the host of heaven and among the inhabitants of the earth; and none can stay His Hand or say to Him, 'What doest Thou?'"* (Dan. 4:35).

In the New Testament, we come across an impressive example of the Divine Will resisted by human unbelief, when Christ uttered His agonizing cry over Jerusalem: *"How often would I have gathered your children together*

NOTES

as a hen gathers her brood under her wings, and you would not!" (Mat. 23:37). Nevertheless, the sovereignty of God ensures that all will be overruled ultimately to serve His Eternal Purpose, and that ultimately Christ's petition: *"Thy Will be done on earth as it is in heaven"* shall be answered.

THERE IS NO SUCH THING AS A PERMISSIVE WILL FOR THE BELIEVER

While God definitely has a permissive will for the world, even as we have already established, with sin being permitted as an example.

Another example is the discussion that Jesus had with the Pharisees concerning divorce.

He said to them, *"What therefore God hath joined together, let not man put asunder."*

They then brought up to Him that Moses allowed divorce.

"He saith unto them, Moses because of the hardness of your heart suffered you to put away your wives: but from the beginning it was not so" (Mat. 19:6-8).

In other words, divorce was not the perfect will of God as should be obvious, but because of sin and hardness of heart, the Lord did permit such, even as he does now under certain circumstances. Nevertheless, the Believer is to want and desire only the perfect Will of God. To say it another way, there is no such thing as a permissive Will of God for the Believer.

Paul addressed this by saying, *"That ye may prove what is that good, and acceptable, and perfect, Will of God"* (Rom. 12:2).

Functioning under the idea that the Believer is desiring to be led by the Spirit of God, one must conclude that the Spirit of God will direct one in no other manner except the *"Perfect Will of God."*

So, while there is a permissive will for the overall Plan of God, and for the obvious reasons, there is no such thing for the Believer.

It is true that we are not able to reconcile God's Sovereignty (all His Ways) and man's responsibility, because we do not understand the nature of Divine Knowledge and comprehension of all the Laws of God that govern human conduct.

The Bible throughout teaches us that all life is lived in the sustaining Will of God *"in Whom we live and move and have our being,"* and that as a bird is free in the air, and a fish in the sea, so man has his true freedom in the Will of God Who created him for Himself. In fact, man will never find true freedom outside of the perfect Will of God.

HIS SUBSISTENCE

In His essential life, God is a fellowship. This is perhaps the supreme revelation of God given in the Scriptures. By that we mean that it is that God's Life is eternally within Himself a fellowship of three equal and distinct Persons; Father, Son, and Holy Spirit, and that in His relationship to His moral creation God was extending to them (extending to man) the fellowship that was essentially His Own.

That might perhaps be read into the Divine dictum that expressed the deliberate Will to create man: *"Let Us make man in Our Image, after Our Likeness,"* that it was an expression of the Will of God not only to reveal Himself as a fellowship, but to make that life of fellowship open to the moral creatures made in His Image and so fitted to enjoy it.

While it is true that man through the Fall lost his fitness to enjoy that holy fellowship, it is also true that God willed to make it possible to have it restored to him. It has been observed, indeed, that this was probably the grand end of Redemption, the Revelation of God in Three Persons acting for our Restoration, in electing love that claimed us, in redeeming love that emancipated us, and in regenerating love that created us for His fellowship.

Oh dear reader, I sense the Presence of God even as I dictate these words. To think that One so lofty, so great, so wonderful as God, would condescend to poor fallen man, is beyond our comprehension.

A PERSONAL QUESTION

Many years ago, as a boy of about eight or nine years of age, I asked my Sunday School teacher as to why God actually made man in the first place? I don't recall her answer, only that it did not satisfy my question.

After beginning to preach the Gospel, I ultimately learned that it was God's love that created man, and at the same time it was God's love which would not allow fallen man to stay in this condition without an opportunity of Redemption.

Many would ask the question as to why God did not do away with Adam and Eve after the Fall, and start over. The answer is twofold:

1. Had He done that, He would have had the same difficulty with the next pair He created.

2. Above all, love would not allow Him to throw that creation aside, it must be redeemed.

HIS FATHERHOOD

Since God is a Person, He can enter into personal relationships, and the closest and tenderest is that of Father. It was Christ's most common designation for God, and in theology it is reserved specially for the First Person of the Trinity. There are four types of relationship in which the word Father is applied to God in Scripture.

CREATIONAL FATHERHOOD

The fundamental relation of God to man whom He made in His Own Image finds its most full and fitting illustration in the natural relationship which involves the gift of life. The Prophet Malachi, in calling his people to faithfulness to God and to consideration of one another, asks: *"Have we not all one Father? Has not one God created us?"* (Mal. 2:10).

Isaiah, in a plea to God not to forsake His people, cries: *"Yet, Oh Lord, Thou art our Father; we are the clay, and Thou art our potter; we are all the work of Thy Hand"* (Isa. 64:8).

But it is more particularly for man's spiritual nature that this relationship is claimed. In the Book of Hebrews, God is called *"the Father of spirits"* (Heb. 12:9), and in the Book of Numbers *"the God of the spirits of all flesh"* (Num. 16:22).

Paul, when he preached from Mars Hill, used this argument to drive home the irrationality of rational man worshipping idols of wood and stone, quoting the Poet Aratus (*"For we are indeed His offspring"*) to indicate that man is a creature of God.

The creaturehood of man is thus the counterpart of the general Fatherhood of God. Without the Creator — Father — there would be no race of man, no family of mankind.

However, the Fatherhood of God is to be used only in His creational capacity, and never of relationship. It is only those who are truly born again who can claim God as their Father, even as we shall see in the fourth relationship.

THEOCRATIC FATHERHOOD

This is God's relationship to His Covenant-people, Israel. In this, since it is a collective relationship that is indicated, rather than a personal one, Israel as a Covenant-people was the Child of God, and she was challenged to recognize and respond to this filial relationship: *"If then I am a Father, where is My honor?"* (Mal. 1:6).

But since the Covenant relationship was redemptive in its spiritual significance, this may be regarded as a foreshadowing of the New Testament Revelation of the Divine Fatherhood.

However, one might say there were always two Israel's, even as there are presently two Churches. Even though God had a Covenant relationship with the entirety of Israel, still, it was only those who kept that Covenant who truly belonged to God. The others were lost the same as the Pagans.

However, the keeping of the Covenant was not done through performance, as it could not be done through performance. That always failed, even with the Godliest, as fail it must. Consequently, the keeping of the Covenant was judged by God as by the root of a *"broken and contrite spirit"* (Ps. 51:17).

In effect, all were saved in Old Testament times by Faith, even as we are presently (Rom. Chpt. 4).

GENERATIVE FATHERHOOD

This belongs exclusively to the Second Person of the Trinity, designated *"the Son of God,"* and *"the Only Begotten Son."* It is, therefore, unique, not to be applied to any mere creature.

Christ, while on earth, spoke most frequently of this relationship which was peculiarly His. God was His Father by eternal generation, expressive of an essential and timeless relationship that transcends our comprehension. However, the Fatherhood of God as it pertains to Jesus, Who is God as well, pertains exclusively to the Incarnation, God becoming man, all for Redemptive purposes.

It is significant that Jesus in His teaching the Twelve, never used the term *"Our Father"* as embracing Himself and them. In the Resurrection Message through Mary, He indicated two distinct relationships: *"My Father and your Father"* (Jn. 20:17), but the two are so linked together that the one becomes the ground of the other. His Sonship, though on a level altogether unique, was the basis of their (Believers) sonship as well.

NOTES

ADOPTIVE FATHERHOOD

This is the redeeming relationship that belongs to all Believers, and in the context of Redemption it is viewed from two aspects, that of our standing in Christ and that of the regenerating work of the Holy Spirit in us.

This relationship to God is basic to all Believers, as Paul reminds the Galatian Believers: *"For in Christ Jesus you are all sons of God through Faith"* (Gal. 3:26). In this living union with Christ, we are adopted into the family of God, and we become subjects of the regenerative work of the Spirit that bestows upon us the nature of children: one is the objective aspect, the other the subjective.

Objective pertains to the legal work done by God upon the evidence of Faith on the part of the Believer which justifies the sinner. Subjective pertains to the experience that one receives in the Lord, in other words a *"know so Salvation."*

Because of our new standing (Justification) and relationship (Adoption) to God the Father in Christ, we become partakers of the Divine Nature and are born into the Family of God. John made this clear in the opening Chapter of his Gospel: *"To all who received Him, who believed in His Name, He gave power* (authority) *to become Children of God; who were born, not of blood nor of the will of the flesh nor of the will of man, but of God"* (Jn. 1:12-13).

And so we are granted all the privileges that belong to that filial relationship: *"if children, then heirs"* is the sequence (Rom. 8:17).

AS STATED, ONLY WITH BELIEVERS

It is clear that Christ's teaching on the Fatherhood of God restricts the relationship to His believing people only. In no instance is He reported as assuming this relationship to exist between God and unbelievers.

Not only does He not give a hint of a redeeming Fatherhood of God towards all men, but he said pointedly to the Jews: *"You are of your father the Devil"* (Jn. 8:44).

REVERENCE AND HUMILITY

While it is under this relationship of Father that the New Testament brings out the tenderest aspects of God's character, His Love, His Faithfulness, His Watchful Care, it also brings out the responsibility of our having to show God the reverence, the trust, and the loving obedience that children owe to a Father. Christ has taught us to pray not only *"Our Father,"* but *"Our Father Who art in heaven,"* thus inculcating reverence and humility.

(Bibliography: T. J. Crawford, *"The Fatherhood of God"*; J. Orr, *"The Christian View of God and the World"*; A. S. Pringle, *"The Idea of God"*; J. I. Packer, *"Knowing God."*)

(21) "NOW HE WHICH STABLISHETH US WITH YOU IN CHRIST, AND HATH ANOINTED US, IS GOD;"

The phrase, *"Now He which stablisheth us with you in Christ,"* refers to the reliability of God in keeping and preserving His children who place their trust in Him. He is capable of keeping the people He saves.

"Stablisheth" in the Greek is *"bebaioo,"* and means *"to confirm, to stabilitate, make firm, make steadfast."* As well, it is a continuous action, meaning that God is in the process of making us dependable servants in Christ which, of course, is the Sanctification process.

The phrase, *"And hath anointed us, is God,"* presents the Father as both establishing and anointing us in Christ. In other words, we have these benefits because of what Christ did at Calvary and the Resurrection.

THE ANOINTING

The word Paul (and John, in I Jn. 2:20) used is related to *"Christ"* (*"Anointed One"* — Christos).

The Kings, Priests, and Prophets of Old Testament times were Anointed with oil as an external symbol of the fact that the Holy Spirit would enable them to fulfill the responsibilities of their Offices. Hence, it was said of David after he was Anointed by Samuel, *"And the Spirit of the Lord came upon David from that day forward"* (I Sam. 16:13).

Paul claimed this Anointing, and so can every other servant of God. It does not come because we deserve it, but it is available because God is true to His Word (Rossier).

TWO TYPES OF ANOINTING

There are two Greek words, both meaning *"to Anoint,"* and as used in the New Testament, referring to different kinds of Anointing, and for different purposes.

These are translated by the one English word *"Anoint."* In order to arrive at a full-orbed

NOTES

accurate interpretation of the passages in which the word *"Anoint"* occurs, it is necessary to know what Greek word lies back of the English translation.

THE FIRST ANOINTING SPEAKS OF OIL

The Greek word is *"aleipho."*

As an example, it was used in Greek culture of applying grease to the yoke-band, the purpose of which was to keep it from chafing the ox. It also refers to the practice, common in the Orient, of giving the body an olive oil massage. Olive-oil was used in the East for medicinal and remedial purposes in the case of illness. It provided an excellent rubdown for the tired athlete after exercise. It prevented skin dryness in the hot dry climate of the Orient.

NEW TESTAMENT EXAMPLES

We see this use of the word *"aleipho"* in Mark 6:13 and James 5:14, where the word is used of the application of oil, one might say for medicinal purposes. The idea is that the sick were Anointed with oil, which is a type of the Holy Spirit, and His Restorative and Healing Powers.

The word is also used of the application of Ointment. Such was a type of oil which was highly scented.

We can better understand the words of our Lord to the discourteous Pharisee (Lk. 7:46), *"My head with oil thou didst not Anoint: but this woman hath Anointed My Feet with Ointment."*

The Hebrew equivalent of this Greek word *"aleipho"* is used in Ruth 3:3; II Samuel 12:20; 14:2; Daniel 10:3; Micah 6:15. Actually, *"aleipho"* is the only word used for Anointing with oil in the New Testament, there being no exceptions to this.

ANOINTING AS IT APPLIES TO THE HOLY SPIRIT

The other Greek word used in the New Testament for Anointing is *"Chrio."* It is never used in connection with oil as the former, but uniformly of the Anointing with the Holy Spirit.

"Chrio" is used in *"The Spirit of the Lord is upon Me, for He hath Anointed Me"* (Lk. 4:18), which is a quotation from Isaiah 61:1, where the same Hebrew equivalent is used. It is also used in Acts 4:27; 10:38, of the Anointing of our Lord by the Holy Spirit.

NOTES

In II Corinthians 1:21, even as we are now studying, the word is used in connection with the Anointing of the Believer by the Spirit.

Hebrews 1:9 presents a seeming deviation of the rule that *"Chrio"* is never used in the New Testament in connection with the anointing with oil. We have *"God hath Anointed Thee* (the Lord Jesus) *with the oil of gladness,"* with *"Chrio"* being used.

How true the inspired writer was to the genius of the two words as they are used in the New Testament, for the word *"oil"* here does not refer to literal oil, but is symbolic of the Holy Spirit. In I John 2:20, 27, *"Unction"* and *"Anointing"* are from the noun form that comes from *"Chrio,"* and referred to the Anointing of the Believer by the Holy Spirit.

THE OLD TESTAMENT TYPES

The Hebrew equivalent of *"Chrio"* is used in the Old Testament, to which we have already alluded, of the Anointing of the Priests and Kings at their induction into office. The Anointing is with oil, but this oil is symbolic of the Anointing by the Spirit, which is not for medicinal purposes.

The Priest was Anointed once only, at the time of his induction into the Priest's Office, the Anointing being symbolic of a reality, the Anointing by the Holy Spirit Who by His Presence with him, equipped the Priest for his service.

Believers in this Christian era are Priests in the New Testament sense. One could say they are Anointed by the Holy Spirit once and once only at the moment they are saved. This Anointing is the coming of the Spirit to take up his permanent residence in their hearts, thus providing the potential equipment for their service as Priests.

However, the full potential for that Anointing cannot at all be realized until the Believer is baptized with the Holy Spirit, which is always according to Acts 2:4, the evidence being *"speaking with other tongues as the Spirit of God gives the utterance."* Hence, Jesus *"commanding them that they should . . . wait for the Promise of the Father"* (Acts 1:4).

The Baptism with the Holy Spirit, which can come only to Believers, is for the purpose of *"power,"* through which the Anointing by the Holy Spirit serves its full purpose, that is if given proper latitude by the Believer (Acts 1:8).

This was something for which the Old Testament Economy had no comparison, simply because the Holy Spirit in this capacity had not yet been given (Jn. 7:39), hence, Jesus saying, *"For He* (the Holy Spirit) *dwelleth with you* (Old Testament Times), *and shall be in you* (after the Day of Pentecost)."

MANY PURPOSES

The Anointing by the Holy Spirit serves many purposes and is efficient in these purposes only as the Believer allows Him proper latitude. In fact, it is all potential, meaning that it can be, but it is not necessarily that it will be. As stated, the *"Anointing"* is by and large predicated on the consecration of the Believer, hence, Paul saying, *"Be filled* (be being filled) *with the Spirit"* (Eph. 5:18). The following may provide some help:

1. All Believers are Anointed by the Holy Spirit at Salvation, even as the Kings and Priests of Old Testament Times.
2. The Anointing by the Holy Spirit comes into full flower as the Believer is Baptized with the Holy Spirit with the evidence of speaking with other tongues (Acts 2:4).
3. The Anointing functions in the *"Power"* of the Holy Spirit, as it is made evident in the Believer's life.
4. It's potential is reached according to the fullness of the Spirit within our lives, i.e. being controlled by the Holy Spirit (Eph. 5:18).
5. The Holy Spirit Anoints the Believer to recognize false doctrine and correct doctrine, i.e. *"the same Anointing teacheth you of all things, and is Truth, and is no lie, and even as it (Anointing) hath taught you, ye shall abide in Him"* (I Jn. 2:27). So, if Believers fall for false doctrine it is because they are not giving the Holy Spirit latitude in their lives respecting His Anointing in this capacity. In other words, self-will is predominant instead of the Will of God, in which alone the Holy Spirit can function (Rom. 8:27).

JESUS AND THE HOLY SPIRIT

Inasmuch as Jesus is the Baptizer with the Holy Spirit (Mat. 3:11), and that the Anointing is His as our Representative Man (Lk. 4:18-19), I think one can say that the more that Jesus is resident in one's heart (has total latitude), the more the Holy Spirit can work, and the more the Holy Spirit works, the more that Jesus is glorified in one's life (Jn. 16:13-15). So, the more prominent that Jesus is in one's life, the more Anointing there is for service.

NOTES

POTENTIAL IN ITS NATURE

Even though we have mentioned this, due to its vast significance, please allow us to deal with it again.

The Anointing by the Spirit forms the basis of all His Ministry to and on behalf of the Believer. Let us remember that it is potential in its nature.

The mere indwelling of the Spirit does not guarantee the full efficacy of His Work in us, since that indwelling is not automatic in its nature. God's ideal for the indwelling of the Spirit is found in the word translated *"caused to take up His residence."* Its root is in the word *"home."* The Spirit was sent to the Believer's heart to make His home there. That means that the Christian must make Him feel at home.

He can do that by giving the Holy Spirit absolute liberty of action in his heart, the home in which He lives. This means that the Believer is to yield himself, all of himself, to the Spirit's control, depend upon the Spirit for guidance, teaching, and strength. Then will the potential power resident in the Presence of the Spirit in the heart of the Believer be operative in the Believer's life.

(22) "WHO HATH ALSO SEALED US, AND GIVEN THE EARNEST OF THE SPIRIT IN OUR HEARTS."

The phrase, *"Who hath also sealed us,"* refers to a seal of ownership. Sealing is the act by which someone designates something as his or her own property.

THE SEAL

A seal is affixed for various purposes, for security, concealment, distinction, authentication, attestation, and confirmation. Several purposes are sometimes combined.

The idea is here, as stated, that of ownership: by the Seal God marked us for His Own. We are also shown how God did this.

God's giving the Spirit in our hearts is His sealing of us for Himself. We know of no sealing except by the Spirit.

It means: A. We belong to God; B. We will continue to belong to God, and no one else can stake a claim on us; and, C. Great and wonderful things are even yet to come.

"Sealed" in the Greek is *"sphragizo,"* and means *"a stamp impressed of genuineness, a fencing in or protecting from misappropriation."*

In other words, God says to the Devil, *"He* (the Believer) *is Mine, evidenced by Faith exhibited in the Finished Work of Christ, and you cannot have him."* To guarantee that protection, the Lord by the Spirit of God, fences in the Child of God, i.e. *"Job's hedge"* (Job 1:10).

The phrase, *"And given the earnest of the Spirit in our hearts,"* presents a guarantee that God will ultimately give us the balance of all He has promised (Rom. 8:23).

"Earnest" in the Greek is *"arrhabon,"* and means *"a pledge, i.e. part of the purchase money or property given in advance as security for the rest."*

What is God's down-payment to us? It is the Holy Spirit. His Presence in our lives, as stated, tells us that all the great Promises of the coming Resurrection (Rapture of the Church), Marriage Supper of the Lamb, Second Coming, Thousand Year Reign with Christ, the new Heavens and new earth, will be, and in fact are, a reality. It will all come to pass.

THE HOLY SPIRIT

It should be readily noticed that Paul makes much of the Holy Spirit in all of his teaching, and to be frank, he does so because the Holy Spirit is the One Who is inspiring him.

The Doctrine of the Holy Spirit, judged by the place it occupies in the Scriptures, stands in the foremost rank of Redemption Truths. With the exception of the Books of II and III John, every Book in the New Testament contains a reference to the Spirit's work; every Gospel begins with a Promise of His outpouring.

Yet it is admittedly the *"neglected doctrine."* Formalism and fear of fanaticism and just plain unbelief have produced a reaction against emphasis on the Spirit's Work in personal experience.

Naturally this has resulted in spiritual deadness, for there can be no vital Christianity apart from the Holy Spirit. Only He can make actual what Christ's Work has made possible. In the words of Ignatius, a leader of the ancient church:

"The Grace of the Spirit brings the machinery of Redemption into vital connection with the individual soul. Apart from the Spirit the Cross stands inert, a vast machine at rest, and about it lie the stones of the building unmoved. Not till the rope has been attached can the Work proceed of lifting the individual life through Faith and Love to the place prepared for it in the Church of God."

NOTES

THE NATURE OF THE SPIRIT

Who is the Holy Spirit? The answer to this question will be found in studying the names He bears, and the symbols which illustrate His Workings.

THE NAMES OF THE SPIRIT

In this, we will learn much about the Spirit of God, Who He is, what He does, and, above all, His relationship to God the Father, God the Son, and the Believer.

As we have already stated, the Holy Spirit sadly and regrettably is almost totally neglected in the Modern Church. Most of the old line Denominations, such as the Baptist, Methodist, etc., have rejected Him, at least in the New Testament manner. In other words, they have gone little farther than the Baptism of John, even if that.

Sadder still, many of the Pentecostal Denominations, which were founded on the very premise of the Moving, Working, and Operation of the Holy Spirit, in other words a vital force within our lives and ministry, are in effect ignoring Him, and one might even say rejecting Him. I realize these are strong words, but I sadly believe them to be true.

As a case in point, it is impossible for anyone who truly knows and understands what Jesus did at Calvary and the Resurrection, and how the Holy Spirit affects that great Work within our hearts and lives, could at the same time recommend humanistic psychology respecting the needs of man. The two are totally antagonistic to each other. In other words, it is impossible to believe this humanistic lie and at the same time believe in the Christ of Calvary and the Power of His Resurrection, made real to us regarding all its benefits, by the Holy Spirit. It is the same as trying to believe in evolution and creationism at the same time. It simply cannot be done.

As we look at the Names of the Holy Spirit, hopefully we will gain a better understanding of His Work within our lives.

THE SPIRIT OF GOD

The Spirit is the executive of the Godhead — in other words, the One who executes that which is to be done, working in every sphere, both physical and moral. In fact, we see Him at the very outset of creation where it says, *"And the Spirit of God moved upon the face of the waters"* (Gen. 1:2). To be sure, He is the vital driving force thereafter.

Through the Spirit, God created and preserves the universe. Through the Spirit — *"the Finger of God"* (Lk. 11:20) — God works in the spiritual sphere, converting sinners, sanctifying, and sustaining Believers.

DIVINE

Is the Holy Spirit Divine in the absolute sense? His Deity is proved from the following facts: Divine attributes are ascribed to Him; He is eternal, omnipresent (everywhere), omnipotent (all-powerful), and omniscient (knows all things, past, present, and future) (Ps. 139:7-10; Lk. 1:35; I Cor. 2:10-11; Heb. 9:14).

Divine works are ascribed to Him such as Creation, Regeneration, and Resurrection (Gen. 1:2; Job 33:4; Jn. 3:5-8; Rom. 8:11). He is placed in co-ordinate rank with the Father and the Son (Mat. 28:19; I Cor. 12:4-6; II Cor. 13:14; Rev. 1:4).

A PERSON

Is the Holy Spirit a Person or just an influence?

The Spirit is often described in an impersonal way — as the Breath that fills, the Unction that anoints, the Fire that lights and heats the Water that is poured out, the Gift of which all partake. However, these are merely descriptions of His operations.

The Spirit is described in such a way as to leave no doubt as to His Personality. He exercises the attributes of personality — mind (Rom. 8:27), will (I Cor. 12:11), feeling (Eph. 4:30). Personal activities are ascribed to Him: He reveals (II Pet. 1:21), teaches (Jn. 14:26), witnesses (Gal. 4:6), intercedes (Rom. 8:26), speaks (Rev. 2:7), commands (Acts 16:6-7), testifies (Jn. 15:26). He may be grieved (Eph. 4:30), lied to (Acts 5:3), and blasphemed (Mat. 12:31-32).

His personality is indicated by the fact that He was manifested in visible form, like a Dove

NOTES

(Mat. 3:16) and also by the fact that He is distinguished from His Gifts (I Cor. 12:11).

A BODY OR SHAPE?

Perhaps some have denied personality to the Spirit because He is not described as having body or shape. But personality and corporeality (possessing a body) must be distinguished. Personalty is that which possesses intelligence, feeling, and will; it does not necessarily require a body. Moreover, lack of definite form is no argument against reality. For instance, the wind is real though without form (Jn. 3:8).

It is not difficult to form a conception of God the Father or of the Lord Jesus Christ, but some have confessed to an inability to form a clear conception of the Holy Spirit. The reason is twofold:

First, throughout the Scriptures, the Spirit's operations are invisible, secret, and internal.

Second, the Holy Spirit never speaks of Himself, or represents Himself; He always comes in the name of and as representing another. He is hidden behind the Lord Jesus Christ and in the depths of our inner man. He never calls attention to Himself, but to the Will of God and the Saving Work of Christ. *"He shall not speak of Himself"* (Jn. 16:13).

And yet, John the Beloved, regarding his Vision as given in the Book of Revelation, said, *"And there were Seven Lamps of Fire burning before the Throne, which are the Seven Spirits of God"* (Rev. 4:5).

First of all, we know there are not seven Spirits of God respecting a number, but that *"Seven"* denotes the totality, completion, and perfection of the Holy Spirit.

The point is, John saw something, or else he could not have described what he saw. This is not to say that the Holy Spirit has a bodily form, i.e. *"a Spirit Body,"* but it's not to say that He doesn't either.

SEPARATE AND DISTINCT

Is the Holy Spirit a personality separate and distinct from God the Father?

Yes; the Spirit proceeds from God the Father, is sent from God the Father, and as well, is the Gift of God the Father to men. Yet, the Holy Spirit is not independent of God the Father.

He always represents the one God acting in the spheres of thought, will, and activity. How the Spirit can be one with God the Father and yet distinct from God the Father is part of the mystery of the Trinity.

THE SPIRIT OF CHRIST

Romans 8:9 speaks of the *"Spirit of Christ,"* Who in reality is the Holy Spirit.

There is no essential distinction between the Spirit of God, the Spirit of Christ, and the Holy Spirit, all being different names for the same Person. For there is only One Holy Spirit, as there can only be one God the Father and One God the Son. But the One Spirit has many Names, descriptive of His various Ministries.

Why is the Spirit called the Spirit of Christ?

1. Because He is sent in the Name of Christ (Jn. 14:26).

2. Because He is the Spirit sent by Christ. The Spirit is the principle of Spiritual Life by which men are born into the Kingdom of God. This new life of the Spirit is imparted and maintained by Christ (Jn. 1:12-13; 4:10; 7:38), Who is also the Baptizer with the Holy Spirit (Mat. 3:11).

This new life is imparted and maintained by Christ because He is the One Who paid the price for our Redemption.

3. The Holy Spirit is called the Spirit of Christ because His special mission in this age is to glorify Christ (Jn. 16:14). His special work is connected with Him Who lived, died, rose, ascended, and Who is now exalted at the right hand of the Father (Mat. 22:44). He makes real *in* Believers what Christ has done *for* Believers. This is so very important because He is the only One Who can make real and viable this great and glorious Work which Christ effected at Calvary and the Resurrection.

4. The Glorified Christ is present in the Church and in Believers by the Holy Spirit. It is often said that the Spirit has come to take the place of Christ, but it is more correct that He has come to make Christ real, which pertains to all that Christ has done for us in His Atoning Work.

The Holy Spirit makes possible and real the Omnipresence of Christ in the world (Mat. 18:20) and His indwelling in Believers.

The connection between Christ and the Spirit is so close, that Both Christ and the Spirit are said to dwell in the Believer (Rom. 8:9-10; Gal. 2:20); and the Believer is Both *"in Christ"* and *"in the Spirit."*

NOTES

Thanks to the Holy Spirit, the Life of Christ becomes our life *in* Christ.

THE COMFORTER

This is the title given to the Spirit in John Chapters 14-17. A study of the background of these Chapters will reveal the significance of the Gift.

The Disciples had taken their last meal with the Master. Their hearts were sad at the thought of His departure, and they were oppressed with a sense of weakness and helplessness. Who will help us when He is gone? Who will teach and guide us? Who will stand by us as we preach and teach? How shall we be able to face a hostile world?

These unspoken fears Jesus quieted with the Promise, *"I will pray the Father, and He shall give you another Comforter, that He may abide with you for ever"* (Jn. 14:16).

The word *"Comforter,"* (*"Paracletos"* in the Greek) bears the following literal meaning:

One called to the side of another for the purpose of helping him in any way, particularly in legal and criminal proceedings.

It was the custom in ancient tribunals for parties to appear in Court attended by one or more of their most influential friends, who were called in Greek *"Paracletes,"* and in Latin *"Advocatus* (Advocates)."

These gave their friends — not for fee or reward, but from love and interest — the advantage of their personal presence and the aid of their wise counsel. They advised them what to do, what to say, spoke for them, acted on their behalf, made the cause of their friends their own cause, stood by them and for them in the trials, difficulties, and dangers of the situation.

ANOTHER

Such was the relationship that the Lord Jesus had sustained to the Disciples during His earthly Ministry, naturally they were dismayed at the thought of His departure. But He comforted them with the promise of another Comforter Who should be their Defender, Helper, and Teacher during His absence. He is called *"Another Comforter"* because He was to be invisibly to the Disciples what Jesus had been to them visibly.

The word *"Another"* distinguishes the Holy Spirit from Jesus, yet puts Him on the same plane. Jesus sends the Spirit, yet Jesus comes spiritually to the Disciples through the Spirit; the Spirit is thus both Christ's Successor and also His Presence. The Holy Spirit makes possible and real the continued presence of Christ in the Church.

THAT OF CHRIST

It is He Who causes the Person of Christ to dwell in them so that they acquire the right to say with Paul, *"Christ liveth in me."* It is, therefore, the Life of Christ, the Nature of Christ, the Sentiments of Christ, the Virtues of Christ, that the Spirit communicates to Believers; it is after the Likeness of Christ that He fashions them, and after the Model which He has left us.

Without Christ, the Spirit has nothing to produce in the heart of the Believer. Take away Christ, and His Word, and it is like removing from the photographer's studio the person whose features are about to be fixed on the plate prepared to receive them.

PARACLETE

The sending of the Comforter does not mean that Christ has ceased to be the Helper and Advocate of His people. John tells us that He still fulfills that office (I Jn. 2:1).

Christ, Whose sphere of work is in Heaven, defends the Disciples against the charges of the *"Accuser of the Brethren"*; at the same time the Spirit, Whose sphere of work is on Earth, *"silences the earthly adversaries of the Church through the victory of Faith which overcomes the world."*

As Christ is *"Paraclete"* in Heaven, so the Holy Spirit is *"Paraclete"* on Earth (Intercessor).

The ascended Christ not only sends the Spirit but also manifests Himself by means of the Spirit. In the flesh Jesus could be in only one place at a time; in His ascended Life He is Omnipresent (everywhere) by the Spirit. During His earthly life, He was external to men; by the Spirit He can dwell in the very depths of their souls. One writer has stated this truth as follows:

JESUS

If Jesus had remained on earth in His physical life, He would have been only an example to be copied; but if He went to His Father and sent His Spirit, then He would be a Life to be lived.

NOTES

If He had remained visibly and tangibly with us, He would have been related to us merely as a model is related to an Artist who chisels his marble, but never as the idea and inspiration which produces the work of art.

If He had remained on earth, He would have been merely the subject of prolonged observation of scientific study, and He would always have been outside of us, external to us; an external voice, an external life, an external example . . . But thanks to His Spirit, He can now live in us as the very Soul of our souls, the very Spirit of our spirits, the very Truth of our minds, the very Love of our hearts, and the very Desire of our wills.

THE SPIRIT'S WORK

If the Spirit's Work is to communicate the work of the Son, what gain could there be in the departing of the One in order to make possible the coming of the Other?

Answer: It is not the earthly Christ that the Spirit communicates, but the heavenly Christ — the Christ reinvested with His eternal power, reclothed with heavenly glory. Employing an illustration suggested by Dr. A. J. Gordon:

"It is as if a father, whose kinsman had died, had said to his children: 'We are poor and I have become an heir. If you will submit cheerfully to my leaving you and crossing the Sea and entering into my inheritance, I will send you back a thousand times more than you could have had by my remaining with you.'"

TEACHES MORE

Christ's life on earth represented the days of His poverty (II Cor. 8:9) and humiliation; on the Cross He secured the riches of His Grace (Eph. 1:7); on the Throne He secured the riches of His Glory (Eph. 3:16).

After His Ascension to the Father He sent the Spirit to convey the riches of the inheritance. By His Ascension Christ would have more to give and the Church would have more to receive (Jn. 14:12; 16:12). *"The Stream of Life will have higher power because of the higher Source from which it proceeds."*

The Comforter teaches only the things of Christ, yet teaches more than Christ taught.

Until the Crucifixion, Resurrection, Ascension, and Exaltation of Jesus, the Christian doctrine was not yet complete and, therefore, could not be fully communicated to the Disciples of Christ.

In John 16:12-13 Jesus says, in effect: *"I have brought you a little way in the knowledge of My Doctrine; He shall bring you all the way."* The Ascension was to bring a larger impartation of Truth as well as a greater impartation of Power.

THE HOLY SPIRIT

The Spirit is called Holy because He is the Spirit of the Holy One, and because His Chief Work is Sanctification.

We need a Saviour for two reasons: to do something *for* us, and something *in* us. Jesus did the first by dying *for* us; through the Holy Spirit He lives *in* us, transmitting to our souls His Divine Life.

The Holy Spirit has come to reorganize the nature of man and to pit Himself against all its evil tendencies.

THE HOLY SPIRIT OF PROMISE

The Holy Spirit is so called because His Grace and Power is one of the outstanding Blessings promised in the Old Testament (Ezek. 36:27; Joel 2:28).

It is the highest prerogative of the Christ, or the Messiah, to impart the Spirit, and this Jesus claimed when He said, *"Behold, I send the Promise of My Father upon you"* (Luke 24:49; Gal. 3:14).

THE SPIRIT OF TRUTH

The purpose of the Incarnation was to reveal the Father; the mission of the Comforter is to reveal the Son.

When we gaze upon a picture, we may for ourselves see much that is beautiful and attractive in its modes of exhibiting color and form; but to understand the inner meaning of the picture and appreciate its real purpose, we need some skilled interpreter to open our eyes.

The Holy Spirit is the Interpreter of Jesus Christ. He does not bestow a new or different revelation, but rather opens the minds of men to see the deeper meaning of Christ's Life and Words. As the Son did not speak of Himself, but spoke what He had received from the Father, so the Spirit will not speak of Himself as from a separate store of knowledge, but will declare what He hears in that Inner Life of the Godhead.

NOTES

THE SPIRIT OF GRACE

This is mentioned in Hebrews 10:29 and Zechariah 12:10.

The Holy Spirit gives man Grace to repent by striving with him; He imparts the Power for Sanctification, Endurance, and Service.

He who does despite unto *"the Spirit of Grace,"* drives away Him Who Alone can touch or move the heart, and thus cuts himself off from God's Mercy.

THE SPIRIT OF LIFE

This is mentioned in Romans 8:2 and Revelation 11:11.

"I believe in the Holy Spirit, the Lord, and Giver of Life," reads an ancient creed.

The Spirit is that Person of the Godhead Whose special function is the creation and preservation of natural and spiritual life.

THE SPIRIT OF ADOPTION

This is mentioned in Romans 8:15.

When a person is saved, he is not only given the name of *"Child of God,"* and adopted into the Divine Family, but he also receives within his soul the consciousness that he is a partaker of the Divine Nature.

Writes Bishop Andrews: *"As Christ is our Witness in heaven, so is the Spirit here on earth witnessing with our spirits that we are the Children of God."*

SYMBOLS OF THE SPIRIT

We have briefly alluded to these elsewhere in our Commentaries, but perhaps a fuller explanation would be helpful.

It has been well said that *"words are often but lame vehicles for the conveyance of Truth. At their best, they but half reveal, half conceal the hidden depths of thought."*

God has chosen to illustrate with symbol of what otherwise, because of the poverty of language, we could never know. The following symbols are employed to describe the operations of the Holy Spirit:

FIRE

This is mentioned in Isaiah 4:4; Matthew 3:11; Luke 3:16.

Fire illustrates the purging, purification, fiery boldness, and zeal produced by the Anointing of the Spirit. The Spirit is compared to fire

NOTES

because fire warms, illuminates, spreads, and purifies. Compare Jeremiah 20:9.

WIND

This is mentioned in Ezekiel 37:7-10; John 3:8; Acts 2:2.

Wind symbolizes the regenerative work of the Spirit and is indicative of His mysterious, independent, penetrating, life-giving, and purifying operation.

Wind symbolizes the Power of the Holy Spirit in carrying out all of these great works in the heart and life of the Believer.

WATER

This is mentioned in Exodus 17:6; Ezekiel 36:25-27; 47:1; John 3:5; 4:14; 7:38-39.

The Spirit is the fountain of Living Water, the absolute pure, the best, because He is a veritable River of Life — flooding, gushing over our souls, cleansing away the dust of sin.

The Power of the Spirit does in the spiritual what water does in the material order. Water purifies, refreshes, quenches thirst, and renders sterility fruitful, in other words, gives Life.

It purifies what is soiled and restores cleanliness; it is an apt symbol of Divine Grace which not only cleanses the soul but adds to it a Divine beauty. Water is an indispensable element of physical life; the Holy Spirit is an indispensable element of spiritual life.

What is the meaning of the expression, *"Living Water"?*

It is that which is alive, i.e., living, in contrast with the stagnant water of cisterns or marshes; it is water that bubbles up, flows along always in communication with its Source and always bearing evidences of Life. If this water is caught in a reservoir, if its flow is interrupted, if it is cut off from its Source, it can no longer bear the name of *"Living Water."*

Christians have the *"Living Water"* only to the extent that they are in contact with its Divine Source who is Christ, and by the Spirit.

OIL

Oil is perhaps the most familiar and common symbol of the Spirit. Whenever oil was used ritually in the Old Testament it spoke of usefulness, fruitfulness, beauty, life, and transformation.

It was commonly used for food, light, lubrication, healing, and soothing of the skin. In like manner, in the spiritual order, the Spirit strengthens, illumines, liberates, heals, and soothes the soul.

It is said that Jesus was *"Anointed . . . with the oil of gladness above thy fellows"* (Ps. 45:7; Heb. 1:9).

THE DOVE

The dove, as a symbol, speaks of gentleness, tenderness, loveliness, innocence, mildness, peace, purity, and patience.

Among the Syrians it is an emblem of the life-giving powers of nature. A Jewish tradition translates Genesis 1:2 as follows: *"The Spirit of God like a Dove brooded over the waters."*

Christ spoke of the Dove as the embodiment of the harmlessness which was characteristic of His Own Disciples.

Even though the Holy Spirit contains and has all the other attributes mentioned in symbol, still, it is through the symbol of the Dove which He inhabits Believers. This speaks of His total gentleness and kindness, in essence one could say, *"Always a perfect gentleman."*

A SEAL

This is found in our subject text, I Corinthians 1:22, as well as Ephesians 1:13 and II Timothy 2:19.

Even though others have concluded this to be a symbol of the Holy Spirit, I really have not considered it so. However, in the event of the possibility, I will include these thoughts.

The *"Seal"* conveys the thought of Ownership. The impress of a Seal implies a relation to the owner of the Seal, and is a sure token of something belonging to him.

Believers are God's property and known to be so by the Spirit dwelling in them. The following custom was common in Ephesus in Paul's day.

A merchant would go to the harbor, select certain timber (or whatever) and then stamp it with his Seal — an acknowledged sign of ownership. Later he would send his servant with his signet who looked for the timber bearing the corresponding impress (II Tim. 2:19).

The idea of security is also involved (Eph. 1:13; Rev. 7:3).

The Spirit inspires the sense of security and assurance in the Believer's heart (Rom. 8:16). He is an earnest or first part of our heavenly inheritance, an assurance of the glory to come. Christians have been sealed, but must be aware of doing anything to break the Seal (Eph. 4:30), for such can be broken.

(23) "MOREOVER I CALL GOD FOR A RECORD UPON MY SOUL, THAT TO SPARE YOU I CAME NOT AS YET UNTO CORINTH."

The phrase, *"Moreover I call God for a record upon my soul,"* is given, along with the subsequent statements, to show them the true reason why he had changed his purpose, and had not visited them according to his first proposal. And that reason was not that he was fickle and inconstant; but it was that he apprehended that if he should go to them in their irregular and disorderly state, he would be under a necessity of resorting to harsh measures, and to a severity of discipline that would be alike painful to them and to him.

BEFORE THE FIRST EPISTLE

It is probably correct that Paul had changed his mind about visiting them before he wrote his First Epistle. He evidently thought it would be better to try the effect of a faithful letter to them, admonishing them of their errors, and in treating them to exercise proper discipline themselves, rather than him personally coming at that present time.

In that Epistle he really did not tell them as yet his change of purpose or the reason of it, but that now, after he had written that Letter, and after it had all the effect which he desired, he states the reason why he had not visited them.

I think he felt if the Letter would not accomplish the task, then nothing would. Actually, it was the Holy Spirit who guided him in this direction, I Corinthians being the actual Word of God, which incidentally, accomplished its intended purpose, even as the Seventh Chapter of II Corinthians proclaims.

LED BY THE HOLY SPIRIT

The Apostle was not guilty of fickleness because he changed his plans. He was not like men of the world who say *"Yes, Yes,"* but in actions say *"No, No"*; but just as God is faithful to His *"Yea"* so was the Apostle. And then, as always with Paul, he lifted small everyday matters into the highest realm of spiritual environment. His argument was — how could he act with fickleness when he proclaimed a God that is faithful to His Promises; and he reminds them that, let the Promises of God be ever so many, yet are they all reliable for they are all deposited in the Son of God, Jesus Christ.

He is the great *"Yes"* of these Promises. The Promises under the First Covenant were deposited in man and depended for realization upon his obedience. There was, of course, complete failure; but the Promises of the New Covenant are all given to Christ, and their realization depends upon Him. There can, therefore, be no failure, for He is the *"Amen"* as well as the *"Yea,"* i.e., He is the Performer as well as the Promisor and all His action in relation to these Promises has for its aim the Glory of God, and the objects of those Promises, the beings in whom they will be exhibited, are redeemed men.

It was only in pardoned sinners that this demonstration of the Grace and Faithfulness of God and of His Son Jesus Christ could have been made.

To these engraced objects of His love He gives His Holy Spirit as a pledge, an earnest, of the Eternal Glory, Splendor, Dominion and Bliss that they are to possess, in order that they may enjoy, while still in this world, in their hearts, a foretaste of the felicity which they then shall have; and all such persons He *"Seals"* for Himself as His Own by that very Spirit which He gives them (Williams).

TENDER AFFECTION

The phrase, *"That to spare you I came not as yet unto Corinth,"* pertains to things he feared he would have to do, such as possibly putting some out of the Church, so he had opted instead to write the Epistle unto them we now refer to as I Corinthians, i.e., was led by the Lord to handle the matter in this way.

He expected to avoid the necessity of these painful acts of discipline, by sending to them a faithful and affectionate Epistle, and thus inducing them to repent, and to avoid the necessity of a resort to that which would have been so trying to him and to them. It was not, then, a disregard for them, or a want of attachment to them, which had led him to change his purpose, but it was the result of tender affection.

This cause of the change of his purpose, of course, he would not make known to them in that Epistle, but now that the Letter had

NOTES

accomplished all he had desired, it was proper that they should be apprized of the reason why he had resorted to this instead of visiting them personally (Barnes).

(24) "NOT FOR THAT WE HAVE DOMINATION OVER YOUR FAITH, BUT ARE HELPERS OF YOUR JOY: FOR BY FAITH YE STAND."

The phrase, *"Not for that we have domination* (dominion) *over your Faith,"* is actually a reference to the previous phrase of *"not sparing them,"* which might have been understood as involving a claim *"to Lord it over their Faith."* He had, indeed, authority as an Apostle (I Cor. 4:21; 10:6; 13:2, 10), but it was a purely spiritual authority. In other words, he could tell them what was right and what was wrong, but he really had no power to enforce such a decree, nor did he desire such.

In other words, had he gone to Corinth and found that it was necessary to excommunicate someone out of the Church, he could say what should be done, but if the Church did not want to carry out that which he said, they did not have to do such. However, had such a thing happened, it would have meant that Paul's usefulness, at least as far as that Church was concerned, would be over, which would mean that the Church would have opted for false doctrine, and would consequently have been destroyed.

CHURCH GOVERNMENT

It should be noted that here, Paul drops back into the plural *"we"* and includes his assistants with himself. This means that as far as lordship over anybody's Faith is concerned, if there were such a thing, it would not belong merely to an Apostle but to all Teachers and Preachers. But no such thing exists.

Everything hierarchical on the part of an Office and on the part of all Officers in the Church is here disavowed. The importance of this fact needs to be stressed in doctrine and in practice, exactly as Paul practiced such here under the guidance of the Holy Spirit.

WHAT DO WE MEAN BY LORDSHIP OR DOMINION OVER ONE'S FAITH?

Human lordship, which is totally unscriptural, is exercised when Faith is made to be or to do what some man demands; the correct Lordship of Christ is exercised when He by His Word and His Ministers tells us what our Faith should be and do. However, that's as far as it should go. The idea of forcing an action is not in the Bible.

The Church still suffers from self-appointed lords and spurious authority. It is easy to detect, for these lords either presume to dispense our Faith and its doing from some word they claim is from the Lord, or they presume to add some requirement to our Faith and our practice that is contrary to or beyond the Word of the Lord (Deut. 4:2; Rev. 22:18-19).

THE LOCAL CHURCH

This means that the Local Church carries the highest spiritual authority as it refers to its government. In other words, no outside governmental control such as denominational leadership, etc., is to exercise authority over the Local Church, that is if they desire to remain Scriptural. As we've already stated, the Word of God is to be given regarding all matters, and is to ever be the rule of conduct; however, it is up to the Pastors and people of the Local Church to enforce this, and their decision is not to be abrogated right or wrong.

Unfortunately, most modern Religious Denominations pretty much ignore the spiritual autonomy of the Local Church. It is forced in any and all matters to adhere to Denominational policy, irrespective as to what the Word of God says about the matter. In other words, it is not the Bible that guides such organizations, but rather Denominational policy which is changed at will. Consequently, any Pastor who yields to such, and that means to yield to anything which is unscriptural, has begun down a road of compromise that will only worsen with time.

THE WORD OF GOD

Regarding Church Government which is so very important, perhaps the single most important aspect of the Work of God on earth, the Word of God must ever be the criteria in all things.

The method used by the Holy Spirit to instruct regarding this all important work, is found more so in practice than in instruction. Consequently, we see the Holy Spirit at work in the Book of Acts and the Epistles, even as here in the words of Paul, carrying out the practice of Church Government.

Because it is given to us, in the capacity of practice, does not mean that the Church is free to set up its own Government, as many have claimed. We should observe closely as to what the Holy Spirit did in all matters regarding the Church, and make every attempt to follow accordingly. To do otherwise is to invite disaster, which actually abrogates the Headship of Christ. The Holy Spirit takes orders from God the Father and God the Son. He does not take orders from denominational heads or any other human being for that matter.

AN EXAMPLE

For instance, in the major Religious Pentecostal Denominations, if there is failure of any sort on the part of any Preacher, that Preacher has to resign his Church, or stop his Ministry of whatever capacity, and cease preaching altogether for some two years, or some such period of time.

While such foolishness may look good to the world, and may appeal to self-righteousness, it has absolutely no validity whatsoever in the Word of God. Actually, it is a form of penance and does despite to the Spirit of Grace. Its very action says that what Jesus did at Calvary is not enough, and other things need to be added, etc.

As stated, there's nothing in the Bible which substantiates such action, but in fact, mitigates in the opposite direction. If repentance before God is not enough, then the Bible is a lie. Whenever God forgives, He does totally and completely. The transgression is forgiven and forgotten. As a result, there is no such thing as punishment of such sorts, nor does God justify one partially. Such a thing, or even the hint of such, is a Scriptural travesty, which makes a mockery of what Jesus did at Calvary and the Resurrection.

Some claim that this portrays that such organizations are hard on sin, etc. No, it actually proclaims the opposite. It in effect says that what Jesus did is not enough and that man must add something to His Finished Work. Nothing could be of greater insult to God.

DOES GOD PUT PEOPLE ON PROBATION?

There is no such thing in the Word of God. What if the Lord did such a thing regarding our Salvation? What if He said, *"I forgive your sins, but it will be a period of two years, or some such period of time, before that forgiveness actually takes affect."*

NOTES

That would not be forgiveness, it would be a joke. While the world may applaud such, and while self-righteousness may applaud such, the actual fact is, that such is grossly unscriptural, and, in effect, makes a mockery of the Grace of God.

PUNISHMENT?

It is regrettable at the number of Christians who desire to see other Christians punished, except when it comes to themselves.

In fact, no Believer irrespective as to whom he may be, has the right to punish another Believer. No Christian is worthy to do such. James addressed that very succinctly when he said, *"There is one Lawgiver, Who is able to save and to destroy: who art thou who judgest another?"* (James 4:12). In other words, he is saying, *"Who do you think you are, thinking you are qualified to judge or punish another Believer?"*

Any sin or failure within itself is punishment enough. Besides, whenever a Believer repents, and irrespective as to what the sin may have been, according to the Word of God that Believer is instantly forgiven (I Jn. 1:9). Consequently, the penalty of the broken law is instantly suspended. There is no such thing in the Bible of the Lord forgiving someone, and then continuing to punish that person. Such is ridiculous!

As I have stated, such Believers who desire to inflict punishment on others, never desire such for themselves.

As well, if chastisement is needed, it is always the Lord who does such, and He never, and I mean never, places such prerogative in the hands of others, always keeping it in His domain (Rom. 12:19; Heb. 12:5-11).

WHAT DOES A BELIEVER OWE TO ANOTHER BELIEVER?

Only one thing!

I owe my brother and sister in the Lord, and you owe your brother and sister in the Lord only one thing, and that is Love. Paul wrote, *"Owe no man anything, but to love one another: for he that loveth another hath fulfilled the Law"* (Rom. 13:8).

If I truly love my brother and sister, I will not do anything that will harm them, but only that to help them, which is exactly what Paul is speaking about in the 24th Verse of this First Chapter of II Corinthians. I owe the same thing to the newest convert in our Church, as I do religious heads, whoever they may be, and that one thing is love.

The Scripture teachers a mutual submission, which is always horizontal and never vertical. Paul said, *"Submitting yourselves one to another in the fear of God"* (Eph. 5:21).

By vertical submission, we mean Preachers or Laypersons submitting to hierarchial heads, i.e., religious leaders, etc. Such is not taught in the Word of God. This is the result of religious hierarchies which in fact pretty much dominate modern Pentecostal organizations. It is sad but true. Such is not Scriptural.

Actually the Bible does teach vertical submission in two situations, which are totally unlike that of which we have mentioned.

SUBMISSION

First of all, it teaches submission to God which is demanded of all Believers, and of course, is vertical, which means that He is above us, which certainly should be obvious (James 4:7).

The second case of vertical submission pertains to younger Pastors in the Local Church, submitting to the Senior Pastor (I Peter 5:5). Of course, that as well, would pertain to only that which is Scriptural, as again would be obvious.

The reader may feel that we may possibly devote too much time and space to this particular subject of Church Government. In fact, most Laypersons hardly think that such concerns them at all; however, nothing could be further from the Truth.

I have felt led of the Lord to deal with this subject in detail and even more than once, for the simple reason that Church Government is without a doubt one of the single most important aspects of the Kingdom of God. If Church Government becomes unscriptural in any capacity, it ultimately affects the entirety of the Church, which in fact is the central core of all Apostasy. Men attempt to wrest the leadership of the Church away from the Headship of Christ. This is what ultimately destroyed the Early Church, eventually bringing on Catholicism. Men attempted, and actually did substitute their own government which was not of God, in place of that which was given by the

NOTES

Holy Spirit. It is the primary cause, I believe, of the spiritual wreckage of modern Pentecostal Denominations.

As well, I address this subject simply because there is very little teaching given anywhere regarding this all important aspect of the Work of God. As the Prophet said, *"People are destroyed for lack of knowledge"* (Hosea 4:6).

CHURCH

Where a person attends Church is of vital significance to their Christian Walk. It is there where they receive much of their Spiritual and Scriptural instruction. That is why Paul was so very concerned about the Church of Corinth.

If a Church is unscriptural in any manner, it will have a telling effect on all who are a part of its direction. Consequently, and as should be obvious, it is absolutely imperative that the leadership of the Local Church, endeavor to be Scriptural in any and all matters pertaining to the Work of God, and life in general — in other words, everything.

The phrase, *"But are helpers of your joy,"* presents the main object of Paul's efforts. He had no desire to exercise Apostolic authority, no desire to throw around his weight, which of course would have been unscriptural in any case, but rather, to be a blessing to the Congregation at Corinth.

Would expelling people from the Church have brought joy? The answer is obviously no!

While such may be necessary in remote cases, even as Paul addressed in the Fifth Chapter of I Corinthians; still, the far better way, is that which we will study in the Second Chapter of this Epistle along with the Seventh. The idea always is to work toward repentance or that wrongs be righted. In fact, what Paul says here regarding *"helpers of your joy,"* is the way and means of the Holy Spirit.

Everything the Lord does for us and to us, is in this capacity. It is to help us, bless us, bring us to the rightful place, restore us, to *"help our joy."* What a beautiful statement!

PAUL'S DELAY

Paul's delay in going to Corinth was made in order to give the Corinthians time to right the evils that had crept in, to right them by heeding his first letter. If he had hastened to come in person he would have had to come with a rod (I Cor. 4:21), which could have caused even greater problems, hence, the reason for his delay.

That would have been painful for both Paul and the Corinthians. That was what he wished to spare them by hoping that they would right themselves, which is the way the Lord always works with us.

Let us say that Paul's wise and tactful plan was successful; he had excellent news from Titus, as we shall see. While all was not yet joy in Corinth, it eventually came to be. When he arrived in Corinth, several months after he had written II Corinthians he had an unmarred three month's visit. Such is the wisdom of the Holy Spirit, which all Spiritual Leaders so-called, should attempt to emulate.

CHRISTIAN MINISTRY

Actually, this is the true conception of Christian Ministry. It's great task is to dispense the Lord's Grace and the Gifts of Grace, all of which are productive of the purest and the highest joy, and by that Grace to remove all that would decrease and mar that joy and bring grief. To do both effectively includes wisdom, care, and carefulness such as Paul exercised so that joy may ever be the result. As stated, what an example for us to follow in all things.

The phrase, *"For by Faith ye stand,"* proclaims a general truth. It was by Faith that Christians were to be established and confirmed, and not by rules and regulations, etc. The connection here requires us to understand this as a reason why Paul would not attempt to lord it over their Faith; or to exercise dominion over them.

The reason was, that thus far they had stood firm, in the main that is, in the Faith (I Cor. 15:1) and had adhered to the Truths of the Gospel, and in a special manner now, in yielding obedience to the commands and entreaties of Paul in the First Epistle, they had showed that they were not only in the Faith, but also firm in the Faith. This is the way of the Holy Spirit, which turned a very ugly situation into the Grace of God. Had Paul handled it in any other manner, it would probably have meant the loss of the Church.

This statement, *"For by Faith ye stand,"* is no doubt, the single most important aspect of the Christian Way. Paul knew that forcing people to do certain things, which he would not attempt anyway, was not going to add to their Victory, but would actually have the very opposite affect. The Believer stands or falls regarding his *"Faith."* Consequently, the Preacher of the Gospel must do everything within his power to build the Faith of the individual, and not the opposite. Even at the risk of overly repeating ourselves, this is not done by force, rules, regulations, or any manner of this nature, but actually only by love, which is what Paul made evident.

While there are times that stringent measures have to be taken, such are not done unless there is absolutely no other alternative. In other words, the individual refuses to repent, thereby continuing in the wrongdoing.

WHAT TYPE OF FAITH DOES PAUL MEAN?

Of course, there is really only one type of Faith, at least as it pertains to the Lord, and that is the Faith that we have in God and His Word.

While using Faith to obtain material things, is appropriate, still, by no means is that to be the cardinal direction of our Faith. To use our Faith only in that capacity, to obtain things, or to make that primary, is a corruption of the great Foundation of Faith.

Faith in God and His Word, according to basics is to pertain to our Salvation, and results in Holiness and Righteousness in Him. We are to ever draw closer to Him, thereby acquiring the rudiments of Christlikeness. That is where our Faith should center (Phil. 3:9-10).

It is regrettable that a great portion of the modern Church is teaching people how to be rich, while the Holy Spirit is endeavoring to teach us how to be Holy and Righteous. It is like using a surgeons scalpel to play mumblety-peg. It can be done, but it is a serious waste of such a fine instrument.

"Encamped along the hills of light,
"Ye Christian soldiers, rise,
"And press the battle ere the night
"Shall veil the glowing skies
"Against the foe in vales below,
"Let all our strength be hurled;
"Faith is the victory, we know,
"That overcomes the world."

"His banner over us is love,
"Our Sword the Word of God;
"We tread the road the Saints above

NOTES

"With shouts of triumph trod.
"By faith they, like a whirlwind's breath,
"Swept on o'er every field;
"The faith by which they conquered death
"Is still our shining shield."

"On every hand the foe we find
"Drawn up in dread array;
"Let tense of ease be left behind,
"And onward to the fray;
"Salvation's helmet on each head,
"With truth all girt about,
"The earth shall tremble neath our tread
"And echo with our shout."

"To him that overcomes the foe
"White raiment shall be given;
"Before the angels he shall know
"His name confessed in heaven.
"Then onward from the hills of light,
"Our hearts with love aflame,
"We'll vanquish all the hosts of night
"In Jesus' conquering name."

CHAPTER 2

(1) "BUT I DETERMINED THIS WITH MYSELF, THAT I WOULD NOT COME AGAIN TO YOU IN HEAVINESS."

The phrase, *"But I determined this with myself,"* concerns a settled position. Paul, after seeking the Lord, had come to the conclusion that this was the Will of God respecting the delay of his proposed visit to Corinth.

The phrase, *"That I would not come again to you in heaviness,"* tells us that Paul had been in Corinth on two previous occasions: the first time when he founded the congregation (Acts Chpt. 18) and a second time during his long stay in Ephesus before he wrote I Corinthians.

In regard to this second visit to Corinth we know nothing but the simple fact gathered from II Corinthians 12:14 and 13:1. It occurred, as stated, before I Corinthians was written and may well have taken place more than a year before, or even as much as two years before that writing.

It seems at this particular time, that Paul was badly insulted and hurt, thereby, going back to Ephesus. He then received the information from the *"house of Chloe,"* which seemed to indicate that the situation had not gotten better but rather worse (I Cor. 1:11). More than likely by the time he received this information, he had already determined in his mind to postpone the proposed return trip. He did not want to come to them while such irregularities existed which must have pained his heart, and would have compelled him to resort to measures that he did not at that time desire to take. Being led by the Lord, he resolved, therefore, to endeavor to remove these evils by sending the First Epistle, which he did, praying they would repent, in which then a visit would be mutually agreeable to both. Actually, this is exactly what happened.

"Heaviness" in the Greek is *"lupe,"* and means *"sadness, grief, sorrow."*

THE HEART OF PAUL

Paul, after thoroughly probing the situation, and no doubt seeking the Face of the Lord, had arrived at this verdict. He had decided, and no doubt led by the Lord, what was best in the interest of the Corinthians, namely by delaying his visit in order to spare them. He could not bring himself to the idea of going back to Corinth *"in grief."*

"In grief" certainly refers to grief in Paul's own heart. Grief is, however, always caused by something. So here Paul's grief was due to the deplorable conditions which were found to be the case in Corinth.

Because of his grief-laden heart, Paul, who felt that a true ministry was to bring joy, did not want to appear at that time in Corinth. He did not want to do this on his own account. But this is his secondary motive; his first and primary one had to do with the Corinthians themselves.

If their interests had been best served by Paul promptly getting to them, heavy though his heart was, he would have gone. But this was not the case, thus, he could think also of himself.

More than all, Paul is baring his heart. We shall see that he does this completely. Injury to the Corinthians grieved him, grieved him to tears, as is recorded in Verse 4. The real Paul had his whole heart and soul in his work. Personal suffering and insult were never his real grief, but any injury to the Church was. Consequently, he only defended himself when he felt that not to do so would hurt the Work of God in general.

NOTES

He was ready to suffer, to give up and sacrifice, to do any work to help save souls, to help the Church onward to prosperity and joy. Things had gone wrong in Corinth, and this grieved him to the heart. His hope was that, given a few months of time, the Corinthians would right themselves, which they did.

FOOD FOR THOUGHT

Here is food for thought for all Ministers. What grief do they experience over deplorable conditions in their congregations? How many grieve only over what they must personally suffer?

How many just settle down to the bad conditions, heave a sigh, and let it go at that? How many are more concerned about the numbers and the money than they are the spiritual condition of the people?

(2) "FOR IF I MAKE YOU SORRY, WHO IS HE THEN THAT MAKETH ME GLAD, BUT THE SAME WHICH IS MADE SORRY BY ME?"

The phrase, *"For if I make you sorry,"* presents the heart of this Apostle in a remarkable way.

METHOD OF DISCIPLINE

In the management of the whole case to which Paul here refers, we have an instance of his tenderness in administering discipline. However, even as we shall see, the discipline was simple, and actually was a one or the other situation.

The offending party was to repent, even as outlined in the Fifth Chapter of I Corinthians, and the Second Chapter of II Corinthians, and if so, was to be restored immediately.

Second, if they would not repent, they were to be disfellowshipped; however, even that was to be done, that is if it was necessary, with the intention of bringing the guilty party to repentance. Everything pointed to repentance.

Paul's tenderness was manifested in many ways. He did nothing to wound the feelings of the offending party. He did nothing in the way of punishment which a stern sense of duty did not demand. Actually, all was in obedience to the Word of God. As we shall see, he did it all with many tears. He wept from the necessity of administering discipline at all.

Paul did not even mention the name of the offender. He did not blazon his faults abroad; nor has he left any clue by which it can be known; nor did he take any measures which were fitted to pain, unnecessarily.

NOTES

In fact, if all discipline in the Church were conducted in this manner, it would probably always be effectual and successful, even as it was then.

REPENTANCE

We should cordially receive and forgive an offending brother, as soon as he gives evidence of repentance. We should harbor no malice against him; and if, by repentance, he has put away his sins, we should hasten to forgive him. This we should do as individuals, and as Churches.

God cheerfully forgives us, and receives us into favor on our repentance; and we should hail the privilege of treating all our offending Brethren in the same manner, even as we shall see in Verses 7 and 8.

SORROW

What type of *"sorrow"* is Paul addressing here?

The idea of grief, sorrow, and anguish is closely linked in Hebrew. One Hebrew word is *"yagon,"* which focuses its use of *"sorrow"* on the mental stress and suffering that come with some afflictions.

Another Hebrew word *"makob,"* emphasizes the physical pain, rather than the mental anguish, that comes with affliction.

THE NEW TESTAMENT

In the New Testament, *"sorrow"* is *"lype,"* and *"to be sorrowful"* is *"lypeo."*

The Greek terms suggest both physical pain and emotional suffering. They do not show quite the precision or sensitivity as the Old Testament words.

These Greek words are used repeatedly in three New Testaments passages. In John Chapter 16, Jesus speaks of the grief (lype) that the Disciples would feel at His departure (*"grief,"* vss. 6, 20, 22; *"grieve"* vs. 20; *"pain"* vs. 21).

Their anguish would turn to joy when they would see the resurrected Jesus again, and they would know the experience of answered prayer when they appeal to the Father in Jesus' Name. Thus, here *"lype"* stands in contrast with joy.

NOTES

AS PAUL USES THE WORD *"SORROW"*

In II Corinthians 2:1-7, the Text of our discussion, Paul uses three Greek words, *"lypeo,"* which means *"grieve"* (vss. 2-3, 5) and *"lype"* which means *"painful"* in Verse 1, *"distress"* in Verse 3, and *"excessive sorrow"* which is rendered in Verse 7.

Here Paul uses this word group to discuss the Corinthians' response to his earlier confrontation concerning sin in the Church. The Holy Spirit clearly brought conviction here with *"sorrow,"* experienced as inner spiritual pain unassociated with physical harm, which in fact, is part of the work of the Spirit in His role of conviction of sin (Jn. 16:8-11).

The same words are used in II Corinthians 7:8-11. Paul returns to the same incident and concludes that the sorrow has been beneficial and that it produced a change of heart and a fresh sensitivity to God. This seems to be the basic distinction between *"Godly"* and *"worldly"* sorrow.

Godly sorrow *"brings repentance that leads to Salvation and leaves no regret"* (II Cor. 7:10). Worldly sorrow is resentment and self-pity. A Godly response to *"lype"* involves acknowledging fault and turning from that which generated conviction's discomfort.

One of the most heart-searching examples of sorrow is Paul's *"great sorrow and unceasing anguish"* because of Israel's unbelief (Rom. 9:2-3) (Richards).

The continuing of the question, *"Who is he then that maketh me glad . . . ?"*, refers to the person who has sinned.

THE GUILTY PARTY

Some say this was the same party of Chapter 5 of I Corinthians, while others say it is a different man altogether.

It is my personal thought that it is the same party; however, it really doesn't make any difference respecting the principle of the situation. Who it is does not change that which the Holy Spirit has outlined respecting repentance and restoration, etc.

Paul's grief was caused by the situation at Corinth. Because of his grief he had to grieve the Corinthians in turn, namely by correcting them in no uncertain terms. This correction constitutes a large portion of I Corinthians; and the mission of Titus, no doubt, who also included a good deal of correction. The fact that he was compelled to grieve the Corinthians was also a part of Paul's grief.

Who could remove this grief from him? Only those who had caused it.

The conclusion to the question, *"But the same which is made sorry by me?"*, presents a twofold situation:

1. As previously stated, Paul inflicted this sorrow only as a matter of last resort, and with the idea in mind of bringing the person to repentance. In other words, it was totally for the person's good.

2. This thing being corrected, which it evidently was, would assuage the grief in Paul's heart.

To which we have already alluded, it is obvious as to where the emphasis lay. Paul could not rest until this matter was settled. He realized that the soul of this individual (or individuals) was at stake, and possibly the continuance of the entirety of the Church. If Paul had not been heeded, the Church quite possibly would have continued, but it would have been of no service to the Work of the Lord. In other words, it would have ceased to be a soul-saving station, and would have turned into a hotbed of false doctrine, which characterizes so many Churches presently. Church is truly Church, that is of the Lord, when it is totally following the Word of the Lord, or at least seeking to do so in every capacity. If the Word of the Lord is not its foundation in all things, then it has no real spiritual purpose to continue its existence. Consequently, that being the case, it becomes some type of religious social center, which to be sure, has no spiritual impact whatsoever regarding the True Work of God, and as stated, is sadly the case in most Churches presently. In other words, they are Church in name only!

(3) "AND I WROTE THIS SAME UNTO YOU, LEST, WHEN I CAME, I SHOULD HAVE SORROW FROM THEM OF WHOM I OUGHT TO REJOICE; HAVING CONFIDENCE IN YOU ALL, THAT MY JOY IS THE JOY OF YOU ALL."

The phrase, *"And I wrote this same unto you,"* refers to what he had written to them in the former Epistle, particularly the incestuous person, requiring them to disfellowship him, barring repentance on his part.

The phrase, *"Lest, when I came, I should have sorrow from them of whom I ought to rejoice,"* refers to why he postponed his visit. He now knows that had he kept to his original plans in visiting Corinth, he probably would not have been met with rejoicing, but rather with sorrow. However, his first Epistle to them, had definitely brought about the results which were intended. These results prove he definitely had the mind of the Lord in postponing his visit, thereby letting his First Epistle do its work.

The phrase, *"Having confidence in you all, that my joy is the joy of you all,"* presents the great dictum from the Love Chapter of I Corinthians that love *"thinketh no evil, beareth all things, believeth all things, hopeth all things"* (I Cor. 13:5, 7).

Paul had enemies in Corinth; he knew that there were some there whose minds were alienated from him, and who were endeavoring to do him injury. Yet he did not doubt that it was the general character of the Church that they wished him well, in fact, that they loved him.

CHURCH AND ITS OPERATION

Satan attempts in every way possible to gain an advantage over Churches, and he does it in a variety of ways. Some of them are as follows:

1. In Preachers refusing to preach the Word, which its doing brings about its own discipline, and is the most effective of all. This lack of straight preaching occurs because some in the Church are rich, or talented, or connected with influential families, and to preach the Word without fear or favor, might drive away such families from the Church.

2. Satan gains an advantage regarding discipline, sometimes, by too great a severity of discipline. If he cannot induce a Church to relax altogether, then he excites them to improper and needless severity. He excites a spirit of persecution. He kindles a false zeal, and causes the Church to mistake it for zeal for Truth.

He excites a spirit of persecution against some of the best men in the Church, by personal animosity becoming involved, which makes the sin of the pretender worse than the offenders. In fact, one of the chief arts of Satan has been to cause the Church, in cases of discipline, to use severity instead of kindness. Almost all evils which grow out of such attempts, might have been prevented by a spirit of love.

NOTES

3. Satan gains an advantage in cases of discipline, when the Church is unwilling to re-admit to fellowship an offending but penitent member. Consequently, his spirit is broken; his usefulness is destroyed, and the upshot is, that the sin of the Church becomes greater than the sin of the offending party (Barnes).

(4) "FOR OUT OF MUCH AFFLICTION AND ANGUISH OF HEART I WROTE UNTO YOU WITH MANY TEARS; NOT THAT YE SHOULD BE GRIEVED, BUT THAT YE MIGHT KNOW THE LOVE WHICH I HAVE MORE ABUNDANTLY UNTO YOU."

The phrase, *"For out of much affliction and anguish of heart I wrote unto you with many tears,"* pertains to the writing of I Corinthians. In fact, Paul's pain was caused him by the Corinthians. Mingled with it was his *"anxiety"* about them, namely as to the effect his letter would have on them, whether they would heed him, or whether they would just get angry at his sharp admonitions and perhaps turn completely against him.

PAUL'S FEELINGS

The evil conduct of others gives pain to a good man; and the necessity of administering reproof and discipline is often as painful to him who does it, as it is to those who are the subjects of it.

The word *"anguish"* means, properly, a holding together or shutting up.

The *"tears"* is an instance of Paul's great tenderness of heart — a trait of character which he uniformly evinced. With all his strength of mind, and all his courage and readiness to face danger, Paul was not ashamed to weep; and especially if he had any occasion of censuring his Christian Brethren, or administering discipline.

This is also a specimen of the manner in which Paul met the faults of his Christian Brethren. It was not met with bitter denunciation. It was not met with sarcasm and ridicule. It was not by blazoning those faults abroad to others. It was not with a spirit of rejoicing that they had committed errors, and had been guilty of sin. It was not as if he was glad of the opportunity of administering rebuke, and took pleasure in denunciation and in the language of reproof.

All this is often done by others; but Paul pursued a different course.

How happy would it be if all who attempt to reprove should do it with Paul's spirit. How happy, if all discipline should be administered in the Church in this manner. But, we may add, how seldom is this done! How few there are who feel themselves called on to reprove an offending brother, or to charge a brother with heresy or crime, that do it with tears!

A *PASTOR'S* HEART

This explanation of the personal feelings of the Apostle Paul reveals his Christian humility. It is revealed to us here that it might be reflected through us elsewhere. After all, the purpose of these intimate touches of biography is not merely to record incidental matters belonging to the First Century. The practice belongs to our century as well, and to us who face the responsibility of being Christians in fact as well as in Faith.

These Verses deal with the Apostle's experience in a Pastoral capacity. He had just finished saying in the last Verse of the previous Chapter that he did not want to have dominion over their Faith. He was not craving authority in other people's affairs. He sought only to be a help. Such help as he could render he would be glad to render at the expense of his own comfort and even his own reputation.

In these things Paul stands as an example of an ideal Christian leader. The ideal is not an ecclesiastical autocrat, nor is he a religious hireling who performs a duty. It is not essential that he excels in the intellectual presentation of Truth. All of these, leadership, dutifulness, and preaching, are required of Pastors, but these alone are not enough.

Pastors are to be fellow sufferers and fellow sharers with their flock. They are to feel sorrow and joy. They are to suffer in sympathy. They are to be prayerful in counsel. They are to feel the pulse of human passion and enter into the affairs of their people in the sense of true concern and forthright help. They are to stand before them to preach the Truth and to walk with them in order to practice that Truth.

The phrase, *"Not that you should be grieved,"* presents Paul as the instrument of these words, but the Holy Spirit as the Author.

Whatever the Spirit of God does with us, to us, or for us, is never to grieve us, but rather for our good, and great good at that! Every move, every word, every direction, every pressure, every discipline, every chastisement, every reproof is for that purpose and that purpose alone. He never means us harm, but always help. It is never for bad but always for good.

NOTES

Isn't it wonderful to serve someone like this! Doesn't such love cause us to desire to walk closer to Christ!

The phrase, *"But that ye might know the love which I have more abundantly unto you,"* presents the highest proof of all, that of tears.

LOVE!

It is cruelty to suffer a brother to remain in sin unadmonished; it is also cruel to admonish him of it in a harsh, severe, and authoritative tone; but it is proof of tender attachment when we go to him with tears, and entreat him to repent and reform. No man gives higher proof of attachment to another than he who affectionately admonishes him of his sin and danger (Barnes).

The plain sense is that when Paul wrote, although he himself was so deeply hurt, he was more anxious about the Corinthians, thus writing even amid many tears. It was not, in fact, could not have been done just to hurt them. His was not a penal letter.

To be sure, it hurt, it grieved. Is it pleasant to hear rebuke? When we are confronted with grave wrong and serious moral conditions, our guilt pains us. Contrition without an inner pang has not yet been invented; the deeper the pang, the truer the contrition.

But the grief is never inflicted for its own sake, but for what it is to produce, namely amendment. The Law is not used except in conjunction with the Gospel. The thought is not that the hurt is to be made less by the Gospel, but is to be healed by the Gospel (Lenski).

The very grief which Paul caused the Corinthians when he wrote to them was a manifestation of his love for them. Only a man who had great love in his heart could have written I Corinthians. If one doubts that, recall its imperishable Chapter (the Thirteenth) regarding love itself.

THE GOD KIND OF LOVE

The love that Paul showed for these people, was not mere affection such as we have for people who are congenial to us, as friends. This was the love of understanding and comprehension coupled with corresponding purpose.

God *"loved"* the world (Jn. 3:16).

How could God affectionately embrace this foul, stinking world?

He comprehended what the world was and purposed to cleanse it by sending His Only-Begotten Son. So we are *"to love our enemies."* They would strike us in the face if we came to them with affection; but we are to suffer their state of hate and are to carry out the purpose of freeing them from that state. This, in brief, pictures the New Testament. It is sometimes conceived as seeing value in the object loved. But such a view is too limited.

To love something merely because it has value, contains at least a degree of selfishness. Love, at least as God renders such, does not deny the value of man despite the Fall, due to the fact that he was originally created in the Image of God. In other words, the Breath of God is in man, even fallen man. That's what makes him a *"living soul,"* i.e., will live forever.

However, the price paid to redeem man, is all out of proportion to the worth of man despite the fact that he was created in the Image of God. Consequently, it was not the worth of man which brought about Redemption, but rather love for man. This is the type of love that Paul had for the Church at Corinth, even his enemies, which is overly evidenced in his conduct in his writings. It is the same type of love that we as Believers are to have as well. Otherwise, we can never properly exhibit Christ.

To be frank, Christ cannot be properly presented, in fact, cannot be presented at all, unless He is presented with a God kind of love.

(5) "BUT IF ANY HAVE CAUSED GRIEF, HE HATH NOT GRIEVED ME, BUT IN PART: THAT I MAY NOT OVERCHARGE YOU ALL."

The phrase, *"But if any have caused grief, he hath not grieved me, but in part,"* presents the Apostle dealing with the person who is probably the incestuous one of Chapter 5 of the previous Epistle. Some think not because this seems to be personally against Paul.

However, from the manner in which that Fifth Chapter of I Corinthians reads, it seems the sin was more than immorality, even as serious as that would have been, but was also a matter of erroneous doctrine. The guilty party was literally glorying in what they misconstrued as

NOTES

Christian freedom, when in reality they were turning the Grace of God into lasciviousness (I Cor. 5:6; Jude vs. 4). So, this being the case, it would have definitely been against Paul, actually corrupting the Doctrine of Grace which he had so capably taught.

Nevertheless, whether as previously stated, it was this man or not, is of little consequence. The same admonition which he shall give holds true irrespective as to the sin or infraction.

If it is to be noticed, Paul did not harshly charge him with sin; he did not use any abusive or severe epithets; but he gently insinuates that the man *"had caused grief"*; he had pained the hearts of his Brethren.

As well, Paul is not claiming that the man has grieved him (Paul) more than others, he is actually saying, that he had grieved him only in common with others.

The great reason for his gentleness here, is because the brother has repented. Consequently, it would be wrong to address him otherwise.

FORGIVEN SIN

We should take a lesson here from the Apostle, relative to sins committed by others, yet forgiven by the Lord, in effect, washed clean by the Blood, no longer held against that person. As far as God is concerned, that individual, which includes every single Believer at one time or the other, is totally justified. In other words, God treats him (or her) as though the sin or infraction was never committed. It is never held over his head. He is never addressed as if though there is anything in his past, for in the eyes of God it does not exist. Such is justification by Faith.

However, how many Believers actually conduct themselves accordingly respecting someone who has failed?

The sadness is, every single Believer who has ever lived, has had to go to the Lord not one time, but many times, even with bitter tears, repenting for sin that has been committed in one way or the other. The problem is, we tend to make allowances for our failures, while magnifying others. It should be the reverse!

We now appreciate even the manner, as stated, in which Paul speaks when he advises the congregation to bring this case to its proper Christian close. He no longer dwells on the grievous sin, does not even name it; he is through with it, thank God.

He does not mention the man's name but writes *"such a one"* and generalizes; for every such person, not merely just this one person, should be dealt with as Paul has directed and now further directs. In effect, Paul eliminates himself from the situation; it comes under the jurisdiction of the congregation, which is Scriptural and right. He regarded it so at the beginning (I Cor. 5:3-5) and still regards it so. He guides the congregation, he is not lord of the Church (I Cor. 1:24).

Tact and good sense are combined with refinement and consideration, and these grace the true Christian Principles along which the congregational action is directed. Let us appreciate this; all of it lies on the high plain on which the Church and all her guides should ever remain.

THE GRAVITY OF THE SITUATION

When Paul wrote I Corinthians and corrected so many of the gravest faults found in Corinth, the chief questions were: *"Will the Corinthians favorably respond? Will they change their erroneous ways, or will they resent Paul's letter, repudiate him, thereby causing a terrible division in the whole Church, etc.?"*

The gravity of the situation is often not fully appreciated. In Corinth things were forced to a decision by I Corinthians. It was an either/or — either heed Paul's letter or repudiate Paul and his letter. Everything hanging in the balance, we can readily imagine Paul's concern.

Prominent in the critical situation was this frightful case of incest. The real test would in a way be made in regard to this case. It was so prominent, it was also vicious; it required formal action on the part of the congregation. Paul had written out even the formal resolution which the Church should pass. If Paul had failed in this case, if the congregation had voted adversely on the resolution he had asked it to pass, the awful breach would have been made: Corinth would have been lost to the Church.

GOOD NEWS

II Corinthians shows the happy turn which events took. Two facts are clear: A. The congregation had passed the resolution written out in I Corinthians 5:3-5; and, B. Had expelled the incestuous member; this member had repented most thoroughly, which Paul had hoped would happen.

NOTES

Paul had received this report from Titus. It was vastly more than good news regarding this one case alone, and it should not be considered in this partial light. The acutest issue had yielded to the Truth and the right of the Gospel; that meant Gospel victory as far as the rest of the errors and abuses noted in I Corinthians were concerned as well.

Paul had the brightest prospect that his grief would be completely dissipated. No wonder he writes as he does.

The congregation had not, however, as yet reinstated the repentant member. The details are immaterial. Since this was the first case of so grave a nature, the congregation evidently hesitated to affect too prompt a reinstatement. Whatever these details may have been, Paul now advises the congregation to reinstate the offending member and to do so immediately and wholeheartedly.

APOSTOLIC DIRECTION

The treatment of this case of Apostolic direction has become classic for the Church for all time, the Divine Guide for all grave cases of Church discipline. If the Church is to derive guidance from this case and it certainly can do so, a correct exegesis of I Corinthians 3:1-5 and actually of all that Paul says in II Corinthians is necessary.

The situation is simple, at least as it regards this offending member respecting incest.

He is to repent, and if he refuses to do so, as evidently was the case at the beginning, he is to be expelled (disfellowshipped) from the Church. However, such is to be done, not with the idea of ridding themselves of him, but rather that he will be brought to a state of repentance.

If he repented, which he evidently did, he is to be reinstated immediately, with the past completely forgotten, and the Brother treated accordingly.

HOW CAN ONE KNOW IF REPENTANCE IS SINCERE?

To be frank, that's not difficult at all. Sincerity in a person can be feigned for a short while, but it begins to be obvious very quickly as to the actual reality of the situation.

To give an example, some time ago a young Preacher who attended our Church had a particular problem. I was made aware of the situation and I called in him and his wife.

He admitted to the guilt, and all of us prayed together with his repentance seeming at the moment to be sincere. Actually I think there was some sincerity, but not enough to really address the situation.

The problem was one of long standing, at least according to his admittance. It was not only causing great problems for him spiritually, but in his marriage as well.

In the midst of this, he was an excellent Preacher of the Gospel, and I feel the Lord had actually laid His Hand upon him. In other words, such was obvious.

PRAYER MEETINGS

We have two Prayer Meetings a day at our Church, 10:00 a.m. every morning and 6:30 p.m. each evening, with the exception of Service Times, and Saturday Morning. They are open to anyone who would desire to come, and we generally have anywhere from 7 or 8 people to well over 100.

He came to the Prayer Meetings several times, and I feel really sought the Lord. His wife accompanied him most of the time if I remember. He was faithful in this category only a short period of time, in which I continued to use him in the manner he had been used previously. About six months later the problem cropped up again.

Once again we gathered in my office and once again he sought the Lord, with what seemed to be genuine repentance.

Knowing the problem was one of long standing, this time I really pressed upon him that his only answer was the Lord, and that this thing had to stop. Now we face the dividing line.

The modern Church, at least as a whole, has so left the Ways of God, that council at this particular juncture is the recommendation of a twelve step program, etc. To be blunt, and without going into any type of dissertation, there is no help from that source, no help whatsoever. If the field of Psychology had some type of antibiotics or wonder medicine which would address the situation, I would be all for making the effort. However, there are no wonder medicines for sin. The only thing the Psychologists has is talk. And if sin can be talked out of someone, then Jesus suffered needlessly on the Cross of Calvary. No, the entire business of Psychology is a sham from start to finish. The only answer is the Lord.

NOTES

I strongly related to him how he must take this thing to the Lord in order to gain victory respecting this terrible problem that was threatening to destroy him. I won't go into detail here, but I would encourage the Reader to obtain our Commentary on Romans, and to especially study Chapters 6, 7, and 8. The Holy Spirit through Paul gave the answer to these dilemmas, and irrespective as to how difficult the situation is, the Lord has provided total and complete victory.

SINCERITY?

To make the story brief, he did not pursue that course, but rather turned on me. He and his wife soon left our Church and city, moving to a distant State. The problems only increased; however, to his credit, it seems that he finally began to do what I told him he must do, with the Lord helping him greatly. He came back and apologized for his actions, and as far as I now know, has an ongoing, viable Ministry.

The point of all this is, that after a very short period of time I saw that his repentance was really not sincere, and that at the time he really did not want to give up this particular sin, or else he thought he could do it his way, which had always failed, and in fact, had brought him to near ruin. So, it's not difficult to tell if someone really means business with the Lord. The telltale signs will quickly become obvious one way or the other.

The phrase, *"That I may not overcharge you all,"* means that Paul even though having to correct the situation at Corinth, had by no means placed the entirety of the congregation in the same category. They had shown their willingness to correct the evil by promptly removing the offender when he (Paul) had directed it. More than likely, some or many in the Church had remarked to Titus, that they prayed that Paul would not think that all were in the category of the situations at hand. While it is true that they did not take proper steps to begin with, even while the offender was glorying in his position of immorality, in other words flaunting it, still, they had now passed that hurdle and wanted Paul to know that they desired to do the right thing, and in fact, were doing the right thing. So the Apostle responds to their supplication.

(6) "SUFFICIENT TO SUCH A MAN IS THIS PUNISHMENT, WHICH WAS INFLICTED OF MANY."

The phrase, *"Sufficient to such a man is this punishment,"* means that it had accomplished all that was desired. It had humbled him, and brought him to repentance; and doubtless led him to put away his wife, who in fact, was his stepmother, i.e., *"his father's wife"* (I Cor. 5:1).

WHAT WAS THIS PUNISHMENT?

Because at the outset he had refused to repent and do the right thing, he had been disfellowshipped from the Church. This means he was no longer considered a part of the Church, and actually was not welcome to meet with the people respecting worship, etc. The idea is that while he was going another way entirely (continuing his incestuous relationship), with the Church going in the other direction, there was no basis for fellowship as would be obvious.

Second, he was *"delivered over to Satan for the destruction of the flesh"* (I Cor. 5:4-5).

This by no means meant that the Church quit praying for him in the sense that he would come to his spiritual senses and make things right with God, but rather that they would no longer pray for his health, prosperity, and protection. In effect, they were praying that the Lord would allow Satan enough latitude in his life in order to bring about adverse circumstances, that hopefully he would come to repentance. While of course, Satan means it for the destruction of the individual, the Lord allows such at times, for the very opposite result. Oftentimes, it works, even as here. As someone has well said, *"Man's extremity is God's opportunity."*

RESTORATION

With the man repenting, the situation had come out exactly as Paul had hoped. It was proper now that he should be again restored to the privileges of the Church. No evil would result from such a Restoration, and their duty to their penitent Brother demanded it.

Locke said in II Corinthians, *"Paul conducts this subject here with very great tenderness and delicacy. The entire passage from Verse 5 to Verse 10, relates solely to this offending brother; yet he never once mentions his name, nor does he mention his sin. He speaks of him only in the soft terms of 'such a one' and 'anyone.' Nor does he use an epithet which would be calculated to wound his feelings, or to transmit his name to posterity in a negative sense, or to communicate it to other Churches. So that though this Epistle should be read, as Paul doubtless intended, by other Churches, and be transmitted to future times, yet no one would ever be acquainted with the name of the individual. How different this from the temper of those who would blazon abroad the names of offenders, or make a permanent record to carry them down with dishonor to posterity!"*

Farrar said, *"The Apostle evidently entered into the Jewish feeling that there is a criminal cruelty in needlessly calling a blush of shame unto a Brother's face."*

NOTES

THE TYPE OF PUNISHMENT MENTIONED HERE

The type of *"Punishment"* mentioned here by Paul in the Greek is *"epitimia,"* and means *"a penalty."*

This is the only place it occurs in the New Testament, and is one of the mildest words for *"punishment"* there is. It perhaps, implies that the Corinthians had not resorted to the severest measures. It shows that these Corinthians, despite the terrible problems that had shown themselves in this Assembly, were people after all who attempted to portray the Love and Grace of God.

It is a mystery to me, how that people could call themselves Christians, which within itself speaks of God's Grace and Love, and still desire to punish others, at least that which is beyond what is necessary!

In fact, if the man had repented at the outset, no action would have been taken whatsoever. As it was the punishment tendered by this fellowship, etc., was meant to act only for the purpose of bringing the individual to a state of repentance, which it did. This is punishment, if necessary, which is constructive and designed to come to a successful conclusion. Punishment for the sake of punishment is not taught in the Word of God, and is foreign to the idea of the Grace of God. But yet, many Christians have the mistaken idea that one must *"pay for their sins,"* at least if they are referring to others.

First of all, Jesus has already paid for our sins. As well, if it's proper for one to pay for one's sins, then it's proper for all, which puts everyone in a most unfortunate situation.

The truth is, there is nothing anyone can do to pay for sin. Irrespective as to what one may attempt, what they may undergo, or whatever type of punishment may be heaped upon that person, it pays for nothing in the eyes of God, and for the simple reason that it's already been paid for in Christ. So, why would a great part of the Church desire such unscriptural activity?

Most people take cues from their leaders. If the leaders, as Paul, follow the Word of God, and conduct themselves accordingly, the people generally will follow suit.

If the leaders do otherwise, regrettably and sadly, most people will also do the same.

The phrase, *"Which was inflicted of many,"* seems to be that most in the Congregation obeyed that which Paul had admonished, with only a few abstaining. It seems that Paul still had a few enemies in this particular congregation.

THE ORDER OF EVENTS

This resolution, which had been formulated by Paul, had finally been adopted by the Congregation. The result had been the very best: the sinner had thoroughly repented.

Titus had just reported these things to Paul. These, it seems, were the recent developments in Corinth. I Corinthians had been written about Easter time, Fall was now approaching. Thus, one may conclude, it had taken some time before this result had been obtained in Corinth. It seems also that the repentant sinner had not as yet been reinstated; Paul is asking that this be now duly done.

Even though the action of the Church had not been unanimous, to which we have already alluded, we should, however, note that Paul has nothing to say about the implied minority. Was their dissent innocent, due to absence from the meeting, or to hostility to Paul? We cannot say for certain, but probably there was still some hostility to the Apostle.

(7) "SO THAT CONTRARIWISE YE OUGHT RATHER TO FORGIVE HIM, AND COMFORT HIM, LEST PERHAPS SUCH A ONE SHOULD BE SWALLOWED UP WITH OVERMUCH SORROW."

The phrase, *"So that contrariwise ye ought rather to forgive him, and comfort him,"* we must remember is Authored by the Holy Spirit, even though Paul was the instrument.

NOTES

Consequently, it is not a suggestion but rather a command.

FORGIVENESS

First, they were to *"forgive."*

"Forgive" in the Greek is *"charizomai,"* and means *"to grant as a favor, to show kindness, pardon, or rescue."* It means also *"to give or to grant."* It is actually connected with the word *"Grace* (Charis)*,"* which when we compare the two words (charizomai), becomes obvious. So when we forgive we are manifesting graciousness. Conversely, people who refuse to forgive are conducting themselves as if they have really never been forgiven by God themselves, i.e., *"in other words, they've never been saved"* (Mat. 6:14-15).

Second, Paul told these Corinthians *"to comfort* (parakalesai)*."*

Why are these two steps, forgiveness and comfort, absolutely necessary?

According to the Apostle, piling *"overmuch sorrow"* or *"more abundant grief"* on the person will *"swallow them up."* *"Swallow"* in the Greek is *"katapothe,"* and can be translated *"to devour."* Peter intended the latter meaning when he used the same basic word to describe the Devil's attempt to devour God's people (I Pet. 5:8). In other words, people who refuse to forgive and to comfort are actually assisting Satan in his efforts to devour Christians!

THE MODERN CHURCH

We seem to have it backward in some segments of our contemporary Church society. Discipline is supposed to be administered in order to lead a person to repentance, at least if they refuse to repent at the outset, yet some modern Ecclesiastical leaders want to punish people after they have repented.

How ridiculous!

If the Devil cannot succeed in getting people to continue in sin, he will endeavor to get the Church to refuse to forgive the ones who have sinned. We seem to forget that the Church is nothing but an organism of repentant and forgiven sinners. In fact, heaven will be populated by the same kind of people, simply because there are no other kind.

It is easy to become Pharisaical. It is easy to become sensorial and play the role of the unforgiving servant. It is easy to become critical and appoint ourselves both judge and jury. We must realize, however, that this kind of attitude plays right into the hands of the Devil because it denies the offender forgiveness and encouragement. As well, when we do such a thing, we have just cut ourselves off from the Mercy and Grace of God (Mat. 6:14-15).

WHAT THE CHURCH SHOULD DO

As we have already stated, I Corinthians Chapter 5 and II Corinthians Chapter 2 are the criteria for handling sin in the Church.

If it is a known moral violation, the individual must repent. As we have stated, if repentance is forthcoming, the matter is to be forgotten then and there.

If repentance is not forthcoming, and the individual insists on continuing this course of action, disfellowship is the only answer. However, such is to be done only with the idea of hopefully bringing the person to a place of repentance. It's not to be done as a matter of punishment just for the sake of punishment. When repentance is enjoined, that is if it is, the Church is to forgive the person and comfort him.

There is every reason to think that this man became a sincere penitent. If so, he must have been deeply pained at the remembrance of his sin, and the dishonor which he had brought on his profession, as well as at the consequences in which he had been involved. Consequently, once such is revealed, it can cause deep distress, so much in fact, that it can lead to serious consequences.

As a result, Paul tells them that they ought to comfort him. They should receive him kindly, as God receives to His favor any penitent sinner. They should not cast out his name as evil; they should not reproach him for his sin; they should not bring up the offense by often referring to it; they should be willing to bury it in lasting forgetfulness, and treat him now as a Brother.

It is a duty of the Church to treat with kindness a true penitent, and receive him to their affectionate embrace. The offense should be forgiven and forgotten. The consolations of the Gospel, adapted to the condition of penitents, should be freely administered; and all should be done that can be done to make the offender, when penitent, happy and useful in the community.

NOTES

At one time, this man was grieving many with his sin, now he was grieving himself in deep contrition for that sin — a blessed change. And yet, he should not be abandoned to this excessive grief lest with or by it *"he be swallowed up."*

There is no need to debate about the meaning of the figure of *"swallowed up,"* as to whether it means suicide or what. It means to sink into despair no matter how the despair might manifest itself.

GOD'S FORGIVENESS

It has been asked why Paul says nothing about God's forgiveness of this man's sin.

Paul does not mention this simply because repentance always guarantees God's forgiveness. He is dealing with the Congregation's forgiveness, which must follow that of the Lord. We must not forget the example that is here portrayed.

That which God does, and He always forgives when forgiveness is sought (I Jn. 1:9), must be followed likewise by the Church, and that means down to each individual on a personal basis. By again receiving the repentant sinner through forgiving and comforting him, the Congregation did absolve him in God's Name and by that absolution brought and sealed God's remission to him. To have done otherwise is to deny the Grace of God, which is a serious offense indeed!

On the other hand, every Christian and thus also every Congregation are to forgive a wrong done to them personally at once, the moment it is committed, no matter whether the wrongdoer repents or not, whether he be a Church Member or a bloody persecutor. However, Paul is not speaking about this type of forgiveness; he is speaking about reinstating a repentant Church Member. In a sense, this can be done only by a formal Congregational resolution, or else at least a formal agreement of the Congregation.

Lenski said, *"Who are you, sinner, to hold a sin that is done against you against any sinner? You yourself sin against others daily. Do not place yourself on a level with God! But when, especially as a Congregation, we act in God's Name we convey God's Own absolution, but never to any save to the contrite and repentant."*

The phrase, *"Lest perhaps such a one should be swallowed up with overmuch sorrow,"* presents a strong expression, denoting intensity of grief. We speak of a man being drowned in sorrow, or overwhelmed with grief; of grief preying upon him.

The figure here is probably taken from deep waters, or from a whirlpool which seems to swallow up anything that comes within reach. Excessive grief or calamity, in the Scriptures, is often compared to such waters (Ps. 69:1; 124:2-5).

It was quite possible that this man's life could waste away under the effect of his excommunication and disgrace, and the remembrance of his offense would prey upon him, and sink him to the grave.

(8) "WHEREFORE I BESEECH YOU THAT YE WOULD CONFIRM YOUR LOVE TOWARD HIM."

The phrase, *"Wherefore I beseech you,"* presents the Apostle conducting himself in an entirely different manner than most Church authorities presently.

If any man had the right to demand things, Paul did. He had founded the Church at Corinth, with almost all the people there saved under his Ministry. But yet, he makes no such demands, but rather *"beseeches,"* in other words, *"I beg you!"* This shows that the Church is the highest Spiritual Authority and that Paul, or any other Minister for that matter, can recommend, can point out the right direction, but it is still left up to the local Church to carry out that which is recommended of their own initiative.

OUTSIDE FORCES

How then do modern religious Denominations think they have the Scriptural authority to override Local Churches, in effect, forcing them into an action, at times which is totally against their will?

The truth is, they have no Scriptural authority for such, having made up the rules themselves. In fact, such rules do not agree with the Word of God, which then puts the Church in a political situation instead of that which is Spiritual. Consequently, most modern Religious Denominations are altogether political at the present time, with very little spirituality remaining.

The phrase, *"That ye would confirm your love toward him,"* in effect, means to ratify their love, as of a will (Gal. 3:15).

NOTES

CONFIRMATION

The word here rendered confirm occurs in the New Testament only here and in Galatians 3:15. It means to give authority, to establish as valid, to confirm; and here means that they should give strong expressions and assurances of their love to him; that they should pursue such a course as would leave no room for doubt in regard to it.

Barnes says, *"Paul referred doubtless, here, to some public act of the Church by which the sentence of excommunication might be removed, and by which the offender might have a public assurance of their favor."*

I remind the Reader, that the Leadership of most modern Pentecostal Denominations would probably agree to this, providing the individual would do what they demanded.

And what do they demand?

DEMAND

Regrettably, repentance, which is the primary focal point in these Passages, in fact, is of little concern to these modern Denominations. They are rather more concerned about their particular rulings, which are man-devised, and have no Scripturality in any capacity.

In fact, most of their man-devised rulings concern Preachers. Considering that the offender of I Corinthians Chapter 5 was probably one of the Elders (Preachers) in the Church at Corinth, this should be the example for all to follow, that is if we desire to be Scriptural.

However, unlike the Spirit of God through Paul, the modern variety demands that the Preacher stop all preaching for two years. Some do say that he can preach street services, or minister in jails, or even to children, but he cannot preach behind the pulpit in a Church. I would hope the Reader can see the foolishness of such rulings. What is the difference in preaching on a street corner, and preaching behind the pulpit in a Church?

The point I make is this: whenever men make up the rules, they are foolish and carry no real meaning of any nature.

Oh yes, the major Pentecostal Denominations also demand that the offender spend several months with a Psychologist.

The idea among this so-called Leadership is that they (the leadership) are, in fact,

NOTES

Spiritual Authority, and whatever it is that they demand, the offender should instantly obey and without question, irrespective as to the Scripturality or not. In fact, they actually place themselves in the position of being above question. In other words, as some of them have actually said, *"Whatever we tell you to do, you are to obey without question, irrespective as to whether it is Scriptural or not!"*

I would hope the Reader can understand the total lack of Scriptural foundation for such foolishness, and even the unGodliness of such situations.

THE WORD OF GOD

The Word of God is to be obeyed at all costs. It alone is the criteria. If someone has failed, they are to get back in line with the Word of God, which demands repentance, and if and when that is done, the matter ends then and there. As we have repeatedly stated, God does not put people on probation, nor does He expect any one of His children to obey that which is unscriptural. To do so, only makes a bad matter worse.

For instance, out of the thousands of Preachers in the Assemblies of God who have had the terrible misfortune of coming under these penalties, there have only been a handful, if that, who have made it back into the good graces of the Leadership of that particular Denomination. In other words, when one considers that the Restoration number is almost zero, that should tell us that something is terribly wrong. It is terribly wrong because they really have no Scriptural program for Restoration.

Why?

I have no idea respecting these people, God Alone knowing their hearts; however, I do know that self-righteousness is very easily embarrassed, with the first and only reaction being that the offending party must be disposed of as quickly as possible. Consequently, the situation is developed, with man-devised rulings put in place, which almost automatically guarantees the removal of these individuals, whomever they may be.

As well, they take the position, that if the individual does not agree to their *"punishment,"* and seeks to quietly go elsewhere, they then feel they have the *"right"* to publicly destroy that person, and to use any tactic at their disposal. In other words, he is then branded as *"fair game,"* with almost any punishment inflicted, irrespective as to what it might be, not only not censured, but rather applauded.

In other words, they are not satisfied merely to let the person go his or her way and not be any longer associated with them, they also feel that they have some type of spiritual commission to destroy that person, even though he is no longer associated in any manner. In fact, if businesses or organizations in the secular world conducted themselves accordingly, they would be breaking all types of laws, and would be liable and subject to severe penalties.

SHOULDN'T CHRISTIANS
BE HARD ON SIN?

Most definitely Christians should be hard on sin, but not on sinners! If they feel they must be, the best place to start is with themselves.

Again, self-righteousness is always hard on the sinner, and really not hard at all on the sin. In other words, they very little preach against sin, and rather condone it in most situations.

The Believer, whether in a position of Spiritual Leadership or not, is to always conduct himself toward offending members exactly as God does. In fact, we are not morally qualified to make up our own rules. There is only One Who is thusly qualified, and that is the Lord. We are to as closely resemble Him as is possible in every situation, including the subject at hand. Again, the Word of God must always be the standard, and not man-made rules.

Since God has not made us administrators of Divine Justice, we would be wise to concentrate on what God has actually called us to do. Paul emphasized that obligation by telling the Corinthians that they should validate their love to this repentant offender. In other words, they were to assure him of their unconditional love (agapen).

This kind of love does not *"wait and see what happens,"* nor does it view the person askance. Instead, it accepts the repentant one just as if he or she had never sinned. In fact, that is the way God accepts all of us. As stated, why do we want to treat others in a manner in which God has not treated us? Genuine love must be made a matter of certainty or else it is mere tokenism (Rossier).

WHAT EXACTLY IS BIBLE FORGIVENESS?

Forgiveness is more than a feeling. It should be motivated by a desire to see the penitent offender restored to a place of useful fellowship. It should be inspired with a passion to spare the guilty person from an overwhelming grief and sorrow.

(The word *"penitent"* and *"penance"* are two different things. *"Penitent"* means that one has repented before God, and is, therefore, Scriptural. *"Penance"* is a form of works in which someone is engaged to attempt to earn forgiveness, etc., and is not Scriptural. Regrettably, the Catholics are not the only ones who engage in *"penance,"* most Protestants do the same.)

We can test the sincerity of our Faith and the earnestness of our own convictions by the attitude we have toward those who transgress the peace and purity of God's people. If we gloat over their failings and rejoice in their censure, we have revealed ourselves as coming far short of the Christian ideal. Paul called upon the Corinthians to *"confirm"* their love by the forgiveness of restoration.

In this Second Chapter of II Corinthians, we see the God type of forgiveness in action. Consequently, anything else that one might label as *"forgiveness,"* is in fact, not forgiveness at all, but rather a contrivance of our own making. In fact, forgiveness is very simple. It is only when we add to that which the Lord requires that it becomes complicated.

Many will say, *"It's not a matter of forgiveness!"* What they are really saying much of the time is, *"They haven't done what I demanded them to do."*

Fortunately, the Lord has not required us to do things made up by men, but only what He requires in His Word. We are to sincerely, earnestly, and honestly repent over the wrong action, and cease that action. The matter is to drop then and there. As well, that doesn't mean that the person, even though they have sincerely repented, will not commit that same sin again. In fact, I think it can be said without fear of contradiction, that every single Believer in the world has had to ask the Lord many times to forgive them for a particular wrongdoing, in fact, something which they promised the Lord they would never do again. But they did! But every time they went to the Lord in earnest, honest conviction, the Lord always forgave them, irrespective of how many times He had done so before. Thank God, He does not put a limit on the times He will forgive. So, for someone to point at a repeated infraction, as sad as that may be and as wrong as that may be, as a sign that they really did not repent to begin with, holds no Scriptural validity whatsoever. As repeatedly stated, they should use that judgment on themselves first of all before they use it on others.

NOTES

LOVE

Does the true Love of God condone sin?

Never! But it does condone the sinner, or else none of us would be here.

A Believer cannot be said to actually know the Love of God, until he fully understands the degree of love that God has already shown him, at least as much as we are able to comprehend such, and the proof of our understanding such Love is that we begin to show it to others. That is the only yardstick.

One can claim to love God to any degree, but until that love is expressed toward others, even the most unlovely, we cannot really and truly be said to actually love God.

The idea is, that we emulate or rather imitate our Heavenly Father. He loved us when we were unlovable, and we are to do the same to the unlovable.

The reason many so-called Believers have a problem forgiving others is because they really do not know the Love of God. If they really understood how much God has actually forgiven them, how much He has loved them, how much Compassion, Mercy, and Grace He has shown toward them, they would be quick to show it to others. As it has been repeatedly said, and rightly so, *"If forgiveness is not the quick response on the part of a Believer, it just may be possible that that individual is not really a Believer after all."* In other words, they've never really truly been Born-Again, i.e. truly forgiven; therefore, they are very slow to forgive others, if at all.

To be frank with you, if what we have just said is true, it scares me. If in fact it is true, that we don't forgive very easily because we actually have not really been forgiven ourselves, i.e. *"not saved,"* then that means there aren't a lot of people in the Church who are truly saved. It's a frightening thought!

(9) "FOR TO THIS END ALSO DID I WRITE, THAT I MIGHT KNOW THE PROOF OF YOU, WHETHER YE BE OBEDIENT IN ALL THINGS."

The phrase, *"For to this end also did I write,"* refers to I Corinthians. He had felt led of the Lord to approach the situation in this fashion. He felt the letter would be more profitable than him actually visiting them in person, at least at this time. Consequently, he postponed his visit, sending the letter instead.

The phrase, *"That I might know the proof of you, whether ye be obedient in all things,"* regarded the entirety of I Corinthians; however, the test made in I Corinthians 5:1, etc., was applied to the Corinthians as the most important, I think; this was an eminent situation that would bring out fully whether they would be obedient in all regards.

OBEDIENCE?

Paul wrote about many matters in I Corinthians, any one and all of which were likewise tests. Because it was such an acute, definite case, the case of incest was one which probed and tested the obedience of the Corinthians most completely. If they passed this test — and they did — they proved that they would be equally obedient in other and lesser cases.

The situation is this: the Church had been obedient in removing the unrepentant offender from their midst, and now they were to be obedient in reinstating the repentant former offender, into their midst. For the *"obedience"* to be true, it had to be worked both ways.

Let us note that Paul here acknowledges the genuineness of the Corinthian Congregation in a very open way. We should remember how anxious he had been regarding the tests to which he had put the Corinthians, in particular also regarding this most decisive test.

What a relief it was to find that they were genuine! So the implication is that in regard to what he now bids the Corinthians do, he is fully assured that they will again respond favorably. We feel that saying what he does, and saying it in this telling way, will surely move the Corinthians the more obediently to respond to Paul's bidding, both in now absolving the

NOTES

repentant sinner and in carrying out whatever else Paul may ask.

APOSTOLIC AUTHORITY

Some have thought that this question is one regarding Paul's personal Apostolic authority and obedience to that. However, the only Apostolic authority that existed was that which had been delegated by Christ.

No Apostle and no Apostolic Church knew of any other, or obeyed any other.

In I Corinthians 5:4, where the formulation of the resolution which was submitted to the Corinthians by Paul is given, there follows: *"In the Name of our Lord Jesus Christ."* To that authority Paul bowed, to that he asked, as well, the Corinthians to bow, which they did. *"Obedient in all respects,"* equals *"to Christ in all things."* To be frank, an Apostolic Hierarchy never existed, and does not exist now.

CHRIST AS THE HEAD OF THE CHURCH

This shows that each Congregation is autonomous (free to act), but that it is ever under Christ when it is exercising its autonomy. Expulsion and reinstatement, the ban and absolution are powers conveyed to the Congregation by Christ (Mat. 18:17), but only as long as it remains Scriptural.

Paul treats the Congregation accordingly. Matthew 18:18, and John 20:23 do not make Apostles or Ministers *"Lords"* (I Cor. 1:24) of the Church. In fact, the fivefold Ministry (Eph. 4:11) is given to the Church, and is to act under Christ. However, it is to conduct itself actually as Paul did here, always setting the example. To be sure, and as is overly obvious, there was no such thing as Denominational authority as is now practiced in many religious circles.

Men voted into religious office by popular ballot do not bestow any spiritual authority. In fact, it is not even recognized by God as anything spiritual, at least in that sense. Such is not necessarily wrong if it is held to an administrative level, and can be very helpful for the Work of God. It is only when religious men leave the Word of God, and begin to devise their own rules which have no Scriptural foundation, that the trouble begins.

Corinth was a Church that had many faults, indeed, grievous faults; nevertheless, it was a Church and must be treated accordingly, and thankfully, ultimately came through with flying colors. It proved itself a Church by allowing itself to be cleansed of its faults. In other words, Jesus was the Head of the Church.

(10) "TO WHOM YE FORGIVE ANY THING, I FORGIVE ALSO: FOR IF I FORGAVE ANY THING, TO WHOM I FORGAVE IT, FOR YOUR SAKES FORGAVE I IT IN THE PERSON OF CHRIST;"

The phrase, *"To whom ye forgive any thing, I forgive also,"* in a sense expresses confidence in the Corinthians, that they were so much now on the right track, that whomever they forgave, he would be confident that it was the right thing to do.

PROOF OF CONFIDENCE

In a sense here, Paul is also telling the Corinthian Church that he has forgiven them for their false doctrine, their condoning immorality, and a host of other things that were going wrong. As a Church they have now repented of these things, are attempting to do things right, which inspires Paul's confidence, hence him giving them his complete trust.

Paul now has such confidence in the Congregation that he votes with it in the case of whomever it may absolve for whatever sin. The implication is that the Congregation, which is now awake to its obligation under Christ, need not wait and first submit each case to the Apostle before taking action. It seems to have done this in the case that was pending respecting the incest.

Again, let us note that the action is one of the Congregation alone, of course under Christ; it is not that of an individual apart from the Congregation, be he an Apostle, a General Officer of a Church Body, or a Pastor. As being a part of the Church, these may advise and direct, but they can do no more. It is the Church as a whole that acts. It expels, it forgives, and reinstates under Christ, but always on the Scriptural foundation.

HAD THIS MAN REALLY SINNED AGAINST PAUL?

In whatever manner that Paul needed to forgive this man, he had done what every good Christian should do, he had at once forgiven the hurt which he had caused him and now tells the Congregation so. In fact, the injury done to Paul, which of course was not personal and involved the Apostle only as it involved the entirety of the Body of Christ, was forgiven by Paul from the very beginning. Paul, indeed, felt the injury throughout, but only as one who had wholly forgiven the individual.

Paul had not been withholding his personal forgiveness until the sinner who had offended him should repent. The Corinthians are not to think that before they may reinstate the man, he must first beg Paul's pardon. The man had always had Paul's personal pardon. How the man stood in the sight of God is another matter, one between himself and God. Paul's soul was innocent, he had never harbored resentment, he had prayed the Lord's Prayer aright.

The idea is, this man's sin was not committed against Paul directly; Paul possibly had not even met the man. Therefore, Paul says: *"In a way I had nothing to forgive him; he involved me only distantly and in that manner I was hurt, but only in that manner, in fact only as every Believer is affected by the failure of any fellow Believer."*

The idea is, that when any member of the Body of Christ is truly blessed by the Lord, the entirety of the Body all over the world, in some mystical sense, is blessed as well, even though only a few actually know this individual, at least in most cases.

Conversely, because the Church is one Body, although made up of many members, if one member fails in any way, the entirety of the Body in some mystical way is hurt also. But it's only in an indirect way.

IN THE FACE OF CHRIST

The phrase, *"For if I forgave any thing, to whom I forgave it, for your sakes forgave I it in the Person of Christ,"* actually means that he forgave the man *"in the Face of Christ,"* which implies *"the Presence of Christ."*

This should help point out how heinous a crime it is when we refuse to forgive. We are actually casting disparagement on the Sacrifice of Christ that makes forgiveness possible. In other words, we are *"throwing it in His Face,"* which means that this is serious business indeed!

It is extremely serious in many ways, but the greatest of all is that if we do not forgive, and forgive completely and absolutely, we have cut

NOTES

off all forgiveness of the Lord on our part as well (Mat. 6:14-15).

Also, this doesn't mean to just merely forgive someone in your thinking but continue to shut them out in actual practice. That is not forgiveness. As we have already stated, the forgiveness of which the Holy Spirit here speaks through the Apostle, is the same type of forgiveness that is rendered on the part of our Heavenly Father. Anyone who meets His conditions, which simply means to repent, which also means to turn away from the sin whatever it may be, can expect immediate forgiveness. At that instance, the person is restored in God's sight totally and completely, with the sin not brought up to him by the Holy Spirit ever again. When this is done, all Believers are to follow suit along with the Lord, or else they enter into a tremendous travesty of justice, which to be certain effects themselves in a very adverse way.

We must never forget that our doing these things, or not properly doing them, are all done in the Presence of Christ, which means that He is surveying all situations of this nature and through the Holy Spirit prescribing the conclusion. Consequently, it is incumbent upon the Believer to do exactly what Christ does.

(11) "LEST SATAN SHOULD GET AN ADVANTAGE OF US: FOR WE ARE NOT IGNORANT OF HIS DEVICES."

The phrase, *"Lest Satan should get an advantage of us,"* presents a much larger picture than the situation at hand.

Satan was seeking greater game than the soul of this one man. He was attempting to use the situation any way he could, hopefully to turn the people against Paul causing them to ignore Paul's demands in Chapter 5 of I Corinthians, which would have alienated the Ministry of the Apostle regarding Corinth, at least had it been done. He hoped to frustrate the whole, blessed work that had been done in Corinth, and to deliver a stunning blow to Paul. These evil results would spread to even other Congregations.

Barring that, Satan would attempt to get the people to ignore Paul's admonishment to forgive and restore the Brother, which would have had a terrible effect upon this particular Assembly, and in fact, would have been just as bad as disobeying the first injunction of I Corinthians Chapter 5.

NOTES

Satan's work is gained either way, whether the condoning of open sin, or too needless severity of discipline. An unkind, unforgiving spirit would be just as ruinous as an open condoning of sin.

The phrase, *"For we are not ignorant of his devices,"* regards *"his ways."*

"Devices" in the Greek is *"noema"* and means *"thoughts, purposes, designs."*

WATCHFULNESS

In Luke 4:13, we read: *"And when the Devil had ended all the temptation, he departed from Him* (Jesus) *for a season."* The English words *"for a season"* could imply that there are times when the Saint is free from the temptations of Satan, and thus, he might relax his vigilance. But the Greek words do not permit of such a thought.

The thought in the original Text is that Satan departed from our Lord until a more opportune, propitious, or favorable time, when our Lord would be more susceptible to temptation, when Satan could work more effectively, or so he thought.

The word *"departed"* is from a Greek word which literally means *"to stand off from."* Thus, Satan never leaves the Saint alone.

If he ceases his activities, it is only that he might stand off from him and wait for a time when the Saint is more susceptible to temptation. Therefore, the price of victory over Satan is an everlasting watchfulness, *"lest Satan should get an advantage of us, for we are not ignorant of his devices."*

SATAN

Some people claim there is no such thing as a Devil; but after viewing the evil that is present in the world, simple folk will be excused for asking who is carrying on his business during his absence.

The fact is Satan is a real person, actually an Angel originally created by God, who served Him in faithfulness for a period of time, and then led a revolution against Him, which is briefly described in Isaiah Chapter 14 and Ezekiel Chapter 28. Exactly when this happened we are not told, but this one thing is certain, the earth has certainly felt the effects of this revolution which spread unto this domain, as recorded in Genesis Chapter 3.

HIS ORIGIN

The popular conception of a horned, cloven-footed, hideous-looking Devil (Satan) is taken from pagan mythology and not from the Bible. According to the Scriptures, Satan was originally called *"Lucifer,"* which means *"light-bearer."* In fact, he was the most glorious of all the Angels. But he proudly aspired to be *"like the Most High,"* and one might quickly add, to be like Him in an illegitimate way, and fell into *"the condemnation of the Devil"* (I Tim. 3:6).

To which we have briefly alluded, notice the background of the accounts in Isaiah Chapter 14 and Ezekiel Chapter 28. People have wondered why the kings of Babylon and Tyre are first addressed, before the account of Satan's fall. One answer is that the Prophet described Satan's fall for a practical purpose. Certain of the kings of Babylon and Tyre blasphemously claimed worship as divine beings (Ezek. 28:2; Dan. 3:1-12; Acts 12:20-23; Rev. 13:15), and thereby made their subjects the playthings of their ruthless ambition.

In order to warn such, God's inspired Prophets drew the veil from the dim past and depicted the fall of the rebel Angel, who said, *"I will be like God,"* i.e. *"I will be God."* The lesson was: if God punished the blasphemous pride of this high Angel, He will not fail to judge any king or ruler who dares to usurp the place of God.

Notice how Satan tried to infect the first parents with his spirit (Gen. 3:5; Isa. 14:14). Note how disappointed pride and ambition still consume him, so that he desires to be worshipped (Mat. 4:9) as *"god of this world"* (II Cor. 4:4), an ambition which will be temporarily satisfied when he becomes incarnate in the Antichrist (Rev. 13:4).

As a penalty for his wickedness, Satan was cast out of heaven, together with a group of Angels whom he had enlisted in his rebellion (Mat. 12:24; 25:41; Eph. 2:2; Rev. 12:7). He attempted to gain Eve as his ally, but God thwarted the plot and said, *"I will put enmity between thee and the woman"* (Gen. 3:15).

HIS CHARACTER

The pollution of Satan's character is indicated by the names and titles by which he is known:

NOTES

1. Satan: This name means literally *"adversary"* and pictures his malicious and persistent attempts to hinder God's purposes.

This opposition was especially manifest in his attempts to thwart God's Plan by destroying the chosen line from which the Messiah was to come — an activity predicted in Genesis 3:15. From the very beginning he has persisted in this effort.

Cain, Eve's first son, *"was of that wicked one, and slew his brother"* (I Jn. 3:12). God gave Eve another son, Seth, who became the appointed seed through whom earth's Deliverer should come.

(Actually, Adam and Eve had many sons and daughters who were not listed in the Bible account.)

The serpent's venom was still working in the race, and in the course of time, the line of Seth yielded to evil influences and deteriorated. The result was that condition of universal wickedness which brought on the flood. God's Plan was not thwarted, however, for there was at least one righteous person, Noah, whose family became the fathers of a new race. Thus failed Satan's attempt to destroy mankind and so defeat God's purpose.

CONTINUED OPPOSITION

From Shem, Noah's son, was descended Abraham, the progenitor of a chosen people, through whom God should save the world. Naturally, the Enemy's efforts would be directed against this particular family. One writer traces Satan's hidden opposition in the following incidents: Ishmael's opposition to Isaac; Esau's attempt to kill Jacob; Pharaoh's oppression of the Israelites.

Satan is described as seeking to destroy the Church, in two ways: A. From within by the introduction of false teaching (Mat. 13:38-39; I Tim. 4:1); and, B. From without by persecution (Rev. 2:10). The same was true of Israel, God's Old Testament Church.

The worship of the golden calf at the beginning of their national life is typical of what occurred constantly throughout their history; and in the Book of Esther we have the example of another attempt to destroy the chosen people. But God's chosen people have survived both the taint of idolatry and the fury of the persecutor, because of the Divine Grace which has always preserved a faithful remnant.

NOTES

THE REDEEMER

When, in the fullness of time, the Redeemer was born into the world, His Death was planned by the wicked Herod. But once again, God prevailed and Satan was frustrated.

In the wilderness, Satan attempted to hinder God's Anointed and to divert Him from His saving mission. But he was defeated; and his Conqueror *"went about doing good, and healing all who were oppressed of the Devil."*

This great agelong conflict will reach its climax when Satan, incarnate in the Antichrist, will be destroyed at the Coming of Christ.

2. Devil: This name means literally *"slanderer."* Satan is so called because he slanders both God and man (Gen. 3:2, 4-5; Job 1:9; Zech. 3:1-2; Lk. 22:31; Rev. 12:10).

3. Destroyer: This is the thought conveyed by the name *"Apollyon"* in the Greek and *"Abaddon"* in the Hebrew, recorded in Revelation 9:11. Filled with hatred against the Creator and His Works, the Devil would set himself up as the Destroyer — god.

4. Serpent: *"That old serpent, called the Devil"* (Rev. 12:9) recalls to our minds the one who, of old, used a serpent as the agent to bring about man's downfall.

5. Tempter: (Mat. 4:3). To *"tempt"* means literally *"to try or test,"* and the term is used also in connection with God's dealings (Gen. 22:1). But whereas God tests men for their good — to purify and develop character — Satan tempts them with a malicious design of destroying them.

6. Prince and god of this world: (Jn. 12:31; II Cor. 4:4). These titles suggest his influence over society as organized apart from God's Will.

THE WORLD

"The whole world lieth in wickedness (in the power of the evil one)*"* (I Jn. 5:19), and is animated by his spirit (I Jn. 2:16).

The world in the sense in which it is denounced in the Scriptures, *"is the vast assemblage of human activities, whose triune God is: A. Power; B. Pleasure; and, C. Profit."*

To these three it subordinates everything; the pursuit of these it endeavors by clever arguments to exalt and ennoble. It has as its help for this purpose the vast machinery of literature, business, commerce, and government, which are constantly insinuating reverence for these three, holding them up as the object of honorable desire, and continually lauding those who attain them.

It judges all things by exterior position and success, by false maxims of honor, by false ideas of the purpose of pleasure, and by false estimates of the value and dignity of wealth. It appeals to the lower part of our nature, investing itself with a false and materialistic refinement.

SATAN'S ACTIVITIES THEIR NATURE

Satan opposes God's Work (I Thess. 2:18), hinders the Gospel (Mat. 13:19; II Cor. 4:4), possesses, blinds, deceives, and snares the wicked (Lk. 22:3; II Cor. 4:4; Rev. 20:7-8; I Tim. 3:7). He afflicts (Job 1:12) and tempts (I Thess. 3:5) the Saints of God.

He is described as being presumptuous (Mat. 4:4-5), proud (I Tim. 3:6), powerful (Eph. 2:2), malignant (Job 2:4), subtle (Gen. 3:1; II Cor. 11:3), deceitful (Eph. 6:11), fierce, and cruel (I Pet. 5:8).

THEIR SPHERE

He does not confine his operations to the wicked and depraved. He often moves in the highest circles as an *"Angel of Light"* (II Cor. 11:14).

Indeed, that he attends spiritual gatherings is indicated by his presence at the Angelic convention (Job Chpt. 1), and by such terms as *"doctrines of Devils"* (I Tim. 4:1) and *"the Synagogue of Satan"* (Rev. 2:9). His agents often pose as *"ministers of righteousness"* (II Cor. 11:15).

The reason for his frequenting gospel meetings is his malicious determination to destroy the Church for he knows that once the salt of the earth has been robbed of its savor, mankind becomes an easier prey to his lawless spirit.

HIS MOTIVE

Why is Satan so intent on our ruin? Answers Joseph Husslein:

"He hates the image of God in us. He hates the very human nature we bear, which has been assumed by the Son of God. He hates the external Glory of God, which we have been created to promote and thereby to attain our own unending happiness.

"He hates the happiness itself to which we are destined, because he himself has forfeited it forever. He hates us for a thousand reasons and envies us."

As an ancient Jewish Scribe has said, *"But by the envy of the Devil, death came into the world: and they that follow him are on his side."*

HIS LIMITATIONS

While recognizing that Satan is strong, we should be careful not to exaggerate his power. For those who believe in Christ he is already a defeated foe (Jn. 12:31), and he is strong only to those who yield to him.

Despite his blustering rage he is a coward, for James says, *"Resist the Devil, and he will flee from you"* (James 4:7). Power he has, but it is limited. He can neither tempt (Mat. 4:1), afflict (Job 1:16), kill (Job. 2:6; Heb. 2:14), nor touch a Believer without God's permission.

HIS DESTINY

In the very beginning God predicted and decreed the downfall of the power that had caused man's Fall (Gen. 3:15), and the humbling of the serpent to the dust was a prophetic picture of the final degradation and defeat of *"that old serpent the Devil."*

Satan's career has indeed been downward. He was cast out of Heaven in the beginning; during the Tribulation he will be cast from the Heavenlies to the Earth (Rev. 12:9); during the Millennium he will be imprisoned in the bottomless pit, and after a thousand years he will be cast in the lake of fire, where he will remain for ever and ever (Rev. 20:10).

Thus, God's Word assures us of the ultimate defeat of evil.

FALLEN ANGELS

All Angels in the beginning were created perfect and blameless, and like man, were endowed with the power of choice. Under the leadership of Satan, many of them sinned and were cast out of Heaven (Jn. 8:44; II Pet. 2:4; Jude vs. 6). The sin by which they and their leader fell was pride. Some have thought that the occasion of their rebellion was a Revelation of the coming Incarnation of the Son of God and of their obligation to worship Him.

The present abode of evil Angels is described in Scripture as partly in hell (II Pet. 2:4) and partly in the world, especially in the air around us (Jn. 12:31; 14:30; II Cor. 4:4; Rev. 12:4, 7-9).

By ensnaring men in sin, they have acquired great power over them (II Cor. 4:3-4; Eph. 2:2; 6:11-12); this power has been broken for those who are faithful to Christ, by the Redemption which He has achieved (Rev. 5:9; 7:13-14). Angels have never come under the provision for Redemption (I Pet. 1:12), at least as we know such, but hell has been prepared for their everlasting punishment, and of course we speak of fallen Angels (Mat. 25:41).

NOTES

DEMONS

The Scriptures do not describe the origin of demons, but this we do know, they are not fallen Angels, as some Preachers claim. Fallen Angels have spirit bodies, and demons do not have any type of body, but seek to inhabit a body in order that they may carry out their evil functions.

Even though the Scriptures do not describe their origin, we do know that God did not originally make them in this fashion, for all that He does is always good (James 1:17). The question of their beginning seems to be a part of the mystery surrounding the origin of evil. But the Scriptures testify very clearly to their real existence and activity (Mat. 12:26-27).

In the Gospels we see them as wicked, disembodied spirits, which enter people who are thereupon said to have a demon. In some cases, more than one demon takes up his abode in the same victim (Mk. 16:9; Lk. 8:2). The effects of their indwelling are insanity, epilepsy, and other diseases, chiefly connected with the mental and nervous system (Mat. 9:33; 12:22; Mk. 5:4-5). However, this does not mean that everyone who is insane or has epilepsy, etc., is demon possessed. In fact, most aren't.

The person who is under the influence of a demon is not master of himself; the evil spirit speaks through his (or her) lips or makes him dumb at his pleasure, drives him whether he wills, and generally uses him as a tool, sometimes imparting for this a supernatural strength.

EXAMPLES

Writes Dr. Nevius, a Missionary to China who has made a thorough study of demon-possession, but which in fact could apply anywhere:

"We notice in cases of demon-possession in China and those given in the Scripture, in some instances a kind of double consciousness, or actions and impulses directly opposite and contrary. A woman in Fuchow, though under the

influence of a demon whose instinct was to shun the Presence of Christ, was moved by an opposite influence, evidently of the Lord, to leave her home and come to Fuchow to seek help from Jesus."

The following are some conclusions of the same writer, based upon a study of demon-possession among the Chinese:

"The most striking characteristic of these cases is that the subject evidences another personality and the normal personality for the time being is partially or wholly dormant.

"The new personality presents traits of character utterly different from those which really belong to the subject in the normal state, and this change of character is with rare exceptions in the direction of moral perverseness and impurity . . . many persons while demon-possessed give evidence of knowledge which cannot be accounted for in ordinary ways. They often appear to know the Lord Jesus Christ as a Divine Person, and show an aversion to and a fear of Him."

Mark especially this good news.

"Many cases of Demon-possession have been cured by prayer to Christ, or in His Name; some very readily, some with difficulty. So far as we have been able to discover, this method of cure has not failed in any case, however stubborn and long continued, in which it has been tried.

"And in no instance so far as appears, has the malady returned if the subject has become a Christian and continues to lead a Christian life . . . as a result of the comparison that has been made we see that the correspondence between the cases met with in China and those recorded in Scripture is complete and circumstantial, covering almost every point presented in the Scripture narrative."

MOTIVES OF DEMON SPIRITS

What is the motive that influences demons to possess themselves of the bodies of men? Answers Dr. Nevius:

"The Bible teaches clearly that in all Satan's dealings with our race his object is to deceive and ruin us by drawing our minds from God and inducing us to break God's Laws and bring upon ourselves His displeasure. These objects are secured by demon-possession, at least in the extreme cases. Superhuman efforts are produced which to the ignorant and uninstructed seem Divine.

NOTES

"Divine worship and implicit obedience are demanded and are enforced by the infliction of physical distress and by false promises and fearful threats. In this way idolatrous rites and superstitions, interwoven with social and political, have usurped the place in almost every nation in history of the pure worship of God (I Cor. 10:20-21; Rev. 9:20; Deut. 32:16; Isa. 65:3).

"As regards the Demons themselves, it appears that they have additional personal reasons. The possession of human bodies seems to afford them a much desired place of rest and physical gratification. Our Saviour speaks of Evil Spirits walking through dry places and seeking rest, and especially desirous of finding rest in the bodies of the victims. When deprived of a place of rest in the bodies of human beings, they are represented as seeking it in the bodies of inferior animals (Mat. 12:43-45)."

PARALLELS

Said Martin Luther, *"The Devil is the Ape of God."* In other words, the Enemy is ever counterfeiting God's Works. And surely Demon-possession is a devilish travesty of that most sublime of experiences — the indwelling of the Holy Spirit in man. Notice some parallels:

1. Demon-possession means the introduction of a new personality into the victim's being, making him in a sense a new but worse creature. Notice how the Gadarene Demoniac (Mat. 8:29) acted and spoke as one controlled by another personality.

Conversely, he who is controlled by God has a Divine Personality indwelling him (Jn. 14:23).

2. Demon-inspired utterances are a Satanic travesty on Spirit-inspired utterances.

3. It has been observed that when a person has consciously yielded himself to a Demon-power, he often receives some gift such as fortune-telling, mediumship, etc.

Writes Dr. Nevius, *"In this stage, the demonized subject has developed capacities for use, and is willing to be used. He is the trained, accustomed, voluntary slave of the demon."* It is a Satanic imitation of the Gifts of the Holy Spirit!

4. Demoniacs often manifest extraordinary and superhuman strength — a Satanic imitation of the Power of the Holy Spirit.

Thus, we see that the demonstrated possibility of Demon-possession argues for the possibility of possession by the Divine Spirit, i. e., *"the Holy Spirit."*

The Lord Jesus came into the world to deliver people from the power of evil spirits and put them under the control of God's Spirit.

(12) "FURTHERMORE, WHEN I CAME TO TROAS TO PREACH CHRIST'S GOSPEL, AND A DOOR WAS OPENED UNTO ME OF THE LORD,"

The phrase, *"Furthermore, when I came to Troas to preach Christ's Gospel,"* presents the place he had visited on his second Missionary journey (Acts 16:8-11), but had left it in consequence of the Vision which called him to Macedonia. He now stops there on his journey through Macedonia to Corinth, which he announced in I Corinthians 16:5.

Troas was located on what is now the coast of modern Turkey. It was on the Aegean Sea, actually across that Sea from Greece. By land, it was probably about 150 miles northwest of Ephesus.

Paul did make a later visit to Troas, actually on his way to Jerusalem, where he preached to a group of Believers until midnight. This was the time that a young man fell out of a window and died as a result; however, God miraculously brought him back to life (Acts 20:7-12).

TROAS

For centuries this notable Seaport, located, as stated, across the Aegean Sea from Macedonia, was a major center for traffic between Asia and Europe. It was founded shortly after the death of Alexander the Great, and its full name was Alexandria Troas.

Despite the open door for Ministry there, Paul was so distraught over the Corinthian situation that he could not take advantage of the opportunity. This incident certainly helps demonstrate that this Spiritual giant was subject to emotional highs and lows, just like the rest of us. In this case, even his itinerary was influenced by his state of mind (Rossier).

The phrase, *"And a door was opened unto me of the Lord,"* concerned an opportunity for Ministry in this place.

It seems that a Church had not been established here as of yet, but Acts 20:6, etc., shows that a Church, in fact, was founded in Troas before the next Spring.

Did Paul return from his meeting with Titus in Macedonia and enter the open door and

NOTES

found the Church at Troas? It seems that he did, although we have no information beyond what is given in Acts Chapter 20. This we do know, Paul was not a man to leave such an open door without entering it eventually.

THAT WHICH SEEMS TO HAVE HAPPENED

The picture of what transpired in Paul's spirit during the anxious wait for the return of Titus from Corinth is realistic in every way. According to the plan projected in I Corinthians 16:5, Paul had come from Ephesus as far as Troas in order to go on from there to Macedonia and finally to Corinth. The tour was not rapid, work was to be done along the way.

On arriving at Troas, Paul expected to find Titus there. We see that he had sent Titus to Corinth long enough before, so that Titus might have returned with a full report about conditions in Corinth. It seems that Troas had been agreed upon as the place of meeting.

But when Paul arrived there, Titus had not come, and no news had been sent by him. One can imagine Paul's feelings. Had the worst happened at Corinth? Was Titus detained in Corinth because nothing had as yet been achieved?

We have seen, not only that Paul's very soul was in his work, but also what the great troubles and dangers in Corinth meant to him and to his work.

As a result, Paul found no rest in Troas, thereby he resolved to wait there no longer but to go into Macedonia, thus hoping to be joined by Titus soon and to get the news that, whether good or bad, meant so much and would end his uncertainty.

So it came about that Titus ultimately joined Paul in Macedonia (II Cor. 7:13); we do not know for sure in what city they met, but it probably was Philippi. Here is our evidence that II Corinthians was written in Macedonia (Lenski).

(13) "I HAD NO REST IN MY SPIRIT, BECAUSE I FOUND NOT TITUS MY BROTHER: BUT TAKING MY LEAVE OF THEM, I WENT FROM THENCE INTO MACEDONIA."

The phrase, *"I had no rest in my spirit,"* presents the simple matter of a journey from Troas to Philippi, as always with Paul, lifted up into the highest realm of the Divine purposes and activities. We should gather from these tiny inflections that everything Paul did, and everything we do as well, should always be elevated to the realm of the Spiritual regarding the furtherance of the Work of God. Of course, only one who is totally sold out to the Lord, would function on this level. And yet, despite the difficulties involved, and there are difficulties, this is the most fulfilling, rewarding life that one could ever have — that of being sold out completely to Jesus.

THE HUMAN SPIRIT

Man is created spirit, soul, and body.

With the body, man has world consciousness.

With the soul, man has self-consciousness.

With the spirit, man has God consciousness.

Inasmuch as this was the Work of God, and I speak of the difficulties at Corinth, Paul's spirit was troubled. He knew the implications of the situation if it went wrong, in other words, if the Church did not heed his admonitions in the Epistle sent to them, which we now know as I Corinthians. As previously stated, for all practical purposes the Church would be lost. So, his spirit cannot rest until he knows what has happened with Titus and his visit there.

Here we have the full revelation of Paul's anxiety regarding the outcome of affairs in Corinth. It drove him past that inviting, open door in Troas; it speeded him into Macedonia to meet Titus at the earliest possible moment.

Are we disappointed in not meeting a cool, calm, self-assured Apostle, a spirit that nothing could perturb? Do we think that this would be the ideal Christian spirit? We shall have to revise our ideal, if such be the case.

Paul shed tears, felt grief, was in anxious tension, confesses it in II Corinthians 2:4 and here in Verse 13. But all this emotion concerned not his own person or his earthly welfare, it concerned the Church. That is the point! Sad and dangerous conditions and situations in the Church — do they draw tears, prayer, and anxiety from our hearts?

That the Holy Spirit allowed the Apostle to so portray his feelings, even that which would seem to most as to be weakness, is a comfort to this Evangelist and should be to each Reader as well.

A PERSONAL EXAMPLE

As Paul knew what he was called of the Lord to do, likewise I know also what the Lord has called me to do. It pertains to mass Evangelism respecting Television and Crusades. Consequently, when we lose a particular Station or Cable, or else, we are not able to air the Program in certain areas because of whatever reason, there is a pain in my heart that approaches grief, exactly as Paul said. By the Grace of God we have seen literally hundreds of thousands brought to a saving knowledge of Jesus Christ, through the Telecast and the Crusades. As stated, the Lord has called us for this task, and has given us the Anointing of the Holy Spirit to deliver the Message which touches the souls of men. Of course, Satan will do all within his power to stop this Message, using every tactic at his disposal. Regrettably, he gets his greatest help from those who call themselves *"Christians."*

Due to these things, at times the grief is so severe, that it seems impossible for a human being to bear. I know how much that souls are at stake, and there is nothing more important than that.

The phrase, *"Because I found not Titus my brother,"* evidently refers to a prearranged meeting, but which did not come off because Titus was delayed for some reason.

Paul had several companions laboring with him who contributed greatly to the Work of God. The four most prominent were: Barnabas, Silas, Timothy, and Titus. Luke was also very prominent, but it seems in a little different way. As the Reader knows, Luke wrote the Book of Acts, which cataloged the history of the great Apostle, and of course is valuable beyond compare. In fact, sometimes the party was quite large, with several traveling with Paul (Acts 20:4).

The phrase, *"But taking my leave of them,"* refers to those in Troas who had already accepted the Lord, and evidently saw the great opportunity in Troas for Paul to build a great Church, which evidently he shortly did.

The phrase, *"I went from thence into Macedonia,"* pertains most of all to meeting Titus and hearing news of what had happened at Corinth. He no doubt met Titus at Philippi.

Macedonia is the upper part of modern Greece, probably at that time taking in as well the southern part of the modern country of Albania.

(14) "NOW THANKS BE UNTO GOD, WHICH ALWAYS CAUSETH US TO TRIUMPH IN CHRIST, AND MAKETH MANIFEST THE

SAVOUR OF HIS KNOWLEDGE BY US IN EVERY PLACE."

The phrase, *"Now thanks be unto God,"* presents Paul by the use of the word *"now,"* having received the great news from Titus concerning the Church at Corinth. As the Apostle, writing after the fact, relates all of these things to the Corinthians, even going into great detail respecting his anxiety regarding the situation, he now proclaims his imminent joy. His first *"thanks"* and appreciation are to God. The Lord had dealt with him as to how to deal with the situation, and now he knows it was the Lord especially considering the tremendous victory which has been won.

THE LEADING OF THE SPIRIT

I personally think that some of the consternation on Paul's part regarding Corinth, concerned his method of handling this situation. As we have repeatedly stated, he had postponed his visit to Corinth, feeling that a Letter to them would serve the better purpose. No doubt he had sought the Lord earnestly about this matter, and felt in his spirit this was the right thing to do.

But yet, I think Paul did not have a clearcut picture in his mind respecting this decision. I think it nagged at him after he had sent the Letter by Titus, if he in fact, really had the Mind of the Lord respecting this very important turn of events. Would it have been better for him to have gone to Corinth instead of sending the Letter? This question might not have ever entered his mind, but I personally think it did.

Sometimes it's very easy to ascertain the Mind of the Lord. Sometimes it's not easy at all. For instance, on the second Missionary trip of Paul, he had made plans to go into Asia, but the Scripture says, *"And were forbidden of the Holy Spirit to preach the Word in Asia."*

He then attempted to go into Bithynia, which was farther East, *"but the Spirit suffered them not"* (Acts 16:6-7).

I have every confidence that Paul had sought the Lord earnestly regarding this trip. He evidently thought he had the Mind of the Lord, but found that he didn't. Finally he receives the great Macedonian call which turned him to Europe (Acts 16:9-10).

Why did the Holy Spirit work in this manner? Of course, all the answers would be known only to the Lord. But I suppose that such manner of approach is intended by the Lord to keep the Believer trusting Him, even someone as notable as Paul.

To know the Mind of the Lord, there are two things which must always be done:

1. We must seek the Lord about everything, and I mean everything.

2. We have to seek His Face constantly.

I think that Paul feared that he had possibly taken the wrong course respecting the sending of this Letter, instead of going in person. Satan takes advantage of such thinking and causes us great problems. To be sure, even the great Apostle was not immune from such situations. And neither are we!

Thankfully, he had made the right decision; he had been led by the Holy Spirit, and victory was the result.

The phrase, *"Which always causeth us to triumph in Christ,"* presents a tremendously encouraging statement to say the least. I want to look at several words in this phrase which I think will be a great blessing to us.

ALWAYS

In effect, this tells us that if we continue to trust the Lord, irrespective as to how difficult the situation may be in the meantime, or how much it may presently look like defeat, victory will always be ours. We all know that it is dangerous to use the adverb *"always"*; however, with respect to God, it is very appropriate because *"the Battle is the Lord's"* (I Sam. 17:47), and we do not have to fear about failing to triumph.

This is not just an Evangelical pep talk. It is the Truth. The Lord has never lost a battle, and the Lord can never lose a battle. If one thinks a moment, 100% is a pretty good record, and that is exactly what the Lord promises.

The *"always"* doesn't mean there will not be a battle, doesn't mean there will not be difficulties, doesn't mean there will not be reverses, but it does mean that if we keep believing, keep true, keep trusting, that the Lord will ultimately see us through and in victorious, glorious fashion.

Not for a moment overlooking our own failures, but always looking forward to the enabling Grace of God, this situation with our own Ministry, which within itself is impossible, at least as far as outward circumstances are concerned,

NOTES

still, will ultimately come out to a glorious, successful conclusion. I know that, because of what the Lord *has* done, because of what He *is* doing, and because of what He *shall* do. In other words, I believe He will help us finish this course with joy!

CAUSETH US

The *"cause"* is God and not our own talent, ability, or techniques, etc. That's the reason that Paul was thanking God. He knew that God was directing the situation all along. In view of that being the case, one may ask the question as to why Paul allowed himself to get into such a state of depression, etc.

That is a good question, whether for Paul, or for us as well.

The answer is that Paul, like us, was human. Some may not like that answer; nevertheless, the answer is correct for all of us. That simply means that it is not possible yet for a person to have so much Faith that the human frailties at this time can be laid aside. That will come at the Resurrection, but until then, we are still in this mortal coil.

Consequently, those who actually have far less knowledge than they think they have, can rail out at Paul claiming that it was a lack of Faith on his part if they so desire; however, such foolishness is only priming them for an even greater despondency. The human bonds cannot be slipped at this time. That day, gloriously, will come, but it has not yet arrived. Until then, the Resurrection, we shout, we laugh, we rejoice, but we also weep, grieve, and yes, at times, fear.

But God is overseeing it all, and will not allow anything to come upon us harder than we can bear, and in fact, tailor-makes the entirety of the situation to fit our spiritual need, always with the idea in mind of helping us to grow in the Grace and Knowledge of the Lord.

TO TRIUMPH

The *"Triumph"* of which Paul speaks here was no doubt colored by the triumphant processions quite common in the Roman Empire of that day. But yet, as grand and glorious as those processions were, still they were nothing in comparison to the actual Triumph which we experience in the spirit world, in Christ.

"Triumph" in the Greek is *"thriambeuo"* and means *"to make an acclamatory procession, to conquer, to give victory."* This word is found in only one other place in the New Testament, Colossians 2:15, and there Paul used it of the triumph of Christ over the Devil and all his forces. Through His glorious Work on the Cross, He *"disarmed"* and *"exposed"* them. The metaphor relates directly to the way the defeated enemies of Rome were actually treated. After being disarmed, they would be paraded through the streets of Rome, or whatever principle city in the Empire was favored.

NOTES

THE ROMAN EXAMPLE

As stated, Paul's terminology in II Corinthians no doubt comes from the Roman custom that was familiar to the inhabitants of the Empire. Under certain conditions, a General would be accorded what they labeled a *"Triumph."* If he had won a single battle in which at least 5,000 members of the opposing army were slain, and if he had extended the boundaries of the Roman Empire, he was qualified to receive this grand honor.

Although the comparison would obviously fall very short, Paul was undoubtedly applying this terminology to Christ, the Great Conqueror, Who always leads us in Triumph — leads us, that is if we truly follow Him.

In conjunction with this Triumph, the General would enter the City of Rome in a chariot drawn by four horses. He would be clothed in a purple tunic and would be carrying an ivory Scepter with the Roman Eagle at its apex. A stop would be made at the temple of Jupiter, where he would offer a sacrifice. Many times his small children, that is if he had small children, would ride with him in the chariot and a slave would stand behind him, holding a jeweled crown over his head.

It was a magnificent procession, with certain groups normally preceding the man being honored: the members of the Senate; other Governmental Officials; the spoils of war taken from the conquered nation; portraits of the conquered land and its fortresses, ships, etc.; a white bull to be sacrificed; the captives in chains; the Officers bearing the insignia of the General; the musicians; and the priests.

The General would be followed by his family and his army. The procession would be made even more extravagant by the plethora of garlands that emitted sweet floral fragrance.

NOTES

Incense bearers would also dispense pleasant perfumes. This aroma transmitted the smell of victory far and wide (Rossier).

IN CHRIST

The victories given to us by God, always come to us through Jesus Christ. He is the One Who has paid the price for man's Redemption, purchasing our Salvation with His Own Precious Blood, and defeating the powers of darkness by what He did at Calvary and the Resurrection.

The victory that the Lord had given Paul was over the enemies of the Gospel; it was success in advancing the interests of the Kingdom of Christ; and he rejoiced in that victory and in that success, with more solid and substantial joy than a Roman Victor ever felt on returning from his conquests over nations, even when attended with the richest spoils of victory, and by humbled Princes and Kings in chains, and when the assembled thousands shouted in triumph!

Jesus Christ must ever be the center of all that we do, but not just Jesus Christ as a miracle worker, etc., but rather Jesus Christ the Crucified, Risen, Ascended, and Exalted Lord.

In listening the other day to a Television ad of the Mormons attempting to sell their Religion, they were trying a new tactic, the promotion of Jesus Christ. However, they were extolling the *"teachings"* of Jesus, as they put it, as the wisdom to follow. They missed the entirety of the point.

Of course, everything that Jesus said could be described as nothing other than *"Words of Life."* Most definitely His *"Teachings"* should be followed to the letter; however, it was not His Teachings which delivered mankind from the terrible bondage of darkness and death, but rather His Sacrificial Atoning, Vicarious Offering of Himself on Calvary's Cross which broke the back of Satan, so to speak, and liberated man from the terrible clutches of darkness.

To extol Christ as a great Teacher, Leader, Preacher, or Miracle Worker, is wonderful and good, but those things within themselves will not liberate mankind or set the captive free. So, in effect, the Christ promoted by the Mormons, as untold millions of others, is, as Paul addressed the subject, *"another Jesus"* (II Cor. 11:4). In fact, much of the Church world promotes *"another Jesus!"* He's a Jesus Who makes them rich, or a Jesus Who is the Example, or a Jesus Who did good things. All of these things may or may not have some place in correct Bible Doctrine, but unless it's *"Jesus Christ and Him Crucified,"* plain, pure, and simple, it is *"another Jesus"* (I Cor. 2:2).

The phrase, *"And maketh manifest the Savour of His Knowledge by us in every place,"* once again in the Apostle's mind is drawn from the Roman culture of his day.

A SWEET SAVOUR

The scene before the Apostle's thinking continues to be that of a Roman triumph. The advent and the presence of the victorious General were announced by slaves scattering sweet odors all along the historic way that ended at the Capitol in Rome. The victor was followed by a multitude of captives, even as we have already stated, some destined to life, others to death. On reaching the Capitol, those doomed to death were slain; those assured to life, liberated. The glory of the conqueror was published by the condemnation of the one group and by the liberation of the other.

The scattering of the sweet odors all along the way was a savour of death to the captives condemned to death, and of life to the captives ordained to life.

THE SWEET INCENSE OF THE GOSPEL

The Glory of Christ is the subject and the purpose of the Gospel. It announces everlasting destruction to those who refuse to obey it (II Thess. 1:8-9), but Eternal Salvation to those who accept it (I Thess. 5:9). A Gospel that excludes either of these doctrines is a false Gospel — it is not a Sweet Savour of Christ to God — and it does not glorify, but, on the contrary, it dishonors Him.

So the Apostle here pictures himself at one and the same time as a slave scattering the Sweet Incense of the Gospel, as a willing captive ordained to life, and as a loyal soldier sharing the Great Conqueror's Triumph. In his hands the perfume of the Gospel was pure.

THE KNOWLEDGE OF THE LORD

Paul speaks here of the Knowledge of Christ, which is the greatest knowledge of all, and fills the world with a very pleasant incense and fragrance, at least where His Gospel is preached.

This *"Savour"* of Christ was acceptable to God — as the fragrance of aromatics and of incense was pleasant in the triumphal procession of the returning Roman victor. This is the same as the Sacrifices that were offered in Old Testament times, and it says, *"The Lord smelled a Sweet Savour"* (Gen. 8:21; Ex. 29:18, 25, 41; Lev. 1:9, 13, 17; 2:2, 9; Num. 15:3; 28:8).

The question may be asked as to how a little animal burning on an Altar could provide a *"Sweet Savour"* or a fragrance to the Lord. It was such to Him because He saw in this, as gruesome as it was, the Salvation of man. As Charles Wesley wrote and sang, *"Oh, love that will not let me go."*

The Knowledge of Christ was diffused everywhere by Paul, as it should be by all. The effect of his conquests was to proclaim the Knowledge of the Saviour — and this was acceptable and pleasant to God — though there might be many who would not avail themselves of it, and would perish.

"In every place" whither the Preachers of this Knowledge come, its blessed fragrance is spread.

(15) "FOR WE ARE UNTO GOD A SWEET SAVOUR OF CHRIST, IN THEM THAT ARE SAVED, AND IN THEM THAT PERISH:"

The phrase, *"For we are unto God a Sweet Savour of Christ,"* actually presents Preachers of the Gospel, rather True Preachers who are true to the Word. Such pertains to the Gospel of Christ which we preach.

Paul speaks of this Sweet Savour in Ephesians 5:2; however, the fragrance there is due to the Sacrifice of Christ on the Cross, while it is here due to the Gospel which Christ's Preachers preach among men.

In Philippians 4:18, Paul offers the same thought again respecting *"a sweet smell,"* i.e., *"Sweet Savour,"* with him referring there to all Believers; however, the thought here concerns only Preachers, their being genuine, never chaffering or bargaining with the Word of God, thereby, bringing in an offensive smell.

The phrase, *"In them that are saved, and in them that perish,"* presents the Gospel of Jesus Christ, i.e., the Sacrifice of Christ, dividing mankind into two distinct clusters. The Apostle called them, literally, *"the ones being saved,"* and, *"the ones perishing."*

The idea is that of progressively enjoying Salvation, becoming more and more like Christ,

NOTES

while at the same time, the other group, those who are perishing, digressively going from bad to worse.

TWO RACES OF PEOPLE

Even though there are five color groups in the world respecting human beings, in the Mind of God there are only two groups — those saved and those unsaved, i.e., *"those who have accepted Christ, and those who have rejected Christ."* There is no middle ground, meaning all the Religions of the world hold no consequence with God whatsoever. To be blunt, as regrettably as it may sound, it is either Jesus Christ or Hell!

This tells us that despite the True Gospel of Jesus Christ being preached in all of its power and fullness, still some will reject Christ, in fact most (Mat. 7:13-14). Consequently, yet though this would be the result, the labors of the Ministers of the Gospel of Christ are acceptable to God.

PREDESTINATION?

Incidently, the terminology used here certainly does not fit the idea of being individually predestined to Salvation or damnation at some point in the past. Just as the same Sun melts wax and hardens clay, the same Gospel humbles the ones who yield to it, but hardens the ones who resist it.

Just as the same cloud brought light to the Israelites, and darkness to the Egyptians, Calvary supplies glorious Light to those who accept it, but terrible darkness to those who refuse it. Just as the same Sun bleaches linen and tans skin, the same Sacrifice of Christ cleanses souls who believe and makes unbelievers even worse children of Hell than they were before hearing the Gospel. It has that effect!

The Scripture plainly says, *"The Lord . . . is . . . not willing that any should perish, but that all should come to repentance"* (II Pet. 3:9).

The fault of the perishing is not the fault of the Gospel nor of God. It is the fault of the individual, as they willingly make their decision against Christ.

THE SUFFICIENCY OF THE GOSPEL

There is a sufficiency in the Gospel for all men, and in its nature it is as really fitted to save one as another. Whatever may be the manner in which it is received, it is always in itself the same pure and glorious System; full of Benevolence and Mercy, i.e., *"Good News."* Consequently, the bitterest enemy of the Gospel cannot point to one of its provisions that is adapted or designed to make men miserable, and to destroy them. All its provisions are adapted to Salvation; all its arrangements are those of Mercy.

Thus, if some be saved, though others perish, the Gospel remains its own virtue, and we the Preachers remain just as we are; and the Gospel retains its wonderful, fragrant properties, though some may disbelieve and abuse it and perish.

A DEEPER CONDEMNATION?

It is implied that the Gospel once heard and rejected, will be the occasion of heavier condemnation, and that they would sink into deeper ruin in consequence of it being preached to them. This is implied in the expression in the next Verse, *"To the one we are the savour of death unto death."*

The Gospel compels no one against his will either to go to Heaven or to Hell. However, it is impossible for anyone to hear the Gospel and not be affected in some manner. No man leaves the Gospel as he first heard the Gospel.

Some may then argue, that being the case, it would be better that the Gospel not be preached at all, considering that almost all reject its Message; however, such thinking is foolishness for the simple reason that despite the Christ Rejecters, every iota of Light in the world presently, and in fact always has been, is a direct result of the Gospel. So, all the prosperity, health and healing, education, correct knowledge, inventions, technological advancement, a superior way of life, all, and without fail, stem from the Gospel of Jesus Christ. So, while it does have a negative affect on the Rejecters, with them actually becoming worse, and incidently, which can happen to an entire nation, still, its benefits a million times over outweigh the negative turn.

So, in answer to the Moslems, the cause and reason for all the debauchery, vice, immorality, crime, etc., in America is not because of the Gospel of Jesus Christ, but rather the rejection of the Gospel of Jesus Christ.

I would remind the Moslem world, as well as all others, that to a great extent, the entirety of mankind looks to America as it looks to no other nation, and even though it does not realize such, the Blessing that America spreads out all over the world, despite its failures, is because of the Gospel of Jesus Christ. So, they can attribute their Blessings, such as they should be, to the one they despise, the Lord Jesus Christ.

NOTES

AMERICA AND THE SPREADING OF THE GOSPEL

America's greatest commodity of export is the Gospel of Jesus Christ, that is if one would be permitted to refer to the Gospel as such. Regrettably, America does not realize this of which I have said, but the great basic ingredient that goes from these shores, and one could say the same for Canada, is little that of which we think such as services and goods, but rather that which can change people's lives for the better, and not just better but rather gloriously better, is none other than the Gospel. Wherever the Gospel of Jesus Christ goes, at least if it is accepted, freedom and prosperity always follow. They are the natural outgrowth of the Message of Jesus Christ.

Someone has well said that as long as America's greatest commodity is the Gospel of Jesus Christ, the jackbooted heels of foreign conquerors will never walk on American soil.

That is true!

THE CHURCH AND THE GOSPEL

Called for the very purpose of taking the Gospel to the world, and having attempted to do so through Television and citywide Crusades, along with the building of Churches and Bible Schools, as well as Schools for the Children, I have some knowledge of that of which I speak.

We have aired the Gospel by Television over a great part of the world, and continue to do so until this hour. Consequently, the Lord has helped us to see untold thousands brought to a saving knowledge of the Lord Jesus Christ.

If one properly studies the Book of Acts and the Epistles as well, one will have to come to the conclusion that the taking of this Message to the world is priority with God. This certainly doesn't mean that other things are not important, for they are. It does mean that if it is priority with God, and it certainly is, then it should be priority with the Church as well.

Satan has done several things to hinder this great work in the Church. First of all, he has drawn away great numbers of Believers into the *"Prosperity Message,"* or the *"Political Message,"* which greatly hinders the propagation of the Gospel. Too many Christians are involved with the idea of the *"here and now,"* rather than the eternal destiny of lost souls. In other words, they are trying to use Christ to get rich, or some other foolishness, rather than seeing the picture as it actually is, humanity lost without God, and desperately needing a Saviour. As someone has also said, *"If man's problem had been money, God would have sent an Economist. If education, He would have sent a Teacher."* The list goes on. While those things certainly have their place and are necessary, still, man's need really is Salvation from sin, so God sent a Saviour. That is the most important Message on the face of the Earth.

As well, many of the mainline Pentecostal Denominations, which once touched the world with the Gospel of Jesus Christ, are for the most part at present, sending amateur Psychologists to the mission field. Consequently, at least in these circles, very little true Gospel is being presented.

There are a few Godly Missionaries left in the world presently, but not many. To be frank, that number is diminishing all the time, and simply because the taking of this great Message of Jesus Christ is of little significance anymore to the far greater majority of the modern Church.

It is my prayer that the Church will come back to Calvary, for it is there that it receives its vision and sees itself as it actually is. It is there, and there alone, that it sees lost and dying humanity in desperate need of Jesus Christ.

(16) "TO THE ONE WE ARE THE SAVOUR OF DEATH UNTO DEATH; AND TO THE OTHER THE SAVOUR OF LIFE UNTO LIFE. AND WHO IS SUFFICIENT FOR THESE THINGS?"

The phrase, *"To the one we are the savour of death unto death,"* carries the idea that because Christ is Christ, Grace is Grace, and True Gospel Preachers preach only Christ's Gospel (namely that we are saved by Christ Alone), that this fragrance which is so sweet to God, so full of life because of its very Source, namely Christ, Who is the Life, and so effective for Life to all who believe, its very nature must be the very opposite for all who do not believe.

NOTES

Since there is only one Power and one Source of Life, when that is spurned it becomes for those who do spurn it a Power and Source of death. This only appears to be a paradox; it is no more so than any positive and negative are.

DEATH UNTO DEATH

The thought is wrong which claims that one class of men make Christ Life for themselves while others make Him death for themselves. He is what He is apart from all of us.

As to why some accept the Gospel and some will not, can only be said to be a mystery which lies in the human will, which we will never penetrate to its complete depths. It is not a question as to how some are saved; Christ is the plain answer to that; it is the fact that others reject Him, draw death from Him, refuse the Life He brings them.

Irrespective as to how men would attempt to explain this scenario, no plausible explanation is possible because the rejection is an unreasonable, we might even say, insane act, and no reasonable explanation can be given for what is unreasonable, not even by those who do the reasonable act.

The phrase, *"And to the other the savour of Life unto Life,"* presents as is obvious, those who accept Christ as their Saviour, making Him the Lord of their lives. Such is *"More Abundant Life"* (Jn. 10:10).

LIFE UNTO LIFE

As an example, the word of the Law which proceeded out of the Mouth of God was an odor of Life to the Israelites, at least to those who would accept it, but an odor of death to the Gentiles.

The idea of *"Life unto Life,"* refers to that which produces life. It is used here to denote Salvation. It is as follows:

1. It is life in opposition to the death in sin and which all are by nature.

2. It is life in opposition to death in the grave — as it leads to a glorious Resurrection.

3. It is Life in opposition to eternal death — to the second dying — as it leads to life, peace, and joy in Heaven.

It is a Life which will never cease, never diminish, will in fact always continue to become more and more alive, which of course is difficult to grasp. The unbeliever keeps getting more and more dead, while the Believer keeps getting more and more alive. All of it through Christ as its Source.

The question, *"And who is sufficient for these things?"*, refers to the Gospel, and it so mighty to save so many from death to life, while at the same time in a sense, sending many to death by death, making this tremendous division among men.

SUFFICIENCY

Paul is speaking here about God's Preachers.

The question calls on the Corinthians most closely to examine all who come to them as Preachers and to weigh them as to their sufficiency. Paul also demands that he and his helpers be thus weighed.

False teachers had come into the Church at Corinth, and Paul here demands that they be taken to account. If that were not so, the present question would not be needed. In effect, he is asking the question, *"What Gospel is sufficient?"*

As well, Paul is asking who is worthy of so important a charge, irrespective as to whom they may be. Who can undertake this great task of proclaiming the Gospel of Jesus Christ, which has such far reaching results, without trembling? Who can engage in it without Divine Grace?

We may remark that if Paul felt this, assuredly we should feel it also. If, with all the Divine assistance which he had — all the proofs of the peculiar Presence of God and all the mighty miraculous Powers conferred on him — Paul had such a sense of unfitness for this Great Work, then a consciousness of unfitness, and a deep sense of responsibility, may very well rest upon all others as well.

To be frank, it was this sense of the responsibility of the Ministry which contributed much to Paul's success. It was a conviction that the results of his work must be seen in the joys of Heaven or the woes of Hell, that led him to look to God for aid, and to devote himself entirely to his great work. Men will not feel much concern unless they have a deep sense of the magnitude and responsibility of their work.

The more we understand this responsibility, and the more we understand just how powerful and important the Gospel really is, then we will feel more and more constrained to look to God for aid and help, that we may carry forth this momentous task as we should.

NOTES

(17) "FOR WE ARE NOT AS MANY, WHICH CORRUPT THE WORD OF GOD: BUT AS OF SINCERITY, BUT AS OF GOD, IN THE SIGHT OF GOD SPEAK WE IN CHRIST."

The phrase, *"For we are not as many, which corrupt the Word of God,"* refers undoubtedly to the false teachers at Corinth, and to all who mingled human philosophy or tradition with the pure Word of Truth.

THE WORD OF GOD

Paul had such a sense of the influence of the Gospel, that he did not dare dilute it with any human mixture. He did not dare to preach philosophy or human wisdom. He did not dare to mingle with it the crude conceptions of man. He sought to exhibit the simple truth as it was in Jesus; and so deep was his sense of the responsibility of the Calling, and so great was his desire on the subject, that he had been enabled to do it and to triumph always in Christ.

The idea of *"corrupting the Word of God,"* carries the thought of a person buying wine to resell, and diluting it with water, or for compounding it of other substances than the juice of the grape for purposes of gain — ill-gotten gain.

Wine, of all substances in trade, at least in those days, afforded the greatest facilities for such dishonest tricks; and accordingly the dealers in that article have generally been most known for fraudulent practices and corrupt and diluted mixtures.

It is applied here to those who corrupt the Pure Word of God in any way and for any purpose.

Of course, a diluted Gospel is shorn of its power, and will cease to be mighty in pulling down the strongholds of Satan's kingdom. It is only the Pure Gospel of Jesus Christ which will bring forth the desired results of bringing the sinner from darkness to light.

FALSE GOSPELS

The following will be strong, but I believe it to be the Truth.

The acceptance of humanistic psychology by the modern Church, presents an impossibility of maintaining the Pure Gospel. The two simply cannot be mixed, the one coming solely from man and the other solely from God. Regrettably, the Old-Line Denominations bought into this years ago, with most of the modern Pentecostal Denominations now following suit, and in a wholesale manner. Consequently, young Bible School students are taught that the way to help humanity is to major, more or less, in the field of psychology. Hence, the Course offerings of almost all Schools which in some way go under the guise of Bible, are laced with psychology offerings. Consequently, these Preachers-to-be know little or next to nothing concerning what Jesus did at Calvary and the Resurrection, which in truth holds the only answer for the ills of man. You can't have it both ways, the Work of Christ is either a Finished Work, or it is not and we should turn to something else. I happen to know that it's real and that it works, and so do untold millions of others.

As well, it is my belief that Preachers who fail to Preach the Baptism with the Holy Spirit, with the evidence of speaking with other Tongues (Acts 2:4), are preaching an insufficient, thereby *"corrupt Word of God."* Regrettably, that covers almost all of the Old-Line Churches, and pretty much most of the modern Pentecostals as well.

If the Truth be known, there is not a lot of Pure Gospel being preached and, in fact, that has always been the case. Satan's greatest work is done inside the Church. Rather than a head-on, frontal attack, he apostatizes from within. He used false Prophets in the Old Economy and he now uses false Apostles. Then he denied Truth, while now he perverts Truth. Consequently, he is far more dangerous presently, because the line is not so plainly drawn.

WHAT IS THE PURE GOSPEL?

The phrase, *"But as of sincerity, but as of God, in the sight of God speak we in Christ,"* says several things. They are as follows:

1. *"But as of sincerity"*: This refers to keeping the Word of God pure, and to delivering it in its purity to mankind. *"Sincerity"* in the Greek is *"eilikrineia"* and means *"clearness, purity, tested as genuine, pure as the rays of the Sun."*

This means there is no hidden agenda, no ulterior motives, with only one thing in mind, and that is to hear the Word of the Lord, and deliver the Word of the Lord.

2. *"But as of God"*: This refers to being influenced by the Lord, as under His control and direction, as having been sent by Him, as acting by His Command. It is His Message, and must be faithfully delivered as He desires that it be delivered.

3. *"In the sight of God"*: The Preacher must always feel that the Eye of God is always on him. Nothing is better fitted to make a man sincere and honest than this.

4. *"Speak we in Christ"*: We speak in the Presence of God and in connection with Christ. We and our speaking are joined to Him. It is God who has called the Preacher to Preach, and He has called him to preach *"Christ"* and nothing else.

The Pure Gospel will always bear a certain type of fruit. I speak of souls being saved, lives being changed, bondages of darkness being broken, Believers being Baptized with the Holy Spirit, sick bodies being healed, in other words, mighty changes. If that *"fruit"* is not prevalent, irrespective as to what is being preached, it should be inspected more closely. Something is wrong!

Jesus told us how to spot false prophets and the impure Gospel. It is given in Matthew 7:15-20. In essence He said to *"check the fruit."*

"There's One Who can comfort when all else fails,
"Jesus, Blessed Jesus;
"A Saviour Who saves tho' the foe assails,
"Jesus, Blessed Jesus:
"Once He traveled the way we go, felt the pangs of deceit and woe;
"Who more perfectly then can know than Jesus, Blessed Jesus."

"He heareth the cry of the soul distressed,
"Jesus, Blessed Jesus;
"He healeth the wounded, He giveth rest,
"Jesus, Blessed Jesus:
"When from loved ones we're called to part,
"When the tears in our anguish start,
"None can comfort the breaking heart like Jesus, Blessed Jesus."

"He never forsakes in the darkest hour,
"Jesus, Blessed Jesus;

NOTES

"His arm is around us with keeping pow'r,
"Jesus, Blessed Jesus:
"When we enter the Shadow-land,
"When at Jordan we trembling stand,
"He will meet us with outstretched hand,
this Jesus, Blessed Jesus."

CHAPTER 3

(1) "DO WE BEGIN AGAIN TO COMMEND OURSELVES? OR NEED WE, AS SOME OTHERS, EPISTLES OF COMMENDATION TO YOU, OR LETTERS OF COMMENDATION FROM YOU?"

The question, *"Do we begin again to commend ourselves?"*, proclaims by the use of the word *"again"* that this was an ongoing problem. Consequently, several things are said here. Due to the fact that the Holy Spirit allowed the Apostle to deal with this subject concerning the validity of his personal Ministry to this degree, we know that the problem was acute. Let's look at some of the possible particulars:

1. SELF-APPOINTED LEADERS: It seems there were quite a number of self-appointed leaders in the Early Church who questioned Paul's Apostleship. While this in no way included the original Twelve, it did have the majority of its birth in Jerusalem, i.e., the Mother Church.

2. JAMES: James, the Lord's Brother, was the Senior Pastor in Jerusalem. While in some ways he seemed to respect Paul highly (Acts Chpt. 15), in other ways, he seemed to waiver toward the opposite direction (Acts 21:18-24). The problem was the Law of Moses. Many on the Jewish side of the Church, which of course had its great strength in Jerusalem, sought to add Christ to the Law of Moses, which Paul vigorously opposed, and rightly so. In fact, the decision handed down by James in Acts Chapter 15 concerning this problem respecting the Gentiles, was definitely of the Lord, but I personally believe the fact that James excluded the Jews from this ruling, was not pleasing to the Lord. I think the evidence bears it out.

The Law of Moses was fulfilled in Christ totally and completely. Consequently, the idea of continuing Sabbaths, Circumcision, and various other fundamentals of the Law, were

NOTES

somewhat of a travesty, considering that Jesus had now come fulfilling the Law. Consequently, the symbols, for that's what they were, are now no longer necessary. The New Covenant has replaced the Old Covenant, which Paul will address in the following Scriptures. So, this Law/Grace issue hung over the Early Church.

3. PAUL: Paul did everything within his power to ameliorate these problems, bending over backwards so to speak, in order that there be no breach in the Church. His taking up large sums of money from the Gentile Churches, in order to help with the need in Jerusalem, which Chapters 8 and 9 of this Epistle graphically bear out, was a part of that effort. However, as F. F. Bruce said, *"Paul always greatly respected Jerusalem, but it seems that Jerusalem little respected Paul."*

4. JEALOUSY: As well, I'm sure there was much jealousy involved, especially considering that Paul was claiming that the Lord had given him the New Covenant, which in effect replaced the Old. I'm sure they pondered in their minds as to why the Lord did not give this Covenant to Peter or to John, or to anyone of the other Apostles for that matter. The Truth is, they were not satisfied with God's choice in this matter, as most men aren't, and we're referring to the Church. In other words, religious men, i.e., Leaders of Denominations etc., almost all the time would choose, and in fact do choose others, than those chosen by the Lord. To be frank, the spirit of what we're seeing here in II Corinthians, and elsewhere in Paul's Epistles, is the fact that many in the Church actively opposed the ones chosen by the Lord. Men love to be *"lords"* over the Work of God, and to be a *"Lord"* one must then have the freedom to choose those who will serve in capacities of Leadership. But of course, none of that is of God, with Him ignoring this man-devised leadership, while at the same time they opposed His leadership.

It doesn't happen in this manner all the time, but I think the evidence is clear that it does happen the majority of the time.

5. LETTERS OF RECOMMENDATION: To buttress man-chosen Leadership, it seems Jerusalem was issuing letters of recommendation to certain ones, which did not include Paul. Consequently, Paul's opponents tried to discredit him by saying that he did not possess

adequate credentials. To be facetious, he had not obtained a Commission from the Apostolic Headquarters in Jerusalem. Peter, James, and John had not blessed him with their stamp of approval. On the other hand, there is no evidence whatsoever that any of the original Twelve opposed Paul in any manner, but rather the opposite I think.

Prior to his conversion, Paul had plenty of experience with credentials. Actually, he made use of his credentials in his efforts to destroy God's people (Acts 9:1-2).

In fact, Paul was not opposed to letters of recommendation. In fact, this was a common practice used by Leaders, including himself, in the Early Church (Acts 15:22-29; 18:27; Rom. 16:1; I Cor. 16:11-12; II Cor. 8:22-24; Col. 4:10; Phile. vss. 17-19). What Paul was saying, is that these *"credentials,"* i.e., *"letters of recommendation,"* were not needed to validate someone's Ministry, and in fact did not show any validation, at least that which God would recognize.

Genuine Gospel Ministry is characterized by changed lives, the best possible proof that God is working through someone. If someone doesn't want to recognize that, then they're not recognizing the proof which God recognizes. In essence, they're making up their own rules which men are prone to do.

The question, *"Or need we, as some others, Epistles of commendation to you, or letters of commendation from you?"*, portrays Paul presenting this contention as an absurdity to suppose that he or Timothy should need such letters, either from the Corinthians or to them.

He will not name them, but he is referring here to the Judaisers, who vaunted of their credentials in order to disparage Paul, who in fact was too much of God to need them, and to independent to use them.

AS SOME OTHERS

Who these some were, of course, we do not know. However, from the way Paul uses the word, it is not too difficult to realize the antagonism barely concealed here (I Cor. 4:18; Gal. 1:7; 2:12).

Men are so prone to flaunt earthly recognition, i.e., recognition by other men. However, such recognition is of no consequence whatsoever with God. If we're going to follow the Scriptures, and I'm assuming that is the thought of all of our Readers, then we will find that the Holy Spirit puts little stock in such things, but rather how He functions through a man or woman, with hearts and lives being changed as a result. There is no higher recommendation or commendation than that, i.e., *"souls saved by the Precious Blood of Jesus."*

The Reader must never forget, that the finish line is not the plaudits of men; the finish line is the *"Judgment Seat of Christ."* While no Believer will ever have to answer for sin, that having been taken care of at Calvary and our Faith in that Finished Work, still, every Believer is definitely going to have to answer for motivation and for that which God has called us to do. We are going to have to answer for what we have supported in the realm of the Gospel when it really was not the Gospel, or what we refuse to support, when it really was the Gospel of Jesus Christ, as well as our conduct and action toward others, in other words, a very heavy scene. The criteria then will be the Word of God, and Jesus Christ Himself will be the Judge.

While no Believer at that time will ever lose one's soul, many will lose their rewards. So it's something we should think about very carefully.

(2) "YE ARE OUR EPISTLE WRITTEN IN OUR HEARTS, KNOWN AND READ OF ALL MEN:"

The phrase, *"Ye are our Epistle,"* refers to the Saints in Corinth who had been saved under his Ministry. The sense is plain. The Holy Spirit is saying, that the conversion of the Corinthians (or conversions anywhere for that matter), under the faithful labors of the Apostle, was a better testimonial of his character and fidelity than any so-called letters of recommendation from other men ever could be. So, and to which we have already alluded, this is the real proof of any Ministry.

THE CHARACTERISTICS

The characteristics of this commendatory Epistle he proceeds immediately to state. The general sense is, that they (converted Corinthians) were the letter of recommendation which God had given to him; and that their conversion under his Ministry was the public testimonial of his character, which all might see and read.

What I'm going to say might seem to be self-serving, but due to the fact that the Holy Spirit

NOTES

has taken this occasion to spell out the characteristics of a true Ministry, and that He allowed Paul to do so, I feel the things I'm about to say is that which the Lord would have me say.

This Ministry, and I speak of Jimmy Swaggart Ministries, is of God. It has always been of God, and it is of God presently. The proof of that is in three things:

1. The life I live: I have made some terrible mistakes, but I have taken them to the Lord exactly as it should have been done. Consequently, whatever the past may be, it is not in the present, and even though it may be in the minds of some people, it is not in the Mind of God, and that's what really matters. In other words, it has long since been washed clean by the Precious Blood of Jesus. Consequently, I say as Paul also said, *"I would to God that . . . all that hear me this day, were both almost, and altogether such as I am, except these bonds,"* i.e., *"except this stigma"* (Acts 26:29).

My life is one that is lived in prayer and the Word of God.

2. The Message I preach: It is the pure, uncompromised, unadulterated Word of God. To be frank with you, that's the reason almost all the Church world opposes us as they do, it is the Message. It's a Message that's never been popular, is not popular today, and will not be popular tomorrow.

However, it is not my business as to what people like or don't like, but rather that I hear from the Lord, and do my very best to deliver that which He has told me to deliver.

I can honestly say before God, I have never knowing or intentionally compromised His Word; I have never preached to the Gallery; I have never been a men-pleaser, and I'm too old to start now.

There is nothing in the world more important than the Word of God. Consequently, there is nothing more important than how I Preach that Word. When I stand before the Lord at the *"Judgment Seat of Christ"* of which I have just mentioned, I will answer in that day according to my Faithfulness to the Word, and not what men thought.

3. The souls which have been saved all over the world: the Message we preach, and the results it obtains by the Grace of God, is the proof of my Message and my Character, exactly as it was of Paul so long ago, and every other True Minister of the Gospel for that matter. Anyone who's character is not what it ought to be before God, does not preach the Truth, and sees no results, at least that which God will accept.

NOTES

REPUTATION AND CHARACTER

When such results are forthcoming, which can only be brought about by the True Message of Jesus Christ, that is the most sure sign of one's reputation, one's character, and the very fact that one is of God, irrespective as to what men may say. One must ever remember, that reputation is what men think of you, and character is what God knows of you. They are two different things altogether.

To be frank, Jesus Christ, the Lord of Glory, the only perfect human being who has ever lived, Who just happened at the same time to be God, had a terrible reputation over Israel, but an impeccable character. However, the reputation of being a deceiver was that which had been attached to Him by His enemies, and not by God. The proof of Who He was, was in His Life, His Ministry, and the results of that Ministry. It is no less for Preachers of the Gospel presently.

One can go into any city in the world where we have previously aired our Telecast, or do so presently, and find people in that city, irrespective of the nationality or country, who have been saved under this Ministry. They number into the literal hundreds of thousands all over the world. I'll say it again exactly as Paul said, *"Those souls which have been brought out of darkness to light, are our Epistle,"* therefore, the proof of this Ministry.

AS PAUL

I will use the Apostle once again as an example for my own life and Ministry: *"I am the least of the Apostles, that am not meet to be called an Apostle, because I failed my Lord."*

But then he said, *"But by the Grace of God I am what I am: and His Grace which was bestowed upon me was not in vain; but I laboured more abundantly than they all: yet not I, but the Grace of God which was with me"* (I Cor. 15:9-10).

The phrase, *"Written in our hearts,"* has reference to the fact, that while he does not have letters of recommendation from men, and neither does he desire any; however, that which he does have is of far greater magnitude, *"changed hearts."*

Has anyone ever stopped to think, that's what this thing is all about! If the Gospel we Preach doesn't change hearts and lives, then it is of no consequence or value. As well, such is the power of sin, that a watered-down, compromised Gospel will not change anything. Does the Reader realize, that there are entire Denominations, with millions of members, having literally hundreds of millions of dollars going through their coffers each year, but actually see absolutely nothing done for the Lord? Does the Reader actually realize, that there are scores of Ministries, so-called, which never see anyone saved, never see anyone Baptized with the Holy Spirit, never see anyone truly healed or delivered by the Power of God? Consequently, even though they may be referred to as a *"Ministry,"* by men, they're not referred to as such by God.

... OF THE LORD OR MEN?

These self-important, puffed up detractors of Paul, for the most part, had never seen anyone saved or any hearts and lives changed at all. So the Holy Spirit through the Apostle is telling them and us, and for all time, that a piece of paper claiming men's recommendation is of little consequence. In fact, it is nothing with the Lord. But yet, that is the claim to fame of most Preachers, they are accepted by some Denomination, or some group, etc.

While I definitely want my Brother and Sister to think well of me, and while I would love to have the well-wishes of most, I realize that's impossible. The thing that stays with me 24-hours a day is that I please the Lord Jesus Christ. While I owe my Brother and Sister in the Lord my love, I owe not only my love to the Lord, but also my allegiance. He is my Commander in Chief.

The phrase, *"Known and read of all men,"* plainly says and emphatically so, that this proof, changed hearts and lives, is obvious to all. If Believers do not want to see this, do not want to recognize this, refuse to make this the criteria of a God-accepted Ministry, then there is nothing that can be done as far as credible proof is concerned. Such is obvious to *"all men."* Consequently, if they refuse to see changed hearts and lives as a proof of Ministry, then it's because they are willfully blind and willfully ignoring the Word of God. As well, the manner in which Paul makes these statements in this Second Verse, pertains to something that is continuous. In other words, these changed hearts and lives could be seen, observed, and witnessed at any time. They were not here today and gone tomorrow.

NOTES

(3) "FORASMUCH AS YE ARE MANIFESTLY DECLARED TO BE THE EPISTLE OF CHRIST MINISTERED BY US, WRITTEN NOT WITH INK, BUT WITH THE SPIRIT OF THE LIVING GOD; NOT IN TABLES OF STONE, BUT IN FLESHY TABLES OF THE HEART."

The phrase, *"Forasmuch as ye are manifestly declared to be the Epistle of Christ ministered by us,"* means that not only are the Corinthians his *"Epistle,"* but as well, *"the Epistle of Christ ministered by us through the Holy Spirit."*

CHRIST THE AUTHOR OF THESE CREDENTIALS

Whereas men were the authors of the letters of recommendation of which Paul speaks, it was Christ Who was the Author of this *"Epistle"* of which Paul speaks, i.e., *"souls saved from sin and darkness."* The implication is that credentials from Him are the only credentials which are actually valid.

In effect, Paul is saying this:

"Souls saved, are that which Christ has sent to be our testimonial. He has given this Letter of recommendation. He has converted you by our Ministry, and that is the best evidence which we can have that we have been sent by Him, and that our labor is accepted by Him. Your conversion is His Work, and it is His public attestation of our fidelity in His Cause."

The idea here is, that Christ had employed their Ministry in accomplishing this. They were Christ's Letter, but it had been prepared by the instrumentality of the Apostles. It had not been prepared by Him independently of their labors, but in connection with, and as the result of, those labors.

The phrase, *"Written not with ink,"* carries with it several connotations:

INK

1. Is it wrong to have letters of commendation from others, or to carry credentials with a particular Religious Denomination? No it isn't! That's not what Paul is saying.

However, if one places any type of spiritual meaning to these things, then they are wrong, and because they are thought of improperly. Such are merely pieces of paper which are issued by the faulty judgment of men. It is not something ordained of God. This is what Paul is saying.

2. If one does not have these letters of recommendation, or particular credentials, even as Paul did not have, that means nothing with God, and should mean nothing with man. Unfortunately, most of the Church World I think, places undue importance on that which is *"written with ink."*

3. There are literally hundreds of thousands of Preachers who carry impeccable credentials from men, who have never won a soul to Christ, never seen a life changed by the Power of God, and have never seen people delivered from the terrible bondages of darkness. So, if this *"ink"* had any special spiritual validity, these individuals, whomever they may be, would have the type of manifest proof of which Paul speaks. But of course, most have no proof at all, despite the *"ink!"*

4. When all of us stand before the Lord at the Judgment Seat of Christ, we can flash our credentials before Him written with *"ink"*; however, even though they may have carried weight with men, they will carry none with the Lord. We must keep that in mind!

That written by *"ink,"* are merely traces drawn on a lifeless substance, and in lines that easily fade, or that may become easily illegible, or that can be read by a few, or that may be soon destroyed.

The phrase, *"But with the Spirit of the Living God,"* speaks of the moving on the heart, which produces a variety of Graces which constitutes a striking and beautiful evidence of one's conversion.

THE SPIRIT OF THE LIVING GOD

What does Paul mean by this statement?

Everything God does in this world, He does by Jesus Christ, and through the Person, Office, Ministry, and Work of the Holy Spirit. The idea is this:

Is the Preacher of the Gospel seeking the plaudits of men, or is he seeking the Moving, Operation, and Manifestation of the Holy Spirit in his life and ministry?

NOTES

Which is it? One cannot have both.

Paul was seeking to live such a life, that the Holy Spirit could function in him and through him, in order that the Work of God could be carried out. That is a must for every Preacher of the Gospel.

The Holy Spirit within our lives is really there in the position of potential. In other words, every Believer in the world, even the weakest, has the Holy Spirit. But that which He does in and through us, is dependent on many things, i.e., our consecration, dedication, yielding to Him, and looking to Him.

So, I'll say it again, and even as Paul outlines this Truth, one can have the work of men, or one can have the Work of God, one cannot have both.

That which is done by the Holy Spirit through Believers, is that alone which is valid. As well, every single trace of the Spirit's influences on the hearts of these people, and in any manner, were an undoubted proof that God had sent the Apostles; and was a proof which men would much more sensibly and tenderly feel than they could any letter of recommendation written in ink.

The phrase, *"Not in tables of stone,"* no doubt refers to the Law of Moses.

Probably those who were false teachers among the Corinthians were Jews, and had insisted much upon the Divine origin and permanency of the Mosaic Institutions. The Law had been engraved on stone by the Hand of God Himself; and thus had the strongest proofs of Divine origin, and the Divine attestation to its pure and holy nature. To this fact the friends of the Law, and the advocates for the permanency of the Jewish institutions, would appeal.

So, by Paul using this phrase as he did, he was probably referring to Judaisers from Jerusalem, who claimed that one must keep the Law of Moses as well as accepting Christ in order to be saved. They also carried letters of recommendation from Jerusalem, which they thought gave them great credence. Paul had none of these *"credentials."*

The phrase, *"But in fleshy tables of the heart,"* refers to the changed heart which the Gospel alone can do, and which the Law of Moses could never do. The Apostle is actually referring to Jeremiah 31:33, where the Prophet foresaw that coming day of Grace. Consequently, the credentials given by Christ are vastly superior to the Law of Moses.

THE GOSPEL OF GRACE,
THE TRUE CREDENTIALS

In effect, Paul is saying, *"This letter of ours you are."* It is public before the eyes of all men who look at you, the Corinthian Church in the Capital of Achaia.

The whole thought simply overwhelms! Here come these deceivers who steal into a True Church that was founded by Christ through the Spirit, by the Ministry of men sent out by Him and tried to worm their way in by recommendatory letters from foolish people who place credence in such.

These base proselyters have had many successors. Talk about Paul and his assistants needing such a letter for the Corinthians or needing anything like self-recommendation! Look at what all men read and continue to read when they regard the Corinthian Church!

They read Paul and his assistants written all over that Church. They read what Christ wrote. They read the writing of the Spirit of the Living God. They read our Ministry to you and the fruit of this Ministry. They read it as having been written on a great, monumental, living heart tablet, the greatest ever erected in Corinth, or any other place for that matter, changed hearts and lives.

TO ALL PREACHERS

This Statement as given by the Holy Spirit through the Apostle, applies to the work of any Preacher of the Gospel, who has attempted to bring souls to the Lord, whether in Evangelistic Work or in Pastoring a Church.

The fact that grave faults had recently crept in respecting Corinth and were not yet fully overcome, the fact that deceivers were still present in Corinth, changed nothing in regard to past accomplishment with all of it that still stood so that all men might see it.

It is a shame, that the recommendation of which Paul speaks is often seen by men without the Church, but are perceived by those in the Church sometimes too late, perhaps not until the Faithful Minister's eyes are closed in death.

Here, too, one may think of the pitiful Epistles which some produce by their *"ministry."* The invaders tried to wipe out and rewrite Paul's Epistle in Corinth. However, as is obvious for all to see, the Holy Spirit did not allow such, because it is literally impossible for such a Ministry to be erased. Too many people were walking around who had been changed by that Ministry, and changed gloriously and wondrously!

NOTES

It is sad, but these deceivers would have destroyed Paul's work if they could; however, the Holy Spirit stepped in, even as He always does, and guards the True Ministry. The credentials of men written in *"ink,"* can easily fade, and always does, but that which is done by the Holy Spirit is eternal, and obvious for all to see!

I wonder, did these men, these Judaisers, these deceivers, actually know that what they were doing, was totally opposed to the Lord, actually opposition against the Holy Spirit? Such position, that of opposing the Holy Spirit, is not that which anyone with sanity would want to do.

DID THESE JUDAISERS NOT THINK
THEY WERE RIGHT?

I'm sure they did! And yet, how could they be so deceived?

They were deceived because they were not looking at the proper fruit of Ministry. They were totally ignoring changed hearts and lives, which had been brought about by the Gospel preached by Paul and his associates.

One may wonder how that anyone could be so foolish?

That question is valid; however, the far greater majority of modern so-called Church Leaders, fall into the same category. Their agenda, sadly and regrettably, is little that of the Holy Spirit, but something else altogether. One wishes that one could point to those deceivers of Paul's day, and say they ceased with that time; however, they are just as abundant and even more so presently than they were then.

Once again, are we going to go back to the Foundation, the criteria, and I speak of the Word of God? Is it going to be the Standard or is something else going to be the Standard?

If the Bible is the Standard, and to be sure it is, then the proper credentials for Ministry is not the approval of men, but souls saved and lives changed.

(4) "AND SUCH TRUST HAVE WE THROUGH CHRIST TO GOD-WARD:"

The phrase, *"And such trust have we,"* refers to the personal confidence that Paul had that he was appointed by God, and that God accepted his work.

In effect, he is saying, *"Such evidence have we in the success of our labors — such incontestable proof that God blesses us — that we have trust, or confidence, that we are sent by God, and are owned by Him in our Ministry."* His confidence did not rest on letters of introduction from men, but in the evidence of the Divine Presence, which portrayed the Divine acceptance of his work.

However, due to its great significance, let us say it again, even regrettably, acceptance presently in the Church world, relies almost altogether on the approval of men, and not the Presence of God. If anything, this is the greatest sign of Apostasy, which will captivate the Church at this final time, and in fact, is already doing so.

The phrase as Paul uses it, *"And such trust have we,"* begs the question, in whom is your trust, God or man?

The phrase, *"Through Christ,"* refers to the agency of Christ. Paul had no success which he did not trace to Him; he had no joy of which He was not the Source; he had no confidence, or trust in God, of which Christ was not the Author; he had no hope of success in his ministry which did not depend on Him.

As well, Paul is saying that Christ is the fulfillment of the Law to which he alludes in Verse 3.

A DECLARATION OF CHRIST

Paul faced repeated opposition from the Judaisers, who were proud of propagating the Old Covenant, in other words, that one had to keep the Law of Moses as well as accept Christ in order to be saved. They were obviously distressed that he was teaching Gentile converts that they did not need to become Jewish proselytes in order to be recognized as truly saved individuals. Before looking at the specifics of the glorious New Covenant, Paul reminded his readers of the foundation for his comments.

He did not teach or write as he did with the purpose of undermining the Old Testament or suggesting that it is less inspired than the New. He knew of course, that the Old Testament was inspired by God the same as the New (II Tim. 3:16).

NOTES

Before Paul was saved, he was a zealous proponent of the concept of justification by works, which of course, was impossible. After his Vision of Christ, he then understood the Old Testament as God intended it to be understood. This is why many of his writings emphasize the correct interpretation of the Old Testament. In fact, the instructions he received concerning it came from God Himself.

Furthermore, these instructions came *"through Christ,"* the Mediator of the Covenant. Paul, therefore, could speak with *"trust,"* or, literally, *"confidence"* about the New Covenant. He knew that Jesus was the end of the Law, in other words, that all the Sacrifices and Rudiments of the Mosaic Law pointed to Christ. Consequently, they were fulfilled in Christ, and were, therefore, of no more necessity, as should be obvious. However, the Judaisers did not like such a thing, still trying to hold on to the Mosaic Law, even though it had been fulfilled in Christ.

The phrase, *"To God-ward,"* refers to the fact that the only way to God is through Christ, actually the One to Whom the Law pointed.

So, he is saying, that his confidence relates to God, that He has appointed us, and sent us forth; and confidence that he will still continue to own and to bless us (Barnes).

The idea of Paul's Statement is, that all which are not anchored totally in Christ, God will not accept. Those who add to Christ or take away from Christ, will soon enough stand face-to-face with God, and Christ will disown them, and God's Judgment will be against them.

So, the warning was not only to the Judaisers of old, and to those who would follow them, but it is as well to all, and had better be considered carefully. As we have previously said, the final thought is not the approval of men, but rather of God. Everyone of us, at least True Believers, will one day stand at the Judgment Seat of Christ. That will be the final thought and, in effect, the finish line. It is to Him we will give account, and to be sure, many things in which men trusted in this present life will carry no weight whatsoever at that time. Our trust had better be through Christ to God, with man nowhere in the midst as it regards that *"trust."*

(5) "NOT THAT WE ARE SUFFICIENT OF OURSELVES TO THINK ANY THING AS OF OURSELVES; BUT OUR SUFFICIENCY IS OF GOD;"

The phrase, *"Not that we are sufficient of ourselves,"* reverts to the question asked in II Corinthians 2:16. He cannot bear the implication that any *"confidence"* on his part rests on anything short of the overwhelming sense that he is but an agent, or rather nothing but an instrument, in the Hands of God (Farrar). In other words, his confidence did not originate in his own ability. This is evidently designed to guard against the appearance of boasting, or of self-confidence.

SUFFICIENCY

Paul had spoken of his confidence; of his triumph; of his success; of his undoubted evidence that God had sent him. He says here, that he did not mean to be understood as affirming that any of his success came from himself, or that he was able by his own strength to accomplish the great things which had been effected by his Ministry. He well knew that he had no such self-sufficiency; and he would not insinuate, in the slightest manner, that he believed himself to be invested with any such power (Barnes).

To say this, therefore, is a denial of any claim to any single thing in the way of title, credit, praise, etc., as having its source in our own selves.

The phrase, *"To think any thing as of ourselves,"* refers to the sufficiency needed to be a competent Preacher and incense-bearer, i.e., to spread the Gospel which has a glorious and wonderful fragrance. Paul was confident that in the Sight of God he possessed that competency through Christ, though personally absolutely incompetent, as are all men for that matter (Williams).

The phrase, *"But our sufficiency is of God,"* makes several points:

THE PARTNERSHIP OF GOD AND MAN

1. Paul did not feel that he was sufficient of himself to have reasoned or thought out the Truths of the Gospel. They were communicated solely by God. However, it definitely is the responsibility of the individual to proclaim those Truths exactly as they are given without compromise. This is what we mean by *"partnership,"* at least, if one would refer to such in that manner.

2. Paul had no power by reasoning to convince or convert sinners. The problem of sin is of such magnitude, that the Gospel cannot be used as a philosophy to convert men. Sin is so powerful that it takes the Power of God to break that chain, which the Gospel is, that is, if the Preacher is preaching the Truth, and doing so under the Anointing of the Holy Spirit. Once again, we address the *"partnership."*

3. He had no right to reckon on success by any strength of his own. All success was to be traced to God.

It is the business of the Believer, be he Preacher or otherwise, to be a channel, an instrument, a vessel, in which the Lord can use. What God puts in the vessel, etc., is strictly of Him, with it being our business to make the Vessel what it ought to be in Christ. Even then, we are severely limited, in that we can only provide an obedient heart and willing mind. To be frank, God has to make the vessel, exactly as He supplies the ingredient, i.e., *"The Gospel."*

THE CHURCH AND SUFFICIENCY

This one statement, *"Our sufficiency is of God,"* proclaims a wealth of information, direction, and leading, even as it is given by the Holy Spirit. This is the greatest problem with the Church.

Too often, our sufficiency is in ourselves, in other men, in our plans, in belonging to certain Churches, or Denominations, etc. Total dependence on God for all things, leading, guidance, power, the Anointing, direction, etc., was the hallmark of Paul. It is meant to be an example for us as well.

On whom are we depending? In fact, on what are we depending?

The Spirit of God will function only in the place and position to where we know and realize that our sufficiency is totally of God. He will not anoint, bless, and help otherwise.

The first requirement upon the part of the Believer, is to have a broken and contrite spirit before the Lord. This speaks of humility.

Those who look to themselves are boastful, proud, egotistical, self-sufficient, which portrays only the *"flesh,"* and never the *"Spirit."* To be frank, one must have the leading and guidance of the Holy Spirit in every single thing that one does. When I say everything, I mean everything! The Believer should want and desire the Lord's guidance in all things, even down to the very mundane. In fact, if we do not trust Him for leading and guidance in the small things, to be sure we will not be able to trust Him regarding the more important things. He alone is our sufficiency!

(6) "WHO ALSO HATH MADE US ABLE MINISTERS OF THE NEW TESTAMENT; NOT OF THE LETTER, BUT OF THE SPIRIT: FOR THE LETTER KILLETH, BUT THE SPIRIT GIVETH LIFE."

The phrase, *"Who also hath made us able Ministers,"* is in no way meant to boast, not even in the slightest, but rather to say that which works and moves through them, i.e., the Gospel, is solely of God.

ABLE MINISTERS

It is said that the translation of this phrase does not quite meet the force of the original. On the surface, it would seem to imply that Paul regarded himself and his fellow-laborers as men of talents, and of signal ability; and that he was inclined to boast of it. But this is not the meaning.

It refers properly to his sense of the responsibility and difficulty of the work of the Ministry, to the fact that he did not esteem himself to be sufficient for this work in his own strength, and he says here that God had made him sufficient. In other words, He has supplied our deficiency: He has rendered us competent, or fit: if a word may be coined after the manner of the Greek here, *"He has sufficienced us for this work."*

This is something man cannot do, whether of himself or for others.

It is unfortunate, that in many religious circles, young men and women are made to think they are qualified for Ministry because they have graduated from a particular College or Seminary, etc. While that may or may not help a person learn the Scriptures, depending on the School, still, in no manner does such provide the sufficiency here of which Paul speaks. He is speaking of the Moving, Operation, Leading, and Guidance of the Holy Spirit within one's heart and life. That alone suffices one, thereby making one *"able."*

The phrase, *"Of the New Testament,"* refers to a fresh or New Covenant. Of course, he is speaking of the Covenant of Grace, to which the Old Covenant pointed.

NOTES

THE OLD COVENANT AND THE NEW COVENANT

There were many Covenants in Old Testament times, but Paul is speaking in this Scripture of the Law of Moses. However, all of the Covenants of the Old Testament pointed to the Coming of Jesus in one way or the other, while the New Covenant, of course, proclaims His Coming. In other words, everything in the Bible points to Jesus.

In the New Testament, old and new take on a different coloration. The New Testament, as stated, describes the Coming of Jesus, with many of His Teachings as *"new"* in the sense of being radically different from what the people steeped in the Old Testament expected.

It is not surprising, then, to find that words for both Old and New suddenly become more than merely descriptive. They become terms that make a strong theological statement.

THE NEW COVENANT

The way in which the New Testament uses *"new"* underlines the Message communicated by its uses of *"Old."*

For instance, Believers help put off the old man and put on the new (Col. 3:10). And the Superior Covenant that Jeremiah promised and that is so carefully described by the writer of Hebrews is also *"New"* (Heb. 12:24).

Christ's death, to which the Old Covenant pointed, initiates a New Covenant between God and man — a Covenant that is vastly superior to the old Mosaic Code (Mk. 14:24; Lk. 22:20; I Cor. 11:25; II Cor. 3:6; Heb. 8:8). Through Christ, human beings themselves become new creations (II Cor. 5:17) and discover a realm of life in which all things become new (II Cor. 5:17).

These new creations wrought by Christ Himself live as new people, God's renewed humanity (Gal. 6:15; Eph. 4:24). In effect, Believers form a new community (Eph. 2:15) in which Jesus' New Commandment, to love as He loved us, is borne out (Jn. 13:34; I Jn. 2:7-8; II Jn. vs. 5). One day God will complete His new work of creation and call into being new heavens and a new earth (II Pet. 3:13; Rev. 21:1-2, 5).

Thus, *"New"* in the qualitative sense makes the strongest possible statement about the impact of the Good News that comes to us in Jesus. The Gospel Message is not a message of reform but of transformation. It is a fresh, powerful word from God. In contrast to all that God does in Christ, the *"Old"* is obsolete and inferior indeed.

THE NEW WINE AND OLD BOTTLES

Each of the Synoptic Gospels reports on Jesus' reference to the new wine and old bottles (wineskins). Luke's version reads: "He (Jesus) *told them this Parable: No one tears a patch from a new garment and sews it on an old one. If he does, he will have torn the new garment, and the patch from the new will not match the old. And no one pours new wine into old wineskins. If he does, the new wine will burst the skins, the wine will run out and the wineskins will be ruined. No, new wine must be poured into new wineskins. And no one after drinking old wine wants the new, for he says, 'The old is better'"* (Lk. 5:36-39; Mat. 9:16-17; Mk. 2:21-22).

The Parable explores the relationship of old and new and gives insight into the spirituality of Israel.

THE FIRST PARABLE

The generally accepted meaning of the first Parable is that the new and better garment represents Christ and His Gospel. The old and worn garment represents the Old Testament pattern of Faith and Life.

Jesus did not come to patch the old but to provide a new and superior garment.

THE SECOND PARABLE

The second Parable looks not so much at the reality represented by the two systems (Old and New Covenants) but in human reaction to them.

A fresh squeezing of wine must be put into wineskins that are superior because they are new, able to stretch and respond as the wine matures. New wine poured into the old wineskins will result in burst wineskins, and the fresh crop will be lost.

THE FINAL STATEMENT?

But what about the final statement showing how people evaluate the two wines?

First, it shows a hasty decision, for the new wine has not had time to mature when it is rejected.

NOTES

Second, it shows a foolish decision. Wine is exhausted, even as the pattern of Faith and Life expressed in the Mosaic Code is now exhausted. The old skins are empty! In other words, like it or not, there is nothing left of the Mosaic Law, it having been fulfilled in Christ.

The only wise decision one can make is to put the new crop in superior wineskins in which it can mature and take on its own unique character.

The reason the Old was desired was because it was that with which they were familiar, and not being familiar at all with the New gave occasion for rejection.

However, the main problem was, that Israel was falsely interpreting the *"Old,"* in that they reckoned it as a system complete within itself, and not that it merely pointed to One Who was coming, Who would do what the Old could not do, which is to give Life.

Jesus must be accepted on His Own terms. We cannot cut Him to fit the gaping holes in our garments: we must cast off the old and let Him clothe us completely. And in the same way those old categories that shaped thinking must be set aside, as we let the Gospel Message infuse our lives and give us a fresh, new shape, chosen by God's Spirit, then the new wine of God's Work within us can mature toward beauty and holiness.

As Israel of old misinterpreted the *"Old"* (Law), likewise, many presently are misinterpreting the *"New"* (Gospel).

The phrase, *"Not of the letter,"* is directed doubtless, to the Jews and Jewish Teachers, who insisted much on the letter of the Law, but entered little into its real meaning.

THE LETTER?

Most in Israel, even up to Paul's day, did not seek out the true spiritual sense of the Old Testament; and hence, they rested on the mere literal observance of the Rites and Ceremonies of religion, without understanding their true nature and design, i.e., that they pointed to Jesus.

Their service though, in many respects conformed to the letter of the Law, yet became old, formal, and hypocritical, abounding in mere ceremonies, where the heart had little to do. Hence, there was little pure spiritual worship offered to God; and hence, also they rejected the

Messiah Whom the Old Covenant prefigured, and was designed to set forth (Barnes).

The phrase, *"But of the Spirit,"* represents the difference in the Old and the New.

THE SPIRIT

Both the Law and the Gospel were committed to writing; each Covenant had its own Book; but in the case of the Mosaic Law there was the Book and nothing more; in the case of the Gospel, the Book (New Testament) is made alive by the Power of the Holy Spirit. That is, the Gospel is founded on the pledge and consummation of the Gift of the Holy Spirit (Mat. 3:11; Acts 1:4; 2:4; Rom. Chpt. 8).

The Law, too, was in one sense *"spiritual"* (Rom. 7:14), for it was given by God, and it was, therefore, a Holy Law. But though such in itself, it merely pointed out the right direction, i.e., what is right and wrong, but gave no power to carry out its commands.

The phrase, *"For the letter killeth,"* refers to the Law doing what all Law is designed to do — condemn one if it is broken.

THE MANNER OF THE LAW OF MOSES

Many are confused by the idea that God would give something which can only kill. In fact, why did God give a Code that people could not possibly fulfill?

First of all, the Lord gave the Law in order that it would show man what is right and what is wrong.

Before the Law of Moses, there were all types of laws in the world made up by men. These laws were grossly unfair, and above all did not really address the moral depravity of the human heart. God's Laws set the standard for all moral conduct in the world, which are valid unto this hour, and in fact, will never change, for the simple reason that Truth cannot change.

If it was wrong to steal three thousand years ago, it's wrong to steal presently, etc.

So, the Law was given to establish a foundation of conduct, and as stated, it holds unto this hour.

Of course, God demanded that His Law be kept, because if such is not demanded, it really isn't Law. All Law demands obedience, and all Law, that is if it is to be Law, must have a penalty attached respecting disobedience.

NOTES

IS IT NOT CRUEL TO DEMAND SOMETHING THAT MEN CANNOT DO?

It would be cruel, if God left it at that; however, He did not leave the situation in that manner.

He knew that man could not keep the Law because of man's depraved nature. Yet, God could not lower the standards of Truth and morality, down to the perverted, depraved nature of fallen man. In fact, Truth cannot be altered in any fashion, and if so, it ceases to be Truth.

As well, Law has no power within itself to help one do anything. Once again, if it does, it's not Law. By the very nature of Law, it can only lay out the cold, hard facts, in other words the Commandment, but that's as far as it can go.

THE NEED OF A SAVIOUR

The Lord not only desired to place Truth in the world regarding Morality, but as well, the Law was designed to show man that he needed a Saviour. In other words, as simple as these Commands were (the Ten Commandments), man in his depraved, fallen state, simply did not have the power and strength to obey. Therefore, the idea was, that man would recognize his fallen, perverted, absolute moral bankruptcy, and turn to God for help, which help, incidentally had been amply provided. However, Israel, at least for the most part, turned the doing of the Law into a religion within itself, which they thought could save, but could in no way save.

So, if God in giving the Law, had infused man with power to keep the Law, it would not have resulted in the Law being kept, but only in the pride of man, which is already his problem, being increased, which would have only made the matter worse.

While a few in Israel saw what the Lord was doing, most, regrettably, did not. They tried to justify themselves by the keeping of the Law, with their so-called Justification made up of the *"doing"* of the Law, instead of actually keeping the Law, which in fact they could not do.

Millions presently do the same with the Gospel. Instead of accepting Jesus as He is, the Crucified, Risen Lord, they try to find Salvation in the *"doing"* of the Gospel, which puts them in the same position as Israel of old — unjustified.

THE SACRIFICES

Knowing that man could not keep the Law, the Lord provided a way and means of Mercy and Grace through the Sacrifices. While they within themselves, contained no cleansing agent, and as a result, effected no Salvation, Faith in the One to Whom they pointed, namely the Lord Jesus, could in fact bring Salvation.

Salvation has always come through the Sacrifice of Christ Himself (Gen. 3:15, 21), of which the Sacrifices were a Type. The New Covenant brings Life because it describes in detail the Sacrifice of Jesus on the Cross.

Does this mean that Salvation was not available to people before the Cross?

No. It has always been available to people who would accept it through Faith, all the way back to Adam and Eve. Before the Cross, Believers looked forward to the fulfillment of the Promises of God regarding a Saviour, which brought them Eternal Life (Gen. 15:6). After the Cross, Believers looked back on an already accomplished fact.

The phrase, *"But the Spirit giveth Life,"* presents that which the Law could not do. The Law could only condemn, while the Holy Spirit gives Life. It is what makes the Gospel effective, powerful, life-redeeming, in fact, the most powerful force on the face of the earth.

THE LIFE OF THE SPIRIT

If one is to observe, Buddhism, Islam, Shintoism, Hinduism, Mormonism, Catholicism, etc., in all the thousands of years of their existence, have not set one single captive free from sin. In other words, not one single alcoholic, not one single drug addict, not one single life and heart filled with hate, has ever been changed by these man-devised philosophies.

Conversely, every single person on the face of the earth, and in fact that has ever been, who has been delivered from the terrible bondages of darkness, with new life given to them, which numbers into the untold millions, has all been done by the Power of Jesus Christ, carried out by the Work, Office, and Ministry of the Holy Spirit.

It is the Holy Spirit Who reveals the Finished Work of Jesus Christ to the believing sinner. He is the One Who makes that Atoning Sacrifice of Christ at Calvary available, and makes real its benefits to our heart and life. It is the Holy Spirit Who energizes what Jesus did at Calvary and the Resurrection. He infuses life into the Believer in the form of the Divine Nature, which gives the Believer power which he heretofore did not have (Acts 1:8).

NOTES

This is what Jesus was speaking about when He said, *"If any man thirst, let him come unto Me, and drink. He that believeth on Me, as the Scripture hath said, out of his innermost being shall flow rivers of Living Water."*

John then said, *"But this spake He of the Spirit, which they that believe on Him should receive"* (Jn. 7:37-39).

Consequently, the First and Second Covenants are contrasted in Verse 6. The First Covenant, that of the *"Letter"* could only point the way, but gave no power to follow the way, and in fact condemned, i.e., *"killeth."* However, the Second Covenant, a better Covenant, that of the Spirit, proclaims Life because of Christ's ability to give it, which He did through Calvary and the Resurrection, and by the Power of the Holy Spirit.

The Law demanded obedience, and Jesus as our Representative Man obeyed it in every respect. Faith in Him, therefore, transfers us from the position of *"Law-Breakers,"* to the position of *"Law-Keepers."* The Law demands performance which man could not give. However, Jesus could, and in fact, did render a perfect performance, which performance is granted freely to the believing sinner, upon Faith in Christ. Thereafter, God looks at the Believer through, by, and of Christ, which gives man a perfect Salvation, thereby, *"Justified by Faith."*

(7) "BUT IF THE MINISTRATION OF DEATH, WRITTEN AND ENGRAVEN IN STONES, WAS GLORIOUS, SO THAT THE CHILDREN OF ISRAEL COULD NOT STEDFASTLY BEHOLD THE FACE OF MOSES FOR THE GLORY OF HIS COUNTENANCE; WHICH GLORY WAS TO BE DONE AWAY:"

The phrase, *"But if the ministration of death,"* refers to that only which the Law was capable of doing, i.e., *"administer death."*

THE LAW AND DEATH

The Mosaic Law did bring death, simply because the Law carried a penalty which was death. Furthermore, it still brings death to people who refuse to believe in Christ.

It does so by exposing God's requirements to them. Since Jesus was the only One Who ever fulfilled those requirements (Mat. 5:17-20), the only way we can fulfill them is by accepting His provision for us.

The modern Christian would be shocked to realize how much of the Law we have brought over into our experience with Christ, and it really doesn't matter whether it's the old Law of Moses, or a law of our own making. The results will be the same in either case — death.

The far greater majority of the world, and for all time, will not accept God's Plan of Salvation which is Jesus, but rather invent their own. Consequently, they can only reach spiritual death, simply because it is not God's Way, but rather a law of their own making.

As well, most Christians, I think I can say without exaggeration, sufficiently believe the Lord for Salvation regarding God's Plan in Christ and Him Crucified, but after Salvation attempt to bring about Sanctification by making up their own laws and rules, which again brings failure. Paul dealt with this in Romans Chapters 6, 7 and 8. I would strongly advise the Reader to get our Commentary on Romans (Vol. 12). To deviate from God's Plan in any capacity only invites destruction.

MINISTRATION OF DEATH

The sadness is, that most Christians think they have total knowledge on these subjects, when in reality, not only do they not have the knowledge, but most Preachers do not know as well. I speak of victory over sin after one becomes a Christian. As Paul had to learn this the hard way, so did I. But thank God, by His Grace, I did learn what the Spirit through Him taught. If I had known such at the beginning, it would have saved me untold grief and heartache.

The purpose of the Apostle is to show that the Ministry of the Gospel is more glorious than even the Ministry of Moses, when he was admitted near to God on the Holy Mount; and when such a Glory attended his receiving and promulgating the Law.

It is called the *"ministration of death,"* because it tended to condemnation; it did not speak of pardon; it was fitted only to deepen the sense of sin, and to produce alarm and dread. In other words, that's what it was designed to do, and it did it well.

NOTES

The phrase, *"Written and engraven* (engraved) *in stones,"* speaks specifically of the Ten Commandments, for that was the only part of the Law of Moses written on Tables of Stone (Ex. 24:12; 31:18; 34:1-4; Deut. 4:13; 5:22; 9:9-11; 10:1-3).

The phrase, *"Was glorious,"* pertains to the manner in which the Law was given, attended with magnificence and splendor. The Glory referred to here consisted in the circumstance of sublimity and grandeur in which the Law of Moses was given.

THE LAW WAS GLORIOUS

If one does not properly understand what is being said, one would wonder how something could be of such gravity, i.e., *"administer death,"* and at the same time be *"glorious?"* It was glorious for the following reasons:

1. Everything God does is always for the good of the people, even the Law of Moses which brought death. While it did bring death, even as it was forced to do, the Lord made provision for escape from this dread malady through Jesus Christ. In other words the Law was absolutely necessary for the benefit of the world.

2. The Law was given in the Glory of God, as He was manifested on Mount Sinai, as the Law-Giver and Ruler of the people.

3. The Glory of the attending circumstances, of thunder, fire, etc., in which God appeared was glorious to say the least. The Law was given in these circumstances. Its giving was amidst such displays of the Glory of God.

4. It was a high honor and glory for Moses to be permitted to approach so near to God; to commune with Him; and to receive at His Hand the Law for His people, and for the world. These were circumstances of imposing majesty and grandeur, which, however, Paul says were eclipsed and surpassed by the Ministry of the Gospel.

Still, some would ask, because the Law brought death, how could it be glorious?

It was glorious because these graven Laws, were God's Own and voiced His Judgment on all transgressors. God's Judgment is Glorious, His Righteousness, and His Justice are attributes of His Glory. Nevertheless, it was an external Glory.

Paul never doubted the Glory that accompanied the giving of the Old Covenant, but the

NOTES

Glory of the New Covenant is a different kind of Glory. Different in what way? To prove his point, the Apostle used a story familiar to all Jews. Let's see what he said:

The phrase, *"So that the Children of Israel could not stedfastly behold the face of Moses for the glory of his countenance,"* refers to the time when Moses came down from Mount Sinai with the two Tables of Testimony in his hands, with his face shining from being in the Presence of God (Ex. 34:29-30). There was such a glory on his countenance, such a dazzling splendor, such an irradiation; a diffusion of light, such that they could not look intently and steadily upon it — even as one cannot look steadily at the Sun. This was produced, as stated, by him being in the Presence of God.

The sons of Israel could not endure it to gaze at this Glory-Light even when it was transferred to Moses. How, then, shall sinners endure the Glory-Light that is on God's Own Face when He comes to judge them?

The phrase, *"Which glory was to be done away,"* refers to a glory which was temporary.

TO FADE AWAY

How soon the Divine Light faded from Moses' face, whether suddenly or gradually, is immaterial. The idea was, that God was doing away with it, putting it out of effect, and so it was gone. Paul's addition of his statement is significant.

God intends that the Glory of the Law of Judgment and Death should disappear before another Glory that is to abide forever, the Glory of the Grace in Christ, the Glory of pardon and life which is conveyed in the Gospel of Jesus Christ, by New Testament Ministers, Christ's Apostles.

THE ABRAHAMIC COVENANT

In order that there be no misunderstanding, let us remember that the Covenant given to Abraham some 430 years before Moses (Gal. 3:17), is actually the Covenant in which Israel had her Salvation. In fact, it is the same Covenant in which we presently have our Salvation, simply because it is a Covenant of Faith. Abraham believed the Lord, and God accounted it to him for Righteousness (Gen. 15:6).

It was into this Covenant that the Ministry of Moses was placed. The Law entered in order fully to reveal sin (Rom. 5:20) and thus, to lead to the knowledge of sin (Rom. 3:20) in true contrition so that Faith in the Gospel might follow.

Consequently, it would be incorrect to think that Moses and Israel had only the Commandments of the Law; they had them in conjunction with the Covenant. Every Israelite who was made contrite by the Law found Forgiveness and Salvation in the Covenant.

Now the Covenant that was inherited from Abraham was entirely Promised, simply Promised. All that Moses added to it with his Ministry was the Law set in fixed Commandments; he could not bring the fulfillment which those Promises had to receive, the fulfillment on which all the saving power of the Promises rested. Jesus had to bring that (Jn. 1:17).

The bringing of the Commandments gave Moses a distinct office for the world. It stands ever: *"The Law was given by Moses"* (Jn. 1:16); he and those Stone Tables, which still pronounce death on all sinners, ever belong together in one. We should misconceive God's intention if we should make Moses all Law and only Law, or all Law for Israel. God would never have added this engraved Law if it were not for the sake of the far greater Covenant with its Promise and the future fulfillment of the Promise. But it is ever Moses and his Ministry that function to this day in the Law that was Divinely given to be our guardian slave to lead us to Christ (Gal. 3:24-25).

ISRAEL'S PROBLEM

Israel's problem was that instead of adding the Law to the Covenant, they inverted it. In other words, they made the Law of Moses first and the Abrahamic Covenant second. Consequently, they attempted to find Salvation in the Law, which it did not contain, and ignored the Covenant that guaranteed their Salvation, which was given to Abraham.

Men love to do religion. In the Law there were all types of doing, where in the Abrahamic Covenant, there was only *"believing."* So, they opted for the *"doing"* because it made them feel religious, but ultimately destroyed them, as it will destroy any and all who succumb to such error.

To be more particular, it was not necessarily the doing of the Law that destroyed them, because in fact, this was something they were supposed to do. It was given by God for them to keep, i.e., *"to do."* The wrong came about, as a result of them trying to make Salvation out of the doing of it, which of course could not be done.

Water Baptism or the Lord's Supper, constitute the doing of particular things, even in the Gospel. It is not wrong to do these things, and in fact is very good, even demanded by the Lord. However, the moment the person thinks that these things contain Salvation, which they don't, then he has left the rudiments of Faith and has gone into works, which will ultimately bring death. Regrettably, as Israel of old, much of the Church world falls into this trap.

In fact, the doing of religion, and in whatever capacity, even though it can be truly of God, can become a narcotic, that is if we put the wrong interpretation on the matter. In fact, the doing of religion is the greatest narcotic there is, from which people need deliverance just as much as they do from alcohol or drugs, etc.

(8) "HOW SHALL NOT THE MINISTRATION OF THE SPIRIT BE RATHER GLORIOUS?"

RATHER MORE GLORIOUS

This is an argument from the less to the greater. Several things in it are worthy of notice:

1. The obvious contrast to the *"Ministration of death,"* would have been *"Ministration of Life."* But Paul chose rather to call it the *"Ministration of the Spirit"* — as the Source of Life, or as conferring higher dignity on the Gospel — than to have called it simply the Ministration of Life.

2. By the *"Spirit"* is manifestly meant here the Holy Spirit; and the whole phrase denotes the Gospel, or the preaching of the Gospel, by which eminently the Holy Spirit is imparted.

3. It is the high honor of the Gospel Ministry, that it is the means by which the Holy Spirit is imparted to men. It is designed to secure the Salvation of men by His Agency; and it is through the Ministry that the Holy Spirit is imparted, the heart renewed, and the soul saved.

The work of the Ministry is, therefore, the most important and honorable in which man can engage.

4. It is more glorious because that of Moses tended to death; this to life.

NOTES

5. It is more glorious because that was engraved on stone; this is engraved on the heart.

6. It is more glorious because that was the mere giving of a Law; this is connected with the renovating influences of the Holy Spirit.

7. It is more glorious because that was soon to pass away. All the magnificence of the scene was soon to vanish. But this is to remain. Its influence and its effect are to be everlasting. It is to stretch into eternity; and its main Glory is to be witnessed in souls renewed and saved, and amidst the splendors of Heaven (Barnes).

Dodderidge said, *"The Work of the Spirit of God on the heart of a rational being, is much more important than any dead letters which can be engraved on insensible stones."*

TWO GREAT MINISTRIES

Thus, two great Ministries stand forth: A. One that is centered in Moses for death; and, B. The other that is centered in the Apostles for life. They are only Ministries, neither produces what it brings. In other words, Moses could not personally bring death, and Apostles cannot personally give life.

The death brought by the one is God's Judgment; the Spirit of Life brought by the other is God's Gift of Grace. The Ministers are just *"bearers"* of the Message.

He made the face of the one shine with His Own Glory, with the blinding, unendurable light that shows forth His Holy Righteousness. Paul asks how, having done this, God could leave the other, the great Apostolic Ministry, without Glory. Does not this Ministry minister God's Love, Grace, Mercy; plant Spirit and Life in place of death? Is there no glory in these attributes of God that can reflect itself in the human Ministers of these attributes?

WHAT KIND OF GLORY?

It will not be blinding Glory Light, which accompanies Divine Justice. It will not be a light that shines upon the sinners as judgment comes upon them, but a light that *"shines in our hearts"* even as this Ministry puts Spirit and Life in our hearts; it will match the Love, Mercy, and Grace of God; it will be and is *"The Light of the Knowledge of the Glory of God in the Face of Jesus Christ"* (II Cor. 4:6).

This *"Light"* will never be *"done away with."* This Light shines not only in the hearts of the

Ministers, but likewise in the hearts of all New Testament Believers.

(9) "FOR IF THE MINISTRATION OF CONDEMNATION BE GLORY, MUCH MORE DOTH THE MINISTRATION OF RIGHTEOUSNESS EXCEED IN GLORY."

The phrase, *"For if the ministration of condemnation be Glory,"* once again means that anything God does is *"glorious."* As we have stated, even the Law, which could do nothing but condemn, was given for man's benefit and not his hurt.

SALVATION

If God had given the Law which roundly condemned, and had provided no way of Salvation, it would in fact have been a horrible thing.

The Law within itself contains no provisions of pardon. To pardon is to depart from the Law; and must be done under the operation of another system — since a Law which contains a provision for the pardon of offenders, and permits them to escape, would be a burlesque in legislation. In other words, it would be a joke! The tendency of the Mosaic Institutions, therefore, was to produce a sense of condemnation. And so it will be found by all who attempt to be justified by the Law. It will tend to, and result in, their condemnation.

However, those who allowed the Law to do its work, which it was designed to do, which was to condemn, and then turn to the Lord by Faith, trusting in the Coming Sacrifice, the Coming Redeemer, Salvation would be found.

In its rightful place and setting, the Law was glorious as a manifestation of the Holiness and Justice of God; and glorious in the attending circumstances. No event in history has been more magnificent in the circumstances of eternal majesty and splendor than the giving of the Law on Mount Sinai.

Even though most of the world does not know or understand, nevertheless, every semblance of true law on the face of the earth, has as its foundation the Ten Commandments, in one way or the other. The more those Commandments are respected, the more freedom and prosperity are guaranteed to people. The less they are respected, the less freedom and prosperity.

The phrase, *"Much more doth the ministration of Righteousness exceed in glory,"* proclaims the New Covenant.

NOTES

RIGHTEOUSNESS

The Ministry announcing death, i.e., *"the Letter,"* that is, the Law, came with glory — a glory so great that man could not look upon it, for it judged him, making him conscious that he was a sinner — but the Ministry announcing Life has so much more excellent glory that it eclipses the Glory of the former.

The Law demanded Righteousness; the Gospel provides Righteousness. The Law bartered Righteousness for obedience, and as that obedience was impossible to man, it was unobtainable by him; hence, his condemnation to death.

The Gospel provides man with a spotless Righteousness as a Free Gift; hence the Gospel is the Ministry of Life. Man being guilty, his greatest need is Righteousness. So the one was the ministration of condemnation; the other, the ministration of Righteousness. Both were *"with Glory,"* for they both expressed God's moral Glory demonstrated in Judgment and in Grace. Both demonstrations were Divinely necessary to the manifestation of that Glory (Williams).

JUSTIFICATION

Even though *"Righteousness"* was what man desperately needed, the way to that Righteousness, and the only way for that matter, was by the *"Ministration of Justification."* This is the plan by which God justifies men. The Law of Moses condemns; the Gospel is the Plan by which man is made Righteous by Justification. And if that which condemns could be glorious, much more must that be by which men can be justified, acquitted, and saved. The superior Glory of the Gospel, therefore, consists in the fact that it is a Plan to justify and save lost sinners.

EXCEED IN GLORY

This Glory consists:

1. In the fact that it can be done when all Law condemns.

2. In the showing forth of the Divine Character while it is done, as just, and merciful, and benevolent in doing it — blending all His great and glorious attributes together; while the Law discloses only one of His attributes — His Justice.

3. In the manner in which it is done. It is by the Incarnation of the Son of God — a far more glorious manifestation of Deity than was

made on Mount Sinai, but yet with not near the splendor.

It is by the toils, and sufferings, and death of Him Who made the Atonement, and by the circumstances of awful and imposing grandeur which attended His Death, when the Sun was darkened, and the rocks were rent — far more grand and awful scenes than occurred when the Law was given, but yet in a different way.

It is by the Resurrection and Ascension of the Redeemer — scenes far more sublime than all the external glories of Sinai when the Law was given.

4. In the effects, or results. The one condemns, the other justifies and saves. The effect of the one is seen in the conviction of conscience, in alarm, in a sense of guilt, in the conscious desert of condemnation, and in the apprehension of eternal punishment.

The other is seen in sins forgiven; in peace of conscience; in the joy of pardon; in the hope of Heaven; in comfort and triumph over the bed of death, and amidst the glories of Heaven (Barnes).

THE RIGHTEOUSNESS OF GOD

Christians are apt to be uncomfortable with the Psalmist's claim, *"I have done what is righteous and just"* (Ps. 119:121). However, if they understood this as speaking of the Righteousness of the Messiah, which it does, then it becomes altogether clear.

From the perspective of the New Testament, we are likely to think of Righteousness, at least within ourselves, and rightly so, as an impossibility. Only God is truly Righteous. And only in Jesus can we stand before God as a Righteous people.

How then can a human being appeal, *"Hear, O Lord, My Righteous plea"*? (Ps. 17:1). Once again, when we understand that this as well is the Messiah speaking, then it becomes altogether clear.

So, if all the Psalms portray the Messiah, which they do, how do we correlate Psalms 143:2, *"No one living is righteous before You"*, or in its original translation, *"For in Thy Sight shall no man living be justified"*?

The Messiah is not speaking of Himself here, but humanity as a whole which lacks Righteousness, and in no way can attain Righteousness (Justification), within their own capabilities.

Inasmuch as Righteousness is a basic theme in both Testaments and a keystone in Christian theology, it is important for us to understand the Biblical concept of this word *"Righteousness."*

NOTES

RIGHTEOUSNESS ACCORDING TO MEN

Whether unbelievers voice such or not, the underlying idea of Righteousness among the unsaved is that of conforming to a norm, whatever that may be, with of course the standard set by man. In their thinking, people are righteous when their personal and interpersonal behavior accords with an established moral or ethical norm.

That's one of the reasons that the United States Supreme Court attempted to define morality according to *"the accepted values of any particular community,"* whatever that may be. Of course, such an interpretation changes with the community, and pretty well leaves it up to the lowest possible common denominator. Such a conclusion is absolutely ridiculous to say the least. In other words, God's Laws are ignored, as though they do not exist, or at the very least, man treats God's Word as less than his own prattle or ramblings. However, to be factual, that's about the best that unregenerate man can come up with. That's at least one of the reasons, the giving of the Law was imperative during the time of Moses.

Consequently, in the Old Testament there was only one standard by which Righteousness was to be measured — the Revealed Will of God, particularly as it is expressed in the Law.

WHAT THE OLD TESTAMENT SAYS ABOUT HUMAN RIGHTEOUSNESS

First of all, we must understand that the use of the word *"Righteous"* or *"Righteousness"* in the Old Testament can refer to that which is comparative between human beings, and on other occasions as the Righteousness of God, which of course is altogether different. The following are some of the examples:

COMPARATIVE RIGHTEOUSNESS

Saul, spared by David, was forced to admit, *"You are more righteous than I . . . You have treated me well,"* (I Sam. 24:17).

David's actions were in closer harmony to the Divine Will than were Saul's. Similarly, Judah said of Tamar, *"She is more righteous than I"* (Gen. 38:26).

NOTES

CONFORMITY TO GOD'S REVEALED WILL

Righteousness in the Old Testament also involves conformity to God's Revealed Will. Moses, reviewing God's giving of the Mosaic Law, told Israel, *"If we are careful to obey all this Law before the Lord our God, as He has commanded us, that will be to our Righteousness"* (Deut. 6:25).

But we must never forget that in both the Old Testament and the New Testament, obedience flows from a right and loving relationship with the Lord.

A RELATIONSHIP WITH THE LORD

Righteousness is also closely linked with a warm and personal relationship with the Lord. The Righteous are *"those who serve God"* (Mal. 3:18).

They are glad in the Lord (Ps. 33:1; 64:10; 68:3) and will praise His Name (Ps. 140:13).

MULTIPLIED BLESSINGS

Righteousness is closely linked with multiplied Blessings from the Lord. The person who serves God and chooses to live by His Standards will be blessed (Ps. 5:12) and upheld (Ps. 37:17), will flourish (Ps. 92:12) and be remembered (Ps. 112:6).

The Righteous may have troubles, but the Lord will help them (Ps. 34:19), and they will neither be forsaken nor fall (Ps. 37:25; 55:22).

Even though the Psalms in their entirety speak of Christ, still, as our Representative Man, it is all for us and as us. Consequently, whatever it says of Him, it is in effect, saying of His Body, the Church.

Proverbs add that the home of the Righteous will also be blessed (Prov. 3:33), that they will not go hungry (10:3), and their desires will be granted (10:24). Their prospect is joy (10:28), for God is their Refuge (10:29), and they will never be uprooted (10:30). They will thrive (11:28) as they are rescued from trouble (11:8), and they will even have a refuge in death (14:32).

Isaiah warning of the terrible judgments coming on God's sinning people can still pause to report this Message from the Lord: *"Tell the Righteous it will be well with them, for they will enjoy the fruit of their deeds"* (Isa. 3:10).

CONFIDENCE IN PRAYER

Righteousness is a basis for confidence in prayer, and in fact can be the only basis in essence.

The person who has lived by God's Standards or at least has tried his best to do so, has a better basis for appealing to God.

"Hear . . . my righteous plea," says the Psalmist (Ps. 17:1). Because his request does not *"rise from deceitful lips,"* the Psalmist can expect vindication (II Sam. 22:21, 25; Ps. 7:8; 18:20, 24; 119:121).

FAITH RESPONSE

Righteousness (Imputed Righteousness) is not the ultimate basis of God's favor. While the Old Testament stresses the importance of personal Righteousness obtained through obedience to the Law of the Lord, righteous acts are not the cause of God's choice of Israel, nor anyone for that matter.

This point is stressed by Moses in Deuteronomy 9:4-6. *"After the Lord your God has driven them out before you, do not say to yourself, 'The Lord has brought me here . . . because of my righteousness' . . . It is not because of your righteousness or your integrity that you are going to take possession of their land . . . The Lord your God will drive them out before you, to accomplish what He swore to your fathers, to Abraham, Isaac and Jacob. Understand, then, that it is not because of your righteousness that the Lord your God is giving you this good land to possess, for you are a stiff-necked people."*

In point of fact, it is only the Believer's Faith response to the Lord that permits God to treat us as though we were righteous. As Scripture says of Abraham, *"Abram believed the Lord, and He credited it to him as Righteousness"* (Gen. 15:6).

THE FRUIT OF RIGHTEOUSNESS

Finally, Righteousness also has an impact on the community. The fruit of Righteousness is peace, and its social effect is security (Isa. 32:7).

When God's Kingdom is finally established on earth, Righteousness and Justice will be the foundation of His Throne (Ps. 89:14).

IMPUTED RIGHTEOUSNESS

Coming into the New Testament, Paul addresses this question as to how a person can be Righteous, by laying the basis for a realized Righteousness in the Believer's union with Jesus (Rom. 6:1-14). We died with Jesus and were raised with Him. Raised to new life, we are told, *"Offer yourselves to God, as those who have been brought from death to life; and offer the parts of your body to Him as instruments of Righteousness"* (Rom. 6:13).

Experimentally, Paul finds this impossible when he struggles in his own strength (Rom. Chpt. 7). But when he accepts his helplessness and applies to his daily life the same principle of Faith that brought Judicial acquittal, he finds freedom!

Trust in the Spirit, expressed by a Faith-response of obedience to His promptings (Rom. 8:9), releases Believers so that *"The righteous requirements of the Law might be fully met in* (them)*, who do not live according to the sinful nature but according to the Spirit"* (Rom. 8:4).

This is the surprising Righteousness of which Jesus spoke. God acts within Believers to *"give life to* (their) *mortal bodies through His Spirit"* (Rom. 8:11) Who lives within. Thus, the Believer is free to actually live a righteous life, not because of conformity to an outward standard, but because the inner person is shaped by the Spirit to chose spontaneously what God Himself chooses.

THE ACTUAL MEANING

It is impossible for man to earn Righteousness on his own, at least the kind which God will accept, which must be a spotless, perfectly pure Righteousness. However, upon simple Faith in Christ, and what He did at Calvary and the Resurrection, the Lord freely imputes total Righteousness to the believing sinner, which he has not earned, and in fact cannot earn. As stated, it is Imputed Righteousness, freely given, because in fact it must be freely given.

THE RIGHTEOUSNESS WHICH EXCEEDS

The Righteousness of which Paul speaks in Verse 9, and which he speaks of constantly in his Epistles, is found totally in Christ. Of course, as God, Jesus is Righteousness Personified.

Nevertheless, in the Incarnation, He won a spotless Righteousness by His perfect keeping of the Law of Moses, which no other human being had ever done. Upon Faith in Him, the believing sinner is awarded this Perfect Righteousness won by Jesus Christ, and freely given to sinners who believe.

NOTES

So, all the Righteousness of which we speak, and which the New Covenant proclaims, and which exceeds in glory all that went before, is all wrapped up in Jesus Christ.

Righteousness is perfect morality, but yet perfection as defined by God and not man. To be frank, man does not even know what perfection is, much less hoping to attain such. And yet, the Believer has a perfect Righteousness, because it comes from a perfect Christ, Who purchased for us a perfect Redemption.

(10) "FOR EVEN THAT WHICH WAS MADE GLORIOUS HAD NO GLORY IN THIS RESPECT, BY REASON OF THE GLORY THAT EXCELLETH."

The phrase, *"For even that which was made glorious,"* refers to the Law of Moses. Paul does not deny that it had an honor and majesty, in some respects, such as the Jews claimed for it. It was glorious in the manner in which it was given; it was glorious in the purity of the Law itself; and it was glorious, or splendid, in the magnificent and imposing ritual in which the worship of God was celebrated (Barnes).

The phrase, *"Had no glory in this respect,"* pertained to comparison.

The reason that the New Covenant excels the Old is that the Old was only for a time (Gal. 3:19, 25; 4:30; Heb. 9:9-10), a particular place — Israel (Deut. 5:16; 11:9; 28:8; 31:13), and a particular people, namely the Jews, although others could come in by becoming a proselyte Jew (Deut. 5:3; Rom. 2:12-16).

To the contrary, the New Covenant is for all time, all lands, and all people (Mat. 26:28; Mk. 16:15-16; Lk. 24:47; Jn. 3:16; Acts 1:8; Rom. 10:9-14; I Cor. 12:13).

The phrase, *"By reason of the Glory that excelleth,"* refers to the New Covenant. The Glory of the Old which it undoubtedly had, was eclipsed by the Glory of the New.

It is like the splendor of the moon and stars compared with the bright light of the Sun.

This excelling Glory is in the Gospel; in the Incarnation, Life, Sufferings, Death, and Resurrection of the Lord Jesus; in the pardon of sin; in the peace and joy of the Believer; and in the glories of the heavenly world to which the Gospel elevates dying men.

One can well see how the Judaizers did not at all appreciate Paul elevating the great Covenant of Grace to this place of ultimate superiority over the Law. Of course, it really was not Paul doing this, but actually the Holy Spirit Himself, and for all the obvious reasons. Nevertheless, such did not set well, especially considering that the Law was not given equal billing. However, this stemmed from a lack of understanding on their part of what the Law really was, and as well, that God's Revelation is always of the progressive nature.

In other words, the very Plan of God is to more and more reveal Himself to His people, which He does at the appointed time.

The next great Revelation which is coming, is the Resurrection, which will transport the Child of God into the total likeness of Christ in every respect.

Even though the New Covenant will never be replaced by another, for the simple reason that such is not necessary, still, Believers have not received all the benefits of this great Covenant as of yet. As stated, the final Chapter remains to the time of the coming Resurrection. Even after that, the Revelation of God will continue to expand, but not in the individual, that having reached in the Resurrection its zenith. It is the Plan of God regarding His Government which will continue to be revealed (Rev. Chpts. 21 and 22).

(11) "FOR IF THAT WHICH IS DONE AWAY WAS GLORIOUS, MUCH MORE THAT WHICH REMAINETH IS GLORIOUS."

The phrase, *"For if that which is done away was glorious,"* tells us several things:

DONE AWAY

Paul here plainly says that the Law was never designed to be permanent, and for all the obvious reasons. Everything in it had a transient existence, and was so designed. Yet it was attended, Paul admits, with much that was magnificent and splendid.

In fact, this is what made Israel the greatest nation in the world. They had the Law of God, which was totally fair, addressing every aspect of life, and because it was from God, it was perfect. By contrast, the surrounding nations only had the laws of men which were grossly unfair, and which really did not address man's core problems of morality. So, this is at least one of the reasons Israel was the greatest nation on the face of the earth, at least during the times they were serving God.

NOTES

However, all of that was to be brought to a conclusion, it having served its purpose. Unfortunately, many Jews didn't see it that way, even some who were followers of Christ.

Less fortunate still, many even in the modern Church continue to try to bring the Law over into Grace, which possibly all of us have done in one way or the other, whether unwittingly or knowingly.

So, the Law in any and all of its forms is not incumbent upon Christians, being done away.

THE TEN COMMANDMENTS

Does that mean the Ten Commandments were abolished as well?

Yes! The totality of the Law was fulfilled in Christ and completely abolished, i.e., *"done away."* However, Nine of the Ten Commandments were reinstated in the New Covenant, leaving out the Fourth, *"Remember the Sabbath"* (Ex. Chpt. 20). Actually, this Commandment was the only one of the Ten which had no moral content, but was basically between Israel and God. If one is to notice, the old Jewish Sabbath of Saturday was not observed in the Book of Acts or the Epistles. Rather it was the First Day of the Week which was observed, which was the Day on which the Lord arose.

However, the Nine remaining Commandments although incumbent upon Believers, present themselves in a different way than under the Old Covenant. In fact, Christianity, i.e., *"The New Covenant,"* actually has no Commandments, at least as we think of such.

Even though these Nine Commandments are binding upon all men everywhere, including Christians of course, still, they have already been kept in Christ, with that victory passed on to Believers. As well, it is not really a question of Christians keeping the Commandments, especially considering that they have already been kept, but that the Believer become Christlike, which the Holy Spirit is ever seeking to bring about, which will automatically take care of these Nine Commandments.

It is a Standing which one has in Christ, rather than a State that one is in, in attempting to do certain things, etc.

The phrase, *"Much more that which remaineth is glorious,"* pertains to the Gospel which will remain forever.

THE ETERNAL CONSEQUENCE OF THE NEW COVENANT

1. It is designed to remain immutable through the remotest ages. It is not to be superseded by any new economy or institution. It is the dispensation under which the affairs of the world are to be wound up, and under which the world is to close, at least as we presently know such.

2. Its effects on the heart are permanent. It is complete in itself. It is not to be succeeded by any other system, and it looks to no other system in order to complete or perfect its operations on the soul.

3. Its effects are to abide forever. They will exist in Heaven. They are to be seen in the soul that has been recovered from sin, is being recovered from sin, and shall be recovered from sin. It will be glorious in the Bosom of God forever and ever.

INTRODUCTION

The Mosaic system — glorious as it was — shall be remembered as introducing the Gospel; the Gospel shall be remembered as directly fitting for Heaven. Its most great and glorious results shall be seen in the permanent and eternal joys of Heaven.

The Gospel contemplates a great, permanent, and eternal good, adapted to all ages, all climates, all people, and all worlds. Consequently, it is so much more glorious than the limited, temporary, and partial good of the Mosaic system, that it may be said in comparison to have had no Glory (Barnes).

The idea as well, pertains to the fact that the Old Covenant came *"through Glory"* while the New Covenant came *"in Glory"* meaning that it resides permanently in the realm of Glory (Rossier).

(12) "SEEING THEN THAT WE HAVE SUCH HOPE, WE USE GREAT PLAINNESS OF SPEECH:"

The phrase, *"Seeing then that we have such hope,"* is not speaking of the hope of Paul and his associates, nor the openness of speech he uses, nor the liberty with which he operates; all these are subordinate.

The point is that the Glory inherent in their Ministry is one that brings Glory upon Glory upon us all, upon those who are served by this Ministry, as well as upon those serving in it.

NOTES

WHAT THIS GLORY DOES

Paul once more draws the Corinthians to his heart, as well as all others for that matter. By showing them the true exaltation of his Ministry he is showing them the true exaltation of themselves as affected by that Ministry, an exaltation that goes from Glory to Glory and cannot be obtained by any means other than this Ministry, i.e., *"this Ministry of the Gospel of Jesus Christ."*

Could Paul use a better way to heal the breach that had been made between himself and the Corinthians, a breach that was now almost healed? By turning from his Ministry and by listening to voices that are hostile to it the Corinthians could only lose this Glory; it would fade away instead of increasing. The loss would be fatal. Not, however, on this negative side does Paul dwell; he presents the positive side, which is most effective.

HOPE

Hope properly is a compound emotion, made up of a desire for an object, and an expectation of obtaining it. If there is no desire for it, or if the object is not pleasant and agreeable, there is no hope, though there may be expectation — as in the expectation of pestilence, famine, sickness, etc.

As well, if there is no expectation of it, but a strong desire, there is no hope, as in cases where there is a strong desire for wealth, or fame, or pleasure; or where a man is shipwrecked, and has a strong desire, but no expectation of again seeing his family and friends. In such cases, despondency or despair is the result.

It is the union of the two feelings, desire for an object and expectation of obtaining it, in proper proportions which constitutes hope.

THE FUTURE

The *"hope"* of which Paul speaks, pertains to the future. The Law had no future, because it could not bring about a desired result. The New Covenant does have a future, and, consequently, a *"hope"* as it regards that future.

Hope, as used here, refers to the prospect, confidence, persuasion, and a clear anticipation of the prospect of Eternal Life.

This hope can be had, because it is based on the Ministry of the Holy Spirit, which shows the way of Justification, and which will never be done away, but will abide forever.

The Gospel is not in types and figures, as the Old Covenant, but in a clear and plain presentation which yields an immediate result.

The phrase, *"We use great plainness of speech,"* refers to the manner in which he preaches the Gospel, which is with a holy boldness, i.e., *"preached in a manner which says he knows what he is talking about, and so will all True Gospel Ministers."*

THE LAW VERSUS THE GOSPEL

There was a necessary obscurity buried in the Law which made it somewhat difficult to understand. In fact, the Law in its entirety spoke of Jesus, but such was not so easily seen at that particular time.

By the time of Christ, the interpretation of the Law was left up to the learned doctors, and was carefully concealed from the vulgar, i.e., the masses. All except the initiated were not allowed to attempt to interpret the Law. That is at least one of the reasons why the masses flocked to Jesus. He did not speak in the manner of the doctors of the Law or even the Pharisees. His terminology was clear, plain, easily understood, and which opened up the Law of Moses as they had never heard before. So, the *"initiated"* were not happy with Him at all respecting this particular situation.

Consequently, the presentation of the Gospel by its Ministers, continues in the manner of Christ. They do not use language abounding in metaphor and allegory. The meanings are clear and plain, with the Holy Spirit ever seeking to make them more clear and plain, and they are given to all.

The Gospel is expressed in the language of common life. As someone has well said, *"What is preaching worth that is not understood?"* Why should a man speak at all, unless he is intelligible? Once again, who was ever more plain and simple in His Words and Illustrations than the Lord Jesus?

The Glories attaching to the Person and Redeeming Work of Christ provide a hope which needs not to be veiled, but, on the contrary, proclaimed without reserve. The Apostle could, therefore, say he had fully preached the Gospel of Christ and keep back nothing that was profitable (Acts 20:20; Rom. 15:19; Col. 1:25).

NOTES

All other Preachers must follow that example!

(13) "AND NOT AS MOSES, WHICH PUT A VEIL OVER HIS FACE, THAT THE CHILDREN OF ISRAEL COULD NOT STEDFASTLY LOOK TO THE END OF THAT WHICH IS ABOLISHED."

The phrase, *"And not as Moses, which put a veil over his face,"* does not at all mean to cast dispersions on Moses, but rather to show the difference in the Old and New Covenants. Paul makes the very same point of Moses' Ministry, namely the mystery, but now adds another point of that feature, namely the *"veil."* Thus, he adds the effect made upon the sons of Israel in contrast to the effect of his own Ministry (and all who minister the Gospel of Grace) upon the Corinthians, and all others for that matter. It is so simple and so obvious.

THE COMPARISON

In Verses 7-11 the two Ministries, Paul's and Moses', suffice for the comparisons.

Now the comparison is between the effects of these Ministries as exhibited in the Jews and in the Christian Corinthians. To be sure, the effects are to be found in the people.

In Verse 7, *"The sons of Israel"* are mentioned only incidentally and not for their own sakes but to show what the Ministry of Moses is.

Paul changes nothing in the account given in Exodus 34:29-35, in regard to Moses and the veil. He uses what is said there about the veil as being illustrative of the blindness of the Jews regarding their entire Old Testament and contrasts this with the effect of the Gospel in *"us all."* Regarding the veil, Paul sees and uses the full illustrative possibilities in regard to the Jews and in regard to all of us Christians.

He sees the veil shutting out the Jews from Christ by their refusal to use the glorious Ministry of Moses as God intended them to use it. He sees the veil removed for the Christians by Christ and his Ministry (Paul's Ministry) so that the faces of all Believers now shine with ever-increasing Glory that is reflected from Christ Himself. However, the greater Glory of the New Covenant is internal where it really counts, and to which the Law could not penetrate, rather than external.

THE PROPHETS

We may go farther and include all the Old Testament Prophets. Their Message was preparatory even for Israel. Because of its nature it withheld much, for the fulfillment in Christ had not yet come. But the Apostolic Ministry had that fulfillment, the complete manifestation of Grace and Salvation for all men for all time.

All reason for reserve or for withholding had disappeared. Moses and the Prophets had to leave much to the future when Christ should finally come. As well, Pagan religions had and have their particular Doctrines, which were at best to be communicated only to the initiated, and which were and are of no consequence irrespective. By contrast, the Gospel of Christ ever speaks with *"full openness"* and dispenses all its Blessings on all alike who will dare to believe, be they great, small, rich, poor, male, female, etc.

The phrase, *"That the Children of Israel could not stedfastly look to the end of that which is abolished,"* means that they could not understand all the design, scope, or purpose of the Mosaic Institutions. That *"end"* was the Messiah, and the Glory of His Institutions. *"Christ is the End of the Law"* (Rom. 10:4).

The Law was never designed to be permanent; and Paul speaks of it here as a thing that was known and indisputable that the Mosaic Institutions were designed to be abolished.

WHAT EXACTLY DID MOSES DO?

There is considerable dispute in regard to just what Moses did, and still more in regard to the purpose of what he did respecting the veil.

According to the account given in Exodus Chapter 34, Moses repeatedly put a veil over his face.

It states that Moses spoke the Commandments to Israel with his face unveiled; that whenever he was done speaking he put on the veil, that when he spoke to God he again removed the veil. In Verse 7 of this Third Chapter of II Corinthians, Paul says that the Glory on Moses' face was so great that the Israelites could not gaze upon it, which means that they were compelled to cover their eyes.

It is incorrect to say that Moses had his face covered and spoke to the Israelites only through a veil. All that both Exodus and Paul say is to the effect that the Glory of Moses' face was to be seen by the Israelites, for this Divine Glory gave the effect to the Divine Commandments as they came from Moses' lips.

NOTES

The fact that the eyes could not endure this Glory was due to the death, the killing power, the condemnation of the Commandments which Moses spoke (II Cor. 3:6-9). The Glory on Moses' face was the Glory of the Divine Law and the Judgment that was reflected by God's Minister of Law.

All of this occurred at Sinai, and we hold that it ended there after the communications of the Law to the Israelites were concluded. The opinion that this veiling and unveiling continued for the entire nearly 40 years of the journey until Moses died is not borne out in Scripture (Lenski).

ABOLISHED

Five times in this Chapter the Holy Spirit through the Apostle speaks of the abolishing of the Law, which end came with Christ (vss. 7, 11, 13-14, 16).

I think one should certainly get the message that the Holy Spirit desires all to know that the Law was fulfilled in Christ, and is no more. As well, the number five as claimed by some, is the number which pertains to the Grace of God. At any rate, the 16th Verse, as we shall see, concludes the scenario with Israel finally accepting Christ, when the veil will then be removed, which will be at the Second Coming of the Lord. So, Grace ultimately overcomes the Law, even as it was intended to do.

(14) "BUT THEIR MINDS WERE BLINDED: FOR UNTIL THIS DAY REMAINETH THE SAME VEIL UNTAKEN AWAY IN THE READING OF THE OLD TESTAMENT; WHICH VEIL IS DONE AWAY IN CHRIST."

The phrase, *"But their minds were blinded,"* means that their powers of reason were, so to speak, petrified (Farrar).

BLINDED!

"Blinded" in the Greek is *"poroo,"* and means *"to petrify, to harden."*

The idea is, their thoughts were hardened by God Himself because Israel refused to accept the true purpose of the Mosaic Law. What is meant by that is this:

The idea is, that God has decreed that a willful rejection of His Word, even in the face of incontrovertible evidence, brings on a willful or judicial judgment. God has ordained that judgment to be a further blindness, a further hardening of the heart. So, unbelief breeds unbelief, even as Faith breeds Faith.

Paul devoted Romans Chapter 10, to explaining their rejection of True Righteousness in order that they might establish their own. Of course, the statement here does not denote every single Jew. Some did accept the Truth of God's Word and become Righteous.

"Callousness," "hardness," "petrification," etc., occur when people prefer trying to impress God with their good works rather than accepting the Sacrifice of Christ for their sins. Reading the Old Testament in the Synagogues was an established tradition in New Testament times (Lk. 4:16-19).

When Jesus publicly read Isaiah 61:1-2, in the Synagogue in Nazareth and applied it to His Own Messianic Ministry, the people of the town where He grew up became furious and actually tried to kill Him (Lk. 4:20-30).

That is how calloused they had become to the Messianic Promises of the Old Testament that extend all the way back to Genesis 3:15.

This *"veil"* (blindness) could have been removed if they would only have accepted Jesus as the Messiah. This obtuseness cannot be removed any other way because He is the only Means of Salvation that God has provided (Acts 4:12). This Verse, along with many others, clearly discloses that the Old Testament can only be properly understood in light of Christ as its fulfillment (Rossier).

PAUL'S STATEMENT IS STRONG

Paul refers here to the fact that the understanding of the Jews was stupid, dull, and insensible, so that they did not see clearly the design and end of their own Institutions. He states simply the fact; he does not go into detail referring to its cause.

By resting in the letter, shutting their eyes against the light that was granted to them, they contracted a hardness or stupidity of heart. And the veil that was on the face of Moses, which prevented the Glory of his face from shining *out* may be considered as emblematical of the veil of darkness and ignorance that is on their hearts, and which hinders the Glory of the Gospel from shining *in.*

The phrase, *"For until this day remaineth the same veil untaken away in the reading of the Old Testament,"* pertains to the fact that even to the time when Paul wrote, it was a characteristic of the great mass of the Jewish people, that they did not understand the true sense of their own Scriptures. They did not understand its Doctrines in regard to the Messiah. A veil seems to be thrown over the Old Testament when they read it, as there was over the face of Moses, so that the glory of their own Scriptures is concealed from their view, even as stated, as the Glory of the face of Moses was hidden.

WHY?

This fact is one of the strangest anomalies of history. As a people the Jews are among the most brilliant, and I think one could say, the most brilliant in the world. They excel in Art, Science, and Literature. By a per capita count their skill and attainments far exceed those of other races. They have distinguished themselves in all walks of life.

However, when this national brilliance is brought to the Bible, which incidentally they have given us, there is a mysterious lack of understanding. The Old Testament is from their hand. The Law and the Prophets flowed through the mold of their mind, yet they cannot perceive their meaning. How strange!

Apart from the explanation we have here of this phenomenon, the whole thing would be beyond our comprehension. Truly, their minds are blinded and there is a veil upon their hearts. The Jewish people gave us both the Scriptures and the Saviour, yet their mind is dulled to the Scriptures and their heart is dead to the Saviour.

THE MIND

The veil, it is important to note, is not on the Scriptures but on the mind. It is universally impossible for these people to perceive the transitory character of the Mosaic Institutions. It is equally impossible for them to concede the historical Christ of the New Testament as having any place in the Old Testament system, when in fact, Jesus is the Entirety of that system.

To them Jesus Christ is an imposter. Their Talmud teaches that Jesus was a wicked man, a sorcerer and an idolater. It further teaches that He is in Hell and that His Name should not be mentioned without saying, *"May His Name be blotted out and His Memory."*

NOTES

The New Testament is called *"the margin of evil or a blank page of sin."* But all of this is because of the veil which is upon their hearts.

STRANGE!

How strange all this is! Israelites by the millions have read the Old Testament Scriptures. It is considered Sacred and Holy. They have eulogized its Patriarchs and memorialized its events. In doing this they have completely failed to see the delineation of their Messiah. Yet, Christ stands forth upon every page of the Old Testament. He is typified in its characters and symbolized in its Sacrifices. He could say, *"Lo, I come (In the volume of the Book it is written of Me,) to do Thy Will, O God"* (Heb. 10:7). He walked with two Disciples, *"And beginning at Moses and all the Prophets, He expounded unto them in all the Scriptures the things concerning Himself"* (Lk. 24:27).

The ignorance and antagonism of the Jewish mind to this Sacred Figure has no natural explanation. It is not for want of evidence, nor can it be explained by lack of information. The ignorance is mental but it is more than that, it is volitional. So, that means the problem is not merely intellectual but rather, spiritual. Its solution is not in education but in regeneration (Laurin).

A CONTINUED NEGATIVE RESPONSE

Unbelief is a peculiar thing. It never leaves one as one is found, but always worse. As stated, unbelief breeds unbelief.

Consequently, as they did at Sinai, so they have done through the centuries in the Synagogues when Moses speaks to them. Their thoughts harden like stone with the opposition of unbelief.

The thought is not that they discard the Pentateuch. They read it continually, revere it and laud Moses to the sky; but they do not believe him and his writings (Jn. 5:46-47) nor what the veil on his face tells them so effectively, what his whole Ministry and his Writings ever expound to them: condemnation done away with only by the Righteousness of Faith in the Promised Redeemer.

Paul states this figuratively by using the veil in an illustrative way just as God had Moses use it: *"To this very day the veil remains unlifted,"* literally, *"not being drawn up to reveal."* The original idea of the veil is retained, for Paul says *"the same veil."*

NOTES

THE ACTUAL MEANING OF THE VEIL

The veil does not mean covering the eyes so as to prevent vision and to make people blind. The veil on Moses' face means the end of the Glory of the Law as it is condemnation for the sinner. The Glory soon disappeared from Moses' face, and he discarded the veil. What is meant by that is this:

The abiding Glory of Righteousness in Christ is to extinguish the Glory of the judgment that condemns. But in the case of the unbelieving Jews it is as though the veil still hangs over Moses' face, as though the Glory of the condemning judgment of the Law still burns on Moses' face under that veil. For them his Ministry lies altogether only in that Glory of the Law.

That Glory and the veil ever go together; if it were not for the one, the other would not exist. By leaving the veil the Glory is left. And that Glory ever means condemnation. It is a Glory of judgment, that alone.

So if the veil *"remains,"* which means that the burning Glory of condemnation continues to burn under it with a destructive light that no man can endure, the Jews are lost. The reason is simple, the Law can only kill, it cannot save. Their rejecting the One Who fulfilled the Law, means they have rejected the only Saviour, the One to Whom the Law pointed, Who Alone could satisfy its curse. Consequently, they are still under its curse.

The phrase, *"Which veil is done away in Christ,"* means that for the unbelieving Jews the veil remains unlifted, because only in Christ can it be taken away.

IN CHRIST

Many of the Prophecies, for example, until the Messiah actually appeared, seemed obscure, and almost contradictory.

Those which spoke of Him, for illustration, as man and as God; as suffering, and yet reigning; as dying, and yet as ever living; as a Mighty Prince, a Conqueror, and a King, and yet as a Man of sorrow; as humble, and yet glorious: all seemed difficult to be reconciled until they were seen to harmonize in Jesus of Nazareth. Then they were clear, and the veil was taken away.

Christ is seen to answer all the previous descriptions of Him in the Old Testament; and His Coming casts a clear light on all which was before obscure.

To acknowledge Christ removes the veil, and one might quickly add, not only for the Jews but for the Gentiles as well. Christ is the Answer to all things.

(15) "BUT EVEN UNTO THIS DAY, WHEN MOSES IS READ, THE VEIL IS UPON THEIR HEART."

The phrase, *"But even unto this day,"* refers to the time when Paul wrote this Epistle, which was about 30 years after Christ was put to death. But it is still as true presently as it was in the time of Paul; the character and conduct of the Jews now so entirely accords with the description which he gives of them in his time, as to show that he drew from nature, and as to constitute one of the strong incidental proofs that the account in the New Testament is true. Of no other people on earth, probably, would a description be so accurate over 1900 years after it was made.

The phrase, *"When Moses is read, the veil is upon their heart,"* refers to them not seeing the true meaning and beauty of their own Scriptures — a description as applicable to the Jews now as it was to those in the time of Paul.

Moses and the veil which he wore at Sinai have passed long since; the Pentateuch is fully clear as to how the Law with its condemnation leads us to the Gospel of Righteousness in Christ. On the objective side all has been done.

They refuse to understand what Moses really was and what he really wrote; they are fixed in their own thoughts about him and also about all that he wrote. They keep, as it were, a veil of their own making wrapped around their hearts.

It is without doubt, the saddest spectacle in all of human history.

(16) "NEVERTHELESS WHEN IT SHALL TURN TO THE LORD, THE VEIL SHALL BE TAKEN AWAY."

The phrase, *"Nevertheless when it shall turn to the Lord,"* proclaims the ultimate restoration of Israel, which will take place at the Second Coming, when they finally accept Jesus Christ as their Lord, Master, Saviour, and Messiah (Zech. Chpt. 14). Paul discussed this at length in Romans Chapter 11. (Please see our Commentary on that all-important Chapter.)

NOTES

The phrase, *"The veil shall be taken away,"* denotes the fact that a coming to Christ removes the veil, i.e., which is the only way it can be accomplished.

RESTORATION

The flavor of the Greek implies that *"The moment the heart of Israel shall have turned to the Lord, the removal of the veil begins."* Then *"They shall look on Him Whom they pierced"* (Zech. 12:10); *"He will destroy in this mountain the face of the covering cast over all people, and the veil that is spread over all nations"* (Isa. 25:7). To *"turn to the Lord"* includes turning from sin, falsehood, etc. The turn speaks of repentance and includes contrition and Faith. The title *"Lord"* here denotes Christ.

The effect of this will be to make them acquainted with the true sense of their own Scriptures, and the light and beauty of the sayings of their own Prophets. Now they are in deep darkness on the subject; then they will see how entirely the Scriptures meet and harmonize in the Lord Jesus.

In fact, no one, Jew or Gentile, can know or understand the Bible in any capacity, unless they know The Lord Jesus Christ. Otherwise, it is a closed Book.

WHAT WILL IT TAKE TO BRING ISRAEL TO THIS PLACE?

In essence this is the cause and reason for the coming Great Tribulation period. While this time will embrace many situations, its primary focus will be to turn Jacob back to God. Jeremiah the Prophet saw that coming day and exclaimed, *"Alas! For that day is great, so that none is like it: it is even the time of Jacob's trouble; but he shall be saved out of it"* (Jer. 30:7).

"Saved out of it" doesn't mean to be spared the consequences, but rather that Satan will not have his way in attempting to destroy the entirety of Israel, i.e., *"all Jews."*

Satan knows that if he can destroy the Jews, the Promises of God will fall to the ground, which in effect, would make the Evil One the winner in this great conflict of Light and darkness. In fact, that was the purpose of Satan in the Holocaust of World War II. Hitler did not know the reason for his great hate, but Satan's purpose was to destroy so many Jews that they would not be able to form a nation. He knew the time of the prophecies of their restoration was about to begin, hence his great effort. Consequently, the forming of the nation of Israel in 1948, was not just another happening on the world scene, but rather, a happening of astounding proportions.

In the very near future, the future from 1998, Israel will accept the Man of Sin as their Messiah, hence fulfilling the Prophecy of Christ, *"I am come in My Father's Name, and ye receive Me not: if another shall come in his own name, him ye will receive"* (Jn. 5:43).

Jesus also said, concerning the coming Great Tribulation, which fits exactly with Jeremiah's Prophecy, *"For then shall be great tribulation, such as was not since the beginning of this world to this time, no, nor ever shall be"* (Mat. 24:21).

It will take a bloodletting of unprecedented proportions to bring Israel back to God, actually being brought to the very edge of total annihilation. Only then will they cry for the Messiah to come, knowing that He is then their only hope. He will not disappoint them, coming back in power and great glory (Rev. Chpt. 19).

If all of these things are that close, and they definitely are, how close must be the Resurrection (Rapture) of the Church! Saint of God, if there was ever a time that we should draw closer to the Lord, it is now. When we see that all these things of which the Prophets spoke, and to which Paul pointed, are already beginning to be fulfilled, it should make us realize that time is drawing to a close, at least regarding this particular Dispensation.

THE PRIVILEGE OF THE CHRISTIAN

It is the privilege of the modern Believer to look on the unveiled and unclouded glory of the Gospel. As well, we do not have to look at it through types and shadows. We do not have to investigate it through a veil of obscurity drawn designedly over it. We see it in its true beauty and splendor.

The Messiah has come, and we may contemplate openly and plainly His Glory, in the grandeur of His Work.

The Jews looked upon it in the light of Prophecy; to us it is history. They saw it only through obscure shadows, types, and figures; we see it in open day, having the privilege of surveying at leisure its full beauty, in the contemplation of the fullness of its splendor, this Gospel of our Blessed God. For this we cannot be too thankful; nor can we be too anxious lest we undervalue our privileges, and abuse the mercies that we enjoy.

NOTES

THE OLD AND THE NEW

In reading the Old Testament, we see the importance of suffering the reflected Light of the New Testament to be thrown upon it, in order correctly to understand it. As we've said many times, the Old Testament is the New Testament concealed, while the New Testament is the Old Testament revealed.

It is our privilege to know what the Institutions of Moses meant; to see the end which he contemplated. And it is our privilege to see what they referred to, and how they prefigured the Messiah and His Gospel.

In reading the Old Testament, therefore, there is no reason why we should not take with us the knowledge which we have derived from the New, respecting the Character, Work, and Doctrines of the Messiah; and to allow them to influence our understanding of the Laws and Institutions of Moses. Thus shall we treat the Bible as a whole, and allow one part to throw light on another — a privilege which we always concede to any book.

As well, one cannot really understand the New Testament, i.e., the Gospel of Jesus Christ, unless one understands the Old Testament. We must understand that Jesus was in everything of the Old Testament, actually the One to Whom all the Sacrifices, Sabbaths, Types, and Shadows pointed. Understanding that, the New Testament and His Person take on a brand-new meaning and complexion. In fact, without properly understanding the Old, one cannot have a clear vision of the New.

(17) "NOW THE LORD IS THAT SPIRIT: AND WHERE THE SPIRIT OF THE LORD IS, THERE IS LIBERTY."

The phrase, *"Now the Lord is that Spirit,"* refers to Verse 6, and speaks of the Holy Spirit.

JESUS AND THE HOLY SPIRIT

The greatest comment on this Verse is Romans 8:2, *"For the Law of the Spirit of Life in Christ Jesus hath made me free from the Law of sin and death."*

The *"Lord"* refers to Jesus Christ. *"Spirit"* refers to the Holy Spirit.

Paul linking the two together in this fashion tells us, that the Sacrifice of Christ makes everything possible, but the Holy Spirit effects the work within our lives. He Alone can make real to us, give us the benefits, help us to understand the benefits, bring them about in our hearts and lives and everyday work before the Lord, of that which Jesus did at Calvary and the Resurrection. Romans Chapter 6 tells us what Christ did, and Romans Chapter 8 tells us how the Holy Spirit makes it effective.

The fact that Paul is not fusing the Two Persons of the Deity into One is at once apparent when he writes *"The Spirit of the Lord."* They are Two Persons but of identical Essence and do the same work. Where the Lord is, there is His Spirit, and where the Spirit is, there is the Lord. In the Presence of the Spirit we see the Glorification of the Lord, and in the Presence and the Glorification of the Lord we see the Spirit and His Work (Jn. 16:14).

This is what Jesus told Philip about Himself and about the Father: *"He that hath seen Me hath seen the Father"* (Jn. 14:9-11; 12:45); or still stronger: *"I and My Father are One"* (Jn. 10:30). This is true also with regard to the Lord and the Holy Spirit (Lenski).

The phrase, *"And where the Spirit of the Lord is, there is liberty,"* refers to the *"liberty"* or *"freedom"* to live a holy life, to obey God, to be like Jesus. The implication is that spiritual bondage cannot exist where the Holy Spirit abides.

LIBERTY!

"Liberty" in the Greek is *"eleutheria,"* and means *"freedom."*

What type of freedom?

As should be obvious, it does not imply license to sin, but rather the very opposite. Genuine spiritual liberty affords people the opportunity to live up to their complete potential in Christ Jesus, and it comes only through surrender to God. Jesus Himself exemplified it in His Own conduct, which was totally dedicated to the Will of the Father. We can see, therefore, that the more free we become, the more capable we are of fulfilling His Glorious Will (Rossier).

In the life and under the domination of the Holy Spirit there is no bondage, but, on the contrary, progress from one degree of moral glory to another, for where the Spirit is Lord there is liberty.

NOTES

Paul did not ascribe this liberty to the Lord Alone, but brought in the Holy Spirit. He did this because the Lord ever works through His Spirit. The graven letters of Moses had no power to convert and to give liberty, only the Lord's Spirit can do that. Those letters bind and condemn so that we may flee to Christ and to His Spirit and be freed.

THE WORK OF THE HOLY SPIRIT

Considering that His Work is unending, in that all the Father and the Son do is done through Him, we will only note several aspects of His all-important agency.

In John 16:7-15, we have a very important Passage. Jesus declares to the anxious Disciples that it is expedient for Him to go away, because otherwise the Spirit will not come. He was speaking of the Spirit coming in a new dimension, for in fact, the Holy Spirit has always been here. Being God, He is everywhere.

Jesus said, *"And when He is come, He will convict the world of sin, and of righteousness, and of judgment"* (Jn. 16:8).

CONVICTION OF THE HOLY SPIRIT

The term *"convict"* involves a degree of understanding along with a moral process. The Spirit Who deals in Truth, and makes His appeal through the Truth, shall convict, shall bring the mind on which He is working into a sense of self-condemnation on account of sin. The word actually means more than merely to reprove, or refute, or convince.

Holy Spirit conviction signifies up to a certain point a moral conquest of the mind: *"Of sin, because they believe not on Me"* (Jn. 16:9). Unbelief is the root sin. The Revelation of God in Christ is, broadly speaking, His condemnation of all sin. The Spirit may convict of particular sins, but they will all be shown to consist essentially in the rejection of God's Love and Righteousness in Christ, i.e. in unbelief.

RIGHTEOUSNESS

Jesus further said, *"Of Righteousness, because I go to the Father, and ye behold Me no more"* (Jn. 16:10).

What does this mean?

The meaning is that Jesus, by His Death and Resurrection, made it possible for ungodly men to have a pure, perfect, spotless

Righteousness, which is demanded by God, and that it can be obtained by exerting simple Faith in Christ. It is the business and task of the Holy Spirit to convict man of his lack of such Righteousness, the total necessity of having such, and that it can be obtained in Christ, and Christ Alone.

JUDGMENT

Jesus also said, *"Of Judgment because the prince of this world hath been judged"* (Jn. 16:11).

In the Incarnation, Death, and Resurrection of Jesus, the prince of this world, the usurper, is conquered and cast out.

The idea is that Satan has been defeated, his stranglehold on humanity broken, the grip of sin broken, which translates into the fact that his captives can now be set free. It also refers to the fact that those who do not avail themselves of the Mercy and Grace of God provided by Jesus Christ, will suffer the same effect that Satan will ultimately suffer, eternal banishment in the Lake of Fire (Rev. 20:10-15).

We may sum up the teachings as to the Spirit as follows:

WHAT HE DOES

He is the Spirit of Truth; He guides into all Truth; He brings to memory Christ's Teachings; He shows things to come; He glorifies Christ; He speaks not of Himself but of Christ; He, like Believers, bears witness to Christ; He enables Christians to do greater works than those of Christ; He convicts the world of sin, of righteousness, and of judgment; He comes because Christ has gone away; He is *"Another Comforter"*; He is to abide with Believers forever.

These teachings cover a very wide range of needs. The Holy Spirit is the subject of the entire discourse. In a sense, it is the counterpart of the Sermon on the Mount.

There, the Laws of the Kingdom are expounded. Here, the means of realization of all the ends of that Kingdom are presented. The Kingdom now becomes the Kingdom of the Spirit. The historical revelation of Truth in the Life, Death, Resurrection, and Glorification of Jesus being completed, the Spirit of Truth comes in fullness. The Gospel as history is now to become the Gospel as experience.

NOTES

THE SPIRIT'S ACTION

The Messiah as a fact is now to become the Messiah as a Life through the Spirit's action. All the elements of the Spirit's action are embraced: the charismatic for mighty works; the intellectual for guidance into Truth; the moral and spiritual for producing holy lives. This discourse transfers the Kingdom, so to speak, from the Shoulders of the Master to those of the Disciples, but the latter are empowered for their tasks by the might of the indwelling and abiding Spirit.

The method of the Kingdom's growth and advance is clearly indicated as spiritual; conviction of sin, righteousness, judgment, obedient, and holy lives of Christ's Disciples.

THE HOLY SPIRIT AND THE EARLY CHURCH

The Book of Acts contains the record of the beginning of the Dispensation of the Holy Spirit. There is at the outset the closest connection with the recorded predictions of the Holy Spirit in the Gospels. Particularly does Luke make clear the continuity of his own thought regarding the Spirit in his earlier and later writings. Jesus in the First Chapter of Acts gives Commandment through the Holy Spirit, and predicts the reception of power as the result of the Baptism with the Holy Spirit which the Disciples are soon to receive.

The form of the Spirit's activities in Acts is chiefly charismatic, that is, the miraculous endowment of Disciples with power or wisdom for their work in extending the Messianic Kingdom. As yet, the Work of the Spirit within Disciples as the chief sanctifying agency is not fully developed, and is later described with great fullness in Paul's writings. However, it is by no means totally lacking in Acts. The ethical import of the Spirit's action appears at several points (Acts 5:3, 9; 7:51; 8:18; 13:9; 15:28).

The chief interest in Acts is naturally the Spirit's Agency in founding the Messianic Kingdom, since here is recorded the early history of the expansion of that Kingdom. The phenomenal rather than the inner moral aspects of that great movement naturally come chiefly into view. But everywhere the ethical implications are present.

THE HOLY SPIRIT IN PAUL'S WRITINGS

The teachings of Paul on the Holy Spirit are so rich and abundant that space forbids an exhaustive presentation. In his writings, the Biblical representations reach their climax. Due to what the Holy Spirit gave to Paul, we must come to the idea that he grasped the unity of the Christian Life as no other man. All the parts exist in a living whole and the Holy Spirit constitutes and maintains it.

In fact, a careful study of Paul's teachings discloses three lines, one relating to Faith, another to Christ, and the third to the Holy Spirit. That is to say, his teachings come together, as it were, point by point, in reference to these three subjects.

Faith is the human side of the Divine activity carried on by the Holy Spirit. Faith is, therefore, implied in the Spirit's action and is the result of or response to it in its various forms. But Faith is primarily and essentially Faith in Jesus Christ. Hence, we find in Paul that Christ is represented as doing substantially everything that the Spirit does, even as we are now studying.

However, we are not to see in this any conflicting conceptions as to Christ and the Spirit, but rather Paul's intense feeling of the unity of the Work of Christ and the Spirit. The *"Law"* of the Spirit's action is the Revelation and Glorification of Christ. In his Gospel, to which we have already alluded, which incidently came later, John defined the Spirit's function in precisely these terms. Whether or not John was influenced by Paul in the matter, of that we have no information.

THE CONNECTION

We begin with a brief reference to the connection in Paul's thought between the Spirit and Jesus. The Holy Spirit is described as the *"Spirit of God's Son"* (Rom. 8:14; Gal. 4:6), as the *"Spirit of Christ"* (Rom. 8:9).

He who confesses Jesus does so by the Holy Spirit, and no one can say that Jesus in anathema (cursed), that is, if he is truly led by, and in the Holy Spirit (I Cor. 12:3).

Christ is called a *"Life-giving Spirit"* (I Cor. 15:45); and in II Corinthians 3:17, the statement appears, *"Now the Lord is that Spirit."* All of this shows how completely Paul regarded the Work of Christ and the Spirit as one, not because they were identical in the sense in which some have contended, but because their task and aim being identical, there could be no sense of discord in Paul's mind in explaining Their activities in similar terms.

NOTES

IN TOTALITY

From beginning to end, the Christian Life is regarded by Paul as under the power of the Holy Spirit, in its inner moral and spiritual aspects as well as in its charismatic forms. It is a singular fact that Paul does not anywhere expressly declare that the Holy Spirit originates the Christian Life. The reason being that such originates in Christ.

But yet, the Holy Spirit is definitely involved in all that is done, all the way from conviction of the sinner to revelation of the need regarding Christ. He is then the institute of Regeneration in the heart and life of the believing sinner, which imparts Divine life. However, all of this is done by, upon, through, and because of the Work carried out and accomplished by Jesus Christ (Rom. 8:2).

(18) "BUT WE ALL, WITH OPEN FACE BEHOLDING AS IN A GLASS THE GLORY OF THE LORD, ARE CHANGED INTO THE SAME IMAGE FROM GLORY TO GLORY, EVEN AS BY THE SPIRIT OF THE LORD."

The phrase, *"But we all, with open face,"* describes the fact that we are like Moses because we are committed to enter into the Presence of God; however, at the same time, we are unlike Moses in that we do not need veiled faces because the Holy Spirit actually dwells within us; consequently, we enjoy constant communion with God Himself.

THE PERSONAL EXPERIENCE

Just as Verse 17 describes the legal aspect of the miracle of freedom, this last Verse describes the experiential aspect. In other words, when we believe in Christ, the Holy Spirit ushers us into a legal state of liberty by removing the veil. This initial action, however, is only the entrance into a life of continuous liberty that makes spiritual growth possible (Rossier).

As well, whereas only Moses then had this glory, and only for a short time, all Christians now hold the same status, which status is Christ.

OPEN FACE

The *"we"* of the *"open face"* are none other that those who have believed and received Jesus Christ and are indwelt by the Holy Spirit. No others have this *"open face."* All other faces are veiled, spiritually speaking. Only when we turn to Christ is the veil taken away.

He unveils us that we, like Moses, may behold the Glory of the Lord.

The attitude of the *"open face"* is that of *"beholding."* This means to gaze. It is not glancing but gazing. It is not looking, but seeing. It is a steadfast gaze which takes time to absorb every detail.

The phrase, *"Beholding as in a glass the Glory of the Lord,"* refers in a sense to a *"mirror."* We are all reflecting as mirrors the Glory of the Lord.

The mirrors of the ancients were made for the most part, of burnished metal, and they reflected images with great brilliancy and distinctness.

THE MIRROR

The meaning is that the Gospel reflects the Glory of the Lord; it is, so to speak, a mirror — the polished, burnished substance in which the Glory of the Lord does shine, and where the Glory is irradiated and reflected so that it might be seen by all Believers. There is no veil over it; no obscurity; nothing to break its dazzling splendor, or to prevent its meeting the eye.

Christians, by looking on the Gospel, can see the glorious Perfections and Plans of God, as bright, clear, and brilliant as they could see a light reflected from the burnished surface of a mirror. The idea is this:

The glorious perfections of God shine from Heaven, beams upon the Gospel, and thence reflects to the eye and the heart of the Christian, and has the effect of transforming us into the same image. This passage is one of great beauty, and is designed to set forth the Gospel as being the reflection of the infinite glories of God to the minds and hearts of men.

The Glory of our Lord is so constituted that no one can in the least reflect it without first himself having become transformed into an image of that Glory. Christ's Glory shown fully upon the Jews, but they rejected it, and, therefore, reflected none of it.

The reflection begins at the moment of transformation, and the transformation instantly results in the reflection.

NOTES

First, we constantly reflect the Image of Christ by *"beholding* (Him) *in a mirror."* What is this glass, or mirror?

It is the Scriptures (James 1:22-25). As we look into the Bible, we actually see two images: the Image of Christ and our own image. This mirror shows us how far short we fall from His Likeness.

The phrase, *"Are changed into the same Image from Glory to Glory,"* refers to the fact that the more we cooperate with the Holy Spirit, we are being changed more and more into the Likeness of Christ (Rom. 8:29).

The idea is that the change is a continuous and progressive action made possible by the Holy Spirit. Paul refers to this constantly (Rom. 12:2) as part of God's Will for Christians.

FROM GLORY TO GLORY

"From Glory to Glory" refers to degrees. Actually, it is a beautiful and lifelong process which will not stop until the Resurrection of Believers.

The phrase, *"Even as by the Spirit of the Lord,"* tells us by Whom this is done, and as stated, that it is by the Word of God.

THE BIBLE

To which we have already alluded, twice the Bible speaks of itself as a glass or a mirror. In James 1:23-25, it refers to the sinner and the mirror of the Word. Here (II Cor. 3:18), it refers to the Christian and the mirror of the Word. When the sinner looks into the Bible, he sees his own image, sinful and vile. When the Christian looks into the Bible, he sees Christ's Image. The sinner beholds and believes for Salvation. The Christian beholds and surrenders for Transformation.

One reason why many people do not read the Bible is because it exposes them. A mirror reflects what looks into it. The Bible is a faithful witness to our sins. It reflects every defect and produces an inner conviction of personal deficiency which it is designed to do.

Because many are made uncomfortable by it, many are afraid to see themselves as the Bible sees them.

The image which the Bible reveals to the people of the unveiled face is the Image of Christ. Gazing results in changing. This change is not a superficial or artificial facial reflection. It is

Transformation, not imitation. It is an inherent change of character, not a mere reflection on our faces, such as Moses had. It is an inherent likeness, not a reflected one.

HIS LIKENESS

Our change is unto His Likeness. This is a wonderful thought. Think of a Transformation that gives a character likeness to Christ. Beware of any cheap religious imitation.

The change is gradual. It is from one degree of glory to another. As stated, it is a continuous Transformation. As we momentarily behold, so shall we be momentarily changed. It is not a sudden and instantaneous change that comes in a flash.

However, there is a change which is, in fact, instantaneous. It is the change of Salvation. That is the change of a moment, but this is the change of Sanctification, and is a change of degrees. The change which is Salvation depends on God. The change which is Sanctification depends on us, in the sense that unless we keep a steadfast gaze and maintain an unbroken fellowship, we will not be changed.

There is another sense in which they both depend on God, because Salvation is God's Work *for* us, while Sanctification is God's Work *in* us. Let us never relax our gaze, and we will never lack the charm of a character changed into Christ's Image.

NOT BY SELF-IMPROVEMENT

Self-improvement is the occupation of much of the world, and regrettably, even the Church. It is a hopeless task. Self cannot be improved by self, and can only come into its rightful place when it is hidden and buried in Christ. All change is God's Work in us. We are not changed by human improvement.

It is not the improvement of attainment but rather the result of an inner change of character and is *"by"* the indwelling Holy Spirit.

It is our steadfast gaze into the Bible's mirror of Revelation which brings the Transformation of our character into the Image of Christ. It is this manner in which the Holy Spirit works. Let us be sure we do the gazing and God will be certain to do the changing.

If you, dear reader, desire a changed life, consider Jesus Christ. Fasten the gaze of your attention upon Him and you will become like that

NOTES

which you contemplate. The place of your gazing and contemplation, as we have repeatedly stated, must be the Bible, for that is where He is revealed, and done so by the Holy Spirit.

"Spirit of Power, anoint me for service,
"Spirit of Holiness, cleanse Thou my heart,
"Give to my soul of Thy Self a new vision,
"And a new measure of power impart."

"Never before has my soul had such yearning,
"For Thy infilling, O Spirit of Love!
"Come to the Throne, be my Master and Ruler,
"And fill Thou me with Thy fullness Divine."

"Myself I yield in complete consecration,
"Body and spirit and soul to be Thine;
"Spirit of Power, regard Thou my yearnings,
"And fill Thou me with Thy fullness Divine."

CHAPTER 4

(1) "THEREFORE SEEING WE HAVE THIS MINISTRY, AS WE HAVE RECEIVED MERCY, WE FAINT NOT;"

The phrase, *"Therefore seeing we have this Ministry,"* refers to the great Covenant of Grace given to Paul by the Lord and with all its particulars.

OPPONENTS

In fact, Paul's detractors, of which there seemed to be many, would deny him this Ministry. These were no doubt Judaisers from Jerusalem who in fact did believe in Jesus, but also claimed that one had to keep the Mosaic Law in order to be saved. Even though this problem was addressed in Jerusalem, even as it is recorded in Acts Chapter 15, still, many from that source were continuing to promote this error. It was the Law/Grace issue. Actually, that's one of the reasons that Paul addressed himself so strongly to the Mosaic Law in the previous Chapter. To be sure, him proclaiming that this Ministry of Grace was of far greater import even than the Mosaic Law, did not set well with his detractors at all.

JEALOUSY

Also, along with these false teachers not totally believing the Gospel of Grace, they were also jealous that Paul had been given this New Covenant.

Why should it be given to him? He was not one of the original Twelve, and beside that, he had been a persecutor of the Church before his conversion. So, in their thinking, he was simply not worthy of this particular place and position. Consequently, along with repudiating his Message, they felt they also had to repudiate his character and this they did. It may seem difficult for us to imagine how a spiritual giant like Paul could be accused of dishonesty, but he was. In fact, his opponents falsely accused him of practically everything imaginable, which no doubt grieved the Apostle, but he in no way allowed it to deter or hinder the progress of the Gospel.

If the man of God stops to defend himself against every accusation, or if he allows it to hinder or deter in his responsibilities, then Satan has succeeded in what he had set out to do. Paul was human as we all are; therefore, these accusations hurt him, but he was more concerned about how they hurt the Work of God than being concerned about his own person.

The phrase, *"As we have received mercy,"* proclaims his answer to these opponents, whomever they may have been. The manner in which he answered should be a lesson to us.

MERCY

Considering that he had been a persecutor of the Church, even a rabid persecutor, his detractors were claiming that he was not really an Apostle; therefore, his Message was bogus as well!

In their thinking, how could such a one as Paul claim that he had been given the New Covenant, a Covenant incidentally even greater than that of Moses, which made this Ministry greater as well?

In fact, Paul does not really deny some of the accusations, but merely says that it is the Mercy of God that is responsible for his high and holy calling.

NOTES

How so much this answer must have discomfited his detractors. Only one who is very secure in his position, i.e., *"secure in Christ,"* could answer accordingly.

Once again we emphasize, that Paul was not overly concerned about attacks on his person, which are borne out in the type of answers he gave, but rather the damage done to the Work of God in general.

Satan does his greatest damage from inside the Church, rather than from the outside. These types of situations leave the Saints confused, at times not knowing what to believe. Unfortunately, such did not stop with Paul, but continues unto this present hour. So, Saints of God are going to have to keep themselves close to the Lord, anchored in His Word, or else be led astray, even as are many.

In fact, every single Believer stands in the Mercy and Grace of God. It is not possible for anyone to be worthy of any Blessing from the Lord. Consequently, Paul, was a product of the Mercy of God, as are all Believers.

It is sad, but many Christians are not satisfied with the choice made by God. In other words, they don't like the one or ones He has chosen for certain Ministries. However, it should be quickly noted, that the Lord is not going to change regardless of what people like or don't like. So, the idea is, that every Believer get in line with God's choice, instead of trying to hinder that which He is doing.

The sadness is, most Believers are so unversed in the Word of God, so little led by the Holy Spirit, that they actually find themselves supporting Satan's efforts instead of that which is of God.

When these people opposing Paul stand at the *"Judgment Seat of Christ,"* at least those who were truly saved, what will their answer be then? In fact, that same question should be posed to all Believers. It's an awful thing to oppose the very One we are supposed to be serving. We should ever keep that in mind.

I certainly don't want to accept that which is not of God, but at the same time I certainly don't want to oppose that which is of God.

THE PATH OF MOST BELIEVERS

The Word of God is to be the criteria for all things, not Churches, Preachers, Denominations, etc. Consequently, everything must be addressed according to the Word of God. What does the Bible say about the matter, whatever the matter may be?

Regrettably, most Believers do not follow that route, but rather whatever their Denomination or a particular Preacher might say. In fact, untold millions are in hell right now simply because they did not follow the Word of God, but rather men. That has ever been a problem in the Church, and continues to be a problem unto this moment.

The Believer is to see what the Word of God says about any given situation, and then follow accordingly, irrespective as to what their Church, Pastor, Denomination, etc., may or may not do. This one thing is certain:

When all of us stand before the Lord, the rule by which we will be judged will not be Churches or Religious Denominations, or anything else of that nature, but rather the Bible. So, one had better know what the Word of God says and then determine in his own heart and mind to follow that Word irrespective as to what will be the results.

The phrase, *"We faint not,"* means that God has not necessarily called us to be successful, but rather *faithful*. *"Faint not"* implies the maintenance of a holy courage (I Cor. 16:13) and perseverance (II Thess. 3:13).

FAINT NOT?

We learn from this statement and personal experience, that the Gospel of Jesus Christ alone sets captives free. Consequently, Satan marshals all his forces against its presentation. He uses every tactic at his disposal, and to be sure, discouragement due to these many obstacles, is one of his greatest weapons. As we've already stated, most of the opposition will come not from the world per se, but rather from the Church itself.

Those who compromise the Gospel will greatly oppose those who don't. Those who teach false doctrine will also greatly oppose those who don't, but rather proclaim the True Gospel. Those who have instituted their own type of government respecting the Church, rather than that given by the Holy Spirit, will greatly oppose those who attempt to maintain *"Government"* as given in the Scriptures.

As well, Satan will greatly hinder on a personal basis, oppressing the Preacher of the Gospel, or anyone for that matter who attempts to do anything for the Lord. The manner of oppression of which I speak, is similar to that which Paul underwent in 1:8-11 of this Epistle. Of course, the degree of oppression as suffered by Paul probably would not be allowed by the Lord regarding most Believers; nevertheless, it would be of the same manner.

The type of oppression of which we speak pertains to spirits of darkness which literally attack the Believer in the realm of acute discouragement, and fear, which weigh the person down to such an extent, that they literally cannot function in a normal manner. It is as if though a black cloud descends upon the individual, literally imprisoning the person, which is actually caused by demon spirits. Most of the time, when it lifts it does so immediately.

This is one form of oppression, with Satan taking advantage of particular things which happen whatever they may be, thereby bringing such hinderance.

However, irrespective of these things, Paul said *"We faint not,"* i.e., we will not quit, we will not give in to Satan's suggestions, we will not give place to discouragement, fear, or opposition in any manner.

THE MANNER OF THE HOLY SPIRIT

In Romans, *Salvation* is set forth. In I Corinthians, *Sanctification* is set forth. In II Corinthians, *Service* is set forth. Salvation is God's Work *for* us. Sanctification is God's Work *in* us. Service is God's Work *through* us.

We are not living a normal Christian experience until these three phases of God's Work for, in, and through the Christian are true of us.

Since in a sense, this is a biographical account of a distinguished Believer (Paul), we shall find here not only the inner secrets of this man's soul, but also a cross-section display of motives and virtues for all Christians.

It seems so strange, as stated, that a man of Paul's character should have been hounded by persecution from within the Church. In fact, he probably suffered more from this source than from all the multiplied adversaries without. These experiences were more painful and more difficult to bear than anything he was called upon to suffer in the world. His motives were called into question. His character was vilified. His name was besmirched. His actions were

NOTES

reviewed with a critical scrutiny that had already prejudged and condemned him.

What Paul offered here in response to all this campaign of hatred and hinderance was not a defense, but a declaration. It was a declaration of motives. He reached into his soul and took out his innermost secrets for the inspection of all who cared for the Truth. Many would not be impressed, for there are people who feed only on suspicion, envy, and slander. They thrive on the troubles of others. They live to obstruct the processes of Sanctification in the heart and life of the Believer.

For these, all Paul could do was to state his ideals and leave the issue with God and then go on with his work, no matter what opposition or obstruction he met. It was a wise course, in fact designed by the Holy Spirit. To cease one's constructive work, to engage in debate and conflict with opponents is to play into the Devil's hands.

LET THE RECORD SPEAK FOR ITSELF

As we've already stated, Paul was willing to let his record speak for his character. His motives were according to God's Mercy. He had received great mercy at the hand of God. Once a proud Pharisee, boasting in the attributes of personal excellence and seeking to establish Salvation by religious zeal, he had met the risen Saviour on the road to Damascus. That road for Paul was one of religious duty. He had been dispatched to put Christians in prison, or even worse.

On that road he had met Christ face-to-face, and had become a changed man. He then saw himself as the chiefest of sinners and in his need turned to Christ and found what religion had previously failed to give him.

Paul had a very definite personal experience. It was not a theory gleaned from books. It was not something learned from teachers. It was not even a ceremonial developed by devotion. It was a life, a new life, a saving life received in the converting experience of the New Birth.

Paul called attention to the fact that he received the Gospel, not only as a personal way of life, but also as a Ministry. It came to him as something to pass on to others, in fact, as something that must be passed on to others. Consequently, he was resolved that the greatness of the Mercy he had received would be the measure of the greatness of the service he would render (Laurin).

NOTES

THE HUMBLING PROCESS

Since the glories of the Gospel dispensation are so great, and its effects on the heart so transforming and purifying, the object is to show the effect of being entrusted with such a Ministry on the character of his Preaching.

The idea is, that it was by the mere Mercy and favor of God that he had been entrusted with the Ministry; and the object of Paul is doubtless to prevent the appearance of arrogance and self-confidence, by stating that it was to be traced entirely to God that he was put into the Ministry.

Nothing will more effectually humble a Minister, and prevent his assuming any arrogant and self-confident airs, than to look over his past life, considering the Mercy and Grace extended to him, and then to remember that it is by the mere Mercy of God that he is entrusted with the High Office as an Ambassador of Jesus Christ. Paul never forgot to trace his hope, his appointment to the ministerial office, and his success, to the mere Grace of God.

Consequently, he would not be disheartened by the difficulties which he met; his faith and zeal did not flag; he was enabled to be faithful, and laborious, and his courage always kept up, and his mind was filled with cheerfulness. In fact, he was deterred by no difficulty; embarrassed by no opposition; driven from his purpose by no persecution; and his strength did not fail under any trials. The consciousness of being entrusted with such a Ministry animated him; and the Mercy and Grace of God sustained him.

ON A PERSONAL BASIS

I would like to believe that I have had some personal experience in this same capacity, even as Paul. Many have asked as to how Frances and I have been able to cope, especially considering the opposition of much of the Church world, not to speak of the world as a whole. We have survived, and victoriously so I might quickly add, even stronger in the Lord than we've ever been before, by simply anchoring in Christ and deriving His Leadership in all that we do. In order to have this, we've had to literally live a life of prayer.

Unfortunately, there are many in the Church who feel if there is any failure of any nature, this gives them license to take whatever measures they desire. Of course, these people have little desire to obey the Word of God, but rather to carry out their own self-will. In other words, they will demand a pound of flesh, and for their own reasons, etc.

The Truth according to the Word of God is, that failure of any kind begins and ends with the individual. If it is properly taken to the Lord, the matter stops there. Such gives no right at all for any measures to be taken regarding persecution, punishment, etc. So, even though all persons are personally responsible for their own acts, they are not responsible for how people respond to those acts. In other words, whatever a person does, gives me no latitude to take a wrong action against them.

So, the idea generally perpetrated in the Church that whatever is done is all the fault of the one who has failed, holds no Scriptural water.

A lady wrote me some time back, saying *"I'll admit that many things have been done toward you which are wrong, but it's your fault."*

No, I beg to disagree! While I am personally responsible for any act that I may commit, I am not responsible for whatever anyone else does. That argument is as old as Adam and Eve in the Garden. Adam blamed his fall on God and Eve, while Eve blamed it on the serpent.

My Mother used to say and rightly so, *"Two wrongs don't make a right."*

The truth is we have suffered much because of what we preach, our dependence on the Holy Spirit, and the things for which we stand. Also, it is not Scriptural to take something which happened many years ago and was washed clean by the Blood of Jesus at that time, and continue to use it as a whipping boy. Such is grossly unscriptural, and in fact, ungodly. It is a denial of the Grace of God, in fact, the very purpose for which Calvary and the Resurrection was brought about. At the same time, why don't they apply the same punishment toward themselves!

No, what we have suffered, and continue to suffer, is because of our stand for the Gospel of Jesus Christ. All else is merely an excuse.

This Ministry is of God, which means that I am of God. Consequently, as those people who opposed Paul will have to answer, so will these who have opposed me, and exactly in the same manner.

NOTES

Despite the opposition, and please believe me it can be very severe at times, *"we faint not."* In other words, that which Satan desires and all who work with him, I will not do. I will continue to preach this Gospel as long as the Lord gives me breath, and I will continue to preach it in exactly the manner in which I believe the Lord has instructed me to so do. For that I do not apologize, for such needs no apology. I will stand on our record regarding souls being saved and lives being changed. The moving and operation of the Holy Spirit is the proof. In fact, it is the only proof that God will accept, and it had better be the proof that all others accept as well!

The idea of what Paul is here saying, is, that despite the opposition, *"we know that we cannot fail as long as we attend to our Ministry with God."*

(2) "BUT HAVE RENOUNCED THE HIDDEN THINGS OF DISHONESTY, NOT WALKING IN CRAFTINESS, NOR HANDLING THE WORD OF GOD DECEITFULLY; BUT BY MANIFESTATION OF THE TRUTH COMMENDING OURSELVES TO EVERY MAN'S CONSCIENCE IN THE SIGHT OF GOD."

The phrase, *"But have renounced the hidden things of dishonesty,"* means that everything is rejected that smacks of underhandedness, double-dealing, exploitation, etc. — anything not based on a sincere desire to help souls turn to Christ and to mature in Him (Eph. 5:12). In effect, Paul is saying *"disgraceful as may be the calumnies of my Jewish opponents, I have said farewell forever to everything to which a good man would blush." "Honest"* in its original Greek expression, stands for moral excellence.

MORAL PERFECTION

Of course, the only moral perfection is in Christ, which in Truth is the purpose of the Incarnation, and Imputed Righteousness upon Faith. Nevertheless, anything in the life of the Believer that is not totally Christlike, must be *"renounced,"* i.e., *"disowned," "to put off."* Anything wrong or wicked, must be taken to the Lord, repented of, forsaken, and renounced.

In fact, no person can claim moral excellence except in Christ. To do so shows an improper understanding of who and what one actually is, and Who and What Christ actually is and did. In other words, no human being can stand justified, except in Christ. But yet, sadly and regrettably, much of the Church world attempts to do exactly that — to claim moral excellence other than Christ.

How do I know that?

Anyone who adds to, or takes away from the Finished Work of Christ, is in effect, claiming their own righteousness instead of that which is imputed freely by Christ upon Faith (Gal. 5:3-6).

WHAT TYPE OF MINISTRY WOULD PAUL HAVE WERE HE ALIVE TODAY?

In studying Paul as I have, I think I am at least somewhat familiar with his manner and way. As well, inasmuch as this *"manner"* and *"way"* were inserted into the Word of God, I have to come to the conclusion that it is that which is sanctioned by the Holy Spirit. In other words, even though it is Paul, we're not merely following a man, but rather the work which the Holy Spirit accomplished through and in him. It is to serve as our example, as well as does the other Bible Greats.

IF PAUL WERE LIVING TODAY, I BELIEVE HE WOULD EXPOSE AUTHORITARIAN DEMANDS

By that I speak of Denominational leaders, or anyone for that manner, who demands compliance regarding things which are not Scriptural. In other words, no one, and I mean no one, has the right to tell a Preacher what he can preach, what he cannot preach, or if he can preach at all. Anyone who would assume that position is grossly unscriptural, and anyone who would obey such demands is unscriptural as well. However, the following must be quickly added:

Most Denominational leaders claim Spiritual authority, which of course, is unscriptural, but as such, if they are not obeyed, they will then seek to destroy. The point is this:

If the Preacher of the Gospel sets out fully to follow the Word of God, he should think twice before joining these particular Denominations, and if joined, he must be willing to suffer the consequences should such arise, which most are not willing to do.

NOTES

This is not to say that Denominations are wrong, at least as far as the formation of such is concerned, or belonging to such, for it isn't. The wrong appears in whenever so-called Church leaders adopt an unscriptural form of Church Government, and then try to force compliance.

Also, most Church people have the idea that Church leaders who have been elected by popular ballot, are in fact, Scriptural and Spiritual authority, and thus must be obeyed. In most cases, nothing could be further from the Truth. Scriptural Church Government, which of course was instituted by the Holy Spirit, does not function as a democracy, i.e., *"by popular ballot."* While such individuals can certainly serve in an administrative capacity and be perfectly Scriptural, their so-called authority begins and ends there. Even as we have already addressed, God-called Apostles constitute Spiritual authority, not those elected by popular ballot (Eph. 2:20). However, even the authority held by these true God-called servants, is never over people, but authority only as it governs their Message. In other words, they can proclaim with authority that their Message is right, but they cannot force people to accept what they say, even as Paul could not force compliance to his Message, hence him constantly saying *"I beseech thee."*

So, I think I can say without any fear of contradiction, that Paul would have strongly opposed such unscriptural authoritarian demands.

In some few of the Religious Denominations of the world, Paul definitely could have functioned with liberty to preach the Gospel and follow Christ, for the simple reason that the government and leaders of those respective Denominations, as few as they may be, are more in line with the Word of God; however, with the far greater majority, I think, he would have been unwelcome and strongly so.

UNSCRIPTURAL PROMOTIONAL TECHNIQUES

I speak of anything which is not born and birthed by the Holy Spirit. The moment we begin to use the techniques of the world, we have lost the Moving and Operation of the Holy Spirit. What do I mean by techniques of the world?

I speak of turning the Church into entertainment, i.e., rock groups and others, using worldly

NOTES

techniques to spread their unscriptural message. While there is nothing wrong with clean entertainment in the realm of fellowship, it must be kept at that level. Anything used to attract people to the Church, must be in keeping with the Moving and Operation of the Holy Spirit, and not in techniques used by the world, which tends to fill the Church with unsaved people.

I think that Paul would have cried out against the entertainment mania which grips the modern Church, and which in many cases is so similar to the world as to be indistinguishable.

A short time ago, in a major Religious Magazine, I saw a write-up promoting a particular Church which was advertising its promotional scheme respecting its efforts to attract young people. A big room had been turned into a dance hall, which also sported a *"Christian rock band."* They went on to advertise their *"bar,"* and *"bartender,"* who served up particular drinks with names similar to their worldly counterparts. Even though they were nonalcoholic, still, they were doing all they could to come as close as possible to the world, without it being the same thing.

The Spirit of God is not in such a thing, but in fact, is grossly opposed to such. While such may attract some young people, it will not see their lives changed, which can only be done by the Power of God. The idea, that we will use worldly techniques in order to draw them to the Church, and then preach the right Message to them, with them giving their hearts to Christ, is bogus indeed!

The Spirit of God will not sanction, bless, anoint, or help anyone or anything, in which is not birthed by Him. The Spirit of God is not in such a place, even though it advertises itself as *"Church,"* neither is He in the so-called *"Christian rock shows,"* etc. To be frank, claiming such borders on rank blasphemy!

Regrettably, the Church advertising this of which I have just spoken, was not one labeled *"modernistic"* but rather one that claimed to be *"Spirit-filled."*

I think it should be quickly added, that there is a vast difference in being Spirit-filled, and being *"Spirit-controlled."*

PSYCHOLOGICAL PSYCHOBABBLE

In most Churches in the world presently, and I exaggerate not, very little Gospel of Jesus Christ is preached, but rather the latest psychological pap. The reader must understand, that this is not the exception, but rather the rule. In other words, the far greater majority of the modern Church has bought into the psychological lie — hook, line, and sinker.

Anyone who knows anything about the Word of God, and believes the Word of God, knows that it's impossible to meld the two — the Bible and Psychology. The former is of God, while the latter is totally of man, i.e., *"of Satan."*

As well, if one knows anything at all about psychology, one knows that it's impossible to join the Word of God with that lie. For instance, psychology teaches that man is basically good while the Bible teaches that man is basically evil (Rom. Chpt. 3). So, with that simple statement, the line is drawn.

I know that Paul would have stood up boldly against this lie of darkness, and would have done so in no uncertain terms.

A FALSE DOCTRINE

Paul lambasted Hymenaeus and Philetus for spreading unscriptural doctrines (II Tim. 2:14-18), and I am certain that he would have done the same presently.

It is never pleasant to take such a stand; consequently, one must be willing to suffer the consequences and there definitely will be consequences. All of these things of which we have mentioned, and some we haven't mentioned, have their origin in Satan. To be sure, he does not take lightly the exposing of that which he has so cleverly disguised. But if one is to be honest, one must do exactly that, expose the lies of darkness.

THE EXPLOITATION OF BELIEVERS

Along with other things, this falls under the heading of the modern prosperity message. Regrettably, this is the message for many Churches. Salvation from sin is given little place at all, which means that man's true need is pretty well ignored.

All under the guise of the Blessings of God, money is held up as the foundation of one's Faith, with prosperity being the yardstick.

This is a huckster's gospel which appeals to the baser motives of man, i.e., his greed. The Lord definitely does bless, and does so abundantly. The business of the Holy Spirit, however, is not designed to make us rich but rather holy. Unfortunately, the prosperity message causes the Believer to miss out on both. As an example note the following:

The Preacher stands before a Television Camera, and tells the people that the Lord has told him that all who respond with a certain gift in the next 30 minutes, etc., will receive a hundredfold return.

Another says, if a particular amount is given, all the bills of the individual will be paid in a particular period of time.

Another says, if $1,000 is given, their home will be paid for at the end of the year, etc.

The list is almost endless, with all being grossly dishonest. To be frank, it is much worse than someone walking into a place of business, drawing a gun and demanding money.

At least, the robber does not pull the Lord into his escapade. However, when a Preacher claims that God has told him something, when in fact He hasn't, and as well when that which is claimed is grossly unscriptural, he has then made God a part of his lie, which ultimately will demand judgment. At least the robber of the convenience store, or whatever, doesn't claim that the Lord has told him to do such; consequently, his sin is far less than that of which we have mentioned.

Some may ask, *"Doesn't the Lord speak to people and give them direction?"* He certainly does, and in fact, He will greatly bless all who give to His work and cause. The Bible is full of such! However, there is no hint in the Word of God of the exploitation practiced by many modern Preachers.

The Lord has not anointed anyone to pray a hundredfold prayer over people. The idea smacks of greed and selfishness. It does not develop the person but merely exploits them. Can anyone find an example in the Word of God for such? No they cannot!

As well, the Lord does not tell Preachers that if so much money is given, so much money will be given by the Lord in return. Once again, is there an example in the Word of God of such? Again, no there isn't!

To take advantage of one's Faith, making them believe something which really isn't there, and especially that which tends to enrich the Preacher, constitutes a terrible sin. Consequently, I think Paul would have renounced such in no uncertain terms.

NOTES

So now I think you can see, why Paul was attacked bitterly, and why Jimmy Swaggart is not admired too very much as well. If one wants to know the Truth, that is the reason for 99%, if not all the opposition leveled against this Evangelist. To be sure, any other Preacher who stands for the same thing, will suffer the same opposition. Unfortunately, ours is on a worldwide basis for the simple reason that our Ministry is worldwide so it attracts hostility on a worldwide basis.

The phrase, *"Not walking in craftiness,"* speaks of subtlety.

CRAFTINESS

"Craftiness" in the Greek is *"panourgia,"* and means *"to play the knave, or villain, act like a rogue, to do holy deeds in an unholy way, or to do unholy deeds in a supposedly holy way."*

"Craftiness" comes from the same Greek word used of Satan's subtlety and beguiling of Eve (II Cor. 11:3). Paul's defamers used this same word against him (II Cor. 12:16).

Actually, the very craftiness of which the false teachers at Corinth accused Paul, they were guilty themselves. In fact, the True Ways of God can never be advanced by anything that remotely smacks of trickery or deceit. To be sure these false teachers were tricksters, as are all false teachers, and they certainly practiced deceit, as again do all false teachers.

Paul has already referred to the charge made in Corinth that he was not always upright and truthful (II Cor. 1:12, etc.), that his yea was not always yea (II Cor. 1:17, etc.). He again addresses about this point when he says *"not walking in craftiness."* But it is now not *"I,"* and not a defense against personal slander; it is *"we,"* Paul and his associates who are presented as men who seek greater success by practicing *"craftiness."* The word means the ability to do certain tricky things, and in the New Testament it is always used in an evil sense: trickiness, cunning deception to gain one's end by underhanded and dishonest means and methods. Men of this type had come to Corinth, probably from Jerusalem. Before Paul is through he will reckon with them (II Cor. Chpt. 10).

The phrase, *"Nor handling the Word of God deceitfully,"* refers to using it for one's own purpose and agenda.

NOTES

DECEIT

Crafty conduct is paired with *"adulterating the Word of God."* These two ever go together. He who is not honest with himself will not be overhonest with the Word.

Adulterating the Word of God (handling it deceitfully), refers to not leaving it pure lest people reject it, but falsifying it to catch the crowd. Of all the dastardly deeds done in the world this is the most dastardly. None are more criminal nor more challenging to God Himself.

These individuals at Corinth, were casting aspersions upon the genuineness of Paul's teaching. Preachers adulterate the Word, to commend themselves to people, to get their favor and following.

Preaching should consist in a simple exhibition of the Truth. There is no deceit in the Gospel itself; and there should be none in the manner of exhibiting it. It should consist of a simple statement of things as they are. The whole design of Preaching is to make known the Truth. And this is done in an effectual manner only when it is simple, open, undisguised, without craft, and without deceit.

WAYS OF DECEIT

While there are as many ways of deceit I suppose, as there are Preachers who would engage in such, still, there are some ways which stand out:

1. Any Preacher who attempts to make the Bible fit his doctrine, instead of making his doctrine fit the Bible, is practicing deceit.

2. Placing emphasis where emphasis is not intended, is another form of deceit. I speak of several things, but particularly of the modern prosperity message. While the Lord is definitely a Blesser of people, still, the main thrust of the Gospel is not money, but rather Holiness and Righteousness in Christ. Consequently, those who make the prosperity gospel their theme, even as untold numbers do, are practicing deceit.

3. Those who know certain things in the Bible to be true, but yet will not preach them or practice them, and because of the fear of man or for whatever reason, are practicing deceit. I speak of Preachers who know that the Baptism with the Holy Spirit, with the evidence of speaking with other Tongues is Scriptural, but yet will not preach it simply because they fear the wrath of man. I speak also of those who know their particular Church Government is wrong, at least as practiced by their Denomination, but yet will continue to obey these unscriptural rulings and demands.

4. Anyone who attempts to preach the Word of God in order to please men, is pure and simple *"handling the Word of God deceitfully."*

If one is to notice, these Preachers seldom see anyone brought to Christ. In fact, they make little if any attempt to bring lost souls to Christ. They boast that their ministry is to more fully educate people after they are brought to Christ. In fact, this was the very tactic used by the interlopers at Corinth.

While they reluctantly agreed that Paul's Ministry may have possibly brought these Corinthians to Christ, they now flatter the Corinthians by telling them that they have now outgrown Paul. In other words, they (these false teachers) had now come to present a deeper life ministry.

No, they had come to lead these people astray, and for their own selfish purposes and ends. So do their modern counterparts.

The phrase, *"But by manifestation of the Truth commending ourselves to every man's conscience in the sight of God,"* has reference to the fact that if these Corinthians will just listen to their conscience, they will know that what Paul has preached is true.

Paul's Gospel would stand the acid test of Truth, because it had brought these Corinthians out of paganistic darkness into the Light of the Lord Jesus Christ. They could not deny that.

By Paul saying this, he is at the same time saying that these interlopers cannot in any way point to anything which their ministry has produced which is Christlike.

THE PREACHING OF THE GOSPEL

It is a very material fact that when the Gospel is correctly preached, the conscience and reason of every man is in its favor, and they know that it is true even when it pronounces their own condemnation, and denounces their own sins. Consequently, this passage proves the following:

1. TRUTH: That the Gospel may be so preached as to be seen to be true by all men.

Men are capable of seeing the Truth; and even when they do not love it, they can perceive that it has demonstration that it is from God. It is a system so reasonable; so well established by evidence; so fortified by Miracles and the fulfillment of Prophecies; so pure in its nature; so well adapted to the needs of sinful man; so fitted to his condition, and so well designed to make him better; and, so happy in its influence on society, that men may be led to see that it is true.

2. CONSCIENCE: The consciences of men are on the side of Truth, and the Gospel may be so preached as to enlist their consciences in its favor. Conscience prompts to do right, and condemns us if we do wrong. It can never be made to approve of wrong, never to give a man peace if he does that which he knows to be evil. By no art or device; by no system of laws, or bad government; by no training or discipline, can it be made the advocate of sin. In all lands, at all times, and in all circumstances, it prompts a man to do what is right, and condemns him if he does wrong.

It may be silenced for a time; it may be *"seared as with a hot iron,"* and for a time be insensible, but if it speaks at all, it speaks to prompt a man to do what he believes to be right, and condemns him if he does that which is wrong.

To say it another way, the consciences of men are on the side of the Gospel, that is, if they will only listen to their consciences. In fact, it is their hearts which are opposed to the Gospel.

3. CONVICTION: The way in which a Preacher of the Gospel is to commend himself to the consciences of men, is that which was pursued by Paul. The Preacher must have a clear and unwavering conviction of the Truth himself. On this subject he must have no doubt. He should be able to look on it as into a mirror, and to see its glory as with open face. It is the simple Truths of the Gospel of Jesus Christ.

A Preacher of the Gospel should be frank, open, undisguised, and candid. He should make a sober and elevated appeal to the reason and conscience of man. The Gospel is not *"a cunningly devised fable"*; it contains no trick in itself, and, consequently Preachers should solemnly refuse all hidden things of dishonesty.

4. BEFORE GOD: The Preacher must ever understand, that what he does and what he preaches, is always *"in the sight of God."* It is as in the immediate Presence of God. We must act as if though we know and understand that His eye is always upon us, and as His Ambassadors, that we will one day answer if we improperly proclaim the Message, or do so with deceit in any manner.

NOTES

HONESTY FOR THE HONEST

In a veiled way, Paul is stating that if the heart is pure, it will never be attracted to a dishonest Gospel. For that which *is* dishonest must also at the same time appeal to that which *is* dishonest.

In other words, the prosperity message appeals to greed, while the political message appeals to pride. Those who would succumb to flattery as offered by false teachers, even as they always do, do so because of self-will in their heart, and certainly not because of Christlikeness.

That which is honest will never appeal to that which is dishonest, and that which is dishonest will never appeal to that which is honest. So, Believers who are pulled away from the True Path of the Gospel of Jesus Christ, onto a perverted, twisted path, are brought to such a way because of dishonesty in their own hearts and lives in some fashion. This is the Message the Holy Spirit is proclaiming through the Apostle.

(3) "BUT IF OUR GOSPEL BE HID, IT IS HID TO THEM THAT ARE LOST:"

The phrase, *"But if our Gospel be hid,"* is referred to as the Gospel preached by Paul in contradistinction to that preached by the false teachers.

A HIDDEN GOSPEL?

"Hid" in the Greek is *"kalupto,"* and means *"to cover or veil"* (Mat. 8:24; 10:26; Lk. 8:16; 23:30; I Pet. 4:8).

The Gospel is hidden from some men because they have willfully closed their eyes to it (Mat. 13:14-16).

If the heart of any man who hears the Gospel is veiled, it is definite that he is lost and fully under the power of sin and Satan. Those who refuse to hear the Gospel are proper subjects for Satan's work to increase the darkness and hardness of heart.

It is implied here, that to many the Beauty and Glory of the Gospel *is* not perceived. This *is* undeniable, notwithstanding the plainness and fullness with which its Truths were made known.

The object of Paul here is to state that this fact *is* not to be traced to any want of clearness in the Gospel itself, but to other causes — and thus probably to meet an objection which might be made to his argument about the clearness and fullness of the Revelation in the Gospel. Here Paul says that it was not to be denied that the Gospel was veiled to some. But it was not from the nature of the Gospel. It was not because God had purposely concealed its meaning. It was not from any want of clearness in itself. It was to be traced to other causes.

It may be asked as to how *"a veiled Gospel"* can be at the same time a *"manifested truth"*? The answer is that the Gospel is bright and clear, but the eyes that should gaze on it are willfully closed.

The phrase, *"It is hid to them that are lost,"* plainly tells us that some are lost, and why they are lost.

THE LOST

Why are people lost?

It is because they refuse to hear and receive the Gospel of Jesus Christ.

However, conspicuous the Gospel is in itself, yet like the Sun it will not be visible to the blind. The cause is not in the Gospel, but in those who hear it but refuse to accept it. Consequently, we learn the following:

1. The beauty of the Gospel is hidden from most of the human race. The structure of Paul's sentence in the Greek tells us that this is not on God's part, in other words it is not His desire that any be lost, but rather on the part of the far greater majority who will not believe the Gospel.

There are thousands and millions, in fact the majority of mankind, to whom it is preached who see no beauty in it, and who regard it as foolishness. Paul said as much in I Corinthians 1:23.

2. Most of the world at this moment is lost. It is not that they will in the future be lost, but they are presently lost. The only thing that death will change is the location of the soul and not the soul itself. This can only be changed by their acceptance of Jesus Christ as their Lord and Saviour; however, they are blinded, even as the next Verse proclaims, to this Truth, not really believing they are lost.

I remember asking a particular man if he was saved? *"Saved from what?",* he asked!

He knew what I was talking about, but would not admit that he needed saving, therefore, denying that he was lost.

3. This is not the fault of the Gospel. It is not the fault of the Sun when men shut their eyes and will not see it. It is not the fault of a running stream, or a bubbling fountain, if men will not drink of it, but rather choose to die of thirst. The Gospel does not obscure and conceal its own Glory any more than the Sun does. It is in itself a clear and full Revelation of God and His Grace; and that Glory to be sure, is adapted to shed light upon the benighted minds of men. In other words, the very idea of the Gospel is that it be heard and understood, and it is so conceived that even a child can understand its Message. Therefore, it is never the fault of the Gospel if it is denied.

In fact, Paul used the word *"manifestation"* in Verse 2, which means *"a full clear statement of the Way of Salvation."* Such a statement reaches man's conscience and receives God's approval — but yet is rejected by most!

EXACTLY WHAT IS THE GOSPEL?

The Gospel is the Good News that God in Jesus Christ has fulfilled His Promises to Israel, and that a Way of Salvation has been opened to all. The Gospel is not to be set over against the Old Testament as if God had changed His Way of dealing with man, but is rather the fulfillment of Old Testament Promise (Mat. 11:2-5). Jesus Himself Who is the Gospel, saw in the Prophecies of Isaiah a description of His Own Ministry (Lk. 4:16-21).

To believe the Gospel means Salvation: to reject the Gospel is damnation (Mk. 16:15-16).

While the Gospel came with Jesus (the Christ-event is the Gospel), it was anticipated in God's Promise of Blessing to Abraham (Gal. 3:8) and promised in Prophetic Scripture (Rom. 1:2).

THE MANNER OF THE GOSPEL

The Gospel not only comes in Power (I Thess. 1:5) but is the Power of God (Rom. 1:16). It reveals the Righteousness of God and leads to Salvation all who believe (Rom. 1:16-17).

NOTES

Paul regards the Gospel as a Sacred Trust (I Tim. 1:11). Thus, he is under Divine compulsion to proclaim it (I Cor. 9:16), and requests prayer that he may carry out his task with boldness (Eph. 6:19), even though this involves opposition (I Thess. 2:2) and affliction (II Tim. 1:8).

The Gospel is *"The Word of Truth"* (Eph. 1:13), but it is hidden to unbelieving men, even as we are now studying (II Cor. 4:3-4).

Even as it was by Revelation that the full theological impact of the Gospel came to Paul (Gal. 1:11-12), so also it is by the response of Faith that the Gospel comes with Saving Power (Heb. 4:2).

(4) "IN WHOM THE GOD OF THIS WORLD HATH BLINDED THE MINDS OF THEM WHICH BELIEVE NOT, LEST THE LIGHT OF THE GLORIOUS GOSPEL OF CHRIST, WHO IS THE IMAGE OF GOD, SHOULD SHINE UNTO THEM."

The phrase, *"In whom,"* refers to those who are lost. The design of this Verse is to account for the fact that the Glory of the Gospel was not seen by them. It is to be traced entirely to the agency of him whom Paul here calls *"the god of this world."* And yet, it is an *"agency"* desired by the lost.

The phrase, *"The god of this world,"* presents Satan as designated here by this appellation. In John 12:31, he is called *"the prince of this world."* In Ephesians 2:2, he is called *"the prince of the power of the air."* An in Ephesians 6:12, the same terrible influence is referred to under the names of *"principalities and powers," "the rulers of the darkness of this world,"* and *"spiritual wickedness in high places."*

THE GOD OF THIS WORLD

The name *"god"* is here given to him, not because he has any Divine attributes, but because he actually has the homage of the men of this world as their god, as the being who is really worshiped, or who has the affections of their hearts in the same way as it is given to idols.

By *"this world"* is meant the wicked world; or the mass of men. Satan has dominion over the world at present. Men obey his will; they execute his plan; they further his purposes, and, they are his obedient subjects. He has subdued the world to himself, and is actually adored in the place of the True God. What is meant by the declaration that Satan is the god of this world is according to the following:

NOTES

1. The world at large is under his control and direction, but actually only under limitations imposed by the True God.

Satan has secured the apostasy of man, and early brought him to follow his plan; and he has maintained his scepter and dominion ever since. No more abject submission could be desired by him than has been rendered by the mass of men.

2. The idolatrous world, which includes almost all, particularly is under his control, and subject to him (I Cor. 10:20). He is worshiped there; and the religious rites and ceremonies of the heathen are in general just such as a mighty being who hated human happiness, and who sought pollution, obscenity, wretchedness, and blood, would appoint; and over all the heathen world his power is absolute.

In the time of Paul, all the world, except the few Jews who had accepted Christ and the few Gentiles likewise, was sunk in heathen degradation.

3. Satan rules in the hearts and lives of all wicked men — and the world is full of wicked men. They obey him, and submit to his will in executing fraud, rapine, piracy, murder, adultery, lewdness; in wars and fighting; in their amusements and pastimes; and, in dishonesty and falsehood. The dominion of Satan over this world has been, and is still, almost universal and absolute; nor has the lapse of some 1900 years rendered the appellation improper as descriptive of his influence, that he is the god of this world. The world pursues his plan; yields to his temptation; neglects or rejects the Reign of God as he pleases; and submits to his scepter, and is still full of abomination, cruelty, and pollution, exactly as he desires it to be (Barnes).

WHO IS SATAN?

The name *"Satan"* means *"adversary."*

This individual who heads up the world of darkness and evil, actually in revolution against God, has not always been this way. He was originally created by God as possibly the most wise and beautiful Angel of all (Ezek. 28:11-19). At some point in time in the distant past, he fell from this lofty position, drawing away some one-third of the Angels with him, as stated, leading a revolution against God (Isa. 14; Rev.

12:3-4). Before his fall he was named *"Lucifer,"* which means *"the morning star."* He is referred to by other names as well:

Tempter (Mat. 4:3; I Thess. 3:5); Beelzebub (Mat. 12:24); Enemy (Mat. 13:39); Evil One (Mat. 13:19, 38; I Jn. 2:13-14; 3:12; 5:18); Belial (II Cor. 6:15); Adversary (I Pet. 5:8); Deceiver (literally *"the one who deceives"*) (Rev. 12:9); Dragon (Rev. 12:3); Father of Lies (Jn. 8:44); Murderer (Jn. 8:44); Sinner (I Jn. 3:8). However, in the vast majority of Passages (70 out of 83) either the name Satan or Devil is used.

THE CHARACTER OF SATAN

Satan is consistently represented in the New Testament as the enemy both of God and man. He has an intense hatred and opposition to God (Mat. 13:39), as well as an intense hatred for man, God's prize creation.

The fundamental moral description of Satan is given by our Lord when He described Satan as the *"Evil One"* (Mat. 13:19, 38), that is, the one whose nature and will are given to evil.

Moral evil is his controlling attribute. It is evident that this description could not be applied to Satan as originally created. Ethical evil cannot be con-created. It is the creation of each free will for itself. Actually, we are not told in definite terms how Satan became the Evil One, but certainly it could be by no other process than a Fall, whereby, in the mystery of free personality, an evil will takes the place of a good will.

THE WORKS OF SATAN

The worldwide and age-old works of Satan are to be traced to one predominant motive. He hates both God and man and does all that is within him to defeat God's Plan of Grace and to establish and maintain a kingdom of evil, in the seduction and ruin of mankind. The balance and sanity of the Bible is nowhere more strikingly exhibited than in its treatment regarding the work of Satan.

Not only is the Bible entirely free from the extravagances of popular Satanology, which is full of absurd stories concerning the appearances, tricks, and transformations of Satan among men, but it exhibits a dependable accuracy and consistency of statement which is most reassuring. Almost nothing is said concerning Satanic agency other than wicked men who mislead other men.

NOTES

In the controversy with His opponents concerning exorcism (the casting out of Demons), our Lord rebuts their slanderous assertion that He is at league with Satan by the simple proposition that Satan does not work against himself (Mk. 3:22). But in so saying He does far more than refute the slander.

He definitely aligns the Bible against the popular idea that a man may make a definite and conscious personal alliance with Satan for any purpose whatever.

THE MANNER OF SATAN

The agent of Satan is always a victim. As well, the idea is carried forth in this discussion by Jesus with the Pharisees, that Satan definitely has a kingdom, and unfortunately, most of the world lies in that realm of Satanic bondage.

However, of all that Satan does, it is evident that his power consists principally in his ability to deceive. It is interesting and characteristic that according to the Bible Satan is fundamentally a liar and his kingdom is a kingdom founded upon lies and deceit.

The Doctrine of Satan, therefore, corresponds in every important particular to the general Biblical emphasis upon Truth. *"The Truth shall make you free"* (Jn. 8:32) — this is the way of deliverance from the power of Satan. As well, this *"Truth"* is found only in God:

1. Jesus Christ is *"Truth"* (Jn. 14:6).
2. The Holy Spirit is *"Truth"* (I Jn. 5:6).
3. The Word of God is *"Truth"* (Jn. 17:17).
4. The Anointing of the Holy Spirit is *"Truth"* (I Jn. 2:27).

SATAN AS THE DECEIVER

It would seem that to make Satan preeminently the deceiver would make man an innocent victim and thus relax the moral issue. But according to the Bible man is a willing participant in the process of his own deception. He is deceived only because he ceases to love the Truth and comes first to love and then to believe a lie (II Cor. 1:10).

This really goes to the very bottom of the problem of temptation. Men are not tempted by evil, per se, but by thinking that good can be obtained by doing wrong. The whole power of sin, at least in its beginnings, consists in the sway of the fundamental falsehood that any good is really attainable by wrongdoing. This was the method of attack by Satan against Adam and Eve. They were made to believe that they could obtain *"good"* by disobeying God. Of course, *"good"* or *"good things"* cannot be obtained at all in this fashion. Since temptation consists in this attack upon the moral sense, man is constitutionally guarded against deceit, at least in his core being, he knows that such is wrong; consequently, he is morally culpable in allowing himself to be deceived.

HOW SATAN TEMPTED CHRIST

The temptation of our Lord Himself throws the clearest possible light upon the methods ascribed to Satan. The temptation was addressed to Christ's consciousness of Divine Sonship; it was a deceitful attack emphasizing the good, minimizing or covering up the evil; indeed, twisting evil into good. It was a deliberate, malignant attempt to secure the Truth and induce to evil through the acceptance of falsehood.

The attack broke against a loyalty to Truth which made self-deceit, and consequently deceit from without, impossible. The lie was punctured by the Truth and the temptation lost its power against Christ.

LET'S LOOK CLOSER

At His Baptism, Jesus received from Heaven the final confirmation of His Incarnation as the Messiah, even though He was aware of this fact long before now. It was the greatest conception which ever entered a human mind and left it sane. Under the irresistible influence of the Holy Spirit, He turned aside to seek out in silence and alone the principles which should govern Him in His Messianic Work. As well, the Scripture says, *"And He was there in the wilderness forty days, tempted of Satan"* (Mk. 1:12-13). This forty days and nights of fasting and solitude were absolutely necessary for the wise prosecution of His role as Messiah. Without the slightest precedent Jesus must determine what the Messiah would do, how He would act. By this conflict, Jesus came to that clearness and decision which characterized His Ministry throughout.

It is easy to see how this determination of guiding principles involved the severest temptation, and it is noteworthy that all the temptation is represented as coming from without, and none from within. Here too He must take His stand with reference to all the current ideas about the Messiah and His Work.

NOTES

JESUS, THE ORIGINAL REPORTER

Jesus Alone can be the original reporter of this, for the simple reason that He was alone at this time. The report was given for the sake of the Disciples, for the principles wrought out in the conflict are the guiding principles in the whole work of the Kingdom of God on earth.

HIS FIRST TEMPTATION

The first temptation is not a temptation to doubt His Messiahship, nor is the second either, as some teach. *"If Thou art the Son of God,"* i.e., *"the Messiah,"* as given by Matthew and Luke, should have been translated, *"Since Thou art the Son of God."* In other words, Satan never questioned the Messiahship of Jesus in the slightest, and neither was there the slightest doubt on this point in Jesus' Mind concerning this fact, and Satan knew it. Consequently, there is no temptation to prove Himself the Messiah, nor any hint of such a thing in Jesus' replies.

The first temptation was simple, turn the stones to bread. Jesus is hungry, He has the power, so why not do this thing!

Jesus replies from Deuteronomy 8:3, that God can and will provide Him bread in His Own way and in His Own time. As well, He is not referring to spiritual food, which is not in question here or in Deuteronomy. He does not understand how God will provide, but He will wait and trust. Divinely assured of Messiahship, He knows that God will not let Him perish. Here emerges the principle of His Ministry; He will never use His supernatural power to help Himself. In other words, He will never step out of the revealed Will of God, for that is what all temptation actually is — the solicitation to step outside of what God wants.

So, the first temptation proved Jesus a man of Faith.

THE SECOND TEMPTATION

The pinnacle of the Temple was probably the southeast corner of the roof of the Royal Cloister, 326 feet above the bottom of the Kidron Valley. It seems that the proposition by Satan was not for Jesus to leap from this height into the crowd below in the Temple Courts, as is usually thought, for there is no hint of people in the Narrative. It was rather for Jesus to leap into the abyss outside the Temple. Why then the Temple at all, and not some mountain precipice?

It was the sheerest depth well known to the Jews, and as well there definitely would have been people that would have observed such, for such action surely would not have gone unnoticed.

Inasmuch as the first temptation proved Jesus a man of Faith, the second is for Him to prove His Faith by putting God's Promise to the test, in other words questioning the Word of God. To have done such would have been the wicked sin of presumption, which has been the destruction of many a useful servant of God. It would have been a real *"tempting"* of God. It would have denied His Incarnation in principle, in effect, taking Himself out of the human realm.

The idea is, that Jesus will not, of self-will, run into dangers, but will avoid them except in the clear path of duty. He will be no fanatic, running before the Spirit, but will be led by Him in paths of holy sanity and heavenly wisdom. In other words, Jesus waited on God, which is what we are to do as well.

THE THIRD TEMPTATION

The former tests have proved Jesus a man of Faith, and a man of Trust.

The third test is the easy road to universal dominion which rightfully belonged to the Messiah. Satan offers it, as the prince of this world. The lure here is the desire for power, in itself a right instinct, and the natural and proper wish to avoid difficulty and pain. The idea is to set up a universal Kingdom of God in Righteousness, which only adds to the subtlety of the temptation. But as a condition Satan demands that Jesus shall worship him. However, that must be properly interpreted.

Satan does not refer to the type of worship offered to God, for that would have been no temptation at all for Jesus. It was rather a compromise which Satan suggested — such a compromise that would essentially be a submission to him.

Recalling the views of the times and the course of Jesus' Ministry, we can think this compromise as nothing else than the adoption by Jesus of the program suggested by the Jews of political Messiahship, with its worldly means of war, intrigue, etc. Jesus repudiates the offer.

NOTES

He sees in it only evil, for war, especially aggressive war, is to His Mind a vast crime against love. As well, such a suggestion changes the basis of His Kingdom from the spiritual to that of the flesh (carnal). The means would, therefore, defeat the end, and involve Him in disaster. He will serve God only, and God is served in Righteousness. Only the means which God approves can be used (Mat. 4:8-11; Lk. 4:9-13).

Here then is the third great principle of the Kingdom: only moral and spiritual means must be used to gain moral and spiritual ends. Jesus turns away from worldly methods to the slow and difficult way of Truth-preaching, which can only end with the Cross. Consequently, when Jesus ended this forty days of temptation, it was crystal clear that His Ministry meant a life-and-death struggle with all the forces of darkness. Therefore, His temptations and victories can be summed up according to the following:

1. Jesus proves Himself a man of Faith, i.e., *"The just shall live by Faith."*

2. He proves Himself a man of total Trust in His Heavenly Father, i.e., He will not be presumptuous, but will do only what the Heavenly Father desires.

3. He will not use worldly means in an attempt to achieve spiritual results.

As we have stated, all the temptations by Satan of Christ involve the pressure applied to get Him to step outside the revealed Will of God. Consequently, that is the basis for all temptation by Satan of every Believer. In fact, this is the greatest hindrance to the Church. It attempts to do things other than God's Way:

1. The Church too often attempts to set aside the Faith principle for the principle of works.

2. The Church too often engages in presumption. If Satan cannot get the Church to deny the Miracle-working Power of God, he will attempt to get the Church to presume that which God really has not promised.

3. Instead of going by the way of the Cross, which is God's Way, Satan attempts to get the Church to follow other means. The political message and the prosperity message are excellent cases in point. Humanistic psychology, however, is the greatest case of all! Whenever the Church attempts to bypass the Cross, it is in effect, falling down and worshiping Satan whether it realizes it or not.

AN ANGEL OF LIGHT

Most frequently, Satan's devices (II Cor. 2:11) include human agents. Those who are given over to evil and who persuade others to evil are children and servants of Satan (Mat. 16:23; Mk. 8:33; Lk. 4:8; Jn. 6:70; 8:44; Acts 13:10; I Jn. 3:8). Satan also works through persons and institutions (Churches) supposed to be on the side of right but which are actually evil. Here the same ever-present and active falseness and deceit are exhibited. When he is called *"the god of this world"* even as we are now studying, it would seem to be intimated that he has the power to clothe himself in apparently Divine attributes.

He also makes himself an angel of light by presenting advocates of falsehood in the guise of Apostles of Truth, which has always been one of the greatest problems of the Church (II Cor. 11:13-15; II Thess. 2:9; I Jn. 4:1; Rev. 12:9; 19:20).

In the combination of these Scriptures just given, it is clearly indicated that Satan is the instigator and fomenter of that spirit of lawlessness which exhibits itself as hatred both of Truth and Right, and which has operated so widely and so disastrously in human life.

THE HISTORY OF SATAN

The history of this Evil One, including that phase of it which remains to be realized, can be set forth only along the most general lines. First of all, he belongs to the Angelic Order of beings. He is by nature one of the sons of Elohim (God) (Job 1:6). He has fallen, and by virtue of his personal forcefulness has become the leader of the anarchic forces of wickedness.

As a free being he has immersed his life in evil and has become altogether and hopelessly evil. As a being of very high intelligence he has gained great power and has exercised a wide sway over other beings. As a created being the utmost range of his power lies within the compass of that which is permitted. It is, therefore, hedged in by the providential Government of God and essentially limited, even as Job Chapters 1 and 2 portray.

The Biblical emphasis upon the element of falsehood in the career of Satan might be taken to imply that his kingdom may be less in extent than appears. In other words, it is not nearly as great as he makes it out to be, considering that it is built upon lies, deceit, and falsehood.

At any rate, it is confined to the cosmic sphere and to a limited portion of time. In other words, it is doomed.

In the closely related Passages of II Peter 2:4 and Jude vs. 6 it is affirmed that God cast the Angels, when they sinned, down to Tartarus (at least some of them) and committed them to pits of darkness, to be reserved unto judgment. This both refers to the constant Divine control of these insurgent forces and also points to their final and utter destruction.

SATAN'S DEFEAT

According to the Gospels, our Lord in the crisis of temptation which immediately followed His Baptism, to which we have already alluded, met and for the time conquered Satan as His Own personal adversary. This preliminary contest, however, did not close the matter, but was the earnest of a complete victory.

According to Luke 10:18, when the Seventy returned from their mission flush with victory over the powers of evil, Jesus said: *"I saw Satan fall as lightning from Heaven."* In every triumph over the powers of evil Christ beheld in vision the downfall of Satan. In connection with the coming of the Greeks (possibly Hellenistic Jews) who wished to see Him, Jesus asserted (Jn. 12:31) *"Now is the judgment of this world: now shall the prince of this world be cast out."* In view of His approaching passion He says again (Jn. 14:30), *"The prince of the world cometh: and he hath nothing in Me."* Once again in connection with the Promised Advent of the Spirit, Jesus asserted (Jn. 16:11) that the Spirit would convict the world of judgment, *"because the prince of this world hath been judged."*

In Hebrews 2:14-15, it is said that Christ took upon Himself human nature in order *"that through death He might bring to nought him that had the power of death, that is, the Devil."* In I John 3:8 it is said, *"To this end was the Son of God manifested, that He might destroy the works of the Devil."* In Revelation 12:9 it is asserted, in connection with the Ascension of the 144,000, that Satan was cast down to the earth and his angels with him.

According to the Passage immediately following (Rev. 12:10-12), this casting down was not complete or final in the sense of extinguishing

NOTES

his activities altogether, but it involves the potential and certain triumph of God and His Saints and the equally certain defeat of Satan.

In I John 2:13 the young men are addressed as those who *"have overcome the Evil One."* In Revelation Chapter 20 the field of the future is covered in the assertion that Satan is *"bound a thousand years"*; then *"loosed for a little season,"* and then finally *"cast into the Lake of Fire."*

One must shout *"Hallelujah!"*

THIS MUCH IS CLEAR

A comparison of these Passages will convince the careful student that while we cannot construct a definite chronological program for the career of Satan, we are clear in the chief points. He is limited, judged, condemned, imprisoned, and reserved for judgment from the beginning.

The outcome is certain though the process may be tedious and slow. The Victory of Christ is the defeat of Satan; first, for Himself as Leader and Saviour of men (Jn. 14:30); then, for Believers (Lk. 22:31; Acts 26:18; Rom. 16:20; James 4:7; I Jn. 2:13; 5:4-18); and, finally, for the whole world (Rev. 20:10). The Work of Christ has in fact, already destroyed the empire of Satan.

THE SCRIPTURAL DOCTRINE OF SATAN

The Scriptural Doctrine of the Evil One is actually not systematically developed in Scripture, although it is graphically implied. For materials in this field we are limited to scattered and incidental references. In fact, these Passages, which even in the aggregate are not numerous, yet tell us what we need to know concerning the nature, history, kingdom, and works of Satan, offer scant satisfaction to the merely inquisitive mind.

The comparative lack of development in this field is due partly to the fact that the Biblical Writers are primarily interested in God, and only secondarily in the Powers of Darkness, which is the way it should be; and partly to the fact that in the Bible, Doctrine is only gradually unfolded. Hence, the malign and sinister figure of the adversary is gradually outlined against the Light of God's Holiness as progressively revealed in the worldprocess which centers in Christ. It is a significant fact that the statements concerning Satan become

NOTES

numerous and definite only in the New Testament. The daylight of the Christian Revelation was necessary in order to uncover the lurking foe, dimly disclosed but by no means fully known in the earlier Revelation. The disclosure of Satan is, in form at least, historical, not dogmatic.

SATAN AND GOD

In the second place, the relationship of Satan to God, already emphasized, must be kept constantly in mind. The Doctrine of Satan merges in the general Doctrine concerning Angels. It has often been pointed out that the personal characteristics of Angels are very little insistent upon. They are known chiefly by their functions: merged, on the one hand, in their own offices, and, on the other, in the activities of God Himself.

In the Old Testament Satan is represented as a fallen and malignant spirit, but as well, as one who plays a part in the Divine function. By that, we refer to the fact that he cannot do anything except allowed by the Lord, which of course, continues to hold true to the present time.

For instance, in the accounts of David's numbering of Israel (I Sam. 24:1; I Chron. 21:1) the tempting of David is attributed both to Jehovah and Satan. This can be explained, as Satan doing the actual tempting, but having to receive permission from the Lord to do so. In fact, the Lord does not tempt anyone to commit sin.

In the Book of Job to which we have already alluded, Satan is among the Sons of God and his assaults upon Job are Divinely permitted, which in fact, is the case with all (Job 1:6).

In Zechariah 3:1-2, Satan is shown as well as a servant of Jehovah, that is if we are allowed to use such terminology. In both these Passages, Job and Zechariah, there is the hint of opposition between Jehovah and Satan. In the former instance Satan assails unsuccessfully the character of one whom Jehovah honors (Job), while in the latter, Jehovah explicitly rebukes Satan for his attitude toward Israel (Zech.).

RESERVED FOR THE NEW TESTAMENT

The unveiling of Satan as a rebellious worldpower is reserved for the New Testament, and with this fuller teaching the symbolic treatment of temptation in Genesis is to be connected. The progressive revelation of God's Character and Purpose, which more and more imperatively demands that the origin of moral evil, and consequently natural evil, must be traced to the will of man as manipulated by Satan, which is always in opposition to the Divine, leads to the ultimate declaration that Satan is a morally fallen being to whose conquest the Divine Power in history is pledged. There is, also, the distinct possibility that in the significant transition from the Satan of the Old Testament to that of the New Testament we have the outlines of a biography and an indication of the way by which the Angels fell.

THE LIMITATIONS OF SATAN

In the New Testament delineation of Satan, his limitations are clearly set forth. He is superhuman, but not in any sense Divine. His activities are cosmic (not limited to the earth alone), but not universal or transcendent (everywhere at one time). He is a created being. His power is definitely circumscribed. He is doomed to final destruction as a worldpower. His entire career is that of a secondary and dependent being who is permitted a certain limited scope of power — a timelease of activity (Lk. 4:6).

Satan's empire had a beginning, and as well, it will have a definite and permanent end. Satan is God's great enemy in the cosmic sphere, but he is also God's Creation, and exists by the Divine Will, and his power is relatively no more commensurate with God then that of men. In fact, Satan awaits his doom, for it has already been pronounced (Rev. 20:10).

WHY HAS GOD ALLOWED SATAN TO CONTINUE?

Of course, our knowledge is very limited in this area, but we do know that God does all things well, and has a purpose for all things. In other words, what He does is right, but it is right not just because He does it, but because it *is* right.

To some minds the reality of created wills (that God has created individuals whether men or Angels with a will of their own) is dualistic (a Doctrine that the universe is under the dominion of two opposing principles, one of which is good and the other evil) and, therefore, untenable. But a true Doctrine of unity (the manner in which God has created things) makes room for other wills than God's — namely of those beings upon whom God has bestowed freedom. Herein stands the Doctrine of sin and Satan. The Doctrine of Satan no more militates against the unity of God than the idea, so necessary to morality and true spirituality alike, of other created wills set in opposition to God's will. In other words, man has been given a free will by God as well; consequently, he can will to love God or to rebel against God, the same as Angels. In fact, for God to get what He wanted, man had to be created in this manner, as evidently so were Angels.

In fact, without Angels or men having wills (the ability to reason), they would be little more than a breathing computer. For man to freely love God, as love must have the freedom to do, he must at the same time have the ability to do otherwise.

HOW DOES SATAN THINK HE CAN SUCCEED?

Despite the fact that Satan knows the Omnipotence of God, recognizing Him as his Creator, and actually answering to Him on a constant basis, and that he can read the Bible as well as anyone else, which incidentally announces his doom, still, he actually believes that he can succeed in this rebellion against God. We as Believers know that he is doomed, but he labors under no such knowledge.

How could he think that he could overthrow God his Creator, Who is unlimited in power, while he in fact, is very limited?

He thinks he will ultimately win because he is deceived. The very pall of doom which he casts over all his followers, which incidentally include most of mankind and for all time, which is the doom of deception, he is in that afflicted himself. He is so deceived that he believes his own lie (Jn. 8:44). In fact, his greatest effort lies immediately ahead.

The Book of Revelation graphically spells out the rise of the man of sin, who in a sense, will be the Incarnation of Satan. As God became Man and died on a Cross to redeem lost humanity, and even rose from the dead, likewise, Satan will attempt something similar, at least to the limits of his power. Regrettably, Israel would not accept the True Incarnation, but will accept this false effort of the Evil One (Jn. 5:43) However, when he turns on them in order to utterly destroy Israel as a nation and as a people, with every determination to make this the *"final solution,"* they will then realize their deception, and will begin to call on the True Messiah. Revelation Chapter 19 tells of the coming of the Lord Jesus Christ, which will then spell Satan's doom.

In fact, the genesis of his plan is to destroy Israel. Knowing all the Prophecies of old concerning their Restoration, he knows that if they can be destroyed, then the Word of God falls to the ground, and in fact, if that can happen, he will have won. To be frank, that was his effort in World War II concerning the Holocaust. If he could kill enough Jews, their nation could not be restored, which Bible Prophecy said must happen, and in fact did happen in 1948 (Isa. 11:11; 14:1-2; 27:12-13; 43:5-6; Jer. 3:17-18; 23:5-8; Ezek. 28:25-26; Ezek. Chpt. 37, etc.). He failed then as he has failed many times, and he will fail the last time which is soon to come. However, this last failure will be so cataclysmic that there will be no doubt about his destruction, for the simple reason that it will be precipitated by the Coming of the Lord (Rev. Chpt. 19). Then the *"god of this world"* will be no more!

If it is to be noticed, he is called *"the god of this world,"* and not of the cosmos (the universe). So, it is *"this world"* which is the battleground between darkness and light.

The phrase, *"Hath blinded the minds of them which believe not,"* refers to the Truth of the Gospel, with all mental reactions blind. The mind is confronted with the Divine reality, but instead of reacting as if it sees this reality, all its thinking and reasoning are as if it does not see it at all. The thoughts are blinded.

NOTES

BLINDED

"Blinded" in the Greek is *"tuphloo,"* and means *"to make blind, to obscure, to envelop with smoke."* The insinuation is, that the cause is *"to be lifted up with pride, to be proud."* In other words, pride blinds the spiritual sensitivity of the individual, which causes them to not see their true need and most of all the solution to that need which is Christ.

To be shown God's Grace, Christ's Blood and Righteousness, Justification by Faith, the New Light and Salvation in Christ, and to think of them as nothing is to have been blinded.

To use an example, the Gospel portrays Satan even as we have been discussing here. But yet, by the world he is treated as a joke, even though he is the very one who has blinded the thoughts of men. Clutched in his power, men see him not even when he is fully shown, and likewise, they cannot see Christ. As well, all who are blinded are perishing. If they are rescued from perishing they are rescued also from blindness and from unbelief.

Also, in the blinding that humanity experiences, Satan does not blind all their thoughts so that they act senselessly in all respects. Actually, the blinding has to do with the Gospel, it is the blindness of unbelief of the Gospel, and because as stated, of pride.

THE WORDS OF JESUS

In the great declaration of Christ as given in his hometown of Nazareth, He said among other things, *"The Spirit of the Lord is upon Me, because He hath Anointed Me . . . to preach deliverance to the captives, and recovering of sight to the blind"* (Lk. 4:18).

The recovering of sight as mentioned here, had nothing to do with opening the literal eyes of those who were physically blind even as He did, but rather the recovery of Spiritual sight which had been lost to Spiritual blindness. Only the Gospel preached under the Anointing of the Holy Spirit can effect this release. That's the reason it is futile to try to bring men to Christ through intellectualism. While the intellect is certainly affected, that within itself cannot bring about the desired results. Man's problem is not intellectual but rather spiritual. As such, it takes the Power of God to break through that blindness in order to reach that lost soul.

That's the reason that Satan fights the Moving and Operation of the Holy Spirit to such an extent. He knows, even as most Preachers do not seem to know, and even some entire Denominations for that matter, that it is only by the Power of the Holy Spirit that these results can be brought about.

The problem of infidelity and sin is more than an intellectual one. Consequently, its solution is more than education. We have so secularized our spiritual approach to the world that it amounts to nothing more than mental improvement. However, Christianity is that and much more. It is Spiritual before it is intellectual. Until we see this and get men spiritually right, all our other well-intentioned efforts will be in vain.

This veil of unbelief covers the eyes of much of the world. Such blindness is not the fault of the Gospel; neither is it necessarily the fault of the messenger of the Gospel. The fault, at least much of the time, lies with the hearer whose veil of unbelief identifies him as being unregenerate.

UNBELIEF

Unbelief and unregeneracy go together. Such unbelief as is mentioned here is not the question of mere doubting. It is bold and deliberate opposition. It reveals an incapacity to understand, which has been deliberately created by continuous unbelief.

As we have stated, one cannot educate people into Christianity any more than one can ceremonially induct them into it, as Catholicism and even many Protestant Churches attempt to do. It is a problem of character and nature, which in turn is a problem of spiritual genetics.

This is serious business. It speaks of men being lost. What does the Bible mean by being lost? Is it a state of personal vagueness that is cleared up automatically? Indeed not! It is a matter of eternal destiny.

The word *"lost"* is the one you use when you speak of an article which has disappeared and gone out of your possession.

The Gospel makes another designation and calls other men *"saved."* These are they who were lost, but have since been recovered. The difference between being lost and being saved is the Gospel of Jesus Christ. Our attitude to it is the most serious thing we have ever faced. Our acceptance of it will be the most profitable choice we ever make.

SELF-CHOSEN BLINDNESS

This blindness of which the Scripture speaks, is not arbitrarily imposed by Satan. It is self-chosen. In other words, all the billions who have suffered thusly, were willing subjects of Satanic propaganda. It would be unthinkable that God would permit men to exist in a

NOTES

state wherein they could not believe and be saved, which some teach, but is actually unscriptural in totality. Wherever a state of personal blindness exists, it is because men permit it to be so.

Even as we are studying, Satan is given a unique title — *"the god of this world."* Literally, it means *"the god of this age."* He is not, of course, the god of the universe. He is the self-chosen god of this age. It is a law of the eternal ages that if we do not make room for Jehovah — God — we will by default give room for the evil influence of Satan. If we reject the Light, we will become victims of darkness.

Satan reigns presently. He reigns in the hearts of men, in fashions, in philosophy, in nations, in commerce, in the world of religion, in every enterprise and individual that does not accept the Truth. Because of this, there are two contrary and antagonistic forces in the world — those who are blinded by the god of this world and those who are enlightened by the Gospel of Christ.

In fact, at least as God sees the situation, there are only two types of people in the world, those who are Believers, thereby having accepted Christ, and those who are unbelievers, thereby having rejected Christ.

Christ is declared to be the Image of God. Christians are the image of Christ, or at least we are supposed to be. You may choose your character and your destiny. It is a matter of deliberate decision. To be a Christian takes a decision. Decision determines direction. Direction determines destiny (Laurin).

The phrase, *"Lest the Light of the Glorious Gospel of Christ, Who is the Image of God, should shine unto them,"* tells us several things. They are as follows:

1. THE LIGHT: The only true *"Light"* in the world, and in fact, ever has been, is the Gospel of Jesus Christ. In fact, the entirety of the Bible and its history, proclaims that *"Gospel."* This *"Light"* is the Source of all freedom, all prosperity, all betterment of society, in fact, every good thing that has ever happened to the human race. All can be traced to this *"Light."*

Every other so-called light in the world, be it Buddhism, Shintoism, Islam, Mormonism, Catholicism, Hinduism, etc., has provided no light because they have no light. The same could be said for the vain philosophies of men, be it Communism, Socialism, or even psychology which is the religion of humanism.

As someone has well said, *"Much Bible, much freedom; little Bible, little freedom; no Bible, no freedom."*

2. THE GOSPEL: *"The Glorious Gospel of Christ"*: This is rather the illumination of the Gospel of the Glory of Christ, or rather the Gospel which gives Spiritual Light, which effects in a very positive way all other types of illumination as well.

For example, the nations of the world which have given credence to this *"Glorious Gospel"* have by and large set the standard for the balance of the world. England and America are two examples. These two countries have given the world at least 90% or more of all technological advancement. If one were able to trace the cause and the reason, it would go back in its entirety to the Gospel.

Some may ask why other countries in the world do not fall into that category such as France or Italy or even countries in Central and South America, considering they are *"Christian."* The answer is simple, they aren't Christian, they are Catholic. Catholicism by no stretch of the imagination can be labeled as Christian, that is if one wants to use the Bible as the guide, which it most surely is. There is no Gospel in Catholicism, and because Christ is not its Centerpiece, but rather Mary.

No two words in our language are so full of rich and precious meaning as the phrase *"Glorious Gospel."* It is glorious, for it is full of splendor; makes known the Glorious God; discloses a glorious plan of Salvation; and conducts ignorant, weak, and degraded man to a world of Light.

The Glory of Christ in the Gospel is the sum of His Divine and His human excellencies. It has been well said that this glory makes Him the radiant point in the whole universe, the object of supreme admiration, adoration, and worship.

It should be quickly added that the word *"Glory"* takes us back to II Corinthians 3:7-11, to the Glory Light of the Law of Moses and the Judgement which was reflected on Moses' face, and to the greater and abiding Glory Light of Grace and the Gospel and the Gospel Ministry. This is the Christ Glory that fills the Gospel.

NOTES

Whereas the Glory on Moses' face dimmed, this Glory and its illuminating radiance can, of course, never be dimmed; Satan cannot hurt the Gospel itself or rob it of its Glory Substance or of its illuminating activity. All he can do is to blind men by unbelief so that this illuminating activity is not able to dawn in their minds and hearts. They remain in darkness while the light plays around them and seeks to make them glorious with its power, *"from Glory to Glory"* (II Cor. 3:18).

3. THE IMAGE OF GOD: *"Who is the Image of God"*: This reveals fully Who Christ actually is. Its meaning appears in John 14:9: *"He that hath seen Me hath seen the Father"*; in John 12:45: *"He that beholdeth Me beholdeth Him that sent Me."* Then in Philippians 2:6, *"Christ in the form of God and equal with God"*; and in Hebrews 1:3: *"The effulgence of His Glory and the very Image of His Substance."*

It refers to the exalted Christ: the God-Man on the Throne of Glory as the essential Image of the Father.

In effect, the sole design of the Ministry is to make fully known the Glory of the Lord Jesus Christ as Redeemer, Saviour, Overcomer, Healer, Baptizer with the Holy Spirit, King of kings, and Lord of lords.

Whatever other objects are secured by the appointment of the Gospel, and whatever other Truths are to be illustrated and enforced by the Ministry, yet, if this is not the primary subject, and if every other object is not made subservient to this, the proclamation of Christ, the design of the Ministry is not secured.

The title *"Christ"* properly means *"The Anointed;"* that is, the Messiah, the Anointed of God for this great office. It is used in the New Testament as a proper name, the name that was appropriate to Jesus. Still it may be used with a reference to the fact of His Messiahship, and not merely as a proper name; and in this place it may mean that they preached Jesus as the Messiah, or the Christ, and defended His claims to that high appointment.

The word *"Lord,"* also, is used to designate Him (Mk. 11:3; Jn. 20:25) and when it stands by itself in the New Testament, it denotes the Lord Jesus (Acts 1:24). But it properly denotes One Who has rule or authority or proprietorship; and it is used here not merely as a part of the appropriate title of the Saviour, but with reference to the fact that He has the supreme Headship or Lordship over the Church and the world.

This important passage, therefore, means that the Preachers in the Early Church made it their sole business to make known Jesus the Messiah, or the Christ, as the supreme Head and Lord of His people; that is, to set forth the Messiahship and the Lordship of Jesus of Nazareth, appointed to these High Offices by God. Consequently, this referred to the doing of several things:

THE MESSIAH

To prove that Jesus is the Messiah so often predicted in the Old Testament, and so long expected by the Jewish people, was at least a part of the Message of the Early Church. To do this was a very vital part of the work of the Ministry in the time of the Apostles, and was essential to their success in all their attempts to convert the Jews, or anyone for that matter; and to do this will be no less important in all attempts to bring people to Christ, i.e. *"to the knowledge of the Truth."*

No man can be successful among Preachers who is not able to prove that Jesus is the Messiah. It is not indeed so vital and leading a point now in reference to those to whom the Ministers of the Gospel usually preach; and it is probable that the importance of this argument is by many overlooked, and that it is not urged as it should be by those who *"preach Christ Jesus the Lord."* In fact, it involves the whole argument of the Truth of Christianity.

It leads to all the demonstrations that this Salvation is from God; and the establishment of the proposition that Jesus is the Messiah, is one of the most direct in certain ways of proving that His Gospel is from Heaven.

FULFILLMENT OF THE PROPHECIES

To properly understand this, means that one understands that Jesus is the fulfillment of the Prophecies of old — one of the main evidences of the Truth of Revelation.

As well, it involves an examination of all the evidences that Jesus gave that He was the Messiah sent from God, and of course, an examination of all the Miracles that He wrought in attestation of His Divine Mission. The first object of a Preacher, therefore, is to demonstrate that Jesus is sent from God, in accordance with the predictions of the Prophets.

NOTES

TO PROCLAIM THE TRUTHS THAT HE TAUGHT

The idea is that Preachers, or anyone for that matter, make known His sentiments and His Doctrines, and not our own. This includes, of course, all that He taught respecting God, and respecting man; all that He taught respecting His Own Nature, and the design of His Coming; all that He taught respecting the character of the human heart, and about human obligation and duty; all that He taught respecting death, the judgment, and eternity — respecting an eternal heaven, and an eternal hell.

To explain, enforce, and vindicate His Doctrines is one great design of the Ministry; and were there nothing else, this would be a field sufficiently ample to employ the life; sufficiently glorious to employ the best talents of man.

The Preacher of the Gospel is to teach the Doctrines of Jesus Christ, in contradistinction from all his own sentiments, and from all the doctrines of mere philosophy. He is not to teach Science, or mere morals, but he is to proclaim and defend the Doctrines of the Redeemer.

THE FACTS OF THE SAVIOUR'S LIFE

The Preacher is to show how Jesus lived — to hold up His example in all the trying circumstances in which He was placed. For He came to show by His Life what the Law required; and to show how men should live. And it is the office of the Christian Minister, or a part of their work in preaching *"Christ Jesus the Lord,"* to show how He lived, and to set forth His Self-denial, His meekness, His purity, His blameless life, His spirit of prayer, His submission to the Divine Will, His patience in suffering, His forgiveness of His enemies, His tenderness to the afflicted, the weak, the tempted, and the manner of His Death.

HE WAS AND IS THE ONLY PERFECTLY PURE MODEL

Were this all that Preachers would proclaim, it would be enough to employ the whole of a Minister's life, and to command the best talents of the world. For He was the only perfectly pure model; and His example is to be followed by all His people, and His example is designed to exert a deep and wide influence on all the world.

Morality, prosperity, and freedom flourish just in proportion as the pure example of Jesus Christ is kept before a people; and the world is made happier and better, just as that example is kept constantly in view.

To the thoughtless, Preachers are to show how serious and calm was the Redeemer; to the worldly-minded, to show how He lived above the world; to the avaricious, how benevolent He was; to the profane and licentious, how pure He was; to the tempted, how He endured temptation; to the afflicted, how patient and resigned; to the dying, how He died; to all, to show how holy, and heavenly-minded, prayerful, and pure He was, in order that they may be one to the same purity, and be prepared to dwell with Him in His Kingdom.

THE DESIGN OF HIS DEATH

It is imperative that the Preacher show why Jesus came to die; and what was the great object to be effected by His sufferings and death.

We must show why He died, in other words, the absolute necessity of His death, and what was to be the influence of His death on the destiny of man. We must show how it makes an Atonement for sin; how it reconciles God to man; how it is made efficacious in the Justification and the Sanctification of the sinner.

Once again, if there were nothing else, this would be sufficient to employ all the time and the best talents in the world. For the Salvation of the soul depends on the proper exhibition of the design of the Death of the Redeemer. There is no Salvation but through His Blood; and hence the nature and design of His Atoning Sacrifice is to be exhibited to every man, and the offers of Mercy through that Death to be pressed upon the attention of every sinner.

HIS RESURRECTION

To properly proclaim this Glorious Gospel is to set forth the Truth and the design of His Resurrection. We must prove that He rose from the dead, and that He ascended to Heaven; and to show the influence of His Resurrection on our hopes and destiny. Actually, the whole structure of Christianity is dependent on making out the fact that He rose; and if He rose, all the difficulties in the Doctrine of the Resurrection of the Dead are removed at once, and His people will also rise.

NOTES

The influence of that fact, therefore, on our hopes and on our prospects for eternity, is to be shown by the Ministry of the Gospel; and were there nothing else, this would be ample to command all the time and the best talents of the Ministry.

TO PROCLAIM HIM AS LORD

This is expressly specified in the next Verse.

Christ is called the Image of God in respect to His Divine Nature, His exact resemblance to God in His Divine attributes and perfections and in His moral attributes as Mediator, as showing forth the Glory of the Father to men. He resembles God because He is God, and in Him we see the Divine Glory and perfections embodied, and shining forth.

4. TO SHINE ON MEN: *"Should shine unto them"*: It is an object of especial dislike and hatred to Satan that the Glory of Christ, Who is the Image of God, should shine on men, and fill their hearts. Satan hates that Image; he hates that men should become like God; and he hates all that has a resemblance to the Great and Glorious Jehovah.

The idea of the *"shining"* is that man has lost this Image of God, and now Christ Who is the Image Himself, equal with the Father, shines in the Gospel for us in order that His Grace may restore God's Image in us. That's what the New Birth is all about.

(5) "FOR WE PREACH NOT OURSELVES, BUT CHRIST JESUS THE LORD; AND OURSELVES YOUR SERVANTS FOR JESUS' SAKE."

The phrase, *"For we preach not ourselves,"* has reference to the idea that what Paul and his associates were preaching was the Word of the Lord, i.e. the Gospel of Jesus Christ, and not ideas and philosophies birthed in their own minds.

A WARNING

By the phrase, *"For we preach not ourselves,"* Paul is warning his detractors that resistance to his Message is resistance to God. Every Believer should heed this word very carefully.

That is the reason the Believer should very carefully study the Word of God, should know the Word of God, and should measure everything by the Word of God. That's the only way they can know if the Preacher is preaching his own philosophy or the True Gospel of Jesus Christ.

The sad fact is, most Believers do not know the Word of God, and are, therefore, being led astray by those who are preaching their own philosophies. Among most Christians, there is very little prayer life, in fact, no prayer life at all. As well, there is very little knowledge of the Word.

How do I know that?

When I see the Church accepting entertainment as the Gospel, i.e. *"so-called Christian rock performers,"* I know that these people do not know the Word of God, or else they have rejected the Word of God.

Observing the Church diving headlong into modern humanistic psychology, lets me know that the Word is not known.

When I see an almost total lack of dependence on the Holy Spirit, and almost total lack of desiring His Moving and Operation, but rather the pitiful plans of men being promoted, I know that the knowledge of the Word is thin. The prosperity message (money as the object) and the political message (thinking to change the nation by political means) fall into the same category.

All of these constitute philosophies out of one's own mind, or else a subtle twisting of the Word of God, which means the True Gospel is not being preached.

PERSONAL INTEREST OR THAT OF THE LORD?

Paul here gives a reason for what he has said in the previous parts of this Epistle respecting the conduct of his Ministry. He had said that his course had been open and pure, and free from all dishonest arts and tricks, that he had not corrupted the Word of God, or resorted to any work of the flesh to accomplish his designs (II Cor. 2:17; 4:1-2).

The reason of this he says here, is that he had not preached himself, or sought to advance his own interests. He regarded himself as sent to make known the Saviour; himself as bound by all means to promote His Cause, and to imitate Him. Other men — the false teachers, and the cunning priests of the heathen religions — sought to advance their own interests, and to perpetuate a system of delusion that would be profitable to themselves; and they, therefore, resorted to all arts, and stratagems, and cunning devices, to perpetuate their authority and extend their influence. Regrettably, as it was then, so it is now — to profit themselves.

In effect, Paul is saying that this is not a business of his own, but rather that of another, the Lord Jesus Christ. Therefore, Paul, and all other Preachers for that matter, must attempt to carry out this Ministry as Jesus would do Himself. In other words, we are merely the Ambassadors of another.

NOTES

FROM A PRACTICAL VIEWPOINT, HOW CAN PEOPLE TELL IF PREACHERS ARE PREACHING THEMSELVES AND NOT CHRIST?

1. When their preaching has a primary reference to their own interest; and when they engage in it to advance their reputation, or to secure in some way their own advantage.

When they aim at exalting their authority, extending their influence, or in any way promoting their own welfare.

2. When they proclaim their own opinions, and not the Gospel of Christ; when they derive their doctrines from their own reasonings, and not from the Bible.

3. When they put themselves forward; speak much of themselves; refer often to themselves; are vain of their powers of reasoning, of their eloquence, and of their learning, and seek to make these known rather than the simple Truths of the Gospel.

In one word, when self is primary, and the Gospel is secondary; when they prostitute the Ministry to gain popularity; to live a life of ease; to be respected; to obtain a livelihood; to gain influence; to rule over a people; and to make the preaching of the Gospel merely an occasion of advancing themselves in the world.

Such a plan, it is implied here, would lead to dishonest arts and devices, and to trick and stratagem to accomplish the end in view. And it is implied here, also, that to avoid all such tricks and arts, the true way is not to preach ourselves, but Jesus Christ.

The other day (as I dictate this in July of 1998), a Preacher stood over Television and told the people that the Lord had told him that if they would send in a certain amount of money, they would in turn have all their bills paid by a certain date.

This is not the Gospel of Jesus Christ, but gross dishonesty at the highest level. As we have previously stated, such antics are worse in the Eyes of God, I believe, than a robber going into a store and demanding money. At least the robber does not make the Lord a part of his scheme. To do wrong is bad enough, but to make Christ a part of the wrongdoing by claiming He has told us to do such is about as bad as it can get. Pure and simple, this is *"huckstering the Word of God"* (II Cor. 2:17).

EVER ON GUARD

Since the days of Paul, the Ministry has always had men who, in the last analysis, preached themselves. They offered their own thoughts and their own doctrines, reshaped the Word and what it says about Christ Jesus as Lord according to their own notions so as to gain favor, following, honor, and personal advantage for themselves.

They tried to beat the Devil by selling themselves into his hands, although no one has ever beat him in that way. The temptation to yield something in regard to Christ Jesus with an eye to ourselves is often subtle, and we must ever be on our guard (Lenski).

The phrase, *"But Christ Jesus the Lord,"* presents the only purpose for Ministry.

How many Preachers place doctrine ahead of Jesus? How many Preachers place their Religious Denomination ahead of Jesus?

Jesus Christ is to be the Center and Circumference of all that we do. He is our past, our present, and our future. Our Gospel is Jesus Christ!

Instead of *"Christ Jesus, the Lord,"* as it is here translated, Paul is actually saying *"Christ Jesus as Lord,"* with the designation centering upon *"Lord."* Consequently, He is God and, as well, the Lord of our lives and all that we do.

Christ Jesus as Lord is not only the Center but the entire Sphere; not only the Central Doctrine but the sum of all Doctrine, omitting none. Christ Jesus as Lord means preaching every Word He spoke or gave by His Apostles, dropping not one.

NOTES

To preach Him as Lord means to serve His interests alone; and since this preaching is the preaching of the Gospel, it is serving only the interest of the Gospel. To devote ourselves wholly to His interests and those of the Gospel, that is blessedness indeed; to substitute our own little temporal interest is the height of folly.

The phrase, *"And ourselves your servants for Jesus' sake,"* goes back to the teaching of Christ on the servant principle (Mat. 20:25-28; Jn. 13:12-17).

SLAVES

"Servants" in the Greek is *"doulos,"* and means *"a slave, a bondservant."*

In effect, Paul is saying, *"slaves for you,"* which means *"not slaves owned, commanded, ordered about as slaves to do your will* (will of the people)," but rather slaves of Christ to do His Will.

Because of Him, our Heavenly Lord and Master, Whose slaves we are, because of His Will and gracious order, because of His interest in you, we are slaves *for* you, and preach, advertise, commend ourselves as such.

In these five words *"your servants for Jesus' sake,"* the whole position and work of Christ's Ministers are expressed by one who, because he was such a Minister, knew all. No Minister has ever improved on these five words; many a Minister has not learned their full secret. We are slaves who do nothing but serve Christ's people. Unselfishly, never tiring, never complaining, seeking nothing, giving everything, listening to no allurements or threats, happy only when we heap up profit for others — so we slave. All *"because of Jesus."*

Why did Paul say, *"Jesus"* and not *"the Lord"*? The very word *"Jesus"* recalls that here on earth, where this was His ordinary name, He came, *"not to be ministered unto, but to minister, yea to give His Life, a ransom, for many"* (Mat. 20:28). *"Jesus"* recalls His example; *"Lord"* would bring to mind the reward He has in store for us.

NOT LORDS

"Slaves for you" — not lords over you but helpers of your joy (II Cor. 1:24), debtors to both Greeks and Barbarians (Rom. 1:14), never lording it over God's heritage (I Pet.

5:3). Never slaves of men, ever slaves of Christ (Rom. 1:1; Phil. 1:1; Titus 1:1) without question or hesitation where He speaks and orders, deaf where others would give us orders.

This word should have made all the Roman Popes and the little Protestant Popelets impossible; likewise, all the man-pleasers in the Ministry.

This word, coming from an Apostle of the Lord Himself, surely must have had a strong effect on the Corinthians (Lenski).

Do we, as Preachers of the Gospel, honestly realize how privileged we are to represent our Lord by proclaiming His Gospel? It would be a great honor to represent the President of our nation as his Ambassador, but that honor pales into insignificance when compared to the honor of representing The Lord Jesus Christ (Rossier).

(6) "FOR GOD, WHO COMMANDED THE LIGHT TO SHINE OUT OF DARKNESS, HATH SHINED IN OUR HEARTS, TO GIVE THE LIGHT OF THE KNOWLEDGE OF THE GLORY OF GOD IN THE FACE OF JESUS CHRIST."

The phrase, *"For God, Who commanded the Light to shine out of darkness,"* is a reference to Genesis 1:3. The way this is said is very important.

When the Lord said, *"Let there be light: and there was Light,"* He was not in effect creating light, but actually calling back into existence something that had already been created before this time.

The light, firmament, waters, earth, darkness, and all other things mentioned in the Genesis account regarding the earth were already in existence, but had been thrown into chaos and the laws which previously governed them had been made void. In other words, the very purpose of their existence had been annulled because of sin.

Now, in the restoration to perfection and original usefulness, God merely commands and the Sun again gives light on this planet, as it had previously done.

THE FALL

Consequently, this statement given by the Holy Spirit through the Apostle, proclaims the fact that man had once had *"Light"* in Adam before the Fall, but had lost the *"illumination"* after the Fall. Hence, Paul had previously said, *"For as in Adam all die, even so in Christ shall all be made alive"* (I Cor. 15:22).

NOTES

THE NATURE OF GOD

The idea is, the thing shall be, and there can be no question about it, the Light will shine, and in fact, does shine.

It is not the Power of God that is described here, as many think of Power. It is rather the Nature of God, the fact that He is the God of Light, that is stressed. He shattered the darkness of chaos by bringing in the cosmic light which He had already created. That shows the kind of God He is. The universe has been bathed in Light ever since.

As it is seen and understood here, there is no such thing as an evolution of light. It was brought into existence in a moment's time, and has continued ever since, which is the way of God.

THE DESIGN

The design of this Verse seems to be to give a reason why Paul and his fellow-Apostles did not preach themselves, but Jesus Christ, the Lord. That reason was that their minds had been so illuminated by that God Who had commanded the Light to shine out of darkness, that they had discerned the Glory of the Divine perfections shining in and through the Redeemer, and they, therefore, gave themselves to the work of making Him known among men. The Doctrines which they preached they had not derived from men in any form. They had not been elaborated by human reasoning or Science, nor had they been imparted by tradition. They had been communicated directly by the Source of all Light — the True God — Who had shined into the hearts that were once benighted by sin.

Thus, having been illuminated, they had felt themselves bound to go and make known the Truths which God had imparted to them.

LIGHT

Light is everywhere in the Bible the emblem of knowledge, purity, and Truth; as darkness is the emblem of ignorance, error, sin, and wretchedness. And the sense is here that God has removed this ignorance, and poured a flood of Light and Truth into their minds. This Passage teaches, therefore, the following important Truth in regard to Christians — since it is as applicable to all Christians as it was to the Apostles.

NOTES

THE MIND IS BY NATURE IGNORANT

The mind is by nature ignorant and benighted, at least as it refers to God — to an extent which may be properly compared with the darkness which prevailed before God commanded the Light to shine. Indeed, the darkness which prevailed before the Light was formed, was a most striking emblem of the darkness which exists in the mind of man before it is enlightened by Revelation, and by the Holy Spirit.

For in all minds by nature, as stated, there is deep ignorance of God, of His Law and His requirements. As well, this is often greatly deepened by the course of life which men lead; by their education; or by their indulgence in sin, and by their plans of life; and especially by the indulgence of evil passions.

The tendency of man, if left to himself, is to plunge into even deeper darkness, and to involve his mind more entirely in the obscurity of moral midnight.

"Light is come into the world, and men loved darkness rather than Light, because their deeds were evil" (Jn. 3:19).

THE MINDS OF BELIEVERS ARE ILLUMINATED

That which Paul gave us in this Sixth Verse teaches the fact that the minds of Christians are illuminated. They are enabled to see things as they are. This fact is often taught in the Scriptures (I Cor. 2:12-15; I Jn. 2:20).

They have different views of things than do unbelievers, and different from what they once had. They perceive a beauty in Salvation which others do not see, and a glory in Truth and in the Saviour, and in the Promises of the Gospel, which they did not see before they were converted.

This does not mean that they are superior in their powers of understanding to other men — for the reverse is often the fact; nor that the effect of Salvation is at once to enlarge their own intellectual powers, and make them different from what they were before in this respect.

But it does mean that they have a clear and consistent view; they look at things as they really are; they perceive a beauty in Salvation and in the service of God which they did not see before.

As well, they see a beauty in the Bible, and in the Doctrines of the Bible which they did not see before, and which sinners do not see, and in fact, cannot see.

Even though there may not be an immediate and direct enlargement of the intellect, still, there is an effect on the heart which does produce an appropriate and indirect effect on the understanding. It is at the same time true, that the practice of virtue, that a pure heart, and that the cultivation of oneness with Christ, all tend to regulate, strengthen, and expand the intellect. As the ways of vice, and the indulgence of evil passions and propensities tend to enfeeble, paralyze, darken, and ruin the understanding, so that, other things being equal, the man of Salvation will be the man of the clearest and best regulated mind.

To be frank, this is often strikingly manifested among unlettered and unlearned Christians. It often happens, as a matter of fact, that they have by far clearer and more just and elevated views of Truth than men of the most mighty intellects, and most highly cultivated by Science and adorned with learning, but who do not know Christ.

GOD IS THE SOURCE OF ALL LIGHT

This Sixth Verse teaches us that it is the same God Who enlightens the mind of the Believer, Who commanded the Light at first to shine. He is the Source of all Light. He formed the Light in the natural world; He gives all Light and Truth on all subjects to the understanding; and He imparts all correct views of Truth to the heart.

Light is not originated by man; and man, on the subject of Salvation, no more creates the Light, which beams upon his benighted mind, than he created the Light of the Sun when it first shed its beams over the darkened earth.

"All Truth is from the Source of Light Divine"; and it is no more the work of man to enlighten the mind, and dissipate the darkness from the soul of a benighted sinner, than it was of man to scatter the darkness that brooded over the creation, or that he can now turn the shades of midnight to noonday.

All this work lies beyond the proper province of man; and is all to be traced to the agency of God — the great Fountain of Light.

THE SAME POWER

It is taught in this Sixth Verse that it is the same power that gives Light to the mind of the Christian, which at first commanded the Light to shine out of darkness. It requires the exertion of the same Omnipotence; and the change is often as remarkable and surprising. Nothing can be conceived to be more grand than the calling forth of Light — when by one word, the whole Solar System was in a blaze.

And nothing in the moral world is more grand than when by a Word God commands the Light to beam on the soul of a benighted sinner. Night is at once changed to day; and all things are seen in a blaze of glory. The Works of God appear different; the Word of God appears different; and a new aspect of beauty is diffused over all things.

IN WHAT WAY DOES GOD IMPART THE LIGHT TO OUR HEARTS?

1. He does so by His written and preached Word. All spiritual and saving Light to the minds and hearts of men has come through His Revealed Truth.

Nor does the Spirit of God now give or reveal any Light to the heart and mind which is not to be found in the Word of God, and which is not imparted through that medium.

2. God makes use of His providential dealings to give Light to the minds of men.

They are then, by sickness, disappointment, and pain, made to see the folly and vanity of the things of this world, and to see the necessity of a better way.

3. It is done especially and mainly by the influences of the Holy Spirit. It is directly by His Agency that the heart becomes effected, and the mind enlightened. It is His province in the world to prepare the heart to receive the Truth; to dispose the mind to attend to it; to remove the obstructions which existed to its clear perception; to enable the mind clearly to see the beauty of Truth, and of the plan of Salvation through the Redeemer.

And whatever may be the means which may be used, it is still true that it is only by the Spirit of God that men are ever brought to see the Truth clearly and brightly. The same Spirit that inspired the Prophets and Apostles also illuminates the minds and hearts of men now, removes the darkness from their minds, and enables them clearly to discover the Truth as it is in Jesus (Barnes).

NOTES

The phrase, *"To give the Light of the knowledge of the Glory of God,"* in a sense makes the Believer the source of light, not as its originator, but as its beacon. We are beacons for the world's vast spiritual darkness.

THE GOD OF CREATION AND OF REDEMPTION

The fact referred to here includes two great events. It includes Creation and Redemption. God commanded the Light to shine out of darkness at the creation, or at least to bring it out into its glory. The Light which shined out in a creative way has now been made to shine in, in a redemptive way. The Light of creation has become the Light of Salvation. The Light placed in the heavens has become the Light placed in our hearts. The Light which was material has become moral. The physical Light of the Sun has become the Spiritual Light of the Son. The universal Light has become the personal Light.

Thus, we have the God of creation and the God of Redemption revealed to us as one. It means that having received physical life as a result of creation, we receive Spiritual Life as a result of Salvation. The first birth requires a second birth.

THE CROSS

Here is a revelation of great importance. The Cross was planned as carefully as creation was planned. It is as necessary to our way of life as the Sun is to the Solar System. One's place in the material world is proof of one's responsibility to the moral world. If God is one's Creator, He must also be one's Saviour. The argument is almost endless, but it addresses itself to the conscience of all men and women.

The medium by which the Light of Salvation through the Cross of Jesus Christ is to reach the world is the Christian. The Light that hath shined out, and shined in, is in us that it may be given to others.

How necessary that the Light shine in! Others cannot see it until we have it. We cannot reflect what we do not see. We cannot give what we do not have.

It is important to understand the nature of the Light, as well as the Source of it. It is described as *"the Light of the knowledge of the Glory of God in the Face of Jesus Christ."* Previously, Christ was spoken of as the Image of God. Now He is spoken of as the Light of God. The Light was reflected in the Face of Christ. What is reflected from His Face is intended to be reflected from our faces to the world about us.

Our motives are the most important thing in our efforts. Achievement is robbed of its glory whenever it is prompted by an unworthy motive. Even failure may be a thing of glory, if we go down to defeat with our souls unsullied and our colors flying.

We should inspect the motives which prompt us in doing today's tasks, lest we be found guilty of that which is unworthy of our High Calling.

OPPOSITION

Whatever the motive, we must be prepared for adversity and opposition. One can be prompted by the highest and best ideals and yet find himself opposed by enemies who will impugn those motives and do all they can to obstruct his efforts. This is inevitable. Regrettable, it will be found inside as well as outside the Church. If we are prepared for this kind of opposition, we will save ourselves the jolt of disillusionment later. Adversity lies athwart the advancement of every Godly person. The best efforts you can put forth will be opposed by the worst efforts of both carnal and religious men.

If Jesus and Paul were the victims of such opposition, who are we that we should escape? It is in the very nature and pattern of events that we shall meet resistance, and great resistance!

However, the presence of these things is the Promise of greater things. The very forces that oppose you will be the elements that advance you. The Eagle sets its wings to take advantage of the wind and, by the wind that opposes him, he soars higher than ever before (Laurin).

THE OBJECT

The object or effect of the enlightened mind is that we may behold the Divine Glory.

NOTES

All of this is for the purpose of enlightening and instructing us concerning the Knowledge of the Glory of God. It is the knowledge of the Divine Glory.

THE GLORY OF GOD

The Glory of God was only reflected on the face of Moses, the mediator of the Law; the Glory of God is embodied in Jesus Christ, the Mediator of the Gospel.

The former Glory was that of the Divine Law and its judgment on sin and on sinners, and the face of Moses could only reflect it since he had been with God only for a few days. The other Glory is that of the Divine Gospel and Grace for sinners, and the Face of Jesus Christ radiates this Glory because He is its very embodiment, He Who came from God, the Very Son of God, and returned to God as our Saviour-Lord forever.

The phrase, *"In the Face of Jesus Christ,"* refers to the fact that He is the Source of the Light.

"Face" means that Moses turned to the Israelites; Jesus Christ turns to us. But they could not endure to look even upon that reflected Glory while we receive the Light of this embodied Glory into our very hearts.

The Glory of the Law and the Judgment kills (II Cor. 3:6), the Glory of God on the Face of Jesus Christ makes alive and saves forever.

THE FACE OF JESUS

Some think that when Paul wrote *"the Glory of God on the Face of Jesus Christ"* he had in mind his Vision on the Road to Damascus. Most probably he did!

More should be said: That light struck Paul to the ground. It was the light of the Law like the Glory on Moses' face; for Jesus said to Paul: *"Saul, Saul, why art thou persecuting Me?"* (Acts 9:4), and confronted him with his sin and his crime. Like the sons of Israel, Paul could not endure that light, as can no sinner.

Yet that light of the Glory of God on the Face of Jesus Christ was also the Gospel Light. Jesus also called Saul (Paul) to repentance, and Paul heeded that Gospel Call.

The idea is this: all the argument in the world could not have changed this cold, calculating bigot; however, one glimpse of Jesus Christ, and more particularly, the *"Glory of God on the Face of Jesus Christ,"* could change him totally from sin to Salvation.

If somehow in our preaching, and our witnessing, and our testifying, we can lift up Jesus, portray Jesus, portray Him as the Son of God, portray Him Crucified and Risen, it will have the same effect on all who desire to hear and see, even as it did Paul.

THROUGH AND IN JESUS

That the Glory of the Divine Nature is seen in Him, since He is *"the brightness of His Glory, and the express Image of His Person,"* becomes very obvious (Heb. 1:3). And it is in and through Him that the Glory of the Divine perfections are made known. Also, the Glory of the Divine Attributes is made known through Him, since it is through Him that the work of creation was accomplished (Jn. 1:3; Col. 1:16), and it is by Him that the Mercy and Goodness of God have been manifested to men.

Jesus showed what God is when He became Incarnate (became a man). He lived as the Incarnate God — He was as pure and holy in human nature as God is in the heavens — the only man who has ever done that. And there is not, that we know of, one of the Divine Attributes or Perfections which has not at some period, or in some form, been evinced by Jesus Christ.

WHATEVER GOD IS, JESUS IS

If it be the prerogative of God to be eternal, Jesus is eternal (Isa. 9:6; Rev. 1:8, 18). If it be the prerogative of God to be the Creator, Jesus is also the Creator (Jn. 1:3). If it is to be Omniscient, Jesus is Omniscient (Mat. 11:27; Lk. 10:22). If it is to be Omnipresent, Jesus is Omnipresent (Mat. 18:20). If it is to be Almighty, Jesus is Almighty (Isa. 9:6). If it is to raise the dead, to give Life, Jesus did it (Jn. 5:21; 11:43-44). If it is to still waves and tempests, Jesus did it (Mk. 4:39). If it is to be perfectly holy, to be without a moral stain or spot, then all this is found in Jesus Christ.

There is not one of the Divine Perfections which has not the counterpart in Him; and if the Glory of the Divine Character is seen at all, it has been seen, it is being seen, and it will be seen in and through Him (Barnes).

Jesus Christ is not merely a reflection of the Glory of God, but is and ever shall be the Source of that Glory (Heb. 1:2).

NOTES

PAUL

So the Glory of God was fully revealed in the Face of Jesus Christ — it was unveiled — and the Apostle Paul as a true Minister of that Glory proclaimed it to the world without a veil in his clear and full presentation of the Gospel.

He announced the Glory of God in the Person of Christ. To point to any other Saviour would have been to put aside and declare worthless what Christ had done. For that Work brings the vilest of men into the very Glory of God, placing them there in a Righteousness in which it is impossible to find a flaw.

Once again, when one comes into even a portion of that Light, much less its full orbed Glory, one is left speechless, and yet at the same time, a *"Hallelujah"* shouts from every fiber and core of one's being.

(7) "BUT WE HAVE THIS TREASURE IN EARTHEN VESSELS, THAT THE EXCELLENCY OF THE POWER MAY BE OF GOD, AND NOT OF US."

The phrase, *"But we have this treasure in earthen vessels,"* presents the emphasis on the contrast between this frail vessel of earth as it relates to us personally, and the priceless treasure of power of the Gospel of Christ that dwells in it. This glorious Light that we have to show to the world is, like Gideon's torches, carried in earthen pitchers.

THIS TREASURE

Man can never be more than an earthen vessel, being frail and humble, and the metaphor especially suits an Apostle of Christ (I Cor. 2:3-5; II Tim. 2:20). But when he takes the Word of Life from the earthen pitcher and waves it in the air, it illuminates all on whom the Light Shines.

It is the *"Light"* of which Paul has been speaking exclusively in the last Verses, which constitutes this *"Treasure."* Those who suppose that this *"Treasure"* is gold or silver or something else of value, such as those who preach the Prosperity Message, should refer to Jeremiah 32:14 and I Timothy 6:5-11.

The obvious message presented here lies in the relatively low value placed on the container when compared with the extraordinary value of the contents.

God could have designed His Plan so He only operated through an aristocracy of some kind.

He could have selected a natural aristocracy of only people born within certain families, or He could have chosen an intellectual aristocracy of only members of the intelligentsia. Had He done either, though, the Treasure most likely would have been lost in light of the supposed value of the vessel; hence, He uses ordinary vessels like you and me who are required only to be willing containers (Rossier).

"Treasure" in the Greek is *"thesaurous,"* and means *"wealth or that of great value."*

"This Treasure" is God's shining in our hearts by the knowledge of Faith filling us with His Glorious Grace in Christ Jesus.

"Earthen vessels" in the Greek is *"ostrakinos,"* and is anything made of burnt clay. These vessels are cheap, utterly common, the least valued, used with small care, bound to break sooner or later. All these ideas are touched in Paul's figure.

If it be asked whether just our bodies are meant as being *"earthy"* (I Cor. 15:47), made of clay, the answer is yes, but not apart from our souls as still being in this earthly life.

THE ASTONISHMENT

The Astonishing thing is that such a Divine Treasure, God's Own Presence of Grace, the ultimate of what is heavenly, absolutely priceless, beyond the value of all rubies and diamonds of earth, should be placed into such wretched vessels and be kept in them so long. One could expect that this Treasure would be entrusted only to vessels of the highest value, be placed where they and their Treasure are only admired and are ever handled with utmost care and reverence. But see what God has done!

Yet this is His Way with this Treasure as I Corinthians 1:26-29 shows. He sent His Own Son into our flesh, permitted Him to be born in a stable, in a paltry village, in lowliest surroundings, Him in Whom all the Godhead dwelt Bodily (Col. 1:15-19; 2:9). Astounding, yet a fact.

Paul's purpose here is to show that it was by no excellency of his nature, or the nature of anyone for that matter, that the Gospel was originated; it was in virtue of no vigor and strength which he possessed that it was propagated; but that it had been, of design, committed by God to weak, decaying, and crumbling instruments, in order that it might be seen that it was by the Power of God that such instruments were sustained in the trials to which they were exposed, and in order that it might be manifest to all that it was not originated and diffused by the power of those to whom it was entrusted. The idea is, that they were altogether insufficient of their own strength to accomplish what was accomplished by the Gospel.

NOTES

The phrase, *"That the excellency of the Power may be of God, and not of us,"* presents the purpose of God in doing this in this manner.

GOD'S PURPOSE

God's purpose and His arrangement are to have this Saving Power wholly as being His possessions and in no measure or degree as having their source in us. For this reason He placed the great Treasure into such poor earthen vessels. Consequently, it cannot possibly be true that this superlative power is generated or produced by these vessels. They are so worthless and fragile in themselves that, if He did not protect them during the many shocks they receive, they would at once be broken into potsherds. As it is, these poor vessels endure only for a time.

To be sure, Paul says, *"We have this treasure,"* it is in us as vessels, and God uses us Ministers for the operation of this wondrous Power. The Power comes *"out of us"* but only because it has been placed in us by God and is thus the Power that is wholly of God and in no degree *"from out of us"* as the Source.

POWER!

First of all, of what type of Power is it, of which Paul speaks?

As well, let it be known, that if this *"Power"* is not present and prevalent within the heart and life of the Believer, Preacher, or otherwise, then it is not truly God which is in the person, but rather a mere philosophy. In fact, this *"Power"* works in three different ways:

1. POWER TO LIVE A GODLY LIFE: First of all, it is Power which helps the Believer live a Godly, consecrated, dedicated, sanctified life, victorious over sin, as Paul outlines in Romans Chapters 6 and 8. This is done by understanding the Power over Satan generated by Calvary and the Resurrection. In fact, it is utterly hopeless that this *"earthen vessel"* could within itself gain victory over these terrible Powers of Darkness. There must be a greater Power, and

that greater Power is what Jesus did at Calvary and the Resurrection, which not only satisfies the sin debt, but as well, breaks the terrible grip of sin in the heart and life of the Believer. In other words, this is the only manner in which victory over sin can be attained. This means that Calvary and the Resurrection are not only the pivot point of one's Salvation, but as well, the cause of one's ongoing victory. The Believer never gets away from the benefits of the Cross.

This is what Jesus was referring to when He spoke of *"binding the strong man* (Satan) *and then spoiling his house"* (Mat. 12:29). Jesus did this to Satan's house at Calvary and the Resurrection, and all, one might quickly say, for us.

2. POWER OVER SATAN: The Child of God has *"Power"* over demon spirits and actually over Satan himself. Jesus said, *"Behold, I give unto you Power to tread on serpents and scorpions* (demon spirits), *and over all the power of the enemy: and nothing shall by any means hurt you"* (Lk. 10:19).

This is done through the Power of the Holy Spirit, and by the privilege of the Believer to use the Name of Jesus (Mk. 16:17-18). This speaks of healing the sick, casting out demon spirits, breaking their power over certain areas, etc. All of this has to do with the Holy Spirit, i.e., *"The Gifts of the Spirit"* (I Cor. 12:8-10).

The idea is, that the Church continue to do what Jesus did in His earthly Ministry. Luke in beginning his Book on *"The Acts of the Apostles,"* said as much, *"Of all that Jesus began both to do and teach,"* insinuating, that it was to continue (Acts 1:1).

3. POWER TO TAKE THE MESSAGE: The Power to take this Message of Jesus Christ to a lost world, and the Power of this Message to wondrously and gloriously change lives, is stated here. It is the power of converting the hearts of sinners, of humbling the proud, and leading the guilty to the knowledge of God and the hope of Heaven.

The idea is, that all this was manifestly beyond human strength; and that God had of design chosen weak and feeble instruments in order that it might be everywhere seen that it was done not by human power, but by His Own. The instrumentality employed was altogether disproportionate in its nature to the effect produced.

As in Gideon's day the earthen vessel carried the Light which conquered the foe and brought deliverance, so God has committed the Gospel Message, not to mighty Angels with celestial bodies, but to feeble men with earthen bodies. But His Power enwraps the earthen vessel, so that though it be troubled, perplexed, persecuted, and struck down, it cannot be destroyed.

The Preacher is immortal till his work is done. The Apostle not only carried as a principle in his soul the dying and the Resurrection Life of Jesus, but he also consciously experienced them in his body; for Satan and men were constantly trying to destroy him and would have killed him more than once — as at Lystra (Acts 14:19) and when he was a night and a day in the deep (II Cor. 11:25). So it was made plain to men that the Power which kept him alive, and all others like him, was not human but Divine.

OF GOD

The idea is, that it may be manifest to all that it is God's Power, and not ours, which brings these things to pass. It was one great purpose of God that this should be kept clearly in view.

The major idea of understanding this, pertains to the desired humility on the part of the Believer. If one thinks about the situation even to a small degree, one quickly comes to the conclusion of the frailty and inability of this *"earthen vessel,"* and, consequently, that all done for God, must be of God and not *"of us."*

The following should always be kept in mind:

1. It is always true, whoever is employed, and however great may be the talents, learning, or zeal of those who preach, that it is by the Power of God that men are converted. Such a work cannot be accomplished by man. It is not by might or by strength; and between the conversion of a proud, haughty, and abandoned sinner, and the power of him who is made the instrument, there is such a manifest disproportion, that it is evident it is the Work of God.

The conversion of the human heart is not to be accomplished by man in any manner.

2. Ministers are frail, imperfect, and even sinful, as they were in the time of Paul. When the imperfections of Ministers are considered; when their frequent errors, and their not infrequent moral weaknesses are contemplated; when it is remembered how far many of them live from

what they ought to, and how few of them live in any considerable degree as becometh the followers of the Redeemer, it is wonderful that God blesses their labors as He does; and the matter of amazement is not that no more are converted unto their Ministry, but it is that so many are converted, or that *any* are converted.

Consequently, it is manifest that it is all of God, of His Power, and not of us.

3. The Lord often makes use of the most feeble, and unlearned, and weak of His servants, to accomplish the greatest effects. Consequently, it is not splendid talents, or profound learning, or distinguished eloquence that is always or even commonly most successful. Often the Ministry of such is entirely barren.

On the other hand, some humble and obscure Preachers have constant success, and Revivals shall attend him wherever he goes. It is the man of Faith, and prayer, and self-denial that is blessed; and the purpose of God in the Ministry, as in everything else, is to *"stain the pride of all human glory,"* and to show that He is all in all (Barnes).

(8) "WE ARE TROUBLED ON EVERY SIDE, YET NOT DISTRESSED; WE ARE PERPLEXED, BUT NOT IN DESPAIR;"

The phrase, *"We are troubled on every side, yet not distressed,"* presents that, as well as the following Passages, which are normal. In other words, it will be normal regarding all those who truly do the Work of God. These statements as given by Paul, little fit the modern so-called Faith Ministry, such being described as a *"bad confession."*

However, we must ever understand, if what we teach, preach and live, does not match up to the Word of God, its our Message which needs change, and not that of the Gospel.

TROUBLED

"Troubled" in the Greek is *"thlibo,"* and means *"afflict, to suffer tribulation, and as well has reference to wrestling, or to the contests in the Grecian games."* It properly means, *"to press, to press together, then to press as in a crowd where there is a throng, then to compress together, and then to oppress, or compress with evils, to distress, to afflict"* (II Cor. 1:6; II Thess. 1:6).

Here it means, that he was encompassed with trials, or placed in the midst of them, so that they pressed upon him as persons do in a crowd, or, possibly, as a man was closely pressed by an adversary in the games.

This speaks of *"wrestling"* in the spiritual sense, exactly as it does in the physical sense. It definitely has reference to the Powers of Darkness, where Paul said, *"For we wrestle not against flesh and blood, but against principalities, against powers, against the rulers of the darkness of this world, against spiritual wickedness in high places"* (Eph. 6:12).

Of course, the way we *"wrestle"* is to *"fight the good fight of Faith"* (I Tim. 6:12). The idea is this:

BROKEN

Going back to Gideon and his *"Light"* in the pitchers (vessels), the Light could not become visible until the vessels were broken (Judg. 7:16-25). Consequently a great victory was won!

The *"Light"* within us of which Paul has addressed, is not visible, and in fact cannot be visible, until we are broken, i.e., *"the flesh is subdued."* This can only happen by the difficulties expressed in Verses 8-12. Unfortunately, despite this Treasure being in pitiful, pathetic earthen vessels, still, we are very quick to become lifted up in pride. As well, there is no exception to this.

If Paul of all people, needed such to keep him *"broken"* before the Lord, I am positive that all of us fall into the same category as well. None of us desire the *"troubles"* or *"persecution"*; nevertheless, due to the constant danger of pride, these difficulties are necessary, and allowed by the Lord for that very reason.

DISTRESSED

"Distressed" in the Greek is *"stenochoreo,"* and means *"to hem in closely, to cramp."*

It comes from the Greek word for squeezing grapes. Thus, *"we are being squeezed,"* but are not *"squeezed out." "We are hemmed in,"* but not *"driven to surrender."*

Paul described his experiences in such terms as to leave us with the thought that although he was a victim of adversity, he was also a victor in that adversity.

Although his foes pressed in upon him from every side, he was not hemmed in. With all the activities of his adversaries, he was not straightened in his own activities. It is the picture, as

NOTES

stated, of a wrestler trying to crush his adversary. Paul was never vanquished by any of his adversaries.

In reading these words as written by Paul, and looking at our own Ministry, which the Holy Spirit certainly desires that we do, how so much these words and experiences fit exactly that of which we face on a daily basis. I realize that most of the Church erroneously think that the attitude of Church Leaders against us has to do with something that happened years ago, but that is totally incorrect. That is only an excuse. The attitude is because of what we preach. As well, it is because of the Moving and Operation of the Holy Spirit on that which we preach. It is the same thing that caused Cain to kill Abel.

The Scripture says, *"And the Lord had respect unto Abel and to his offering: but unto Cain and to his offering He had not respect. And Cain was very wroth, and his countenance fell"* (Gen. 4:4-5).

These people, and they number into the literal thousands, do not want or desire the Spirit of God; however, they are not satisfied to stop there. They as the Judaizers of old, who attempted to destroy Paul and hurt his Ministry in any manner, are still at work today. They feel they must destroy the Message *and* the Messenger.

Irrespective, the Lord allows them only so much latitude and no more. Consequently, we may be greatly *"troubled on every side,"* but yet we are *"not distressed."* We still have some room to maneuver, provided to us by the Lord, and for that we give Him thanks and praise.

The phrase, *"We are perplexed, but not in despair,"* means here, that they were often brought into circumstances of great embarrassment, where they hardly knew what to do, or what course to take. They were surrounded by foes; they were in want; they were in circumstances which they had not anticipated, and which greatly perplexed them.

PERPLEXITY

"Perplexed" in the Greek is *"aporeo,"* and means *"to have no way out, a problem without a solution."*

However, such always refers to a solution solely according to the resources of one's thinking of this world. With the Lord, as we shall see, there is no such thing as a problem without a solution. God is able to do all things.

The Lord allows such to His Children, even to His most favored as Paul, that we may learn total dependence on Him. As we have repeatedly stated, unfortunately this cannot be brought about, this Christlike condition, by a mere Commandment. The flesh is always of such occasion that it will resort to measures other than the Lord, if given the slightest opportunity. So, the Lord allows things to come our way which seem to be overly restrictive, with our own resources quickly coming to an end. In these situations, we have to resort to the Lord, which is what the Holy Spirit intends.

DESPAIR

"Despair" in the Greek is *"exaporeomai,"* and means *"to be utterly at a loss."*

Paul is saying that he had never come to this place of despair. Because of his dependence on the Lord, and the help of the Lord which was always given, he would always see victory. The idea of Paul here is, that they were not left entirely without resource. Their wants were provided for; their embarrassments were removed; their grounds of perplexity were taken away; and unexpected strength and resources were imparted to them.

When they did not know what to do, when all resources seemed to fail them, in some unexpected manner they would be relieved and saved from absolute despair. How often does this occur in the lives of all Christians, especially those who truly do the Work of God! And how certain is it, that in all such cases God will interpose by His Grace and aid His people, and save them from absolute despair.

Paul's circumstances often brought him to his wit's end so that he hardly knew which way to go or what to do, but never to the place of ultimate despair.

It is not unnatural to doubt, but it is not necessary to despair. It is possible to be bewildered and confused, but not necessary to give up hope and surrender the fight.

The margin rendering says: *"Not altogether without help or means."* When you feel the weakest and effort seems futile and the cause lost, then remember you have at your command means to extricate yourself from your perplexity — that means is the Power and Promises of God.

NOTES

(9) "PERSECUTED, BUT NOT FORSAKEN; CAST DOWN, BUT NOT DESTROYED;"

The phrase, *"Persecuted, but not forsaken,"* refers to being pursued but not actually caught.

PERSECUTION

Persecution and tribulation are inevitable experiences of Christian Life. Jesus said they would come. He further said that when they came, He too would come to stand with us. Actually, man's persecution means God's Presence; thus, our adversity brings a new advantage.

"Persecuted" in the Greek is *"dioko,"* and means *"to pursue with the intent of overtaking the person pursued, with the idea in mind of hindering or stopping altogether their ability to function."*

Persecution was frequently foretold by Christ, as certain to come to those who were His true Disciples and followers. He forewarned them again and again that it was inevitable. He said that He Himself must suffer it (Mat. 16:21; 17:22-23; Mk. 8:31).

It would be a test of true Discipleship. In the Parable of the Sower, He mentions this as one of the causes of defection among those who are Christians, but with little consecration. When affliction or persecution ariseth for the Word's sake, immediately the stony-ground hearers are offended (Mk. 4:17).

However, on the other hand, persecution would be a sure means of gaining a Blessing, whenever it came to His loyal followers when they were in the way of welldoing; and He thus speaks of it in two of the Beatitudes, *"Blessed are they that have been persecuted for Righteousness' sake: for theirs is the Kingdom of Heaven. Blessed are ye when men shall reproach you, and persecute you . . . for My sake"* (Mat. 5:10-11).

This persecution would take different forms, ranging through every possible variety, from false accusation to the infliction of death, beyond which, He pointed out (Mat. 10:28; Lk. 12:4), persecutors are unable to go. The methods of persecution which were employed by the Jews, and also by the heathen against the followers of Christ, came in different varieties:

Men would revile them and would say all manner of evil against them falsely, for Christ's sake (Mat. 5:11). Contempt and disparagement: *"Say we not well that thou art a Samaritan, and hast a demon?"*, was that posed to Jesus (Jn. 8:48).

NOTES

In the case of Christ, persecution took the form of attempts to entrap Him in His speech (Mat. 22:15); the questioning of His authority (Mk. 11:28); illegal arrest; the heaping of every insult upon Him as a prisoner; false accusations; and a violent and most cruel death.

AGAINST THE APOSTLES

After our Lord's Resurrection the first attacks against His Disciples came from the High Priest and his party. The High Priesthood was then in the hands of the Sadducees, and one reason which moved them to take action of this kind was their *"sore trouble,"* because the Apostles *"proclaimed in Jesus the Resurrection from the dead"* (Acts 4:2; 5:17).

The Gospel based upon the Resurrection of Christ was evidence of the untruth of the chief Doctrines held by the Sadducees, for they held that there is no Resurrection. But instead of yielding to the evidence of the fact that the Resurrection had taken place, they opposed and denied it, and persecuted the Disciples of the Lord.

The Pharisees were as little less hostile for a while, possibly because of their opposition to the Sadducees; however, gradually almost all of the Jewish people became bitter persecutors of the Christians. Thus, in the earliest of the Pauline Epistles, it is said, *"Ye also suffered the same things of your own countrymen, even as the Believers* (in Judaea) *did of the Jews; who both killed the Lord Jesus and the Prophets, and drove us out, and pleased not God, and are contrary to all men"* (I Thess. 2:14-15).

Serious persecution of the Christian Church began with the case of Stephen (Acts Chpt. 7); and his lawless execution was followed by *"a great persecution"* directed against the Christians in Jerusalem. This *"great persecution"* (Acts 8:1) scattered the members of the Church, who fled in order to avoid bonds and imprisonment and even death. At this time Paul (Saul) signalized himself by his great activity, persecuting *"this Way unto the death, binding and delivering into prisons both men and women"* (Acts 22:4). Ironically enough, he was soon to become the target of such, instead of the instigator.

PAUL

During the period covered by the Acts there was not much purely Gentile persecution: at that time the persecution suffered by the Christian Church was chiefly Jewish. There were, however, certain times of great dangers and risks encountered by the Apostles and by all who proclaimed the Gospel. Thus, at Philippi, Paul and Silas were most cruelly persecuted (Acts 16:19-40); and even before that time, Paul and Barnabas had suffered much at Iconium and Lystra (Acts 14:5-19).

On the whole, however, the Roman Authorities were not actively hostile during the greater part of Paul's lifetime. Nevertheless, that ultimately changed, which brought on his death, as well as that of Peter and others. In fact, untold thousands suffered terrible martyrdom at the hands of the Roman Government for several centuries.

After Rome fell, the Church which had been drifting towards Apostasy for quite some time, now became the Catholic Church and, as well, the persecutor. Again, under the Catholic inquisitions, untold thousands gave their lives for the Cause of Christ, which gradually came to an end only after the Reformation finally took hold.

Even since then, in heathen countries which know not Christ, many have suffered for the cause of the Gospel. The greatest example being the former Soviet Union and China, etc.

RESULTS OF PERSECUTION

Persecution is brought about because of antagonism toward Jesus Christ and the Gospel, which extends to His followers. However, there is a persecution which stems from inside the Church instead of without. This was probably more hurtful to Paul even than that from without, inasmuch as it hurt the Work of God to a far greater degree. That from without has to do more so with that which is physical and material, but can definitely extend to that which is deeply humiliating. That from within the Church, however, is far more subtle, and designed to stop the Message and to do so by stopping the Messenger.

WITNESSES

The results of persecution were to raise up witnesses, true witnesses, for the Christian Faith. Men and women and even children were among the martyrs whom no cruelties, however refined and protracted, could terrify into denial of their Lord. It is to a large extent owing to persecution that the Christian Church possesses the testimony of men who gave their all for the Cause of Christ, even their very lives. While those who had adopted the Christian Faith in an external and formal manner only, generally went back from their profession; however, the True Christian, as even the Roman Proconsul Pliny testifies, could not be made to do this.

NOTES

CHRISTIAN FAITH IS IMMORTAL

Persecution showed that Christian Faith is immortal even in this world. Of Christ's Kingdom there shall be no end. *"Hammer away, ye hostile bands, your hammers break, God's Altar stands."*

Pagan Rome tried hard to destroy the Church of Christ; it was literally drunk with the blood of the Saints. God allowed this tyranny to exist for several centuries, and the blood of His Children was shed like water.

Why was it necessary that the Church should have so terrible, and so prolonged, an experience of suffering?

It was in order to convince the world that though the *"kings of the earth gather themselves against the Lord and against His Christ,"* yet all that they can do is vain. *"God is in the midst of Zion; . . . He shall help her, and that right early"* (Ps. 46:5). The Christian Church, as if suspended between Heaven and earth, had no need of other help than that of the unseen but Divine Hand, which at every moment held it up and kept it from falling. Never was the Church more free, never stronger, never more flourishing, never more extensive in its growth, than in the days of its persecution.

And what became of the great persecuting power, the Roman Empire? It fell before the Barbarians. Rome is fallen in its ruins, and its idols are utterly abolished, while the Barbarians who overwhelmed the Empire have become the nations of modern Europe, which for the most part have recognized Christ in one way or the other. As well, their descendants have carried the Christian Faith to North, Central and South America, as well as Australia and Africa and all over the world.

TO PRESERVE THE GREAT DOCTRINES OF THE BIBLE

Persecution became, to a large extent, an important means of preserving the True Doctrines of the Person and of the Work of Christ. It was in the ages of persecution that gnosticism died, as well as other Apostasies, though they died slowly.

Persecution was followed by these important results, for God in His Wisdom had seen fit to permit these evils to happen, in order to change them into permanent good; and thus the wrath of man was overruled to praise God, and to effect more ultimate good, than if the persecutions had not taken place at all.

What, in a word, could be more Divine than to curb and restrain and overrule evil itself and change it into good? God lets iniquity do what it pleases, according to its own design; but in permitting it to move on one side, rather than on another, He overrules it and makes it enter into the order of His Providence. So He lets this fury against the Christian Faith be kindled in the hearts of persecutors, so that they afflict the Saints of the Most High. But the Church remains safe, for persecution can work nothing but ultimate good in the Hand of God. As Tertullian said, *"The blood of the martyrs is the seed of the Church."*

Jesus said He would never leave us or forsake us, and as well, the Holy Spirit through Paul, said that even though we would be persecuted, still, we would not be *"forsaken,"* i.e., *"never forsaken by the Lord."* What a consolation!

The phrase, *"Cast down, but not destroyed,"* refers to the fact that at times we are knocked down but not knocked out.

Paul is describing the experience which was constantly his, and in fact, will be that of anyone who attempts through Christ to push back the darkness of the Satanic kingdom. Paul is describing the ongoing process, and not the conclusion of the matter. The end result of this Christian life, in other words how it will end, will be exactly as the trip there, all by the Lord's Own Will.

CAST DOWN

To be thrown down means to be at death's door, the enemy is over us to administer the last blow; yet the Lord time and time again steps in with deliverance.

NOTES

If one is to notice, there is an order or gradation here: A. *"Trouble"*; B. *"Perplexity"*; C. *"Persecution"*; and, D. *"Cast down."*

However, as it is structured in the Greek, the gradation thus sketched by the Holy Spirit is not intended to be one that follows these steps in order. Sometimes only one of these four happens, sometimes the other. In Acts 14:5, etc., Paul fled from the danger; but in 14:19, etc., Paul was dragged out as dead and yet did not perish.

He was cast down, but not destroyed.

This means to be struck down and beaten to the earth, yet never eliminated or driven from the field of conflict.

By these things we can see how sorely the Christian may suffer and how the multiplicity of adversity may beset him, yet he is still victor.

Here, too, is the Truth that victory is not what we experience, but how we experience it. Triumph is not escape from adversity, as much of the modern Gospel proclaims, but it is bearing it to personal conquest.

Paul found such words in the vocabulary of his experience as stated, as *"trouble, perplexity, persecution, and being cast down,"* but out of these came victory and triumph.

ERRONEOUS MODERN THOUGHT

Presently, the modern Faith man is pictured as someone who has confessed away all of these things mentioned here by the Apostle, with him living as a *"King's Kid,"* in royal style. Consequently, as one modern excuse for a Preacher said, *"I'm not a K-Mart Christian."* Of course, he was insinuating that people with Faith shopped at only the upscale places.

How such drivel, and drivel it is, could pass for Gospel is beyond me. But yet, this particular individual has several thousands of people attending his Church. . . . Church?

Instead of formulating one's own gospel which appeals to greed and base motives in the hearts and lives of those who are so foolish as to listen to such pap, one had better line up his gospel with the Word of God.

Some may think me overly hard respecting my statements; however, considering that we are talking about the single most important thing in the world, the eternal destiny of one's soul, I personally think strong terminology is in order. Our problem today is preaching which says nothing, or else says it in such a way, that the listener does not exactly know what is being said. Regrettably, most Preachers are *"safe Preachers."* In other words, they have *"itching ears,"* which means they are trying to feed the people what the people want to hear, instead of *"thus saith the Lord."* In fact, what the people want has absolutely no bearing on anything. It's what God wants, and only what He wants that is of value.

The Lord told the Prophet Ezekiel that he must warn the people, and in no uncertain terms. If they rejected the warning they would die eternally lost, but the Preacher would have delivered his soul.

However, if he did not warn the people, they would still die lost, but their blood would be required at the hands of the Preacher (Ezek. 3:17-21).

The blood of untold millions is going to be required at the hands of many Preachers!

(10) "ALWAYS BEARING ABOUT IN THE BODY THE DYING OF THE LORD JESUS, THAT THE LIFE ALSO OF JESUS MIGHT BE MADE MANIFEST IN OUR BODY."

The phrase, *"Always bearing about in the body the dying of the Lord Jesus,"* does not present a process of self-salvation as some think, but rather the experience of Sanctification. It was fulfilling what Jesus had said must be true of His Disciples. *"If any man will come after Me, let him deny himself, and take up his Cross, and follow Me"* (Mat. 16:24).

BEARING ABOUT IN THE BODY

"Bearing" in the Greek is *"periphero,"* which means *"to carry about with one."*

"Body" in the Greek is *"soma,"* and means *"the physical body."* It also carries the connotation of a *"slave."* It can be used literally or figuratively. Paul is here using it literally, i.e., *"the physical body."*

The body is not the man, for he himself can exist apart from his body (II Cor. 12:2-3), and in fact, does exist without the body in the form of the soul and the spirit, concerning all who have *"fallen asleep,"* i.e., *"gone on to be with the Lord."* The body, however, is an essential part of the man; therefore, the redeemed will not be perfected until the Resurrection, which in essence is what Paul is here addressing (Heb. 11:40), which refers to our Sanctification. No

NOTES

man in his final state will be without his body, i.e., *"Glorified Body,"* as it regards Saints (Jn. 5:28-29; Rev. 20:13).

THE IDEA OF *"BEARING ABOUT IN THE BODY"* IS TWOFOLD:

The persecution and opposition that one must experience for the *Cause* of Christ, is here proclaimed.

The Glorified Christ is *not* still dying in us, nor is He being put to death in our sufferings. His death and its purpose have been completed; but what His enemies once did to Him they continue to do to His Ministers *"for His Name's sake"* (Jn. 15:18-21) even as Jesus foretold.

The same hatred that pursued and killed Jesus now pursues His Believers who are one with Him by Faith in His Name.

As we've already stated, this language as used by the Holy Spirit through the Apostle reminds us that there is a price connected with being True Ministers of the Lord. Paul would probably not blend in very well with some modern Preachers who claim that if we have enough Faith we will never suffer. According to the Apostle, the more effective we become as vessels of God, the more suffering will occur in our lives. The word *"always"* guarantees that. We will see many concrete expressions of this when we get to II Corinthians Chapter 11. As a vessel for Jesus, Paul knew he was sharing in the death that Jesus suffered. Literally, *"he was delivered over to death,"* just like the Lord was.

What does all this mean?

Basically, it means that we face the same kind of opposition that our Lord faced when He was on earth. Nevertheless, if we truly take on ourselves the attitude He had (Phil. 2:5), we will be practicing self-abnegation for the benefit of others (Phil. 2:7). In other words, we do not glorify ourselves as vessels, but we allow the contents to be manifested through us (Rossier).

SANCTIFICATION

The second meaning has to do with the Sanctification process.

According to Romans Chapter 6, Calvary is an ongoing process. In other words, the benefits of what Jesus did there, pertain not only to the Salvation experience of being *"Born-Again,"* but as well, has to do with our

Sanctification. Jesus not only *"paid the sin debt"* at that time, in effect taking our place, He also *"broke the sin grip."* However, to maintain constant victory over sin, we must appropriate on a continuing basis the benefits of Calvary in this respect. We must understand that we were Baptized into His Death, which means that Satan and sin in all its forms, have been defeated. We were buried with Him, which means all the passion and pride were buried with Him and should never surface again. Also, we were raised with Him in the Resurrection spiritually speaking, to *"Newness of Life."* All of this, as stated, is in Romans Chapter 6.

In effect, this is what Jesus meant by stating that we had to *"daily bear the Cross"* (Lk. 9:23). It is a *"daily"* appropriating of the benefits of the Cross, i.e., *"what Jesus did at Calvary."*

The Cross is more than a pious ancient sentiment. It is to be an ongoing, personal experience. As well, the sphere of this experience is not to be in our imaginations or pious reflections. It is to be in our bodies. Paul said he bore these things in his body. That means he felt the crucifying effects of Christ's Cross in his feelings, appetites, activities, and desires. In other words, the Cross figures in the practical problems of our everyday experience (Laurin).

The phrase, *"That the life also of Jesus might be made manifest in our body,"* has reference to the fact that if we do not understand and properly appropriate, the Death of Jesus on Calvary, we will not be beneficiaries of His *"Life."*

HIS LIFE

The purpose of experiencing Christ's Death in our body is to reveal Christ's Life in our body. When we die to self, He lives. These are not just pretty sayings; they are the Laws of Spiritual Life. Jesus said, *"Except a corn of wheat fall into the ground and die, it abideth alone: but if it die, it bringeth forth much fruit"* (Jn. 12:24). The seed must die if it expects to live.

We, too, must die to all our self, which includes selfish ambitions, that is if we expect the abundant fruitfulness of a Sanctified, Christlike Life. No one can retain his own selfish ambitions and at the same time be inspired by the noble purposes of Jesus Christ. If He is to live through us, we must die in Him.

NOTES

(11) "FOR WE WHICH LIVE ARE ALWAY DELIVERED UNTO DEATH FOR JESUS' SAKE, THAT THE LIFE ALSO OF JESUS MIGHT BE MADE MANIFEST IN OUR MORTAL FLESH."

The phrase, *"For we which live are alway* (always) *delivered unto death for Jesus' sake,"* explains just how this strange effect is accomplished.

DELIVERED UNTO DEATH?

I am sure it has often been true of all of us, that we have passed through experiences we could not understand. In fact, we can understand only in proportion to our place in the Will of God. Paul understood the *purpose* of his experiences very plainly. He shows that by giving us these statements.

It was God's purpose to display through Paul the excellencies of Christ's Life. The immediate object of this display was the people of Corinth. All of Paul's pains and perils were to be the means of exhibiting to these Corinthians, plus all others as well even unto this hour, the Life of Christ.

Here was life at its highest level. It was not life at its easiest, to be sure. The easy way is not necessarily the best way. In fact, Christianity is not a means of higher self-enrichment. It is the means of reproducing Jesus Christ in our lives as well as others.

The *"death"* spoken of here, refers to dying to self and selfish ambitions. As well, it refers to the death of the flesh, i.e., *"seeking to overcome sin and Satan in our own strength."* Unless this *"death"* is brought about, we cannot have His *"Life."*

"Delivered" in the Greek as it is used here, is *"paradidomi,"* and means *"to surrender, to yield up,"* and reflects that it is done by the Holy Spirit. In other words, the Holy Spirit functions on the premise of obtaining for us the benefits of Calvary. We are literally delivered unto His Death (Rom. 6:3).

The Spirit of God is ever seeking to put down the flesh, which has to do with our own religious efforts to overcome sin and Satan, as well as all personal ambition, etc. This is a constant battle, an ongoing battle, and is *"always"* the case. In other words, no Christian is immune from this procedure, which in effect, continues and will continue until the Lord takes us home.

FOR JESUS' SAKE?

Why is it for Jesus' sake, considering that this is all for us?

The Great Price He paid, was entirely for sinners. In other words, God becoming man, and dying on a Cross for the sins of man, had only one view in mind, that of redeeming the sinner. Heaven did not need such, and neither did the Lord.

For someone to pay such a price, they are certainly desirous that the ones for whom the price was paid, take advantage of that which was done. To not do so, is an insult of the highest order, which regrettably includes most of the world. So, even though all of this was all for us, still, it is also for *"Jesus' sake"* that we live as we live and do as we do. It is to show that His Great Sacrifice was not in vain!

The phrase, *"That the life also of Jesus might be made manifest in our mortal flesh,"* has to do with our physical body, which plays out in our everyday walk before God. As we have stated, Christianity is a practical experience, meaning that it is not some mere lofty sentiment, but rather that which lives itself out in us — in our everyday lives.

THE LIFE OF JESUS

This is not so much speaking of His approximate 33½ years of Life as it is with Him being the Life Source. He Alone can make us what we ought to be. He Alone can give us victory over jealousy, envy, malice, greed, racism, temper, slander, concupiscence, etc. It is all done through the Power of the Holy Spirit as made evident in Romans Chapter 8; however, the Holy Spirit will only function and work according to what Jesus did at Calvary and the Resurrection. He makes those benefits real to us on an everyday basis. It comes by Faith, which demands that we at least understand somewhat that of which He did, which necessitates us understanding the Word of God (Rom. 10:17).

This statement by Paul also refers to the coming Resurrection, but has more to do with our present walk before God.

(12) "SO THEN DEATH WORKETH IN US, BUT LIFE IN YOU."

The idea of this Verse is that Paul as a Minister of the Gospel, was to be an example of what Jesus could do in one's life. The *"death"* here of which the Apostle speaks, concerns the Death of Jesus at Calvary, and its benefits as played out in Paul's life. Consequently, the Corinthians had not only his teaching on this very important subject, but his experiences as well in the realm of overcoming. In other words, he set the example by showing that what Christ did at Calvary worked in his life, and it would work in all others as well. Preachers of the Gospel are to be examples. There is another side to this also.

NOTES

THE PRICE TAG OF TAKING THE GOSPEL TO OTHERS

Any Preacher of the Gospel who properly understands the priority of God in getting the Gospel to the lost, and operates in that capacity, will be opposed by Satan with the greatest ferocity of the Evil One. Paul, of course, was one of the champions of World Evangelism. As such, he suffered opposition from the Powers of Darkness as few men ever have suffered. However, the *"death"* he faced constantly and in every capacity, played out to *"Life"* regarding those who heard and accepted his Message. So, while it was *"death"* to him, it was *"Life"* to these converts. It is no less the same presently.

The Lord has called me as well for the task of World Evangelism. That is my Ministry, my Calling, my Burden, which stays with me 24-hours a day, in fact never leaving. The Lord has called me to preach the Gospel by Television, and given me the Message and the Anointing to preach that Message. It has resulted in untold thousands giving their hearts and lives to the Lord Jesus Christ, for which we give Him all the Glory.

That's the reason we labor extensively to get the Telecast on in every city where it is possible to air the Program. This is what God has called me to do, and for the purpose of reaching lost souls.

A PERSONAL EXAMPLE

Just this morning in Prayer Meeting (July 14, 1998) one of the men of our Church who was present, related to us the following testimony. It had been related to him just a few days earlier by the man to whom this had happened.

The man was on drugs, even as millions are, but to the extent that he was actually facing death. There were needle tracks up and down both arms, and his weight had dropped to below 100 pounds. It was a bondage he could not beat despite trying everything to stop.

In his own words, he related how that he had finally come to a place in his despair that he was going to take his own life plus the lives of his wife and two children. Standing in the middle of the floor with a high-powered revolver in his hands, he changed his mind about taking the lives of his family, and zeroed in on himself.

He put the barrel of this high-powered Magnum in his mouth and was ready to pull the trigger, when he looked up at the Television Set over which our Program was then airing. I was preaching.

In the course of the Message, I said, or words to this effect, *"You must not do, what you are about to do. Jesus Christ is your Answer, He can still set the captive free."*

All of a sudden, as he heard those words, the Power of God came all over him, as he slowly took the gun barrel out of his mouth and his finger away from the trigger. He laid the gun down, and in a few minutes time began to pray with me, as I prayed the sinner's prayer.

In a moment's time his life was changed. The bondage of darkness was broken. The terrible grip of sin was loosened. That horrible monster of drugs which he could not whip, was suddenly gone. The amazing thing about the story is this:

As he stood there telling my dear friend what Jesus had done for him, my friend's testimony, now wondrously saved and Baptized with the Holy Spirit, is much the same. He was saved in pretty much the same way. In fact, we have seen thousands saved in the exact same way as the testimony just given.

That's why Satan will go to any lengths to stop the Gospel of Jesus Christ, and those who proclaim its Message.

Anyone who comes to Christ, the Life they now have in them, was brought about by two great Sacrifices. First of all, the far greater Sacrifice of what Christ did at Calvary and the Resurrection. Second, the lesser Sacrifice (far lesser) of those who have in some way brought the Gospel to them. This is in essence that of which Paul speaks.

(13) "WE HAVING THE SAME SPIRIT OF FAITH, ACCORDING AS IT IS WRITTEN, I BELIEVED, AND THEREFORE HAVE I SPOKEN; WE ALSO BELIEVE, AND THEREFORE SPEAK;"

NOTES

The phrase, *"We having the same Spirit of Faith,"* lends credence to the fact that whatever Satan did, whatever type of hardships there may have been, Paul had Faith in God, that ultimate victory was his. This is the idea of the text.

What holds Paul to his Ministry despite the fact that because of it he is constantly being delivered to death, what makes him think only of the life he is thus able to bring to the Corinthians, is now stated. In effect, he is saying, that he has the same Spirit that David had.

The idea is, nothing deters us. Even if we were tomorrow to be killed by the enemies who want to silence us we would go on speaking (preaching Christ) today.

THE SPIRIT OF FAITH

The phrase, *"According as it is written, I believed, and therefore have I spoken,"* is derived from Psalms 116:10.

When the Psalmist uttered these words, he was greatly afflicted. In these circumstances he prayed to God, and expressed confidence in Him, and placed all his reliance on Him. In his affliction he spoke to God; he spoke of his confidence in Him; he proclaimed his reliance on Him; and his having spoken in this manner was the result of his belief, or of his putting confidence in God.

Paul's circumstances were similar to those of David in these respects:

1. That Paul, like David, was in circumstances of trial and affliction.

2. That the language which both used was that which was prompted by Faith — Faith, which led them to give utterance to the sentiments of their hearts: the Psalmist to utter his confidence in God, and the hopes by which he was sustained, and Paul to utter his belief in the glorious Truths of the Gospel, to speak of a risen Saviour, and to show forth the consolations which were thus set before men in the Gospel. The sentiments of both were the language of Faith. Both, in afflictions, uttered the language of Faith; and Paul uses here, as he often does, the language of the Old Testament, as exactly expressing his feelings, and the principles by which he was actuated. The *"same spirit of Faith,"* is objective Faith, that *"which is believed,"* or *"by which one believes."*

3. *"What we believe"* contains a certain *"spirit,"* and that spirit we *"have"* when we believe. *"The Faith"* is identical in both Testaments; both contain the same Truth, the Old Testament in the form of Promise, the New Testament in the form of fulfillment. Hence, the spirit of both is identical in defying persecution and death.

The phrase, *"We also believe, and therefore speak,"* presents Paul in the face of insurmountable odds, having Faith in God exactly as did David. Consequently, they put words to their Faith. They believed and they spoke what they believed.

AND, THEREFORE, SPEAK

From the manner in which the Holy Spirit delivers this word to us through Paul, I think it is obvious that He is saying, that if we actually do have true Faith, we will speak that which we believe. Until it is *"spoken"* I think one would be hard put to say that it is Faith.

When we speak the words, say what is in our heart, proclaim what we believe God has told us, then and then only is it Faith. Consequently, there is no such thing as a silent Faith, at least in this category.

David said, *"I believe, therefore have I spoken"* (Ps. 116:10), therefore, Paul said, *"We also believe, and therefore speak."* One can only shout *"Hallelujah!"*

Even as David and Paul spoke, and untold numbers other than these two, I want to add my voice to this glorious multitude who exclaims the Faithfulness and Power of God. I have believed, and, therefore, I speak as well.

I believe the Lord has told me that He would heal this Ministry totally and completely. I believe He has also told me, that He is going to send a Moving of the Spirit in these last of the last days, totally unlike anything the world has ever known previously. I believe He has told me as well, that we would be a part of this great outpouring of the Holy Spirit. Even though Apostasy will deepen, and many will turn from God, still, there will be many who will turn to the Lord, and will see great things accomplished and brought about in their hearts and lives.

There are many other things I could say, but due to the fact that they are more personal, I think the Lord would not be pleased. Therefore, suffice to say what we have said, and I say it in Faith, because this is what I believe and, therefore, I speak.

NOTES

(14) "KNOWING THAT HE WHICH RAISED UP THE LORD JESUS SHALL RAISE UP US ALSO BY JESUS, AND SHALL PRESENT US WITH YOU."

The phrase, *"Knowing that He which raised up the Lord Jesus shall raise up us also by Jesus,"* pertains to the coming Resurrection.

THE RESURRECTION

Paul was inspired by the glorious hope of the Resurrection. It accounted not a little for the tremendous power of his life. He saw beyond this life with its frustrations and difficulties into another. He did not think of death as something which frustrated one's labor of life, as it does for those who do not know the Lord.

Death for the Christian merely transfers life and labor into a better and more productive sphere.

It is not bravado that animates Paul's words. Men often laugh at death and imagine that they are heros when they plunge into it. In the case of Paul the Resurrection of the Blessed removes all fear of temporal death. The idea is, that a Resurrection is coming, in which He Who raised up the Lord Jesus will raise us up also with Jesus.

The one fact is passed (the Resurrection of Christ), the other future (the coming Resurrection of the Saints), but they are connected at both ends.

It is the same God Who did raise up, will also raise up, and it is the same Lord Jesus Who was raised up, with Whom we shall be raised up.

Those who think that Paul changed his mind about the Rapture because of what he said, *"shall raise up us also by Jesus,"* and now no longer expects to live until Christ's return, overlook the fact that Paul faced just what we are facing today: total uncertainty regarding the time of the Rapture, plus, as well, total uncertainty regarding the arrival of death.

The phrase, *"And shall present us with you,"* proclaims the sure knowledge of Paul of far more than their personal Resurrection. They believe and, therefore, speak and work with all their heart to bring others to believe because these others will also attain the Resurrection of the Blessed.

When God, Who raised up the Lord Jesus, presents us together with you as belonging together and does this by raising you and us from the dead, He presents you and us as what we are by virtue of His Grace. It is the highest possible honor when God thus presents anyone.

It actually means, *"to make stand beside."* The opposite is to order away out of God's Presence: *"Depart from Me."*

(15) "FOR ALL THINGS ARE FOR YOUR SAKES, THAT THE ABUNDANT GRACE MIGHT THROUGH THE THANKSGIVING OF MANY REDOUND TO THE GLORY OF GOD."

The phrase, *"For all things are for your sakes,"* records the fact that Jesus died that sinners may be saved, and called Preachers to proclaim this Great Word. All of it is for the sake of sinners. He wants all, a great host, to stand together with us, all to raise the everlasting Psalm of thanksgiving for His Glory.

The phrase, *"That the abundant Grace might through the thanksgiving of many redound to the Glory of God,"* presents God's present purpose as to multiply His Grace in Christ Jesus. This multiplication is to be effected *"by means of the multiplied number,"* of all the Believers who are filled with His Grace by the Ministry. Grace cannot be multiplied in itself; it is multiplied by being put into more and more hearts by Faith.

When we and you stand forth glorified on Resurrection Day, a great symphony of Thanksgiving will rise from our lips. God is now planning His Work of Grace toward this end.

THE THANKSGIVING OF MANY

Here Paul again draws all his readers into fullest union with himself. How sad if any of them will not be among the Blessed number of those standing together at God's side at that day; how glorious that all of them and even still others with them should be in company with Paul and his fellow workers when the final Thanksgiving for God's Glory is raised!

Thus, it is that now *"all these things are because of you,"* on your account for your sakes.

"For all things," pertains to the persecutions and all the delivering over to death which Paul and his helpers endured.

The word *"redound"* here means *"to abound, or be abundant."* It means *"that the overflowing Grace thus evinced in the Salvation of many would so abound as to promote the Glory of God."*

NOTES

PREDESTINATION?

While predestination is a viable Biblical doctrine, that is if understood correctly, this passage shoots down the incorrect interpretation of this word which is said to proclaim the fact that some are predestined by God to be eternally lost while others are to be eternally saved. The structure of the Greek Text lends no credence whatsoever to that erroneous conclusion.

The idea is, for God to receive Glory regarding His *"Abundant Grace,"* there must be an abundant number of people who accept that Grace. Inasmuch as it is *"Abundant Grace,"* its very nature demands an *"abundant number."* The more who receive, for that is the way Grace is designed, the more Glory there is for God.

All will conclude one mighty day, with a throated roar of *"thanksgiving,"* for this *"Great Salvation"* afforded by Jesus Christ.

Like Paul's Master he suffered all *"these things"* for their sakes, that Grace might abound to them, and that they might have a life of joy and thanksgiving; but all the Glory of such Grace should be wholly given to God and nothing attributed to him (Williams).

(16) "FOR WHICH CAUSE WE FAINT NOT; BUT THOUGH OUR OUTWARD MAN PERISH, YET THE INWARD MAN IS RENEWED DAY BY DAY."

The phrase, *"For which cause we faint not,"* presents the same thing he said in Verse 1.

With such an object in view, and sustained by such elevated purposes and desires, then the purpose of trying to save as many as possible would make toil easy, privations welcome, and would be so accompanied by the Grace of God, as to gird the soul with strength, and fill it with abundant consolations.

Despite all the problems, all the difficulties, the near death experiences, Paul was not discouraged. What a testimony!

The phrase, *"But though our outward man perish,"* presents the Apostle as not being blind to what was happening to him regarding the persecutions, etc. He has stated it at length in Verses 8 and 9 and now restates it with a condition of reality: *"Even if our outward man is being destroyed."*

NOTES

THE OUTWARD MAN

By *"outward man,"* Paul evidently means the physical body. By using the phrases, *"the outward man"* and *"the inward man,"* he shows that he believed man was made up of two parts, the *"outward"* being the physical body, and the *"inward"* being the soul and the spirit. Paul here describes these two parts as constituting man, so distinct, that while the one perishes, the other is renewed; while the one is enfeebled, the other is strengthened; while the one grows old and decays, the other renews its youth and is invigorated.

Of course, the soul and the spirit are not dependent on the body for their vigor, since they expand while the body decays; and, as well, the soul and the spirit may exist independently of the body, and in a separate state, even as they shall as previously stated, when the Lord calls us home.

Irrespective as to how much Faith a Believer may have, nevertheless, the physical body, as time goes on, will grow old, become weak and feeble and lose its vigor under the infirmities of advancing years. It is a characteristic of the *"outward man"* that it thus perishes. Great as may be its vigor in its youth, yet it must decay and die. It cannot long bear up under the trials of life, wear and tear of constant action, and must soon sink it to the grave.

The phrase, *"Yet the inward man is renewed day by day,"* presents that which is entirely different from the *"outward man."*

THE INWARD MAN

The soul and the spirit is the undecaying, the immortal part of the human being.

As it is renewed day by day, this means the powers of the mind expand, the courage becomes bolder, the great Truths of the Word of God become clearer, and one is more filled with the joys and triumphs of the Gospel.

This Verse is an ample refutation of the doctrine of evolution, and proves that there is in man something that is distinct from decaying and dying matter, and that there is a principle which may gain augmented strength and power, while the physical body dies.

HOW IS IT RENEWED?

The soul and the spirit are renewed on a day-by-day basis, by prayer, study of the Word of God, and constant praise to the Lord. However, this *"inward man"* is renewed *"day-by-day,"* if the Spiritual nourishment is provided *"day-by-day."*

While such could surely be said for Paul, and all others who follow accordingly, still the sad fact is, there is precious little spiritual nourishment taken in by most modern Christians.

The Truth is that most Christians have no prayer life at all, and very little Bible study. Most go to Church once a week and whatever it is they know about the Bible, and whatever little spirituality there is, is what they encounter in Church, which in most Churches is painfully little.

So, with most Believers (and I exaggerate not), the *"outward man"* is perishing and then, regrettably, the *"inward man"* is perishing as well!

(17) "FOR OUR LIGHT AFFLICTION, WHICH IS BUT FOR A MOMENT, WORKETH FOR US A FAR MORE EXCEEDING AND ETERNAL WEIGHT OF GLORY;"

The phrase, *"For our light affliction,"* presents an interesting outlook by the Apostle.

LIGHT AFFLICTION

One need only look at Verses 8 and 9, along with the *"perils of waters," "perils of robbers," "perils by mine own countrymen,"* and *"perils by the heathen," "in weariness and painfulness,"* etc. (II Cor. 11:26-27), to see what type *"affliction"* of which the Apostle speaks. And yet he calls these things *"feathery lightness,"* for that's what the word means.

I suspect that we would be inclined to call it a dreadful load. But the severest tribulation and affliction are as nothing compared with the Glory awaiting us.

It is not sufficient to say that the affliction was *"light,"* or was a mere trifle; but he says that it was to endure but for a moment. Though trials had followed him ever since he began to make known the Redeemer, and though he had the firmest expectations that they would follow him to the end of life and everywhere (Acts 20:23), yet all this was a momentary trifle compared with the Eternal Glory before him. The word rendered *"light,"* means that which is easy to bear, and is usually applied to a burden.

PAUL'S ATTITUDE AND SPIRIT

Even though the Holy Spirit did desire that Paul enumerate these tribulations and difficulties, even life threatening difficulties, still it was done for a purpose and reason. The idea is not that the tribulations are to be glorified, but rather that the Apostle's outlook be held up as an example. Anyone who can take these types of things in stride cannot be beaten. This is what the Holy Spirit is portraying. He is also saying something else:

The Lord gauges each affliction, allowing Satan only so much latitude. Never think that the Evil One is allowed free rein. His way with the Believer is carefully measured (Job Chpts. 1-2). Of course, the idea on the part of Satan is that we give up and quit, while that on the part of the Lord is that we be taught trust and obedience, and in effect, drawing closer to the Lord. These things are designed by the Lord to draw us ever nearer to Him.

To which we have previously addressed, one may wonder as to why the Lord would see the need of the great Apostle having to endure such. I think the answer is relatively simple for Paul and all of us, for that matter.

Faith must always be tested, and great Faith must always be greatly tested. As well, lacking difficulties, it is so easy for the human being to become quickly lifted up in himself. In fact, the manner of the Lord's leading goes all the way back to the Garden of Eden, which has to do with the Fall of man. It concerns the reason why he fell, which consists of pride, i.e., dependence on self instead of God. So, everything is designed by the Lord in order to cause the Believer to look exclusively to God, and to continuously do so. Unfortunately, troubles and difficulties are the only manner which will sufficiently carry out this task.

The phrase, *"Which is but for a moment,"* presents everything weighed by comparison. In other words, this life, ever how long it may be, is nothing in comparison to eternity, i.e., *"time without end."*

BUT FOR A MOMENT

Whatever affliction we face in this earthly life is nothing compared to the Glory we will experience after this earthly life is complete. This Verse contains an interesting Hebraism which is typical of Jewish superlatives.

NOTES

Paul actually used the same word, *"hyperbole,"* twice as a way of saying *"excess on top of excess."* Naturally, the affliction does not seem light when a person is facing it; however, it must be compared with the *"excessively excessive Glory"* that will result later. Regarding time, it is a moment when contrasted with eternity. Regarding magnitude, it is very light when contrasted with that which is very weighty. Regarding character, it is affliction contrasted with Glory (Rossier).

"Moment" in the Greek as used here is *"pararrhueo,"* and means *"to flow by, to carelessly pass."* In other words, when we arrive in the Glory, we will look back and it will leave so little impression that it may be called levity itself.

The Greek word used here occurs no where else in the New Testament. It qualifies the word *"light,"* and is used in the sense of that which is momentary, transient. Consequently, the Holy Spirit, through the Apostle, is expressing two ideas in as emphatic a manner as possible:

1. That the affliction is *"light,"* irrespective as to what it may be, and we should think of it accordingly.

2. It is transient, momentary, and will soon pass away.

The phrase, *"Worketh for us,"* means exactly what it says, it's for our good.

WORKETH FOR US

The effect of these afflictions is to produce eternal glory. This they do according to the following:

1. By their tendency to wean us from the world.

2. To purify the heart by enabling us to break off from sins on account of which God afflicts us.

3. By disposing us to look to God for consolation and support in our trials, in other words, to learn to depend on Him completely.

4. By inducing us to contemplate the Glories of the heavenly world, and thus winning us to seek Heaven as our home.

5. Because God has graciously promised to reward His people in Heaven as the result of their bearing trials (bearing them properly) in this life. It is at least partly by affliction that He purifies us (Isa. 58:10), and by trial that He takes our afflictions from the objects of time

and sense, and gives them a relish for the enjoyments which result from the prospect of perfect and Eternal Glory. In other words, to cause us to look forward to that coming time with tingling anticipation.

The phrase, *"A far more exceeding,"* contrasts the there and then with the here and now.

Greek Scholars say this is the most energetic expression found in the New Testament.

EXCEEDING

In the New Testament this word means *"excess, excellence, eminence."* The entire phrase means *"exceedingly, supereminently"* (Rom. 7:13; I Cor. 12:31; II Cor. 1:8; Gal. 1:13).

This expression would have been by itself seemingly sufficient. But it was not sufficient to express Paul's sense of the Glory which is laid up for Believers. So he uses a greater superlative, in effect coining an expression, *"far more exceeding."* In other words, it is not merely eminent, but it is eminent into eminence; excess unto excess; a hyperbole unto hyperbole — one hyperbole heaped on another; and the expression means that it is *"exceedingly glorious, glorious in the highest possible degree."*

The idea is that, in the Glory, Believers although passing from one degree to another, from one sublime height to another, but still, an infinity remains beyond. It will never be exhausted.

Consequently, nothing can describe the uppermost height of that Glory; nothing can express its infinitude.

The phrase, *"And eternal weight of Glory,"* stands in contrast with the affliction that is for a moment. The one is momentary, transient — so short, even the longest life, that it may be said to be an instant; the other has no limits to its duration. It is literally everlasting.

WEIGHT OF GLORY

This *"weight of Glory"* stands opposed to the *"light affliction."* That was so light that it was a trifle. It was easily borne. It was like the most light and airy objects which constitute no burden at all. Consequently, *"affliction"* as Paul uses the word is not even here called a burden, or said to be heavy to any degree.

On the other hand, Paul likens the Glory as *"weight"* which in the Greek means *"abundance, extent, depth."* It does not at all carry the idea of a heavy load to be borne, but rather the very opposite, that to be immensely enjoyed. It is speaking of the overabundance of Glory which will be *"eternal."* It refers here to the splendor, magnificence, honor, and happiness of the coming eternal world.

In this exceedingly interesting passage which is worthy of the deepest study by Christians, Paul has put in most beautiful and emphatic contrast, the trials of this life and the glories of Heaven (Barnes).

When we reach that Glory, we shall wonder why we ever even sighed during the Tribulations; we shall then say, if the Tribulation has been a thousandfold greater and longer, it would even then have amounted to no more than lightness, at least when compared to this Glory.

(18) "WHILE WE LOOK NOT AT THE THINGS WHICH ARE SEEN, BUT AT THE THINGS WHICH ARE NOT SEEN: FOR THE THINGS WHICH ARE SEEN ARE TEMPORAL; BUT THE THINGS WHICH ARE NOT SEEN ARE ETERNAL."

The phrase, *"While we look not at the things which are seen,"* refers to this present world, and the trials and tests we presently endure.

THINGS WHICH ARE SEEN

Emphatically the Holy Spirit is telling us through the Apostle not to get our eyes on the present difficulties. In fact, that is what Satan desires to do — to cause us to become so engrossed in our present problems, that we will get discouraged and quit. Consequently, the design of this is to show in what way the afflictions which are endured become in our view light and momentary. It is by looking to the glories of the future world, and thus turning away our attention from the trials and sorrows of this life.

If we look directly at our trials — if the mind is fixed wholly on them, and we think of nothing else — they often appear heavy and long, even more than we can bear. But if we can turn away the mind from them, and contemplate future glories; if we can compare them with eternal blessedness, and feel that they will introduce us to perfect and everlasting happiness, they will appear to be transitory, and will be easily borne. As a result, Paul here has stated the true secret of bearing trials with patience.

NOTES

It is to look at the things which are unseen, to anticipate the glories of the heavenly world.

What are the things which are seen?

They are the things of this life — poverty, want, care, persecution, trial, etc. To regard them and to let them fill our eyes and our hearts is folly. Their brief season will soon be over, at least for the Child of God.

Tragically, the only thing the unredeemed can look to is this present world. That's the reason to them that life has little meaning. Consequently, pain is a bandit of the soul — a bandit that robs them of pleasure, because pain in one way or the other is always with us.

The phrase, *"But at the things which are not seen,"* presents a brand-new explanation of life.

THINGS NOT SEEN

There is something exceedingly sensible about this. It is the reverse of the usual idea about life. Materialism bases its hopes on what is tangible to the five senses, yet everything we touch ultimately crumbles and everything we see ultimately passes away. Only that which Faith sees, and sees from the Word of God, is eternal. Consequently, the Christian bases his hopes on the unseen. This and this alone will last. It will endure when all else fades and fails. Money, time, and talent invested in the unseen will remain, while all of that invested in that which we see, will soon perish.

However, this does not mean to suggest that for the rest of our natural lives we should sit down and stare off into space. We are still in a world of practical reality. While we handle that which is *"seen,"* we do it in the spirit of the *"unseen."* While we build houses, mend clothes, and keep books, we do it with the devotion of the unseen. Thus, we transfer the material into the spiritual and the seen into the unseen and the temporal into the eternal.

If we glorify our present difficulties and troubles as Paul is doing here, and magnify labor in the light of these facts, life will then hold a different meaning, even as the Holy Spirit intends.

What are the things which are not seen?

It is the glories of Heaven. It is the eternal Presence of God, which within itself is of such magnitude as to be beyond comprehension. It is the privilege of being close to the Person of Jesus Christ, the One Who redeemed us, and to be with Him forever and forever. It is the privilege of living in an environment free from want, care, poverty, pain, loneliness, death, dying, sickness, hunger, disease, aging, jealousy, murder, racism, envy, malice, etc. It is a place free of sin.

As well, it is a tangible place, that which is real, even material. Revelation Chapters 21 and 22 give us a general idea of what it is going to be like. To be frank, it is beyond compare, but yet it is guaranteed.

Not only is all of this given to the redeemed, plus that which I could not even remotely begin to relate, but as well, it will be eternal. In other words, it will be *"forever and forever."* While they are unseen, still they definitely are real, and will be ours momentarily. Jesus said so (Jn. 14:1-4).

The phrase, *"For the things which are seen are temporal,"* presents an emphatic statement by the Holy Spirit.

TEMPORAL

"Temporal" in the Greek is *"proakairos,"* and means *"for the occasion only, temporary, for a while, to endure for a time, for a season."*

Even though Paul is addressing things which may be suffered, still, it is true of all things that pertain to this present world. Those of the world strive for Power, Pleasure, and Profit; however, for the few who do get such, it is only temporary. They will all soon vanish away. So will the pain, sorrow, and tears, at least for the Child of God. All that we enjoy, and all that we suffer here must soon vanish and disappear. The most splendid palace will decay; the most costly edifice will ultimately molder to dust. The most magnificent city will fall to ruin; the most exquisite earthly pleasures will soon come to an end; and the most extended possessions can be enjoyed but for a little time.

On the other side, for the Child of God, the acutest pain will soon be over; the most lingering disease will soon cease; the evils of the deepest poverty, want, and suffering will soon be past.

There is nothing on which the eye can fix, nothing the heart can desire here, which will not soon fade away; or if it survives, it is temporary in regard to us. We must soon leave it to others; and, if enjoyed, it will be enjoyed while our bodies are slumbering in the grave,

NOTES

and our souls engaged in the deep solemnities of eternity.

How foolish, then, to make these our portion and to fix our affections supremely on the things of this life! How foolish also to be very deeply affected by the trials of this life, which at the furthest can be endured but a little longer before we shall forever be beyond their reach! (Barnes)

The phrase, *"But the things which are not seen are eternal,"* pertains to the things of God.

ETERNAL

The Greek word for *"eternal"* is *"aionios."* Its roots in the Old Testament concept form the background for the New Testament teaching involving this word. It means *"that which is forever, everlasting."*

In the New Testament, *"eternal"* and *"eternity"* come into focus. Essentially, the eternal is that which is not limited by time. The eternal has no beginning and no end but stands outside of and beyond time.

God is like this. His Nature (Rom. 1:20) and His Purposes (Eph. 3:11) are timeless, for He created the material universe and set in motion the processes by which time is measured.

Paul points out that everything that can be seen is temporary. It is subject to change within the flow of time's passing stream. But there are realities that exist outside of and uncorrupted by time — realities not perceived through the senses. *"For what is seen is temporary, but what is unseen is eternal."*

The Christian makes a commitment to act on the basis of the conviction that what cannot be seen has far greater reality than the things that can be seen. Thus, we live as citizens of an eternal kingdom (II Pet. 1:11). We accept by Faith an Eternal Life (Mat. 25:46), won in an Eternal Redemption (Heb. 9:12). We are sure that because of Jesus we are no longer in danger of going to Hell and being eternally lost.

Faith hears God's Word announce unseen, but eternal realities, and then believes.

And when all these things are contemplated, well might Paul say of the things of this life — the sorrows, trials, privations, and persecutions which he endured — that they were *"light"* and were *"for a moment."* How soon will they pass away! How soon shall we all be engaged amidst the unchanging and eternal realities of the things which are not seen!

NOTES

THE DUTY OF THE PREACHER OF THE GOSPEL

Even though these statements as given by Paul apply to the entirety of the Body of Christ, still, the basic foundation of this Fourth Chapter pertains more so to Preachers of the Gospel.

Ministers of the Gospel have no cause to faint or to be discouraged. Whatever may be the reception of our Message, and whatever the trials to which we may be subjected, yet there are abundant sources of consolation and support in the Gospel which we preach. We have the consciousness that we preach a system of Truth; that we are proclaiming that which God has revealed; and if we are faithful, that we have His smiles and approval.

Even, therefore, if men reject and despise our Message, and if we are called to endure many privations and trials, we should not faint. It is enough for us that we proclaim the Truth which God loves, and that we meet with Him approbation and smiles. Trials will come in the Ministry as everywhere else, but there are also peculiar consolations. There may be much opposition and resistance to the Message, but we should not faint or be discouraged. We must do our duty and commit the result to God.

In other words, the Lord has not called us to be successful, but rather to be faithful.

THE SUSTAINING POWER OF CHRIST

We have in this Chapter an illustration of the sustaining power of the Lord Jesus Christ in the midst of trials. To be sure, Christians have been called upon to endure every form of suffering. Poverty, want, tears, stripes, imprisonments, and deaths have been our portion. We have suffered under every form of torture that men could inflict upon us. And yet, the Power of Christ has never failed us. It has been amply tried, and has shown itself able to sustain us always, and to enable us always to Triumph.

Though troubled, we have not been so close pressed that we have no room to turn; though perplexed, we have not been without some resource; though persecuted by men, we have not been forsaken by God; though thrown down in the conflict, yet we have recovered our strength, and been prepared to renew the fight, and to engage in new contentions with the foes of God.

Who can estimate the value of an experience like this? Who does not see that it is adapted to man in a state of trial, and that it furnishes him with everything he needs in this world?

LIKE CHRIST

Christians should be willing to endure anything in order that we may become like Christ on earth, and be like Him in Heaven. It is worth all our efforts and our self-denials. It is the grand object before us; and we should deem no sufferings too severe, no self-denial or sacrifice too great, if we may become like Him here below, and may live with Him above.

THE INFLUENCE OF OUR HOPE

Under the influence of this hope and expectation of eternal life, Paul was willing to encounter any danger and to endure any trial, and so must we. The prospect of being raised up to Eternal Life and Glory was all that was needed to make trials welcome, and to uphold him and us in the midst of privations and toils. And so we, if we are assured of this great Truth, shall face whatever we must face, and shall be able to endure afflictions and persecutions. They will soon be ended; and the Eternal Glory in the morning of the Resurrection shall be more than a compensation for all that we shall endure in this life.

Christians should have such a belief in the Truth of their experience in Christ as to be willing to speak of it at all times, and in all places. If we have such a belief, we shall be willing to speak of it. We cannot help it. We shall so see its value, and so love it, and our hearts will be so full of it, and we shall see so much of the danger of our fellowmen in their lostness without God that we shall be instinctively prompted to go to them and warn them of their danger, and tell them of the Glories of the Redeemer.

THE BEARING OF AFFLICTIONS

We learn from this Chapter how to bear affliction in a proper manner. It is to be looking at eternity and comparing our trials with the eternal weight of Glory that awaits us. In themselves, afflictions often seem heavy and long. Human nature is often ready to sink under them. The powers of the body fail, and the mortal frame is crushed. The day seems long while we suffer; and the night seems often to be almost endless. But compared with eternity, how short are all these trials!

NOTES

Compared with the weight of Glory which awaits the Believer, what a trifle are the severest sufferings of this life. Soon the ransomed spirit will be released and will be admitted to the full fruition of the joys of the world above. In that world, all these sorrows will seem like the sufferings of childhood, that we have now almost forgotten, and that now seem to us like trifles.

How vain and foolish, therefore, the attachment to earthy objects! How important to secure an interest in that future inheritance which shall never fade away! (Barnes)

That's why Paul said, *"We walk by Faith, not by sight"* (II Cor. 5:7).

"Beyond the sunset, oh blissful morning,
"When with our Saviour Heav'n is begun.
"Earth's toiling ended, O Glorious dawning; beyond the sunset when day is done."

"Beyond the sunset, no clouds will gather,
"No storms will threaten, no fears annoy;
"Oh day of gladness, oh day unending, beyond the sunset eternal joy!"

"Beyond the sunset a hand will guide me
"To God, the Father, Whom I adore;
"His Glorious Presence, His words of welcome, will be my portion on that fair shore."

"Beyond the sunset, oh glad reunion,
"With our dear loved ones who've gone before;
"In that fair homeland we'll know no parting, beyond the sunset forevermore!"

CHAPTER 5

(1) "FOR WE KNOW THAT IF OUR EARTHLY HOUSE OF THIS TABERNACLE WERE DISSOLVED, WE HAVE A BUILDING OF GOD, AN HOUSE NOT MADE WITH HANDS, ETERNAL IN THE HEAVENS."

The phrase, *"For we know,"* presents the accent of certainty found only in Bible writers.

The reason for their certitude is the inspiration afforded by the Holy Spirit. In other words, even though Paul and other writers were the instruments, the Holy Spirit was the Author.

NOTES

A SURE KNOWLEDGE

Outside of God and His Word there is no certitude of anything. Those without Christ have no knowledge of life beyond death. In fact, to them death ends it all, and if somehow they think it doesn't, still they have no sure word whatsoever respecting eternity.

While these questions definitely are in the heart of man, still, they have no knowledge as to what exactly that world holds, irrespective of their intelligence or education in this world. It is only those who know the Lord who have a knowledge of eternity, Heaven, Hell, the judgment, eternal life or eternal damnation. We can say for a certainty, *"we know!"*

In fact, the expression *"we know"* is the language of strong and unwavering assurance. Paul had no doubt on the subject of eternity. And it proves that there may be the assurance of Eternal Life; or such evidence of acceptance with God as to leave no doubt of a final admission into Heaven.

This language was often used by the Saviour in reference to the Truths which He taught (Jn. 3:11; 4:22) and it is used by the Sacred writers, as stated, in regard to the Truths which they recorded, and in regard to their own personal piety (Jn. 21:24; I Jn. 2:3, 5, 18; 3:2, 14, 19, 24; 4:6, 13; 5:2, 15, 19-20).

When Paul used the phrase *"we know,"* it was not in the sense of *"you do not know."* The fact is that all true Christians know what is so comforting and strengthening for all of us, that our true home is with the Lord. Yet it is only by way of an application, accepting Christ, that one can add, *"we, too, know,"* to Paul's *"we know."*

EARTHLY HOUSE

The phrase, *"That if our earthly house,"* refers to the physical body, as the habitation, or the dwelling place, of the spirit and soul. It refers to that which is *"upon earth, terrestrial, belonging to the earth, or on the earth"*; and is applied to physical bodies, (I Cor. 15:40).

The phrase, *"Of this Tabernacle,"* does not present a mere redundancy, i.e., *"earthly house."* The idea is, that this tabernacle or *"tent"* is not permanent. It was set up for a temporary purpose. It refers here to the body as the frail and temporary abode of the soul and spirit.

In fact, the idea is a beautiful one, that the body is a mere unfixed, movable dwelling place; liable to be taken down at any moment, and not designed, any more than a tent is, to be a permanent habitation. (Tabernacle in the Greek means *"tent."*)

The phrase, *"Were dissolved,"* actually refers to death.

DISSOLVED

"Dissolved" in the Greek is *"kataluo,"* and means, *"to throw down, to destroy, come to nought."* It refers to the human body dying and going back to dust.

In the previous Chapter, Paul referred to *"this tabernacle"* as the *"outward man."* There it is perishing, while here it is dissolving, which is the same. The tragedy is, mankind spends almost all his energy, time, and attention, on that which is perishing and dissolving, and next to nothing on the *"inward man,"* this *"Building of God,"* which is eternal. In fact, I think one can say without exaggeration, that most Christians fall into the same category.

Too much time and attention are lavished on that which is perishing, and too little on that which is eternal.

A BUILDING OF GOD

The phrase, *"We have a Building of God,"* refers to the Glorified body which all Saints will gain at the Resurrection and have for all eternity. It will be incorruptible and immortal.

When he says it is a *"Building of God,"* he evidently means that it is made by God; that He is the architect of that future and eternal dwelling.

The phrase, *"An house not made with hands,"* means that it is not constructed by man whatsoever. This coming habitation is not like those which are made by human skill, and which are, therefore, easily taken down or removed, but one that is made by God Himself.

This does not imply that this *"earthly house"* which is to be superseded by that in Heaven is made with hands, for it isn't. But it does mean that this *"earthly house"* is temporary, frail, easily taken down, and removed. But that which is coming, is permanent, fixed, eternal, as if made by God, and in fact, definitely made by God.

The phrase, *"Eternal in the heavens,"* actually means that this coming Glorified Body will last and live forever. The future body shall never be taken down or dissolved by death. It is eternal, of course, only in respect to the future, and not in respect to the past.

As well, this eternal body is never to be subjected to sin, suffering, or death. Those things will have forever been done away.

This Coming Glorified Body will be like the one Christ now has (I Jn. 3:2).

"IF," AS IT CONCERNS THE RAPTURE

In the first part of this Verse Paul used the word *"if"*; however, it is not meant to suggest if these things will take place, but rather if he would still be physically alive at the Resurrection of the Church or if his body will already be dead.

Paul practiced a sound balance relative to death and Resurrection. He looked for the latter to occur at any moment, but he also realized that it might not transpire during his earthly lifetime. It obviously did not. We would all be wise to develop this same Scriptural balance about death and Resurrection (Rossier). When the Rapture will happen we do not know, but that it will happen, of that we are certain. In other words, *"we know!"*

(2) "FOR IN THIS WE GROAN, EARNESTLY DESIRING TO BE CLOTHED UPON WITH OUR HOUSE WHICH IS FROM HEAVEN:"

The phrase, *"For in this we groan,"* speaks not of that which is temporary, but rather a continuous *"groaning."* The *"groaning"* is due to the life here, the longing to the Glory beyond. The sense is simple and clear: in our present life and existence, filled, as they are, with affliction, we can only groan and long to enter this Blessed, heavenly existence which is prepared and awaiting us.

GROANING

"Groan" in the Greek is *"stenazo,"* and means *"to be in straits, to sigh."*

The idea is not in complaining about one's present lot, for the entirety of the Text proclaims the very opposite, but rather the seeing by Faith that which is to come, and, thereby, longing for it to arrive.

NOTES

As well, it certainly does not mean that one wants to die, for that is not the idea at all, but rather that there is no fear of death for the Believer, considering that the Lord will usher him into the Glory beyond. Actually, this is the tenor of the Text.

The phrase, *"Earnestly desiring to be clothed upon with our house which is from heaven,"* concerns the coming Resurrection when the corruptible shall put on incorruption, and the mortal will put on immortality (I Cor. 15:53). If one knows what will be, and we do know from the Word of God, then one looks forward to such with tingling anticipation.

The *"house"* of which Paul here speaks is the *"house not made with hands, eternal in the heavens."*

In the last Chapter as well as this Chapter and as is obvious, Paul blows to pieces the bankrupt theory of evolution. Even though the following only touches a part of the evolutionary lie, the fossil record, perhaps the information contained therein will be helpful. For other information on evolution please see our Commentary on the Gospel according to John Chapter 1.

EVOLUTION

Creationists and other nonevolutionary Scientists argue that evolution cannot logically be considered factual apart from any real evidence: *"all the hard data in the life sciences show that evolution is not occurring today, all the real data in the earth sciences show it did not occur in the past, and all the genuine data in the physical sciences show it is not possible at all."* Nevertheless, despite evidence to the contrary, evolution is almost universally excepted as a fact in all the natural sciences.

Consider the comments of the late Canadian Scholar, Arthur C. Custance, Ph. D. in Anthropology and author of the Seminal 10-Volume *"The Doorway Papers."* He was a member of the Canadian Physiological Society, a fellow of the Royal Anthropological Institute, and a member of the New York Academy of Sciences. In *"Evolution: An Irrational Faith,"* he observes, *"virtually all the fundamentals of the orthodox evolutionary faith have shown themselves either of extremely doubtful validity or simply contrary to fact.*

"So basic are these erroneous (evolutionary) assumptions that the whole theory is now

NOTES

largely maintained 'in spite of' rather than 'because of' the evidence. As a consequence, for the great majority of students and for that large ill-defined group, 'the public' it has ceased to be a subject of debate. Because it is both incapable of proof and yet may not be questioned, it is virtually untouched by data which challenges it in any way. It has become in the strictest sense irrational. Information or concepts which challenge the theory are almost never given a fair hearing."

THE FOSSIL RECORD

What about all the alleged evidences for evolution? It is generally admitted that the fossil record contains the most cogent evidence for the evolution hypothesis. So, if we discover this evidence to be nonexistent, then perhaps the other alleged evidences don't exist either. (In fact, they don't.)

The fossil record is continually heralded as *"proof"* of evolution and conceded to offer the primary scientific evidence that evolution has really occurred.

In attempting to prove evolution by the fossil record, eminent French Biologist and Zoologist, Pierre P. Grasse correctly points out:

"Zoologists and Botanists are nearly unanimous in considering evolution as a fact and not a hypothesis. I agree with this position and base it primarily on documents provided by paleontology (the fossil history of the living world).

"Naturalists must remember that the process of evolution is revealed only through fossil forms. A knowledge of paleontology is, therefore, a prerequisite; only paleontology can provide them with the evidence of evolution and reveal its course of mechanisms. Neither the examination of present beings, nor imagination, nor theories can serve as a substitute for paleontological documents.

"If they ignore them, Biologists, the philosophers of nature, can only indulge in numerous commentaries and can only come up with hypotheses. This is why we constantly have recourse to paleontology, the only true science of evolution . . . the true course of evolution is and can only be revealed by paleontology."

Thomas Huxley also realized the importance of this issue when he wrote, *"If it could be shown that this fact (gaps between widely distinct groups) had always existed, that fact would be fatal to the doctrine of evolution."*

Now let's look further at the fossil record as proof of evolution.

TIME

The problem here is how evolutionary theory can ever be demonstrated when it necessarily postulates immense periods of time. It can't. Here, Biologist Theodosius Dobzhansky criticizes Creationists for asking evolutionists to do the impossible, that is, provide real evidence for the occurrence of evolution. But to our way of thinking, he only points out that the theory of evolution should not be accepted as a proven scientific fact, as no Scientists have ever lived long enough to observe the evolution of major life forms.

He said, *"These evolutionary happenings are unique, unrepeatable, and irreversible. It is as impossible to turn a land vertebrate into a fish as it is to effect the reverse transformation. The applicability of the experimental method to the study of such unique historical processes is severely restricted by the time intervals involved, which far exceed the lifetime of any human experimenter. And yet, it is just such impossibility that is demanded by anti-evolutionists when they ask for 'proofs' of evolution which they would magnanimously accept as satisfactory."*

We beg to disagree with Dr. Dobzhansky. If Scientists cannot observe evolution as ever having taken place, how can they categorically state evolution is a fact of science? They attempt to do so by pointing to the fossil record as claimed by Dr. Grasse. They believe it provides the critical evidence for evolution by preserving the record of the past that demonstrates gradual evolutionary change has occurred between the lower and higher life forms.

But even Darwin was concerned about the fossil record. In thinking the geologic record incomplete, Darwin himself confessed the following: *". . . (Since) innumerable transitional forms must have existed, why do we not find them imbedded in countless numbers in the crust of the earth? (And) Why is not every geological formation and every stratum full of such intermediate lengths? Geology assuredly does not reveal any such finely graduated organic change; and this perhaps is the most obvious and gravest objection which can be urged against my theory."*

Again, Darwin asked, *"... Why if species have descended from other species by insensibly fine gradations, do we not everywhere see innumerable transitional forms?"* And, *"... the number of intermediate and transitional lengths, between all living and extinct species must have been inconceivably great."*

DARWIN

Incidentally, Charles Darwin, the father of modern evolution, reflecting on his work near the end of his life, confessed:

"I was a young man with unformed ideas. I threw out queries, suggestions, wondering all the time over everything; and to my astonishment the ideas took like wildfire. People made a religion of them."

Being bedridden many months before his death, Darwin was often reading. When one visitor asked what it was he was studying, he replied: *"Hebrews, still Hebrews, 'The Royal Book,' I call it."*

After speaking on *"the holiness of God"* and *"the grandeur of this Book,"* Darwin declared: *"Christ Jesus and His Salvation. Is not that the best thing?"*

So I think it is obvious that Darwin renounced his evolutionary prattle in his closing years.

NO EVIDENCE AT ALL

Now, over one hundred years after Darwin's death, despite wild claims, it has become clear that further research has not filled in the unexpected and extensive gaps in the fossil record. This is conceded by many leading evolutionary Scientists as the following citations demonstrate.

Noted Paleontologist Stephen Jaygould of Harvard points out, *"The fossil record with its abrupt transitions offers no support for gradual change... All Paleontologists know that the fossil record contains precious little in the way of intermediate form; transitions between major groups are characteristically abrupt."*

With an estimated 250 million catalogued fossils of some 250,000 fossil species, the problem does certainly not appear to be one of an imperfect record. Nevertheless, many Scientists have claimed that the fossil data are sufficiently complete to provide an accurate portrait of geologic record. However, University of Chicago Professor of Geology, David Raup points out the following: *"Well, we are now about 120 years after Darwin and the knowledge of the fossil records has been greatly expanded. We now have a quarter of a million fossil species but the situation hasn't changed much. The record of evolution is still surprisingly jerky and, ironically, we have even fewer examples of evolutionary transition than we had in Darwin's time...."*

THE TRUTH

Again, the Truth is that the fossil record is composed *entirely* of gaps, not evidence of evolutionary transitions. The claimed transitions, of which there are very few, can all be rationally challenged. This means there isn't even a *single* proven evolutionary transition that exists anywhere in the fossil record. Evolutionary Scientists themselves agree that the fossil record is comprised almost entirely of gaps. How, then can it logically offer Scientific evidence of evolution?

Dr. George Gaylord Simpson who was one of the world's best known evolutionists, and Professor of vertebrate paleontology of Harvard University, in his book, *"The Major Features of Evolution,"* admitted, *"... it remains true, as every paleontologist knows, that most new species, general, and families appear in the record suddenly and are not led up to by known, gradual, completely continuous transitional sequences."*

Perhaps this explains why Dr. Austin Clark, once Curator of paleontology at the Smithsonian Institute in Washington, D. C., wrote in 1928, *"Thus so far as concerns the major groups of animals, the creationists seem to have the better of the argument."*

However, this continues to remain true unto today. In his book, *"Biology, Zoology and Genetics,"* Thompson agrees when he writes, *"Rather than supporting evolution, the breaks in the known fossil record support the creation of major groups with the possibility of some limited variation within each group."*

NO GRADUAL EVOLUTION

In his article *"The Nature of the Fossil,"* Dr. Derek Ager also points out what every informed Scientist knows, that *"if we examine the fossil*

NOTES

record in detail, whether at the level of orders or of species, we find — over and over again — not gradual evolution, but the sudden explosion of one group at the expense of another."

However, Simpson thinks that the fossil record is almost complete for the larger terrestrial forms of North America and yet, he says, *"The regular absence of transitional forms is an almost universal phenomenon among all orders of all classes of animals and analogous categories of plants."*

Consequently, it is not surprising to hear Professor E. J. H. Corner of the Botany Department of Cambridge University say that, although he believes there is evidence for evolution in other fields, *". . . I still think that, to the unprejudiced, the fossil record of plants is in favor of special creation . . . Can you imagine how an orchid, a duck weed, or a palm have come from the same ancestry, and have we any evidence for this assumption? The evolutionists,"* he went on to say, *"must be prepared with an answer, but I think that most would break down before an inquisition."*

EVOLUTIONISTS UNABLE TO PROVIDE SCIENTIFIC DATA

Indeed, if, in the words of several evolutionary Scientists, the fossil record *"fails to contain a single example of a significant transition,"* then we are correct in concluding that paleontological histories of the plants and animals simply do not exist.

Ichthyologist Dr. Donn Rosen, Curator of fish at the American Museum of Natural History in New York, noted that evolution has been *"unable to provide scientific data about the origin, diversity and similarity of the two million species that inhabit the earth and the estimated 8 million others that once thrived."* In fact, this complaint has thus been registered for almost every species of plants, animals, insects, birds, and fish known to man.

Thus, the remark of Stephen J. Gould on Darwin's dilemma remains valid: *"New species almost always appeared suddenly in the fossil record with no intermediate lengths to ancestors in older rocks of the same region."* Dr. Gould even concedes that the lack of fossil evidence is the *"trade secret of paleontology."* He went on to say, *"The evolutionary trees that adorn our textbooks have data only at the tips and nodes of their branches; the rest is inference, however reasonable, not the evidence of fossils . . . Most species exhibit no directional change during their tenure on earth . . . In a local area, a species does not arise gradually by the steady transformation of its ancestors; it appears all at once and 'fully formed.'"*

All this is why Creationist Scientists feel justified in doubting that the fossil record provides any genuine evidence for evolution. For example, Dr. Kurt Wise, who received his Ph.D. in paleontology from Harvard University, in his essay *"The Creation Hypothesis,"* shows that the alleged evidences for evolution in the areas of similarity, are either poorly or not at all explained by evolution, or else better explained by creation.

OUGHT TO BE ENTIRELY ABANDONED

The fossil evidence is so poor that even the accomplished Swedish Botanist and Geneticist, Nils Heribert-Nilsson made the following confession and offered an amazing alternate theory.

After 40 years of attempting to find evidence for the theory of evolution, he concluded that the task was impossible and that the theory was even *"a serious obstruction to biological research."*

In his 1,200 page book, *"Synthetic Speciation,"* he declared the theory *"ought to be entirely abandoned,"* in part because it *"obstructs — as has been repeatedly shown — the attainment of consistent results, even from uniform experimental material. For everything must ultimately be forced to fit this speculative theory. An exact Biology cannot, therefore, be built up."*

In other words, if evolution is to be considered a true scientific fact, it must be able to explain the origin of developed life forms by recourse to proven methods of evolutionary change. Can it do so?

It would seem that most Scientists who have examined this subject critically are honest enough to say *"No,"* even though they continue to believe in evolution. The problems of natural selection, mutation, and newer theories attempting to explain how evolution occurs are, put simply, too expansive to be resolved by current knowledge. Indeed, some Scientists have confessed there is little hope that any conceivable breakthrough in this area will ever be forthcoming.

NOTES

NOTES

The Truth is, the fossil records, nor any other record of study for that matter, portray any form of evolution even in the slightest degree. The simple fact is, evolution is a farce, with no credible scientific proof whatsoever to give it substance. It is a lie from beginning to end.

The idea that everything has come from nothing is a bit hard to swallow, even for many Scientists. Reflecting Darwin's own concerns, leading evolutionists such as Ernest Mayr have conceded that the idea that systems such as the *"eye," "feather,"* or *"instinct"* could evolve and be improved by random mutations, represents *"a considerable strain on one's credulity."*

The Truth is, that many materialistic Scientists are now being forced to consider God and Biblical ideas concerning the origin of the universe.

WHAT THE BIBLE TEACHES

This is exactly what Romans 1:20 teaches — that the creation itself provides evidence that is clearly seen and understood concerning God's existence. Thus, the evidence for a finely tuned universe has led many to conclude that there must be a mind behind it all. Remarkably, many professed Atheists have been forced by the weight of 20th-Century discoveries in Astronomy and Physics to concede the existence of an intelligent designer behind the creation of the universe.

For example, Paul Davies once a leader for the Atheistic, materialistic world view, now asserts of the universe, *"There is for me powerful evidence that there is something going on behind it all . . . It seems as though somebody has fine-tuned nature's numbers to make the Universe... The impression of design is overwhelming. Further, the laws of Physics themselves seem to be the product of exceedingly ingenious design."*

Astronomer George Greenstein observed, *"As we survey all the evidence, the thought instantly arises that some supernatural agency must be involved. Is it possible that suddenly, without intending to, we have stumbled upon scientific proof of the existence of a Supreme Being? Was it God Who stepped in and so providentially crafted the Cosmos for our benefit?"*

Statements like this could be multiplied many times over. They prove beyond a doubt that the best Science by some of the most brilliant scientific minds leads us back, not to dead matter, but to a living God.

The esteemed late Carl Sagan and other prominent Scientists have estimated the chance of man evolving at roughly one chance in 10 — 2,000,000,000 — 57. In mathematical computations this is a figure with two billion zeros after it. According to what is termed *"Borel's Single Law of Chance,"* this is no chance at all.

Thus, it is not surprising to hear famous Astronomer Sir Fred Hoyle concede that, the chance that higher life forms might have emerged through evolutionary processes is comparable with the chance that a *"tornado sweeping through a junkyard might assemble a Boeing 747 from the material therein."*

Because God has created us as rational creatures, it may even be argued that sin against reason is a sin against God. Scientists should know better. And, generally in their rational moments they do. They know the universe didn't arise from literally nothing. The suppression of Truth is to try and make it seem as if it did. Most Scientists, it seems, prefer to disguise their belief in magic by making the idea of chance origins appear scientific and rational. Why?

Because they do not personally like the consequences of having to seriously consider the implications of a Creator God.

But in the end, a Creator God is our only logically possible explanation for origins. If we reject the laws of logic, we reject everything and all knowledge becomes impossible. But if we accept the laws of logic, as we must, then this leaves us only one valid option for explaining the origin of the universe: Creation by God.

Of course, there is much more going on here than poor Science. In Romans 1:18-25, we are told that the unregenerate deliberately suppresses the Truth of God as Creator. Consequently, the Scripture is clear on the subject: *"And even as they did not like to retain God in their knowledge, God gave them over to a reprobate mind, to do those things which are not convenient"* (Rom. 1:28). (The material on evolution was provided in part by Ankerberg and Weldon, *"Ready With An Answer."*)

(3) "IF SO BE THAT BEING CLOTHED WE SHALL NOT BE FOUND NAKED."

The phrase, *"If so be that being clothed,"* refers to the future Resurrection body, i.e., *"the Glorified Body."*

The phrase, *"We shall not be found naked,"* means that in the coming future state the soul will not be naked; that is, destitute of any body or covering. The present body will be laid aside. It will return to corruption, and the disembodied spirit will ascend at death to God and to Heaven. It will be disencumbered of the body which it has been so long clothed. But we are not thence to infer that it will be destitute of a body, for it will be given a Glorified Body at the Resurrection.

THE INTERMEDIATE STATE

Paul's statements as given here, do not deal so very much with this intermediate state, but rather looks forward to the coming Resurrection. However, many Christians are unclear on the subject respecting the intermediate state between the death of the Christian and the coming Resurrection. Even though the conclusion of that particular state will not be long in coming at the present time, it has involved a considerable period of time for Old Testament Saints, at least as we presently think of time.

The Scriptures teach that there is to be what is properly termed an intermediate state of life between the Christian's earth-life and his heaven-life. It is that phase of his existence which immediately follows death on earth and precedes life in Heaven. That is to say, it is a life in Heaven, but not the final life in Heaven.

By intermediate, we mean something in between. When death occurs to the Christian, it separates him from the temporal, although it does not immediately unite him with the eternal. The immediate effect of death is to release the person (soul and spirit) from the body. That redeemed person is then immediately brought into the presence of Christ. It says in Verse 8 of this Chapter, *"to be absent from the body, and to be present with the Lord."* This present with the Lord is not a bodily presence, because that will not occur until the Resurrection. In other words, we do not receive our new bodies, as Paul is here discussing, until the dead shall be raised incorruptible (I Cor. 15:51-54).

Between the time the body is buried and the time it is resurrected, the Christian is in this intermediate state. Where he is, is described only by such words as we find here, *"to be absent from the body, and to be present with the Lord."*

NOTES

THERE IS NO SUCH THING AS
PURGATORY OR SOUL SLEEP
AS TAUGHT BY SOME

The Bible is not being rightly interpreted when it is claimed to teach either a purgatory of purification or an oblivion of unconsciousness, which claims that when the Christian dies, his soul and spirit sleep in the grave until the Resurrection. Such is not taught in the Bible.

At death, we do not cease to be. In fact, our bodies are only a tent or tabernacle for the real person of the soul and the spirit. The body and the person are as building and occupant. Bodies die and are buried and passed through dissolution (corruption). The occupant moves out, i.e., *"the soul and the spirit."*

Paul is giving us a contrast between our old and our new habitations. He is telling us the difference between our body of corruption and our body of Glory. He calls our body a tabernacle. This tent-body is the one in which we are making our pilgrimage from earth to Heaven. Someday it will be taken down and laid away and covered up. At that time it is to be dissolved, or loosed. It will be loosed from its present form and shape and will return to the elements from which it sprang at the Creation — dust. In its place we will have, not a tent, but a building. The tent was temporary. The building will be eternal. The tent will be left on earth. The building (the Glorified Body, a Building of God) will be eternal. The tent is left on earth. The building will inhabit the heavens. The tent passes through disintegration which reduces it to its original chemical state of common soil. The building possesses the qualities of Christ's Resurrection which are incorruptibility and immortality.

AN INTERVAL OF TIME

Of necessity, there must be an interval of time between our departure from our dissolving earth-body and our inhabitance of our eternal heaven-body. During this interval (between death and the Resurrection) we are in conscious existence, although we are not yet in our Resurrection bodies. However, we are not floating around in space as invisible spirits without the capacity of speech or action. Neither are we asleep or unconscious in a temporary lethargic state. Actually, we are to be very much alive and very near to Christ in soul and spirit form, for the Scripture says, as we have stated, for to be *"absent from the body"* means to be *"present with the Lord."*

To simplify the matter we can put it this way: while death disembodies us, it does not immediately embody us with this *"house not made with hands."* This *"house not made with hands"* is not another temporary body, and for that reason it is called *"eternal."* It is our final habitation, but will not come to realization until the Rapture and the Resurrection.

A NEW DESIRE

This new desire we have, as Paul mentioned in Verse 2, is not the desire for death which dissolves or unclothes the spirit. That would be unnatural. The Christian is looking beyond death for the time when he will be clothed with his new body.

Death as a natural process, is not the hope of the Christian, for death disembodies and disrobes. It is the Resurrection and the Rapture (both are the same) which the new desire longs for, because the Resurrection and the Rapture will bring us this building which is *"an house not made with hands."*

(4) "FOR WE THAT ARE IN THIS TABERNACLE DO GROAN, BEING BURDENED: NOT FOR THAT WE WOULD BE UNCLOTHED, BUT CLOTHED UPON, THAT MORTALITY MIGHT BE SWALLOWED UP OF LIFE."

The phrase, *"For we that are in this tabernacle do groan, being burdened,"* does not pertain to the Christian desiring death, for death is a curse. It answers no questions and settles no problems. However, for the Christian, there is a hope that came through the Death and Resurrection of Christ, our Saviour. It is this hope that sustains us. It is what the Resurrection will accomplish that we yearn for. It is the ultimate answer for all the aspirations of Faith.

Christians are not Stoics, we feel the burden and we groan; not because we are cowards and just want to escape our burden, but because we want to put on the Heavenly life.

NOTES

NO LONGING TO ESCAPE, BUT RATHER A LONGING TO ATTAIN

This is not the idea of the Christian desiring to escape this life, but rather a longing to attain that which is coming. It is not cowardice and neither is it fear, but rather, glorious hope.

There are many who tire of life and it's excessive burden; that is a morbid state which Christians should conquer. Some also quail at the thought of death, but this, too, is not the normal Christian feeling. Worldly men prefer anything to the great vicissitudes of this life and then simply throw life away with a thought that the hereafter (whatever that is, they think) cannot be worse.

However, this negative motive is wholly foreign to Paul and to all true Believers for that matter. When we groan under this heavy burden, the reason is, *"not that we want to put off, but that we want to put on."* We as Believers, unlike the world, know what is coming, and what is coming is so glorious, so far beyond what we presently have, that even though we want to live this present life to the fullest, still, there is an obvious yearning for that which is to come.

The phrase, *"Not for that we would be unclothed,"* means we do not desire to die, nor are we unwilling to bear these burdens as long as God shall appoint. It is not that we merely wish to lay aside this mortal body. We do not desire to die and to part merely because we suffer much, or because the body here is subjected to great trials. This is not the ground of our wish to depart. We are willing to bear trials. We are not impatient under afflictions. The sentiment here is, that the mere fact that we may be afflicted much and long, should not be the principal reason why we should desire to depart. We should be willing to bear all this as long as God shall choose to appoint.

So, the anxiety of Paul to enter the eternal world was from a higher motive than a mere desire to get away from trouble.

The phrase, *"But clothed upon, that mortality might be swallowed up of life,"* refers to putting on immortality, as explained in I Corinthians 15:35-54. This will take place at the Rapture (I Cor. 15:35-54; Phil. 3:21; I Thess. 4:13-16).

CLOTHED UPON

"To be clothed upon" refers to our Spiritual Body. We desire to be clothed with that body.

We desire to be with the Lord, and to be clothed with immortality. We wish to have a body that shall be pure, undecaying, ever glorious and eternal. It is not, therefore, a mere desire to be released from suffering; it is an earnest wish to be admitted to the glories of the future world, and partake of the happiness which he would enjoy there. This is one of the reasons why Paul wished to be in Heaven.

There are other reasons he has stated elsewhere. Thus, in Philippians 1:23 he says he had *"a desire to depart, and to be with Christ."*

And then in II Timothy 4:6-8, he speaks of the *"Crown of Righteousness"* laid up for him as a reason why he was willing to die.

So, *"But clothed upon, that mortality might be swallowed up of life,"* speaks of the coming Resurrection, when this mortal body will be changed to that which is immortal. Paul desired to pass away from the mortal state to one that shall be immortal — a world where there shall be no more death (Barnes).

ORIGIN AND DESTINY

No one can take an indifferent attitude to what the Bible says of our origin and our destiny, and expect in that indifferentism to have an intelligent and practical view of life.

We cannot escape the connection between origin and destiny. We cannot be wrong about one and right about the other. If we mistrust the Bible's declaration about origin, how can we believe what it says about destiny? In the Bible, both are linked together. Origin is contained in a process of creation, while destiny is contained in a process of redemption. The Creator is revealed as the Redeemer.

The materialism of our age would persuade us to believe in an origin of force. The logical end of that kind of a creation is to begin as a beast and to die as a beast; to come out of oblivion and to go out into oblivion; to come up from the soil and to go back to the soil.

The Bible speaks differently. While man's body came up from the soil, because God made it from dust, his soul, or his personality, came down from God. He was made in God's Image and likeness. His creation was after a Divine pattern. Having lost the image of that pattern it produced the necessity of Redemption.

Redemption is man's re-creation after a Divine pattern. Having been created in the Image of God, man is redeemed and regenerated in the Image of God's Son.

NOTES

The spiritual part of that new Image comes through Redemption, while the physical part of that new Image comes through Resurrection (Laurin).

(5) "NOW HE THAT HATH WROUGHT US FOR THE SELFSAME THING IS GOD, WHO ALSO HATH GIVEN UNTO US THE EARNEST OF THE SPIRIT."

The phrase, *"Now He that hath wrought us for the selfsame thing is God,"* means *"this very thing,"* i.e., the thing to which he had referred — the preparation for Heaven, or the Heavenly Dwelling.

WROUGHT

The word *"wrought"* here means, that God has formed, or made us for this; that is, He has by the influences of the Spirit, and by His Agency on the heart, created us, as it were, for this, and adapted us to it. God has destined us to this change from corruption to incorruption; He has adapted us to it; He has formed us for it.

This does not refer to the original creation of the body and the soul for this end; but it means that God, by His Own renewing, and sanctifying, and sustaining agency, has formed us for this, and adapted us to it.

All of this has to do with the Redemption process, which is ever leading toward the coming consummate change which will take place at the Resurrection.

The object of Paul in stating that it was done by God, is to keep this Truth prominently before the mind. In other words, this was in the mind of God from the very beginning. The entire credit belongs to God. He made us what we are and shall be; He did it by giving us His Spirit.

PREDATED

The Christian's assurance of the time when mortality will be swallowed up of life is not postdated. It is, in fact, predated. We have the assurance of that hope now. It is something in which we live. We live for it and He lives by it. It is not something away off in a mystic future, but something within, i.e. *"The Holy Spirit."*

The Resurrection is the consummation of Regeneration. In fact, it is the final phase of God's plan of Redemption. We were redeemed with all of this in mind and God Who is working out this Redemption is in us at this present moment and has not left us without a very definite assurance. He has, in fact, given us a guarantee that we will be brought to the consummation of His plan.

The phrase, *"Who also hath given unto us the earnest of the Spirit,"* presents the guarantee.

THIS EARNEST IS A PLEDGE

The word *"earnest"* means *"surety"* or *"pledge."* A surety is security which one gives for the performance of a promise. It is making one's self legally liable for the performance of a contract. In other words, it is a pledge to consummate what one has commenced.

In Bible times when a man bought a piece of land he would be given a handful of its soil as the assurance of its ultimate possession. In turn he would deposit a consideration of money as the assurance of its ultimate payment.

The earnest money of any transaction or agreement was a part payment of the whole sum promised. It became the pledge to the receiver by the giver that the contract or promise would be carried out in due time. According to Blackstone, the prepayment of a mere penny would legally bind a contract.

THIS PLEDGE IS A PERSON

It is the Holy Spirit Who has been given to us as the pledge.

As a rule, the pledge given and received was the same in kind as the ultimate payment. In this case, the ultimate contract which God made with us was life and the pledge which He has given that He will fulfill that contract is the Person of the Holy Spirit (Jn. 7:37-39).

A pledge is always a preview and a foretaste of what is to come. In this case, we can expect to have the presence of a Heavenly Life on earth.

The Christian is not to pursue his Discipleship merely because he expects to get to Heaven. The end of the Christian life is not only life hereafter. It is life here. It is not a means to an end. It is the end itself. It is something for this world, as well as for the next.

The proof and pledge of this intention is the Presence of the Holy Spirit Who resides in all who are Children of God (I Cor. 3:16).

Here is the ultimate purpose of the Holy Spirit. He is God presently with us. He is God powerfully with us. He is God reverently with us. Let us not prostitute this sacred relationship by fanatical orgies of hysteria and hypocrisies. Let us not treat the Holy Spirit as some phenomenon of emotion which we can reproduce at will in a state of ecstasy. The Holy Spirit is God come to His Temple. He is God as the present guarantee of our coming consummation. He is God Who comes to us the moment we come to Him. He is God as the indwelling Presence of every Christian at the moment of the New Birth.

As such an indweller at such a moment of birth, He is the foretaste of what we shall have and what we shall be at the Resurrection.

IT IS ETERNAL LIFE RIGHT NOW

Because of this fact, Christian experience is not something that merely gives us the expectancy of Eternal Life. It is Eternal Life. It is that right now. It is so because every pledge is the same in kind as the ultimate payment. It is a foretaste of the coming life. Therefore, what we are to be is what we have now. What God is going to do *for* us He is doing *in* us.

The coming physical transformation of the Resurrection has its anticipation in the spiritual transformation of Regeneration. We, who are to be changed into His Likeness, are now being changed *"into the same Image from Glory to Glory, even as by the Spirit of the Lord."*

In this way the Spirit Who is the present pledge of the future Resurrection of the Christian, is also the present power of the daily transformation of the Christian.

A PLEDGE AND NOT A PROMISE

If you will remember that the Holy Spirit is a pledge and not a promise, you will never find yourself in any spiritual difficulty concerning which many err. Even though He was a Promise, and a Promise made by the Heavenly Father, He is not now a Promise to be expected. He is a pledge already given (Acts 1:4).

He was promised and in fulfillment of that Promise, He was given. The Promise thus became a Gift and the Gift a fact. The fact is something to be enjoyed. We do not seek Him but we should yield to Him. We cannot rightfully seek what has already been given, and we should yield and surrender all our faculties and members to His transforming Power.

NOTES

When we do this we will experience that transformation of character which is the anticipation of the transformation of body that will occur at the Resurrection.

THE PRESENT AND THE FUTURE

In this light, the pattern of Christian experience becomes very clear and beautiful. It becomes a complete and glorious picture. It balances the present with the future. It gives the present, in a limited sense, an equality with the future. It puts experience and expectation on the same level. It dignifies the Christian life to the degree of nobility.

We have been told that the only thing of assurance is the present. The future has been described as vague, a fluctuating uncertainty. It is all of this to the natural mind, but not to the Believer. Christianity is a philosophy of Faith which reduces the future to the present. It is not so to sight, of course, but it is so to Faith. It is not something which is going to happen. It has already happened. It has happened in a personal and individual sense.

Notice how confidently Paul spoke of death and what follows. In the First Verse he used the words, *"For we know,"* while in the Sixth Verse he used the words, *"We are always confident."* It is the knowledge and confidence which Paul had.

He did not have all the facts of the experience before him, but he had the Faith of a spiritual experience in him. Until the facts materialize, Faith is sufficient. Faith is *"the highest act of reason"* (Laurin).

(6) "THEREFORE WE ARE ALWAYS CONFIDENT, KNOWING THAT, WHILST WE ARE AT HOME IN THE BODY, WE ARE ABSENT FROM THE LORD:"

The phrase, *"Therefore we are always confident,"* joined with *"for we know"* of Verse One, proclaims a guarantee, and all because of the *"Earnest of the Spirit."*

OF GOOD CHEER

The word *"confident"* means *"to be of good cheer; to have good courage; to be full of hope."*

The idea is, that Paul was not dejected, disheartened, or discouraged, despite the fact of all the difficulties and problems. He was cheerful and happy. He was patient in his trials, and diligent in his calling.

NOTES

As well, this *"good cheer"* was not occasional and transitory, but constant and uniform. In other words, it always existed.

This is an instance of the uniformed cheerfulness which will be produced by the assured prospect of Heaven. It is an instance, too, when the hope of Heaven will enable a man to face danger with courage; to endure toil with patience; and to submit to trials in any form with cheerfulness.

Why not? Irrespective as to what the situation is now, we know that tomorrow a grand change is coming. A change, so prolific, so cataclysmic, so powerful, so total, so glorious, as to defy all description. Therefore, with that prospect, and a guaranteed prospect at that, every Christian ought to be and do exactly what Jesus said, *"Be of good cheer; it is I; be not afraid"* (Mat. 14:27).

The phrase, *"Knowing that, whilst we are at home in the body,"* makes an important distinction between the person and his body.

THE BODY AND THE PERSON

Paul's body was not Paul anymore than your house is you. Paul was a spiritual personality who lived in a physical body just as you live in your house. The body is the vehicle of the soul — the vehicle which makes it possible for the person to act, speak, and live a normal earth-life.

Someday we will have no more use for the body. We will be disengaged from it. We shall go on while it goes back to the soil out of which it came.

The idea that Paul here expresses, is not that of being *"at home"* — for this is an idea which is the very opposite of that which the Apostle wishes to convey. His purpose is not at all to represent the body here as our home, and the original word does not imply that. It means here simply to be in the body; to be present in the body; that is, while we are in the body. In other words, we are dwelling in this present physical body temporarily.

The phrase, *"We are absent from the Lord,"* refers to the Lord Jesus.

WITH THE LORD

In effect, the Apostle is saying that he is in a strange world, and among strangers. His great desire and purpose was to be with the Lord; and hence he cared little how soon the frail tabernacle of the body was taken down, and was cheerful amidst all the labors and sufferings that tended to bring it to the grave, and to release him to go to his eternal home where he would be present forever with the Lord.

But the good courage of Paul and of his associates is not like that of worldly men who face misfortunes and dangers with head erect and flying colors and march right into the jaws of death. They face eternity blindly and rush to their doom. Paul and his associates are not like that, and neither is any Believer.

He has already shown us the solid ground on which his assurance and courage rest. So this does not call for further repetition; it is enough to say how they have come to view their present situation in the light of their assurance regarding death and eternity.

Why should they grow faint and discouraged while in the body, considering they are away from the Lord only for a little while and are soon to join Him forever?

THE FIGURE OF THE TENT

Paul has not dropped the figure of a tent, house, or building, as an habitation which he used in Verses One and Two. He advances it and makes it more personal when he speaks of putting on and putting off. And he does so still more when he uses *"to be at home"* and *"to be away from home."* This is typical of Paul's mind; he sees all the different angles and facets of the thought, all the ways in which he may turn and adapt a metaphor.

One is at home in a house that really belongs to him. The body is a house that belongs to us in its present state, only for the time being; the Heavenly Glory is our everlasting habitation and home.

So Paul says that we have come to know *"that while we are at home in the body,"* in this our distressful earthly existence, *"we are away from home from the Lord,"* away from that blessed existence in the visible company of our Lord, the true home of all God's blessed Children (Lenski).

(7) "(FOR WE WALK BY FAITH, NOT BY SIGHT:)"

The phrase, *"For we walk,"* refers to our daily walk or life before the Lord. It has reference to the fact that life is a journey, or a pilgrimage, and that the Christian is traveling to another country.

NOTES

The sense here is, that we conduct ourselves in our course of life with reference to the things which are unseen, and not with reference to the things which are seen.

The phrase, *"By Faith,"* presents the belief in those things which we do not see. We believe in the existence of certain things which are invisible, and we are influenced by them.

TO WALK BY FAITH

To walk by Faith, is to live in the confident (cheerful) expectation of things which are to come; in the belief of the existence of unseen reality, and suffering them to influence us as if they were seen.

The people of this world are influenced by the things that are seen. They live for wealth, honor, splendor, praise, for the objects which this world can furnish, and as if there were nothing which is unseen, or as if they ought not be influenced by the things which are unseen.

The Christian, on the contrary, has a firm conviction of the realities of the Glories of Heaven; of the fact that the Redeemer is there; of the fact that there is a Crown of Glory; and he lives and acts as if that were all real, and as if he saw it all. The simple account of Faith, and of living by Faith is, that we live and act as if these things were true, which in fact they are, and suffer them to make an expression on our mind according to their real nature. It is the opposite of existing simply under the influence of things which are seen.

GOD

God is unseen — but the Christian lives, and thinks, and acts as if there were a God, which there is, and as if he saw Him. Christ is unseen now by the bodily eye; but the Christian lives and acts as if He were seen; that is, as if His Eye were known to be upon us, and as if He was not exalted to Heaven, and was the only Saviour, in which He is!

As well, the Holy Spirit is unseen; but the Believer lives and acts as if there were such a Spirit, and as if His influences were needful to renew and purify the soul.

Also, Heaven is unseen; but the Christian lives, and thinks, and acts as if there were a Heaven, and as if he now saw its glories. He has confidence in these and in kindred truths, and he acts as if they were real.

FAITH IS EVERYTHING

For this life *"Faith"* is everything, the all-sufficient substitute for *"sight."* It deals with the unseen as if it were the seen: *"seeing it afar off"* as strangers and pilgrims on the earth (Heb. 11:13). By dealing with *"the things not seen"* in this way Faith really has them, and sight will follow.

Even the world, in its worldly affairs, goes on Faith or Trust. If no man trusted another, earth would be an earthly hell. Let men mock at Christian Faith, these very mockers have faith in handling their own affairs. The trouble with the world is that its Faith is in itself and, therefore, misplaced. It trusts where it ought to mistrust, and it mistrusts where it ought to trust, and thus cheats itself both ways.

Take these mockers at Christian Faith: they will not trust Christ and consequently cheat themselves in that way; they do trust in religious fakes and so cheat themselves once more. The Faith by which we walk, as did Paul, rests on the Rock of Ages. Unseen, it holds Christ and Salvation, and soon These shall be fully seen. They who demand sight too soon will also have to wait, but then they shall have more sight than they want, enough to terrify them forever.

There are many ways of being convinced of the existence and reality of objects besides seeing them; and it may be as rational to be influenced by the reason, the judgment, or by strong confidence, as it is to be influenced by sight. Besides, all men are influenced by things which they have not seen. They hope for objects that are future. The aspire to happiness which they have not yet beheld. They strive for honor and wealth which are unseen, and which are in the distant future, if at all!

SO WHY NOT THE CHRISTIAN?

Men live and act concerning the things of this world — influenced by strong faith and hope — as if these things were attainable; and they deny themselves, and labor, and cross oceans and deserts, and breathe in foul air, to obtain those things which they have not seen, and which to them are in the distant future. And why should not the Christian endure like labor, and be willing to suffer in like manner, to gain the unseen crown which is incorruptible, and to acquire the unseen wealth which the moth does not corrupt?

NOTES

And further still, the men of this world strive for those objects which they have not beheld, without any promise of any assurance that they shall obtain them. No being, able to grant them, has promised them; no one has assured them that their life shall be lengthened out to obtain them. In a moment they may be cut off, and all their plans frustrated; or they may be utterly disappointed even as most are, and all their plans fail; or if they gain the object, it may be unsatisfactory, and may furnish no pleasure such as they had anticipated. But not so the Child of God.

THE GUARANTEES OF FAITH

The Faith held by the Believer is of far greater substance than that of the world. Our Faith is of substance regarding the future, simply because of what has preceded us in the past. God has been true to His Word, and the past proves that. Consequently, He will be true to His Word in the future. Of that we can be certain!

The following is that which is promised:

1. The promise of Eternal Life.

2. We have the promise and assurance that sudden death cannot deprive us of Eternal Life. In fact, death will remove us to the object of pursuit, not from it.

3. We have the assurance that when obtained, it shall not disgust, or satiate, or decay, but that it shall meet all the expectations of the soul, and shall be eternal.

The phrase, *"Not by sight,"* refers to these things which we can presently see. It is Faith that controls us, and not sight.

SIGHT?

Until we go on, and while we are here awaiting that summons which will cause us to vacate the body, we walk by Faith. Sight is the common way. Faith is the uncommon way. Sight is the way of flesh. Faith is the way of the Spirit. Sight is the world's way. Faith is the Word's Way. Whatever is common to sight is uncommon to Faith.

Sight relates to the temporal, Faith to the eternal. Sight relates to the seen, Faith to the unseen. Besides this, Faith not only sees the unseen, it also sees the seen. It is a spiritual sense for two worlds. If you walk by Faith, you can walk in two worlds at once, whereas if you walk only by sight, you walk only in this world.

Faith is not only a way to Life, it is a walk through life. Whosoever walks by Faith has the most comprehensive and practical way of life. He is not an impractical religious visionary, as some claim, but one who has linked hands with God.

To walk by Faith does not mean to walk in blindness. It means to walk with another sense of sight. It is not walking in the dark, but walking in the light. It is exchanging eyesight for God-sight.

(8) "WE ARE CONFIDENT, I SAY, AND WILLING RATHER TO BE ABSENT FROM THE BODY, AND TO BE PRESENT WITH THE LORD."

The phrase, *"We are confident, I say,"* once again proclaims the cheerfulness and courage of the Faith-filled Child of God.

THE CHEERFUL BELIEVER

Twice Paul has mentioned *"groaning"* (vss. 2, 4), so now he twice mentions cheerfulness, i.e., *"confident"* (vss. 6, 8).

He who lives a life of Faith and not sight will be able to say *"I know,"* and, *"I am always confident* (cheerful)*,"* for Faith makes Divine facts real, and illumines the mind with certitude.

Satan and men might do their best to destroy the clay-tent in which Paul lived, but that did not trouble him; for he knew he had not a *"tent"* but a *"house,"* a building from God, not made with hands, eternal, in the heavens.

Our longing is to be satisfied by realization. What Faith now embraces as being unseen it shall presently embrace as seen. *"The things not seen"* now (II Cor. 4:18) shall presently turn to things seen.

Certainly, then, we are of good courage as we go on here in the body, walking by Faith. Why should we not be?

The phrase, *"And willing rather to be absent from the body,"* refers to the soul and the spirit escaping this body, which it will do at death. This is what Paul means by being *"absent from the body."* As should be obvious, it does not present a cessation of being or existence, but rather a change of location.

THE WILL OF GOD

"Willing" in the Greek is *"eudokeo,"* and means *"to approve an act, to think well, to approve."* The idea is, that Paul had no personal preference referring to his dying or living, but rather that he wanted the Will of God, whatever that Will may be.

NOTES

He wanted to stay on this earth as long as the Lord desired such, but the moment the Lord wanted otherwise, he wanted that. Such portrays total trust in the Lord, which place the Holy Spirit is attempting to bring all Believers.

Death cannot hold any terror for one like this, and neither can life. Everything is in the Lord. If the situation is difficult at the present time, it is going to change in the near future — and what a change that will be!

This is the only real way to live, which is a life totally guided by Faith — Faith in God. It is truly a *"peace that passeth all understanding."*

The phrase, *"And to be present with the Lord,"* proclaims what the transition will bring.

PRESENT WITH THE LORD

To die and be absent from the body means we go to Heaven to be with the Lord (Phil. 1:21-24; Heb. 12:23; James 2:26; Rev. 6:9-11).

This is proof that the inward man does not go to the grave at death, but to Heaven, that is if one is right with God. If one is wicked he goes to hell awaiting the resurrection of his body, which will take place one thousand years after the Resurrection of Life for Believers (Lk. 16:19-31; Rev. 20:11-15).

The idea of Paul is, that the Lord Jesus would constitute the main glory of Heaven, and that to be with Him was equivalent to being in a place of perfect bliss. He had no idea of any Heaven where the Lord Jesus was not; and to be with Him was to be in Heaven.

The world where the Redeemer is, is Heaven. This also proves that the spirits of the Saints, as we have stated, when they depart, are with the Redeemer; that is, are at once taken to Heaven. This means the following:

1. That they are not annihilated.

2. That they do not sleep, and remain in an unconscious state, as some claim.

3. That they are not in some intermediate state — either in a state of purgatory, as the Papists suppose, or a state where all the souls of the just and the unjust are assembled in a common abode, as some have thought.

4. That they dwell with Christ; they are with the Lord. They abide in His Presence; they partake of His Joy and His Glory; they

are permitted to sit with Him on His Throne (Rev. 3:21).

This is the same idea the Saviour expressed to the dying thief, when He said, *"Today shalt thou be with Me in Paradise"* (Lk. 23:43).

THE SOUL

Some ancient Philosophers taught that at death the soul is absorbed into a universal world-soul. The Bible teaches the very opposite, that we will remain individuals for eternity. Actually, we are at present incomplete individuals, but at the Resurrection we will be made complete, because we will be like Him, *"The Lord Jesus Christ"* (I Jn. 3:2).

What a contrast from the approach of unbelievers who view physical death with absolute terror. James described this earthly life as a vapor or mist (James 4:14), and the Psalmist compared it to a few days full of trouble and sorrow (Ps. 90:9-10). Then he encouraged us to use these days wisely (Ps. 90:11-12).

The Jewish mind considered being without a body as one of the worst things that could happen to an individual. They actually considered that condition as being without a personality. Paul, of course, did not accept that philosophy. Christians know that their spirits are not dependent on physical bodies for this existence.

We need to be careful to develop a Biblical balance relative to this matter. Some contemporaries take the same approach that the ancient Greek Philosophers did and make too sharp a distinction between the physical and the spiritual. They end up actually torturing the human body in order to conquer it.

The Gnostics went even further because they considered all matter to be evil. They even claimed that the God of the Old Testament and the God of the New Testament as two different Beings. That way they could ascribe the creation of *"evil matter"* to some lesser *"god."* This is what happens when people take the separation of the material and the spiritual to an extreme.

At the other end of the spectrum we see people who make no distinction between the physical and the spiritual, and they classify humans as a higher order of *"animals."* The Bible in no instance classifies man as a part of the animal kingdom.

NOTES

The Bible does teach that God will ultimately redeem both body and spirit. The latter occurs at conversion; the former will take place at the Resurrection of the Church. The end result will be redeemed souls and redeemed bodies living in a redeemed universe (Rev. 21:1-5).

(9) "WHEREFORE WE LABOUR, THAT, WHETHER PRESENT OR ABSENT, WE MAY BE ACCEPTED OF HIM."

The phrase, *"Wherefore we labour,"* actually means, *"we are ambitious."* It comes from the combination of *"love* (philos)*"* and *"honor* (time)*,"* so it speaks of the love of something honorable. It was used commonly of *"aim," "ambition,"* or *"purpose"* in a positive sense (Rom. 15:20) (Rossier).

WHEREFORE

By the use of the word *"wherefore"* Paul is speaking of the prospect of a Resurrection and of future Glory. Since we have the assurance that there is a house not made with hands, eternal in the heavens; and since God has given us this hope, and has granted to the earnest of the Spirit, we make it our great object to please the Lord in all things, to be accepted by Him.

The idea is, that this alone is what matters, all else being of no sufficient consequence. John addressed this, the coming Resurrection, by saying, *"Those who have this hope purify themselves even as He is pure"* (I Jn. 3:3).

The thought of approaching nearer and nearer to the Lord and of soon seeing Him face to face, makes us ashamed to do anything that is displeasing to Him, and spurs us on to do everything that is well-pleasing to Him. It is to act merely from the love of honor, but rather, honor that the Lord bestows.

LABOUR

"Labour" in the Greek is *"philotimeomai,"* and means *"eager or earnest to do something, to be ambitious."*

There are two different Greek words translated *"ambition"* in the New Testament. One word is strongly negative, the other just as strongly positive.

SELFISH AMBITION

The word *"eritheia,"* is translated *"selfish ambition"* in Galatians 5:20; Philippians 1:16;

2:3; James 3:14, 16. It appears elsewhere in the New Testament only in Romans 2:8 (*"self-seeking"*) and II Corinthians 12:20 (*"factions"*).

It portrays a contentious struggle for personal profit or power, with no redeeming hint of service to others. Romans 2:8 suggests that such ambition demonstrates not only a wrong attitude but also wrong goals. Selfish ambition battles others for immediate gains and empty honors, which have no eternal value.

Regrettably, this problem persists not only in the world but also in the Church. Too often, those in religious Denominations, maneuver, jockey, and manipulate others or situations, in order to gain ascendancy in that particular Denomination. Consequently, it becomes very political, which regrettably characterizes most religious Denominations presently.

In this atmosphere, the Lord is little the leader in any capacity, and conversely, the Preachers little labor for the Lord, but rather for themselves or for the Denomination.

GODLY AMBITION

The Greek word for Godly ambition (philotimeomai) and which we have already given, is used only three times in the New Testament (Rom. 15:20; II Cor. 5:9; I Thess. 4:11). The word suggests eager, continuing efforts for something that is good.

Paul aspired to preach the Gospel where Christ was not known (Rom. 15:20) and always tried eagerly to please the Lord (II Cor. 5:9).

The Apostle urges Believers to strive to live a quiet life, filled with the honest work that wins the respect of outsiders and maintains independence (I Thess. 4:11). Each of these ambitions is closely linked with the idea of service to others. Each calls us to focus our life on things that have eternal value, with the general idea being to please the Lord. Consequently, there is no striving for place or position. There is no manipulation, no political effort. Paul belongs to the Lord, and the Lord will do with him what He desires, and that is what Paul desires as well. Such is meant by the Holy Spirit to be our example.

The phrase, *"That, whether present or absent,"* refers to being present with the Lord, which will take place when we die or are raptured, or absent from Him, that is, whether in this world or the next.

NOTES

WHEREVER

Wherever we are, or may be, it is and will be our main purpose and object so to live as to secure His favor. Paul did not wish to live on earth regardless of His favor, or without evidence that he would be accepted by Him. He did not make the fact that he was absent from Him, and that he did not see Him with the bodily eye, an excuse for walking in the ways of ungodly ambition, or seeking his own purposes and ends.

The idea is, that so far as this point was concerned, it made no difference with him whether he lived or died; whether he was on earth or in Heaven; whether in the body or out of the body; it was the great fixed principle of his nature so to live as to secure the approval of the Lord.

And this is the true principle on which the Christian should act, and will act. The fact that we are now absent from the Lord will be to us no reason why we should lead a life of sin and self-indulgence, anymore than we would if we were in Heaven; and the fact that we are soon to be with Him is not the main reason why we seek to live so as to please Him.

It is because this has become the fixed principle of the soul; the very purpose of life; and this principle and this purpose will adhere to us and control us wherever we may be placed, or in whatever world we may dwell (Barnes).

The idea is, no matter in which state we find ourselves, at home (with the Lord) or away from home (on this earth), all we want is to have the Lord pleased with us. The implication is also that we belong wholly to the Lord; He is the One Who is guiding our lives and, therefore, orchestrates our condition, so we must conduct ourselves rightly in every situation in order that He ever be pleased with us.

The phrase, *"We may be accepted of Him,"* means to be approved by Him (Rom. 12:1; 14:18; Eph. 5:10; Phil. 4:18; Titus 2:9).

ACCEPTANCE

Paul is not speaking here of his Salvation, for that was settled on the road to Damascus long before. We do not labor or work to earn Salvation, for such cannot be accomplished in that fashion. Salvation is a free Gift, and is secured by Faith (Eph. 2:8-9).

Paul is speaking of his service for the Lord, the manner in which he uses his life for the Lord, in other words, the stewardship of this priceless possession of Salvation.

Are we making our life count for the Lord? Or rather is our service and life a hit or miss proposition?

If the Lord has blessed us with money, are we properly using it for the Glory of God? Is our driving ambition to reach others with the Gospel of Jesus Christ?

What is it that takes up most of our time? What is it that our minds and thoughts dwell on?

Is the Lord no more than one hour on Sunday morning? Do we think we have done our *"duty"* when we pay our Tithe?

Is Jesus Christ preeminent, paramount, foremost and total within our hearts and lives?

How we may ever please Him need not be said here; it has been indicated throughout this Epistle. In the case of the Corinthians, however, the point to be noted is that they should understand and fully appreciate the motives of Paul and those with him, these motives and these aims in all that they have been doing with the situation in Corinth, yea, and all that they will yet do.

Paul and those with him were pleasing neither themselves nor men, but ever only the Lord. Do the Corinthians not want them to do that? Will they themselves not want to join Paul and his associates in that?

In other words, the Holy Spirit is using Paul to set the example, and it is not for the Corinthians only, but for all who claim the Name of Christ.

It is not that we be accepted of men. Regrettably, many if not most Preachers fall into that category, seeking to be accepted by men, i.e., Denominational heads, or peers of renown, etc. While we would like for all men to think well of us, that is by no means the overriding factor and is really not that important. It is God Alone Who knows that counts.

We had better ask ourselves as to whom we are attempting to please? Is it man or is it the Lord?

(10) "FOR WE MUST ALL APPEAR BEFORE THE JUDGMENT SEAT OF CHRIST; THAT EVERY ONE MAY RECEIVE THE THINGS DONE IN HIS BODY, ACCORDING TO THAT HE HATH DONE, WHETHER IT BE GOOD OR BAD."

The phrase, *"For we must all appear before the Judgment Seat of Christ,"* refers to the time after the Resurrection of the Saints, when we shall be judged of the things done in the body, whether they be good or bad (Rom. 14:10; I Cor. 3:11-15). This will take place in Heaven, and will probably be immediately before the Second Coming (Rev. Chpt. 19).

As well, this has nothing to do with one's Salvation, that having been settled at Calvary, but rather what we did with our life as it pertains to the Lord.

NOTES

FOR WE MUST

This fact to which Paul now refers is another reason, and at least one of the greatest reasons of all, why it is necessary to lead a holy life, and why Paul gave himself with so much diligence and self-denial to the arduous duties of his office. As stated, the Holy Spirit intends for him to serve as an example.

There is a necessity or a fitness that we should appear there to give account, for we are here on trial; we are responsible moral agents; we are placed here to form characters for eternity.

Before we receive our eternal allotment, it is proper that we should render an account of the manner in which we have lived, and of the manner in which we have improved our talents and privileges. In the nature of things, it is proper that we should undergo a trial before we receive our reward, or to lose that reward; and God has made it necessary and certain, by His direct and positive appointment, that we should stand at the bar of the final *"Judge."*

Let it be clearly understood, to which we have already mentioned, that this process is not to discover whether we are Christians, but rather to reveal the true character of our Christianity. This judgment will not be held to determine whether our characters are good or bad, but whether the deeds done in the body are good or bad.

All this is very solemn. It is something that should give us no carefree ease until we are determined to live today according to the pattern of this coming Judgment.

ALL

This means every single Believer who has ever known the Lord, going all the way back to Adam. It speaks of old and young, bond and free, rich and poor, all of every class, and every age, and every nation. None shall escape by being unknown; none by virtue of their rank or wealth; none because they have a work too pure to be judged.

In fact, Paul is actually saying that he will stand there himself, and so will all others.

That being the case, and to which we have already referred and will continue to refer, should not this coming time ever be before us, thereby modeling our life and actions toward this coming day? In other words, we are going to give account, and of that we may be sure.

APPEAR

The word properly means *"to make apparent, manifest, known; to show openly,"* etc. Here it means that we must be manifest, openly shown; that is, we must be seen there, and be publicly tried.

Knowing this, it should serve as an incentive to prompt and inspire us in our labor for the Lord. In fact, regarding Paul, and all of us as well, this incentive went behind his labor to his ambitions, because the word translated *"labor"* as we have already stated, is the word for *"ambition."* His ambitions were prompted and energized by a great thought. Whether it was life or death, prosperity or adversity, health or sickness, he labored to be well-pleasing to God.

Paul, like every other Christian, was already accepted in Christ, but now he expressed himself as being ambitious to be accepted of Christ. The first acceptance was the result of God's Work for us; the second acceptance will be the result of our work for God. One acceptance indicates our Standing, the other indicates our State. The one was God's responsibility, the other is our responsibility.

It is impossible to go through life selfishly and recklessly, giving no consideration to God, and then expect to have His approval.

Paul believed in this coming appearance, and he determined to let the future have a practical bearing on his life. He realized that at that time his life and deeds would be reviewed and he ordered his life accordingly. If we really believe as Paul believed, we too will live with the same thing in view. What a vastly different world this would be if every Christian began to order his life, from this day on, with that in mind. *"For we must all appear before the Judgment Seat of Christ."*

NOTES

THE JUDGMENT SEAT OF CHRIST

At this point we must be clear in understanding that the Judgment spoken of now is the judgment of Christians and not sinners. The judgment of sinners will take place at the Great White Throne (Rev. 20:11), which will take place approximately a thousand years after the Judgment Seat of Christ.

As well, we must also clearly understand that here the Christian will not be judged for sin in respect to Salvation. As we have already stated, that took place at the Cross. Here, it is a judgment in the form of a review or adjustment. It is a judicial judgment for the purpose of making such adjustments that were not made before. Here the Believer must face unconfessed sin. Here he must adjust all the differences with fellow Christians which were not settled in the flesh. Here he must be brought into a perfect relationship with God as a prelude to the life of the eternal ages. Here any uncompleted work of Sanctification must be finished.

Christ is our Saviour, our Baptizer with the Holy Spirit, our Healer, our Overcomer, our Strength, our Anointing, our Life; then He will be our Judge.

The phrase, *"That every one may receive the things done in his body, according to that he hath done, whether it be good or bad,"* concerns this present life, and what we did *"through the body,"* or through this *"tent"* or *"tabernacle."*

THINGS DONE IN HIS BODY

These are things done by means of the body. The body with its five senses is the vehicle of the soul, and whatever has been done through this medium will be reviewed in the light of the Standards of the Gospel.

If our deeds have been of the character of gold, silver, and precious stones (symbolically speaking), we shall receive a reward. If, on the other hand, they have been of the character of wood, hay, and stubble, we shall *"suffer loss"* (I Cor. 3:11-17). However, the loss suffered is not the loss of our Salvation, but the loss of our reward.

THE ROMAN EXAMPLE

The Judgment Seat of Christ is an expression which had a local significance to these early Christians. It referred to the Tribunals of the Roman Magistrates — Tribunals which were august representations of justice.

It was, first of all, a place. The technical word used here is *"Bema"* or *"Bema Seat"* which was a Tribunal. The *"Bema"* was a lofty seat on an elevated platform usually at the end of the Judgment Hall, so that the figure of the Judge could be seen towering above the crowded room.

It is also a process.

As a result of our appearance before this *"Bema,"* we shall be seen in our true light. We shall be stripped of all disguise and pretense. All the trappings and gaudy coverings of religious hypocrisy will have been dissolved and we shall be seen as we are. There will be no further pretense or sham. This last great reckoning will reveal us in the blaze of reality.

As well, this place and process has a time.

It will be when Christ comes. We do not go immediately from death to judgment, nor to our reward. There is an interval of time between.

ACCORDING TO THAT HE HATH DONE

There is no more probation after death or after the Resurrection. The probation is now, this present life. All beyond the grave is either reward or punishment; it is not probation. The destiny is to be settled forever by what is done in the world of probation. It is to be for all the deeds done in the body; for all the thoughts, plans, purposes, words, as well as for all the outward actions of the man. All that has been thought or done must come into review, and the Believer must give account for all.

The reward or lack of reward will be measured by what has been done in this life. Every man shall receive just what, under all the circumstances, he ought to receive, and what will be impartial justice in the case. The Judgment as given by Christ will be such that it will be capable of being seen to be right; and as the individuals themselves will see, ought to be rendered.

In this Judgment life's labor will be reviewed to discriminate and separate those parts of our lives which have been lived for eternity or for time. Only the eternal will survive. Only the labor and the deeds of common occurrence about the home and shop which have been done in consecrated surrender will have the quality of survival.

NOTES

All of this is very solemn.

It is something that should give us no carefree ease until we are determined to live today according to the pattern of this coming Judgment.

WHETHER IT BE GOOD OR BAD

What is meant by good or bad?

In what way can the works of Believers be *"bad,"* or *"worthless?"*

In the sense of motivation.

This issue relates directly to Paul's statement in the previous Verse that his ambition was to please God. If a Christian's ambition is to please self, or even others, that person cannot expect the Anointing of the Holy Spirit on his efforts. Furthermore, unless the Holy Spirit works through us, our efforts will not stand the examination of the Judgment Seat of Christ.

On the other hand, what we have accomplished because of the Anointing, Leading, and Guidance of the Holy Spirit, will stand the test. It all boils down to motive and desire.

Why are we doing what we are doing? Are we men-pleasers or God-pleasers?

There will be a Judgment.

Every act leaves its mark upon our souls. In the natural world there are ample evidences of this. *"Every part of the material universe contains a permanent record of every change that has ever taken place therein, and there is no limit to the power of minds like ours to read and interpret the record. A shadow never falls upon a wall without leaving thereon a permanent trace, a trace which might be made visible by resorting to proper processes."*

If this is true in our material world, consider how much more it is true in our moral world.

Having presented the future and its consequences of life, Paul next reviewed the present and its responsibilities of life.

If the foregoing matters of death and judgment are true, we must do something about them. In the following verses Paul has told us we must do something about these matters right now. Thus, we have the compelling motive of Evangelism, personal and public.

After all, death should not be considered as some isolated part of life, or as something appended to the end of an earth-existence, or even as some sort of executioner. In the Christian scheme of things, death should be considered as belonging to life. It is that which ushers us from one phase of life to another — but a good phase only if one is a Believer. It is also that which shuts off opportunities that will never come again. Death, therefore, gives a new imperative and incentive to life. We must live right if we expect to die right.

WILL THE SINS OF BELIEVERS BE BROUGHT UP AT THE JUDGMENT SEAT OF CHRIST?

All sins committed before conversion, are washed and cleansed at the time of conversion (II Cor. 5:17).

All sins committed by Christians after conversion are as well washed and cleansed and promptly forgotten, if in fact they are properly confessed before the Lord (I Jn. 1:9). Proper confession always guarantees proper forgiveness. Proper forgiveness by the Lord demands that these sins be remembered against us never again (Ps. 103:12; Isa. 43:25; 44:22; Acts 3:19).

However, if sins of the Believer have not been properly confessed before the Lord, and that means sins of any nature, it will then have to be settled at the Judgment Seat of Christ, and done so publicly.

To which we have already also briefly alluded, our treatment of fellow Christians if not done according to the Word of God, will have to be settled there. This all comes under the heading of those things which are *"bad."*

The Believer should take stock of his life, and see there what is actually *"good"* and what is actually *"bad."* As well, the Word of God is the Standard, and not man-made rules or public opinion.

We can settle it here, or we will settle it there, but settle it we shall! If it is settled here correctly, that means according to the Word of God, we will suffer no loss. However, if it has to be settled at the Judgment Seat of Christ, whatever the situation may be, the loss of some reward, which will be a great loss indeed, could very well be the result.

(11) "KNOWING THEREFORE THE TERROR OF THE LORD, WE PERSUADE MEN; BUT WE ARE MADE MANIFEST UNTO GOD; AND I TRUST ALSO ARE MADE MANIFEST IN YOUR CONSCIENCES."

The phrase, *"Knowing therefore the terror of the Lord, we persuade men,"* does not refer

NOTES

to blind fear which fills the world, but rather the intelligent view of the final ending and final inspection and final sifting that will most surely come.

THE TERROR OF THE LORD

"Terror" in the Greek is *"phobos,"* and should have been translated *"fear."* Together with the Love of God this *"fear"* controls the Christian during his whole life.

Only the Godly have this holy fear. Its distinctive mark that it is always combined with trust in God and love toward God, is thus differentiated from the fear and dread of God which at last overwhelms the ungodly.

The fear of God ever shrinks from offending Him, from calling forth His Judgment and Retribution. It ever feels and speaks as Paul does in Verse Ten. How it keeps from sin is shown by the fine example of Joseph (Gen. 39:9).

Paul understood God not as some vacillating Deity Who could be moved back-and-forth between wrath and love by man's prayers, etc. Paul knew Him as a God of Love and Justice with His Justice grounded in His Love. He was a God Who demanded sincerity, honesty, and integrity in His people. Paul knew it.

While Paul knew it was possible to live a deceitful life of service here, deluding the people and serving for gain, he knew it was impossible to deceive God. He knew the *"terror* (fear) *of the Lord."* That is to say, he had a holy and a wholesome respect for God's opinion of his life and he purposed to adjust his life to that opinion, or better, *"God's Will."*

IS THERE ANYTHING TO FEAR IN GOD?

At this point personal opinion is worthless. Let God speak. The Bible says, *"The fear of the Lord is the beginning of wisdom."* It further says, *"It is a fearful thing to fall into the hands of the Living God."*

Does it mean that God is a dread tyrant? Not at all. It is one side of the question only.

Through your house flows an invisible current of power. It lights your lamps, heats your toaster, and powers your washer. That is one side of this current. If, under adverse circumstances, you were to take hold of the naked electrical wire through which that invisible current flows, it could cause instant death. That is the other side of this current. Knowing God is Life.

Not knowing God is death. Yes, there is something to fear in God.

As well, there is something for the Christian to fear. He should fear the consequences of a misspent Salvation, i.e., *"life."* He should fear the inspection of the judgment if his life and service are insincere and hypocritical.

From this wholesome and holy fear of God, Paul moved to win men.

WE PERSUADE MEN

The statement means, literally, *"to win men."* Henceforth every thought, word, and act of Paul's life were to be part of a campaign of persuasion. At all cost he would win men from the slavery of sin and the kingdom of Satan.

So far, the motive was personal. It was because Paul wanted no blood on his skirts that he sought to persuade men. It was because of the answer he must make at the Judgment that he wanted his life to be free from blame.

Persuading men to do what?

Paul is not alluding to slander that was uttered in Corinth to the effect that he and his helpers were no more than persuasive talkers. Nor is the sense that Paul and his helpers seek to allay suspicion regarding themselves by persuading people in regard to their good and honest intentions. No such ideas are developed here.

"Men we are engaged in persuading" is broad and general and signifies: bringing them to Faith. Persuasion is still the great task of the Gospel Ministry. It is not done with human argument, with *"persuasive wisdom words"* (I Cor. 2:4), but with the greatest persuasive force which men have ever used, the Gospel of Jesus Christ told and preached under the Anointing of the Holy Spirit.

We must endeavor to persuade men to flee from the wrath to come. Notice: it is not, we drive men; or we endeavor to alarm men; or we frighten men; or we appeal nearly to their fears; but it is, *"we persuade men"* — we endeavor to induce them, by all the arts of persuasion relative to the Gospel and the Holy Spirit, to flee from the wrath to come.

Having said that, is it proper for the Preacher to preach and declare hellfire and perdition?

It certainly is, for Jesus did this very dramatically (Lk. 16:19-31). However, that is only a part of the Message, and not all of the Message.

NOTES

THE TRUE EFFECT

The knowledge that there will be a judgment, and that the wicked will be sent to hell, was a powerful motive for Paul, and should be for us, to endeavor to *"persuade"* men to escape from this wrath; and was a motive for the Saviour to weep over Jerusalem, and lament its folly and its doom (Lk. 19:41).

But they who fill their sermons with denunciations of wrath; who dwell on the words hell and damnation for the purpose of rhetoric or declamation, to round a period, or merely to excite alarm; and who *"deal damnation around the land"* as if they rejoice that men were to be condemned, and in a tone and manner as if they would be pleased to execute it, have yet to learn the true nature of the way to win man to God, and the proper effect of those awful truths on the mind.

The true effect is to produce tenderness, deep feeling, and love; to prompt to the language of persuasion and of tender entreaty; to lead men to weep over dying sinners rather than to denounce them; to pray to God to have mercy on them rather than use the language of severity, or to assume tones as if they would be pleased to execute the awful Wrath of God.

Yes, the Preacher should preach hellfire, but he should ever do so with the looming idea of God Who sent His Only Son to die on Calvary, to redeem men from the potential of this awful place. We must never forget, it is love that motivates God and all that He has done, not the threat of eternal hell and eternal judgment, even though these things are very real.

The phrase, *"But we are made manifest unto God,"* means that what we do, we do before Him, seeking only to have His leading, guidance, direction, and approval.

MANIFEST UNTO GOD

The Lord knows if we are sincere and upright in our aims and purposes. He is acquainted with our hearts. All our motives are open to Him, and He sees that it is our aim, or not our aim, to promote His Glory, and to save the souls of men.

This could have been said, to counteract the charge which might have been brought against him by some of the disaffected in Corinth, that he was influenced by improper motives and aims. To meet this, Paul says that God knew that he was endeavoring to save souls, and that he was actuated by a sincere desire to rescue them from the impending terrors of the coming Day of Judgment.

God knows all and sees all; consequently, He cannot be fooled, as should be obvious. So, everything we do should be done knowing and understanding that it is *"manifest"* in totality to the Lord. It is what God knows that counts, and only what God knows that really counts.

The phrase, *"And I trust also are made manifest in your consciences,"* means that if the work is manifested before God, and is accepted by Him, and proven so by proper fruit, then such will be *"made manifest in your consciences"* as well!

THE CONSCIENCE

The idea is this: If the conscience of the Christian is right before God, one will properly know that which is of God. That is quite a statement, but that which I believe to be true.

The Believer should ever be seeking to know that which God honors and blesses, instead of that which man honors. The trouble is, too many Believers are looking to see what man approves and not God.

The Holy Spirit is saying through the Apostle to these Corinthians, and all others for that matter, that the Believer is to earnestly seek to know the proper fruit of a Ministry. If that fruit is forthcoming, which is the Salvation of souls, Believers being Baptized with the Holy Spirit, sick bodies being healed, bondages of darkness being broken, people being properly drawn to Christ — if the conscience of the Believer is right before God, he will know that the manifestation is proper and, therefore, of God.

This is extremely important, in that we are told here how that Ministries should be judged and accepted. If it is accepted of God, it must be accepted by the Body of Christ.

If it is accepted of God, there will be manifestations which are obvious, such as souls being saved, lives being changed, etc. In other words, that is the proof of the Holy Spirit working within a Ministry, which is the highest approval that a Ministry can have.

Regrettably, too many Believers make their judgment on other criteria. They go by what other men say, what public opinion is, in other words, what Satan wants them to believe. If he can get Believers, which he is very adept at doing, to reject a True Ministry such as that of Paul, he has won a great victory. The reasons should be obvious.

NOTES

If God has specifically called someone for a particular purpose, and has greatly anointed them for that purpose, and the Church refuses that person, which Corinth had been on the very verge of doing regarding Paul, the people will greatly hinder their spiritual walk by rejecting that which is of God. As well, there will be no other Preacher or Apostle who can take the place of that which God has intended. In such a case, the Work of God and the Body of Christ suffer greatly — all because of not following the Word of God, but rather men. Could anyone have taken Paul's place?

THE GOSPEL AS PREACHED BY PAUL

Paul's heart filled with pity and love for perishing men. He showed to them the Grace that had been shown to himself, and did his best to persuade them to flee from the wrath to come. He preached the True Gospel of the Wrath of God and His Love in Christ; and, as in Romans 1:18, he in faithfulness to Truth first announced the coming wrath, and then proclaimed the virtue of the Atoning Blood (Rom. 3:25).

Modern religious thought denies the Wrath of God and does not believe in conversions motivated by fear of that Wrath. But the human race would have utterly perished had not one man been *"moved with fear"* (Heb. 11:7) when he heard of the approaching judgment of the flood.

The Apostle knew that the purity of his Doctrine and of his motives were manifest to God, and he hoped that they were manifest also to the Corinthians' conscience, and as we have stated, they certainly should have been.

(12) "FOR WE COMMEND NOT OURSELVES AGAIN UNTO YOU, BUT GIVE YOU OCCASION TO GLORY ON OUR BEHALF, THAT YE MAY HAVE SOMEWHAT TO ANSWER THEM WHICH GLORY IN APPEARANCE, AND NOT IN HEART."

The phrase, *"For we commend not ourselves again unto you,"* refers to what Paul had said in the previous Verse.

A CONSCIOUSNESS OF INTEGRITY

In essence Paul is saying that he should not have to commend himself to these Corinthians at all. Why was it necessary for him to do such? How could anyone turn against Paul, especially considering that he had brought the Gospel of Jesus Christ to their beleaguered souls? Why would he of all people have to prove himself to the Corinthians?

Even though many of the problems had been settled at Corinth, still, there were still some detractors there to the Ministry of Paul. As well, Paul knew that others could come in, fueled by their own self-will, actually as he will later say, presenting *"another Jesus,"* by *"another Spirit,"* which in effect, was *"another Gospel"* (II Cor. 11:4). Consequently, he would once again in a sense, defend himself.

In the previous Verse he had in essence said that he had such a consciousness of integrity that he could appeal to God, and that he was persuaded that the Corinthians also approved his course, and admitted that he was influenced by right motives. He here states the reason why he had said this.

It was not to commend himself to them. It was not to boast of his own character, nor was it in order to secure their praise or favor. Some might be disposed to misrepresent all that Paul said of himself, and to suppose that it was said for mere vainglory, or the love of praise. He tells them, therefore, that his sole aim was necessary self-defense, and in order that they might have the fullest evidence that he, by whom they had been converted, was a True Apostle; and that he whom they regarded as their friend and father in the Gospel was a man of whom they need not be ashamed (Barnes).

AMAZED!

Once again I am amazed that anyone could question the integrity of Paul. How could people be induced to turn against him, especially considering as stated, that they were saved because of his Ministry? How could they doubt his Apostleship?

Naturally, all of this was being fueled by Paul's detractors who were attempting to peddle their legalism. They were attempting to wed the Law with Grace, which Paul denounced totally, and to do such they felt they had to denigrate the character of the Apostle. They questioned his character, motives and Apostleship. In so doing, they caused many of the Corinthians to doubt the Apostle, to doubt

NOTES

his Gospel, which in effect, was the Gospel of Jesus Christ. In other words, they were thrown into a state of confusion, which is never of the Lord, but always of Satan.

The dignity and aplomb with which Paul answered these charges, presents an example for us all. How humiliating! And yet, he did not feel humiliated simply because self was properly hidden in Christ. Consequently, he could answer in a righteous manner, touching on himself only as it was needed.

In the scenario, we are observing a man so hidden in Christ, so totally absorbed in Christ, so fully Christlike, that he can respond to everything in a Christlike manner.

The phrase, *"But give you occasion to glory on our behalf,"* does not carry the connotation of boasting that it would today. What he was offering his supporters in Corinth was *"an occasion"* to assist him.

TO GLORY

The picturesque terminology which follows shows that he was making it possible for these Corinthian supporters to have the true facts to present to the opposition who were glorying in themselves. These people, whoever they were, were boasting in what they perceived rather than what was actually in Paul's heart. Regrettably, too many Christians follow suit. They form conclusions on what they perceive things to be, instead of how things really are.

The sense is, *"You have been converted under my labors. You profess to regard me as your spiritual father and friend. I have no reason to doubt of your attachment to me.*

"Yet you often hear my name slandered, and hear me accused of lacking the evidence of being an Apostle, and of being vainglorious, and self-seeking. I know your desire to vindicate my Character, and to show that you are my friends; I therefore say these things in regard to myself in order that you may be thus able to show your respect for me, and to vindicate me from the false and slanderous accusations of my enemies. Thus doing, you will be able to answer them; to show that the man whom you thus respect is worthy of your confidence and esteem."

This was for their benefit, and of the Gospel, and not of himself.

TO SET THE RECORD STRAIGHT

In effect, Paul is once more referring to this matter of self-recommendation. In II Corinthians 3:1, etc., he has already said most emphatically that he and his assistants need no letters of commendation and recommendation to the Corinthians or from the Corinthians, since the Corinthians themselves were the grandest letter of recommendation which Paul could wish, one that is inscribed as on a public monument so that all men in Corinth, and elsewhere if so desired, may read it.

He is, in effect, saying, *"We founded this congregation; it stands as a public monument in Corinth; whoever passes by can read upon it the fact that God has helped us to found this Church."*

What are letters of papyrus or parchment which are secured from persons far away, compared with a monumental letter like this which is open to the eyes of all men in all Corinth?

GENUINE RECOMMENDATION

This is Paul's answer to the slanders that he had no letters of recommendation, or that he does no more than to recommend and to glorify himself. In II Corinthians 4:2 he adds that he and his helpers in fact do recommend themselves after a fashion, do it by putting away all tricks and all falsifications of the Word, by publishing the Truth, and by thus recommending themselves to every man's conscience. If that is not genuine recommendation, then what is? So he again says: *"We are certainly not again trying to recommend ourselves to you."*

After founding the Corinthian Church, after building it up so strongly, does Paul still have to recommend himself to the Corinthians? Is he not as yet manifest in their consciences as to what he really is?

WHY SHOULD THEY HAVE NEEDED THIS FROM PAUL?

What Paul is saying about himself and those with him, their work and their way of working, is intended to give the Corinthians the information which they need so they may defend or even praise Paul and by this praise stop the mouths of these false slanderers.

In fact, the Corinthians should really have had no need of being given such ammunition against such men. The moment these detractors came to Corinth and began their attacks upon Paul, the Corinthians should have hushed them up with their own loud boasts of what Paul was and what he had done for them. Not even one ear should have taken in one slanderous word against Paul.

NOTES

But sadly, that is too often the way some Church Members act. Instead of defending the best Pastors or Evangelists that God ever gave them, they are often inclined to listen to evil-minded men who want to destroy the work of such Preachers of the Gospel. It is the Devil's cunning: he cannot stop the work, so he inspires men to tear it down and finds that those who ought to prevent such tearing down, in fact let it proceed, perhaps at times, even lending a hand.

The phrase, *"That ye may have somewhat to answer them,"* presents Paul as desiring no false praise from anyone; but he does want true recognition. As he strives to obtain it from God, so he strives to have it in men's consciences.

It is spurious humility to regard the conscientious recognition which we receive as True Ministers of Christ as nothing. In fact, our very success in the Ministry depends on securing proper recognition in men's consciences (II Cor. 4:2).

VITAL!

This was vital in Corinth because of the opponents who had been busy trying to turn the Church against Paul and against his work. The way in which he characterizes these opponents shows that they were not Corinthians but had come to Corinth and had been trying to attain leadership. They had letters of recommendation. From whom they had received them we do not know; they had certainly not received them from any of the other Churches. Probably these letters had come from Jerusalem.

These letters seemed to have impressed the Corinthians, who thus foolishly listened to these strangers. Paul calls them *"those who make a business of glorifying themselves."*

Regarding my own Ministry this hits close to home. To do the work that God has called me to do, I must have the help of others. To be sure, the Lord has definitely commissioned as many people as it takes to get this work done, even as He has commissioned me to do the work. Of course, I speak of World Evangelism, at least as it pertains to our Ministry.

Seeing almost the entirety of the Church attempting to tear us down, even as these were doing such to Paul, I can only depend on people abiding by the Word of God, and appealing to their own consciences. If they abide by the Word of God and their consciences, they will support us. They will help us get this task done, and they will not listen to the detractors and those who would tear down this Ministry.

Regrettably, to do that, they will have to go against public opinion, against most of the Church, and many times against their own loved ones, friends, and relatives. Most are not able to do that. They bow to public opinion, simply not able to take the abuse that one must take, to support this Work and Ministry.

Consequently, how grateful we are, how thankful we are, how so much we thank the Lord for those few who do stand with us, both prayerfully and financially, to help us take this Gospel of Jesus Christ to a lost and dying world. To be sure, their reward will be great!

The phrase, *"Which glory in appearance, and not in heart,"* presents the very thing of which I have just spoken.

APPEARANCE

Face and heart, appearance and real inner purpose do not always agree. On the surface these opponents look like good and reliable men, but if the Corinthians would compel them to manifest what is really in their hearts they would be shocked and horrified.

Paul stops with this brief characterization. The commentators at times supply more. On their face these invaders are said to be born Jews, advocates of legalism and Law observance, eloquent, boasting of Scripture knowledge, of possible acquaintance with the other Apostles (the original Twelve), perhaps even of personal acquaintance with Jesus during His earthly Ministry. But it seems more important to ask how Paul can speak so confidently of what is in the hearts of these men when he had not been in Corinth, at least at this time, and had not himself seen them.

IS PAUL GUILTY OF JUDGING?

I will ask the question again, *"Is Paul guilty of this dangerous business of judging men's hearts?"*

Paul had received full accounts from Titus who had just returned from Corinth (II Cor. 2:13; 7:6, 13). It was no longer a question as to what was in the hearts of these invaders; they had exposed that from the beginning by using even foul means (slander, etc.) to break down what Paul had built up at such cost of labor.

NOTES

The sin of judging the heart consists in imputing base motives to another person's heart even when he does what is right. These men were tearing down the true work of God undercover of praising themselves by an outward display as reliable men. The Corinthians looked at the latter and became impressed thereby and failed to note the former which revealed what was really in the hearts of these men.

Paul also bids the Corinthians to look at what has come out of their hearts (the hearts of Paul and his associates).

PAUL'S HEART

Paul wants to be judged and can properly be judged only in the same way that he judges these men. The Corinthians must look at Paul's heart through the window of what he has wrought among them and is still trying to work as he states in II Corinthians 4:2 and, in fact, throughout also the rest of these Chapters where he once more enters into the very heart of the Gospel and of his own Ministry.

This entire Epistle more than the others bears Paul's inmost heart, all his deepest motives and inner purposes, and does all this by means of what he has done and is still doing.

When in Chapters 10 to 12 he is compelled to compare himself with others in an outward way, he says that he feels like a fool for doing so. His glorying was in his infirmities, for which men would despise him. It is his glorying to be nothing but a clay vessel in order to make the treasure of the supreme Power of God stand out the more by contrast (II Cor. 4:7, etc.).

He thus indicates to the Corinthians what they may use in regard to himself and those with him, for silencing and for getting rid of the impostors who had come to trouble them.

A PERSONAL STATEMENT

Once again I will add that this hits so close to home, that I pray the Reader will allow me latitude regarding the similarity.

Even as Paul is here addressing, it is not very pleasant to be maligned, caricatured, made fun of, in other words, ridiculed by others — especially by those who should be holding you up. It is not pleasant to have impure and even ungodly motives ascribed to one. To be branded a fake, even a hypocrite, is a load heavy to bear.

Of course, the instant response to my statements is a quick pointing to failure which took place years ago. However, if such is going to be the basis for such an attitude, then in one way or the other all fall into the same category. No, that is no excuse at all!

So why does the Church take such a position? Have such an attitude?

I suppose to answer that question, one would have to go to the heart of each individual person, which of course, only God can do. As we have previously stated, it is always easier to follow the crowd.

The proof otherwise is abundantly obvious.

The Gospel we preach is the pure, undiluted, uncompromising Word of God, that still gets people saved as it always has. In fact, at least not to my knowledge, no one has accused us of not preaching the Gospel.

As well, the Anointing of the Holy Spirit is obvious regarding both the Message and the Messenger, that is, for those who care to be honest. As should be known, the Anointing of the Holy Spirit is the highest recommendation that God can give. To be sure, and as I am certain all would know, God will not anoint sin, hypocrisy, or false doctrine. The Message I preach, and the Anointing upon that Message, has resulted in literally hundreds of thousands being brought to a saving knowledge of Jesus Christ. As stated, it continues unto this hour. So why the rejection?

SCRIPTURAL?

Once again, I am certain that many would have an instant answer to that question; nevertheless, if they will be honest with themselves, their answer will not be Scriptural. And if it is not Scriptural, then it is of no validity and is not recognized by God.

As there was no Scriptural reason for the attitude of the Corinthians against Paul, there is no Scriptural reason for the attitude of the majority of the Church against us. As that against Paul was unscriptural and wrong and greatly hurtful to the Work of God, so is that against us. Irrespective as to what it does against me personally, it is greatly hurtful to the Work of God, and that's what really matters.

NOTES

Many may quickly retort even as one woman did, when she admitted the wrong against me and this Ministry, but quickly stated, *"It's your fault."*

No, it is not my fault. Whatever wrongdoing I have committed is my fault, but the wrongdoing that others commit is not my fault. That fault lies with them alone. That excuse is as old as time.

Adam blamed God and Eve for his failure, as Eve blamed the serpent. The Lord recognized none of these excuses.

My wrong cannot be blamed on anyone else, and neither can the wrong of others be blamed on anyone else. Everyone must take personal responsibility for their own actions. To blame it all on me may make a good excuse, but it will not stand up in the court of God's Word.

RESPONSIBILITY!

Let's look at the word *"responsibility"* just a moment.

To take responsibility for anything, we must abide strictly by the Word of God, thereby taking the situation to the Lord. If sin is involved, it must be properly confessed to the Lord of which instant forgiveness is assured (I Jn. 1:9). The matter stops then and there, at least if one wants to abide by the Word of God.

There is absolutely nothing in Scripture which states that such a person should be forced then to abide by unscriptural demands — in other words, things made up by men which have no Scriptural validity. In fact, to yield to such man-devised demands whatever they may be, abrogates the Grace of God. God does not require penance, and if one thinks He does, let them begin by applying such to themselves.

When Church Leaders or anyone else for that matter take it upon themselves to apply punishment to another Believer, they have just overstepped their bounds. In fact, none are worthy to do so, and James plainly says so (James 4:12).

The Truth is, too often, so-called Church Leaders use these occasions to hinder or hurt, or even destroy Ministries with which they do not agree, or of which they are jealous. And please believe me, there is no jealousy in the world like religious jealousy. That is the reason the Word says that *"jealousy is as cruel as the grave"* (Song of Sol. 8:6).

THE FALSE TEACHERS IN CORINTH

Probably they boasted of their rank, their eloquence, their external advantages such as living in Jerusalem and being a part of the First Church. As stated, maybe they knew some of the original Twelve and who knows, quite possibly one or more of them may have even seen Jesus during His earthly Ministry. As also stated, they had letters of recommendation, evidently from someone of repute, or else these letters would not have been held up as proof of preeminence. However, their boasting was only of external things, that which carried no weight with the Lord, and did not consist of the things that really mattered such as souls being saved and lives being changed. In other words, these people were parasites, feeding off those who had been won to the Lord by others, in this case, Paul.

Paul, on the other hand, gloried mainly in his sincerity, his honesty, his desire for salvation of souls; in his conscious integrity before God; and not in any mere external advantages or professions, rank, eloquence, or talent.

Of course, these false teachers denied the Apostle the very thing he actually was — a man of integrity and called of God to be an Apostle to the Gentiles. Nevertheless, even as all of their acceptance would not have made Paul Godly and upright, if in fact that were not the truth, likewise, all of their denial did not take away from him that which God had ordained him to be. What men say is one thing; what God says is what really matters.

(13) "FOR WHETHER WE BE BESIDE OURSELVES, IT IS TO GOD: OR WHETHER WE BE SOBER, IT IS FOR YOUR CAUSE."

The phrase, *"For whether we be beside ourselves, it is to God,"* pertained to the idea that his detractors were accusing him of being mentally unbalanced.

BESIDE OURSELVES

"Beside ourselves" in the Greek is *"exestemen,"* and means *"to be insane."* So, it is altogether probable that he was charged with being deranged, which means they were trying to destroy the Apostle. Actually, this is a favorite accusation used by the world and some so-called Christians. Festus thought Paul was deranged, when he said, *"Paul, thou art beside thyself; much learning doth make thee mad"* (Acts 26:24) and the Saviour Himself was regarded by His immediate relatives and friends as beside Himself (Mk. 3:21).

And at all times there have been many, both in the Church and out of it, who have regarded those singly touched by the Lord, and, therefore, singly dedicated to God's Work, as being insane.

The object of Paul here is to show, whatever be the appearance or the estimate which they affixed to his conduct, what were the real principles which actuated him. These principles were, a zeal for God, a love for souls, and as well, the constraining influences of the Love of Christ.

THE FLESH AND THE SPIRIT

In fact, this very thing here of which the Apostle speaks, is a far greater problem than presently meets the eye.

Naturally, it is obvious that the world and its system knows nothing about God; consequently, they are quick to affix the epithet of derangement, mental imbalance, weak minds, etc., to those who serve God. Actually, the whole thing, this serving the Lord, is *"crazy"* as far as they are concerned. However, this problem does not begin and end with the world. Most Christians operate so little in the Spirit, and so much in the flesh, in other words like the world, that they too conduct themselves as these false teachers of Corinth, quickly affixing the same epithets to those who truly walk in the Spirit. Actually, that is the greatest problem in the Church presently, and in fact, always has been.

The believing sinner immediately upon being brought into the Born-Again experience, is brought as well into a realm in which all things are judged and measured and viewed in the Life and Light of the Holy Spirit as measured by the Word. Prior to spiritual birth the Believer was in a realm in which everything was judged by the wisdom of the carnal mind. Unfortunately, many Believers grow little in the Lord; consequently, they shift back and forth from the Spiritual to the carnal, with some remaining almost exclusively in the carnal. As a result, they do not see things correctly; thereby,

NOTES

causing great problems for themselves and especially for the work of God.

The problem is, that oftentimes this afflicts not only those who might be referred to as *"carnal Christians,"* but as well those who claim to be Spiritual, even as these false teachers at Corinth.

The Truth is, that if the Believer does not have a constant prayer life and study of the Word of God, his relationship with Christ is going to be seriously impaired, irrespective of his claimed Spirituality, which will always result in the individual flowing in the carnal instead of the Spiritual.

Paul was not beside himself, in fact, he was one of the most balanced, sane men who ever lived. That definition applies to all who truly walk in the Spirit, and, consequently, after the Spirit (Rom. Chpt. 8).

INSANITY AND SIN

To be frank, there is a certain insanity to sin. Its very nature tends toward imbalance, i.e., *"missing the mark."* In fact, the closer one walks with the Lord, the more one sees the imbalance, mentally speaking, in the world.

This mental imbalance centers up in deception more so than anything else. In this deception, a mental blindness covers the soul, which causes the sinner to view the Lord and His Word in a jaundiced, false way. Consequently they don't think right — and I speak primarily of things which pertain to God, but which definitely flow over into every aspect of life.

Admittedly, there are so-called religious quacks and spiritual kooks, but all of that has to do with the Believer not following after the Spirit, but rather his own notions, etc. The Truth is, the only proper illumination, be it spiritual or otherwise, is found in those who truly serve the Lord, endeavoring to walk wholly after His Word. This *"Light"* and *"Salt,"* have provided every iota of freedom and prosperity that the world has ever known. Of course, the world does not recognize that, and in fact, cannot recognize that; nevertheless, such does not alter the truth of the matter (Mat. 5:13-16).

The phrase, *"Or whether we be sober, it is for your cause,"* refers to being of sound mind and to be thought of as such.

NOTES

SOBER

"Sober" in the Greek is *"sophroneo,"* and means *"to be of sound mind, sane, moderate, soberly minded."*

Nobody would advance as a charge against a man the fact that he is too sober-minded, except in one instance. Sober-minded is never used in an evil sense like calculating, at least if it is interpreted correctly.

However, the evidence is that some of Paul's detractors were accusing him of being too stern, too demanding of Truth, too uncompromising. In other words, he would not give place for a moment to the great New Covenant being compromised by adding other things such as the Law, etc.

If one is to notice, concerning the charge of *"derangement,"* he points to God, meaning that God's True Ways, do seem to be derangement to the world and to many Christians. However, to the charge of being too sober-minded, he says that if he appears to be that way, *"it is for your cause,"* i.e., meaning that the Gospel must be delivered to them pure and unsullied.

Consequently, we should look at the irony in this Verse. Some of them accused him of being insane; others said he was too sober.

(14) "FOR THE LOVE OF CHRIST CONSTRAINETH US; BECAUSE WE THUS JUDGE, THAT IF ONE DIED FOR ALL, THEN WERE ALL DEAD:"

The phrase, *"For the Love of Christ constraineth us,"* literally means, *"The Love of Christ overmasters us."*

OVERMASTERED BY CHRIST

When we are overmastered by Christ, it means that His Life is ours, His Love is ours, His Truth is ours, His Will is ours and His Passionate Concern for Men is ours.

Actually, this does not refer to some type of insipid religious love for Christ, but it rather speaks instead of Christ's Love for the great lost and dying world. In other words, those who claim to love Christ, and have little or no concern for the lost, little regard for attempting to reach them for Christ, little thought as to pulling these souls out of darkness, which tragically fits most professing Christians, are more so a professor of Christ rather than an actual possessor of Christ.

Paul was consumed with the taking of the Gospel to a lost world. He was gripped by this unshakable conviction, that he must do all within his power to shove back the darkness.

He brings into view the principle which actuated him; the reason of his extraordinary and disinterested zeal. That was, that he was influenced by the love Christ had shown in dying for all men, and by the argument which was furnished by that death respecting the actual character and condition of man, and, consequently, the obligation of those who professed to be His Followers.

The actual strain of the phrase is the Love of Christ for us, i.e., *"for sinners,"* which facilitated His Death, and which should facilitate us on His behalf.

The idea is, that the only real way we can properly show our love for Christ, is by telling this grandest story ever told to others. Consequently, any so-called Ministry which places anything above souls being brought to Christ, the taking of the Gospel to others, the evangelizing of the world, is not a True Gospel, but rather a hybrid.

If the Ministry of Paul is a pattern, and it certainly should be, the order always must be the Salvation of Souls first, those saved being Baptized with the Holy Spirit, and then the Healing of the Sick and other particulars, following thereafter. While it is certainly true that some Ministers have a Calling that may bend more toward a certain other direction, which refers to some planting and some watering, still, there will be some souls saved by these Ministries, at least if they are properly being led by the Spirit. Ministries that care little for souls, irrespective of their show or their seeming effectiveness, in fact, are not Biblical.

THE LOVE OF CHRIST

Here it means, that the impelling, or exciting motive in the labors and self-denials of Paul, was the Love of Christ — the Love which He had shown Himself to the children of men. Christ so loved the world as to give Himself for it. His love for the world was a demonstration that men were dead in sins. And we, being urged by the same love, are prompted to like acts of zeal and self-denial to save the world from ruin.

NOTES

The Lord operates the entirety of His Kingdom from the principle or foundation of Love. God does not merely contain Love, He in fact, is Love. Consequently, it was Love that created man, and, therefore, Love that redeemed man. While God has force and power, and functions constantly in the realm of judgment, still, all is done from the basis of Love. That is His modus operandi, so to speak. Even when He uses force, and His Wrath is exhibited, as it often is, at least in a subdued manner, still, it is from the principle of Love.

THE WORLD AND THE LOVE OF GOD

Because of Satan's slanderous attacks against God, the world doesn't think of God as Love, but something else entirely. In fact, if they believe there is a God, they want absolutely nothing to do with Him, thinking that any type of involvement will bring on His Judgment. Consequently, they have it in their minds, that if there is no involvement there will be no judgment. Of course, all of that is basely false.

Regarding the world, the Scripture plainly tells us how much God loves sinful men. While He hates the sin, He loves sinful men so much, that He gave His Only Begotten Son, in order that men might be saved (Jn. 3:16). Consequently, the greatest act of Love in human history, an act incidentally which will never be surpassed, was Calvary.

JESUS AND THE LOVE OF GOD

If it is to be noticed, the three Gospels of Matthew, Mark, and Luke, do not mention that Jesus ever says that God loves, although John did plentifully. The idea is, whereas John portrayed the teaching by and large of Christ, the other three Gospels portray His Life and Actions. Consequently, rather than preaching sermons on the Love of God, He portrayed that Love, which is the greatest example of all.

The general impression of what Jesus did teach about God through His lifestyle and acts of healing and deliverance, is most surely that of Infinite Love, invincible in resources, altogether perfect in its good purposes. The two great Commandments, *"Love the Lord your God . . . Love your neighbor as yourself"* (Mk. 12:30-31; Mat. 19:19) depend on the prior assumption that God is, in fact, lovable and loving. Jesus reminded the Jewish Religious

Leaders that God preferred lovingkindness to a sacrificial cult (Mat. 9:13; 12:7).

As the Galileans soon recognized, there was in His Message a new note which may be summed up as the Doctrine of God as Father (Mat. 5:16; 6:9; 11:25-27; 16:17; 23:9; Mk. 1:27; 8:38; 11:25; 13:32; 14:36; Lk. 6:36; 12:32; 22:29; 23:46). The intimate tone of *"Abba Father"* implies a deep fellowship of understanding and affection as well as obedience. Hence the idea of God's Kingdom, imminent in His mission and already effective for the Work of Salvation, was transformed.

THE MESSAGE OF JESUS

Jews were summoned, not by the judgment blasts of John the Baptist or the warrior Psalms of the Old Testament, but by the gentle words of the Prophet from Nazareth — Prophet to them, and Prophet in reality, but as well, the Son of God. He proclaimed their fathers' God (Mk. 12:26), the High and Holy One, the Creator of Heaven and Earth; and yet the Way of Life demanded by the Father's incoming reign of Righteousness to be far different from the outward so-called holiness of the Priest, or the legalism of the Pharisees. God, said Jesus, cares for His creatures and for mankind: He clothes the grass and feeds the ravens (Lk. 12:24, 28); He makes His Sun rise on the evil and the good, and sends rain on the just and the unjust (Mat. 5:45); the cheapest sparrow does not die without God's remembrance, and the very hairs of our heads are all numbered (Lk. 12:6-7).

This is not quaint, poetic hyperbole as the Pharisees were prone to do, so much as Jesus bringing down to the level of all men the tender declaration of the universal and intimate character of the Divine Love of God as shown to the human family.

Man is dependent; God is independent, the Self-existent, without beginning or end, and yet God cares!

There are three words which may describe briefly what this Love is:

PATIENCE

The parable of the fig tree teaches the Divine goodness that allows another chance and at the same time the awful judgment if the opportunity is rejected; for God is God, and

NOTES

He is to be scorned and hated at our peril (Lk. 13:6-9; Mat. 18:35; Lk. 12:5).

MERCY

The parables of Luke Chapter 15 (lost coin, lost sheep, lost boy) demonstrate the wonder of that gracious Mercy from which forgiveness springs (Mk. 2:3; Lk. 7:36; 18:13).

Grace elicits love in return; this is the lesson of the incident in Luke 7:47 (*"For she loved much"*). But we must not press (Lk. 7:42-43) as if Jesus implied that love is in proportion to the sins forgiven; for instance, God's generosity is illustrated in the story of the laborers in the vineyard, which is not intended to apply to industrial wage disputes, but rather to show the Mercy and Grace of God (Mat. 7:11; 20:1-16; Lk. 11:13; 12:32).

GENEROSITY

This Divine love is an active benevolence that will go to any length to do good to the beloved object and to secure its well-being. Jesus, however, does not analyze the nature of love; His Mind was concrete rather than speculative. In other words, that the Love of God fluctuates, which it does not.

Nevertheless, it would be true to His teaching to affirm that the Divine Love of God is sovereign, unmotivated save by the necessity to be itself, spontaneous, and redemptive. Again in other words, that God's Love is not motivated by man's actions, but is rather the fact of Who God actually is.

DIVINE LOVE AS MANIFESTED TO MAN

Love more than all is revealed at the Cross, and in the character of Jesus Christ. *"God shows His love for us in that while we were yet sinners Christ died for us"* (Rom. 5:8).

This declaration is set in the context of the Divine Wrath against sin and sinners (Rom. 1:18; 2:5; 9:22; 12:19; Col. 3:6; I Thess. 1:10). In I Thessalonians 2:16, Paul says that the Divine Wrath has already overtaken the Jews, who crucified Jesus and now hinder the preaching of the Gospel. God, Who is Holy, requires moral integrity and obedience from men, both Jew and Gentile, and He rewards them according to their deeds (Rom. 2:6-11).

Yet, Christ has been made a Sin-Offering (II Cor. 5:21), and through the Crucified Lord, God

Himself has provided a way of escape from the ultimate consequences of His Wrath. *"Christ died for us"* means that Jesus chose to die and did this to redeem us; that somehow in Him were concentrated the horror, the anguish, and pain of human guilt.

Paul does not quite say that Christ bore our guilt. In fact, the Atonement springs from the Love of God and Christ's own Love, so that there is an unfathomable mystery in the sin-bearing.

THE SYMBOL OF WATER BAPTISM

The other side of this Doctrine is the symbol of Water Baptism. In this symbolic gesture, the man who believes in Jesus as the Risen Christ and trusts in Him is united with the Lord Who died. Water Baptism symbolically portrays a kind of spiritual death, a con-crucifixion (Gal. 2:20); and on rising out of the waters of death, the Believer is portrayed as being renewed by the Divine Spirit. He is clothed upon with Christ and becomes a new man in Christ, a new creation, a limb of His spiritual body, the Church. Now he is a Son of God, who should be led by the Spirit and live in the same love that Christ exhibits (Rom. 6:3; 8:2-16; 13:14; I Cor. 12:12; II Cor. 5:17; Gal. 5:16; Col. 1:18, 22; 2:11; I Thess. 3:12).

THE WONDER OF THE CROSS

The Cross of Jesus Christ, which produces an astounding wonder, was the great new word announcing the Holy God Whose wrath men fear. Of course, Salvation being all of the Lord, God was solely responsible for the Cross of Redemption, He in fact, making the enmity of men His tool. He had done what the Law could not do in Judaism, nor any system of Gentile men outside the Law. He had renewed Adam.

Paul's Gospel, which was given to him by Christ, rests on the idea that Adam, as the representative man, plunged humanity into a depth of sin and depravity, and that Jesus, as the Second or Last Adam, lifted man from that morass of sin and shame. Still, Jesus becoming the Second or Last Adam, which He did, in no way lifts moral responsibility from the redeemed life, in other words, that one may *"continue in sin that Grace may abound"* (Rom. 6:1), nor did he conceive of Jesus Christ as a mere scapegoat.

Rather, he had discovered that sin is primarily a rebellion against Divine Love and that

NOTES

Atonement results from the Sacrificial Ministry of this love personally present in the human life of God's Son, which is meant to evoke the gratitude and loyalty of those who perceive the Glory of God in the Face of Jesus Christ.

In view of that, it is not surprising that with such a grasp of what Christ is as Love incarnate, Paul seldom spoke about repentance and *never* of penance. Instead, he called men and women to have *"faith"* — a loving, trustful attitude that involves the total personality in the acceptance of a Free Gift of Grace (Rom. 4:16-25; 5:6-21).

LOVE IS ALMIGHTY

Because the Cross stands for victory over sin and evil (princes and powers of evil, the Apostle would have said), love is almighty. Divine Providence means that God's care is constantly exercised for the good of mankind. This was a truth that Christians needed over and over again to hear, because love also involved them in suffering. By tribulations, even as we are now studying, are the Sons of God to enter the Kingdom (II Cor. 11:23-12:10; I Thess. 2:14; 3:3-4; II Thess. 1:5).

Whatever threats there might be in this world, whether from natural disaster, from the onset of the Devil, or from any other source, Believers can take courage from the assurance that Love reigns and that God will never desert them; for God's Love is precisely the same as Christ's Love (Rom. 8:28-39).

The phrase, *"Because we thus judge,"* refers to the firm conviction and belief of the Apostle.

THUS JUDGE

In essence, Paul says, *"We have arrived at this judgment."* The word *"judge"* denotes a finality.

This means that this is not a mere theoretical, logical conclusion or just a subjective opinion; it is the judgment which finds this a fact and so accepts and declares it as a fact.

As a Judge declares what the fact in the case is, so Paul does as well.

When they first came to this judgment need not be said; it was when the whole significance of Christ's death dawned upon them. *"Christ"* is also the proper name because it designates Him according to His Messianic Office. Consequently, this one phrase, *"Because we thus judge,"* is significant vastly beyond our powers of comprehension. How a person judges Calvary and the Resurrection, for this is what Paul is addressing, has everything to do with their Salvation and continued victory over sin. If an individual is deficient in other things respecting the Word of God, there will be negative consequences as should be obvious; however, those consequences are nothing in comparison to a lack of knowledge and understanding regarding the Finished Work of Christ at Calvary. Above all, the Believer must be crystal clear on that and all that it means, at least as far as possible to do so. The tragedy is, most Believers do not have near the understanding of Calvary and the Resurrection as they should.

The phrase, *"That if one died for all,"* presents unquestionably this *"One"* as the Lord Jesus Christ.

DIED FOR ALL

If *"One"* died for all, then it follows that all were dead, i.e. *"dead in trespasses and sins."*

The word *"for"* means in the place of, in the stead of. It means that Christ took the place of sinners, and died in their stead; that He endured what was an ample equivalent for all the punishment which would be inflicted if they were to suffer the just penalty of the Law; that He endured so much suffering, and that God by His great substituted sorrows made such an expression of His hatred of sin, as to answer the same end in expressing His sense of the evil of sin, and in restraining others from transgression, as if the guilty were personally to suffer the full penalty of the Law.

If this was done, and it was, of course, the guilty might be pardoned and saved, since all the ends which could be accomplished by their destruction have been accomplished by the substituted sufferings of the Lord Jesus. In other words, He was our Substitute in all things. As we identify with Him, we gain Salvation.

THE ATONEMENT

The phrase, *"for all,"* to which we have already alluded, obviously means for all mankind; for every man. This is an exceedingly important expression in regard to the extent of the Atonement which the Lord Jesus made; and while it proves that His death was vicarious, that is, in the place of others, and for their sakes, it demonstrates also that the Atonement was general, and had in itself considered no limitation, and no particular reference to any class or condition of men, and no particular applicability to one class more than to another.

NOTES

There was nothing in the nature of the Atonement that limited it to any one class or condition; there was nothing in the design that made it, in itself, any more applicable to one portion of mankind than to another. And whatever may be true in regard to the fact as to its actual applicability, or in regard to the purpose of God to apply it, it is demonstrated by this passage that His Death had an original applicability to all, and that the merits of that Death were sufficient to save all. Consequently, the argument in favor of the general Atonement, from this passage, consists in the following points:

CHRIST DIED FOR ALL

Paul assumes this as a matter that was well known, indisputable, and universally admitted, that Christ died for all. He did not deem it necessary to enter into the argument to prove it, nor even to state it formally. It was so well known, and so universally admitted, at least as far as the Church was concerned, that he made it a first principle — an elementary position — in other words, a maxim on which to base another important doctrine — to wit, that all were dead, i.e. *"dead in trespasses and sins."*

It was a point which he assumed that no one would call into question; a Doctrine which might be laid down as the basis of an argument — like one of the first principles or maxims in Science.

NO SUCH THING AS A LIMITED ATONEMENT

It is the plain and obvious meaning of the expression — the sense which strikes all men, that the manner in which Paul makes the statement concerning *"all,"* that it shoots down the erroneous doctrine of a limited Atonement — in other words, that Jesus died only for those who will be saved.

If a man is told that *all* the human family must die, the obvious interpretation is that it applies to every individual. If told that all the passengers on-board a steamboat were drowned, the obvious interpretation is that every individual was meant. If told that a ship was wrecked, and that all the crew perished, the obvious interpretation would be that none escaped. If told that all the inmates of a hospital were sick, it would be understood that there was not an individual that was not sick.

Consequently, such is the view which must be taken by all men, that if told that Christ died for all, then it is meant that He died for all, whether they accept His Redemption or not.

Consequently, this cannot be consistent with the statement that Jesus died only for the elect, and that the elect was only a small part of the human family.

THE DECLARATION

This interpretation is in accordance with all the explicit declarations on the design of the Death of the Redeemer. Hebrews 2:9 says, *"That He, by the Grace of God, should taste death for every man."* John 3:16 says, *"For God so loved the world, that He gave His Only Begotten Son, that whosoever believeth in Him should not perish, but have everlasting life."* Paul said in I Timothy 2:6, *"Who gave Himself a ransom for all."* And then John wrote (I Jn. 2:2), *"And He is the propitiation for our sins; and not for ours only, but also for the sins of the whole world."*

THE OFFER IS TO ALL

The fact also, that on the ground of the Atonement made by the Redeemer, Salvation is offered unto all men by God, is a proof that He died for all. The Apostles were directed to go *"into all the world, and to preach the Gospel to every creature,"* with the assurance that *"he that believeth and is baptized shall be saved"* (Mk. 16:15-16); and everywhere in the Bible the most full and free offers of Salvation are made to all mankind (Isa. 55:1; Jn. 7:37; Rev. 22:17).

These are offers of Salvation through the Gospel, of the pardon of sin, and eternal life to be made *"to every creature."*

But if Christ died only for a part as some contend, if there is a large portion of the human family for whom He died in no sense whatever; if there is no provision of any kind made for them, then God must know this, and then the offers cannot be made with sincerity, and God is tantalizing them with the offers of that which does not exist, and which He knows does not exist. It is of no use here to say that the Preacher does not know who the elect are, and that he is obliged to make the offer to all in order that the elect may be reached. For it is not the Preacher who offers the Gospel. It is God Who does it, and He knows who the elect are, and yet He offers Salvation to all. And if there is no Salvation provided for all, and no possibility that all to whom the offer comes should be saved, then God is insincere; and there is no way possible of vindicating His character.

NOTES

ALL ARE SINNERS AND ALL, THEREFORE, CAN BE SAVED

If this interpretation is not correct, and if Christ did not die for all, then the argument of Paul here is worthless. The demonstration that all are dead (in trespasses and sins), according to him, is that Christ died for all.

But suppose that he meant, or that he knew, that Christ died only for a part — for the elect — then how would the argument stand, and what would be its force?

"Christ died only for a portion of the human race, therefore, all are not sinners. Medicine is provided only for a part of mankind, therefore, all are not sick. Pardon is offered to part only, therefore, all are not guilty."

I think it is obvious as to how ridiculous such thinking is. But Paul never reasoned in this way.

He believed that Christ died for all mankind, and on the ground of that, he inferred at once that all needed such an Atonement; that all were sinners, and that all were exposed to the Wrath of God. And the argument is in this way, and in this way only, sound.

But still, it may be asked, what is the force of this argument? How does the fact that Christ died for all prove that all were sinners, or dead in sin?

IN THE FIRST PLACE, WHY THE OFFER IF THERE IS NO NEED?

To offer medicine to all proves that all are sick. To offer pardon to all who are in a prison proves that all there are guilty.

What insult is it to offer medicine to a man in health; or pardon to a man who has violated no law! And there would be the same insult in offering Salvation to a man who was not a sinner, and who did not need forgiveness.

THE PRICE PAID PROCLAIMS THE NEED

The dignity of the Sufferer, and the extent of His sufferings, prove that all were under a deep and dreadful load of guilt. Such a Being would not have come to die unless the race had been apostate in totality; nor would He have endured so great sorrows unless a deep and dreadful malady had spread over the world.

The deep anxiety, the tears, the toils, the sufferings, and the groans of the Redeemer show what was His sense of the condition of man, and proved that He regarded them as degraded, fallen, and lost. And if the Son of God, Who knows all hearts, regarded them as lost, they are lost.

He was not mistaken in regard to the character of man, and He did not lay down His life under the influence of delusion and error.

If to the view which has been taken of this important passage it be objected that the work of the Atonement must have been to a large extent in vain; that it has been actually applied to but comparatively a small portion of the human family, then it is unreasonable to suppose that God would suffer so great sorrows to be endured for nought, we may reply.

IT WAS NOT IN VAIN

Even though the majority of mankind has rejected what Jesus did at Calvary, which in effect, is the answer and the only answer to the sin of mankind, Calvary is still not in vain. They have had the opportunity to accept, and that is what is so very important.

As well, there no doubt have been other purposes accomplished by Calvary besides the direct Salvation of men. It was doing much when it rendered it consistent for God to offer Salvation to all; it is much that God could be seen as just, and yet pardoning the believing sinner; it was much when His determined hatred of sin, and His purpose to honor His Law, were evinced; and in regard to the benevolence and justice of God to other beings and to other worlds, should there be such, much, very much was gained, though all the human race had rejected the Plan and been lost. In regard to all these things, and even many things of which we have no knowledge, the Plan of God was not in vain, and the sufferings of the Redeemer, despite the fact that most have rejected His Salvation, were not for nought.

NOTES

GOD'S WAYS ARE BEYOND THE INTELLIGENCE OF MEN

All of this is in accordance with what we see everywhere, when much that God does seems to our eyes, though not to His, to be in vain. How much rain falls in vain, at least to our eyes, on ever sterile sands or on barren rocks. How many pearls lie useless in the ocean; how much gold and silver in the earth; how many diamonds amidst rocks to us unknown, and apparently in vain!

How much medicinal virtue is created by God each year in the vegetable world that is unknown to man, and that decays and is lost without removing any disease, and that seems to be created in vain!

Year after year, and age after age, they existed in a suffering world, and men died perhaps within a few yards of such medicine which would have relieved or saved them, but it was unknown, or, if known, disregarded. However, the times ultimately come when their value is appreciated, and then they are applied to benefit the sufferer. So with the Plan of Salvation. It may be rejected, and the sufferings of the Redeemer may seem to have been for nought. However, we shall see at the end, that none of what Christ did was in vain, and that the results will be commensurate with the price paid.

The phrase, *"Then were all dead,"* refers to all men everywhere, and for all time, being dead in sin. That is, all were sinners. The fact that He died for all proves that all were transgressors.

DEAD

The word *"dead"* is not infrequently used in the Scriptures to denote the condition of sinners (Eph. 2:1). It means not that sinners are in all senses and in all respects like a lifeless corpse, for they are not. They are still moral agents, and have a conscience, and are capable of thinking, speaking, and acting. It does not mean that they have no more power than one in the grave, for they definitely do have more power.

But it means that there is a striking similarity, in some respects, between one who is dead and a sinner. That similarity does not extend to everything, but in many respects it is very striking.

The idea is that the sinner is totally dead to God and all things of God. Consequently, all overtures, spiritually speaking, must be made from God to man.

SPIRITUALLY INSENSIBLE

The sinner is as insensible to the Glories of the Heavenly World, and the appeals of the Gospel, as a corpse is to what is going on around or above it. The body that lies in the grave is insensible to the voice of friendship, and the charms of music, and the hum of business, and the plans of gain and ambition; and so the sinner is insensible to all the Glories of the Heavenly World, and to all the appeals that are made to him, and to all the warnings of God.

He lives as though there were no Heaven and no Hell; no God and no Saviour.

DIVINE POWER

There is as much need of the same Divine Power to convert a sinner as it is to raise up the dead. The same cause does not exist, making the existence of that power necessary; but it is a fact that a sinner will no more be converted by his own power than a dead man will rise from the grave by his own power.

No man ever yet was converted without direct Divine Agency, any more than Lazarus was raised without Divine Agency. And there is no more just or melancholy description which can be given of man, than to say that he is dead in sins.

He is insensible to all the appeals that God makes to him; he is insensible to all the sufferings of the Saviour, and to all the glories of Heaven; he lives as though these did not exist, or as though he had no concern in them; his eyes see no more beauty in them than the sightless eyeballs of the dead do in the material world; his ear is as inattentive to the Calls of God and the Gospel as the ear of the dead is to the voice of friendship or the charms of melody; and in a world that is full of God, and that might be full of hope, he is living without God and without hope.

(Much of the material above on the Atonement was derived from Albert Barnes.)

(15) "AND THAT HE DIED FOR ALL, THAT THEY WHICH LIVE SHOULD NOT HENCEFORTH LIVE UNTO THEMSELVES, BUT UNTO HIM WHICH DIED FOR THEM, AND ROSE AGAIN."

NOTES

The phrase, *"And that He died for all,"* again brings the reader back to the supreme sacrifice paid by Christ.

SUBSTITUTION

When Christ bowed His Head on the Cross, in perfect correspondence with His death, all men died then and there. All who had ever lived, all who will yet live until time ends, died in Christ's death, died in Christ, their substitute.

One mere man may substitute for another man when equivalence is more inexact, one man might substitute for several. But one mere man could not substitute his death and have it equal the death of the universe of men in all ages. Only the God-Man could be this substitute. Even though He was very man (fully man), still, without Christ's Deity His effective substitution becomes fiction. If Christ is not true God, He might die a thousand times, and despite all the deaths, it would not suffice for lost humanity.

However, He as Very Man and Very God could lay down the price, and that price was reckoned as though we had laid it down. Each of us might die a thousand times, and this would amount to nothing. We are sinners who are doomed to die. However, the death of the sinless Son, the Lamb without spot or blemish, this, and this death alone, equals the death of all for whom He died.

Erase the Substitution, and Paul's judgment and statements become fiction, in effect, ceasing to be fact. Christ's Death ransomed all, atoned for all, satisfied for all, made Sacrificial expatiation for all, paid for all. Consequently, the Death of Christ, in which all died, changed the relation of all to God.

UNNECESSARY REPETITION?

The casual reader may look at these statements and reckon that this phrase, *"And that He died for all,"* is a needless repetition. However, it is impossible that these statements could ever be regarded as an unnecessary repetition. The fact stated is so tremendous, so awesome, so all encompassing, that it cannot be stated too often. Repetition emphasizes, and if emphasis is ever in place, it is so here. As usual, it will introduce a new Truth.

The phrase, *"That they which live,"* refers to those who accept this which Christ did and

NOTES

thereby gain Eternal Salvation. The statement at the same time, of course, proclaims the fact that many, even most, will not accept and be saved.

THEY WHICH LIVE

The word *"live"* is set over against the word *"dead"* as it was used in the previous Verse.

In fact, these who *"live"* were once dead to God, but now have yielded to the appeals of the Holy Spirit, thereby taking unto themselves the Eternal Life of Redemption. Whereas sinners are dead in sins, Christians are alive to the worth of the soul, the Presence of God, the importance of all that God does, even the solemnities of eternity. Those who *"live"* do so only because of the Life of Christ which has been imparted unto them upon Faith, and they, consequently, act and feel as if these things had a real existence, which they do.

It is observable that Paul makes a distinction here between those for whom Christ died, and those who actually *"live."* As we have already stated, the Atonement was for all, but only a part are actually made alive to God.

Multitudes reject it; but the fact that He died for all, that He tasted death for every man, that He not only died for the elect but for all others, that His benevolence was so great as to embrace the whole human family in the design of His Death, is a reason why they who are actually made alive to God should consecrate themselves entirely to His Service.

The fact that He died for all, and that we have been privileged to accept all the benefits which His Death and Resurrection have brought about, we certainly should devote all that we have to His Service.

The phrase, *"Should not henceforth live unto themselves,"* now presents the manner as to how all Believers should observe and conduct themselves toward this *"Gift of God."*

A SALVATION FROM SIN AND SELF

The idea is, in this Christian Life the Believer should not seek his own ease and pleasure; should not make it his great object to promote his own interests; but should make it the grand purpose of our lives to promote His honor, and to advance His Cause. This is a vital principle in our experience with the Lord; and it is exceedingly important to know what is meant by living to ourselves, and whether we do it.

There is a new view of life when one becomes a Christian. One does not stay in the same place. One does not live the same way. One does not have the same ideas. With the new nature there comes new activities. It would be impossible to conceive of the Christian Life continuing on the same basis as the old life. There is a new person indwelling us. There is a new pattern for the old ways. There is also a new power for the old weaknesses.

WHAT DO WE MEAN BY SALVATION FROM SIN AND SELF?

Most Believers understand very well what we mean by Salvation from sin; however, very few understand what we are speaking about when we say, *"Jesus died that we might be saved from sin and self!"*

As we have previously stated, the human body is that which responds to the world, the soul is that which responds to self, and the spirit (of man) is that which responds to God. So, when we deal with our *"self,"* we are at the same time dealing with our *"soul."* It is impossible to deal with one without dealing with the other.

Self is the seed of our passions, appetites, desires, love, and hate, etc. It is our personality.

Through the Fall, all of this has been warped, twisted, perverted, and depraved. In other words, it doesn't function properly. Appetites crave that which is ungodly, passions run wild, desires become evil effected, as well, we love the wrong things and at times hate the wrong things.

Upon conversion, all of this changes; however, whereas the sin question is settled immediately, the *"self"* question is in fact a process. It is called Sanctification, and remains a process until we die, or else the Rapture takes place.

We have to learn to deny self, in effect, to properly place self in Christ. This and this alone is the only safe place, hence Jesus speaking of one denying oneself, taking up the Cross daily, following Him (Lk. 9:23).

In the last few years, we have heard much of high self-esteem or low self-esteem. In fact, some Preachers have foolishly held up high self-esteem as the answer to all the problems of mankind. How ridiculous!

Whether it's high or low, it is still *"self,"* and that presents the problem. As stated, self must be properly placed in Christ, which is meant to be done at the Cross, and can only be done at the Cross.

HOW IS IT DONE?

We must go back to Luke 9:23-24:

1. Deny himself: This means that Christ now becomes preeminent in our lives, with self not all paramount anymore in anything.

2. Take up his Cross daily: This refers to an ongoing process, which will never stop, at least until death or the Rapture.

It refers to understanding that Jesus not only paid the sin debt with His Death at Calvary, but as well, broke the grip of sin. Consequently, we are to appropriate the victory of Calvary everyday within our hearts and lives. We are to understand that it was there that the great work was done and in effect, finished. We must also know that when He died, we were baptized into His Death, buried with Him, and arose with Him in newness of life (Rom. 6:1-11).

The *"Cross"* is to die on, and as it regards the Child of God, it refers to self dying there. However, it is a death that must be done on a *"daily"* basis. Even though Salvation is a once for all thing, Sanctification, as stated, is a process, even a daily, unending process. As well, Sanctification, hence the self-life is tied totally to the Cross, and one's understanding of what Jesus did there for lost, dying humanity.

3. Follow Me (Jesus): The following Him has to do with the Cross. By that we mean that Jesus redeemed humanity by way of the Cross, and we are to understand that our victory, in fact all of our victory in every respect, comes through the Cross. As we have already stated, but due to its vast significance we will reiterate. Most understand the Cross and Salvation, but few understand the Cross and Sanctification. (Please see our Commentary on Romans Chapters 6, 7, and 8, in respect to this all-important subject.)

4. We must lose our life (self) for His sake: However, in the doing of such, we will *"save it,"* i.e. *"find it."*

PERSONAL WILL INSTEAD OF GOD'S WILL

Whenever Christians jockey for position, manipulate others to their own end or satisfaction, play religious politics, i.e. *"you scratch my back and I'll scratch yours,"* one can be certain that self-will is predominant and not the Will of God.

Those who ardently seek God's Will, and ascertain His Will as to where they presently are, will then seek to do the very best job they can in that particular capacity. Staying open to His Will and Leading, they make no effort for self-promotion, but leave all of that in the Hands of the Lord. At His time, He does what He desires, and promotion comes; however, it is not promotion engineered by human hands, but exclusively by the Lord. He leads, directs, moves, and is in control of everything.

The individual who is in this position, is the most fulfilled, the most rewarded, the happiest, simply because he is seeking the Will of God, and not his own purposes or desires.

The phrase, *"But unto Him which died for them, and rose again,"* refers of course to the Lord Jesus Christ. To live unto Him is the opposite to living unto ourselves.

UNTO HIM

We are to seek His honor; to feel that we belong to Him, which in reality we do; that all our time and talents — all our strength in intellect and body — all the avails of our skill and toil — all belong to Him, and should be employed in His Service, irrespective as to whether we are a Preacher or otherwise.

If we have talents by which we can influence other minds, they should be employed to honor the Saviour. If we have skill, or strength to labor, by which we can make money, we should feel that it all belongs to Him, and should be employed in His Service in one way or the other.

If we have property, we should feel that it is His, and that He has a claim upon it all, and that it should be honestly consecrated to His Cause.

A servant, a slave, does not live to himself, but to His master. His person, his time, his limbs, his talents, and the avails of his industry are not regarded as his own. He is judged incapable of holding any property, or anything for that matter, which is not at the disposal of his master. If he has strength, it is his master's. If he has skill, the avails of it are his master's.

He is regarded as having been purchased with money; and the purchase-money is supposed to give a right to his time, his talents, his

NOTES

services, and his soul. Such as the slave is supposed to become by purchase, and by the operation of human laws, the Christian becomes by the purchase of the Son of God, and by the voluntary recognition of Him as the Master, as having a right to all that we have and are. To Him, all belongs; and all should be employed in endeavoring to promote His Glory, and in advancing His Cause.

WHICH DIED FOR THEM

The effect of the Death of Christ was the same as a purchase. In fact, it was a purchase (I Cor. 6:20; 7:23; I Pet. 1:18-19).

What compels Paul to sacrifice himself to the Work of God, and which should compel us as well, is the conviction, that One, even Christ, died on behalf of all men a redeeming death (Rom. 5:15-19). That was the greatest Sacrifice, the greatest Gift, the greatest Work, in all of human history.

As well, in that death, all potentially died with Him — died to their life of sin and rose to the life of Righteousness. Paul even said, and which identifies with all, *"I have been crucified with Christ"* (Gal. 2:19-20). When Christ died, all humanity, of which He was the Federal Head, died potentially with Him to sin and self, which guarantees Eternal Life to all who will believe (Jn. 3:16).

AND ROSE AGAIN

The Resurrection of Christ ratified all that was done at Calvary. To this fact, Paul traced all his hopes of Eternal Life, and of the Resurrection from the dead for all Saints (Rom. 4:25).

As we have the hope of the Resurrection from the dead only from the fact that He rose; as He has *"brought life and immortality to light,"* and hath in this way *"abolished death"* (II Tim. 1:10), as all the prospect of entering a world where there is no death and no grave is to be traced to the Resurrection of the Saviour, so we are bound by every obligation of gratitude to devote ourselves without any reserve to Him. To Him, and Him alone, should we live; and in His Cause our lives should be, as Paul's was, a living sacrifice, holy and acceptable in His sight (Barnes).

"Oh happy day, Oh happy day,
"When Jesus washed my sins away."

NOTES

(16) "WHEREFORE HENCEFORTH KNOW WE NO MAN AFTER THE FLESH: YEA, THOUGH WE HAVE KNOWN CHRIST AFTER THE FLESH, YET NOW HENCEFORTH KNOW WE HIM NO MORE."

The phrase, *"Wherefore henceforth know we no man after the flesh,"* refers to looking at people in the exact opposite manner as they are viewed by the world.

AFTER THE FLESH

"After the flesh" pertains to any and all things which characterizes humanity in this present world. It speaks of riches, fame, education, knowledge, ability, place, position, etc. It is the manner in which the world recognizes its own. It is the system of the world, the way of the world, the attitude of the world.

Unfortunately, such attitude and action too often characterizes the Church as well. Men are elected to some Church office by popular ballot, which is not necessarily wrong, though it be *"after the flesh."* The wrong comes in, when the Church attempts to make spiritual that which is of the flesh. These people oftentimes are lauded, revered, and even feared, even though in spiritual reality, they have contributed little if anything to the Cause of Christ. As stated, too much of the organizational structure of modern Religious Denominations fall into the category of *"after the flesh."* As well, this would include many Independent Churches, for the simple matter that this problem of the *"flesh"* is rather a spirit than a particular denomination, etc.

Also, one is not to read these statements thinking they are meant to demean organization, for they are not. In fact, there is no organization like that of the Lord. Everything He has and does is organized, but the secret is that it is His organization and not man's.

NO MAN

What a person is in Christ, is what that person is. In other words, it is what God says about the person, which shows itself in the operation of the Holy Spirit within one's life. Regrettably, the Church little goes by that criteria, but rather after *"the flesh."*

This of which Paul speaks, has the effect of changing all our feelings, and giving us an entirely new view of men, of ourselves, and even of the Lord.

As Paul makes this statement, his mind seems to have been thrown back to the period when these new views burst upon his soul; and the sentiment is, that from the time when he obtained those new views, he had resolved to know no one after the flesh.

The idea of Paul's statement is that our estimate of man is formed by other views, that according to the flesh. What was in Paul's mind was one thing, what the Holy Spirit is portraying is that which we want to know. However, what the Holy Spirit desired that we know, as well, had root in the heart of the Apostle. Possibly the following may include these things which were in his mind.

BIRTH OR COUNTRY

Paul was no more influenced in his estimate of men by regard to their birth or country. He did not form an attachment to a Jew because he was a Jew, or to a Gentile because he was a Gentile. He had learned that Christ died for all, and he felt disposed to regard all alike.

If the color of one's skin becomes apparent, then the person is not conducting himself as Paul mentions here. In fact, there are only two types of people in the world, at least as far as God is concerned, those who are Believers, and those who aren't! Consequently, any individual ought to be welcome in our Churches, whomever they may be, or whatever they may have been in the past, or whatever they are at present. There is inestimable worth in the heart and life of every individual, irrespective as to their person. In other words, Jesus died for all, which is the foundation of all that Paul is here saying. So the question remains, do we look at men after the flesh or after the Spirit?

RANK, WEALTH, OR OFFICE

Paul was not influenced in his estimate of men by their rank, and wealth, and office. Before his conversion, he had been; but now he learned to look on them after the mind of Christ, and to regard that as making the only permanent and really important distinction among men. He did not esteem one man highly because he was of elevated rank, or of great wealth, and another less because he was of a different rank in life.

NOTES

MAYBE EVEN HIS OWN RELATIVES

It may also include the idea that he had left his own kindred and friends on account of superior attachment to Christ. He had parted from them to preach the Gospel. He was not restrained by their opinion; he was not kept from going from land to land regarding their desires.

It may be that they were opposed to him, and there is evidence that they were, especially as it regarded his efforts in the Cause of the Lord Jesus Christ.

It may be that they would have set before him the advantages of his birth and education; would have reminded him of his early brilliant prospects; and would have used all the means possible to dissuade him from embarking in a Cause like that in which he was engaged.

The passage here means that Paul was influenced by none of these considerations.

THAT WHICH HAPPENED TO HIM

In early life Paul had been very much influenced by *"the flesh."* He had prided himself on rank, and on talent. He was proud of his own advantages as a Jew; and he estimated worth by rank, and by national distinction (Phil. 3:4-6).

He had despised Christians on account of their being the followers of the Man of Nazareth; and there can be no reason to doubt that he partook of the common feelings of his countrymen, and held in contempt the whole Gentile world. But his views were changed — so much changed as to make it proper to say that he was a new creature, which the next Verse spells out.

When converted, he did not confer with flesh and blood (Gal. 1:16), and in the School of Christ, he had learned that if a man was His Disciple, he must be willing to forsake father, mother, sister, and brother, and in effect, to hate his own life that he might honor Him exclusively (Lk. 14:26).

He had formed his principle of action now from a higher standard than any regard to rank, or wealth, or national distinction, and had risen above them all; and now estimated men, not by these external and factitious advantages, but by a reference to their personal character and moral worth.

The phrase, *"Yea, though we have known Christ after the flesh, yet now henceforth know we Him no more,"* could very well be a rebuke to those members of the Christ party at Corinth, who may have boasted that they were superior to all others because they were following the teaching of some particular Teacher who may have even personally seen or known Christ during His earthly Ministry. Or it may be possible that even someone in the Church at Corinth, a Jew perhaps, had personally seen Christ. At any rate, if in fact that was the case, this idolizing of Christ in the flesh, it was a spirit which Christ Himself not only discouraged (Jn. 16:7) but even rebuked (Mat. 12:50).

CHRIST AFTER THE FLESH

To Paul, Christ is now regarded as far above all local, national, personal, and Jewish limitations. Even though he was the Jewish Messiah, He did not come to this world solely for Jews, but in fact, for the entirety of mankind. Consequently, Paul had banished all Jewish particularism for Gospel Evangelism. He regards Christ, not in the light of earthly relationships and conditions, but as the risen, glorified, eternal, universal Saviour of all men (Farrar).

This mention of not knowing Christ after the flesh would have been very special to Paul, and particularly peculiar to him as a Jew.

There can be no doubt that Paul, in common with his countrymen, had previously expected a Messiah Who would be a magnificent temporal Prince and Conqueror, One Who they supposed would be a worthy successor of David and Solomon. The coming of such a Prince, Paul had confidently expected. In fact, he expected no other type of Messiah. He had fixed his hopes on that. This is what is meant by the expression *"to know Christ after the flesh."*

It does not mean that he had seen Him in the flesh, but that he had formed, so to speak, carnal views of Him, and such as men of this world regard as grand and magnificent in a Monarch and Conqueror. However, he had no correct views of His Spiritual Character, and of the pure and holy purposes for which He would come into the world.

WE KNOW HIM NO MORE IN THIS FASHION

We know Him no more in this manner. Our conceptions and views of Him are changed. We no more regard Him according to the flesh; we no longer esteem the Messiah Who was to come as a temporal Prince and Warrior; but we look on Him as a Spiritual Saviour, a Redeemer from sin. The idea is, that his views of Him had been entirely changed.

It means that from the moment of Paul's conversion he had laid aside all his views of Jesus being a temporal sovereign and all his feelings that He was to be honored only because he supposed that Jesus would have an elevated rank among the Monarchs of the earth.

However, upon conversion his views are changed. He is seen to be the chief among tens of thousands, and altogether lovely; as pure, and holy, and benevolent; as mighty, and great, and glorious; as wonderful in His precepts, wonderful in His life, wonderful in His death, wonderful in His resurrection, and as most glorious as He is seated on the Right Hand of God. He is seen to be a Saviour exactly adapted to the condition and wants of the soul; and the soul yields itself to Him to be redeemed by Him alone.

There is no change of view so marked and decided as that of a sinner in regard to the Lord Jesus Christ at his conversion; and it is a clear proof that we have never been Born-Again if our views in reference to Him have never undergone any change.

WHAT THINK YE OF CHRIST?

This question, *"What think ye of Christ?"*, is a question the answer to which will determine any man's character, and demonstrate whether he is or is not a Child of God.

Tindal translated Paul's statement in this manner, *"Though we have known Christ after the flesh, now henceforth know we Him so no more."*

This statement of Paul is so large that it transcends all national hopes, and even brings itself to our present hour. The Reader must understand, that there is no such thing as a Baptist Jesus, or Pentecostal Jesus, or Catholic Jesus, or Holiness Jesus, etc.

As well, Jesus is above all Doctrine, all theory, all teaching, all revelation. We dare not bring Him down to the level of particulars.

Also, He is not a Name to merely be used in the rite of Water Baptism, or the symbol of the Lord's Supper, or to be associated with a particular Church.

The moment we do this, and much we have not named, we trivialize Him, decrease His

NOTES

stature, insult His Deity, and weaken His Redemption. When we do these things we are doing exactly what Paul said not to do, *"Though we have known Christ after the flesh* (before we gave our heart to Christ, thereby having foolish notions of Him), yet now (after conversion) *henceforth know we Him no more,* (in these trivial ways)."

AS CHRIST, SO MEN!

If we properly judge Christ, properly understand His Deity, His universal Salvation, then we will properly judge men. We will realize that the old judgments and measurements are out-of-date.

From now on we measure a man by a new standard, not by the flesh, but by the Spirit; not by social birth, but by the New Birth; not by his advantages, but by his activities; not by himself, but by Christ. In Christ we judge a man, not by what he has, but by what he does; not by what he was, but by what he is.

Why is all of this so? In fact, how is all of this so? How do we come by this measurement?

The next Verse gives us the answer in crystal clarity.

(17) "THEREFORE IF ANY MAN BE IN CHRIST, HE IS A NEW CREATURE: OLD THINGS ARE PASSED AWAY; BEHOLD, ALL THINGS ARE BECOME NEW."

The phrase, *"Therefore if any man be in Christ,"* refers to being united to Christ by Faith; or to be in Him as the branch is in the vine — that is, so united to the vine, or so in it, as to derive all its nourishment and support from it, and to be sustained entirely by it (Jn. 15:2).

IN CHRIST

"As the branch cannot bear fruit of itself, except it abide in the vine; no more can ye, except ye abide in Me" (Jn. 15:4). To be *"in Christ"* denotes a more tender and close union; and implies that all our support is from Him. All our strength is derived from Him; and denotes further that we shall partake of His fullness, and share in His Glory, as the branch partakes of the strength and vigor of the parent vine.

UNIVERSAL

The affirmation here is universal, *"if any man be in Christ"*; that is, all who become true Christians, irrespective as to race, color, nationality or social position, undergo such a change in their views and feelings as to make it proper to say of them that they are new creatures.

NOTES

No matter what they have been before, whether moral or immoral; whether infidels or speculative Believers; whether amiable, or debased, sensual, and polluted, yet if they become Believers, thereby placed *"in Christ,"* they all experience such a change as to make it obvious as to that change.

This means that the Gospel of Jesus Christ is not a *"Western Gospel,"* but rather is a Gospel for the entirety of mankind and for all the world. In other words, it is a *"Western, Eastern, Southern, and Northern Gospel." "For God so loved the world . . ."* (Jn. 3:16).

WHAT DOES IT EXACTLY MEAN TO BE IN CHRIST?

First of all let's see what it is not.

It is not mental affirmation. In other words, millions of people believe in Jesus Christ, believe that He was the Son of God, believe all the right things, but yet aren't saved. So, merely mentally affirming something carries no weight.

Regarding the matter of *"true believing,"* at least as the Bible speaks of such, one must take upon oneself the nature, character, processes, leading, and direction, of the philosophy, object, or person in which or whom one is believing. In this case we are speaking of Christ; therefore, it means to fully accept Him, in all that He is and all that He did. Actually, this is not difficult to understand.

Hundreds of millions of people follow Mohammed. They believe in him and the teachings of the Koran. It doesn't save them, because there is no Salvation from that source. Nevertheless, they do believe. One could name many other religions in the same manner. These people believe who and what they are following, and do so, at least many of them, with all their ardor and strength. So, merely believing is not enough.

Regarding Christ, the believing must be total, meaning that He becomes our all in all, our everything, and to be sure when this is done, a change takes place in one's heart, which cannot be brought about by these other religions, etc.

NOTES

Fully accepting Christ as well, has little to do with joining a particular Church, or prescribing to a particular Doctrine, or engaging in a particular ceremony such as Water Baptism, or the Lord's Supper, etc. Untold millions are very religiously engaged in the ceremony of the Church, but do not know Jesus at all, are not saved, and in fact, are just as lost as those who make no profession of Faith whatsoever.

Being *"in Christ,"* is first of all and foremost, a heartfelt experience. In other words, one accepts Christ in their heart, exhibiting Faith in Him, and the moment this is done, wherever or whomever the person may be, that individual is saved, i.e., *"in Christ"* (Rom. 10:9-10, 13; Eph. 2:8-9; Rev. 22:17).

AN INNER CONNECTION WITH CHRIST

To be constrained by Christ's love and to live unto Him alone evidently involves an inner connection with Christ. This is what is meant by being *"in Christ."* In fact, this is a phrase, or else similar, which is used by Paul in many varied connections.

The picture is that of a sphere or a circle. Christ fills that circle as Christ, as our Saviour, our Lord, etc., with all His love for us, His Life, the fount of Life for us. We, too are placed into this sphere.

How?

By the means of Faith which is wrought in us by the Word, meaning that we hear the Word of God and the Holy Spirit quickens it to our heart, we believe, and are saved, i.e., *"in Christ."* We are thus in a living, spiritual connection with Christ which means that our emptiness and need are filled up with Christ.

A NEW CREATURE

The phrase, *"He is a new creature,"* proclaims in the Greek, that he definitely is a new creature. In other words, there is no *"maybe so"* about the situation.

The word *"creature"* is interchangeable here with the word *"creation."* Either or both are correct. We have then a new creation as against the old creation.

The fountainhead of life of the old creation was Adam. From him sprang the physical race down to our present day, but it was and is a race of sinners. It was a race, if you will, of living dead men. They lived physically but were dead spiritually. The need was for a brand-new creation. It called for the introduction of a new kind of Life. That kind of Life came in and through Jesus Christ. Now we have, according to the law of spiritual genetics, a new creation of which Christ is *the* fountainhead. It is a race of new people. They are people with a new nature (Laurin).

HOW IT CREATES

The word *"creature"* means the act of creating and is then applied also to what the act creates. A Creator is implied, and of course, the Creator is the Lord Jesus Christ, Who carries forth His work by the Power, Agency, Person, and Ministry of the Holy Spirit.

As we've already stated, *"Creation"* leads us to think of what God did when He created the world. In fact, the two acts are comparable, but yet in one way vastly different.

We are not made a new creation by Omnipotence (Almighty Power) but by Grace. The two are distinct and are never confused in Scripture. The one is God's power as much as the other, but the first created that which was the world and the universe, which is physical, while the other creates that which is spiritual.

We are *"a new creation"* (*"creature"* is less exact) by virtue of the spiritual life created in us, the life by which we live not to ourselves but to Christ, meaning He is totally the Source.

REGENERATION

In other words, becoming a *"new creature"* involves the miracle of regeneration.

Paul also said, *"Not by works of righteousness which we have done, but according to His Mercy He saved us, by the washing of regeneration, and renewing of the Holy Spirit"* (Titus 3:5).

In trying to find the cause of evil, and being forced to admit that it does exist, Medical Scientists are closely observing and endeavoring to understand the genetic make-up of man. Genetics is a branch of biology that deals with the heredity and variation of organisms, in other words as it relates to man, who we are, what we are, and why we are. It has to do with *"genes"* which are an element of the germ plasm that controls transmission of a hereditary character by specifying the structure.

The word *"genealogy"* is derived from the word *"genes"* or *"genetic make-up"* which refers to the account of the descent of a person, family, or group from an ancestor.

To make it simple, Scientists are endeavoring to ascertain if the person who is a serial killer, or an alcoholic, a homosexual, pathological liar, etc., has a different type of *"gene"* than those who are not of these particular aberrations. In fact, Medical Scientists are closer to the truth than they realize, but yet only closer, and not actually the Truth.

Their idea is, if the genes of these particular individuals are in fact different, then possibly the gene can be altered or changed, thereby changing the person, etc. Once again, even though they are closer to the Truth, they are merely treating symptoms, that is, if they are in fact able to do such a thing. In other words, even if they could do such, it would not change the person.

THE FALL

The Truth goes back to the Fall of man in the Garden of Eden. When this happened, all of his *"genes"* were altered in a negative sense, i.e., *"perverted."* It is referred to theologically as the *"depraved nature."* In other words, it is not a physical problem as our good Scientists think, but rather a spiritual problem.

At the *"Fall"* man was cut off from his Life Source, spiritually speaking, which is God. Man was created by God to depend on God for his Life Source. When this is cut off, which it was, the source that took its place was that of Satan, which in fact is, perversion, evil, aberration, pollution, i.e., *"death,"* i.e., *"spiritual death."*

That's why Jesus said, *"The thief* (Satan) *cometh not, but for to steal, and to kill, and to destroy: I am come that they might have Life, and that they might have it more abundantly"* (Jn. 10:10).

That's why Jesus also said, *"Except a man be born again, he cannot see the Kingdom of God"* (Jn. 3:3).

The *"born again"* experience, involves *"regeneration,"* which actually means, that a person is then *"re-gened."* The *"Life Source"* is now flowing back into the individual, which constitutes this miraculous change, hence as Paul said, *"He is a new creature."*

THIS PARTICULAR TRUTH

The Truth is, that due to the Fall, even as we have stated, all are born with irregular or perverted genes. And if the Scientists keep probing, they probably will find that there are particular *"aberrated genes"* peculiar to the Homosexual, pathological liars, etc. However, even though they may possibly find such, they will not be able to alter this situation by changing the *"gene."* They have no way to insert Spiritual Life into the genes; consequently, they cannot and will not be able to alter this situation of evil by this method. So, what else am I saying?

I am saying that homosexuals were definitely born with a proclivity toward that disposition, and so were pathological liars, murderers, etc.

In theologically arguing this position, some may then contend that if that is in fact the case, then these people are not responsible, and for the obvious reasons. However, that is true but at the same time not true.

The Truth is, all are born in original sin, and all are thereby, born lost. While all do not turn out to be homosexuals, or serial killers, etc., all are in fact depraved. That's the reason Paul said, which we've already studied, *"That if One* (Jesus) *died for all* (all of mankind), *then we're all dead,"* i.e., *"born in this condition of spiritual deadness."*

Again, the Truth is, that God does not actually banish sinners from His Presence, for the simple reason that they are sinners. He certainly knows that mankind is in this condition, because of something one man (Adam) did at the dawn of time. Therefore, the condemnation and eternal banishment comes about, and will come about, because men reject the Solution to this terrible problem, the Lord Jesus Christ. That's why Jesus said concerning the Holy Spirit, *"And when He is come, He will reprove the world of sin, and of Righteousness, and of Judgment: of sin, because they believe not on Me"* (Jn. 16:8-9).

So, men are eternally lost, not just because they are sinners (although they are definitely lost on that account), but primarily due to the fact that they reject and refuse the Solution to this terrible sin problem, Who is Jesus Christ. It is only through Him that men can reach God, and only through Him that man can be Born-Again, i.e., *"new creatures,"* i.e., *"re-gened."*

A MORAL CREATION

The *"new creature"* here of which Paul speaks, is a new creation in a moral sense; and

NOTES

the phrase, *"new creature"* is equivalent to the expression in Ephesians 4:24: *"The new man, which after God is created in Righteousness and True Holiness."* It means, evidently, that there is a change produced in the renewed heart of man that is equivalent to the act of creation, and that bears a strong resemblance to it — a change, so to speak, as if the man were made over again, and had become new. Even though the words are here figurative, still, at the same time they are literal. The phrase implies the following:

DIVINE POWER

There is an exertion of Divine Power in the conversion of the sinner as really as in the act of creating the world out of nothing, and this is as indispensable in the one case as in the other. However, this Divine Power is in the realm of Enabling Grace.

That's the reason that the foolishness of psychological counseling (psychology) is of no value whatsoever. Psychology has no power, no wonder drug, no proper medicine, only talk. And if the Psychologists can *"talk"* these problems away, then why did not God do the same, when He in fact, did speak everything else into existence (Gen. Chpt. 1).

The Truth is, that the condition of man is of such magnitude, that even God could not speak Redemption into existence, but first had to pay the sin debt by Jesus dying on Calvary, and even then there had to be an infusion of power into the heart and life of the believing sinner in order for him to be saved.

As well, even after the individual comes to Christ, Jesus continues to be the answer to any and all following sin, aberrations, etc. The idea that we must believe Christ in order to be saved, but not continue to trust Him for any following problems, but rather resort to Psychologists, as the far greater majority of the Church teaches, is a spiritual travesty of the highest order. In fact, it borders on blasphemy!

If Jesus is the answer to the sin question of man as it regards Salvation, He is also the answer regarding any future problems. All sin, moral failure, or aberrations spring from the same source, namely Satan, i.e., *"the sin nature."* So, if Jesus is the answer for the former, He is definitely the answer for the latter as well.

NOTES

The major problem is twofold as it regards the modern Church and humanistic Psychology, etc.:

1. Unbelief: Most in the Church have drifted so far away from the Word of God, that they simply no longer believe that Jesus is the answer, despite what they may say. In other words, if they did believe, they would not recommend humanistic wisdom, i.e., *"psychological counseling."*

2. The second major reason, is a lack of understanding respecting all the benefits of Calvary and the Resurrection. Many Preachers believe in the effect of Calvary regarding one's Salvation, but think it starts and stops there.

However, Calvary while definitely having to do with our Salvation, also has to do with our Sanctification, which pertains to our everyday walk with the Lord, which of course, will continue until we die or else the Rapture takes place. As the sinner must believe in what Jesus did at Calvary in order to be saved, likewise, the Believer must also believe that Calvary and the Resurrection provided and does continue to provide, power for our continued walk. I dare say that not one out of a thousand Christians actually understand this as they should. So, meeting these problems after one is saved, and not understanding the benefits of Calvary which guarantees victory over any and all problems of this nature after Salvation, thereby not receiving its benefits, many Preachers resort to the recommendation of the Psychologists. However, this will not help the person, but in fact, will make the situation worse, pulling him away from the only answer, which is Calvary and the Resurrection.

(Please see our Commentary on Romans, Chapters 6, 7, and 8, which deals with this situation at length.)

A TOTAL CHANGE

The change which is produced at conversion is so great as to make it proper to say that the individual is a new man or a new woman. He has new views, new motives, new principles, new objects and plans of life. He seeks new purposes, and he lives for new ends.

If a drunkard is saved, there is no impropriety in saying that he is a new man. In fact, he no longer has to say as Alcoholics Anonymous claims, *"I am an alcoholic,"* or words to that effect. He is no longer an alcoholic, etc.

If a man who was licentious becomes pure, there is no impropriety in saying that he is not the same man that he was before. There is in fact such a change as to make the language proper.

So in the conversion of a sinner, there is a change so deep, so clear, so entire, and so abiding, that it is proper to say, here is a new creation of God — a work of the Divine Power as decided and as glorious as when God created all things out of nothing.

A short time ago, someone mentioned to me a particular man (whom I did not know) who was supposed to have gotten saved at a particular Church. The individual relating the account went on to say, *"But there has been no change, he is continuing to do the same things he has always done."*

That being the case, and which is the case with untold millions, this man really was not saved. Because when someone truly comes to Christ, the very symbol of Christianity is the moral change which instantly takes place in that person's life. That doesn't mean that he or she becomes perfect, for such will not be until the coming Resurrection, but it does mean that the change is so radical that it is obvious.

OLD THINGS

The phrase, *"Old things are passed away,"* means literally everything of the old life before conversion. That has been cast aside, which are *"the old things"* of the flesh, in which we one time lived, which at one time were our love and our delight, which at one time filled our whole being.

Actually, there are two kinds of old things which pass away. They are as follows:

THE OLD MAN

The spirit, nature, and power of sin — the old man, which is nothing more nor less than the spirit, nature, and power of the Devil working in men of disobedience, was (is) buried with Christ (Rom. 6:3-7).

This is what the Bible calls, as stated, *"the old man"* (Rom. 6:6; Eph. 4:22; Col. 3:9), *"sin"* (Jn. 1:29; 8:34; Rom. 6:4; 8:2), *"the body of sin"* (Rom. 6:6), *"the power of Satan"* (Acts 26:18), *"the body of this death"* (Rom. 7:24), *"the lust of the flesh"* (Eph. 2:3), *"the lust of the eyes"* (I Jn. 2:15-17), *"the pride of life"* (I Jn. 2:15-17), *"the works of the flesh"* (Gal. 5:19), *"the world"* (I Jn. 2:15-17; James 4:4), *"vile affections"* (Rom. 1:26, 29), *"the lusts of the mind"* (Eph. 2:3), *"the lusts of sin"* (Rom. 6:11-12), *"the motions of sins"* (Rom. 7:5), *"the law of sin and death"* (Rom. 7:7; 8:2), *"the carnal mind"* (Rom 8:1-13), *"the god of this world"* (II Cor. 4:4), *"spiritual wickedness in high places... rulers of darkness"* (Eph. 6:12), *"the lusts of your father"* (Jn. 8:44), *"sin that dwelleth in me"* (Rom. 7:17), *"the course of this world"* (Eph. 2:2), *"the body of the sins of the flesh"* (Col. 2:11; Rom. Chpt. 8; Gal. 5:24).

NOTES

ALL OUTWARD SIN

Both outward and inward sin must pass away or one cannot claim to be in Christ. The theory that only outward transgressions are forgiven and one is still under control of the old man, the Devil, is one of the most erroneous doctrines in Christendom (Rom. 6:6-23; 8:1-13; II Cor. 5:17-18; Eph. 4:24; I Jn. 5:18).

That doesn't mean that there will not be future problems, which in fact there always are, and without exception. Those problems come about through the *"sin nature"* which still remains in the Believer, but which within itself is of no harm or consequence. But yet, if the Believer yields to the flesh and sins, and then tries to overcome that sin by efforts of the flesh, which almost all of us attempt to do, then the sin nature springs into life, with the Christian finding himself under the dominion of sin again. This doesn't mean that he's lost, but does mean that he is not properly interpreting Calvary and the Resurrection regarding his everyday walk with the Lord. In fact, until he learns how to appropriate the benefits of Calvary and the Resurrection to himself on a daily basis, he will not in fact, overcome these evil impulses and sin.

The moment the believing sinner comes to Christ, at that moment every sin and weakness is instantly addressed, with the sin question totally taken in hand and the sin debt completely paid. In other words, the new Believer starts out with a clean slate, carrying no baggage of the past life. However, sadly and regrettably, Satan does not cease his temptation and pressure.

The Evil One knows our ignorance regarding what Christ has done for us at Calvary, in this Finished Work. He takes advantage of that ignorance and causes us great problems. If not handled properly, we find the *"old things"* coming back. Paul dealt with this at length in Romans Chapter 7, even as he faced this problem himself after conversion. Thankfully, the Lord gave him the answer to this problem, which is given to us in Romans Chapters 6 and 8.

NOTES

ATTACHMENT TO RITES AND CEREMONIES

When a person is truly Born-Again, all religion passes away, and by that I mean attachment to rites and ceremonies, thinking that such brings Salvation. All of these things are renounced along with dependence on such, with Christ Alone looked at as the Saviour, which He is.

The tragedy of much of modern Christianity is, that untold millions look to the Church to save them, or some particular doctrine, when in reality, they've never really had a personal relationship with Jesus Christ. In other words, they're not saved. However, the moment that true conversion happens, all of these other things are put in their proper perspective, in reality dependence on such passing away, with Christ now becoming the total object.

THE LOVE OF SIN

The love of sin is a powerful factor, with the individual unable to change that situation unless he comes to Christ. Then strangely enough, the appetites, passions, and loves greatly and wondrously change. The sins which once brought pleasure and satisfaction, now no longer do so. Actually, this is what confuses many unsaved people.

They have it in their minds that if they come to Christ, they will still love their old sins but just simply won't be able to do them. Contemplating that in their heart, they reject Christ. However, what they do not understand is, that upon coming to Christ, everything changes, plus the things they once loved such as sin, they no longer do.

That's one of the reasons that oftentimes people have to be flat on their back, proverbially speaking, before they will say yes to Christ. This means that many have to get sick as the result of their sin before they will finally surrender to the Lord.

LOVE OF SELF PASSES AWAY

In fact, the change of attitude toward *"self,"* is one of the greatest changes which takes place at conversion. The supreme love of self passes away. Self is then seen as by and large selfish; consequently, with no more provisions made for the flesh, but everything toward Christ.

This is a change which is instantaneous at the New Birth, which is carried on by progressive Sanctification, and will be consummated at death and in Heaven.

ALL THINGS ARE BECOME NEW

The phrase, *"Behold, all things are become new,"* means that the old things could not be renewed, and had to be cast away entirely, with new things, completely new and fashioned, to take their place. This new life brings an entirely new set of appetites, desires, ideals, inclinations, etc. If the Believer will nourish this new Life of the Spirit which has come by the New Birth, these new appetites, desires, ideals, and inclinations will grow and develop and become the controlling factor of life. What is true *of* the Believer will be true *in* the Believer.

This is a crucial point of Christian experience. Someone will say that when he became a Christian he did not immediately get rid of a bad temper or a quick tongue, etc. However, we must understand the following:

The New Birth does not annihilate the old nature, but actually brings in a new nature to control it. Henceforth, the old tempers and the old tongues have a new master and are under a new control. Their passing away is both a crisis and a process. The crisis of the passing away comes at the New Birth when the New Nature is implanted to displace these faults from their old seats of control.

POTENTIAL CONTROL

Potential control and conquest lie within us the moment we are Born-Again. However, actual control and conquest depend on the degree to which we yield ourselves to the transforming power of our new nature, which has to do with our understanding of the benefits of Calvary and the Resurrection. We have to understand that Jesus not only paid the sin debt there, but as well, broke the sin grip within our heart and life. Even though Salvation as it regards the sin debt being paid and our Faith in that, is instantaneous, the other is not instantaneous, and in fact is a process.

In other words, most of us go through a trial and error period regarding overcoming certain things within our life, in other words, our Sanctification. We know how to appropriate Faith for Salvation, that being a once for all thing at the time of the New Birth; however, it is not so easy appropriating Faith for this daily walk before the Lord, for the simple reason that we tend to lean on the arm of flesh, thinking all the time it is the Spirit. As well, this is a daily process and experience.

We still have to contend with some of the *"old things"* while we live in the *"new things,"* but control and conquest is the result of the indwelling new nature of Christ.

Do not think for a moment that the statement, *"Old things are passed away,"* means that there is no more evil in you or in the world about you. Were this true it would belie the consistent teaching of the Bible as well as the facts of life. The Truth is that a new kind of life in Christ has come and it has within it the power and blessing of new things.

It is a new relationship with God. He becomes our Father instead of merely being our Creator. It is a new rule of action, a new object in life, a new experience of pleasure, a new thrill of living and a new satisfaction of heart. This and a multitude of other new things come in the wake of this new life. However, we have to learn to live in this new set of things, appropriating Life from Christ, while at the same time some of the old things keep trying to make a reentrance.

This new life gives us a new set of ideals. Now they are Bible ideals. As someone has well said, *"Ideals are like stars; you will not succeed in touching them with your hands, but, like the seafaring men on the desert of waters, you choose them as your guides, and following them, reach your destiny."*

THIS NEW LIFE BEGINS WITH CHRIST

It is very important to be clear on this one point. This new creation begins with Christ Alone. The Bible says, *"If any man be in Christ, he is . . ."* What he is depends on where he is. His new manhood is the result of a new relationship. His new existence and experience do not begin with a new resolution to be good or with a new course of studies in religion. They begin in Christ.

NOTES

It is important to know that of all God's creatures man is the only one who has the capacity to understand Him. Man was originally made in God's Image and for God's Presence. Man possessed an affinity of life by which there was instant and perfect understanding. He did not have to try to decipher a message from the stars, nor labor in agonizing prayer, nor make long and holy pilgrimage to some sacred spot. Man was not Divine but the Presence, the Light and the Knowledge of God were in his soul. Because of these, we read in the early Chapters of Genesis of God's communications to Adam and of Adam's conversation with God.

Due to the Fall, the curtain is drawn on that picture and following it is man hiding in fear and finally fleeing from that trysting place under condemnation. Instead of communication it is now condemnation.

Now we have another picture since communication has been broken by condemnation, we are presented with a possibility of Reconciliation. The hiding and fleeing man is invited to stop beside a Cross, and be reconciled. With Reconciliation will come the communication of a new life, and new relationship and a new experience with God.

There can be no communication with God on the creature-basis. That basis has short-circuited the lines of the soul. But when one comes to God on the child-basis, having been Born-Again, he is in instant contact with the Infinite.

You can get clearance for your soul at a place called Calvary (Laurin).

AND YET, ALL IS NEW

There are new views of God and of Jesus Christ; new views of this world and of the world to come; new views of Truth and of duty; and everything is seen in a new aspect and with new feelings.

Nothing is more common in young converts than such feelings, and nothing is more common than for them to say that all things are new. The Bible seems to be a new Book; and though some few may have even read the Bible previously, yet now, there is a beauty about it which they never saw before, and which before conversion, was actually impossible to perceive.

The whole face of nature seems to them to be changed, and they seem to be in a new world.

The hills, and vales, and streams; the sun, the stars, everything, seems to be new.

The heavens and the earth are filled with new wonders, and all things seem now to speak forth the Praise of God. Even the very countenances of friends seem to be new; and there are new feelings towards all men; a new kind of love to kindred and friends; a love before unfelt for enemies; and a new love in fact, for all mankind.

(18) "AND ALL THINGS ARE OF GOD, WHO HATH RECONCILED US TO HIMSELF BY JESUS CHRIST, AND HATH GIVEN TO US THE MINISTRY OF RECONCILIATION;"

The Gospel announces that God because of the Person and Work of His Beloved Son, is reconciled to sinful man, and He commits the proclamation of these glad tidings, not to sinless Angels, but to redeemed sinners.

AND ALL THINGS ARE OF GOD

The phrase, *"And all things are of God,"* pertains to the fact that since conversion, all things are for God, of God, pertaining to God, through God, by God, and is God.

Paul now makes this statement in general, showing that not only these things pertaining to Salvation were produced by God, and solely by God, but that all things were and are under His direction, and subject to His control.

Nothing that is done, at least that is of the Lord, is to be traced to man's own agency or power, but God is to be acknowledged everywhere. This great Truth Paul never forgot; and he never suffered himself to loose sight of it. It was in his view a cardinal and glorious Truth; and he kept its influence always before his mind and his heart.

In the important statement which follows, therefore, about the Ministry of Reconciliation, he deeply feels that the whole plan, and all the success which had attended the plan, was to be traced not to his zeal, or fidelity, or skill, but solely to the agency of God.

THE HOLY SPIRIT

Even though the Holy Spirit is inspiring Paul to say these very things, still, all of this played very heavily in the heart, life, and ministry of the Apostle.

Paul now looks back before his conversion, and realizes that all that he did in the name of the Lord, in fact originated in his own mind, and was carried out by his own zeal. In other words, even though he claimed it to be of the Lord, in fact, it was not of the Lord at all. Regrettably, such characterizes much of the modern Church.

For something to be *"of God,"* it must first be birthed and borne by the Holy Spirit. The Holy Spirit will attend to nothing which is birthed by man. In fact, this is the great area of conflict in the Sanctification process. Religious men either purposely set aside the Word of God, depending on their own resources and ingenuity, or else it is ignorantly done, thinking it is the Spirit, when all the time it is the flesh. However, if it is *"of God,"* it cannot be *"of the flesh."*

RECONCILIATION

The phrase, *"Who hath reconciled us to Himself by Jesus Christ,"* refers to the fact that this was done through and by the Death and Resurrection of the Lord Jesus Christ.

The pronoun *"us"* includes all who are Christians — whether Jews or Gentiles, or whatever nationality. They have been brought into a state of reconciliation, or agreement with God, through the Lord Jesus Christ. Before, they were opposed to God. They had violated His laws. They were his enemies. But by the means of the Plan of Salvation they have been brought into a state of agreement, or harmony, and were united in feeling and in aim, with Him.

For instance, two men who have been alienated by prejudice, by passion, or by interest, are reconciled when the cause of their alienation is removed, on whichever side it may have existed, or if on both sides, when they lay aside their enmity and become friends. Thence forward they are agreed, and live together without alienation, heartburnings, jealousies, and strife. So it is between God and redeemed man.

WHAT EXACTLY DOES RECONCILIATION MEAN?

The term *"reconciled"* is found infrequently in the New Testament. Yet it remains a basic theological term that defines vital aspects of the Salvation that God offers us in Christ.

The Bible pictures sin as an impenetrable barrier to personal relationship with God. Sin has destroyed our harmony with God, making us hostile toward this One Whom we sense must be our Judge. Objectively and spiritually we are placed in a position of hostility, at enmity with One Whose only desire is to express His Love.

Romans Chapter 5 calls the Death of Jesus for us a demonstration of God's Love. By that Death, Believers are justified (declared legally innocent by God).

But Jesus' Death also reconciles, restoring Believers to a harmonious relationship with the Lord (Rom. 5:10-11). Our other key New Testament passage regarding *"Reconciliation"* is found in the passages we are now studying, II Corinthians 5:17-19.

GREAT TRUTHS EXPRESSED

Several important Truths about Reconciliation are expressed in these passages:

1. It is human beings who need Reconciliation; their sinful attitude toward God must change.
2. God has acted in Christ to accomplish Reconciliation, so that without sins no longer counted against us, Believers no longer have a basis for counting God as an enemy.
3. When we come to believe the Gospel, we experience a personal and spiritual change, as our attitude is brought into harmony with the Divine reality. We who once were enemies now *"rejoice in God through our Lord Jesus Christ"* (Rom. 5:11).

In pagan religions, human beings might bring offerings designed to win the affection of some wounded deity. Only in Christian Faith, however, does God take the initiative to win, at terrible cost, the affection of those who have wounded Him by their sins.

RECONCILIATION BETWEEN HUMAN BEINGS

Ephesians 2:11-21 looks at one special aspect of the Work of Jesus at Calvary. Mankind is now a divided race, shattered by hostilities that are precipitated by such distinctions as color, religion, sex, social status, and cultural background.

Paul points out that Jew and Gentile, separated by multiplied hostilities and diverse outlooks are now joined *"in this one Body"* (Eph. 2:16). In Christ, both are reconciled to God. From being strangers and foreigners, those now united in a common Faith have become *"fellow citizens"* and *"members of God's household"* (Eph. 2:21).

NOTES

All who have been brought into harmony with God are, by that reality, brought into harmony with one another. Christ provides the basis for loving personal relationships.

The importance of our new unity is seen in the New Testament's stress on love. It is also seen in references as to a person-to-person Reconciliation in Scripture (Mat. 5:23-24).

THE DISPLEASURE OF GOD

Man was alienated from God. He had no love for Him. He disliked His Government and Laws. He was unwilling to be restrained. He sought his own pleasure. He was proud, vain, self-confident. He was not pleased with the character of God, or with His claims or His plans.

And in like manner, God was displeased with the pride, the sensuality, the rebellion, the haughtiness of man. He was displeased that His Law had been violated, and that man had cast off His Government. Now Reconciliation could take place only when these causes of alienation could be addressed and should be laid aside, and when God and man should be brought to harmony; and when man should lay aside his love of sin, and should be pardoned, and when, therefore, God could consistently treat him as a friend.

In the New Testament *"Reconciliation"* means, to change one person towards another; that is, to reconcile to someone.

It conveys the idea of producing a change so that one who is alienated should be brought to friendship.

THE CHANGE

Of course, all the change which takes place must be on the part of man, for God will not change, and in fact, does not need to change, and the purpose of this plan of Reconciliation is to affect such a change in man as to make him in fact reconciled to God, and at agreement with Him.

There were indeed obstacles to the Reconciliation on the part of God, but they did not arise from any unwillingness to be reconciled; from any reluctance to treat His creature as His friend; but they arose from the fact that man had sinned, and that God was Just; that such is the perfection of God that He cannot treat the good and the evil alike; and that, therefore, if He should treat man as His friend, it was necessary that in some proper way he should maintain the honor of His Law, and show His hatred of sin, and should secure the conversion and future obedience of the offender. For we must ever realize and remember, that it is not man who has been offended, but rather God.

All this God purposed to secure by the Atonement made by the Redeemer, rendering it consistent for Him to exercise the benevolence of His Nature, and to pardon the offender.

GOD IS NOT CHANGED

The Plan of Reconciliation, totally devised by God, has made no change in the Character or Nature of God. It has not made Him a different Being from what He was before. There is often a mistake on this subject; and men seem to suppose that God was originally stern and unmerciful, but that He has now been made mild and forgiving by the Atonement. But it is not so!

No change has been made in God; none needed to be made; none could be made. He was always mild, merciful, and good; and the Gift of the Saviour and the Plan of Reconciliation is just an expression of His original willingness to pardon.

When a father sees a child struggling in the stream, and in danger of drowning, the peril and the cries of the child make no change in the character of the father; but such was his former love for the child that he would plunge into the stream at the hazard of his own life to save him. So it is with God.

Such was His original love for man, and His disposition to show Mercy, that He would submit to any Sacrifice, except that of Truth and Justice, in order that He might save drowning man. Hence, He sent His Only Son to die — not to change His Own Character; not to make Himself a different Being from what He was, but in order to show His love and His readiness to forgive when it could be consistently done.

BY JESUS CHRIST

Jesus was the Mediator to interpose in the Work of Reconciliation. And He was abundantly qualified for this work, and was the only Being Who has lived in this world Who was qualified for it. These qualifications among others are as follows:

NOTES

HE WAS GOD AND MAN

Jesus was endowed with a Divine and human nature — the nature of both the parties at issue, God and man, and thus, in the language of Job, could *"lay His hand upon us both"* (Job 9:33).

HIS INTIMATE ACQUAINTANCE WITH BOTH

He was intimately acquainted with both the parties, and knew what was needful to be done.

He knew God the Father so well that he could say, *"No man knoweth the Father but the Son"* (Mat. 11:27). And he knew man so well that it could be said of Him He *"needed not that any should testify of man, for He knew what was in man"* (Jn. 2:25).

No one can be a mediator who is not acquainted with the feelings, views, desires, claims, or prejudices of both the parties at issue.

THE FRIEND OF BOTH PARTIES

Jesus was and is the Friend of both parties, in that He loved God, and He loved man enough to die for him. He was always desirous of securing all that God claimed, and of vindicating Him and He never abandoned anything that God had a right to claim.

As well, His love for man showed in all His Life. He sought man's welfare in every way possible, and gave Himself for him. Yet no one is qualified to act the mediator's part who is not the common friend of both the parties at issue, and who will not seek the welfare, the right, or the honor of both.

WILLING TO SUFFER

Jesus was willing to suffer anything from either party in order to produce Reconciliation. From the Hand of God He was willing to endure all that He deemed to be necessary, in order to show His hatred of sin by His vicarious sufferings, and to make an Atonement; and from the hand of man He was willing to endure all the reproach, and scorn which could be possibly involved in the work of inducing man to be reconciled to God.

HE REMOVED ALL THE OBSTACLES

Jesus removed all the obstacles which existed to a Reconciliation. On the part of God, He has made it consistent for Him to pardon. He has made an Atonement so that God can be just while He justifies the sinner. He has maintained His Truth and Justice, and secured the stability of His moral Government, while He admits offenders to His favor.

And on the part of man, He, by the agency of His Spirit, overcomes the unwillingness of the sinner to be reconciled, humbles his pride, shows him his sin, changes his heart, subdues his enmity against God, and secures in place a harmony and purpose between God and man, so that they shall be reconciled forever (Barnes).

The phrase, *"And hath given to us the Ministry of Reconciliation,"* pertains to announcing to men the nature and conditions of this plan of being reconciled. We have been appointed to make this known, and to press its acceptation on men.

The simple meaning of this statement, *"The Ministry of Reconciliation,"* may be put into six words: He reconciled us to reconcile others. This is every Christian's Ministry. It belongs to all and not to some. It is the simple plan that underlies the whole scheme of World Evangelization. Our Reconciliation should lead to others being Reconciled.

There is a dignity of Deity about this that lifts it above ordinary religious service. It is a cause that proceeds from Christ and was not invented by a Church committee.

MINISTRY

The word *"Ministry"* has a very significant meaning. It really means *"Charter."* Charters are certain rights granted and guaranteed by the sovereign power of the State. It may be a charter to carry on a certain kind of business or a benevolent organization. In any case, this specifies the purpose of the business and then states certain lines and limitations under which this business is to be carried on.

In this same sense the Christian Church and the Christian in general have been chartered to conduct the King's Business. The Charter of the Church is the New Testament. The Business under this Charter is described here, in part, as *"the Ministry of Reconciliation."*

This means that it is the responsibility of every single Believer to take the Gospel of Jesus Christ to others. This is not merely a part of one's Christian experience, but is rather designed by the Holy Spirit to be paramount. If this is not foremost with the Christian, irrespective as to whom he may be, then his life is not as it ought to be with the Lord.

NOTES

Man is in a terrible dilemma, and his only hope is for someone to tell him about Jesus, at least giving him a chance to be reconciled to God. That is our Business, or should be, even as we've already stated.

THE NEED FOR RECONCILIATION

The need for Reconciliation begins in the fundamental wrong of life. That wrong is sin. Reconciliation presupposes separation and separation presupposes an obstruction. In other words, there is a separation between God and man. This is not a religious myth. The New Testament says, *"The carnal mind is enmity against God: for it is not subject to the Law of God, neither indeed can be"* (Rom. 8:7). This *"neither indeed can be"* means that there is a spiritual obstruction between God and man. Until that obstruction is removed there can be no Reconciliation. Until there has been a Reconciliation there can be no communication. We cannot enjoy God. We have no basis for a real prayer life. We have no place of satisfaction.

GET RID OF THE OBSTRUCTION

The thing to do then is to get rid of this obstruction between man and God. In the first place, what is it?

For one thing, it is not ignorance. One does not have to be made wise. The obstruction is sin. It is not merely a defect in one's nature, it is an obstruction. It is an obstruction between man and God, between man and his fellowman, between man and himself.

The fact of this obstruction goes back to Verse 14 where it says, *"Because we thus judge, that if one died for all, then we're all dead."* The dead need Life and the process of giving that Life is by Incarnation and Regeneration. By Incarnation Christ partook of our nature. Through His passion as one of us He brought Reconciliation. Then by Regeneration we partake of His Nature. Thus, by His sharing our life we are able to share His Life (Laurin).

ENEMY OF GOD

The Bible tells us bluntly that sinners are *"enemies of God"* (Rom. 5:10; Col. 1:21; James 4:4). We should not minimize the seriousness of these and similar Passages. An enemy is not

NOTES

someone who comes a little short of being a friend. He is in the other camp. He is altogether opposed. As well, the New Testament pictures God in vigorous opposition to everything that is evil, and this includes the evil of man.

Now the way to overcome enmity is to take away the cause of the quarrel. We may apologize for the hasty word, we may pay the money that is due, we may make what reparation or restitution is appropriate; however, that within itself will not suffice.

But in every case the way to Reconciliation lies through an effective grappling with the root cause of the enmity, which is sin. Christ died to put away our sin.

In this way, He dealt with the enmity between man and God. He put it out of the way. He made the way wide open for men to come back to God. It is this which is described by the term *"Reconciliation."*

NO RECONCILIATION OF GOD TO MAN

Even though we have already made these statements in another way, due to their vast significance, please allow us to address them again in the following manner.

It is interesting to notice that no New Testament Passage speaks of Christ as reconciling God to man. Always the stress is on man being reconciled. This in the nature of the case is very important.

It is man's sin which has caused the enmity. It is man's sin that has had to be dealt with. And yet man may very well be called on in the words of II Corinthians 5:20 to be *"reconciled to God."* Some students go on from this to suggest that Christ's reconciling activities are concerned only with man. However, it is difficult to harmonize this with the general New Testament position.

That which set up the barrier was the demand of God's Holiness for uprightness in man. Man, left to himself, does not see this. In fact, he is not particularly worried by his sin. Certainly he feels no need of God on account of his sin, at least as we think of such. The barrier arises because God demands Holiness in man. Therefore, when the process of Reconciliation has been affected it is impossible to say it is completely manward, and not Godward in any sense. There must be a change from God's side if all that is involved in such expressions as *"the Wrath of God"* is no longer exercised towards man, but yet this change is not in God, for God cannot change, for the simple reason that God does not need to change. It pertains to a change in the situation.

THE LOVE OF GOD

Of course, this does not refer to a change in God's Love. The Bible is very clear that God's Love to man never varies no matter what man may do. Indeed, the whole Atoning Work of Christ stems from God's great Love. It was *"while we were yet sinners"* that *"Christ died for us"* (Rom. 5:8).

This Truth must be zealously guarded. But at the same time we must not allow ourselves to slip into the position of maintaining that Reconciliation is a purely subjective process.

Reconciliation in some sense was affected outside man before anything happened within man. Paul can speak of Christ *"through Whom we have now received our Reconciliation"* (Rom. 5:11).

A Reconciliation that can be *"received"* must be proffered (and thus, in some sense accomplished) before men receive it. In other words, we must think of Reconciliation as having effects both Godward and manward.

Man's sin is dealt with, and that makes it possible for God to change the way He deals with man — at least those who believe.

(19) "TO WIT, THAT GOD WAS IN CHRIST, RECONCILING THE WORLD UNTO HIMSELF, NOT IMPUTING THEIR TRESPASSES UNTO THEM; AND HATH COMMITTED UNTO US THE WORD OF RECONCILIATION."

The phrase, *"To wit, that God was in Christ,"* means that God by Christ, by the means of Christ, by the Agency or Mediatorship of Christ, brought about this great Work.

GOD IN CHRIST

Christ was the Mediator (the go-between) by means of Whom God designed to accomplish the great Work of Reconciliation. The Apostle and all others for that matter, were to announce the fact of this Reconciliation, and that its proclamation had been committed to him as an Ambassador, and to us as well. He, therefore, besought men to be reconciled to God; and he told them that because the sinless Saviour was made to personate sin itself, and because He had offered up Himself as a Sin-Offering of infinite value, God was thereby reconciled, His Justice vindicated, all the claims of His Throne satisfied, and a spotless Righteousness provided for guilty men.

The phrase, *"Reconciling the world unto Himself,"* represents the Atonement as the work of the Blessed Trinity, and as being the result of love, and not of wrath.

RECONCILING THE WORLD

To which we have already addressed, this phrase, plus scores of others similar, ought to have been a sufficient warning against the hideous error, which claims that the Atonement did not embrace all of mankind, but rather an elect few. The *"world"* here evidently means the human race generally, without distinction of nation, age, rank, or gender.

The whole world was alienated from Him, and He sought to have it reconciled. This is one incidental proof among many, that God designed that the Plan of Salvation should be adapted to all men. It may be observed further, that God *sought* that the world should be reconciled. Man did not seek such. Man had no plan for such. Man did not desire such. Man had no way to affect such. It was the offended party, namely the Lord, not the offending, that sought to be reconciled; and this shows the strength of His Love.

It was love for enemies and alienated beings, and love evinced to them by a most earnest desire to become their friend and to be at agreement with them, hence *"reconciling the world unto Himself."*

IMPUTATION

The phrase, *"Not imputing their trespasses unto them,"* refers to the fact that the penalty for these trespasses were imputed to Christ instead.

"Imputing" in the Greek is *"logizomai,"* and means *"to number, reason, reckon, or conclude."*

God not reckoning or imputing trespasses to transgressors, means that He forgave them, pardoned them, that is upon one's Faith in Christ.

The idea here is, that God did not charge sinners with the stern justice their offenses demanded, but graciously provided a Plan of Pardon, and offered to remit their sins on the conditions of the Gospel. The Plan of Reconciliation demonstrated that He was not disposed to impute their sins to them, as He might have done, or to punish them with unmitigated severity for their crimes, but was more disposed to pardon and forgive.

And it may be asked here, if God was not disposed to charge with unrelenting severity their own sins to their account, but was rather disposed to pardon them, can we believe that He is disposed to charge on them the sin of another, namely Adam?

The sentiment here is, that God is not disposed or inclined to charge the transgressions of men upon them; He has no pleasure in doing it; and, therefore, He has provided a Plan by which they may be pardoned. At the same time it is true that, unless their sins are pardoned, Justice will charge or impute their sins to them, and will exact punishment to the uttermost.

As we have stated, men are lost not nearly as much for committing sin or sins, as they are for rejecting God's solution to that sin, the Price that Jesus paid at Calvary for man's Redemption.

THE WORD OF RECONCILIATION

The phrase, *"And hath committed unto us the Word of Reconciliation,"* means, that the Office of making known the nature of this plan, and the conditions on which God was willing to be reconciled to man, has been committed to Ministers of the Gospel.

WHAT IS THAT WORD?

First, the trespasses that men have committed and accumulated had to be removed. To do this, Christ removed them by dying in our stead, by expiating them with His Blood. This changed the whole world of men and its objective relation to God.

It was then and there a redeemed world, meaning every sinner from Adam onward to the end of time was possible to be redeemed. To receive this Redemption, man has to undergo a subjective change, which refers to being changed in their hearts. Individually they have to be brought to contrition, Faith, and obedience. God does this by means of the Word of Reconciliation that is preached to the world by His Ministers, or in fact, told and testified by any Believer.

This *"Word"* is the *"grandest story ever told!"* It is the simple Message that man is a

NOTES

sinner, but that he can be saved through Faith in Jesus Christ.

The *"Word of Reconciliation"* which we possess and are to pass on to others is the disclosure of a wonderful thing. It is not a Word about rules to follow. It does not speak of a long list of penances. It is not full of abstract religious sayings. It is not centered about some mystical idea of God. It is the simple and understandable fact that *"God was in Christ, reconciling the world unto Himself."*

INCARNATION

God being in Christ, means Incarnation. None of us can completely comprehend God as a Spirit, but all of us can comprehend or understand God as a Man. Thus, it came to be when Christ came, for *"God was in Christ."* This puts Salvation on human terms.

On God's side there was Incarnation in order that there might be Reconciliation. But what about man's side?

Man had nothing to do with providing the means of Reconciliation, but he must provide something which is necessary for the operation of Reconciliation. That one thing is Faith and includes repentance and trust. It is a willingness to leave the old life and a readiness to take the new life.

The immediate result of this Reconciliation is twofold. One is described here in the words, *"not imputing their trespasses unto them."* This means the canceling of the record of transgressions of which all men are guilty.

God not only cancels the record of evil, He also commences a new record of good. He puts to our credit by imputation (by assignment) the Righteousness of Jesus Christ. This is our new capital of character on which we may draw for the needs of our life.

THE NATURE OF CHRIST

This is not all, for a Righteousness imputed, without a righteous nature imparted, would be an abortive and futile Christianity. Consequently, we are not only given Christ's Righteousness, but as well, His Nature.

This high view of Christian experience should lead each of us to an earnest review of his life. There can be no place in such a life for willful and known sin. After all, Christianity is more than a creed. It is conduct. To be in Christ means to be out of sin. To be reconciled to God means to be settled in a New Life and separated from an old life.

NOTES

We as Believers, and especially Preachers, are to tell this story using every means at our disposal. The Lord has called me for Mass Evangelism, which includes Television, Radio, and Crusades.

When I say that *"He has called me,"* I am meaning that He has specifically directed that I do this thing. In other words, I don't have a choice as to whether I should preach over Television or not. It is a task that I must do. It is why as well, we have seen so many people brought to Christ through this medium. Inasmuch as He has *"committed"* this Calling and task to me, it behooves me to do all within my power, to carry out this which is most important — actually, the most important thing in the world.

The Truth is, if we who are Believers do not tell this grand story, who will?

(20) "NOW THEN WE ARE AMBASSADORS FOR CHRIST, AS THOUGH GOD DID BESEECH YOU BY US: WE PRAY YOU IN CHRIST'S STEAD, BE YE RECONCILED TO GOD."

The phrase, *"Now then we are Ambassadors for Christ,"* presents the ones whom Christ has sent forth to negotiate with men in regard to their reconciliation to God.

AMBASSADORS FOR CHRIST

The word *"Ambassadors,"* as it is used here, refers to one who is empowered to deliver a message for another, without being able to do anymore other than to explain or enforce it. He is sent to do what the Sovereign would Himself do were He present. They're sent to make known the will of the Sovereign, and to negotiate matters of commerce, of war, or of peace, and in general everything affecting the interests of the Sovereign among the people to whom they are sent.

At all times, and in all countries, an Ambassador is a sacred character, and his person is regarded as inviolable. He is bound implicitly to obey the instructions of his Sovereign, and as far as possible to do only what the Sovereign would do were he himself present.

The four following basic matters apply to Ambassadors.

NOTES

COMMISSIONED BY THE HEAD OF STATE

One does not decide to become an Ambassador. The Chief of State is extremely selective with respect to Ambassadors because they have the ability to cement international relationships or sever them.

In contrast, every Believer is an Ambassador for Christ. It would be difficult to overemphasize the importance of Ambassadors. If political Ambassadors play such consequential roles in the affairs of nations, how much more significant are Christ's Ambassadors to deal with eternal souls.

As well, we must understand that it was not Paul who actually chose this word *"Ambassadors,"* but rather, the Holy Spirit.

REPRESENTS THE PRESIDENT OR KING WHO SELECTS HIM

Whatever happens to that representative has a direct impact on the one being represented. Wars have started over the action and treatment of Ambassadors. Do we honestly recognize who we are representing as Christ's Ambassadors?

Even though as stated, all Believers in a sense are Ambassadors for Christ, still, it is Ministers of the Gospel who are more particularly Ambassadors. Ministers are to make known, and to explain, and enforce the terms on which God is willing to be reconciled to men. They are not to negotiate on any new terms, nor to change those which God has proposed, nor to follow their own plans or devises; they are simply to urge, explain, state, and enforce the terms on which God is willing to be reconciled.

Of course, they are to seek the honor of the Sovereign who has sent them forth, and to seek to do only His Will. They go not to promote their own welfare; not to seek personal honor, dignity, or wealth, etc.; but they go to transact the business which the Son of God would engage in were He again personally on the earth.

THE AMBASSADOR PROPAGATES THE MESSAGE ASSIGNED BY THE CHIEF OF STATE SHE OR HE REPRESENTS

The Ambassador cannot afford to interject purely personal views into the messages he conveys. How conscientious are we about proclaiming God's Word and not our own concepts?

What is the Message?

As should be obvious, the Message is the Word of God. It was faithfully delivered by the Holy Spirit through various Prophets and Apostles, and it is meant to be followed to the letter. Some years ago, the National Religious Broadcasters sent out a questionnaire to all of its members of which I was then a part, as to what these members thought the people wanted to hear as it regarded the Gospel?

I wrote back kindly, but I tried my best to make certain that they did not misunderstand what I said.

"I have no interest in what the people want to hear, I only seek to know what the Lord wants me to tell them!", I said.

AN AMBASSADOR IS AN ALIEN IN A FOREIGN LAND

The Ambassador is not a citizen of the country to where he is sent. He is not a part of its culture, its political spectrum, nor its decision making. He is there but for one purpose, and that is to properly represent the Sovereign who sent him.

We as *"Ambassadors for Christ"* are to ever understand that we are not truly citizens of this earth, we do not march to its tune, or function according to its precepts. In other words, we are aliens, sent by the Lord to convey the Message He desires, no more, no less!

One day, at the *"Judgment Seat of Christ"* each of us will be called to account before the Sovereign of all the ages, the King of kings and the Lord of lords, the Lord Jesus Christ, to give account for our Ambassadorship. Consequently, we must conduct ourselves with the understanding that such a day is soon to come.

GOD PLEADING FOR SOULS

The phrase, *"As though God did beseech you by us,"* is to be understood that our Message is to be regarded as the Message of God. It is God Who speaks. What we say is said in His Name and on His authority, which should be received with the respect which is due to a Message directly from God.

This Gospel Message is God speaking to men through the Ministry, and entreating them to be reconciled. This invests the Message which the Ministers (Ambassadors) bear with infinite dignity and solemnity; and it makes it a fearful and awful thing to reject it.

As we've already stated, an Ambassador represents his government in all its dignity, whatever that may be. To scorn an Ambassador or to mistreat him is to scorn and to mistreat the government which sent him. To send him away is to break off relations with the government and the ruler whom he represents.

An Ambassador speaks wholly for his ruler, he is his ruler's mouthpiece. He is to never utter his own thoughts, offers, promises, demands, but only those of his ruler.

In fact, an Ambassador's person lends no weight to what he says. They to whom he is sent see and hear in him only the king who sent him.

No potentate is as high as is He Who commissioned us. In essence we work for the Lord Jesus Christ, King of kings and Lord of lords.

BESEECH

The word *"beseech"* as it is used here, means *"to beg."*

This word is remarkable in everyway in this connection. Here is the God of Heaven and of earth and Christ, His Son, Who by His death, reconciled all to God (or rather made it possible for men to be reconciled), and here are Their high Ambassadors representing God in Christ.

The ones to whom they are addressing are transgressors, actually *"enemies."* And yet, these Ambassadors are sent by God and Christ to beg these transgressors: *"be reconciled!"* Yet here there is a secret.

It is love, condescending love alone that wins enemies, overcomes their enmity and hostility and thus works reconciliation in them. No threats of Law can do that, no demands but only the Gospel voice that admonishes and begs.

IN CHRIST'S STEAD

The phrase, *"We pray you in Christ's stead,"* actually means we are doing, or rather we are supposed to do, what Jesus did when on earth, and what He would do were He here presently.

That's the reason we must adhere strictly to the Word of God. For instance, the Book of Acts is the pattern for the Church; consequently, our modern Churches should line up with the Book of Acts, simply because it is the same Holy Spirit working in both, or at least should be. That means, if our Church is not similar to the Book of Acts Church, then we cannot honestly

NOTES

say it is *"Church,"* for the simple reason that we are misrepresenting the One Who has sent us, in effect, making up our own rules.

All that we do regarding our lives and Ministry, is to be done *"in Christ's stead,"* i.e., *"as if though He were performing the task."*

RECONCILED TO GOD

The phrase, *"Be ye reconciled to God,"* presents the plea.

The Truth is, that man has no power to reconcile himself to God, but in fact, can only furnish *"a willing mind and obedient heart."*

It would seem that since God tells men to be reconciled, men must have the ability to obey. However, they do not, at least according to their own ability and strength. Nevertheless, the Truth is according to the following:

Every Gospel imperative is full of the Divine Power of Grace to affect what it demands. In other words, and as stated, if the sinner will be willing, power will be granted. The Truth is, if the Gospel counted on even the least power in the sinner it would never secure the least effect. Jesus calls this the Father's drawing (Jn. 6:44; 6:65; 12:32).

Every reconciled sinner is reconciled by God to God in Christ — by God Alone. In fact, *"Be reconciled to God"* is *"the Word of Reconciliation."*

This is the sum and burden of the Message which the Ministers of the Gospel bear to their fellowmen.

MAN IS TO SUBMIT

In order to be reconciled, man has to give up his opposition. He is to submit to the terms of Mercy. All the change in the case is to be in Him, for God, as stated cannot change. God has removed all the obstacles to Reconciliation which existed on His part. He did it through the Lord Jesus Christ. He has done all that He will do, all that needed to be done, in order to render Reconciliation as easy as possible. And now it remains that man should lay aside his hostility, abandon his sins, embrace the terms of Mercy, and become in fact, reconciled to God.

And the great object of the Ministers of Reconciliation is to urge this duty on their fellowmen. They are to do it in the Name of Christ. They are to do it as if Christ were Himself present, and were Himself urging the Message.

They are to use the arguments which He would use; evince the zeal which He would show; and present the motives which He would present, to induce a dying world to become in fact reconciled to God (Barnes).

(21) "FOR HE HATH MADE HIM TO BE SIN FOR US, WHO KNEW NO SIN; THAT WE MIGHT BE MADE THE RIGHTEOUSNESS OF GOD IN HIM."

The design of this very important Verse is to urge the strongest possible reason for being reconciled to God. This is one of the most tremendous statements written by Paul's pen. It is so tremendous because it so completely and in such striking form reveals what God has done for us.

A SIN OFFERING

The phrase, *"For He hath made Him to be sin for us,"* refers to Jesus becoming a *"Sin-Offering"* at Calvary, thereby taking the penalty for sin in our place.

God did not *"make"* Jesus a sinner. God did less, and at the same time He did more. God left Jesus as sinless as He was. The idea of God making anyone a sinner, to say nothing of His Own Son is unthinkable. James plainly said, *"Let no man say when he is tempted* (tempted to evil), *I am tempted of God: for God cannot be tempted with evil, neither tempteth He any man"* (James 1:13).

God did something else entirely: He laid on Him the iniquity of us all (Isa. 53:6) so that He bore our sins in His Own Body on the tree (I Pet. 2:24), so that He was made a curse for us, which means He suffered the curse of the Law which was death (Gal. 3:13, *"in our stead"*), so that He died for all.

God made Christ sin or rather a Sin Offering by charging all that is *"sin"* in us against Him, by letting Him bear all this burden with all its guilt and penalty *"in our stead"* in order to deliver us from that penalty.

DID CHRIST ACTUALLY BECOME A SINNER ON THE CROSS AS SOME TEACH?

1. He was not sin in the abstract, or sin as such, simply because if such had been, He could not have served as a *"Sin-Offering."* That particular Offering, which was a type of Christ giving Himself at Calvary had to be *"without blemish unto the Lord for a Sin Offering"* (Lev. 4:3).

NOTES

2. It cannot mean that Jesus was a sinner, or even became a sinner on the Cross, for it is said in immediate connection that He *"knew no sin,"* and it is everywhere said that He was holy, harmless, undefiled.

3. As well, it cannot mean that Jesus being made to be sin, can in any proper sense be misconstrued as Him being guilty. For no one is truly guilty who is not personally a transgressor of the Law; and if He was, in any proper sense, guilty, then He deserved to die, and His death could have no merit than that of any other guilty being; and if He was properly guilty, it would make no difference in this respect whether it was by His Own fault or by imputation: a guilty being deserves to be punished; and where there is a just desert of punishment there can be no merit in sufferings.

The Truth is, all such views which tend to make the Holy Redeemer a sinner, or guilty, or deserving of the sufferings which He endured, border on blasphemy, and are abhorrent to the whole strain of the Scriptures. In no form, in no sense possible, is it to be maintained that the Lord Jesus was sinful or guilty, or made to be a sinner on the Cross. In fact, it is the Cornerstone of the whole system of Salvation, that in all conceivable senses of the expression He was holy, and pure, and the object of the Divine Approbation (approval). And every view which leads to the statement that He was in any sense guilty, or which implies that He deserved to die, is prima facie a false view, and should be at once abandoned, because it violates all Scripture.

4. If the declaration that He was made *"sin"* does not mean that He was sin itself, or a sinner, or guilty, then it must mean that He was a *"Sin-Offering"*— an Offering or a Sacrifice for sin; and this is the interpretation which the Scripture bears out.

GOD TREATED HIM AS IF HE WERE A SINNER

This means that He had to bear the penalty for sin. God subjected Him to sufferings which, if He had been personally a sinner, would have been a proper expression of His hatred of transgression, and a proper punishment for sin. It means that He made an Atonement; that He died for sin; that His death was not merely that of a martyr; but that it was designed by substituted sufferings to make Reconciliation between man and God. Consequently, it can be translated, *"For God hath made Him subject to suffering and death, the punishment and consequence of sin, as if He had been a sinner, though He were guilty of no sin"* (Locke).

THE LAW OF THE SIN-OFFERING

In fact, Jesus fulfilled all five of the Sacrificial Offerings when He died on Calvary. Those Offerings were: A. Sin-Offering; B. Burnt-Offering; C. Trespass-Offering; D. Peace-Offering; and, E. Meat-Offering (actually a Thanksgiving Offering which basically contained only bread and no flesh.) However, the greater structure concerning the Sacrifice of Christ at Calvary, concerned the *"Sin-Offering."*

Without going into great detail, the Sin-Offering was a Sacrifice of a special kind, actually of special value as an expiatory Sacrifice (to atone for, to pay the penalty).

This Sacrifice was to be killed on the north side of the Great Altar, which was of course a type of the coming Crucifixion of Christ, and the Judgment of God poured out on Him, instead of the ones who rightly deserved it.

The Sin-Offering was most holy, and the Priests alone might eat what was left of the animal in the Holy Place. Whatever touched it was to be holy, any garments sprinkled with its Blood must be washed in a holy place, earthen vessels used in the process must be broken, and brazen vessels thoroughly scoured and rinsed. As stated, all typified the absolute holiness of the Lord Jesus Christ, and as well, the Holiness of what He did at Calvary and the Resurrection.

THE GREAT DAY OF ATONEMENT

Even though the Sin-Offering was used constantly by the people of Israel and by the Priests regarding themselves as well, it was also one of the Offerings used on the Great Day of Atonement (Lev. 16:1-28).

The other Offering was the Whole Burnt Offering, which was in effect, a *"Consecration Offering."* Both beautifully typified Christ, Who offered up Himself as a Sin-Offering which was the penalty in our stead, and a Burnt-Offering which means that He gave His all.

On the Great Day of Atonement, which came about once a year, Aaron must take a Bullock for himself and his house, two he-goats for the people, and present the Goats at the Sanctuary. He was to cast lots regarding the Goats, one of them to be used as a Sin-Offering and the other as a Scapegoat, to be sent into the wilderness.

The Bullock was killed, sweet incense was burned within the Veil, with blood sprinkled once on the Mercy Seat in the Holy of Holies and before it on the ground seven times. The seven times denoted the Perfect Redemption effected by Jesus Christ at Calvary and the Resurrection. (All of this was done twice, first for himself, second for Israel.)

The Scapegoat was then presented, hands laid on it, the sins of all confessed and put upon the goat, with it then sent into the wilderness. The carcass of the Bullock and the he-goat which were offered in Sacrifice, were burned without the camp. As well, the writer of Hebrews wrote concerning Jesus, *"Wherefore Jesus also, that He might sanctify the people with His Own Blood, suffered without the gate. Let us go forth therefore unto Him without the camp, bearing His reproach,"* (Heb. 13:12-13).

THE SACRIFICE OF CHRIST

The Sacrifice of Christ is one of the chief themes of the New Testament. His Saving Work is sometimes spoken of in ethical, sometimes in penal, but also often in Sacrificial terms. He is spoken of as the slain Lamb of God, whose Precious Blood takes away the sin of the world (Jn. 1:29, 36; I Pet. 1:18-19; Rev. 5:6-10; 13:8) — a lamb being the animal most often used in various Sacrifices.

More specifically, He is spoken of as the True Passover Lamb (I Cor. 5:6-8), as a Sin-Offering (Rom. 8:3; II Cor. 5:21; Lev. 5:6-7, 11; 9:2-3; Ps. 40:6, etc.), and in Hebrews Chapters 9 and 10 as the fulfillment of the Covenant Sacrifices of Exodus Chapter 24, the Red Heifer of Numbers Chapter 19, and the Day of Atonement Offerings.

The New Testament constantly identifies our Lord with the Suffering Servant of Isaiah Chapters 52 and 53, Who is a Guilt-Offering (Sin-Offering, Trespass-Offering, Burnt Offering) (Isa. 53:10), and with the Messiah (Christ) of Daniel Chapter 9, Who is to Atone for iniquity (Dan. 9:24).

The New Testament uses the terms *"propitiate"* and *"ransom"* (Propitiation, Redeemer)

NOTES

of Christ in a Sacrificial sense and the idea of being cleansed by His Blood (I Jn. 1:7; Book of Hebrews).

BOOK OF HEBREWS

In fact, the Doctrine is most fully worked out in the Epistle to the Hebrews. The writer stresses the importance in Christ's Sacrifice, of His Death (Heb. 2:9, 14; 9:15-17, 22, 25-28; 13:12, 20), and the fact that His Sacrifice is done and complete (Heb. 1:3; 7:27; 9:12, 25-28; 10:10, 12-14, 18).

The Epistle to the Hebrews confines Christ's Priesthood and Sanctuary to Heaven (Heb. 8:1-5; 9:11, 14), but it emphatically does not confine His Sacrifice there. It states indeed that He offered there (Heb. 8:3), but *"offer"* is a word used equally of the donor who brings and kills a Sacrifice outside the Sanctuary and of the Priest who presents it, either there on the Altar or within.

The reference here is doubtless to the sprinkling or *"offering"* of Blood in the Holy of Holies on the Day of Atonement by the High Priest (Heb. 9:7, 21-26), a typical action fulfilled by Christ when He offered His Blood on the Mercy-Seat of Heaven, which of course, was after His Resurrection (Heb. 9:12).

THE CROSS AND THE BLOOD

All that was costly in the Sacrifice — the part of the donor and the victim — took place at the Cross. There remained only the Priestly part — the presentation to God by an acceptable Mediator — and this Christ performed by entering into His Father's Presence at the Ascension, since then His Sprinkled Blood has remained there (Heb. 12:24).

There is no call to think of any other presentation of Himself or of His Blood after it was once presented: It is enough that He entered as the Priest of the Sacrifice slain once for all at the Cross, was immediately welcomed in Heaven, and sat down in Glory. His everlasting Priestly intercession in Heaven (Heb. 7:24; Ps. 99:6; Joel 2:17) is not some further activity, but is all part of His *"now appearing in the Presence of God on our behalf"* (Heb. 9:24).

On the basis of His Finished Work on the Cross and with His Sufferings now all past, His simple appearance in God's Presence on our behalf, is both continual intercession for us and

NOTES

continual *"expiation"* or *"propitiation"* for our sins (Heb. 2:10, 17).

In other words, His Work was and is a Finished Work, which requires nothing else on His Part or on our behalf. His simple Presence in Heaven makes Intercession for us, and all else that is needed for that matter, without Him having to do anything else whatsoever.

THE SACRIFICES OF THE OLD TESTAMENT A TYPE OF HIS PERFECT SACRIFICE

Due to the fact that the blood of bulls and goats could not take away sin, what the Sacrifices of the Old Testament represented, contained the great spiritual value — the Atoning Offering of Christ.

For the body of the animal, we have the Body of God's Son (Heb. 10:5, 10). For the Altar, we have Calvary. For the fire, we have the Judgment of God upon His Only Son, typified by the slain animal. For spotlessness, we have the sinlessness of the Son of God (Heb. 9:14; I Pet. 1:19). For a sweet smell as it regards the incense, we have true acceptableness (Eph. 5:2). For the sprinkling of our bodies with blood, we have forgiveness (Heb. 9:13-14, 19-22). For symbolical Atonement, we have real Atonement (Heb. 10:1-10).

OLD TESTAMENT SACRIFICES IN THE NEW

The Old Testament Sacrifices were still being offered during practically the whole period of the composition of the New Testament, and it is not surprising, therefore, that even their literal significance comes in for some illuminating comment. Important examples are to be found in Matthew 5:23-24; 12:3-5 and parallels, Matthew 17:24-27; 23:16-20; I Corinthians 9:13-14.

It is noteworthy that our Lord has Sacrifice offered for Him or offers it Himself at His presentation in the Temple, at His last Passover and presumably on those other occasions when He went up to Jerusalem for the Feasts.

The practice of the Apostles in Acts removes all ground from the opinion that after the Sacrifice of Christ the worship of the Jewish Temple is to be regarded as an abomination to God. We find them frequenting the Temple and Paul, himself, goes up to Jerusalem for

Pentecost, and on that occasion offers the Sacrifices (which included Sin-Offerings) for the interruption of vows (Acts Chpt. 21; Num. 6:10-12).

THE OLD COVENANT READY TO VANISH AWAY

However, in principle, due to Jesus' Death and Resurrection, these Sacrifices were now unnecessary, for the Old Covenant was now indeed *"old"* and *"ready to vanish away"* (Heb. 8:13), so that when the Romans destroyed the Temple even the non-Christian Jews ceased to offer the Sacrifices.

The Epistle to the Hebrews, to which we have already alluded, contains the fullest treatment of the Old Testament Sacrifices. The teaching of Paul, that is if he actually wrote Hebrews, has its positive side (Heb. 11:4), but his great concern is to point out their inadequacy except as types. The fact that sacrifices cannot gain for men entrance into the Holy of Holies proves that they cannot free the conscience from guilt, but are simply carnal ordinances, imposed until a coming time of Reconciliation (Heb. 9:6-10). Their inadequacy to atone is shown also by the fact that mere animals are offered (Heb. 10:4), and by the very fact of their repetition (Heb. 10:1-2). Consequently, they are not so much remedies for sin as reminders of it (Heb. 10:3).

(Bibliography: Commentaries on the Epistle to the Hebrews; V. Taylor, *"Jesus And His Sacrifice,"* B. B. Warfield, *"The Person And Work Of Christ,"* N. Dimock, *"The Doctrine Of The Death Of Christ."*)

WHO KNEW NO SIN

The phrase, *"Who knew no sin,"* refers to the fact and graphically so, that He was not guilty. He was perfectly holy and pure. This idea is thus expressed by Peter when he wrote, *"Who did no sin, neither was guile found in His mouth"* (I Pet. 2:22). As well, Hebrews 7:26 says, *"He was 'holy, harmless, undefiled, separate from sinners'."* In all respects, in every way, and in all conceivable senses, the Lord Jesus was pure and holy. If He had not been, He would not have been qualified to make an Atonement. Hence, the Sacred writers are everywhere at great pains to keep this idea prominent, for on this depends the whole superstructure of the Plan of Salvation.

NOTES

The phrase, *"knew no sin,"* is an expression of great beauty and dignity. It indicates His entire and perfect purity. He was altogether unacquainted with sin; He was a stranger to transgressions; He was conscious of no sin, He committed none. He had a mind and heart perfectly free from pollution, and His entire life was perfectly pure and holy in the Sight of God.

SHOOTS DOWN THE JESUS DIED SPIRITUALLY DOCTRINE

In brief, this particular doctrine teaches that Jesus became a sinner on the Cross, the same as any other sinner, died and went to Hell (the burning side), and was Born-Again in Hell, thereby being the *"Firstborn of many brethren."*

This teaching is wholly fiction and contains no Scriptural substance whatsoever.

First of all, as stated, Jesus bore the sin penalty in our place, but did not become an actual sinner. While the penalty for transgression can be transferred to another, it is impossible to transfer the transgression itself to another. Besides, the Scripture plainly says, on which we are here commenting, *"Who knew no sin."* How much plainer could it be?

As well, while Jesus did definitely go into the Paradise side of Hell (Lk. 16:19-31; Eph. 4:9), and also *"preached unto the spirits in prison,"* which were fallen angels (I Pet. 3:19), there is no Scriptural record that Jesus went into the burning side of Hell whatsoever.

Also, that He was Born-Again in Hell, is pure fiction as well. In the first place, anyone *"who knew no sin,"* doesn't need to be Born-Again.

And finally, *"The Firstborn among many brethren,"* does not refer to being Born-Again as a sinner, but is intended to suggest Jesus' supreme rank and uniqueness of His special relationship with the Father. In the case of Jesus, it is referring to the Incarnation. As such, He is the Firstborn in the new creation by being raised first from the dead, and is thus Lord over the Church (Col. 1:18; Rev. 1:5). He is thus the Firstborn in a whole family of Children of God who are destined to bear His Image (Rom. 8:29).

As well, God's People, both living and dead, can be described as the *"Firstborn"* who are enrolled in Heaven, since they share the privileges of the Son (Heb. 12:23).

STRIKES AT THE ATONEMENT

The *"Jesus died spiritually doctrine"* is dangerous because it strikes at the Atonement, completely misconstruing the great Sacrifice of Christ. Carried to its completion, this doctrine places no credence at all in the Sacrifice of Jesus at Calvary, thereby paying the sin debt and satisfying the curse of the Law, neither in the shedding of His innocent Blood, but rather places all emphasis on Him being in Hell as a sinner, and there being Born-Again. As a result, many of the Churches that teach this doctrine, and they number many, do not teach the Cross or the Blood, referring to these as *"past miseries."* So, as should be obvious, the end of this doctrine is heresy. Any misunderstanding of the Cross, the price that Jesus paid at Calvary, the shedding of His Life's Blood, the satisfying of the curse of the Law, strikes at the very heart of the Salvation Message, which is the reason these Churches see precious few people saved, but rather parasite off those who in fact do bring people to Christ.

THE RIGHTEOUSNESS OF GOD

The phrase, *"That we might be made the Righteousness of God in Him,"* proclaims a spotless Righteousness provided for guilty men.

In that Righteousness, no flaw can be found. He has gone into the very Holiest, and has been accepted before the Throne of God. Christ is the Righteousness of God (Jn. 16:10). In that Righteousness, God stands, and in that same Righteousness, the Believer stands.

God and the Believer stand in the one and selfsame Righteousness; so, the Believer can say, *"I have a Righteousness in which no flaw can be found; it has preceded me into Heaven and has been accepted there."*

This great fact contradicts the doctrine of Purgatory — for Believers only are said to go to Purgatory — but the Believer's Righteousness is the Righteousness of God, and how could a supposed Purgatory (incidently, which does not exist) make that Righteousness more pure?

ON ACCOUNT OF WHAT JESUS HAS DONE

We who believe in Christ, are accepted as Righteousness, and treated as Righteous by God on account of what the Lord Jesus has done. There is here an evident and beautiful contrast between what is said of Christ, and what is said of us.

NOTES

He was made sin — we are made Righteousness; that is, He was treated as if He were a sinner, though He was perfectly holy and pure — we are treated as if we were Righteous, though we are defiled and depraved.

The idea is that on account of what the Lord Jesus has endured on our behalf, we are treated as if we had ourselves entirely fulfilled the Law of God, and had never become exposed to its penalty.

HIS PLAN

In the phrase, *"Righteousness of God,"* there is a reference to the fact that this is His Plan of making men Righteous or of justifying them. They who thus become Righteous, or are justified, are justified on His Plan, and by a system which He has devised.

Lock renders it in this manner, *"That we, in and by Him, might be made Righteous, by a Righteousness imputed to us by God."* The idea is that all our Righteousness in the sight of God we receive in and through a Redeemer. All is to be traced to Him. In fact, this 21st Verse contains a beautiful epitome of the whole Plan of Salvation, and the peculiarity of the Christian system.

On the one hand, One Who was perfectly innocent, by a voluntary substitution, is treated as though He were guilty; that is, is subjected to pains and sorrows which, if He were guilty, would be a proper punishment for sin. And on the other hand, they who are guilty, which includes all of us, and who deserve to be punished, are treated, through faith in His vicarious sufferings, as though we were perfectly innocent; that is, in a manner which would be a proper expression of God's approbation if we had not sinned.

SUBSTITUTION AND IDENTIFICATION

The entire Plan, therefore, is one of Substitution and Identification. Without such Substitution, Christ taking our place, and our Identification with Him, there can be no Salvation. Innocence voluntarily suffers for guilt, and the guilty by Faith are thus made pure and holy, and are saved.

The greatness of the Divine Compassion and Love is thus shown for the guilty; and on the ground of this it is right and proper for God to call on men to be reconciled to Him. It is the strongest argument that can be used.

When God has given His Only Son to the bitter suffering of death on the Cross in order that we may be reconciled, it is the highest possible argument that can be used why we should cease our opposition to Him, and become His friends (Barnes).

Christ identified with man's sin in regard to its penalty, and man identified with Christ's Righteousness, in regard to Faith. And thus, in Christ, God becomes *"Jehovah-Tsidkenu,"* which means *"the Lord our Righteousness."*

MORE ABOUT THE SIN-OFFERING

Due to the fact that the King James translators incorrectly translated the phrase, *"for He hath made Him to be sin for us,"* when they should have translated it *"for He hath made Him to be a Sin Offering for us,"* — from this error much false doctrine has sprung up. I personally think excellent scholarship is here required.

The following is taken from the expository work of Adam Clarke, one of the foremost Greek Scholars of our age, and should prove helpful.

He says that the Greek word here used for *"sin,"* signifies a *"Sin-Offering"* or Sacrifice for sin, and should have been translated accordingly. As well, and which is so very important, it answers to the *"chattaah"* and *"chattath"* of the Hebrew Text; which signifies both sin and Sin-Offering in a great variety of places in the Pentateuch (Genesis through Deuteronomy). In other words, the same Hebrew word can be translated either *"Sin"* or *"Sin Offering,"* so the associating texts have to be considered to arrive at the proper meaning.

The Septuagint (Greek translation of the Old Testament) translates the Hebrew word as *"Sin-Offering"* in some 94 places in Exodus, Leviticus, and Numbers. Had the King James translators attended to their own method of translating the word in other places where it means the same as here, they would not have given this false view of a passage which has been made the foundation of much blasphemous doctrine. Doctrine such as *"our sins were imputed to Christ, and that He was a proper object of the indignation of Divine Justice, because He was blackened with imputed sins."*

NOTES

Some have proceeded so far in this blasphemous manner as to say that *"Christ may be considered as the greatest of sinners, because all the sins of mankind,"* as they say, *"were imputed to Him, and reckoned as His Own."*

One of these writers said, *"God accounted Christ the greatest of sinners, that we might be supremely Righteous."* Thus, they have confounded sin with the punishment due sin.

The Truth is, *"Christ suffered in our stead; died for us; bore our sins,* (the punishment due us) *in His Own Body upon the tree, for the Lord laid upon Him the iniquities of us all; that is, the punishment due us; explained by making His soul — His life, an Offering for sin; and healing us by His stripes."*

SCRIPTURAL PROOF

That it may be plainly seen that *"Sin-Offering"* not *"Sin"* is the meaning of the word in II Corinthians 5:21, I shall set down the places from the Septuagint where the word occurs; and where it answers to the Hebrew words already quoted; and where the translators did render it correctly what they rendered in II Corinthians 5:21 incorrectly.

Exodus 29:14, 36; Leviticus 4:3, 8, 20-21, 24-25, and 29 twice, 32-34; 5:6-8, 9 twice, 11 twice, 12; 6:17, 25 twice, 30; 7:7, 37; 8:2, 14 twice; 9:2-3, 7-8, 10, 15, 22; 10:16-17, 19 twice; 12:6, 8; 14:13 twice, 19, 22, 31; 15:15, 30; 16:3, 5-6, 9, 11 twice, 15, 25, 27 twice; 23:19; Numbers 6:11, 14, 16; 7:16, 22, 28, 34, 40, 46, 52, 58, 70, 76, 82, 87; 8:8, 12; 15:24-25, 27; 18:9; 28:15, 22; 29:5, 11, 16, 22, 25, 28, 31, 34, 38.

II Chronicles 29:21, 23-24; Ezra 6:17; 8:25; Nehemiah 10:33; Job 1:5; Ezekiel 43:19, 22, 25; 44:27, 29; 45:17, 19, 22-23, 25.

Consequently, the same word being used, and carrying forth the same sense, the translators should have translated II Corinthians 5:21, *"For He hath made Him to be a Sin Offering for us, Who knew no sin; that we might be made the Righteousness of God in Him."*

"Jesus, Thy Blood and Righteousness my
beauty are, my glorious dress;
"Midst flaming worlds, in these arrayed,
with joy shall I lift up my head."

"Bold shall I stand in Thy great day, for
who aught to my charge shall lay?

"Fully absolved thru these I am, from sin and fear, from guilt and shame."

"Lord, I believe Thy Precious Blood which at the Mercy Seat of God,
"Forever doth for sinners plead, for me, e'en for my soul was shed."

"Lord, I believe we're sinners more than sands upon the ocean's floor,
"Thou hast for all a ransom paid, for all a full Atonement made."

CHAPTER 6

(1) "WE THEN, AS WORKERS TOGETHER WITH HIM, BESEECH YOU ALSO THAT YE RECEIVE NOT THE GRACE OF GOD IN VAIN."

The phrase, *"We then, as workers together with Him,"* refers to working with God. It refers to being a joint-worker with the Lord in securing the Salvation of men.

WORKERS

"Workers" in the Greek is *"sunergos,"* and means *"fellow workers or fellow laborers,"* and should have been translated accordingly.

The manner in which the Holy Spirit structures this word through Paul is that it includes every single Believer, whether Preacher or otherwise. Everyone is to be a *"worker"* for the Lord. In what way can this be done?

First of all, the Lord has a task, a life, a work, a position if you will, for every single Believer irrespective as to whom they may be. It is the business of the Child of God to walk close enough to the Lord, that the Holy Spirit may be able to bring the Saint into his allotted place.

The Work of God is like a giant jigsaw puzzle, with every piece having a place. Every single Believer has a place and position in the Work of God, and if they do not find that place and position and labor therein, whatever it may be, the work as a whole suffers, as would be obvious. While we see only our place and position, and possibly a little further, God of course, sees all. That's the reason that things get out of harmony when individuals do not have the Mind of the Lord, but rather launch out on their own. It would be somewhat like having a mechanic working for an airline, suddenly, decide that he wants to fly the plane. While he does a great job as a mechanic, even with his service being indispensable, still, flying the airplane is not his task. But yet, many Christians take it upon themselves to chart their own course, which as should be obvious, always causes problems.

NOTES

CONSECRATION

The major difficulty with most Believers is a lack of consecration. They don't know their part, place, and position in this great Christian experience, simply because they don't walk close enough to the Lord for Him to lead or guide.

As the Believer consecrates to the Lord, the Holy Spirit will begin to direct him according to the Will of God. With some few He calls them to preach the Gospel, but with most they fit into one or more the categories listed by Paul in Romans Chapter 12. As well, Paul did not list all the places and positions which the Holy Spirit carves out for Believers, but he did give us an idea as to what the Holy Spirit is saying.

Any Christian who consecrates Himself to the perfect Will of God for his life, will find Himself productive, fruitful, useful, as well as fulfilled, developed, happy, and joyous in the Lord. Every Believer is to be a worker for the Lord.

LABORERS INTO HIS HARVEST

Irrespective as to what position in which the Lord places us, in one way or the other, all are to fall out unto *"laborers into His harvest."* This refers in some way, to bringing people to God.

While the task the Lord has assigned us may not seem to flow in that direction, to be sure, if what we are doing is the Will of God, which constitutes our place and position in the Work of God, whether we can see such or not, it will have a positive effect in some way on the *"harvest,"* i.e., *"the Salvation of souls."* However, Jesus also said, *"The harvest truly is plenteous, but the laborers are few"* (Mat. 9:37-38). The tragedy is, most Believers contribute little or nothing toward this great harvest.

For instance, a great segment of the modern Body of Christ, places their priority on the use of the Scriptures to get rich. Of course, they are not going to get rich but actually poorer, both in material assets and spiritually; however, I suppose there is enough greed in all of us, to make us believe that such can come to pass.

While it's not wrong for a person to be rich, should the Lord desire such, it is wrong to make that the goal of one's life in the Lord.

As I dictate these notes (7-24-98) most of the major Ministries, and I speak of those who have some type of worldwide impact, make little effort at all to get anyone saved. Also, it seems that the major Pentecostal Denominations are more concerned presently about protecting property and their particular place, whatever that may be, than they are about taking the Gospel to a lost world.

Satan is little concerned, about us being in the *"Work,"* if our emphasis and priorities are wrong.

To be a worker for the Lord is the greatest privilege that anyone could ever know; however, we must make very certain that the work we are doing, is Scriptural, and where God has placed us and not we ourselves.

TOGETHER WITH HIM

The word *"together"* refers not only to God, but as well to fellow Christians. We are to work together as a team, being led and guided by the Lord. When Believers are not functioning in their assigned place, a place incidently which only the Holy Spirit can designate, the results are everyone pulling in different directions, or as is the case with most, not pulling at all. This is probably the greatest problem in the Church presently, and in fact always has been.

Using Paul as an example, it is very obvious as we study the Book of Acts, and his Epistles as well, that this problem was severe at that time, even as it is now.

The Lord had called the Apostle for a particular task which included the Message (the New Covenant), and the propagation of that Message all over the world, i.e., *"World Evangelism."* If there is anything obvious in the Word of God, this is obvious concerning Paul.

But yet, a great segment of the Church was pulling in the opposite direction, with some espousing other doctrines, and above all making little effort to get anyone to Christ, but rather trying to wrongly indoctrinate those won to the Lord by Paul. Due to their false Gospel they could not get anyone saved, so they had to resort to the place and position of parasites.

I'm certain the reader can understand that these people, whomever they may have been, and as numerous as they may have been, certainly were not doing the Work of God, and in fact were greatly hindering the Work of God. How much better and easier and more productive for that matter it would have been, if they had been flowing with the Holy Spirit, instead of being opposed to Him. This one thing is certain, had that been the case, they would have been helping Paul, or at least not opposing him.

NOTES

WORLD EVANGELISM

As I hope we have adequately stated, irrespective of the place and position in Christ desired for us by the Holy Spirit, in some way, the effort will lead to the taking of the Gospel of Jesus Christ to a hurting world.

Using our own Ministry as an example, the Lord has called me for this task. I speak of Mass Evangelism, whether by Television, Radio, or Crusades. We have aired Television programming in many nations of the world, actually translating the program into quite a number of different languages. The Lord has helped us to see untold thousands through this effort, brought to a saving knowledge of Jesus Christ.

With the call that God has given me, He has also called the appropriate number of people to support this work and Ministry, both prayerfully and financially, that the task may be done. In fact, I must have these people, whomever they may be, working together with me, as we all work together with the Lord, to carry out this task. I need them and they need me, and we all need the Lord. In fact, our task is basically to *"plant and to water,"* with Him giving the increase (I Cor. 3:7).

And yet, if the people assigned by the Holy Spirit to help us take this Gospel to the world fall by the wayside, and for any reason, the work will suffer to the degree that that particular help is lacking.

Second, it is Satan's business to try to stop anything that is of God. And regrettably, even as he did in the days of Paul, he has his greatest success in using Christians to hinder the true Work of God. In doing that, he has succeeded on two fronts:

First of all, any person opposing that which is of God, and in any manner, as should be obvious, is hindering the Work of God. In fact, there is no such thing as an individual staying neutral respecting this of which we speak. Jesus plainly said, *"He that is not with Me is against Me; and he that gathereth not with Me scattereth abroad"* (Mat. 12:30).

The structure of the sentence demands an active participation, and if such is not forthcoming, the Lord places that person in the minus column as *"against Me."*

Second, Satan not only succeeds in placing such Believers in a very negative position, but as well, greatly hinders the spread of the Gospel all over the world. So, as stated, his success is *"twofold."*

The idea of this text as given by Paul, *"Workers together with Him,"* is that if we are properly working together with the Lord, being led by Him, guided by Him, we will at the same time work in union with fellow Believers who are truly doing the Work of God. The first proper union (the Believer and the Lord) guarantees the proper union of the latter (Believers working with other Believers).

The phrase, *"Beseech you also that ye receive not the Grace of God in vain,"* tells us by its very structure that such definitely can be done.

BESEECH YOU

"Beseech you" actually means *"to beg."*

In fact, Paul frequently uses this phrase, which shows us his own nature of humility, but as well, gives us an idea as to what the Holy Spirit desires respecting Ministerial Leadership. We as Ministers of the Gospel are always to function in the position of servants. Jesus plainly portrayed this in John Chapter 13.

Regrettably, this is a far cry from the dictatorial spirit of many modern Preachers, and especially those in positions of so-called leadership, as it regards particular Denominations. All too often, the opposite spirit prevails which says, *"You do what I tell you to do, whether it is Scriptural or not, and if not, we will destroy you."* This is a sad state of affairs, and I trust that the Reader can see, if in fact such is the case, just how unscriptural is such a position.

THE GRACE OF GOD

The *"Grace of God"* means evidently the gracious offer of reconciliation and pardon.

As important as the Grace of God actually is, and considering that it has to do with the entirety of the great Plan of Salvation, let's take a closer look at this all-important subject.

NOTES

One could say that the work of Grace, at least as it deals with the sinner, has a fourfold aspect. They are as follows:

THE SOVEREIGN ASPECT AND THE ACT OF FORGIVENESS

In the act of forgiveness, as it regards Grace, God is to be regarded as Sovereign, as He deals with rebels as it pertains to sinners. However, upon appeal, the rebellion has been broken and the rebel sues, in effect, for mercy.

This is granted on the grounds of what Jesus did at Calvary, and the soul receives a pardon which is abundant, full, and free (Isa. 55:7; Eph. 4:32).

This moment in the life of the believing sinner is of such magnitude, such moment, in fact the greatest moment in human history as it regards that precious soul — and as such, is beyond the pale of human comprehension. It is great and wonderful! To be totally, fully, completely, and absolutely forgiven by God, forgiven of all sin, forgiven of all rebellion, forgiven of all wickedness, forgiven of all hostility toward our Saviour, presented, as stated, a full, absolute, and complete pardon, is so wonderful that it makes the Angels in Heaven shout, and it should cause us to do the same (Lk. 15:10).

THE JUDICIAL ASPECT AND THE FACT OF JUSTIFICATION

Justification has to do with the sinner in his legal relationships. The word at once carries us into the Court of Divine Justice, before which he is arraigned, and wonder of wonders, the verdict goes in his favor and he is honorably discharged, although he has been proved guilty and has confessed to all the charges laid against him.

What, then, is the secret here?

On the basis of the following Scriptures (Acts 13:38-39; Rom. 1:17; 3:19-31; 5:1; 8:33-34; I Cor. 6:11; Gal. 2:16; 3:11, 24), the Doctrine may be stated thus:

Justification is that judicial act by which God, on account of a new Faith relationship to Jesus Christ, declares the sinner to be no longer exposed to the penalty of the broken Law, but restored rather to the Divine favor. It is a reversal of the Divine attitude, bringing the sinner into harmony with the Law of God, and thereby securing peace.

Justification presupposes some preliminary facts, namely:

THE PAST

Concerning the past: A radical repentance, with all that this involves. It is a complete renunciation of the old life. The sinner has now turned his face in an opposite direction, and refuses even to consider the things left behind (Gal. 2:17-18).

Repentance demands a willing restitution. By that we mean, if wrongs toward others exist, the penitent one makes an honest effort to make those things right (Lk. 19:1-10).

It is a full reliance on the Calvary Work of Jesus (Rom. 3:25-26).

THE PRESENT

Concerning the present: An honesty of purpose as to a daily walk with God.

Justification is predicated on the sinner confessing the fact that he is a sinner, and the Believer confessing particular sins.

It is not for the sinner coming to God to attempt to confess particular sins, as such would be literally impossible. He is merely to confess that he is a sinner, which carries with it the weight of all sins committed, and forgiveness, cleansing, and justification instantly granted.

Regarding the person who is already a Believer, who is no longer in a sinful state, if sin is committed, that sin must be confessed before the Lord as quickly as possible (Ps. 32:5; I Jn. 1:9).

Justification cannot be retained while there is a conscious present committing of sin, with the idea that Grace covers all (Gal. 2:17-18; I Jn. 3:8). Conscious sinfulness and Divine favor never coexist. The Lord does not save in sin, but rather from sin.

While it is true that no Believer is perfect, at least as it regards sinlessness, still, the true Believer hates sin, and will cooperate with the Lord that all sin be removed from his life.

The actual Plan of God, as it regards Salvation, is that no state of Grace admits of committing sin. A state of Justification implies freedom from the guilt of sin by pardon, and freedom from the commission of sin by renewing, assisting Grace. At least, that is the ideal, which all true Christians struggle toward.

One could say that the minimum of Salvation is Salvation from sinning. The maximum is Salvation from pollution — the inclination to sin, which is a process, in fact, the process of Sanctification.

The conditions of receiving Justification and of retaining it are the same. Christ is received by penitential submission and Faith. *"As ye have received Christ Jesus, so walk ye in Him."* Consequently, it should go without saying, that Justification cannot be retained with less consecration and Faith than that by which it was received.

SURRENDER

Conscious confidence and conscious guilt cannot coexist in the same heart. There is a vital union between justifying Faith and an obedient spirit. While obedience makes Faith perfect, disobedience destroys it. Salvation is by appropriating Faith (Faith in Christ and what He did at Calvary and the Resurrection), and such Faith or Trust can be exercised only when there is a consciousness of complete surrender to God. Consequently, a justified state can exist only in connection with a serious, honest intention to obey all the commands of God, even though at times we do fail.

Justification is interpreted wrongly by many. Some think it gives a license to sin, which of course, it never does. Others, going to the far side of the spectrum, claim sinless perfection. Both directions are wrong.

There is no license to sin in Justification, inasmuch, as stated, that the Lord saves from sin and not in sin.

As well, Justification demands that the Believer work with the Holy Spirit in removing all sin from our lives, even the inclination to sin; however, as also stated, to that place of perfection, no Christian has ever come, and in fact, will not come, until the Resurrection. But yet, that must be the goal, for how could God demand less?

Justification has been stated as being fivefold in its aspect:

1. The spring of our Justification is Grace (Rom. 3:24).

2. The principle of our Justification is Faith (Rom. 5:1; Gal. 3:24-26).

3. The ground of our Justification is *"His Blood"* (Rom. 5:9).

4. The guarantee of our Justification is His Resurrection (Rom. 4:25).

NOTES

5. The outcome of our Justification is Holiness (II Cor. 7:1).

THE PARENTAL ASPECT AND THE WORK OF REGENERATION

Thus far, we have dealt with *"Divine Acts"* on the sinner's behalf, having to do with his standing before God. These, however, are not wrought alone, but are complementary to a Divine operation within the soul itself, by which the Believer is *"begotten again."* It is called *"born again," "quickened,"* also *"passing from death unto life"* (Jn. 1:13; 3:1-8; 5:24; Eph. 2:1; Titus 3:5; I Pet. 1:3, 23; I Jn. 3:14; 5:4, 13).

Lee said, *"Regeneration is a renewal of our fallen nature by the power of the Holy Spirit, received through Faith in Jesus Christ, whereby the regenerate are delivered from the power of sin which reigns over all the unregenerate.*

"Regeneration reverses the current state of the affections, and so renews the whole soul in order that the Christian Graces may exist.

"The power of sin is broken; the principle of obedience is planted in the heart."

Foster said, *"With respect to Regeneration, it is a work done in us, in the way of changing our inward nature; a work by which spiritual life is infused into the soul, whereby he (the regenerate) brings forth the peaceable Fruits of Righteousness, has victory over sin, is enabled to resist corrupt tendencies, and has peace and joy in the Holy Spirit; a radical change by which the preponderating tendencies of the soul are turned towards God, whereas they were previously turned from Him — by which the love of sin is destroyed, its dominion broken and a desire and relish for and longing after Holiness implanted."*

Wood said, *"Regeneration is the impartation of spiritual life to the human soul, in which God imparts, organizes, and calls into being the capabilities, attributes, and functions of the new nature. It is a change from death to life, from the dominion of sin to the reign of Grace, and restores the spiritual life which was lost by the Fall. It is instantaneously wrought by the Holy Spirit, and always accompanies Justification."*

John Wesley said, *"From hence it manifestly appears what is the nature of the New Birth. It is that great change which God works in the soul when He brings it into life; when He raises it from the death of sin to the Life of Righteousness.*

NOTES

"It is the change wrought in the whole soul by the Almighty Spirit of God when it is 'created anew in Christ Jesus'; when it is renewed after the Image of God in Righteousness and True Holiness; when the love of the world is changed into the Love of God; pride into humility; passion into meekness; and hatred, envy, malice, into a sincere, tender, love for all mankind.

"In a word, it is that change whereby the earthly, sensual, devilish mind is turned into the 'Mind which was in Christ Jesus.' This is the nature of the New Birth: 'so is everyone that is born of the Spirit.'"

This experience of the New Birth is set forth in John's First Epistle as having seven decided characteristics:

1. A righteous life (I Jn. 2:29).
2. Victory over sin (I Jn. 3:9).
3. Brotherly love (I Jn. 3:14).
4. A compassionate spirit (I Jn. 3:17).
5. Recognition of the Lordship of Jesus (I Jn. 5:1).
6. Victory over the world (I Jn. 5:4).
7. The Spirit's inward witness (I Jn. 5:10).

THE FAMILY ASPECT AND THE POSITION OF ADOPTION

The thought behind the position of Adoption, as it pertains to Grace, is the putting of a stranger in the place of a son. Its relation to Regeneration differs from that of Justification, although, like Justification, it is a legal idea or work.

In the case of Justification, the thought is that of the criminal being treated as righteous, whereas in Adoption, it is the stranger being treated as a son. This is the legal privilege of the Second Birth, the heritage of Saving Grace.

This *"Adoption"* was familiar among both Greeks and Romans at the period in which the New Testament was penned, and Paul, ever on the lookout for current illustrations of the Gospel which he preached, seized upon the fact as illustrative of that act of free Grace whereby the soul, pardoned, justified, and twice born, becomes a member of the Divine Family and is made an heir of God by Faith.

The term *"Adoption"* is found five times in the Pauline Epistles, but nowhere else in the entirety of Scripture. It is distinctly a

Revelation of God to the Apostle Paul as it regards the New Covenant (Rom. 8:15, 23; 9:4; Gal. 4:5; Eph. 1:5).

Here, then, under these four great aspects, we have this magnificent *"Work of Divine Grace."* The soul's relation to sin is now such that most extraordinary figures are used to express it:

1. Sins are pardoned, forgiven, covered (Ps. 32:1; Isa. 55:7; Jer. 33:8; I Jn. 1:9).
2. Removed as far as the east is from the west (Ps. 103:12).
3. Cast into the depth of the Sea (Micah 7:19).
4. Cast behind God's back (Isa. 38:17).
5. Blotted out (Isa. 44:22-23).
6. Sought for and not found (Jer. 50:20).
7. Remembered no more (Jer. 31:34).

IN VAIN

The word *"vain"* means *"into emptiness," "to no profit,"* or *"to no purpose."*

The word *"vain"* can refer to two directions:

1. It can refer to the Believer falling far short of his actual potential in Christ, in effect, much of the Grace of God being in *"vain"* respecting his spiritual growth.
2. It can refer to the Believer veering off into false doctrine, or else ceasing altogether to live for God, and if continuing in that state, will lose his soul.

Consequently, the word *"vain"* as it is used here could refer to either direction, and as should be obvious, completely shoots down the unscriptural doctrine of Unconditional Eternal Security.

UNCONDITIONAL ETERNAL SECURITY

This doctrine is taught by several major Religious Denominations, consequently, believed by many millions of people. The Doctrine, pure and simple, is unscriptural. Untold millions have believed this lie, and that's what it is; consequently, many even a majority I think who believe this false doctrine, make little pretense at living for God, their lives are not changed, in fact, they are living a life of open sin. Most of them, because of this false way, will die in that condition, and be preached into Heaven at their funeral. Due to the seriousness of this situation, and serious it is, I think it is incumbent upon us to address

NOTES

the subject, and do so in some detail, where the Word of God gives the opportunity.

There are several words which are very similar in meaning, which pertain to the Eternal Security question, and are very Biblical if used correctly. However, much of the time they are not used correctly. I speak of *"election," "foreknowledge," "predestination,"* all which have a bearing on Eternal Security. In the following statement on this particular subject, these words will be used quite often.

I believe in Eternal Security, but I believe in this doctrine as the Bible teaches it, and not as many have claimed it to be. One is secure as long as one stays in Christ. And one can stay in Christ if one so desires. However, the will of man is never violated by God, which is necessary for entrance into Salvation, and can be used for an exit out of Salvation, if one so foolishly desires. There is no danger of one being lost if one wants to be saved, and attempts to obey and follow the Lord, despite all the many failures that all of us seem to incur. However, the idea that one can make a profession of Faith in Christ Jesus, and then live any way they desire thereafter, in other words, and as stated, in open sin, and then expect to be right with the Lord when they die, is a fool's hope. Untold millions, in fact, are now in Hell because of this pernicious doctrine.

Even though we are dealing with II Corinthians, the following material will be from Romans Chapter 9.

ROMANS CHAPTER 9

Romans Chapter 9 is the stronghold Chapter of Augustine, Calvin, and the Eternal Security teachers. This is the passage most argued by them in defense of their Predestination doctrine. So, let us give them a fair hearing. Let us not evade or twist anything, but rather examine the passages by fair rules of interpretation, and let Truth be whatever it is. If Salvation is unconditional, even as they teach, and that's what the Bible teaches, then that's what we should believe. However, that is *not* what the Bible teaches, as we shall see.

As we have previously stated, it is never proper to try to force a particular meaning into a passage of Scripture, even though it may seem to indicate a certain thing, especially if all the other Scriptures on that particular subject lend in the opposite direction. A few Scriptures do not disprove many Scriptures. The Bible is not a house divided against itself. The whole Bible is a unit of Truth, and is meant to be studied in that fashion. In other words, a true interpreter will impartially seek the Truth in all parts of this unit. He will see what the Scriptures say in their entirety concerning any given subject, not just two or three. Each part must fit into the whole unit.

It is a vicious system of interpretation that picks and chooses those parts of Scripture that seem to affirm a particular doctrine but ignores the balance of the Word of God on that particular Subject. Every false doctrine in Christianity today is defended by this method of interpretation — which lifts particular Scriptures out of their proper context.

THE MISINTERPRETATION OF SCRIPTURE

Romans Chapter 9 does not teach differently about Election or Predestination than do other Scriptures about this doctrine. We must understand Paul in Romans Chapter 9 by comparing Paul and his other Epistles. Paul is not at variance with himself, nor is he at variance with Moses, or any of the other Apostles or Prophets. When all the Scriptures on a Doctrine are fairly examined, a single thought emerges and predominates.

This rule of unity, we think, has been grossly violated by Augustine, Calvin, and the modern Eternal Security teachers. And if they are allowed to do this, then as Young says in the preface of his *"Literal Translation of the Bible"*: *"We cannot deny the same privilege to others who may twist other passages in like manner."* The hopeless mass of doctrinal confusion among Christian denominations today is the result of distorted interpretation.

Dr. F. W. Farrar, Dean of Canterbury, stands in the first rank of Bible Scholars. He spent twenty years on his valuable work, *"History of Interpretation."*

He said on page 39 of that particular work:

"The misinterpretation of Scripture must be reckoned among the gravest calamities of Christendom."

The misinterpretation of Election and Predestination in which Eternal Security figures, is among these grave calamities. Let us now get the facts and see why this is true.

NOTES

PROPER DEFINITIONS

First, it is highly important that we establish the definitions of Election, Predestination, and Foreknowledge. Everything hangs on the meaning of words, and often they are dangerous things. Recently, a news commentator said: *"The United Nations has been trying to define the word 'aggression' for fifteen years."*

Many people, even some who call themselves Calvinists, do not know what Election actually is. This is also true of many Ministers.

WHAT THE WORD ELECTION MEANS

In Scripture, there is not the slightest hint to an election of God whereby one person is chosen to be saved and another is not. There is no teaching that a man is saved because of God's choice alone; there must also be the choice of the individual to meet God's terms of Salvation.

It is the *"Plan of God"* that is elected, chosen, foreknown, and predestined — not the individual or natural choice of man to conform to that Plan. The Plan is the same for all alike; and everyone is invited, chosen, elected, foreknown, and predestined to Salvation, without exception on the sole basis of the individual's choice and total conformity to the Gospel, simply because Jesus died for all. Otherwise, one will be lost, and there is no exception, nor can there be an exception to this, the Divine Plan.

God's part in Salvation for all men has been completed, and whoever meets His terms will be saved. The whole program of Salvation is simply that of being Born-Again — becoming a New Creature in Christ (Mat. 18:3; Jn. 3:1-8; 14:17; II Cor. 5:17-18). And the door is open to all (Rev. 22:17).

The *"International Standard Bible Encyclopedia"* is widely referred to as *"the best Bible Encyclopedia."* It says:

"Election never appears as a violation of human will. For never in the Bible is man treated as irresponsible. In the Bible, the relation of the human and Divine wills is inscrutable; the reality of both is assured. Never is the Doctrine presented apart from a moral context."

THE MEANING OF PREDESTINATION

The words *"foreordain"* and *"predestinate"* come from the same Greek word, *"prooridzo,"* and means *"to determine beforehand."*

The meaning of the word *"Predestination"* means that God's Law is the thing that is predestinated, and not the individual conformity to that Law. All Scripture is clear that men are absolutely free to choose for themselves whether they conform to the predestined plan or not (Jn. 3:16-20; Rev. 22:17, etc.). Those that do conform will enjoy forever the predestined blessings and those who do not will suffer eternally the predestined judgments of the Plan.

This, and this alone, is all that the Bible teaches concerning Predestination in connection with free moral agents, even as we have seen regarding *"Election."*

In the Plan of God, it was predestinated that Christ would die for the world (Acts 4:28); that some (it is not stated who or which ones) would be saved by believing on Jesus as their Saviour (Rom. 8:29-30); that those who would freely choose to be saved were predestinated to be holy and to be Children of God through Christ (Eph. 1:5); that these Children of God have a predestinated inheritance according to the Eternal Purpose (Eph. 1:11); that they were predestinated to be enlightened with wisdom kept secret from of old (I Cor. 2:7); but no statement is made that God's predestined Plan and Purpose includes the free acts of free moral agents nor does it name those who will conform to the Plan.

THE MEANING OF THE WORD FOREKNOWLEDGE

The word *"foreknowledge"* simply means the Omniscience of God, which means that God has the ability to know any and all things, past, present, and future. He has a Plan, and He knows His Plan from the beginning to the end.

However, having the ability to know what will happen in the future, even as God does, in no way means that the free wills of men are necessarily violated. In fact, according to Scripture, they are not violated at all.

THE FIRST ARGUMENT FOR UNCONDITIONAL SALVATION

"For this is the word of promise, At this time will I come, and Sarah shall have a son.

"And not only this; but when Rebecca also had conceived by one, even by our father Isaac;

"(For the children being not yet born, neither having done any good or evil, that the purpose of God according to election might stand, not of works, but of Him that calleth;)

"It was said unto her, The elder shall serve the younger.

"As it is written, Jacob have I loved, but Esau have I hated" (Rom. 9:9-13).

Our opponents, using these Verses to support their doctrine of unconditional salvation, say it was God's elected purpose to love Jacob and hate Esau. They point out that God predestinated them to be loved and hated when they were *"not yet born, neither having done any good or evil."* The reason for this elected choice, they say, lies in the mysterious sovereign Will of God, and is, therefore, beyond the power of human thought to penetrate. Augustine said, *"The more difficult this is to understand, the more laudable is the Faith that believes it."*

Calvin said there is a deep mystery to this *"horrible decree"* that caused God to love Jacob and hate Esau, without regard to anything they could do or could not do for their Salvation. And Calvin held that God's love and wisdom was the cause of His predestinating choice in loving and hating them, without regard to anything they could do or could not do.

God's love and wisdom, Calvin said, then issued this *"horrible decree."* In response to that I ask the following question, *"Could human love and wisdom do such a horrible thing?"* Here in Romans 13:10, Paul said: *"Love worketh no ill."* Then, can Divine Love work such horrible ill to men?

WHY THEN DID GOD LOVE JACOB AND HATE ESAU?

Why then did God have this *"relative preference"* for Jacob, and this *"relative disregard"* for Esau?

God's reasons for His choice of Jacob over Esau are reasons found in the characters of these two men, and not reasons in a mysterious sovereign will. Let us take a glance at the characters of these two men and see if this could be true.

God appeared to Jacob and revealed Himself to him; and Jacob vowed a vow to serve God (Gen. 28:10-22). Jacob honored his father and mother and obeyed their wishes not to marry a heathen woman. His conscience protested against participating in the tricks his mother taught him (Gen. 27:11-13). Despite his problems, Jacob was a man of Faith (Heb. 11:21). This means he simply believed God. He was mighty in prayer and prevailed with God, and was changed from Jacob (*"supplanter"*) to *"Israel,"* which is the great Covenant name of the Jews. Jacob was a man who saw God *"face to face"* (Gen. 32:24-30).

There were defects in his character, but he was changed into a great Saint and Covenant partner with God. Throughout the Scriptures, Jehovah is referred to as *"the God of Abraham, Isaac, and Jacob."*

IN CONTRAST TO JACOB, CONSIDER ESAU

Esau *"despised"* his birthright and sold it for *"one morsel of meat"* (Heb. 12:16). This indicated his low estimate of spiritual values and his desire for the pleasure of appetite.

He married heathen wives which was a *"grief"* to his parents (Gen. 26:34-35). He was a man of unbelief and debased character. His whole evil character was gathered and flashed at us in two words: *"fornicator"* and *"profane."*

The word *"profane"* means *"unclean"* and *"Godless."* It also means *"that which lacks all relationship or affinity to God."*

Our opponents argue that God made His choice between Jacob and Esau before they were born — before they had done good or evil. However, God foreknows all things, and knew exactly what type of men both Jacob and Esau would be. He would not be God if He did not have this foreknowledge.

IS THERE UNRIGHTEOUSNESS WITH GOD?

God forbid! God is not unrighteous for choosing Jacob, who as a *"prince"* had *"power with God"* and *"prevailed"* — a man who was transformed into the mighty *"Israel"* when God revealed Himself to him face to face. Nor was God unrighteous for rejecting the fornicator and profane Esau who joined himself to the heathen.

The next point that Eternal Security teachers stress is Romans 9:15, *"I will have mercy on whom I will have mercy, and I will have compassion on whom I will have compassion."* This statement is a context between Jacob, Esau, and Pharaoh. We have seen what an evil character Esau was, and Pharaoh was worse.

NOTES

Dr. Robertson, in his *"Word Pictures in the New Testament,"* pointed out that *"Pharaoh hardened his own heart also"* (Ex. 8:15, 32; 9:34).

In fact, God gives men up to *"their own"* hardness of heart (Rom. 1:24-28). Pharaoh wasn't born hardened, nor was Hitler, Joseph Stalin, or any other person for that matter. They reach the hardened state through regressive stages of unbelief and disobedience.

DO NOT ERR, MY BELOVED BRETHREN

Everything moves ever onward to its climax. Every cancer has a small beginning. Every hardened heart began with *"his own lust"* and develops by the same Satanic means until it is full grown. One should not think it began in some predestinating council of God. There are many speculative ideas about the origin of sin, but James set us straight, and said it begins when the sinner follows Satan's lure *"of his own lust."* Sinners love sin, as Esau and Pharaoh loved sin.

This hardening of heart, through the free volition of the individual, is given repeated emphasis in Scripture. Nehemiah said the Israelites *"hardened their necks . . . And refused to obey"* (Neh. 9:16-17). They continually disobeyed the warnings of the Prophets and *"hardened their necks, like the neck of their fathers . . . And rejected His statutes, and His Covenant"* (II Ki. 17:14-15).

Solomon said a sinner *"hardeneth his neck"* after being *"often reproved"* (Prov. 29:1).

Acts 19:8-9 says that many Jews were *"hardened"* after hearing Paul for *"three months."* Hebrews 3:13 says sinners are *"hardened through the deceitfulness of sin"*; and Verses 8, 15-17: *"To day if ye will hear his voice, harden not your hearts, as in the provocation . . . in the wilderness."* Unbelievers harden their hearts after they hear the Voice of God, and reject the Voice. This was true of Pharaoh.

THE MERCY OF GOD

Some claim that God did not have mercy on Esau or Pharaoh. In one sense, that is true; however, it is because these men did not ask for mercy, did not want mercy, in fact, were constantly rebelling against God.

In fact, God will always grant Mercy to any who call upon His Name. But for those who rebel against Him, fight against Him, and seek to hinder His Cause, no mercy is given, simply because it is not wanted or desired.

The Word of God says that the Lord shows *"mercy unto thousands of them that love Me, and keep My Commandments"* (Ex. 20:6). Loving God and keeping His Commandments are conditions for receiving His Mercy.

Mary said, concerning Jesus, that *"God's Mercy is on them that fear Him from generation to generation"* (Lk. 1:50). Clearly, Mary understood that Fear of God was a condition of His Mercy.

The writer of Hebrews also said, *"He that despised Moses' Law died without Mercy"* (Heb. 10:28). Disrespect for Moses' Law was a cause for not receiving Mercy. Those who respected it received Mercy. Respectful obedience was a condition. Those who obeyed Moses could have disobeyed, and those who disobeyed could have obeyed, if they had only desired to have done so. God does not give His Mercy to *"them that hate Me"* (Deut. 5:9), and neither is He expected to do so and neither should He do so.

Esau could have obeyed God and received Mercy. But he despised his birthright. He despised his parents, he despised God. His evil life was not the result of his acting under the impulses of a mysterious predestination. His profane acts were not the working of foreordained damnation. It was Esau who was profane, and, therefore, rejected by God, and rightly so! It was Pharaoh who continued to oppose God, even after being given many opportunities to repent. Consequently, God could not grant Mercy to one who did not desire such.

THE WILL OF MAN

The Eternal Security teachers press hard on Romans 9:16 in relation to Jacob, Esau, and Pharaoh. Actually, this has been one of the most disputed Texts in 16 Centuries of doctrinal debate. The Scripture says:

"So then it is not of him that willeth, nor of him that runneth, but of God that sheweth mercy" (Rom. 9:16). This means simply that Salvation cannot be earned, but is a Gift of God (Eph. 2:8-9).

We consider first: *"Not of him that willeth."* Opposing teachers say this means that the wills of Jacob, Esau, and Pharaoh had no part in their eternal destinies. All is determined, they say, by sovereign will.

NOTES

As supporting evidence, they quote John 1:13: *"Which were born, not of blood, nor of the will of the flesh, nor of the will of man, but of God."* But the preceding Verses, which they neglect, upset this interpretation.

"He came unto His own, and His own received him not. But as many as received him, to them gave He power to become the sons of God, even to them that believe on His Name" (Jn. 1:11-12).

To receive Him and to believe on His Name were conditions for becoming sons of God. Can anyone do this without *"willing it"*? One must wreck the laws of language and logic to deny it.

Whether it be Jacob, Esau, Pharaoh, Jews, or Gentiles, none are predestinated without regard to the free acts of his own will. These texts they quote do not prove unconditional Salvation. They do not rule out *"human wills"* as a condition for Divine Mercy.

God commanded that all Israel's worship, Sacrifices, and Offerings had to be of their *"freewill."* They offered unto the Lord *"Freewill Offerings"* (Lev. 22:18). This Freewill Offering was a *"sweet savour unto the Lord"* (Num. 15:3). This Freewill Offering is also specified in Deuteronomy 12:6; 23:23; II Chronicles 31:14. The worship of religious puppets would not be to God a *"sweet savour."*

When the Israelites brought their gifts to God, it was required that they come from *"every man that giveth it willingly with his heart"* (Ex. 25:2). It was repeatedly stated by Moses that a condition of acceptance for their Offering was that it come from *"whosoever is of a willing heart"* (Ex. 35:5) — that it come from *"every one whose heart stirred him up, and every one whom his spirit made willing"* (Ex. 35:21).

"As many as were willing hearted" brought Offerings to the Lord (Ex. 35:22).

The Psalmist said, *"Accept, I beseech Thee, the Freewill Offerings of my mouth, O Lord"* (Ps. 119:108).

The Spirit through Isaiah said, *"If ye be willing and obedient, ye shall eat the good of the land: but if ye refuse and rebel, ye shall be devoured with the sword"* (Isa. 1:19-20).

SALVATION BY GRACE

The next part of the opposing argument in Romans 9:16 uses the word *"nor of him that runneth* (that worketh), *but of God that sheweth mercy."*

NOTES

It is argued from this that our efforts have no part in our Salvation. In other words, that God just arbitrarily chooses some to be saved and others to be lost. But this interpretation cannot stand up to the test of facts that we shall apply to it.

These words do not mean that Salvation is unconditional. They mean that men cannot originate nor earn their Salvation by works — and that is all Paul intended them to mean.

Calvin and the Eternal Security interpreters used the important Rule of Comparison on other Bible Doctrines, so we shall use it on this Scripture. We shall compare and interpret Paul in Romans by Paul in his other Epistles.

"The Structural Principles of the Bible," written by F. E. Marsh, is widely considered a Bible Study Classic. On page 238, Marsh wrote:

"The careful comparison of one Scripture with another will generally explain a seemingly contradiction."

Dean Alford, an eminent Scholar, wrote:

"It should be a maximum for every Expositor and every student, that Scripture is a whole, and stands or falls together."

Leading Biblical and legal interpretation experts agree with this comparative rule. And if it is not allowed, then we cannot answer the critics who say, *"The Bible is self-contradictory* (which it is not), *and can be made to prove anything."*

So we place in comparative position with Romans 9:16 other statements by Paul on running or working as it relates to our Salvation.

MORE ON PAUL

Paul also said in conjunction with Romans, *"Know ye not that they which run in a race run all, but one receiveth the prize? So run, that ye may obtain. I therefore so run, not as uncertainly; so fight I, not as one that beateth the air"* (I Cor. 9:24, 26).

He also said, *"I have fought a good fight, I have finished my course* (finished running the race), *I have kept the faith: Henceforth, there is laid up for me a Crown of Righteousness. . . ."* (II Tim. 4:7-8).

Paul told the Romans that God's Mercy is not to him that runneth, but he told the Corinthians to run that they may obtain the prize. And he told Timothy, after he had finished the race, that the Lord would give him the victor's crown. In Hebrews, the Apostle told the people to run the race, and to lay aside every encumbrance that they might run it better.

Is there a contradiction between Paul in Romans and Paul in Corinthians and Timothy? Certainly not!

Different subjects were under consideration in these Epistles. What Paul was addressing in Romans is not what he is addressing in Corinthians and Timothy. It is required in interpretation that *"language must be understood according to the subject matter of discourse."*

All the willing and running and efforts and works of man cannot save him. He cannot, as it regards his own strength, and irrespective of his great effort, be his own Savior. Without God's unmerited and unearned Love and Grace, no sinner can ever be saved, not even the heathen religious fanatics who torture themselves all their lives. However, God's free Grace, undeserved as it is, does not dispense with conditions for man's Salvation. In fact, predestinating Grace requires Faith, Repentance, Obedience, willing and running as conditions. Further evidence of this will appear as we proceed.

BACK TO ROMANS CHAPTER 9

The main thrust of the opposing argument in Romans Chapter 9 is in Verses 19-24.

These passages are: *"Thou wilt say then unto me, Why doth He yet find fault? For who hath resisted His will?*

"Nay but, O man, who art thou that repliest against God? Shall the thing formed say to Him that formed it, Why hast thou made me thus?

"Hath not the potter power over the clay, of the same lump to make one vessel unto honour, and another unto dishonour?

"What if God, willing to shew His wrath, and to make His power known, endured with much longsuffering the vessels of wrath fitted to destruction:

"And that He might make known the riches of His glory on the vessels of mercy, which He had afore prepared unto glory,

"Even us, whom He hath called, not of the Jews only, but also of the Gentiles?"

The argument for Eternal Security from these Verses goes like this: *"As the potter is sovereign in forming vessels, so God is sovereign in forming moral agents . . . He loves one and hates another. He exercises mercy towards some and hardens others, without reference to anything save His Own Sovereign Will."*

It is fair to say that all Calvinists do not accept the above quotation. In fact, I have read quite a number of messages, although promoting the Eternal Security doctrine, nevertheless, would repudiate this extreme Calvinism. In other words, one might say that Semi-Calvinists do not agree with extreme Calvinists. However, if one is going to teach Unconditional Eternal Security, then in all fairness one must embrace the totality of Predestination or Election as it is taught by Calvin.

(John Calvin, as most know, was one of the great advocates of the Unconditional Eternal Security doctrine even to the extreme of claiming that God ordains some to Heaven and some to Hell. Much of his teaching came from Augustine.)

Going back to the potter-clay Verses, Paul was quoting from Jeremiah Chapter 18. However, it was not within the purpose of Paul's thought to quote the context of the potter-clay Verses. So we now go to Jeremiah to get the whole thought.

THE LAW OF FIRST MENTION

There is another rule of interpretation called *"The Law Of First Mention,"* which can be decisive and in fact is decisive, in interpretation of Scripture. It says:

"The first mention of a thing, the very first words of any subject of which the Holy Spirit is going to treat, is the keystone of the entire matter."

Let us now use this rule and we will see that the Calvinist potter-clay argument is easily refuted by the context (all the Scriptures dealing with that subject are in Jeremiah Chapter 18).

Jeremiah said, *"Then the Word of the Lord came to me, saying,*

"O house of Israel, cannot I do with you as this potter? saith the Lord. Behold, as the clay is in the potter's hand, so are ye in Mine Hand, O house of Israel.

"At what instant I shall speak concerning a nation, and concerning a kingdom, to pluck up, and to pull down, and to destroy it;

"If that nation, against whom I have pronounced, turn from their evil, I will repent of the evil that I thought to do unto them.

NOTES

"And at what instant I shall speak concerning a nation, and concerning a kingdom, to build and to plant it;

"If it do evil in My sight, that it obey not My voice, then I will repent of the good, wherewith I said I would benefit them.

"Now therefore go to, speak to the men of Judah, and to the inhabitants of Jerusalem, saying, Thus saith the Lord; "Behold, I frame evil against you, and devise a device against you: return ye now every one from his evil way, and make your ways and your doings good.

"And they said, There is no hope: but we will walk after our own devices, and we will every one do the imagination of his evil heart" (Jer. 18:5-12).

Here at the source of Paul's potter-clay quotation, the Potter (the Lord) pled with the Clay (Israel) to repent of their evil and obey His Voice. But the Clay, stubborn and rebellious, refused the Potter's offer of Mercy and said they would walk in their own way and do the evil of their own hearts. The Potter (the Lord) twice told them that if they would repent, He would spare them the judgment soon to fall upon them.

I ask the Reader, *"Do these Scriptures as given in Jeremiah seem as if though God is arbitrarily choosing some for Heaven and others for Hell?"* No! In fact, He is doing the very opposite. He is giving them an opportunity to repent, and if they will, he will spare them. To be frank, that same plea has always gone forth and continues to go forth even unto this hour (Jn. 3:16).

With the Holy Spirit through the Prophet using *"Clay"* as a symbolism for Israel, we must understand that it was not a lifeless thing. With its own spirit of rebellion, it rejected God's conditions. In fact, if the Reader will read the balance of God's conditional dealings with Israel to the end of the Book of Jeremiah, he will see why they were *"vessels of wrath."*

These facts should be sufficient to convince an unprejudiced mind that in Romans Chapter 9, Paul was not dealing with unconditional Salvation. Now let us take another look at Romans 9:22.

WILLING?

Paul said, *"What if God, willing to shew His wrath, and to make His power known, endured with much longsuffering the vessels of wrath fitted to destruction."*

This quote, *"God willing"* does not mean that the Potter (the Lord) predestinated the Clay to be *"vessels of wrath."* Dr. A. T. Robertson, top Greek authority, wrote and I paraphrase: *"God being willing to show His wrath, does not mean it was an arbitrary decision on His part, but rather that Israel was responsible for the wrath being poured out upon them because they refused to repent. That they are responsible may be seen from I Thess. 2:15."*

Concerning the phrase, *"fitted to destruction"* as given in Romans 9:22, Vine, another Greek Scholar, says that Paul speaks here of *"men persistent in evil."* He went on to say that the word *"fitted"* in the Greek Text means *"that the vessels of wrath fitted themselves for destruction."*

Again using the *"Rule of Comparison,"* Paul said, which we have already quoted, *"Hath not the potter power over the clay, of the same lump to make one vessel unto honour, and another unto dishonour?"* (Rom. 9:21).

He also said in II Timothy, *"But in a great house there are not only vessels of gold and of silver, but also of wood and of earth; and some to honour and some to dishonour.*

"If a man therefore purge himself from these, he shall be a vessel unto honour, sanctified, and meet for the Master's use" (II Tim. 2:20-21).

Comparing these Scriptures, we learn that there is an *"if"* connected to this *"vessel of honour"* and it is not that God arbitrarily makes one such and the other the opposite. The spirit of the Text is that to be an honorable vessel (a Believer approved by the Lord) it is necessary that one purge himself from all that is displeasing to the Potter. If that is not obvious, I don't know what is obvious.

LET'S CONTINUE WITH PAUL

Follow Paul through the rest of Romans Chapter 9 and get his complete thought. Don't stop at Verse 23 as Eternal Security expositors do, for in Verses 30-33 he expands his thought and throws further light on the subject of the vessels of mercy and wrath.

He said, *"What shall we say then? That the Gentiles, which followed not after Righteousness, have attained to Righteousness, even the Righteousness which is of Faith.*

"But Israel, which followed after the Law of Righteousness, hath not attained to the Law of Righteousness.

NOTES

"Wherefore? Because they sought it not by faith, but as it were by the works of the Law. For they stumbled at that stumblingstone;

"As it is written, Behold, I lay in Sion a stumblingstone and Rock of offence: and whosoever believeth on Him shall not be ashamed" (Rom. 9:30-33).

The words *"Faith"* and *"Righteousness"* stand large in these Texts. The Gentile-Clay (Gentile Believers) *"attained to Righteousness, even the Righteousness which is of Faith."* But Israel-Clay (the nation of Israel) did not attain to this Righteousness. And Paul asks, *"Wherefore?"*

Was it because they were predestinated not to attain to it? Paul answers:

"Because they sought it not by Faith . . . For they stumbled at that Stumblingstone." In their unbelief, they stumbled over Christ. To Gentile Faith, Christ was the Stone (the Rock of Salvation). To Jewish unbelief, He was the Stumblingstone.

Paul extends this truth about Jews and Gentiles into Chapters 10-11. Actually, the three Chapters of Romans 9, 10, and 11, are a unit of Thought. Consequently, to properly understand them, one must disregard the Chapter divisions.

UNIT OF THOUGHT

One cannot rightly understand Paul in these three Chapters without this *"Unit of Thought"* principle. In fact, the entirety of the Bible must be understood in this fashion. In other words, it's not proper to take one or two Scriptures out of this *"Unit of Thought"* and force them into a particular Doctrine. The entirety of the *"Unit of Thought"* must be addressed for a proper interpretation.

Paul also said in the connecting link in Chapter 10:

"Brethren, my heart's desire and prayer to God for Israel is, that they might be saved.

"For I bear them record that they have a zeal of God, but not according to knowledge.

"For they being ignorant of God's Righteousness, and going about to establish their own righteousness, have not submitted themselves unto the righteousness of God" (Rom. 10:1-3).

It isn't necessary that anyone be a Theologian to see from these Verses that Israel, in establishing their own righteousness (or attempting to do so), refused God's Righteousness which is by Faith in Christ. The Righteousness of God which is by Faith in Christ is the center of the whole matter.

Israel refused to confess with their mouth the Lord Jesus Christ, and to believe in their hearts that God had raised Him from the dead. Therefore, they could not be saved. They had not *"obeyed the Gospel."* God pled long with Israel, and *"endured with much longsuffering"* these vessels of wrath.

"But to Israel He saith, All day long I have stretched forth my hands (pleading) *unto a disobedient and gainsaying* (contradicting) *people"* (Rom. 10:21).

In Chapter 11, we now see the last part of Paul's *"Unit of Thought"* about the Jews and Gentiles.

"I say then, Hath God cast away his people? God forbid. For I also am an Israelite, of the seed of Abraham, of the Tribe of Benjamin.

"God hath not cast away His people which He foreknew. Wot ye not what the Scripture saith of Elias? how he maketh intercession to God against Israel, saying,

"Lord, they have killed Thy Prophets, and digged down Thine Altars; and I am left alone, and they seek my life.

"But what saith the answer of God unto him? I have reserved to Myself seven thousand men, who have not bowed the knee to the image of Baal.

"Even so then at this present time also there is a remnant according to the Election of Grace" (Rom. 11:1-5).

THE REMNANT

Paul dealt here with questions about the Jewish people. His questions were much discussed in Paul's day, and serious meaning was attached to them. Had God cast off His people, the Jews? Paul's answer was an emphatic, *"No."* He then referred back to Jewish history. God always had a faithful *"Remnant"* in Israel. Remnant means *"A faithful and believing minority."*

There was such a Remnant in Elijah's day. Elijah, during the apostasy of his time, thought he alone had remained true to Jehovah's Covenant. But God told him there was a Remnant of 7,000 in Israel who had not bowed to the heathen Baal. It was through the Remnants that God fulfilled His Covenant Promise to Abraham and David.

NOTES

The Remnant did not bow to Baal — when there was powerful pressure upon them to do so. The faithless majority yielded to this pressure and bowed. God cast off the majority and *"reserved"* the minority to Himself. *"God hath not cast away His people* (the Remnant) *which He foreknew."* God foreknew they would not bow to Baal, thus they are His predestinated Remnant *"according to the Election of Grace."* Observe that *"foreknew"* and *"Election of Grace"* are in a context about a Remnant who were faithful to God's Covenant of Salvation.

The disobedient majority were not elected because they bowed to Baal, killed God's Prophets, and digged down God's Altars. God foreknew that, too.

It should be obvious here, that it was the Plan of God which was foreknown and elected, actually predestinated, rather than the people in that particular Plan. The Plan was that those who disobeyed would be rejected, and those who obeyed would be accepted, i.e., *"the Remnant."* So, it becomes very obvious that God did not arbitrarily select some to be lost and some to be saved. The facts are, these Jews were either saved or lost according to their own personal will in the matter.

IT IS THE SAME PRESENTLY

At this present time also there is a Remnant. They refuse to bow to the *"god of this world."* Sometimes the Remnants are really small. In fact, there is much interesting Truth in the Bible about Remnants for those who will study the subject.

If the Remnant of Elijah's time had bowed to Baal, would they have been predestinated to God's Grace?

Moreso still, did God force these people to obey Him and not bow to Baal, while at the same time, He forced the majority to bow to Baal?

The answer to those questions is obvious.

God has a faithful Remnant in every generation. They could bow to the gods of this world but they will not, and it is not because they are being forced to take this particular route, but simply because they will to do so. Faithfulness to God's Covenant is a true mark of every Remnant. All God's elect have this mark of identification. In other words, they purposely choose to obey the Lord, a choice incidentally of their own volition. In fact, they have the ability to choose either way, but they purposely chose the Lord. The nonelect as well had the same power of choice, but chose rather to disobey God. That has always been the case, and is the case now.

THE SYMBOL OF THE OLIVE TREE

Paul, in Romans 11:17-24, extended the range of his thought on the Jewish and Gentile questions raised in Romans Chapters 9 and 10. Here, he set forth the subject with the symbol of an olive tree.

"And if some of the branches be broken off, and thou, being a wild olive tree, wert grafted in among them, and with them partakest of the root and fatness of the olive tree;

"Boast not against the branches. But if thou boast, thou bearest not the root, but the root thee.

"Thou wilt say then, The branches were broken off, that I might be grafted in.

"Well; because of unbelief they were broken off, and thou standest by Faith. Be not highminded, but fear:

"For if God spared not the natural branches, take heed lest He also spare not thee.

"Behold therefore the goodness and severity of God: on them which fell, severity; but toward thee, goodness, if thou continue in His goodness: otherwise thou also shalt be cut off.

"And they also, if they abide not still in unbelief, shall be grafted in: for God is able to graft them in again" (Rom. 11:17-23).

Paul, greatest of Theologians, stressed this *"if-condition"* in dealing with questions about God's purposes of Salvation for Jews and Gentiles.

Paul taught that the Jewish branches were broken off their Covenant tree *"because of unbelief."* The cause was Jewish unbelief — not a mysterious sovereign predestination. The Gentiles were grafted into the Jewish Covenant tree because of their *"Faith."* It was all a matter of faith and unbelief, and not that God purposely caused the Jews to be damned and the Gentiles to be saved. Paul answered that by saying *"God forbid"* (Rom. 11:1).

The specified *"if-condition"* lies deep in Paul's Doctrine. The Jews would be grafted in again *"if they abide not still in unbelief,"* which in fact will happen, at the Second Coming (Zech. Chpt. 12).

As well, Paul said that the Gentiles would also be broken off *"if"* they did not *"continue in the Faith."* Jesus said: *"If a man abide not in Me, he is cast forth as a branch, and is withered . . . and they are burned"* (Jn. 15:6).

Here in Romans Chapter 11, Paul gave the *"if-condition"* its full force. As he made Salvation conditional in Chapter 11, it follows that he did not teach it was unconditional in Chapter 9. There is Salvation in God's Covenant tree for those who *"abide"* in it. Paul had no doctrine such as *"once in the Tree, always in the Tree."*

FOREORDINATION (PREDESTINATION) IS ACCORDING TO FOREKNOWLEDGE

The evidence we have seen justifies our conclusion that God's foreknowledge is not casual — in other words, a casual selection of some to be saved and some to be lost. Foreordination is according to foreknowledge, which means that God knew beforehand what would be done and as well, done by the free will of the individual, and not because God forced the issue. *"Jesus knew from the beginning who they were that believed not. . . ."* (Jn. 6:64).

God knew all things from the beginning and designed His eternal Plans according to what He knew about men from the beginning. The words *"predestination"* and *"election"* in no way alter the fact that God formed His eternal Plans for men according to what He foreknew they would do with their free power of decision.

John 2:23-25 says that *"many believed in His Name, when they saw the miracles which He did. But Jesus did not commit Himself unto them, because He knew all men, And needed not that any should testify of man: for He knew what was in man."*

Jesus knew from the beginning what was in man. He knew the characters of men, whether they had faith or unbelief; whether they would accept or reject Him; whether they would continue in Faith or be temporary Believers like the *"many"* with a casual excitement about His Miracles. However, we say again, that all of this was according to the free wills of these people, and not because God forced their wills in any capacity.

God, from the beginning, knew what was in Jacob, Esau, Pharaoh, and all of us. He is a *"discerner of the thoughts and intents of the heart"* (Heb. 4:12). But these thoughts and

NOTES

intents are *"what was in man,"* in other words, of man's own choice.

PREDICTIVE SCIENCE

Specialists working in the field of human behavior have developed a predictive science that is often amazingly accurate. After a character analysis, they often predict success in marriage or failure in business. Crime experts study the past record of a criminal and capture him by foreknowledge of his next move.

Wars have been won by Generals who knew the opposing General's habits of thought. We could go on down the line about school teachers and pupils, parents and children, husbands and wives, etc. How much more then does God know about human thoughts and intents and what is in man?

The interpretation of unconditional Salvation from Romans Chapter 9 tramples over established interpretive Laws. Our interpretation of conditional Salvation from this Chapter satisfies these Laws. It would be a sad day for Christianity if other Bible doctrines had to be defended with the same method of interpretation that is used by some to defend Calvinistic Predestination.

That which we have given you does not pick and choose from a few Texts in Romans Chapter 9 or elsewhere, but reasons from Paul's complete Unit of Thought in the three Chapters of 9, 10, and 11. The *"if-evidence"* we saw in this unit overturns our opponent's conclusion drawn from a few selected Verses in Chapter 9. In fact, we could have presented further evidence from Romans. Example:

"For if ye live after the flesh, ye shall die (be lost)*: but if ye through the Spirit do mortify the deeds of the body, you shall live* (be saved).

"For as many as are led by the Spirit of God, they are the sons of God" (Rom. 8:13-14).

The *"ifs"* presented here in these two Verses are obvious for all to see, and clear and plain respecting their meaning.

The *"if-evidence"* in Romans is convincing for conditional Salvation. A proved fact is a proved fact, and no amount of misinterpretation can make it anything else. Let the Reader examine the evidence. There is always hope when people look fairly at all sides.

(Almost all the material on Unconditional Eternal Security, i.e. *"Election, Predestination, Foreknowledge,"* was provided by Guy Duty.)

NOTES

(2) "(FOR HE SAITH, I HAVE HEARD THEE IN A TIME ACCEPTED, AND IN THE DAY OF SALVATION HAVE I SUCCOURED THEE: BEHOLD, NOW IS THE ACCEPTED TIME; BEHOLD, NOW IS THE DAY OF SALVATION.)"

The phrase, *"For He saith,"* is derived from Isaiah 49:8.

In that Passage, the declaration refers to the Messiah, and the design is there to show that God would be favorable to Him; that He would hear Him when He prayed, and would make Him the medium of establishing a Covenant with His Own people, and of spreading the true Word of the Lord around the earth.

THE MESSIAH

Even though Paul is not dealing with this primarily at this time, one can read the previous seven Verses of Isaiah Chapter 49, and we there find another proof of Who and What the Messiah of Israel would be. Consequently, there was no excuse for Israel not knowing these things. They did not know them, simply because of their own self-will, in other words, they did not want to know them. The Word of God was clear and plain respecting the Messianic description.

It is the same presently with all men. The Gospel Light has gone out to the entirety of the world. Admittedly, it is known to a far greater extent by some than others; nevertheless, there is enough Light for the heart of most to accept. Men do not accept Christ because they do not want or desire Christ, or else they desire Him on their own terms, exactly as Israel of old, but which God of course cannot accept.

Paul quotes the Passage here, not as affirming that he used it in exactly the same sense, or with reference to the same design for which it was originally spoken, but as expressing the idea which he wished to convey, or in accordance with the general principle applied in its use in Isaiah. The general idea there, or the principle involved was that under the Messiah, God would be willing to hear; that is, that He would be disposed to show Mercy to the Jew and to the Gentile. This is the main idea of the Passage as used by Paul.

Under the Messiah, it is said by Isaiah, God would be willing to show Mercy. It would be an acceptable time. That time, says Paul, has arrived.

The Messiah has come, and now God is willing to pardon and save. And the Doctrine in this Verse is, *"that under the Messiah, or in the time of Christ, God is willing to show Mercy unto all men."* In Him Alone is the Throne of Grace accessible; and now that He has come, God is willing to pardon, and men should avail themselves of the offers of Mercy.

I HAVE HEARD THEE

The phrase, *"I have heard Thee,"* refers to God hearing the prayers of the Messiah. It is a prayer for the Salvation of the heathen world.

The Promise to the Messiah was, that the heathen world should be given to Him; but it was a Promise that it should be an answer to His prayers and intercessions: *"Ask of Me, and I shall give Thee the heathen for Thine inheritance, and the uttermost parts of the earth for Thy possession"* (Ps. 2:8).

The fact is, the Salvation of the heathen world, and of all who are saved, which includes you and me, is to be, and in fact is, in answer to the prevalent Intercession of the Lord Jesus.

This is carried out through His Body, the Church. In other words, whenever any and all Believers intercede according to the Holy Spirit for souls, for different parts of the world, for Revival, for an outpouring of the Holy Spirit, for Saving Grace on men, they are entering into the intercessory role of Christ. As His Body, we have this privilege, but as well, we must never forget that it is more than a privilege, but rather a responsibility.

A TIME ACCEPTED

The phrase, *"In a time accepted,"* has reference to the great Plan of God. As well, it is far more involved than one would immediately think.

The Apostle immediately points out that all Christians should engage in this activity of Grace, for it is a time, or Day of Grace in which God is accepting sinners and saving them. It is a day of Salvation because of the Death and Resurrection of the Lord Jesus. This is the force of the quotation from Isaiah 49:8, where God is heard speaking to His Beloved Son on the Morning of the Resurrection. He succoured Him out of the abyss, and accepted Him and His Atoning Work — for the Resurrection demonstrated that acceptance. The fruit of that succour and acceptance is for man's benefit and blessing; and, consequently, the present Dispensation is for him a day of Grace and acceptance. And all those who have experienced this Grace should seek to make it known to others though it be at the cost of the shame and suffering described in the coming Verses 4 through 10.

NOTES

The idea is that the time had now come when God would show Mercy, and because He could show Mercy. The great Price of Redemption has now been paid, the sin debt settled, the grip of sin broken, the evil one defeated. Now the great Salvation Message can be extended to the whole world. It is a time which He had fixed as the appropriate period for extending the knowledge of His Truth and His Salvation, and because of the great Work of Christ which had been carried out.

As well, it proves that there was to be a period which was the favorable period of Salvation, again, favorable because of what Jesus had done.

While it is true that people could be saved before Christ, nevertheless, it was not easy. In effect, they had to come under the Abrahamic Covenant, and to do that, they would have to become a proselyte Jew. As stated, it was not a simple thing for Gentiles; consequently, there were very few Gentiles who actually were saved during all of this period of time. Sadder still, there was only a small *"Remnant"* of Jews who were actually saved, even as we have already discussed.

So, this *"time accepted"* was not an arbitrary decision fostered by God, but was rather predicated on the Finished Work of Christ.

TIME

It is difficult to treat *"time"* philosophically. Scripture does not encourage our speculation. But the Bible does have a viewpoint about the meaning of time.

Experienced time is simply that span of time available for an individual or generation to experience. It contrasts with the past and future that are now outside of that span.

The Old Testament has a number of ways of perceiving experienced time. The Hebrew word *"et"* conceives of time as a series of recurring seasons or as a moment that is particularly appropriate or opportune. Often this word is closely linked with meeting the Lord. In effect, this is what Paul is speaking about as he quotes Isaiah.

EXPERIENCED TIME

The Old Testament does see a rhythm to time. It has recurring cycles of days and weeks, of months and seasons and years. Life itself follows the pattern of seasonality, as Solomon points out in Ecclesiastes Chapter 3, so there is even an appropriate time for dying (Gen. 29:21).

But time also flows toward a future determined by God, even as we are now studying. An individual or nation may find that personal experience intersects with an *"appointed time."* This may be a time when God acts in the stream of time to keep history on its appointed course.

As well, it may also be an appointment with God, such as to keep one of the annual festivals that recalls one of His decisive acts in history, as it relates to the Old Testament.

TIME BEYOND PERSONAL EXPERIENCE

The Old Testament accepts the reality of past and future time that is beyond the possibility of personal experience by a living generation. This time is real, for it stands within the span of God's Own endless *"lifetime,"* and He, the Lord of history, is able to speak about it.

The appointed times of history are in His Hand and develop according to His purposes.

THE RIGHT TIME

In the New Testament, the Greek words *"chronos"* and *"kairos"* are the two basic words translated *"time." "Chronos"* designates a period or space of time. It is very close in meaning to the rather scientific way in which Westerners speak of time.

The function of *"kairos,"* also often translated *"time,"* is to characterize the content and the quality of the time it indicates. *"Kairos,"* whatever the duration of the *"chronos"* involved, highlights the significance of that brief or extended moment.

For instance, it was at the *"right time"* that Christ died for the ungodly (Rom. 5:6; Eph. 1:10) and forever changed the character of time.

Not only must all of history be reinterpreted by that moment, but time itself has become different as well. We live now in an *"acceptable time,"* and *"Day of Salvation,"* a *"Day of opportunity"* (II Cor. 6:2).

A SUMMARY

Time is significant in the Old Testament and the New Testament. Scripture locates the significance of time outside the experience of any individual. Time, like the rest of the environment in which human beings move, has been ordered and designed by God. It is marked by cycle and repetition, and yet flows from a beginning toward a culmination.

Time is also marked by significant moments. The greatest of all significant moments are significant because God sets them aside as times of His Own action in history. These moments are also significant because they provide opportunity for each of us to confront the reality of God and to respond to Him.

Spans of time may be remembered as troubled or peaceful, but the truly significant points in each person's life are those in which he or she senses the Call of God and responds to Him — with rejection or with joyful obedience.

The New Testament focuses on the fact that all time finds its focus and fulfillment in Christ. His Coming transforms every moment into opportunity; and when He returns, the fulfillment of every Promise God ever made will be achieved.

How important, then, that we sense and use our moments of time wisely, sensing the eternal significance that our relationship with Jesus brings to all time (Richards).

THE DAY OF SALVATION

The phrase, *"And in the Day of Salvation,"* presents the time when Salvation has been afforded through Christ, therefore, much easier to obtain by any and all.

It doesn't mean that the requirements for Salvation change, for that is impossible. It does mean that the opportunity for Salvation is much more pronounced, and because of what Jesus did at Calvary and the Resurrection.

It is in regard to this great *"Day of Salvation"* that Paul encourages us to be *"workers together with Him."* However, to a large degree we have ceased being workers, to become religious drones.

NOTES

What tragic words were in the requiem which Marshal Petain pronounced over fallen France when Germany overran that nation in 1941: *"Our spirit of enjoyment was stronger than our spirit of sacrifice. We wanted to have more than we wanted to give. We tried to spare effort and met disaster."*

The cause of Christ languishes in a wounded world for lack of valiant workers who might, if they would, bring such a flood of truth as would sweep out the evil forces of this moment. However, we prefer enjoyment, it seems, to sacrifice. We would rather have than give.

We, like Paul, should not merely be working for God, but with God. This indicates a place of great honor. There are many who can say they work for a particular industrialist, but only a few who can say they work with him. To realize this is to realize the exalted place of Christian Service.

The work to be done has just been described in the closing Verses of the previous Chapter as *"Reconciliation."* As such, it is primarily a spiritual work to be done with individuals. It is not a social work to be done with the masses. Reconciliation is an Ambassadorial mission to men as individuals. It is this phase of our work which we must keep clear and pure. We must never allow ourselves to be employed in anything less than this.

PAUL'S WARNING

When Paul besought the Corinthians that they *"receive not the Grace of God in vain,"* he suggested a peril possible to a great many professing Christians. This remark, remember, was addressed to the Corinthians and not the Pagans, and it concerned their failure to enter into all the advantages of Grace.

Grace provided Reconciliation and with it a life of fruitful employment with God. One might receive this Grace in vain by accepting it without appropriating it or by failing to live so as to show he was a new creature with old things passed away and with all things new.

That which Paul said which was quoted from Isaiah, requires us to remember that the Apostle was speaking to Christians. He was reminding us that this whole age is both the *"accepted time"* and the *"Day of Salvation."* Whoever is not concerned with his work as Ambassador is receiving the Grace of God in vain. Such a one is failing in his mission. He is misusing his life.

NOTES

God has here and now provided Reconciliation through Christ. This Reconciliation is waiting for Ambassadors to carry it far and wide. It is waiting for acceptance by those who need to be reconciled.

THE AGE OF GRACE

The other aspect of what Paul is saying is equally allowable. If this is the Day of Reconciliation's offer, it is also the Day of its acceptance. If *"the day"* is an age of Grace, then it is equally true that the age has its days.

Man lives a total of approximately 25,000 to 30,000 days, more or less. Of all these days, there is a great day of decision that marks the shape of destiny. That day is now. Grace is offered now. Christ is available now.

As it regards these *"days,"* the following Verses point out a description of experiences which come to one man in the course of his life and labors. These experiences run the gamut of pleasure to pain. They enroll a broad expanse of circumstances, which we will see, that follow one's fidelity to duty. They summarize the total feelings of a man who is all-out for God.

It will take courage to read this recital and say at its end, *"God helping me, I too, will live so that my life will be the best credential Christ has in the world"* (Laurin).

HAVE I SUCCOURED THEE

The phrase, *"Have I succoured Thee,"* refers to the Messiah. In effect, the Lord is saying regarding the Messiah, *"I have sustained Thee, that is, in the effort to make Salvation known."* God speaks here of there being an accepted time, a limited period, in which petitions in favor of the world would be acceptable to Him. That time Paul says has come; and the idea which he urges is, that men should avail themselves of that, and embrace now the offers of Mercy.

This tells us that the entirety of the Plan of God, which is wrapped up in Christ, at least as it refers to man's Salvation, is done for the express purpose of the Salvation of the souls of men. Considering the great expense involved concerning Christ, even the very giving of His Own Life, one is able to understand the urgency of the moment.

Carried in the idea of this phrase, is the veiled threat of judgment to all who refuse this great offer of Salvation. In effect, this will come about in the coming Great Tribulation, which is going to break over the world with a ferocity it has never known before in its history. Jesus called it *"Great Tribulation, such as was not since the beginning of the world to this time, no, nor ever shall be"* (Mat. 24:21).

In fact, this coming terrible time proclaimed by the Prophets, and predicted by Christ, is upon us, even at the very door at this present hour.

NOW

The phrase, *"Behold, now is the accepted time,"* means that the time referred to by Isaiah has now arrived. It is now a time when God is ready to show compassion, to hear prayer, and to have Mercy on mankind. Only through the Messiah, the Lord Jesus, does He show Mercy, and men should, therefore, now embrace the offers of pardon.

The Doctrine taught here, therefore, is, that through the Lord Jesus, and where He is preached, God is willing to pardon and save men; and this is true wherever He is preached, and as long as men live under the sound of the Gospel.

MERCY

It is not the idea that God has more Mercy now than He once did, for God does not change. In other words, He has and exhibits the same Mercy presently, as He always has.

However, the time will come, and in fact does come for all men, when no more Mercy will be shown, and that is the time of their death. First, second, and third opportunities, actually, unlimited opportunities, are on this side of the grave. At death, the door of Mercy closes forever. Then the period of trial is ended and men are removed to a world where no Mercy is shown, and where compassion is unknown.

The general Doctrine is, that men should seek reconciliation with God. To enforce that, he says here, that it is now the acceptable time, the time when God is attempting to be reconciled to men, and if they will only heed His clarion call, such reconciliation can be effected.

SALVATION

The phrase, *"Behold, now is the Day of Salvation,"* presents in fact the conclusion of two double statements. Twice it is said that it is the *"accepted time,"* and twice it says that it is the *"Day of Salvation."* Whenever the Holy Spirit says something twice, it is of extreme importance. When He in fact, doubles the double, it is meant to be understood as something of extreme importance. Of course, nothing could be more important than the Salvation of souls, especially considering the price that was paid for that Salvation.

By using the word *"Day"* twice, we are pointing not only to a span of time, but as well to that which is the opposite of darkness.

If men grieve away the Holy Spirit; if they continue to reject the Gospel; if they go unprepared into eternity, no Mercy can be found. God does not design to pardon beyond the grave. He has made no provision for forgiveness there; and they who are not pardoned in this life must be unpardoned forever.

Martin Luther pointed it out to the German nation of his day when the Gospel ran through that country and beat down upon the land like a great shower of rain. He bade the Germans prize the Gospel while they had it and warned them that the time might come when it could no longer be had. He bade the Germans to look at the lands and cities of Asia Minor where the Gospel once flowed so freely, but where now the Turk rules, and the Gospel has disappeared.

The lives of individuals pass through a similar experience. Salvation's day comes, God's accepted time. Make fullest use of it, despise it not as though it might continue forever and wait on our pleasure. A time may also come, and in fact will come, when it is too late, that is if rejection continues.

(3) "GIVING NO OFFENCE IN ANY THING, THAT THE MINISTRY BE NOT BLAMED:"

The phrase, *"Giving no offence in any thing,"* actually uses in the Greek that which is referred to as a double negative, *"no nothing,"* which is not acceptable in English.

NO OFFENCE

"Offence" in the Greek is *"proskope,"* and means *"that which causes one to stumble, an occasion of sin."* The idea is, of *"giving no occasion for condemning or rejecting the Gospel."* And the idea is presented as well, that Paul and his fellow-Apostles so labored as that no one

NOTES

who saw or knew them should have occasion to reproach the Ministry, or the Gospel which they preached. The opposite was to be the case, that their lives would be so pure and so self-denying, that the strongest argument would be seen for embracing the Gospel. How they conducted (themselves) so as to give no offence he states in the following Verses.

The truth is, Paul was blamed often enough, but wrongfully, never for a cause that he gave but only for a cause that was invented by the enemies of the Gospel. As a man is known by the friends he has, so he is known by those who blame him.

As someone has well said, *"Get friends of whose praise you can be proud and thus enemies who blame of you is equal to a compliment, of which you as well, can be proud."*

DAVID

There is nothing worse for a Preacher of the Gospel than to fail the Lord, and to thereby hurt the Cause of Christ.

After David's great sin Nathan said to him, *"Because by this deed thou hast given great occasion to the enemies of the Lord to blaspheme"* (II Sam. 12:14).

Upon the occasion of such, one can only take the thing to the Lord, even as did David. Nevertheless, even though Forgiveness and Grace are shown to the truly penitent heart of the offender, still, much damage is done to the Cause of Christ.

THE MINISTRY BE NOT BLAMED

The phrase, *"That the Ministry be not blamed,"* refers here not merely to the Ministry of Paul, or any other Preacher for that matter, but that the Ministry itself which the Lord Jesus had established would be blamed, or would be reproached by the improper conduct of anyone who was engaged in that work.

The idea is, that the misconduct of one Minister of the Gospel would bring a reproach upon the Work of God itself, and would in a sense, prevent the usefulness and success of others, just as the misconduct of a Physician exposes the profession to reproach, etc.

The errors, follies, misconduct, or bad example of one Minister of the Gospel bring a reproach upon the Sacred Calling itself, and hinder in some way, either more or less, the usefulness of many others. Ministers do not stand alone.

NOTES

And though no one can be responsible for the errors and failings of others, yet no one can avoid suffering in regard to his usefulness by the sins of others.

WHAT CAN ONE DO?

There are actually only two things one can do respecting failure:

1. One must take the situation to the Lord, whatever it is, in humble, broken repentance, seeking for Mercy and Grace. The Word of God promises that such will always be given, that is, if the individual is sincere and honest before the Lord (I Jn. 1:9).

One in such a situation, will be besieged by many demanding certain things which are often unscriptural. In fact, this problem is widespread as it regards Denominations. Irrespective, the penitent one, must go strictly by the Word of God, and nothing else. To engage in any act which smacks of penance (trying to earn one's forgiveness, etc.), can in fact, nullify the Grace of God, if such a course is demanded (Gal. 5:2-4).

It has been my experience in observing Preachers who have had the misfortune of failing the Lord in some manner, that they very seldom made it back, that is if they followed the demands of most Denominations, which in fact, are demands of penance, which in effect, make a mockery out of the Grace of God. If an unscriptural course is set upon, it will only add misery to woe.

Don't listen to men; listen to God. Do exactly what His Word says to do, no more, no less. If it means that one loses the favor of the Denomination, so be it. It is better to obey God rather than men.

2. Set about thereafter to live as close to God as is humanly possible. There is no way that wrongdoings of the past can be rectified, but there is a way that the present and the future can glorify God. To be sure, such will little undo much of the damage that's been done, but it will point to the Grace of God, and show His Love and Mercy regarding those who fail.

The actual truth is, that every single Believer and even every single Preacher, has failed in one way or the other. Maybe their failing was not public. In fact, maybe it was known by no

NOTES

one but God and the individual involved. Maybe the failing was not as bad as the failing of others, for some things are definitely worse than others; however, irrespective, the point I am attempting to make is, that every single Believer in one way or the other, has had to go to the Lord many times, even with burning tears, seeking forgiveness for something that was wicked, sinful, or wrong. That people do not know of such, does not make it any less wicked in the Eyes of God, although of course, such is definitely less hurtful to the Cause of Christ. But one should never make the mistake of thinking that because something has not been made public, that that somehow legitimizes the act, or else it is less bad.

Even though as Paul has plainly said, we should ever think of those who are watching us, which in fact, is the entirety of the world in one measure or the other; still, the One we must actually answer to, is the Lord. If we please all others and do not please Him, in effect, we have little pleased anyone who really matters. If we please Him, and displease all others, it is by far the better choice.

A life of Dedication, Godliness, and Holiness, after one has failed, does not in any way make up for the failure, nor is it implied that it can; however, it can and does show that the Lord is a kind, merciful, compassionate, forgiving God, which is the kind of God that all men want to face at one time or the other.

WHAT SHOULD THE CHURCH DO IN SUCH A SITUATION?

I am assuming that the Reader wants to know what the Bible says about these matters, and not rulings made up by men.

First of all, the Church must ever understand that it is made up totally and completely of forgiven sinners. In other words, every single individual in the Church, irrespective of whatever type of Church it may be, and irrespective as to how Godly they may be, were sinners when God saved them, and they were saved by the Grace of God, and not for any other purpose or reason.

As well, since their conversion, and whoever they may be, they have had to go to the Lord many times, asking Forgiveness and Mercy for wrongdoing of one nature or the other. And as well, until they die or the Rapture takes us home to be with the Lord, they will continue to have to ask the Lord for Mercy and Grace for certain wrongs committed. There is no such thing as a perfect Christian. All of us are dependent totally and completely on the Mercy and Grace of God, and if we are depending on anything otherwise, we have sealed our doom.

Understanding these things, the Church must abide by the Word of God regarding any member, whether Preacher or otherwise, respecting these matters. As well, it is not difficult to know and understand what the Bible says about these matters.

I Corinthians Chapter 5 tells us, that if a person has committed sin of a moral capacity, if they will not repent, they are to be disfellowshipped. However, even then, such is not to be done with the idea of destroying the person, but with the motive of bringing the individual to a state of repentance, and, thereby, back into the Church. In other words, make every effort, but be redemptive.

II Corinthians Chapter 2, plainly tells us that if a person has repented, they are to be restored in totality.

SHOULD THERE NOT BE A PROBATION PERIOD?

Once again, I am assuming that the Reader wants to know what the Word says.

There is no such thing in the Word of God as a probationary Forgiveness or Salvation. To be frank, such is an insult to the integrity of the Lord and the great price that He paid at Calvary for our Redemption.

There is no such thing as a 50 percent Justification, or 50 percent Forgiveness, or some such foolish thinking. When the Lord forgives a person, He does so totally and completely, with the past sin or infraction completely washed away and forgiven. He then treats us as though we have never sinned. That is called *"Justification by Faith."* Believers are to conduct themselves toward that person exactly as God does (II Cor. 2:7-9; I Jn. 1:9).

Rules made up by men, that say if a Preacher does something wrong he cannot preach for two years, or some such span of time, are not of God, and in fact, are wicked. There is absolutely nothing in the Word of God that even remotely sanctions such a travesty.

In the first place, such an action is hypocritical. Men are not capable of making such judgments and neither are they qualified (James 4:12).

Furthermore, God is the One Who calls men to preach, and not other men. Consequently, no man has the right to tell another Preacher what he can preach, when he can preach, or how he can preach. That prerogative belongs entirely to the Lord, and woe be unto any man who thinks otherwise. To be frank, the major Pentecostal Denominations are destroying themselves in this very manner, which abrogates the Headship of Christ.

HOW CAN ONE BE CERTAIN IF A PERSON IS SINCERE REGARDING THEIR REPENTANCE?

We have addressed this in the Second Chapter, but I will touch on it again briefly.

How could people be certain if you were sincere when you came to Christ, or anyone for that matter?

Sincerity will quickly show itself. There are certain telltale signs which show up regarding sincerity, and likewise for insincerity.

The Church is filled with people who desire to demand things of others, that they do not demand of themselves. In other words, double standards are rampant. If everyone would apply the same standards to themselves, things would be quite different. There is much hypocrisy in the Church, and sadly it is fostered and nurtured too often by those who call themselves Leaders. Anytime we leave the Word of God, and make up rules on our own, the results will never be good. In fact, this *"leaven"* will ultimately corrupt the whole, which is exactly what is happening now to modern Pentecostal Denominations.

WHERE IS SPIRITUAL AUTHORITY IN THE CHURCH?

If one carefully reads the Book of Acts and the Epistles, it becomes obvious very quickly, that spiritual authority resides in essence in the Local Church. That means it does not reside in Denominational Headquarters, or any such outside effort.

While outsiders may advise and counsel, even as Paul did to the Church at Corinth and all others for that matter which he had founded, that is as far as it should go. The Pastor or Pastors and people of the Local Church should

NOTES

Prayerfully and Scripturally make decisions respecting circumstances and situations in their own particular Church. For so-called outside authority to come in and force their will, is totally unscriptural. Such, as well, abrogates the Headship of Christ.

This means that if a Pastor of a Local Church, or any of the Church Leaders in that Church, or any of the people for that matter, do something wrong, that Local Church should evaluate the situation prayerfully, seek the Leading of the Holy Spirit, and do all within their power to abide strictly by the Word of God. Each case would have to be dealt with according to its own merits or lack thereof. But again, it is the Local Church who must make the decision, and not outside influences.

If a congregation is Scriptural in their decision, Jesus plainly said, *"Verily I say unto you, whatsoever ye shall bind on earth shall be bound in Heaven: and whatsoever ye shall loose on earth shall be loosed in Heaven"* (Mat. 18:18).

The Lord within the confines of Scripture, has given great latitude to the Local Church (Mat. 18:20). But of course, the admonition of total Scripturality is always demanded.

WHAT ABOUT ACCOUNTABILITY?

Accountability is a favorite word used by many at this particular time; however, we should make it clear as to what their definition of accountability actually is.

When most Preachers talk about accountability, most are meaning something entirely different than what the Bible says about the matter. They are claiming that if a person is *"accountable,"* which means that they are attempting to do right, then they will obey whatever they are told to do. Consequently, the person is judged as having no accountability, if they do not obey certain demands.

First of all, and again being Scriptural, accountability means accountability to the Word of God. In other words, whatever the matter, it must be judged Scripturally.

Personally, I will do what anyone asks me to do, providing it is Scriptural. If it is not Scriptural, I am not going to abide by such demands irrespective as to what the cost may be.

If wrongdoing is involved, the person must take it to the Lord seeking Mercy and Forgiveness. As well, they must do all within their power to get victory over the problem, whatever that problem may be. When proper repentance is engaged, according to the Bible the situation stops then and there. If it is a Preacher involved, the idea that some so-called Church Leader is going to then step in and demand that the Preacher quit preaching for two years or some such span of time, is totally unscriptural. There is nothing in the Bible that even remotely places a seal of approval on such, but actually, the very opposite.

The Lord did not tell David that he had to step down from being king for a certain period of time, after he found himself in this terrible situation of immorality.

If such unscriptural demands are not obeyed, then certain men are very fond of tacking a label on such a one as *"lacking accountability."* However, one must understand that the definition of accountability is what God says it is, and not man. If one obeys the Word of God, one is accountable, for that is the highest accountability there is.

SHOULD THERE NOT BE A DIFFERENT STANDARD FOR PREACHERS?

Again we are assuming that the Reader wants to be Scriptural.

Does God have one standard of Salvation for Preachers and another standard for laypersons?

Does the Lord have two standards or more regarding forgiveness for different types of sins?

Of course, the answer to these questions is obvious. God's Standards are the same for all. All sin is taken to the Lord in the same fashion. So, the idea that there is a different standard of Forgiveness and Mercy for Preachers than there is for others is ludicrous.

While it is certainly understood, that the failure of some has far greater effect than others, even as we are now studying, still, that in no way impacts God's Standards to any degree. David had to ask forgiveness (Ps. 51) in the same manner as a person would ask forgiveness for lying, or for slander or gossip.

While all sin is terrible, and some sins are definitely worse than others, still, the Church has a habit of ignoring many sins while coming down sharply on others. To be frank, anything done in this fashion, shows terrible self-righteousness.

Even though all sin is wicked, ungodly, and evil, still, if we want to know exactly how God labels sin, we should look at Proverbs 6:16-19.

NOTES

WILL GOD FORGIVE MORE THAN ONCE?

Of course, anyone who would ask such a question, has little knowledge of the Word of God or of themselves for that matter.

The Truth is, that every single Believer who has ever lived, has had to go to the Lord several times for the same sin or wrongdoing. If the person sincerely asks forgiveness, the Scripture plainly tells us that the Lord is always faithful and just to forgive (I Jn. 1:9).

I heard a part of a Sermon the other day entitled, *"The God of the Second Chance."* The Truth is, He is the God not only of the Second Chance, but the third and fourth and fiftieth for that matter.

The Lord places no time limits on His Mercy or Grace, which are obvious in Scripture. As well, the idea that if someone fails a second time, they were not sincere the first time regarding repentance, is silly to say the least. Once again, every Believer who thinks that way, should apply the same ruling to themselves.

As someone said a long time ago, when we judge ourselves we should judge harshly, but when we judge others, we should judge leniently. Unfortunately, the reverse is the case most of the time.

SHOULD NOT PEOPLE BE PUNISHED FOR SIN?

Once again, if a person thinks such a thing, they should first of all apply it to themselves.

To be sure, even if a person goes exactly according to the Word of God, all failure carries with it a terrible punishment. In fact, to enumerate all of the different types of hurt, sadness, pain, and suffering that such causes, would probably be impossible. If a person loves the Lord, such as David loved the Lord, and anyone else for that matter, the idea of failing Him is a punishment that is beyond imagination. So, for anyone to think that sin does not carry punishment, even though the person receives total and complete forgiveness, simply has little understanding of the Word of God.

Regarding punishment, one should always understand that *"whatever measure we mete, shall be measured to us again"* (Mat. 7:1-2).

Three things must be addressed regarding punishment for sin. They are as follows:

1. God never in His Word gives the right or authority to a Believer, irrespective as to whom

they may be, to punish another Believer. Such is never allowed in Scripture.

While the Lord may use outside forces such as Nebuchadnezzar to punish Israel (II Chron. 36:16-17). They are always an unwitting instrument. In other words, Nebuchadnezzar did not know he was being used by God for this purpose. As well, even in this situation, we find that Babylon overplayed their hand, in other words, they overdid the situation, and suffered punishment themselves from God (Jer. 50:17-20).

The Lord plainly said that all punishment is reserved unto His Hands (Rom. 12:17-21).

2. In the second place, no Believer is qualified to punish another. This goes as well for so-called Church Officials or any other Believer for that matter.

James plainly said, *"There is one Lawgiver, Who is able to save and to destroy: Who art thou that judgest another?"* (James 4:12).

In other words, who does a Believer think he is, thinking he is qualified to judge another Believer?

So, any Believer who would take it upon himself to ladle out punishment to another Believer, is in fact, placing himself on a very high level of perfection. In other words, he is saying that he is worthy to do such, which smacks of hypocrisy and gross self-righteousness. To be completely honest, anyone who would take such authority upon themselves, which is completely unscriptural, that person, be he Church Official or otherwise, is committing a far graver sin than the one who he is punishing. These individuals should know and understand, that all who engage in such, are inviting the sure Judgment of God upon their own heads (Mat. 7:1-2; Gal. 6:1-3).

3. And last of all, and far more important, Jesus took the punishment for our sins at Calvary (Isa. Chpt. 53). For any Believer, be he Church Official or otherwise, who thinks he must add something to what Jesus has already done, in fact says, that what Christ did at Calvary was not enough. In other words, he is impugning, maligning, and making less of Calvary than it really is. Such is a gross sin!

It is the same as saying that Faith in Christ is not enough for one to be saved, but something else must be added. Other than blaspheming the Holy Spirit, there could be no worse sin. Consequently, when a so-called

NOTES

Church Official attempts to add punishment, they are in effect saying, *"We must beat Jesus more, He has not suffered enough. We must drive the nails deeper, for He has not experienced enough pain."*

Looking at the situation in that light should give us pause.

SHOULD THERE NOT BE DISCIPLINE IN THE CHURCH?

There is discipline in the Church. That is if it abides by the Word of God. In fact, the discipline is the Word of God.

Most modern Pentecostal Denominations have so strayed from the Word of God, that for anyone to obey what they demand, will have the very opposite effect. In other words, instead of restoring them spiritually, it will destroy them.

First of all, if it is a Preacher, and a problem of morals is involved, they will demand that he stop preaching for a period of time, normally two years. They will also demand that he undergo months of psychological counseling, in other words that he visit a Psychologist for several months. As well, they will not reinstate him respecting their particular Denomination, until he is signed off by a Psychologist.

There are a myriad of other man-devised rules, unscriptural as well, too numerous to mention. Also, they are constantly changing these rulings.

My question is, *"If their rules are Scriptural to begin with, how can they be changed?"*

To the carnal, unspiritual mind, the mind incidentally which does not regard the Word of God, these rules I have just mentioned will meet with their wholehearted approval. But to those who know the Word of God, it is quickly obvious as to how unscriptural these things are, and, therefore, ungodly.

Any sin, any failure, is a terrible business. It brings heartache and suffering of unimaginable proportions. The only answer to such is Jesus. In fact, it is easy to ascertain how bad that sin really is, when we properly understand the terrible price that was paid at Calvary's Cross to save man from sin. Also, I will quickly remind the Reader, that if Jesus is the Answer for sin, then why do we need Psychologists? And if the Psychologist is the answer, then why did Jesus have to come and die?

I must also remind the Reader, that the only thing the Psychologist can do, is to talk to the individual. They have no wonder drugs, no medicine, or anything of that nature, only talk. I again remind the Reader, that if sin or failure of any nature can be *"talked away,"* why did not God speak sin out of the way and Redemption into existence? I also remind the Reader that if God with all of His Power could not speak these things out of existence, then how does a poor pitiful man, a Psychologist, think that he can do so?

Most of the time, the Laity takes the position that these things are between Preachers and Church Officials, etc.; consequently, it does not affect them. The answer to that is simple:

THE WORD OF GOD

Anything that affects one in the Body of Christ affects all, even as Paul graphically described in I Corinthians Chapter 12. So, that excuse won't hold water.

In thousands of Pentecostal and Charismatic Churches presently, the Spirit of God is completely absent. Those particular Churches have degenerated into little more than a social center, if that. The reasons may be manyfold; however, at least part of the reason is that the Church has instituted for the most part, government devised by man, and thrown out the Government of God. As we have already stated, any leaven if not rooted out, will ultimately corrupt the whole. Churches, even entire Denominations, cannot ignore the Word of God and fail to pay the penalty. We must always remember, the Word of God is the criteria and nothing else. When other things are inserted, even as we have attempted to portray, in effect it is being said, that we are wiser than God, in fact, the same sin committed by Adam and Eve in the Garden of Eden.

Whatever it personally costs me, I am going to make every effort to obey the Word of God and not man. My heart grieves over any sin or failure; however, I know that such can only be handled at the Cross, and not by the foolish prattle of religious men functioning in an unscriptural manner. I will say as Joshua of old, *"As for me and my house, we will serve the Lord"* (Josh. 24:15).

(4) "BUT IN ALL THINGS APPROVING OURSELVES AS THE MINISTERS OF GOD, IN MUCH PATIENCE, IN AFFLICTIONS, IN NECESSITIES, IN DISTRESSES,"

NOTES

The phrase, *"But in all things approving ourselves as the Ministers of God,"* means, in every respect, in all that we do, in every way, both by words and deeds.

APPROVING OURSELVES

The actual translation should be *"commending ourselves."*

As well as speaking of the responsibility which all Preachers of the Gospel should have, as well as listing the hardships which True Ministers will have to go through, even as we will study, Paul is no doubt referring to the insinuation, which had evidently caused him deep pain, that he was not authorized to preach, as his Judaic opponents were, by *"letters of commendation"* (II Cor. 3:1-3). These letters probably came from James or from the Elders at Jerusalem. However, Paul has plainly said, and rightly so, that his credentials came from God, Who had enabled him to be faithful (Farrar).

The idea is, that even though he does not have any *"letters of commendation,"* still, the proof of his office is obvious. The sense is: We want people always to see in us true Ministers of God, whose one recommendation it is that we act as such in every respect. We recommend ourselves by letting our entire conduct as God's Ministers speak for us. It always does that, and people always listen to what that conduct says.

Ministers often fool themselves on that point, and some people are also fooled by them. But True spirituality and devotion to Christ, the Gospel, and the Ministry are hard to imitate. In other words, what is really there, will sooner or later surface.

MINISTERS

What Paul says about himself and his associates as being *"God's Ministers"* can easily be applied to God's people whom this Ministry serves. The beautiful word *"Ministry"* must be noted: rendering service to others freely so that the benefit may be wholly theirs. The Corinthians had abundantly enjoyed these benefits through Paul and those with Him.

Paul is saying a great deal here; just how much he is saying the following shows. It is not a boast but a catalog of concentrated facts, an elaboration of *"in everything."* Each item could be elaborated by many details.

Those who find merely a loose array of phrases, etc., in the following statements do Paul an injustice. Paul never writes loosely. His series of items is most carefully arranged. His rapid mind has often been noted, generally to prove that he outruns his expressions and his language; however, a true rapid mind never does that but sees in advance and has the end present to the mind when the mind begins a thought or a list of items. This is evident here (Lenski).

This phrase, *"In much patience, in afflictions, in necessities, in distresses,"* when added to the next Scripture, lists ten testings, all somewhat negative.

Before we begin the Commentary on each of these *"testings,"* it should be noted that the Holy Spirit is portraying here the fact through the Apostle, that such *"testings"* will properly show if the individual is truly God-called or not! As someone has well said, it is not so much the action that counts, but rather the reaction.

How does the man or woman of God hold up under these testings?

PATIENCE

Actually *"patience"* probably should not be listed as one of the *"testings,"* simply because, patience is in fact, the thing to be developed in the worker. It is the object of the testings. The nine things which follow are the means by which patience is developed.

Biblical patience is a God-exercise, or God-given, restraint in face of opposition or oppression. However, it is not passivity. The initiative lies with God's Love, or the Christian's, in meeting wrong in this way.

THE OLD TESTAMENT

In the Old Testament, the concept is denoted by the Hebrew word *"arek,"* meaning *"long."* God is said to be *"long"* or *"slow"* to anger (Ex. 34:6; Num. 14:18; Neh. 9:17; Ps. 86:15; 103:8; 145:8; Joel 2:13; Jonah 4:2).

In fact, the idea of patience is exactly represented in the New Testament, as in the Old, with the Greek word *"makrothymia."* It is often translated *"longsuffering,"* and defined by Trench as *"a long holding out of the mind"* before it gives room to anger.

NOTES

Such patience is characteristic of God's dealings with sinful men, who are fully deserving of His Wrath (Isa. 48:9; Hos. 11:8). His protective mark on the murderer Cain (Gen. 4:15), His providential rainbow sign to a world that had forfeited its existence (Gen. 9:11-17; I Pet. 3:20), His many restorations of disobedient Israel (Hos. 11:8-9), His sparing of Nineveh (Jonah), His repeated pleadings with Jerusalem (Mk. 12:1-11; Lk. 13:1-9, 34; Rom. 9:22), His deferment of Christ's Second Coming (II Pet. 3:9) — these are all expressions of His patience.

CHRISTIANS AND PATIENCE

Christians are to show a like character of the Lord in their patience (Mat. 18:26, 29; I Cor. 13:4; Gal. 5:22; Eph. 4:2; I Thess. 5:14). In Proverbs the practical value of patience is stressed; it avoids strife, and promotes the wise ordering of human affairs especially where provocation is involved.

The Patience of God is a *"purposeful concession of space and time."* It is opportunity given for repentance (Rom. 2:4; 9:22; II Pet. 3:9). In fact, God's forbearance has always been a *"truce with the sinner"* (Rom. 2:4; 3:25), in a sense, awaiting the final Revelation and Redemption in Christ (Acts 17:30).

Prayer on the part of the Saints may prolong the opportunity for repentance regarding the unsaved (Gen. 18:22; Ex. 32:30; I Jn. 5:16).

The Christian's patience in respect of persons must be matched by an equal patience in respect of things, that is, in face of the afflictions and trials of the present age (Rom. 5:3; I Cor. 13:7; James 1:3; 5:7-11; Rev. 13:10). God is the God Who gives such Christlike patience (Rom. 15:5; II Thess. 3:5), and Jesus is the great Example of it (Heb. 12:1-3). He who thus endures to the end, by his patience will gain his soul (Mk. 13:13; Lk. 21:19; Rev. 3:10).

AFFLICTIONS

The word *"afflictions"* means *"to press,"* or *"to squeeze."*

The common Old Testament word for affliction is usually a translation of some form of the Hebrew *"anah."* The word expresses a sense of helplessness and distress. It is at times associated with poverty and may imply that the afflicted person is socially and economically defenseless, subject to the oppression by others.

God not only permits affliction but He also uses it. Although affliction is sometimes a punishment (II Ki. 15:5), it is actually intended as a Blessing. When Solomon dedicated the Jerusalem Temple, he expressed that thought.

He called on God to respond to the people *"when they pray toward this place and confess your Name and turn from their sin because You have afflicted them"* (I Ki. 8:35).

Affliction is never pleasant. But the Godly will say, *"It was good for me to be afflicted so that I might learn Your decrees"* (Ps. 119:71).

COMPASSION ON THE AFFLICTED ONES

We cannot, however, dismiss the devastating impact of the pain suffered by the afflicted in society. We sense something of that helplessness when Isaiah twice uses the word *"afflicted"* to describe the Sufferings of the Messiah as He is crushed for our sins and burdened with the weight of our iniquities (Isa. 53:4, 7).

The Psalmists often cried out to God, expressing the despair of the afflicted. Isaiah responds with a Promise: *"The Lord comforts His people and will have compassion on His afflicted ones"* (Isa. 49:13).

The Greek word *"thlipsis"* is rendered *"affliction."* However, this word is not linked with social vulnerability as affliction is in the Old Testament. It focuses attention here on external conditions as the cause of emotional pressures. Paul's thought in Colossians as well as the Text of our present study, is that the afflictions and the suffering that have come to him in the course of his Ministry should not be viewed as discipline or as punishment. Instead, such suffering is an extension of the suffering experienced by Jesus, for it comes from the same source.

Following Jesus, Paul also willingly chose a course of action that would bring him into conflict with human society. We, too, have the privilege of making such choices, knowing that the pain that comes to us is far outweighed by the benefits our suffering will bring to others. This is the gist of Paul's thought.

NECESSITIES

This is a stronger term than afflictions, and denotes the distress which arose from want. Paul everywhere endured adversity. It denotes unavoidable distress and calamity.

NOTES

It could refer to needs unsupplied.

Is not this in contradiction to the statement, *"My God shall supply all your need. . . ."* (Phil. 4:19)?

It is not, when it is placed as a part of the classroom of patience. It is for a higher purpose that God sometimes withholds.

For instance, there is a higher purpose in Grace than merely granting contentment. Character does not grow out of gratification. To withhold is sometimes more beneficial than to be bestow.

DISTRESSES

These are those compressing experiences that put us into straits. We get into the narrows of confining circumstances and then wonder why. It is to develop what would not come, and in fact, could not come any other way.

The word used here denotes, properly, *"straightness of place, want of room."* As well, it is a stronger word than either *"afflictions"* or *"necessities."*

Paul means that in all these circumstances he had evinced patience, and had endeavored to act as became a Minister of the Gospel.

These problems listed here, do not cause the spirit in us which reacts, but only brings out what is already there. Consequently, we as Believers are to allow these things, as distasteful as they may be, to be what God intends for them to be: A. To prove us; B. To show us what is already there, for God already knows; and, C. To teach us trust in Him, and to ask for His help in correcting that which is not Scripturally proper.

(5) "IN STRIPES, IN IMPRISONMENTS, IN TUMULTS, IN LABOURS, IN WATCHINGS, IN FASTINGS;"

I think these thing as listed by Paul, would little fit into much modern Theology. Men are told today that if they have enough Faith, they can abolish or sidestep all of these distasteful things. However, such teaching is that of man and not of God.

Some of these things are in fact, required, even as listed here, and for our good. As stated, they are distasteful, but necessary.

In this Verse, Paul proceeds to specifications of what he had been called to endure. In the previous Verse, he had spoken of his afflictions in general terms. Now he specifies.

NOTES

STRIPES

He and his fellow-laborers were scourged in the Synagogues and cities as if they had been the worst of men. In fact, in II Corinthians 11:23-25, as we shall see, Paul says that he had been scourged five times by the Jews, and had been thrice beaten with rods. The Apostle lists these things, attempting to show that none but True Ministers of the Gospel would undergo such. This was the proof of his Ministry, not some *"letters of recommendation."* In fact, during times of great persecution, there aren't many false Apostles and for the obvious reasons.

IMPRISONMENTS

Paul was imprisoned for a short period of time at Philippi (Acts 16:24), and for at least two years at Caesarea (Acts 24:27), plus several years in Rome (Acts 28:30).

Why did the Lord desire that this Apostle remain in prison these several years? To the natural mind, it would surely seem that the great Apostle could certainly do more for the Lord outside the prison rather than in these confines. Paul was a great Evangelist, and the great builder of Churches, but yet, there was little he could do, at least in this regard, confined to a prison cell, or other types of confinement.

Actually, the Lord never did give Paul a reason and seldom does He give us reasons for similar circumstances.

We do know that the Lord could have had Paul released at any time, or even have prevented him from ever going to prison in the first place. Paul knew this to such an extent, that he referred to himself not as a prisoner of Nero, but rather *"a prisoner of Jesus Christ"* (Phile. vs. 1).

Whatever the reason, the Lord always knows best. Whatever He does is right, and it's right not simply because He does it, but because in fact, it *is* right.

It must have been very difficult for Paul in prison, especially that his detractors were no doubt trumpeting loudly, that if Paul was really who he said he was, an Apostle of the Lord, he would not be in prison. There is evidence this was happening; however, the Lord did not bother to justify His Apostle, but to be sure, the *"Judgment Seat of Christ,"* will definitely bring it all to light.

TUMULTS

The Greek word denotes, properly, *"instability, disorder."*

Here it means that in the various tumults and commotions which were produced by the preaching of the Gospel, that Paul endeavored at all times, to act as became a Minister of the Gospel. Such *"tumults"* are listed at Corinth (Acts 18:6), at Philippi (Acts 16:19-20), at Lystra and Derbe (Acts 14:19), at Ephesus (Acts Chpt. 19), and in various other places.

The idea is, that if Ministers of the Gospel are assailed by a lawless mob, they are to endeavor to show the Spirit of Christ, and to evince all patience, and to do good, at least if it is possible, even in such a scene.

A few experiences of flogging by Jews or by Roman lictors, a taste of abominable jails, and a riot or two, will quickly denote as to whether the man is truly called of God or not. What one suffers for the Cause of Christ, is the credentials the Holy Spirit provides, for such quickly separates those who really are and those who really aren't.

LABOURS

This speaks of toil. Real Christian service is arduous labor. It knows no hours and brings a weariness to mind and body. I remind the Reader, that the Lord told us to *"pray ye therefore the Lord of the Harvest, that He would send forth laborers into His harvest"* (Lk. 10:2). He did not say *"loafers!"*

Although I would not even attempt to compare my personal efforts to that of Paul, nor the times in which we live; however, as an example, as poor as it may be, my day begins a little bit after 5 a.m. each morning, and that is seven days a week. I finish up each evening at about 8 p.m., and that is seven days a week as well.

In fact, there is no work any harder, but yet at the same time, no work anymore satisfying than that of the Gospel of Jesus Christ. As difficult as it may be, and that which Paul here epitomizes, it is a privilege to serve the Lord in any capacity, and especially the Ministry.

WATCHINGS

These were nights of sleeplessness. They were night vigils caused by an agonized heart. A mind working overtime considering and planning, at times burdened, often found no rest in sleep.

Much travel is never easy; however, travel was extremely difficult in the times of Paul. First of all, there were no hotels as we think of such presently. Accommodations were often very sparse, if any at all. No doubt, the Apostle and all with him, spent many a night under the stars, sometimes with weather that was very inclement. In fact, there was absolutely no comparison in then and now — and yet, none of this deterred him, not even the beatings and imprisonments.

What an example!

FASTINGS

The *"fastings"* mentioned here, point more so to the involuntary doing without food, rather than fasting as we commonly think of such. The idea is, that he was often destitute of food. As stated, there were few restaurants in those days, at least as we think of such, and besides that, there were times it seems, that they simply had no money to buy food. Here is self-denial and sacrifice. It was hunger and thirst willingly endured that the Message might be taken to those who had not heard.

What testings these were! How they must have tried every nerve and fiber of body and soul. They were the testings of patience. Whoever is willing to pay their price can have their profit.

In all of this, the Preacher constantly finds himself challenged by the Bible he endeavors to preach and teach to others. It is a constant source of personal measurement.

FOLLOWING PAUL

It is not a simple thing, following Paul through the maze of his experiences. The Preacher stands ashamed that he has been so unwilling to take the hard way. Too oftentimes we find ourselves selfishly saying that we will not do certain things because it means difficulty. However, in the face of Paul's experiences we blush for shame. The easy way is unworthy of any real servant of Christ.

And yet, it is natural to want the easy way. We unconsciously choose it. Colonel Lawrence of Arabia told of two Arab Chieftains who had been brought to London by the British Government. It was a goodwill gesture to win their allegiance to the British cause in the Near East.

NOTES

They had been given many honors and entertained with lavish luxuriance. As they were about to return to Arabia, Colonel Lawrence asked what they would like to take back with them as a typical memento of their visit.

One of them quickly replied, *"We would like to have two hot water faucets to take home with us. It would be nice in Arabia to turn them on and have hot water anytime one wished."*

Of course, they saw the easy side of the hot water. It was the bright and shiny faucet. Back of that faucet were pipes, valves, reservoirs, and fire. In fact, without the fire, the faucet was of no use.

Many of us would like the convenient gadgets of Godliness. We like to gather our Salvation on the run and enjoy ourselves. That is the easy way. However, back of all True Godliness there is consecration; consecration means fire and fire means purging and pressure. We can wish for the nice shiny faucets of religious ecstasy, but the service that the faucet represents means fire (Laurin).

(6) "BY PURENESS, BY KNOWLEDGE, BY LONGSUFFERING, BY KINDNESS, BY THE HOLY SPIRIT, BY LOVE UNFEIGNED."

Paul, having in the previous Verses grouped together some of the sufferings which he endured, and by which he had endeavored to commend and extend the True Salvation, proceeds here to group together certain other influences by which he had sought the same object.

BY PURENESS

The substance of what he says here is, that it had not only been done by sufferings and trials, but by a holy life, and by entire consecration to the great Cause to which he had devoted himself. He begins by stating that it was *"by pureness,"* that is, by integrity, sanctity, a holy and pure life.

All preaching and all labors would have been in vain without this; and Paul well knew that if he succeeded in the Ministry, he must know and have the pureness of God. Consequently, this speaks of moral purity.

The greatest personal credential of the worker is his personal purity of character and conduct, not his brilliance or his ability. At this present time, we have laid altogether too much stress on what a man does without a proportionate emphasis on what a man is.

The previous nine or ten testings, according to the way they are grouped, were what the worker found outside. These listed now are what the worker should find inside. They are not to be merely artificial religious equipment, but actual life attainments. They are to represent character and to reflect the man inside.

If previously we were shown the lengths required to develop patience, we are now shown how this patience is to be manifested.

"Pureness" is listed first because God desires and requires pureness first. If we are not pure, nothing else will be right either.

Second, it is not only *"purity of morals,"* but as well *"purity of motive."* This speaks of all that we do and suffer. However, motive, when it is ill-informed though it be ever so pure in itself, leads to many a wrong deed as Jesus Himself says in John 16:2. Consequently, *"knowledge"* is joined with purity in motive. These two constitute a pair.

We at once see what a lack of either of these two would mean, and often enough one or both are lacking even in Ministers of the Gospel. In fact, the insertion of *"knowledge"* has puzzled some, yet this is done only because the right motive must have also the right information (Lenski).

BY KNOWLEDGE

The *"knowledge"* spoken here, refers to two things:

1. Knowledge of the Word of God: A Preacher, or anyone for that matter, is ill-equipped, if their knowledge of the Bible is insufficient. Sadly it is insufficient in the hearts and lives and Ministries of most. So, the motive can be ever so pure, but if the knowledge of the Word of God is insufficient, one can well see how great damage can be done.

2. The *"knowledge"* mentioned here, also refers to the Holy Spirit. We must have knowledge concerning His Leading, Guidance, and Direction. This can only be done by familiarity with Him, which insists upon a constant communion with Him. This is done through the Word of God, and nearness to Christ.

BY LONGSUFFERING

The patient endurance of insults, of which Paul shows a practical specimen in this Epistle, and still more in Philippians 1:15-18, is evident.

NOTES

We endeavor to obtain and keep a control over our passions, and to keep them in subjection. In other words, *"longsuffering"* is the opposite of being short-tempered.

If one is pure of heart, and has the proper knowledge of the Word of God, the heart will exercise patience with men, will not be hasty to give up, to turn away, to cast off.

BY KINDNESS

This characterized the Ministry of Jesus; it was one of kind, mild, gentle, helpful treatment of poor sinners.

Actually, the first proof of the True Love of God in a person's heart, is *"longsuffering and kindness"* (I Cor. 13:4). What a wonder!

To serve as an exhibition of the great Love of God one could think of many things, but yet the Holy Spirit labels *"longsuffering and kindness"* as the greatest example of all. In other words, the True Love of God operates in the simple practicalities of life. It is not something high and majestic, beyond the reason of us poor mortals, that is if we know God.

BY THE HOLY SPIRIT

The Holy Spirit is placed here right in the middle of all of these things mentioned by the Apostle and placed there for a particular reason.

It is to draw our attention to the fact that everything we truly accomplish in the Lord is done by the Power of the Holy Spirit — and that means everything.

In fact, He Alone can produce these sanctifying influences. He Alone can produce the Graces and Virtues which is His office peculiarly to produce in the heart.

I think that Paul here is not so much referring to the Miraculous Agency of the Holy Spirit, as much as he is referring to the Working of the Holy Spirit which he and his fellow-Ministers manifested. The idea is, that they were able to carry out these things, this longsuffering, this kindness, to stand the great trials and tests, as the Holy Spirit helped them to do so. If one is to notice, Paul constantly points to the Holy Spirit as the One Who Alone can bring to pass all that Jesus afforded at Calvary and the Resurrection. However, He is not only the great Revelator, but as well, the great Helper (Jn. 16:7-15). In fact, Paul is proclaiming here the Holy Spirit as *"Helper,"* more so than *"Revelator."* This *"help"* is absolutely indispensable for the Child of God, and yet sadly, most Church people little know or understand anything about the Holy Spirit.

Regrettably, the Book of Acts experience regarding the Holy Spirit (Acts 2:4), is denied by most Churches, and ignored by most of the balance. Consequently, these Churches are devoid of Spiritual Life, and the help that the Holy Spirit Alone can give as Paul here portrays.

BY LOVE UNFEIGNED

This is love that is genuine, not hypocritical. It is not a mere mask. In I Corinthians Chapter 13 is Paul's own wonderful description of genuine love that is wrought by the Holy Spirit.

What good can a Preacher do, if he does not love his people and the souls of men? The prominent characteristic in the life of the Redeemer was love — love to all. So if we are like Him, and if we do any good, we shall have love, His Love within our hearts, love which will be shown to all men.

He who shows that he truly loves Me has access at once to My heart; he who does not, cannot make a way there by any argument, eloquence, denunciation, or learning. No Minister is useful without it; no one with it can be otherwise than useful.

One could say that this is the surest Fruit of the Spirit, and the best of all Spiritual Gifts (Rom. 12:9; I Cor. 8:1; Chpt. 13; II Cor. 12:15).

(7) "BY THE WORD OF TRUTH, BY THE POWER OF GOD, BY THE ARMOUR OF RIGHTEOUSNESS ON THE RIGHT HAND AND ON THE LEFT,"

This particular Scripture proclaims to the Believer the tremendous armaments made available by the Holy Spirit to all who follow Christ. It is as follows:

THE WORD OF TRUTH

The phrase, *"By the Word of Truth,"* refers of course, to the Word of God, which *"Truth"* (Jn. 17:17).

It was Paul's obligation, and the obligation of every single Preacher, and Believer for that matter, to make known this simple Truth of the Word of God. He did not corrupt it by false mixtures of philosophy and human wisdom, but communicated it as it had been revealed to him.

NOTES

The object of the appointment of Christian Ministry is to make known this great Truth. That is why Paul would later write to Timothy, saying, *"Preach the Word"* (II Tim. 4:2).

The great sin of the age is Preachers who simply don't know the great Truth of the Word, or else they simply do not believe the Truth of the Word. Either way, their Message will spell death to those who are unfortunate enough to sit under them.

The question could be asked, *"How many Preachers are proclaiming all the Truth of the Word of God, and nothing but the Truth?"* How many are diluting it with men's philosophy, i.e., *"the wisdom of this world,"* or by their own false interpretation?

TRUTH

Jesus Christ as the Truth of God becomes the Standard and Test for Truth regarding the Faith of men. However, Jesus Christ is not to be summarized as a mere mental affirmation, to be accepted and contended for, but in the subjective way of experience, in a series of ideals to be realized and propagated. In other words, Jesus Christ is to be looked at as the Central Core of all Truth as it is embodied in the Word of God. If the Believer does not understand that everything in the Bible leads ultimately to Jesus and to Jesus as Truth, then the intent of the Word is being missed. Jesus Christ is the Central Figure of all Truth. All the Prophets of the Old Testament pointed forward to Him, while all the Apostles of the New point backward to Him. As stated, He Alone is the Truth of God.

If Christ in any way, in any manner, is relegated to any position other than this Central Core, this epitome, this ultimate goal, then the person through his or her own volition, or else being led astray by others, is missing the entirety of the point of the Word of God.

So, we do not explain Truth as we would a philosophy, which within itself is a search for Truth, but we recognize Truth primarily as a Person, i.e., *"The Lord Jesus Christ."* To the degree that He is misunderstood in the Word, to that degree will the Word of God be misunderstood.

THE HOLY SPIRIT AND TRUTH

In fact, even as Christ, the Holy Spirit is Truth (I Jn. 4:6).

Inasmuch as the Holy Spirit is Truth, and in fact, is the illumination of Truth in the Word of God, He will always glorify Christ as the Central Truth (Jn. 16:13-15). Consequently, the Holy Spirit even though He is God, will never glorify Himself, but will always glorify Christ; however, the manner in which He glorifies the Son of God, is His position as the Central Core of Truth.

When one is properly led by the Holy Spirit, one will see Jesus in every aspect of the Word of God. He will see Christ in all the Promises, the Sacrifices, the Tabernacle, the Temple, the Law of Moses, all the Covenants, in all the Feast Days, Sabbath-keeping, etc. He will see Jesus as the True Israel, as He is also the True Church.

We see Him now as the Fulfillment of all the Old Testament Promises, in His Atoning, Vicarious Work at Calvary and the Resurrection, in the fulfillment of those Promises, consequently, as our Saviour, the Baptizer with the Holy Spirit, our Lord, our King, our Victory, our Overcomer, our Strength, our Light, our Life. It is the Work of the Holy Spirit to reveal this to the Believer, i.e., *"the Word of Truth."*

THE POWER OF GOD

The phrase, *"By the Power of God,"* proclaims the fact that there is a Divine Power in the *"Word of Truth."* In other words, when it is fully preached, fully lived, therefore, fully believed, it is always attended by the *"Power of God."*

That is the reason Paul also said, *"For I am not ashamed of the Gospel of Christ: for it is the Power of God unto Salvation to every one that believeth"* (Rom. 1:16).

No philosophy or religion in the world contains any power, but the *"Word of Truth"* which is the *"Gospel of Christ,"* contains the Power of the ages, *"the Power of God."* That is why drunkards upon hearing this Word, if they believe, can be set free from the ravages of that bondage. The same goes for drug addicts, or the bondage of sin in general. It alone can set the captive free.

This means that every single person in the history of man who has ever been set free from the terrible bondages of darkness, and millions have, it has all come about through this *"Word of Truth,"* Which is, and Who is, Jesus Christ. That means that Buddhism has never set one single captive free, and neither has Islam, or Mormonism, or Catholicism, or Hinduism, or Shintoism, or any other philosophy that has ever existed, or presently exists.

NOTES

In fact, there are millions of people in the world at this very moment, who are a walking testimony to the Gospel of Christ. They have experienced Jesus Christ, i.e., *"the Word of Truth,"* and they have been forever changed by the Miracle-Working Power of God.

Some have attempted to limit this to the power of working Miracles; however, the structure of the Text points to the inclusion of all displays of Divine Power which attends the propagation of the Gospel, whether in the working of Miracles, or in the conversion of men. Neither is to be weakened.

Another idea here is, that the Apostles used this great Power entrusted to them not for the purposes of gain and ambition, or for vain display, but solely for the furtherance of the Gospel and the Salvation of men. This as should be obvious, is extremely important.

THE USE OF THE POWER OF GOD

Several things are involved here. Most Preachers do not preach the entirety of the Word of God, with much of that false direction headed up in a failure to believe or proclaim Jesus as the Baptizer with the Holy Spirit. Consequently, there is no power in their Ministry, it being reduced mostly to platitudes, etc. And then others do preach the entirety of the Word, but attempt to use the Power therein, for their own selfish gains.

To be sure, such is always masked under the guise of greater enlightenment, a Blessing for the people, etc. Nevertheless, this misuse of Power is obvious. This can fall under many headings:

When the Preacher builds himself up instead of Christ, that is a misuse of the Power of God, even though he may be preaching all the Truth, at least as far as the letter is concerned. If he is attempting to build up his Denomination instead of Christ, that is another blatant misuse of Power. To be frank, the two just mentioned, are pandemic in the world of religion. The Prosperity Message is another case in point. It is cloaked under the guise of greater enlightenment which will greatly enrich the participants, but the Truth is, that this message is false, simply because it places emphasis on that other than Christ.

However, having said all of that, the glorious Message is still portrayed in the Scripture as saying, *"For the Kingdom of God is not* (only) *in Word, but in Power"* (I Cor. 4:20).

THE ARMOR OF RIGHTEOUSNESS

The phrase, *"By the Armour of Righteousness on the right hand and on the left,"* speaks of being completely armed.

One could say, in the right hand is the Sword of the Spirit which is the Word of God, and in the left hand the Shield of Faith. The former is for our offensive warfare, while the latter is for defensive measures.

MILITARY TERMS

If one is to notice, Paul frequently uses terms which are indicative of the military. He does this for a purpose, in that the Holy Spirit is helping us to understand that this is a conflict in which we are engaged, and furthermore, a military conflict one could say.

While the Old Testament examples were mostly physical, still, they were symbols of the spiritual conflict we now face constantly on an everyday basis in our walk with the Lord. A perfect example is found in Exodus Chapter 17. It speaks of the Children of Israel in the wilderness, which is a type of the world. There was no water to drink, even as the world is bereft of the Water of Life respecting Salvation.

Moses was told by the Lord to smite the Rock which was a Type of Jesus, and more particularly, a type of Jesus as the Baptizer with the Holy Spirit. Upon the Rock being smitten, the water gushed out in a veritable river, which slaked the thirst of the Israelites.

However, immediately upon that happening, the Eighth Verse of the 17th Chapter of Exodus says, *"Then came Amalek, and fought with Israel in Rephidim."* The idea is this:

The reception of the Holy Spirit immediately causes war. Up to this point God had fought for Israel. Israel was to stand still and see His Salvation; but the command now is to go out and fight.

There is an immense difference between Justification and Sanctification. The one is Christ fighting *for* us; the other, the Holy Spirit fighting *in* us. The entrance of the new nature is the beginning of warfare with the old.

NOTES

Amalek pictures the old carnal nature. He was the Grandson of Esau, who before and after birth tried to murder Jacob, and who preferred the mess of pottage to the Birthright. The carnal nature wars against the Spirit, *"It is not subject to the Law of God neither indeed can be"*; and God has decreed war against it forever (Ex. 17:16).

The victory over Amalek hung upon the intercession of Moses, and upon the wisdom and valor of Joshua. Christ is both Moses and Joshua to His people — excepting that His Hands never grow weary.

God did not destroy Amalek, but determined to have war with him from generation to generation. He was to dwell in the land, but not to reign in it. Romans 6:12 says, *"Let not sin therefore reign in your mortal body."* The command would be unmeaning if sin were not existing in the Christian. In fact, sin does dwell in a Believer, but is not supposed to reign. Sin both dwells and reigns in an unbeliever.

THREE KINDS OF ARMOR FOR THREE KINDS OF FOE

The Scriptures speak of three kinds of armor for three kinds of foe. We face the three foes of the world, the flesh and the Devil:

1. There is the Armor of Righteousness referred to here by Paul in order that we may fight the foe which is of the world.
2. There is the Armor of Light referred to in Romans 13:12 in order that we may fight the foe which is the flesh.
3. Then there is the Armor of God referred to in Ephesians 6:11 in order that we may fight the foe which is the Devil. Of course, all of this is carried forth as the *"good fight of Faith"* (I Tim. 6:12).

Thus, the soul is fully armored for its necessities.

Sometimes we try desperately to reconcile certain of our experiences with justice and with Scripture. It is often impossible because Christian experience has its paradoxes (that which is seemingly contradictory or opposed to common sense and yet is perhaps true). Actually, there can be no reconciliation to sight, only to Faith. There are contradictions that will always contradict. There are paradoxes that will always be paradoxical. That simply means, that there are some things which happen to us and with us, that seem to have no explanation.

Consequently, we are thrown back time after time upon a statement in this Epistle, *"We walk by Faith, not by sight."* By Faith, a paradox does not become more understandable, but it does become a part of the picture that completes the whole. There are some things which we will never fully understand, at least short of the Resurrection, while there are others that work out to glorious conclusions before our wondering eyes (Laurin).

(8) "BY HONOUR AND DISHONOUR, BY EVIL REPORT AND GOOD REPORT: AS DECEIVERS, AND YET TRUE;"

This Scripture portrays to us that which will happen to Godly Believers. Inasmuch as this is given by the Holy Spirit, this is not something that possibly will happen, but something that definitely will happen, and we are here forewarned.

BY HONOUR AND DISHONOUR

The phrase, *"By honour and dishonour,"* presents the paradox of which we have just mentioned. Why would it be this way?

Why will some honor and praise the man or woman of God, while from others come dishonor and infamy? Some will approve your work and others will disapprove. How can we reconcile the two? You cannot, so do not try. Go on, without being elated over your honor nor deflated over your dishonor.

Quite possibly, among all the other reasons, the Holy Spirit allows such — the honor and the dishonor — for a particular reason. Few are the men who are not injured by honor; few who are not corrupted by flattery. Most Preachers do more to *"give offense"* in times when they are greatly honored by the world than when they are despised. So, if the Apostles were sometimes honored, they were often dishonored. If the world sometimes flattered and caressed them, it often despised them, and cast out their names as evil.

As we have already stated, the *"honour"* is perhaps far more dangerous to the Believer, and especially the Apostle, than the *"dishonour."* So, for those who truly know the Lord, and are truly working for the Lord, the Holy Spirit allows the *"dishonour"* in order to keep us on even keel. The flesh loves the *"honour,"* while of course, it despises the *"dishonour."* And yet, that which is invigorating to the flesh, is usually very harmful to the spirit. Conversely, that which is normally helpful to the spirit, is grievous to the flesh. So, perhaps one could say that the *"dishonour"* does us more good than the *"honour,"* for the simple reason, it keeps us on our knees.

NOTES

BY EVIL REPORT AND GOOD REPORT

On the one hand a worker is met with praise and on the other hand with the opposite. One upholds him, another debases him. One credits him with good motives while another defames his character.

We must learn to balance these reports so as not to be dependent on the one nor despondent over the other. Remember, men may bandy your reputation about but they cannot touch your character. It is character that will count in the long run.

As we've previously stated, reputation is what people think you are, while character is what God knows you are.

Regarding the *"evil report"* it is very trying to human nature to have one's name slandered and cast out as evil when we are conscious only of a desire to do good. But it is sufficient for the Disciple that he be as his Master; and if they call the Master of the house Beelzebub, we must expect that they will also slander those of His household. So, that being the case, a man should be willing to be anything if it will make him like the Redeemer — whether it be in suffering or in Glory (Phil. 3:10; I Pet. 4:13).

Concerning *"good report"* for which we are all thankful, the truth is, few men can withstand the influence of flattery, hence it has happened, that God has so ordered it that His faithful servants have but little of the *"good report"* but that they have been generally subjected to persecution and slander.

However, Believers must be very careful, that they do not become a tool of Satan in becoming a part of the *"evil report"* respecting the slander of others. It is so easy to be caught up in popular opinion, in other words, toward what something is perceived to be. When this happens, however, we are always wrong, actually becoming Satan's tool. It is sad, but he uses the Church to spread his *"evil reports,"* more so than he does any other medium.

AS DECEIVERS, AND YET TRUE

The phrase, *"As deceivers, and yet true,"* presents another paradox of being branded as a deceiver but vindicated as true. We must not read into this that it is as an actual deceiver that one extends the Cause of Christ. Rather, it means that even though some may slander you with the epithet of a deceiver, you will be vindicated as being true by continuing to be His servant in sincerity and simplicity. The best vindication is the fruit of your life (Laurin).

The Jews called Christ *"a deceiver,"* which means *"a deliberate and misleading imposter"* (Mat. 27:63; Jn. 7:12). This is an illustration of the *"evil report."*

Regarding the phrase, *"And yet true,"* there is no *"yet"* in the original, and its omission gives more force to these eloquent and impassioned contrasts.

The closer that one is to God, the heavier and deeper the Calling upon his life, the more that such will be opposed by the world and the Church. It is regrettable, that the Church joins with the world, but oftentimes it does.

It is not a pleasant thing to see yourself caricatured and lambasted over worldwide Television, branded as a deceiver, as dishonest, as crooked, but yet, this is exactly what Paul spoke about. I have every confidence, that had the Apostle been alive now rather than then, that he definitely would have been the target of both the News Media and the Church. He was opposed by the world and great segments of the Church then, so it stands to reason, that he would be similarly opposed presently.

Paul seldom turned aside to vindicate himself from such charges, but pursued his Master's work, and evidently felt that if he had a reputation that was worth anything, or deserved any reputation, God would take care of it. A man, especially a Minister, who is constantly endeavoring to vindicate his own reputation, usually has a reputation which is not worth vindicating.

A PERSONAL EXPERIENCE

It seems that ever so often, one of the major News Networks, one incidentally which covers much of the world, will take it upon themselves to denigrate this Evangelist. Thankfully, all they can do is to drag up that which the Lord has long since forgiven and forgotten; however, they do their best to make it seem as if though it is a part of the present, and as well, that this Ministry deceives the people, and, consequently, should be put out of business, etc. They paint their piece as ugly as they know how, and they are very adept at their business. It is designed after their father the Devil, *"to steal, kill and destroy"* (Jn. 10:10). Regrettably, many people, even Christians, believe their carefully crafted lies. As I have stated, it is not a very pleasant thing to see yourself handled in such a manner.

Regarding one of these recent episodes, one casts about in one's mind trying to figure out what to do. Of course, we made it a matter of prayer, constantly seeking the Lord that He would give us direction.

During the midst of this, driving from the Office to our house, and with these things weighing heavily upon my mind, wondering how in the world that it would be possible for any Ministry to survive such an onslaught, irrespective as to the falseness of the reports. This was in 1997.

Coming down the Interstate, only about five minutes before I was to reach our house, the Lord spoke to me and said, *"Don't do anything. You have been wondering what to do, and now I'm telling you as to what you should do. Don't do anything."*

And then He said, *"Let Me handle the situation in its totality. Do not defend yourself, let Me defend you."*

I remember saying to the Lord, *"But what about Christians who believe these things, and especially the few who support this Ministry?"*

He then said again, *"For everyone who stops their support, I will raise up someone to take their place."*

I knew it was the Lord, and in a moment's time I fully yielded in my heart to do exactly what He said. At that moment, the Peace of God filled my soul, like I have seldom experienced. Actually, that Peace of God did not leave for days, giving me a strength that I had not previously known.

We did exactly what the Lord told us to do, and He has taken care of the situation exactly as He has said He would.

Did some Christians believe the garbage that was portrayed by this Network concerning

NOTES

this Ministry? I'm certain that some did, but that's between them and the Lord. The main thing is this:

Though we are branded as a deceiver, I know what the true report really is, and that is all that matters. What one actually is, is not what people think, but what one is in Christ.

(9) "AS UNKNOWN, AND YET WELL KNOWN; AS DYING, AND, BEHOLD, WE LIVE; AS CHASTENED, AND NOT KILLED;"

Once again the Holy Spirit paints the picture as to what the true Child of God actually is. As the Lord helps us to dissect these words and phrases, perhaps they will be a blessing to the Reader.

AS UNKNOWN, AND YET WELL KNOWN

The phrase, *"As unknown, and yet well known,"* refers to the obscurity into which true Christian character often passes in the world. The world will little note nor long remember, its greatest souls. A man is well-known in the world because of his public relationship, yet his position alone is not always the measurement of true greatness.

However, what does it matter then if you are ignored by men as long as you are recognized by God? What does it matter if men depreciate so long as God appreciates? What does it matter if men forget so long as God remembers?

The manner in which Paul makes this statement tells us that the true heart of the Apostle, and as with all who are truly Godly, is certainly *"unknown"* by the world, and pretty much *"unknown"* by the Church. Regrettably, oftentimes that which is *"well-known,"* is not actually an accurate portrayal of reality.

There is no way for the world to properly discern anything, at least as it relates to the Lord; however, the Church does not have that excuse.

There was no reason for anyone to misjudge Paul. No reason for anyone to attribute to him wrong or base motives. No reason for anyone to think of him as a deceiver or imposter. So, why did some who claimed to be followers of Christ, engage in this type of activity, especially considering that this is one of the greatest men of God who has ever lived?

Who knows why Christians do certain things. Perhaps the reasons or excuses are as varied as the number of people involved. However, these reasons or excuses are not acceptable to God.

NOTES

To lend a voice to such destruction, makes one a tool of Satan, which is the worst place that any Christian would want to be. And yet this is the place occupied by many.

AS DYING, AND, BEHOLD, WE LIVE

The idea of the phrase *"as dying, and, behold we live,"* is that the Apostle and those with him, had gone through many things which by all common reasoning, should have occasioned their death. But yet, they still live. In other words, God has protected them.

This portrays the fact, that they had long since given up their lives for the Cause of Christ. While they were not foolhardy or reckless, still, they ventured constantly into situations and places, and because the Lord led them to do so, which without God's help they could not have survived.

The point is, they did not consider their lives. They reckoned that the one Who numbers the very hairs of our head, could definitely see them through whatever the situation. In other words, as long as they trusted the Lord, they would not die until their work was finished, even though they stared death in the face constantly.

The manner in which Paul makes this statement, seems as well, that there were some who claimed to be followers of Christ, who actually wished that the Apostle would die. But he says, *"Behold we live!"*

I think such would have to be the case, especially considering that many slandered and reviled him. Those who would do such a thing, would at the same time relish his death. One cannot separate the first evil from the latter. Such a spirit and attitude characterizes many at present as well.

However, the lives of the Apostle and his associates, were not in the hands of these detractors, but rather in the Hands of the Lord. Consequently, there could be no greater protection.

AS CHASTENED, AND NOT KILLED

The phrase, *"As chastened, and not killed,"* refers to that which is extremely interesting.

The word *"chastened"* means *"corrected, chastised."* It is applied to the chastening which God causes by affliction and calamities (I Cor. 11:32; Heb. 12:6; Rev. 3:19).

It refers here, not to the scourgings to which they were subjected in the Synagogues and elsewhere, but to the *"chastisements"* which God inflicted, the trials to which He subjected them. And the idea is, that in the midst of these trials they endeavored to act as became Ministers of God. In other words, they bore them with patience. They submitted to them as coming from His Hand. They felt that they were right, and they submitted without a murmur.

WHY WOULD ONE SUCH AS PAUL NEED CHASTENING?

I can certainly understand my need, and I am certain that the Reader considers likewise; however, there have been few men in history with the dedication, consecration, and love for God as Paul. Why would he need chastening? Quite possibly, those who are used the most by the Lord, are subjected to greater chastening than all. In the midst of reasons which we do not know, the looming factor of personal pride always casts a shadow over the horizon. As distasteful as these things are, the flesh is *always* in need of chastening.

As well, the *"chastening"* is not because of a lack of love on God's part, but rather because of the very opposite, His Great Love (Heb. 12:6).

The idea is, that the chastening at times was so severe, that he wondered if it could be survived. But yet, looking back, the idea presents itself, that the Lord is doing this with no intention of killing us, but rather the very opposite. While certain things in our lives are definitely *"killed,"* which is the intention of the Holy Spirit, other things are made more abundantly alive, i.e., *"our relationship with Christ."*

That is the general idea!

(10) "AS SORROWFUL, YET ALWAY REJOICING; AS POOR, YET MAKING MANY RICH; AS HAVING NOTHING, AND YET POSSESSING ALL THINGS."

Most all of this Chapter carries on the subject of not receiving the Grace of God in vain, i.e., to no purpose; for Grace saves (vss. 4-10); sweetens (vss. 11-13); and separates (vss. 14-7:1).

It seeks to save others; it fills the heart with the sweetness of Christian Love; and it separates to a life of holy fellowship with God. It animates to association with Christian workers and separation from world-servers — not isolation from perishing sinners but separation from defiling connections.

NOTES

AS SORROWFUL, YET ALWAYS REJOICING

The phrase, *"As sorrowful, yet alway rejoicing,"* seems to be a contradiction in terms, but yet it isn't.

Here is an evidence of an inner triumph that puts tears to flight by the smiles of Praise. Who dares to rejoice in sorrow? A fanatic? A lunatic? Must one be totally devoid of all sense of reason and be so emotionally unstable and so reckless as to actually laugh in the face of disaster?

This is not hysteria. It is the Christian's way to reconcile the paradoxes of life. It is balancing the budget of experience. It is putting Faith into the blackout of sight (Laurin).

That of being *"sorrowful,"* as it pertains to the Believer, addresses itself to the condition of the world. The world lays under a dark cloud of captivity, which of course, is engineered by Satan and the world of darkness, and causes untold heartache in every capacity. To those who truly know the Lord, consequently knowing the cause of the evil and the heartache, and observing the rejection of Christ by most of the world, Who is the only solution, creates sorrow.

Knowing that things are not right, and in fact, cannot be right, until Jesus comes back, are grounds for sorrow. And yet, in the midst of all of this, even the difficulties that come one's way simply because they are a follower of Christ, still, there is *"rejoicing."* Salvation has a power not only to sustain the soul in trial, but to fill it with positive joy. The sources of such joy are the assurances of the Divine favor, and the hopes of Eternal Glory. There is always, an internal peace and joy which the world may not see or appreciate, but which is far more than a compensation for all the trials which the Christian endures. To attempt to explain this *"rejoicing"* is not easy or simple.

JOY

It comes from deep within, and, consequently, is not subject to the variances and circumstances of life. That is how Paul and Silas could *"pray and sing praises unto God,"* in the midst of a Philippian jail — even after they had been beaten almost to death and then *"thrust into the inner prison, with their feet made fast in the stocks"* (Acts 16:23-25).

This is a joy that literally gushes forth at times, that provides the most wonderful feeling of security, of well-being, in fact, of oneness with God. It is the *"peace which passeth all understanding."*

As stated, there are circumstances and difficulties, though at times alarming, and which do cause sorrow, still, the joy and *"rejoicing"* never leave. It is a constant bubbling up, even as a spring of water, which has as its source a subterranean river.

If one is to notice, Paul uses the word *"rejoicing,"* which speaks of Praise, in other words, an active participation, but rather more than that. The word speaks of something bubbling up to such an extent, that it cannot be contained, and there must be a recognition. That recognition is Praise, Worship, and all toward the Lord Who is the True Source.

This is God's Way and Method of *"therapy,"* that is, if one would desire to use such a word. The world has nothing that is similar, and that's what makes it so ridiculous for Christians to leave this which is tried and true, for that which is the very opposite, and I speak of psychological counseling, etc. It is understandable as to the world resorting to such, but not understandable at all to those who name the Name of Christ.

The modern Church should know and understand, that the Lord has been giving such joy, bringing about such *"rejoicing,"* even from the very beginning. He was doing this before there was such a thing as modern *"psychology,"* and He continues unto this hour.

AS POOR, YET MAKING MANY RICH

The phrase, *"As poor, yet making many rich,"* once again, speaks of a contrast.

I think there is little doubt that the Apostles were poor, at least as far as this world's goods were concerned. The little property which some of them may have had, had all been forsaken in order that they might follow the Saviour, and go preach His Gospel. And there is little doubt as well, that the great mass of Preachers of the Gospel fall into the same category.

And yet the Preacher of the Gospel, makes many *"rich,"* and by that we speak of the Preaching of the Gospel, and men accepting this Gospel, which changes the entirety of their lives.

NOTES

The Apostle was speaking in the vernacular of the world regarding *"poor"* and *"rich."* And yet, what is the true definition of *"poor"* and of *"rich"* for that matter?

If a man has all the money in the world, all the property he could ever desire, all the power he could muster, still, if he does not know Jesus Christ as his Lord and Saviour, that man is *"poor,"* i.e., *"absolutely poverty-stricken."*

Conversely, if a person has none of this world's goods, none of its power, none of its accolades, and doesn't even know where food will come from the next week, other than provision by the Lord, still, if that man knows Jesus, has experienced Saving Grace, has a close, warm, personal relationship with the Lord Jesus Christ, that man is *"rich"* beyond one's wildest dreams.

If we measure riches only in silver or gold, only in things of this world that men count as riches, then we are missing the point altogether.

The rich man of Luke Chapter 16 died and went to Hell, while the beggar died and went to Paradise. I will ask the question, *"Which one was actually rich?"*

The Preacher of the Gospel and any Believer for that matter, has the distinct privilege and honor of presenting the Gospel, which *"makes many rich,"* with the *"true riches."*

AS HAVING NOTHING, BUT YET POSSESSING ALL THINGS.

There are those who own many things and yet possess nothing. In fact, they are possessed by what they have. They are controlled, body, mind, and soul by their possessions. They are slaves to the master of money.

Yet, there is another class who have nothing, at least as far as this world is concerned, yet possess all things.

This is not a call that one should despise wealth, for with it one can be a blessing to the world, that is if it is used correctly. However, we must learn to appreciate the greater riches which are spiritual wealth, for such is greater than all other forms of possessions.

This last phrase tells us as well, that we must not set our affections on the things of this world. They are fleeting, and even if we are able to amass great quantities of money and great possessions of real estate, still, it can only be used a short time, and then it is left to others, oftentimes to destroy them or to be squandered and wasted.

While it is not wrong to be wealthy, that is if the Lord would see fit to do such as He sometimes does, still, the greater pursuit, the enlarged effort, the thrust of activity, the consuming desire, must always be in the direction of spiritual wealth. Of course, this goes for all Believers whether Preachers or otherwise.

When many, stand at the *"Judgment Seat of Christ"* at that coming day, all the things they counted so dear down here, such as wealth, riches, money, place, position, power, etc., will count for nothing there, with one exception — did we use it for the Cause of Christ?

The things that will really count, and that which will be eternal in scope and condition, which will never die but rather gain dividends forever and forever, will be the spiritual wealth that comes only through and in Christ Jesus.

A very wealthy man died. As his funeral train was passing by, one man was overheard asking another, *"How much did he leave?"*

The answer was quick, *"He left it all!"*

That is why Jesus said, *"Lay not up for yourselves treasures upon earth, where moth and rust doth corrupt, and where thieves break through and steal: But lay up for yourselves treasures in Heaven, where neither moth nor rust doth corrupt, and where thieves do not break through nor steal; For where your treasure is, there will your heart be also"* (Mat. 6:19-21).

(11) "O YE CORINTHIANS, OUR MOUTH IS OPEN UNTO YOU, OUR HEART IS ENLARGED."

In this very short Verse of Scripture, we find one of the most beautiful statements in the entirety of the Word of God. In it we will see the Power of the Gospel of Jesus Christ, and the Love of God, as well as the great heart of the Apostle Paul.

O YE CORINTHIANS

The phrase, *"O ye Corinthians,"* presents a statement that is astounding in concept, miraculous in content, and is the answer to the ills of man.

The city of Corinth, i.e., Corinthians, was noted to be one of the most jaded cities on the face of the earth of that day. It was given over to licentiousness, lust, unbridled passions, the very epitome of wickedness. Immorality was its staple, of which a great convergence of humanity merged in these pits of vice. Consequently, if one desired to speak of another in a most jaded way, he would say, *"He has been Corinthianized."* The meaning was understood immediately in the world of that day. There was nothing lower, more immoral, more jaded, than to fall under this spell of evil, i.e., *"to be Corinthianized."*

And yet, the Gospel of Jesus Christ as it was preached by Paul in this very city, this den of iniquity, had made such an impact, had touched so many hearts and lives and had seen them gloriously and miraculously changed by the Power of God, that now the entirety of the complexion changes. Paul can say, *"O ye Corinthians,"* and it now means something entirely different than what it had formerly meant.

It now spoke of the Grace of God, the Love of the Lord Jesus Christ, changed lives, men and women lifted up above the shadows, bondages of darkness broken, broken homes put back together, marriages heading for oblivion now salvaged — all because of the Gospel of Jesus Christ.

Even though the city of Corinth is no more, yet its jaded past is recognized not at all as it regards the name *"Corinthians."* If it is spoken of presently outside of the Gospel, and it is often, it is mentioned in the context of *"Corinthian Architecture,"* which speaks of *"Corinthian Columns."* No hint of its jaded past is now attached, and because of the great Gospel of Grace brought to that city by Paul the Apostle.

What a Testimony!

OUR MOUTH IS OPEN UNTO YOU

The phrase, *"Our mouth is open unto you,"* represents the fact that the Apostle had spoken frankly, clearly, and straight to these Corinthians. Nothing was hid from them. He exposed the innermost secrets of his soul.

In fact, this is a rare and very personal form of loving appeal, which occurs nowhere else in these Epistles.

Regarding the things he had said to them, it flowed in two particular directions. First of all, he pulled no punches, laying it out straight regarding problems in the Church and false Doctrine. None in the Church at Corinth would be able to say that they did not have the right word

NOTES

on the subject. As the Holy Spirit led and guided him, Paul had dealt with each problem specifically, which not only gave direction to the Corinthians, but to all Churches and Believers which would follow, even unto this hour.

As well, even though he had used strong terminology, and at times was very frank, still, the other direction of the things said to them regarded his great love for them. There is no way that anyone could read both Epistles and not sense strongly the love and concern of the Apostle for these people.

How many Preachers are as honest as Paul? How many talk out of both sides of their mouth? How many trim their Message to fit the occasion or the person? How many proclaim truly, *"Thus saith the Lord!"*

To preach the Gospel is a weighty task. As should be obvious, it has eternal consequences. Consequently, the *"mouth must be open"* to the people at all times, preaching and proclaiming, as well as living, this great Gospel of Jesus Christ.

THE ENLARGED HEART

The phrase, *"Our heart is enlarged,"* has reference to the fact, that even though his *"mouth"* had been forced to say some strong things, it was only because his *"heart"* went out to them in love and affection.

Paul had founded this Church. Almost all the people there were his converts. He had watched their spiritual growth as they had been brought out of heathenistic darkness. Even though he had now been away for some time, his interest and love for them never waned, but felt for them with a true Shepherd's heart.

In fact, he had loved them so much that he was willing to be reproached, to be persecuted, even to be poor and to have his name cast out as evil, in order to speak to them the Truth. In effect, he was saying, *"I am full of ardent attachment, and that naturally vents itself in the strong language which I have used."* True attachment will find means of expressing itself. A heart full of love will give vent to its feelings. There will be no dissembling and hypocrisy.

(12) "YE ARE NOT STRAITENED IN US, BUT YE ARE STRAITENED IN YOUR OWN BOWELS."

The Apostle had a large heart. So large that there was room in it for all at Corinth. Therefore, he spoke to them without reserve, for such is the nature of love.

NOTES

STRAITENED

The phrase, *"Ye are not straitened in us,"* refers to the fact that they did not possess a narrow or contracted place in Paul's affections. His heart was totally open to them without any restrictions.

The idea is that the Apostle had not withheld anything from them. He had bared his heart and his soul. There were no ulterior motives in his heart of any nature, and to be sure, this was obvious in his writings.

Once again, how many Preachers can say the same concerning the people to whom they minister, and that which is ministered unto them? In fact, if a Preacher truly loves the people, truly cares for them, is truly concerned about their eternal destiny, he will say the things to them that need to be said, even though it may cause animosity and anger toward him. He has no choice in the matter, that is, if he desires to follow the Lord and be a true Preacher of the Gospel.

The sadness is that many Preachers oppose only that which is popular to oppose. If its not popular, they say nothing. In effect, they are addressing the situation backwards. They fall under the heading of teachers with *"itching ears"* (II Tim. 4:3). They are *"hirelings."*

The idea is that the man of God hear from the Lord and deliver to the people what is heard. As well, he will also see and observe the difficulties in the Church regarding false doctrine or false direction, and will address those issues in no uncertain terms, whether he has had a Revelation from the Lord or not regarding these particular things. If the bridge is out, we don't have to have an Angel appear to us in order to warn the people. The need should be obvious!

CONFINED IN THEIR AFFECTIONS TOWARD HIM

The phrase, *"But ye are straitened in your own bowels,"* should have been translated, *"Ye are straitened in your own hearts."* The word *"bowels"* by no means expresses the idea of the word used here in the Greek.

The idea here is that despite the fact that Paul was completely open with them, the Corinthians had not been so in return with him, meaning that they were confined in their affections for him. In effect, he is asking them to make room in their affections for him.

His statement is the language of reproof, meaning that he had not received from them the demonstrations of attachment which he had a right to expect, and which was a fair and proportionate return for the love bestowed on them.

For the Apostle to have to appeal to the Corinthians that they love him in return is almost unthinkable! Had it not been for Paul, these people would have been eternally lost, never knowing the great delights of Salvation or the Person of Jesus Christ. Consequently, they owed more to him than words could ever begin to express.

In this Epistle, he, in effect, tells them the price that had been paid for him to bring the Gospel their way. It had not been without price, but in fact, at great cost. Along with the terrible hardships encountered, he even risked his life in this great endeavor.

To be sure, it was not to gain anything from them, but totally in obedience to what the Lord had told him to do. But yet, that he would have to appeal to them for their love and affection, causes pain to even read the words.

WHY?

Paul had been forced to correct the Corinthians, and rather harshly at times. It was done with love, in fact, it dripped with love, but yet it was totally straightforward, pulling no punches. Consequently, some evidently had been offended. There is evidence that most had repented, but still, there seemed to be some holding back on the part of a few.

The Truth, i.e., *"Word of Truth,"* at times, offends. People do not take kindly to being told they are wrong. Some few repent, but many grow angry and then fight out at the Preacher who has delivered that Truth. So, that is at least one of the reasons why few Preachers are willing to take a stand. It is not pleasant being the target of the response.

(13) "NOW FOR A RECOMPENCE IN THE SAME, (I SPEAK AS UNTO MY CHILDREN,) BE YE ALSO ENLARGED."

Paul asked that the Corinthians reciprocate by expanding their hearts wide in the same way as he and his associates are expanding theirs. Then nothing will remain between them to cause restraint, a feeling of not being considered and treated right.

NOTES

Wide open is the heart of the Apostle to embrace the Corinthians, will they not in the same way reciprocate and open theirs wide again to embrace him with the old warmth?

A RECOMPENSE IN THE SAME

The phrase, *"Now for a recompence in the same,"* in effect, is asking them to put the past behind them and begin afresh.

The word *"recompence"* refers to the reward or compensation which one gives or receives.

He is, in effect, saying, *"I do not ask silver or gold, or any earthly possessions. I ask only a return of love, and devotedness to the cause which I love, and which I endeavour to promote."*

The manner in which he says this, could very well refer to the false teachers demanding sums of money, which they no doubt did. The Apostle in answer to that, even though in a veiled way, is saying, *"I don't want your money, just your love."* The position he takes here, should be glaringly obvious to all as to who are the True Apostles. Almost always, money plays a big part in these situations, but not with Paul!

MY CHILDREN

The phrase, *"I speak as unto my children,"* is given as a parent addressing his children.

In effect, he is saying, *"I sustain toward you the relation of a spiritual father, and I have a right to require and expect a return of affection."* He had said in his first letter to them, *"For though ye have ten thousand instructors in Christ, yet have ye not many fathers: for in Christ Jesus I have begotten you through the Gospel"* (I Cor. 4:15).

Once again, the Apostle is addressing himself to particulars of which the Corinthians would have been aware.

Some had evidently questioned his right to address them, to correct them, as he had done. He is, in effect, telling them that in fact, he is the only one who really does have that right. The false apostles certainly don't have that right. Actually, if he had not taken the steps which he did take toward their correction, he would have been woefully failing in his duty to them and the Lord. As their spiritual parent, he was obligated toward them, and had every right to do and say the things which had transpired.

As well, and going much beyond his *"right,"* he loved them dearly as any true Parent should love his Children. So, his position was twofold: A. His right as a spiritual parent toward them; and, B. His love for them.

ENLARGED

The phrase, *"Be ye also enlarged,"* simply means, *"Love me as I love you."* Give to me the same proofs of attachment which I have given you. As a spiritual parent, he loved them, and as his spiritual children, they should love him as well.

(14) "BE YE NOT UNEQUALLY YOKED TOGETHER WITH UNBELIEVERS: FOR WHAT FELLOWSHIP HATH RIGHTEOUSNESS WITH UNRIGHTEOUSNESS? AND WHAT COMMUNION HATH LIGHT WITH DARKNESS?"

There are two fellowships in the world, and only two, and all men belong either to the one or to the other. No one can belong to both and claim to be a Christian, for God only recognizes as His Children those who walk in fellowship with Him.

These fellowships are in opposition. The one is fellowship with God; the other is fellowship with the world. The world is the assemblage of all unconverted people.

Christians are the companions of the Living God. He dwells with them and walks about among them. Therefore, they must have no fellowship with the world, and only on this condition will God recognize them as His sons and daughters. God will not have worldlings in His family. He will not recognize those whose affections are in the world.

The world rejected and crucified His Beloved Son, and whoever will be the friend of the world must be the enemy of God.

THE UNEQUAL YOKE

The phrase, *"Be ye not unequally yoked together with unbelievers,"* sets forth a very important principle of Christian practice and behavior. It is not creating a set of religious taboos, nor is it laying down the Law. It is a clear statement of principle which is to govern the Christian as he walks on this earth.

In the first place, it speaks of two separate spheres of life based upon the Christian concept of life. That concept is clearly stated in

NOTES

II Cor. 5:17: *"Therefore if any man be in Christ, he is a new creature: old things are passed away; behold, all things are become new."*

One sphere is in Christ, and the other sphere is out of Christ. One is the sphere of old things, and one is the sphere of new things. One is the sphere of the Christ, and the other the sphere of the world.

It is exceedingly important to understand this conception of life, for it will affect the whole course of our Christian conduct.

IN KEEPING WITH THAT SPHERE

The Christian who belongs to the sphere of new things is to think, act, and live in keeping with that sphere. He is not to shuttle back and forth between one and the other. If he does, he will be destroying his experience and his influence.

When a Christian understands this, his life will take on new meaning and importance. He will see himself as one who belongs to Christ for high and holy things. It will be something more than a legalistic regulation of his life. Instead, it will be the high purpose of living for the best and noblest things.

There was an important reason why this should have to be true of the Corinthians. The world of their day was wholly idolatrous. To have followed Christ out of that kind of world meant a clear break. One could not be half-Christian and half-pagan. It required a clean-cut separation.

PRESENT OCCUPATION

There is also an important reason why the same should be true of modern Christians. The entire scheme of Christian experience is based on a new life. It is something more than a religious profession.

In fact, Christianity is not actually meant to be a better human life in the strict sense of the word. It is not something that seeks to improve the present world life, even though this is the direction taken by much of the modern Gospel. Actually, it is a new life that moves in a new sphere. Because this is so, we are warned not to lose our identity as Christians in this world. We are to maintain our intercourse in the world socially, commercially, and professionally, but without making common cause with the world's system.

The world system and the Christian system are two separate and distinct operations. One springs from the material realm and the other from the spiritual. One is controlled by the mastership of Satan and the other by the Mastership of Christ. One is conducive to the flesh and the other to the spirit.

For this reason we are cautioned and warned, *"Be ye not unequally yoked together with unbelievers."* The yoke would be unequal because it would link the new and the old, which must *not* be done.

PAUL'S STATEMENT HAS ITS ROOTS IN THE OLD TESTAMENT

God forbade Israel to make international alliances for defensive or even economic purposes — a practice common among other nations. Israel, as God's peculiar people, was to be distinctly different from the surrounding nations. Israel was warned a number of times against forming alliances (Ex. 23:32; Josh. 23:12).

The primary reason for this prohibition was spiritual. Treaty relationships would involve contact with pagan religions and call for toleration of pagan practices. This proved exactly what happened when Solomon adopted this strategy of interlinking international alliances.

Solomon avoided war during his lifetime; but the alliances were sealed by royal marriages. Through the foreign women Solomon married, his heart was turned from the Lord to idolatry, and pagan worship centers were established in Jerusalem itself (I Kings Chpt. 11).

GOD'S PROMISES

That the principle of nonalliance extended beyond international treaties to trading relationships may be inferred from II Chronicles 20:35-37. Jehoshaphat made a trade alliance with Israel's wicked king, Ahaziah. A Prophet came to Jehoshaphat and announced, *"Because you have made an alliance with Ahaziah, the Lord will destroy what you have made"* (II Chron. 20:37). A subsequent storm wrecked the ships provided for the joint venture.

Perhaps the most significant reason to reject alliances was found in God's Promises to Israel. God committed Himself to protect His people and to give them victory over their enemies when Israel was obedient and followed His Law (Deut. 7:12-24; 28:7). In a very basic sense, making an alliance in a search for security was failure to trust God.

NOTES

THE SAME GENERAL PRINCIPLE

This same general principle of nonalliance is restated in the New Testament, actually the very Scriptures we are now studying (II Cor. 6:14-18). Faith and unbelief can never be yoked together. Believers are to be separated (as far as alliances are concerned) from all that is unclean and to live lives characterized by Righteousness.

Exactly to what relationships this principle of separation should extend must be determined by each individual. But it is clear that all our relationships and associations are to be carefully scrutinized.

EXACTLY WHAT DOES IT MEAN TO BE UNEQUALLY YOKED?

Even though there are boundaries which should be clearly obvious to all true Believers, still, the individual Christian must be led by the Holy Spirit and not Law. This is the ideal and the only direction which really works. A long list of do's and don'ts constitute Law, which is not a part of the Christian experience; however, the Holy Spirit most definitely specifies *"do's and don'ts,"* but such are always tailored for the individual Believer. It is not a matter of particular Church Commandments. Nevertheless, perhaps the following will be of some help and should be the obvious of which we have already spoken:

1. Believers should not marry unbelievers. It is even unwise for two Believers to marry who are of different so-called Faiths.

However, if a Believer has in fact married an unbeliever, these statements should not be taken as a call to break up the marriage. That which is done cannot be undone. The Believer should work diligently to seek the Salvation of the unsaved mate, as no doubt they do.

2. The Believer should be very careful, earnestly seeking the leading of the Lord, before entering into any type of business arrangements with unbelievers and for the obvious reasons.

3. A Christian is to have no *"fellowship with the unfruitful works of darkness, but is rather to reprove them"* (Eph. 5:11). Amusements and pleasures that are entirely worldly, and sinful in their nature, and which cannot be brought

under Christian principles must be avoided. In fact, many amusements fall into this category.

In fact, the modern method of attempting to reach the youth by using worldly methods, such as so-called Christian rock music shows, displays either a desire to be like the world, or else an ignorance of the Word of God.

We do not reach people for the Cause of Christ by aping the world. People are reached whether they be young or old, by the Word of God being preached under the Anointing and convicting power of the Holy Spirit. To employ any other tactics, presents a spiritual travesty of the highest order. The idea of yoking up with unbelievers in order to win them to Christ is a direct contradiction of the Word of God, even as Paul speaks here.

The idea that we will win the youth by becoming *"rockers,"* is facetious to say the least, or the gamblers by gambling with them, or the drunks by drinking with them, etc.

4. Preachers must be very careful that they do not yoke up with particular religions which contradict the Word of God. For instance: In citywide Crusades, or any meetings for that matter, if I am to have Catholic Priests on my platform in association with me, that means I have compromised my message, or else they would not be there. For Preachers to send new converts to Churches with obviously unscriptural Doctrine, is tantamount to spiritual suicide. In effect, it is yoking up with unbelievers. Even though the *"unity"* thing may sound good to the ears of the world and to a carnal Church, it has no place in Godly Christian Service.

Even though we must at all times be kind and gracious to all, still, a line must be drawn when it comes to the Word of God. It must not be compromised in any degree.

PROPER DIRECTION

There is no principle of Christianity that is more important than that which is stated here by the Apostle; and none in which Christians are more in danger of erring, or in which they have more difficulty in determining the exact rule which they are to follow. The questions which arise are very important.

Are we to have no intercourse with the people of the world? Are we to cut loose from all friends who are not Christians? Are we to become monks and live a recluse and unsocial life? Are we never to mingle with the people of the world in business, in innocent recreation, or in the duties as citizens and as neighbors and friends?

It is important, therefore, in the highest degree to endeavour to ascertain what are the Principles on which the New Testament requires us to act in this matter. And in order to have a correct understanding of this, the following Principles may be suggested.

There is a large field of action, pursuit, principle, and thought over which infidelity, sin, heathenism, and the world as such, have the entire control. It is wholly without the range of Christian Principles and, in fact, stands opposed to Christian Principles. It pertains to a different kingdom, is conducted by different principles, and tends to destroy and annihilate the Kingdom of Christ. It cannot be reconciled with Christian Principles, and cannot be conformed to but by an entire violation of the Word of God. Here the prohibition of the New Testament is absolute and entire.

Christians are not to mingle with the people of the world in these things, and are not to partake of them.

THE SPIRIT OF THIS WORLD

That's the reason that Christians should be very careful of the Movies they view, whether in a theater or by television. Hollywood is given over completely to the spirit of the world, which should be overly obvious. In other words, if anything is obvious, that is. Consequently, they have no regard for Christian Principles, Biblical Morality, or anything that pertains to the Word of God. In fact, they are openly opposed to such, which again should be obvious. Consequently, why would a Christian desire to support such and be influenced by such? Once again, it is not a matter of making rules, but rather of being led of the Holy Spirit. If the Believer truly and sincerely desires to follow the Lord, openly seeks His leading and guidance, he won't have any trouble knowing what to do and what not to do. The Spirit of God will be very bold in giving direction. In fact, His giving direction is not the difficulty, but rather obedience on the part of the Believer.

This world is not our friend. Its spirit is totally antichrist, and as a result, we should be very careful about our involvement with its

NOTES

direction in any capacity. While as Christians we must be in the world, and in this world we are to let our light shine, still, we are to never be *of* the world. *"In"* the world, and *"of"* the world, are two different things altogether.

SEPARATION AND NOT ISOLATION

Many Christians have misunderstood the words of Paul, thinking he was demanding isolation. No so!

Jesus was with sinners; He ate with them and conversed with them. In fact, while He never condemned them with His speech or actions, still He never compromised His Principles of total Righteousness and Holiness.

Actually, Jesus contemplated that His people would have such intercourse with the world, and that in it they would do good. But in none of these is there to be any compromise of principle; in none to be any yielding to the opinions and practices that are contrary to the Word of God.

As we have already stated, if we isolate ourselves, we cannot let our light shine. So, it is not isolation that is demanded, but rather separation. As well, *"separation"* must be that which is guided and direction by the Holy Spirit and not legalism. Nevertheless, having said that, one can be certain that the Holy Spirit is not going to place a seal of approval upon that which is obviously wrong. In fact, in all of this, the boundaries are not difficult to locate, nor are they difficult to obey. Jesus plainly said, *"My yoke is easy, and My burden is light"* (Mat. 11:30).

THE YOKE

Inasmuch as Paul used the word *"yoke"* or *"yoked,"* let's see what the Bible says about this matter.

The yoke is a powerful symbol in the Bible. It refers to a cattle yoke, which bound animals to a plow, often together so they could work in tandem.

In the Old Testament, the yoke is often used figuratively of bondage and of the burden borne by slaves (Ex. 6:6-7; I Tim. 6:1). The image is used powerfully by the Prophets to portray the fate of disobedient generations (Isa. 10:27; Jer. 27:11; Ezek. 34:27).

The same image is used in unique ways in the New Testament. For example: Jesus' invitation attracts us, even to which we have already alluded: *"Come to Me, all you who are weary and burdened, and I will give you rest. Take My yoke upon you and learn from Me, for I am gentle and humble in heart, and you will find rest for your souls. For My yoke is easy and My burden is light"* (Mat. 11:28-30).

Is this a reference to the cattle yoke, a symbolic invitation to join Jesus and find in His strength release from our own unbearable burden?

Or is this Jesus' call to people to become His slaves and find in their new Master release from the crushing weight they experienced when Law was their master?

In either case, the theme and the invitation are central. Jesus calls, *"Come,"* and He promises us rest for our souls.

IN JESUS SOMETHING TOTALLY NEW

The Rabbis did not feel that being under the yoke of the Law was burdensome. In fact, it wasn't burdensome until the Pharisees added a myriad of man-devised laws to the original. Then it became very burdensome.

But with Christ came a fresh perspective. When some in the Early Church demanded that the Mosaic Law be imposed on Gentile converts, a Council at Jerusalem refused to comply. Law had been a burden, at least in the manner in which it had now been perverted by men, *"that neither we nor our fathers have been able to bear,"* Peter told the Council (Acts 15:10).

In Galatians, Paul develops his own distinctive grasp of the nature of Law. Because of the weakness in human nature, Law could neither justify a person nor provide power for a righteous life. All who try to live under the Law do, by that choice, turn their backs on the Principle of Grace, which alone brings *"the Righteousness for which we hope"* (Gal. 5:5). No wonder that Law offers no one freedom but instead is a *"yoke of slavery"* (Gal. 5:1).

That is the reason that Churches are never successful in their efforts to legislate Holiness. Such cannot be done, because it reverts to Law, which cannot accomplish the desired result. In fact, there is no *"Law"* in Christianity, at least not as we think of such according to the Old Testament pattern. That was all addressed by Christ, kept perfectly by Christ, and then its demands satisfied on the Cross of Calvary.

NOTES

Consequently, it is not a part of the Christian Faith, nor is it intended to be.

THE MODERN PRINCIPLE

In our Verse which we are studying, Paul speaks of being *"yoked together with unbelievers."* In such a relationship, there can be no agreement or harmony, and it is to be avoided. The verdict is prefigured in Old Testament Law, which forbids mating different kinds of animals (Lev. 19:19) and even plowing with an ox and a donkey together (Deut. 22:10).

Paul called his co-laborers in the Gospel *"true yoke-fellows"* (Phil. 4:3), but it is inconceivable that any enterprise calling for total unity of heart and purpose can mix Believers and unbelievers.

The extent to which this Principle is to be applied may be discovered by studying the issues Paul explores in his correspondence to the Believers in Corinth, especially in discussing lawsuits and marriage (I Cor. 6:1-6; 7:12-39).

FELLOWSHIP

The question, *"For what fellowship hath Righteousness with unrighteousness?"*, is posed so as to fall out to the obvious answer — none.

Five questions are propounded to reveal how unequal this yoking of the new and the old would be:

1. What fellowship hath Righteousness with unrighteousness?
2. What communion hath light with darkness?
3. What concord hath Christ with Belial?
4. What part hath he that believeth with an infidel?
5. What agreement hath the Temple of God with idols?

Here are two kingdoms of Truth and two spheres of light.

One Kingdom is described by the terms of Righteousness, Light, Christ, Believer, and the Temple of God. The other kingdom is described by the words unrighteousness, darkness, Belial, infidel, and idols.

These two kingdoms are so different and diverse that the Scriptures declare that between them there can be neither fellowship, communion, concord, part, or agreement. These words which the Scriptures employ indicate how impossible it is for the Christian to live in both spheres and retain his distinction. Any attempt to do so will cause a loss of personal blessing and influence.

SEPARATION

Everything in this world tends to revert unless protected by separation. To obtain the best roses, they must be separated by grafting and cultivation. If allowed to grow by themselves, they revert to scrawny and unlovely blooms. Likewise, the new life implanted in us must be protected and nurtured by the Principle of Separation. It must be lived in the sphere of new things. If we feed it on the things of the old life, it will starve and become ineffectual and we will revert ultimately to the old way of life.

WHAT TYPE OF FELLOWSHIP WAS PAUL ADDRESSING?

In the Old Testament, fellowship with the Lord could probably be described better by the *"Peace Offering."* This particular Sacrifice was a fellowship offering in two senses:

1. The Offering was made by those at Peace with God, in contrast with the Sin Offering which was designed to restore Peace.

Thus, the fellowship (Peace) Offering represented the blessing of wholeness, which comes through a right relationship with God.

2. The Offering was a Communion Sacrifice. That is, the Priests and the worshipers ate of this Offering. By this shared meal, the worshipers expressed their fellowship with each other and the bond of their common faith.

In the New Testament, Acts 2:42-47 gives us a beautiful picture of participation in the life of the believing community at Jerusalem. It portrays a mutual commitment to God that helps us sense the deeper meaning of fellowship.

"They devoted themselves to the Apostles' teaching and to the fellowship, to the breaking of bread and to prayer. Everyone was filled with awe, and many wonders and miraculous signs were done by the Apostles. All the Believers were together and had everything in common. Selling their possessions and goods, they gave to anyone as he had need. Every day they continued to meet together in the Temple Courts. They broke bread in their homes and ate together with glad and sincere hearts, praising

God and enjoying the favor of all the people. And the Lord added to their number daily those who were being saved."

A NEW REALITY

The Greek Philosophers chose the word *"koinonia,"* which means *"association," "fellowship,"* or *"participation"* — to depict the ideal of a harmonious secular society. But such a utopia has never been realized.

Sin always twists the reality of interpersonal relationships, leaving mankind hungry for the realization of its dreams. Consequently, there is hope only in that provided by the Lord.

Paul uses the same word *"koinonia"* some 15 times. However, his usage does not echo the Philosopher's dream. Instead, the New Testament affirms a new reality. God has called us *"into fellowship with His Son Jesus Christ"* (I Cor. 1:9).

We are drawn into relationship with God and participate in a unique fellowship won for us by the Blood of Christ (I Cor. 10:16). Everything in life is an expression of our mystical but real participation in all that Jesus is.

This mystical union is what overflows into our relationship with other Believers. Recognizing that others are also in Christ, we extend to them the right hand of fellowship (Gal. 2:9), sensing a partnership in the Gospel (Phil. 1:5). Even Christian giving must be understood in the context of fellowship. In this context, financial gifts become sharing, not actually *"giving"* (Rom. 15:26; II Cor. 8:4; 9:13; Heb. 13:16).

OUR MYSTICAL UNION WITH CHRIST

Paul's use of *"koinonia"* emphasizes the reality of our mystical union with Christ. But John in his First Epistle focuses on our experience of fellowship. John begins with the fact that fellowship *"is with the Father and with His Son, Jesus Christ"* (I Jn. 1:3). But we do not have (experience) fellowship with God if we walk in darkness.

Here darkness represents not sin but self-deceit, as light represents not sinlessness but dishonesty in our relationship with the Lord. When we do live honestly in our relationship with God, we have fellowship with God and with God's people as well (I Jn. 1:7).

The bonds that link us to Jesus bond us to one another. The fellowship we experience in the community of Faith goes far beyond friendship.

NOTES

In the New Testament, then, fellowship begins with our relationship with the Lord in mystical union with Jesus. We experience that union as we live close to the Lord and with honesty in our dealings with Him. Our union with Jesus is the basis for a bond with our fellow Christians. Because that bond is so vital and real, we can live with each other in an intimacy impossible in every other setting.

Understanding these things and especially our relationship with Christ, hopefully we can see how impossible it is to mix Righteousness with unrighteousness. The two have no fellowship, and in fact, can have no fellowship. They are total opposites.

RIGHTEOUSNESS

The Righteousness of the Believer is that which he has by Faith, the imputed Righteousness of Christ which is so pertinently mentioned in II Corinthians 5:21 in connection with Reconciliation: *"That we might be made the Righteousness of God in Him."* Due to God's verdict of acquittal, this quality belongs to the Believer.

Righteousness is *"moral rightness,"* but with the definition given by God. In other words, it is a perfect moral righteousness, to which man within himself and on his own, could never hope to attain. It is freely imputed to the believing sinner upon one's Faith in Christ.

UNRIGHTEOUSNESS

The unbeliever has no such acquittal from God. He is entirely that of unrighteousness, i.e., *"lawlessness."* That is God's verdict in regard to him. *"Thou hatest all workers of iniquity"* (Ps. 5:5; Rom. 8:7-8).

In Romans Chapter 2 Paul convicts all of the moralists, both Pagan and Jewish, by means of the very Law which they use to reform men; that Law (Law of Moses) condemns even the moralists as being full of lawlessness.

So, the *"lawful"* can have no fellowship with *"lawlessness."* The *"Righteous"* can have no fellowship with *"unrighteousness."* The idea of mixing the two, which many in the Church attempt to do, is presented here as a spiritual impossibility. There can be no basis for sharing between people who have yielded to the

Righteousness of God and those who are rebelling against it.

COMMUNION

The question, *"And what communion hath light with darkness?"*, adequately represents the impossibility of attempting to mix the two. Light and darkness in their nature have nothing in common, and likewise, Believers and unbelievers have nothing in common.

"Communion" has basically the same meaning as *"fellowship."*

The idea of Paul in using the words *"light"* and *"darkness,"* is that they exclude each other by their very nature; where the one is, it drives out the other.

LIGHT AND DARKNESS

God Himself is *"Light,"* and in Him is no darkness at all (I Jn. 1:5). Christ is the True Light (Jn. 1:9), the Light of the world (Jn. 8:12), and His Word is the Light of Life. This Light Power has entered the Believer and makes him a Child of Light (Mat. 5:14; Jn. 12:36; Eph. 5:8), and so the Believer walks in the Light (Jn. 12:35-36; I Jn. 1:7), although there is still some darkness in him because his old nature has not been entirely put off.

He is also a *"partaker of the inheritance of light"* (Col. 1:12). Light — the Divine, Saving Truth, concrete and full reality in God, Christ the Word; but always active, powerful, streaming out.

Its opposite is *"darkness,"* lie, falsehood, which are concreted in Satan, demons, the world; it is always active, powerful, seeking to envelop and to penetrate.

In the beginning God separated Light from darkness (Gen. 1:4), and this separation is typical also of Light and darkness in the spiritual sense. *"Ye were once darkness but are now Light in the Lord"* (Eph. 5:8).

"Have no fellowship with the unfruitful works of darkness" (Eph. 5:11).

The Devil and his Angels are *"the rulers of the darkness of this world"* (Eph. 6:12), all his followers walk in spiritual darkness (Jn. 3:19), and shall be cast into outer darkness unless they turn from Satan to Christ (Mat. 22:13; 25:30; II Pet. 2:17). Out of this spiritual darkness God has called the Believers (I Pet. 2:9); from it He delivered them (Col. 1:13). Light brings Life, darkness is death (Lenski).

NOTES

(15) "AND WHAT CONCORD HATH CHRIST WITH BELIAL? OR WHAT PART HATH HE THAT BELIEVETH WITH AN INFIDEL?"

Christ intended to set up a Kingdom that should be unlike the Kingdoms of this world. And He designed that His people should be governed by different principles from the people of this world.

CONCORD

The question, *"And what concord hath Christ with Belial?"*, presents another name for Satan. It means *"worthlessness."* It is the equivalent of the Hebrew *"beleyahal,"* which means *"without profit, worthlessness, wickedness"* (Deut. 13:13; Judg. 19:22; 20:13; I Sam. 1:16; 2:12; 10:27; 25:17, 25; 30:22; II Sam. 16:7; 20:1; etc.).

In every reference in the Old Testament, it is used of evil men being sons of Belial in the same sense the New Testament speaks of them being children of the wicked one and of the Devil (Mat. 13:38; Acts 13:10; I Jn. 3:10).

The word *"concord"* means *"harmony or accord."* The word does not occur elsewhere in the New Testament. It refers, properly, to the unison or harmony produced by musical instruments, where there is a chord.

The idea is, then, there is as much that is discordant between Christ and Belial as there is between instruments of music that produce only discordant and jarring sounds. It is the same as the left hand playing the G chord on the piano, and the right hand playing the C chord. There is no unison because there cannot be any unison.

What is there in common between Christ and Belial? Implying that Christians are governed by the Principles of Christ, and that they must follow the example of Christ as well.

The idea is, that the persons to whom Paul referred, the heathen, wicked, unbelieving world, were governed by the principles of Satan, and were *"taken captive by him at his will"* (II Tim. 2:26), and that Christians should be separate from the wicked world, as Christ was separate from all the feelings, purposes, and plans of Satan. He had no participation in them; He formed no union with them; and so it should be with the followers of the One in relation to the followers of the other.

BELIEVERS AND INFIDELS

The question, *"Or what part hath he that believeth with an infidel?"*, has reference to the fact that those who make a profession of Salvation, should resolve to separate themselves from the world. Salvation cannot exist where there is no separation. As well, those who are unwilling to forsake infidel companions, and find their chosen friends and pleasures among the people of God, can have no evidence that they actually are Christians.

The world, with all its wickedness and pleasures, must be forsaken, and there must be an effectual line drawn between the friends of God and the friends of sin.

"Infidel" in the Greek is *"apistou,"* and means *"an unbeliever."*

As we've already said, the idea here is not isolation, but rather that the Believer must not participate in the sins or the direction or attitude of the unbeliever, i.e., *"infidel."*

The Believer and the unbeliever are governed by different principles; have different feelings, are looking to different rewards, and are tending to a different destiny.

(16) "AND WHAT AGREEMENT HATH THE TEMPLE OF GOD WITH IDOLS? FOR YE ARE THE TEMPLE OF THE LIVING GOD; AS GOD HATH SAID, I WILL DWELL IN THEM, AND WALK IN THEM; AND I WILL BE THEIR GOD, AND THEY SHALL BE MY PEOPLE."

Paul is going to give us another reason in this Verse as to why the lack of separation is so devastating to the Believer. To be frank, the Holy Spirit through the Apostle, leaves no room for doubt respecting what God expects of Believers. We should read it carefully and read it prayerfully.

THE TEMPLE OF GOD

The question, *"And what agreement hath the Temple of God with idols?"*, now joins God and the Believer; consequently, we have the persons in their ultimate relation.

The point of the question here is misunderstood when it is said that nothing can be asked beyond God because He is supreme. In fact, the subject here is not God. The question is not one about God and idols. We have what is more than that already in Christ and Satan (Belial).

NOTES

This question is one about *"God's Sanctuary,"* God united with us.

It rises above Christ and the Believer, with the question pointing to the ultimate cause, Who is God. To such a one God Himself descends and dwells in Him. This is the ultimate. *"God's Sanctuary"* is absolutely for God Alone. *"I am the Lord thy God; thou shalt have no other gods before Me."* God's Ways have ever been directed toward union with man. Of course, this could only be done under certain conditions. A thrice holy God could not be in the presence of unholy man, without a mediator, or else man would die. So, the entirety of the Plan of God has been to provide this Mediator, of which the Great High Priest was a Type, with Jesus ultimately coming as the Mediator, the Fulfillment of all the Prophecies.

First of all, God dwelt between the Mercy Seat and the Cherubims in the Tabernacle. He said, *"And there I will meet with thee, and will commune with thee. . . ."* (Ex. 25:22).

Despite the Sacrifices which covered sin, the sin debt against man remained, because the blood of bulls and goats could not take away sin; consequently, God could not at that time reside in man as He presently does.

When Solomon's Temple was completed, the Lord transferred to that Edifice (I Ki. 8:11).

However, on the Day of Pentecost, due to the sin debt being settled at Calvary by the Lord Jesus Christ, upon Faith in Him, man is now judged by God as being 100 percent pure and clean; consequently, God could now literally come into this temple, i.e., man, and take up His abode in him. Inasmuch as God now dwells in us, Paul refers to Believers as *"the Temple of God"* (I Cor. 3:16).

For God to literally live within a person, which He does in the Person of the Holy Spirit, is without a doubt the greatest honor, the greatest privilege that anyone could ever know or have.

AGREEMENT

Paul has lifted this entire scenario to greater heights by the presentation of the sheer fact, that God literally lives with us, i.e., *"makes His abode within our hearts and lives."* As well, it is not a mere philosophic union, but rather a spiritual union, with the Holy Spirit in His Own mysterious way living in us, even as He once did in the Tabernacle and the Temple. Consequently, whatever is done is literally done in His Face. By the sheer fact that He lives with us, He becomes a party by His very Presence, to all that we do, be it good or evil. Even though He is a thrice holy God, still, He by His very Presence, becomes a part of us in all activity, even though He cannot be in agreement with that which is ungodly. And yet He must suffer the presence of evil, if evil is present. This is the reason for Paul's admonitions.

IDOLS

The idea is, that it is just as wrong for a Believer to mix and mingle with the infidel world, as it was to erect the image of a heathen god in the Temple of Jehovah during the old economy of God.

Idols are objects which God hates, and on which He cannot look but with abhorrence. The sense is, that for Christians to mingle with the sinful world — to partake of its pleasures, pursuits, and follies — is as detestable and hateful in the sight of God, as if His Temple in olden times, were profaned by erecting a deformed, shapeless, and senseless block in it as an object of worship. And assuredly, if Christians had such a sense of the abomination of mingling with the world, they would feel the obligation to be separate and pure.

Modern idols are anything that come between the Believer and God. It can be something unholy or something innocent; however, if it takes the place in one's affection which should belong only to God, it then becomes an idol. Why do you think John said, *"Little children, keep yourselves from idols"* (I Jn. 5:21)?

John wasn't addressing himself to figures made of wood, stone, or anything else for that matter, but rather, of the affections of the heart.

As an example, sports have become various idols to untold millions of Americans. Stars and Starlets of Hollywood, plus Entertainers of every description, fall into the same category. Money is another idol. To be frank, religion is the biggest idol of them all.

An idol is anything that replaces Christ, that vies for the supreme place in our hearts, which makes Christ lesser.

ACTUAL IDOLS?

Some feel that Paul is thinking only of actual idols as he does in I Corinthians Chapter 8 where he speaks about attending idol's feasts, etc. However, that is not the case here.

NOTES

He tells us that he is speaking of *"all defilement of flesh and spirit"* and of its opposite, *"holiness in God's fear." "Idols"* is a concrete expression for this double defilement; this expression at the same time indicates the seriousness of such defilement.

No, Paul is speaking here of anything which attempts to replace Christ.

LIVING GOD

The phrase, *"For ye are the Temple of the Living God,"* again points to the fact that Paul is not speaking of a mere philosophy, but rather God Who is alive, and, consequently, works, moves, acts, leads, guides, judges, etc. The implication is, that even though He is patient, longsuffering, kind and gracious, still, He will not tolerate willful wrongdoing in His Temple forever. If we insist upon attempting to mix unrighteousness with Righteousness, or idols with God, there will be repercussions. We should well understand that!

As an example, the vignette of the Ark of the Covenant being placed in Dagon's Temple shows how incongruous it would be to combine the two (I Sam. 5:1-5). When the two are in fact combined, as it is in the hearts and lives of many Believers, ultimately one or the other will have to go — but not until there has been a fierce struggle. To be sure, in this struggle, the Temple is going to be damaged, and at times, severely.

DWELLING

The phrase, *"As God hath said, I will dwell in them,"* is taken in part from Exodus 29:45; Leviticus 26:12; and Ezekiel 37:27. They are not literally quoted, but Paul has put together the substance of what occurs in several places.

The word *"dwell"* in both Hebrew and Greek suggests being in a residence. As it is used in the Old Testament, it most often is used in the ordinary sense of dwelling or living in a particular city or place. But the Old Testament raises a theological question, which the New Testament answers in an exciting way.

The Old Testament word in the Hebrew is *"yasab,"* and means *"to sit," "to remain,"* or *"to dwell."* It is found some 1,090 times in the Old

Testament; when used of God, it usually indicates His residence in the Heavens.

As Solomon asks: *"Will God really dwell on earth? The Heavens, even the highest Heaven, cannot contain You. How much less this Temple I have built!"* (I Ki. 8:27).

The other Hebrew word translated *"dwell"* is *"sakan."* This word occurs 129 times and suggests a permanent stay. It is used 43 times with God as the subject and emphasizes His Faithfulness to His Commitments.

The Tabernacle and the Temple were constructed, as stated, as Divine dwelling places so that God's people might always approach Him (Ex. 25:8; 29:45-46; II Chron. 6:1). Still, God announces, *"I live* (sakan) *in a high and holy place, but also with him who is contrite and lowly in spirit"* (Isa. 57:15).

THE NEW TESTAMENT

It is in the New Testament that this last theme is developed. And in the New Testament the emphasis shifts from God dwelling *with* His people to His dwelling *in* them.

Two Greek words are used in this special sense. *"Enoikeo,"* meaning *"to take up residence,"* is used in this connection in four of its five occurrences in the New Testament (Rom. 8:11; II Cor. 6:16; Col. 3:16; II Tim. 1:14).

The New Testament tells us that God now settles down in the hearts of His people. It is no longer the Old Testament Temple, nor is it the modern Church building, but it is the personality of the Believer that is the residence filled with God's Living Presence.

But there is another word translated *"dwell"* in the New Testament. It is *"katoikeo."* The word means *"to establish permanent residence,"* implying a permanence that stands in contrast to the making of occasional visits.

In the Gospels this word is used in its ordinary sense, as when it is said that one dwells in Nazareth (Mat. 2:23) or Jerusalem (Lk. 13:4). But in the Epistles the word has special theological significance.

Through Faith, Christ takes up permanent residence in our hearts (Eph. 3:17). *"In Christ all the fullness of the Deity lives* (katoikeo) *in bodily form, and you have been given fullness in Christ"* (Col. 2:9-10).

Consequently, the permanent, Living Presence of Jesus and His Spirit (James 4:5) is

NOTES

now established in the hearts of His people (Richards).

WALK

The phrase, *"And walk in them,"* refers to activity. Of course, this is speaking of the Person of the Holy Spirit.

He has come into our lives, as a result of our Salvation; however, He has come for a specific purpose. The following is only a small portion of what He does:

1. First of all, He produces Spiritual Life within us. This is the energy of God which consistently and continually flows in, through, and from the Believer, as a result of the quickening Power of the Spirit (Rom. 8:10).
2. He quickens our mortals bodies, which means He also gives aid and help to the physical man (Rom. 8:11).
3. He mortifies the deeds of the body, which means that He gives us victory over all sin, that is if we properly understand what Christ did for us at Calvary and the Resurrection which is outlined in Romans Chapter 6 (Rom. 8:13).
4. He leads us through this life's journey according to the Will of the Father, telling us what we should do and should not do (Rom. 8:14).
5. He bears witness with our spirit, that we are Children of God. This is a beautiful assurance that stays with the Believer constantly (Rom. 8:16).
6. He helps our infirmities, which speaks of physical, mental, and even moral weaknesses or flaws (Rom. 8:26).
7. He makes intercession for the Saints according to the Will of God. This means to act as an agent or manager in all phases of Salvation and dealings with God. As well, He is in our hearts and lives not to do our will, but to carry out the Will of God as it pertains to us (Rom. 8:27).
8. He is our Comforter and Helper in all things, which we desperately need (Jn. 16:7).
9. He guides us into all Truth (Jn. 16:13).
10. He shows us things to come (Jn. 16:13).
11. He glorifies Christ within us, which means to make real to us all the benefits of Calvary and the Resurrection (Jn. 16:14).

Those things constitute His *"walk,"* plus many more we have not named. Nevertheless, I think it should be obvious as to the absolute necessity of His Presence.

"Walk" in the Greek is *"emperipateo,"* and means *"for the sake of"* and *"to give self wholly to."* Isn't that beautiful!

THEIR GOD

The phrase, *"And I will be their God,"* is said in the realm of communion, fellowship, companionship, strength, help, protection, etc.

In essence, He is saying that He will not only be the God Whom they worship, but the God Who will protect and bless them. I will take them under My peculiar protection, and they shall enjoy My favor.

The Holy Spirit in using Paul to say these things, is to impress upon Believers the solemnity and importance of the Truth that God dwells among them and with them; that they were under His care and protection; that they belong to Him, and that they, therefore, should be separate from the world.

The idea is, that He is our God, meaning that we will have no other gods (idols) before Him, in connection with Him, or beside Him. Let's look at this a little closer.

The Prophet Samuel said to Israel at one particular time, *"If ye do return unto the Lord with all your hearts, then put away the strange gods and Ashtaroth from among you, and prepare your hearts unto the Lord, and serve Him only: and He will deliver you out of the hand of the Philistines"* (I Sam. 7:3).

One should notice the phrase, *"Serve Him only,"* which means, that Israel was attempting to serve both God and idols. In fact, this is the problem that every single Believer faces constantly.

If Satan cannot get the Believer to throw the Lord over completely, he will attempt to bring other things in, which will be conjunction with the Lord. In other words, the modern Believer has the same problem as Israel of old, in that too often we serve both the Lord and idols. We don't think of it in that way, but that is exactly what is happening. This can fall into the category of almost anything, especially if we allow it to dominate us, and to take the place within our heart which only God should occupy.

As we have already briefly mentioned, of all the things we could name, Religion is probably the greatest culprit of all. People serve God and their Church, they serve God and a particular Doctrine. They serve God and their Denomination, etc. Satan uses Religion to such a great extent, because it is difficult for many people to distinguish between the Lord and Religion, thinking that both are one and the same. They are not!

NOTES

Look at the Catholic Church for instance. Catholics are taught to serve the Church, be faithful to the Church, and they will be saved. Well of course, there is no Salvation in the Church, which in that capacity is no more than a man-devised organization. So, Catholics serve both God and a Church, which of course, God cannot accept. Regrettably, that goes for quite a number of Protestant Denominations as well.

When the Holy Spirit said through Paul, *"I will be their God,"* He meant, *"all in all,"* in effect, *"everything."*

We need look no further, because He supplies everything we need. In fact, He is the only One Who can supply everything, so why look elsewhere?

MY PEOPLE

The phrase, *"And they shall be My people,"* refers to us giving our all to Him, because He has given His all to us.

It is in this context that He spoke to Israel long centuries ago, and speaks accordingly to us today, *"For thou shalt worship no other god: for the Lord, Whose Name is Jealous, is a jealous God"* (Ex. 34:14).

As well, that's the reason that the Holy Spirit through James said, *"The Spirit that dwelleth in us lusteth to envy"* (James 4:5).

What do the words *"lusteth to envy"* mean? We are not accustomed to linking these two words *"lusteth"* and *"envy"* to the Holy Spirit. But here it is done, and correctly.

The word *"lusteth"* is the translation of a Greek word that means *"to earnestly or passionately desire."* The indwelling Holy Spirit possessing all the potential power and help a Saint needs, has a passionate desire to the point of envy. Of what is He envious, and what does He passionately desire? The context makes this clear.

It is speaking of Christians who are not living in separation from the world and unto God. In effect, they are committing spiritual adultery and playing false with their Lord and because of their fellowshipping with the world.

They are allowing evil natures to control them. Consequently, the Holy Spirit is envious of any control which that fallen nature might have over the Believer, and passionately desires Himself, to control our thoughts, words, and deeds. He is desirous of having the Believer depend upon Him for His Ministry to him, in order that He might discharge His responsibility to the One Who sent Him, namely, that of causing the Believer to grow in his Christian Life.

(17) "WHEREFORE COME OUT FROM AMONG THEM, AND BE YE SEPARATE, SAITH THE LORD, AND TOUCH NOT THE UNCLEAN THING: AND I WILL RECEIVE YOU,"

The Holy Spirit through the Apostle now gives the requirements which the Believer should heed diligently. The statements here are emphatic; therefore, it means, this is the way it is, and it's not going to change.

COME OUT

The phrase, *"Wherefore come out from among them,"* refers to idolaters and unbelievers.

These words are taken, with a slight change, from Isaiah 52:11. They are there applied to the Jews in Babylon, and are a solemn call which God makes on them to leave this place of exile, to come out from among the idolaters of that city, and return to their own land.

Babylon, in the Scriptures, is the emblem of whatever is proud, arrogant, wicked, and opposed to God; and Paul, therefore, applies the words here with great beauty and force to illustrate the duty of Christians in separating themselves from a vain, idolatrous, and wicked world.

It also has to do with all types of Religions which are not of God, and of which Babylon was also a symbol. When one comes to Christ, they must come out totally and completely from the Religions of the world, from false doctrine, from false interpretations of the Bible, from all ways which are not strictly Biblical.

For instance, in 1982 the Lord spoke to my heart concerning a Message to the Catholics. At that time our Telecast was aired over a great part of the world, translated into several languages. In fact, it pretty much covered Central and South America, which is Catholic dominated, and of course, the United States and

NOTES

Canada, which also have a heavy concentration of Catholics.

CATHOLIC CHARISMATICS

This was the heyday of Catholic Charismatics, i.e., those who had been Baptized with the Holy Spirit with the evidence of speaking with other tongues, but were still in the Catholic Church.

The Lord told me to say two things in my Message to these people:

1. The just shall live by Faith, which means Faith in Christ exclusively, in other words, that the Church cannot save.
2. Catholics who had truly given their hearts to the Lord, must come out of that unscriptural system.

I did my best to be as diplomatic as possible, but I little realized before the fact as to the furor that my Message would cause. It seemed like the whole world exploded, when I began to preach over our Telecast what I believed the Lord had given to me.

Almost all the Preachers of that day of the Pentecostal and Charismatic persuasion, at least those in any position of Leadership, had advised the Catholic Charismatics the very opposite of what I was preaching. In other words, they told them to stay in the Catholic Church.

I sometimes think that most Preachers don't know too much about the Bible, or else they have little interest in following its direction. How can the Holy Spirit lead one into all Truth, if one is immersed in error?

As well, it does not apply merely to Catholics, but to everyone for that matter. He leads us into Truth, not error, not falsehood, not that which is obviously wrong, as should be overly obvious.

The animosity toward me regarding my stand was venomous to say the least. To be frank, I think there was greater anger against me from my so-called Pentecostal and Charismatic friends than even the Catholics themselves.

However, despite that particular attitude, we saw many thousands of Catholics brought to a saving knowledge of Jesus Christ, and continue to do so unto this hour.

THE PENTECOSTAL WAY

As we are dealing with this particular subject, perhaps it would be profitable to make another statement also.

I have used the word *"Charismatics,"* which has several different meanings; however, as it relates to the Church, it simply refers to people of particular religious persuasions other than Pentecostal, who have been Baptized with the Holy Spirit, with the evidence of speaking with other tongues. In other words, it speaks of Baptists, Methodists, Nazarenes, Lutherans, Catholics, etc. Taken to its conclusion, the word means that Baptists, Methodists, etc., retain most if not all their beliefs respecting these particular Denominations, with one exception, that they have been Baptized with the Holy Spirit, with the evidence of speaking with other tongues (Acts 2:4).

For the most part, that as well is wrong. Even though there are some few Charismatic Churches, which are Biblically straight, for the most part, many of their Doctrines are unscriptural.

THE BAPTISM WITH THE HOLY SPIRIT

As someone has well said, Salvation separates people from the world, while the Baptism with the Holy Spirit, separates them from cold, formal, dead religion. That is true, and hanging on to some of that dead, cold religion, hinders the Holy Spirit greatly.

First of all, the Spirit-filled and Spirit-led life, is Biblical, and in fact, the only lifestyle that is Biblical. As well, if one is still holding on to unscriptural Doctrines, the truly Spirit-filled life cannot function as it should.

What do we mean by the Spirit-filled life?

One need only read and study the Book of Acts, and the Epistles to understand what the Spirit-filled life actually is. In every manner, every way, if what we have now does not coincide with that which is given to us in the Book of Acts, then something is wrong.

There was a time when all, I suppose, of the Pentecostal Denominations attempted to follow that pattern, but regrettably, most of these particular Denominations at present, and for all practical purposes, have pretty much abandoned the direction they once maintained. In other words, their pattern is not the Book of Acts, or the Spirit-filled life. While there are certainly exceptions in these particular ranks, for the most part, it is as I have said.

NOTES

WHAT IS THE SPIRIT-FILLED LIFE?

For the most part, it was prophesied by Joel and quoted by Peter on the Day of Pentecost. In brief, it is as follows:

1. First of all, the Spirit-filled Life is a sign to the world, especially as it relates to the *"Latter Rain"* that time is about up, we are nearing the end of this Dispensation, and Jesus is about to come (Joel 2:1).

2. It is a Life of fasting (not only of food occasionally, but as well of separation from the world), prayer, supplication and intercession for a lost world (Joel 2:12-17).

3. It is a Life of gladness and rejoicing in the Lord Jesus Christ (Joel 2:21-27). There is no joy on the face of the earth, no gladness on the face of the earth, like that of the Spirit-filled life.

4. It is a Life that believes in the poured-out Spirit on all flesh, and which attempts to proclaim it to the entirety of the world. Due to the Holy Spirit, Who glorifies Christ, it is the Message of Evangelism and of Missions (Joel 2:28-29).

5. It is a Life that believes in signs, wonders, and miracles, in other words, that God is doing great things today among His people (Joel 2:30).

6. It is a Life which proclaims the last-day events, of the Rapture of the Church, the rise of the Antichrist, and the Second Coming of the Lord (Joel 2:31).

7. It is a Life that proclaims the Good News of Salvation, that *"Whosoever shall call on the Name of the Lord shall be saved"* (Joel 2:32). It believes that Jesus died for all, and will save all who will come to Him.

In brief, that is the Spirit-filled Life. As stated, it is what Peter quoted on the Day of Pentecost (Acts 2:16-21), and what characterizes the Book of Acts. If the Believer has anything less, than he is not living the Spirit-filled Life, as the Lord intends.

SEPARATION

The phrase, *"And be ye separate, saith the Lord,"* means separate from the world, and all its corrupting influences.

However, and as we have already said, this separation does not mean isolation, and neither does it mean segregation.

To live a separated life does not mean that we have to segregate ourselves from the world. One may move among one's fellowmen in all the necessary and proper social, professional, and commercial contacts, but still retain his identity and integrity as a Christian. One can live in one's sphere and still be living by the other sphere. One can walk in the world and still walk as a Christian.

Separate in the Greek is *"aphorizo,"* and means *"to set off by boundary, by limit, to exclude certain things."* It also means, *"to appoint, decree and specify."*

So, there are certain things that the Lord does not want the Believer to do, certain places He does not want the Believer to go, certain things He does not want the Believer to watch, and certain things He does not want the Believer to engage. The idea here is not rules and regulations, but rather being *"led by the Spirit."* Rules and regulations tend toward legalism, and have really never helped anyone. To be led by the Spirit is always personal, total, complete, and right for the particular individual.

WHAT THE BIBLE SAYS ABOUT SEPARATION

"Separation" is a word used in some Christian communities in ways that may or may not square with its Biblical intent. One of our problems in building a contemporary concept of separation is rooted in the fact that different Hebrew and Greek terms are translated by the same English word.

Another problem is that factors shaping the life of Believers in one era may be dramatically different from those in another.

THE HEBREW WORDS

A number of different Hebrew words and expressions are translated *"separate"* and *"separation"* in the Old Testament. In some places the verb simply means *"to part"* (II Sam. 14:6). In I Kings 5:9 the thought is one of being discharged, as from a contract or military service. Sometimes the Hebrew simply means *"to be scattered"* (Jer. 52:8; Ezek. 46:18).

Two Old Testament Passages (II Ki. 15:5; II Chron. 26:21), speaking of the isolation of a leprous ruler, use a word (*"hapsit"*) found only in these two places in the Old Testament.

NOTES

There are three other Hebrew words that have special significance. They are *"badal," "parad,"* and *"nazar."*

TO SEPARATE

"Badal" means *"to separate"* (i.e., to remove something from something else and thus to make a distinction between them).

This is the word used in Genesis Chapter 1, as the Creator established order in the universe, dividing day from night, land from sea, the waters on the earth from the waters above. The word is also often used of Israel's separation from other nations (Ezra 6:21; 9:1; Neh. 9:2).

In a significant sense, Israel was set apart from all other people, the critical distinction being that God had chosen Israel and had entered into Covenant relationship with them.

SET APART

Separation is also at the root of many of Israel's ritual practices and laws: *"I am the Lord your God, Who has set you apart from the nations. You must therefore make a distinction between clean and unclean animals and between unclean and clean birds"* (Lev. 20:24-25).

In this Passage, both *"set apart"* and *"make a distinction"* are *"badal."* Thus, the peculiar practices designated by God to Israel, served to constantly remind God's people that they were different — because of their relationship with Him.

The same kind of distinction existed within Israel, as God consecrated the Levites, setting them apart from the other Tribes to serve Him in worship (Num. 16:9; Deut. 10:8; I Ki. 8:53; I Chron. 23:13).

TO DIVIDE — TO ABSTAIN FROM

The Hebrew word *"parad"* tends toward physical description. It means *"to separate"* or *"to divide,"* as rivers separate into streams. It is also used in Proverbs to speak of divisive actions that separate friends.

The last Hebrew word *"Nazar"* means *"to separate"* and is often followed by a preposition that gives it the meaning *"to abstain from"* or *"to keep away from."* In Leviticus 15:31, even without this preposition, the meaning is clear:

"You must keep the Israelites separate from things that make them unclean, so they will not

die in their uncleanness for defiling My Dwelling Place, which is among them."

This Hebrew word, used in another Passage with another preposition, suggests *"separation to."* This Passage (Num. 6:1-21) speaks of consecration to the Lord on the part of those who took the special Nazarite vow. The vow involved refraining from specific things as an act of special devotion to the Lord.

THE CONTEXT OF SEPARATION IN THE OLD TESTAMENT

In the Old Testament, the believing community existed as a nation that was socially and geographically separated from its Pagan neighbors. The Mosaic Law regulated the total lifestyle of Israel, not simply its religious practices. Many aspects of Israelite life were neither *"right"* nor *"wrong"* morally but were still regulated by Old Testament Statutes and Laws.

As the Passages quoted above make clear, the reason for the regulations that serve to set Israel apart from other nations was a spiritual one. Israel was different. Israel had been called into a relationship with the Lord God, and both Israel and the nations around her had to be constantly reminded of the distinction that God Himself had made.

THE GREEK WORDS IN THE NEW TESTAMENT

Two Greek words are found in the New Testament which read *"separate"* or *"separation."* They are *"chorizo"* and *"aphorizo."*

TO SEPARATE OR TO DIVIDE

"Chorizo" means *"to separate"* or *"to divide,"* and is often used in the sense of separating oneself. When physical separation is in view, it may speak of being parted or of departing.

But there are a number of figurative uses as well. God's commitment to us is so great that nothing imaginable can separate us from the Love of Christ (Rom. 8:35, 38-39).

God's Plan for marriage calls for a similar commitment. No one should separate those so joined (Mat. 19:6; Mk. 10:9).

A related word (choris) is also used in Ephesians 2:12, which describes the unsaved Gentile as one who is separated from Christ.

NOTES

TO SET APART, OR SEPARATE

"Aphorizo" means *"to set apart, or separate."* It is a strong term, often carrying with it an implication of Divine determination. Thus, God will act at history's end to separate the evil and the good (Mat. 13:49; 25:32). This is the word Paul used when rebuking Peter for wrongfully separating himself from Gentile Believers when Jewish Brothers visited Antioch (Gal. 2:12).

This is also the word found in II Corinthians 6:17, the Verse of our study. Appealing to the principle of separation from unbelieving nations around Israel, Paul quoted the Old Testament (Isa. 52:11), and said, *"Come out from among them and be separate."* The context makes the issue very clear. Paul was writing specifically about yoked relationships with unbelievers.

THE CONTEXT OF SEPARATION IN THE NEW TESTAMENT

The Believing Community of the New Testament era exists as clusters of Believers within the larger, secular society. It is clear that the separation by total lifestyle appropriate for Israel may not be appropriate for those who must live as members of differing cultures. In fact, separating elements of the Law were done away with when the Old Covenant was superseded by the New Covenant at Christ's Death and Resurrection.

What then can we carry over from Old Testament Principle into New Testament Practice?

Paul says specifically that being yoked with unbelievers is a violation of the ancient separation principle. But in an earlier letter to the Corinthians he clarified the idea of separation: they were to associate with the immoral and ungodly of the world, not to withdraw from them (I Cor. 5:9-13).

As we have stated, separation does not imply isolation of the Christian from his or her culture and society, nor from the lost neighbor.

OUR SEPARATION IS TO GOD

Certainly the principle of separation to God has contemporary application to the Christian. But we must apply this principle with great care. As Jesus' representatives in the world, we are called to live within our society and in the company of sinful people.

In its most significant sense, our separation is to God.

NOTES

We are to be different from those around us, not withdrawn from them. The distinction that God seeks to draw in and through our lives is simply that we are to walk as Jesus walked when He was here (I Jn. 2:6). As Jesus sought and helped the lost, so will we. As Jesus suffered the accusations of those who criticized His association with the sinners of His day, so we may suffer the accusations of the religious among us when we reach out to draw others with and to God's Love.

So the idea is, as the Holy Spirit proclaims it: Separation from the world's system, and unto God.

THE UNCLEAN

The phrase, *"And touch not the unclean thing,"* refers to Christians avoiding all unholy contact with a vain and polluted world. The idea is, that the Standard of the Believer is totally different than that of the unbeliever.

"Unclean" in the Greek is *"akathartos,"* and means that which is *"impure, lewd, foul."*

The Scriptures nowhere make a list of what is *"unclean,"* but they define most perfectly: everything in body and in spirit that is contrary to our Righteousness in Christ, to the Light (Word), to Christ, to our Faith to ourselves as the living Sanctuary of God.

The *"unclean thing"* as the Holy Spirit uses the phrase through Paul, refers by and large to that which is *"immoral."* In other words, the state of *"morals."*

THE TEN COMMANDMENTS

Going back to Exodus Chapter 20, one finds God's Standard of morality. It is the *"Ten Commandments."* It covers every moral aspect of society, of the human heart, and of interpersonal relationships between human beings. It is and they are as follows:

1. Thou shalt have no other gods before Me: This refers to the idols of which Paul has mentioned in these Passages.

2. Thou shalt not make unto thee any graven image: this refers not only to the idols carved by hand, but as well can definitely refer to statues of Saints, etc.

3. Thou shalt not take the Name of the Lord thy God in vain: This speaks of any and all profanity, or any irreverent use of the Name of God, the Lord Jesus Christ, or the Holy Spirit.

4. Remember the Sabbath Day, to keep it holy: This Commandment was not brought over into the New Testament. Actually, it is the only one which does not have a moral content.

But yet, inasmuch as the Sabbath was a day of rest, and actually pointed to Jesus Who would in fact give us spiritual rest, one could bring this Commandment over into the great Plan of Salvation as it regards Redemption. When we found Jesus, we found *"rest"* from all of our struggle otherwise to be what we ought to be.

5. Honor thy Father and thy Mother: The love we should have for our parents is supposed to parrot the love we have for God. Actually, the symbolism of the parents is to refer to our Heavenly Father.

6. Thou shalt not kill: The word *"kill"* should actually have been translated *"murder."* The sanctity of life is ever held up in the Word of God, and because it is given by God. Inasmuch as man is made in the *"Image of God,"* he is to be respected accordingly. As well, this Commandment also covers the murder of one's reputation or influence by gossip, slander, or whispering.

7. Thou shalt not commit adultery: This is obvious respecting its moral content.

8. Thou shalt not steal: That which does not belong to us is to be left alone.

9. Thou shalt not bear false witness against thy neighbor: Lying is immoral!

10. Thou shalt not covet: This covers every unholy desire of the human heart.

These Commandments are given in the sense of the positive. In other words, they are given as though man is keeping them, even though he hasn't. Consequently, God is saying that this was the moral way and moral right before man fell. As well, his fall has not changed that moral right and moral way.

These Commandments as they are, point to the *"clean,"* while the breaking of them, points to the *"unclean."* To say it another way, it means that one who keeps them is *"clean,"* while one who breaks them is *"unclean."*

However, it must be quickly said, that these Commandments cannot be kept, at least all of them, and in spirit any of them, except in Christ. We are made clean by Christ, and kept clean by Christ. That is the only way, there is no other! The Believer can only keep these

Commandments as Christ keeps them through him. There is no other way. That means the unbeliever cannot keep them at all.

TOUCH

"Touch" in the Greek is *"haptomai,"* and means *"to attach oneself to — in many implied relations."*

The idea is, that we not only not involve ourselves in that which is spiritually unclean, but as well, that we do not even *"touch"* those types of things. It is not actually speaking of a physical *"touch,"* even though it could definitely refer to that, but that we don't have anything to do with such situations in any capacity. They don't enter our minds; they are not a part of our thinking; they have no part or place in us; they are totally foreign to our thinking and way of doing things. We don't *"touch"* them in any capacity, whether with the thought life, personal life, or action life.

Israel of old was not even to discuss the doings of the wicked, and modern Believers would do well to take a page from their book. To discuss that which is ungodly, unholy, immoral, can cause a mental attachment to be formed. So, Christians who gossip about the wrongdoing of others, are in effect, *"touching the unclean thing,"* which in some cases, makes them just as guilty as the one of whom they speak.

I WILL RECEIVE YOU

The phrase, *"And I will receive you,"* at the same time means that if the person disobeys what the Lord has said, that He will not receive us.

The Lord receiving those who claim His Name, cannot be done until they are separated from an idolatrous and wicked world. The fact of their being received by God, and recognized as His Children, depend on their coming out from the world system.

These words, with the Verse following, though used evidently somewhat in the form of a quotation by Paul, yet are not to be found in any single place in the Old Testament. In II Samuel 7:14, God says of Solomon, *"I will be his Father, and he shall be My son."* In Jeremiah 31:9, God says, *"For I am a Father to Israel, and Ephraim is My firstborn."*

It could well be the case that Paul had such Passages in his eye, yet he doubtless designed rather to express the general sense of the Promises of the Old Testament than to quote any single Passage.

NOTES

Or it may be, that Paul is speaking directly of Inspiration. He was inspired as well as the Prophets; and it may be that he meant to communicate a Promise directly from God. Grotius supposes that it was not taken from any particular place in the Old Testament, but was a part of a Hymn that was in use among the Hebrews.

It is more fully explained in the next Verse exactly as to what it means for the Lord to *"receive us."*

(18) "AND WILL BE A FATHER UNTO YOU, AND YE SHALL BE MY SONS AND DAUGHTERS, SAITH THE LORD ALMIGHTY."

This Scripture is freighted with Glory, and contains a Promise not found in any of the other Epistles.

FATHER

The phrase, *"And will be a Father unto you,"* means that God will assume all responsibility of parental concern and give Himself to the eternal care of His family (Mat. 7:11; Eph. 3:14).

Earthly parents may lack the power and the means to supply all things for their families, but this is not true of God Who owns all and rules all.

A Father is the protector, counsellor, and guide of his children. He instructs them, provides for them, and counsels them in time of perplexity. No relation is more tender than this.

In accordance with this, God says, that He will be to His people their Protector, Counsellor, Guide, and Friend. He will cherish towards them the feelings of a Father; He will provide for them, He will acknowledge them as His Children. No higher honor can be conferred on mortals than to be adopted into the Family of God, and to be permitted to call the Most High, *"our Heavenly Father."*

SONS AND DAUGHTERS

The phrase, *"And ye shall be My sons and daughters,"* constitutes the most elevated rank that one could ever have — that of being the sons and the daughters of the Lord Almighty.

Yet this is the common appellation by which God addresses His people; and the most humble in rank, the most poor and ignorant of His friends on earth, the most despised among men, may reflect that they are the children of the Ever-Living God, and have the Maker of the heavens and the earth as their Father and their Eternal Friend. How poor are all the honors of the world compared to this! How this trivializes all other so-called awards and honors! The very greatest thing that anyone could ever say is *"I am a son or daughter of the Lord!"*

JEHOVAH SHADDAI

The phrase, *"Saith the Lord Almighty,"* presents the greatest Promise, at least in this capacity, found in the Epistles.

The appellative or title, *"Lord Almighty,"* actually means *"Jehovah Shaddai,"* or *"El Shaddai."* It occurs nowhere else in the New Testament except in the Book of Revelation (Rev. 1:8; 4:8; 11:17; 15:3; 16:7, 14; 19:6, 15; 21:22).

The Hebrew words *"shad"* means *"a woman's breast."* The title *"Shaddai"* suggests love and unfailing benevolence. Satan had his imitation of this in Diana of the Ephesians (Acts Chpt. 19), who was pictured as a many-breasted divinity.

"Lord Almighty" or *"El Shaddai,"* means One Who has all Power and is applied to God in contradistinction from idols that are weak and powerless. God is able to protect His people, to provide for His people, and they who put their trust in Him shall never be confounded. What has he to fear who has a Friend of such Almighty Power?

A CHILD OF GOD

What an estimable privilege it is to be a Believer! To be a Child of God! To feel that He is a Father and a Friend! To feel that though we may be forsaken by all others, though poor and despised, yet there is One Who never forsakes, One Who never forgets that He has sons and daughters dependent on Him, and who need His constant care!

Compared with that, how small the honor of being permitted to call the rich our friends, or to be regarded as the sons or daughters of Nobles and of Princes! Let the Christian then most highly prize his privileges, and feel that he is raised above all the elevations of rank and honor which this world can bestow.

All these shall fade away, and the highest and the lowest shall meet on the same level in the grave, and alike return to dust. But the elevation of the Child of God shall only begin to be visible and appreciated when all other honors fade away.

NOTES

THIS, LET US SEEK

Let all seek to become the sons and daughters of the Lord Almighty. Let us aspire to this rather than to earthly honors; let us seek this rather than to be numbered with the rich and the great.

All cannot be honored in this world, and few are they who can be regarded as belonging to elevated ranks here. But all may be the Children of the Living God, and be permitted to call the Lord Almighty their Father and their Friend.

Oh! If men could as easily be permitted to call themselves the sons of monarchs and princes; if they as easily be admitted to the palaces of the great, and sit down at their tables, as they can enter Heaven, how greatly would they embrace it! And yet how poor and paltry would be such honor and pleasure compared with that of feeling and knowing that we are the adopted children of the Great and the Eternal God! (Barnes).

"Spirit of Eternal Love, guide me, or I
blindly rove;
"Set my heart on things above, draw me
after Thee!
"Earthly things are paltry show,
phantom charms, they come and go;
"Give me constantly to know fellowship
with Thee!"

"Come, O Spirit, take control where the
fires of passion roll;
"Let the yearnings of my soul Center all
in Thee.
"Call into Thy fold of peace thoughts
that seek forbidden ways;
"Calm and order all my days, hide my life
in Thee."

"Thus supported, even I, knowing Thee
forever nigh,
"Shall attain that deepest joy, living
unto Thee.
"No distracting thoughts within, no
surviving hidden sin!
"Thus shall Heaven indeed begin, here
and now in me!"

CHAPTER 7

(1) "HAVING THEREFORE THESE PROMISES, DEARLY BELOVED, LET US CLEANSE OURSELVES FROM ALL FILTHINESS OF THE FLESH AND SPIRIT, PERFECTING HOLINESS IN THE FEAR OF GOD."

This Verse should have actually been Verse 19 of the preceding Chapter, because it has to do with that which Paul had been saying beginning with the 14th Verse.

At this point it is well to remember that we have in this Second Epistle to the Corinthians what one might call a biographical record of its writer. He has given a simple account of his own experiences. They add up to the grand total of Godliness. They reveal the simplicity of the Christian Faith. They show how the ordinary events of ordinary people may be made into a noble pattern of life.

PROMISES

The phrase, *"Having therefore these Promises, dearly beloved,"* goes back to the previous Chapter in which the Christian was challenged to live a separated life. In living such a life he would experience the Presence and Blessings of God in a very marked manner. The Promise was, *"Wherefore come out from among them, and be ye separate, saith the Lord, and touch not the unclean thing; and I will receive you, and will be a Father unto you, and ye shall be My sons and daughters, saith the Lord Almighty."*

We should notice that the Promise is conditional. If we will come out from evil alliances, God will come unto us in intimate Blessing and Power. If we will walk with God in separation, God will walk with us in greater Blessing. In other words, if we will obey the Laws of the spiritual life, we will receive the profit of such obedience.

This refers to the responsibility which is the Christian's with regard to his own development and advancement in character and life. There can be no progress outwardly until there is cleansing and correction inwardly. Christian experience begins within.

The basis for all experience is found in the Scriptures. Here it is specifically stated as *"these Promises."* And *"these Promises"* hold out to every Christian a noble ideal. It is the ideal of a life lived in the close companionship of God. It is life freed from the dragging liabilities of evil alliances (Laurin).

NOTES

God will dwell in us, will be our God, and will be to us a Father, which is a privilege beyond compare; nevertheless, we must remove from us whatever is offensive in His Sight.

CLEANSE OURSELVES

The phrase, *"Let us cleanse ourselves from all filthiness of the flesh and spirit,"* presents an extremely significant process as it regards our Sanctification.

There are two kinds of cleansing:

1. The first is positional, and is something which only God can do. In fact, it is our Sanctification which automatically takes place at Conversion, which is done instantly and which comes about simply by Faith (I Cor. 6:11). This is inward and can only be done by the Grace of God. It is our *"position"* in Christ, which comes about at Conversion, and which is not dependent upon performance, etc., but rather Faith, and, therefore, does not change.

2. The second kind of cleansing, and actually that of which Paul speaks here, is conditional, and in a sense is outward. It is something each of us is charged with. It is the cleansing of our actions, our deeds, and our words.

While the first is our actual *"position,"* this is our actual *"condition,"* with the Holy Spirit working with us, to bring it up to our *"position."*

We are too prone to pray for God to cleanse us when there is much that depends upon us. The words here are very plain, *"Let us cleanse ourselves."* If there is in us at this moment a known sin or an un-Christian habit, its cleansing is our responsibility. While only God can cleanse us from the moral pollution of sin, we *can* cleanse ourselves from the habitual practice of sins, that is if we properly depend on Christ, and secure the help of the Holy Spirit.

While our positional cleansing depends strictly on our Faith in what Christ did for us at Calvary and the Resurrection, this cleansing depends upon our cooperation with the Holy Spirit. He will definitely help us, but He will not do what needs to be done, at least in this sphere without our cooperation and help.

Also, the Believer must properly understand what Christ has done for him at Calvary and the

Resurrection, by not only paying the sin debt which man could not pay, but as well, breaking the sin grip. So, in this respect, we can cleanse ourselves, but only according to certain guidelines. Romans Chapter 6 tells us what Christ has done, while Romans Chapter 8 portrays to us the help of the Holy Spirit, on which we are totally dependent. As well, His help is predicated on what Jesus did at Calvary and the Resurrection. He will not veer from that direction.

Most Christians do not understand the fact that Calvary not only pertains to our Salvation, but our Sanctification as well. They understand the first part, but little understand the second.

While it is true that all purifying influence and all Holiness proceed from God, it is also true that the effect of all the influences of the Holy Spirit is to excite us to diligence, to purify our own hearts, and to urge us to make strenuous efforts to overcome our own sins, which, however, can only be done the Bible way.

He who expects to be made pure without any effort of his own, will never become pure; and he who ever becomes holy, will become so as a result of strenuous efforts to resist the evil of his own heart, and to become like God.

PAUL INCLUDES HIMSELF

Some also express surprise that Paul includes himself; but this is unwarranted. In fact, Paul writes plainly about himself in Philippians 3:12-14. As that which he said in Philippians bears out, he did not consider himself a perfectionist.

The idea is, that Believers cooperate with God, and one of the activities in which we do this is in keeping ourselves clean, *"keeping ourselves unspotted from the world"* (James 1:27). We are to refuse to touch anything unclean (II Cor. 6:17). We must resist temptation. It is about this self-cleansing that Paul speaks. With it goes repentance for sin that we still commit, which brings God's cleansing, Who is *"faithful and righteous to forgive us our sins and to cleanse us from all iniquity"* (I Jn. 1:9). We are, indeed, clean (Jn. 13:10; 15:3; I Cor. 6:11), and yet we need to continually wash our feet, spiritually speaking (Jn. 13:10); every branch must be purged to bear more fruit (Jn. 15:2), and as well we must ever fight sin and temptation.

NOTES

FILTHINESS OF THE FLESH

These are the sins of our bodily members. They are the sins of the five physical senses. They belong to the physical part of us and include any practice, habit, or indulgence which will cause uncleanness or defilement.

Filthiness, and by that we speak of moral uncleanliness, is something that soils and whatever soils us is wrong. It should be put away. It is not a question of whether it is conventional, but whether it is Biblical. Christianity stands for all that is clean. Any habit, practice, or indulgence of the physical senses that soils us and causes uncleanness is wrong and, therefore, un-Christian. Concerning it, we have a very definite responsibility — cleanse ourselves.

The physical body is the Temple of the Holy Spirit, and should be kept holy — which refers to all such passions and appetites as the Holy Spirit of God would not produce.

FILTHINESS OF THE SPIRIT

By *"Filthiness of the spirit,"* the Apostle means, probably, all the thoughts or mental associations that defile the man. Thus, the Saviour (Mat. 15:19) speaks of evil thoughts, etc., that proceed out of the heart, and pollute the person.

As well, one may be scrupulously Christian in habit but very decidedly un-Christian in disposition. A person may neither smoke, drink, be immoral or guilty of the violent pollution of the flesh yet be most unattractive in his nature.

This filthiness of the spirit, therefore, refers to hatred, malice, jealousy, animosity, ill-temper, pride and a host of companion evils.

It is not enough to cleanse ourselves of defiling habits. There are also defiling traits of character. One can defile and soil home life by a selfish disposition. He can spoil the lives and peace of other people by a contentious and troublesome spirit.

There is just as much reason to be clean in spirit as to be clean in body. There should be as much evidence of Christ in our disposition as there is in our activities. Unless Christ has made us more agreeable and more sociable and more decent to live with, we have not experienced the fullest measure of His Grace.

SQUARELY UP TO THE BELIEVER

All of this, remember, is something which is put squarely up to us. It says, *"Let us cleanse ourselves."* Do not wait for God to do what He expects you to do. Do not sit around piously wishing to be someone better than you are, but get up in the strength of Christ and become that better person. Do not wish to do what you must will to do.

As someone has said, *"Here is your responsibility. The Bible is your challenge. Christ is your Master. The Holy Spirit is your Strength."*

HOLINESS

The phrase, *"Perfecting Holiness in the fear of God,"* means *"to bring to a state of completion."* It is not an optional matter; we are to do it *"in the fear of God."*

Once again we find ourselves faced with a great responsibility. We are charged with the responsibility of perfecting Holiness. Many of us have considered that to be a passive Work of Grace. We have said, with a great deal of spiritual laziness, that Holiness is something God will do for us. That is as true in one sense as was true of moral cleansing.

At the same time, one can say of Holiness exactly as is said of Sanctification. There is a *"Positional Holiness"* which is the same as *"Positional Sanctification."* As well, there is a *"Conditional Holiness,"* the same as a *"Conditional Sanctification."* In fact, one might could say that both Sanctification and Holiness are for all practical purposes one and the same.

What we are before God in our *"Standing"* is by His Grace. But what we are before man is our *"State,"* and is by our own determination to a great degree. (Standing and State are the same as Position and Condition.)

The first in all cases is by God's Will and the second by our will. The Holiness of our Standing will only become the Holiness of our State as we yield to the means of Grace which God provides for our growth. That the Holy Spirit seeks to bring our *"State"* up to our *"Standing,"* is the same as saying that He desires to bring our *"Condition"* up to our *"Position."*

THAT WHICH IS CERTAIN

One thing is eternally certain. There can be no perfecting of Holiness unless there is a cleansing of moral filthiness. Filthiness recedes as Holiness proceeds. Filthiness goes out as Holiness comes in. Even so, Holiness is not merely the absence of filthiness. It is not the state of a religious vacuum. It is not what is left when you have removed the filthiness of flesh and spirit.

NOTES

Instead, it is the indwelling Spirit. It is the increasing stature of Christ. Holiness is, in fact, the very Life of Christ. So long as that Life is stifled by filthiness, it cannot grow. Give it room and area by cleansing what is foreign to it and it will grow and increase. This is Holiness. It is the Life of Christ making holy the life of the Christian.

THE FEAR OF GOD AND PERFECTION

The unceasing and steady aim of every Christian should be perfection — perfection in all things — in the Love of God, of Christ, of man; perfection of heart, and feeling, and emotion; perfection in our words, and plans, and dealings with men; perfection in our prayers, and in our submission to the Will of God. No man can be a Christian who does not sincerely desire it, and who does not constantly aim at it, even though we cannot arrive at that place until the Resurrection. Still, it should ever be our goal.

No man is a friend of God who can acquiesce to a state of sin, and who is satisfied and contented that he is not as holy as God is holy. And despite our shortcomings, frailties, and failures, any man who has no desire to be perfect as God is, and who does not make it his daily and constant aim to be as perfect as God, may set it down as demonstrably certain that he is not really saved, or else he has drifted far from what he should be in the Lord.

How can a man be a Christian who is willing to live in a state of sin, and who does not desire to be just like his Master and Lord?

Out of fear and reverence of God, our life is to be planned. It is to be done from a regard to His Word, and a reverence for His Name.

The idea seems to be, that we are always in the Presence of God; we as Believers are professedly under His Design, Will, and Law — yes Law, *"The Law of the Spirit of Life in Christ Jesus"* (Rom. 8:2). As a result, we should be awed and restrained by a sense of His Presence from the commission of sin, and from indulgence in the pollution of the flesh and spirit.

There are many sins that the presence of a child will restrain a man from committing; and so should the conscious presence of a Holy God keep us from sin; if the fear of a man or a child will restrain us, and make us attempt to at least be better, how should the fear of the all-present and the all-seeing God keep us, not only from outward sins, but from polluted thoughts and unholy desires!

IN FEAR AND NOT BY FEAR

This cleansing and perfecting is to be accomplished by Faith and in fear. Be careful to notice that it says *"in fear"* and not *"by fear."* It is something which is done by Faith while we have a reverent respect for God. Whoever lives reverently before God will find its effect in life. The fear of God is not fright but such reverence and regard for God as will cause us to be what He desires.

The person who properly fears God is one who has cleansed himself from the spoiling defilements of life and is perfecting a holy character.

Take God out of life and men live to no good or intelligent purpose. It is this very fact that makes so much of our modern life evil and senseless.

As well, having God in life is something more than believing in a Supreme Being. A person may believe in such a Being and still be as pagan as a Roman.

There is a difference between belief and Faith. Many people believe in God who do not have Faith in God. One is simply an attitude of mind while the other is an act of will. One may believe in the necessity of food, but believing does not supply the body with nourishment. One must act on that belief and take food into the body before belief is of any practical value.

So it is with one's belief and Faith in God. You may believe that God is necessary to your life, but until your Faith acts upon your belief, God will be no practical part of your life.

Belief in God requires a conception whereas Faith in God requires a decision. Belief results in a conclusion; Faith results in a conversion. It is conversion which puts God into life. Belief is a state, while Faith is an act.

One can believe in God, in other words that there is a God, and have little or no fear of Him; however, the moment one begins to exhibit Faith in God, at that moment the Believer begins to have a *"fear of God,"* which is an absolute necessity, and is spiritually healthy.

NOTES

There is, indeed, one kind of fear, a base and servile fear, which is not of God, and is cast out by Perfect Love; but the fear of which Paul speaks here, is reverential awe which always remains with the true and wisely instructed Christian. Consequently, such a one will never be guilty of the profane familiarity adopted by some so-called ignorant Believers who speak of God *"as though He were someone on the next street"* (Heb. 12:28; I Pet. 3:15).

For instance, one Preacher of my acquaintance was heard referring to the Lord Jesus Christ as *"Jeez!"* Such proclaims gross irreverence, and as well, gross ignorance.

THE METHOD OF PAUL

In this whole letter we find what 7:1 again reveals: Paul joins the Corinthians to himself: *"Let us cleanse ourselves."* He does not pose as a Saint who rebukes them because they are unclean. He wins them by doing what he asks them to do.

The full beauty of this course reveals itself in the balance of this Chapter, as the Corinthians themselves find themselves in Paul's heart, and then bring themselves to his side.

(2) "RECEIVE US; WE HAVE WRONGED NO MAN, WE HAVE CORRUPTED NO MAN, WE HAVE DEFRAUDED NO MAN."

The phrase, *"Receive us,"* links, and in essence is a repeat of 6:13. However, it also connects with 6:14 and following Verses.

THE GREAT DIFFERENCE

In 6:14 the Corinthians are not to put their necks under the yoke of unbelievers; now, however, Paul does not add: *"Put your necks under our yoke, come and join us!"* No; he delicately states it the other way: *"Make room for us — let us come to you and be received in your hearts!"*

Paul assumes that the Corinthians had repudiated the foreign yoke, and as well, have shunned the stain of flesh and spirit which he has pointed out in 7:1. So the Corinthians will, indeed, make room, most expansive room in their hearts for him and for his fellow workers. In fact, *"make room"* is not said with a doubt on Paul's part but with the assurance that the Corinthians will answer: *"We certainly will!"*

Consequently, in this statement we are given an example of the terrible bondages which the world imposes upon its followers in the form of *"yokes,"* and the freedom given and guaranteed by Christ. While there is a *"yoke"* that one must bear or wear respecting Christ, called *"His Yoke"*; still, it is a yoke which is *"easy and light,"* which makes it totally unlike that of the world. So, what Paul was asking of these Corinthians was simply that they love him as he loved them. I hardly think that was too much to ask.

RELIGIOUS YOKES

In the simple words *"Receive us,"* even as they were spoken by the Holy Spirit through the Apostle, we are witnesses of True Christianity. Unfortunately, the demeanor that Paul here exhibits, is totally foreign to much modern-day Christianity.

For instance, Religious Denominations much of the time demand allegiance as they exercise control. By control, I speak of control in every facet, be it economic, material, physical, and spiritual. It is not a *"Receive us,"* but rather, *"You do as we say, or else!"*

However, this is not a spirit necessarily of Denominations, but rather of the so-called Leaders in these Denominations. Denominations are mere things, which within themselves carry no strength or power one way or the other. By that I mean, that it is not unscriptural or sin to form a Religious Denomination, or to be associated with one. The wrongdoing comes about as unscrupulous men attempt to insert government which is foreign to the Word of God, which they usually do. Then they exercise control.

However, let it not be thought that this spirit of control is indicative of Denominations only, for the simple reason that such permeates the majority of independent Church structures, as well. It is an attitude and spirit which is fostered by Satan himself, which has been the bane of the Church almost from its very beginning. Actually, Jesus warned His Disciples in no uncertain terms, pointing to the fact that men love to control other men, and religious men love to control other men most of all (Mat. 20:24-28).

AN EXAMPLE

Some years ago I was made aware of a particular problem in which a young Evangelist of my acquaintance had encountered. I know very little about the problem, so will not attempt to deal with that. I did know that God was using him, with his Ministry touching many hearts and lives. In fact, this young man was not associated with any particular Religious Denomination, but was rather associated with a group of particular Independent Churches, Charismatic incidentally.

He occasioned to write me about the problem, stating in his letter that he had placed himself under the authority of the leadership of this particular Church, which they in fact, demanded that he do.

In essence, there was no problem with that, providing their demands were not unscriptural. However, as he began to relate to me those demands, it immediately became obvious that they were unscriptural.

Among other things, he could not preach for two years, or some such protracted period of time. As well, that is if I remember correctly, he was not to travel even with his wife and family, over a certain distance away from this particular city. There were other foolish and silly demands as well.

In their demands, which were pretty well indicative of all such demands, regarding such situations, be they ordered by Denominations or otherwise, there was no mention of repentance, a daily prayer life, in other words, the very things which would solve the problem.

I wrote him back and kindly suggested to him that what these people were demanding was not Scriptural, and that it would fall out to no good. He answered insisting that he knew this was the right way and that he was going to adhere to their demands to the letter, etc.

HOW DID I KNOW IT WOULD NOT WORK?

Anything that is unscriptural won't work. Even though such may sound good to the world, and to those in the Church who have a carnal mind and ear; still, such constitutes the ways of the world being brought over into the Church.

The world has judges, juries, law officers, prisons, and punishment. These things are necessary in the world, because it is unregenerate. However, when we bring these things over into the Church, we are making a mockery of everything Jesus did at Calvary.

I will ask this simple question.

What in the world does the punishment of not preaching, which the Bible in no way demands, and in fact is totally opposed, have to

NOTES

do with the problem at hand, whatever that problem may be? As well, how can not traveling but so many miles away from this particular city, effect anything good?

Of course, the answer to those things, plus much more suchlike foolishness we could name, is obvious. Such is not meant to solve any problem, but rather to serve as punishment.

The first thing these people should do is exert such upon themselves, for the simple reason that Preachers who demand such of other Preachers, are sinning far worse than whatever it is the other individual has done. Their sin is the abrogation of the Headship of Christ in the Church, and a denial of what Christ did at Calvary for sinners. When Jesus forgives, He forgives, and it is done totally, with no mention again of the past. No penance is required or further Atonement. He did all of that at Calvary's Cross, and how dare any man attempt to add to what He has done and finished.

Incidentally, it is a great sin for any Preacher be he Church Leader, so-called, or what, to tell another Preacher whom God has called, if he can preach, where he can preach, why he can preach, or what he can preach. One will look in vain in the New Testament for any such action. It simply does not exist. So why do most so-called Religious Leaders engage in such foolishness presently, and in fact in one way or the other, always have?

CONTROL

It goes back to control. Men are not willing to allow the Lord to control the Church, they feel they must take such out of His Hands. As we have stated, the carnal mind applauds such, but the spiritual mind knows better.

(I have used the short phrase *"so-called"* several times, and will continue to do so, for the simple reason that most of these individuals are Religious Leaders in name only. In other words, they occupy a man-devised position, which is not recognized by God, hence, *"so-called."*)

Incidentally, this young Evangelist went about a year under this unscriptural regimen, when other unscriptural demands began to be made of him as well, if I remember correctly, these so-called Leaders telling him, that they were going to lengthen the time he would be unable to preach. Why did they do this?

NOTES

Of course, I do not know all the reasons, but it is my understanding that he and his wife and family had traveled at one particular time a further limit outside the city where he had been imprisoned — imprisoned by their demands, etc. At that time he finally broke away, and commenced his Ministry, even as he should have done at the very beginning.

Anything that is unscriptural, can only get worse until it is changed to that which is Scriptural. However, in doing such, becoming Scriptural, one may very well lose the plaudits of men, and in fact definitely will. However, the Preacher of the Gospel and all others for that matter who serve the Lord, must settle it in their minds once and for all, that they are going to obey God rather than men.

I will do anything my Brother ask that I do, providing it is Scriptural. However, and irrespective as to what it may cost, if it is unscriptural, I am not going to engage myself in those demands, irrespective as to what the outcome may be. For me to do what I must do for the Lord, I must have His Blessings and not man's. While I love and respect my Brother and Sister in the Lord, I am not Scripturally obligated to obey them, and especially if the demand is unscriptural (Rom. 13:8).

RECEIVE US

The phrase, *"Receive us,"* as Paul uses it here, means, properly, *"give space, place, or room."* It means here, *"Make room for us in your affections; that is, admit or receive us as your friends."* As stated, it is an earnest entreaty by the Apostle that the Corinthians would do what he had exhorted them to do in 6:13.

Here he returns to the subject and asks an interest in their affections and their love.

Here is an intimate touch of Christian fellowship. How natural it was for Paul to desire the love and fellowship of the Corinthians. He asked them to receive him. There were some evidently, who had sought to spoil this fellowship by maligning Paul's character, therefore, he reminded them of his careful life. He had not wronged anyone; he had not defrauded anyone; he had been careful to live so as not to injure others, and consequently merited the most intimate fellowship and approval of his fellow Christians.

Paul did not say these things in condemnation of the Corinthians. He had spoken of them in highest terms. He had boasted of the Work of Grace that had taken place in Corinth. As a matter of fact, so great was his confidence in the converted lives of his Corinthian friends that he declared himself as determined to live and die for them.

A NEW KIND OF LOYALTY

This kind of loyalty is refreshing. It was loyalty based on the new order of life. That order was the new life of conversion, which meant controlled by Christ. It was the result of the new creation.

The old paganism had given way to the new Christianity. The old lasciviousness had gone and a new Righteousness had come. Here was a solid basis for confidence and fellowship, which actually makes up the foundation of the Church, both then and now.

No matter what age we may live in, the greatest need is for converted lives. The solution of our problems, according to Jesus, is the transformation of character. *"The human drama is not playing itself out very well, and no shifting of the scenery can fix the drama up. Something profound must happen to the actors if it is to come out right."* That *"something profound"* is the profound necessity of becoming Christlike.

For this reason the Gospel Plan of Life is indispensable to our day and to our social order. *"Christianity in Christ is not a cosmetic to adorn the spiritual externals of our society. It is the medicine which can cure the inner wrongness that ruins life."* This is so because conversion goes to the very root of the human wrong, which is sin.

THE REMEDY

If the Bible's idea of sin is right, then we are equally sure its idea of the remedy for sin is right. If it is true that men are born sinners, then we will find it true that men must be Born-Again. Sin is something associated with the first birth and Salvation is something associated with the second birth.

Discipline is an important part of Discipleship. An undisciplined Disciple will find himself an unprepared, undeveloped, and unfit Disciple. Without discipline there can never be conspicuous Christianity.

Today we find ourselves in the midst of an undisciplined Christianity. In the First Century Christianity was unpopular and the Disciples suffered unmentionable persecution, but the discipline of those days gave the Church a triumphant life. Today Christianity is popular. The Christian is scarcely distinguishable from the non-Christian. There is no discipline in his life. There is none from without and none from within and in consequence he is soft and ineffectual.

DISCIPLINE

The disciplined Christian is the one who follows Christ all the way. There is a Christ-given and self-chosen distinction in habits and activities. He determines to mark himself by what he does and does not do. This is not legalism; it is loyalty. It is not narrow-mindedness; it is Christianity at its best. Jesus said, *"If any man will come after Me, let him deny himself, and take up his Cross and follow Me. For whosoever will save his life shall lose it: and whosoever will lose his life for My sake shall find it"* (Mat. 16:24-25). That is discipline.

Denial is not indulgence. Following Jesus is not following the world. Finding one's life is not spending it or squandering it on the whims of selfishness. Following Christ means disciplined discipleship.

The danger of an undisciplined life is sin in the life, which in fact, occasioned this breach between Corinth and Paul. Their sin was twofold: First they listened to false teachers which turned them against the Apostle, and then they began to fellowship with the world. The two go hand in hand.

A PERSONAL APPEAL

Consequently, as the Apostle of old, I am going to make the same appeal to the modern Church: *"Receive us; we have wronged no man, we have corrupted no man, we have defrauded no man."*

Rather than go into a long explanation, suffice to say that such is true in the Eyes of God, irrespective of the slander and the accusation of others, and that's all that really matters.

WRONGED NO MAN

The phrase, *"We have wronged no man,"* means we have done injustice to no man.

This is given as a reason why they should admit him to their full confidence and affection.

NOTES

It is not improbable that Paul had been charged with such action — having wronged some individual. This accusation could very well have been brought against him by the false teachers at Corinth.

However, irrespective as to what his enemies might insinuate, there was no single member of their Church who could complain of injury, moral harm, or unfair treatment from him. Clearly he is again thinking of definite slanders against himself.

Whenever the Preacher is forced to correct false doctrine, as Paul was here forced to do, many men take umbrage at such. I know what I'm talking about, having been the victim of such.

On a personal basis, as I preach what I know God has called me to preach, I realize perfectly well that it affects some in a negative way. For instance, when I preach the wrongness of modern humanistic Psychology as it is brought into the Church, those who believe and practice such are not happy with my remarks, to say the least. Regrettably, this covers almost all of the modern Church Leadership.

When we speak strongly against the Prosperity Message, this as well strikes chords of anger for those who preach and practice such. Again, this false message permeates a great part of the Charismatic and even the Pentecostal world. So, those who would practice such, are not happy with this particular Ministry.

As well, when we denounce unscriptural Church Government, of which most Church Denominations are engaged, that Message as well strikes fire. Also, our call for a strict adherence to the Word of God, and a dependence on the Holy Spirit, while not openly rebutted, and because of the obvious reasons, still, strikes fire in the heart of those who do not follow that direction.

With those things in their hearts, many while not voicing such, are quick to point back to previous failure, when the real reason is the Message that we preach. Never mind that that Message has seen literally hundreds of thousands brought to a saving knowledge of Jesus Christ, and continues to do so unto this very hour. Never mind that this is the fruit: the Salvation of souls, bondages of darkness being broken, Believers being Baptized with the Holy Spirit, sick bodies being healed, etc. This and this alone should be the criteria for the acceptance of a Ministry (Mat. 8:20).

NOTES

CORRUPTED NO MAN

The phrase, *"We have corrupted no man,"* pertains to bringing one into a worse state or condition. It can refer to morals or direction.

Inasmuch as the Apostle surely had not done anything to corrupt the morals of these people, he is more than all speaking of wrong doctrine. In other words, he had preached to them the Truth, and not error which would have corrupted them. To be frank, the false teachers had *"wronged"* these people by preaching unto them error, which always has the tendency to *"corrupt"* the individual, and which then *"defrauds"* them. Such is the direction of all false gospel.

For instance, the modern Prosperity Message, which places money at the core of the Christian experience, is none other than a corruption of the Truth.

While the Lord certainly does bless His people in a monetary and material sense, still, that is certainly not the primary Message of the Gospel, or anywhere close to its primary Message. Jesus came to save men from sin, and an improved financial picture is not the fruit of His Finished Work at Calvary.

AN EXAMPLE

Frances and I along with a friend happened to be in London, England for a couple of days in the late Summer of 1998. We were on our way to minister at a particular Church about 200 miles north of that great city.

While we were there, we received a phone call from a dear friend who along with his wife, was also in London to attend a particular meeting regarding World Evangelism. On the day in question we had dinner with he and his party that night.

He mentioned the Service the night before, along with the lineup of Preachers who had been invited to address this Conference. I was acquainted with only one or two of the Preachers, and that only in a very limited way.

However, he mentioned the Service the night before, and the Preacher in question, with whom I was acquainted by way of his Doctrine, but not on a personal basis.

His Message was, they said, *"Money Cometh,"* or words to that effect. In other words, he was going to tell the several thousands assembled, how they could get rich.

They were upset about the Message, asking me if I knew the Preacher? As stated, I had never met the man, but I was acquainted with his Message — a Message incidentally, which is not Scriptural.

We have before us a world going to Hell, men dying without God, with their only hope being Jesus Christ, and this Preacher standing before this congregation shouting to them that *"Money Cometh."* Even though the morals of these people were not corrupted regarding this Message, their Faith definitely was.

To even an elementary student of the Word of God, they know that such is wrong, at least if they are honest with themselves and the Bible. While prosperity is definitely a Blessing from the Lord and definitely, I believe, was included in the Atonement, still, that is not the primary Message of the Gospel. If it is presented as the primary Message, it will corrupt the listeners.

Admittedly, the Churches which espouse such, and they are many, for the most part are full and running over. The reason is simple. There is enough greed in all of our hearts to desire such, especially when it is ladled out under the guise of being one's spiritual right in Christ.

While there in London, my wife and our friend visited Westminster Abbey, and strangely enough, they saw in the foyer of the Church a little sign which said, *"Beware of pickpockets in the Church."*

Even though they were speaking of the many visitors and tourists who visited that ancient Church daily, still, the warning applies to all. There are many pickpockets behind modern pulpits.

DEFRAUD NO MAN

The phrase, *"We have defrauded no man,"* means to take advantage, seek unlawful gain, to circumvent, defraud, deceive.

When the Preacher fails to preach the True Gospel of Jesus Christ, he is guilty of Scriptural and Spiritual *"fraud."*

The idea is, that Paul had taken advantage of no circumstances to extort money from them, to overreach them, or to cheat them, or to take advantage of them in any way.

As I have mentioned elsewhere in these Volumes, the Lord spoke to my heart many years

NOTES

ago, saying, *"If you ever exploit the people, I will take My Anointing from you."* In fact, exploitation is the great sin of the modern pulpit.

The people are exploited (defrauded) by making them believe that Salvation consists of them belonging to a certain Church, or at least, they will be spiritually deprived if they discontinue their association with that particular Church, whatever it may be. To be factual, the Church world is full of that type of exploitation.

Many Baptists are told that if they do not continue in that particular Doctrine they will be lost. The same goes for many Pentecostals, etc. Of course, Catholicism openly advocates such, claiming that the Catholic Church is the Saviour.

Fraudulent activities also consist in Preachers referring individuals with serious spiritual problems to humanistic Psychologists. Even though many of these Psychologists may claim to be Believers and claim to join the Bible with Psychology, still, that which they are peddling is a lie. It cannot heal any hurt, wash away any sin, break any bondage of darkness, in other words, all such efforts are useless. When such is being promoted, it amounts to defrauding the people, for the simple reason that there is no help from that source. Jesus Christ Alone holds the answers to the aberrations, sins, malformities, idiosyncracies, quirks, bondages, and emotional disturbances of the human race.

Going back to money, when the Preacher stands before the Television camera (or anywhere else for that matter), and tells the people that God has told him, that all who send in sizable offerings in the next 30 minutes, or whatever period of time, will receive a hundredfold return, is fraud pure and simple. As well, any variation of that falls under the same category.

God never appeals to baser motives in order to carry on His Work, but only to the highest motives. Such as this which we have just mentioned, appeals to greed. It does not appeal to a love for God.

THE DIFFERENCE

If one is to notice Paul's Ministry, he never attacked people, even though he did attack, and strongly so, false doctrine. As well, I do not attack Preachers, but I do attack Doctrine which I believe to be wrong, in other words, not according to the Bible.

The difference is, these false teachers at Corinth attacked Paul personally, which is generally always the case with false doctrine. They attempted to destroy Paul by accusing him of whatever, and regrettably, many of the Corinthians were swayed toward such thinking. What a travesty!

This shows us that if people who had been saved under Paul, could be turned against the great Apostle, with him now importuning them to *"receive him,"* we find just how insidious this evil actually is.

Whenever one's person is being attacked, one overhearing such efforts should ask themselves, as to why such is being done.

As a Believer I do not have the right to attack the person, which refers to the character of anyone. Not being God, I do not know their motives, or much of anything about them for that matter. So, if such is being done, one could almost all the time chalk it up to a grievous sin against that person.

George Whitefield was one of the greatest Preachers of the Gospel who ever lived. He helped turn this nation in the 1700's toward God. He was so vilely attacked on a personal basis, that one poet said of him —

"His sins were such as Sodom never knew,
"And Calumny stood up to swear all true."

PERSONAL!

George Whitefield saw untold thousands turn to Jesus Christ, and with two or three other Preachers such as Finney and Wesley, literally turned this nation toward God.

So, whenever Preachers, or anyone for that matter, are personally attacked, such is never Scriptural, and, therefore, sin.

And yet at the same time, as a watchman appointed by the Lord, it is my sworn duty to the Lord Jesus Christ, to not only preach the Truth of the Gospel, but as well, to point out error. We are to do it in no uncertain terms, leaving the listener knowing full well what has been said, that no one will be able to stand up and say, *"I did not know."*

It is the business of the Preacher of the Gospel to point out error, in fact, any danger to the spiritual welfare of the Child of God.

NOTES

This is dealt with in Ezekiel, where the figure of a watchman is used.

"If the watchman sees the sword coming and does not blow the trumpet to warn the people and the sword comes and takes the life of one of them, that man will be taken away because of his sin, but I will hold the watchman accountable for his blood" (Ezek. 33:6).

The Believer-watchman is responsible to the wicked to *"speak out to dissuade him from his ways"* (Ezek. 33:8). But the watchman is not responsible for how the person warned responds.

Yet the responsibility to warn remains. However, and as stated, such will always result in the Preacher doing the warning, being attacked vigorously. That's the reason not many Preachers are willing to pay the price, willing to preach what God says preach, for the simple reason, that almost all will turn against them.

(3) "I SPEAK NOT THIS TO CONDEMN YOU: FOR I HAVE SAID BEFORE, THAT YE ARE IN OUR HEARTS TO DIE AND LIVE WITH YOU."

The phrase, *"I speak not this to condemn you,"* means, *"I do not speak this with any desire to reproach you."* I do not complain of you for the purpose of condemning, or because I have a desire to find fault, though I am compelled to speak in some respect of your want of affection and love towards me.

It is not because I have no love for you, and wish to have occasion to use words implying complaint and condemnation. Paul rather knew, that their attitude of refusing his fellowship would ultimately damage them. This is probably why he spoke as he did in the preceding Chapter (6:11-13).

God's people cannot refuse to fellowship with other Believers without causing definite problems for themselves. In fact, what type of damage would have occurred if the Church at Corinth had not heeded Paul's admonition? What if they had shut out him and his Ministry?

To be blunt, the results would have been catastrophic. People would have lost their souls, and as is overly obvious, false doctrine would have prevailed, which would have ultimately destroyed the Church.

Any time one who is called of God is cut off, especially if that person is doing all within their power to abide by the Word of God, and to do so in humility and brokenness, and especially considering that they have a Message, in fact a very important Message for the Church, the Church as a whole will suffer great loss because of failing to receive such a one. If such were not possible, the Holy Spirit through the Apostle would not have gone to such great lengths to portray this which was happening at Corinth.

IN OUR HEARTS TO DIE AND LIVE

The phrase, *"For I have said before, that ye are in our hearts to die and live with you,"* refers to the Corinthians having such a place in his affections.

In effect, the Apostle is saying that if it is the Will of God, he would be glad to spend his life, even to give his life for these Corinthians. This is an expression of the tenderest attachment, and portrays such Christlikeness which is seldom seen.

It was true that the Corinthians had not shown themselves remarkably worthy of the affections of Paul, but from the beginning he had felt towards them the tenderest attachment.

The Apostle is saying, *"You are in our hearts"* — how could we ever think of doing any of you a wrong or damage or seek advantage of you? *"In our hearts"* — in the bosom of our love — how could we thus now utter covert accusation or condemnation? In fact, it was not possible for him to be of what these detractors were accusing him.

Thus, one marvels at Paul when one notes how he brings the strongest appeals to bear upon his readers. Censoriousness does not draw, love does. And Paul's love never strikes a wrong note. Having delighted in sharing the same life, this is union and fellowship indeed!

UNITY WITH CHRIST

By our (all Believers) unity with Christ and in the love which He has implanted in us we are, indeed, spiritually bound together (Jn. 13:34-35): we are in each other's hearts.

We died the same death to sin, and we are living the same Spiritual Life.

Even though one can stretch the statement to refer to dying a natural death or living a natural life, such is not actually the true meaning.

The striking feature of this statement is the order: death first and then life. The meaning is not *"so that we are together in life and death."*

NOTES

Even if the thought were considered ideally, even as it can be and as stated, this really is not the actual sense of the statement.

In the Greek structure of the Text, the sense is plain: You died with us when you were severed from sin, the world, etc., in repentance and Faith; you have ever since been living together with us in the true Spiritual Life. This is what makes you and us one. This should keep you from every alien yoke (Lenski).

In making this statement, Paul is no doubt thinking of the Words of Jesus, *"I am the good Shepherd: the good Shepherd giveth His life for the sheep."*

He then said, *"But he that is an hireling and not the Shepherd, whose own the sheep are not, seeth the wolf coming, and leaveth the sheep, and fleeth: and the wolf catcheth them, and scattereth the sheep."*

And finally, *"I lay down my life for the sheep"* (Jn. 10:11-12, 15).

(4) "GREAT IS MY BOLDNESS OF SPEECH TOWARD YOU, GREAT IS MY GLORYING OF YOU: I AM FILLED WITH COMFORT, I AM EXCEEDING JOYFUL IN ALL OUR TRIBULATION."

BOLDNESS OF SPEECH

The phrase, *"Great is my boldness of speech toward you,"* proclaims the Apostle having the right to say these things to the Corinthians. He was their shepherd under Christ, i.e., *"under-shepherd."* Consequently, he loved them dearly. Such love would never exploit them or take advantage of them. In fact, such love could not do so, because it was the Love of God shed abroad within his heart for them.

The Lord never exploits people, nor does He merely *"use"* them. In fact, it was love and not need which occasioned the creation of man by God. God did not need anything much less man. It was love that created man, and it is love that saves man, and love alone.

In fact, God always gives the True Preacher of the Gospel great *"boldness of speech"*; however, He will not do so, unless the heart of that Preacher is filled with love, the God kind of Love.

I have had many people to become upset with me because of my boldness in preaching the Gospel. Catholicism is an excellent example.

Many have claimed, and some vigorously so, that I should not be so bold toward the Catholics in telling them that *"The just shall live by*

Faith," and not by rituals and ceremonies, etc. My answer is always after this fashion:

I have suffered much because of the stand I've taken relative to preaching that which I felt that God told me to preach. I may have done it poorly, but I've done my very best to say what He wanted me to say, and to say it in the way He wanted it said. I lay on my face daily seeking His Face, asking Him direction along with leading and guidance. The Word of God is of such import, of such value, of such power, of such eternal consequence, that we as Preachers of the Gospel, must without fail and without compromise proclaim to the people, *"Thus saith the Lord,"* and only what *"Thus saith the Lord."*

I preach to the Catholics, and all others for that matter, with great boldness of speech, in order that they have absolutely no doubt as to what I am saying, even though it may bring their wrath down upon my head, for the simple reason that I love them. It is only love that would cause me to endure such attacks upon my person, such vilification upon my efforts, etc.

Paul as an Apostle had the right of *"boldness of speech,"* and not only the right, but the absolute necessity. And yet, *"boldness of speech"* is seldom heard among modern Preachers. They are afraid they will make someone angry, or will upset the powers that be.

IT CANNOT BE BOTH WAYS

Men are either going to Heaven or Hell, there is no in-between. They are either lost or saved, there is no in-between. It is one or the other.

While it will definitely make many people angry in using *"boldness of speech,"* at the same time many will be convicted, and will be saved.

We have seen literally hundreds of thousands, among them many Catholics, brought to a saving knowledge of Jesus Christ. That and that alone is the proof of my Message.

GLORYING OF YOU

The phrase, *"Great is my glorying of you,"* refers to the fact, that even though he used boldness of speech when addressing them personally, that behind their backs he *"gloried"* in them by praising them.

To them personally he spoke without reserve and sternly. Behind their backs he boasted of them. All Christians should obey this principle.

NOTES

How could Paul glory in these Corinthians, especially considering the many problems which they had, and even that many of them had turned against him?

That is a good question. He did so because he had Faith in them. He believed that they would ultimately come to the right way. He believed that his admonitions to them would not be long discarded, but would ultimately be taken to heart, which they were. In other words, his Faith saw them victorious instead of defeated. It saw them on fire for God instead of cold and lukewarm. It saw them heeding his Gospel, instead of the error of the false teachers. Only Faith could do such.

A GREATER LESSON

Whenever Christians speak of a fellow Christian, they should do so with Faith and confidence. Irrespective of the problems some may have, out of the mouth of the Believer as he speaks of that particular individual, should always flow forth that which is positive, profitable, and helpful. James addressed this beautifully when he said:

"Therewith bless we God, even the Father; and therewith curse we men, which are made after the similitude of God."

And then, *"Out of the same mouth proceedeth blessing and cursing. My brethren, these things ought not so to be."*

And finally, *"Doth a fountain send forth at the same place sweet water and bitter?"* (James 3:9-11).

And then the clincher, *"And the tongue is a fire, a world of iniquity: so is the tongue among our members, that it defileth the whole body, and setteth on fire the course of nature; and it is set on fire of Hell"* (James 3:6).

The idea is, that when the Believer speaks, especially considering that he is a Temple of the Holy Spirit, his words carry weight and effect, whether they are positive or negative. In fact, whenever a Christian, considering the power he possesses in the Holy Spirit, begins to speak evil on a personal basis of a fellow brother or sister in the Lord, or even those of the world for that matter, he is, in effect, practicing witchcraft. In other words, he has the power with his tongue to help or hinder.

Whenever he speaks words which are positive about a particular individual, it has an effect in the spirit world, to bring help and solace to the person in question. The person in question may never know the kind words spoken, and in fact, may not even know the one doing the speaking, but he definitely does know the benefits he receives in his own spirit.

Sadly and regrettably, it has the same effect whenever negative words are spoken, but in the opposite direction. In other words, when the Believer begins to speak negative of a fellow Believer, he in effect, *"sets on fire the course of nature."* Such is spawned by Hell itself, actually *"set on fire of Hell,"* i.e., *"is meant to destroy, and, consequently, authored by Satan"* (James 3:6).

So, Paul would *"glory of you,"* i.e., *"concerning the Corinthians,"* believing that his positive words on their behalf, would fall out to ultimate victory, which it did.

COMFORT

The phrase, *"I am filled with comfort,"* actually refers to consolation.

He is actually speaking of the good report which had been given to him by Titus, concerning their response to his letter written to them (I Corinthians).

Paul was human as the rest of us. Had the Message from Titus been the opposite, the Apostle would not have been filled with comfort or consolation. However, Paul's admonition had been received favorably by them, thereby, averting a spiritual tragedy. Consequently, he is *"filled with comfort."*

Comfort in the Greek is *"paraklesei,"* and has to do with the Holy Spirit, Who in fact, is our *"Paraclete,"* i.e., *"One called alongside to help, to comfort, etc."*

So, the *"comfort"* the Apostle was now enjoying, was generated not only by the good report received by the mouth of Titus, but more so by the work and operation of the Holy Spirit within his heart. In other words, the Holy Spirit poured through the Apostle a sense of well-being, security, positive results, a favorable conclusion, as only the Holy Spirit can do. So, this means that Paul's attitude and spirit at this time, i.e., *"his comfort,"* was more than just a reaction to good news, but rather a work of the Holy Spirit which was taking place at that time within his heart.

"This is the rest wherewith ye may cause the weary to rest; and this is the refreshing," as was prophesied by Isaiah so long ago (Isa. 28:12).

NOTES

Countless times, in these last few years, I have left one of our prayer meetings filled with this same type of *"comfort."* Whereas I may have fallen on my face before the Lord (spiritually speaking) at the beginning of that prayer session, imploring the Lord concerning a multitude of problems, when I arose some time later, oftentimes it was with an entirely different spirit and attitude. The Holy Spirit had comforted me, and had done so with such strength and beauty, that it literally flowed throughout my very being.

Countless times, I have gone home after such prayer meetings at night, or even after those in the mornings back to my office, with such a feeling of euphoria, of blessing, of well-being, that it actually defies all description. This is the *"comfort"* of which the Apostle speaks.

In fact, maybe the problems had not gone away, but by Faith I knew that ultimately they would go away, or would be handled as the Lord so desired. At any rate, there was no more fear from that direction.

EXCEEDING JOYFUL

The phrase, *"I am exceeding joyful in all our tribulation,"* does not proclaim the taking away of the *"tribulations,"* but rather the *"exceeding joy"* in the midst of these tribulations.

What type of tribulations?

There was opposition in every manner to Paul's efforts to proclaim the Gospel. One could use an old adage, that the tribulation came from the world, the flesh, and the Devil. Naturally the world was in opposition to Paul's Message for the simple reason that it was governed and in fact is governed, by the prince of the powers of the air, i.e., Satan. And yet it probably was the cause of the least tribulation of all.

We know that Paul had difficulties with the *"flesh,"* for the simple reason of the things that he said in Romans Chapter 7. While he certainly had victory and total victory at that, still, it did not come easy, and as well, the ongoing victory necessitated a constant appropriation of the benefits of Calvary, even on a daily basis.

Satan himself engineered all of this opposition, but I suspect that the greatest opposition of all, came oddly and strangely enough, through the Church. Of course, the opposition was fierce from the nation of Israel, with them even trying to kill him on a constant basis. However, I think the opposition from his own ranks, from the Church in Jerusalem, from those who professed Christ, who in fact should have been aiding and abetting Paul, instead were rather trying to hinder his Ministry. In fact, the situation at Corinth, caused by false teachers, had been some of the worst tribulation of all, but which now had experienced victory.

It was this victory at Corinth which had brought him *"exceeding joy."*

Beautifully enough, the phrase *"exceeding joyful"* occurs nowhere else in the New Testament, except in Romans 5:20, where it is translated *"abound."* It is a word which Paul evidently compounded, which means to *"superabound over,"* to superabound greatly or exceedingly. It is a word which would be used only when the heart was full, and when it would be difficult to find words to express its conceptions.

Paul's heart was full of joy; and he pours forth his feelings in the most fervid and glowing language. In other words, he is saying *"I have a joy which cannot be properly expressed."*

(5) "FOR WHEN WE WERE COME INTO MACEDONIA, OUR FLESH HAD NO REST, BUT WE WERE TROUBLED ON EVERY SIDE; WITHOUT WERE FIGHTINGS, WITHIN WERE FEARS."

This Verse is called a *"bad confession"* by many in the modern Church. Paul is here admitting to, and confessing *"troubles," "struggles,"* and *"fears."* In fact, some of these purveyors of their false gospel, even claim that if Paul had had the Faith they have, he would not have uttered such things, in fact, would not even have had to undergo such.

The utter, absolute senselessness of such drivel, and drivel it is, is not really worthy of an answer. The Truth is never a bad confession. How could Bartimaeus have been healed of blindness, if he had not first confessed that he was blind? (Mk. 10:51-52).

Jesus did not reprimand him for confessing such, but rather said, *"Thy Faith hath made thee whole."*

No, this was not a bad confession on the part of Paul, but rather that which will prove to be a great comfort to us, even as we shall see.

NOTES

MACEDONIA

The phrase, *"For, when we were come into Macedonia,"* presents the area of Thessalonica, Berea, and Philippi. It is across the Aegean Sea from Asia Minor.

This was detailed in 2:12-13, with Paul very anxious about the situation at Corinth, having traveled to Troas from Ephesus where he hoped to meet Titus. This associate had been sent to Corinth with Paul's first letter (I Corinthians), and then was scheduled to meet Paul at Troas where he would give him information respecting the response of the Corinthians to this particular letter. However, for reasons unknown, Titus did not keep to this schedule, with Paul now going into Macedonia, hoping to meet Titus there, which he did. He probably met Titus at Philippi, and it was probably from that city that he wrote II Corinthians.

THE FLESH

The phrase, *"Our flesh had no rest,"* presents the Apostle looking back a short time earlier to this occasion. In 2:13 he had said, *"I have no relief for my spirit,"* while he now says, *"No relief for my flesh."* What did he mean by this latter statement?

Some think that in addition to the problems at Corinth, Paul and Timothy and whoever else was with him, encountered a mass of trouble in Macedonia. If that is correct, we are not told what that trouble was; nevertheless, it seemed to afflict them bodily.

Here is a common pattern of experience. It is outward foes and inward fears. The flesh is the arena of suffering. With Paul it was an endless succession of bitter conflicts centered around him. He was constantly troubled and hindered by these distressing afflictions.

His fears were inner concerns and they represent an experience common to any Christian. We all have conflicts of one kind or another. We all have our fears and concerns. We find ourselves at times fretfully wondering how things will go.

To say this is not a fact, is just plain dishonesty. It is better to admit it and plan for its defeat than to try piously to avoid the issue even as some do.

Of one thing we may be sure, Paul did not succumb to his fears. He may have experienced them, but he was not conquered by them. Fear was conquered by Love and Faith.

As well, and which much modern gospel will not admit, there is always a good use for adversity. The fightings and fears of Paul were some of the means of making a better Paul. If we would recognize this, then we would take a different attitude to the adversities we suffer. The Lord allows such not for our harm, but rather for our spiritual growth and thus for our benefit.

To be sure, such things are painful to the flesh even as here stated; nevertheless, they are invigorating to the spirit, for the simple reason that they drive us to our knees, and, consequently, closer to the Lord.

To be sure, no one wants or desires such and neither did Paul. Irrespective, every Believer is designated, I believe, a certain amount of trouble.

TROUBLED ON EVERY SIDE

The phrase, *"But we were troubled on every side,"* simply means there was no rest from any quarter.

The style, in its picturesque irregularity, almost seems as though it were broken by sobs.

Paul's feelings of distress are reflected in the way in which he writes about it. He intends merely to indicate the miserable situation and not to tell about it at length. I think the Holy Spirit allowed the Apostle to pen these words dealing with his own situation, to show that even the great Apostle faced the same kind of weaknesses and anxieties that confront all of us.

We make a dreadful mistake when we elevate people like him to a superhuman level. In fact, the Bible describes these individuals, as stated, to help encourage us. They were people with feelings just like our own (James 5:17). The fact that they overcame these difficulties of life by God's Grace, should spur us on to do the same (Rossier).

FIGHTINGS

The phrase, *"Without were fightings,"* could very well have referred to Pagan Jews, and false Brethren (II Cor. 11:26). In fact, Tumults were usually excited wherever Paul went. Actually, he preached the Gospel commonly amidst violent opposition most of the time.

NOTES

When the True Gospel of Jesus Christ is preached in all of its power and glory, it will not only bring forth tremendous results of Salvation and Deliverance, but as well, will arouse great opposition. Naturally, the Gospel confronts all false doctrine and false apostles. Consequently, anger is aroused with the first thought being, as stated, stop the Message, which is done by stopping the Messenger.

Years ago preaching a citywide Crusade in a particular State, the Pastor of the Church who was our Chairman, informed me almost immediately upon arriving, that he played golf every Monday (I believe he said) with the Catholic Bishop in that city. He was letting me know that they were on very good terms, and I should soften my Message accordingly, etc. Two things here are brought out:

First of all, if this man had been preaching the Gospel as he should have been preaching the Gospel, it is a guaranteed certitude that he and the Catholic Bishop would not have been on such a friendly basis.

As well, I did not temper my Message, as I have never tempered by Message, and by the Help and Grace of God, I will never temper my Message. In fact, the far greater majority of that particular Pentecostal Denomination (Pentecostal so-called), pretty well falls into the same category. They have made friends and come to an alliance, with the world, the flesh, and the Devil. Consequently, even though they may be *"rich and increased with goods, and think they have need of nothing,"* the Truth is, *"They are wretched, miserable, poor, blind and naked"* (Rev. 3:17).

Satan will do everything he can to stop the Gospel, and compromise is one of his greatest methods. Paul was constantly engaged in *"fightings,"* for the simple reason that he never trimmed his Message.

FEARS

The phrase, *"Within were fears,"* could have referred to many things, but probably referred to the success of the Epistle which he had sent to the Church at Corinth. He had felt great concern on the subject, as he now looks back.

It seems that these fears had increased when Titus did not meet him at Troas as expected.

In such a situation, the mind can expect the worst. Why was not Titus there? Had his

Epistle been totally rejected, with Titus attempting to salvage the Church?

I have no doubt that all of these thoughts went through the mind of the Apostle, just as such thoughts go through our minds as well. However, it must be understood that Paul's fears were not for his own personal safety or well-being, but rather for the Work of God. Thank the Lord, those fears never materialized, even as he will momentarily say.

Did this not show a lack of Faith on the part of the Apostle?

I think one would have to say that it possibly did; nevertheless, do any of us have any room to talk. I suspect, if we had to presently face what the Apostle then faced, that we would not come out near as well.

Also, the Apostle is steadfast enough, secure enough, strong enough, anchored in Christ enough, that he can confess these things openly, without fearing what people will think. So, in one sense, these admissions show a greater stability rather than less.

To be frank, any Believer who claims to never have *"fightings without and fears within,"* I greatly suspect, is not telling the Truth, or else are doing so little for the Lord, that Satan little bothers with them. I think the latter would probably be the case in most situations.

"Fears" as used here by Paul in the Greek is *"phebomai,"* which means *"to be put in fear, alarm or fright."*

(6) "NEVERTHELESS GOD, THAT COMFORTETH THOSE THAT ARE CAST DOWN, COMFORTED US BY THE COMING OF TITUS;"

This Verse, plus those that follow, change the complexion entirely. Titus had brought great news.

NEVERTHELESS GOD

The phrase, *"Nevertheless God,"* is literally, *"But God."*

In these two words several things are said:

1. God is ever mindful of *everything* that is going on, and especially as it pertains to His Children.

2. He is not only aware, but is actually superintending events down to the finest detail.

3. Paul always looked to God and never man, which must be our criteria as well.

NOTES

COMFORT

The phrase, *"That comforteth those that are cast down,"* in a sense presents one of God's wonderful names: *"He Who comforts the lowly."* How could He comfort the proud, the self-satisfied? The idea is that God gives consolation to those who are anxious and depressed. All Paul's consolation was in God; and by whatever instrumentality comfort was administered, he regarded and acknowledged God as the Author.

It is sad that the modern Church little regards the Lord in this capacity. If the situation becomes very acute, Psychologists are oftentimes recommended. There is no hope in these directions, all such being totally of man and not of God. As someone has well said, *"When we look to man we get the help that man can give, which is precious little, and when we look to God, we get the help that He gives, which is ever all-sufficient."*

A PERSONAL EXAMPLE

As I dictate these notes (8-17-98), Frances and I have just arrived home from the great country of England. While there, we had the privilege of ministering in one of the great Churches of that country, in the city of Norwich, a little over 200 miles Northeast of London.

One of its Pastors, Alan Pimlott mentioned to Frances and me something that had happened to him personally a short time before.

He told of a particular need with seemingly no way to solve the problem. He went on to relate as to how the concern had been very pronounced, and then there came a beautiful moving of the Holy Spirit.

He went on to convey as to how a great peace filled his heart, as if though the load had shifted from his shoulders to those of the Lord, which in reality is exactly what happened.

This is the comfort of which I speak, and which every Believer has undergone countless times, and which is one of the greatest joys of the Christian experience. The old song says:

"Lift me up above the shadows
"Lift me up and let me stand
"On the mountaintops of glory,
"Let me dwell in Beulah land."

The word *"comfort"* as it's used in the New Testament, means *"to call alongside of,"* or *"to summon for assistance."* To comfort is to cheer and encourage. It contains a positive force as it indicates the dispelling of grief by the impartation of strength.

So in the Old Testament, *"Comfort ye My people"* (Isa. 40:1), is much stronger than the mere word *"console,"* which affords only the power of calm endurance of affliction, while *"comfort"* as given by God, proclaims the brightest hopes of the future and the highest incentives to present activity, all given by the Divine Grace that is here bestowed.

COMFORTED US

The phrase, *"Comforted us by the coming of Titus,"* refers to the fact that Titus came to Macedonia. Paul rejoiced not only in again seeing him, but especially in the intelligence which he brought respecting the success of his Epistle, and the conduct of the Church at Corinth (Barnes).

This tells us that the Lord used Titus to bring about this comfort. In fact, God uses many and varied things respecting such, but at times does so solely by the Moving and Operation of the Holy Spirit Who in fact, is the great Comforter.

Although not mentioned in Acts, Titus was one of Paul's companions in which he placed a considerable amount of trust. He is first heard of at the time of the Gentile controversy when he accompanied Paul and Barnabas to Jerusalem (Gal. 2:1).

He provided a test case, since he was a Gentile, but he was apparently not compelled to be circumcised (Gal. 2:3). Titus probably accompanied Paul on his subsequent journeys, but no definite information of his work is available until the time of the Corinthian crisis. He had evidently been acting as Paul's representative at Corinth during the year preceding the writing of II Corinthians (8:16) with a special commission to organize the collection scheme there. The task was evidently unfinished, for Titus is later urged by Paul to return to Corinth to see its completion (II Cor. 8:6).

A STRONG PERSONALITY

A more delicate task was the smoothing over of the tense situation which had arisen between Paul and the Corinthians, a task which clearly demanded a man of great tact and force of character. He appears to have been a stronger personality than Timothy (I Cor. 16:10; II Cor. 7:15) and possessed ability as an administrator. A comparison of II Corinthians Chapters 2 and 7 suggests that he carried I Corinthians from Paul to the Church at Corinth, in which the Apostle took them to task with much anguish of heart for their high-handed attitude (or as some suggest, it could have been an Epistle which has since been lost.)

Titus eventually rejoined Paul in Macedonia with good news, which we are now studying, and as a result II Corinthians was written and was willingly carried by Titus (II Cor. 8:16), who seems to have possessed a particular affection and serious concern for the Corinthians.

He is described by the Apostle as his *"partner and fellow worker"* (II Cor. 8:23), who would not think of taking advantage of those entrusted to his care (II Cor. 12:18).

From the Epistle addressed to him it may be surmised that Titus accompanied Paul to Crete subsequent to the latter's release from the Roman imprisonment and was left there to consolidate the work (Tit. 1:5). The letter urges the use of authority in establishing a worthy Ministry, in overcoming opposition, and in the teaching of sound Doctrine.

He was summoned to rejoin Paul at Nicopolis when relieved by either Artemas or Tychicus (Tit. 3:12), and may possibly have been further commissioned at Nicopolis for an Evangelistic Mission to Dalmatia on which he was engaged at the time when Paul wrote II Timothy (II Tim. 4:10).

Later tradition, however, assumed his return to Crete and described him as Bishop there until his old age.

It is evident that he was an ardent, able, active fellow-worker, and most beloved friend of the Apostle (Gal. 2:1, 3; II Tim. 4:10; Tit. 1:4; 3:12). We learn most about him from this Epistle.

(7) "AND NOT BY HIS COMING ONLY, BUT BY THE CONSOLATION WHEREWITH HE WAS COMFORTED IN YOU, WHEN HE TOLD US YOUR EARNEST DESIRE, YOUR MOURNING, YOUR FERVENT MIND TOWARD ME; SO THAT I REJOICED THE MORE."

As we have already stated, II Corinthians is in a brief sense of the word, an autobiography of the Apostle. In none of his other Epistles does he open his heart as he does in this Epistle.

HIS COMING

The phrase, *"And not by his coming only,"* means not merely by the fact that he was restored to me, that my anxieties in regard to him were now dissipated.

It is the arrival of Titus as such that is stressed as being a comfort for Paul and for those with him. Note that *"with the arrival of Titus"* is repeated: *"Not only with his arrival."*

It seems that Paul may have been worried about the safety of Titus. When he did not find his friend at Troas, after waiting he then went on into Macedonia and still waited, the fear grew that perhaps something had happened to the man. Things were either in a terrible condition in Corinth so that Titus dare not leave, or he had left and had been injured on the way (robbers, thieves, accident, etc.) or had taken sick, or maybe even had lost his life.

The last appeared the more probable, for surely, when Titus could not get back in proper time as had been agreed, he would, if he were alive, have sent some message, and he would have done this the more since he knew Paul's great concern. However, he is now at last here! (Possibly he did send a message, but it did not reach Paul.)

THE CONSOLATION

The phrase, *"But by the consolation wherewith he was comforted in you,"* refers to the visit by Titus to Corinth. He had been kindly treated, and he had seen all the effect produced by the letter which he had desired. He had, therefore, been much comforted by his visit to Corinth; and this was a source of additional joy to Paul.

Titus rejoiced at what he had witnessed among the Corinthians, and he imparted that same joy to Paul as well.

The joy of one friend will diffuse itself through the heart of another. Joy within itself is diffusive; and one Christian cannot well be happy without making others happy also.

The idea of Paul's statement is, *"He who comforts — comforted us — with the comfort — with which he was comforted."* This is Paul's way of ringing the changes on a word; it conveys the thought that a flood of comfort poured in on those who so much needed it. As to Titus, he did not only bring comfort, he brought it out of a heart that had drunk in all the comfort while he was in Corinth. He conveyed all of it like a full vessel.

NOTES

WHY IS THIS SO IMPORTANT?

The stakes here were high. Not only was the Church at Corinth at stake, for had they rebelled against Paul's Epistle which we now know as I Corinthians, it would have meant their destruction, and possibly could have spread to other Churches.

Satan had engineered an all-out attack against the Church, and had done so by seeking to pervert and twist the True Gospel of Jesus Christ which had been conveyed by Paul. He was using false teachers to accomplish this task. He almost succeeded!

Even though the Scripture is not overly clear on this point, it is my contention that these interlopers were from Jerusalem. This we do know, the flashing of their credentials as outlined in 3:1, were such that they impressed the beholder. All during this time, and the establishing of Churches over that part of the Roman Empire, Paul was constantly engaged in a balancing act. He was trying to maintain at least some type of harmony with Jerusalem, without having to compromise the great Covenant of Grace, which he of course, sternly refused to do. Consequently, if these false teachers had succeeded in turning the Corinthians, the fallout could have been disastrous; therefore, the significance of all of this is weighty indeed.

THEIR EARNEST DESIRE

The phrase, *"When he told us your earnest desire,"* refers to the desire of the Corinthians to comply with that which Paul had written and stated. In other words, they instantly set about to reform the abuses which existed in the Church, and which had given him so much pain. This is what so gladdened the heart of the Apostle.

In effect, they recognized by their action his Apostleship, which the detractors had caused to be brought into question; therefore, they recognized what he wrote in I Corinthians as the Word of the Lord. Actually, this is what it was all about.

They would either recognize the false doctrine of the false apostles, or the Word of the Lord as given to Paul. They could not have both.

In reality, this is the great battleground of the ages and always has been. Cain would change the Word of the Lord, while his brother Abel would adhere to the Promise. Consequently, that conflict has raged ever since, and rages unto this hour.

Satan's efforts presently are to pull people away from the Word, and to use any means at his disposal to do so. He desires that men substitute their own gospel, or else they subtly twist and pervert the True Word of God.

"Earnest desire" in the Greek is *"epipothesin,"* and means *"eager longing."*

MOURNING

The phrase, *"Your mourning,"* speaks of deep repentance over the sins which had prevailed in the Church. They had a sincere sorrow for what had been done, and a strong desire to rectify the situation, which is a perfect blueprint for repentance, or what repentance actually is.

The word *"mourning"* in the Greek is *"odurmon,"* and means *"lamentation."*

This has reference to the fact that the Light broke through, and all of a sudden they began to see the direction in which they had been going, a direction incidentally, which would have destroyed them had it continued. It is the moment when the wayward Christian sees his wrong and desires to straighten out the situation.

THIS IS THE WAY IT MAY HAVE HAPPENED

When Titus arrived at Corinth, no doubt, the news spread fast that he had come directly from Paul, and as well, had brought a long Letter with him addressing all the problems of the Church. Quite possibly the largest home was selected, for all the Believers to gather in one place.

I personally feel that the Holy Spirit was moving mightily upon the scene and in every heart and life. In other words, it was not just another gathering, and the significance of all that was happening could no doubt be felt by the Corinthians.

Once they had all gathered, the floor was given to Titus. He no doubt began his remarks by greeting them on behalf of Paul, and giving news of the great Apostle. The Lord, no doubt, attended his words. The crowd of possibly several hundreds of people must have leaned forward so as to catch every word, themselves feeling the greatness and the poignancy of the moment.

NOTES

Titus then tells them how that this Letter contains answers to the questions they had asked, plus it addresses other very serious concerns which had come to Paul's ears. Titus would then have probably bowed his head and prayed along with the congregation, and then proceeded to read this Letter from Paul.

He begins, *"Paul, called to be an Apostle of Jesus Christ through the Will of God . . . unto the Church of God which is at Corinth. . . ."*

A holy hush fills the place as Titus continues to read. Paul first of all addressed the party spirit at Corinth, which was threatening to destroy the Church, and then he addressed the terrible problem of incest (I Cor. Chpt. 5).

By this time, the convicting power of the Holy Spirit is moving strongly through the hearts and lives of the people, as faces begin to be wet with tears. There must have been a stifled sob here and another there. Others could be heard quietly weeping, as the Holy Spirit drives home the words of the Apostle.

When Titus at last comes to the great 15th Chapter of I Corinthians which details the great Resurrection, by now the pureness of this Message hits home, with it striking to the very depths of the hearts of all who were present. In a few minutes time as the Spirit of God moves, error and wrong thinking are swept away. And then Titus reads the closing words of the Apostle, *"My Love be with you all in Christ Jesus. Amen"* (I Cor. 16:24).

The word *"mourning"* as it refers to *"lamentations"* means that the entirety of the proceeding was broken up by loud sobs as men and women began to repent and to call on God. As the Spirit of God sweeps the place, there is a possibility that the Service may have lasted all day or all night, with scores of people repenting before the Lord, even asking God to forgive them for the anxiety they had caused the Apostle, and their wrong direction.

As Titus relates all of this to Paul, the comfort that fills his heart knows no bounds, even as is evidenced in the things he says here. One can well imagine his feelings. In fact, he probably wrote II Corinthians almost immediately after this particular incident.

How many Churches in the land, just as Corinth of old, need to once again hear the

Word of God and be brought to a place of repentance? As at Corinth, it would be the greatest thing that ever happened to them.

TOWARD PAUL

The phrase, *"Your fervent mind toward me,"* speaks volumes.

It is impossible to separate the Message from the Messenger. If they would not accept Paul, they would not accept his Message. They are now faithful to him, since repentance, because now they fully recognize his place and position in Christ, and that his great interest in them is not for his own personal satisfaction, but rather for their own sakes and the Cause of Christ. Woe to the Preacher who thrusts his person ahead of Christ and succeeds in getting people to cling to him and not above all to Christ!

The idea is, that their genuine repentance had changed their focus on life, toward God's man, and God in general. The idea denotes that they evinced great ardor of attachment to him, and an earnest desire to comply with his wishes.

Previously he pleads with them to recognize his Apostleship. As well, he pleads with them to love him as he has loved them (7:2-3).

But now all of this has changed and wondrously so! The Holy Spirit has performed the task; He has accomplished the work in their hearts, something no mortal could have done. Paul was the instrument, but the Holy Spirit was the Author.

REJOICING

The phrase, *"So that I rejoiced the more,"* refers to the fact that his rejoicing increased, as Titus began to give him the details of what had happened. Under any circumstances the coming of Titus would have been an occasion of joy; but it was especially so from the account which he had given to Paul.

This was joy beyond all comfort. Comfort was precious indeed; but to be able to rejoice was like comfort being crowned. Forget not that all this came just when Paul was deepest in concern and in other troubles.

(8) "FOR THOUGH I MADE YOU SORRY WITH A LETTER, I DO NOT REPENT, THOUGH I DID REPENT: FOR I PERCEIVE THAT THE SAME EPISTLE HATH MADE YOU SORRY, THOUGH IT WERE BUT FOR A SEASON."

NOTES

The remainder of this Chapter details the repentance of Corinth. Paul did not want to come to Corinth in grief and delayed his coming for that very reason. Now he indeed rejoices and can go to Corinth in joy, which he did later.

What had so deeply grieved him was what compelled him to grieve the Corinthians, to grieve them in love. In 2:2 he says that only he who grieved him could remove that grief and rejoice him again. This is what happened, he is now voicing that joy.

SORRY

The phrase, *"For though I made you sorry with a Letter,"* no doubt, refers to I Corinthians which had been delivered by Titus, and had occasioned the repentance. This *"Letter"* was and is the infallible, unchangeable, unalterable Word of God.

(Some think that he is referring to another Epistle which is now lost; however, even though there may have been an Epistle lost or maybe even two, still, the terminology of I Corinthians fits the idea of all that is being here said and done. Consequently, I feel that I Corinthians is the *"Letter"* of which he speaks.)

The word *"sorry"* here is actually referring to *"Godly sorrow,"* which will be detailed in Verse 10, which speaks of true repentance.

The word *"repent"* in the Greek is *"metanoeo,"* and in classical Greek means *"to change one's mind or purpose, to change one's opinion."*

The noun *"metanoia,"* means *"a change of mind on reflection."* These two words used in classical Greek signified a change of mind regarding anything, but when brought over into the New Testament, their usage is limited to a change of mind in the spiritual sphere. They refer to a change of moral thought and reflection which follows moral delinquency.

This includes not only the act of changing one's attitude towards an opinion of sin but also that of forsaking it. Sorrow and contrition with respect to sin, are included in the Bible idea of repentance, but these follow and are consequent upon the sinner's change of mind with respect to it.

THE ACT OF REPENTANCE

The act of repentance is based first of all and primarily upon an intellectual apprehension of the character of sin, man's guilt with respect to it, and man's duty to turn away from it. The emotional and volitional aspects of the act of repentance follow, and are the result of this intellectual process of a change of mind with respect to it.

This means that the correct approach of the Christian worker to a sinner whom he wishes to lead to the Lord is that of clearly explaining the issues involved. When the unsaved person is made to clearly understand the significance of sin, the intellectual process of changing his mind with respect to it can follow, with the result that sorrow, contrition, and turning away from it will also follow.

A mere emotional appeal to the sinner is not the correct one. The Greek word *"metanoeo"* tells us that the intellectual appeal must come first, since the act of repenting is basically a mental one at the start. In other words, man has to come to the realization in his mind that he is a sinner and that he needs a Saviour. Of course, the Holy Spirit all the time is working upon the heart of the sinner as the Gospel is being given to him.

In some way, the sinner has to know why he needs to repent, why he needs a Saviour, and why sin is destroying him. Even though all of this originates in the heart, still, it must affect the mind, or else the person cannot be saved. That doesn't mean that he has to understand everything about the Gospel, but it does mean that he has to understand some things.

In I Corinthians Paul felt it necessary to reprove the Corinthians for their dissensions and other disorders which had occurred, and which were being tolerated in the Church. That Epistle was fitted to produce pain in them — as severe and just reproof always does; and Paul felt very anxious about its affect on them.

It was painful to him to write it, and he was well aware that it must cause deep distress among them to be thus reproved.

CONVICTION OF THE HOLY SPIRIT

In effect, what we're speaking of here by the word *"sorrow,"* in a sense, is the convicting power of the Holy Spirit. He convicts of sin, Righteousness and of judgment (Jn. 16:7-11). As recorded here, He convicts the hearts of Christians just as much as He does the hearts of sinners. Sin is sin wherever it is found.

NOTES

It is regrettable, but most Preachers (and I exaggerate not) never preach a corrective Message. Consequently, there is no repentance in their Churches such as it was at Corinth.

Even as Paul emphasizes here, it is never pleasant to preach such a Message, even though at times they are desperately needed. Consequently, if the Preacher is not led by the Lord and determined to obey Him, he in fact will never preach a Message of this nature. Consequently, he becomes little more than a hireling.

Worse still, many Believers do not desire a Church where the Word of God is preached accordingly, and the Holy Spirit convicts of sin and wrongdoing. They don't like to be made to feel uncomfortable, even as the Corinthians were made to feel at that particular time. As a result, they seek Churches where the Message never convicts them and they can, consequently, continue to feel comfortable in their sin and wrongdoing. Such, however, is the road to spiritual ruin, and every other type of ruin for that matter.

While the Holy Spirit definitely makes the Saint of God happy and glad, in fact, in a way that the world can never compare; however, He can also make the wayward Christian, even as at Corinth, feel like he's hanging over Hell on a rotten stick. As stated, some Christians don't like that, so they seek a Church where such does not exist.

THE FEELINGS OF THE APOSTLE

The phrase, *"I do not repent, though I did repent,"* presents Paul using the word here which does *not* denote repentance in the sense in which the word is commonly understood, as if any wrong had been done. It is not the language of remorse.

It can denote here nothing more than *"that uneasiness which a good man feels, not from the consciousness of having done wrong, but from a tenderness for others, and a fear lest that which, prompted by duty, he had said, should have too strong an affect upon them."*

Here it is not to be understood that Paul meant to say that he had done anything wrong. He was an inspired man, and what he had said to the Corinthians, because it is that of which we speak, was proper and right. He was a man of deep feeling, and of tender affections, and was pained at the necessity of giving reproof.

And there is no improbability in supposing that after the Letter had been sent off, and he reflected on its nature and on the pain which he knew it would cause to those whom he tenderly loved, that there might be some misgiving of heart about it, and the deepest anxiety and regret at the necessity of having to do such.

I have some empathy for the Apostle, even as any Preacher would have, inasmuch as I have felt led of the Lord to preach a particular Message, or even to write an article, which I knew would be overly strong. Countless times, I have grieved after doing so, wondering if I had been too strong? However, even as the Apostle of old, every single time, at least if my memory serves me correctly, it has always been of God.

SCRIPTURAL INSPIRATION

There are some who have difficulty in putting statements such as this together with inspiration. Consequently, they try all kinds of fantastic hypotheses and tortuous exegesis to explain away this phrase as though it were inconsistent with Paul's inspiration; however, the Doctrine of Inspiration is not the fetish into which it has been degraded by formal systems of scholastic theology.

Inspiration was not a mechanical dictation of words, but the influence of the Holy Spirit in the hearts of men who retained all their own natural emotions.

Inspiration is that special influence of the Holy Spirit in the lives of holy men, which qualified and enabled them to make an infallible record of Divine Truth concerning the Will of God to man.

The purpose of Inspiration is to secure Truth and unity in record and not sameness of words or statements. Revelation discovers new Truth; Inspiration superintends the communicating and recording of that Truth.

The Spirit use the faculties, abilities, talents, and personalities of the writers to record things, past, present, and future. He gave direct Revelations, guided them to choose records of men, and superintended the writers in all their work until we now have a perfect and infallible record of the origin and destiny of all creation.

NOTES

TO WHAT DEGREE WERE WRITERS INSPIRED?

1. Some of Scripture give the exact Words of God (Ex. 32:16; Deut. 5:4, 24; Mat. 3:1).

2. Some words were put into the mouths of the speakers who spoke as the Spirit inspired them (Ex. 4:12; Num. 23:5; Ezek. 2:7; 3:10-11; Acts 3:21).

3. Some words were written as the Spirit moved men (Ex. 34:27; II Pet. 1:21).

4. In some parts of Scripture it was left up to the writers to choose their own words and relate truth by the inspiration and guidance of the Spirit (Dan. 12:8, 9; Lk. 1:1-4; Jn. 20:30-31; Acts 1:1-2).

WHAT IT PRODUCED

The phrase, *"For I perceive that the same Epistle hath made you sorry, though it were but for a season,"* proclaims the good effect of the Epistle. It produced the kind of sorrow which Paul desired — a sorrow that brought them to repentance. Consequently, it produced permanent good results.

As well, the sorrow which is caused was only for a season; nevertheless, the good effects will be abiding.

Consequently, Paul is saying, *"I have, therefore, great occasion to rejoice that I sent the Epistle. It produced permanent repentance and reformation, and thus accomplished all that the Holy Spirit wished and desired, which overly gladdens my heart."*

In effect, Paul is saying, *"Even though I felt I may have been too strong in my Letter toward you after it was sent, now of course, I know it was the right thing. It did what it should have done, it made you sorry and brought you to repentance; however, the sorrow was only for a short time, while the joy will be everlasting."*

(9) "NOW I REJOICE, NOT THAT YE WERE MADE SORRY, BUT THAT YE SORROWED TO REPENTANCE: FOR YE WERE MADE SORRY AFTER A GODLY MANNER, THAT YE MIGHT RECEIVE DAMAGE BY US IN NOTHING."

All of that temporary regret which was due to being so far away from Corinth, so completely in the dark until Titus came, so plagued with uncertainty in regard to the manner in which his letter would be received, has now entirely disappeared.

REJOICING

The phrase, *"Now I rejoice, not that ye were made sorry,"* means that Paul was not happy or rejoicing simply because they were made sorry, but by what the sorrow produced, which was repentance. Paul rejoices, *"not that you were grieved,"* not that I merely hurt you deeply — how could he rejoice because of that? — *"but that you were grieved unto repentance."* The fullest stress is on this phrase.

A surgeon may cause severe pain; he rejoices when he sees the cure that this pain has produced. It is not the pain as such but the pain as being productive of the cure that rejoices him.

SORROWED TO REPENTANCE

The phrase, *"But that ye sorrowed to repentance,"* indicates that it was not mere grief; it was not sorrow producing melancholy, gloom, or despair; it was not sorrow which led one to be angry at him who had reproved them for errors — as is sometimes the case with the sorrow that is produced by reproof; but it was sorrow that led to a change and reformation. It was sorrow that was followed by a putting away of the evil for the existence of which there had been occasion to reprove them.

"Repentance" here is not the same word that is used in Verse 8. The sense here is, that it produced a change, a reformation. This *"repentance"* denotes a change for the better; a change of mind that is durable and productive in its consequences; a change which amounts to a totally different direction, i.e., *"a permanent reformation."* It was such sorrow for their sin as to lead them to put away the evils which had existed among them. It was this fact, and not that they had been made sorry, that led Paul to rejoice.

The way to true repentance even in the case of Christians who have sinned and erred as at Corinth, is the way of deep grief and sorrow. The mistake made by many a Preacher is the endeavor to induce a painless, griefless repentance. In fact, such repentance does not exist.

Peter wept bitterly. A broken and a contrite heart is not a pleasant sensation, but it definitely does lead to a pleasant sensation.

NOTES

Much repentance presses out tears. The peaceable Fruit of Righteousness grows from the pain of chastisement (Heb. 12:11).

Repentance expresses the vital inner change that is wrought by the Law in conjunction with the Gospel when the heart turns from its sin and guilt to God and His pardon in Christ Jesus. When repentance is used alone, as it is here, it denotes the whole act which speaks of contrition (sorrow) plus Faith — Faith in Christ. It signifies a renewal of the heart's inner change. In Corinth the congregation as a whole, in a great change of heart, turned back from the wrong and sinful course which it had followed, and now proceeded down the right path of the True Gospel.

A GODLY MANNER

The phrase, *"For ye were made sorry after a godly manner,"* in effect, means *"According to God."*

The being grieved *"unto repentance"* should be distinguished from being grieved otherwise. The grief or sorrow mentioned here, refers to *"a way that accords with God."*

One usually grieves over a grave loss; this grief which led to a repentance that was in harmony with God (a godly manner) is the very opposite. The Corinthians were not thereby made to suffer loss in any way.

NO DAMAGE

The phrase, *"That ye might receive damage by us in nothing,"* presents the grief of repentance as never a loss in any way. It is always the very opposite, the greatest spiritual gain.

The Greek word rendered *"receive damage"* means properly, to bring loss upon anyone; to receive loss or detriment.

The sense here seems to be, *"So that on the whole no real injury was done you in any respect by me. You were indeed put to pain and grief by my reproof. You sorrowed. But it has done you no injury on the whole. It has been a benefit to you, and a great benefit at that. If you had not reformed; if you had been pained without putting away the sins for which the reproof was administered; if it had been mere grief without any proper fruit, you might have said that you would have suffered a loss of happiness or you might have given me occasion to inflict severer discipline. But now you are gainers in happiness by all the sorrow which I have caused."*

No man suffers loss by being told of his faults if he repents; and men are under the highest obligations to those faithful Ministers and other friends who tell them of their errors, and who are the means of bringing them to true repentance.

(10) "FOR GODLY SORROW WORKETH REPENTANCE TO SALVATION NOT TO BE REPENTED OF: BUT THE SORROW OF THE WORLD WORKETH DEATH."

It is amazing to the degree that Paul deals with the subject of repentance, and as well repentance as it pertains to Believers, and yet, many in the Charismatic world do not even believe in repentance, claiming it is an Old Testament Doctrine exclusively. The problem in that particular category of Churches is that they have an improper knowledge, in other words, a skewed interpretation of the Plan of Redemption, which as should be obvious, is a very serious thing. There are times that Christians need to repent, just as it was with ancient Corinth, and as well, this is God's manner of dealing with the problem of sin. He has devised no other. In other words, if men repudiate His Plan of Redemption, they are guilty of substituting their own salvation which of course, God can never accept.

GODLY SORROW

The phrase, *"For Godly sorrow,"* refers to the right type of sorrow. It is sorrow which understands that one has sinned against God, has insulted God, and, therefore, has made a mockery of Righteousness. It is sorrow that takes full responsibility and blame for ones actions, which means not casting blame elsewhere.

The first sin in the Garden exhibited no Godly sorrow. Adam and Eve blamed others for their predicament, even God (Gen. 3:12-13).

"Godly sorrow" presents a very important expression in regard to true repentance, and shows the exact nature of that sorrow which is connected with a return to God. The phrase may be regarded as implying the following things:

THE SORROW THAT GOD APPROVES

Such sorrow as God approves, or such as is suitable to, or conformable to His will and desires. It cannot mean that it is such sorrow or grief as God has, for He has none; but such as shall be in accordance with what God demands in a return to Him.

NOTES

It is a sorrow which His Truth is fitted to produce in the heart; such a sorrow as shall appropriately arise from viewing sin as God views it; such sorrow as exists in the mind when our views accord with His in regard to the existence, the extinct, the nature, and the ill-desert of sin.

Such views will lead to sorrow that sin has ever been committed; and such views will be *"according to God."*

SORROW EXERCISED TOWARD GOD

Such sorrow as shall be exercised towards God in view of sin is that of which we speak. It should arise from a view of the evil of sin as committed against a Holy God. It is not mainly that it will lead to pain; that it will overwhelm the soul in disgrace; that it will forfeit the favor or lead to the contempt of man; or that it will lead to an eternal hell; but it is such as arises from a view of the evil of sin as committed against a Holy and just God, deriving its main evil from the fact that it is an offense against His infinite majesty.

Such sorrow David had (Ps. 51) when he said, *"Against Thee, and Thee only have I sinned"*; when the offense regarded as committed against man, enormous as it was, was lost and absorbed in its greater evil when regarded as committed against God.

So all true and genuine repentance is that which regards sin as deriving its main evil from the fact that it is committed against God.

IT IS A SORROW THAT LEADS TO GOD

It leads to God to obtain forgiveness — to seek for consolation. A heart truly contrite and penitent seeks God, and implores pardon from Him. Sorrow in view of sin, other than that which is genuine repentance, leads the person away from God.

Such seeks consolation in the world; he endeavors to drive away his serious impressions, or to drown them in the pleasures and the cares of life. But genuine sorrow for sin leads the soul to God, and conducts the sinner, through the Redeemer, to Him to obtain the pardon and peace which He only can give to a wounded spirit.

In God Alone can pardon and true peace be found; and Godly sorrow for sin will seek them there.

WORKETH REPENTANCE

The phrase, *"Worketh repentance,"* proclaims that which produces a change that shall be permanent; a reformation.

It is not mere regret; it does not soon pass away in its effects, but it produces permanent and abiding changes. A man who mourns over sin as committed against God, and who seeks God for pardon, will reform his life, and truly repent.

He who has grief for sin only because it will lead to disgrace or shame, or because it will lead to poverty or pain, will not necessarily break off from it and reform. It is only when it is seen that sin is committed against God, and is evil in His sight, that it leads to a change of life.

As well, this which *"worketh repentance"* constitutes no penance whatsoever. In other words, it is not possible for a human being to atone for sin in any manner by works, by doing religious things, by giving money, by punishing oneself or being punished — all such effort is scripturally irresponsible. In effect, such action is an insult to God, actually saying by its very nature that what Jesus did at Calvary to atone for sin was not sufficient, and other things must be added. Regrettably, much of the Church world falls into that category. God does not require a person to repent before Him and also say 100 Hail Mary's, or do some such other silly thing.

Jesus paid it all at Calvary; consequently, as bad, as evil, as horrible as sin is, the only manner in which it can be covered, washed, cleansed, and forgiven by God, is for the believing sinner to exhibit Faith in what Christ did at Calvary and the Resurrection. John said it clearly:

"If we confess our sins (confess them to God), *He is faithful* (will never turn us away) *and just* (has satisfied His justice by what Jesus did at Calvary) *to forgive us our sins* (to justify us), *and to cleanse us* (sanctify us) *from all unrighteousness"* (I Jn. 1:9).

SALVATION

The phrase, *"To Salvation not to be repented of,"* means that such action will never be regretted. It is that which the mind and heart approves, and which it will always approve, for the simple reason that it restores the individual to God and God to the individual.

Whoever yet repented of having truly repented of sin? Who is there, who has there ever been, who became a true penitent, and a true Christian, who ever regretted it? Not an individual has ever been known who regretted his having become a Christian. No one who regretted that he had become one too soon in life, or that he had served the Lord Jesus too faithfully or too long.

This brings a glad heart and because the load of sin and guilt is lifted, with fellowship restored.

Sin destroys fellowship with God; it destroys the ability of the person to praise God; it creates a wall between God and man. When all of this is removed, and it can only be removed by true heartfelt repentance, peace is instantly restored.

THE SORROW OF THE WORLD

The phrase, *"But the sorrow of the world worketh death,"* presents a sorrow that is merely remorse, often despair, actually the direct forerunner of death.

It is sorrow that regrets that it was caught and not sorrow over the sin itself. It is regret over the effects of sin, and not sorrow over the fact of sin. Such sorrow is always selfish and is never Godward. In other words, it has no concern that it has offended God, only offended itself.

Such is seen in the suicide of Judas Iscariot. It is the false repentance of Cain, Saul, and Ahithophel and untold numbers of others.

WHAT IS THE SORROW OF THE WORLD?

All sorrow which is not toward God, and which does not arise from just views of sin as committed against God, or lead to God, is the sorrow of the world.

When such sorrow arises from a view of worldly consequences merely, and when there is no looking to God for pardon and consolation, such defines worldly sorrow. Thus men, when they loose their property or friends, often pine in grief without looking to God. Such sorrow arises from the world, and it terminates there. It is the loss of what they valued pertaining to this world, and it is all which they had, and it produces death.

This type of sorrow always tends to death, and never toward life. It produces distress only. It is attended with no consolation. It tends to break the spirit, to destroy the peace, and to mar the happiness. It often leads to death itself, and in fact, will always ultimately lead to death.

In fact, such sorrow produces murmuring, repining, complaining, fretfulness against God, and thus leads to His displeasure, and to the condemnation and ruin of the soul.

THE SALVATION OF MAN

Even though Paul is only dealing here with one aspect of Salvation, that of repentance, still, due to its vast significance, I think it would be proper here to address ourselves to the total Plan of God regarding the single greatest thing that man could ever know, the Salvation of the soul, i.e., *"to be restored to God through faith in Jesus Christ."*

The Lord Jesus Christ, by His atoning death, purchased man's Salvation. How is this Salvation applied by God and received by man, and so realized in experience?

The Truths relating to the application of Salvation may be grouped under three headings: Justification, Regeneration, Sanctification.

The Truths relating to man's acceptance of Salvation may be grouped under the headings: Repentance, Faith, Obedience.

THE NATURE OF SALVATION

1. Justification is a judicial term bringing to our minds a courtroom scene. Man, guilty and condemned, before God, is acquitted and declared righteous — that is, justified.

2. Regeneration is that which takes place in the heart of the believing sinner. The soul, dead in trespasses and in sins, needs a new life, which new life is imparted by a Divine act of Regeneration. The person then becomes a Child of God and a member of His household.

3. Sanctification suggests a Temple scene, for the word is connected primarily with the worship of God. Set right in relation to God's Law and Born-Again to a new life, the person is henceforth dedicated to the service of God.

Bought with a price, he is no longer his own; he departs not from the Temple (figuratively speaking) but serves God day and night (Lk. 2:37). He is sanctified by God, which means to be made clean and set apart to God, and is self-given to God.

A saved man, then, is one who has been set right with God, adopted into the Divine family, and is now dedicated to God's service. In other words, his experience of Salvation, or state of Grace, consists of Justification, Regeneration (and adoption), and Sanctification. Being justified, he belongs to the Righteous, in fact is Righteous; being Regenerated, he is a Child of God; being Sanctified, he is a *"Saint"* (literally, a holy person, made so by faith in Christ).

FULL SALVATION

Do these blessings follow one another or are they simultaneous as to time?

There is indeed a logical order: the sinner is first set right in relation to God's Law; his life is disordered, therefore, he must be changed; he has been living for sin and the world, and, therefore, must be separated to a new life and service. Yet, the three experiences are simultaneous in the sense that they cannot be separated actually, although we separate them for the purpose of study.

All three (Sanctification, Justification, and Regeneration) constitute *"full Salvation."* The outward change called Justification is followed by the inward change called Regeneration, and this is followed by dedication to God's service. We cannot conceive of a truly justified person being unregenerate; neither can we conceive of a truly regenerate person being unsanctified (although in actual life a saved person may at times violate his consecration). However, there can be no full Salvation without these three experiences anymore than there can be a real triangle without three sides. They represent the three-sided foundation on which the subsequent Christian life is built. From these three beginnings the Christian life progresses to its consummation.

This threefold distinction regulates the language of the New Testament down to the finest detail. Let us illustrate:

SANCTIFICATION

Paul gave us the order of Salvation when he said, *"But ye are Washed, but ye are Sanctified, but ye are Justified in the name of the*

NOTES

Lord Jesus, and by the Spirit of our God" (I Cor. 6:11).

If one is to notice, Sanctification is placed first for the simple reason that one must be made clean and set apart unto God, which defines Sanctification, before one can be Justified. This is done instantly upon one believing in Christ.

However, the Sanctification process continues throughout the life of the Christian.

The Christian life is a life dedicated to the worship and service of God, that is, a Sanctified life. In relation to the Sanctified life, God is the Holy One; Christ is the High Priest; sin is defilement; repentance is consciousness of defilement; the Atonement is an expiatory Sacrifice; the Christian life is dedicated on the Altar (Rom. 12:1); the perfection of this aspect is progressive Sanctification from sin and separation to God.

JUSTIFICATION

God is the Judge, and Christ is the Advocate; sin is transgression of the Law; Atonement is satisfaction; repentance is conviction; acceptance is pardon or remission; the Spirit's witness is a pardon; the Christian life is obedience and its perfection the fulfillment of the Law of Righteousness.

Sanctification makes one not guilty, while Justification declares one not guilty, in other words, a legal work.

REGENERATION

Salvation is also a new life in Christ. In relation to this new life, God is the Father (begetter), Christ, the Elder Brother and Life; sin is self-will, choosing our will rather than that of the Head of the household who is Christ; Atonement is Reconciliation; acceptance is Adoption; renewal of life is Regeneration, being born of God; the Christian life is the crucifying or mortifying of the old nature, which is opposed to the new nature, and the raising up of the new; the perfection of this life is the perfect reflection of the Image of Christ, the Only Begotten Son of God.

Even though these things take place in succession, still it is all in a single act, and is done totally by the Lord, with the Believer only furnishing Faith.

All three Blessings of Grace, Sanctification, Justification, and Regeneration, were procured by the Atoning Death of Christ, and the virtues of that death are imparted to man by the Holy Spirit. As stated, it all comes by Faith.

NOTES

As satisfying the claims of the Law, the Atonement secured man's pardon and Righteousness; as abolishing the barrier between God and man, it made possible our regenerate life; as a Sacrifice for purification from sin, its benefit is Sanctification and Holiness.

Note also that all three blessings flow from our union with Christ. The Believer is one with Christ in virtue of His Atoning Death and in virtue of His Life-giving Spirit. We have become the Righteousness of God in Him (II Cor. 5:21); and through Him have the forgiveness of sins (Eph. 1:7); in Him we are new creatures, Born-Again to a new life (II Cor. 5:17); we are sanctified in Him (I Cor. 1:2), and He is made unto us Sanctification (I Cor. 1:30). He is *"the Author of Eternal Salvation."*

SALVATION — OUTWARD AND INWARD

Salvation is both objective (outward) and subjective (inward):

1. Righteousness is first of all a change of position, but it is followed by a change of condition. Righteousness must be both imputed and imparted, which is done by Christ.

2. Adoption refers to the conferring of the privilege of Divine Sonship; Regeneration is the inward life that corresponds to our calling and makes us *"partakers of the Divine Nature."*

3. Sanctification is both external and internal. Outwardly it is a separation from sin and dedication to God; inwardly it calls for purification from sin.

The outward aspect of Grace is provided by the Atoning Work of Christ; the inward aspect is the Work of the Holy Spirit.

THE CONDITIONS OF SALVATION

What do we mean by the conditions of Salvation?

God has requirements regarding the man on whom He freely bestows the Blessings of the Gospel of Grace.

The Scriptures set forth Repentance and Faith as the conditions for Salvation; Water Baptism is mentioned as the outward symbol of the convert's inner Faith (Mark 1:15; Acts 2:38; 3:19; 16:31; 22:16).

Turning from sin and turning to God are the conditions and preparations for Salvation.

Strictly speaking, there is no merit to repentance or Faith; for all that is necessary for Salvation has already been done for the penitent. By repentance the penitent removes the obstacle to the receiving of the Gift; by Faith he accepts the Gift. But though repentance and Faith are obligatory because commanded, the helping influence of the Holy Spirit is implied. Blasphemy against the Spirit drives away Him Who Alone can move the heart to contrition, hence, there is no pardon.

WHAT IS THE DIFFERENCE BETWEEN REPENTANCE AND FAITH?

Faith is the instrument by which we receive Salvation, which is not true of repentance. Repentance is concern with sin and misery while Faith dwells upon God's mercy.

Can there be Faith without repentance?

No; only the penitent feels the need of a Saviour and desires the Salvation of his soul.

Can there be Godly repentance without Faith? No one can repent in the Scriptural sense without Faith in God's Word, without believing His threats of judgment and promises of Salvation.

Are Faith and Repentance simply preparatory to Salvation?

No, they also follow the Believer into the Christian life; Repentance develops into zeal for soul-purification, and Faith works in love and continues to receive from God.

REPENTANCE

Even though we have previously dealt with this subject, still, perhaps the following thoughts will add to what we have already said.

Repentance is true sorrow for sin, with sincere effort to forsake it. In other words, it is a godly sorrow for sin, even as we are now studying.

The conviction of guilt produced by the Holy Spirit's application of the Divine Law to the heart, constitutes the groundwork for repentance. It is being sorry enough to quit, as someone has said.

Three elements constitute Scriptural Repentance: an intellectual, an emotional, and a practical. They may be illustrated as follows:

1. A traveler learns that he is on the wrong train; this knowledge corresponds to the intellectual element by which a person realizes through the preaching of the Word, that he is not right with God.

2. The traveler is disturbed at his discovery; he is annoyed, perhaps fearful. This illustrates the emotional side of Repentance which is a self-accusation and sincere sorrow for having offended God (II Cor. 7:10).

3. He leaves the train at the first opportunity and boards the right train. This illustrates the practical side of Repentance, which involves a complete *"about face"* and a traveling in God's direction.

One Greek word for *"Repentance"* means literally *"a change of mind or a change of purpose."* The convicted sinner purposes to mend his ways and turn to God; the practical result is that he brings forth fruits meet for Repentance (Mat. 3:8).

Repentance honors the Law as Faith honors the Gospel. How does Repentance honor the Law? In contrition it mourns over its departure from the Holy Commandment and over personal defilement revealed in its light; in confession it acknowledges the justice of the sentence; in amendment it turns from sin and makes what reparation is possible and necessary under the circumstances.

How does the Holy Spirit help a person to repent? By applying the Word to the conscious, touching the heart and by strengthening the will and determination to turn from sin.

FAITH

Faith in the Scriptural sense means belief and trust. It is the assent of the mind and the consent of the will. In regard to the intellect it is belief in certain revealed Truths concerning God and Christ; in regard to the will it is the acceptance of these Truths as directing principals of life.

Intellectual Faith alone is not sufficient for Salvation (Acts 8:13, 21; James 2:19); a person may give intellectual assent to the Gospel without committing his life to it. Belief in the heart is essential (Rom. 10:9).

Intellectual Faith means the acknowledgement that the Gospel facts are true; heart Faith means the willing dedication of one's life to the obligations which those facts involve. Faith as trust implies also an emotional element; thus saving Faith is an act of the entire personality, involving intellect, emotion, and will.

NOTES

THE ENTIRE BODY OF TRUTH

The meaning of Faith may be determined by the manner in which it is employed in the original Greek. Faith sometimes denotes not only the act of believing a certain body of Truth but the entire body of Truth itself, as in the following expressions:

"Preacheth the Faith which he once destroyed"; "shall depart from the Faith"; "the word of Faith which we preach"; "the Faith once delivered unto the Saints." This is sometimes called objective (or outward Faith). The act of believing these Truths is known as subjective Faith.

The word *"believe"* conveys the thought of reposing or resting on a sure foundation, as for example in John 3:16. It also means a trust which makes a person one with its object. Thus, Faith is the connecting link between the soul and Christ.

IS FAITH A HUMAN OR A DIVINE ACTIVITY?

The fact that man is commanded to believe implies the ability and obligation to do so. All men have the capacity to place their confidence in somebody and something, so that, for example, one may put his trust in riches, in man, in friends, etc. When belief is directed to the Word of God, and the confidence reposed upon God and Christ, we have saving Faith.

However, the assisting Grace of the Holy Spirit, in co-corporation with the Word, is implied in the producing of saving Faith (Jn. 6:44; Rom. 10:17; Gal. 5:22; Heb. 12:2).

WHAT IS SAVING FAITH?

The following definitions have been given: *"Faith in Christ is a saving Grace whereby we receive and rest upon Him Alone for Salvation as it is offered to us in the Gospel."*

It is *"the act of the penitent only, as especially aided by the Spirit, and is resting upon Christ."*

"That act or habit of mind in the penitent by which, under the influence of the Divine Grace, he puts his trust in Christ as the only and sufficient Saviour."

"A sure trust and confidence that Christ died for my sins, that He loved me, and gave Himself for me."

NOTES

"It is to believe, to rely on the merits of Christ, that for His sake God is certainly willing to show mercy to us."

"The flight of a penitent sinner to the Mercy of God in Christ."

CONVERSION

In its simplest meaning, conversion is turning from sin unto God (Acts 3:19). The term is used to denote both the critical period of a sinner's return from the ways of sin to the path of Righteousness, and also repentance for some particular transgression on the part of those already in the path of Righteousness (Mat. 18:3; Lk. 22:32; James 5:20).

It is closely related to Repentance and Faith, and occasionally is stands for either or both, as representing the sum total of the activities by which man turns from sin to God (Acts 3:19; 11:21; I Pet. 2:25).

The Westminster Catechism, in answer to its own question, gives the following well-rounded definition of conversion:

WHAT IS REPENTANCE UNTO LIFE?

"Repentance unto life is a saving Grace, whereby the sinner, out of a true sense of his sin, and apprehension of the Mercy of God in Christ, doth with grief and hatred of his sin, turn from it unto God, with full purpose of, and endeavor after, new obedience."

Notice that this definition shows how conversion involves the whole personality — intellect, emotion, and will.

How is conversion to be distinguished from Salvation? Conversion describes the human or manward side of Salvation. To illustrate:

It is observed that a notorious sinner no longer drinks, gambles, or frequents haunts of vice; he hates the things he once loved and loves the things he once hated. His acquaintances say, *"He's converted, he's changed."*

They are describing what they see, namely, the manward side of the event. But from the Godward side, we would say that God has pardoned his sin and given him a new heart.

DOES THIS MEAN THAT CONVERSION IS ENTIRELY A MATTER OF HUMAN EFFORT?

Like Faith and Repentance, which it includes and involves, conversion is a human activity; but it is also a supernatural effect in that it is man's reaction to the drawing power of God's Grace and God's Word. Thus, conversion is produced by the co-corporation of Divine and human activities.

"Work out your own Salvation with fear and trembling. For it is God which worketh in you both to will and to do of His good pleasure" (Phil. 2:12-13).

The following Scriptures relate to the Divine side of conversion (Jer. 31:18; Acts 3:26). The following refer to the manward side (Ezek. 33:11; Acts 3:19; 11:18).

WHICH COMES FIRST, REGENERATION OR CONVERSION?

The operations involved in conversion are deep and mysterious, and, therefore, not to be analyzed with mathematical precision.

It is told of a candidate for ordination who was asked which came first, Regeneration or Conversion. He replied: *"Regeneration and Conversion are like the cannonball and the hole — they both go through together."*

(11) "FOR BEHOLD THIS SELFSAME THING, THAT YE SORROWED AFTER A GODLY SORT, WHAT CAREFULNESS IT WROUGHT IN YOU, YEA, WHAT CLEARING OF YOURSELVES, YEA, WHAT INDIGNATION, YEA, WHAT FEAR, YEA, WHAT VEHEMENT DESIRE, YEA, WHAT ZEAL, YEA, WHAT REVENGE! IN ALL THINGS YE HAVE APPROVED YOURSELVES TO BE CLEAR IN THIS MATTER."

This Verse tells us what actually constitutes true repentance. There should be, and there will be, deep feeling. The true penitent hates nothing so cordially as he does his sin. He hates nothing but sin. And his warfare with that is decided, uncompromising, inexorable, and eternal.

THIS SELFSAME THING

The phrase, *"For behold this selfsame thing,"* refers to the happy effects of godly sorrow.

The Corinthians had previously treated sin with careless indifference. They had let it pass and did nothing, considering neither the sin nor the sinner involved. They disregarded what this sin did to the soul, and considered not themselves, and what this indifference and inaction did to them as a congregation.

NOTES

Then Paul took them to task in I Corinthians Chapter 5. He even thought it necessary to send Titus.

Upon the occasion of his Epistle and it, no doubt, being read to them by Titus, there came the conviction of sin which resulted in Repentance, which means that the Corinthians dropped their indifference and got thoroughly busy and earnest concerning their condition.

SORROWED AFTER A GODLY SORT

The phrase, *"That ye sorrowed after a Godly sort,"* means they did what true repentance required. It was not fake, or a sham, or something of their own contrivance. It was the way of the Holy Spirit, i.e., *"Godly sorrow."*

I think the Scripture is emphatic that this Godly sorrow must be present in the heart and life of the Believer, irrespective as to the manner in which it conveys itself. The person may weep or mourn, but whatever the case, there will be a deep contrition in one's heart concerning the sin committed which has offended God. This is the *"Godly sort."*

In the following explanation given by the Apostle, we find seven proofs of Repentance, or seven things which happen when one truly repents.

Inasmuch as these were enumerated by the Holy Spirit, and the number seven denotes perfection and completion as it pertains to God, we must understand the significance of what is being said here.

CAREFULNESS

The phrase, *"What carefulness is wrought in you,"* properly denotes speed, haste, diligence, earnest effort, and forwardness.

Here it is evidently used to denote the diligence and the great anxiety which they manifested to remove the evils which existed among them. They went to work to remove them. They did not merely sit down to mourn over them, nor did they wait for God to remove them, nor did they plead that they could do nothing; but they set about the work as though they believed it might be done, and in fact, must be done.

When men are thoroughly convinced of sin, they will set about removing it with the utmost diligence. They will feel that this can be done, and in fact, as stated, must be done, or that the soul will be lost.

This no doubt referred to the case of incest, as well as possibly other situations of which we are not aware.

CLEARING OF YOURSELVES

The phrase, *"Yea, what clearing of yourselves,"* properly means an apology for their laxness in respect to these problems left unattended.

I think that one could say that they admitted to their wrongs, owned up to the wrong direction, clearly and publicly stated that what Paul had proclaimed must be done.

This does not refer to merely one or two people, but rather the entirety of the Church. In other words, even those who were not guilty of wrongdoing, or had not succumbed to false doctrine, in some way owned up to their own culpability, thereby taking blame, consequently, *"clearing themselves."*

To say it another way, it doesn't mean that some in the Church disavowed any part in the wrongdoing, but rather that all took at least some responsibility, thereby not blaming others for their own involvement, whether it had been little or large.

The way to clear oneself as the Holy Spirit through the Apostle here proclaims, is not the way of the world which is to try to attach blame elsewhere, but rather to take personal responsibility for one's wrongdoing, irrespective as to what others have done. In other words, the wrongdoing of someone else is no excuse for my wrongdoing. It is what is called *"taking personal responsibility."*

INDIGNATION

The phrase, *"Yea, what indignation,"* refers to a decided hatred of sin. It is not mere regret, or sorrow; it is positive hatred. There must be a deep indignation against sin as an evil and a bitter thing. As well, it would have been an indignation against themselves for their neglect in allowing the Church to get into this condition. In fact, if we were indignant as Christians over our personal spiritual laxness, our lukewarmness, our unconcern for lost souls, etc., our relationship with Christ would greatly improve.

FEAR

The phrase, *"Yea, what fear,"* speaks of the fear they should have had of God all along, but did not.

NOTES

The word probably refers to the anxious state of mind that the whole evil might be corrected, and to the dread of having any vestige of the evil remaining among them. In other words, they had come to see the awfulness of sin, the danger of its presence, the destruction that it afforded, and even above that, how that God cannot abide sin in any form. A proper fear of God is an absolute necessity, if we are to have a proper evaluation of things.

This does not mean a slavish fear, but rather a knowledge of Who God actually is, and what His Nature demands.

God is our Heavenly Father, at least to those who are Born-Again, and as a member of the family there need be no fear involved whatsoever except for disobedience. We should understand that God says what He means, and means what He says. His Word is not to be taken lightly.

VEHEMENT DESIRE

The phrase, *"Yea, what vehement desire,"* refers to their fervent wish to carry out that which Paul had proclaimed, in other words, to do what they should do, and what they should have done all along.

It refers to their anxious wish to remove the sin, and all the things which were wrong in the Church. The Holy Spirit had opened their eyes when they had heard I Corinthians read to them by Titus. The Word of God had garnished its desired effect. Now there was an eagerness to get things done, to set things straight.

All of this is the sure sign of Revival.

ZEAL

The phrase, *"Yea, what zeal,"* refers to them setting about the work of reformation in great earnest.

There was a *"zeal"* to get this work done, to get it done quickly, to get it done thoroughly, to leave no doubt about it being done. As well, the Holy Spirit is the Author of this thoroughness, this readiness, this great effort, this zeal.

REVENGE

The phrase, *"Yea, what revenge,"* probably refers to a determination to right the wrongs perpetrated against Paul.

As well, *"revenge"* as portrayed here, is an expression of displeasure against all that was wrong in the Church. The true penitent hates nothing so cordially as he does his sin. His warfare with that is decided, uncompromising, inexorable, and eternal, i.e., *"revenge."*

The *"revenge"* that one can exact against the Devil, is the cleaning out of every nest of sin within our lives, irrespective as to how large or little it may be. This is the revenge of which the Apostle speaks, not against people, or even the offenders in the Church, as some have claimed. Thus concludes the seven.

APPROVED YOURSELVES

The phrase, *"In all things ye have approved yourselves to be clear in this matter,"* means that the repentance was sincere, which resulted in these particular things taking place. So, if one wants to know the sincerity of any repentance, one need only look at the seven earmarks listed by the Holy Spirit through the Apostle.

(12) "WHEREFORE, THOUGH I WROTE UNTO YOU, I DID IT NOT FOR HIS CAUSE THAT HAD DONE THE WRONG, NOR FOR HIS CAUSE THAT SUFFERED WRONG, BUT THAT OUR CARE FOR YOU IN THE SIGHT OF GOD MIGHT APPEAR UNTO YOU."

In this Verse, Paul is stating that the main reason for his strong rebuke is not mainly the perpetrator of I Corinthians Chapter 5. Even though that definitely was a part of the reason, it was only a part.

He wrote his rebuke so that his sincere concern for all the Corinthian Believers would be manifested. In other words, he was concerned about the entirety of the Church.

To which we have already alluded, the situation at Corinth was of far greater significance than meets the eye. If Corinth had fallen, in other words if Paul had been repudiated as an Apostle, which meant that his Ministry would no longer be accepted, such could easily spread to other Churches, which no doubt, was Satan's original intentions.

Paul was ever attempting to keep a working balance between the Churches and Jerusalem. He knew that they looked at him as somewhat of a maverick, a lone ranger, in other words not a part of the original group. And yet, there is no hint that the original Twelve felt this way at all; nevertheless, there were problems which Paul was forever attempting to assuage.

NOTES

The interlopers or detractors who had come brandishing their *"letters of commendation,"* were no doubt, from Jerusalem. While they maybe were not the cause of all the problems at Corinth, they definitely were the cause of most, especially the efforts to undermine Paul and denigrate his Ministry. So, had they been successful, a severe blow, as should be obvious, would have been dealt to the entirety of the Church, and especially the great Covenant of Grace.

Satan's attack was ingenious and wide, hence, the reason for Paul's deep concern. But thankfully, the Holy Spirit had grandly come upon the scene, and great victory had been the result.

I CORINTHIANS

The phrase, *"Wherefore, though I wrote unto you,"* refers to I Corinthians.

If one is to notice, most of Paul's Epistles were written as a result of particular problems in the Church, I Corinthians being but one and are, therefore, corrective. Consequently, the Holy Spirit used such to not only deal with the problems at hand at that particular time, but as well to serve as instruction for the entirety of the Church for all time. Therefore, that which was written, was and is the Word of God, which means it is error free and perfect in direction.

NOT FOR ONE PURPOSE ONLY

The phrase, *"I did it not for his cause that had done the wrong,"* probably refers to the person of I Corinthians Chapter 5.

Why did Paul say this?

Even though that problem was very severe, still, there were other problems in the Church as well, which Paul dealt with at length. However, I think that the Apostle made the statement for reasons other than what I've just said.

I personally believe that he was reaching out to that individual, trying to let him know, that he wasn't the only one in the world who had done wrong, and that there were other problems as well. In other words, I think he was trying to encourage the man.

Satan takes advantage of these situations, and attempts to make such a one believe that they have done so bad that there is no more hope. Or else, their wrong is far worse than that of anyone else; consequently, there is not much hope for them if any at all. Condemnation is a terrible thing, and to be sure, Satan does his best to heap upon the person all the condemnation he can.

While sin or wrongdoing in any capacity is never to be condoned, still, every effort must be made to salvage the individual in question. In other words, every effort must be that of Redemption and never of punishment, etc.

THE TACT USED BY THE APOSTLE

The phrase, *"Nor for his cause that suffered wrong,"* is no doubt speaking of the man against whom the wrong was committed. It was the wrongdoer's father, actually the one he had sinned against by taking his wife, who evidently had been his stepmother.

If one is to notice, the Apostle handles the entirety of the situation very gently, using great tact. It is only the self-righteous who would do otherwise.

The great purpose of Christian discipline is to benefit the entirety of the Church. It is not merely on account of the offender, nor is it merely that the injured may receive a just recompense. It is primarily that the entirety of the Church may be pure, and that the Cause of Christ may not be dishonored.

When the work of discipline is entered on from any private and personal motives, it is usually attended with bad feeling, and usually results in evil. However, when it is entered on with a desire to honor God, and to promote the purity of the Church, and as well, to salvage all parties concerned, then the matter will be prosecuted with good temper, and with right feeling, and will always lead to happy results. As someone has well said, let no man institute a process of discipline on an offending Brother from private, personal, and revengeful feelings. Let him first examine his own heart, and let him be sure that his aim is solely the Glory of Christ, before he attempts to draw down the censure of the Church on an offending Brother. How many cases of Church discipline would be arrested if this simple rule were observed? While the case before us shows that it is important in the highest degree that discipline should be exercised respecting an offending member of the Church, and while no consideration should prevent us from exercising that discipline, still, this case shows that it should be done with the utmost tenderness, in other words, as though we were passing sentence on ourselves.

NOTES

It is unfortunate, but many Believers take such an opportunity to settle private scores, or to vent negative personal feelings, for whatever reason. As someone has well said:

"When a person is down, and anyone can do just about anything to him they so desire, and without fear of censure or reprimand but rather applause, then one quickly finds out what people really are."

A SHEPHERD'S HEART

The phrase, *"But that our care for you in the sight of God might appear unto you,"* speaks of the Church at large, and not singling out one particular incident. The idea of this phrase is:

While there were other problems in the Church, still, Paul mentions this at hand which pertains to I Corinthians Chapter 5; but the idea is that this problem of incest was so weighty, that if it wasn't handled correctly, it could cause the Church to be destroyed.

At this stage of the game, the man had truly repented, even as Chapter Two of this Epistle bears out, and now it is the obligation of the Church to properly restore the Brother in question. If they did not do so, but rather take a harsh view toward him, or else place him as some type of secondary Christian in their treatment and thinking, it would not only hurt the man in question, but it would hurt the entirety of the Church. I think this is what Paul is attempting to press home. If things are handled right, which means to be handled Scripturally, then the entirety of the Church is blessed. If not, the results are always hurtful and negative. Paul wanted the people to see this, and that the things he had done respecting instruction, were for their good and not their harm.

The phrase, *"In the sight of God,"* actually means *"Under God's Eyes."* In other words, everything must be handled Scripturally, with all personal feelings and vendettas laid aside. Consequently, such is very serious, as can well be imagined.

If every Church handled every problem in this capacity, understanding that what they do is *"under God's Eyes,"* and that such is to be taken literally, quite possibly, many things would be done differently. Regrettably, the Headship of Christ has been so abrogated in many Denominational circles, and even in independent capacities, that the fear of God carries little place in the thinking of most people. Nevertheless, and irrespective as to what people think, or how much they ignore the Word of God, the Truth is, everyone will be called to account ultimately.

That's the reason that back in Chapter Two, Paul in effect tells the Corinthians, that whereas this man who had done this terrible deed had previously been on trial, now in view of his repentance, it is the Church which is now on trial. They are to *"confirm their love toward him,"* with Paul then saying, *"For to this end also did I write, that I might know the proof of you, whether ye be obedient in all things"* (II Cor. 2:8-9).

Every Christian must always remember, that sin must not be condoned in any manner, whether regarding our own person, or the Church in general; nevertheless, in dealing with offenders, we must abide strictly by the Word of God and never attempt to insert man-devised rules. We must never forget, that whoever the offender may be, and whatever his sin, that first of all that person belongs to the Lord, and we must conduct ourselves toward him or her accordingly.

The entirety of this scenario shows us exactly what should be done in these situations, and the Holy Spirit demands that these guidelines be followed. If a sinning member refuses to repent, they are to be disfellowshiped. However, the moment they repent, they are to be fully restored. As well, Verse 11 of this Chapter tells us what the earmarks of true repentance actually are.

(13) "THEREFORE WE WERE COMFORTED IN YOUR COMFORT: YEA, AND EXCEEDINGLY THE MORE JOYED WE FOR THE JOY OF TITUS, BECAUSE HIS SPIRIT WAS REFRESHED BY YOU ALL."

Titus had just come from Corinth, and of course, he has given Paul the good news which occasioned Paul's great joy. He is now to go back to Corinth, bearing this Second Epistle. Paul very fittingly speaks of the part he had in bringing the comfort and the joy.

COMFORTED IN YOUR COMFORT

The phrase, *"Therefore we were comforted in your comfort,"* refers to the joy and comfort the Corinthians experienced, when they obeyed the Word of the Lord. The indication seems to be, that they were now a happy people and rightly so, and would continue to be happy by obeying the Commands of God.

This fact gave Paul additional joy; and he could not but rejoice that they had removed the cause of the offense, and that they would not thus be exposed to the displeasure of God. Had they not repented and put away the evil, the consequences to them would have been deep distress. As it was, they were happy and blessed.

EXCEEDING JOY

The phrase, *"Yea, and exceedingly the more joyed we for the joy of Titus,"* refers to the fact that Titus was glowingly happy and rejoicingly uplifted because of what had taken place at Corinth, especially considering that he had had some small part to play in the matter.

The idea is, that Titus was so overjoyed at the results at Corinth, that as he gave the report to Paul, the overflowing joy of Titus only increased the joy of the Apostle. On all counts, the sending of the Letter (I Corinthians), and the manner in which Paul handled the situation, shows that he was led exactly by the Holy Spirit, and the proper results followed.

As one reads these words, one likewise literally feels the joy of the Apostle. How much more wonderful is this stance than that of Verse 5, when he spoke of *"fightings and fears."*

A REFRESHED SPIRIT

The phrase, *"Because his spirit was refreshed by you all,"* refers to Titus being so kindly received, and hospitably entertained.

In effect, in the manner in which they received Titus, which evidently was with abundant graciousness, Paul knew that in essence by their doing this, they were at the same time receiving him accordingly. I think this as well, is what contributed to his *"exceeding joy."*

It was not so much that he was concerned about his own personal feelings, but that this questioning of his Apostleship was now laid aside, which means that Satan's attack in this sector had failed.

There is nothing that refreshes the spirit like a Move of God. It is without a doubt, the greatest thing that could ever happen to an individual.

NOTES

NOTES

When Titus came into Corinth bearing I Corinthians, it was probably with some consternation. How would they receive him? How bad actually was the situation at the present?

And then, when he was received with open arms, which resulted in a great Move of God, which put the Church back on the right course, his spirit was truly refreshed, encouraged, strengthened, and lifted up.

(14) "FOR IF I HAVE BOASTED ANY THING TO HIM OF YOU, I AM NOT ASHAMED; BUT AS WE SPAKE ALL THINGS TO YOU IN TRUTH, EVEN SO OUR BOASTING, WHICH I MADE BEFORE TITUS, IS FOUND A TRUTH."

The idea of this Verse is, that everything for which Paul had believed the Lord respecting Corinth, had now been brought to pass. His Faith had been greatly rewarded. His confidence had been upheld. Satan had given the Church his greatest blow, but had failed on all fronts.

BOASTING

The phrase, *"For if I have boasted any thing to him of you, I am not ashamed,"* pertains to the things the Apostle had said to Titus about the Believers at Corinth, and his Faith in them that they would pass this terrible test. Despite the problems, despite the difficulties, despite even those who had turned against him personally, he still believed that they would come through and boasted accordingly to Titus.

It had all turned out to be true. Titus had found the situation exactly as Paul said it would be. So, the Apostle was not shamed.

It could be said in this way, *"One reason of my exceeding gladness was that you fully justified that very favorable picture of you which I had drawn for Titus when I was urging him to be the bearer of my Letter."*

However, the grand scheme in all of this effort goes beyond even that which has been said. Paul was saying all of these things by Faith, simply because the outward circumstances looked otherwise. There was very little if anything concerning the reports from Corinth, that would have given Paul the occasion to think or believe such in the natural. His *"boasting"* was purely by Faith, and from which we should take a lesson.

It is not easy to speak words of Faith, even to the extent of *"boasting,"* when circumstances look to be the very opposite. One's spirit seeks to do otherwise, actually the very opposite. The flesh desires to speak words of gloom, of doubt, of unbelief, which coming from the mouth of a Believer, carries tremendous weight, even if it's in the negative sense. However, when the Believer, even in the face of negative circumstances, begins to boast of what he believes that God can do and will do, and all of that despite what the outward circumstances may look like, these things have, I believe, a tremendous positive effect upon the outcome. God honors Faith, He never honors unbelief.

Even as I dictate these words I sense the Presence of God. Out of the mouth of the Believer, should come nothing but *"boasting"* as it concerns the Work of God. Whatever the circumstances, God is able. As the mighty Angel Gabriel told Mary, the Mother of our Lord, *"For with God nothing shall be impossible"* (Lk. 1:37). Paul would also write, *"And whosoever believeth on him shall not be ashamed"* (Rom. 9:33).

TRUTH

The phrase, *"But as we spake all things to you in Truth, even so our boasting, which I made before Titus, is found a truth,"* refers to the fact that Faith is never idle boasting, but rather *"Truth,"* i.e., *"the Truth of God's Word."* It is *"calling those things which be not as though they were"* (Rom. 4:17).

Inasmuch as Paul's *"boasting"* was *"Truth,"* Titus, as well, *"found it to be a Truth."*

Also, the idea seems to be, that Titus at the beginning was not sure that Paul's direction was correct, or that the Corinthians would respond favorably. There seems to be hesitancy on the part of Titus, but now that he has seen that Paul was right, he is overjoyed. Paul is saying, *"You Corinthians more than verified my words to Titus."*

(15) "AND HIS INWARD AFFECTION IS MORE ABUNDANT TOWARD YOU, WHILST HE REMEMBERETH THE OBEDIENCE OF YOU ALL, HOW WITH FEAR AND TREMBLING YE RECEIVED HIM."

This Verse portrays that which Titus had not actually expected. But really, the picture is of far broader scope than here meets the eye. It actually had to do with the Apostleship of Paul.

NOTES

INWARD AFFECTION

The phrase, *"And his inward affection is more abundant toward you,"* carries the idea that Titus had not always felt this way. He had no doubt been previously hurt regarding the opposition from this source against Paul. He, even as we do presently, no doubt wondered how these people could turn against the man who had brought them the Gospel, in fact, had saved their very lives.

Occurrences of the word *"affection"* in modern translations usually reflect one of several common Old Testament terms for love. In the New Testament, such references translate a single, uncommonly powerful Greek word.

THE DEEPEST OF DIVINE EMOTIONS

The verb form of this Greek word, *"splanchrizomai,"* is found only in the Gospels. There it is used to communicate the deepest of Divine emotions called out of human needs. We can sense best the meaning and power of this emotional term by reading such stories as the one that reveals the lonely agony of the man with leprosy (Mk. 1:41) or the confusion of the harassed and hungry crowds (Mat. 9:36).

In response to both needs, Jesus was *"moved with compassion."* The Lord is portrayed as being so moved also elsewhere in the Gospels: (Mat. 9:36; 14:14; 15:32; 18:27; 20:34; Mk. 1:41; 6:34; 8:2; 9:22-27; Lk. 7:13; 10:33).

THE SAME COMPASSION AS THE LORD

The noun form of the Greek word *"splanchna"* is found nine times in the Epistles. We discover that Christ's Own affection invades the heart of Paul (Phil. 1:8). The Apostle expects those of us who are now united to Christ to have Jesus' Own compassion for each other (II Cor. 7:15; Phil. 2:1; Col. 3:12; Phile. Chpts. 7, 12, 20; I Jn. 3:17).

Originally the word *"splanchna"* was a physical term, encompassing all vital inner organs. Extended, it became a powerful emotional word, expressing the total involvement of one's being at the deepest possible level.

The complete caring and deep love projected by this word are possible only for God. But God makes it possible for Believers to begin to share this quality, for we are being transformed to share Jesus' Own Likeness (II Cor. 3:18).

Consequently, the two words *"inward affection"* as are used of Titus by Paul, tell us that this associate of the Apostle is learning much out of this situation himself. He is now sensing and sharing the compassion and love for the Corinthians, which Paul always had, and which is so Christlike.

OBEDIENCE

The phrase, *"Whilst he remembereth the obedience of you all,"* speaks of acquiescing to what Paul had said in his First Epistle to them, but more particularly, obedience to the Lord.

According to Scripture, God demands that His Revelation be taken as a rule for man's whole life. Thus, obedience to God is a concept broad enough to include the whole of Biblical spirituality and morality. The Bible is insistent that isolated external acts of homage to God cannot make up for a lack of consistent obedience in heart and conduct (I Sam. 15:22; Jer. 7:22).

DISOBEDIENCE AND OBEDIENCE

The disobedience of Adam, the first representative man, and the perfect obedience of the Second, Jesus Christ, are decisive factors in the destiny of everyone. Adam's lapse from obedience plunged mankind into guilt, condemnation, and death (Rom. 5:19; I Cor. 15:22).

Christ's unfailing obedience *"unto death"* (Phil. 2:8; Heb. 5:8; 10:5-10) won Righteousness (acceptance with God) and life (fellowship with God) for all who believe on Him (Rom. 5:15-19).

In God's promulgation of the Old Covenant the emphasis was on obedience as His requirement if His people were to enjoy His favor (Ex. 19:5). In His Promise of the New Covenant, however, the emphasis was on obedience as His Gift to them, in order that they might enjoy His favor (Jer. 31:33; 32:40; Ezek. 36:26; 37:23-26).

FAITH, HOLINESS, AND OBEDIENCE

Faith in the Gospel, and in Jesus Christ, is obedience (Acts 6:7; Rom. 6:17; Heb. 5:9; I Pet. 1:22), for God commands it (Jn. 6:29; I Jn. 3:23).

Unbelief is disobedience (Rom. 10:16; II Thess. 1:8; I Pet. 2:8; 3:1; 4:17). A life of obedience to God is the fruit of Faith (Gen. 22:18; Heb. 11:8, 17; James 2:21).

Christian obedience means imitating God in Holiness (I Pet. 1:15) and Christ in humility and love (Jn. 13:14, 34; Eph. 4:32-5:2; Phil. 2:5).

It springs from gratitude for Grace received (Rom. 12:1), not from the desire to gain merit or to justify oneself in God's sight. Indeed, Law-keeping from the latter motive is not obedience to God, but it's opposite (Rom. 9:31-10:3).

Obedience to Divinely-established authority in the family (Eph. 5:22; 6:1; II Tim. 3:2), in the Church (Phil. 2:12; Heb. 13:17), and to the State (Mat. 22:21; Rom. 13:1; Tit. 3:1; I Pet. 2:13), is part of the Christian's obedience to God.

When claims clash, however, he must be ready to disobey men in order not to disobey God (Acts 5:29) (Mundle).

FEAR AND TREMBLING

The phrase, *"How with fear and trembling ye received him,"* suggests he had not expected to be received accordingly.

There is a good deal back of this *"fear and trembling,"* namely the fact that the Corinthians had returned to their allegiance to Paul, that they felt deeply that they had deserved the severest rebuke, and that they expected to receive chastisement when Titus came from Paul.

It is not clear as to whether this state prevailed upon his arrival, or after the reading of the Epistle and, consequent repentance.

I personally think that the weight of the evidence falls on the side of the latter. Their *"receiving him,"* had to do, I think, with receiving the Message that he brought from Paul in the form of I Corinthians. In other words, they received the admonition of the Epistle, which resulted in their repentance, and as well, which resulted in affection toward Titus, and above all, toward Paul. When their hearts got right with God, their hearts got right with the Apostle as well!

(16) "I REJOICE THEREFORE THAT I HAVE CONFIDENCE IN YOU IN ALL THINGS."

This Verse portrays the fact that the dark clouds have been dispersed. To be of good cheer implies that some things still need adjustment, but also that all misgivings have disappeared in regard to such adjustments as are yet to be made.

NOTES

REJOICING

The phrase, *"I rejoice therefore,"* presents the reason for the rejoicing of the Apostle. What had begun so dark has now turned to Light. What at first had seemed all but hopeless, now seems all but miraculous. To be sure, it is an occasion for rejoicing, in that Satan has been defeated and his effort shoved aside. The Word of God has prevailed, which is always an occasion for rejoicing.

In this, it is easy to observe that which brings joy to the Apostle. Pure and simple, it is that and that alone, which pertains to God.

CONFIDENCE

The phrase, *"That I have confidence in you in all things,"* refers not only to the present, but the future.

In effect, the Apostle is saying that he has proof now that they are disposed to obey God, and to put away everything that is offensive to Him.

The address of this part of the Epistle, says Dodderidge, is wonderful. It is designed, evidently, not merely to commend them for what they had done, or to show them the deep attachment which he had for them, but in a special manner to prepare them for what he was about to say in the following Chapter respecting the collection which he had so much at heart for the poor Saints at Jerusalem.

What he here says was admirably adapted to introduce that subject. They had thus far showed the deepest regard for him. They had complied with all his directions, i.e., *"the Lord's directions."* All that he had said of them had proved to be true.

As he had boasted of them to Titus, and expressed his entire confidence that they would comply with his requirements, so he had also boasted of them to the Churches of Macedonia which we will now study, and expressed the utmost confidence that they would be liberal in their giving.

"More like the Master I would ever be,
"More of His meekness, more humility;
"More zeal to labor, more courage to be true,
"More consecration for work He bids me do."

"More like the Master is my daily prayer;
"More strength to carry crosses I must bear;

"More earnest effort to bring His Kingdom in;
"More of His Spirit, the wanderer to win."

"More like the Master I would live and grow;
"More of His Love to others I would show;
"More self-denial, like His in Galilee,
"More like the Master I long to ever be."

"Take Thou my heart, I would be Thine alone;
"Take Thou my heart and make it all Thine Own;
"Purge me from sin, O Lord I now implore,
"Wash me and keep me Thine forevermore."

CHAPTER 8

(1) "MOREOVER, BRETHREN, WE DO YOU TO WIT OF THE GRACE OF GOD BESTOWED ON THE CHURCHES OF MACEDONIA;"

Chapters 8 and 9 of this Epistle present the greatest dissertation on the matter of *"giving"* and the support of the Work of God, than anything else found in the entirety of the Word of God. The Holy Spirit uses the Apostle to address just about every nuance of giving, respecting our motives, the amount we give, and how and what our giving should be. As stated, it is exhaustive in its instruction, which means that it is important enough that the Holy Spirit devoted more space to this subject, than He did many others. Prayerfully, the following two Chapters will provide a wealth of information concerning this all-important aspect of the Kingdom of God.

A WITNESS

The phrase, *"Moreover, Brethren, we do you to wit,"* actually means *"We cause you to know,"* or *"We desire you to be a witness."*

The purpose for which Paul informs the Corinthians, and all others for that matter, of the liberality of the Churches of Macedonia was done in order to excite them to similar liberality. We are speaking here, as stated, of the collection he wishes to receive for the Church at Jerusalem. From this we learn, that he is attempting to receive offerings from all the Churches which he had planted, or over which he had influence.

NOTES

We as well learn from this, that the Lord uses the giving of some to serve as a witness or example for others, in order to encourage them to give.

In our Campmeetings which we conduct each year at Family Worship Center, in these Meetings we will raise funds for World Evangelism. Many times, individuals giving a certain amount will encourage others to follow suit, or at least in some capacity. So, we find from this example, that the Holy Spirit uses such in a positive way, in order that all may have a part in helping to support the great Work of God. To be sure, the Lord could have used many and varied methods in order to finance His Work. Being God He doesn't need anything we have being totally Self-sufficient; however, this is the method He has used, the giving of our financial resources to help support His Work, which He in turn then blesses. This is not a man-devised method, but rather that originated by the Holy Spirit, consequently, extremely important.

WHY WAS PAUL RECEIVING OFFERINGS FOR THE CHURCH IN JERUSALEM?

Of course, as is known, the Day of Pentecost, in effect, was the beginning of the Church. We know this from Acts 1:4. In fact, about 3,000 people gave their hearts and lives to Christ that very day (Acts 2:41). A day or so later, about 5,000 men were added to the Church, beside the women and children (Acts 4:4). Consequently, within a week of the Day of Pentecost when the Holy Spirit came down, probably between 10,000 and 20,000 people gave their hearts to Christ. Of course, people continued to be saved thereafter.

Due to the great animosity of the Religious Leaders of Israel against Christ, in fact recently having crucified Him, they held no less animosity for His followers. Consequently, the moment that any Jew in Jerusalem gave his or her heart to Christ, they were summarily excommunicated from the Synagogue.

EXCOMMUNICATION

There were three types of excommunication practiced in Israel during the time of Christ:

1. The Niddin: This was a 30-day excommunication during which offenders were prohibited from public worship, and men were not allowed to shave, and as well, were required to wear garments of mourning. Of course, this pertained to something they had done which the Religious Leaders considered to be wrong, etc.

2. The Cherem: This was pronounced on those who continued in rebellion. The offender was formerly cursed, was excluded from all intercourse with other people, and was prohibited from entering the Temple or a Synagogue. This could last as long as the Religious Leaders thought necessary.

3. The Shammatha: This was pronounced on those who persisted in rebellion. They were cut off from all connection with Jewish people, and were consigned to utter perdition. In other words, this last excommunication was for life.

With Israel being a religious State, there was no such thing as a separation of Church and State. Their religious Government, was their Government in totality, Civil and otherwise. In effect, the Religious Leaders controlled the country.

WHAT EXCOMMUNICATION MEANT IN THE CASE OF FOLLOWERS OF THE LORD

If the Jew who came to Christ during those times, which lasted until Israel was destroyed in A.D. 70, was not privileged to own his own home, he was generally evicted from his place of abode, with little likelihood of getting anywhere else to go. As well, in most of the cases he lost his job, which cut off his means of support. Synagogues serving as a central point for all social, educational, and religious worship in Israel, the children of parents who had accepted Christ, were expelled from school, for Synagogues served that purpose as well, and could not return. Also, the families of new converts would disown the individual, never mentioning their name again, and would treat the person as though they were dead and cursed by God.

In view of all of this, one can see the tremendous problems which instantly accrued with thousands of people who had accepted Christ, deprived of livelihood, and in effect, out on the street. In fact, this is the reason for the statement, *"Neither said any of them that ought of the things which he possessed was his own; but they had all things common . . . neither was there any among them that lacked: for as many as were possessors of lands or houses sold them, and brought the prices of the things that were sold . . . and laid it at the Apostles' feet"* (Acts 4:32-37).

NOTES

The Early Church was not practicing Communism as some have claimed, but was rather addressing the problem of trying to take care of the thousands who were destitute due to being excommunicated, etc.

So, in view of this, Paul was attempting to help by receiving offerings from all the Churches, for the problem continued as stated, until the destruction of Jerusalem by Titus in A.D. 70.

GIVING AS DESIGNED BY THE HOLY SPIRIT

First, we make a dreadful mistake when we perceive of Christian giving as only financial. While it is true that stewardship of finances does enter the picture in a definite way, it consists of only one aspect of True Christian giving. Actually, Jesus dealt with this in Luke 6:27-45. As well, in Matthew 6:19-34, He proclaimed the fact that when the Believer comes to the Lord, he then enters the Economy of God, which is the greatest guarantee of blessing, security, and prosperity, that the world has ever known.

As well, in Luke 6:38, Jesus gave a pregnant promise, and it is thus:

It is impossible to outgive God. The metaphor, as Jesus used it, speaks of the loose flowing outer garment of the day but also doubled as a container when necessary. Jesus definitely taught that the person who truly practices Christian giving as a way of life will always have a *"bosom,"* or *"lap,"* that is full, pressed down, shaken together, and running over with plenty.

The problem comes when false teachers take this Verse out of context just to teach giving in order to get. That concept is completely contrary to the total Passage in Luke Chapter 6.

In fact, Jesus condemned such a mind-set (giving to get) by calling it the world's concept of giving (Lk. 6:32-34). Such basically consists of loving only those people who love us in return. Even unbelievers do that, Jesus said. In fact, the unsaved world practices giving in order to get something in return.

On the contrary, genuine Christian giving entails loving our enemies. It consists of a way of life that includes loving the ones who do not love us, doing good to the ones who hate us, blessing the ones who curse us, praying for the ones who mistreat us, and giving without expecting anything in return. This kind of concept stems from people whose lives have been regenerated and who prove their regeneration by the fruit they produce (Lk. 6:43-45). They do not judge or condemn other people; instead, they forgive (Lk. 6:37-42). Giving, therefore, includes far more than just dropping money into an offering plate.

THE GREAT GIVING PRINCIPLE

The Apostle Paul obviously derived that which he gives us concerning giving in Chapters 8 and 9 of this Epistle, as a result of Revelation directly from the Lord. As we have stated, he outlined this teaching more thoroughly in these two Chapters than any other segment of his writings, dealing with just about every aspect of giving.

It is important, though, to realize that these two Chapters reside in the context of valid Gospel Ministry, in which every single Believer must be involved. Legitimate Christian service is definitely Gospel Ministry. Some people may not realize it, but the Lord does not force Believers to serve Him anymore than He forces individuals to become Christians. A careful study of Jesus' Teaching about developing a servant attitude will show the Bible Student that Jesus encourages His followers to adopt such an attitude, but He does not force it on them as a requirement for Salvation (Mat. 20:20-28; Mk. 10:35-45).

Consequently, it is, in a sense, possible to avoid total commitment to Christian service and still remain a Believer, as regrettably, characterizes most.

On the other hand, it is not possible to avoid the consequences such a lukewarm person will face at the Judgment Seat of Christ, when the reward will be lost.

A SERVANT'S HEART

We see, therefore, that all Christians do not really get involved in Gospel Ministry because they do not follow the Lord's injunctions about having a servant's heart. That is why II Corinthians Chapters 8 and 9 are an integral segment of the total theme of this Epistle. A giving heart is definitely foundational to Christian service. Without this attitude of making ourselves available for God to work through us for the benefit of others, especially for the unsaved, we really are not candidates for authentic Gospel Ministry.

Look carefully at the way the Apostle approached this serious issue that underlies all we do throughout our Christian lives on earth (Rossier).

NOTES

THE MANNER IN WHICH THIS PRINCIPLE WAS INSTITUTED

Our first information regarding the great collection is stated in I Corinthians 16:1, etc. In their letter to Paul the Corinthians had requested directions regarding it, and Paul sends these in I Corinthians Chapter 16. There we learn that the Galatian Churches were already following the method proposed to the Corinthians, namely that on each Sunday each person lay by what he could.

When Paul wrote I Corinthians he expected to get to Corinth eight or nine months later and so asked that the whole collection be completed by that time so that men who were approved by the Church might then carry the funds to Jerusalem. Just when, where, and how this movement toward a collection started we cannot say, for all we have is the remark made in Galatians 2:10 about remembering the poor, which Paul promised to do.

The next information we have is found in these two Chapters of this Epistle. In II Corinthians 9:2 we see that the collection was begun in Corinth a year before II Corinthians was written, and that means five or six months before I Corinthians was written.

Paul boasts to the Macedonians about the early start that was made in Corinth and in Achaia regarding this matter; but he now boasts to the Corinthians about the wonderful response he had found in Macedonia and writes in detail about the Macedonians in order to enthuse also the Corinthians.

The danger is that the Corinthians will fall behind, that when representatives from Macedonia come to Corinth to join the party that is to convey the collection to Jerusalem, they will find Corinth unready although here in II Corinthians Paul is boasting that Corinth began already a year ago. So Paul tries to speed up the collection in Corinth by sending back Titus to help direct matters. Paul himself will get to Corinth in two or three months, the Macedonian representatives will accompany him.

LUKE'S ACCOUNT

We can follow the main events from Luke's report in Acts 20:4, where he names the whole party which started from Corinth in the Spring of the next year and carried the collection from the European Churches to Jerusalem. Luke describes the whole journey.

How the funds gathered in Asia and in Galatia were combined with those which had been collected in Europe we are not told. They were perhaps brought when the Ephesian Elders met Paul and his party at Miletus (Acts 20:17).

The collection must have been turned over to James and to the Elders at Jerusalem when they received Paul and his party (Acts 21:17, etc.). In his defense before Felix in Acts 24:17 Paul mentions the fact that he had come to Jerusalem to bring alms to his nation.

SATAN HAD HINDERED

We now go back to the six months that intervened between I and II Corinthians. The relation between the Corinthians and Paul had become severely strained. All that we know about this is what we are able to gather from the two Epistles themselves. We have this much in the way of facts.

I Corinthians is filled with rebuke and corrections in every Chapter. Conditions were bad, very bad in Corinth: party factions; the whole wisdom-folly; the case of incest; litigations; harlotry not considered wrong; wrong notions regarding marriage and celibacy; attending idol feasts; ruining the Agape in the celebration of the Lord's Supper; the folly concerning gifts, forgetting love; and, capping this list, the denial of the bodily resurrection. No wonder Paul shed tears while he was writing this letter (II Cor. 2:4).

THE WORK OF GOD HAD ACTUALLY STOPPED AT CORINTH

Just consider this array of evils, all of which were found in one congregation. Timothy arrived in Corinth after Paul had been given the information concerning the situation. We know that after Timothy returned to Paul in Ephesus. Paul then sent Titus to Corinth. From II Corinthians we gather that things had, indeed, looked bad in Corinth, and that Paul had feared even the worst. Judaizers had come in, and a movement to disown Paul was begun.

NOTES

But the Corinthians thoroughly righted themselves with the help of Titus. Titus so reported to Paul in Macedonia, of which account we have in the previous Chapter, with Paul then writing II Corinthians.

But we see that because of all this disturbance the collection had fared badly. We may well suppose that it had gone by the board for the time being. It is with this background that Paul writes about it in order to set it going again.

Paul had perhaps been attacked also on the score of this collection. We shall see how he guards his expressions. These two Chapters regarding the collection are again a sample of how in a situation, that is by no means simple, Paul knows exactly the right thing to say, to touch only the purest motives, to avert every wrong implication, and to deprive every hostile mind of the least opening for an attack.

THE MANNER OF THE HOLY SPIRIT THROUGH THE APOSTLE

Paul does not write: *"I hear that the matter of the collection has stopped in Corinth; you must start it again."* As well, he does not put this matter into diplomatic language by sugarcoating it with smooth words. Paul issues no command of authority.

He knows only one principle for giving, and that is the giver's own free will. He takes it for granted that the Corinthians, who have now returned through repentance to their true allegiance and love, will desire to join in the movement of the collection (II Cor. 9:1). His aim in writing these two Chapters on the subject is to make their participation pure and true in every respect, a product of the Gospel Spirit in every way, a delightful task that is performed in the fullest Gospel consciousness.

For this reason he starts with the Macedonians, who are busy gathering their contributions in the finest Christian spirit.

THE GRACE OF GOD

The phrase, *"Of the Grace of God bestowed on the Churches of Macedonia,"* proclaims the Apostle using these as an example, and that the Corinthians were to be a witness of their faithfulness.

It is Paul's delight and manner to praise where praise is due. He cannot write on this subject without glorying in what the Macedonians are doing. He would glory thus no matter to whom he might write. Invidious comparisons do not enter his mind. Legalistic promptings are impossible to him. All these beautiful fruits are pure *"Grace of God."*

As far as the Corinthians are concerned, the only stimulation which Paul knows is that of rich Gospel Grace. He wants nothing from the Corinthians but a repetition of the delight which he is now experiencing among the Macedonians.

GRACE INSTEAD OF LAW

That he secured what he desired from the Corinthians we see from Romans 15:26-28, which probably was written later in Corinth just before he and the selected delegates started for Jerusalem with the collection. The secret of Paul's success in this field is still hidden from many who now manage the finances of Churches.

A little Law, often just Law, seems to them to be much more promising than pure Gospel. When they do try to use the Gospel they do it awkwardly because down in their hearts they do not trust it for complete effectiveness with Paul's full trust. In other words, giving is never to be a matter of Law, but always a matter of Grace.

When Paul used the word *"Brethren,"* this made it very personal for the Corinthians.

As well, the collection of the Macedonians should not be called *"the Grace of God."* It is not the collection that is the *"Grace of God,"* but rather the *"Grace of God"* is something the Macedonians have received (and thus possess) *from* God.

THAT WHICH GRACE ACTUALLY IS

Right here we have the full depth of Paul's view. All of our fruit of good works, all our beneficence and contributions of money are God's unmerited favor to us, His undeserved Gift to us.

HOW SO?

Every good work is the fruit of God's operative Grace. It is a treasure that He in His Grace deposits in our basket. Blessed is he who has his basket overflowingly full of such Gifts of God! Those who refuse to give turn their basket away when God wants to place another gift into it.

They keep their gift and lose the gift to themselves which their gift might have been. Poor where Grace would make them rich in good works, to come with rejoicing bearing their sheaves (Ps. 126:6), to stand among those whom the King shall call *"the blessed of My Father"* (Mat. 25:34-40) (Lenski).

The actual meaning of the phrase *"Grace of God,"* means that God had bestowed on them Grace to give according to their ability in this cause.

THIS GRACE AS GIVEN BY GOD

According to this the following is implied:

1. That a disposition to contribute to the cause of Christ is to be traced to God. He is its Author. He excites it. It is not merely a plant of native growth in the human heart; but a large and liberal spirit which is one of the effects of His Grace, and is to be traced to Him.

2. It is a favor bestowed on a Church when God excites in it a spirit of Giving. It is one of the evidences of His Love. And indeed there cannot be a higher proof of the favor of God, than when by His Grace He inclines and enables us to contribute largely in regards to His Work, and above all, to take the Gospel to the world.

In other words, it is a privilege to give to the Work of God.

3. God would only bestow Grace on those who will be open, liberal, and generous with His Work. Consequently, this *"grace"* will function in many and varied ways.

First of all, it will enable that person to give, in other words make such possible by blessing him, and as well, the giver, when giving in this fashion, will enjoy all the other benefits of Grace, which actually knows no boundaries, and affects the giver in every capacity, be it emotionally, financially, materially, domestically, physically, and above all spiritually.

THE CHURCHES OF MACEDONIA

Paul wants to tell the Corinthians how extremely liberal the Macedonians had been, since it was his custom to stir up one Church by the example of another (II Cor. 9:2). He

NOTES

begins by speaking of their generosity as a proof of the Grace which they are receiving from the Holy Spirit.

The only Macedonian Churches of which we have any details in the New Testament are those of Philippi, Thessalonica, and Berea. In modern Greece, the area would extend across the northern part of that country.

Of these Churches, Philippi seems to have been most distinguished for their liberality (Phil. 4:10, 15-16, 18).

(2) "HOW THAT IN A GREAT TRIAL OF AFFLICTION THE ABUNDANCE OF THEIR JOY AND THEIR DEEP POVERTY ABOUNDED UNTO THE RICHES OF THEIR LIBERALITY."

This Verse proclaims to us that a giving attitude does not depend on circumstances. In fact, the Holy Spirit through this example teaches us an invaluable lesson.

A GREAT TRIAL OF AFFLICTION

The phrase, *"How that in a great trial of affliction,"* probably refers to the Civil Wars which had taken place in this locality shortly before this time. This had greatly impoverished that area, which had brought on economic hardships, which had of course, affected the Churches as well.

"Affliction" in the Greek is *"thlipsis,"* and comes from the metaphor of *"squeezing grapes."* Consequently, these Macedonians knew what it was to be *"squeezed"* (I Thess. 1:7; 2:14; II Thess. 1:4).

WHY DOES GOD ALLOW AFFLICTION?

The Hebrew mind did not dwell on secondary causes, but attributed everything, even afflictions, directly to the great First Cause and Author of all things: *"Shall evil befall a city, and Jehovah hath not done it?"* (Amos 3:6); *"I form the light, and create darkness: I make peace, and create evil* (calamity)*: I am Jehovah, that doeth all these things"* (Isa. 45:7).

Thus all things, including calamity, were referred to the Divine Operation.

For instance, Job's calamities are ascribed to Satan, but even he receives his word of command from God, and is responsible to Him, like the other *"sons of God"* who surround the Heavenly Throne. He is thus *"included in the Divine Will and in the circle of Divine Providence."*

In New Testament times, physical and mental maladies were ascribed to the agency of evil spirits called demons, whose prince was Beelzebub or Satan (Mat. 9:32; Mk. 1:23; 3:22; 5:2, etc.). Christ gave His assent to this belief when He spoke of the woman under infirmity, *"whom Satan hath bound"* (Lk. 13:16). As well, Paul attributed his difficulties to an evil angel sent by Satan (II Cor. 12:7), though he recognized that the evil agent was subordinate to God's purpose of Grace, and was the means of moral discipline.

Thus while evil spirits were regarded as malicious authors of physical maladies, they were not, thought to act in complete independence; rather, they had a certain place assigned to them in the Divine Providence.

The Truth is, that God is over all. Satan never works independently of permission from God. Consequently, God is in a sense the cause of all things, but yet under certain guidelines. For instance, God does not cause sin, iniquity, wickedness, etc. However, He does allow Satan, Demon Spirits, Fallen Angels, and even humanity certain latitude, due to the manner of their creation. Consequently, evil is the result of those who are evil, but yet with the permission of God. However, such permission has limitations, and there is coming a day when all evil will be stricken from existence, which means that all perpetrators of evil will be locked away (I Cor. 15:24-28; Rev. 20:10-15).

THE MEANING AND PURPOSE OF AFFLICTION

Why does God afflict men or rather allow men to be afflicted? How is suffering to be explained consistently with the Goodness and Justice of God? In fact, this was an acute problem which weighed heavily upon the Hebrew mind. Consequently, we can only briefly indicate the chief factors which the Scriptures contribute to the solution of this problem:

1. The traditional view in early Hebrew Theology was that afflictions were the result of the Divine Law of Retribution, by which sin was invariably followed by adequate punishment. However, even though this certainly is correct in many cases, the logic of facts prove that such is not the case on a constant basis.

For instance, Jeremiah's sufferings were

due, not to sin, but to his faithfulness to his Prophetic vocation. So was the *"suffering servant"* in Isaiah. Job, as well, despite his many woes, was firm in the conviction of his own integrity. Actually, to prove the inadequacy of the view that all affliction is caused by sin, is the main purpose of the Book of Job.

2. Afflictions are allowed by God at times to test the character or Faith of the sufferer. This idea is especially prominent in Job, to which we have already noted. God allowed Satan to test the reality of Job's piety by overwhelming him with disease and misfortunes. Consequently, for those who are able to stand the test, suffering has a purification or disciplinary value. Actually, the purificatory function of trials is taught in such Passages as Isaiah 1:25; Zechariah 13:9; Malachi 3:2-3, where the process of refining metals in fire and smelting out the dross is the metaphor used.

3. Suffering and affliction are also looked at in the Old Testament as a vicarious and redemptive process. In other words, one suffers for another. The classical Passages are Isaiah Chapters 52 and 53, which deal with the woes of the oppressed and afflicted Servant of God, which of course, speaks of the Messiah.

The idea is that Jesus suffered, but it was not for any sins which He had committed, or wrongdoing of any nature, but rather for the sins of others.

As well, it stands to reason that Believers can at times, enter into suffering and affliction, which are brought on them by the Holy Spirit, and are totally vicarious in nature, therefore, on behalf of others. Paul is a perfect example, and in fact, every Believer who suffers persecution as a result of the Gospel of Jesus Christ, is in a sense, suffering for others. Actually, the idea of vicarious and redemptive suffering has a far deeper significance in the New Testament even than in the Old, and finds concrete realization in the Person of Jesus Christ. Consequently, the Passion of Christ fulfills a unique purpose in the Plan of God, of course, which is overly obvious.

Yet in a sense, His followers, as stated, partake of His vicarious sufferings, and *"fill up . . . that which is lacking of the afflictions of Christ"* (Col. 1:24; Phil. 3:10; I Pet. 4:13). Here, surely, is a profound thought which may throw a flood of light on the deep mystery of human affliction.

NOTES

The Cross of Christ furnishes the key to the meaning of sorrow as the greatest redemptive force in the universe.

THE ENDURANCE OF AFFLICTION

The Scriptures abound in words of consolation and exhortation adapted to encourage the afflicted. We are in effect told in the Word of God, that love is on the Throne of the universe, and we may rest assured that all things are meant for our good (Rom. 8:28). Consequently, tribulation although at times present, is of brief duration, in comparison with the joy that shall follow (Ps. 30:5; Isa. 54:7; Jn. 16:22).

Even though the Old Testament gives a faint and flickering light toward this insight, still, it is the New Testament postulate of Faith, by which the Christian is able to fortify himself in affliction, remembering that his affliction is light and momentary compared with the *"far more exceeding and eternal weight of glory"* which is to issue out of it (II Cor. 4:17; Mat. 5:12; Rom. 8:18).

Akin to all of this is the comfort derived from the thought of the near approach of Christ's Second Coming (James 5:7-8). In view of such Truths as these, the Bible encourages Believers in trouble to show the spirit of patience (Ps. 37:7; Lk. 21:19; Rom. 12:12; James 1:3-4; 5:7-11; I Pet. 2:20), and even the spirit of positive joy in tribulation, which in fact, characterizes these Macedonians.

Above all, the Scriptures recommend the afflicted to take refuge in the supreme blessedness of fellowship with God, and of trust in His Love, by which we may enter into a deep peace that is undisturbed by the trials and problems of life (Ps. 73; Isa. 26:3-4; Jn. 14:1-27; Phil. 4:7).

THE ABUNDANCE OF JOY

The phrase, *"The abundance of their joy,"* is connected with the *"great trial of affliction."* The idea is, that if the Lord allows *"affliction,"* He will compensate with an *"abundance of joy."*

In reality, their joy overflowed their affliction, and their liberality overflowed their poverty (Mk. 12:44). This is called Divine bookkeeping.

POVERTY

The phrase, *"And their deep poverty,"* refers

to extreme poverty, far beyond the norm, and which was caused as previously stated, by the circumstances of the region. However, as we will see in the next Chapter, the Lord would attend to this situation, with it changing.

However, at this particular time, the structure of the Greek words is that so deep was the poverty that you could not dip it out; but yet, so great their joy that it poured itself out in a tide of wealth.

This is astonishing when it is put this way, but Paul labels all of the facts with exact terms. Every term states a fact and is evident in the Greek language.

THE RICHES OF THEIR LIBERALITY

The phrase, *"Abounded unto the riches of their liberality,"* refers to the abundance of their giving. This is the mark of great Grace. It points to the development of Christian experience beyond the ordinary run of Discipleship. It was more than merely being consecrated, as important as that is, it was being victoriously Christian.

These people gave according to their present ability and did not wait until they became affluent. Whoever waits for abundance before giving, will never give at all. Those who give in the times of poverty to be sure will ultimately be blessed with an abundance, for that is the sure Word of the Lord (II Cor. 9:6).

"Liberality" in the Greek is *"haplotetos,"* and comes from the Greek term meaning *"single,"* which refers to a *"single-minded attitude"* (Mat. 6:22) and is a mind-set of giving without ulterior motives (Rom. 1:28).

This excess of joy in so severe a test of affliction, which brought them so great poverty exceeded *"for the riches of their single-mindedness."* This excess did its exceeding in this direction; it just bubbled over into this beautiful channel, namely *"the wealth of their single-mindedness."*

It is the moral, spiritual quality which Paul sees in the contribution which these Macedonians were making with such joy, despite the affliction of poverty which had struck them. This quality stood the great test and was proven genuine. Paul calls it, as stated, sincerity or *"singleness"* of heart, *"single-mindedness."*

Paul says that the Macedonians fixed their minds on a single thing. And we know what that is: to let God's Grace give them its gift, namely this blessed work of helping in the collection. There was no doubleness in their minds; in other words, no one stood up and said: *"Why, we are so poor that somebody ought to take up a collection for us instead of asking us to give to others!"*

That crooked *"single-mindedness,"* I fear, would appear in many Churches presently that have members who are not nearly as poor as these Macedonians were. So the Grace of God would be wasted by them.

Despite the poverty which the affliction had brought to the Macedonians they had kept, yea increased, their greatest wealth and their joy with it. Grace of God, indeed!

LAW OF PROSPERITY

First of all, I think that one can say, and with the Word of God as our source, that it is the Will of God for all Believers to enjoy financial, physical, domestical, and above all, spiritual prosperity. The Holy Spirit through John the Beloved said, and I quote from THE EXPOSITOR'S STUDY BIBLE, *"Beloved, I wish above all things that you may prosper* (refers to financial prosperity, and should be the case for every Believer) *and be in health* (speaks of physical prosperity), *even as your soul prospers* (speaks of spiritual prosperity; so we have here the whole Gospel for the whole man)*"* (III Jn., Vs. 2).

As it regards domestic tranquility and prosperity, Paul gives us the Scriptural admonition in Ephesians 5:22-33.

However, rather than giving a dissertation on financial prosperity per se, or prosperity in general, I want to look at the foundation, in other words, that on which all prosperity must be based and, as well, that which is absolutely necessary as it regards prosperity, irrespective of the type of which we speak. Unfortunately, there is all type of teaching prevalent presently as it regards this subject, with most of it being wrong. In other words, all prosperity must be based entirely, totally, and completely on the foundation of the Cross of Christ. Otherwise, it's a prosperity that God cannot honor.

THE FOUNDATION DOCTRINE OF THE CROSS

The Doctrine of the Cross, that is if one

NOTES

would use such terminology in reference to the Cross, is in reality, the Foundation Doctrine of the entirety of the Word of God. In other words, it was the very first Doctrine formulated by the Godhead and, consequently, is meant to serve as the foundation of all Biblical Doctrine. In other words, if all corresponding doctrines aren't built squarely on the foundation of the Cross, then in some way the interpretation will be specious. Listen to what Simon Peter says:

"Forasmuch as you know that you were not redeemed with corruptible things, as silver and gold (presents the fact that the most precious commodities [silver and gold] could not redeem fallen man)*, from your vain conversation* (vain lifestyle) *received by tradition from your fathers* (speaks of original sin that is passed on from father to child at conception)*;*

"But with the Precious Blood of Christ (presents the payment, which proclaims the poured out Life of Christ on behalf of sinners)*, as of a Lamb without blemish and without spot* (speaks of the lambs offered as substitutes in the Old Jewish economy; the Death of Christ was not an execution or assassination, but rather a Sacrifice; the Offering of Himself presented a Perfect Sacrifice for He was Perfect in every respect [Ex. 12:5])*:*

"Who verily was foreordained before the foundation of the world (refers to the fact that God, in His Omniscience, knew He would create man, man would Fall, and man would be Redeemed by Christ going to the Cross; this was all done before the Universe was created; this means the Cross of Christ is the Foundation Doctrine of all Doctrine, referring to the fact that all Doctrine must be built upon that Foundation, and as stated, or else it is specious). *But was manifest in these last times for you* (refers to the invisible God Who, in the Person of the Son, was made visible to human eyesight by assuming a human body and human limitations)*"* (I Pet. 1:18-20).

In fact, if one traces all false doctrine down to its root cause, even though many things enter into such a false interpretation, still, the foundation problem will be found, I think, to be a false or improper interpretation of the Cross.

THE STORY OF THE BIBLE

In fact, the entire story of the Word of God, can be pulled down to one simple sentence, *"Jesus Christ and Him Crucified"* (I Cor. 1:23). Immediately after the Fall, the Lord told Satan through the serpent, and I quote from THE EXPOSITOR'S STUDY BIBLE, which will characterize all Biblical quotes in this article:

"And I will put enmity (animosity) *between you and the woman* (presents the Lord now actually speaking to Satan, who had used the serpent; in effect, the Lord is saying to Satan, *"You used the woman to bring down the human race, and I will use the woman as an instrument to bring the Redeemer into the world, Who will save the human race"*)*, and between your seed* (mankind which follows Satan) *and her seed* (the Lord Jesus Christ)*; it* (Christ) *shall bruise your head* (the victory that Jesus won at the Cross [Col. 2:14-15]*, and you shall bruise His heel* (the sufferings of the Cross)*"* (Gen. 3:15).

The Apostle John gives us the order of Biblical events in just three particular Scriptures found in the First Chapter of his Gospel. The Apostle said:

"In the beginning (does not infer that Christ as God had a beginning, because as God He had no beginning, but rather refers to the time of Creation [Gen. 1:1]) *was the Word* (the Holy Spirit through John describes Jesus as *'the Eternal Logos'*) *and the Word was with God* (*'was in relationship with God,'* and expresses the idea of the Trinity)*, and the Word was God* (meaning that He did not cease to be God during the Incarnation; He *'was'* and *'is'* God from eternity past to eternity future)*"* (Jn. 1:1).

This tells us that the entirety of the Bible points exclusively to the Lord Jesus Christ. In other words, if one traces each Scripture, each Passage, each illustration back to its Source, Christ will there be found. That's the reason we keep saying that Christ is the Source.

Then John said, *"And the Word was made flesh* (refers to the Incarnation, *'God becoming man'*)*, and dwelt among us* (refers to Jesus, although Perfect, not holding Himself aloft from all others, but rather lived as all men, even a peasant)*, and we beheld His glory, the glory as of the only begotten of the Father,* (speaks of His Deity, although hidden from the eyes of the merely curious; while Christ laid aside the expression of His Deity, He never lost the possession of His Deity) *full of Grace* *and Truth* (as *'flesh,'* proclaimed His Humanity, *'Grace and Truth'* His Deity)*"* (Jn. 1:14).

As one cannot understand the Bible unless one understands Jesus Christ, as outlined in Verse 1, likewise, one cannot understand His reason for coming to this world, without understanding the Fourteenth Verse.

Now the Apostle John will tell us in no uncertain terms, and in plain language, as to exactly why Jesus came to this world. While He would do many things, would perform many miracles, would minister as no one had ever ministered, would bring about countless healings, still, His main Purpose was the Cross, for that was the only way that man could be redeemed.

John the Beloved records the fact of John the Baptist introducing Christ, and saying, *"Behold the Lamb of God* (proclaims Jesus as the Sacrifice for sin, in fact, the Sin-Offering, Whom all the multiple millions of offered lambs had represented), *which takes away the sin of the world* (animal blood could only cover sin, it could not take it away; but Jesus offering Himself as the Perfect Sacrifice took away the sin of the world; He not only cleansed acts of sin but, as well, addressed the root cause [Col. 2:14-15])*"* (Jn. 1:29).

So, in these three Verses found in this First Chapter of John, we find out in plain language, that the entirety of the Bible addressed itself to the Lord Jesus Christ, and the reason that God became flesh and dwelt among us. It was to go to the Cross, where there the fallen sons of Adam's lost race would be redeemed, at least for all who would believe (Jn. 3:16).

THE CROSS OF CHRIST

All of this tells us, that every single thing received by the Believer, irrespective as to who the Believer is, comes to us strictly through Christ as the Source, and the Cross as the means. In other words, Salvation, the Baptism with the Holy Spirit, Divine Healing, prosperity, Fruit of the Spirit, Gifts of the Spirit, in fact, the help of the Holy Spirit rendered to us, plus every single thing of which one could ever begin to think, all, and without exception, are made possible by the Cross of Christ. This speaks not only of our Salvation, but as well, of our Sanctification.

HOW TO LIVE FOR GOD

Tragically and sadly, the modern Church, at least as a whole, simply doesn't know how to live for God. That doesn't mean they aren't Saved, it doesn't mean they can't be Saved, it just simply means, that what Jesus did for us at the Cross, the great price there paid, and the great victory there won, most Christians only have a part of that of which Jesus paid such a price. Considering the price that He paid, which was His Own Perfect Life, it stands to reason, that He would want us to have all for which He has paid this great price. I think everyone would agree to that; however, the truth is, and as the heading states, most Christians simply do not know how to live for God; therefore, not knowing how to live for the Lord, which means they do not know how to order their behavior, do not know how to live this life, do not know how to take advantage of what He did for us at the Cross, most Christians live a life, at least in some way, of spiritual defeat. That is tragic, but true!

In fact, if the Believer doesn't understand God's Prescribed Order of Victory, he will find the sin nature in some way exactly as it did before he came to Christ. First of all, let's look at that which is God's Prescribed Order of Victory.

GOD'S PRESCRIBED ORDER OF VICTORY

God has an order into which man must enter, that is if he is to walk victorious, meaning to live victorious over the world, the flesh, and the Devil. And those three things, *"the world, the flesh and the Devil,"* sum up, I think, the hurdles that every Believer must face and thereby conquer or be conquered.

God's Prescribed Order of Victory is found in the great Sixth Chapter of Romans. Of course it's found elsewhere in the Apostles' Epistles, but is outlined perfectly in the Sixth Chapter of the great Epistle to the Romans.

First of all, it must be understood that it was to Paul that the meaning of the New Covenant was given, which in actuality is the meaning of the Cross. The Apostle said:

"But I certify you, Brethren (make known), *that the Gospel which was preached of me* (the Message of the Cross) *is not after man.* (Any Message other than the Cross is definitely devised by man.)

NOTES

"For I neither received it of man (Paul had not learned this great Truth from human Teachers), *neither was I taught it* (he denies instruction from other men), *but by the Revelation of Jesus Christ* (Revelation is the mighty Act of God whereby the Holy Spirit discloses to the human mind that which could not be understood without Divine Intervention)" (Gal. 1:11-12).

Before this Revelation was given to Paul, no one else knew nor understood the Message of the Cross, i.e., what the Cross actually meant. In fact, the Apostles at that time preached the Resurrection of Christ more so than anything else. When the Lord gave this great Revelation to Paul, who then gave it to us in his fourteen Epistles and, as well, related it to all of the Apostles, this was the first time that this great Truth was known, at least in this fullness.

THE SIXTH CHAPTER OF ROMANS

We find in the first two Verses of Romans Six that sin is the real cause, the real problem. While the Church may put a different face on the problem, if the face is pulled off, whatever type of face it might be, one will find that the problem is sin.

Whenever the Christian comes to the erroneous conclusion that now since he is a Child of God, he has no more problem with sin, that's when he is being deceived. Let me say it again:

The problem that every Believer faces, is the problem of sin.

And then on the other hand, the Holy Spirit has been given to us for many glorious reasons, all made possible by the Cross; however, the main purpose of His taking up abode within our hearts and lives, is that He would help us to overcome sin and all of its effects, in other words, to root out all sin in our lives (Rom. 8:2). Our Lord did not save us <u>in</u> sin, but rather <u>from</u> sin.

Now Paul tells us in Verses 3 to 5 of this great Sixth Chapter as it regards the answer to the sin problem, it is, and without exception, the Cross of Christ. He said:

"Know ye not, that so many of us as were baptized into Jesus Christ (plainly says that this Baptism is into Christ and not water [I Cor. 1:17; 12:13; Gal. 3:28-29; Eph. 4:5; Col. 2:11-13]) *were baptized into His Death?* (When Christ died on the Cross, in the Mind of God, we died with Him; in other words, He became our Substitute, and our identification with Him in His Death gives us all the benefits for which He died; the idea is that He did it all for us!)

"Therefore we are buried with Him by baptism into death (not only did we die with Him, but we were buried with Him as well, which means that all the sin and transgression of the past were buried; when they put Him in the Tomb, they put all our sins into that Tomb as well)*: that like as Christ was raised up from the dead by the Glory of the Father, even so we also should walk in newness of life* (we died with Him, we were buried with Him, and His Resurrection was our Resurrection to a *'newness of Life'*).

"For if we have been planted together (with Christ) *in the likeness of His Death* (Paul proclaims the Cross as the instrument through which all Blessings come; consequently, the Cross must ever be the Object of our Faith, which gives the Holys Spirit latitude to work within our lives), *we shall be also in the likeness of His Resurrection* (we can have the *'likeness of His Resurrection,' i.e., 'live this Resurrection Life,'* only as long as we understand the *'likeness of His Death,' wh*ich refers to the Cross as the means by which all of this done)*"* (Rom. 6:3-5).

The idea of the Sixth Chapter of Romans, which, as stated, gives God's Prescribed Order of Victory, is how that the Christian can have victory over the sin nature.

THE SIN NATURE

Some seventeen times in this Sixth Chapter alone, the Apostle Paul mentions the word *"sin."* Fifteen of those times, in the original Greek, in which the Text was originally written, Paul uses what is referred to now as the *"definite article,"* making the Text read in those instances, *"the sin."* The words *"the sin"* refer to the fact that Paul is not speaking of acts of sin, but rather the cause or the root of sin, i.e., in other words, the sin nature.

In the Fourteenth Verse, the definite article is not included, but inasmuch as the word *"sin"* is used here as a noun and not a verb, this tells us that Paul as well, is using the word as referring to the sin nature, and not acts of sin.

The only time that acts of sin are mentioned by the use of the word in this Sixth Chapter is in the Fifteenth Verse. So, the Apostle is dealing with the sin nature, and how the Believer can have victory over this terrible problem.

WHAT IS THE SIN NATURE?

The sin nature pertains to the nature of the individual, which is directed toward sin, toward transgression, toward iniquity, etc. It is a result of the Fall. Man fell from the lofty heights of total God consciousness, down to the low, low level of total self-consciousness. In other words, all unsaved people are ruled constantly and continuously by the sin nature.

Whenever the believing sinner comes to Christ, the sin nature is made ineffective. Paul said:

"Knowing this, that our old man is crucified with Him (all that we were before conversion), *that the body of sin might be destroyed* (the power of sin broken), *that henceforth we should not serve sin* (the guilt of sin is removed at conversion, because the sin nature no longer rules within our hearts and lives)*"* (Rom. 6:6).

The Greek word translated *"destroyed"* in the Sixth Verse, would have been better translated *"made ineffective."* In other words, at the moment of conversion the sin nature was not and is not removed from the Believer, but is rather made ineffective, or dormant. As long as the Believer keeps his faith exclusively in Christ and the Cross, understanding that all benefits comes to us from Christ by the means of the Cross, then the sin nature will remain ineffective; however, if the Believer, which most all do at one time or the other, makes something else the object of their faith instead of the Cross of Christ, then the sin nature will quickly have a revival, in other words, be resurrected. Then in some way, it will begin to control the Believer, with him not quite understanding what is happening. Unfortunately, most Believers have been taught that once they are now a Christian, that Satan cannot force them to do anything. In other words, that God has greatly strengthened their willpower, and all they have to do now is simply say *"no"* to the Devil, etc.

That is basely wrong!

In the first place, the Lord does not strengthen the willpower of the Believer.

In other words, the Believer does not live a victorious, overcoming, Christian life, by the use of willpower. He is to live such a life by Faith; however, it is to be Faith placed exclusively in the Christ and what Christ has done for us at the Cross.

NOTES

Concerning willpower, the Apostle Paul said, *"For I know that in me, that is, in my flesh, dwells no good thing* (speaks of man's own ability, or rather the lack thereof in comparison to the Holy Spirit, at least when it comes to spiritual things)*: for to will is present with me* (Paul is speaking here of his willpower; regrettably, most modern Christians are trying to live for God by means of willpower, thinking falsely that since they have come to Christ, they are not free to say *'no'* to sin; that is the wrong way to look at the situation; the Believer cannot live for God by the strength of willpower; while the will is definitely important, it alone is not enough; the Believer must exercise Faith in Christ and the Cross, and do so constantly; then he will have the ability and strength to say *'yes'* to Christ, which automatically says, *'no'* to the things of the world)*; but how to perform that which is good I find not"* (outside of the Cross, it is impossible to find a way to do good)*"* (Rom. 7:18).

As we have already stated, in this one Verse, the Apostle Paul tells us that willpower within itself, even though important, is not enough, and if a Believer is depending on such, the Believer is going to be sadly disappointed.

THE HOLY SPIRIT

To cut straight through to the bottom line, the Believer cannot be what he ought to be, cannot be what he should be, and cannot be what he must be, without the empowerment of the Holy Spirit. But the sadness is, most Christians, even Pentecostals, do not really know how the Holy Spirit works. In other words, they just simply take Him for granted.

How does He work?

First of all, the Holy Spirit works exclusively within the boundaries or parameters of the Finished Work of Christ, i.e., *"The Cross of Christ."* Listen again to Paul:

"There is therefore now no condemnation (guilt) *to them which are in Christ Jesus* (refers back to Romans 6:3-5 and our being baptized into His Death, which speaks of the Crucifixion), *who walk not after the flesh* (depending on one's personal strength and ability or great religious efforts in order to overcome sin), *but after the Spirit* (the Holy Spirit works exclusively

within the legal confines of the Finished Work of Christ; our Faith in that Finished Work, i.e., *'the Cross,'* guarantees the help of the Holy Spirit, which guarantees Victory).

"For the Law (that which we are about to give is a Law of God, devised by the Godhead in eternity past [I Pet. 1:18-20]; this Law, in fact, is *"God's Prescribed Order of Victory"*) *of the Spirit* (Holy Spirit, i.e., *'the way the Spirit works'*) *of life* (all life comes from Christ, but through the Holy Spirit [Jn. 16:13-14] *in Christ Jesus* (anytime Paul uses this term or one of its derivatives, he is, without fail, referring to what Christ did at the Cross, which makes this *'life'* possible) *has made me free* (given me total Victory) *from the Law of Sin and Death"* (these are the two most powerful Laws in the Universe; the *'Law of the Spirit of Life in Christ Jesus'* alone is stronger than the *'Law of Sin and Death'*; this means that if the Believer attempts to live for God by any manner other than Faith in Christ and the Cross, he is doomed to failure)" (Rom. 8:1-2).

As stated, for the Holy Spirit to help us, which help we must have, that is if we are to live a victorious life, and do so perpetually, our Faith, due to the fact that the Holy Spirit works exclusively within the parameters of the Atonement, must be anchored squarely in Christ and the Cross, with us not allowing it to be moved. That being the case, the Holy Spirit will then work on our behalf, will assure us the victory, meaning that the sin nature will no longer be able to rule us in any way. That is, in brief, God's Prescribed Order of Victory. That is the foundation, and we continue to speak of the Cross of Christ, on which all doctrine must be built.

ANOTHER JESUS

The problem with the modern Church is that it is preaching *"another Jesus."* What do we mean by that?

If the Cross is omitted, if it's given lesser place, this shows that we do not understand what the mission of Christ actually was. God became Man, and came to this world for one purpose, and that was to go to the Cross, which was demanded by a thrice-Holy God, in order that man be redeemed. While our Saviour did many things, still, it was the Cross that was His destination. This means that the Cross of Christ was not an incident, an accident, an execution, or an assassination. It was a Sacrifice, in fact, a Sacrifice planned from before the foundation of the world (I Pet. 1:18-20).

Second, it was at the Cross, even as we've already stated, that every victory was won, that the broken law was addressed, with Satan and all his minions of darkness totally and completely defeated (Col. 2:14-15).

When Jesus said that He *"must go into Jerusalem and suffer many things of the Elders and Chief Priests and Scribes, and be killed, and be raised again the third day,"* the Scripture also says, *"Then Peter took Him, and began to rebuke Him."*

Jesus did not at all take kindly to this, but instead said to Peter, *"Get thee behind Me, Satan* (Jesus used nearly the same words in rebuking Peter, and the other Disciples that He had used to the Devil, in His temptation [Mat. 4:10]; all denial of the Cross in any form, is of Satan)*: you are an offense unto Me* (speaks directly to Peter, because he is now being used by Satan)*: for you savor not the things that be of God, but those that be of men* (if it's not the Cross, then it's of men, which means it is of Satan)*"* (Mat. 16:21-23).

Jesus then said, *"If any man will come after Me, let him deny himself* (not asceticism, but rather the denial of one's own strength and ability), *and take up his Cross* (the benefits of the Cross, which Jesus did there [Col. 2:14-15], *and follow Me.* (If Christ is not followed by the means of the Cross, He cannot be followed at all)*"* (Mat. 16:24).

Jesus also said, *"And whosoever does not bear his Cross* (this doesn't speak of suffering as most think, but rather ever making the Cross of Christ the Object of our Faith; we are Saved and we are victorious, not by suffering, although that sometimes will happen, or any other similar things, but rather by our Faith, but always with the Cross of Christ as the Object of that Faith), *and come after Me* (one can follow Christ only by Faith in what He has done for us at the Cross; He recognizes nothing else), *cannot be My Disciple.* (The statement is emphatic! If it's not Faith in the Cross of Christ, then it's Faith that God will not recognize, which means that such people are refused [I Cor. 1:17-18, 21, 23; 2:2; Rom. 6:3-14; 8:1-2, 11, 13; Gal. 6:14; Eph. 2:13-18; Col. 2:14-15])*"* (Lk. 14:27).

So, if the modern Church is not preaching

NOTES

Christ and the Cross, they are, in effect, preaching *"another Jesus."*

This *"other Jesus"* draws on opposition, raises no fuss, simply because it is a manufactured Jesus, in other words, a Jesus that's not in the Bible.

In essence, Paul told the Corinthians that if they preached anything other than Jesus Christ and Him Crucified, they would not be preaching the Gospel, would not be truly proclaiming Christ, and would be, in effect, proclaiming another Jesus (II Cor. 11:4).

Let me say it again: The Jesus of the Bible, the Son of the Living God, the Christ of Glory, is the Jesus Who died on the Cross and, as stated, Who came to die on a Cross and, thereby, accomplish Redemption, which was planned by the Godhead from before the foundation of the world (I Pet. 1:18-20).

Once again we state with the Apostle Paul: *"We preach Christ Crucified"* (I Cor. 1:23).

PROSPERITY

The prosperity of which I have spoken is based squarely on the foundation of the Cross of Christ, and unless any and all prosperity is based on that foundation, in truth, there is no true prosperity, at least that which will last.

(3) "FOR TO THEIR POWER, I BEAR RECORD, YEA, AND BEYOND THEIR POWER THEY WERE WILLING OF THEMSELVES;"

Men are often most liberal when in circumstances of distress, perplexity, and affliction. Prosperity often freezes the heart, while adversity at times opens it. Success in life often closes the hand of unselfishness, but adversity at times opens it.

We are taught to feel for the sufferings of others by suffering ourselves; and in the school of adversity we learn invaluable lessons of generosity which we could never acquire in prosperity. If one needs sympathy, if one needs help, go to a man in affliction, and his heart is open. And hence it is, that God often suffers His people to pass through trials in order that they may possess the spirit of large and active benevolence and sympathy (Barnes).

A PERSONAL EXAMPLE

Using myself as an example, I do not look at people as I once did. In the first place, the self-righteousness is gone and in the second, one who has suffered much, even though some of the cause was his own, still has empathy for others. When I hear a Christian or anyone for that matter, denigrate someone else, even though what has happened to them may be their fault, I cringe inside. At great price, the Lord has given me, I think, much more love for the human race and much more patience with weakness and failure.

But isn't that the Spirit of the Lord? Isn't that the manner in which He deals with us?

As we said in earlier commentary regarding affliction, I think affliction and suffering are allowed at times by the Lord, in order that we might have proper feeling for others. It's very easy to point a finger of accusation and blame someone else. It costs nothing to do that, and it rolls off the lips easily. However, that finger of accusation always comes from the pit of self-righteousness, which is the very spirit and sin that crucified the Lord of Glory.

THEIR POWER

The phrase, *"For to their power, I bear record,"* refers to the fact that the Apostle knew the financial circumstances of these Macedonians. Paul had founded these Churches, and had spent much time with them. He was, therefore, well qualified to bear testimony in regard to their economic situation.

BEYOND THEIR POWER

The phrase, *"Yea, and beyond their power,"* means they did not measure their gift according to their ability. They gave more than they comfortably could afford. They gave beyond the limits of their ability.

In effect, their giving was beyond what could have been expected of them, even beyond that which Paul expected of them. Actually it was beyond as we shall see, what would have been thought possible according to their condition.

The sense is, they were willing to give more than they were well able. It shows the strong interest they had in the Work of God, and the desire to please the Lord.

The idea is, and even as we have already stated, that the Holy Spirit chose the Macedonians, the least economic viable of all the Churches, to serve as an example of generosity, of obedience, and of the road to Blessing.

NOTES

It must be remembered, that these people were what we refer to today as *"dirt poor."* They were not merely somewhat short regarding finances, they were actually in *"deep poverty."* In other words, they were having problems putting food on the table and clothes on their children's backs. And yet, these people responded so much to Paul's request, that the Holy Spirit would single them out as the prime example of all time.

Please note, He did not choose the wealthy Churches which no doubt gave far more, at least as far as an amount was concerned, but rather these who gave out of their deep poverty, which reflected the greatest gift of all.

It must ever be remembered, that giving is not measured in dollars and cents. There are many things that go into this factor. For some people to give $10.00, it is a great sacrifice. For others to give $10,000, it is no sacrifice at all. So, it is relative, and to be sure, the Lord looks at the entirety of the situation, regarding motives, the amount we give, but more particularly, the amount we have left.

A BEAUTIFUL EXAMPLE

A Businessman and a Lawyer, both Christians, were traveling in Korea. One day they saw in the field by the side of the road a young man pulling a crude plow, while an old man held the handles. The Lawyer was somewhat amused and took a snapshot of the scene.

"That's a curious picture! I suppose they are very poor," he said to the Missionary who was the interpreter and guide to the party.

"Yes," was the quiet reply. And then the Missionary said, *"That is the family of Chi Boui."*

He then went on to say, *"When the Church was built a short time ago, they were eager to give something to it, but they had no money, so they sold their only ox and gave the money to the Church. This spring they are pulling the plow themselves, because they have no ox."*

The Lawyer and the Businessman by his side were silent for some moments. Then the Businessman said, *"That must have been a real sacrifice."*

"They did not call it that," said the Missionary. *"They thought it was fortunate that they had the ox to sell."*

The Lawyer and the Businessman had not much to say. When they reached home the Lawyer took the picture that he had taken of this Korean man and his son and showed it to his Pastor and told him about the situation. He then said, *"I want to double my pledge to the Church."*

He then added, *"In all of my life, I have never really given anything to the Lord that actually cost me anything."*

That's quite a statement! A long time ago, David said, *"Neither will I offer . . . unto the Lord my God of that which doth cost me nothing"* (II Sam. 24:24).

I'm afraid it is true of most Christians, and possibly all of us at one time or the other, that we are accustomed to giving to God that which cost us nothing.

WILLING

The phrase, *"They were willing of themselves,"* means they were acting from choice, and not because someone had pressured them into doing so.

Not only did they do so willingly, but they rejoiced in the opportunity in doing it. They came forward of their own accord and made the contribution. The idea is, that they made a joy of robbing themselves.

"Willing of themselves" in the Greek is actually a combination of two words. One means *"self* (autos)*"* and the other *"I choose* (haireomai).*"* This speaks of giving willingly without pressure. The truth is, if we do not give willingly, it really cannot be classified as Christian giving. Unfortunately, some people give to the Work of God for totally unscriptural reasons.

UNSCRIPTURAL GIVING

1. Giving to get. While the Lord certainly does give back and grandly so to all who give to Him, even promising such in His Word; however, if in fact our giving is only for the purpose of getting something in return, it really cannot be classified as giving; consequently, such is not pleasing to God, will not be blessed, and because it is the wrong motive.

2. Responding to appeals which guarantee a hundredfold return, or some such amount at a particular time, once again, is wrong, simply because the motivation is wrong, which means the person is not actually giving. They are in fact making an investment, but it should be quickly said, an investment that God will never

honor. Any Preacher who promises such is grossly unscriptural, and in fact, is resorting to manipulation and exploitation.

For instance, a Preacher of my acquaintance some time back, told the people in his audience that particular night, that the Lord had told him that all who would give $1,000 in the offering, would have their home paid for free and clear at the end of the year. Of course, quite a number of people responded.

Did the Lord tell this to this Preacher?

Unequivocally, no! The Lord never appeals to base motives or to greed. The man lied about the situation, and due to the type of lie it was, it was extremely evil, because it sought to make the Lord a part of the scheme.

Incidentally, if I remember correctly, two or three people who walked up that night lost their homes because of the $1,000 gift they could ill afford. Actually, that they could ill afford such did not enter into the picture. These Macedonians could not afford what they did either, but there the similarity ended.

The Macedonians were giving out of love, while these people were responding to a lie, i.e., *"fraud."*

3. One should not give unless one knows where the money is going. In doing that, one should not merely take the word of the one receiving the offering. Maybe what is being said is totally true and honest, but sadly and regrettably, much of the time it isn't.

Is a Ministry winning souls? Is it seeing Believers baptized with the Holy Spirit? Is it seeing people delivered by the Power of God? Is it seeing people truly healed, and not merely a part of hype? Is it truly proclaiming the uncompromised Word of God?

Jesus plainly told us that we should look at the fruit of the Ministry before we support that work (Mat. 7:15-20). To be frank, the far greater majority of the money supposedly given to the Cause of Christ, does little or nothing for the Work of God, and in fact, is given to that which is really not the Work of God, but rather that which is false.

In this very Church at Corinth, before their repentance, the people there were heavily supporting the false teachers who had come in. Does anyone actually think that particular giving was of the Lord? The answer is obvious, no it wasn't!

NOTES

Paul's Ministry was a legitimate Ministry, and its support is consequently heralded in the Word of God. To be sure, that given to the false teachers and false apostles receive no positive mention at all.

ARE YOU WILLING?

I think the Believer should ask himself the question regarding giving to God, *"Am I willing?"* Even though the question is simple, still, spiritually speaking it is quite heavy.

Many would quickly answer in the affirmative without really thinking the thing through. Their thoughts would be, *"I am willing, but I simply don't have the money. When I have the money, then I will give."*

That's not what the Holy Spirit is saying here.

If you are truly *"willing,"* irrespective of your present financial situation, you will immediately begin to give, and I trust to that which is right, Scriptural, and legitimate.

As well, the word *"willing"* here actually means, *"to give beyond one's ability."* Are you willing to do that?

Now we see as to how the simple question, *"Are you willing?"*, is quite heavy with its content and meaning.

I suppose one could say, and drawing from the illustration just given, are you willing to sell the ox and pull the plow yourself?

The Lord does not require such giving on a constant basis. But He does occasionally require such. The question is, when He does ask for such a sacrifice, are we willing to obey?

(4) "PRAYING US WITH MUCH INTREATY THAT WE WOULD RECEIVE THE GIFT, AND TAKE UPON US THE FELLOWSHIP OF THE MINISTERING TO THE SAINTS."

We will find several beautiful examples and at least one great Truth in this particular Scripture. It will be and is greatly refreshing to say the least!

MUCH INTREATY

The phrase, *"Praying us with much intreaty,"* tells us several things:

1. Their gift was far larger than Paul ever dreamed possible.

2. It was so large that Paul did not want to receive it, especially knowing and understanding their economic situation.

3. They had to literally demand that Paul take the Offering. The evidence is, that he wanted to give some back, but they steadfastly refused.

RECEIVE

The phrase, *"That we would receive the Gift,"* in effect, means that they begged Paul to take the gift.

They wanted *"this Grace,"* i.e., *"the Grace of God"* mentioned in Verse 1 and as has already been explained, they considered their Gift a Grace and a Gift of God to themselves. They gave to the very limit in order to get into the communion of giving to the fullest possible extent.

THE FELLOWSHIP

The phrase, *"And take upon us the fellowship of the ministering to the Saints,"* refers here to the Saints in Jerusalem.

Paul viewed giving as a matter of *"fellowship,"* which was a means of ministering to these people in Jerusalem. Most of the times, our modern giving is not thought of in this fashion. We should think of it accordingly, then our giving would be far more personal.

As an example, most of my personal efforts to raise funds pertains solely to World Evangelism. We air the Telecast in foreign countries all over the world, at least where we have the funds to do so. Of course, these are people who the giver never sees, and in fact does not know, except by Faith.

In other words, we should always understand, at least in the case of our Ministry, that giving always boils down to people. Some of them as a result of our Telecast will find Christ as their Saviour. As such, those who give in order to make it possible for the Gospel to reach these people, are literally ministering to them in the highest sort of way — the Salvation of their souls. Paul referred to such as a *"fellowship."*

COMMUNION OR FELLOWSHIP

From the very beginning the early Christians experienced a peculiar sense of unity. Christ is at once the center of this unity and the origin of every expression of fellowship.

Sometimes the fellowship is essentially an experience and as such it is scarcely susceptible of definition. It may rather be regarded as a mystical union in Christ. Actually that is how it is defined respecting money given to win souls to Christ. Their becoming a part of Christ, means that they become a part of the Body of Christ as well. As such, fellowship and communion are enjoined, even though the giver and the recipient of the gift may never see each other, in fact may never know each other.

NOTES

In its various relations, fellowship is represented accordingly:

1. As a communion between the Son and the Father. The Gospel record represents Jesus as enjoying a unique sense of communion and intimacy with the Father. Among many such expressions those of Matthew 11:25-27; Luke 10:21-22; John Chapters 14 and 15 are especially important.

2. As our communion with the Father which is through the Son and by the Holy Spirit. *"Our Fellowship is with the Father, and with His Son Jesus Christ"* (I Jn. 1:3; Jn. 14:6, 23-26).

Giving to win souls to Christ, enables the person brought to the Lord, to then have Communion with the Father and with the Son. So, the Fellowship or Communion, actually refers to a far greater sort than merely person to person, but rather person to God.

So, even though Paul is here speaking of ministering to Saints, and more particularly Saints in Jerusalem, still, this principle also holds true as it regards ministering to the unsaved.

(5) "AND THIS THEY DID, NOT AS WE HOPED, BUT FIRST GAVE THEIR OWN SELVES TO THE LORD, AND UNTO US BY THE WILL OF GOD."

If Christians desire to be liberal they must first devote themselves to God. If this is not done they will have no heart to give, and they will not give. They will have a thousand excuses ready, and there will be no ground of appeal which we can make to them. True liberality is always based on the fact that we have given ourselves wholly to God.

BEYOND WHAT WAS HOPED

The phrase, *"And this they did, not as we hoped,"* rather means, *"not as we expected,"* but rather beyond our expectations.

In other words, they were so poor that it was impossible for Paul to expect much from them, but they surpassed his expectations in every way.

GAVE THEMSELVES TO THE LORD

The phrase, *"But first gave their own selves to the Lord,"* presents the key to this scenario.

In effect, they were giving themselves. To give oneself when one gives a gift is the highest form of Christian Giving. To use a metaphor, it refers to giving far more than the fat, but down to the muscle and the ligament.

The idea is not, however, that of giving themselves for the Work of the Gospel, which it definitely is, but here is far greater.

It is giving like that of the widow whom Jesus commended so highly. When she dropped in her last coin, which was all her living, she gave herself into God's hands in absolute dependence on His care. For her living she then had God alone. And no gift can please God as much as that.

As someone has said, the surrender of self to the Lord involves the surrender of the purse. It is God Who makes the heart willing to such a surrender.

AND UNTO US BY THE WILL OF GOD

The phrase, *"And unto us by the Will of God,"* means they had thorough confidence in Paul and his Ministry.

The manner in which the Greek is structured, has reference to the fact that it was by one act that the Macedonians *"gave themselves"* to both *"the Lord and to us."* However, the act had two sides, one was directed *"to the Lord,"* the other was directed *"to us"* (Paul and his associates). They gave themselves to the Lord Who was their Master, who purchased and won them and to us Who are the Lord's Ministers. This was *"God's Will."*

This is said to the Corinthians who had of late turned away from devotion to Paul. What a contrast the Macedonians are affording! Here is the example which the Corinthians should follow, and no doubt now will, inasmuch as Repentance has now been enjoined.

The idea is, that if they first gave themselves to the Lord, and then to the Lord's Ministers, in this case Paul and his associates, then whatever money they would give would be acceptable to God.

The Macedonians knew that Paul was doing the Will of God and, consequently, willingly gave themselves to him. It is crucial, even as we have already stated, to discern whether specific Ministries are in accord with God's Plan before committing ourselves to them.

How can we tell if Ministries are doing the Will of God? We do so by evaluating them according to the Scriptures. If they are truly fulfilling the Will of God, as stated, they will be concentrating on worshipping God (Eph. 1:3-14), on reaching the unconverted (Mat. 28:19), and on training Believers so they can minister effectively (Mat. 28:20; Eph. 4:11-16).

NOTES

EXTREMELY IMPORTANT

Even as we have already stated, the Reader should very carefully take these things to heart. We have a perfect example here of the Macedonians giving themselves to Paul, but the Corinthians ceasing to do so, at least for a time. Satan had been successful through false teachers, in getting the people of Corinth to believe that Paul in essence was not of God. Never mind, that they were saved because of his Ministry, consequently, brought out of heathenistic darkness. In some foolish way, they allowed Satan to turn their heads, even as the false doctrine of the false apostles turned their hearts.

It is Satan's business to get Christians to believe that which actually is of God, isn't, and that which isn't of God, is. He is very successful in his efforts. Consequently, much if not most of the money given for that which purports to be for the Cause of Christ, is rather being wasted. To be sure, the money given to these false apostles at Corinth certainly did not enhance the Work of God, but had the very opposite affect. Actually, at least in this case, Satan succeeded in getting Christians to support his work. The far greater majority of modern Christians do the same — support the work of Satan thinking it is of God.

Giving money is a very special thing in the Eyes of God, even as the Holy Spirit brings out in these two Chapters. It is far more than merely giving to some type of charity. It incorporates one's consecration, or the lack thereof. It speaks to our motives, our intentions, and above all, our consecration to the Will of God. Actually, the entirety of these proceedings hinge on the *"Will of God."*

Unfortunately, most Believers do not arrive at the Will of God regarding their giving, for the simple reason that they do not properly evaluate the *"fruits"* of the Ministry they are supporting (Mat. 7:15-20).

(6) "INSOMUCH THAT WE DESIRED TITUS, THAT AS HE HAD BEGUN, SO HE WOULD ALSO FINISH IN YOU THE SAME GRACE ALSO."

This Verse deals with the very thing which we have just mentioned. Due to the Church at Corinth getting off track, the Work of God had actually ground to a halt. Now it is back on course.

THAT WHICH HE HAD BEGUN

The phrase, *"Insomuch that we desired Titus, that as he had begun,"* refers to this collection having begun over a year before, for it is mentioned in the last chapter of I Corinthians. However, and as stated, due to the problems at Corinth, everything had ground to a halt which is exactly what Satan had wanted.

The purpose of citing the example of the Macedonians in the matter of giving was to incite the Corinthians to the same spirit and action. Now that the Corinthians had gotten back on track, the Work of God could proceed forward, even as it should have continued.

GRACE

The phrase, *"So he would also finish in you the same Grace also,"* by the use of the word *"Grace,"* places Giving in a very sacred position. This means that true giving to God is one's own spiritual enrichment.

We need not look askance at the statements that Titus began and is to finish this Divine Grace and then change the word into something human, namely the favor which the Corinthians extend by their contributions of money. Even God's Saving Grace is extended through means, the Word and the Ministry. As God's Minister, Titus *"began,"* as such he is to *"finish"* this *"Grace"* from God, to the great enrichment of the Corinthians.

THE MANNER IN WHICH GIVING IS GRACE

Here we have the right view of the work of the Ministry in collecting money for the Work of God. When we induce the people to give as these Macedonians gave, and as the Corinthians had begun to give and were to continue giving, we act as God's means for bestowing additional measures of God's Grace upon them. We are helping them to new measures of priceless Grace.

In other words, we are enriching them and not impoverishing them. As to more and more bestowals of God's Grace, read the Salutations to Paul's other Epistles, in which he wishes for his readers *"Grace from God, our Father,"* etc.

Grace does not exhaust itself in the one gift of Righteousness when Faith is kindled. Even greater measures of Grace are to become ours. This is what the Apostle is talking about here.

LOOK AGAIN AT MACEDONIA

These people were the poorest of the poor, even in *"deep poverty,"* but yet Paul asked that they give a certain amount as poor as they were. He did not excuse them, because he realized this was the key to Blessing.

And yet, the Holy Spirit, even as we have seen, went even further than Paul, even much further, in asking of them that which seemed impossible for them to do — to give completely beyond their means. This they did and gladly so, which brought a tremendous Grace of God upon them, which strengthened them, developed them, matured them, and blessed them in every way. Consequently, we have here a beautiful example of the means by which God does two things by our giving to His Work:

1. He uses our giving as a springboard to funnel more Grace to us, which is the crown of God's Blessings to His people.

2. He uses our giving, to bless us. Even as we shall see in the next Chapter (9:6), the Lord blessed these Macedonians *"bountifully,"* which speaks of material or economic Blessing.

One has to shout *"Hallelujah!"*

(7) "THEREFORE, AS YE ABOUND IN EVERY THING, IN FAITH, AND UTTERANCE, AND KNOWLEDGE, AND IN ALL DILIGENCE, AND IN YOUR LOVE TO US, SEE THAT YE ABOUND IN THIS GRACE ALSO."

This Verse as given by the Holy Spirit to the Apostle, places Giving in its proper role and place in the great attributes of God. However, we must ever be careful that we do not rob giving of its spiritual characteristics, by relegating it to the far lower level of merely giving to get, which I'm afraid characterizes much giving presently.

NOTES

ABOUND IN EVERYTHING

The phrase, *"Therefore, as ye abound in everything,"* presents these great Graces of Christianity, but which had previously fallen by the wayside due to the Corinthians' spiritual declension, but had now been renewed.

The idea is presented by the use of the word *"everything,"* that Believers not fall short in any complement, any quality, any Grace of the Holy Spirit within our lives. If our growth is proper, all of these Graces will grow accordingly.

The sadness is that at this present time, the Church in many quarters has gone overboard respecting giving, making it the primary Message, thereby attaching all of these other qualities (Faith, etc.), to that one Grace, which is wrong. In other words, giving is very important, even as Paul here brings out, even to a degree far above that thought by most, actually equal to Faith, etc., as we shall see. But when all the other Graces are made subservient to the one Grace of giving, as it's being done in many circles presently, heresy is then the result.

To use an example, the Grace of Giving is somewhat like the dessert regarding our meal; however, if we neglect the other ingredients of our meal, such as potatoes, beans, meat, etc., eating dessert almost exclusively, in a short period of time the individual is going to suffer physical malnutrition. Regrettably, this is what is presently happening in much of the modern Church.

IN FAITH

The phrase, *"In Faith,"* refers to the full belief of the truth and obligation of the Gospel. It is actually the foundation of this prepared meal, which one might call the *"meat of the Word."*

As well, it covers every single aspect of our Christian experience, not merely Faith in God to obtain money, etc. Faith in its proper setting, pertains to one's Salvation, one's victory in Christ, one's spiritual Growth, in other words, the complement of the entirety of the Word of God and as it is applied to our hearts and lives on a daily basis.

AND UTTERANCE

The phrase, *"And utterance,"* refers to the Word of God (logo), which pertains to Doctrine and our presentation of that Doctrine.

Some have attempted to reduce this word to *"speaking with Tongues,"* which it does definitely include; however, it only includes this particular Grace, with the word *"utterance"* carrying a far greater connotation, actually pertaining to the entirety of the Word of God.

AND KNOWLEDGE

The phrase, *"And knowledge,"* pertains to knowledge of the Word of God, which of course, is the single most important thing in which anyone could ever excel.

As well, the *"knowledge"* given here, pertains to a knowledge of the entirety of the Word of God, and not just part. For instance, many modern Charismatics little study the Old Testament, claiming it's not necessary presently, except only in a limited sense. Such thinking is foolish!

The Truth is, if one does not properly understand the Old Testament, it is literally impossible to understand the New — hence the reason for so many unscriptural doctrines in these particular circles.

AND IN ALL DILIGENCE

The phrase, *"And in all diligence,"* refers to readiness in the discharge of every Scriptural and spiritual duty.

With many Christians, all types of diligence are shown regarding the things of this world in our own personal lives, but not too much regarding the things of God. The Truth is, and by all means, this is where our diligence must prevail. Paul here calls *"diligence"* a *"Grace,"* with most Believers probably not thinking of it as such.

In other words, the Lord is intently watching, looking, and searching our lives, respecting our diligence in His Cause. For instance, are we very quick to go to a ball game, irrespective of the inclement weather, because we love that particular sport; but with Church, the slightest weather problem, keeps us at home?

YOUR LOVE

The phrase, *"And in your love to us,"* presents the Apostle as *not* issuing orders to the Corinthians as a Commander who is simply to be obeyed. He is doing a far deeper thing, he is using the loving earnestness of others, in this case the Macedonians, as a simple means for testing the genuineness of the love of the Corinthians. In other words, he is giving the Corinthians an opportunity to compare their love with the love the Macedonians manifested in their great earnestness to carry out this important Grace — the Grace of Giving.

As well, the Apostle means to test the love of the Corinthians for him and his associates as God's Ministers. The context shows clearly that this love, love for them, is referred to and not just love in general or love for the needy in Jerusalem.

Actually, in this Verse, Paul acknowledges this love toward him; it had declined but had revived and would now be tested by being asked to do something that would call it fully into action, namely this collection. In Verse 5 he states that the Macedonians gave themselves to him in complete devotion by the way in which they responded in the matter of this collection.

We should not be surprised that Paul makes this collection a test of love toward himself. Love for Paul and his associates was love for the great work in which they were engaged, which of course, was the Work of God. Through this collection the Corinthians would participate in this work; their hearts would be knit together in purest love with these Preachers of the Gospel who literally lived in this work.

Coldness and indifference in the matter of the collection would show how little they loved these Ministers. It is just that simple!

Paul has no fear that contributions might be made only for his sake. He ever conducted his work so that this could not be done. He so completely merged himself and his work in the Lord that one could show genuine love to him only by loving the Lord and genuine love to the Lord only by loving also Paul and those who helped Paul. That is quite a statement, but I believe it to be true in every aspect.

The Lord has so meshed His Work and His Ministers together, that it is literally impossible to separate the two. Of course, I am speaking of those who are truly called of God, and are truly anointed by the Lord to do the Work of God. As we have repeatedly stated, this will be evident by the Scriptural *"fruit"* of the Ministry in question.

THIS GRACE ALSO

The phrase, *"See that ye abound in this Grace also,"* completely, absolutely, and totally, places the Giving of our money to the Work of God, at the high, high level of a *"Grace,"* actually in the same category as *"Faith,"* etc. However, it is a *"Grace"* even as we have already stated, only as it is kept in this position, and not lowered to the far lower level of merely giving to get.

NOTES

The idea here is, that eminence in spiritual endowments of any kind, or in any of the traits of the Christian experience, should always lead to a spirit of *"giving"* whether of our time, our ability, our consecration, or our money. The idea goes further by suggesting that the character of the Child of God is not complete unless this Grace of Giving manifests itself toward every good object that may be presented.

In fact, the entirety of the economy of God is wrapped up in the one word *"give."* The Scripture says, *"For God so loved the world, that He gave . . ."* (Jn. 3:16).

As we have stated, God has nothing for sale, and as well, He operates His Kingdom on this great and wonderful basis of *"giving,"* which is the direct opposite of the spirit of the world.

If the world gives at all, it is only to get something in return. In fact, selfishness and greed are the twin spirits of the world. The Christian is to be the very opposite.

The moment we come into the great Salvation of Christ, we come into His Economy, and this refers to every aspect of our lives. Consequently, we are to take upon ourselves the very aspect of this Economy. God is constantly giving to us and in every manner; consequently, we are as well to be constantly *"giving"* to others. That is why Paul refers to this beautiful complement as a *"Grace."*

The very word *"Grace"* means *"unmerited favor."* In other words, God doesn't give to us because we deserve it, but because He is good. Likewise, our giving is not to rest solely upon merit — the merit of others — but because we are functioning in the Goodness of God. If God gave to us only because we deserved it, to be frank, we would receive nothing. That's what *"Grace"* is all about. All it asks is a broken and contrite spirit, and Grace will be abundantly supplied in every capacity (Lk. 18:14).

(8) "I SPEAK NOT BY COMMANDMENT, BUT BY OCCASION OF THE FORWARDNESS OF OTHERS, AND TO PROVE THE SINCERITY OF YOUR LOVE."

In this Verse three great Truths are presented; consequently, we should study them very carefully.

NOT BY COMMANDMENT

The phrase, *"I speak not by Commandment,"* does not mean that he had no express Command of God in this case, for he did, but that he did not mean to command them. The idea is this:

The Grace of *"giving,"* cannot be by *"Commandment"* or else it is no longer giving, etc.

This means that the Believer must never give out of a sense of fear, in other words, if he doesn't give something bad will happen to him, etc. If one thinks such, one is functioning totally outside of the Economy of God. In that case, giving becomes a Commandment, which in reality is a *"tax,"* which is a total perversion of the Word of God. If our giving is no more than a mere *"tax,"* we are robbed of all joy, all Faith, and all Blessing. In other words, God cannot bless a *"tax,"* for the simple reason that a tax is something owed. We do not give to God because we *"owe"* Him, which in reality we actually do; however, the Holy Spirit does not treat us as servants or slaves, but rather as members of the Family of God (Rom. 8:14-18). In fact, Jesus addressed this beautifully when He said, *"What thinkest thou, Simon? Of whom do the kings of the earth take custom or tribute? Of their own children, or of strangers?*

"Peter saith unto Him, Of strangers. Jesus saith unto him, Then are the children free" (Mat. 17:25-26).

So, the Believer should never allow himself to be maneuvered into the position of giving to God simply because he feels he must do so. If such a spirit or feeling persists, that shows that we are not where we ought to be with the Lord, in fact, do not see or properly understand our place and position in Christ as children and not strangers. To be frank, the world owes God and big time, even though they do not recognize such. And in every strict sense of the word, Believers owe Him as well, and even in a greater way than the world; however, even though that should always be our feeling toward Him, that we ever owe Him which we certainly do, the Lord never treats us accordingly. There is never a spirit or idea on His part, that addresses us in this manner. He addresses us as members of the Family, which is entirely by Love and Grace. Consequently, He really asks nothing in return; nevertheless, at all times, we are to willingly and gladly give our all to Him. That is the basis on which Christianity functions.

NOTES

This attitude and spirit is epitomized beautifully in the *"Whole Burnt Offering"* of the Old Testament. As God gives His all to us, the *"Whole Burnt Offering,"* as it was sacrificed by the offerer, in effect, a *"Consecration Offering,"* said, *"In turn I give my all to You."*

FORWARDNESS OF OTHERS

The phrase, *"But by occasion of the forwardness of others,"* proclaims grandly that Giving inspires Giving. In other words, when people begin to give to God, such inspires others to give to God, which the Holy Spirit intends. In its truest sense of the word, it means that Faith is contagious, just as one might quickly add, unbelief is also contagious.

As an example, and to which we have already alluded, in our Campmeetings which we conduct at Family Worship Center in Baton Rouge, Louisiana, in each of these Meetings we raise funds for World Evangelism. It is to help pay for the placing of the Telecast around the world.

Even though we very seldom ask as to who will give so much, at times we will state a certain amount we would like for the people to give.

Time and time again, I've seen people step out and begin to give, with a spirit of giving then begin to come over the congregation, and because others have seen such giving, they will step out and give likewise. In fact, they probably would not have done so, unless they had seen the *"forwardness of others."*

Thank the Lord, for those who are used of the Lord to be *"forward"*; consequently, their giving, due to their faithfulness, is multiplied many times over, for the simple reason that it inspires others to give as well.

Consequently, we do wrong when we complain about some who walk forward and give certain amounts. Whatever the motive of their hearts might be, that is between them and God. But the fact is, what they have done, at least within itself, is not wrong, but rather right. God uses this *"forwardness,"* even as Paul here plainly and clearly says, and by the inspiration of the Holy Spirit.

I say these things, because I have seen some Christians refuse to give, or else claim that people who walk forward with such amounts, were doing so only for show. While that certainly may be true in some cases, as stated, that is not our business, but rather between God and that person. Even though at times, some few may have a wrong motive in this capacity; nevertheless, the Lord will still use that which they have done to inspire others, even as He says here. As well, if in fact their motive is wrong, He will deal with that as well, but that is not our business. That is between that person and the Lord. The Truth is, there is no way that we can ascertain the motive of one's heart, that being the domain of God Alone. So for us to judge one accordingly, does a great disservice to that person and to God, and to ourselves as well. What measure we mete, will be measured to us again (Mat. 7:1-3).

The Truth is, that the *"forwardness of others"* has caused untold millions of dollars to be raised for the Cause of Christ, which possibly might not have come in otherwise. To be sure, if this was not important, the Holy Spirit would not have brought it out as plainly as He did through the Apostle.

TO PROVE THE SINCERITY OF YOUR LOVE

The phrase, *"And to prove the sincerity of your love,"* presents the third great Truth of this Scripture. It tells us several things:

1. Giving must be from the basis and foundation of love, or else it is not giving.
2. The Holy Spirit through the Apostle is bluntly saying, that if we truly love God, we will give to His Work. It is just that simple!
3. Giving to God proves our sincerity. Words are cheap, but giving proves the validity of our words. In other words, if we refuse to give to God, and for any reason, irrespective as to what we may claim or profess, our actions in this capacity prove that we really do not love the Lord.
4. The Holy Spirit by using the word *"prove,"* has placed *"giving"* as the acid test. *"Prove"* speaks of the process of placing impure ore into a crucible and burning out the dross so that the pure metal would remain. When God places people into His crucible, and this is one of the ways that He does such, which is the test of our Giving, He burns out all that is spurious so that only the *"genuine"* or *"real"* is left. The idea is this:

NOTES

The Holy Spirit judges this in two ways: first of all our *"giving,"* and second, our *"motivation."* Many people give, but the motivation is wrong, which means that such giving is looked at by the Holy Spirit as *"dross,"* and will consequently burn up. As well, some will not give at all, which makes their claims and profession empty, i.e., *"dross."* However, those who give to God as they should, and to prove the sincerity of their love for Him, the Holy Spirit looks at that as the pure gold of consecration.

(9) "FOR YE KNOW THE GRACE OF OUR LORD JESUS CHRIST, THAT, THOUGH HE WAS RICH, YET FOR YOUR SAKES HE BECAME POOR, THAT YE THROUGH HIS POVERTY MIGHT BE RICH."

This freighted Passage presents Jesus as our Example and as well, proclaims other great Truths.

THE GRACE OF OUR LORD JESUS CHRIST

The phrase, *"For ye know the Grace of our Lord Jesus Christ,"* presents this great thing that Jesus did in the Salvation of lost humanity, as *"a Grace."* This was *"Grace"* which did something, and which in fact, always does something. It is in the fullest sense of the word, *"wholly undeserved favor,"* and wholly undeserved favor upon sinners. In this, the full name, *"Lord Jesus Christ"* is used. He is our Lord (His relation to us whom He purchased and won) Jesus (His Personal Name, which itself means Saviour) Christ (His official Name, the Anointed One sent us by God and anointed as our Prophet, High Priest, and King).

The Apostle Paul was accustomed to illustrate every subject, and to enforce every duty, where it could be done, by a reference to the Life and Sufferings of the Lord Jesus Christ. The design of this Verse is obvious.

It is to show the duty of giving liberally to the Work of God, in order that we may follow the example of the Lord Jesus Christ Who gave so liberally of Himself. The idea further expressed is, that He was willing to become poor in order that He might benefit others, i.e., *"that we might become rich,"* i.e., spiritual riches.

Paul is saying, that He Who was Lord and Proprietor of the universe, and Who possessed all things, was willing to leave His exalted station in the Bosom of the Father and to become poor, in order that we might become rich in the Blessings of the Gospel, in the means of Grace, and in heirs of all things; and that we who are thus benefitted, and who have such an Example, should certainly be willing to part with some of our earthly possessions in order that we may benefit others for Christ.

EVER-EXPANDING GRACE

Five times Paul uses the word *"Grace"* in this Chapter (vss. 1, 6, 7, 9, 19).

This presents a new measure of favor each time from God, when we respond to Him by giving to His Work and Cause. In other words, each time it is a new measure of His Grace to us. In fact, the Corinthians already had this Grace, but are to desire and to receive a new measure of it just as did the Macedonians.

Now, be it far from the Reader's mind, that Grace or anything can be purchased from the Lord by the giving of money or any other way. The entire warp and woof of Paul's Teaching, drive toward the very opposite. We are to give because we love the Lord, not because He will give back to us more money, or even Grace. And yet, He has promised to do all of these things, which He amply does; consequently, *"giving"* provides one of the greatest tests for the Believer.

Will the Believer succumb to the giving-to-get spirit? Will the Believer give in order to earn something? This is designed in this fashion, that it might prove the heart of the Believer. What is in our heart regarding our giving? Outward particulars might fool people, but they do not fool God, Who sees and knows the human heart. Consequently, *"giving"* is one of the greatest tests of all, as it measures our love for God, our consecration, and our proper motives.

THE RICHES OF THE LORD

The phrase, *"That, though He was rich,"* stands opposed to that poverty which He assumed and manifested when He dwelt among men. Following are among the Truths implied:

1. The phrase implies His preexistence, for He became poor. In other words, He was not always poor, and in fact, is not poor at the present time.

He had been rich; yet not in this world. He did not lay aside wealth here on Earth after He had possessed it, for He had none. He was not first rich, and then poor on Earth, for He had no earthly wealth. Consequently, this refers to a state of antecedent riches before His assumption of human nature; and the expression is strikingly parallel to that in Philippians 2:6-7, *"Who, being in the form of God, thought it not robbery to be equal with God: But made Himself of no reputation,"* etc.

2. He was rich as the Lord and Proprietor of all things. He was the Creator of all (Jn. 1:3; Col. 1:16) and as Creator He had a right to all things, and the disposal of all things.

The most absolute right which can exist is that acquired by the act of creation; in this right the Son of God possessed over all gold, and silver, diamonds, and pearls; over all earth and land; over all the treasures of the oceans, and over all worlds for that matter.

DOMINION

The extent and amount of His riches, therefore, is to be measured by the extent of His Dominion over the universe; and to estimate His riches, therefore, we are to conceive of the Scepter which He waves and sways over the distant worlds.

In fact, what wealth has man that can compare to the riches of the Creator and Proprietor of all? How poor and worthless appears all the gold man can accumulate, compared with the wealth of Him Whose are the silver, and the gold, and the cattle upon a thousand hills?

In other words, we are speaking of *"riches"* so beyond the ability of man to compare, that it is actually impossible for us to grasp or comprehend.

FOR OUR SAKES

The phrase, *"Yet for your sakes,"* presents the total and complete purpose of Calvary and the Resurrection.

This entire Plan of Salvation, with Jesus actually being that Plan, which included His Incarnation, His Perfect Walk, His Death at Calvary, His Resurrection, His Ascension, and His Exaltation, which proclaims His Position at the Right Hand of the Father — all in its entirety, totally and completely, was for sinners. In other words, this great thing done by Christ was not for Angels, Himself, or Heaven to any degree, but altogether for lost and dying humanity.

NOTES

So, if He did this wonderful and noble thing, this great thing, the greatest of all greatness, it should stand to reason that He wants us to avail ourselves of this which He did, i.e., *"purchased at such great price."* It was all for *"our sakes."*

Such represents a love which cannot be comprehended by mere mortals. It was His Love that gave, that caused Him to give, and it is to be Love which motivates our giving as well.

HE BECAME POOR

The phrase, *"He became poor"* literally says, *"Because of you He became poor while being rich,"* — because of you, *"In order that you by means of His poverty may become rich."*

What was this *"poor,"* or *"poverty?"*

It was not the Incarnation by which Christ became poor although this idea is often expressed. In fact, He is Incarnate now, and with indication that He ever will be, and is certainly not presently poor in His Glorified, Incarnate State.

When He came to this world, He willingly chose a condition of poverty, a rank of life that was usually that of poverty. He *"took upon Himself the form of a servant"* (Phil. 2:7). He was connected with a poor family. Though of the family and lineage of David (Lk. 2:4), yet the family had fallen into decay, and was poor.

In the Old Testament He is beautifully represented as a shoot or seedling that starts up from the root of a decayed tree (Isa. 53:2).

His whole life was a life of poverty. He had no home (Lk. 9:58). He chose to be dependent on the charity of the few friends that He drew around Him, but yet repaying them with enumerable miracles, rather than to create food for the abundant supply of His Own wants, which He had the power to do. He had no farms or plantations; He had no splendid palaces; He had no money hoarded in useless coffers or in banks; He had no property to distribute to His friends. His Mother He commended when He died to the charitable attention of one of His Disciples (Jn. 19:27), and all His personal property seems to have been the raiment which He wore, and which was divided among the soldiers that crucified Him.

THAT WHICH HE TAUGHT

He formed no plan for becoming rich, and He always spoke with the deepest earnestness of the dangers which attend an effort to accumulate property. He was among the most poor of the sons of men in His Life; and few have been the men on Earth who have not had as much as He had to leave to surviving friends, or to excite the cupidity of those who should fall heirs to their property when dead.

He died poor. He made no will in regard to His property, for He had none to dispose of. He knew very well the effect which would follow if He had amassed wealth, and had left it to be divided among His followers. They were *very* imperfect; and even around the Cross there might have been anxious discussion, and perhaps strife about it, as there is often now over the coffin and the unclosed grave of a rich and foolish father who has died.

Jesus intended that His Disciples should never be turned away from the great work to which He called them, by any wealth which He would leave them; and He left them not even a keepsake as a memorial of His Name. All this is the more remarkable from two considerations:

HE HAD THE POWER TO DO ANYTHING

He had the power to choose the manner in which He came to this world. He might have come in the condition of a splendid prince. He might have rode in a chariot of ease, or have dwelt in a magnificent palace. He might have lived with more than the magnificence of an oriental prince; and might have bequeathed treasures greater than those of Croesus or Solomon to His followers. But He chose not to do it.

What is right for Him should have been right for them. Men often mistake on this subject; and though it cannot be demonstrated that all His followers should aim to be as poor as He was, yet it is undoubtedly true that He meant that His Example should operate constantly to check their desire of amassing wealth.

In Him it was voluntary; in us there should be always a readiness to be poor, if such be the Will of God; nay there should be rather a preference to be in moderate circumstances, that we may thus be like the Redeemer.

HUMILIATION

In summing up all the things we have said, and as well much unsaid, He became poor by

NOTES

entering into a state of humiliation. He entered this state simultaneously with His Incarnation, but the two should not be confused or made identical. Christ entered the state of humiliation in order to be able to work out our Redemption. In fact, even though He could have done all of these other grand and glorious things of princely splendor, still, He could not have done so, and at the same time saved humanity.

Pride was the cause and result of man's Fall in the Garden of Eden; consequently, He literally had to become the opposite of pride and ostentatiousness which expressed poverty.

The Scripture says that *"He emptied Himself"* (Phil. 2:7). This speaks of His Deity, i.e., *"riches."* However, it must ever be noted, that while He did purposely set aside the expression of His Deity, He never for a moment set aside His Possession of Deity. Christ was and remained God, blessed forever (Rom. 9:5) during the entire state of His humiliation. This state pertained only to His human nature, and ended at the time of the Resurrection. His human nature then entered the state of eternal exaltation.

MIGHT BE RICH

The phrase, *"That ye through His poverty might be rich,"* refers to the riches of Eternal Life, found only in Christ, and is obtained by Faith.

This speaks of the durable and eternal riches, the riches of God's everlasting favor. They include:

1. The present possession of an interest in the Redeemer Himself. He who has an interest in the Redeemer has a possession that is of more value than all that Princes can bestow.

2. We have the heirship of an eternal inheritance, the prospect of immortal glory (Rom. 8:17).

3. We have everlasting treasures in Heaven. Thus, the Saviour compares the heavenly blessings to *"treasures"* (Mat. 6:20). Eternal and illimitable wealth is ours in Heaven; and to raise us to that blessed inheritance was the design of the Redeemer in consenting to become poor.

A DESCRIPTION OF TRUE RICHES

He designed by His Example to counteract the effect of the wealth of this world. He taught men that this was not the thing to be aimed at; that there were more important purposes of life than merely to obtain money; and to furnish a perpetual reproof of those who are aiming to amass riches.

The example of the Redeemer thus stands before the whole Church and the world as a living and constant memorial of the Truth that men need things other than wealth; and that there are objects that demand their time and influence other than the accumulation of property. Consequently He said, *"Take heed, and beware of covetousness: for a man's life consisteth not in the abundance of the things which he possesseth"* (Lk. 12:15).

There was no way to properly teach man this invaluable lesson, without Jesus actually living the part, which was His necessary humiliation.

THE MODERN PROSPERITY GOSPEL

This modern Doctrine, but yet not so modern, for this is the first temptation that Satan posed to Jesus, when he proposed that Jesus turn the stones to bread (Mat. 4:3-4). He wanted Jesus to use the Word of God and His Power to benefit Himself and not others. In other words, to use such for His Own enrichment. The Prosperity Message is the same tactic.

It is obvious from the Word of God that the pell-mell pursuit of money is condemned (I Tim. 6:6-11). So Satan does with the modern Church what he attempted to do with Jesus. He has lured much of the Church into the position of attempting to acquire riches by Faith in God, which on the surface seems to legitimize the effort; however, it does not legitimize the effort, but only makes it worse.

Satan's approach is subtle. The Truth is, God does bless His people. He is the Giver of good things. In fact, prosperity is a part of the Atonement, i.e., *"your* (Heavenly) *Father knoweth that you have need of these things."* His Word actually is filled with Promises concerning His Blessings upon His Children. However, these things are all secondary and will come, if we seek first the Kingdom of God and His Righteousness. That is the Promise of God (Mat. 6:33).

So, what is the subtle difference?

The difference and the wrong is, that men make these things primary instead of the Kingdom of God. In other words, and irrespective as to how much it is denied, the sole thrust, effort, proclamation, and message, is the

NOTES

acquiring of riches, i.e., *"things."* Every Scripture is twisted into this unfortunate direction. All interpretation is placed on this elusive goal. In the doing of this several things happen:

1. A person's Faith is measured by the model of their car or the price of their clothes. To be sure, such is foolishness. Those of this stripe boast that they are not *"K-Mart"* Christians, implying that they purchase only the finest things, because this is the lot of the Child of God.

2. In this headlong lust, the true riches are ignored, which are Holiness and Righteousness. These Preachers claim they can make you rich, while the Holy Spirit is attempting to make us Holy and Righteous. The two directions have no similarity.

3. Such a gospel (another gospel) appeals to the baser motives of man such as greed and pride. Anything that appeals to these motives is not of God.

4. As a proof of His Apostleship, Paul gave the following, *"In labours more abundant, in stripes above measure, in prisons more frequent, in deaths oft."*

He then said, *"Of the Jews five times received I forty stripes save one. Thrice was I beaten with rods, once was I stoned, thrice I suffered shipwreck . . ."* etc. (II Cor. 11:23-27).

The proof of these false Apostles, and false they are, is *"things."*

It is a heady gospel for the simple reason that it appeals to greed and pride, which all of us seem to have some at least. It does not develop the Believer, but has the effect of doing the very opposite.

Worse still, no money is obtained in this fashion, because God cannot bless that which is obviously unscriptural. To be sure, the Preachers may enrich themselves, but that is about the extent. As well, their enrichment, if in fact it does come, is based on exploitation, which presents them yielding to Satan's suggestion, which Jesus refused.

As an example of which there are many, at one particular Church, a man was told he could not put one of the Church stickers on the bumper of his car, because the car was too old. In fact, these Churches are Churches in name only. They are actually motivation workshops which *"use"* certain parts of the Bible. Those who attend such Churches will not win the lottery as they are led to believe, but will rather

NOTES

lose what little bit they do have. Regarding spiritual growth, there is none but rather the opposite.

(10) "AND HEREIN I GIVE MY ADVICE: FOR THIS IS EXPEDIENT FOR YOU, WHO HAVE BEGUN BEFORE, NOT ONLY TO DO, BUT ALSO TO BE FORWARD A YEAR AGO."

We will find as we pursue this Scripture, that it follows that said by Paul in Verse 8. Its meaning as we shall see, is totally different than that from which most people think.

ADVICE

The phrase, *"And herein I give my advice,"* which means he is not undertaking to command them, even as he said in Verse 8, or to prescribe how much they should give. And yet, this phrase as given by Paul, is just as much the Word of God as anything else in this Epistle. Some have thought that this was only his personal opinion, which equates it with not being inspired; however, that is totally incorrect. While it is his advice, such is couched in this way, because as it pertains to giving, it cannot be expressed in any other manner.

Let's look at this word *"advice"* a little closer.

The New Testament Church was a close-knit fellowship. Believers were deeply involved in other's lives. Yet the New Testament says almost nothing about giving advice — or acting on another's advice.

LET'S LOOK AT THIS WORD FIRST FROM THE PERSPECTIVE OF THE OLD TESTAMENT

At times, context suggests that a general word such as *"speech"* which in the Hebrew is *"dabar,"* or *"mouth"* which in the Hebrew is *"peh,"* should be translated *"advice"* or *"counsel"* (Num. 31:16) (Dabar); (Josh. 9:14) (Peh). But the Hebrew word that best communicates the concept is *"ya'as,"* with its derivative *"esah."* The root means *"advice, counsel, purpose, or plan."* It is used both of God's counsel and of human counsel, and the ways in which it is used reflect the Old Testament's view both of God and of human beings.

TAKING COUNSEL

Two incidents from Old Testament history illustrate this use of *"ya'as."* The rebellion of

Absalom against his father David is told in II Samuel, Chapter 17. Ahithophel, Absalom's advisor, presented Absalom with a plan to take the fleeing David. Hushai, David's undercover agent in Absalom's camp, presented another plan, which was actually designed to give David time to escape. The young usurper wavered — and then chose Hushai's plan.

In this situation, *"counsel"* is used of each advisor's plan. The word clearly means to give one's opinion on how to best deal with the specific situation. *"Ya'as,"* then, is a plan for dealing with the problem. But a plan presented is only an option. The one given the counsel must decide which option to act on.

NOTES

THE PLAN OF GOD

We see the same interplay in I Kings, Chapter 12. Solomon's son and successor, Rehoboam, was confronted by his overtaxed people. His older advisors counselled him to reduce taxes and win the people's hearts. The fiery younger men of Rehoboam's own age saw complaint as rebellion and urged stern repression. Rehoboam followed the advice of the younger men and tried to implement their plan. He succeeded only in splitting the Kingdom into two separate nations.

In each of these cases, there is also a relationship of the Purpose of God to the counsel given and accepted. The rebellious Absalom and the hasty Rehoboam each freely chose the course of action that fit the Plan of God, even though the Plan of God was not their concern.

Usually the Old Testament portrays counsel as being given to kings (I Chron. 13:1; II Chron. 25:17). Proverbs suggests that one should seek counsel from many. The thought is that human beings are limited and need many contributors to be sure all alternatives are thought of and explored (Prov. 11:14; 15:22; 20:18; 24:6).

When we face important decisions, we need counsel (ya'as) to help us explore all the options. However, no advice frees the person of responsibility from the necessity of making his or her own choice.

GOD'S COUNSEL: PURPOSING

Although *"ya'as"* is used of both the counsel of humans and the Counsel of God, when God is the subject there is a definite shift of meaning. God's Counsels are not options. They are sure purposes that He has determined. So Psalms 33:10-11 says: *"The Lord foils the plans* ('esah) *of the nations; He thwarts the purposes of the peoples. But the Plans of the Lord stand firm forever, the Purposes of His Heart through all generations."*

This is the critical difference between the counsel of humans and the Counsel of the Lord. Human beings may sort through options suggested by advisers, but there is no certainty to be found in the best of human plans. Nor can any human plan alter what God has purposed (Isa. 14:24-27). God's Counsel is sure: what He purposes will come to pass.

A SURE WORD

The implication is exciting. God knows the future, and He knows the best course for His Child to follow in every situation. Thus the Psalmist expresses joy when he said, *"I will praise the Lord, Who counsels me"* (Ps. 16:7).

And the Psalmist also gives us this Promise, a Promise for all who trust the Lord: *"I will instruct and teach you in the way you should go; I will counsel you and watch over you"* (Ps. 32:8). Our one infallible Counselor is God, Who shows us how to make our choices in harmony with His Purpose and Will, according to His Word.

ADVICE OR COUNSEL FROM THE PERSPECTIVE OF THE NEW TESTAMENT

The Greek word that conveys the idea of giving advice is *"vouleuo,"* and means *"to take counsel, or deliberate,"* or from a compound, *"symbouleuo,"* which means *"to take counsel together."*

When used of God, *"vouleuo"* is a theologically significant term and has the impact of *"to will"* or *"to purpose."*

GIVING COUNSEL

There are only a few New Testament examples of giving advice. When Paul says, *"Here is my advice about what is best,"* even as we are now studying, it is his advice, but it is anchored in inspiration, and fits the occasion of the moment, which is the subject of giving.

The same tone of mature consideration is found in Acts 5:38-39: Gamaliel, when advising

NOTES

the Sanhedrin regarding Jesus' followers, said, *"In the present case I advise you: Leave these men alone! Let them go! For if their purpose or activity is of human origin, it will fail. But if it is from God, you will not be able to stop these men."*

This was advice, exactly as stated, but as well, it was the Word of the Lord, whether Gamaliel knew it or not.

THE COUNSELOR: DIVINE GUIDANCE

The Old Testament views God's Counsel as His fixed Purpose. It was important that Israel, when facing national crises, receive guidance from God. His Word provided instruction concerning the pattern of normal living. But when God's people were facing crisis situations, the Prophets often provided special direction (Deut. 18:14-21; Jer. 49:30).

The New Testament picks up this same theme of guidance. God wants to guide His people with His Counsel. John is actually the one who develops this thought. His Gospel reports Jesus' Promise that after He would return to the Father, He would send the Holy Spirit as Counselor (Helper).

"Counselor" is an appropriate translation of the Greek word *"parakletos,"* which has many shades of meaning. In context, the Spirit is seen as the One Who interprets God's Truth by helping the Disciples recall needed teaching (Jn. 14:26; 16:14) and also by introducing more Truth (Jn. 16:12-15).

The emphasis in this Ministry of the Spirit is on His helping Believers relate God's Truth to present situations, thus guiding them in action they are to take.

Although the Spirit may use any number of avenues to sense His Direction, it is clear that the Spirit Himself takes on the roles given the Old Testament Prophet. The Spirit guides us to decisions that are in harmony with what God purposes for us.

So, considering the paucity of instruction given in the New Testament respecting advice, we learn from this that the Lord does not put much stake in such guidance. The Truth is, as stated, the Holy Spirit is to be our Teacher, Leader, Guide, and Counselor (Jn. 16:13-15).

That does not mean that we are to totally ignore advice given by others, but that it should be weighed heavily against the Word of God. Unfortunately, the modern Church has pretty much taken the role of ignoring the Holy Spirit in His major role as Counselor to the Believer, in favor of men, i.e., *"Psychologists and/or Denominational Heads."*

EXPEDIENT

The phrase, *"For this is expedient for you,"* means, *"It will be profitable."* The idea is, that they were bound by a regard to consistency and to their own welfare, to perform what they had purposed. As well, there would have been manifest disadvantages if it had not been done. Of course, we are speaking of this Collection for the situation in Jerusalem.

As we have previously stated, the problems in the Church at Corinth had caused everything to be brought to a halt, at least as far as the Work of God was concerned. Of course, that is one of the large things that Satan desires. He wants the Church to become embroiled in quarrels, dissention, false doctrine, etc. If he can bring this about, which he did at Corinth, and has in untold numbers of other Churches, everything grinds to a halt, at least everything that is of God.

A GOOD BEGINNING

The phrase, *"Who have begun before,"* concerns them beginning the Collection approximately a year before.

Paul points out a special additional reason that this judgment of his should have special weight. Of course, this fact should have decisive weight that our giving is really a Grace and an undeserved gift bestowed upon us Givers by God and by our Lord Jesus Christ. But in addition to this general consideration there is the special advantage that will accrue to the Corinthians since they had already begun this work a year ago.

TO BE WILLING

The phrase, *"Not only to do, but also to be forward a year ago,"* refers to the fact that they were willing at that time, but had allowed the problems to interfere.

It was good for them to now take a new look at this blessed work, to see it with Paul's eyes, to note that it was not merely a work of doing something for other people, but really a bestowal of a new Measure of Grace upon themselves by

God and by Christ. They should have a great desire for this Grace as should all, and accordingly, such should move them mightily to now finish this work, to finish it so that it will be Grace and enrichment for themselves from God and from their Lord Jesus Christ.

For this reason Paul states it in this significant way: You began a year ago *"not only the doing but the willing."* He places the willing in the second place because this is the essential thing.

No mere doing, even if it were completed, would make this work a Grace from Christ, for one might do the giving only outwardly, only because others were also giving, or for improper reasons. No, Paul says, you also began the willing, the essential thing in this matter; consequently, it is a *"willing"* that is to remain operative all the time. In other words, the *"willing"* or *"forward"* says that you will give to God all the days of your life. To have such willing is to have Grace and enrichment from God, the Giver of all Grace, and from Christ, the Mediator of all Grace Who become poor for our enrichment (Lenski).

(11) "NOW THEREFORE PERFORM THE DOING OF IT; THAT AS THERE WAS A READINESS TO WILL, SO THERE MAY BE A PERFORMANCE ALSO OUT OF THAT WHICH YE HAVE."

Little by little the Holy Spirit leads us into deeper depths in the carrying out of the Will of God for our lives. We must always remember, that all of this is for our good, and ours alone.

PERFORM THE DOING OF IT

The phrase, *"Now therefore perform the doing of it,"* actually means, *"Let our completed deed measure up to our readiness and our will!"* Oftentimes when the deed is finished it falls far below our well-intentioned readiness. He is speaking of the person who starts out with high resolve and often ends with only partial execution.

Paul used the Greek word for *"complete"* twice in this same Verse (perform and performance). It comes from the basic root for *"purpose"*; therefore, the injunction is for these Believers to get back on track relative to God's Purpose for them. Jesus had a stinging rebuke for people who begin to do God's Will but allow themselves to look back (Lk. 9:62).

NOTES

A READINESS TO WILL

The phrase, *"That as there was a readiness to will,"* simply means that if the *"willing"* is genuine, true, deep, and effective, then they will follow through to completion. The doing to completion is the evidence and the proof of the right willing.

One may will with a loud voice; however, unless one's will produces the corresponding deed, it is hollow, no Grace of God and of Christ will come whatever, no enrichment for one's spiritual life (I Jn. 3:17-18).

PERFORMANCE

The phrase, *"So there may be a performance also out of that which ye have,"* proclaims that for which the Holy Spirit is looking.

The intention within itself is not sufficient, and neither does a willing mind release one from the obligation.

The idea is this:

If God has called a person to do something, even as He had called the Church at Corinth to help with this Offering for Jerusalem, that which He desires, is never laid aside. Even though there had been a fight in the Church, which had stopped all progress for about a year, what God had originally called them to do respecting this particular situation, had not changed. They must now obey and do that which He originally called them to do.

Paul plainly wrote, *"For the Gifts and Calling of God are without repentance"* (Rom. 11:29).

That means that God does not change His Mind respecting that which He had called one to do. While it is true that some men, particularly some Denominational Leaders, and even others, will attempt to claim that God's Gifts and Callings are to be set aside because of circumstances or events; however, none of that is Scriptural. If a person gets off track, even as these Corinthians had done, the answer is not in abrogating the Calling, even as Paul proclaims here, but rather getting right with God, and then carrying out what He had originally called one to do. Circumstances, events, situations, sin, wrongdoing, failure, disobedience, rebellion, hardship, etc., does not change God nor His Plans, as should be obvious, and in fact is obvious, if one knows the Scriptures. He plainly said a long, long time ago, *"God is not a man, that He should lie* (about our mission);

neither the son of man, that He should repent (change His Mind)*: Hath He said, and shall He not do it* (carry it through to completion)? *Or hath He spoken, and shall He not make it good* (His Word cannot change)*?"* (Num. 23:19).

The phrase, *"Which ye have,"* actually means, *"according to your ability."* It should be in proportion to your means.

(12) "FOR IF THERE BE FIRST A WILLING MIND, IT IS ACCEPTED ACCORDING TO THAT A MAN HATH, AND NOT ACCORDING TO THAT HE HATH NOT."

Another great Truth materializes here, which makes it possible for every Believer to have a part in the great Work of God.

A WILLING MIND

The phrase, *"For if there be first a willing mind,"* has reference to the fact that if the heart is in it, then the Offering will be acceptable to God, whether one is able to give much or little. A willing mind is the first consideration.

Actually, this is a principle that is applicable to everything we do for the Lord. A willing mind is the first and main thing. It is that which God chiefly desires, and that without, everything else will be offensive, hypocritical, and vain.

The great Truth here presented by the Holy Spirit, is that no poor man should ever grieve because he has little to give. Let him not think that, because his Gift has been small, that he is deprived of the Grace of God and the enrichment which his giving will bring to him.

God does not count dollars, but in actuality many things are looked at regarding our giving, even as the entirety of this Teaching as given by Paul brings out. In fact, most of the Gifts given to the Work of God, fall into the category of small. However, even though they may be small, when many of these Gifts are added up, they become quite significant. So let no one think that his small Gift, and for the reason that he simply doesn't have more to give, is inconsequential. Not at all! In fact, in the Eyes of God, even as the widow's mite, it may be the largest Gift of all.

ACCEPTED

The phrase, *"It is accepted according to that a man hath,"* means that God will approve of it, and will receive it favorably. One's obligation is

NOTES

proportioned according to one's ability. The Offering is acceptable to God according to the largeness and willingness of heart, and not according to the narrowness of one's fortune. If the means are small, if the individual is poor, and if the Gift shall, therefore, be small in amount, yet it may be proof of a larger heart, and of more true love to God and His Cause, than when a much more ample Gift is tendered by one in better circumstances. As already stated, this sentiment the Saviour expressly stated and defended in the case of the poor widow (Mk. 12:42-44; Lk. 21:1-4).

WHAT WE HAVE OR DON'T HAVE

The phrase, *"And not according to that he hath not,"* means that our obligations to the Lord in all cases are limited by our ability. This is obviously the rule of equity; and this is all that is anywhere demanded in the Bible, and this is everywhere demanded.

Thus our love to Him is not in proportion to how much we give, but in proportion to our ability to give.

None but a tyrant ever demands more than can be rendered; and to demand more is the appropriate description of a tyrant, and cannot appertain to the Ever-Blessed God. If there is any service rendered to God, according to our ability, it is accepted of Him. It may not be as much or as valuable as may be rendered by others of higher power; it may not be as much as we would desire to render, but it is all that God demands, and is acceptable to Him.

However, it should always be understood, that most of the time, most Believers can give more than they think they can give, even as the Macedonians surprised Paul by doing. If we really want to do something, we generally find a way to do that which is desired, and as well, we find ourselves doing far more than we originally thought could be done.

(13) "FOR I MEAN NOT THAT OTHER MEN BE EASED AND YE BURDENED."

We see from this Verse that the system of proportional giving is based on the matter of equality. Let's see what the Holy Spirit says!

EQUALITY

The phrase, *"For I mean not that other men be eased,"* refers to the fact that no person is to be exempt from doing what they can.

The Truth is, most Believers, and I think I exaggerate not, are in fact, *"eased."* In other words, they do not share, they see no responsibility, they give little or nothing, and soothe their conscience by making excuses. However, what they do not realize is, that they deprive themselves of added Grace, which is a Gift beyond compare, as well as all other Blessings of the Lord. I think as we proceed in this Chapter plus the following, it will become more and more obvious just how important this Grace of Giving actually is with God and should be with us.

As an example let us look at World Evangelism, which is priority with God, and which is the responsibility of every single Believer. And yet the average giving toward this all-important cause in the United States by all who profess to be Believers, is about one cent a day per person. Yes, I said *"One penny a day per person."* The Truth is, that the far greater majority give nothing, with about one or two percent taking unto themselves the responsibility.

That is very sad when we consider that most of the people mentioned here, have money for other things, with some of it even being wasted. And yet, the first great sign of a terrible spiritual declension, is the lack of concern for a lost world, and the taking of the Gospel to dying men.

(The numbers given above are based on an approximation of the amount of money actually given for World Evangelism on an annual basis, from the approximate 100 million in the United States who claim to be Born-Again.)

BURDENED?

The phrase, *"And ye burdened,"* implies that as commendable as generous giving is, even as proven by the Macedonians, God does not intend that people impoverish themselves in the process. The Biblical Plan includes an equality that spreads out the responsibility to all Believers. Unfortunately, even as we have stated, some Christians do not take this responsibility very serious, so that the burden often falls on a percentage of individuals (and a small percentage at that) rather than on the entire body of Believers, which is intended.

Probably the Corinthians were able to contribute more than many of the Churches, certainly more than the Churches of Macedonia, and Paul, therefore, presses upon them the duty of giving according to their means, yet he by no means intended that the entire burden should rest upon them.

NOTES

This matter of Christian Giving is not one of furnishing all possible relief to others even to the point of leaving ourselves in distress. The perfection of Giving does not include that. Consequently, we should not so understand from Verse 4, the Macedonian Giving as being *"beyond their ability."* This is not Paul's point, and as such, it is not that of the Holy Spirit.

As stated, the Lord does not require of us what we do not have, but He does require of us what we can do, and as stated, most of the time most of us, can do more than we think we can do.

(14) "BUT BY AN EQUALITY, THAT NOW AT THIS TIME YOUR ABUNDANCE MAY BE A SUPPLY FOR THEIR WANT, THAT THEIR ABUNDANCE ALSO MAY BE A SUPPLY FOR YOUR WANT: THAT THERE MAY BE EQUALITY:"

This Verse seems at first glance to be somewhat contradictory; however, as it is unfolded, we will see, I pray, exactly what the Holy Spirit is saying to us.

JUST AND EQUAL PRINCIPLES

The phrase, *"But by an equality,"* proclaims that which the Holy Spirit intends for the entirety of the Body of Christ. As our heading states, it is based on just and equal principles.

The Greek conception is, *"drawn from"* equality; and the noun means *"sameness,"* two sides are even, alike, balanced. In True Christian Giving the ledger is always balanced, at least that's the way the Holy Spirit intends for such to be. Regrettably, that is the ideal and not the actual reality. However, that is not the fault of the Lord, but that of disobedient Christians. How embarrassing that will be when these people stand at the Judgment Seat of Christ!

ABUNDANCE AND SUPPLY

The phrase, *"That now at this time your abundance may be a supply for their want,"* referred to the problem at hand. Jerusalem was in dire need because of the problems previously discussed (excommunication from the Synagogue), while Corinth and the other Churches, were not plagued with this particular problem.

Consequently, they were expected to balance the situation.

The idea presently is somewhat different, but yet carries the same principle.

Every Believer presently, has an abundance, and because of the Grace bestowed upon us by the Lord Jesus Christ. As we have previously stated, the moment the believing sinner comes to Christ, he enters into God's Economy and is guaranteed of supply (Lk. 12:22-32). A regrettable percentage of the world goes to bed hungry each night, and because they do not have the benefit of the Economy of God, but rather of this world and its selfishness. So, millions are hungry.

However, the very first requirement of the Church, is to get the Gospel to those of the world who do not know Christ. While charitable and humanitarian efforts have their place, it should be obvious, the great need is spiritual rather than otherwise. If that is not handled first, the other problems will never be solved. That's the reason Jesus said, *"Seek ye first the Kingdom of God and His Righteousness; and all these* (other) *things shall* (will) *be added unto you"* (Mat. 6:33).

The real *"want,"* of the unbeliever is Jesus Christ, whether they realize such or not. In fact, they don't realize that; nevertheless, that is their real *"want,"* actually their real *"need."* So it is up to us as recipients of the Grace of God, of the *"abundance"* of the Lord, to *"be a supply for their want of Salvation."* In fact, there is no other way for them to obtain such, than by and through Believers, who were once just as they now are.

The idea is, that if we do not supply their want from our abundance, the abundance may not be such very long.

PERHAPS THE GREATEST DANGER

As I dictate these notes (8-24-98), there is not very much of the abundance of the Church going out to supply the want of those without God, i.e., *"the taking of the Gospel to a lost world."* In fact, the 1990's have seen a paucity of True World Evangelism. There is precious little effort being made presently.

Tragically, many of those presently called Missionaries, are little more than glorified Psychologists or social workers. Thankfully, there is one here and there who is truly called of God, and full of the Holy Spirit, and will definitely make a difference wherever they are sent by the Lord. But on the whole, those are as scarce as the proverbial hen's teeth.

NOTES

In the early 1990's the Lord made it possible for us to air our Telecast, translated into Russian, over the largest single network in Russia, and actually the world, TV ONE. Actually, this was the old Communist propaganda channel, which reached the entirety of the 15 Soviet Republics, as they were then known. The Lord allowed us to air the Gospel over this Channel for about two years.

(I would be remiss if I did not give Jim Woolsey the credit for having the faith to pursue this almost impossible endeavor, until it became an actual reality.)

The Lord used the Telecast to an amazing degree, with untold numbers finding Christ as their Saviour. Even our enemies, of which there seemed to be many, admitted that of which I have just said. Actually, one Pastor who I knew somewhat, called me some time back, after coming back from Moscow.

He related to me that each year his Church along with others, raised certain amounts of money, which they used to bring Preachers in from all over the former Soviet Union to Moscow, where they would undergo a rigorous week of intensified Bible training.

He told me how that he just happened to ask the Preachers at the beginning of the last session to stand and tell how they had been saved. He said, *"Brother Swaggart, over half of those Preachers, some of them pastoring Churches running over a thousand, etc., had been saved as a result of your Telecast."*

And yet, to keep our Program on that particular Channel out of Moscow, even though it was reaching untold millions of people with tremendous results, we struggled severely to pay for the airtime and the production costs, even to the place of bringing the Ministry close to bankruptcy. Yes, we appealed again and again for help, but with little success.

MANY ADVERSARIES

The Denomination to which we formerly belonged, told their people not to support our Ministry, as well as most, if not all other Pentecostal Denominations. Because of our stand on other particular issues, most Charismatics fell into the same category. Consequently, the task was very hard, but the Lord helped us somehow to remain on the air until the Program was taken off, due to the demands of the Greek Orthodox Church. (They were indignant over its popularity, and demanded of the Government that it be removed, which it ultimately was.)

Even though at the present time, we are still airing in some parts of Russia, and in about 30 other countries of the world, with the Program translated into several languages; still, in most countries of the world, while there is much religious activity, there is very little Gospel being presented which carries with it, the Anointing and Convicting Power of the Holy Spirit, which are an absolute necessity, that is if people are to be saved. Due to this problem, I feel that the United States is facing great problems, which we find in the next phrase.

A SUPPLY FOR YOUR WANT

The phrase, *"That their abundance also may be a supply for your want,"* seems to be a contradiction, but it isn't.

Most of the world has an abundance of sin, failure, poverty, ignorance, superstition, bondage, etc. So, we may ask as to how *that* could be a supply for our want?

Inasmuch as God has chosen this method, the giving of our abundance to the Cause of Christ, to pronounce Grace and Blessing upon His people, the Lord then balances out the situation by blessing all who give to meet the terrible spiritual need of the lost. So, in a peculiar sort of way, but which is God's Way, the abundance of the spiritual need of the world's lost, serves as a vehicle to supply the want and need of all Believers, as we give to supply their spiritual need.

In simple terms, they have a great spiritual need which we are to supply, which in turn, brings great Blessings upon the Giver.

EVERYTHING EQUALS OUT IF DONE GOD'S WAY

The phrase, *"That there may be equality,"* makes the second time the Apostle has used this phrase in this one Verse.

There is a huge need in the world for the Gospel of Jesus Christ. In fact, it is the greatest need of all mankind. Believers are blessed with an abundance of this Gospel, and it is our duty to get the grandest story ever told, to those who have not had the privilege to hear. When that is done, great Blessings from the Lord ensue. Thus, there is an equality. The lost are blessed by hearing and receiving the Gospel, while the Believer is blessed for giving the Gospel.

NOTES

(15) "AS IT IS WRITTEN, HE THAT HAD GATHERED MUCH HAD NOTHING OVER; AND HE THAT HAD GATHERED LITTLE HAD NO LACK."

Once again, a Great Truth is opened up to us in this particular Passage. In effect, the Holy Spirit takes us from Truth to Truth, which actually is His method.

THE WORD OF GOD

The phrase, *"As it is written,"* is taken from Exodus 16:18.

The Apostle, in his typical fashion, cited the Old Testament to indicate that his Teaching was based on the Word of God.

There it referred to the gathering of Manna in the wilderness. Through Moses, God instructed the Israelites to gather only the amount of Manna they needed for each particular day with the exception of the day before the Sabbath, when they were to gather enough for that day and for the Sabbath as well. Despite these clear instructions, there were a few people who paid no attention and tried to hoard some of the Manna. Of course, it spoiled, exactly as the Lord said it would.

There were also individuals at first who tried to gather Manna on the Sabbath, but found none (Ex. 16:27), for the simple reason that it was not given on those particular days.

NOTHING OVER

The phrase, *"He that had gathered much had nothing over,"* means that it did no good to hoard, for the excess did breed worms and stink (Ex. 16:29).

The idea was, that the people would trust the Lord each day for their sustenance and supply, which was actually to be a type of Christ.

The manner in which Paul uses this statement is revealing to say the least. The Holy Spirit through him is telling us, that if Believers hoard money, it will ultimately be taken through taxes, waste, theft, lawyers, etc. The implication is, that they should have given all over and above their actual needs, which includes one's family, to the Cause of Christ. In fact, the giving will bring great Blessing, while the hoarding will ultimately come out to nothing.

NO LACK

The phrase, *"And he that had gathered little had no lack,"* portrays trust. They gathered as much as they needed of the Manna on that respective day, trusting the Lord to bring about another supply tomorrow, which He always did.

So, the Holy Spirit is saying through the Apostle, that if we give generously to the Cause of Christ, He will see to it that there is *"no lack,"* respecting our own needs, or those of our family. So, if in fact, the Lord would see fit to bless one with an excess, he can place his trust in the State, Lawyers, the variances of the Stock Market, or in the Lord.

I think it should be obvious as to the guaranteed security. It is always in the Lord. But sadly, many Believers who are blessed accordingly, opt for that other than the Lord, which most of the time does harm instead of good.

These are great Truths which the Reader should take to heart.

(16) "BUT THANKS BE TO GOD, WHICH PUT THE SAME EARNEST CARE INTO THE HEART OF TITUS FOR YOU."

Paul thanks God for filling Titus with such earnestness for the Corinthians because he is sending Titus back to Corinth, whence he had just come.

THANKS TO GOD

The phrase, *"But thanks be to God,"* proclaims the Apostle as regarding every right feeling, every pure desire — every inclination to serve God or to benefit a fellow-mortal — as the Gift of God. He, therefore, ascribes praise to the Lord that Titus was disposed to show an interest in the welfare of the Corinthians (Barnes).

In fact, Titus was far more than just a messenger for Paul. This associate also loved the Corinthians as deeply as the Apostle did. In essence, the burden of the Apostle for lost souls which made him such a striking force for the Lord, was as well, the burden of Titus, and all of the associates of Paul for that matter. In Truth, this is one of the great principles of Christianity.

NOTES

As God calls Apostles, and He definitely continues to do so, whatever Message He gives them, is meant to be multiplied in the hearts and lives of associates or fellow Ministers who are influenced by that particular Apostle, exactly as Titus and others were by Paul. Actually, there is every indication that Titus was also an Apostle, which we shall see in next to the last Verse of this Chapter.

THE SAME EARNEST CARE

The phrase, *"Which put the same earnest care into the heart of Titus for you,"* presents this Brother as being far more than a mere helper of Paul. This *"earnest care"* for the Corinthians, and all others for that matter, made Titus willing to take Paul's strong letter of rebuke (I Cor.) to them. It also enabled him to rejoice over their sincere repentance. His care for them was truly a matter of *"the heart"* (Rossier).

Paul could trust this man, because he had the same concern for the Work of God as Paul, the same diligence, the same burden. To be frank, these are not easy to find.

When Paul was in prison in Rome, he needed to send a Preacher to Philippi, but none there could be found (in Rome); consequently, he said, *"For I have no man likeminded, who will naturally care for your state. For all seek their own, not the things which are Jesus Christ's"* (Phil. 2:20-21).

(17) "FOR INDEED HE ACCEPTED THE EXHORTATION; BUT BEING MORE FORWARD, OF HIS OWN ACCORD HE WENT UNTO YOU."

The idea of this Verse and those following, has to do with the tremendous change which has taken place at Corinth, a change altogether for the good we might quickly add, which as well changed the entirety of the situation.

THE EXHORTATION

The phrase, *"For indeed he accepted the exhortation,"* means that Titus had no qualms whatsoever about going back to Corinth regarding the collection which was to be received for the situation in Jerusalem.

The idea is, even though Paul does not say such here, that Titus was somewhat reluctant to go the first time when he took I Corinthians to the Church there, which actually was instrumental in their repentance. However, the reluctance was only in the manner of him feeling he may not be able to cope with the situation, providing it turned ugly. Thankfully, it had the opposite result.

OF HIS OWN ACCORD

The phrase, *"But being more forward, of his own accord he went unto you,"* presents an eagerness on the part of Titus, and for all the obvious reasons.

Actually, Titus would carry this Second Epistle to the Corinthians, exactly as he had carried the First, but with much more joy this particular time. Then he was not certain as to what the outcome would be, but now he is eager to go, and because of the great Revival which has taken place at Corinth. There is a good possibility that he read II Corinthians to the Church at Corinth, as he had probably read to them I Corinthians. But this time, things were altogether different. It was important for the Corinthians to know this. It was actually the best recommendation which Paul could send along with Titus.

(18) "AND WE HAVE SENT WITH HIM THE BROTHER, WHOSE PRAISE IS IN THE GOSPEL THROUGHOUT ALL THE CHURCHES;"

This Scripture continues regarding the Collection to be received.

THE BROTHER

The phrase, *"And we have sent with him the Brother,"* presents this man as unnamed, but for no negative reason. As the clause reads, he was not one of Paul's own assistants like Timothy, Titus, Silas, or Luke, but rather it seems, an Evangelist on his own account. Whoever it was, it was someone well-known, and in whom the Church at Corinth could have entire confidence.

Even though we very much would have desired to have known his name, the Holy Spirit did not desire that it be given. As stated, that reason is not negative.

I personally think that the idea presents itself, and is intended by the Holy Spirit, that our work and service belong to the Lord. Everything is done for Him and as well, He is the Judge of all things.

This Brother's name is not known to the many centuries which have followed, nevertheless, it definitely is known to the Lord, and that is all that matters. If we strive for recognition here, in effect, we have received our reward, but if what we do is solely unto the Lord, then a great reward will be forthcoming (Mat. 6:1-4)

THE GOSPEL

The phrase, *"Whose praise is in the Gospel throughout all the Churches,"* proclaims him, I think, as an Evangelist. The Greek I think bears it out, that he was known for preaching the Gospel throughout the Churches of Macedonia, and perhaps elsewhere as well.

Paul chose this Brother along with a second Brother mentioned in Verse 22, to accompany Titus to Corinth. This was all done to secure the proper precautions regarding the funds collected.

The men whom Paul chose were beyond reproach, so much so that Paul could unhesitatingly say wonderful things about them.

(19) "AND NOT THAT ONLY, BUT WHO WAS ALSO CHOSEN OF THE CHURCHES TO TRAVEL WITH US WITH THIS GRACE, WHICH IS ADMINISTERED BY US TO THE GLORY OF THE SAME LORD, AND DECLARATION OF YOUR READY MIND:"

Paul arranged that the purse of money for Judea should not be entrusted to him alone but that he should have companions in the trust, so as to avoid the possibility of a suspicion or accusation of maladministration, etc.

CHOSEN OF THE CHURCHES

The phrase, *"And not that only, but who was also chosen of the Churches,"* records the fact that the Churches agreed with Paul relative to the individuals he had chosen. This refers to the entirety of the journey by which the great Collection is finally to be carried to Jerusalem. Acts 20:4 names seven men, and no doubt all of them were appointed in this manner. This Evangelist was one of the seven. Being from Macedonia it seems, he could have been either Sopater of Berea, or Aristarchus, or Secundus of Thessalonica.

The Greek word for *"chosen"* is *"cheirotoneo,"* and means *"to vote by raising the hand."* So, the idea is, that Paul evidently chose these individuals and then presented their names to the Churches, with the Churches voting to ratify what Paul had already done.

Considering that money was coming from all the Churches, this would undoubtedly have been quite a sum, which Paul wanted to take care that it was handled in the right manner.

THIS GRACE

The phrase, *"To travel with us with this Grace,"* once again places the Offering on a very high level of spirituality. The whole movement of the Collection is a Grace of God and of Christ to those engaged in it, a part of the enrichment which Christ wants the Givers to have.

As we have already stated, Paul took everything, even that which seemed to be mundane, to a high spiritual level. The idea is, that everything a Child of God does, even that which seems to be ordinary, is in fact very spiritual, because of who the Believer is, i.e., *"a Child of God."* Consequently, all Believers must understand this accordingly.

Everything the Believer does, even to simple mundane, seemingly insignificant things, even our secular work, is to be understood as something spiritual. The Believer is *"salt"* and *"light,"* and as such, everything done is to come under the scrutiny of spirituality, i.e., *"the Word of God."* That's the reason Paul also said, *"With good will doing service* (secular work) *as to the Lord, and not to men"* (Eph. 6:7), *"And whatsoever ye do in word or deed, do all in the Name of the Lord Jesus, giving thanks to God and the Father by Him"* (Col. 3:17).

ADMINISTRATION

The phrase, *"Which is administered by us to the Glory of the same Lord,"* means that Paul had been the instrument regarding this Collection. The design was to promote the Glory of the Lord, by showing the Love of God respecting this particular need.

In a sense, *"being administered by us"* (by Paul and his helpers) means administered for God.

Most Commentators refer to the Grace and favor which the Givers bestow upon the poor Saints at Jerusalem and hence say that Paul and his helpers administer this kind of human favor for these Givers. However, how they can say this we really cannot understand, since the word *"Grace"* is used five times in succession in the same sense, and two of those times (vss. 1 and 9) so decisively, once with reference to God, once with reference to Christ.

NOTES

In the consciousness that he and his helpers are ministering this Grace as a Gift from God and Christ to the Givers, Paul twice makes the statement *"being administered by us,"* which means that God and Christ were employing them (Paul and his associates) to minister and not that the Givers were employing them.

In other words, what we are saying is that the Lord had laid this Grace, this act of benevolence, on the heart of Paul who then took the lead in the matter. Actually, this is the manner in which the Holy Spirit works. He speaks to His Apostles, etc., and then they tell the Church or Churches what the Lord has said, with the Churches then helping to carry out these very important works.

If done in this way, which is actually the only way it can be done if it is to be Biblical, it will bring Glory to the Lord, which it is supposed to do. However, in most modern religious circles, the order is reversed — the Church attempts to tell the Apostles, which is an unscriptural manner.

READY MIND

The phrase, *"And declaration of your ready mind,"* proclaims the Corinthians plus the other Churches, joining together, carrying out this which the Lord had already given to Paul. This is the ideal way that the Work of God should be carried out.

Here it denotes the readiness of Paul and of his associates to minister this Grace to the Churches by moving their willingness to action. There is not the least inconsistency or incongruity, but the fullest harmony between *"the Lord's Glory"* and *"our own readiness"* when it is a matter of Divine Grace that is ministered.

The Holy Spirit has a way and manner regarding all things. It is our business as Believers, whether Preachers of the Gospel or Laypersons in the Church, to follow as closely to the Word of the Lord as possible. To be sure, the example set in the Book of Acts and the Epistles, as here, provides the pattern which should be followed closely.

(20) "AVOIDING THIS, THAT NO MAN SHOULD BLAME US IN THIS ABUNDANCE WHICH IS ADMINISTERED BY US:"

Along with this great Grace of Giving, the Holy Spirit uses the Apostle to portray the proper administration of finances in the Church.

NOTES

NO BLAME

The phrase, *"Avoiding this, that no man should blame us in this abundance,"* presents the fact that every precaution is to be taken regarding the management of these funds, which was not only an example then, but meant to be an example for all time.

The blame which Paul intends to avoid is by no means that he and his personal assistants might be charged with dishonesty. He is speaking about something else.

The arrangement which he is making is that he is asking the congregations in the different provinces to elect *"travelling companions,"* a delegation in other words, to carry the bounty to Jerusalem. This delegation and not necessarily Paul is to make the presentation in Jerusalem. Since it is made by elected representatives from all the Churches, these Churches will receive the credit for the bounty and not Paul. The money comes from the Churches and not from Paul. The credit belongs to them, and Paul's arrangements are made so that it will be given to them.

As well, and as should be obvious, he wanted these funds handled in such a way, that not even the slightest suspicion could be cast toward any hint of dishonesty.

ADMINISTERED BY US

The phrase, *"Which is administered by us,"* proclaims the fact that he is responsible.

The entire delegation as we have stated, is named in Acts 20:4. These Representatives made the presentation. When Paul wrote I Corinthians 16:3-4 he had this plan of a delegation in mind. At that time he had not yet decided as to whether he himself would accompany the delegates; he might only give them letters that would accredit them to Christians with whom they might stop en route, accredit them also in Jerusalem. Paul eventually went with the delegates. However, from the way it was handled, no one could cast a reproach on Paul that he was stealing honor or credit from the Churches, or that anything was handled improperly regarding the money.

(21) "PROVIDING FOR HONEST THINGS, NOT ONLY IN THE SIGHT OF THE LORD, BUT ALSO IN THE SIGHT OF MEN."

It was not enough that honesty should be practiced in the Lord's sight; it must be visibly practiced in the sight of men as well.

HONESTY

The phrase, *"Providing for honest things,"* is also given to us in Romans 12:17.

In that place, however, it refers to the manner in which we are to treat those who injure us; here it refers to the right way of using property; and it seems to have been a rule or measure by which Paul regulated his life — in other words, that honesty was applicable to everything, which most surely it was.

The sentiment is, that we are to see to it beforehand, that all our conduct shall be comely and honest.

The word rendered *"providing for,"* means foreseeing, or perceiving beforehand; and the idea is, that we are to make it a matter of previous calculation, a settled plan, a thing that is to be attended to of set design.

"Things honest" mean, properly, beautiful, or comely.

IN THE SIGHT OF THE LORD

The phrase, *"Not only in the sight of the Lord,"* presents that which is supposed to be a given. In other words, the structure of the sentence takes it for granted that the Christian will always do things honest in the sight of the Lord. Regrettably that is not always the case, but ideally it is supposed to be the case.

His idea is, that he meant so to conduct himself in the whole transaction, as that his conduct should be approved by God, but that it should also be regarded as beautiful or correct in the sight of men.

IN THE SIGHT OF MEN

The phrase, *"But also in the sight of men,"* proclaims where the major problem is regarding the Church and as well, which is mostly caused by a lack of wisdom.

"In a field of melons," says the Chinese Proverb, *"do not stoop to tie your shoe; for that will look as if you wanted to steal one of the melons."* In other words, as Believers, and especially as Preachers, every precaution must be taken that things will not only be honest in the sight of God, but as well, appear honest in the sight of men.

However, irrespective of precautions taken, even as here with Paul, seemingly there will always be slanderous remarks and aspersions cast upon one's character by those who seek to find fault, and if they cannot find such they will simply manufacture fault.

A PERSONAL EXAMPLE

Jimmy Swaggart Ministries is a Church, but it is also a Worldwide evangelistic effort as it regards World Evangelism. to carry out this Call of God we air our Telecast all over the world, and as well, conduct Citywide or Church Crusades.

Regarding the airing of Television Programming, we have to pay for all of this airtime, which in the aggregate costs a lot of money, but reaches a staggering number of people. The money is handled in the following fashion:

1. All the money given at the Church is handled by the Deacons and the Accounting Department. I never see the funds, neither does any member of my family. As well, all the money that comes in through the mail for the support of our Telecast is handled in a similar fashion.

It goes to a mail room where there are several people, again, none who are members of my family, who open the envelopes and attend to whatever is needed, whether the sending of product, etc. All of the orders and accounts are entered into the computer, which must match up at the end of the day, with it then going to the Accounting Department where it is deposited in the bank. Hopefully we get enough to meet the expenses, which most of the time it seems we don't. Again, I never see these funds.

2. Jimmy Swaggart Ministries which includes the Church, has a Board of Directors, made up of Businessmen from all over the United States. We have three Board Meetings a year, where the business of the Ministry is handled during these particular times. I do not attend the Board Meetings, and in fact, have been in only one of the meetings for about 25 or 30 minutes during the entirety of the last seven years. The individuals comprising the Board are very strong business people in their own right, and are perfectly capable of directing anything which needs to be handled.

3. We have an outside accounting firm (actually located in Texas) which oversees the accounting practices of the Ministry. In fact, this has been our practice for the last 20 or so years.

NOTES

My wife and I receive a salary from the Ministry; however, we have taken only a portion of that salary, actually, a small portion on my part, for the simple reason that the Ministry needed the funds. Also, my wife and I have no stocks, bonds, or investments. However, the Ministry does provide for us a home and a car, for which we are very thankful.

Fortunately, Paul did not have the News Media breathing down his neck trying to make something sinister out of every action. Unfortunately, we do have that problem.

Many years ago and somewhat naive I might quickly add, I had the mistaken idea that if I would open up the Ministry to the News Media, showing them anything they desired, providing any information they wanted, that they would give us a fair report. How wrong I was!

I found out to my dismay, that they had already made up their minds before they ever wrote the articles or portrayed their programs over Television. They have no regard for our honesty, only desiring to try to make us look dishonest to the people, thereby destroying our credibility. The sad fact is some Christians believe these things; nevertheless, that is a thorn in the flesh which we must bear. While it is true that there are some dishonest Preachers and Ministries, this Preacher and this Ministry do not fall into that category.

Because of the good graces of the Lord, and the talent He has given us, we have sold over 15 million Recordings all over the world. I'm glad I can say, that all of the funds from the sale of this product went in its entirety to help us take the Gospel of Jesus Christ all over the world. None of the money has come to my family, and it is still carried on in the same manner presently.

One day I will stand before the Lord, as will all, and will give account for this Ministry. I'm glad that I can say, that I look forward to that coming time.

(22) "AND WE HAVE SENT WITH THEM OUR BROTHER, WHOM WE HAVE OFTENTIMES PROVED DILIGENT IN MANY THINGS, BUT NOW MUCH MORE DILIGENT, UPON THE GREAT CONFIDENCE WHICH I HAVE IN YOU."

The men whom Paul chose were beyond reproach, so much so that Paul could unhesitatingly say, *"They are . . . the Glory of*

Christ." What a beautiful tribute, especially considering that it was sanctioned by the Holy Spirit. These men were an honor to the cause they served. They brought glory to the Christ they followed.

OUR BROTHER

The phrase, *"And we have sent with them our Brother,"* presents another in conjunction with the Brother mentioned in Verse 18. Again, and as stated, who this was is wholly unknown, and conjecture is useless. Consequently, two men, both approved by the Churches, would accompany Titus to Corinth.

As well, *"Our Brother,"* as distinguished from *"The Brother"* referred to in Verse 18, means that this second man could definitely be one of Paul's close associates, while the other man is not.

DILIGENCE

The phrase, *"Whom we have oftentimes proved diligent in many things,"* lends more credence to the thought, that he had been the companion and fellow-laborer of Paul.

If it is to be noticed, Paul was very quick to praise those who proved themselves with him, even to the place of giving them equal billing with him, even as he did Timothy in the salutation of this Epistle and Sosthenes in the First Epistle to the Corinthians.

Paul was working for the Lord, so he did not desire any praise from men. And the Truth is, he received very little from others. But yet he wanted others to know of the faithfulness of those who labored with him, and as here was quick to say so.

What an honor it was to be mentioned by Paul in any capacity but above all to know and realize that the Holy Spirit sanctioned his words. Nothing could be greater than that!

GREAT CONFIDENCE

The phrase, *"But now much more diligent, upon the great confidence which I have in you"* proclaims this Brother joining with Titus, and no doubt others with Paul, who were overjoyed and happy concerning the turn of events at Corinth.

The idea is, that due to the recent Revival at Corinth, that this Brother had great confidence in the Corinthians that they would give liberally, which made the Work of God a joy, for the simple reason that the work was now being done with diligence, with which it should have been done all along.

NOTES

(23) "WHETHER ANY DO ENQUIRE OF TITUS, HE IS MY PARTNER AND FELLOW-HELPER CONCERNING YOU: OR OUR BRETHREN BE ENQUIRED OF, THEY ARE THE MESSENGERS OF THE CHURCHES, AND THE GLORY OF CHRIST."

The Holy Spirit through Paul places a seal of approval upon these three Brethren, and as well gives us further information concerning them and the Call of God in general.

TITUS

The phrase, *"Whether any do enquire of Titus,"* presents Paul placing Titus in charge respecting the three who were to go to Corinth. The idea is not that Paul endorses Titus above the others, but that the Corinthians are to regard Titus as the leader of this small commission.

"About Titus" the matter is clear: As Paul's special associate he has been working together with the Corinthians and continues in this status. However, the third Brother as seems to indicate, is also an associate of Paul's as Verse 22 shows; it seems that only the second has been voted as a delegate to Jerusalem. So Paul adds a third to his own party, to make the situation even more responsible.

PARTNER AND FELLOWHELPER

The phrase, *"He is my partner and fellowhelper concerning you,"* refers as stated, to Titus not only being a very close associate with Paul, but more knowledgeable than anyone else concerning Corinth other than Paul.

When Titus was called by the Lord to help Paul, I wonder if he had even an inkling of the significance of this Calling and task? Did he realize that his name would be read by untold millions down through the centuries and with great love and appreciation, concerning his very important part in the establishing of the Early Church? Several things are said here:

1. Anything that anyone does for the Lord is eternal, while all things done otherwise are abruptly temporal. I doubt very seriously if most Believers fully understand that. Many Christian Businessmen devote 99 percent of

their time to making money, which within itself is not wrong if done properly; however, with many of them their devotion to Christ is small by comparison which is a shame, considering the eternal consequences. Thank the Lord for the few who put Christ first.

2. The Lord has a place for every single Believer. Titus was appointed by the Holy Spirit for the task of serving as the *"partner and fellowhelper"* of one of, if not the greatest Apostle who ever lived, Paul. He served faithfully in this assigned task, as is obvious.

However, please allow us to make it crystal clear, that it is not just a few who are designated by the Holy Spirit such as Titus, but in fact, every single Believer. It is the business of the Believer, or rather should be, to find what that task is and then perform it diligently. If the Believer will ask, the Lord will always respond accordingly.

3. In this great work, the Lord does not judge places or positions as small or large. He judges faithfulness exclusively. In other words, the Lord has not called us, as we have previously stated, to be successful, but rather faithful. In fact, faithfulness is success with God. God has called some Believers to a life of prayer. They should be faithful to that task. Others to giving. Whereas all are to give, even as these two Chapters in II Corinthians portray; still, *"giving"* with some is a Ministry to a far greater degree than others. In fact, the Holy Spirit through Paul even labels *"hospitality"* as a Calling of the Lord (Rom. 12:8, 13).

APOSTLES

The phrase, *"Or our Brethren be enquired of, they are the Messengers of the Churches,"* actually means that these three were Apostles as well. The word *"Messengers"* in the Greek is *"apostoloi,"* and means as should be obvious, *"Apostles."*

Some claim that these were not Apostles in the technical sense, that they did not stand in the Office of the Apostle as Paul. However, there is no indication in Scripture that such is correct. While the word *"Apostle"* means *"a delegate, one sent with full power of attorney to act in the place of another, the sender remaining behind to back up the one sent,"* every indication is that these men were sent by God, and not merely by Paul. We know this

NOTES

from Verses 16, 19 and 23, even as the next Phrase proclaims.

Even though their Calling as Apostles may not have carried the same responsibility as that of Paul, still, that made them no less Apostles. However, even as we have already said, responsibility is a word that is relative to the task at hand, and is looked at accordingly by the Lord. In other words, each place and position, whatever that may be, is extremely important to Him. So, to say that one is more important than the other may not possibly be the manner in which such should be described. Without these men, Paul's task would have been immeasurably harder, and perhaps even impossible in certain circumstances. In fact, the manner in which the Church is led and directed by the Holy Spirit, is through Apostles. The Holy Spirit through Paul said concerning the great Work of God, *"And are built upon the foundation of the Apostles and Prophets, Jesus Christ Himself being the Chief Corner Stone"* (Eph. 2:20).

The problem with the Church which prevails presently, and in fact, has always been one of Satan's great means, is that it is not led by the Holy Spirit through Apostles, but mostly by Denominational Heads who hold an unscriptural office, at least in the manner in which they have made that office, through which the Holy Spirit will not function. Apostles are Called of God, and not elected by popular ballot.

THE GLORY OF CHRIST

The phrase, *"And the Glory of Christ,"* proclaims Jesus as the Head of the Church, Who through the Holy Spirit was directing Paul regarding this particular situation.

Some have concluded from this phrase, that the Holy Spirit is speaking here solely of the character of these particular individuals and how they brought honor to the Christian name, etc. While this certainly enters into the situation, it is by no means the meaning of the Text.

The idea is, that Christ is upheld as the Head of the Church, Who is directing the situation through the Holy Spirit, and the Holy Spirit through the Apostles. This order must never be abrogated, especially considering its vast significance.

This doesn't mean that the Lord does not speak to, or work through other Callings such as that of the *"Prophet, Evangelist, Pastor, or Teacher"* (Eph. 4:11). In fact, He works and moves through these constantly, as well as Laypersons in the Church, who do not stand in any office regarding the Fivefold Calling. One will not find a Hierarchy in the Work of God, at least that God institutes, for such does not exist. Regrettably there definitely are Hierarchies in modern Church functions, and save for the Early Church have always existed; nevertheless, they are of man, i.e., *"of Satan,"* and never of God. In fact, this of which we speak here, has done more to hurt the Work of God than anything else Satan has devised.

Religious men are not satisfied to abide by the Word of God, in which the Book of Acts and the Epistles give us direction regarding this all-important subject, but feel they must institute their own type of government, which has no Scriptural foundation. Consequently, they make up their rules, which can never be sanctioned by the Holy Spirit. It is for *"the Glory of Christ,"* or the glory of man; it cannot be both!

This doesn't mean that Denominations or belonging to Denominations are wrong. It does not mean that the administrative offices in these Denominations are wrong, for they aren't. In fact, all of that can be very useful for the Cause of Christ. It is when men make more of these Denominations and these offices than they should, in other words, attaching a spiritual significance to them in the realm of spiritual authority, which makes for the wrong.

It is the same in a sense with Water Baptism and the Lord's Supper. These things are definitely of God as should be obvious; however, when men attempt to make them a part of Salvation, in other words that the doing of one or the other constitutes Salvation, such is very wrong.

Satan very seldom totally disavows or denies the Truth. His greatest tactic is to simply twist or pervert the Truth.

(24) "WHEREFORE SHEW YE TO THEM, AND BEFORE THE CHURCHES, THE PROOF OF YOUR LOVE, AND OF OUR BOASTING ON YOUR BEHALF."

This Passage is to awaken the full consciousness in the Corinthians that they are one Church among all these their sister Churches.

NOTES

BEFORE THE CHURCHES

The phrase, *"Wherefore shew ye to them, and before the Churches,"* pertains to Paul requesting a liberal contribution in the cause in which they are engaged, which as well will be an example to the other Churches even as Macedonia was an example (8:1-5).

All three of these men are Apostles who were sent by Paul, but by him as connected with all these Churches. Whatever treatment the Corinthians accord these three men will thus be *"in the sight of the Churches."* This is stated as we have said, that Corinth may understand that this endeavor is not just one Church, but actually all the Churches.

Paul is pressing for unity, for a concentrated direction and a like burden, which will definitely exist if all of those of like Faith, are following the Lord as they should.

Regrettably, such unity presently and fellowship between congregations or Churches are often ignored and set aside. Too often, one Church cares little or nothing as to how its action affects its sister Churches. It boldly outrages not only the feelings but the Scriptural direction as well of its sister Churches that are, perhaps, located in the same City. Thus, inner unity is destroyed. Such disregard exhibits a low moral condition, a deep decline in spirituality. How can one love God, Whom one has not seen, who does not love his Brother, whom he sees? (I Jn. 4:20). Does this not apply also to the relation between Churches?

As well, some Bible Commentators write as if the Apostle had nothing good to say about the Church at Corinth. As I think by now should be obvious, nothing could be further from the Truth. He thought so highly of them, especially after the great Move of God which had taken place, that he implores them to be an example to the other Churches.

PROOF OF LOVE

The phrase, *"The proof of your love,"* concerns love for God, love for Paul (in this instance), love for the other Churches, and love for those in Jerusalem who were in need. The idea is, that it's impossible to love God, if we do not love the Brethren. To say we love is one thing, but the proof of love rests in the action it must produce.

To bring it down to a fine point, the proof of love is in Giving. The proof of loving God is not necessarily in praying as important as that actually is. As well, the proof of loving God is not necessarily in worship. Worship may be for the sake of religious respectability. The actual proof of loving God is in giving oneself to God.

It is so with loving man. Love is peculiarly expressed by our gifts. The first act of love is giving what you are to another in love's troth. The next and continuing act of love is giving what you have.

Love thrives on giving and dies in withholding. Love shrivels and atrophies when confined.

The greatest example of Love is of course, God. He *"so loved the world, that He gave."* Divine Love was proved by the Divine Gift. We are no exception to the rule. Our Love will be proved by our Gifts.

In essence, Paul is saying that the thing to do is not to talk about it, but prove it.

Look about you. Do your eyes meet the appeal of someone's need? Do not content yourself by saying, *"I would if I could."* Say, *"I will do what I can."* Let affection respond to affliction. Only by the practical display of it can we prove the actual possession of it.

The Scripture addresses this pointed question to us, *"Whoso hath this world's good, and seeth his Brother have need, and shutteth up his bowels of compassion from him, how dwelleth the Love of God in him?"* The proof of its possession is Love in action.

BOASTING

The phrase, *"And of our boasting on your behalf,"* pertains to Paul boasting that the Corinthians would surely do their part.

In effect, he is saying, *"Let it now be seen that my boasting was well founded, and that I properly understood your character, and your readiness to contribute to this particular need."*

As well, we learn from this, even as we have previously stated, that it's not improper or wrong for Preachers of the Gospel, or anyone for that matter, to *"boast"* about the generosity of certain Churches or certain Believers for that matter. If the person is right with the Lord, it will not swell the ego nor contribute to pride. It will rather constitute a thankfulness in the heart that one is able to respond to the need. All the Glory will go to God and not man.

NOTES

"It was for you the Saviour died, for you
the fountain opened wide;
"The crimson Blood flow'd from His
Side; For you, yes, for you; For you,
yes, for you."

"It was for you the price was paid, the
Wrath of God in Mercy stayed,
"For you the Saviour low was laid; For
you, yes, for you; For you, yes,
for you."

"It was for you the Saviour sought, your
soul that wondrous price was bought,
"For you Salvation's Plan was wrought;
For you, yes, for you; For you, yes,
for you."

"It was for you He gave His all, redeemed
you from the curse and fall;
"O, hear and heed His loving Call: For
you, yes, for you; For you, yes, for you."

CHAPTER 9

(1) "FOR AS TOUCHING THE MINISTERING TO THE SAINTS, IT IS SUPERFLUOUS FOR ME TO WRITE TO YOU:"

In this Chapter the Apostle continues the subject which he had discussed in the previous Chapter — the Collection which he had purposed to make for the situation in Jerusalem. The deep anxiety which he had, that the Collection would be generous; that it should not only be such as to be really a help to those who were suffering, but be such as would be an expression of tender attachment to those in need on the part of these Gentiles.

Paul's primary wish undoubtedly was to furnish aid to those who were suffering. But in connection with this, I think he also wished to excite a deep interest among the Gentile converts on behalf of those who had been converted to Christianity among the Jews. He wished that this Offering should be so liberal as to show that they felt that they were united as Brethren, and that they were grateful that they had received the true Plan of Salvation which in essence, had come from the Jews.

And he doubtless wished to cement as much as possible the great body of Christian Brotherhood, and to impress upon their minds the great Truths, that whatever was their national origin, and whatever were their national distinctions, yet in Christ they were one.

In fact, Satan at this time was working strongly to affect a split between Jewish and Gentile Christians. Actually, most of Paul's difficulties respecting the Churches, and a great part of the problem at Corinth had been from this very source. It was the Law/Grace issue, with many of the Jewish Leaders (not the Apostles), claiming that Gentiles must as well keep the Law of Moses along with accepting Christ, that is if they were to be good Christians, etc. Of course, Paul fought this thing strenuously because he knew it would destroy the Church if allowed to gain a foothold. And yet, by no means did he want a split to be effected; therefore, I personally believe this Offering was meant to show the love of the Gentiles for the Jews, and, hopefully, to ameliorate these difficulties. Regrettably, there is little evidence that it actually helped, despite the efforts of the Apostle.

MINISTERING TO THE SAINTS

The phrase, *"For as touching the ministering to the Saints,"* continues with the subject at hand, which refers to the Offerings being received in all the Churches concerning the need in Jerusalem.

Following as well, for the subject matter continues in the same vein, the Holy Spirit through the Apostle continues to give a wealth of teaching on this all-important Doctrine, i.e., *"Grace."*

As we've already stated, about every question that could be asked and answered is addressed in these two Chapters concerning the Giving of our financial resources to the Work of the Lord. And yet, in all of this Teaching, Paul does not one time mention *"Tithing."*

Why?

First of all we do know that it was not an oversight on his part. He wrote what the Holy Spirit inspired him to write, and only what the Holy Spirit inspired him to write.

The Bible teaches Tithing as the foundation of all Giving, whether in the Old or New Testaments.

NOTES

Tithing did not originate with the Law of Moses as many think, but actually began with Abraham, at least as far as we know. The Scripture says that Abraham gave him (Mel-chizedek King of Salem) *"Tithes of all"* (Gen. 14:18-20). This is the first mention of Tithing in Scripture. Consequently, we learn several things from this:

1. The Melchizedecian Priesthood is eternal, of which Priesthood is Christ (Heb. 6:20). Inasmuch as this Priesthood is eternal in Christ, and that Abraham paid Tithes to this man, the example was set that it might continue even as it still does.

2. Abraham paid Tithes to Melchizedek because he was instructed by the Lord to do so. We as Abraham's children are to continue to do what the Patriarch Abraham did as our example (Heb. 7:1-11, 17, 21; Gal. 3:7-9).

3. The Lord designated the Tithe as it regards the amount, which is a tenth; therefore, it serves as a foundation for all Giving including that which is Christian. Nowhere in the Bible is this changed.

Seeing this is eternal and not to be changed, Paul, I think, built on this. His premise is, that we are not to turn Giving into a Law, which many have done with the *"Tithe."* In fact, everything the Believer has belongs to the Lord and should be available to Him at all times. This is the spirit that the Holy Spirit is promoting, which goes far beyond Tithing, as should be obvious. While Tithing serves as the foundation, it by no means is to be the end of our Giving, but actually the beginning.

TO WRITE TO YOU

The phrase, *"It is superfluous for me to write to you,"* means that he believes they (the Corinthians) are already very much aware of their obligations and have already purposed to meet them with responsibility. It is unnecessary for him to urge arguments as to why it should be done, but rather that he will offer some suggestions in regard to the manner in which it shall be accomplished.

As well, the Holy Spirit is no doubt using this occasion to bring forth this teaching which is the most comprehensive on this subject — the subject of Giving — as found anywhere in the Bible. Consequently, that given is not only for the Corinthians, but all the other Churches at that particular time, and in fact, for all Churches for all time.

THE MANNER IN WHICH THE BIBLE IS WRITTEN

We have here a striking specimen of the manner in which the Bible is written. Instead of abstract statements and systematic arrangement, the principles of Christianity are brought out in connection with a case that actually occurred. But it follows that it is important to study attentively the Bible, and to be familiar with every part of it.

In other words, the Word of God deals with circumstances and situations, actually everyday happenings, in fact, all things which pertain to Life and Godliness (II Pet. 1:3-4).

In other words, the Bible deals with life as it is, and seeks to make it better, but above all, with a view to Eternal Life.

(2) "FOR I KNOW THE FORWARDNESS OF YOUR MIND, FOR WHICH I BOAST OF YOU TO THEM OF MACEDONIA, THAT ACHAIA WAS READY A YEAR AGO; AND YOUR ZEAL HATH PROVOKED VERY MANY."

These two Chapters are of special importance, due to the fact that the Spirit of God presses upon Believers the duty of giving liberally to the need at hand. The principles on which this should be done are fully developed here. The motives which it is lawful to urge are urged here by Paul. Consequently, both these Chapters are worthy of our profound study, and because of their great significance.

The Holy Spirit taught Paul well the rudiments of human nature. Well he knew the motives which would influence others to give. And well he knew exactly how to shape his arguments and adapt his reasoning to the circumstances of those whom he addressed.

THE FORWARDNESS OF YOUR MIND

The phrase, *"For I know the forwardness of your mind,"* presents Paul speaking about the readiness with which his first proposal some time back of a grand Collection for the relief of the poor in Jerusalem met, not only in Corinth, but in all the Churches in Achaia.

"Forwardness," in the Greek is *"prothumian,"* and means *"eagerness to help."* Regrettably, Satan attempts to destroy this *"forwardness"* in the mind of the Believer, which he nearly succeeded doing at Corinth. This *"forwardness"* was for the Work of God, the things of God, in this case, the needy Saints in Jerusalem.

NOTES

The question should be asked of us all, as to how forward and eager we are presently to carry out the Work of God.

I BOAST

The phrase, *"For which I boast of you to them of Macedonia,"* presents Paul then being in Macedonia, probably Philippi.

So well assured was the Apostle that the Church at Corinth would make the Collection as it had been proposed, that he boasted of it to the Churches of Macedonia as if it were already done, and made of this an argument to stimulate them to make a greater effort. He had mentioned this as well in II Corinthians 8:24.

READY A YEAR AGO

The phrase, *"That Achaia was ready a year ago,"* presents the part of Greece of which Corinth was the capital. It is no doubt probable that there were Christians in other parts of Achaia besides Corinth, and indeed it is known that there was a Church in Cenchrea (Rom. 16:1), which was one of the ports of Corinth.

Him mentioning *"a year ago,"* carries a heavy meaning. Several points must be noted here.

The *"year ago"* speaks only about the beginning that had been made, and made with great zeal as here implies; however, the problems at Corinth had halted all of this. We have nothing after that up until now, with *"a year ago"* limiting us to that past time.

Concerning that particular time, Paul had boasted to the Macedonians as to what the Corinthians were going to do, with of course, it not having yet been done. How much the Macedonians knew about the problems at Corinth, we are not told; nevertheless, Paul is now treating the Corinthians as though this problem had never happened, in effect, picking up where they had originally left off.

As we have previously stated, all positive and forward activity had pretty well ground to a halt during this intervening year — consequently, time wasted.

Before this problem, the Corinthians had a *"readiness of mind"* regarding this effort, and now they surely have the same inasmuch as they have now experienced repentance. So, Paul's boasting then was not in vain, and it is not in vain presently.

PROVOKED MANY

The phrase, *"And your zeal hath provoked very many,"* means it had aroused, excited, even impelled others to give.

We use the word *"provoke"* commonly now in the sense of *"to irritate,"* but in the Scriptures it is confined to the signification of exciting, or arousing.

From this one Phrase, although others are not lacking, we learn that the Corinthian Church was in fact a great Church. Due to its location, its Light did shine brightly. Consequently, this is one of the reasons, I believe, that Satan singled out this particular congregation. He did so with a three-pronged attack: first of all from the world, hence Paul telling them to *"come out..."* Second, false doctrine had been introduced by the Judaizers, who were a constant source of irritation to Paul and a great hindrance to the Work of God. Third, these interlopers caused the person of Paul to be attacked vigorously, even calling into question his Apostleship. Consequently, seeing the potential for spiritual greatness, Satan mustered an all-out attack against the Work of God in this City.

To be sure, such does not excuse their wrongdoing, but before our judgment becomes too harsh, we had best first consider ourselves. Satan hated their *"zeal"* for the Lord, their *"forwardness,"* and their example! Thank the Lord, due to Paul using much wisdom in the situation, therefore, being led by the Holy Spirit, the Church had been salvaged.

(3) "YET HAVE I SENT THE BRETHREN, LEST OUR BOASTING OF YOU SHOULD BE IN VAIN IN THIS BEHALF; THAT, AS I SAID, YE MAY BE READY:"

This Letter (II Corinthians) was taken by Titus to Corinth, even as the First Epistle had been sent. There is a good possibility as well, that Titus personally read this Epistle to them. Concerning this Collection, which Chapters 8 and 9 are all about, he is preparing the Believers at Corinth, in effect, preparing to receive an Offering.

I and II Corinthians present the greatest amount of instruction given by the Holy Spirit to any one Church. Even though much of the instruction was as the result of problems, still, such gave occasion to the opportunity for much teaching. In fact, at least half of Paul's Epistles fall under the category of being *"corrective."* To be frank, this does not fit with most modern Teaching and Preaching, which claim to be altogether positive; however, if being *"corrective"* is done in the right spirit, it will turn out to a positive result. Consequently, from this pattern laid down by the Holy Spirit, we learn that the Preacher must function in this mode at times, or else he is not being Scriptural. Regrettably, false apostles and false doctrine abound. As Paul here did, such must be addressed.

THE BRETHREN

The phrase, *"Yet have I sent the Brethren,"* refers to those mentioned in II Corinthians 8:18, 22-23.

We should readily understand that all of this was very important, or the Holy Spirit would not have gone into such detail. Paul's writings show us two things:

1. The Lord is always very concerned about His people. As we've already stated, due to thousands of Jews having accepted Christ and, therefore, being excommunicated from the Synagogue, the need there was great, as should be obvious. The Lord certainly cares about this and makes preparation for the need to be met, even as we are now studying. Unfortunately, it had been hindered by the onslaught of Satan.

Nevertheless, all of this is not merely to go about the mechanics of receiving an Offering, or any such type things, but rather, the Love of God for His Children, and His means of meeting these needs. This should be a great comfort to all of us as well.

2. Paul's writings proclaim constantly, the taking of the Gospel to those who have never heard. This was ever his thrust, his burden, his obedience to the Call of God.

BOASTING IN VAIN

The phrase, *"Lest our boasting of you should be in vain in this behalf,"* simply means that he believes they will now finish what they had grandly started.

Paul is speaking about the preparation which he made a year ago and not about a preparation which the Corinthians have made

NOTES

recently or are now making. The preparation made by Paul a year ago was thorough and effective. Verse One states that it would be superfluous to make it anew; Verse Two adds that, when Paul made this preparation, it produced *"readiness."*

To go into more detail, he no doubt at that time told them exactly what they should do, and how it should be done. As he closed out I Corinthians, and on the premise that they would heed his admonitions, he said to them, *"Upon the first day of the week let every one of you lay by him in store, as God hath prospered him, that there be no gatherings when I come"* (I Cor. 16:2).

The point of interest here is the practical human measures which Paul used to insure the success of his mission. He employed both Faith and works. He trusted God and used means.

There are many occasions where Divine help is the only hope we have, but I am quite sure God does not intend our Faith to be a substitute for our works. Faith is the cause and works are the effect. It seems to be a cooperative engagement and effort. What is Evangelism but God's Word sounded forth by human means?

Paul undoubtedly had great Faith in the success of his financial mission in raising funds in Corinth for the Christians at Jerusalem, but he had only asked God to provide these funds and he asked the Corinthians to give them. Furthermore, he not only asked the Corinthians to give, but he organized a financial mission of three trusted men to go before him as a precautionary measure to take such steps as were necessary to gather these funds.

DESIRABLE AND SCRIPTURAL

All of this was both legitimate and proper. It was that desirable combination of God and man, the Divine and the human, Faith and works, Trust and action. It was the balancing of God's Power and the human instrument. We fail in not understanding that God works through the human instrument and not apart from it.

YE MAY BE READY

The phrase, *"That, as I said, ye may be ready,"* presents Paul employing particular measures, but being very careful to have the Corinthians understand that it was not to be by coercion, but by cooperation. Paul sought these funds as an expression of Corinthian generosity and Grace and not as something extorted from them.

NOTES

The length to which we hear some modern Ministers go in receiving Offerings, to which we have already alluded, is often a disgrace to the dignity of the Word of God. They ask people to make large gifts claiming that they will receive so much in return, which in its pure and simple form is nothing but greed. As well there are appeals of the auctioneer type, appeals by psychological tricks, appeals to carnal vanity so that Christianity is demeaned and disgraced.

If these Corinthians were to give on the principle of readiness, if they were to be ready to meet the need of others, they must be sensitive to that need. They could not be sensitive to the need unless they were sympathetic to their fellow Christians.

Believers must feel the same way about the lost. They must empathize with the lost. They must realize that they too were once lost without God, and, therefore, on that basis realizing that the Lord sent someone to tell them the Grand Story, in turn they will do the same for others.

ARE YOU READY?

These people were ready to give to the Cause of Christ. Revival had broken out in their midst, occasioned by great Repentance. Now they desire to do something for the Lord.

Television presently has made it possible to reach untold millions with the Gospel of Jesus Christ. By this method, which God has called us to do, we have seen literally hundreds of thousands brought to a saving knowledge of Jesus Christ, which fruit remains all over the world. And yet, there are many areas around the world where we could instantly begin preaching the Gospel by Television, which would instantly begin to garner results in the realm of souls being saved, but we simply do not have the money to do so. It is because many Christians are not ready! They are distracted by other things, by personal pleasures, or by pursuits of their own inventions. Irrespective, while a few definitely are ready, and are doing all they can, the far greater majority give only a token amount, or nothing at all for the greatest cause on earth, the bringing of souls to Jesus Christ.

WHAT KIND OF PREACHER AND WHAT KIND OF MESSAGE?

Many Christians have the mistaken notion that any Preacher will do. That is not true.

Paul was called of God for the task of World Evangelism among other things. Others were called as well, but not all, in fact, not even a majority. While all are certainly called to do their part, the part of all is not the direct proclamation of the Message, that part pertaining only to a few.

While every Preacher can certainly preach to anyone and everyone and should do so; still, they will not have near the results as someone who is truly called for that particular task. So, just any Preacher will not accomplish the task. It must be the one(s) whom God has sent.

Also, not only must that individual even as Paul, be Divinely sent, there must be a heavy Anointing of the Holy Spirit on his or her life. This can only come about by great consecration and dedication to the Lord. It involves a heavy prayer life, a constant study of the Word, in order that the Spirit of God may have proper access to that particular Temple, and that the person may be used effectively. Without the Holy Spirit nothing is going to be done, with the Holy Spirit, all things can be done.

And last, if false doctrine is being preached, even as the Judaizers were doing in the Churches founded by Paul, most certainly that is not going to be blessed but rather the opposite. In fact, such gospel which Paul referred to as *"another gospel,"* is not only not going to get anybody to Christ, it is going to corrupt those who have already been brought to Christ, which actually is the intention of Satan to start with (II Cor. 11:4).

The point is, every single Believer is responsible to God to do his and her part in World Evangelism, no one is excepted or excused. However, every Believer must also seek the Lord incessantly as to who they are to support. It must be one who God has truly called for this task, and which the True Gospel of Jesus Christ is truly being preached, accompanied by *"signs following."*

By *"signs following,"* I mean souls being saved, lives being changed, sick bodies being healed, bondages of darkness being broken, and Believers being Baptized with the Holy Spirit. It will also include the demons of darkness being cast out, along with all the works of Satan being destroyed. The criteria should always be the following:

1. The Call of God.
2. The Word of God.
3. The Power of God.

Again I ask, *"Are you ready?"*

(4) "LEST HAPLY IF THEY OF MACEDONIA COME WITH ME, AND FIND YOU UNPREPARED, WE (THAT WE SAY NOT, YE) SHOULD BE ASHAMED IN THIS SAME CONFIDENT BOASTING."

Regarding this need at Jerusalem, it is so easy to become calloused by the frequency and the commonness of human tragedy. It is so easy to become wrapped up in the comfortable garments of our own circumstances and to build around ourselves and our domiciles the high wall of selfish indifference. World Evangelism falls into the same category.

To be saved and not care respecting others who aren't, who possibly have not even had the privilege to hear, is the greatest tragedy of all. And yet sadly and regrettably, I think I exaggerate not when I say that most Believers have little concern for the lost of this world.

The reasons are varied and many; improper burden or no burden at all on the part of the pulpit, another gospel, and most of all a lack of personal consecration on the part of the individual Believer.

To those of you who have read our Commentaries to any degree, you are probably aware of the Prayer Meetings conducted daily at this Ministry and Family Worship Center. We have visitors quite often; however, a short time ago some visiting Christians came into one of the Prayer Meetings, who really did not even know what a Prayer Meeting was. Outside of Church, and then only in a formal manner, they had never heard anyone pray. What am I saying?

I am saying that today's Church, even among those who claim to believe all the Bible and be filled with the Spirit, is not a praying Church; consequently, there is little fertile ground spiritually speaking, in which the Holy Spirit can work, in order to nurture these all-important aspects of Christianity.

NOTES

NOTES

UNPREPARED

The phrase, *"Lest haply if they of Macedonia come with me, and find you unprepared,"* carries with it a far greater import than embarrassment for Paul or failure respecting the Offering for Jerusalem. That which the Holy Spirit is teaching us here, is *"preparation,"* and the way the word and the sentence are structured, *"constant preparation."*

Regrettably, and I think I exaggerate not, most of the Church world today is *"unprepared!"* Some may ask, *"Unprepared for what?"*

The answer is simple, unprepared for anything which pertains to God and His Work, the very purpose for which the Church is supposed to function. An army is prepared to fight, or at least it is supposed to be. Government is prepared to govern, or at least it is supposed to be. So, for what is the Church supposed to be prepared?

1. The preparation must be on the part of the individual Believer in respect to his personal readiness concerning the shining of the Gospel Light which in reality he is supposed to be and do (Mat. 5:13-16).

2. He is to be prepared, even as Paul is here addressing, to carry out the basic function of the Church, which is to take the Gospel to a lost world.

3. The Believer, i.e., *"the Church,"* is to be prepared for the Coming of the Lord, i.e., *"the Rapture of the Church"* (I Thess. 4:13-18; 5:4-8).

ASHAMED

The phrase, *"We* (that we say not, ye) *should be ashamed in this same confident boasting,"* once again carries a far greater significance than the matter at hand. The Believer who is unprepared, the Church which is unprepared, will of necessity come to shame at a point in time. While such may not show up presently, to be sure, it definitely will show up at the *"Judgment Seat of Christ"* (II Cor. 5:10).

The idea presents itself further, that if the Church at Corinth would not prepare itself regarding this matter under the prodding of Paul, they would not prepare themselves at all. Of all the leaders they would have down through the years, as should be obvious, none I think, would be of the caliber of this Apostle. So, what am I saying?

Paul was merely the instrument, although a finely-tuned instrument spiritually speaking, while the Holy Spirit was the actual Author of this which was being done. I am saying that the Moving and Operation of the Holy Spirit through the Apostle to the Church at Corinth, and all other Churches for that matter, would have the greatest latitude of all. It is a frightful thing for the Church to lose its way in any case, but worse still, when the Message is delivered through an instrument such as the Apostle.

WHAT COULD PAUL SAY IN THE FACE OF POOR RESULTS?

Even if he asserted anew what he had done, the Macedonians would have their doubts. Should Paul chide the Corinthians in the presence of these Macedonians and say that the fault for this lack of proper results was theirs? Would the Corinthians want Paul to do that?

Then let them remember that whatever preparation Paul had made in Macedonia had yielded the very greatest results (8:1-5). That would certainly justify the conclusion that similar preparation made by Paul in Corinth should have produced somewhat similar results, the other alternative being that Paul had not made the preparation as he claimed he had.

Consequently, the Apostle writes: *"Lest perhaps we be put to shame — not to say you."*

Every evidence is, that Corinth did come through, with Paul's confidence being justified.

PAUL

The Reader may wonder at the emphasis placed here on the feelings of Paul respecting this matter.

The idea is that the Holy Spirit is the Author of this thrust and all that is done, but that He works very closely through His Messengers, in this case Paul. If Paul is made ashamed, the Holy Spirit is as well.

I think that most Believers have little idea as to the union of the Believer and the Spirit of God. One must consider that it is very close especially understanding that the Holy Spirit has actually taken up abode within our hearts and lives (I Cor. 3:16).

The idea is, that whatever feelings are registered in the heart and life of the Believer is predominant as well in the Holy Spirit. Of course, that does not hold true on a constant basis, for the simple reason that we at times lapse into that which is not of Faith, such as Paul when he said, *"Within were fears"* (II Cor. 7:5). As should be obvious, there is no fear on the part of the Holy Spirit.

Nevertheless, during these times or lapses we might say, the Spirit of God does not leave us at all, but rather goes into a mode of helping us to overcome these particular situations (Jn. 16:7).

The perfect example of this of which I speak, is the Lord Jesus Christ. His every emotion, action, feeling, thought, direction, etc., were the same as that of the Holy Spirit. They were perfectly one in all things, and because the Temple of Christ was perfect in every respect.

No Believer can boast such, not even Paul; however, the Holy Spirit is ever seeking to bring us as close as possible to this total oneness within our hearts and lives, which most definitely will full take place at the coming Resurrection (I Cor. 15:51-54).

(5) "THEREFORE I THOUGHT IT NECESSARY TO EXHORT THE BRETHREN, THAT THEY WOULD GO BEFORE UNTO YOU, AND MAKE UP BEFOREHAND YOUR BOUNTY, WHEREOF YE HAD NOTICE BEFORE, THAT THE SAME MIGHT BE READY, AS A MATTER OF BOUNTY, AND NOT AS OF COVETOUSNESS."

This Verse proclaims the necessity of preparation, and not taking things for granted. It also extols the absolute necessity of proper leadership. In other words, most Believers will do what they ought to do when they are properly led, and not before.

NECESSITY

The phrase, *"Therefore I thought it necessary to exhort the Brethren, that they would go before unto you,"* refers to the three Brethren which included Titus.

The triple repetition of the word *"before"* in this Verse, shows how earnest Paul is in the matter. The Corinthians had promised largely, yet there seems to be some evidence that there had been, or that there was ground for fearing that there might be, some slackness of performance, even after the recent Move of God. I think had not that been the case, the amount of attention here shown would not have been done.

NOTES

But again, the Holy Spirit may have used the Apostle in this manner regarding instructions to the Corinthians, in order to produce in all Believers and for all time, the absolute necessity of being prepared at all times to carry out the Work of God.

YOUR BOUNTY

The phrase, *"And make up beforehand your bounty,"* should have been translated *"Blessing."* The Greek word is *"eulogian,"* from which we get our word *"eulogy."* Consequently, the word as used here, means *"Blessing, and Praise applied to God."* It is *"that which blesses,"* whether of God to men, or of one man to another. Here it refers to the contribution of the Corinthians and the other Churches as well, as that which would be adapted to confer a Blessing on others, or fitted to produce happiness.

Whatever one wants to do concerning *"a Blessing"* will, of course, be bountiful in quantity, but in this connection the word means more than quantity, but rather a *"Blessing"* bestowed upon those in need in the Name of the Lord, which in effect, praises Him. In other words, our Gifts to the Lord are never a mere exchange of money, or even a charitable work, but rather a *"Praise to the Lord."* Consequently, this is the reason that the Apostle referred to this as a *"Grace"* (II Cor. 8:6-7).

So, when we *"give"* to the Lord, we are at the same time *"praising"* the Lord! Consequently, it should stand to reason that we would not want to be conservative in our Praises but rather liberal, i.e., *"giving generously."*

A LIBERAL BLESSING

The phrase, *"Whereof ye had notice before, that the same might be ready, as a matter of bounty,"* is better understood *"as a matter of generous blessing."* Three things were to be understood here:

1. The Corinthians were to understand that this Offering was a *"Blessing"* which would not only bless others, in this case those in Jerusalem, but in turn, would bless the Giver as well.
2. It was to be generous, especially considering that it was in reality a Gift to God.
3. It was not to be looked at as the mere giving of money, but rather as a *"Praise Offering."*

How so much this takes our giving to God out of the mundane, out of the mere handing over of money, into the spiritual realm, with the Lord looking at such exactly as He observed the Sacrifices of old.

COVETOUSNESS

The phrase, *"And not as of covetousness,"* refers not so much to the small quantity given, but the mean spirit which wants more for self, and is actually giving for that reason. This blows to pieces the modern Prosperity Message, where people are encouraged to give not as a spirit of Praise, or as an Offering to the Lord, but rather to get. In other words, it is a matter of greed.

I am certain that the Reader can see the absolute difference in giving properly to the Lord, than this modern gospel which induces men to give on the basis that they're going to get so much in return. Of course, it is true that God blesses and blesses grandly His people for their giving, even as the next Verse proclaims. Still, our motive for giving, for that's what it's all about, must ever be in the realm of a Sacrificial Offering unto the Lord, and not from the spirit of covetousness.

THE TERRIBLE SIN OF COVETOUSNESS

The Hebrews visualized the soul as full of vigorous desires which urged it to extend its influence over other persons and things. Consequently there are several Hebrew words for *"covetousness."*

There is *"hamad,"* which pertains to *"desiring a neighbour's possessions"* (Deut. 5:21; Micah 2:2). As well there is *"besa,"* which is *"a desire for dishonest gain"* (Prov. 28:16; Jer. 6:13) and *"awa,"* which is *"selfish desire"* (Prov. 21:26). Covetousness is a grievous sin, and is actually the last *"Thou shalt not,"* of the Ten Commandments (Ex. 20:17).

There are several Greek words describing *"covetousness,"* with the first being *"epithymia,"* which *"expresses any intense desire,"* which if misdirected may be concentrated on money, as in Acts 20:33; Romans 7:7; I Timothy 6:9.

Another Greek word *"pleonexia"* generally expresses *"ruthless self-assertion"* (II Cor. 2:11; 7:2), which is applied to possessions in Luke 12:15, and repudiated by Christ in Mark 7:22. As well, the word is often associated with immorality and lists of vices (Eph. 4:19), and, being in essence the worship of self, is characterized as the ultimate idolatry in Ephesians 5:5 and Colossians 3:5.

NOTES

It can be rendered *"avarice"* in II Corinthians 9:5, actually the Scripture of this particular study, and II Peter 2:3.

Another Greek word *"zelos"* is used to inculcate an intense desire for spiritual gifts which is legitimate as in I Corinthians 12:31; but it describes a very sordid carnal strife in James 4:2.

(6) "BUT THIS I SAY, HE WHICH SOWETH SPARINGLY SHALL REAP ALSO SPARINGLY; AND HE WHICH SOWETH BOUNTIFULLY SHALL REAP ALSO BOUNTIFULLY."

We are here shown at length how our giving can, indeed, be *"a Blessing,"* a Blessing all around, a Blessing also to ourselves.

Of course, there dare then be no *"covetousness"* about it. If such indeed does exist, there will be no Blessing concerning our giving, with this particular Promise so glowing and wonderful, actually made void.

SOWING AND REAPING SPARINGLY

The phrase, *"But this I say, He which soweth sparingly shall reap also sparingly,"* was probably taken by Paul from Proverbs 11:24-26.

Paul says here that it is in giving as it is in agriculture. A man that sows little, must expect to reap little. If he sows a small piece of land, he will reap a small harvest; or if he does not sow enough seed, wishing to save his seed and will not commit it to the earth, he must expect to reap little as well. So it is in giving.

Money given to the Work of God, and the Believer must actually know that it is the Work of God, is in a way similar to the act of committing seed to the earth. It will be returned again in some way with an abundant increase. It shall not be lost. The seed may be buried long. It may lay in the ground with no indication of a return or of increase. One who knew not the arrangements of Providence might suppose it was lost and dead. But in due time it shall spring up and produce an abundant increase.

So with money given to the Work of God. To many, and especially to the world, it may seem to be a waste, or may appear to be thrown away. But in due time it will be repaid in some way with abundant increase.

And the man who wishes to make the most out of his money for future use, will give liberally to the Work of God — just as the man who wishes to make the most out of his grain will not suffer it to lie in his granary, but will commit the seed to the fertile earth. *"Cast thy bread upon the waters: for thou shalt find it after many days"* (Eccl. 11:1).

The idea is, that one reaps in proportion to what is sowed. This everyone knows is true in regard to grain that is sowed, so it holds true in respect to that which we give to God as well.

As well, God looks at our giving in many ways. He looks at our faithfulness, our motivation, etc. And with God, some people giving a hundred dollars is far more in His Sight, than some who would give fifty thousand dollars, and for the obvious reasons.

SOWING AND REAPING BOUNTIFULLY

The phrase, *"And he which soweth bountifully shall reap also bountifully,"* in effect could be translated, *"He which soweth great Blessings shall reap also great Blessings."* If the principle of sowing and reaping holds true on the small amounts, it also holds true on the large amounts, as would be obvious.

We have already seen the Greek word for *"Grace* (charis)*"* used over and over in the teaching on this subject (II Cor. 8:6-7). In fact, II Corinthians 8:9 linked with all the other Passages in these two Chapters, describes the most beautiful set of twins the world ever has seen — *"Grace and Gratitude."* God has manifested His marvelous Grace to us by giving the Lord Jesus Christ as our Perfect Sacrifice. He has, in addition, added manifold Blessings to this glorious Salvation.

A truly gracious person is one who will want to reciprocate with gratitude to God for all of these wonderful benefits. Such is the kind of person who has the proper foundation for genuine Gospel Ministry. God has an inexhaustible store of provisions for His people. The receipt of those provisions should, in turn, elicit constant gratitude from them. Indeed, it will always spark thankfulness from the ones who are standing on the correct foundation. Hence, the first principle of True Christian Giving is that God has an inexhaustible supply (Rossier).

The *"reaping"* here of which the Holy Spirit speaks through the Apostle, is of far greater magnitude than a single return of money. It speaks of physical blessings, i.e., *"the health of our family."* It speaks of well-being and peace of mind. It speaks of spiritual growth and economic blessings. To be frank, the Blessings are unending.

NOTES

The Apostle begins this Scripture with a demonstrative pronoun, *"this,"* in the Greek being *"touto."* Being in the position of emphasis, therefore, this first principle dominates the rest of the Passage.

The verb *"will reap"* is future tense, so it indicates the inevitable outcome of either a miserly approach or a generous liberality. As already stated, it obviously refers to far more than just money. The realm of Blessings is much broader than that, which in effect, speaks of multiple types of Blessings.

On all accounts, therefore, we have every inducement to give liberally to the Work of the Lord.

SHOWERS OF BLESSINGS

If every Christian Giver knew what a Showers of Blessings he starts through his giving he would be like the Macedonians referred to in II Corinthians 8:4 begging to let him give. Review what Paul calls it in II Corinthians 8:1, *"The Grace of God,"* i.e., Grace and thus a great Blessing to the Giver himself. Here this is extended by the significant word *"Blessing"* — others are blessed, by means of their thanks, God is blessed, and thus we ourselves are blessed most of all. *"It is more blessed to give than to receive"* (Acts 20:35).

In this Scripture we are shown two classes of sowers; and the question is to which of the two do we belong, to which do we desire to belong?

The idea is not merely one who sows bountifully, but one who *"keeps on sowing bountifully."* This is Paul's picture of the True Christian Giver. As well, the very word *"sowing"* implies that a harvest is coming. So all our good works are a sowing; ever and ever a harvest is coming.

God designed grain to be sown and to yield its return; God arranged Christian life and good works and giving in the same way. It is He Who wants us to have the Blessing of the harvest. This is His beautiful way of bestowing His Blessing. It is His Economy (Lk. 12:31).

WHY IS IT SO HARD FOR US TO CATCH THIS VISION?

Every farm and every garden reveals it every Spring, Summer, and Fall. God is a God of showers of harvest riches. He is the same God of Showers of Blessings in the Christian Life. He does not intend that we shall be poor; all His arrangements are designed to fill us with riches. It is not because of His lack of generosity that so many of us remain poor. It is either because we give sparingly, or we give with the wrong motivation.

God correlates the two, sowing and harvesting. If He is to give us much, we must give much. How can God pour 1,000 bushels into a receptacle that holds no more than a hundred? If, despite all that God wants to give us, we insist on taking only a little, perhaps nothing at all, shall He upset the entire generous arrangement which He has made in letting sowings produce rich harvests in order to give us abundance in some other way?

What other way that accords with God's generosity could you suggest? The only other way which the world has ever found is mostly to enrich oneself by robbing others, by grinding the faces of the poor, by withholding the workman's wages, etc. In fact, the world is full of that.

But God does not operate His Kingdom on that basis. He has designed the Law, and a Law it is, of sowing and reaping. What a man sows he shall reap (Gal. 6:7).

By the way in which you sow, God lets you yourself say in advance in what way, what kind of harvest, and how much you want to reap. Sow *"sparingly"* if you will, just a few grains — what a pity to throw more into the ground! *"Sparingly you will also reap."* You certainly do not expect a few grains to produce barn-fulls. You certainly know at sowing time for what size of harvest you are sowing.

AN EXAMPLE

Let me give you an example which I have given in other of these Volumes; therefore, I will be brief.

Years ago I was preaching a meeting in a Church in Albuquerque, New Mexico. In one of the Services I casually made the statement, *"Don't give to God according to what you are presently making, but give to Him according to what you want to make."*

About two years later, if I remember correctly, I went back to that city for a convention. A man met me at the airport with whom I was

NOTES

not acquainted. As we were driving to the hotel, he said to me, *"Brother Swaggart, I asked if I could pick you up, because I wanted to give you a Testimony."*

He told how he had been in our Meeting some two years before, and had heard me make the statement, *"Don't give to God according to what you are making, but give to Him according to what you want to make."*

He said, *"Brother Swaggart, that got down into my spirit. It was God's Rhema Word to me."*

He went on to tell how that at that particular time he and his wife were close to bankruptcy, actually not knowing what they were going to do. Beginning that very week, he said, they began to give to God, at least as they were able to do so, according to what they wanted to make.

A few weeks later a man approached him about taking over a Dairy Queen in the city of Albuquerque. Actually, the man offered to sell it to him with nothing down. On those terms he bought that particular business.

To make the story short, he said (if I remember correctly), *"Brother Swaggart, I now own three Dairy Queens, and I am in the process of buying two more. It all started with that Word of Truth that you gave that night and God made real to my heart. I acted on that which I heard. I began to sow according to the harvest I wanted, and God was faithful to His Word, and has blessed me abundantly. That is the reason I wanted to pick you up and just say 'Thank you!'"*

Even as I dictate these words I sense the Presence of God. If you the Reader, will take to heart what has been said, make it a Rhema Word to your heart and life, you can be certain that God will always do exactly what He has said. If we sow bountifully, we shall reap bountifully. (A Rhema word is a special word given by God to you.)

THE PLURAL

The Greek Scholars tell us that the plural is real in these Texts. It pluralizes the singular, which actually speaks of multiplication, which is the principle of grain. He who sows *"on the basis of, on the principle of blessings,"* he shall reap on this basis and this principle.

This sowing is ever done on one idea alone, on the idea of Blessings — Blessings, Praises to God; Blessings, Blessings to men; returned Blessings to ourselves. On no other basis or principle does this sower operate. On this basis he reaps. He reaps all the Blessings to God and all those to men, and he reaps the returned Blessings that God pours out on him.

It is all very wonderful, yet also true.

The Catholic exegesis finds in this a works-righteousness, namely the harvest as a reward of merit. However, no man ever earned a harvest. God makes seed, soil, sunshine, growth, ripening, and even the brain and the hand to place the seed into the soil and to bring the increase home. No, it is God Who gives the increase, and not we ourselves (I Cor. 3:6-7).

FAITH

As always, Faith enters into all of this which we are saying. In fact, God uses all of these things to teach us Trust, confidence in Him, dependence on Him, and Faith in His Word. We must believe that God honors His Word, but to be frank, that's not difficult to do.

Why is it difficult to believe God, when we can look at all the things He does, such as the rotation of this earth every 24 hours, the rising of the Sun, etc., plus a million other things which could be named, which always function without fail, and because God is the Creator. If He can do all of that, we should understand by the things we see, that He'll have no problem keeping His Word in these matters (Rom. 1:19-20).

Admittedly, the Lord at times tests our Faith, consequently, allowing or bringing about circumstances which at the outset seem difficult; however, it is irrespective all for our good. In the overall scheme of things, it is easy to believe God. He is One in Whom one can trust. He has a record of thousands of years of Faithfulness, and the evidence as stated, which is abundant before us at all times.

So, obey Him, believe Him, and the results will be great. He promised it, and He will do it.

(7) "EVERY MAN ACCORDING AS HE PURPOSETH IN HIS HEART, SO LET HIM GIVE; NOT GRUDGINGLY, OR OF NECESSITY: FOR GOD LOVETH A CHEERFUL GIVER."

We are given here additional instructions, which at the same time, bring out additional Truths. In other words, the Lord makes it so easy for us to obey Him, and the reason is that

NOTES

He desires to bless us. Nevertheless, it must be on His terms, and not ours.

FREEWILL

The phrase, *"Every man according as he purposeth in his heart,"* refers to freewill giving. It means giving without compulsion. In fact, it means giving without regulation or constraint or force of any kind. It is giving by one's own individual intention. It is something free from assessment. The amount of our gift cannot be assigned to us by another, at least as far as man is concerned. It is solely our choice, relative to God's Will.

The Greek structure of the Text, brings out the idea that the Believer idea chooses freely what he wants and would like to have for himself, whether he wants a sparing return or one that is running over with all kinds of Blessings.

WHAT IS TO DETERMINE OUR CHOICE, AS TO THE AMOUNT OF OUR GIFT?

Are we free to say that we will give a dollar when we are able to give ten? The proportion of our giving is subject to the need and also subject to the Lord. The Law of the Tenth, as we have already explained, is a wise and fair proportion, but even this is not the final standard, as should be obvious in these two Chapters. The highest Standard is the Holy Spirit Whose promptings will give sensitive Christian souls the most accurate measurement of choice. But, remember, it is to be by our choice and by our freewill.

Paul wants nothing but voluntary gifts for his great Collection. Consequently, he here sets forth voluntariness as being the only true motive and principle of Christian giving. If it is anything other than that, it is not actually giving. Such actuated the Apostolic Church (Acts 2:44-45; 4:22); it has ever distinguished true Christian Giving.

SO LET HIM GIVE

The phrase, *"So let him give,"* actually speaks of that which is dictated by the heart.

As someone has said, the heart is usually more concerned in the business of giving than the head. If liberality is evinced, it will be the heart which prompts to it; if it is not evinced, it will be because the heart has some bad passions to gratify, and is under the influence of avarice, or selfishness, or some other improper attachment.

Very often a man is convinced he ought to give liberally, but a narrow heart and a stingy spirit prevent it.

Of course, what we are stating here, is the exact opposite of what many will say. They will claim that one should give according to their head and not their heart. That may be true respecting things of this world, but it is never true regarding things of God.

The Truth is, that God has implanted the generous feelings in the heart that would prompt us to do good; and he who acts most in accordance with them is most likely to do what he ought to do; and in general it is the safest and best rule to give just what his heart prompts him to give when a need concerning the Work of God is presented.

Man at best is too selfish to be likely to give too much, or to go beyond his means; and if in a few instances it should be done, more would be gained in value in the cultivation of this great principle, than would ever be lost in money. In fact, no one has ever lost anything by giving to God.

NOT GRUDGINGLY, OR OF NECESSITY

The phrase, *"Not grudgingly, or of necessity,"* actually says, *"If it is not willing giving, it is not really Christian Giving!"*

This refers to giving for a reason such as circumstances, fear of criticism, custom, external peer pressure, commercial motives, greed, etc. When giving has a view only to reward, it ceases to be Christian Giving!

A CHEERFUL GIVER

The phrase, *"For God loveth a cheerful giver,"* actually means *"a hilarious giver."*

From this we gather that God's approval and our profit are not to be determined by the amount of our gift, but rather by the spirit in and the motive behind the gift. This is so because in giving, God is seeking to develop and enlarge the resources of the giver.

Giving is not merely a means of distributing money or even charity. It is a means of developing character. For this reason God seeks our cooperation in the spirit of joy and love, rather than from compulsion and constraint.

NOTES

In fact, in this last analysis it is a question of Christ's Lordship and our loyalty.

As valuable as any gift may be in itself, yet if it is forced and constrained, who can esteem it as desirable? God as stated, desires the heart in every service. No service that is not cheerful and voluntary, none that does not arise from true love to Him, can be acceptable in His Sight.

God loves a cheerful giver because it shows a heart like His Own — a heart disposed to give cheerfully, and to do good on the largest scale possible; and because it shows a heart attached from principle to His Service and Cause.

In nothing, therefore, is it more important than to examine the motives by which we give, for this is the intent of this phrase. However, liberal may be our giving, yet God may see that there is no sincerity, and may even hate the spirit with which it is done.

Israel was never at a higher spiritual level than when Moses actually had to call a halt to their hilarious giving for the Tabernacle (Ex. 35:4-36:7). The Lord instructed that it was to be a willing Offering (Ex. 25:2), and that's exactly what it was, and that's exactly why God blessed it so abundantly.

(8) "AND GOD IS ABLE TO MAKE ALL GRACE ABOUND TOWARD YOU; THAT YE, ALWAYS HAVING ALL SUFFICIENCY IN ALL THINGS, MAY ABOUND TO EVERY GOOD WORK:"

We were told in the previous Verses as to what the Believer should do, with Paul now saying what God will do.

GOD IS ABLE

The phrase, *"And God is able to make all Grace abound toward you,"* presents the ability of God, and that His Gift to us is of far greater magnitude than mere money, i.e., *"Grace."* This *"Grace"* refers to all kinds of favor. He is able to impart to us those things which are needful for our welfare.

As well, the word *"Grace"* glaringly portrays another great Truth.

Our giving, no matter how generous it may be, within itself cannot earn anything from God. As we have said repeatedly, the Lord has nothing for sale.

Also, God needs nothing, so all of this is for our benefit and definitely not His.

All of this is to teach us trust and confidence in Him. In effect, it is an entering into God's Economy, which is an Economy of *"giving"* (Jn. 3:16; Lk. 12:22-32).

Furthermore, the *"Grace"* which God gives us, is *"abounding Grace!"*

In the Greek the verb is placed emphatically forward: *"Able is God."* Paul first presents His Ability, what God *can* do, which implies His Willingness; and then in Verse 10 what God *will* do.

The idea of the statement as Paul used it, is not reliance based on his own ability to move the Corinthians as they ought to be moved, but on God's Ability alone. He tells the Corinthians that, and thereby, turns their hearts to God. Thus Paul excludes the idea that he is belaboring the Corinthians with appeals of his own, for this is far from his mind. Abounding Grace as given by God is to bring abounding good works.

ALL GRACE

"All Grace" could be translated *"Every Grace."* It denotes, as previously stated, multiplicity. Grace is a unit, but as an active attribute of God He bestows many different Gifts of Grace, and each exhibits a certain form. John 1:16 says *"Grace for Grace." "Every Grace"* is comprehensive in its multiplicity; it omits not a single Gift of Grace that we may need. Since it is *"Grace,"* every Gift is totally undeserved — pure, sweet Grace through and through.

ALL SUFFICIENCY

The phrase, *"That ye always having all sufficiency in all things,"* does not limit Grace merely to money or even to earthly possessions. The Child of God is to be sufficient in *"all things,"* which includes the physical, mental, economical, and spiritual.

The sense is, if you give liberally, you are to expect that God will furnish you with the means, so that you will be able to abound more and more in it. You are to expect that He will abundantly qualify you for doing good in every way, and that He will furnish you with all that is needed for this. The man who gives, therefore, should have Faith in God. He should expect that God will bless him in it; and the experience of the Christian world may be appealed to in proof that men are not made poor by liberality.

NOTES

ABOUND

The phrase, *"May abound to every good work,"* refers to the Believer taking the bounty that God has given him, and liberally dispensing it out to needs in every area.

Note the heaping up of *"every,"* or *"all."* In essence it is *"Every Grace," "Every Sufficiency," "Every Good Work."* God, indeed, knows no limit.

The main feature is, however, to see that God's bestowal of *"Every Grace"* in abundance means our *"having in everything every sufficiency in abundance for every good work." "Every Grace"* is thus practically defined for us. Here there is a stream that is full to the banks.

All these many good works we need in our hearts: Faith, Love, Tenderness, Pity, Strength, Courage, Energy, Zeal, Enlightenment, Wisdom, etc. All the sufficiency God is able to supply.

IMPROPER INTERPRETATION

Some Commentators claim that Paul borrowed the word *"sufficiency"* from Greek Philosophy, which limits its meaning, i.e., *"only having barely enough, and expecting nothing beyond it."*

To be sure, Paul did not invent the word; however, in the way he uses it in the common Greek, it rather means *"a complete supply, one, however, that is provided by God."*

The idea is, that God is able to provide us with such abundance that none of us ever need to hesitate about dispensing it with full hands in all manner of good works. In fact, that we rely on His supplying us and thus engage to the limit in good works — this is His intention.

The entire Structure of the Greek Text upholds this view in every circumstance of its meaning.

(9) "(AS IT IS WRITTEN, HE HATH DISPERSED ABROAD; HE HATH GIVEN TO THE POOR: HIS RIGHTEOUSNESS REMAINETH FOR EVER."

The purpose of Divine Grace is to increase the resources of the hilarious giver so that he may be able to respond in other cases of need. God's Gifts to us are not intended for selfish consumption. They are intended to serve others.

There is a great challenge in this principle of giving. Whoever will dare to step out upon this Promise of Divine Grace will have a sufficiency for another's deficiency; he will have an abundance for another's lack.

The problem is not on the Divine Side, but the human. With God there is always sufficient ability. He waits only for enterprising children who will dare to believe and act upon this challenging Promise. Our sufficiency will be through His supply. This means that by the Law of Faith we will tap the resources of God and turn them into practical good, which is the Lord's intention.

The only reason we do not have *"all sufficiency"* for all emergencies is because we do not believe it is possible. It is easy for us to say the words in these Verses, but it is another thing to put our lives into the place of their power.

IT IS WRITTEN

The phrase, *"As it is written,"* is taken from Psalms 112:9.

Once again, Paul bases everything on the Word. The Psalmist is describing the character of the Righteous Man. Actually, as do all the Psalms, this speaks of the Messiah.

His Righteousness *"remaineth for ever,"* that is, God does not tire, as men do, of giving largely and continuously.

Most have taken Verse 9 to refer to Believers. However, if we understand that the Psalms speak in their entirety of Christ, and that Verse 8 refers to God and the first part of Verse 10, then we must come to the conclusion, that Verse 9 does not refer to Believers giving to the *"poor,"* but rather the Lord giving to the poor, etc.

DISPERSED ABROAD

The phrase, *"He hath dispersed abroad,"* refers to the Promises of God applying to all of mankind and for all time. God is no respecter of persons, what He does for one, He will do for another, providing the conditions of Righteousness and Faith are met (Acts 10:34).

THE POOR

The phrase, *"He hath given to the poor,"* refers to the fact that Jesus Christ is the only hope of the *"poor,"* or anyone else for that matter.

Back in the 1980's we were conducting citywide Crusades all over the world, but with most being conducted in Central and South America. The Lord specifically spoke to my heart concerning these Meetings, that I should tell the people, and without fail, that Jesus and Jesus Alone is their Answer. If they are looking toward Government to help them, or even America, or any other source for that matter, they are going to be sadly disappointed; however, if they will look to the Lord, He Alone is able to meet their need.

I preached that Message basically all over the world, with great hope being given to these many thousands, and with great numbers responding to the invitation to accept Christ. The directions by the Holy Spirit were straightforward and to the point. *"Tell them that Jesus is their only Answer, and that refers to every facet of their lives."*

Regrettably, the *"poor"* are exploited all over the world. Very few truly care about them, but Jesus does! He is able to bring the *"poor"* out of poverty, out of ignorance, and above all out of spiritual darkness.

HIS RIGHTEOUSNESS

The phrase, *"His Righteousness remaineth for ever,"* refers to the Righteousness of Christ.

"Righteousness" speaks here of the fact that God will never change. He will always *"do right."*

As well, His Promises are based on His Righteousness; therefore, they cannot change. What He promised yesterday, He continues to promise today, and will promise tomorrow. As well, His Righteousness demands, that these Promises be kept. If God at any time, failed to keep even one Promise, that would mean that His Righteousness has failed, which is impossible!

IN THE PLACE WHERE THE TREE FALLETH, THERE IT SHALL BE

Ecclesiastes 11:1-6, gives one of the greatest Promises found in the entirety of the Word of God, regarding the provision of the Lord claimed and received by Faith.

In the Third Verse it says, *"And if the tree fall toward the south, or toward the north, in the place where the tree falleth, there it shall be."*

The idea is, that millions of people think that due to their situation they cannot be blessed. They live in the North while the Blessings are falling in the South, or vice versa.

The Holy Spirit is saying, that irrespective as to which way the tree falls, if the person will believe God, stand upon His Promises, sow bountifully, that irrespective as to where the person may be, what proverbial strikes are against that person, what difficulties there may seem to be, God is bigger than all of that, and can work in any type of situation, thereby bringing prosperity, if man will only believe Him.

In regard to the harvest, if the person has sowed bountifully, the harvest will be bountiful as well. God's Righteousness is at stake, and stands behind every single Promise. We can rest assured, that there is no time limit, it *"remaineth for ever."*

(10) "NOW HE THAT MINISTERETH SEED TO THE SOWER BOTH MINISTER BREAD FOR YOUR FOOD, AND MULTIPLY YOUR SEED SOWN, AND INCREASE THE FRUITS OF YOUR RIGHTEOUSNESS:)"

Even though these two Chapters deal primarily with economic prosperity, as well, the tenor of the Text encompasses the entirety of one's relationship with the Lord.

In view of this, the Holy Spirit last night in Prayer Meeting (8/31/98) began to move upon my heart to believe God for a harvest of souls, actually a great harvest. At the time of this writing our Prayer Group, for about seven years, has been meeting together daily for many and varied reasons; however, the greatest intercession by far is for this harvest of which we speak, actually a Worldwide harvest of souls. In a powerful manner the Holy Spirit impressed upon me that II Corinthians 9:6 encompasses that as well, and actually anything for that matter which pertains to the Lord. In this respect we have sowed bountifully, and I believe with all of my heart that the Lord has told us that we are going to *"reap also bountifully."*

THE MINISTRY OF GOD

The phrase, *"Now He that ministereth seed to the sower,"* speaks of the Lord, and harks back to Verse 9.

From what God is *able* to do the thought proceeds to what God *will* do. His ability, of course, already implies His willingness even as His willingness implies His ability. God's Purpose is *"that you abound in every good work"* (vs. 8); this Purpose carries out, for Paul now says we shall see: *"He will increase the fruits of your Righteousness."* Thus, the final object is attained.

"Ministereth" in the Greek is *"epichoregeo,"* and means *"to supply, to aid."*

What God does in the domain of nature (for this is the symbolism He uses), He will in a higher, richer way do in the domain of Grace. Actually no greater illustration could be used. We see this every time a man sows grain. It is God Who provides that *"seed,"* and the means for it to germinate.

As well, the word *"ministereth"* also carries the idea of a great, free generosity. It is, indeed, with a lavish hand that God supplies seed and bread for mankind.

NOTES

A PRACTICAL ILLUSTRATION

Continuing the theme of God supplying seed to the sower, and looking at it in the natural, we are told that this present earth, even now under the curse, has the wherewithal to supply food for a hundred billion people. However, there are many things which hinder this, namely war, religion, a lack of Faith in God, and plain ignorance — all which have their origination in Satan. So, the idea that the population explosion is going to tax the food supply is ridiculous to say the least.

While there definitely is hunger in this world at the present time, it is not caused by God's lack of supply, but rather by destructive forces (Jn. 10:10).

The same holds true in the sense of the spiritual. God has provided all the *"seed"* that is needed, even an overabundant supply, as it regards money, victory over sin, spiritual growth, means of Worldwide Evangelism, physical healing, prosperity in every capacity, etc.; however, even as war, religion, and ignorance, hinder the growth of natural food and in a great way we might quickly add, it does the same in the spiritual sense. In other words, all of us, and I speak of those who truly believe the Lord, only attain a portion (and sometimes a very small portion) of what we could actually have in abundance, if we would only follow the Lord with all of our heart, soul, and strength. Whatever it is we are lacking, the fault is not on the part of the Lord, for He has supplied enough *"seed"* in every capacity, and for every circumstance, for every situation, not only to have victory, but an abundant supply of victory, even to such an extent that it beggars description. The entirety of this Text is literally loaded with these guarantees.

So why don't we believe God, even with a runaway Faith, for God loves Faith, and take advantage of this abundant supply, which the Lord actually delights in us doing.

BREAD FOR YOUR FOOD

The phrase, *"Both minister bread for your food,"* presents the first part of God's Laws of the spiritual world. The idea is, that God has given everything that is needed, and an abundant supply at that, that we may be and do what He desires in our hearts and lives.

Christ and the Apostles see these beautiful and instructive correspondences between nature and Grace and use them most effectively. Men generally and even Christians so often fail to see them. In fact, worldly men fail even to see the Hand of God in the domain of nature and talk only about the *"laws of nature,"* etc., and thus fail to let the Goodness of God lead them to repentance (Rom. 2:4) and furthermore, do not even thank Him (Rom. 1:21-22).

Paul is probably deriving this Verse from Isaiah 55:10. The spirit of the Text is, that God is the Source of all increase. Satan subtracts while the Lord multiplies (Jn. 10:10).

So, the Believer must first of all look to God as the Source and not only the Source, but the Source of all increase as well. In other words, God is not dishing out the seed in tight-fisted amounts, but rather in an overabundant supply. Actually, the entirety of the tenor of Scriptures points to this. The Holy Spirit said through Malachi, *"Prove Me now herewith, saith the Lord of Hosts, if I will not open you the windows of Heaven, and pour you out a Blessing, that there shall not be room enough to receive it"* (Mal. 3:10). Regarding spiritual things, Joel prophesied and Peter quoted, *"And it shall come to pass in the last days, saith God, I will pour out of My Spirit upon all flesh"* (Acts 2:17). Here again we have the words *"pour out!"* Jesus said, *"But seek ye first the Kingdom of God, and His Righteousness; and all these things shall be added unto you"* (Mat. 6:33). Notice, He said *"added,"* and not *"subtracted!"*

The word *"food"* as it is used in this Tenth Verse, of course, first of all speaks of natural food, for this is the symbolism being used; however, it was symbolism used for a purpose, meaning for the Reader to understand that it applies in the spiritual as well, and actually in every capacity.

A MISTAKE!

Men make a mistake when they limit God in any manner. As we have already stated, when a person comes to Christ, they enter into God's Economy (Lk. 12:22-32). This speaks of God's Way, and His abundant supply for everything. In other words, it is the whole Gospel for the whole man. This speaks of the spiritual (Salvation and the Baptism with the Holy Spirit), the physical (this speaks of Divine health and Divine healing), mental (this speaks of peace of mind, sense of well-being, peace with God) and financial (this speaks of prosperity in an abundant way).

NOTES

If we had to supply the seed, of course, the situation would be hopeless. But God supplies the seed and abundantly so, and all that is required for us to reap the harvest of that seed, is to properly sow it, which speaks of giving in every capacity, because *that* is the Economy of God. Have Faith in God, and then reap a bountiful harvest. It is just that simple!

MULTIPLICATION

The phrase, *"And multiply your seed sown,"* presents the harvest. Notice that He said, *"multiply!"* As we have previously stated, Satan subtracts, but God multiplies.

How much multiplication do we desire? Whatever it is, it is limited only by the seed that we sow. Let's look at that a moment.

If it is spiritual growth that we desire, and most certainly all and above all, should desire that, we must sow the seed of close relationship with the Lord, which can only be done by the means of prayer, study of the Word, and a hunger and thirst for Righteousness. If we are speaking of the physical, we must use our Faith to believe God to keep us in health, and to give us healing if such is needed.

The Lord wondrously healed me when I was about ten years old. Without going into detail, for all practical purposes I have not been sick since, and that has been over fifty years ago at the time of this writing. The same is true for the entirety of my family. We give the Lord all the Praise and Glory. We have done our best to sow the seed of physical well-being, despite the fact that the outward man is slowly perishing.

Regarding the mental, we must sow the seed of Faith in God respecting this *"more abundant life."* This is by and large anchored in the Word of God which produces Faith, moreso than anything else. Once again, it is God's Economy.

Concerning financial resources, we must sow the seed which speaks of giving. Our giving must be a motivation of love for God. As well, we must give to that which is truly of God, of which there will be proper fruit.

So, it is all a matter of sowing the seed which God has already provided. Unfortunately, millions of Christians sit around moaning and complaining about a lack of harvest, when in spiritual reality they have not sowed any seed for a harvest.

As I mentioned in a previous paragraph, the Holy Spirit last night in Prayer Meeting impressed this upon me greatly. Regarding the harvest of souls of which we so much desire, He said to my heart, *"You have been sowing seed for this for several years, now believe Me that this harvest is going to be great."*

This I do believe!

THE FRUITS OF YOUR RIGHTEOUSNESS

The phrase, *"And increase the fruits of your Righteousness,"* speaks of the results and effects. God will not only *"furnish"* in the domain of Grace, He will even *"multiply,"* He will even *"augment."* To keep men alive with bread is a smaller matter for God than to load His Christians with the abundance of His Grace. The bread which He furnishes to men in the natural is only *"food that perishes"*; He wants us to have the *"food that endures to Eternal Life"* (Jn. 6:27).

As we are studying here, Paul calls this *"the fruits of your Righteousness,"* actually of that Righteousness which *"remains for ever,"* meaning, that God will never change His Economy. John 15:8 adds that the Father is glorified when we bear much fruit of this kind, and thereby show that we are Christ's Disciples. In other words, the Holy Spirit through the Apostle, is telling us that we should be victorious in every capacity.

The idea of all of this is that God will not only supply the *"seed,"* but as well, the means for the *"seed"* to develop, grow, and to produce a crop. The only thing He requires of us is to properly *"sow"* the seed, and have Faith in Him to bring forth the harvest.

The structure of the Greek Text is that God will do these things now. It is not something that is merely futuristic, and that presents another hindrance for the Child of God.

A NOW GOD

While God definitely does promise great things for the future, that is not what is being described here. God is a *"now"* God! He works now; He provides now; He wants us to believe Him now.

While it should be obvious that it takes a while for seed to germinate and grow; still, the duration should not be long regarding any harvest Please understand, that the symbolism carries on out in every capacity.

While in the natural some particular crops may take a little longer to come to fruition than others, still, it is not that much longer. The great delays, if there is a delay, are caused by our lack of Faith, or disobedience on our part, or sowing the seed in bad ground. In other words, the fault is not God's but ours.

On God's part the will is always there to provide this increase of fruits of Righteousness in the way indicated. If the increase is not forthcoming, this is due to our unwillingness in some capacity. We do not let God multiply the crop we have or we do not even care to obtain the fruits.

What a delight it is to any farmer to have many fields growing toward harvest! How pitiful it is if he has but a tiny patch! So it is with regard to me and you in our spiritual life. Now God's Will for us is literally to multiply our sowings, to increase the resultant fruits to the utmost.

If one is to notice, the Lord puts all of this on a spiritual plain, hence calling it *"the fruits of Righteousness."* That means, that every Believer must understand, that everything he does, all that pertains to him, even that which seems to be altogether secular, still, are actually in the domain of God's Economy, thereby spiritual. The Believer is to *never* separate anything from this. In other words, there is no such thing, at least in the true sense of the word, of anything being outside the spiritual domain of the Believer. If we allow such to happen, we invite disaster.

This means that our job of driving a truck to provide for our family, or whatever for that matter, is not in the Eyes of God, just a job. It is where He has placed us, that is if He has truly placed us there, and we are to always look at this task in a spiritual sense, doing it as unto the Lord.

RIGHTEOUSNESS

Everything in the life of the Believer comes under the heading of *"Righteousness,"* which

NOTES

means that it passes under the scrutiny of the Word of God. If one is to notice, Paul placed everything on a spiritual level, irrespective as to how mundane, insignificant, or seemingly unspiritual it may be.

In fact, the great crime of Believers is leaving God at the Church door. In fact, we are the Temple of God, not some particular building made out of wood or stone, etc. So, our speech must be in the realm of Righteousness, our actions in the realm of Righteousness, our thoughts in the realm of Righteousness, our doings in the realm of Righteousness and irrespective as to whatever that may be. Everything comes under *"Righteousness."*

That's the reason that Jesus said, *"Blessed are they which do hunger and thirst after Righteousness: for they shall be filled"* (Mat. 5:6). Notice, He said, *"filled!"*

As well, He said, *"But seek ye first the Kingdom of God, and His Righteousness; and all these things shall be added unto you"* (Mat. 6:33).

God's Kingdom is that of *"Righteousness,"* which means, *"The way things are,"* and His Economy is Righteousness as well, which means, *"the way things are done."*

This Economy is based on three basic things:

1. God will supply seed for the one who desires to sow.
2. He will cause that seed to multiply abundantly so the harvest will expand constantly.
3. In all of this He will provide for the basic needs of the sower.

Unfortunately, many people concentrate on the third item — the satisfaction of their own needs — that they forget the other two. Consequently, when they do this they step outside the Economy of God, which then destroys the harvest. Let us say it again:

God's Economy is based on *"Giving." "God so loved the world that He gave. . . ."* (Jn. 3:16). However, this *"Giving"* must be based on the realm of Righteousness, which demands the right motivation and the right purpose.

(11) "BEING ENRICHED IN EVERY THING TO ALL BOUNTIFULNESS, WHICH CAUSETH THROUGH US THANKSGIVING TO GOD."

The Bible completely contradicts the notion that if we give our finances to God, He will reward us financially for the sole purpose of our own personal benefit. This He will not do, and for all the obvious reasons.

NOTES

Just yesterday (8/31/98) Frances and I, along with Donnie and Debbie, had lunch with a young man and his wife who are members of our Church, actually some of the pillars of the Church.

They have a particular type of business which the Lord has begun to bless abundantly. To be sure, they have properly sowed the seed, and have actually caught the vision here of which Paul speaks.

The lady remonstrated as to how the Lord had spoken to their hearts that He was going to bless them; however, that Blessing was not to be hoarded. While they were to provide a good living for themselves, they were to bless the Kingdom of God. They both were adamant and rightly so, that the Lord had specifically instructed them in this. In other words, they were to take this harvest and give it to others, which is God's Economy. In this case, and as they related, it speaks of helping us to take this Gospel of Jesus Christ to a lost and dying world. They have caught the vision and the burden of that. The Salvation of souls has now become a part of their spiritual and mental make-up. This is the *"Righteousness"* of which the Holy Spirit speaks here through Paul.

As long as they stay in that capacity, and which I believe they always will, God will always give an abundant harvest. However, this is the area which destroys the harvest in most lives. We become selfish and greedy, even though we always cover ourselves with pious-sounding phrases.

For instance, God blesses the businessman abundantly, but he gives little to the Lord, claiming that he's investing everything in other business operations in order to have much more to give later on. Sorry, but it doesn't work that way!

Whoever does such a thing, steps outside of God's Economy. If we will properly give, and to the right Ministry, the Lord will see to the increase of the harvest, i.e., *"other business opportunities."* However, if we hoard and refuse to give, consequently investing everything in things other than God's Work, the system breaks down. In fact, this is where many Believers go astray. When they then meet trouble down the road, they are quick to exclaim that this of which the Bible teaches, simply doesn't work.

Oh yes, it works! It's just that we don't do right many times. If we do it God's Way, which must be done without fail, the harvest will come despite circumstances or situations.

ENRICHED IN EVERYTHING

The phrase, *"Being enriched in every thing to all bountifulness,"* proclaims the fact that this great Plan of God for our prosperity, must not be limited to money alone, but must include everything regarding life and Godliness (II Pet. 1:3-4).

That is one of the great mistakes of the so-called *"Prosperity Message".* While what they teach regarding sowing and reaping is by and large correct, the motivation and end result are wrong, simply because they have made financial prosperity the goal. That is not the Scriptural idea as taught here by Paul. While such is a part of the whole, it is only a part. The Holy Spirit is interested in developing us totally and completely, and this means in every respect. The idea of a Believer giving money to the Lord strictly in order to get money from the Lord, misses the point entirely.

Some may ask as to how I know this is being done in that particular system?

The old adage is true when it says, *"If it walks like a duck, quacks like a duck, etc., it just might be a duck."* If the emphasis is placed on money, to the neglect of Righteousness and Holiness, all that we are saying quickly becomes obvious.

It is not the purpose of the Holy Spirit to make us rich at least in the realm of silver and gold. His purpose is to develop in us *"fruits of Righteousness,"* of which the other is but a part. I'll say it again:

The goal in mind regarding the Holy Spirit is not mere money, but rather "Righteousness." If we lose sight of that, we've lost sight of everything.

The *"riches"* of which the Holy Spirit through Paul speaks here, consist in God providing everything for the Corinthians so that they could put their minds on one single thing without having other conflicting considerations. That one thing is twofold:

THANKSGIVING TO GOD

The phrase, *"Which causeth through us thanksgiving to God,"* presents the second Work of the Holy Spirit, the first being the development of *"fruits of Righteousness"* (vs. 10). That is the twofold work which the Holy Spirit is carrying out.

The idea in this phrase concerning *"thanksgiving to God,"* is to have as many people as possible thanking Him, which means that He wants to bless people. The more He blesses, the more thanksgiving there is.

Belay the thought that God is egotistical and desires praise on that score. Such thinking is ridiculous!

The idea is, that the individual know and realize that it is God Who does all of this, and not man. Due to the Fall, man has a problem of self-dependency and self-sufficiency, which of course, is false. Man was created to draw sustenance and life from God and not from himself or other sources. In other words, everything that man needs comes from the Lord.

But due to the Fall as stated, man has a tendency, even Godly Believers, to start thinking that maybe their consecration or dedication or ability, etc., are the cause of these Blessings. Understanding that God is the One Who supplies all things to us, and properly thanking Him for these things, abrogates the cause and direction of the Fall. The Believer must ever understand that the Lord is the Source, is the Supply, is the Benefactor, is the One Who does all things. Proper thanksgiving to Him goes back to the manner in which man was originally created.

TOTAL DEPENDENCY

The closer one gets to God, the more one enjoys His Blessings, the more one realizes one's total dependency in everything on the Lord. As stated, this is the manner of man's original creation, and we fulfill our creaturely role only when we have a proper understanding of such, which in effect, guides our lives. We are to have a single-mindedness in this matter. In other words, nothing is to hinder a constant thanksgiving to God, with a constant knowledge that we derive all things from Him.

Romans 1:21 combines Glorifying God and Thanking God, for we glorify Him best when we thank His Holy Name. The highest aim for all of us should be this single purpose, to multiply thanksgivings to God. In fact, the Preacher's highest work is to aid those who sit under him in attaining this aim.

That's at least one of the reasons that the Psalmist said, *"Enter into His gates with thanksgiving, and into His courts with praise: be thankful unto Him, and bless His Name."*

And now he gives the reason, *"For the Lord is good; His Mercy is everlasting; and His Truth endureth to all generations"* (Ps. 100:4-5).

I have noticed in my own prayer life, that the Holy Spirit always leads me into thanksgiving and praise to the Lord. In other words, a great part of my prayer time is spent in this function. Little by little and more and more I learn that everything I am, everything I have, everything I hope to be, is wrapped up in my relationship with the Lord.

So, the efforts of the Holy Spirit are to produce *"fruits of Righteousness,"* and *"thanksgiving to God."*

THANKSGIVING

The Old Testament has no concept parallel to the English word *"thanks,"* that is, simply an expression of appreciation to other persons or to God. What do the words *"thanks"* and *"thanksgiving"* mean in the Old Testament?

The Hebrew word is *"yadah,"* which with its derivative *"totah,"* often translated *"thanks"* or *"thanksgiving."* It means *"to declare publicly"* or *"to acknowledge."*

It is used of the confession of human sin and also of public confession of God's Character and Works.

In the latter usage (todah), the Hebrew concept is that of praise, not thanksgiving.

The New Testament words translated *"thank* (eucharisteo)," *"thankful* (eucharistos)," and *"thanksgiving* (eucharistia)" signify a thankful attitude and a demonstration of gratitude. Only in three Passages (Lk. 17:16; Acts 24:3; Rom. 16:4) are these words used of thanks given to human beings.

THREE PRIMARY ASSOCIATIONS

In the New Testament, the swelling sense of gratitude and appreciation expressed in thanksgiving has three primary associations:

1. Thanks is given at the eucharist (Communion Service) for the broken Body and the Blood of Jesus (Mat. Chpt. 26; Mk. Chpt. 14; Lk. Chpt. 22; I Cor. Chpt. 11).

2. Thanks is given for the Blessings that have come to us through Christ, which we are even now studying (I Cor. 15:57; II Cor. 2:14; 9:11, 15).

3. Thanks is given for those who come to know Christ and who bring joy to Paul's heart (I Cor. 1:4; Eph. 1:16; Phil. 1:3; Col. 1:3; I Thess. 1:2; 2:13; Phile. vs. 4). Remembering all that Jesus has done for us and in us, it is appropriate to address every prayer with thanksgiving (Phil. 4:6).

NOTES

CAUSE

The Holy Spirit through the Apostle used the word *"causeth,"* which not only speaks of an act, but as well, that of purpose. Consequently, I think it would be profitable to look at this word a little further.

There are two senses in which the word *"cause"* is used in the Bible. One (a noun) is reflected in the Psalmist's cry, *"Defend the cause of the weak"* (Ps. 82:3).

The other is reflected in this dramatic question: *"When disaster comes to a city, has not the Lord caused it?"* (Amos 3:6).

THE JUST CAUSE

The Bible speaks of God as One Who *"defends the cause of the fatherless and the widow"* (Deut. 10:18; Isa. 1:17; Jer. 22:16). The Psalmists often call on God to act to uphold the cause of the weak (82:3), the needy (140:12), and the oppressed (146:7).

A number of different Hebrew words are translated *"cause"* in such Passages. But each implies a dispute, controversy, or law suit that must be brought to someone to settle.

Typically, appeals to God to defend or uphold a cause are made by those who are powerless, or who are being unjustly persecuted. Such appeals are based on the Old Testament Believers' firm conviction that God is faithful to those who keep His Covenant and that He is fully able to act in the world of men.

CAUSATION

All of us can look at a given situation and isolate factors that are causes of events. This is also common in Scripture. For example, according to John 12:18, *"Many people, because they had heard that He* (Jesus) *had given this miraculous sign, went out to meet Him."* A Miracle performed by Jesus was the proximate cause of the curious crowd going out to see Him for themselves.

NOTES

The Old Testament is full of similar expressions. Exodus 23:33 gives God's warning against letting the Canaanites remain after Israel was conquered. Contact with their religion would cause them to sin against God. Elisha purified the tainted waters of a poisonous spring and gave the people God's Promise: *"Never again will it cause death or make the land unproductive"* (II Ki. 2:21).

Judah's King Amaziah was warned against the pride that prompted him to attack Israel, for it would cause his own downfall (II Ki. 14:10).

CAUSE AND EFFECT

In each of these cases, Scripture looks at a given situation and points to choices or to events that cause other events. Cause and effect clearly do operate in our world of space and time. Anyone looking at a given situation will often be able to identify those things that serve as causes of subsequent events.

In both Testaments, cause and effect are spoken of within the framework provided by specific situations. But Scripture does not take the logical leap of Faith made by many Philosophers.

Scripture never suggests that the idea of proximate cause (immediate cause within the given situation) can be extended to forge some endless chain in which every event can and must be explained only in terms of preceding causes. When the notion of cause and effect is so extended, we are left with a mechanical universe. In such a universe, human beings would be trapped, having neither freedom nor responsibility.

There is a great difference between, on the one hand, seeing cause and effect operate within the framework of specific situations and, on the other hand, imagining that history is nothing more or less than an unfolding chain of effects, each predetermined by preceding causes.

HUMAN RESPONSIBILITY

The Bible makes it clear that individuals are responsible for their own actions and thus no mechanistic *"cause/effect"* theory can explain away human choice.

Each of us has the freedom to choose, and the exercise of that freedom is not determined by circumstance.

At the same time, the Gospels repeat a warning of Jesus to His Disciples: *"Things that cause people to sin are bound to come, but woe to that person through whom they come"* (Lk. 17:1; Mat. 18:7). It is a serious thing to *"cause one of these little ones to sin"* (Lk. 17:2).

Romans 14:21 helps us sense the way in which *"cause"* is used in this and similar Passages. Romans Chapter 14 deals with a dispute between those who felt that eating certain meat was wrong and those who believed it was right. Such personal convictions are not part of the Gospel (Rom. 14:14). But, even so, it would be wrong for a person holding a conviction to act against it.

A QUESTION

In this context, Paul raises the question of our responsibility toward those with whom we differ. Paul gives no clear-cut answer, but he does say that if eating meat in front of a Brother *"causes"* him *"to stumble," "it is better not to eat meat"* (Rom. 14:21).

Here *"cause"* is not used in either the sense of force or the sense of releasing the individual from responsibility for his own action. Paul's thought is that eating meat before such a Brother might prove a proximate cause of leading him to start *"passing judgment"* or else to violate his conscience.

There is a delicate balance here. Each individual is responsible to God for his choices and for his actions. However, others within the context of the situation in which the choices are made may influence the individual — for good or ill. Jesus' warning and Paul's reminder in Romans are intended to make us sensitive to the fact that our actions do have an influence on others.

While each individual is accountable to God for his own choices, all of us are called by God to influence others toward that which is truly good.

GOD BEYOND ALL CIRCUMSTANCES

The universe is never portrayed in Scripture as mechanical, with events determined by some endless cause-and-effect chain. Cause and effect, as we have stated, do operate within specific situations. But, even here, human beings exercise personal freedom of choice, and it is the moral choice of individuals that most significantly effects the sequence of events.

But Scripture does provide a non-situational view of the universe. Far from being dead and mechanical, the universe that the Bible describes is infused by the power of a Living, Moral Creator and Sustainer.

To the writers of the Old Testament and New Testament, cause and effect can be found only beyond our material universe. The principles that govern events on earth are moral in nature and flow from the Character and the Purpose of God. Only when we see history in a perspective provided by our knowledge of God can we understand what has happened and why.

THE BIBLICAL VIEW

Essentially, a Biblical view of cause and effect affirms that the universe operates on moral principles and that God ultimately (although at times indirectly) guides the course of history. The moral nature of the universe and of history is often seen in the Old Testament. It is seen when Moses warns Israel, *"If you turn away from following Him, He will again leave all this people in the desert, and you will be the cause of their destruction"* (Num. 32:15).

The moral choice of the adults of a generation will lead to preservation or to destruction, for God will shape history according to the Righteousness of their acts. In the same way, Moses explained that obedience to Law would bring Blessing, but if Israel should disobey, *"The Lord,"* he told them, *"will cause you to be defeated before your enemies"* (Deut. 28:25; Ezek. 32:12).

GOD IS INVOLVED IN THE SHAPING OF EVENTS

The moral, rather than the mechanical, theory of causation is the one found in Scripture, and it demands that God be actively involved in the shaping of events. Again, the conviction that God is just this kind of Being is expressed in both Old Testament and New Testament.

At times His intervention is miraculous and clear. But generally His intervention is quiet, and His causative actions are unnoticed by people. Only when we have the perspective of Daniel, who recognized God's Presence in every situation, are we able to perceive in our own lives a principle that was true in Daniel's: *"Now God had caused the official to show favor and sympathy to Daniel"* (Dan. 1:9).

NOTES

The Message of the Bible is that there is a hidden supernatural aspect to cause and effect. God is beyond, and yet within, every circumstance. He acts to shape and to mold. The greatest impact that we can have on the shape of our future is to make truly moral personal choices, choices that express obedience to God's Leading and His Word. It is our responsibility to obey. It is God's part to shape the results of our actions to fit His good Purposes and His Plan (Richards).

(12) "FOR THE ADMINISTRATION OF THIS SERVICE NOT ONLY SUPPLIETH THE WANT OF THE SAINTS, BUT IS ABUNDANT ALSO BY MANY THANKSGIVINGS UNTO GOD;"

It is a mistake on the part of the Corinthians to think that, as far as their participation in this Gift is concerned, that it means no more than that they are only adding something to fill up the deficiencies of the Saints in Jerusalem. They are, of course, doing this, but they are doing vastly more by doing this, they are causing an overflow of many Thanksgivings to God. The latter should especially delight their hearts and make them eager to participate.

THE ADMINISTRATION

The phrase, *"For the administration of this service not only supplieth the want of the Saints,"* in this case, and as stated, speaks of Jerusalem, but could in fact, pertain to anything as it regards the Work of God.

"Administration" as it is used here in the Greek is *"diakonia,"* and means *"attendance as a servant, a Teacher or Minister, a waiter on tables or other menial duties."*

In a sense, the manner in which Paul uses the word here, applies to the spiritual gift of administration (I Cor. 12:28). Peter used the same word, although it is there translated *"Minister"* (I Pet. 4:10); however, it means the same thing. It speaks of Elders (Preachers of the Gospel) administering the Grace of God within the Church.

Let's look at the word a little further and perhaps we'll get a little better understanding:

OLD TESTAMENT TERMINOLOGY

A number of different Hebrew words or phrases are translated *"administer"* in modern English Versions. Such phrases in the original as *"do justice"* and *"execute judgment"* are so translated (I Ki. 3:28; Jer. 21:12).

At other times, the Hebrew word indicating *"administrator"* means *"one who is over or above."* Daniel apparently borrowed a foreign word for use in Daniel 6:2-3 to identify the administrators in the Persian bureaucracy; it is a word that tells us little of the administrative system or the administrators' roles and responsibilities. Other Old Testament words and phrases simply serve as general references to governing: they encompass the full range of legislative, executive, and judicial functions without clear definition.

NEW TESTAMENT TERMINOLOGY

The New Testament words and their usage are no more precise than those of the Old Testament. Three times the Greek words translated *"administer"* or *"administration"* are *"oikonomos"* or *"oikonomia"* (Eph. 3:2, 9; I Pet. 4:10). An *"oikonomos"* was a slave who served as manager of a man's property and household.

In most New Testament occurrences, the Greek word involved refers to such a manager or managerial responsibility (Lk. 12:42; 16:1-4, 8; Gal. 4:2). In some Passages it is applied to the exercise of Leadership in the Church (I Cor. 4:1-2; Tit. 1:7).

When Paul in II Corinthians 8:19 speaks of an Offering, he uses *"diakoneo,"* which means an act of service or a ministry. When he speaks of a Gift of Administration in I Corinthians 12:28, the word is *"kybernesis"* (used only here in the New Testament). This is a nautical term that signifies the steersman, who holds the ship on the course directed by the Captain.

THE REASON THE WORD IS VAGUE

It is clear that Leaders of the New Testament Church were called to *"administer"* the Body of Christ. But just how they administered is not clear-cut and cannot be established by the general terms used in the original Text, which is posed in this manner by the Holy Spirit for purpose and reason. In other words, from the particular word *"administer"* or *"administration,"* we have little clue as to the manner in which God expects Leaders to lead.

The reason these words are somewhat nebulous in the New Testament Text is because the Holy Spirit does not consider Administrators as the Leaders of the Church. While it is certainly true that all Leaders administer or administrate, it is definitely not true that all administrators are Leaders.

The Leadership of the Church functions after the fivefold calling, *"Apostles, Prophets, Evangelists, Pastors and Teachers"* (Eph. 4:11). In regard to the Leadership affected by these individuals, whomever they may be, administration is, of course, involved.

However, there are Church Administrators of every type, with many of them actually Called of God to do such and which is labeled a *"spiritual gift"* (I Cor. 12:28). However, this speaks of Administrative Leadership and not necessarily Spiritual Leadership (Eph. 4:11).

THE MODERN CHURCH

The Modern Church has by and large confused this issue, especially in Denominational ranks, attempting to force in many cases, Administrative Leadership into Spiritual Leadership.

For instance, most all Religious Denominations regard their elective offices such as Superintendent, General Superintendent, Overseer, President, Moderator, Bishop, etc., as Spiritual Offices, which in most cases they aren't. Elective offices are those devised by man and filled by popular ballot.

In fact, in some cases these offices could definitely be filled by one who is truly Called of God to be an Apostle, but seldom. If these offices in the Church are looked at as administrative only which they are, they can be of great service to the Work of God, and of course, occupied by Godly men and women. However, if more is made of these offices than is Scripturally intended, then the Church is strapped with an unscriptural form of Government, which is presently the case in many Religious Denominations, and in fact, mostly always has been.

When I use the word *"always,"* I do so in a limited sense. In fact, this problem did not persist in the Early Church, even as we read in the Book of Acts and the Epistles, even as we are now studying. Nevertheless, after the First Century, Satan began to push strongly in the realm of Church Government, with him ultimately succeeding, with a gradual process of God's Government being replaced with man's Government. It didn't happen overnight, but gradually deteriorated in this regard until we

NOTES

now have what is known as the *"Catholic Church."* In fact, the title *"Pope,"* did not come into full use until the early Seventh Century, with the effort beginning some two centuries before. As stated, it was a gradual process of spiritual degeneration, which ultimately resulted in the *"Dark Ages."*

As well, if one is to notice, Paul uses the word *"Saints,"* in this 12th Verse, signifying all Believers as Saints, and immediately so upon conversion, in fact made that way by Christ. Consequently, this completely abrogates the Catholic contention that the Catholic Church has the power to label certain individuals as *"Saints,"* after they have died. Of course, this follows the contention of the Catholic Church as well, that it is the Church which is the final authority on all things and not the Scriptures. In other words, the Scriptures are what the Catholic Church says they are and no more. I would hope the Reader can understand the absolute blasphemy of such a position.

ABUNDANT THANKSGIVINGS

The phrase, *"But is abundant also by many thanksgivings unto God,"* proclaims the fact that the more that is done for the Lord which blesses people, the more thanksgivings come up from these hearts, as should be obvious.

Whenever the Saints in Jerusalem would receive this help, one can well imagine the *"many thanksgivings unto God"* regarding this need being met. In fact, this is true not only in these types of situations, but as well, from the hearts of people who are brought to Christ.

As an example, Jimmy Swaggart Ministries had the privilege according to the help of many dear Saints, and the leading of the Holy Spirit, to build approximately 176 Schools in Third World Countries. Most of these were Elementary Schools, but provided a tremendous service for impoverished children.

If I remember correctly, we built about 35 or 40 in the little country of Haiti. I remember going to one of those Schools after it was built, which was so far back, that there was not even a road to this particular area. In fact, it took us some two or three hours of walking to get there.

I'll never forget the reaction on the part of these children, people incidently who were very, very poor. They kept thanking us and thanking the Lord for this School, as would be understandable. In fact, I was told that they had a Prayer Meeting each day, thanking the Lord that their children would have an opportunity to at least get some education.

The point is, they were constantly thanking the Lord for this, even as Paul here proclaims.

Inasmuch as Paul mentions *"thanksgiving to God"* in both Verses 11 and 12, we must come to the conclusion that these *"Thanksgivings"* are much more important than the mere act itself which expresses gratitude.

NOTES

THE SPIRIT WORLD

Inasmuch as the Holy Spirit has designated that these Blessings as given by the Lord respecting our support of His Work, are designed to do two things, first *"the increase of the fruits of our Righteousness,"* and, second, *"to cause through us thanksgivings to God,"* we learn something of its great significance.

Just this morning over the News, the Reporter stated that very shortly the population of the world would reach six billion. The far, far greater majority of these people do not know the Lord; consequently, from their lips by and large come a constant stream of profanity, vulgarity, blasphemy, i.e., *"in effect, praise for Satan."* Satan must in fact gloat over this, as would be obvious.

However, regarding the Child of God, the Scripture tells us that *"Five of you shall chase an hundred, and an hundred of you shall put ten thousand to flight"* (Lev. 26:8). In this we see several things:

First of all, the Praises of God's people as they come up in thanksgiving to the Lord, carry far greater weight than the curse is of the unredeemed. Taking the Scripture literally, five Saints giving thanks to the Lord, cancel out a hundred blasphemies in the spirit world. And the Praises and Thanksgivings of a hundred Saints, cancel out the blasphemies of ten thousand of the unredeemed. In fact, even though the number in the aggregate may be small in any given city concerning those who truly know the Lord, still, only a few Saints truly praising the Lord and giving Him thanksgiving, which all certainly should do, can cancel out the blasphemies of an entire city regarding the spirit world.

So, in many cases, Satan gets no praise at all, for the simple reason that Saints are praising God. This is at least one of the reasons, for the great significance of these *"many thanksgivings unto God,"* and of course, that which brings about these *"thanksgivings."* While it shows gratitude on the part of the Believer which it certainly should, it also has, as I hope we have amply demonstrated, an even higher purpose.

(13) "WHILES BY THE EXPERIMENT OF THIS MINISTRATION THEY GLORIFY GOD FOR YOUR PROFESSED SUBJECTION UNTO THE GOSPEL OF CHRIST, AND FOR YOUR LIBERAL DISTRIBUTION UNTO THEM, AND UNTO ALL MEN;"

We will find in this particular Scripture the Holy Spirit through the Apostle giving us even added and deeper meaning respecting this *"Thanksgivings unto God."* It is as follows:

THE EXPERIMENT

The phrase, *"Whiles by the experiment of this ministration they glorify God,"* refers to the evidence or proof of the spirituality of the Corinthians, and all others who participate as well. The idea is this:

Paul is not speaking about how the poor Saints at Jerusalem will thank the Corinthians for the alms bestowed upon them, nor how these Saints will thank God for these alms, which of course, they certainly shall do. Such thanks are self-evident to Paul.

As Paul conceives their reaction, the Saints will glorify God in a much higher way. Induced *"by the test of this your Ministry"* to them, they will glorify God for the spiritual results which God has produced in the Corinthians. This *"test"* or *"experiment"* is not one which these Saints have originated; it is one that God is applying to the Corinthians. In other words, God tests out *"the Ministry"* of the Corinthians in this case in order to see how genuine it is as men test out the metal and the weight of coins. In fact, this phrase speaks about a completely successful test which proves *"this Ministry"* of the Corinthians a genuine Ministry indeed, that is in no way to be discounted.

When the Saints in Jerusalem receive the alms, they will see this Ministry, not only from the amount given to them, but from the entire

NOTES

spirit which produced that amount. Impelled by what they thus see, they glorify God.

BY FAITH

However, Paul, even though speaking with great assurance regarding the Corinthians, in fact knows, that the test is yet to be made. Consequently, how can he be so sure? What if the Corinthians fail in this test?

Paul's trust is not placed in the Corinthians but in God Who will move them. He trusts that God will surely bless the efforts he is making in writing to the Corinthians as he does and in sending them three good men to help them (II Cor. 8:16-24). Because he uses God's means, Paul is not the man to speak as though these means would fail. We fail when we resort to other means, when we do not trust the true ones which God furnishes us, and when we do not trust God enough to bless these means.

THE TEST

Actually, every single thing that happens to a Believer falls under the heading of *"experiment"* or *"test."* The entirety is designed by the Holy Spirit.

How will the Believer react to certain situations? What will be his response? How will he conduct himself?

The idea is, that everything must be brought under the judgment and light of the Word of God. In other words, the Believer is to have his life guided by the Word, which is the only basis from which the Holy Spirit will function.

Many Believers desire the help of the Holy Spirit, but are not abiding by the Word of God, so the Holy Spirit cannot help, even though He desires to do so. It is up to us to get in line with the Word, know what the Word says, make the Word a lifelong work, because the Holy Spirit always leads us to the Word, and functions only through and by the Word.

These Saints at Corinth had recently had a great Revival. The Lord had brought them back to the foot of the Cross; consequently, they were now ready to commence the Work of God, and the Offering which Paul proposes, serves as a Test.

The question might quickly be asked, as to how you the Reader are responding to the Tests which the Lord brings your way constantly. To be sure, these Tests are not generated that

NOTES

He may know, for as God He already knows. They are designed that we may know, and that we may grow in Grace and the knowledge of the Lord.

Many claim to be Believers, thereby claiming to be saved, but the Truth is, there are no *"fruits of Righteousness"* resident within their lives, which means they are professing only and not really possessing Salvation, or else they have drifted sorely from the Lord.

The idea is, that there definitely will be righteous works which will issue forth from the Child of God as a result of his Salvation, which directs attention to every phase and facet of our lives. In other words, it deals with money, how we treat others, our concern for the Work of God, our involvement, our obedience in following the Lord, etc.

SUBJECTION UNTO THE GOSPEL OF CHRIST

The phrase, *"For your professed subjection unto the Gospel of Christ,"* proclaims the fact that if one professes Christ, that the actual possession will always play out to such righteous activity. In effect, it says, *"You profess to be Christians and that you love your Brethren. Your bountifulness is proof of it"* (I Jn. 3:17).

Paul sees two things happening here regarding the Corinthians, and all other Believers for that matter. They are as follows:

1. First of all, *"For the submissiveness of your confession in* (or in regard to) *the Gospel of Christ."* It is the actual submissiveness that shows that we are confessing the Gospel aright.

In this case, the gathering of alms for the Saints (and it could be anything) in the manner and the spirit set forth by Paul presents the proper submissiveness that belongs to the confession of the Corinthians in regard to the Gospel. This part of submissiveness is evidence that the rest of the submission is also present.

2. Secondly, the Saints are seen as glorifying God *"also for the single-mindedness of fellowship with all other Saints."* The idea is, that the contribution to the Saints at Jerusalem is as good as a contribution to all Saints everywhere; by helping some really all are helped.

Paul is speaking about something that is far higher than *"the liberality of the contribution."* The Saints at Jerusalem are pictured as glorifying God for the single-mindedness of the fellowship directed by the Corinthians toward them. It plays out to spiritual fellowship and communion. It is this fellowship of the Corinthians which extends not only to those Saints who are being helped at present but to all God's Saints, whether they are actually helped in a literal sense or not. This could actually be referred to as *"the communion of Saints."*

The idea is, that profession means fellowship, and fellowship means profession.

For this reason Paul says *"confession"*(profession) and not merely Faith. We know and recognize each other by our mutual and our identical confession. We cannot see each others' Faith, but we do hear each others' confession. Confession is, however, the voice of Faith even as fellowship is the evidence of this Faith.

LIBERAL DISTRIBUTION

The phrase, *"And for your liberal distribution unto them, and unto all men,"* proclaims exactly what we have been saying, that this fellowship projected by the Corinthians not only blesses the Saints in Jerusalem, but has a positive effect on the entirety of the Body of Christ.

A confession that is not wholly and truly submissive to the Lord is one that submits not only to the Gospel but also to something else besides the Gospel. In other words, it divides its allegiance. It tries to serve two masters. On one occasion we confess with our Brethren, then we turn around and confess with others who are not our Brethren. At one time with those who accept all the Gospel as Christ gave it, then with those who alter that Gospel at least in part. This is what we call *"unionism."* It is a sin that is in the heart, which will compromise the Gospel in order to have the approval of others. Christ ever requires complete submission to Him Alone, to His Word and Gospel Alone.

SINGLE-MINDEDNESS

This is true with regard to the *"single-mindedness in the fellowship"* with the Saints and True Believers. *"Single-mindedness"* is exactly the proper word.

It means a cloth that is spread out with no fold under which something may hide. Its opposite is *"double-mindedness."* Read Paul's own description of the latter in II Corinthians 6:14-18.

NOTES

Single-minded fellowship is found where the mind and the heart want only this one fellowship with the true confessors of the Gospel of Christ. The other kind wants to fellowship the true confessors but at the same time also those who are not such confessors. Such fellowship is worthless. It has been likened to a harlot who is not for a husband but for several, perhaps, many men. He who can brother beyond the true confessors thereby reveals that his brothership means too little. Christ requires *"single-mindedness"* in our fellowship.

If the True Gospel of Jesus Christ is proclaimed, it will always center on bringing people to Christ, the One Who can save them from sin. This kind of Ministry does not just talk about Christ, it presents the Gospel of Christ. It proclaims the life-changing Message that Jesus died, was buried, and rose again according to the Scriptures.

Fellowship is destroyed if there is a lack of single-mindedness. In other words, the central theme of the Gospel must be Jesus. He is the Saviour, Baptizer with the Holy Spirit, Healer, Overcomer, Victor over sin and Coming King.

By the sheer nature of the Gospel and what it represents, I cannot have fellowship with those who advocate another way such as Psychology or Humanism in any form. Likewise, it is difficult to have fellowship with those who give little place or prominence to the Holy Spirit. If one studies Paul's Epistles, one quickly comes to the conclusion as to the prominence of the Spirit of God in all that is done, respecting the great Redemption afforded by Christ at Calvary and the Resurrection. Whenever the Church adopts the ways of the world in attempting to ape secular rock music, claiming that such wins the youth to Christ, I have to part company. For I know that the Lord does not borrow from the world to do anything. People are won to the Lord, the youth included, by the Word of God being preached unto them, i.e., *"the Gospel of Christ,"* on which the Holy Spirit moves.

THE MINISTRY OF PAUL

There were many in Paul's day who were advocating *"another gospel"* even as we will study in the 11th Chapter, but it was Paul's Ministry and others like him who preached the same Message, which got people saved. This is the proof. While many others made great claims, it was the Salvation of souls which Paul held up as the proof of his Message (II Cor. 3:1-2). A false gospel will not bring people to Christ, and simply because the Holy Spirit Who is absolutely required for the Salvation of souls, will not, and in fact, cannot function or work respecting that which is error. Consequently, there may be much religious activity and many claims; however, if it's a false Message, there will not be any people who will truly be saved, except maybe some few in a peripheral way which we will not take the time now to explain.

I will say the same thing regarding this particular Ministry (JSM). The proof of its certitude is found in the tremendous numbers of people which have been brought to Christ and continue to be brought to Christ unto this very hour.

(14) "AND BY THEIR PRAYER FOR YOU, WHICH LONG AFTER YOU FOR THE EXCEEDING GRACE OF GOD IN YOU."

The Gospel of Jesus Christ carried out in the hearts and lives of Believers, is a continuous proof of its reality and its moral power in the heart of the Believer. The Gospel changes lives and miraculously so one might quickly add.

PRAYER FOR YOU

The phrase, *"And by their prayer for you,"* refers to those in Jerusalem who will begin to pray for the Corinthians even in a greater way, after they receive the help the Corinthians will give. This is human nature!

Almost everyday I pray for the partners and supporters of this Ministry. While I certainly pray for others as well, naturally my heart goes out to those who believe in what we are doing, and are doing their best to help us do that which God has called us to do. We pray for them constantly asking the Lord that His Face would constantly shine upon them.

So, the Corinthians, and all others of that time for that matter who participated in this event, would be doubly blessed by the Saints in Jerusalem calling out to God on their behalf, thanking Him for the kindness which had been exhibited on their behalf.

As well, we learn here the tremendous significance of Prayer, how powerful it is, and how much it should be a part of the physical, mental, and spiritual make-up of the Child of God.

THE EXCEEDING GRACE OF GOD

The phrase, *"Which long after you for the exceeding Grace of God in you,"* proclaims the fact that the Believers in Jerusalem, as a result of the gift tendered by the Corinthians and others, would know that such was the result of the *"Grace of God"* in the hearts and lives of these who had not long been snatched from the jaws of Paganism. In other words, their Christianity was real. They had the same Salvation as did their Jewish friends in Jerusalem. All of it was because of the *"exceeding Grace of God."*

This is what is meant by the profession or confession of Faith in Verse 13, and the True *"Gospel of Christ."* That which is truly of Christ, will always have certain earmarks, one of those earmarks being the *"Grace of God."*

The idea is, that the Corinthians had the means with which to promote this Work for the Lord and the heart to do it, but God's Grace was the Author of it.

Considering what the Corinthians and others would do for those in Jerusalem, there would naturally develop a longing for personal acquaintance to be made. However, this is not possible; Corinth and Jerusalem are too far apart. So this Intercession of Prayer bridges the gap.

To be sure, this longing is not superficial, just desiring to meet their benefactors. The reason behind it is spiritual: *"because of the exceeding Grace of God upon you."* Those who live in the Grace of God long in brotherly fellowship to meet those who also live in this Grace, the more so when personal gratitude for benefactions produced by this Grace seeks for expression.

This very idea moved Paul to plan and to carry through this work respecting the Offering for Jerusalem. He had a higher object in view than the relief of personal suffering. He had that, too, in mind in fullest measure. But here was the opportunity to achieve far more, namely to cement the bond of confessional unity and fellowship and the bond of Christian love and attachment.

The Saints in Jerusalem were Jewish Christians, the majority of those in Paul's Churches were Gentile Christians. How easy it was for these two to drift apart in thought and in feeling. What a blessed thing to keep them in closest fellowship, which the Holy Spirit is here intending to do.

NOTES

CHURCH POLITICS?

This is not Church politics in any sense of the word. This is spiritual statesmanship of the highest and the purest kind. It has nothing to do with outward organization in which Church politics and mere ecclesiastical statesmanship spread themselves today. Would that more Church leaders would feed on this Text and then turn it into action for the present Church!

"Church politics" have to do with things which are strictly secular and have no spiritual meaning whatsoever. As stated, the Church is full of such. This of which Paul does, is the very opposite. It is meant to bridge this gap, which the Holy Spirit no doubt told him to do. While it did help the needy Saints in Jerusalem, and while that was very necessary and desirable, still, the Holy Spirit always has a higher view in mind. It's up to us to find what that higher view is, and then to function accordingly.

How beautiful all of this is when we see it in its purest light. How wonderful that things are when the Holy Spirit has a proper vessel such as Paul, through whom He can work. How so unselfish was the Apostle, how so desirous He was to know exactly the mind of the Lord, and then to carry out that which the Lord intended. How so in tune he was to the slightest move of the Spirit of God. What an example for us presently!

(15) "THANKS BE UNTO GOD FOR HIS UNSPEAKABLE GIFT."

The Apostle closes this particular teaching on the Grace of Giving by speaking of the greatest Gift of all, our Lord Jesus Christ.

THANKS BE UNTO GOD

The phrase, *"Thanks be unto God,"* presents the Apostle closing this part of his Epistle and the grand thought expressed in Verses 12-14 in a beautiful manner.

Note how *"God"* is found throughout this paragraph (vss. 6-15). Paul turns all the thoughts of the Corinthians upward to God and describes the thoughts and the feelings of the Saints at Jerusalem as likewise being turned to God. This is due to the fact that all of Paul's own thoughts are turned upward as well.

I think the idea of the Apostle is, that irrespective of what we might do for the Lord, even at its greatest it is small in comparison with the great gift which God has imparted in His bestowal of the Saviour. I think this, the coming of Jesus Christ, His great Sacrifice, was never far from Paul's mind. I think he dwelt on this constantly and rightly so! Consequently, looking at that as the example, makes anything we do pale by comparison.

HIS UNSPEAKABLE GIFT

The phrase, *"For His unspeakable Gift,"* pertains exclusively to the Lord Jesus Christ. This indescribable Gift fills Paul's entire vision. This is the immensity of God's Gift of Grace to all of the Church and to all its members, and in fact, to the entirety of the world. Such a *"Gift"* God gave. But now let us *not* make the trivial application: *"So we, too ought to give."*

From II Corinthians 8:1 onward Paul speaks of our giving, of all our good works, of all our motives in such giving and such works, of all our aims and our purposes in them, and of all the results and the fruits produced by them as being nothing but a part of God's Grace to us, riches for us, blessing for us. All these are a part of this Divine unmerited Grace which includes even vastly more.

So, Paul extends the Gift of Christ by God the Father, to include the Grace that enables us to give, which in turn brings upon us great blessings. Therefore, I'm not even sure, if it is proper to refer to our gifts to the Lord as such. In fact, the Holy Spirit through the Apostle steers the entire concept away from such a thought, referring to it as a *"Grace"* (8:1, 6, 7, 9; 9:8, 14) even with other words lending toward that principle.

So, I hardly think it would be proper for us to talk about how much we give to the Lord, when in reality such *"sowing,"* for this is how the Holy Spirit labels such, is in reality a great benefit, which in turn will reap a great harvest. God is the One Who originally gives us the *"seed,"* and then He germinates the seed after it is *"sowed,"* so, how can we rightly label such as a *"gift"* to Him, unless we understand it properly. In fact, every single thing we have is a pure gift from God in toto. When we rise to that

NOTES

pure plain as Paul did, the spirit of what he has said will shine in its full glory.

INDESCRIBABLE

"Unspeakable" should have been translated *"indescribable,"* for that is what it really means. Consequently, the fitting conclusion of this Chapter on giving is this word about thanksgiving. Giving and gratitude are a proper cause and effect. It is gratitude to the Divine Giver Who is the original Giver and Who's bounty makes it possible to supply others.

Jesus Christ is God's Great Gift and the source of all Christian Grace.

Nothing ever seemed so much to disburden the full heart of Paul after deep emotion as an utterance of thanksgiving (Rom. 7:25; 9:5; 11:33; I Cor. 15:57; Gal. 1:5; I Tim. 1:17).

The thanksgiving here supplied by the Apostle is like a great sigh of relief. The subject of it is perfectly general. It is not a mere *"Amen"* uttered as it were by Paul at the end of the thanksgivings of the Saints at Jerusalem which he has been presupposing; but an offering of thanks to God for the issues of Grace in general, all summed up in the one act of God's *"inestimable love"* in the giving of His Son, the Lord Jesus Christ (Jn. 3:16; Rom. 6:23; 11:33; Eph. 3:19) (Farrar).

Incidentally, the phrase *"His unspeakable Gift,"* or *"His indescribable Gift,"* occurs nowhere else in the New Testament. The idea is, that no words can properly express the greatness of the Gift thus bestowed on man. It is higher than the mind can conceive; higher than language can express.

THE GREATEST GIFT OF ALL

On this Verse we may observe the following:

1. The Saviour is a Gift to men. So He is uniformly represented. Man had no claim on God. He could not compel Him to provide a Plan of Salvation; and the whole arrangement — the selection of the Saviour, the sending Him into the world, and all the benefits resulting from His work, are all an undeserved Gift to man.

2. This is a Gift indescribably great, which value no language can properly express, no heart fully can see. It is so because of His Own greatness and glory. It is so as well because of the inexpressible love which He evinced. Also,

one must not forget the unutterable sufferings which He endured.

Going to the conclusion of His work, we must not forget the inexpressibly great benefits which result from that which He has done for humanity. No language can do justice to this work in either of these respects; no heart in this world fully conceives the obligation which rests upon man in virtue of His Work.

3. Thanks should always be rendered to God for this. We owe Him our highest praises for this. It is something we must never forget.

It is given to us strictly because of the Love of God and nothing else. We had no claims; we could not compel Him to grant us a Saviour. The Gift might have been withheld, and His Throne would have been spotless. In fact, we owe no thanks where we have a claim; but where we deserve nothing, then He Who benefits us has a claim on our thanks.

All of us have received inestimable benefits from Him. Who can express this? All our peace and hope; all our comfort and joy in this life; all our prospect of pardon and salvation; all the offer of eternal glory are to be traced to Him. Man has no prospect of being happy when he dies, except in the virtue of this *"unspeakable Gift"* of God.

And when one thinks of his sins, which may now be freely pardoned, when he thinks of an agitated and troubled conscience, which may now be at peace, when he thinks of his soul, which may now be eternally happy, when he thinks of a hell from which he is delivered, and of the heaven which eternal glories he may now know, and all by the Gift of a Saviour, his heart should overflow with gratitude, and the language should be continually on his lips and in his heart, *"Thanks be unto God for His indescribable Gift."*

Every other mercy seems small when compared to this; and every manifestation of right feeling in the heart should always lead us to contemplate the Source of it, and to feel, as Paul did, that *all* is to be traced to this *"indescribable Gift of God"* (Barnes).

"Now thank we all our God with heart
and hands and voices,
"Who wondrous things hath done, in
Whom His world rejoices;
"Who from our mother's arms hath
blessed us on our way,
"With countless gifts of love and still is
ours today."

"Oh may this bounteous God through all
our life be near us,
"With every joyful hearts and blessed
peace to cheer us;
"And keep us in His Grace, and guide us
when perplexed,
"And free us from all ills in this world
and the next."

"All praise and thanks to God the
Father now be given,
"The Son, and Him Who reigns with
them in highest heaven,
"The One Eternal God, Whom earth and
heaven adore;
"For thus it was, is now, and shall be
ever more."

NOTES

CHAPTER 10

(1) "NOW I PAUL MYSELF BESEECH YOU BY THE MEEKNESS AND GENTLENESS OF CHRIST, WHO IN PRESENCE AM BASE AMONG YOU, BUT BEING ABSENT AM BOLD TOWARD YOU:"

Someone has said that the first nine Chapters of this Epistle involve what the last four contain to such an extent that the nine cannot be properly understood without the four. The reverse is also true: the last four rest upon the preceding nine to such an extent that these four cannot be understood without the nine.

All the hints found in the first seven Chapters in regard to opposition and opponents in Corinth leave us at sea until the last four Chapters bring the complete answer to the questions raised by those hints.

The last four Chapters reveal why the Collection for the Saints in Jerusalem began to lag, and why Paul wrote Chapters eight and nine in order to expedite the matter of the Collection.

Already this shows why the three parts of the Epistle are arranged in the order in which these parts appear. The first seven Chapters must come first; then must come Chapters eight and nine in regard to the Collection, and not until then the last four Chapters about the Judaizers and their personal attacks on Paul, which included also Paul's associates but chiefly the Apostle himself (Lenski).

VINDICATION OF HIMSELF

Paul, having finished the subject of the duty of our giving of our financial resources in the previous two Chapters, enters in this Chapter on a vindication of himself from the charges of his enemies. His general design is to vindicate his apostolic authority, and to show that he had a right, as well as others, to regard himself as sent from God. Actually, this vindication is continued through Chapters 11 and 12.

In this Chapter, the stress of the argument is, that he did not depend on anything external to recommend him — on any *"carnal weapon"*; on anything which commended itself by outward appearance; or on anything that was so much valued by the admirers of human eloquence and learning. In fact, he seems willing to admit all that his enemies could say of him on that score, and to rely on other proofs that he was sent from God.

In Chapter 11 he pursues the subject, and shows, by a comparison of himself with others, that he had as good a right certainly as they to regard himself as sent from God. In Chapter 12 he appeals to another argument, to which none of his accusers were able to appeal, that he had been permitted to see the glories of the heavenly world, and had been favored in a manner unknown to other men.

FALSE TEACHERS

It is evident that there was one or more false teachers among the Corinthians, who called and questioned the Divine authority of Paul. These teachers were evidently Jews from Jerusalem, and they boasted much of their own endowments. It is impossible, except from the Epistle itself, to ascertain the nature of their charges and objections against him. However, whatever the charges, their actual desire was to tag the Law of Moses onto the Grace of God. This is mentioned in Acts Chapter 15, with the matter settled at that particular Council in Jerusalem; however, there were some it seems, who insisted on continuing down that perilous road, of attempting to force the Gentiles to keep the Law, which in effect, repudiated Grace. The two, Grace and Law, are opposites, as should be obvious. However, old habits die hard. They believed in Christ, but they also desired to continue with the Law, which is what is referred to presently as an *"oxymoron."* In other words, the two principles oppose each other to such an extent, that only a moron would attempt to wed the two.

It is not that the Law of Moses was wrong, but simply that Jesus had fulfilled that Law, making it now unnecessary. Who needed the symbolisms, the types, the shadows, etc., when the reality was now present!

This was just another of Satan's efforts, and a powerful effort at that, to demean and hopefully destroy the work that Christ had brought about by His Death and Resurrection.

WHY THE DEFENSE?

Some may wonder as to why Paul even bothered to answer these critics. Why should he stoop to such a level?

First of all, one can be certain that he did so, simply because the Holy Spirit desired that he do so. The reasons should be obvious.

First, these individuals, whoever they may have been, were teaching false doctrine and such has to be exposed. As well, they were denigrating the person of Paul and actually his Apostolic Calling. Had they succeeded, and they almost did at Corinth, the entirety of Paul's work and ministry would have been placed in jeopardy, which as well would have placed in jeopardy the New Covenant. One of Satan's favorite tactics, is to attempt to deny the Calling of a man or woman of God, or else to claim that it has been forfeited, etc. In other words, they will go to any lengths to keep people from hearing the one who is definitely called of God. When I say *"they,"* I am speaking of the Church and not the world. Satan always raises up the greatest hindrances in the Church. In fact, the Church even as Israel of old, has always been made up of two branches — the apostate, which makes up the far greater majority, and the genuine, i.e., *"Remnant,"* which makes up the much smaller part.

To be sure, the two are not easily discernable at times, with some similarities existing in both. However, the Lord knoweth those who are His (Jn. 10:14).

NOTES

I BESEECH YOU

The phrase, *"Now I Paul myself beseech you,"* presents the Apostle appealing to the Corinthians.

For what is he appealing?

First he is appealing to the Corinthians from a basis of love as it regards the false apostles who had come into the Church. These individuals, whomever they may have been, were questioning his Apostleship, and as well, were corrupting the faith of the converts. That they were of commanding presence and gifted with eloquence, we shall see in Verse 10. As well, we shall see in Verse 5 that they were highly cultivated and that they were personally attractive, for they had a large following in the Church (II Cor. 11:18). Also, I think that II Corinthians 11:15 will show that they announced an *"ethical Gospel"* instead of the Gospel of the Cross of Christ.

These individuals had demeaned the person of Paul, spoken with contempt of his authority and demeaned his claims of Apostleship. He is appealing to the Corinthians to deal with them according to the rules of the Gospel, which means to deny them and their false message.

Inasmuch as Paul often uses the word *"beseech,"* which means *"to beg or to appeal,"* I think it would be profitable for us to look at this word in a more extended manner.

APPEAL

In the Old Testament, appeal is generally used in the sense of making a request. It translates a variety of Hebrew phrases, such as *"to cry to"* or *"to seek."*

In the New Testament, *"appeal"* is used in several senses. Acts tells us that Paul appealed to Caesar (Acts 25:11-12, 21, 25; 26:32; 28:19). This involved Paul's invoking his right as a Roman citizen to be tried before Caesar's court in Rome rather than by an inferior court — a right called *"provacatio."* The Greek word that Luke chose is *"epikaleomai."* It means to *"call out to"* or *"appeal to."* It was not normally used in the New Testament world in the technical sense of a legal appeal, and only in the above-mentioned Verses is it translated *"appeal"* in the New Testament.

Besides signifying appeal as we have just mentioned concerning Paul, it is also used to express comfort and exhortation. Typically

NOTES

Paul's appeals are made to Believers and are based on his readers' experience of his own and of Christ's Love. Typically too the appeals focus on a call to a distinctively Christian life.

There are two other Greek words which are rendered *"appeal."* In Romans 11:2, Paul speaks of Elijah's historic *"appeal to God against Israel."* The word here is *"entynchano."* It means *"to approach, to meet with a person, or to intercede for or against someone."*

When Peter speaks of false teachers *"appealing to the lustful desires of sinful human nature"* (II Pet. 2:18), he uses the word *"deleazo,"* which means *"to allure."*

GOD'S APPEALS

How striking, then, that God's appeals through the Apostle are significantly different. Paul's words reflect the difference. *"By the meekness and gentleness of Christ, I appeal to you . . . ,"* as it addresses the Verse of our study.

In essence Paul says, *"Although in Christ I could be bold and order you to do what you ought to do, yet I appeal to you on the basis of love"* (Phile. vss. 8-9).

God appeals to people in a variety of ways, especially by addressing the highest capacities enjoyed by redeemed human beings. God's appeals never coerce but always invite people to experience what is best for them, for other people, and for God's Kingdom (Richards).

THE MEEKNESS AND GENTLENESS OF CHRIST

The phrase, *"By the meekness and gentleness of Christ,"* refers to Paul making every effort to imitate the gentleness and kindness of the Master. In fact, he desired at all times to imitate and to exhibit the general feelings of the Saviour.

The way the sentence is structured in the Greek, it makes a unit of *"the meekness and gentleness of Christ."* Jesus was ever *"meek and lowly in heart"* (Mat. 11:29; 21:5). *"Meekness"* is the quality in the heart, and its expression is *"gentleness"* in dealing with poor sinners. Both qualities were manifested by Jesus during His entire life. He is ever, also now, the gentle Shepherd Who leads His flock, Who gently carries the lambs in His Bosom, Who goes out and finds the lost sheep and bears it back to the fold.

PAUL KNEW

Let no one tell you that Paul did not know how meek and gentle Jesus was during His earthly ministry; the very words he uses here regarding Him show how fully he knew.

Yet do not misunderstand this meekness and gentleness of Christ, as some do, when they think that Christ could never be anything but meek and gentle. He twice drove the traffickers out of the Temple. The woes with which He denounced the Scribes and Pharisees to their very faces are no less than terrific (Mat. 23:13). In other words, Christ could be severe, scathing, fiery, and crushing. He was not an anemic Jesus, Whose every word was soft. The thunders of His denunciations are terrible. Even though this is true, He used severity only when He had to use it; He ever longed to use only gentleness.

In view of this, we understand the appeal which Paul is making to the Corinthians. Think of that meekness and gentleness of Christ, Paul tells them, how sweet it is to you. Surely, you Corinthians want such meekness and gentleness extended to you and not their opposites. Let my reminding you of this meekness and gentleness draw you wholly away from these false apostles, who will be treated with severity, if necessary.

Paul is following the example of Christ in treating the flock with meekness and with gentle hands; but he also follows Christ's example when he is dealing with deadly severity with arrogant enemies and with those who second their enmity. May none of the Corinthians invoke that severity when Paul gets to Corinth.

BASE?

The phrase, *"Who in presence am base among you,"* probably presents the Apostle using the actual taunts of his adversaries.

Even though Corinth has experienced a Revival, which account is given us in Chapter 7, still, if this problem of the false apostles is not dealt with, the Corinthians can very well revert right back to their previous predicament. Revival in its truest sense of the word demands two things:

1. Repentance, which brings Believers back to the Cross.
2. A riddance of all that is wrong.

NOTES

Satan does his greatest work from inside the Church. Regarding these detractors of the Apostle, it was not enough for them to oppose his Message, which in reality they could not successfully do; therefore, they opposed him personally, denigrating his character and denying his Calling. This continues to pretty much be the tactic of Satan. Little able to successfully attack the true Biblical Message, he resorts to attacking the person. His goal is to destroy the person's influence and by using whatever tactic is at his disposal, which will then make invalid his Message, which is desperately needed by the Church.

THE REASON IT IS SO SUCCESSFUL

Sadly and regrettably as it regards most Believers, the determination to do right is not as strong as it should be. In other words, the True Biblical Message preached under the Anointing of the Holy Spirit, generally offends most people, even most Believers. Many times such a Message is corrective, and even if it is not corrective, its Truth clashes with the error contained in the hearts of many if not most. Upon such an event, the pull is toward repentance, even as it is intended to be; however, most not wanting to set things right at any rate, if an excuse can be found, will leap in that direction. So, if something can be found wrong with the Messenger, then in their minds, they are free from obeying the Message, even attempting to make themselves believe that their wrong direction is now right. As well, far too often, Religious Leaders oppose the true Apostles, which then gives even added excuse to the greater majority of the Church to disavow the Message, and continue the erroneous direction. If Pastors join in this course, which the greater majority always will do, that is if Denominational Leaders set the course, the people then feel they are justified in rejecting the Message. Consequently, Satan has then been successful in carrying out his design — making null and void the Word of the Lord.

In these situations which have happened countless times in the past, the Church goes deeper and deeper into apostasy. The Word sent to them by the Holy Spirit, which is always by Apostles and Prophets, and almost never by Denominational Leaders so-called, unless by chance an Apostle or Prophet happens to occupy one of those positions, which has happened but seldom, then that word never reaches its intended destination.

Consequently, Satan's tactics are very successful, in that the Prophets of old were stoned to death, with the Apostles for the most part being bitterly opposed, who would also be stoned if the law of the land allowed such (Mat. 23:37).

It is ironical! Rome started killing Preachers not long after Paul wrote this Epistle (he was one of the first), while the Church took up that gruesome task several centuries later.

BOLD!

The phrase, *"But being absent and bold toward you,"* no doubt once again has the Apostle parroting his detractors. They are referring to his Letters. The idea of his slanderers is that when he is face to face with them Paul is a lamb and a lion only when he is at a safe distance; he turns tail when you face him, he roars only when he is far off in the woods. These statements are not actually referring to his personal appearance, as some have claimed.

DID PAUL ACTUALLY HAVE SPIRITUAL AUTHORITY?

In other words, did the Apostle have the spiritual power and authority to tell people what they must do, and if such is not obeyed judgment will then come? To properly answer that question, one must understand what spiritual authority actually is. The Truth is, Paul definitely did have spiritual authority. That should be obvious to all concerned; however, spiritual authority as held by the Apostle Paul, and all others of the fivefold calling but especially Apostles, is never authority over other people, but only over evil spirits and the powers of darkness, which of course, covers a wide range of circumstances. But over people, no!

In this authority which he held, and which all Apostles hold, he was given the Word of God, which he passed on to the people, but that's all he could do — pass it on. He could not force them to obey, as should be obvious in all his dealings with the Churches. He can warn them, even threaten them, but in the final analysis the decision had to be theirs.

He had no power to excommunicate rebellious Christians from their Salvation, and

NOTES

neither does any other man, that being the domain strictly of the Holy Spirit, under the tutelage of Christ as the Head of the Church.

Jesus plainly told His Disciples, that such authority (dominion over people) was the way of the world, *"But it shall not be so among you: but whosoever will be great among you, let him be your servant"* (Mat. 20:26-27).

MODERN CIRCUMSTANCES

So, when Denominational Leaders, or any Preacher for that matter, steps over the sacred boundary of violating the freedom in Christ of another person, irrespective as to what they have done, they have then violated the Word of God, which God can never sanction. If any man had the right to do such, at least as it's looked at in the natural, Paul surely had that right. He had planted these Churches, nurtured these Churches, with most all of the converts saved under his Ministry. As well, he had been sent to these places by the Holy Spirit, had been Anointed by the Holy Spirit, with tremendous works raised up; however, the Apostle as is overly obvious in his writings, never used his authority in a dictatorial manner, but always in a Christlikeness, which is what the Holy Spirit desired.

In the mind of Paul, Jesus was always the Head of the Church, and an active Head at that, which means He was working in and among His people. Consequently, the Apostle always conducted himself, even as we always must conduct ourselves, as undershepherds. He knew that the Lord through the Holy Spirit would handle the situations, even as He always did. To be sure, if the people will not allow the Holy Spirit to have His way, there is certainly no way in which a mere man can achieve desired results by using forceful authority.

(2) "BUT I BESEECH YOU, THAT I MAY NOT BE BOLD WHEN I AM PRESENT WITH THAT CONFIDENCE, WHEREWITH I THINK TO BE BOLD AGAINST SOME, WHICH THINK OF US AS IF WE WALKED ACCORDING TO THE FLESH."

In this Verse, we will see Truth further enlarged, and other Truths presented.

In these last four Chapters of this Epistle, we have a continuance of Paul's biographical account of himself. It is such an account as will find its application in all Christian thinking and living. It points out to us those things which commend a Christian.

Actually, the sense of this Tenth Chapter is found in the last Verse, *"For not he that commendeth himself is approved, but whom the Lord commendeth."*

The problem before us is the oft recurring problem of human relations, but with a deeper thrust against the very Plan of God. Going back to the former, it presents itself frequently in our experience. It is found in the home in the relation of one family member to another. It is found in the community in the relation of one neighbor to another. It is found in the Church in the relation of one Christian to another.

The relation of one Christian to another has the possibilities and prospects of the sweetest fellowship on earth, but if we are not careful it can turn into the bitterest experience on earth. Former Brethren can become bitter, recriminative, and vicious. They can completely forget their Master Who exercised the greatest tolerance and forbearance.

As stated, when wronged He never sought vengeance. In fact, the injustices against Him were more useful in furthering His Ministry than if all men had been fair to Him. These things Christians are prone to forget; they allow carnality the ascendancy and thus seek to establish their personal cause at the expense of the Master's. All the time their personal animosities are being fought, their Master's cause is suffering and languishing.

THE PERSONAL EXPERIENCE OF PAUL

Paul found himself the victim of injustice, ill-treatment, false report and personal abuse. The circumstances of this attack grew out of his residence and labors in Corinth. For the space of a year and one half he had given himself, his time and his energy in prayer and teaching. Through God's Blessing upon his indefatigable labors he had seen a little colony of Christians grow in a truly remarkable manner. When the Church reached the stage of maturity where they could carry on what Paul had commenced, under the guidance of the Holy Spirit he moved on to other and larger fields of activity.

Since leaving Corinth Paul had heard of a preconceived effort on the part of certain enemies to sabotage his character and reputation. They had succeeded in turning at least some of Paul's converts away from confidence in him. They had succeeded in destroying the friendship of some of Paul's old friends. What was worse, these personal enemies were stopping at no lengths to so effectively damage Paul's reputation as a servant of Christ as to make it difficult for him to carry on his Ministry.

NOTES

A SAD STATE AMONG CHRISTIANS

What a sad state of affairs this was. How lamentable that weapons of hatred, animosity, and wickedness were being turned upon this man of God in a diabolical attempt to hinder his usefulness and service. And yet, we can be grateful that the Holy Spirit allowed this unpleasant experience in Paul's life to be given to us, because the lessons in personal conduct and Christian behavior which it teaches will enable us to meet situations of a similar nature whenever they arise in our life.

Paul's experience presents not only a cross-section of Christian experience, but also the ideals of Christian behavior. It is for our profit that Paul suffered. It will be to our credit and ultimate vindication and triumph if we heed these lessons.

SATAN'S TACTICS

Notice what happened. Paul moved out and other leaders moved in who were neither of the spiritual stature or nature of the great Apostle. They immediately set about to build up their own reputations by destroying Paul's reputation. They set about to win the affection of these Corinthians by destroying their affection for Paul. In order to be loved, they insisted on Paul being hated. In order to be liked, they insisted on Paul being disliked. In order to be held in esteem, they insisted on Paul's person and labors being held in contempt.

In their desperate search for a case against Paul with which to carry on their sabotage they could find nothing wrong with his preaching, his doctrine, or his moral conduct, so they took up purely personal matters. It was a perfect revelation of their own diminutive stature and their own ignoble character. They attack Paul purely on differences of opinion. They took certain characteristics of the Apostle and magnified them out of all proportion and sought to use these to destroy him.

How did Paul meet this challenge to his life's usefulness? What he did indicates more than anything else the genuineness of his Christian character. Paul's most effective vindication would not come by means of the approval of many, but by following the example of His Master. In this crisis Paul determined to be Christian. As we have seen, he might have employed force or used the authority of his Apostleship or established his claims before some tribunal. Instead, he appealed to Christ. If they thought well of Christ, they would think well of Paul. If they were eager to follow Christ and give a genuine exhibition of Christlikeness, they would withdraw their carnal and childish differences and seek to establish Christ's Cause in the world.

WHY CHRISTIANITY IS SO DIFFERENT

Someone has said that *"Christianity as it works in the heart, is mightier than it is when explained and enforced in a thousand volumes. Christianity in books is like seed in the granary, dry and all but dead. It is not written, nearly as much as it is living character, which has the power to convert men. In effect, the lives of good men and not the library of intellectuals, is the converting power."*

Much, though not all truth, lies in that declaration. While our example does not convert others, it at least attracts them to the Word which does convert them.

We continue to see Paul in action under abuse and malediction. He did not lose his self-control because he was controlled by Christ. He did not lose his spiritual dignity, nor his equilibrium, nor his awareness of being Christ's servant (Laurin).

BEG YOU

The phrase, *"But I beseech you,"* introduces a stronger verb than the *"beseech"* in Verse One, and actually means *"I beg,"* or *"I beg you."* Paul urges, yes, begs the Corinthians.

His reason for taking this position, and I speak of an even deeper servile approach, is twofold:

1. This was the Way of the Lord, therefore, the right way.

2. If they did not heed this approach, they would then be face-to-face with Christ, with Him definitely not assuming the position of

NOTES

meekness and gentleness. Such a position no sane person desires to occupy.

I am persuaded that there are untold numbers of Christians presently, who have ignored this manner of the Holy Spirit regarding correction, continuing on the path of rebellion, and are consequently sick, with many even dying prematurely (I Cor. 11:29-31).

MAY I BE ALLOWED TO BE PERSONAL!

Not for a moment excusing wrongdoing on my part, but yet knowing that such never excuses wrongdoing on the part of others, I make the following statements.

First of all, and exactly as the Apostle said of himself, *"I am nothing"* (II Cor. 12:11). So the statement I will make has little bearing on me personally, but rather as it regards the Word and Work of God.

I believe the possibility at least exists, that our situation has served as a test not only for me personally, but as well for the Church. I say that not at all because I am more than anyone else, for it is obvious that I'm not; however, due to the fact that I am known all over the world, what I'm about to say I believe has validity.

Is it possible that the Lord has pulled back, allowing the Church to do to me whatever it likes (up to a point), in order to portray its true heart? When there is no restraint, at least when men think there is no restraint, it is shocking at times as to what people will actually do, even Christians. When a person is in a position to where anyone can do any negative thing to him they so desire, without any fear of condemnation but rather applause, one quickly finds out what actually resides in the hearts of individuals. That's the position we have been in for the last ten years, and regrettably, millions have taken their turn. It has not been a pretty picture.

No, I do not flatter myself, but I do know what Jesus said:

"Inasmuch as ye have done it unto one of the least of these My Brethren, ye have done it unto Me" (Mat. 25:40).

We must never forget that the Word of God is the criteria, not the word of men, or of Religious Denominations, or anything else for that matter. And if in fact the Word of God is actually the criteria, which it definitely is, the situation then is ugly indeed! According to that criteria, the Church desperately needs to repent.

BOLD AGAINST SOME

The phrase, *"That I may not be bold when I am present with that confidence, wherewith I think to be bold against some,"* refers to the fact that Paul did not want to use boldness or severity against all the Corinthians, even though it may possibly have to be used against some. In effect he is saying, that he will challenge certain ones if need be. He will not bluff, he has complete confidence.

What did he actually mean by this statement?

These detractors were claiming that in person, even as we've already stated, Paul would be as meek as a lamb. In other words, he would not hold to his bold contentions, would not declare unequivocally the Word of God, but would rather hem and haw, seeking compromise.

The Apostle is telling them that as strong as he is in his letters, as straightforward, as to the point, even as bold as he is, he will be the same in person as well, and even more so. In fact, anyone who knew the Apostle even to a small degree, would have never ventured such foolish opinions. In fact, they had picked on the strong point of this Apostle. His courage even in the face of what looked like certain death, was perhaps unequalled in human history. I realize that's quite a statement, but I believe it to be true.

So, these people impugning the courage of the Apostle, is like claiming the Sun has no heat, that water is not wet, that fire is not hot. Only very foolish people would make such ridiculous assertions.

This does not present a challenge; it causes him no sleepless nights, at least the part about himself; however, understanding the attack against the Word and Work of God, knowing what Satan's aims were, did definitely cause him concern, even as it should have.

WALK ACCORDING TO THE FLESH

The phrase, *"Which think of us as if we walked according to the flesh,"* means that he is not addressing the situation as they are — in the flesh. The Holy Spirit is working through him, the Word of God is on his side, Jesus Christ the Head of the Church stands with him, which proclaims a mighty force to say the least, while his opponents have none of this, because God cannot aid and abet on the side of error. While it may look for a while as though the *"flesh"* side is winning, ultimately, it will always lose.

NOTES

WHAT IS THE FLESH AS THE WORD IS HERE USED BY PAUL?

To cut through all the explanations that could be given, in its most simplified form, the *"flesh"* pertains to anything which is not berthed, led, guided, and carried out by the Spirit of God through the Believer. That's the reason the sin of Abraham and Sarah was so great respecting their *"helping God"* bring about the fulfillment of the Promise concerning the child that was to be born to them.

In fact, and as should be obvious, the Revelation and Promise they were given concerning this great thing which was to be, was definitely of the Lord, i.e., *"berthed by the Spirit."* However, they grew impatient at the delay, and then fearful that it could not be brought about at all due to their advanced ages and the barrenness of Sarah, concocted a scheme whereby Hagar would take Sarah's place, thereby bringing the child into the world (Gen. Chpt. 16). The result was *"Ishmael,"* which has caused problems for Israel from that day even unto the present. (Ishmael is the father of all the Arab nations.) So, while the Promise definitely was from the Lord, the manner in which it was initially carried out was definitely not of the Lord.

In fact, the Promise of God regarding Abraham and Sarah could not be carried out, which goes as well for all other Believers, until all hope of the flesh had died. To say the least, this is not an easy process (Gen. Chpt. 21).

MANY TIMES WE THINK IT'S THE SPIRIT WHEN IN REALITY IT'S THE FLESH

Being taught some things from the experience of Abraham and Sarah, we learn that not only the Promise (and in whatever variety) must originate with God, but as well the carrying out of that which is to be done, is to be totally of God as well. Consequently, we should look at these two situations.

First of all, the far greater majority of all that which goes on and is carried out in the realm of religion, is totally of man, planned by man, thereby carried out by man because it was berthed by man and not God. In other words, what is being done is a work of the flesh in its entirety. As stated, this covers almost everything done in the realm of religion.

In fact, many Religious Denominations do not even believe that God speaks to people presently, so of necessity everything they do, at least for the far greater majority of those in these particular Denominations, is of the flesh. As well, most Pentecostals whereas they once relied totally on the Holy Spirit (or at least many did), now have pretty much abandoned the ways of the Spirit, consequently, carrying out all they do in the flesh. So, the far greater majority of the modern Church little seeks the Lord about anything, thereby proceeding solely on human wisdom, which in effect, is evil (James 3:15).

And then all of us, even the best of us whoever that may be, even though hearing from God, exactly as Abraham heard from God, still have a tendency to want to *"help God"* carry out that which He has told us to do. However, the flesh in that capacity cannot be blessed by the Lord, anymore than Ishmael could be blessed by the Lord, at least in a true spiritual capacity. Regarding the Promises of God, and I speak of those which are given to us personally, all of us have a tendency to become impatient, or to resort to human ingenuity, which we cover amply with Scriptures, attempting to make ourselves think that what is done is in the Spirit, when in reality, it's in the flesh. This latter comes about because of failure to wait on the Lord as we properly should, failure to know and understand His Word as we should, and failure to trust God as we properly should. The flesh is the result of all of this, simply because it is done in our own strength and power rather than that of God, which God cannot bless. Paul plainly said, *"So then they that are in the flesh* (operating in their own strength and ability) *cannot please God"* (Rom. 8:8).

What makes it so bad is, that *"We are in the flesh, but yet have the Spirit,"* in other words, we do not have to rely upon our own strength and ability, but have the Holy Spirit to help us in whatever capacity is needed (Rom. 8:9). To use the phrase from an old song *"Oh what needless pain we bear,"* presents an apt illustration.

NOTES

THERE CANNOT BE A MIXTURE OF THE FLESH AND THE SPIRIT

To learn to function, to work, to do, to be totally in the Spirit, after the Spirit, and of the Spirit, is the greatest victory that any Believer could ever win. In fact, this is the great struggle in every Christian life — to function totally in and after the Spirit of God.

The closer one gets to the Lord, the easier it is to look back at previous experiences, realizing how much of the flesh was involved, which we at the time thought was the Spirit. During these times, the Lord blessed whatever was of the Spirit, but did not, and in fact, cannot, bless that which is of the flesh. Nevertheless, the privilege of His Blessings in some capacities, makes us think at times, that He has placed His approval upon all that we are doing. That is not the case at all! Thank God, He does use what can be used (that which is totally of the Spirit), or else, I'm afraid that He would never be able to use anyone.

The secret is, as we grow in Grace and the Knowledge of the Lord, that we more and more recognize the flesh for what it is and as well recognize the Spirit of God. As stated, the closer one gets to the Lord, the more obvious the flesh becomes and the uglier it becomes, which is the intention of the Holy Spirit as He works with us (James 4:5).

In fact, the great struggle of the Spirit within our hearts and lives has to do with control — but control which must be freely given by the Believer to the Holy Spirit, for He will never take such by force. He desires to control every function of our lives and in every capacity, which brings about Blessings of untold worth. It is so sad that all of us little use His vast resources which are available to us. We fail in that respect, and we too often lean on the frail arm of flesh.

THINGS I HAVE LEARNED

Since 1991 we have been forced into a position of which we have had to trust the Lord for everything, and I mean everything. That speaks of finances for the Ministry, the continuing of our Call regarding World Evangelism, our own personal lives, and in fact, any and all things. Instead of getting any help from the Church world, for the most part, it was and is virtually attempting to put us out of business.

So, if the Lord did not provide, there was no way any situation could be handled and addressed. During this time I have learned more than ever to trust Him, believe Him, look to Him, depend on Him, which is the greatest place and position in which one could ever be.

No, it hasn't been easy, but it has been glorious and wonderful all along the way. Every time our finances would get in such a state that I could not see how we could continue, the Lord always works a Miracle. I now stand back in amazement, as I watch Him work. At times, the situation looks impossible, but He always comes through, which is teaching me more and more to lean on Him.

I realize that many will quickly retort by saying, *"Well it's all your fault!"* No, it isn't all my fault. Any wrongdoing I have committed, was definitely my fault and my fault alone; however, the negative position that much of the Church has taken is not my fault. In fact, that's one of Satan's oldest tactics, to get people to blame others for their wrongdoing.

EVERYTHING IS A TEST

The Believer must understand, that everything he faces each and everyday, and on a continual basis, is always a test. How will we react? What will be our position? What will we do?

While Job was being tested, his three friends plus his wife, and all others for that matter, were being tested as well!

In fact, the struggle between the flesh and the Spirit plays out in the form of testing as well. Will we rely on the Spirit, look to the Spirit, be guided by the Spirit, depend on the Spirit, or the arm of flesh, which constitutes not only our own strength, but the looking to other men and women for help as well? The sadness is, most Preachers I think, look to their Denomination for all their leading, instead of the Holy Spirit. The Lord is no more pleased with that than He is any other type of flesh, for *"flesh"* it is!

So, we see that this struggle, this conflict, this thing referred to as the *"flesh"* and the *"Spirit"* plays out in every facet of our lives. We are either looking to the Lord, or else we are looking to other sources. Whatever those other sources are, and even how well intentioned they may be, still, constitute the flesh, because whatever is not of the Spirit is of the flesh, for there is no in between.

NOTES

(3) "FOR THOUGH WE WALK IN THE FLESH, WE DO NOT WAR AFTER THE FLESH:"

What does Paul mean by *"walking in the flesh"* and *"warring after the flesh"*?

WALKING IN THE FLESH

The phrase, *"For though we walk in the flesh,"* refers to the fact that we have not yet experienced the Resurrection, consequently, do not yet have Glorified Bodies; therefore, our daily living, even though we be led totally by the Spirit of God, is still in the flesh, as is obvious. Actually, this one phrase, *"Walking in the flesh,"* is where all the trouble develops.

This means we are mortal, like other men. We dwell in mortal bodies, and necessarily must devote some care to our temporal wants. And the fact that we are in the flesh, makes us conscious of our imperfections and frailties like others. The sense is, Paul, and neither do we, claim exemption from the common wants and frailties of nature. Consequently, the best and Godliest of men are subject to these wants and frailties and the best of men are liable to err. In fact, the closer to God we get, the more this becomes very obvious within our lives. In other words, because we are *"walking in the flesh,"* which we must do until the Resurrection, presents the reason for this constant struggle. This means, we are simply poor, weak, human beings, who have constant need of constant leading and guidance by the Holy Spirit.

WE DO NOT WAR AFTER THE FLESH

The phrase, *"We do not war after the flesh,"* presents the fact that even though we are *"in the flesh"* (human beings with mortal bodies), still, the struggle of which we speak, is not done in the energy of the flesh at all, that is if we are to have victory, but rather by the Power of the Holy Spirit. These mighty weapons afforded us, of which we will address to a greater degree momentarily, are the source of our strength and victory, and not those things of the flesh. Whatever conflict or controversy in which Paul was engaged, was fought on this basis. Whatever difficult task he was confronted with was attacked by this means. Whatever service he was to render was done by this method. It is something for us to follow.

None of us is exempt from conflict, difficulty, or obligation. We can meet these things either as Spirit-controlled Believers, or as Pagans, either as new men or the old way, either as spiritually minded or carnally minded, either with the weapons of the flesh or the weapons of the Spirit.

Paul said that he walked in the flesh but did not war after the flesh. He was compelled to walk as a man walks, by sight and sound, to use his five senses, and to meet the problems of the world of men and women of flesh. While this was a necessity by force of unchangeable circumstance, and will be until the Resurrection, Paul did not forget that he belonged to a new race and a new people. He was a Believer, a Christian and, consequently, a new creation. He was indwelt by God and united to powers and forces of superhuman capacity and ability.

HIS STRENGTH

His strength did not lie in his flesh but in his spirit, which was indwelt by the Holy Spirit. His conflict was not to be one of force against force, flesh against flesh, anger against anger, feeling against feeling. His strategy was that and that alone of the Spirit. His was not the blitzkrieg of the flesh but the power of Faith.

WHAT TYPE OF WARFARE IS IT OF WHICH PAUL SPEAKS?

1. It is a warfare with the corrupt desires and sensual propensities of the heart; with spiritual corruption and depravity; with the remaining unsubdued propensities of the fallen nature.

2. It is warfare with the powers of darkness — the mighty spirits of evil that seek to destroy us, which are outlined in Ephesians 6:11-17.

3. It is warfare with sin in all forms; with idolatry, sensuality, corruption, intemperance, profaneness, wherever they may exist.

The Christian is opposed to all of these, and all of these are opposed to the Christian. It is the aim and purpose of the Believer, as far as he may be able, to resist and subdue these things. However, they can only be subdued by the power of the Spirit, and never by the arm of flesh.

THE MANNER OF THIS WARFARE

The idea of this warfare is that the Believer allow the Holy Spirit to do the things which need to be done against the powers of darkness. Of course, there are things the Believer must do as well, such as putting on the whole armor of God (Eph. 6:11-17), and a proper understanding of the Word of God; however, the understanding of which we speak concerns the manner in which the Holy Spirit works. I suspect that most Believers are not too clear on that subject.

The Spirit of God works strictly from the legal work and position of what Jesus did at Calvary and the Resurrection. In fact, it was this, the paying of the sin debt, that made it possible for the Spirit of God to come dwell in the hearts and lives of Believers (I Cor. 3:15).

As Paul outlines in Romans Chapter 8, the Holy Spirit works from that premise and that premise alone. He is resident within our hearts and lives, and can easily defeat all powers of darkness, but He will do so only from the principle of *"Truth"* as it regards what Jesus did in the Atonement. However, if the Believer is lacking in knowledge respecting this all-important work, as regrettably most are, the Holy Spirit although always doing all He can, is limited. He will not help an individual outside the legal boundaries of Calvary, which makes it imperative for the Believer to know what those boundaries are.

The Reader may not think this is very important; however, it is all-important. To misunderstand this is to misunderstand everything. The trouble is most of us little know all that Christ did at Calvary and the Resurrection, thereby, inserting our own works and efforts, which the Holy Spirit cannot bless. Consequently, Satan defeats us, and we don't know why, especially considering that we have tried so hard. Please believe me, this Writer knows what he's talking about, for he's been there.

(For an extended dissertation on this all-important subject, please see our Commentary on Romans Chapters 6, 7 and 8.)

(4) ("FOR THE WEAPONS OF OUR WARFARE ARE NOT CARNAL, BUT MIGHTY THROUGH GOD TO THE PULLING DOWN OF STRONG HOLDS;)"

This Verse presents that which is the very opposite of the weak weapons of the flesh. In other words, they are not of this world.

Paul was surrounded by all sorts of philosophies and systems of religion. They were weak

NOTES

and impotent to help men, exactly as the world of humanistic psychology is presently. The weapons of the Apostle were those of great power, because they were weapons of the Holy Spirit. With them and them alone, could victory be gained, and it holds true presently.

THE WEAPONS OF OUR WARFARE

The phrase, *"For the weapons of our warfare are not carnal,"* instantly cuts down all those which are of the flesh, i.e., *"philosophies, wisdom of the world, humanistic psychology in any form, etc."*

These weapons are from God Alone, are of God Alone, and cannot be mixed with those of the flesh.

Herein lies potential power for each of us. Frankly, we have failed to fully appreciate the great power at our disposal. It is our shame that in times of conflict and difficulty we have turned away from this arsenal of the soul to use the ineffectual weapons of the flesh. It has always been to our sorrow. In the light of past failures, let us turn to our present opportunities with a new determination to avail ourselves of these mighty weapons and instruments of God.

CARNAL?

"Carnal" in the Greek is *"sarkikos,"* and means *"that pertaining to flesh, mere human nature."* It is the lower side of man as apart from the Divine influence, which of course, is no match for the spirit world in any fashion. The sad fact is, that most Christians do in fact depend totally upon *"carnal weapons."* They know almost nothing about the spirit world, almost nothing about the Spirit of God. These are just words to them, but actually using such is beyond the thinking of most.

Paul had learned these things the hard way, even as Romans Chapter 7 proclaims; however, irrespective of the way it was learned, he had learned, consequently, passing the information on to us (Rom. Chpts. 6-8).

In the far greater majority of Churches in the land, if problems of any nature are addressed such as alcohol, gambling, immorality, perversion, etc., these people, whomever they may be, are instantly pointed toward a 12-step program of psychological counseling, which is not only worthless but actually harmful.

NOTES

In the January 8th, 1997, issue of the *"Pentecostal Evangel,"* the official weekly organ of the Assemblies of God, for problems of the nature mentioned, they were recommending that the individual find a Church which had access to a good *"12-step program,"* as they put it. In fact, almost all of the so-called Pentecostal Denominations have all but abandoned the Word of God and the Power of the Holy Spirit, at least for all practical purposes, in favor of humanistic psychology, i.e., *"carnal weapons."* Of course, there are exceptions in those ranks, but not many.

This is tragic, and even worse than tragic, considering that these are organizations which purport to believe in the mighty Power of God, i.e., *"The Holy Spirit."* The Truth is, they no longer believe, or else they simply do not understand the rudiments of Calvary and the Resurrection, which I suspect is the case with many. Consequently, not knowing what to do, and feeling they have to do something, they have resorted to Humanism.

There is very little opposition to this direction for the simple reason that most of the Church World, even those who claim to believe in the Holy Spirit, have long since abandoned the tremendous help which He Alone can give. As we've already stated, there definitely are exceptions out there, but not many. In fact, this, the neglect or even outright abandonment of the Holy Spirit is the greatest danger in the Church presently.

LAST NIGHT IN PRAYER

Last night (9/10/98) the Lord began to impress this upon me to a degree that I have not previously experienced. Of course, knowing this Truth, and doing my best to understand this Truth, I have sought the Lord earnestly for the Moving and Operation of the Holy Spirit within my life. In fact, the hundreds of thousands of people we have seen brought to a saving knowledge of Jesus Christ, has all been because of the Moving and Operation of the Holy Spirit. That goes for everything else done for the Lord for that matter. It also goes for the tremendous victory that the Lord has given me in my own life over the powers of darkness, a total and complete victory I might quickly add, which is so grand that it defies all description. This came about exactly as I have been relating to you in previous paragraphs,

NOTES

concerning what Jesus did at Calvary and the Resurrection, and the Holy Spirit utilizing that great Truth. So, what I am writing and you are reading, is something that I've experienced, so I know that of which I speak.

Even though what I am about to say I have known, and known succinctly, the Holy Spirit seemed to impress this upon me in prayer last night even in a greater way than ever before. It was simple and to the point.

Nothing will be done for God, absolutely nothing, unless it is done through the Person, Power, Agency, and Ministry of the Holy Spirit. If the Lord uses any talent we may have, it will only be as the Holy Spirit overshadows that talent and carries it out according to His intended purpose. So, let no one think that their talent or ability in any manner, can bring about that which can only be brought about by the Holy Spirit. Jesus said it succinctly, dogmatically, and to the point:

"The Spirit of the Lord is upon Me, because He hath anointed Me to preach the Gospel to the poor; He hath sent me to heal the brokenhearted, to preach deliverance to the captives, and recovering of sight to the blind, to set at liberty them that are bruised, to preach the acceptable year of the Lord" (Lk. 4:18-19).

This of which Jesus said, covers ever single aspect of the needs of humanity. Even in the Life and Ministry of Christ, Who was and is the Son of God, the Holy Spirit was needed in all His Power, in order that these great victories may be won. So the question may be asked, if Jesus had to have the Holy Spirit in this fashion, where does that leave us? Of course, the answer is obvious, if we do anything at all for the Lord, it will be by and through the Power and Anointing of the Spirit of God.

Jesus, Alone, holds the answer for the alcoholic, for the gambler, for the immoral and unclean, for the thief, the murderer, or any other sin, perversion, or aberration. There is no other answer!

EXACTLY HOW IS IT DONE?

Beautifully enough, we are given a perfect description in illustration form in Exodus Chapter 16.

The Children of Israel had just been brought out of Egypt, with the song and dance of triumph hardly dying on their lips, when they faced the bitter waters of Marah. Needing water to drink, and to make the story brief, Moses *"cried unto the Lord."*

BITTER WATERS

These *"bitter waters"* are a symbolism of the terrible difficulties of life, whether brought on by personal sin, or else one being the victim of sin. In fact, life is full of such.

Now, to face these difficulties, to seek help for these problems, we can do one of two things, resort to carnal measures, or *"cry unto the Lord"* (Ex. 15:25).

However, the only help that one will receive will be from the Lord. Thankfully, He invites all, excluding none, irrespective of their problem, irrespective of their failure, to come to Him (Mat. 11:28-30).

The offer is so general, so widespread, so open-ended, so all-inclusive, that none need turn away — all may come. So why would one, especially a Believer, and especially a Spirit-filled Believer, desire to resort to other measures?

The only answer is, that they do so because they do not know the Truth of the Word of God, having been led astray by their leaders whether intentional or otherwise.

THE TREE

The Scripture plainly said in answer to Moses' petition, *"And the Lord shewed him a tree"* (Ex. 15:25).

The tree was a representation, a symbolism, a type of Calvary. In fact, the whole of history, which means the whole of humanity, has ever functioned, at least as far as Salvation is concerned, around this *"Tree."* It is the answer to the dilemma of the Garden of Eden, and was promised by the Lord at that dark time (Gen. 3:15).

All Salvation and Victory come through what was done by Christ on that *"Tree."* It is the Source of all Victory, all Healing, all Forgiveness, all Mercy, all Grace, all Life, in effect, the answer to everything, and without which there is no answer. That's why the *"preaching of the Cross,"* is an absolute necessity for wasted, hurting, broken humanity (I Cor. 1:18).

WERE MADE SWEET

The Lord told Moses to *"cast* (the tree) *into the waters,* (and) *the waters were made sweet"* (Ex. 15:25).

NOTES

There is your answer!

This is the only way the bitter waters of life can be healed. Considering the terrible price paid by Christ at Calvary, it is an insult of the highest proportions, of the most egregious calumny, the most despicable character, the most utter blasphemy, to ignore what He did. Jeremiah said it very succinctly, *"For My people have committed two evils; they have forsaken Me the Fountain of Living Waters, and hewed them out cisterns, broken cisterns, that can hold no water"* (Jer. 2:13).

I AM THE LORD THAT HEALETH THEE

Strangely enough, it was sweet water and not healing that the people needed, considering that all had been healed on coming out of Egypt, with not a *"feeble person among their tribes"* (Ps. 105:37). However, God used this occasion, to give them the great Covenant of Healing by revealing Himself to them as *"Jehovah-Ropheka,"* which means *"Jehovah the Healer, or Jehovah your Physician Who heals you"* (Ex. 15:26).

Even though this great Promise speaks of physical healing, it even more so speaks of inner healing, which incorporates Grace, Forgiveness, Mercy and all that pertains to Deliverance and Forgiveness of sin.

We are told here emphatically, that Salvation, Healing, Deliverance, Forgiveness, Justification, Sanctification and in fact, every attribute of God, comes through *"the Tree,"* i.e., *"Calvary."*

Consequently, we can trust in the *"broken cisterns,"* or we can trust in the *"weapons of warfare"* provided by the Lord. We cannot trust both!

CALVARY AND THE RESURRECTION

Most of the Church hardly believes the Lord in any capacity, resorting totally and completely to the things and ways of the world. Sadder still, even those who claim to believe that God can do great and mighty things, if asked about these *"weapons,"* would point to great Faith, or the Gifts of the Spirit, or the laying on of hands, etc., all which are right and valid in their place. However, these things as powerful as they are in their own right, still cannot be used or utilized regarding all their potential, unless we understand how they fit into Calvary. Our problem is, we've tried to take Faith away from Calvary, forcing it to stand alone. It will not work in that fashion.

One of the first rewards we have of Faith being utilized is Genesis 15:6. The Scripture says, *"And he* (Abraham) *believed in the Lord; and He counted it to him for Righteousness."* The *"believing"* and *"Faith"* of Abraham pertained to Calvary and the Resurrection (Jn. 8:56). The Believer must understand, that every single thing comes through and from Calvary. Nothing is excluded. The *"weapons of our warfare"* are anchored in that event.

MIGHTY THROUGH GOD

The phrase, *"But mighty through God,"* refers to the fact that the only way spiritual victory can be obtained and assured, and that means in any capacity, is through and by the Power of God (II Cor. 1:18). Anything that man has or does within himself, irrespective of its claimed potency, is doomed to failure. The sin question in any form and the powers of darkness, can only be addressed by the Power of God. And that's where the Church runs aground. It trusts God as a general rule, little more than the worldling.

WHAT DOES IT MEAN *"THROUGH GOD"*?

To give the answer in brief, the Holy Spirit through the Apostle is speaking of the Lord Jesus Christ, and more particularly, what Jesus did at Calvary and the Resurrection. It was Jesus Who redeemed man from the awful clutches of sin and Satan. It was Jesus Who broke that terrible chain. It was Jesus Who paid the price at Calvary. That's the reason that Paul said, *"For I determined not to know anything among you, save Jesus Christ, and Him crucified"* (I Cor. 2:2).

Jesus as the great Miracle-Worker was not enough. Likewise, Jesus as the great Teacher, the great Preacher, the great Prophet, even Jesus as the Son of God Virgin-born, was not enough. He had to go to the Cross where He there became a Sin-Offering, which satisfied the demands of heavenly justice and at the same time, made Satan's claims invalid, thereby breaking the terrible grip of sin. Once again and ever, it is always Christ and Him crucified, which is held up as the Answer for sinful man, which takes in all the aberrations, perversions, and sins of mankind.

NOTES

MIGHTY

The Holy Spirit through the Apostle tells us that these *"weapons of our warfare"* are *"mighty!"* What does he mean by *"mighty"*?

First let's look at the weapons. Even though Paul lists other particulars in Ephesians Chapter 6, that of which he speaks here are foundational. They are as follows:

1. The Holy Spirit: Jesus said and it is recorded in John Chapter 16 that the Holy Spirit would be sent as our Helper. Thank God on the Day of Pentecost, He came. Inasmuch as He is God, therefore, *"All-powerful, All-knowing, and All-present,"* I think one can easily say that He is not only *"mighty,"* but *"All-mighty."*

2. The Word of God: When Jesus faced Satan in the wilderness of temptation, His two weapons were the Holy Spirit and the Word of God (Mat. Chpt. 4).

3. The Name of Jesus: That Name is so powerful, so great, so All-mighty, so glorious, so magnificent, that at its very mention, Satan and all his demon hosts literally tremble (James 2:19).

4. The Blood of Jesus: The Precious Shed Blood of the Lamb of God, is not only a cleansing agent (I Jn. 1:7), it is a protective agent as well (Ex. 12:13).

However, all of this, the Holy Spirit, the Word of God, the Name of Jesus and the Blood of Jesus, of necessity, are tied to what He did at Calvary and the Resurrection. As we've already stated, the Holy Spirit functions from that premise, the legal work done at Calvary and the Resurrection. As well, the Word of God throughout its entirety, points to the central and focal point, which is Calvary. Likewise, the Name of Jesus is powerful only on the basis of that Finished Work. And of course, the Blood of Jesus literally speaks of the price that was paid at Calvary.

IGNORANT OF THE WORD

If one is to notice, Paul said over and over again, *"Brethren, I would not have you ignorant"* (Rom. 1:13; 11:25; I Cor. 10:1; 12:1; 14:38; II Cor. 1:8; 2:11; I Thess. 4:13). The sad Truth is, most Christians are ignorant of the most basic, fundamental foundation of their Christian experience, Calvary and the Resurrection. To be sure, most think they know all about it, but actually most don't.

Millions of Christians experience precious little help from the Holy Spirit, at least by comparison as to what they could have, for the simple reason they do not know and understand the legal boundaries from which He works. As well, millions use the Word of God, and actually receive few results and are thereby left, somewhat confused. The Name of Jesus as well, is hurled constantly at Satan, with him most of the time paying little notice, and the Blood of Jesus, most Christians simply take for granted, if they think of such at all.

Satan full well knows and understands if you properly know the ground on which you stand. He knows your knowledge of the things of which we speak, or the lack thereof. He knows when you are functioning in the flesh, thinking you are in the Spirit. He knows when you are depending on self, thinking it is Christ. He also knows if you have the Truth and will back away accordingly. (Once again, I would urge you to get our Commentary on Romans which spells this out, and especially in Chapters 6, 7 and 8 of that great Epistle.)

THE PULLING DOWN OF STRONGHOLDS

The phrase, *"To the pulling down of strongholds,"* refers properly to a fastness, fortress, or strong fortification erected by Satan in one's life.

As well, the word for *"pulling down,"* which implies the entire clearance of an obstacle, is only found in the New Testament, in fact, in this Epistle (II Cor. 10:4, 8; 13:10). It is translated *"destruction"* in the latter two Verses.

Even though Paul is basically speaking of philosophic strongholds of which we will address in the next Verse, it also stands for passions and sins of any nature which Satan attempts to fasten onto the Child of God, in effect, making a stronghold of evil in one's life. In fact, this is a common occurrence. These *"strongholds"* function in many capacities: uncontrollable temper, lust, greed, pride, jealousy, envy, gambling, alcohol, nicotine, drugs, etc. We fool ourselves if we think that Christians do not battle with these things, with Satan attempting to erect a stronghold in their lives which will ultimately destroy them, if it (the stronghold) is not destroyed.

A BEAUTIFUL OLD TESTAMENT EXAMPLE

Over and over again, most of these things of which are mentioned in the New Testament in spiritual form, are given to us in the Old Testament in literal form. That's at least one of the reasons that a Believer must avail himself of learning the Old Testament just as much as the New.

When David was anointed to be King over Israel, the very first thing he did was to dislodge the Jebusites from the *"stronghold of Zion,"* i.e., *"Jerusalem"* (II Sam. 5:6-7).

Right in the middle of Israel, in fact, in the very city where God was to place His Name, Satan erected a stronghold which was occupied by the Jebusites, who were fierce enemies of Israel. Even though Saul won many battles concerning the Philistines and others, he was never able to dislodge the Jebusites. During the entirety of his 40-year reign as King, that stronghold existed in the very midst of Israel.

As someone has well said, *"If one does not defeat the enemies within he will ultimately be defeated by the enemies without."* Saul was ultimately destroyed by the Philistines without.

DAVID

Immediately upon David becoming King, the first thing he did was to take out this stronghold. In fact, he made Jerusalem his headquarters, with this very stronghold of Satan, becoming the actual site of the Temple which was built by Solomon (II Chron. 3:1).

Concerning this great victory, the Scripture says, *"And David went on, and grew great, and the Lord God of Hosts was with him"* (II Sam. 5:10).

There was no way that Israel could be what she should be with the Jebusites her sworn enemy, occupying in a stronghold in her very midst. Likewise, there is no way a Believer can be what he ought to be in Christ, as long as there is any type of stronghold in his life. As David rooted that thing out, our heavenly David, by the Power and Agency of the Holy Spirit, seeks to do the same in our lives. In fact, every single stronghold must be defeated, i.e., *"pulled down, destroyed."*

When David set out to destroy the Jebusites, they literally taunted him, in effect saying, *"We are so strong, that even the lame and the blind among us can defeat you"* (II Sam. 5:6). Likewise you dear Reader have possibly been taunted by Satan, respecting a particular stronghold that he has erected in your life. You have tried again and again but seemingly to no avail. The stronghold remains. Oftentimes you have teetered on the edge of despair, because despite your best efforts, the thing remains.

NOTES

However, to be sure, you *can* have total and complete victory. When Jesus died on that Cross, He produced a Finished Work, which means that every single, solitary power of darkness of every description, was totally and completely defeated. In other words, nothing was left undone, nothing left for us to finish, nothing left for us to contribute but our Faith.

Even though the following is overly brief, which means it is overly simplified, still, I would not feel right in my soul if I did not give at this time at least an abbreviated account of how total victory can be brought about in one's life. In the last few minutes even as I dictate these notes I have sensed the Presence of God greatly. The reason is simple. I have experienced what I'm writing about. So did the Apostle Paul (Rom. 7:24-25), and so have untold millions of others.

VICTORY THROUGH JESUS CHRIST TOTALLY ON OUR BEHALF

The great Plan of Redemption with God becoming man, was carried out totally on our behalf. In other words, Heaven did not need this great Redemption, only man. So, He did it all for us.

AT GREAT PRICE

Considering the great price that He paid, and considering that it was totally on our behalf, one would surely understand that He would desire that we avail ourselves of these great victories that He has won for us.

CALVARY AND THE RESURRECTION

This victory was won at Calvary and the Resurrection. In effect, when Jesus died that day, sinners were literally *"Baptized into His Death"* (Rom. 6:3). That means He took our place, in effect, becoming a Sin-Offering. Faith in that on our part reckons us with God as receiving its benefit. In other words, it is the same as if though we would have died for our sins; however, if we had personally died in that fashion, it would not have done any good, for the simple reason that it would have been a Sacrifice that God could not accept, due to it being polluted and stained by sin. The Sacrifice of Christ was utterly spotless, perfect, therefore, acceptable by God.

As well, we were *"buried with Him by Baptism into death,"* which again speaks of Calvary, and does not really have anything to do with Water Baptism. It speaks of the old man with all its passion and pride being crucified and buried with Him (Rom. 6:4-6).

We were then raised with Him in *"newness of life,"* which speaks of His Resurrection (Rom. 6:4-5).

Of course, we actually did not do any of this, but our Faith in Him, which simply means that we believe in what He did, and that it paid the price for our Redemption, immediately affords us a spotless Righteousness freely given to us by Jesus Christ (Jn. 3:16).

BELIEVING ON A DAY TO DAY BASIS

We did when we got saved, we must continue to believe on a daily basis that Calvary affords not only our initial Redemption, but as well, it keeps us on a day-to-day basis. It is called *"Sanctification."* In other words, the Believer must continue to appropriate the benefits of Calvary on a daily basis, and continue to do so until he dies or else until the Rapture takes place. That's why Jesus said, *"If any man will come after Me, let him deny himself, and take up his Cross daily and follow Me"* (Lk. 9:23).

If one is to notice, He said *"daily."* This simply means that we trust totally and completely in what Jesus did at Calvary and the Resurrection for our Redemption and continued victory over sin. It was all done at Calvary, and the Victory continues through Calvary, even on a daily basis.

Actually, that's what bearing the Cross actually is. It is trust and confidence in what the Cross brought about, which is victory over the powers of darkness.

That's why Paul said, *"But God forbid that I should glory, save in the Cross of our Lord Jesus Christ, by Whom the world is crucified unto me, and I unto the world"* (Gal. 6:14). Paul is saying here that the world is conquered and overcome, not by our abilities, strength or willpower, but rather through what Christ did on the Cross, and our Faith in that Finished Work.

NOTES

CHRISTIANS AND CONFLICTS

It is sad, but we Christians are too often attempting to fight battles which Jesus has already fought and won. Consequently, our efforts, be they ever so noble or sincere, are still an insult to Christ, because in effect they say, that He really did not finish the task. Once we properly understand Calvary, and that it pertains not only to the sin debt being paid, but as well the terrible grip of sin being broken, and on a daily basis, we will then find that these *"strongholds"* which were so formidable to us and which we have never been able to defeat, will simply and easily be *"pulled down."* The reason is because the Holy Spirit is now doing this thing, and because we are trusting in that which Jesus did at Calvary and not in ourselves (Rom. 8:1-3). The difference is the difference between us and God.

As sincere as I may be, as holy and righteous as I desire to be, within myself I am no match for Satan, and neither is any other person. However, Satan is no match for the Holy Spirit, and when He comes on the scene, which He always will do when we cease our own pitiful efforts, the *"strongholds"* easily fall. What is impossible to us (and impossible it is), is nothing to Him. He is God!

Even as I write these words I sense the Presence of God so strongly! Consequently, I believe that He has helped me say these things and to say them in the right way, which will mean victory to you if you will only believe.

That means that the Christian who has struggled with cigarettes for years can lay them down and never pick them up again. It means that the Christian who has come to the edge of seeing his marriage destroyed because of an uncontrollable temper, can see instant victory in this respect. In fact, it doesn't matter what it is, whether it's a stronghold of alcohol, gambling, or gossip, etc., or even religion, which is the greatest stronghold of all, they will instantly come tumbling down.

"Standing on the Promises of Christ my King,
"Through eternal ages let His praises ring;

"Glory in the highest I will shout and sing,
"Standing on the Promises of God."

(5) "CASTING DOWN IMAGINATIONS, AND EVERY HIGH THING THAT EXALTETH ITSELF AGAINST THE KNOWLEDGE OF GOD, AND BRINGING INTO CAPTIVITY EVERY THOUGHT TO THE OBEDIENCE OF CHRIST;"

Even though we primarily dealt with sins of passion respecting the last Verse, this particular Verse deals with sins of pride, which are far more subtle and, therefore, far more deadly. In fact, it was not the sins of passion as wicked as they may be, which nailed Christ to the Cross, but rather these *"sins of pride."*

By that I am not speaking of the fact that Jesus died to cleanse us from all sin, but rather of the individuals who put Him there. Religious evil is the most cruel evil there is, for the simple reason that it is hidden under a cloak of self-righteousness. It is that which opposed Christ more than anything else, and it is that which opposes the Gospel of Christ more so than anything else presently. In fact, that's why Jesus said to the Pharisees, *"Verily I say unto you, that the Publicans and the Harlots go into the Kingdom of God before you"* (Mat. 21:31).

It was not that Jesus was condoning those wicked sins, but that those sins were obvious, and not too difficult to bring to repentance. But the *"sins of pride"* are another story altogether. There is seldom repentance concerning that (Mat. 21:32).

CASTING DOWN IMAGINATIONS

The phrase, *"Casting down imaginations,"* actually could be translated *"reasonings."* It speaks of *"philosophic strongholds."*

These *"imaginations"* or *"reasonings"* speak of every effort that man makes outside of the Cross of Jesus Christ, with an effort to meet the human need. It speaks of all the philosophies of man, which attempt to understand man, but which is not of God. It speaks of all the religions of the world, which have attempted to devise their own ways of Salvation, which of course, God cannot honor. It speaks of man's efforts to assuage this terrible problem of sin through intellectualism or education, or even with riches, place, and position. It speaks of man's reasonings.

NOTES

Paul in Romans Chapter 1 graphically tells us where all of this leads. He said, *"Because that, when they knew God, they glorified Him not as God, neither were thankful; but became vain in their imaginations. . . ."* (Rom. 1:21).

Man *"reasons"* that his so-called good morals, which in fact are not good at all, should make him acceptable to God. Others imagine that their good works should purchase for them a ticket. The Spirit of God is opposed to the spirit of the world, in which He must be opposed. He throws it aside, shoves it out of the way, pointing directly to the Cross of Christ as the answer to man's dilemma, and in fact, the only answer!

"Casting down" in the Greek is *"kathairountes,"* which means *"to tear down fortresses."* The term was used of Roman soldiers demolishing military strongholds by removing one rock at a time. Spiritually, the Holy Spirit works through God's people to overthrow these sanctuaries of the enemy, and does it totally and completely. Let me give you an example:

THE PROOF

Intellectualism, or man's philosophies, or man's religions, cannot point to one single soul in all of the world and for all time, that has ever been set free from this terrible malady of sin and bondage, despite all their efforts. However, there are multiplied millions even now, beside all the many millions of the past, who have found Freedom in Jesus Christ, Deliverance from their bondages, Healing for their sicknesses, Life for their death, Salvation for their sin, in other words, deliverance from all of Satan's kingdom of darkness. If that's not proof, then I don't know what proof is!

At this very moment, there are untold numbers who were once alcoholics or drug addicts, or whatever, in Satan's darkness of destruction, but today are shouting the Praises of God, totally free from that bondage of death which once possessed them. There is no power on earth that can do such a thing as that, only the Power of God.

So, in effect, the Holy Spirit is saying, *"Out with your vain philosophies, out with your imaginations, out with your reasonings, out with your pitiful effort!"* The answer is Jesus Christ, and more than all, *"Jesus Christ and Him Crucified."*

In fact, we serve a Miracle-Working God. Let me give you just one example from World War II. It was written by a Correspondent.

DUNKIRK

"I am still amazed about the whole Dunkirk affair. There was from first to last, a queer, medieval sense of miracle about it. You remember the old quotation about the miracle that crushed the Spanish Armada, 'God sent a wind.' This time 'God withheld the wind.' Had we had one on-shore breeze of any strength at all, in the first days, we would have lost a hundred thousand men.

"The pier at Dunkirk was the unceasing target of bombs and shellfire throughout, yet it never was hit. Two hundred and fifty thousand men embarked from that pier. Had it been blasted. . . .

"The whole thing from first to last was covered with that same strange feeling of something supernatural. We muddled, we quarreled, everybody swore and was bad-tempered and made the wildest accusations of inefficiency and worse in high places. Boats were badly handled and broke down. Arrangements went wrong.

"And yet out of all that mess we beat the experts, we defied the Law and the Prophets, and where the Government and the Board of Admiralty had hoped to bring out 30,000 men, we brought away 335,000. If that was not a miracle, there are no miracles left."

And now I will say in addition to what Arthur Divine the Correspondent wrote, *"What a Mighty God we serve."*

HIGH THINGS AND THE KNOWLEDGE OF GOD

The phrase, *"And every high thing that exalteth itself against the Knowledge of God,"* speaks of every exalted opinion respecting the so-called dignity and purity of human nature; all the pride of the human heart and of the understanding. All of this is opposed to the Knowledge of God, and all exalts itself into a vain self-confidence.

Men entertain vain and unfounded opinions respecting their own excellency, and they feel that they do not need the provisions of the Gospel, and are unwilling to submit to God.

NOTES

Paul was surrounded by all sorts of philosophies and systems of religion. They were weak and impotent to help men. It is the same presently, and in fact always has been.

Men keep attempting to bring out that from their own intellectualism which they think will address itself to the human problem. The following are examples:

HUMANISTIC PSYCHOLOGY

Some small part of the following has been printed in other Volumes of our Commentaries; nevertheless, due to the information given here, and the necessity of the Reader understanding the *"lie"* of psychology, and especially considering that most Churches have accepted this lie, I think it is worthwhile reprinting the information given here, at least in part.

When you read the following, I think it will become obvious as to why we are not too very much appreciated in many Christian circles. Nevertheless, if the Truth is worth anything, then it is worth defending.

WHAT IS PSYCHOTHERAPY?

The primary Greek word *"psycho"* is the root from which we derive the English terms *"Psychology"* and *"Psychologist."* Interestingly, the word *"psycho"* is utilized in the New Testament for *"soul."*

A specific distinction should be made, however. The secular Psychotherapist considers himself a worker with *"minds,"* while the so-called *"Christian Psychologist"* considers himself a worker with *"souls."*

Proponents of Psychotherapy call it Scientific and camouflage its discrepancies with Scientific jargon and medical argot. However, the questions must be asked: *"Is Psychotherapy science or superstition? Is it fact or fabrication?"*

SCIENCE

These questions must be asked, because we have come to venerate almost anything labeled as *"Science."* If, indeed, Psychology and Psychotherapy are Scientific, they should command our respect and should be used within every community. However, if they are not, we have valid grounds for questioning the propriety of intruding them into the Preacher's methodology.

In Martin and Deidre Bobgan's book, *"The Psychological Way/The Spiritual Way,"* they state:

"In attempting to evaluate the status of Psychology, the American Psychological Association appointed Sigmund Koch to plan and direct a study which was subsidized by the National Science Foundation. This study involved 80 eminent Scholars in assessing the facts, theories, and methods of Psychology.

"The results of this extensive endeavor were then published in a seven-volume series entitled 'Psychology: A Study of Science.'"

Koch concludes:

"I think it is by this time utterly and finally clear that Psychology cannot be a coherent Science."

He further declares that such activities as perception, motivation, social psychology, psychopathology, and creativity cannot be properly labeled *"Science."*

In his book *"Psychological Seduction,"* William Kirk Kilpatrick had this to say:

"True Christianity does not mix well with Psychology. When you try to mix them, you end up with a watered-down Christianity instead of a Christianized Psychology. But this process is subtle and is rarely noticed . . . it was not a frontal attack on Christianity . . . it was not a case of the wolf at the door: the wolf was already in the fold, dressed in sheep's clothing and from the way it was petted and fed by some of the shepherds, one would think it was the prize sheep."

MAN MUST CHANGE HIMSELF?

Jacob Needleman, writing in *"Consciousness, Brain, States of Awareness, and Mysticism,"* says:

"Modern Psychiatry arose out of the vision that man must change himself, and not depend for help on an imaginary God. Over half a century ago, mainly through the insights of Freud, and through the energies of those he influenced, the human psyche was wrested from the faltering hands of organized religion and was situated in the world of nature as a subject of Scientific study."

Martin Gross, in his book *"The Psychological Society,"* says:

"When educated man lost faith in formal religion he required a substitute belief that would be as reputable in the last half of the 20th century as Christianity was in the first. Psychology and Psychiatry have now assumed that special role."

NOTES

DEEPLY ANTI-CHRISTIAN

Modern-day Psychotherapy has its root in Atheism, Evolution, and Humanism. Psychology pretends to have a cure for troubled souls. It is taught in Atheistic Universities, oftentimes by Atheistic Professors. And this same subject, with the same foundations and influences, is accepted today as an integral part of the Christian curriculum in most Bible Colleges and Seminaries.

There aren't two kinds of Psychotherapy; there is only one. As Paul Vitz says, *"It is deeply anti-Christian."*

Someone once said, *"America's problem is not ignorance; America's problem is that she accepts a lie."*

Psychotherapy is not Scientific; it is not even an *"art"* as claimed. It is a lie, purely and simply, and has no basis in Scientific or Biblical fact. When Bible Colleges offer it, they are offering a bald fabrication. When Seminaries teach it, they are teaching a lie. When would-be Preachers immerse themselves in it, they are immersing themselves in falsehood. When individuals accept a doctorate in this nefarious shamanism, they are receiving a certificate without Scientific validity.

I say that Preachers of the Gospel (what Gospel?), attempting to meld Psychotherapy with the Word of God, will help no one. They will deliver only confusion. There may be a temporary illusion of help, but that only leads people away from the true help that is available only through the Word of God.

The two, Psychology and the Bible, are as immiscible and as antagonistic as oil and water.

DIFFERENCES THAT CANNOT BE BRIDGED

1. The Bible is the word of God (Jn. 1:1). The *"Bible"* for Psychology is man's opinion which changes almost on a daily basis.

2. The Bible holds all answers relative to human behavior (II Pet. 1:3). Psychology claims to hold all answers relative to human behavior.

3. The Bible says man is an eternal soul (Jn. 3:16). Psychology has its roots in evolution.

4. The Bible says man is a sinner (Rom. 3:23). Psychology says man is a victim.

5. The Bible says the problem is man's evil heart (Jer. 17:9). Psychology says man's problem is his environment.

6. The Bible says man is inherently evil (Jer. 17:9). Psychology says man is inherently good.

7. The Bible treats the core of man's problem, which is an evil heart (Jer. 17:14). Psychology treats man's symptoms only.

8. The Bible says that Jesus Christ is the Answer (Mat. 11:28-30). Psychology says Psychotherapy is the answer.

9. The Bible says that we should deny self (Mat. 16:24). Psychology says we should love self.

10. The Bible directs us to the Spirit of God (Zech. 4:6). Psychology directs us to the flesh.

11. The Bible directs us to Faith in God (Mk. 11:22). Psychology directs us to self-effort.

12. The Bible directs us to repentance (Acts 26:20). Psychology directs us to remorse.

13. The Bible directs us to restoration (Gal. 6:1). Psychology directs us to referral.

14. The Bible directs us to Truth (Jn. 17:17). Psychology directs us to man's opinions.

15. The Bible directs us to relationship with Christ (Jn. 3:16). Psychology directs us to idolatry.

16. The Bible directs us to personal responsibility (Rev. 22:17). Psychology directs us to irresponsibility.

17. The Bible directs us to free will (Rev. 22:17). Psychology directs us to determinism (causes other than oneself).

18. The Bible deals with a *"cure of souls"* (Mat. 11:28-30). Psychology deals with a *"cure of minds."*

19. The Bible says God's Truth is unchangeable (Ps. 119:89). Psychology says Truth is determined by majority and culture.

20. The Bible says it is sufficient (II Pet. 1:3). Psychology says the Bible is insufficient.

21. The Bible leads to love for God and man (Mat. 22:37-39). Psychology leads to love for self.

HUMANISM

Psychology is actually the religion of Humanism. Humanism puts man in the center of all things. Hence, Psychology puts man in the center of all things. Conversely, the Bible puts Christ in the center as the only Answer for man. Psychology (Psychotherapy) and the Bible, therefore, are total opposites and cannot be reconciled.

NOTES

THE TREE OF THE KNOWLEDGE OF GOOD AND EVIL

If one goes back to the true roots of Psychotherapy, one has to go back to the *"Tree of the Knowledge of Good and Evil."*

"But of the Tree of the Knowledge of Good and Evil, thou shalt not eat of it: for in the day that thou eatest thereof thou shalt surely die" (Gen. 2:17).

The *"evil"* part of this *"Tree of the Knowledge of Good and Evil"* is readily obvious to all the world, even as it enslaves billions. However, the *"good"* part of the *"Tree of the Knowledge of Good and Evil"* is not so readily obvious. And because it is *"good,"* at least to the natural mind, it is readily accepted. Yet its enslavement is just as deadly, or even more so, than the *"evil"* side of the Tree.

The *"good"* part of this Tree comes under the heading of *"The Pride of Life,"* and, as such, it camouflages its evil, which is even more insidious than its opposite (which is openly evil).

Psychotherapy comes from the *"good"* side of the *"Tree of the Knowledge of Good and Evil."* And just as the *"good"* side snared Eve (Gen. 3:6), so has this *"good"* side snared most of the billions who have lived since Eve. Psychotherapy is just one of the products of this *"good"* side of the *"Tree of the Knowledge of Good and Evil."*

CHRISTIAN PSYCHOLOGISTS

The term *"Christian Psychologist"* is a misleading term causing unsuspecting seekers of help to think that such individuals have a body of learning that is not available to secular Psychologists — or to Preachers of the Gospel for that matter.

The Truth is, there is no such thing as *"Christian Psychology"* or *"Christian truck drivers"* for that matter, or *"Christian pilots,"* etc.

There are Psychologists who claim to be Christians, and truck drivers who are Christians, and airplane pilots who are Christians, etc., but there definitely is not any type of training for Christians who wish to be pilots other than the same type of training for non-Christians who wish to be pilots, etc.

Likewise, there is no training or education that *"Christian Psychologists"* receive that is any different from secular Psychologists. The education that is given to a Christian who aspires to be a Psychologist is the same education that is given to the individual who has no regard for Christianity whatsoever.

The term *"Christian Psychologist"* subtly leads the seeker of help to believe that the practitioner has a body of knowledge that is not given in the Word of God. In other words, there is an implication that the Word of God does not hold the answer to the problems that beset modern man.

In fact, the Word of God alone holds the answers for modern man, for the simple reason that the problems of modern man are the same as they have always been respecting things that pertain to Life and Godliness (II Pet. 1:3).

ALL TRUTH IS GOD'S TRUTH?

Those in Christendom who promote the Psychological Way rather than the Bible Way, claim that Truth is Truth wherever it is found, and that if Freud and those like him have stumbled upon these great *"Truths,"* of Psychoanalysis, then we should avail ourselves of the help they afford, for *"All Truth is God's Truth."*

To unsuspecting minds that statement may seem plausible; however, the Truth is, there is no Truth in that being claimed.

JESUS IS TRUTH

Truth is not a philosophy as some think. Actually, philosophy is a search for Truth. Truth is, in fact, a Person, and that Person is the Lord Jesus Christ (Jn. 14:6). In fact, the Bible teaches a fourfold Truth:

1. Jesus is Truth (Jn. 14:6).
2. The Holy Spirit is Truth (I Jn. 5:6).
3. The Word is Truth (Jn. 17:17).
4. The Anointing is Truth (I Jn. 2:27).

It must be understood that this fourfold completion does not merely contain Truth, but in fact, is Truth.

In view of that, it is impossible for anyone to find *"Truth"* respecting *"Life and Godliness,"* unless they first find and accept the Lord Jesus Christ, Who is Truth. Were that not true, then Jesus needlessly came down to this earth, thereby suffering horribly the humiliation of Calvary. No, there is no Truth outside of Christ.

NOTES

THE NATURAL MAN RECEIVETH NOT THE THINGS OF THE SPIRIT OF GOD

Paul in his first Letter to the Corinthians said, *"But the natural man receiveth not the things of the Spirit of God: for they are foolishness unto him: neither can he know them, because they are spiritually discerned"* (I Cor. 2:14).

How much plainer can it be.

The Holy Spirit through the Apostle plainly says, that it is not possible for *"the natural man"* (a man outside of Christ) to receive these great Truths concerning the human condition. In fact, Paul emphatically states, *"Neither can he know them, because they are spiritually discerned."* Once again, how much plainer can it be!

Anyone who would claim that unconverted, unredeemed men can understand spiritual Truths, simply does not know what he is talking about. He does not know nor understand the human condition and neither does he know and understand God. So, the idea that *"all Truth is God's Truth,"* irrespective as to where it is found, is not only plainly unbiblical, but downright silly. And yet, this is what is being espoused by many so-called Pentecostal and Charismatic Leaders!

THE PSYCHOLOGIZING OF THE CHURCH

A subtle and deadly process is at work in the Church today in which the Christian Faith is being *"psychologized."* This word speaks of the redefining of the Christian Faith by the intrusion of Psychological thinking into the Church of the Lord Jesus Christ.

It is related to Secularism and Humanism running rampant in much of the world over recent decades. The Secularists are attempting to remove God from our thinking and our values. The Humanists are at the same time trying to establish man as the source of all values and all necessary adequacy. These perspectives on life have helped establish Psychology as a cultural religion for multitudes of people (Hoekstra).

Regrettably, the Church has bought into this fabrication in totality. This is at least one of the reasons that the Leaders of the major Pentecostal Denominations have done everything within their power to destroy our Ministry. They have bought this lie of Psychology, and they fear if my voice is heard it will expose this *"lie of darkness,"* among other things, even as it once did. Consequently, they do everything within their power to keep our Telecast from being aired.

THE CHURCH AND THE WORLD

Along with all these developments in the thinking of the world, the Church has for decades been weakening in its calling to be Salt and Light in the world. Consequently, instead of us affecting the world as we are supposed to be doing, the world is affecting the Church. Instead of the people of God telling the world about Him and about His Ways in all things, the world is now teaching the Church the ways of man, as worldly thinking makes increasing inroads into the Church.

This process is bringing us a new vocabulary and a new way of thinking about God and man. Actually, this means we are being given a new Theology that is in conformity to this world. In this worldly Theology, the Word of God is not forsaken altogether. However, the Scriptures get twisted and tortured in order to protect and propagate this new message.

Foundational elements of *"the Faith, once and for all, delivered to the Saints"* (Jude vs. 3) are given a new, popular, earthbound, psychological meaning. I believe, and many others are coming to believe with me, that the Church desperately needs a warning call to come back to the Lord and to His Word.

COUNSELING

The Word of God declares, and our lives illustrate the fact that every Christian needs counseling regularly. However, this does not mean that we should seek an appointment with some professional counselor. It merely means that we need the direction of God time and time again, and actually on a constant basis. We are sheep who must have a Shepherd to guide us through life, with all its dangers and dilemmas (Isa. Chpt. 53; Jn. Chpt. 10).

God's Word also reveals that every Christian is responsible to give counseling to others periodically. This Truth can be seen in Romans 15:14 and Colossians 3:16, where the term *"admonishing"* can be rendered *"counseling."* We are to be *"counseling one another."* Counseling is one of the many strategic *"one another"* Ministries in the Family of God whereby we each serve the other in a mutual and reciprocal way (Gal. 6:1; Eph. 4:32; Heb. 10:24-25).

NOTES

THE LORD IS THE COUNSELOR OF COUNSELORS

The heart of the Counseling Ministry lies in Christ. Isaiah 9:6 points us in that direction: *"For unto us a Child is born, unto us a Son is given; and the Government will be upon His Shoulder. And His Name will be called Wonderful, Counselor. . . ."* This Child to be born, this Son to be given would be the Son of God come as a man. This would be God in the flesh.

The authority and responsibility to rule the Kingdom of God would be upon His Shoulders. Now, Christians know that this is the Lord Jesus Christ. He is to rule over the lives of the people of God. He is to guide every issue of thought and life for us.

Notice this title that declares one of the great Ministries that Jesus is to have among His people. *"His Name shall be called Wonderful, Counselor."* From this Prophetic Word of the Old Testament to the declarations of the Gospels and Epistles of the New Testament, it is clear that Jesus Christ is to be our Wonderful Counselor.

Even though at times He uses us as His instruments as He gives His counsel, however, He is actually the Counselor. We are not really the counselors. The Pastor is not the true counselor. The staff member is not the counselor. The experts of the world are certainly not the counselors.

Jesus is the True Counselor for the Body of Christ. Any Christians who are actually Counseling well are doing such by passing on the counsel of the Lord Jesus. In fact, it is the Lord Who is Counseling right through their lives to the one who is seeking Counseling. This is the fundamental Truth in the matter of Godly Counseling. The Lord is the Counselor. He is the Wonderful Counselor.

ALL TREASURES OF WISDOM AND KNOWLEDGE

Now, just how wonderful is Jesus as our Counselor? Can he handle the task fully? Does

He have all that is necessary to thoroughly carry out this important responsibility?

A powerful answer to these questions is found in Colossians 2:3, *"In Whom* (in Christ) *are hidden all the treasures of Wisdom and Knowledge."*

Knowledge and Wisdom are generally what people are seeking when they look for Counseling. They are needing to know more and/or how to properly use or implement what they already know. All of this Wisdom and Knowledge is available in the Lord Jesus, and the Lord Jesus Alone. All of the necessary Wisdom and Knowledge that is needed for *"Life and Godliness"* (to borrow an important phrase from II Peter 1:3) is all found in Christ. Every heavenly treasure of Knowledge and Wisdom for man to live as he should is all hidden in our Lord. That is how Wonderful He is as our Counselor!

IN CHRIST

However, we do well to remember that these treasures are hidden in Christ. They are not lying around to be automatically picked up at Church meetings or in visits to Christian Counseling Clinics or from sessions of a recovery group, or by reading the latest Christian self-help book. They are hidden in a Person. They are not hidden there so that we cannot find them. Rather, they are hidden there so that we will know where the One and only place that we are to be looking.

These treasures can only be found by seeking after the Lord Jesus, discovering the wonders of Him and His Work on our behalf and His provisions for us. The Christian Life is a relationship with the Living God. In order to allow the Son of God to counsel us, we must be developing a growing relationship with Him.

GOD'S WORD

How do we dig into these heavenly treasures? How does the Lord get His wonderful counsel to us?

Psalm 119:24, speaking of God's Word, tells us how. *"Your Testimonies are my delight and my counselors."* God wants us to delight in His Word, to seek Him in His Word, and thereby let Him counsel us through His Word. As we eagerly dig into the Word of God, seeking after Him, His Holy Spirit brings forth the heavenly treasures of our Wonderful Counselor for our lives.

NOTES

However, it should be quickly stated, that an understanding of the Word of God, cannot be brought about successfully unless there is a proper relationship with Christ.

BUT INSTEAD, WHAT IS HAPPENING IN THE CHURCH?

Instead of the Ministry of Counseling being the Lord Counseling us with His Treasures of Wisdom and Knowledge through His Word, here is what is happening.

When hurting or needy people seek help, their Churches often refer them to the human experts (so-called) of the world who have been trained in psychological theory. This new, predominant trend involves sending troubled folks to the Christian Therapist or, more and more, to the Christian Counseling Clinic. The difficulty here is that these Christian Counselors generally have been trained in the same psychological theories as the secular therapists of the world. In fact, that is their training.

Such Counselors may be well-meaning. They may have tender hearts of compassion with great desire to help people. They may even be spiritually gifted by God in the area of Counseling. However, their approach to Counseling typically involves integrating the human speculations of Godless theoreticians like Sigmund Freud, Carl Jung, Abraham Maslow, Erich Fromm, and others with the Divine Revelations of our Wonderful Counselor, The Lord Jesus Christ. Some of the larger Churches even have their own psychologically-educated therapists on staff. This is going on even though the very core of these theories is contrary to Christ and to His Word.

HUMAN WISDOM?

This is not to say that these individuals, whomever they may have been are not intelligent; however, their wisdom is not from God, but rather from this world, and as James said, *"is earthly, sensual, devilish"* (James 3:15).

Whatever these men may do, they are doing it from a philosophical perspective on life that purposely left God out of the equation. Only God can look on the heart of man, evaluate it, and supply the remedy for the needs of the heart.

Some Believers may claim at this point that they have received help from Christian Psychological Counselors. However, if the Truth actually be known, that is incorrect.

They may have received so-called help which is temporal, but the real root of their problems have not been addressed, because the theories of Psychology *cannot* address these problems. In other words, such is impossible from that source.

These individuals are using the humanistic approaches of man. In doing so, they are neglecting the Commands, Provisions, and Warnings of God, whether they think so or not. In other words, the two cannot be mixed. It is impossible to mix heavenly wisdom and worldly wisdom, Faith in God and faith in man, the Ways of God and the ways of man. In fact, this is not something new.

Man has been attempting to do this very thing from the very beginning. Cain did not ignore God completely. In fact, he offered up a Sacrifice, but it was not the kind that God demanded; consequently, it could not be accepted by God, as these modern ways cannot be accepted by God either.

SIN

If the psychological influence of the world upon the Church were limited only to the Ministry of Counseling, this would still be a very serious situation for the Family of God to face. However, the psychologizing of the Faith is consistently and increasingly reaching into far more fundamental issues than Counseling. One example of this can be seen in the problem of sin.

Romans 3:23 speaks of what this problem is and how extensive it is. *"For all have sinned and come* (fall) *short of the Glory of God."* The word for sin here is *"missing the mark."* If God's Holy Standard were a target right in front of our face, we could not hit it even if we tried with all of our might. If the Glorious Character of God (seen in His Laws and Commandments) were a measuring rod reaching from the earth to the highest point of the heavens, could anyone measure up?

The Law says, *"You shall be holy, for I the Lord your God am holy"* (Lev. 19:2; I Pet. 1:16). To measure up we must be as holy as God. However, we have all fallen dreadfully short on the basis of our own righteousness. This is the problem of sin. It is a universal problem. It affects all who exist or have ever existed or will yet exist.

NOTES

THE CONSEQUENCES OF SIN

Romans 6:23 elaborates on this matter by describing the drastic consequences of this sin problem. *"For the wages of sin is death."* All of us have sinned, and what we have earned from our sinning are some very serious wages — death. This not only involves physical death, but, far more critical, it involves spiritual death. Alienation from God, relational deadness toward God was what we earned through our sin. On our own we could not know the Lord, please Him, walk with Him or serve Him. We were all *"dead in trespasses and sins"* (Eph. 2:1). If these consequences of sin are not properly addressed and taken care of by God's One and only remedy, we would have to stay forever in that dead, alienated condition, never able to fellowship with the Lord.

ETERNAL LIFE

God has a glorious solution, and it is given in the balance of Romans 6:23, *"But the Gift of God is Eternal Life in Christ Jesus our Lord."*

What we earn from God on even our best efforts is death, for all our own works of self-righteousness are polluted with sin. God is willing to give us as a gift that which we desperately need, but could never acquire on our own, that is, Eternal Life. It is a living, lasting relationship with the One, True and Living God.

It comes only through the wondrous work of another, the Lord Jesus Christ. What a glorious Gift we have in Eternal Life. What a costly work the Lord undertook on our behalf to provide this Gift for us. Jesus went to the Cross to pay the debt we owed for our sins. He died in our place, drinking the cup of sin and death that was our appropriate judgment, that the Father *"might be just and the justifier of the one who has Faith in Jesus"* (Rom. 3:26). So, the holy Justice of God is satisfied, and He is freely able to offer forgiveness of sins and life eternal to all who believe.

GOD'S GRACE

These rich Gifts of God's Grace, as His remedy for the problem of sin, are unfolded even more in the Fifth Chapter of Romans. Herein we see not only forgiveness and new life available through Christ, but also how His provision includes the resources of God for living a fruitful and victorious Christian Life. *"Therefore, just as through one man* (Adam) *sin entered the world, and death through sin, and thus death spread to all men, because all sinned"* (Rom. 5:12).

This Verse is speaking of Adam's sin, which introduced into the family of man the devastations of sin (rebellion against God, going our way instead of His Way). Then, along with that rebellion came the alienation and spiritual deadness toward God that we are now considering. This death was then passed on to all mankind generation by generation.

ALL ARE INCLUDED!

All of us who have only been born once (natural birth, through the family of Adam's race) had passed on to us the condition of Adam. We too were existing in sin and death. This death rules as a tyrant dictator over all who do not yet have a second birth (a supernatural birth into the Family of God). *"For if by the one man's offence death reigned through the one. . . ."* (Rom. 5:17).

The deadness of sin rules over the lives of the unredeemed. It is evidenced by spiritual blindness, fear, pride, selfishness, deceit, prejudice, sensuality, jealousy, etc. Herein lies the explanation of why lives are so troubled, broken and bound. *"Death reigned through the one."*

GOD'S REMEDY IN CHRIST

However, God's Remedy in Christ is abundantly more than our sin problem in Adam. *"Much more those who receive abundance of Grace and of the Gift of Righteousness will reign in life through the One, Jesus Christ"* (Rom. 5:17).

We all start out in Adam, in all of his sin and death. The only hope available, and the only hope we will ever need for time and eternity, is to become one who is *"in Christ"* (like a branch is in a vine) by Faith in Him. When we humbly repent of our way and call upon the Lord for cleansing and forgiveness, we receive the Gift of His Righteousness that we may stand accepted before a Holy God. Though this is a glorious introduction to His Grace, it is merely our first step into the abundance of His Grace.

NOTES

This abundance of Grace in Christ makes it possible for us to *"reign in life."* Reigning in life is being a Christlike overcomer. It is growing and maturing in the things of Christ. It is living above circumstances instead of under them. It involves walking increasingly in the liberty of the Lord instead of in the bondage of the world. It involves walking in the wholeness of Christ instead of in the brokenness of man, but it can only be done *"through the One, Jesus Christ."*

Such cannot be produced in any way by the religious efforts of man, even the dedicated and zealous attempts of a serious Christian. It is only *"through the One, Jesus Christ,"* and more importantly, through what He did at Calvary and the Resurrection by paying the sin debt, and as well, breaking the terrible grip of sin for all who believe.

Reigning in life comes from trusting in, depending on, abiding in, counting on the One Who walked upon this earth and overcame the world, the flesh, and the Devil. It comes from looking to the One Who always did those things which were pleasing to the Heavenly Father.

Then, as we draw life and strength from Him, we become more and more like those who display His Love, Joy, Peace, Longsuffering, Kindness, Goodness, Faithfulness, Gentleness, and Self-control.

OF SPIRITUAL FRUIT

Such Spiritual Fruit comes from the Grace of God at work in and through us, because it is the Life of Christ flowing into and through those who do not deserve it, could never earn it, and could never produce it on their own.

This is what Life in Christ is all about. Jesus came *"full of Grace and Truth"* (Jn. 1:14). *"And of His fullness we have all received, and Grace for Grace* (or, Grace upon Grace)*"* (Jn. 1:16).

The True Christian life is by Grace from the moment of New Birth right on into Eternity. Christian living involves one layer of Grace upon another, upon another, upon another, upon another, etc. Oh, how we underestimate the overwhelming abundance of the Grace of God. Everyday is to be lived by the sustaining Grace of God, and in fact, that is the only way it can be lived.

NOTES

Every step of progress and change into greater heights of New Life in Christ is to be taken by the transforming Grace of God. Only God's abundant Grace can take people from death reigning over them, to them reigning in life.

The problem that man faces is sin. First, it is our own sin. Then, at times, it is the sins of others toward us, or the sins of the world that come hard against Believers in Jesus.

The basic problem of mankind is sin. The Remedy of God for all sin is the abundance of His Grace to forgive, sustain, set free, transform, make whole, mature, guide, and make us fruitful. This is one of the foundation stones of the Faith that the Church of the Lord Jesus Christ is to guard, stand upon, and proclaim.

THE PSYCHOLOGIZING OF THE CHURCH

This problem which we are attempting to address, this *"high thing that exalts itself against the Knowledge of God,"* is more, much more, than one merely going to a Psychologist regarding their problems instead of taking them to Christ. The entirety of the belief system of the Word of God is subtly (and sometimes not so subtly) being changed, in fact as it must be changed, at least if that course and way are continued.

What is going on in much of the Church world today concerning the basic problem of man which is sin and God's basic Remedy?

Instead of sin, man's problems now, at least in the manner in which they are being redefined, are dysfunctionalism or codependency or victimization or various types of so-called Psychological diseases and disorders. This sort of psychologized thinking in the Church is redefining in new, inadequate, humanistic terms what man's problems are all about.

The concept of *"dysfunctionalism"* is a prime example. Man observes or learns of a troubled family, and decides to call it *"dysfunctional."* That is, this family is not functioning in a manner that we or the participants would desire. In that sense, however, *"All have dysfunctioned and have fallen short of their desired level of human functionality."* We can understand where such a term comes from. It is describing some actuality in human experience.

However, it is using the wrong standard, and it does not go deep enough in its analysis. As a standard, dysfunctionalism says that I cannot function in a manner that I desire, or others did not function toward me in a manner that I desired. However, the True Standard is what God desires, and not we or someone else. He says that *"All have sinned and fall short of the Glory of God,"* which actually means, that the entirety of the human race is dysfunctional. In fact, that's what the story of Redemption is all about!

CODEPENDENCY

Codependency also is another word used in the world of Psychology, and is woefully inadequate as a diagnosis of man's problem.

While it is certainly true that some people can wrongly attempt to find meaning for their lives by becoming dependent upon helping others who are wrongly dependent upon drugs, alcohol or whatever. However, the problem is not that we are sacrificing for others, in fact, the Lord calls us to lay down our lives for one another (I Jn. 3:16).

Jesus tells us that greatness in His Kingdom is measured in servanthood (Mat. 20:25-28). The problem is that we either serve self, or we serve others out of self-interest. The remedy is to learn to serve others by the Grace of God and for the Glory of God. Then it takes on an entirely different meaning altogether.

VICTIMIZATION

Victimization is another insufficient term that people often turn to in trying to understand their deepest problems. It explains, and often justifies, our shortcomings as being a consequence of wrongs done to us, so we thereby find justification for our condition and/or place blame on others. Sure, everyone has been wrongly treated and has wrongly treated others, but we cannot build a relationship with God on the basis of *"they all made me this way,"* in other words, "my problem was caused by others." Neither can we relate to others on the basis of blame, which in effect, Psychology teaches.

The problems that we can deal with before God are our own wrongs against Him and against others. We can find that His Remedy is Forgiveness, Cleansing, Transformation, and Reconciliation (between God and man).

DISEASE

Another psychologized evaluation of man's need is seen in trying to turn every aspect of sin and carnality into a disease or a disorder. So we are now treating the disease of alcoholism and the disorder of compulsive eating, instead of dealing spiritually with the sins of drunkenness and gluttony.

The Scriptures do not deny that we can have physiological needs, like chemical imbalances, etc. In fact, God's Word does not disallow medical treatment for physical problems. *However, this does not mean that we can turn the spiritual problem of sin into mental or emotional diseases, and then treat them by drugs and individual or group therapy.*

The ultimate problem that man faces is sin. Only God can deal with sin. Sadly, the problem of sin is being psychologically redefined in many Churches today, which changes the entire complexion of how we deal with man and man's problems. Consequently, as I think should be obvious, and as stated, the problem is far more involved than merely sitting down in a chair and talking to a Psychologist.

THAT WHICH IS ACTUALLY HAPPENING

If we are honest with ourselves and with the Word of God, I think we should by now see that a subtle and deadly process is at work in the Church today in which the Christian Faith is being *"psychologized."* This word speaks of the redefining of the Christian Faith by the intrusion of psychological thinking into the Church of the Lord Jesus Christ. It is related to Secularism and Humanism running rampant in much of the world over recent decades.

The Secularists are attempting to remove God from our thinking and our values. The Humanists are at the same time trying to establish man as the source of all values and all necessary adequacy. These perspectives on life have helped establish Psychology as a cultural religion for multitudes of people, and which has been basically accepted by most of the Church.

ENLIGHTENMENT?

Many people would view Psychology's influential position as an inevitable result of living in an enlightened scientific age, to which we have already briefly alluded. However, only a minor portion of Psychological Theory is capable of Scientific verification (the fact that repeated experiments will always give the same results, which should be obvious). Actually, the overwhelming portion of Psychological Theory is philosophical in nature, in other words a search for answers.

Psychology happens to be a way to view life. It amounts to an attempt to explain man (who he is, what he is here, and how to develop him, how to solve his problems, how to meet his needs, and how to help him get to where he thinks he needs to go).

It is a philosophy of life with man at the center and with man as his own basic hope. Colossians 2:8 gives a strong warning about the philosophies of man.

TWO EVILS

God's rebuke to His people of old is so timely today, and that which we have previously mentioned: *"For My people have committed two evils: they have forsaken Me, the Fountain of Living Waters and hewn themselves cisterns, broken cisterns that can hold no water"* (Jer. 2:13). Many of the people of God today are in the process of repeating Israel's shocking sins of old. The True and Living God had pledged to be to them their constant flowing supply of life and reality. However, instead of looking to the Lord Alone to be and to provide all that they needed, they got involved in the religious systems in the world around them. How sad! How could they do this in light of all the Lord had done for them and had promised to them?

However, the Church world is doing the same thing presently. Jesus Christ is our all-sufficient Lord, our life, our all in all, yet many are turning from Him to the broken cisterns of psychological theories.

These theories are clever and ingenious (high things), but there are holes in their cisterns. They do not hold water. You cannot live by them, in the true sense of God's promised abundant life. So it all brings shame upon the Name of our forsaken Lord as it brings spiritual deadness to His people.

THE SERPENT

One of Paul's concerns for the Early Church was that it might be enticed to drift away from the God-ordained simplicity that pertains to

NOTES

Christ. His concern was related to the craftiness of our enemy: *"But I fear, lest somehow, as the serpent deceived Eve by his craftiness, so your minds may be corrupted* (or, led astray) *from the simplicity that is in Christ"* (II Cor. 11:3).

In the Garden, Eve succumbed to subtle trickery, not some obvious frontal attack on her relationship with God. By enticing the Church to follow after psychological insights and theories, the enemy of our souls may have unleashed one of his craftiest tactics ever. It all sounds so scientific, so wise, so beneficial, so justifiable, so compatible with the things of Christ. It all appears to supply those contemporary perspectives and sophisticated remedies that modern man assumes are not available in the *"ancient writings of the Prophets and Apostles."* In fact, some so-called Christian Psychologists are even claiming that modern man is facing problems which are not addressed in the Word of God.

For one to make such a statement, especially one who claims to know the Lord Jesus Christ, either shows a gross ignorance of the Word of God, or else it is rank blasphemy.

Whenever we make statements of this nature, some have challenged the simplicity of saying that in Christ, His Word, works and provisions to us, we have all that we need (that is, *"all that pertains to Life and Godliness"*).

Remember, the danger facing the Early Church (and the Church ever since) was that their minds would be corrupted and led astray from the simplicity that is in Christ.

JESUS CHRIST

Probably what people are afraid of are things that are simplistic, things that are so simple that there is no significant substance to them. However, the Message of the Scriptures is that the whole Kingdom of God is wrapped up in Jesus Christ. That is the simplicity. Follow Him, and He changes us! Follow Him, and all the fullness is in Him! Follow Him, and we are complete in Him! Follow Him, and find everything that pertains to Life and Godliness. Follow Christ, and we will grow in a fruitful, useful, purposeful life as we become instrument in the Hands of Almighty God.

It is all found in following Jesus. That is the simplicity, the lack of complication. However, it is not simplistic, in the sense of lacking sufficient substance. If we think the simplicity in Christ indicates inadequacy on His part, then we greatly underestimate Who He is and what He has done. If we told a fish that all it needed was simply the ocean, and the fish felt that we were being too simplistic, then we would know that the fish was unfamiliar with or was underestimating the resources of the ocean.

Christ is far deeper than the deepest ocean. In fact, we are offered in the Person and Work of Jesus *"the unsearchable* (unfathomable) *riches of Christ"* (Eph. 3:8).

People saying that they need more than the simplicity of Christ is like a fish saying it needs more than the ocean. The depths of the riches of Christ can never be exhausted or be shown as insufficient.

THE DECEIT OF HUMAN PHILOSOPHY

Colossians 2:8 gives us this additional viewpoint: *"Beware, lest anyone cheat you* (or, take you captive) *through philosophy and empty deceit, according to the tradition of men, according to the basic principles of the world, and not according to Christ."*

We are to watch out for and sound the alarm about these perspectives on life. We are not to welcome them into the Church. We are not to integrate them into our Message and Ministry. This certainly includes the psychological theories of man.

We must not allow anyone to lead us into these directions. The warning and prohibition applies no matter how well educated, intended, popular, or influential in the Church a Leader may be. Beware, lest anyone captivate your thinking through any of these matters.

Philosophy is man's way of viewing man and life and how to help and/or change people. Empty deceit involves humanly contrived ways of thinking that originate in spiritual deception and, therefore, are not built upon True Godly realities.

The tradition of man is another area of dangerous enticement, because it is merely man passing on to man that which seemed to be useful or desirable. Closely related to these traditions are the basic principles of the world which represent the contemporary, conventional wisdom and accepted procedures of society, but which yet are not Scriptural, and, therefore, worthless!

NOTES

THE ANSWER IS NOT OF THIS WORLD

Jesus said, *"My Kingdom is not of this world"* (Jn. 18:36). How can we mix the wisdom of the kingdom of man with the Kingdom of God? God's pronouncement on the wisdom of this world is given in I Corinthians 3:19-20, *"For the wisdom of this world is foolishness with God. For it is written, 'He catches the wise in their own craftiness'; and again, 'The Lord knows the hearts of the wise, that they are futile.'"* God says man's wisdom is foolishness.

All of these psychological theoreticians who have intrigued the Church in our day seem so brilliant, when measured against other humans. However, before God, they are foolish, because they did not learn from God, but rather, from their own vain imaginations.

Also the Lord is fully aware of the thoughts of the wise. He knows all about the theories of those who claim to hold the answer for mankind, like Freud, Adler, Jung, Maslow, Fromm, Rogers, and on and on. He says their thoughts are futile.

That word means *"useless, vain, empty."* They are of no value to God in developing His Kingdom and building the lives of His people. We must be watching out for anything that is not according to Christ. Only Jesus Christ and His Ways and His Truth are to be guiding and shaping our lives.

THE PROCLAMATION OF THE WORD OF GOD

With these warnings from God laid out before us, it is so clear that we must be proclaiming only the Message of God's Word: *"Preach the Word! Be ready in season and out of season. Convince, rebuke, exhort, with all longsuffering and teaching. For the time will come when they will not endure sound doctrine, but according to their own desires, because they have itching ears, they will heap up for themselves teachers; and they will turn their ears away from the Truth, and be turned aside to fables"* (II Tim. 4:2-4).

We are called in the Family of God to proclaim the Word of God, not man's theories. Included in this fundamental exhortation is a Prophecy that the time was coming when people would not settle for sound doctrine. They would not be interested in healthy, life-giving, Biblical Teaching. Rather, they would desire to hear those things which please their flesh, even if it involved fables and myths and theories, instead of the Truth.

NOTES

Surely these Words speak of the days in which we live. Many Church Leaders are turning away from the Truth to proclaim a Message that is heavily integrated with mythic, humanistic, psychological concepts, which titillate fleshy ears.

HOLDING FAST TO THE FAITH

God has entrusted into our care and use of His Word, *"The Faith once for all delivered to the Saints."* We are to guard it by staying away from all the human systems of philosophical knowledge. We are to adhere strongly to the exact pattern of spiritually healthy teaching given to us through the Prophets and Apostles in the Scriptures.

The Lord made this very clear in His Message through Paul to Timothy: *"Oh Timothy! Guard what was committed to your trust, avoiding the profane and idle babblings and contradictions of what is falsely called knowledge; by professing it some have strayed concerning the Faith . . . Hold fast the pattern of sound words which you have heard from Me, in Faith and Love which are in Christ Jesus. That good thing which was committed to you, keep by the Holy Spirit Who dwells in us"* (I Tim. 6:20-21; II Tim. 1:13-14).

We must not do this in a self-righteous, know-it-all attitude. It must be humbly in the love that is in Christ Jesus, but, it must be done. We must keep this good deposit of absolute, Divine Truth that has been given to us. However, we can only do it by the powerful working of the Holy Spirit Who lives in God's people.

This is another great, indispensable Ministry of the Spirit. The only way to guard this treasure of the Word of God and keep it pure in our lives, Churches and Ministries is by giving ourselves to the Guidance, Teaching, and Power of the Holy Spirit working in our lives through the Word. No other approach will stand up against the onslaught that is trying to redefine the Faith. He Alone can give us the insight, discernment, wisdom, courage, alertness, and love that we need for this critical task. He is fully able!

May the Spirit of the Lord give us eyes to see what is happening in the psychologizing of the Faith. May He give us hearts to be instruments in His Work of spiritual restoration.

(Most of the material on counseling and the psychologizing of the Faith, was derived from material written by Bob Hoekstra.)

THE CAPTIVITY OF OUR THOUGHTS

The phrase, *"And bringing into captivity every thought to the obedience of Christ,"* contains the idea that every thought of the Believer is to be of God, by God and for God.

The figure here is evidently taken from military terminology. The idea is, that all the strongholds of heathenism, worldly wisdom, pride, and sin, would be demolished; and that when this was done, like throwing down the walls of a city, or making a breach, all the plans and purposes of the soul, the reason, the imagination, and all the powers of the mind, would be subdued or led in triumph by the Gospel, like the inhabitants of a captured city.

Christ was and is the great Captain in this warfare. In His Name the battle was and is waged, and by His Power the victory was and is won. All captives are to be under His authority, and subject to His control.

Every power of thought, all the systems of philosophy, all forms of opinion among men, all the purposes of the soul, all the powers of reason, memory, judgment, fancy, in an individual, are to come under the Laws of Christ. In other words, and as stated, Christ is to be in every thought.

ACCORDING TO HIS WILL

All Doctrines are to be in accordance with His Will; philosophy should no longer control them, but they should be subject to the Will of Christ. All the plans of life should be controlled by the Will of Christ, and formed and executed under His control — as captives are led by a conqueror, which Christ is!

All the emotions and feelings of the heart should be controlled by Him, and led by Him as a captive is led by a victor. The sense is, that it was the aim and purpose of Paul to accomplish this, and that it would certainly be done. All the opinions, plans, and purposes of the world must become subject to the all-conquering Redeemer.

NOTES

THE MIND, THE GATEWAY TO THE SPIRIT

This Verse, and more particularly this phrase, portrays God's Power to demolish every physical force and every intellectual force arrayed against His Will.

Satan first plants the thought in the mind of the individual, which is his beginning of temptation and seduction. The Believer, even though he cannot stop the thought from coming, by the Power of Christ does not have to dwell on that thought, but has the power instead to throw it aside. In other words, it is not strong willpower on the part of the individual which accomplishes this task, even though one's will is definitely brought into play as should be obvious; however, it is the Power of Christ which garrisons the mind of the Believer. That's why Paul also wrote, *"Finally, Brethren, whatsoever things are true, whatsoever things are honest, whatsoever things are just, whatsoever things are pure, whatsoever things are lovely, whatsoever things are of good report; if there be any virtue, if there be any praise, think on these things"* (Phil. 4:8).

The Believer has the power in Christ to *"think on these things,"* and to shut out all things that are not of these things, i.e., *"of Satan."*

THE TRIBES OF ISRAEL

One may wonder how in the world the ancient Tribes of Israel would have anything to do with this question at hand?

In fact they do, and for the simple reason that they provide a perfect illustration regarding this particular problem of *"our thoughts."*

As it pertains to the wilderness, whenever Israel was instructed by the Lord to change locations, they were instructed by the Lord to be led by Judah which means Praise (Num. 2:9). In other words, Israel was to be led by *"Praise."* That should be as well, the revelation of a great secret regarding victory in the Lord. The Believer should be constantly praising the Lord, which holds back the powers of darkness.

The Tribe of *"Dan,"* was to be the last Tribe, in fact making up the rearguard.

"Dan" means *"judging."*

So, *"Dan"* was to judge Israel's enemies which came up from the rear attempting to attack the people of God.

Jesus Christ is our Heavenly *"Judah,"* and in fact, our Heavenly *"Dan."* He leads us in praise, making it possible for us to praise even on a continual basis, which should fill the heart of every Believer, and as well, judges (garrisons) by His great power, every *"thought"* which is not of God. Properly understanding this, the mind is closed off to that which is ungodly, bringing everything to the *"obedience of Christ."*

Of course, all of this is done by the Power of the Holy Spirit, in effect, bringing the Believer into the *"Law of the Spirit of Life in Christ Jesus"* (Rom. 8:2).

In other words, it is a *"Law,"* which cannot be broken, that is if the Believer fully is trusting Christ, understanding the great benefits of Calvary and the Resurrection.

(6) "AND HAVING IN A READINESS TO REVENGE ALL DISOBEDIENCE, WHEN YOUR OBEDIENCE IS FULFILLED."

Paul continues in the military manner, which in effect, spoke of imperial armies subjecting particular nations. When this happened, garrisons were installed and were ever on the alert to squelch any incipient disobedience, to nip in the bud any revolt. In the same spirit, the Apostle carries this through in the spiritual sense.

A READINESS TO REVENGE ALL DISOBEDIENCE

The phrase, *"And having in a readiness to revenge all disobedience,"* refers to that which is opposed to the True Gospel of Jesus Christ. The Gospel must not be compromised, must not be weakened, must not be subject to addition or subtraction. The idea is to judge between the counterfeit and the genuine.

Everything genuine has its counterfeit. It seems as though almost all things exist in double; not duplicates but doubles. One is the substance and the other is the shadow. There is the Saint and the hypocrite, the doctor and the quack, the merchant and the faker, the statesman and the demagogue, the Preacher of Truth and the charlatan. So it is that truth and error, illumination and illusion are to be found throughout our life. Our judgment and decision are required in these things.

NOT A SIMPLE MATTER

As we have previously stated, Satan is a master at making that which is of God seem as though it isn't, and that which isn't of God, seem as though it is. Circumstances and situations often cloud the issue, which means that on the surface things are not often what they are perceived to be. Actually, perception (that which seems to be on the surface), is one of Satan's greatest ploys. That means that untold millions accept a false gospel preached by false apostles, while at the same time rejecting the True Gospel as preached by True Apostles. The error is followed for a variety of reasons:

As we have stated, perception, a lack of knowledge of the Word of God, swayed by popular opinion, etc.

The reason that erroneous gospel is so easy to follow is because Satan does not oppose such, considering he is its author; consequently, the crowd generally goes in that direction. Most people follow the crowd for the simple reason that it's easier to do so. As well, they find it very difficult to take the heat of not doing so. So they follow to their doom!

PREACHERS OF THE GOSPEL

It is not an easy thing to have a readiness to revenge all disobedience of the Word of God, which is done by pointing out the error and then proclaiming the Truth. Such always upsets many people, and especially many Religious Leaders; consequently, most Preachers do not desire to rock the proverbial boat, so they say little or nothing, even though they know better, preferring instead to compromise their Ministry.

In effect, Paul is saying that he will not tolerate the false message of the Judaizers, will not brook the denial of any part of the Gospel Message, but will stand strongly against all *"disobedience."*

"Disobedience" in the Greek is *"parakoe,"* and means, *"inattention, to mishear, to neglect to hear, to disobey."*

"Revenge" in the Greek is *"ekdikeo,"* and means *"to vindicate, retaliate, to carry out justice."*

So, we are not actually speaking here of misdeeds, nearly so much as a twisting and distortion of the Gospel, which is the worst sin of all.

OBEDIENCE FULFILLED

The phrase, *"When your obedience is fulfilled,"* refers to the Church at Corinth bringing most everything in line with the Gospel, but still

NOTES

lacking in one or two areas, which evidently referred to a certain false doctrine.

The point of this phrase is obvious. *"Disobedience"* had showed its head in Corinth. Rebels had broken into the congregation. Paul would have been a foolish Commander if he had not taken measures to frustrate this movement and if he had not planned to bring those rebel invaders to summary justice. He purposely speaks only about disobedience and about bringing to justice. He does not specify who the disobedient are or what the justice will be.

The phrase, *"As soon as your own obedience shall be completed,"* answers the question as to why Paul did not at once rush to Corinth when he first heard of the problems there. He did send I Corinthians with Titus, with Titus nearly a year later taking II Corinthians as well.

He had refrained from coming himself because he did not desire to bring to justice any of the Corinthians themselves — a most painful task for him. He trusted that the Corinthians would right themselves under the measures he was taking so that only the opponents who had come to Corinth would need to be served with due justice, if they, indeed, had courage enough to stay and finally to face Paul when he actually would come. He is giving the Corinthians time to correct this situation which was wisdom.

Christians often right themselves under proper advice and counsel if they are given time; they thus obviate the need of extreme measures. Actually, this is the way the Lord intends for things to be. The Holy Spirit through the Apostle had previously said, *"For if we would judge ourselves, we should not be judged"* (I Cor. 11:31).

OBEDIENCE

In respect to Paul using the word *"obedience,"* as it is used here, perhaps a more thorough investigation of the word would be profitable.

Often our understanding of the Bible is subtly colored. When we read the Bible, we often import a tone of voice into our reading. The words we read may seem harsh or impersonal, or strident and demanding, not because they are so used in the Bible, but because we intuitively feel this way about the words themselves. This is particularly a danger when we read of *"obedience"* or *"disobedience."*

NOTES

All too often the warmth and love that infuse the Passages that speak of them are replaced by a cold impersonality that we bring with us and that robs Scripture of its meaning.

TO HEAR AND OBEY

The basic word translated *"obey"* in the Old Testament is *"sama,"* which means *"to hear."* The Biblical concept stresses effective hearing: one who truly hears will comprehend and will respond with obedience.

The Old Testament portrays obedience as the appropriate response of God's Covenant people to His Revelation, i.e., *"His Word."* In this sense, obedience is the outward expression of a heart that has turned to God.

Throughout the Old Testament, obedience is intimately associated with Blessing. The person and generation that lives in intimate relationship with the Lord will experience the Blessing He yearns to extend to His people. So God promises, *"Follow My Decrees and be careful to obey My Laws, and you will live safely in the land. Then the land will yield its fruit, and you will eat your fill and live there in safety"* (Lev. 25:18-19; Deut. 4:30).

God's Call to obedience is, at the same time, a Call to Holiness and an invitation to Blessing: *"Hear O Israel, and be careful to obey so that it may go well with you and that you may increase greatly in a land flowing with milk and honey"* (Deut. 6:3).

DISOBEDIENCE

Obedience enabled God to bless His people, but disobedience led necessarily to discipline. *"See,"* God told them, *"I am setting before you today a blessing and a curse — the blessing if you obey the Commands of the Lord your God that I am giving you today; a curse if you disobey the Commands of the Lord your God and turn from the way that I command you today by following other gods"* (Deut. 11:26-28). The consequences of obedience and disobedience were fully explained for Israel in Deuteronomy Chapters 28 and 30.

THE WARMEST TONES

We need to hear both the Promises and the Warnings as they were uttered — i.e., in the warmest and most loving of tones. This is how the Old Testament Believer who truly loved and

NOTES

trusted the Lord heard God's instructions on obedience and His warnings about disobedience.

Thus, the Psalmist did not regard God's Call to obedience as a cold command that aroused resentment. Instead, his deep love for God enabled him to hear God's Call as the loving invitation it truly was, an invitation filled with Promise: *"Do good to your servant according to Your Word, O Lord. Teach me knowledge and good judgment, for I believe in Your Commands. Before I was afflicted I went astray, but now I obey Your Word. You are good, and what You do is good; Teach me Your Decrees . . . The Law from Your Mouth is more precious to me than thousands of pieces of silver and gold"* (Ps. 119:65-68, 72).

THE NEW TESTAMENT

Two different families of Greek words are linked with *"obedience"* and *"disobedience."*

"Peitho" means *"to convince"* or *"to persuade."* It is logically linked with obedience; a person who is persuaded to obey a demand obeys it. This root is translated *"obey"* only three times (Rom. 2:8; Heb. 13:17; James 3:3).

Another word from the same root is much stronger and is used of obeying a superior. That word is *"peitharcheo."* It occurs four times in the New Testament (Acts 5:29, 32; 27:21; Tit. 3:1).

Disobedience is expressed by negative forms of this root: *"apeithei," "apeithes,"* and *"apeitheo."* In most usages in the New Testament, disobedience is viewed as a disobedience to God (except in Rom. 1:30; II Tim. 3:2).

Strikingly, disobedience does not stand in contrast in the New Testament with obedience but in contrast with Faith. The reason for this critical linkage is explored by the writer of Hebrews.

AN ATTITUDE

The other family of Greek words for obedience and disobedience is, like the Old Testament concept, linked with hearing. The emphatic form of *"akouo,"* which means *"to hear,"* is *"hypakouo,"* which in all its forms means *"to obey."* The sense here as in the Old Testament is that of understanding and responding.

Obedience can be spoken of as an attitude (II Cor. 2:9; Phil. 2:12) and most particularly as a Faith-rooted disposition. In many contexts obedience to Christ or the Gospel has the same meaning as Faith in Christ and a Faith response to the Gospel (Rom. 15:18; 16:26; II Thess. 1:8).

OBEDIENCE AND DISOBEDIENCE IN THE TEACHING OF JESUS

In Jesus' Teaching, as in the Old Testament, obedience is a relational term. Obedience flows out of a personal relationship and is motivated only by love. The reality of a relationship with God is demonstrated by one's obedience to Him.

This theme is developed in several key Passages, particularly in the Last Supper discourse (Jn. 14:17). The following are key statements in that discourse:

"Whoever has My Commands and obeys them, he is the one who loves Me . . . If anyone love Me, he will obey My Teaching . . . He who does not love Me will not obey My Teaching . . . If you obey My Commands, you will remain in My Love, just as I have obeyed My Father's Commands and remain in His Love" (Jn. 14:21, 23-24; 15:10).

The picture provided here is vital. Obedience flows from a love relationship with God and cannot be generated by any other motivating force. Jesus maintained His Own unique fellowship with the Father through that responsive relationship with Him portrayed as obedience. We too maintain our fellowship with Jesus and the Father by responding to His Words and Teaching with obedience.

Later the Apostle John picks up this theme and develops it. Obedience is one of those qualities that gives the Believer evidence that he is living in close fellowship with the Lord (I Jn. 2:3; 3:22, 24; 5:3).

THE OBEDIENCE OF JESUS

In His discourse on obedience, Jesus held Himself up as an example. Two Passages from the Epistles examine Jesus' obedience. Philippians Chapter 2 is a call to the Christian to adopt a Christlike attitude. Jesus, devoid of pride, took on human nature. Then, *"Being found in appearance as a man, He humbled Himself and became obedient to death — even death on a Cross!"* (Phil. 2:8). Subsequently Jesus was raised from death and was exalted to the highest place in our universe.

The Passage has two lessons. First, if we maintain this attitude of Jesus, we will be able to work out the fullest possible expression of our Salvation (Phil. 2:12). Only when we live in full accord with God's Will can our actions be in accord with His good purpose (Phil. 2:13).

In Jesus' full commitment to God's Will for Him, He demonstrated the level of commitment we are to achieve. And He showed us the result: exaltation.

This is the second lesson about obedience. It produces blessing, but this blessing may not be experienced until the Resurrection occurs.

JESUS LEARNED OBEDIENCE

Hebrews 5:7-10 also speaks of Jesus' obedience, especially His *"learning"* obedience and His *"being made perfect"* through it.

If one is to notice, it did not say that Jesus learned to be obedient, for that would have meant that He had been disobedient, which He never was.

The thought is that Jesus established His integrity by living a normal human life in which obedience was demanded. By actually living out obedience He was *"perfected"* in the sense of being demonstrably qualified to become *"the Source of Eternal Salvation for all who obey* (believe in) *Him"* (Heb. 5:9).

OBEDIENCE AND FAITH

Jesus spoke of our personal relationship with the Lord in terms of a love that generates obedience. The writer to the Hebrews examines the relationship of obedience to the responsive hearing of God's Word that expresses Faith and Trust in Him.

First, disobedience stems from a hard heart (Heb. 3:7-11). The heart is further characterized as *"a sinful, unbelieving heart that turns away from the Living God"* (Heb. 3:12). The modern reader is warned not to hear God today with a similarly hard heart. Both the attitude and the resulting disobedience of the earlier generation regarding Israel was located in unbelief (Heb. 3:19).

God has spoken in Scripture. One response to the Word is an expression of the sinful heart, which simply will not trust God. This response is disobedience. The other response, obedience, comes from a heart that trusts God, being persuaded that He is able to guide His people into rest (Heb. 4:1-11).

NOTES

OBEDIENCE AND RELATIONSHIP

Greek and Hebrew words view obedience as a response. One hears, grasps what is communicated, and acts on it. Thus, obedience is essentially linked to God's Revelation. God initiates by speaking; creatures respond by obeying.

In both Testaments, obedience is also closely linked with relationship. It was God's intention to guide His Old Testament people to blessing by speaking to them in Statute and Commandment. If they obeyed, they would find the blessing He yearned to give. If they disobeyed, they would find only tragedy and necessary discipline. Thus, the call to obedience in the Old Testament is God's loving invitation to blessing, and not some cold, impersonal command.

OBEDIENCE AND LOVE

In the New Testament, obedience is further demonstrated and analyzed. Jesus lived a life of obedience and in doing so demonstrated the exaltation that comes at last to the person who obeys God. Jesus' Teaching linked obedience to love; only the person who loves God will truly obey Him.

The New Testament goes on to link obedience with Faith; only the person who trusts God will obey Him. Thus, Biblically speaking, there is a definite and vital connection between Faith in God, love for God, and obedience to God, and all are a result of God's Work in a person's life.

FELLOWSHIP AND OBEDIENCE

The New Testament testifies that today as well as in sacred history, an obedience that is motivated by love and exists as an expression of Faith is necessary in order to stay close to God. We live in fellowship with God only as we obey Him.

So obedience, properly understood, is never a cold or impersonal thing. God's Call to obedience is a loving invitation to experience His best. Our response flows from a growing love for God and expresses our confidence that God is living and able. Only in a deep and loving relationship can the Biblical import of obedience be fully understood.

(The material on obedience provided by Lawrence O. Richards.)

(7) "DO YE LOOK ON THINGS AFTER THE OUTWARD APPEARANCE? IF ANY

MAN TRUST TO HIMSELF THAT HE IS CHRIST'S, LET HIM OF HIMSELF THINK THIS AGAIN, THAT, AS HE IS CHRIST'S, EVEN SO ARE WE CHRIST'S."

This Verse deals with perception, which refers to things as they seem to be but actually aren't. Paul's teaching here is extremely important, and should be taken to heart and in an extensive manner.

OUTWARD APPEARANCE

The question, *"Do ye look on things after the outward appearance?"*, simply means that one is not to judge something by eye or ear value. It is a poor and inaccurate way to judge. And yet, that's the way most people form judgments, even Christians, who ought to know better. In fact, things are seldom as they seem to be on the surface. And what does that mean respecting surface?

It means what one sees with the eye or hears with the ear, or that which circumstances provide. That's the reason that the Scripture says of the perfect judgment of Jesus Christ, *"And He shall not judge after the sight of His Eyes, neither reprove after the hearing of His Ears: but with Righteousness shall He judge. . . ."* (Isa. 11:3-4).

Satan maneuvers things in order to get people to believe what he desires that they believe. Of course, what he desires, as would be obvious, is always wrong. And yet, the way it is presented oftentimes is made to seem to be right.

As someone has rightly said, *"All that glitters is not gold,"* and yet it fools most!

FRUIT

That's the reason that Jesus commanded all concerned to judge the *"fruit"* of any claims (Mat. 7:15-20). Fruit is the result of a Ministry and cannot actually be faked, that is if it is properly observed.

Actually, the way this question is posed by Paul in the original Greek, points to the fact of what the Corinthians should have seen all along. So why did they not see that which was obvious?

That question should be asked about a lot of things. The Truth is, people most of the time see what they want to see.

What Paul was meaning is that there was no excuse for them being led astray by false

NOTES

teachers. It was obvious as to what Paul had taught as to its rightness. The fruit was obvious for all to see, even in their very lives. But yet they were swayed by the false teachers.

THIS MINISTRY

If I may be allowed to be personal, there is no reason for anyone, even despite situations of the past, not to know of the veracity of this Ministry. The Anointing of the Holy Spirit is obvious regarding the Church Services, and the Telecast. Likewise, there are hundreds of thousands of people who have been brought to a saving knowledge of Jesus Christ, which continues unto this hour. That, the Moving and Operation of the Holy Spirit and souls, are the *"fruit"* of which we speak. It is obvious to all! So why the rejection?

The modern Church, and especially the Pentecostal and Charismatic variety, has never been so bogged down in false doctrine as presently. As well, there is something about false doctrine that puts people into a drugged stupor spiritually speaking. It's almost as if they are in a trance, no longer thinking for themselves. In fact, that is the case!

Not only do we preach a Message that brings people to Christ and edifies the Saints, but as well, it is also corrective. In their spiritual stupor, many of them do not want to hear that which is corrective. If so, that means they will have to do something about the situation in which they now find themselves.

Consequently, it is easier for them to believe any number of lies that Satan produces, and regrettably so, for the most part, through Christians. Some of those lies are as follows:

That we once were of God but no longer are. Consequently, what we now say is of no consequence and should not be heeded.

Others claim while I might be a Christian, it is not right for me to Preach the Gospel. Reasons for that would vary almost to the number of people making these claims.

Many claim that what is happening is not the Spirit of God, but rather talent or ability, etc. Inasmuch, as it's not the Spirit of God, they are to ignore what is being said and done.

To be frank, I could continue to fill pages with excuses of this nature, and not a single one of them would be Scriptural. In other words, all of these excuses are patently unscriptural, and yet they are believed by most Christians.

Not only does most of the world desire to push Truth aside, but many Christians likewise follow suit. They can believe *"appearances"* or they can believe the *"Spirit of God,"* they cannot believe both! Unfortunately, it is much easier presently to believe *"appearances."*

AN OLD TESTAMENT EXAMPLE

When Samuel was sent by the Lord to anoint David as the future king of Israel, Samuel evidently not being acquainted with the family, would have anointed *"Eliab,"* if the Lord had not stopped him. The Scripture says, *"That he looked on Eliab, and said, 'Surely the Lord's anointed is before Him,'"* meaning that this young man looked like a king from all outward appearances (I Sam. 16:6).

However, *"The Lord said unto Samuel, Look not on his countenance, or on the height of his stature; because I have refused him: for the Lord seeth not as man seeth; for man looketh on the outward appearance, but the Lord looketh on the heart"* (I Sam. 16:7).

Shortly thereafter, David was brought in, and *"The Lord said, Arise, anoint him: for this is he"* (I Sam. 16:12).

APPEARANCES ARE DECEIVING

Samuel was no doubt at this particular time, the Godliest man on the face of the earth. And yet, even though this was true, without the Leading of the Lord, he would have chosen the wrong man to have been king. It was all because of outward appearances. Eliab looked like a king, and had the appearance of a king. But his heart was not right with God.

Regrettably, most are not presently led by the Lord, thereby judging according to appearances, thereby, choosing *"Eliab."* So the Church is filled with Eliabs.

The point I'm making is, if Samuel the great Prophet of God, in fact one of the Godliest men who ever lived, could not make a proper choice according to outward appearances, how in the world do we think we can?

Our judgment of people and situations should be twofold: First of all we should judge spiritually instead of carnally (outward appearances), and above all, be led by the Holy Spirit.

NOTES

TRUST TO HIMSELF

The phrase, *"If any man trust to himself that he is Christ's, let him of himself think this again,"* actually refers to the false teachers who laid claims to being followers of Christ by way of eminence. Whomever these teachers were, it is evident that they claimed to be on the side of Christ and to be appointed by Him. They were probably Jews, and one or two of them may have even possibly seen Christ during His earthly Ministry.

The phrase, *"Trust to himself,"* seems to imply that they relied on some special merit of their own, or some special advantage which they had.

The fact is, all false teachers claim to be of Christ, sent by Christ, and anointed by Christ. So that is nothing new!

The fact was and is, they were false apostles, deceitful workers, pretending to be Apostles of Christ. They beguile as the serpent beguiled Eve, simply put, they are snakes to poison simple minds. The Truth is, they preach another Jesus, have another spirit, offer another gospel, even as Paul will outline in II Corinthians 11:4.

Once again, the phrase *"Trust to himself,"* means these men were not of God, were not of Christ, had not been sent by the Lord, and were in reality, false messengers. The world is full of them presently as well!

HOW DO YOU TELL THE FALSE FROM THE REAL?

These men, whomever they were, were subtle enough to fool and pull astray some of these Corinthians from the ways of the Lord. Considering that these people had been brought to Christ under Paul, which means that they had been given the greatest foundation and the finest of Biblical Teaching. And yet, these false teachers had the power to draw some of them astray.

How could this be?

Many people are drawn astray simply because they do not know the Word of God; consequently, they fall for that which seems to be proper, but in reality isn't. However, these individuals of whom we speak, were well-grounded in the Word, considering that Paul was their father in Christ (I Cor. 4:15).

The reason that Believers go astray from sound doctrine, thereby falling for the lures of the Evil One as presented by his false apostles, is probably as varied as the number of people involved. However, I feel there are two major situations which always apply to this problem:

1. Many discontinue judging from a spiritual basis, and make decisions according to outward appearances. I think I can say without fear of exaggeration, that one will always be led astray following this method.

2. One's relationship with Christ must be maintained on a constant basis. If it weakens, and it will weaken unless the individual has a strong prayer life and Bible study, which regrettably, most don't have.

WE ARE OF CHRIST

The phrase, *"That, as he is Christ's, even so are we Christ's,"* presents the Apostle claiming that he is of Christ, and that he has the proof to back up what he says.

The whole Corinthian congregation received Christ according to the Ministry of Paul and his associates. They learned from Paul what really makes a Christian. Any man in Corinth who thus judged himself a Christian would certainly not deny that Paul and his associates were likewise Christians — unless he had been so deceived by these outside enemies of Paul's as to count them as not of God. However, if they do that, which some few evidently had been doing, they were also repudiating their own experience, which they do not seem to realize. It is inconceivable that anyone would claim that Paul was not of the Lord, especially those who had been brought to Christ by the Apostle; however, the lies of Satan, the fabrications of that Evil One, are so subtle, even as Paul will address in the next Chapter, that many Christians are fooled into believing that which is preposterous.

AN OLD TESTAMENT EXAMPLE

During the early times of David, Israel had what one might refer to at that time as the *"Saul Church,"* and the *"David Church."*

Both these men were Israelites as is obvious. Both were supposed to be under the Abrahamic Covenant and the Law of Moses. However, Saul was not of God, not chosen by God, at least in the strict sense of the word, and was, therefore, of the flesh, so to speak.

NOTES

And yet, Saul, hence the *"Saul Church,"* was favored by the people and, therefore, of the people, which meant that it was not of God (I Sam. 8:4-7).

By contrast, David was of the Lord, actually anointed of God to be the true king of Israel (I Sam. 16:1-13). And yet, even though David was of the Lord, Saul tried every way to kill him, even as the false church always tries to kill those of the true Church (I Sam. 18:12, 29; 19:9-10).

Even though most of Israel went to the *"Saul Church,"* with David's Church being very small. Actually, the Scripture says, *"And every one that was in distress, and every one that was in debt, and every one that was discontented, gathered themselves unto him"* (I Sam. 22:2).

Of course, David ultimately became the king of Israel, even as the Lord had anointed him, but it did not come quickly or easy, with the *"Saul Church"* ever trying to destroy him, as is always the case.

THE APOSTATE CHURCH AND THE TRUE CHURCH

In the Work of God, even as the time of Paul, there have always been two directions, that which is fostered by Satan, and that which is truly of the Lord. The Believer must make a choice between the two, because it is Satan's business to pull Believers from the True Church. He does so in many and varied ways, all seeming to be right, but in Truth, all actually being wrong.

As we continue in this Chapter, and especially in the next Chapter, we will see more distinctly as to how Satan operates his *"church."* We will find that it will be so similar to that which is true and real, that it will not be easy to distinguish the difference. However, considering what is at stake, the very soul of man, we must constantly do as Paul wrote in the latter part of this very Epistle, *"Examine yourselves, whether ye be in the Faith; prove your own selves. Know ye not your own selves, how that Jesus Christ is in you, except ye be reprobates?"* (II Cor. 13:5).

(8) "FOR THOUGH I SHOULD BOAST SOMEWHAT MORE OF OUR AUTHORITY, WHICH THE LORD HATH GIVEN US FOR EDIFICATION, AND NOT FOR YOUR DESTRUCTION, I SHOULD NOT BE ASHAMED:"

It seems that the Corinthian Church, with its inflated factions, reeked with boasting, and Paul is driven, with utter distaste, to adopt in self-defense language which, to the uncandid and indiscriminating, might seem to wear the same aspect. The word which is infrequent in other Epistles, occurs 13 times in these Chapters alone.

SPIRITUAL AUTHORITY

The phrase, *"For though I should boast somewhat more of our authority,"* speaks of Spiritual Authority which automatically comes with the Calling of the Apostle. Such authority is also resident in *"Prophets, Evangelists, Pastors and Teachers,"* although possibly, on a somewhat lesser scale (Eph. 4:11).

However, this authority is not to tear down, nor is it even to be exercised over people, but rather to smash the power of the enemy, i.e., demon spirits, etc. Paul had no reason to be ashamed, because he had not been guilty of exercising his authority in an unlawful manner, i.e., *"for destructive purposes."* The only time he would do so is if he recognized the power of the Evil One working in their midst, and even then, this authority would be directed at the spirits of darkness operating through these people.

Contemporary Ecclesiastical Leaders would do well to follow his practices. He used his authority to build up the Kingdom of God and to tear down the kingdom of Satan. How many times has this order been reversed by some modern clerics who seem more concerned about preserving their positions then preserving the Church of the Lord Jesus Christ (Rossier).

Our whole authority as given by the Lord, Paul says, is *"for upbuilding, not for wrecking you. In this way we use this authority, with this as the aim and object, ever to build you up spiritually in the Lord, never to tear you down and to wreck you spiritually. It is the aim which the Lord set for us; and when we boast of our authority, it is as having accomplished this blessed purpose, and no one can put us to shame for boasting thus."*

THE FALSE APOSTLES

Here we have a direct blow against the false apostles. What Paul and his assistants had built up so beautifully, a very Temple of God, these false apostles, stealing and later when Paul and his associates were far away, went on to tear down, to wreck. Paul puts it personally: for upbuilding and not for wrecking *"you."* The false apostles reversed that.

They used their spurious authority *"not for upbuilding but for wrecking you."* These false apostles wrecked the Lord's building, yea, wrecked it by stealthy undermining (Lenski).

Paul and his assistants were also to do some *"wrecking,"* some tremendous wrecking with great engines of war, but it would be the wrecking of false doctrine and works of Satan and not people.

Spiritual Authority is a strong subject in the modern Church. Exactly what is Spiritual Authority, and who has this power and responsibility?

WHAT IS SPIRITUAL AUTHORITY?

The Greek word for *"authority,"* is *"exousia,"* and means *"delegated power or freedom of choice."*

When speaking of secular authority, it means the *"power to give orders,"* but which we are not studying here.

Concerning *"Spiritual Authority,"* it refers to the power *"to give orders,"* which is limited to demon spirits, and never to people.

USING JESUS AS AN EXAMPLE . . .

A Roman soldier came to Jesus to ask for help. His statement then penetrated to the heart of the authority issued. He expressed the belief that if Jesus would simply speak the word, his servant would be healed, because *"I myself am a man under authority, with soldiers under me. I tell this one 'Go' and he goes; and that one 'Come,' and he comes. I say to my servant, 'Do this,' and he does it"* (Mat. 8:9).

The point is this: As a military officer this man derived his authority from Rome, i.e., from the empire itself, which had chosen to extend to him the freedom of action he enjoyed in controlling the behavior of his troops.

The Officer's request for Jesus to simply speak a healing word was a confession of Faith. The Officer recognized that the authority Jesus derived from God was so complete that He was able to exercise control even over diseases. Jesus spoke and acted with full Divine authority and authorization.

NOTES

THE SON OF MAN HAS AUTHORITY

The Gospels tell us that Jesus' very freedom of action in teaching and healing stunned and disturbed the Jewish people (Mk. 1:22, 27; Lk. 4:32-36). Instead of constantly referring to tradition as the authority for His actions, Jesus relied on His Own unmistakable aura of power. When Jesus scandalized His listeners by pronouncing the sins of a paralyzed man forgiven, He proved His authority to do so by healing him: *"So that you may know that the Son of Man has authority (exousia, freedom of action) to forgive sins. . . ."* (Mat. 9:6-8; Mk. 2:10; Lk. 5:24).

Despite Jesus' Miracles, at the end of His Ministry on earth He was still being challenged by the Religious Leaders who were unwilling to accept Him as God's Son and Messenger (Mat. 21:23-29; Mk. 11:28-33; Lk. 20:2-8).

The Gospels, however, report many statements made by Jesus that define His authority, and the Epistles extend the authority of the now-risen Lord. While Jesus was on earth, His Miracles showed His authority over nature, sickness, sin, demons, and even death itself. However, He never used that authority over people if one is to carefully notice.

THAT WHICH THE FATHER GRANTED HIM

Jesus has authority to judge all humankind (Jn. 5:27). The Father has *"granted Him authority over all people that He might give Eternal Life to all those You* (the Father) *have given Him"* (Jn. 17:2).

Human beings might appear to have the power to snatch Jesus away from His friends and to take His life. But Jesus claimed, *"I lay down My life — only to take it up again. No one takes it away from Me, but I lay it down of My Own accord. I have authority to lay it down and authority to take it up again"* (Jn. 10:17-18).

After His Resurrection Jesus told His followers, *"All authority in Heaven and on earth has been given to Me"* (Mat. 28:17).

This means that Jesus now has total freedom to act (Col. 2:10), and He does act on behalf of His Body, the Church (Eph. 1:21-23).

Ultimately Jesus will exercise His freedom to act and will destroy every competing power, making everything subject to the direct, active Will of God the Father (I Cor. 15:24-28).

So, Spiritual Authority is the freedom of the Child of God to act against the powers of darkness, which includes all demon spirits as they affect man.

NOTES

Jesus said, *"And these signs* (this authority) *shall follow them that believe; in My Name they shall cast out devils; they shall speak with new tongues; they shall take up* (put away) *serpents* (evil spirits)*; and if they drink any deadly thing it shall not hurt them; they shall lay hands on the sick, and they shall recover"* (Mk. 16:17-18). All of this speaks of Spiritual Authority.

When Jesus said, *"All power is given unto Me in Heaven and in earth,"* He was speaking of *"authority"* (Mat. 28:18).

When He said, *"Go ye therefore, and teach all nations, baptizing them in the Name of the Father, and of the Son, and of the Holy Spirit: teaching them to observe all things whatsoever I have commanded you: and, lo, I am with you alway, even unto the end of the age,"* He was speaking of delegated power given to Believers, i.e., *"authority"* (Mat. 28:19-20). In other words, He was delegating His Power (authority) to all Believers.

That's the reason He also said, *"But ye shall receive power* (*'dunamis,'* inherent power capable of reproducing itself like a dynamo)*, after that the Holy Spirit is come upon you"* (Acts 1:8). This speaks of the power of the authority granted.

WHO HAS SPIRITUAL AUTHORITY?

Every Believer has Spiritual Authority (Mk. 16:15-18; Acts 1:8).

He also said, *"Behold, I give unto you* (all Believers) *power* (authority) *to tread on serpents and scorpions* (demon spirits)*, and over all the power of the enemy: and nothing shall by any means hurt you."*

He then said, *"Notwithstanding in this rejoice not, that the spirits are subject unto you; but rather rejoice, because your names are written in Heaven"* (Lk. 10:19-20).

In the 20th Verse, we are plainly told that our authority is over *"spirits"* which speaks here of evil spirits, and never over human beings. So, all Believers have Spiritual Authority, that is if they are baptized with the Holy Spirit (Acts 1:8).

REGARDING DOCTRINE

Regarding Doctrine, I think that the Holy Spirit has delegated greater authority to

"Apostles, Prophets, Evangelists, Pastors and Teachers" (Eph. 4:11).

In other words, this particular authority, even of which Paul speaks in II Corinthians 10:8, comes with the Call.

It is for the *"perfecting of the Saints, for the Work of the Ministry, for the edifying of the Body of Christ"* (Eph. 4:12).

However, again this authority is not to be leveled at people, in other words to give orders, but rather to proclaim Sound Doctrine. Of the fivefold Calling, I think the Scripture bears out that the Apostle bears the greater authority, with the Prophet doing so in Old Testament times. Paul said as much, *"And are built upon the foundation of the Apostles and Prophets, Jesus Christ Himself being the Chief Cornerstone* (Chief Authority)*"* (Eph. 2:20).

WHAT ABOUT DENOMINATIONAL HEADS AND SPIRITUAL AUTHORITY?

These Administrative Offices in the Church are definitely Scriptural, as they come under the headings of *"helps and governments"* (I Cor. 12:28). However, they are administrative only, and carry no spiritual authority whatsoever within themselves.

I realize that some Denominational Leaders in the last few years, have made attempts to claim that they had Spiritual Authority by reason of their elective office (voted by popular demand into office); however, Spiritual Authority and the fivefold Calling of Ministry, are not elected by men, voted on by men or appointed by men, but rather called of God.

These individuals were claiming, even as many have down through the centuries, that due to their having this so-called Spiritual Authority they were to be obeyed, irrespective of what they demanded. In other words, they were giving orders to people, and demanding obedience.

Even at first blush, this should be obvious as to it being totally unscriptural. There is no precedent for such in the Word of God.

While those particular elective offices may in fact be of the Lord, that is if they are conducted Scripturally, they in fact carry no Spiritual Authority. As well, even those who are of the fivefold Calling, although having Spiritual Authority, will never use it in that particular fashion, and if they do, it is not of God, and should not be obeyed.

NOTES

As stated, true Spiritual Authority is never over people, but rather over demon spirits and as well, has its place in the realm of Sound Doctrine.

(This becomes more understandable when we recognize the fact that demon spirits are also the instigators of all false doctrine. I Tim. 4:1)

PAUL'S EXAMPLE

If one is to notice, even though Paul definitely had Spiritual Authority, he always dealt very kindly with people, never ordering them around, never actually giving orders period. He would constantly say, *"I beseech you,"* which actually means, *"I beg you."* That's a far cry from some Ecclesiastical Leaders who demand things which are totally unscriptural, and then claim they must be obeyed. Of course, such is foolishness, and more foolish still, for people to believe such pap.

EVEN IN THE REALM OF DOCTRINE, HOW FAR DOES SPIRITUAL AUTHORITY EXTEND?

All Spiritual Authority is subject totally and completely to the Word of God. In other words, it must never violate the Word, irrespective as to who says what. If it does violate the Word, it must not be obeyed. A perfect example is Simon Peter.

First of all, this man was one of the Godliest men who ever lived. He was not only the spokesman for the original Twelve, but was used by the Lord to preach the inaugural Message of the Church on the Day of Pentecost (Acts Chpt. 2). As well, he was used mightily of God concerning the forming of the Early Church as recorded in Acts Chapters 3, 4, and 5. As well, he first of all, ministered to Gentiles (Acts Chpt. 10).

But yet, while at Antioch, the Scripture says, *"that certain came from James . . . but* (and) *when they were come, he withdrew and separated himself, fearing them which were of the circumcision."*

The Scripture even says that *"Barnabas also was carried away with their dissimulation,"* which speaks of *"hypocrisy"* (Gal. 2:11-14).

Some may think this to be a minor thing; however, it was anything but minor. In fact, it was a frontal attack on the great Covenant of Grace.

However, even though Peter was definitely an Apostle, in fact, one of the greatest of the

Apostles, still, what he was doing at that particular time was Unscriptural, and Paul *"withstood him to the face, because he was to be blamed"* (Gal. 2:11).

If Paul had not been there, even the newest convert, whoever that may have been, should have stood his ground in the face of the great Apostle, and said *"No! This is not right!"* Of course, it would have taken much courage for one to have done that, especially one of far less statue; however, the Scripture demands that every single Believer do his very best to abide according to the Word of God. If it's according to the Word, then it ought to be obeyed, at least if it applies to the individual. If it is not according to the Word, it must not be obeyed.

In fact, this very issue, obedience, has soaked the earth with blood, with millions down through the centuries refusing to obey Civil Governments which demanded something unscriptural, and even religious governments. To be sure, they had to pay with their lives, but better that than to lose one's soul.

The Word of God is to always be the ultimate authority. Consequently, even if a true Apostle of the Lord erroneously demands something regarding Doctrine, it must not be obeyed, much less those who impose their self-appointed authority.

HOW IS SPIRITUAL AUTHORITY TO BE USED?

In fact, this has actually already been answered.

Spiritual Authority is totally unlike Civil Authority which can *"give orders,"* which demands obedience, and rightly so — that is, if it does not violate our conscience or the Word of God. Spiritual Authority carries no such demand. In fact, Spiritual Authority, as already stated, extends its authority only over Demon Spirits, and as well sets the standard for Doctrine according to the Word of God. As we've already stated, this goes hand-in-hand, for the simple reason that demon spirits are the instigators of all false doctrine (I Tim. 4:1).

The New Testament teaches through the example of Christ and as well the Apostle Paul, that whatever authority Christian Leaders actually may have, their freedom of action does not include the right to control the actions and choices of their brothers and sisters.

NOTES

In fact, the more we study Paul, even II Corinthians 10:8, the Scripture of our study, this and other Passages, tell us that the style of leadership practiced by Paul, and sanctioned by the Holy Spirit, suggests strongly that in the Church God limits the authority given to leaders. The leader's authority is not an authority to control, but an authority to help the Believer use his or her freedom to respond willingly to Jesus, which is a far cry from the dictatorial authority evidenced by some presently!

This means that no Preacher, be he Denominational head or whoever, be he an Apostle or otherwise, has the right to tell another man or woman what he can preach, if he can preach, and where he can preach. There is no evidence given whatsoever for such anywhere in the New Testament. God, not other men, calls men to preach. Consequently, even though I owe my brother and sister in the Lord the privilege and opportunity of loving them, there is nothing in Scripture that says I must obey them (Rom. 13:8).

CONTROL

The further away that religious denominations get from God, the more they attempt to exercise control over the members of the Denomination, and especially its Preachers, which in effect, removes the leadership from the Headship of Christ, into the hands of frail men. Evidently, they are fearful of allowing Christ to be the Head of the Church. However, the moment His Headship is abrogated in any manner, the Holy Spirit vacates the premises. He will only operate under the legal guidelines of the Headship of Christ and never of men.

In fact, even though it is a common thing for us to use terminology such as *"Spiritual Leaders,"* and within a narrow sense, that is correct; however, in reality, Christ is the Head, with the Holy Spirit serving as the Administrator, and the Heavenly Father serving as the Parent. Therefore, all true Spiritual Leadership resides in the Trinity. That's the reason it is wrong to refer to any man as a *"Pope,"* or even a *"Priest."* We have one Father, and that is God, one Lord, and that is Jesus. As well, Jesus is our Great High Priest, Who serves as the Mediator between God and men. No other is needed!

As well, the idea of men being appointed as *"Bishops"* over certain areas incorporating many Churches, etc., is unscriptural. There is nothing in the New Testament to verify such. In fact, the title Bishop, Pastor, Shepherd, Elder, and Presbyter, all mean the same thing, that of the Pastor of a *Local* Church. Once again, to do otherwise constitutes a man-made office, which cannot be sanctioned by the Holy Spirit. Regrettably, men love to be lords, and religious men most of all, and, therefore, to lord it over others. Jesus said, *"But it shall not be so among you"* (Mat. 20:25-26).

GOVERNMENT?

I have been accused of not believing in *"government"*; however, the very opposite is true. Actually, our strong suit, our foundation, the very thing we preach and teach strongly so, is *"Government."* However, it is *"Government"* according to the Bible, in other words, that which is given to us by the Holy Spirit in the Book of Acts, and the Epistles.

In fact, much if not most Church Government is totally unscriptural, for the simple reason that worldly men have attempted to bring Civil Government over into the Church. It won't work because it's the ways of the world.

Anytime anything differs from the Word of God, even to the slightest degree, *"leaven"* is then being instituted and inserted. If that happens, and the *"leaven"* is not removed, which speaks of man's ways and not God's Ways, the *"leaven"* will ultimately corrupt the whole (I Cor. 5:6).

EDIFICATION AND NOT DESTRUCTION

The phrase, *"Which the Lord hath given us for edification, not for your destruction,"* gives us the purpose for Spiritual Authority. As we have already stated, it is never to be used by true Apostles to destroy somebody, but rather the very opposite.

"Edification" in the Greek is *"oikodome,"* and means *"architecture, a structure, building, to build up." "Destruction"* refers to the very opposite.

Paul had no ulterior motives in mind as should be obvious. He only wanted these people to be built up in the Lord, to grow close to the Lord, to be led by the Lord. By contrast, these false teachers had other motives in mind. They wanted power, or money, or both! To obtain this, they would seek to draw these people after themselves, and would seek to denigrate the Apostle Paul to do so.

NOTES

WHY NOT ORIGINATE SOMETHING THEMSELVES?

That's a good question. They did not originate anything themselves, i.e., *"plant a new Church,"* for the simple reason that their message being false, therefore, not anointed by the Lord, could not get anyone saved. So it was virtually impossible for them to start anything new; consequently, they had to parasite off something that had been started by others, in this case Paul. In fact, this is the manner of false teachers.

They very seldom make any efforts whatsoever to get people to Christ and for the obvious reasons. One said just the other day over Television, *"We do not attempt to get people saved, that's not our ministry."*

First of all, it is the ministry of anybody in the Work of God, who is truly called by Christ, to get people saved. Even though some callings will certainly have more success than others, still, the idea that Bible Teachers never see anyone saved, is erroneous indeed!

The Truth is, the only way those false teachers then, and these false teachers now, can exist is by parasiting on something built up by others, which will always fall out ultimately to *"destruction."* That's one of Satan's oldest tricks.

He comes in to unsuspecting converts, claiming that they are now ready for greater enlightenment. Regrettably, it's not enlightenment they will get, but the very opposite. Sadly, much of the Charismatic world falls into this category, as it pertains to the *"prosperity message,"* etc.

NOT ASHAMED

The phrase, *"I should not be ashamed,"* means simply that Paul was not ashamed of the manner in which he had presented the Gospel, had dealt with the Corinthians, and had conducted himself.

In effect, he is saying, *"No shame shall ever accrue to me from my 'boast' being proved false."*

CRITICS!

These false teachers were criticizing Paul, just as every true Believer will experience criticism. Of course, as we all know, there is such a thing as constructive criticism and such a thing as destructive criticism.

Irrespective, it's a good thing to know what one's critics say, for in this way we may discover weaknesses in ourselves that our own judgment does not see. Someone has called his critics the unpaid sentinels of his soul.

Another has said, *"Men know not themselves by themselves alone."* May grace bring us then to the place where we shall be thankful for the criticism as well as the commendation.

Of course, and as stated, there is harmful as well as helpful criticism. If we are in this way to wash one another's feet, we must be careful that the water is not too hot. Bitter criticism of another's actions may proceed from ignorance of his motives. Criticism, in other words, may scald rather than cleanse.

None of us is beyond the place of improvement. Knowing this, we should seek that state of growth in Grace where we may profit and learn by the adversities, injustices, and criticisms that come our way.

Paul answered his critics by challenging the method of their criticism. He said, and to which we have already referred, *"Do ye look on things after the outward appearance?"* He tells them, his critics, that this is not the proper way to judge anything.

One person is no better than another just because he looks better or has more. There is an equality of birth — this time the New Birth. There is an equality of place — this time our place in Christ. Disciples are not to be judged by appearances, but by character. However, character is what God knows you are, while reputation is what people think you are.

(9) "THAT I MAY NOT SEEM AS IF I WOULD TERRIFY YOU BY LETTERS."

The *"Letters"* of which he speaks, at least as it concerned the Corinthians, were the Epistles we now know as I and II Corinthians.

LETTERS

Even though it was done in a somewhat left-handed way, his critics were casting aspersions on his *"Letters."* I wonder if they knew or understood that these *"Letters"* were actually the *"God-breathed Word of God!"*

No, they did not realize that, because the next Verse proclaims them as *"his Letters."*

NOTES

How awful to have in one's hands the very Word of God, in fact, a Word (Letter), which will be read by untold millions down through the centuries, and is actually that given by God, and not have enough spiritual sense to recognize it for what it is. In other words, it is the same as Genesis, or Exodus, or the Psalms, etc.

I think the evidence is clear that these men would have laughed if someone had mentioned this fact to them; nevertheless, it was true!

HOW MANY TIMES IS THIS ACT PRESENTLY REPEATED?

Since John the Beloved closed out the Canon of Scripture on the Isle of Patmos by the writing of the Book of Revelation, no further Word of God has been added, nor will anymore be added. And yet, anytime God truly does something, truly uses someone, and it is ridiculed, such critics fall into the same category as those who criticized Paul's Epistles, in effect criticizing Paul. In fact, it's impossible to criticize that which is of God, without criticizing the person whom God is using. We should get an idea from Paul's writings as to exactly what the Lord thinks of such.

While Believers are to definitely *"try the spirits"* (I Jn. 4:1), and check everything against the Word of God (Mat. 4:1-11), and as well check the *"fruit"* (Mat. 7:15-20), if those litmus tests are passed, tendering any type of criticism endangers the Believer. When such is done, one is actually criticizing God.

Paul was accused by his critics of *"terrifying"* the people by his weighty Letters. The Truth is, Paul was not intending to terrify anyone. He was writing exactly what the Holy Spirit wanted written, and which was written, which constituted the Word of God, should in fact, cause people to *"tremble."* The Holy Spirit, through the Prophet Isaiah, said, *"But to this man will I look, even to him that is poor and of a contrite spirit, and trembleth at My Word"* (Isa. 66:2).

At the same time, Paul, at least as far as his thoughts were concerned, had no desire whatsoever to terrify anyone. He begins the statement by saying, *"That I may not seem...."* But yet at times, I think it is obvious, that some of the statements made did *"terrify,"* and because the Holy Spirit meant for them to do so.

THE WORD OF GOD

The Bible is not a novel. It is not just another book. It is the Word of God. Consequently, God says what He means, and means what He says. That's why Jesus said, *"Till heaven and earth pass, one jot or one tittle shall in no wise pass from the Law, till all be fulfilled"* (Mat. 5:18).

The Word of God should console, comfort, strengthen, edify, lead, guide, and direct, but it also at times, should *"terrify."*

(10) "FOR HIS LETTERS, SAY THEY, ARE WEIGHTY AND POWERFUL; BUT HIS BODILY PRESENCE IS WEAK, AND HIS SPEECH CONTEMPTIBLE."

We now begin to catch a glimpse of the type of slander leveled against Paul. His person and appearance were denigrated. His mannerisms suspect, at least according to these experts. So exactly what was the Truth?

LETTERS, WEIGHTY AND POWERFUL

The phrase, *"For his Letters, say they, are weighty and powerful,"* presents the description given by his critics. However, even though they referred to them as such, they did not believe the content of these *"Letters,"* or else, they would have repented.

Even though the word *"Letters"* is used in the plural, by this time, at least as far as we know, only one *"Letter"* had been sent to the Corinthians, with II Corinthians to be sent shortly. So, they were either talking about other *"Letters,"* which have been lost to us, which many believe at least one other was written to the Corinthians, or else Paul's other Epistles, of which they were no doubt familiar.

THE MANNER IN WHICH PAUL WROTE

As we should know, Inspiration as given by God does not pertain to automatic writing, but rather that the Holy Spirit use the talents, abilities, education, and personality of the writer in question. There is evidence, that the Holy Spirit even structured the sentences down to each word, actually helping the writer to find the correct word, while at the same time not departing from the writer's personality, etc. Of course, only God could do such a thing, but that is exactly what God did.

As a result, the entirety of the Bible is God-breathed, which actually means it is error free.

NOTES

Paul wrote somewhat in the style of a lawyer. His Epistles abounded with strong argument, manly appeals, and impressive reproof. This even his enemies were compelled to admit, and this no one can deny whoever read them.

Paul's Letters comprise a considerable portion of the New Testament; and some of the most important Doctrines of the New Testament are those which are advocated and enforced by him; and his Letters have done more to give shape to the Theological Doctrines of the Christian world than any other cause whatever. Counting Hebrews, he wrote 14 Epistles to Churches and individuals on various occasions and on a great variety of topics; and his Letters soon rose into very high repute among even the inspired Ministers of the New Testament (II Pet. 3:15-16), and were regarded as inculcating the most important Doctrines of Christianity.

GENERAL CHARACTERISTICS

The general characteristics of Paul's Letters are:

1. They are strongly argumentative. See especially the Epistles to the Romans and the Hebrews.

2. They are distinguished for boldness and vigor of style.

3. They are written under great energy of feeling and of thought — a rapid and impetuous torrent that bears him forcibly along.

4. They abound more than most other writings in parentheses, and the sentences are often involved, even greatly so.

5. They often evince rapid transitions and departures from the regular current of thought. A thought strikes him suddenly, and he pauses to illustrate it, and dwells upon it long, before he returns to the main subject. The consequence is, that it is often difficult to follow him.

6. They are powerful in reproof — abounding with strokes of great boldness of denunciation, and also with specimens of most withering sarcasm and most delicate irony.

7. They abound in expressions of great tenderness and pathos. Nowhere can be found expressions of heart more tender and affectionate than in the writings of Paul.

8. They dwell much on great and profound Doctrines, and on the application of the

Principles of Christianity to the various duties of life.

9. They abound with references to the Saviour. Paul illustrates everything by His Life, His Example, His Death, His Resurrection. Is it not wonderful that Letters composed on such subjects and in such manner, by an inspired man, produced a deep impression on the Christian world; nor that they should be regarded now as among the most important and valuable portions of the Word of God. Take away Paul's Letters, and what a chasm would be made in the New Testament! What a chasm regarding Doctrines and especially in the consolations of the Christian world! Of course, that should be obvious, inasmuch as Paul was given the entirety of the New Covenant by the Holy Spirit.

(The material on Paul's Epistles and his manner of writing was derived from the scholarship of Albert Barnes.)

THE BODILY PRESENCE
OF THE APOSTLE

The phrase, *"But his bodily presence is weak, and his speech contemptible,"* presents the slander concerning his person.

Is it correct?

Liars cannot tell the truth, and even when they do tell the truth, it is somehow turned into a lie.

The phrase, *"His speech contemptible,"* not only denigrated his delivery, but also the substance of his Message. In other words, they didn't believe what he wrote or preached.

Rather than paying heed to these windbags, we should do better to get our picture from the hints which Paul himself furnishes and which Luke gives (Acts 14:12).

Barnabas evidently looked more imposing, but Paul was the superior speaker. In the next Verse of this Chapter, Paul says that he and his associates would show themselves as being mighty in act as they showed themselves mighty in writing.

The fact is, the man who gave the addresses which Luke sketches in Acts, which on occasion were very dramatic, some of them impromptu at that, was indeed no shallow, glittering, Tertullus (Acts 24:1-8), but a real speaker. What else could a man be who stormed the citadels of the great pagan world with indomitable courage and established Churches everywhere

NOTES

despite fierce opposition? Let no slander deceive us in regard to Paul.

Paul is speaking about one of the Corinthians who is impressed by this slander, who himself also repeats it, silly though it is. Derogatory flings find such easy lodgement. People who ought to know better repeat them and often act as if they had to be true (Lenski).

No one can read Paul's defense before Agrippa or Felix, and not be convinced that as a speaker he deserves to be ranked among the most distinguished of ancient times. No one who reads the account in the Book of Acts can believe that he had any remarkable impediment in his speech, or that he was remarkably deformed in any manner as claimed by some.

Judged by their standard, it may be that Paul had not the graces in voice or manner, or in the knowledge of the Greek language, which they esteemed necessary in a finished speaker or orator; but judged by his power of thought, and his bold and manly defense of Truth, and his energy of character and manner, and his power of impressing Truth on mankind, he deserves, doubtless, to be ranked among the first orators of antiquity. No man has left the impress of his own mind on more other minds than Paul. And yet, irrespective as to the ability of his speaking, it was the Holy Spirit Who anointed him, helped him, inspired him, and empowered him. That was the secret of his preaching!

(11) "LET SUCH AN ONE THINK THIS, THAT, SUCH AS WE ARE IN WORD BY LETTERS WHEN WE ARE ABSENT, SUCH WILL WE BE ALSO IN DEED WHEN WE ARE PRESENT."

Paul could speak in this manner because he was depending on Christ and the power of the Holy Spirit, and not himself. His detractors were counting on their eloquence, or the fact that they had recommendations from Jerusalem, or something, which of course in the Eyes of God, were of no consequence.

SUCH AN ONE

The phrase, *"Let such an one think this,"* refers directly to the one who is speaking in Verse 10.

We know that the Holy Spirit inspired Paul to write these words, consequently, allowing him to defend himself. To be sure, there was a far greater purpose and reason behind that which the Holy Spirit allows, than the Apostle merely defending himself. To be frank, the evidence is overwhelming that Paul was not troubled in the least, at least on a personal basis, as to what people said about him. He was not on an ego trip. Neither was he thin-skinned. There are other reasons:

1. First of all, I think the Holy Spirit is proclaiming here the Spiritual Authority of the Apostle, which means that such a Calling actually pertains to the leadership of the Church. This means that the Holy Spirit was discounting the claims of those who were from Jerusalem, if in fact they were from Jerusalem. Irrespective, these detractors were not spiritual leaders despite their claims, whatever they had told the Corinthians.

2. To which we have already dealt, this tells us how true Spiritual Authority operates. It is not the idea that Paul would personally do anything to these people, whomever they may have been, but that the Lord ultimately would, if they did not cease and desist their false direction. When the Lord would do such, of course, would be left up solely to His discretion; however, one can be certain that measures would ultimately be taken.

3. As should be obvious by now, we here see the true manner of Church Government. And we also see Satan's efforts to hinder that Righteous Government, or replace it altogether.

So, the issues at stake here were of far greater consequence than Paul merely defending himself against personal slander.

IN WORD AND DEED

The phrase, *"That, such as we are in word by Letters when we are absent, such will we be also in deed when we are present,"* proclaims absolutely the Spiritual Authority of the Office of the Apostle, which pertained not only to Paul, but all who follow in this Office, even unto this present hour. Of course, as should be obvious, this is a God-called Office and not that appointed by man.

The idea of all of these statements, and especially the phrase we have just mentioned, is that an individual is setting himself directly against God when he places himself in opposition to Heaven directed Spiritual Authority. Again we emphasize, it's not that Paul would personally do anything to these individuals, but that the Lord would take measures, that is if the person did not repent.

NOTES

GOD'S ORDER

Now as then, it seems that very few people in the Church fully understand what true Spiritual Authority actually is, and if they think about it at all, they place such in the hands of Denominational heads who have been elected by popular ballot, or appointed by man. As we have already stated, those particular administrative offices contain no Spiritual Authority whatsoever, despite the claims of most of the modern Church. One must remember that a million people claiming something does not make it true, unless in fact, it is true. It is God Who is the Author and to be sure, the Church belongs directly to Jesus Christ, and not man or any earthly order (Mat. 16:18).

To give some examples, and to use the vernacular, not many people would have bought stock in Joseph's company when he was sold into Egypt, but Joseph ultimately prevailed for the simple reason that Spiritual Authority, granted by God, was on his side, even though not recognized by his Brothers.

Likewise, not many would have put much faith in David when he was being hounded by Saul, but he ultimately prevailed, because again, Spiritual Authority, i.e., *"the Call of God,"* was on his side. It may take a while, but Truth will ultimately triumph, irrespective of the odds arrayed against its survival.

At a very dark time in this Ministry, with major religious Denominations doing all within their power, even enlisting the aid of the News Media to destroy this Ministry, the Lord spoke to both Frances and me saying, *"The Lord shall fight for you, and you shall hold your peace"* (Ex.14:14). That He has done and wondrously so.

I realize that the world thinks, and even most all of the Church, that the reason for this fierce opposition by particular Pentecostal Denominations was because of my own failure; however, that was actually only an excuse. The real reason was what we stood for, and what we preached. To be frank, it was the same with Paul of old.

Many in those days, were not satisfied with God's choice respecting the person of Paul, so they attempted to set him aside; however, in attempting to do this they were also at the same time attempting to set God aside, which of course, could not be done.

Once again, that which is at stake is not merely the feelings of an individual, but rather a frontal assault on God's Plan. If God's Order which is amply portrayed in Scripture, is set aside to any degree, spiritual ruin will always be the results. In fact, this is Satan's greatest area of attack, God's Governmental Order.

(12) "FOR WE DARE NOT MAKE OURSELVES OF THE NUMBER, OR COMPARE OURSELVES WITH SOME THAT COMMEND THEMSELVES: BUT THEY MEASURING THEMSELVES BY THEMSELVES, AND COMPARING THEMSELVES AMONG THEMSELVES, ARE NOT WISE."

In this statement Paul exposes graphically so, the unscriptural position of what these people are doing. He is speaking of self-appointed spiritual authority.

THE NUMBER

The phrase, *"For we dare not make ourselves of the number,"* proclaims the Apostle severing himself totally and completely from the political power play of these individuals. In other words he is saying, *"These people are not of God, are not doing the Work of God, are not sent by God, irrespective of their claims, and I will not be a party to their efforts."* The reason was simple, all of this was man-instituted, man-directed, man-appointed, etc.

From this one statement by Paul, *"For we dare not make ourselves of the number,"* we find the dividing line of the Church. Concerning you the Reader, on what side are you? Are you a part of that *"number,"* or that which belongs to God?

CHURCH HISTORY

After Paul and his associates, and the original Twelve went home to Glory, that particular *"number,"* ultimately prevailed. Church Government was gradually taken over by these religious politicians, and even though it took several centuries, the ultimate result was the Catholic Church, which is entirely man-directed and man-appointed, which means it is not of God. Consequently, as the Bible was taken from the common people, the world was plunged into the dark ages. In fact, that's the way its always been. Religious men desire you to ignore the Word of God, and to follow them, whatever they may say or do.

NOTES

Truth ultimately triumphed as Truth always does, with the advent of the Reformation; however, it did not come quickly or easily.

The *"number"* of which Paul mentions here, are *"the certain ones"* mentioned in Verse 2, the false apostles.

COMMEND THEMSELVES

The phrase, *"Or compare ourselves with some that commend themselves,"* means that these individuals, whomever they may have been, were not called by God, but had rather called themselves. To be sure, the Church is full of this type.

The verb rendered *"commend"* is that from which is derived *"the commendatory letters"* of II Corinthians 3:1. In other words, as then noted, these false apostles had letters of recommendation from someone who was known enough to impress the Corinthians. Or else the letters may have been merely from Jerusalem, whoever signed them. Of course, anything from Jerusalem would have carried weight, if in fact, the origination was Jerusalem. Whatever the case, the Corinthians were impressed, which started them down a wrong road, which if continued, could have caused the loss of their eternal souls, or at least weakened them seriously in a spiritual sense. To be frank, that's where most of the Church is presently.

MAN'S APPROVAL

Despite nearly 2,000 years of Church History, and the terrible damage this has ever caused, the fact remains, that man's approval still carries great weight, even as it did with the Corinthians of old.

While man's approval is certainly to be appreciated in certain cases, and even desired; still, the fact remains, if something is demanded which violates the Word of God, in other words it is unscriptural, even if it has the approval of all men, it is to be rejected out of hand.

The Truth is, that most Preachers put the approval of men first, with God given little thought. Regarding Laypersons, most are not directly involved in whatever is happening in

Ministerial ranks; therefore, they just somewhat go along with whatever is being advocated.

When it comes to the true Work of God, it is seldom that man's approval can be obtained, at least to any degree. There will always be a few who will do their best to please the Lord and not man, but not many.

To be frank, the situation is far worse presently even than it was during Paul's day. Jerusalem then had some sway, but not much; whereas, at the present time, Denominations or even Independent groups, are very powerful. As well, they pretty much take the position, that if one is not sanctioned by them, one is then blacklisted, i.e., every effort made to destroy. So, if a Preacher or even a Layperson in many cases, attempts to stand up for that which is right, they will suffer consequences. In view of that, most back down. In fact, most ardently seek man's approval.

THE WORD OF GOD

However, having said all of that, the Reader must understand, that it is not man's approval which is the criteria, but rather the Word of God. What does the Bible say about the matter, whatever the matter may be?

The sad truth is, most Preachers and especially Laypersons, don't know their Bibles very well. Or else the Bible takes second place, if any place at all.

To be frank, the Leadership of the major Pentecostal Denominations, as a general rule, do not even consult the Word of God about situations, but only their own Constitution and Bylaws. In other words, most everything they do is for the preservation of that particular Denomination, with the Scripture given very little credence if any at all. I realize that most Laypersons would have difficulty believing that, but it is true.

MEASUREMENT

The phrase, *"But they measuring themselves by themselves, and comparing themselves among themselves, are not wise,"* actually pertains to self-righteousness. In other words, they made themselves the standard of excellence instead of Christ, which sadly and regrettably, characterizes much if not most of the modern Church. This is a graphic description of pride and self-complacency.

NOTES

A MEASUREMENT HATED BY GOD

In fact, this characterizes almost all the world. So, when the Church falls in line with this method of righteousness, which in fact, is no righteousness at all, they are merely taking upon themselves the ways of the world. Paul said it is *"not wise,"* which actually means *"stupid and foolish."*

Why?

1. The Truth was, they had no such excellence as to make themselves the standard and neither does anyone else.

2. Such is always an indication of acute pride.

3. Such an attitude and spirit makes one blind to the true Righteousness of Christ. In fact, these types are deadly opposed to the Righteousness of Christ.

4. The requirements of God, and the character of the Redeemer, are the proper standard of conduct. Consequently, nothing is a more certain indication of folly than for a man to make himself the standard of righteousness. Such an individual must be blind to his own real character; and the only thing certain about his attainments is, that he is inflated with pride. And yet, how come? How self-satisfied such persons are! How pleased with their own character and attainments! How much they enjoy comparing themselves with others, which somehow makes them feel superior.

The idea is, they do not understand their own character or their inferiority.

A MODERN EXAMPLE

The modern Church little believes in true Biblical repentance, which instantly imputes, thereby, restoring Righteousness. In other words, they do not actually believe that a person can be unclean one moment and perfectly clean the next by having Faith in Christ. The modern Church demands a probationary time, actually, a form of *"penance."*

There's nothing in the Bible that teaches penance, probation, partial forgiveness, or part justification. Such does not exist in real Biblical terms. When God forgives, He forgives totally and completely. When He justifies, He justifies totally, in other words, 100%.

In fact, that's the very nature of Christianity! That's why Jesus died on Calvary, paying the price for man's Redemption, thereby, satisfying the claims of Heavenly Justice.

Whenever anyone demands penance or probation, etc., they are in effect saying that what Jesus did at Calvary is not enough, and there must be other things added. In fact, the vocabulary to properly explain the utter absurdity of such action, such fabrication, such error, is probably beyond any language on earth. Such is an insult of the highest order to God.

A PERSONAL EXAMPLE

Sometime back a friend of mine went into a Christian Bookstore, and asked the clerk if they had one of our particular Recordings. The clerk, so the lady said, indignantly stated that they did not carry them, and in fact, would not think of doing such.

My friend very respectfully then asked if they had a Bible. The clerk said, *"Of course we have all types of Bibles!"*

My friend then asked, *"Do these Bibles contain the Psalms?"*

The lady replied, *"Of course!"*

My friend then said, *"I'm surprised that you would carry anything written by David!"*

I would trust that the point is well taken.

What people do not realize is, when they take such a position, which in fact, almost all the Church does, they are in effect judging themselves; however, they seem not to realize this. I guess they are so busy *"measuring themselves by themselves, and comparing themselves among themselves,"* that they forget that such measurements God will not recognize.

PROPER MEASUREMENT

In fact, what measurement does God recognize?

Of course, we are referring to the measurement of Righteousness.

God demands a perfect, pure, spotless, absolutely certain Righteousness, which man, irrespective of his efforts, cannot produce. In other words, it doesn't really matter what a man may try to do in the realm of earning such Righteousness, he is hopelessly defeated before he even begins. Nevertheless, almost all the world tries to measure up by standards they have drawn themselves, consequently, ignoring God's Standards. In fact, that is the reason for all the Religions of the world.

NOTES

If you will notice, when the unsaved speak of those who have just deceased, they will normally point out their good points, plus good things they have done (supposedly), or other so-called particular qualifications and then will probably say, *"If there is a Heaven, he* (or she) *is there!"* It is somewhat like a brownie point system, or else a merit and demerit system. In other words, one's so-called good things outweigh the bad things, and that means one is saved, etc.

Regrettably, the Church has pretty much bought into the same foolishness, which is so unscriptural that it beggars description.

The Truth is, that the world's worst sinner can fall at the feet of the world's Redeemer, the Lord Jesus Christ, asking for Mercy and Grace, and as Faith in Christ is exhibited, by which the very act of coming to the Lord proclaims, instantly, that person is washed, cleansed, and forgiven, which means they are justified by Faith, and immediately granted a perfect, pure, spotless Righteousness — the Righteousness of Jesus Christ. It is done in a moment's time.

That is the same with a Believer who goes to the Lord asking forgiveness (I Jn. 1:9). As the Believer exhibits Faith, the sin, whatever it may have been, is instantly washed, cleansed, and forgiven, with Communion instantly restored by the Lord.

WHAT DO WE MEAN BY THE RIGHTEOUSNESS OF CHRIST?

The nature and justice of God demanded that sin be addressed, atoned for, in effect, with justice satisfied. There is no way that man could do that, at least and stay alive. The wages of sin is death, so automatically man is shot down before he ever begins.

Admittedly, the justice of God would have been satisfied upon the death of man, but the Love of God definitely would not have been satisfied. So, justice demanded the full penalty, with love paying that penalty in the Form of Christ.

In other words, God became man, and did for man what man could not do for himself.

Jesus walked perfectly the entirety of the 33 2 years of his life, which means that He as our Representative Man, was a perfect Law-keeper. Faith in Him by the believing sinner, also makes the seeking soul a perfect Law-keeper.

Jesus then went to the Cross, providing by His spotless, sinless body, a perfect Sacrifice, an Offering for Sin, in other words, a *"Sin-Offering,"* thereby paying the price, a price which God would accept and in fact, did accept.

Now, the nature and justice of God are completely satisfied with the terrible debt of sin totally paid. As the Believing sinner reaches out in Faith toward Christ, believing in what Jesus did at Calvary and the Resurrection, God awards that believing sinner the perfect Righteousness of Christ, just as though he had been on the Cross himself.

But of course, it would not have done man any good to have been crucified on the Cross, simply because of his fallen, sinful condition. In other words, it would have been a Sacrifice that God could not accept.

THAT WHICH GOD WILL ACCEPT

If He would not have accepted man's sacrifice in any capacity, which He would not, then how do we think that He will accept our good works presently as payment for Salvation? In fact, if man could atone for his sins in some way, why did Jesus have to come down here and suffer such a brutal death on Calvary's Cross?

Every person in the world is faced with a choice. You can accept the measurements of man, or you can accept the measurement of God — you cannot have both.

Which measurement are you? That of yourself, or that provided by the Lord Jesus Christ?

(13) "BUT WE WILL NOT BOAST OF THINGS WITHOUT OUR MEASURE, BUT ACCORDING TO THE MEASURE OF THE RULE WHICH GOD HATH DISTRIBUTED TO US, A MEASURE TO REACH EVEN UNTO YOU."

Paul continues to use the word *"measure,"* but now enlarging its meaning to include one's Ministry.

We will find in this Scripture much Truth, which should be looked at very carefully by the Church.

OUR MEASURE

The phrase, *"But we will not boast of things without our measure,"* refers to the Call of God on his life.

Those who operate on the measurement of self-righteousness, in that self-righteousness attempt to control the ministries of others, or even deny that Ministry outright, even as the false apostles were doing with Paul. In other words, they were denying that he was an Apostle, which was patently absurd to say the least. If he wasn't an Apostle as he claimed, then his Ministry was not valid, and the Churches he had built were not valid as well. Were that so, these parasites would not have had any victims to exploit. In fact, the evidence is that these individuals were boasting of what had been done in Corinth as though it were really their work, though it had been done by the Apostle himself.

One commentator said, *"It is probable that they boasted of what had been done by the mere influence of their name. Occupying some type of central position, they supposed that their reputation had gone abroad, and that the mere influence of their reputation had had some type of important effect."*

Not so with Paul. He made no boast of anything but what God had enabled him to do by his labors.

THE MEASURE OF THE RULE

The phrase, *"But according to the measure of the rule,"* refers to God's measurement as it concerned Ministry.

Here it means the limit, boundary line, or sphere of action assigned to anyone. Paul means to say that God had appropriated a certain line or boundary as the proper limit of his sphere of action; that his appropriately extended to the Corinthians; that in going to them, though they were far distant from the field of his early labors, he had confined himself within the proper limits assigned him by God.

The idea seems to be, that these false apostles were claiming that Paul had no right to minister in Corinth, in fact according to them, he had no right to minister anywhere.

Why?

Once again we come back to the self-righteousness mode. If someone doesn't measure up to the standards they have proposed, in other words man's standards, that person is automatically ruled as unqualified. The actual Truth is, that they do not accept God's Standard of Righteousness, and they are opposed to anyone who does.

GOD HATH DISTRIBUTED TO US

The phrase, *"Which God hath distributed to us,"* in effect, says by Paul, that the Lord had assigned him his Ministry as it respected his Calling.

The Greek word here rendered *"distributed"* means, properly, *"to measure"*; and the sense is, that God had measured out or apportioned their respective fields of labor; that by His providence He had assigned to each one his proper sphere; and that, in the distribution, Corinth had fallen to the lot of Paul. In fact, and as we shall see in Verse 16, he is stating that his sphere of Ministry goes much farther than Corinth.

Paul's Calling came from God. As well, every place he went was that which was designated by the Holy Spirit. The Truth was, that these false apostles were intruding upon his Ministry, instead of him intruding on theirs. In fact, they really did not have a Ministry. They actually had not been called by God, or if they originally had, they had long since departed from the ways of the Lord, consequently, devising their own ways.

If these men could have stopped Paul from preaching they would have done so. They put every blockade and obstacle in his path which they could muster. To be frank, their breed did not die with these individuals, but continues to thrive even at the present time.

One of the leaders of one of the major Pentecostal Denominations, made the statement to one of my associates, *"We will get him off Television, and will use any means at our disposal to do so."* Why did they want me off Television?

Was I saying things about them personally? Was I saying derogatory things about their Denomination? Was I preaching something that was false or unscriptural?

The answer is *"No,"* on all counts. I was preaching what I had always preached, which has brought untold thousands of people to a saving knowledge of Jesus Christ.

The only answer I can give is, as these men did not like Paul, these individuals did not like me. I don't know why, inasmuch as I had never had a cross word with any of them, in fact, no problems whatsoever. Of course, I actually do know the answer.

They did not like what I preached, or the Spirit of God which rested on my Ministry. Even though the faces change, the attitude and spirit are the same. As Satan worked through those individuals of Paul's day, causing him tremendous difficulties, Satan continues to do the same presently.

I am on Television, because God told me to preach over Television. I conduct Meetings and Crusades all over the world, because that's what the Lord has called me to do. I did not ask man if I could do so, and neither will I ask man if I can do so. My Ministry is not for sale, and as well, it is not subject to control by others. And neither is any truly God-called Ministry!

NOTES

TO REACH EVEN UNTO YOU

The phrase, *"A measure to reach even unto you,"* in effect is meant to say, *"Aren't you glad that it did!"*, as it addressed the Corinthians.

God had specified what Paul called *"the measure of the rule."* In other words, He had marked off a specific area of Ministry for Paul, who was determined to fulfill that Call by the Grace of God.

He did not claim to be the only one preaching the Gospel, but he knew God had called him to take the Gospel to as many souls as he could possibly reach. Had this *"Apostle to the Gentiles"* not been confident of the definite call of God, he probably would never have overcome all the insults that were heaped on him.

The argument of Verses 13-16 is that Corinth was within the field of labor apportioned to the Apostle; that he was the first to preach the Gospel there; that God had delegated punitive power to him in relation to Corinth; and that, therefore, he was authorized to act toward them as he did both by Letter and by visitation.

He will point out, as we shall see, that no Preacher no matter how successful, should boast of his ability or of his success, and that Christians have only one legitimate subject of boasting, and that is the Lord Jesus Himself and the perfection of His Person and Work. Further, that self-commendation does not prove Divine ordination, and that where spiritual results follow they demonstrate that the Preacher enjoys the commendation of the Master. In other words, the *"fruit"* of his claims, was obvious to all. But of course, the fruit of people being saved and lives being gloriously changed, was not fruit that these false apostles would accept, and neither does the modern variety.

(14) "FOR WE STRETCH NOT OURSELVES BEYOND OUR MEASURE, AS THOUGH WE REACHED NOT UNTO

YOU: FOR WE ARE COME AS FAR AS TO YOU ALSO IN PREACHING THE GOSPEL OF CHRIST:"

We learn from these Passages, that the call to preach the Gospel involves an initial summons from God, but it also includes constant direction as to where He desires us to minister. In other words, He doesn't merely call someone, and then allow them to shift on their own. Such is facetious to say the least.

It is amazing that some Preachers in the Charismatic Community, have the mistaken idea, that they are free to go anywhere they like. In other words, after God calls them, their field of labor is strictly their own choice. Nothing could be further from the Truth.

These Passages proclaim to us in no uncertain terms, that God has literally *"measured off,"* the field of Ministry for every person He has called. To be sure, the Lord is involved in the hearts and lives of every Believer to a total extent, even down to minute details. Jesus had, *"But the very hairs of your head are all numbered,"* telling us exactly as to the involvement of our Heavenly Father.

To those who truly love the Lord, such involvement, such detail, such inspection, are not a negative but rather a grand positive (Mat. 10:30).

BEYOND OUR MEASURE?

The phrase, *"For we stretch not ourselves beyond our measure,"* in effect, says that Corinth was not out of bounds.

Whomever these detractors were at Corinth, they evidently were very much lifted up in their own importance. They somehow thought they had the right to delegate ministry, or in other words, to say who could preach and who could not preach.

There are certain Denominations, which have an unscriptural central type of Government. In other words they operate the Denomination by placing the Preachers where they desire them to be, with the Will of God given little or no latitude at all.

In these particular Denominations, I don't know how much their Preachers get on their knees and ask the Lord as to His direction, but I do know that they court the Central Headquarters, in order that they may get the good Church, etc.

NOTES

It would seem to me that the unscripturality of such a position would be obvious; however, the truth is, many Preachers do not actually desire to seek the face of the Lord regarding direction, but would rather be told what to do. In their minds, it seems they think this absolves them of all responsibility. However, that is not the case at all, with the Lord holding all responsible.

UNTO YOU

The phrase, *"As though we reached not unto you,"* presents Paul's calling as not only including Corinth, but even the individuals who had been saved under his Ministry. In other words, the Call of God went so far as to detail the sphere of operation, but as well, to define even the individuals in that operation.

I am so glad that in the year 1939, two women who were then in Mobile, Alabama, felt the Call of God to come to our little backward community by the name of Ferriday, Louisiana.

I was born into a home that knew not God. In fact, my Dad had never even seen a Bible until he was 25 years old, which meant he had never been in Church of any nature. My Mother was pretty much in the same situation.

However, to make the story brief, these two women came to our little town to build a Church. They had very little money, knew no one in Ferriday, and had the backing of no particular Denomination, even though they were at that time ordained with the Assemblies of God. However, that particular organization at that time, had very little money, if any at all, to help start pioneer Works. In other words, they had to depend strictly on the Lord.

GOD WORKS IN MYSTERIOUS WAYS

Ferriday in those days was a small town of approximately three to four thousand people. There may have been several millionaires in the city, but I was only acquainted with two, my Uncle and another gentleman. In fact, I was born in my Uncle's home on March 15, 1935. Consequently, I was four years old when this Church was built.

The Lord brought about this situation in a most beautiful manner. These two ladies, actually the Mother and Sister of Lester Sumrall, were attempting to prepare a lot for the erection of a tent. My Uncle, Lee Calhoun, happened to pass in his pickup truck at that particular time.

Knowing that this lot belonged to the other millionaire in town, my Uncle stopped his truck, approached the women, asking what they were doing.

As they looked at my Uncle, at that moment they probably could not even begin to realize that this was the man who would furnish the money to build the Church.

They told him what they were doing, and he was somewhat nonplused, two women trying to build a Church, and claiming that God had sent them to do so. Somehow or the other, this statement intrigued my Uncle.

As stated, he loaned the money for the Church to be built, in which the entirety of my family came to Christ. How so much I thank God, that the *"measure"* which the Lord had drawn out for these two ladies, reached even unto me, plus my Mother, Dad, my Sister, plus my Grandparents, etc.

PREACHING THE GOSPEL OF CHRIST

The phrase, *"For we are come as far as to you also in preaching the Gospel of Christ,"* presents the purpose for all this, the greatest purpose, the greatest reason there could ever be, the Salvation of Souls, through the Gospel of Jesus Christ.

This is the purpose of the entirety of the Work of God, the Gospel of Christ. This was not the purpose of the false apostles. They had another agenda in mind altogether. Paul had but one purpose, and that is to preach this glorious Message to sinners, in order that they may find Jesus, and, consequently, Eternal Life.

WHAT IS THE GOSPEL?

Of course, as most all know, the Gospel is *"good news."* Men are lost with no way to save themselves. As we've already stated, Jesus paid that price, in order that men might be saved and have Eternal Life. If that's not *"good news,"* then I don't know what good news actually is.

Every true Preacher of the Gospel has one thing in mind, get people saved, and then nurture them in Christ.

That is not the agenda with many. They are instead attempting to build their Denomination, protect their Denomination, i.e., *"protect themselves,"* or to build some type of personal kingdom of their own. When the Salvation of Souls matter little, such a ministry is not valid. And to be sure, one can easily observe a Preacher's ministry and actions, to see how much it really matters.

NOTES

PARASITES

Still more important is the fact that the false apostles broke into other men's work, where these other men (Paul and his associates) had first built up the work. Their efforts would not have been so damnable if they had gone out into new territory as the first ones to preach their false Jesus; but no, they made it their business to invade other men's work. Modern parasites continue to do the same.

The whole world is open to them in order to spread their errors if they must do so; but they make it their business and their delight to invade the congregations which were long ago built up in the True Gospel. The Devil could not remain in Hell, he had to break into Eden (11:3).

Of course, the reasons are obvious, and as we have previously stated, their Gospel, which in fact, is no Gospel at all, cannot actually get people saved. So they are forced to prey on others.

(15) "NOT BOASTING OF THINGS WITHOUT OUR MEASURE, THAT IS, OF OTHER MEN'S LABOURS; BUT HAVING HOPE, WHEN YOUR FAITH IS INCREASED, THAT WE SHALL BE ENLARGED BY YOU ACCORDING TO OUR RULE ABUNDANTLY,"

Even though it is unsaid, quite possibly these false apostles were denying Paul's ministry, claiming that he was not part of the original Twelve, so how could he make all of these boastful claims? The manner in which Paul addresses this issue lets us know that these people were pulling some pretty big names out of the hat. Of course, this in no way meant that the original Twelve Apostles were party to this. On the contrary, every evidence is, that all of them held Paul in very high regard.

NOT BOASTING

The phrase, *"Not boasting of things without our measure, that is, of other men's labours,"* proclaims Paul stating that his ministry has not overlapped into the field of endeavors of others.

NOTES

In fact, Paul was *"boasting"* in the Lord Jesus Christ and what He had called him to do. The Corinthians were a part of that, with Paul having endured trials and persecutions in order to reach these precious souls in this pagan city. As well, he had labored there for a year and a half (Acts 18:11). However, these despicable false apostles never started a single new congregation of their own. Noxious parasites, they feasted on what other men, true men, had built up with arduous, wearying labors.

Again, these fellows boast *"in regard to the things that no one can measure."* They, of course, have to do that, for otherwise people would measure them and would soon see through them. Craftiness is their game: their measure, which is in no sense a measure, so that the things which they do, cannot really be measured at all.

Paul's Ministry, and as well every other true Ministry, can be measured by souls being saved, lives being changed, Christians growing in Grace, Believers being baptized with the Holy Spirit, sick bodies being healed, people being delivered from bondages of darkness, etc.

All other types of measurement such as Denominationalism, education, money, plaudits of men, acceptance by Religious Orders, etc., presents that which God will not accept.

THE INCREASE OF FAITH

The phrase, *"But having hope, when your Faith is increased,"* presents the Apostle desiring the Corinthians to mature in the Lord, to where they would not fall for the pap of those who were false, but could stand on their own two spiritual feet. Please note, that maturity is here measured or gauged by the *"increase in Faith."*

What did he mean by that?

The *"increase of Faith"* as here designed, pertains little to believing God for *"things,"* but rather has to do with the foundation of the Faith.

He is speaking of Faith in Christ relative to the Salvation of these Corinthians, and all others for that matter. This is the type of Faith of which he speaks.

All Christians must understand that their Salvation and continued victory, resides in the Cross of Jesus Christ. It was what He did at Calvary and the Resurrection, which purchased our Redemption, and as well, guaranteed our continued victory over sin. The stronger the Believer is in that knowledge, the less likely he can be pulled astray by weird doctrines. As well, Satan fights this particular Gospel of Grace, the Gospel of the Cross, moreso than he does anything else. If Believers are weak in their understanding of the Cross and what it affords, then it stands to reason that they will be weak in all else as well.

PENTECOSTALS AND THE CROSS

Inasmuch as I am Pentecostal, I think I can speak with at least some authority respecting this subject.

Pentecostals of old, were strong in the Cross and all it represented. They understood the rudiments of the Cross, what it meant to Believers as well as sinners.

I remember years ago when Frances and I first began in Evangelistic Work, I heard A. N. Trotter make a statement that at that particular time I really did not understand.

He said, *"If we go beyond the Cross, we backslide, we lose our way."*

What he meant was, that every single thing we have in the Lord, and I mean everything, comes through the Cross. Salvation comes through the Cross. The Baptism with the Holy Spirit was made possible by Jesus paying the terrible sin debt at the Cross. It was the Cross that made possible our healing, our deliverance, our victory, our prosperity, and all hinges on the Cross. It is the intersection of humanity, the foundation of the Church.

Regrettably, many modern Pentecostals are going beyond the Cross, or ignoring the Cross, claiming that what Jesus did there is not sufficient for the sins and aberrations of man. In other words, and to which we've already addressed, they're claiming that humanistic psychology is needed as well.

Pure, plain, and simple, this is going beyond the Cross, or as stated, ignoring the Cross, which is tantamount to blasphemy.

Many in the Charismatic Community, claim that the Cross was necessary for our Salvation, but thereafter it is not needed. Consequently, many of them will not sing songs about the Blood in their Services, will not preach on the Cross, in fact refer to the Cross as *"past miseries."* Those who do this, have purely and plainly, gone beyond the Cross, which means they have lost their way with God.

So, this is the Faith of which Paul speaks — Faith in the Cross and what it represents.

ENLARGED BY YOU

The phrase, *"That we shall be enlarged by you according to our rule abundantly,"* has reference to the fact that upon the increase of Faith among the Corinthians, they would then be a help to Paul, instead of him having to nurture them. He wanted them to be enlarged spiritually so they could pray for him, hold him up before God, in other words intercede on his behalf, and as important, he would not have to be concerned about their spiritual welfare. He would know that they were properly grounded and rooted in the Faith.

THE ROLE OF THE MINISTRY

True Ministry, and especially the type carried forth by the Apostle Paul, which invades the very strongholds of darkness, is far more than meets the eye. That which can be observed, is like the tip of the iceberg.

Naturally Satan does not desire to give up any part of his kingdom. When the Gospel comes in, he marshals every force against its presentation, levelling every type of attack against the Messenger, in this case, Paul. To be sure, very few Christians in the world know or understand the degree of oppression that comes against a Minister of the Gospel, who is so to speak, on the front lines. The type of oppression, of opposition, of attacks by the powers of darkness, could probably be summed up best in Paul's own words, *"We were pressed out of measure, above strength, insomuch that we despaired even of life"* (II Cor. 1:8). That is the type of oppression of which we speak.

I know somewhat of that which Paul speaks, and so do others. The *"measure of Ministry"* which the Lord has allotted to me, falls into the same category, which attacks Satan and his strongest citadels. I speak of proclaiming the Gospel by Television all over the world.

There is no way that I could properly explain the degree of the powers of darkness and their opposition to stop us from carrying out this work. Satan uses every means at his disposal, be it the News Media, fellow Christians, who ought to be helping but oftentimes prove to be Satan's greatest allies, and one's own flaws and failings. So, the Preacher of the Gospel, irrespective as to what type of ministry he has, but more particularly if it is a front-line ministry such as that of Paul's, desperately needs the intercession, the prayers, even the travail of Faith-rooted Believers. To be frank, such is absolutely imperative, and is that which Paul mentions here.

NOTES

There is no way that I can properly express myself regarding my appreciation for those who lift up Jimmy Swaggart in prayer. As far as I'm concerned, that's the greatest thing that anyone could ever do for me.

(16) "TO PREACH THE GOSPEL IN THE REGIONS BEYOND YOU, AND NOT TO BOAST IN ANOTHER MAN'S LINE OF THINGS MADE READY TO OUR HAND."

In this passage, Paul outlines his sphere of Ministry given to him by God, in other words his *"measure,"* which actually includes all virgin territory — those regions where the Gospel had not been preached.

REGIONS BEYOND YOU

The phrase, *"To preach the Gospel in the regions beyond you,"* proclaims to us his burden, and it was his burden because this is what God had called him to do. As well, it tells us what priority is respecting the Lord. In fact, the Book of Acts bears it out, the taking of the Gospel of Jesus Christ to the entirety of the world.

For every person who does not know that Jesus died for them, as far as that person is concerned, Jesus died in vain. There are two factors about the Gospel:

1. What Jesus did at Calvary and the Resurrection.

2. The telling and proclaiming of this grandest Story every told, to all of mankind.

In a nutshell, that is it! What He did, must be told, must be preached, must be proclaimed, and in fact, must be told again and again. Were it one of many answers to the terrible ills of man, that would be different; however, it is the only answer to the ills of hurting humanity.

PRIORITY

Whatever the Church does, if its burden is not missions, if its burden is not the lost, if its burden is not the taking of this great Message to others, then whatever it is doing is second best or third best, etc. Whenever Churches, Denominations, or even the individual Christian, lose that burden for the lost, this is the first sign of spiritual deterioration, which will ultimately conclude in spiritual wreckage. The Story must be told, and it must be told with a burning passion, which will not take no for an answer.

What *"regions"* are here referred to can only be a matter of conjecture. He could be speaking at this time of Italy or Spain, or maybe both (Rom. 15:24, 28).

ANOTHER MAN'S LINE OF THINGS

The phrase, *"And not to boast in another man's line of things made ready to our hand,"* refers to areas where others were not preaching. To be frank, that could hardly be a problem.

Even in the Early Church, there were not many who would endure the hardships of going into virgin territory with the Gospel. So, when one considers that the entirety of the world is actually the field, for Jesus died for all, the infringement of territory should never be a problem.

Paul is not saying that it's wrong for one Preacher to minister where others have ministered, he is rather answering the charges against him made by these false apostles, that he did not have any right to preach and to build Churches in these areas, etc. So, the Holy Spirit takes the occasion to teach us valuable things about Ministry.

THE CUNNING OF THE FALSE APOSTLES

These false apostles let Paul go ahead, build up Churches in Pagan cities, and then would steal after him and do their nefarious work in those Churches. Actually, this was one of his greatest problems.

Would they, for instance, be the first to go to Pagan Spain? That thought would not enter the heads of these parasites. That's why deep scorn throbs in Paul's stunning phrase.

These parasites make their soft nest in these Churches, eat their way in farther and farther, and boast about it, trying to get praise and honor for it. Disgusting!

Cannot the Corinthians see at all?

(17) "BUT HE THAT GLORIETH, LET HIM GLORY IN THE LORD."

Paul probably derived this particular Passage from the following, *"Thus sayeth the Lord, let not the wise man glory in his wisdom,*

NOTES

neither let the mighty man glory in his might, let not the rich man glory in his riches:

"But let him that glorieth glory in this, that he understandeth and knoweth Me, that I am the Lord which exercise Lovingkindness, Judgment, and Righteousness, in the earth: for in these things I delight, sayeth the Lord" (Jer. 9:23-24).

GLORY IN THE LORD

Note the emphasis. Let him make the Lord his boast. When the Lord sends and blesses him, when he really does the Lord's work according to the Lord's rule and method, then he may boast, not, indeed, as taking glory for himself but as praising the Lord. This is the true principle.

Paul follows it in all of his Apostolic work. But it applies to every one of us wherever the Lord has placed us, and whatever He gives us to do. Thus the Apostle brings his discussion to a focus and a resting point. It is his way of doing throughout (Lenski).

Paul was disposed to trace all to the Lord, and to regard Him as the Source of all blessing and all success.

PERSONAL GLORY

As someone has said, *"There is nothing so worthless that it does not constitute a subject of glorying, provided it be ours."* If it belongs to others, it may be valueless.

The idea is, that no mortal man has anything to glory about. If in fact, there would be *"wisdom,"* or *"might,"* or *"riches,"* these things, though helpful in their place, cannot actually deal with man's real problem which is sin. Only the Lord can do that. So, if we glory at all, it must be that we know the Lord, and we know Him relative to His *"Loving kindnesses, Judgment, and Righteousness."* That alone is worth glorying.

In essence, Paul is here saying, that all the glorying these false apostles had done, regarding their place and position, whatever that may have been, is in reality of no consequence. As well, the Corinthians were foolish for listening to such! However, it seems that such pompous braggarts always find willing ears.

As well, if one is to notice, this Passage as given in Jeremiah leaves no room for a prideful boasting of how great one is in the Lord. If we inspect these Verses closely, we learn that it is only to the one who is *"poor in spirit"* to whom the Lord reveals Himself (Mat. 5:3). His *"Lovingkindness"* is extended only to those, and He judges them as *"Righteous."*

To the prideful, He has nothing but abasement (Lk. 18:14).

(18) "FOR NOT HE THAT COMMENDETH HIMSELF IS APPROVED, BUT WHOM THE LORD COMMENDETH."

In this one Verse of Scripture, we find the true ingredient of Gospel Ministry. It is regrettable, but many Christians, and especially Preachers, seek the approval and the plaudits of men, little thinking of God. Consequently, the great Work of God, then becomes political instead of spiritual.

COMMENDETH HIMSELF

The phrase, *"For not he that commendeth himself is approved,"* proclaims God's standard of approval. In this phrase we also find the ingredient of personal Salvation.

The individual who is attempting to commend himself, i.e., *"Righteous in his own eyes,"* will always at the same time, seek the approval of other men. The two go hand in hand. He will work long and diligent attempting to secure man's approval. That is his goal, his agenda, his standard. As stated, the whole thing becomes merely political.

Those who truly know themselves, who truly understand that they have no personal Righteousness of their own, in other words, that all of us are spiritually and morally bankrupt, and must have the Grace of God, also know that without this, we are doomed. Those in that category, do not seek the commendation of man. If it comes, well and good; however, in all likelihood it won't. The major effort is always to please the Lord.

"Approved" in the Greek is, *"dokimos,"* and means *"acceptable, but only after being assayed, even as metal is assayed."* So I guess one should ask himself the question as to whose *"approval"* he seeks?

THE LORD COMMENDETH

The phrase, *"But whom the Lord commendeth,"* tells us that He does not accept man's recommendations or commendations; they mean nothing to Him.

NOTES

"Commendeth" in the Greek is *"sunistao,"* and means *"to approve, with whom to stand, to travel in company with, companionship."* In other words, the Lord will not have as companions, those who ignore His approval, rather opting for that of man.

I suppose that's the reason that Jesus said, *"Blessed are ye, when men shall revile you, and persecute you, and shall say all manner of evil against you falsely, for My Sake."*

"Rejoice, and be exceeding glad: for great is your reward in Heaven: for so persecuted they the Prophets which were before you" (Mat. 5:11-12).

Thus Paul seriously shows that we should be mainly anxious to obtain the Divine Favor. It must be our grand aim and purpose of our life; and we should repress all disposition for vainglory or self-confidence; all reliance on our talents, attainments, or accomplishments for Salvation. Our boasts is that we have such a Redeemer; and in that we all may glory, and that alone!

"What a wondrous Message in God's Word!
"My sins are blotted out, I know!
"If I trust in His Redeeming Blood, my sins are blotted out, I know!"

"Once my heart was black, but now what joy,
"My sins are blotted out, I know!
"I have peace that nothing can destroy, my sins are blotted out, I know!"

"I shall stand someday before my King,
"My sins all blotted out, I know!
"With the ransomed host I then shall sing: My sins are blotted out, I know!"

CHAPTER 11

(1) "WOULD TO GOD YE COULD BEAR WITH ME A LITTLE IN MY FOLLY: AND INDEED BEAR WITH ME."

This section is unique in all Paul's writing. It has been well called the most magnificent and yet destructive thing that Paul has done in the way of irony. Like an actor on the ancient stage he puts on a mask in order to act a part, and the part which he acts is that of a fool, of a fellow who has no sense. But it is only he himself who feels that he is acting a fool.

He asked his readers for once to allow him to do this. He feels that he is inflicting something on them, something senseless, but yet something that is needed. He asked them to tolerate it for a little while.

What makes Paul feel that he is acting the role of a fool is the fact that he boasts about his own person. This is what he dislikes. But the Corinthians themselves have crowded him into assuming so unpleasant a role.

He takes this role because of his great concern for them, because of the attacks made upon his person in order to injure not merely him but, most of all the Corinthians themselves, their Faith and their entire spiritual life.

Paul's whole motive and aim are not self-aggrandizement but complete frustration of the attempts of the false apostles who have already done much to hurt the Corinthians.

HIS FEELINGS

He feels like a fool also because he seems to descend to the level of the false apostles whose great asset was self-recommendation and boasting about themselves. Is Paul now not advertising himself in the same way, in that the more after he has exposed these men's folly as being senseless?

Ah, but these men are not playing a role as is Paul, their whole life and activity are this very folly. Paul only apparently stoops to their level by now boasting about himself. Their boasts are entirely hollow. Behind the great show which they make is not only nothing, mere empty air; behind that show and pretense of great excellence and power is, in stark reality, only secret viciousness which they would not dare to let the Corinthians see.

When Paul now takes the boaster's role, it is only a role, just a role, because all that he will say and boast of himself is not sham, not pretense, not false and lying, but the straight fact and the simple reality from beginning to end, something which the false apostles cannot say.

In fact, the Corinthians cannot verify a single boast of the false apostles; they have nothing but the simple word of these boasters, whose greatness lies in comparing themselves with themselves.

NOTES

Every word of Paul's boasting the Corinthians can verify, yea, most of what he will say they have long ago verified. Truth does not like to boast, lies must boast. Truth can truly boast, lies can boast only by lying (Lenski).

BEAR WITH ME

The phrase, *"Would to God ye could bear with me a little in my folly,"* expresses earnest desire; however, the appeal is not to God, but to the Corinthians.

The idea seems to be, *"I know that boasting is generally foolish, and that it is not to be indulged in; but though it is to be generally regarded as folly, yet circumstances compel me to it, and I ask your indulgence."*

THE HOLY SPIRIT ALLOWED THIS FOLLY

As we've already stated this situation was far more than a Preacher merely defending himself. Actually, in most circumstances we should not defend ourselves, leaving that to the Lord. He is our defense. And yet, the Holy Spirit not only allowed this by Paul, but sanctioned it as well!

Whatever it may look like to the Reader, the facts are, that this was an attack by Satan against the prescribed order of God, in essence, the Government of God. It was an attack against the one the Lord had chosen, namely Paul in this instance. The Truth is, the Church is very seldom satisfied with the ones chosen by God, and for the simple reason that most Religious Denominations, have long since abrogated the Headship of Christ, consequently, serving as the head themselves. So, if they do not choose the person, they automatically oppose the person. And to be sure, those in that particular unscriptural position of so-called leadership, will never choose that which God has chosen, and for all the obvious reasons. Basically, the abrogation of the Headship of Christ, is Satan's means of destroying Denominations, even those which begin correctly.

To be led by the Lord demands a consecrated prayer life, a constant study of the Word of God, which maintains a broken and contrite spirit. Many do not desire to do that, so they either attempt to take over the Headship of Christ themselves, or else they look to other men for leadership, which makes up virtually most of the modern Church.

A SUBVERSION OF THE GOSPEL

Along with the abrogation of the Headship of Christ, almost, if not always, a subversion of the Gospel takes place as well.

These false apostles were Judaisers, who were attempting to attach Law to Grace, which of course is basely unscriptural. So, I personally think it is impossible for the Government of God to be replaced, without at the same time, the Gospel being subverted. So, there was far more here, than just a Preacher merely defending himself.

NECESSITY

The phrase, *"And indeed bear with me,"* presents the Apostle repeating himself, for the simple reason that he doesn't enjoy the tact he is forced to take.

The things about which he was writing were the subject of scrutiny at Corinth. Certain workers (false apostles) had come to Corinth after Paul left and had set about to institute their own false gospel, and to do this, they felt they had to discredit Paul and his work, which is generally the tact taken by such who do Satan's work. Paul's appeal for the approval of the Corinthians was the sincerity of his service. As we have repeatedly stated, it's an insult of the highest order, for this man of God to have to prove himself to the very people he has brought to Christ.

JUSTIFICATION

There is a sense in which our Justification is twofold. In God's sight, Faith justifies. In man's sight, work justifies. In fact, the Scriptures say, *"Faith without works is dead."* This is the point at which Law and Grace are reconciled. The New Testament way of life is not the Old Testament way. We are saved by Grace, but when Grace saves it produces in its place the fulfillment of the Law.

This does not mean that the old Mosaic Commandments are revived and that we are to be regimented as Israel of old, by a system of legalistic obedience. It does mean, however, that the inner Law of Grace supersedes the outer Law of Commandments. At the same time the evidence of Faith is in works, but it is works inspired by Faith. Works are the effect of Faith and not the cause of it.

NOTES

FAITH

Thus, the only way to show our Faith to men, is by our works. God sees the quality of our Faith by His Own Divine Knowledge while man sees the reality of our Faith by his human observation.

The saving element of Faith is in our believing, while the evidential element of Faith is in our doing. When Abraham believed God, he was justified in God's sight. But not until Abraham offered Isaac in sacrifice, or at least proceeded to do so but was stopped by the Lord, did he prove his Faith. Faith is not only a feeling; it is an act.

We must be careful to preserve the distinction between Faith and works. We are justified when we believe, but not until we live out that inner Justification will men count us as just men. The cause of Justification is Faith, while the effect of Justification is works.

So far as God was concerned, He accepted Paul's service because of its Faith, but so far as man was concerned, He accepted Paul's service because of its works.

One of the most convincing evidences was the Apostle's sincerity. His motives were not personal. He was actually jealous for the spiritual progress of his converts. He had espoused them to Christ and could not be content unless he saw them continuing in blessing and growth.

As well, he knew if they bought into this doctrine of Law being added to Grace, it would ultimately destroy them spiritually (Laurin).

(2) "FOR I AM JEALOUS OVER YOU WITH GODLY JEALOUSY: FOR I HAVE ESPOUSED YOU TO ONE HUSBAND, THAT I MAY PRESENT YOU AS A CHASTE VIRGIN TO CHRIST."

In this Verse Paul give us the reason for his actions. It is, as stated, the Corinthians themselves. They must not be lost to false doctrine.

JEALOUS

The phrase, *"For I am jealous over you with Godly jealousy,"* refers to the *"jealously of God"* (Ex. 20:5; 34:14; Nahum 1:2).

In both the Old and New Testaments, jealously can refer to an exclusive single-mindedness of emotion which may be morally blameworthy or praiseworthy depending on whether the object of the jealousy is self or some cause beyond self.

In the former case the result is envy, or hatred of others (Gen. 30:1; Prov. 3:31; Ezek. 31:9), which for the New Testament is the antithesis of love, and hence, the enemy of true Christian fellowship (I Cor. 13:4; II Cor. 12:20; James 3:14).

The Bible, however, also represents the other possibility, of a *"Divine jealousy,"* which is actually the subject of this Scripture, which is a consuming single-minded pursuit of a good end, which Paul exhibited toward the Corinthians (Ex. 20:5; I Ki. 19:10; I Cor. 12:31).

This positive usage is frequently associated with the marriage relationship, which in a sense Paul uses here, where a jealousy for the exclusiveness of the relationship is the necessary condition of its permanence (Num. 5:11; Ezek. 16:38; II Cor. 11:2).

GOD IS A JEALOUS GOD

Jealousy, as stated, is referred to God as well as men (Ex. 20:5; 34:14; Nahum 1:2). Difficulty is sometimes felt with this, due to principally the way in which the negative connotations of the term have come to predominate in common English usage.

Scripture, however, also witnesses to a positive application of jealousy and finds in this idea a highly relevant term to denote God's holy zeal for the honor of His Name and the good of His people who are bound to Him in the marriage of the Covenant — whether the Old, which represented Israel, or the New, which represents the Church (Deut. 32:16, 21; II Ki. 19:31; Ezek. 36:5; Zech. 1:14; Jn. 2:17).

In this sense the jealousy of God is of the essence of His moral character, a major cause for worship and confidence on the part of His people and a ground for fear on the part of His enemies.

BECAUSE HE LOVED THEM

It was because Paul loved these Corinthians, and because he feared that they were in danger of being seduced from the simplicity of the Gospel, that he writes these words and takes this tact. Actually, the phrase, *"I am jealous,"* means, properly, I ardently love you; I am full of tender attachment to you. In fact, the word was usual and common among the Greeks to denote an ardent affection of any kind.

In making these statements, Paul reverts in his mind to the tenderness of the marriage relation, unto the possibility that in that relation the affections might be estranged. Consequently, he makes use of this figure.

NOTES

HIS MOTIVE

Back of the proposed foolishness, which Paul mentioned in the first Verse, as we see here, lies the deepest seriousness. Paul reveals his motive and his aim at once and thus excludes all wrong ideas about *"a little something of foolishness"* that is now to be employed.

When the purpose is so serious, any folly or foolishness which serves that purpose will certainly not be frivolous, superficial, or objectionable in any way.

Three parties are most deeply concerned: Paul, the Corinthians, and Christ. What unites them is Paul's great and holy office. As well, we have that office shown here in a new and most lovely light. Here there are the three that are concerned in that Office, all in their actual relation. Here are the motives, here the purposes, all intertwined, so supreme for all concerned — shown for the welfare of the Corinthians.

THE ONE HUSBAND, CHRIST

The phrase, *"For I have espoused you to one husband,"* proclaims the fact that the Apostle was not jealous of the affection of the Corinthians for himself, but of their affection for Christ.

The picture is that of a father who has betrothed his daughter to the noblest of bridegrooms. Soon the nuptials will be celebrated. Soon the father is to lead his daughter to the Altar (we use our modern language).

This father can lead her there only as a pure virgin. The point and pivot of the whole imagery lies in this term: *"a virgin pure."* Hence, we have the preamble: *"I am jealous over you with God's jealousy."* I watch over you with jealous eyes and see that you ever remain pure for that great day of presentation to Christ.

As far as we are able to say, this imagery is borrowed from the Oriental style betrothal in which the Bride was pledged to the Groom by the parents, which made the two man and wife, yet so that a longer or a shorter interval intervened before the Groom came to claim his Bride, to carry her to his own home in grand state, there to consummate his marriage.

The word *"espoused"* as Paul uses it here, means, properly, to adapt, to fit, to join together.

Hence to join in wedlock, to marry. Paul is here forming a connection, similar to the marriage connection, between the Corinthians and the Saviour in which actually all Believers fit. Jesus is the *"husband,"* and the Church is the *"Bride,"* at least as Paul uses the analogy here.

A CHASTE VIRGIN

The phrase, *"That I may present you as a chaste virgin to Christ,"* tells us several things:

1. They were not to befoul themselves with spiritual adultery, which is what would happen, if they accepted the teaching of the false apostles.

2. *"Present you,"* actually refers to a *"presentation,"* which will take place at the Rapture of the Church, and more particularly, at the *"Marriage Supper of the Lamb"* (Rev. 19:7-9).

Even though Paul was Jewish, but more particularly an Apostle to the Gentiles, still, his thinking was in Jewish terms, hence the manner in which he presents this subject.

To hopefully shed more light on that which he is saying, the following is a presentation given by Zola Levitt, as it regards a Jewish wedding of old.

THE FLAVOR OF THE ENTIRETY OF THE BIBLE IS JEWISH

Our Lord was Jewish and He did things like a Jew. So often, if we consult the Jewish Law and custom, we find many of the motivations for particular actions of our Lord.

For example, *"the Miracle of Passover,"* and *"the Spirit of Pentecost,"* presents that, which were originally purely Jewish Feasts days. However, the Communion or Lord's Supper has its roots in the *"Passover."* Likewise with *"Pentecost,"* we find that this is not only the day on which the Holy Spirit came, but as well, it is an apt symbol of the calling out of the Church — a festival devoted to planting and harvesting. Now, let us look at the Jewish custom of matrimony.

Obviously, wedding customs varied from nation to nation and from time to time. Even in today's world we see different traditions of marriage taking place at the same time in different countries. The Jews had their own peculiar ways, based on the Old Covenant, and the Lord as we shall see, followed those traditions in choosing a Bride.

NOTES

A PRACTICAL LEGAL MATTER

We should appreciate that the Jews had no dating or courtship as we now think of those things. Marriage to them was a practical legal matter, established by contract and carried through by exacting procedure. These customs exist in a form today in the Jewish wedding ceremony and in Jesus' time they were most fascinating and complex.

THE MANNER IN WHICH IT WAS DONE

When the young man of Israel in Jesus' time saw the girl he wanted (or the girl his father said he wanted), he would approach her father with a marriage contract. He would come to her house with a Covenant — a true legal agreement — giving the terms by which he would propose marriage. The most important consideration in the contract was the price the bridegroom would be willing to pay to marry this particular bride.

THE BRIDE PRICE

The *"bride price"* is still utilized today in parts of the Mediterranean and African worlds and while it seems most archaic to us now, it had some useful purposes.

First of all, if the bridegroom was willing to sacrifice hard cash for his bride, he was showing his love in a most tangible way.

Second, it was a favor to his future father-in-law. We must recall that in those days of farming and heavy labor, it was something of a liability to raise a daughter. A family with sons would prosper more because of the built-in work force; but a family with daughters would expect to *"consolidate their losses"* when the girls were mature enough to attract bridegrooms.

And so the father of the bride was more or less paid off for his earlier expenses and for his patience and skill in raising a girl to be good marriage material.

The bridegroom would present himself to the bride with this agreement, offering to pay a suitable price for her, and she and her father would consider his contract. If the terms were suitable, the bride and groom would drink a cup of wine together and this would seal the bargain. This cup was most significant.

It signified the bridegroom's willingness to sacrifice in order to have this bride. It was offered as a toast to the bride, and of course, it showed the bride's willingness to enter into this marriage.

Then the groom would pay the price. It should be said that this price was no modest token but was set so that the new bride would be a costly item — that was the idea. The young man had no delusions that he was getting something for nothing. He would pay dearly to marry the girl of his choice.

I GO TO PREPARE A PLACE FOR YOU

When that matter was settled the groom would depart. However, before he departed, he would make a little speech to his bride, saying, *"I go to prepare a place for you,"* and he would then return to his father's house. Back at his father's house, he would build her a bridal chamber, a little mansion, in which they would have their future honeymoon.

We should appreciate that this was a complex undertaking for the bridegroom. He would actually build a separate building on his father's property, or add a room or entire floor to his father's house. The bridal chamber had to be beautiful — one doesn't honeymoon just anywhere; and it had to be stocked with provisions since the bride and groom were going to remain inside for seven days.

This construction project would take the better part of a year, ordinarily, and the father of the groom would be the judge of when it was finished. (We can see the logic there — obviously, if it were up to the young man, some would probably throw up some kind of modest structure and go get the girl!) But the father of the groom, who had been through this previously and was less excited, would be the final judge on when the chamber was ready and when the young man would go to claim his bride.

A LADY-IN-WAITING

The bride, for her part, was obliged to do a lot of waiting. She would take the time to gather her trousseau and be ready when her bridegroom came. Custom provided that she had to have an oil lamp ready in case he came late at night in the darkness, because she had to be ready to travel at a moment's notice.

During this long period of waiting, she was referred to as *"consecrated," "set apart,"* or *"bought with a price."* She was truly a lady-in-waiting, but there was no doubt that her groom would return.

NOTES

Sometimes a young man would depart for a very long time indeed, but of course he had paid a high price for his bride; even though there were other young women available, he would surely return to the one with whom he had made a Covenant.

THE COVENANT AND THE VEIL

The bride would wear her veil whenever she stepped out of her house so that other men would realize she was spoken for and would not try to approach her with another contract. (Today, the Bride of Christ wears a veil — those not understanding of our Covenant try to make other contracts with us that would violate the one we have with our Bridegroom. We are to resist those other offers and wait only for the One Who paid for us, the Lord Jesus Christ.)

As the year went on, the bride would assemble her sisters and bridesmaids and whoever would go with her to the wedding when the bridegroom came, and they would each have their oil lamps ready. They would wait at her house every night on the chance that the groom would come, along with his groomsmen, and sweep them all away to a joyous and sudden wedding ceremony.

Meanwhile, the bridegroom would be building and decorating with all that he had. His father would inspect the chamber from time to time to see if it were ready. If we came along the road at this point and saw the young man working on his bridal chamber, we might well ask, *"When's the big day?"* But the bridegroom would say, *"Only my father knows that."*

THE COMING OF THE BRIDEGROOM

Finally, the chamber would be ready and the bridegroom would assemble his young friends to accompany on the exciting trip to claim his bride. The big moment had arrived and the bridegroom was more than ready, we can be sure. He and his young men would set out in the night, making every attempt to completely surprise the bride.

And that's the romantic part — all the Jewish brides were in a sense *"stolen."* The Jews had a special understanding of a woman's heart. What a thrill for her, to be *"abducted"* and carried off into the night, not by a stranger but by one who loved her so much that he had paid a high price for her.

Over at the bride's house, things had better be ready! To be sure, the bride would be surprised since the groom would try to come at midnight while she was sleeping. But the oil lamps were ready and the bride had her veil. And while she might be sleeping in her wedding dress, she definitely could be surprised. It's a wonder she would sleep at all as the year went on!

THE SHOUT

Now there were rules to be observed in consideration of a woman's feelings. The groom couldn't just rush in on her. After all, she might be fixing her hair, etc.! Actually, as the excited party of young men would get close to her house, they were obliged to give her a warning. Someone in the wedding party would shout.

When the bride heard that shout, she knew her young man would be there momentarily. She had only time to light her lamp, grab her honeymoon clothing and go. Her sisters and bridesmaids who wanted to attend also had to have their lamps trimmed and ready, of course. No one would try to walk through ancient Israel, with its rocky terrain, in the dark of night without carrying a lamp.

THE ARRIVAL!

And so the groom and his men would charge in, grab the bride, plus all the other girls, and make off with them! The father of the bride and her brothers would look the other way — perhaps just making one quick check to see that this was the young man with the contract — and the wedding party would be off.

People in the village might be awakened from their sleep by the happy voices of the young people carrying the oil lamps through the streets, and that's how they knew a wedding was going on. Today, we hear car horns — back then, they saw the lamps late at night.

Those looking on would not know who the bride was because she was still wearing a veil, of course. But she would be returning through these same streets a week later with her groom and then her veil would be off.

At the return of the bride with her bridegroom, all the people would know just who got married and they would realize the total significance of this wedding.

NOTES

When the wedding party reached the house of the groom's father, the bride and groom would go into their chamber and shut the door. No one else would enter. The groom's father, meanwhile, would have assembled the wedding guests — his friends — and they would be ready to celebrate the new marriage.

Since the wedding was actually going to take seven days (until the appearance of the bride and groom out of the chamber), it was hard to plan for. Occasionally, the host would run out of wine, as we can well imagine. The Lord Himself graced a wedding at Cana with His Presence and replenished the wine (grape juice) for the celebrants as told in John Chapter 2.

THE CONSUMMATION OF THE MARRIAGE

But the celebrating wouldn't start right away. First, the marriage had to actually be consummated. The Jews were a most Law-abiding people and the Law provided that the bride and groom become one before their marriage was recognized. Thus, the friend of the bridegroom — the individual we might refer to as *"the best man"* — would stand near the door of the bridal chamber, waiting to hear the bridegroom's voice. When the marriage was consummated, the bridegroom would tell his friend through the door and the friend would then go to the wedding guests and announce the good news. The celebration would then begin and would continue for an entire week!

THE APPEARANCE

At the end of the week, the bride and groom would make their long awaited appearance to the cheers of the crowd. There would then be a joyous meal — a marriage supper, which we might refer to as the wedding reception — to honor the new couple.

At this point, the bride would have discarded her veil, since she was now a married woman, and all would see exactly who it was the bridegroom had chosen.

The new couple and the guests would enjoy a magnificent feast to conclude the entire matrimonial week.

After the marriage supper, the bride and groom would depart, not remaining any longer at the home of the groom's father. They would go instead to their own house, whether it was a room onto the father's house, or a house of their own on the property, which had been prepared by the bridegroom. (The Bride of Christ will spend seven years in Heaven at the home of the groom's Father, and then we shall return with our Bridegroom, the Lord Jesus Christ, to occupy the Kingdom He has prepared for us.)

As the bride and groom would travel back through the village, it would be appreciated by all onlookers just who the couple was and where their permanent home would be.

And that was a complete Jewish wedding in Jesus' time, and all its glory. Readers of the Gospel can easily see the beautiful analogies between this complex procedure and the manner in which the Lord Himself called out His chosen Bride.

THE GREEKS

The Greeks had another custom which appointed an Officer whose business it was to educate young women, especially those of rank and figure, designed for marriage. And then to present them to those who were to be their husbands; and if this Officer through negligence permitted them to be corrupted between the espousals and the consummation of the marriage, great blame would fall upon him.

Such a responsibility Paul felt. So anxious was he for the entire purity of the Church which was to constitute *"the Bride, the Lamb's wife"*; so anxious that all who were connected with the Church should be presented pure in Heaven (Barnes).

(3) "BUT I FEAR, LEST BY ANY MEANS, AS THE SERPENT BEGUILED EVE THROUGH HIS SUBTILTY, SO YOUR MINDS SHOULD BE CORRUPTED FROM THE SIMPLICITY THAT IS IN CHRIST."

Paul has just compared the Church to a Virgin, soon to be presented as a bride to the Redeemer. The mention of this seems to have suggested to him the fact, that the first woman, Eve, was deceived and led astray by the Tempter, and that the same thing might occur in regard to the Church which he was so desirous should be preserved pure.

I FEAR

The phrase, *"But I fear,"* as it correlates with the following statements, presents the grounds of his fear. They were:

NOTES

1. That Satan had seduced the first woman, thus demonstrating that the most holy were in danger of being led astray by temptation.

2. That special efforts were being made to seduce them from the faith. The persuasive arts of the false teachers, the power of philosophy, and the attractive and corrupting influences of the world, he had reason to suppose, might be employed to seduce them from simple attachment to Christ.

3. All other deceptions are the repetitions of the original in the Garden of Eden, and are very effective. Its practitioners will use the basest means, any and all such means, to gain one's evil ends — *"craftiness."*

SEDUCTION

The phrase, *"As the serpent beguiled Eve,"* goes back, as we have stated, to the original seduction (Gen. 3:1-11).

The word *"serpent"* here refers to Satan, who was the agent by whom Eve was beguiled (Jn. 8:44; I Jn. 3:8; Rev. 12:9; 20:2).

Paul did not mean that the Corinthians were in danger of being corrupted in the same way, but that similar efforts would be made to seduce them. Satan adapts his temptations to the character and circumstances of the tempted. He varies them from age to age, and applies them in such a way as best to secure his object. Hence, all should be on their guard.

No one knows the mode in which he will approach him. But all may know for certain that he will approach them in some way.

SUBTILTY

The phrase, *"Through his subtilty,"* refers to the strategy of Satan.

"Subtilty" in the Greek is *"panourgia,"* and means *"shrewdness, cunning, and craft."* A tempter always employs cunning to accomplish his object. This can fall out to many directions. If one is lying, they can go in any direction, after any manner. Truth has only one direction, while lies can chart its own course. This is the method Satan used against Eve (Gen. 3:1).

We will find in this Chapter, that Satan is to be dreaded as a lion (I Pet. 5:8); more to be dreaded as a serpent, even as this Verse proclaims; and most to be dreaded as an angel (vs. 14).

Jesus referred to this in John 8:44. It is so effective because it is the first deception that entered our world, and because its results were so terrible. All other deceptions are the repetitions of this original, most fatal one, which are the outcome of radical deception.

Paul says *"Eve"* and not *"Adam"* in this connection because he wants to designate the *"serpent"* as the deceiver, as he dealt with Eve. He says *"the serpent"* and not *"Satan"* because he desires to bring out the full baseness of the act in its similarity to what the false prophets were doing in Corinth. They crawled into Corinth as Satan did into Eden, they were like serpents.

They used the same *"craftiness,"* they, too, intended to slay the innocent. Consequently, these deceivers in Corinth were doing the Devil's serpent work. Paul desires to arouse all the horror of the serpent in the Corinthians. Like a flash this word *"serpent"* reveals all the deadly danger from which the Corinthians should flee.

ERROR

Late Jewish fiction and speculation regarded the fall of Eve as a sexual sin. In other words, that Satan as a fallen angel had sexual intercourse with the first woman.

Some of the commentators collect all the Jewish statements on this subject on the supposition that they cast light on Paul's reference to Eve, that Paul might at least have had such in mind, since he pictures the Corinthians as a pure virgin who may not be found pure at her presentation to her bridegroom. We decline to follow them.

There is nothing of sex in Paul's words. Nor does his statements even slightly hint at such a thing. Eve's seduction had nothing to do with sexual immorality, but rather an immorality of the spirit, which fell out to disobedience regarding the Word of God.

CUNNING!

The *"subtilty"* mentioned here by Paul, assumed an attractive form to be sure. It was a fascinating manner, a manner fitted to charm, in order to seduce these Corinthians. To be frank, it almost succeeded! In fact, considering that these people had been saved under Paul, and that he was without a doubt one of the greatest men of God in the world of that day, that these people could be turned against Paul which they almost were, tells us how powerful this *"subtilty"* was and is.

NOTES

THE SIMPLICITY THAT IS IN CHRIST

The phrase, *"So your minds should be corrupted from the simplicity that is in Christ,"* proclaims the fact that Paul feared for his own converts that they may be turned away from Christ, as Eve was beguiled by Satan to turn away from God.

The idea is that all the individual members of the Church should be holy. They, as individuals, are soon to be presented in Heaven as the fruit of the labours of the Son of God, and as entitled to His eternal love. How pure should be the lips that are soon to speak His praise in Heaven! How pure the eyes that are soon to behold His Glory! How holy the feet that are soon to tread His courts in the heavenly world!

YOUR MINDS

As Paul uses the word *"minds"* it speaks of the thoughts being perverted. The mind is corrupted when the affections are alienated from the proper object, and when the soul is filled with unholy plans, purposes, and desires.

This speaks of devotion to Christ, and Christ alone. Satan will try to use the world, or false doctrine, to turn people away from their love for Christ. However, anyway it is sliced, a departure from the ways of Christ, impacts of necessity our love for Christ.

Jesus said in connection with *"false prophets"* which would arise, and *"deceive many,"* that *"the love of many shall wax cold"* (Mat. 24:11-12).

To be sure, the time of which Jesus spoke in this 24th Chapter of Matthew, pertains to the very times in which we presently live.

The word *"minds"* as well refers to *"single-mindedness,"* as it refers to Christ. The mind and all its thoughts are set solely and singly upon Him in love, loyalty, devotion, and there is no duplicity which secretly turns to another.

As well, the word *"purity"* can be added to this meaning, as it refers back to the figure of *"a virgin pure."* The thoughts are to be without a stain or a smudge of disloyalty of any kind.

In his craftiness the serpent aims to introduce duplicity into our thoughts which are directed to Christ and thereby to defile our thoughts regarding Him. In other words, we are no longer to be Christ's Alone in our thoughts; secretly in our hidden thoughts we are to hanker after another or something else.

Figuratively we should thus no longer be a bride loyal and pure in heart for our blessed marriage presentation to Christ.

Consequently, an admonition underlies Paul's words which urges the Corinthians to flee any contact with false apostles. What a shame to pretend to be loyal to Christ while disloyalty has crept into the heart through the serpent's agency which used the false apostles.

CORRUPTED

"Corrupted," in the Greek is *"phthio,"* and means *"to spoil by any process, or shrivel or wither, to ruin, to destroy."*

The facts are, there is a great danger concerning all Believers of being corrupted from the simplicity that is in Christ. Satan desires to destroy us; and his great object is readily accomplished if he can seduce Christians from simple devotion to the Redeemer; if he can secure corruption in doctrine or in the manner of worship, and can produce conformity in dress and in the style of living to this world.

Formerly, he excited persecution; but in that he was foiled. The more the Church was persecuted, the more it grew. Then he changed his ground. What he could not do by persecution he sought to do by corrupting the Church, and in this he has been by far more successful.

This can be done slowly, but certainly, even effectually, but without exciting suspicion. And it matters not to Satan whether the Church is crippled by persecution or its zeal destroyed by false doctrine and by conformity to the world. His aim is secured; and the power of the Church destroyed. In fact, the form in which he *now* assails the Church is by attempting to seduce it by simple and hearty attachment to the Saviour. To be frank, he is by and large successful!

SIMPLICITY

One of the greatest tricks of Satan presently, and in fact, that which he has always used, even as Paul outlines here, is the pretense at leading Believers into higher enlightenment.

One propagator of the prosperity message made the statement the other day, *"our ministry is not to get people saved, but to enlighten them after they get saved."* However, his so-called enlightenment is pure and simple, *"another Jesus, another spirit, and another Gospel"* (II Cor. 11:4).

NOTES

The following will provide some of the means by which Satan attempts to destroy the simplicity that is in Christ:

1. From the Pure Doctrines of the Word of God: by the admixture of philosophy, by the opinions of the world, there was danger that their minds should be turned away from their hold on the simple truths which Christ had taught.

2. Christ had a single aim; was free from all guile; was purely honest; never made use of any improper arts; never resorted to false appearances, and never deceived. His followers should, in like manner, be in the same capacity.

There should be no cunning, no tricks, no craft in advancing our purposes. There should be nothing but honesty and truth in all that we say.

Paul was afraid that the Corinthians would lose this beautiful simplicity and artlessness of character and manner; and that they would insensibly be led to adopt the maxims of mere cunning, of policy, of expediency, of seductive arts, which prevail so much in the world — a danger which was imminent among the shrewd and cunning people of Greece, but which is confined to no time and place.

Christians should be more guileless than even children are; as pure and free from tricks, as was the Redeemer Himself.

3. From the simplicity in worship which the Lord Jesus commended and required:

The worship which the Redeemer designed to establish was simple, unostentatious, and pure — strongly in contrast with the gorgeousness and corruption of the pagan worship, and even with the imposing splendor of the Jewish Temple-service.

The Lord through the Holy Spirit, intended that worship should be adapted to all lands, and such as could be offered by all classes of men — a pure worship, claiming first the homage of the heart, and then such simple external expressions as should best exhibit that homage.

How easily might this be corrupted, and in fact, has been corrupted!

What temptations were there to attempt to corrupt it by those who had been accustomed to the magnificence of the Temple-service, and who would suppose that this of the Messiah could not be less gorgeous than that which was designed to shadow forth His coming. As well, those who had been accustomed to the splendid rites of the pagan worship, might well suppose also that the worship of Christ must be at least as splendid as these false religions had been!

Sadly, according to the history of the Church, for a considerable part of its existence, its beautiful, simple worship of the Lord, instituted by the Redeemer, has been corrupted until all that is left is ceremony and ritual. Or else, we have thought that great noise and activity constituted such, when it really doesn't.

So, I think one could easily say that this which Satan attempts to corrupt regarding simplicity, is our *love* for Christ, the Pure *Doctrine* of Christ, and the *Worship* of Christ. He seeks to alienate the love, infiltrate the doctrine, and adulterate the worship.

(4) "FOR IF HE THAT COMETH PREACHETH ANOTHER JESUS, WHOM WE HAVE NOT PREACHED, OR IF YE RECEIVE ANOTHER SPIRIT, WHICH YE HAVE NOT RECEIVED, OR ANOTHER GOSPEL, WHICH YE HAVE NOT ACCEPTED, YE MIGHT WELL BEAR WITH HIM."

Why does Paul then not attack these false apostles on what would thus be the chief issue, their false gospel? Why does Paul fight about the issue of his own person, as he does in these Chapters, as if this were the chief issue? He tells us throughout.

These false apostles made Paul's person the supreme issue. They used *"craftiness"* in this. They intended to establish themselves as the genuine apostles of Christ. Paul will later say that this is no marvel, for Satan tries to appear as well, as an angel of light (vs. 14).

There is some evidence that they may have held their real teaching, which was no doubt Judaism, in abeyance until they should have destroyed Paul's standing in Corinth, and have fully established themselves. This accomplished, they planned, it seemed, to come out into the open with their false gospel. For this reason Paul compares them to the serpent and to Satan.

It seems that the Corinthians were still in the dark as to what these liars really taught in regard to the Gospel. Paul rightly joins the issue which they drew on his own person. This alone stood in the open, the other was concealed, could thus be evaded if it were attacked by Paul.

NOTES

HE THAT COMETH

The phrase, *"For if he that cometh,"* is not meant to portray a hypothetical situation, but rather a particular individual who had come into the Church at Corinth with devious purposes in mind, or else the ringleader of several.

Perhaps several such had come to Corinth, and many others who may yet come are included in Paul's indictment. As well, that which he says is meant not only for that particular time, but in fact, as an admonition for the Church for all time. As false prophets were rife during the old economy of God (the Old Testament), false apostles fit that category now under the New.

ANOTHER JESUS

The phrase, *"Preacheth another Jesus, whom we have not preached,"* presents the core effort of Satan's deception. If *"another Jesus"* is preached, *"another spirit"* will be received, and *"another gospel"* believed, all, bogus.

What does Paul mean by *"another Jesus"*?

Paul preached *"Jesus Christ and Him crucified,"* as the answer for hurting, dying humanity. In fact, he said, *"But God forbid that I should glory, save in the Cross of our Lord Jesus Christ, by Whom the world is crucified unto me, and I unto the world"* (Gal. 6:14).

So, to preach Jesus in any other capacity than the Crucified, Resurrected One, is to preach another Jesus. This means that a historical Jesus is bogus. It means that if we make Jesus the provider of money as our primary message, we are plainly and simply preaching another Jesus. In other words, to preach Jesus in any capacity except Him crucified, which means that the Offering of Himself satisfied the claims of heavenly justice, making it possible for sinners to be saved, we are preaching a bogus gospel. It is not just Jesus, but rather, *"Jesus and Him Crucified"* (I Cor. 2:2).

Jesus is not an Economist, He is a Saviour. Jesus is not a Psychologist, He is a Saviour. Jesus is not a Doctor, He is a Saviour. Jesus is not a Sociologist, He is a Saviour. Jesus is not a Politician, He is a Saviour. In fact, He is *the* Saviour, which means there is no other.

While all these other things are definitely affected in a positive way, that is not His primary objective, it being the salvation of the soul.

The Jesus that Paul preached, *"Christ and Him Crucified,"* sets captives free. It saves souls, while at the same time destroying the powers of darkness. Man's real problem is sin and that's the problem Jesus addressed as Saviour, and did so by the Cross.

THE FALSE APOSTLES

The false apostle, whom Paul describes, preached *"another Jesus"*; he speaks of the same Person and uses the same Name, but makes Him altogether *"other"* than Paul does. Thus, *"another"* is in place. Such a Jesus would send a *"different spirit,"* Who would also employ a *"different gospel."* This is the major problem in the Church presently.

Much of the Charismatic world, whether through ignorance or otherwise, repudiates the Cross. While they admit its necessity for Salvation, they repudiate its effectiveness thereafter. In other words, they go beyond the Cross, which means it is *"another Jesus."*

As well, when most Pentecostals, and I am Pentecostal, opt for Humanistic Psychology, in place of the Cross which is the answer for all of the ills of man, they are pure and simple preaching *"another Jesus."* Regrettably, almost the entirety of the Church world has fallen for this humanistic lie. That Jesus saves no one or delivers no one. Consequently, we have Churches full of unconverted people.

THE GOSPEL AS PREACHED BY PAUL

By Paul using the phrase, *"Whom we have not preached,"* proclaims the fact and the truth that the Holy Spirit gave him his Message, and thereby sanctioned his Message of the Cross. In other words, if we do not preach the Gospel that Paul preached, which is *"Jesus Christ and Him Crucified,"* the fact is, we are not preaching the Gospel. We should think this over very carefully, and as Paul also said, *"examine yourselves, whether ye be in the Faith"* (II Cor. 13:5).

ANOTHER SPIRIT

The phrase, *"Or if ye receive another spirit, which ye have not received,"* proclaims the ultimate result of *"another Jesus."* If *"another Jesus"* is presented, it is guaranteed that *"another spirit,"* will be the result. In other words, even though it may look like it's the Holy Spirit, in fact it will not be the Holy Spirit, but rather a spirit of darkness.

By Paul using the phrase, *"Which ye have not received,"* he is referring to the fact that what set them free from the terrible bondages of sin, was the Holy Spirit of God, and not some bogus spirit. However, the insinuation is, if they keep listening to these false apostles preaching *"another Jesus,"* they would find themselves back in the bondage from whence they had previously been delivered. It is a frightening prospect!

THE PRESENT TIME

Many things are happening presently which purport to be *"Revival,"* or a *"Moving of the Holy Spirit,"* etc. While the Believer definitely does not want to reject something which is actually of Christ, neither does he want to accept something which is not of Christ.

As we've already stated, Satan coming as a roaring lion is overly obvious, and does not pertain to deception (I Pet. 5:8). However, him coming as a *"serpent,"* definitely does pertain to deception (II Cor. 11:3), and he is most dangerous as *"an angel of light"* (II Cor. 11:14).

We are hearing reports at this time of people who are supposed to be in the Spirit, who are barking like dogs, roaring like lions, or crowing like roosters, etc. Women are supposedly going through some type of spiritual labor, actually imitating a physical birth, claiming that it's giving birth to Revival, or a Moving of the Holy Spirit, etc.

Let the Reader understand, that the Holy Spirit does not bark like a dog, or roar like a lion, or crow like a rooster. Neither does He go through indecent contortions claiming that it is a *"spiritual birthing."* All of this is bogus. In fact, it is *"another spirit."*

One will look in vain in the Word of God, which must always be the criteria, for such antics. However, if that is not bad enough, to claim that such is of the Spirit of God, makes the sin even worse, and sin it is, even gross sin.

In fact, even with something that may possibly be Scriptural, if it is taken out of context, or undue preeminence is given, the Holy Spirit simply will not function in that capacity. Paul said, *"If therefore the whole Church be come*

NOTES

together into one place, and all speak with tongues," or one might quickly add, *"all convulse in laughter,"* or any number of things, *"and there come in those that are unlearned, or unbelievers, will they not say that ye are mad?"* (I Cor. 14:23).

While the Lord at times definitely can come upon a person until they can no longer stand, or come upon one with laughter, etc., if in fact, the Believer goes to Church solely for such to happen, they will soon get into *"another spirit."*

THE ANOINTING OF THE HOLY SPIRIT

It is regrettable, but most in the modern Church little understand anymore, nor are they able to recognize if what is happening is the true Anointing of the Holy Spirit or not! So much of that which is totally of the *"flesh,"* is labeled as the *"Anointing"* when it obviously isn't. Many in the Church have been led to believe that a certain mood is the *"Anointing,"* whether it is fast music or slow music, or whatever.

To be frank, *"mood"* has absolutely nothing to do with the Holy Spirit, and neither can He be conjured up by our incantations. In fact, while we certainly should do all we can to provide a proper atmosphere for the Moving and Operation of the Holy Spirit, and in fact, to be very careful to do that; still, that is about all the Believer can do. Such atmosphere is provided by having a clean temple, a worshipful attitude, and a stifling of all things that pertain to the flesh.

ANOTHER GOSPEL

The phrase, *"Or another gospel, which ye have not accepted,"* means that the Gospel that first came to you set you free, and if you revert to this *"other gospel,"* you will go back into bondage.

The false apostle comes and preaches another Jesus — you thus get a different spirit, one that you did not get from us — and a different gospel, which you did not receive from us.

The true Gospel of Jesus Christ, which is the Message of the Cross, gets people saved, lives changed, bondages broken, sick bodies healed, Believers Baptized with the Holy Spirit, which radically changes everything for the better. There is no higher enlightenment than that, which these liars profess to have. That goes for now as well as then. Any Ministry that does not fit in somewhere with the things we have stated, which is a mirror of the Book of Acts and the Epistles, is not a true Ministry. And to be sure, I do not speak of fake claims which some throw around at random.

NOTES

BEAR WITH HIM?

The phrase, *"Ye might well bear with him,"* proclaims a touch of irony.

In effect, the Apostle is saying, *"He comes and preaches to you another Jesus, whom we did not preach"* to you. You Corinthians know that it is not the same Jesus. What do you do? Avoid that man? No, you did nothing of the kind; you tolerated him, *"Well do you bear him!"* You have done it already, and you thus show that you are this kind of people. Let another, let others come and do the same, and you will, no doubt, accept them also. That is the reason, I'm afraid you may be corrupted from a single-mindedness and purity of heart toward Christ.

"Another Jesus" — as if there were another! You Corinthians know there is but One, the *"One"* to Whom *"as Husband"* I did espouse you, the *"One"* to Whom you know that you belong as a bride to her betrothed.

WHAT KIND OF JESUS?

These false apostles were offering a different picture of Jesus as He lived and walked on Earth, most probably a Judaistic picture which stressed the Judaism of Jesus in a false way. The idea probably was, since Jesus lived as a Jew, so they preached, all His followers ought also to live as Jews. This is what the foolish Corinthians bear so well instead of rising up against it in indignation. By means of this Jewish Jesus these false apostles played themselves up as *"the superlative apostles"* who were vastly superior to Paul and his associates, whom they then vilified in all manner of ways.

From *"Jesus"* Paul advances to the *"Spirit"* and then to the *"Gospel"* because it is the Spirit through Whom Jesus works among men, and because it is the Gospel by means of which the Spirit does this work. The three occur in their natural and proper order.

This false apostle, or false apostles, whom Paul describes, preaches *"another Jesus"*; they speak of the same Person and use the same Name but make Him altogether *"other"* than Paul does. Thus, *"another"* is in place. Such a

Jesus would send *"a different spirit,"* who would also employ a *"different gospel."*

These two are not just *"other"* with a different look and complexion as was the case in regard to Jesus but actually *"different"* from the Holy Spirit and the Christian Gospel, namely a spirit who is only called so, a gospel that is such only in name, each actually being nothing but fiction (Lenski).

(5) "FOR I SUPPOSE I WAS NOT A WHIT BEHIND THE VERY CHIEFEST APOSTLES."

This statement about *"Super-Apostles"* makes the picture a little clearer. Apparently, this instigator was claiming that Paul was not one of the original Twelve, so he was not as important as they were, that is if he had any importance at all.

Could it be that the doctrine of the primacy of Peter was already being circulated?

I SUPPOSE?

The phrase, *"For I suppose,"* is used in somewhat of a haphazard manner. It is as though he is not very interested in making this statement, which no doubt is the case. However, the Holy Spirit allowed him to say this, simply because it was true. For him to make these particular statements, and especially considering that the Holy Spirit sanctions such, the attack upon his person must have been severe. As we've already stated, but because of its vast significance, we will allude to this premise one more time.

This was more than a mere attack against Paul, but rather an effort by Satan to hinder the New Covenant of Grace. Considering that Paul was the one to whom this great Covenant was given, which evidently aroused great jealousy in the hearts of some, if he could be put down or even destroyed, his Gospel would fail as well.

These were Judaizers who claimed to be upholding a gospel that was superior to the one Paul preached. He was saying that people could be delivered from sin by the Grace of God through simple Faith in the finished work of Christ on the Cross. They, on the other hand, were saying that Salvation was not complete until a person was circumcised and kept the regulations of the Old Testament Law.

These Judaizers were preaching a gospel of works and using the historical Jesus to do so. Their philosophy, probably was something like this: Live a good life just like Jesus did, fulfill the Mosaic Law just like He did. As well, these false apostles observed the rite of Circumcision, so they are superior to Paul, or so they claim.

NOTES

The argument could go on and on, but the bottom line is that they were preaching a gospel of works, not a Gospel of Grace that operates through Faith. These Corinthians were being sucked into a vortex of legalism, the same kind that Paul lived in before his conversion. That is why he could recognize it so easily. The only major difference in what he had once lived and what they were presently preaching, was that Jesus was not used to justify his former life of legalism (Rossier).

PRESENTLY?

As these were demeaning the leadership of Paul, which history has proved to be one of the most stupid positions that anyone could ever take, the counterparts of these self-righteous legalists are presently alive and well. As they were then quick to disclaim Paul's Calling, and his qualifications for leadership, the modern variety continues to do the same.

In fact, the major dividing line in the Church has always been over leadership. Religious men love to disavow those whom they have not approved, and to be sure, they very seldom approve anyone that's called by the Lord. And those who are truly called by the Lord, which are the only ones who will actually do anything for the Lord, are constantly being pressured to compromise that Calling, by demands made upon them by either self-appointed leaders, or those who have been elected by popular ballot to some man-devised office. Rivers of blood have flowed over this one thing.

These self-appointed leaders (for they are certainly not God-appointed), are never satisfied to merely deny the Call of God on the lives of others, they also feel they must do everything within their power to hinder that person, in essence, to stop him (or her) from preaching the Gospel. This within itself shows how wrong they are.

If the person is not Called of God as they claim, why are they so fearful of His Ministry?

While most Laypersons in this country are not aware of what I say, the truth is, that the far greater majority of Preachers, if it lay within their power, would stop everyone in the world

NOTES

from preaching the Gospel, except those of whom they approve. If they had the power, they would shut up all the Churches of which they did not approve, deny access to any Radio or Television Stations, and in fact, if the Law of the land allowed such, some would actually kill the individuals in question.

I realize that many may think that my statements are to the extreme; however, I remind the Reader that these are the Words of Jesus. He said, *"O Jerusalem, Jerusalem, which killest the Prophets, and stonest them that are sent unto thee . . . !"* (Lk. 13:34). As well, Church history has witnessed a river of blood over this very thing, especially by the way of the Catholic Inquisitions, which brought about the torture and slaughter of untold thousands.

I remind the Reader, that the only thing that stops such presently is the Law of the land, for the spirit in the hearts of such individuals presently or in the time of Paul, is the same spirit of darkness that has murdered possibly millions down through the ages.

CHIEFEST APOSTLES

The phrase, *"I was not a whit behind the very chiefest Apostles,"* probably alludes to the original Twelve, but is not meant in any way as a reflection upon them.

He merely means that, even if any with whom he was unfavorably contrasted were *"Apostles ten times over,"* he can claim to be in the front rank with them. This is no more than he has said with the utmost earnestness in I Corinthians 15:10; and Galatians 2:6.

There is no self-assertion here; but, in consequence of the evil done by his detractors, Paul, with an utter sense of distaste, is forced to say the simple truth (Farrar).

Considering that Paul was entrusted by the Holy Spirit to write about half the New Testament, and was given the great Covenant of Grace, one would have to conclude that if anything, his words comprise an understatement instead of otherwise. He certainly was not *"behind"* anyone!

(6) "BUT THOUGH I BE RUDE IN SPEECH, YET NOT IN KNOWLEDGE; BUT WE HAVE BEEN THROUGHLY MADE MANIFEST AMONG YOU IN ALL THINGS."

In the legal profession, it is said that if the opposing lawyer cannot find fault with the evidence, he should vehemently attack the messenger. So, this is the method these hypocrites used on Paul.

RUDE IN SPEECH?

The phrase, *"But though I be rude in speech,"* is not an admittance by Paul as some claim, that he in fact was a poor speaker, but actually the very opposite. No, this is not such an admission, it is refutation. The idea is this:

What a silly thing to quibble about a man's speech while disregarding what that speech contains in the way of knowledge!

As stated, this is an old trick: draw attention to the surface in order to withdraw attention from the golden things underneath the surface; fuss about the wrapping so that nobody will look at what is wrapped up. In fact, the Jews tried this trick on Jesus in John 7:15 in order to turn the people away from Him because He was not graduated from the schools of their Rabbis, but Jesus exploited their cunning; consequently, the same thing is tried against Paul. He uses only a slight blow or two to render the trick innocuous.

WHAT KIND OF SPEAKER ACTUALLY WAS PAUL?

From his various addresses recorded in Acts we know what kind of speaker Paul was. Those addresses show the same ability which his Letters reveal.

However, it must quickly be said, that the art which Paul employed is not the artificial techniques of the Greek orators and rhetoricians (Lenski).

The truth is, Paul did not depend upon oratorical skills in order to move people toward God, or any other *"trick of such trade."* He depended totally and exclusively upon the Moving and Operation of the Holy Spirit upon his Message, in other words the Anointing, for that which he said to have its intended impact.

As Farrar said, *"His eloquence, depended on conviction and emotion."*

KNOWLEDGE!

The phrase, *"Yet not in knowledge,"* is speaking of the knowledge of the Word of God, and in effect, actually says in the Greek, *"Yet not in the knowledge."* So, he limits the word *"knowledge"* to the necessities of the Gospel, in effect, saying that he has little interest in Greek philosophy, etc.

The truth is, it could no doubt be said that Paul was the greatest scholar in the world of that particular time in the Mosaic Law. Of course, he had more knowledge of the New Covenant than anyone else, due to the fact that he was the one to whom this Covenant was given by the Lord Jesus Christ (Gal. 1:12).

It might be asked as to how much *"knowledge"* that you the Reader would have respecting the Word of God? The very fact that you have secured this Commentary, tells me that you have a hunger for God and His Word. Consequently, the road you travel respecting the seeking of *"knowledge"* as it regards the Word of God, is the most rewarding road and direction on which anyone could ever embark. Sadly, most Christians I think, have very little knowledge of the Word of God. If they happen to attend a good Church, where the Gospel is faithfully preached, which is scarce to say the least, they are most blessed. But as stated, most do not have that privilege; consequently, most are led astray.

THE AGE OF APOSTASY

The very word *"apostasy"* means *"a departure from truth,"* a departure from the Word of God. Paul plainly wrote to Timothy, *"Now the Spirit speaketh expressly, that in the latter times* (the times in which we now live) *some shall depart from the Faith, giving heed to seducing spirits, and doctrines of Devils"* (I Tim. 4:1).

He also said, *"For the time will come when they will not endure sound doctrine; but after their own lusts shall they heap to themselves teachers, having itching ears;*

"And they shall turn away their ears from the truth, and shall be turned unto fables" (II Tim. 4:3-4).

ONE OF THE REASONS FOR THESE COMMENTARIES

I believe that the Lord has instructed me to write these Commentaries for several reasons; however, I have come to believe that the most primary reason of all is that of *"sound doctrine."* As stated, there is a terrible departure from truth at the present.

There was a time that one pretty well knew what particular Churches taught by the name on the door. That little applies at the present. Consequently, if the Believer is attending a Church simply because it is of the same Denomination to which they have always attended, or because they like particular sports or social programs offered by the Church, on that score the Believer is inviting disaster.

NOTES

Churches are to be attended for two reasons, and two reasons alone:

1. The Word of God is faithfully preached behind the pulpit, without fear, favor, or compromise.

2. The Spirit of God moves upon the services.

The tragedy is, however, that most Believers, and I exaggerate not, anymore little know what the true Word of God actually says, and actually little know what is the genuine Moving and Operation of the Holy Spirit. All Preachers claim to be preaching the Word, and most claim that what is happening in their midst, irrespective as to what it is, is the Holy Spirit. So, that means that the Believer on a personal basis, is going to have to have a close walk with the Lord, and also a deep consecration to the Lord, which refers to a concentrated study of the Word, and prayer life, which without, relationship with Christ cannot be maintained.

How many are on such a course of concentration?

I'm afraid that the answer would have to be *"not many!"*

Considering that we're talking about the single most important thing that one could ever know or understand, the Salvation of the soul, I think the Reader should make it his or her business to attend to this which is of such vast significance — actually, eternal consequence.

MANIFEST AMONG YOU

The phrase, *"But we have been throughly made manifest among you in all things,"* presents an appeal to the transparent openness and sincerity of all his dealings, as in II Corinthians Chapter 1:20 and 12:12.

"Manifest" in the Greek is *"phaneroo,"* and means *"to render apparent, manifestly declare, make manifest, or to show self."*

No Church as Corinth, as well as all the other Churches planted by Paul, ever had the opportunity of such profound teaching of the Word, and that powerfully anointed by the Holy Spirit. Exactly as he said, the great rudiments of the Faith, the great Gospel of Jesus Christ, the great Plan of Salvation, the great Work of the Spirit, had truly *"been throughly made manifest among* (them) *in all things."* The Word *"all things"* means that every single aspect of the Gospel had been covered. They were not deficient in any rudiment of the Faith, and if in fact they were, it was their fault and not that of Paul.

WHY THE DEPARTURE FROM THE FAITH?

Considering the expert teaching in the Word these people had, actually the greatest that anyone could ever have, and especially considering that it was not *"in Word only, but also in Power, and in the Holy Spirit"* (I Thess. 1:5), how is it possible that some of these Corinthians, and anyone for that matter exposed to such truth, could go astray?

Deception is a powerful factor, so powerful in fact, that it can invade the heart of even the Godliest, that is if they slack in their consecration.

What the true Word of God and the true Operation of the Holy Spirit can do within a heart and life, and I speak of Believers, are predicated on the consecration of the particular Believer, and more particularly, their personal relationship with Christ. These things I say, do not pertain to merit, or that one can earn something from the Lord by consecration, etc., but it does pertain to the provision of fertile spiritual soil where the seed of the Gospel can germinate, which cannot be done without Consecration and Relationship.

As well, Consecration and Relationship with Christ, cannot be brought about or maintained, without a strong prayer life (which regrettably, most Believers don't have), and a strong, habitual study of the Word of God. I personally think the two go hand in hand. If one doesn't have a strong prayer life, one is not going to have much of a *"Word life"* as well, and the same goes in the opposite direction.

If an individual is lacking in Consecration and Relationship, the Spirit of God can move ever so mightily upon the Word being delivered to the people, and they will be relatively unmoved. I have seen it happen countless times, and so have other true Preachers of the Gospel.

If people could lose their way under Paul's Teaching and Preaching, one surely is made to grasp the fact, that it can be done under any circumstance if one is not careful.

When spiritual dry-rot sets in, such a person does not see, feel, or sense the Moving and Operation of the Holy Spirit when it is happening all around them. As well, the Word of God, and irrespective as to how much power with which it is preached, falls basically on deaf ears, at least as far as they are concerned. Many times this happens to those who call themselves the most spiritual. The truth is, they have no spirituality at all, but only a pious, self-important, self-righteousness. In other words, such people are totally bereft of humility, which is always the hallmark of the consecrated Believer, and an absolute requirement for closeness to God (Lk. 18:14).

(7) "HAVE I COMMITTED AN OFFENCE IN ABASING MYSELF THAT YE MIGHT BE EXALTED, BECAUSE I HAVE PREACHED TO YOU THE GOSPEL OF GOD FREELY?"

The idea of this Verse, and several following, is that the false apostles of this situation at Corinth, attempted to turn Paul's consecration against him, and to do so in a most unusual way.

The idea is, that he had not taken any maintenance or material support from the Corinthians, of which we hope to explain why in a moment, with his detractors claiming that he received nothing in this capacity, because he was worth nothing. It is amazing at the length to which liars will go, in attempting to buttress their claims!

AN OFFENCE?

The beginning of the question, *"Have I committed an offence . . . ?"*, in effect says, *"Have I committed a sin by supporting myself when I ministered to you, instead of being a burden to you?"*

Paul uses this type of terminology, in effect, in the form of a question, simply because these detractors were reading something sinister in this act of love and generosity which he performed.

The word for this is *"malignity,"* which in the Greek is *"kakoetheia."* It means *"malignity of the mind, which leads its victim to put the worse construction on every action; ascribing to the best deeds the worst motives."* Of course, many in the world function in this capacity, but it is awful when those who profess to be Believers, are guilty of such.

How this must have hurt the Apostle Paul to have to defend himself regarding such matters! How it must have stung!

ABASING MYSELF

The phrase, *"In abasing myself that ye might be exalted,"* refers to the trade of tentmaker which was despised, tedious, and mechanical.

The Greeks considered anyone who would perform such tasks, as simply not having enough intelligence to do something more worthwhile. Consequently, such people who earned their living by such means, were looked down upon in that day, by the educated, etc. That's what Paul meant by *"abasing myself."*

Why did he do this?

First of all, from the terminology used in the 10th Verse, we must come to the conclusion that the Lord instructed him to act accordingly. Among the reasons why the Holy Spirit would have directed Paul to act in this manner, could very well have had to do with the heathen temples at Corinth.

The Priests in these temples, made constant and heavy demands for money on the devotees to these particular gods. By and large, it was money to be used for the enrichment of these Priests. As well, they lived far above the people in every capacity, and would not have dared to dirty their hands in any manner with any type of menial labor.

Consequently, the Holy Spirit desired that Paul conduct himself in the very opposite manner. He would make or repair tents, which was dirty, menial labor, and as well, would ask nothing of the Corinthians regarding his personal support.

(However, as it regarded money for other projects, such as help for the Church in Jerusalem, even as Chapters 8 and 9 of this very Epistle proclaim, Paul would make heavy appeals. However, it was not for himself but for others, and it was basically done after the Church had been planted, and had sufficiently matured, or at least should have.)

What a consecration and an example for us to follow!

PREACH THE GOSPEL OF GOD FREELY

The conclusion of the question, *"Because I have preached to you the Gospel of God freely?"*, doesn't mean that this should be a rule, even as the next Verse proclaims the opposite.

In effect, Paul is asking the question, *"Are you Corinthians, to whom I gave so much in order to exalt you so highly, going to call me a sinner for doing this for you for nothing?"*

Conversely, the idea seems to be presented, that the false apostles did the very opposite, making heavy demands upon the people for money, which it seems was readily given. If in fact that was the case, and it no doubt seems to have been, what a travesty! What an injustice!

What these Corinthians did or did not do, was not the thought in question, as wrong as it may have been. The Lord had told Paul to take this position, therefore, this is what he did.

Nevertheless, to use his consecration against him, even as we have stated, insinuating that he made no effort to receive support from them, and neither was he given any, and because he was worth nothing, is an insult of the highest order. These people had been saved under Paul. The Gospel which he brought to them, and freely as he added, was that which brought them out of heathenistic paganism which was spiritual darkness of the worst sort. In effect, they owed everything to him, with some seemingly thinking, that they owed nothing.

They had come to this place, because of believing the false doctrine, i.e., pap and drivel, of these liars.

IS IT PROPER FOR THE PREACHER OF THE GOSPEL TO BE PAID?

Yes it is, even as the next Verse proclaims.

Paul himself wrote, *"For it is written in the Law of Moses, thou shalt not muzzle the mouth of the ox that treadeth out the corn"* (I Cor. 9:9). He said the same thing again in I Timothy 5:18.

So, by the Lord instructing Paul to do what he did at Corinth, relative to not receiving any support for himself from the converts, was strictly a personal thing, and seemingly was intended for the Church at Corinth only. As well, it seemed that it pertained only to Paul, and not to others who followed him. Also, it pertained only to the time he was planting the Church, and not thereafter.

(8) "I ROBBED OTHER CHURCHES, TAKING WAGES OF THEM, TO DO YOU SERVICE."

NOTES

In this scenario we are given a portrayal as to how the Work of God should be carried forth, respecting Missions endeavors.

SUPPORT

The phrase, *"I robbed other Churches,"* tells us several things:

1. *"Robbed"* in the Greek is *"sulao,"* and means *"to take from, to take away."* It simply means that he took wages or material help from other Churches as their Missionary so that his needs might be supplied.

The word *"robbed"* as here used by the Apostle, does not have the same meaning as at present. The idea is, that he did not preach for them at this particular time or supply any other service; consequently, their gift to him was not for what he had done for them at this time, but that he may help others. They supported him when he was laboring for other people.

2. By the use of the plural *"Churches"* we know that more than one Church supported him somewhat while he was raising up the Church at Corinth.

3. In fact, this is the manner used by the Holy Spirit respecting Missions endeavors all over the world. In many parts of the world, the poverty is so severe, that very little material help is forthcoming, at least from that particular source; consequently, in order to carry out a Work in those places, the Missionary or Evangelist must have support from another source, i.e., other Churches which are developed and mature.

OUR MINISTRY

In 1975 the Lord gave me instructions respecting the airing of the Gospel by Television. In other words, I was called for this task. As well as airing the Telecast here in America and Canada, He gave me instructions to do the same in countries all over the world where the door would be opened. In fact, we were to translate the Program into whatever language that was indigenous to the people where it was being aired, which we did and continue to do. As a result, we have seen literally hundreds of thousands (which I can say without exaggeration) brought to a saving knowledge of Jesus Christ.

However, our only manner of being able to do this, is that we can receive help from people who already know the Lord, which enables us to minister to those who are not yet saved. In fact, what we can do, at least in one sense of the word, is limited to the help that we receive to accomplish this task. As a result, Paul would say in Romans 10:14-15, that the *"sender"* is just as important as the one *"sent!"* In other words, you who send me to accomplish this task, are quite a necessary part of this Work of God, as should be obvious.

While Paul supported himself, at least as far as possible by the making or repairing of tents, still, without the extra help from the *"Churches,"* his situation would possibly have been perilous. In other words, the tent-making effort, was hardly enough to keep body and soul together, hence him saying earlier, *"even unto this present hour we both hunger, and thirst, and are naked"* (not having sufficient clothing) (I Cor. 4:11). So, no one could say that Paul enriched himself at the expense of others.

TO DO YOU SERVICE

The phrase, *"Taking wages of them, to do you service,"* refers to taking the support of these Churches, whatever it may have been, while the Corinthians at that time contributed nothing. Of course, he was speaking of the raising up of this Church, which took over a year. In effect, Corinth owed not only Paul a debt of gratitude, but these Churches as well, wherever they may have been, which helped Paul to bring the Gospel to Corinth.

It sounds as though Paul is speaking disparagingly of the entire scenario respecting support and giving, etc.; however, that is not the case at all. In fact, what these Churches did was right and proper. The Apostle is simply trying to show the Corinthians that what they have came at great price; consequently, they should not throw it away by becoming embroiled in false doctrine which if continued, would constitute labor expended on them *"in vain"* (I Cor. 15:2).

Thankfully, according to II Corinthians Chapter 7, there had been a great Revival at Corinth, with repentance forthcoming concerning many things; however, the Apostle continues to warn them, even in no uncertain terms, respecting false apostles, either because there were still one or two continuing to peck at the Church, or else he was attempting to warn them sufficiently that they would not become embroiled in such again. Of course, the Holy Spirit had him to say these things as well for the benefit of all, even unto this hour.

(9) "AND WHEN I WAS PRESENT WITH YOU, AND WANTED, I WAS CHARGEABLE TO NO MAN: FOR THAT WHICH WAS LACKING TO ME THE BRETHREN WHICH CAME FROM MACEDONIA SUPPLIED: AND IN ALL THINGS I HAVE KEPT MYSELF FROM BEING BURDENSOME UNTO YOU, AND SO WILL I KEEP MYSELF."

Paul's sincerity was never in such conspicuous evidence as when it revealed his attitude concerning remuneration for his service. Of course there were economic requirements which must be met and these were not to be viewed in an impractical manner.

Paul refers here to his own carefulness in desiring to be chargeable to no man. As stated, he even labored with his own hand so as to be economically independent. When it was necessary to have support, he accepted it from other sources so as to preach gratuitously to the Corinthians.

How far should a modern servant of Christ go in expecting support for himself concerning his service?

I think the answer would be, certainly not so much as a payment for service rendered, even though the workman is worthy of his hire, but rather as a means of continuing in service. Christian service must never be computed by the dollar value. Whatever is received is not to be considered as a wage, but as a support. It is for the sake of creating economic freedom so as to release all the worker's time and talents for his service.

WANTED?

The phrase, *"And when I was present with you, and wanted,"* seems to point to particular times at Corinth, when his economic situation became perilous. He was there for 18 months.

From all of this we learn that Paul's Missionary endeavors, were not an easy task to say the least. To establish the Church, and I speak of the Church in general and not the one merely at Corinth, it took a man of much courage and character, of which the breed is in short supply. His life was in danger almost constantly and beside that, even as we are studying here, his economic situation was anything but stable.

NOTES

And then on top of all of that, he had the constant problem of false apostles coming into the works which he raised up.

Along with all of this, I think it is obvious that he received little or no help whatsoever from Jerusalem, probably even hindrance. As F. F. Bruce said, *"It seems that Paul always respected Jerusalem, but Jerusalem little respected Paul."* Of course, he was speaking of the Church in Jerusalem, as well as the nation as a whole, etc.

So, the task marked out for him by the Lord was anything but easy. Consequently, the world owes a debt to Paul, that it will never be able to repay. As no other man, he is responsible for what we presently refer to as *"Western Civilization,"* especially considering that our culture is based squarely on the Life, Ministry, Death, and Resurrection, of the Lord Jesus Christ. As the Baptist Preacher, George W. Truett said, *"Paul was the greatest example for Christ that Christianity ever produced."* If in fact that was the way in which he made this statement, it would have been better said, *"Paul was the greatest example for Christianity that Christ ever produced."*

DEPENDENT ON NO MAN

The phrase, *"I was chargeable to no man,"* means that he was burdensome to no one; or more literally, *"I did not lie as a dead weight upon you."*

According to Jerome, its use here is typical of Paul. The idea is, that he did not lead a torpid, inactive life at the expense of others. He did not expect support from them when he was doing nothing; nor did he demand support which would in any sense be a burden to them.

However, even as the following phrases will show, this is not meant to be misconstrued as an independence of thought and support. In fact, if such had been done, it would have been unscriptural, even according to Paul's own words (Chpts. 8-9). Paul is speaking here of Corinth, and this one particular situation, which he felt demanded a certain course of action, which we have already attempted to explain. Different situations call for different tactics, even as Paul here explains. No doubt, the Lord led him respecting this particular position, and for particular reasons.

MACEDONIA

The phrase, *"For that which was lacking to me the Brethren which came from Macedonia supplied,"* pertains to him accepting help from them, and for which he was very grateful, and to which he had just alluded concerning the *"Churches."*

It is ironical that the Lord used the Brethren from Macedonia, who in fact, were in deep poverty themselves (II Cor. 8:2). In fact, much of the money given to the Work of God, comes from those mostly of the economic disposition of those in Macedonia. While there are certainly some wealthy people who contribute to the Work of God, probably now more than ever (because of the Blessings of God), still, I think it can be said without fear of contradiction, that the greatest percentage of money given to the Work of God comes from those who have little of this world's goods.

And yet that is not as strange as one may think, due to the fact that the Lord uses the principle of giving according to two particulars:

1. Giving is the manner in which He blesses His people (Mal. 3:8-12; Lk. 6:38; II Cor. 9:6). Actually, this is the economy of God, i.e., *"His method of increase"* (Lk. 12:22-32).

2. Believers, whether rich or poor, give out of gratitude, because so much has been given unto us. That's why Paul said, *"I am debtor both to the Greeks, and to the Barbarians; both to the wise, and to the unwise"* (Rom. 1:14).

Being a *"debtor"* does not mean that we can pay the Lord for what He has done for us, for such is impossible. It does mean, that in view of the fact that He has done so much for us, that we should at least desire to give all we can to help take this glorious Message to others. In fact, if we have little concern for these particulars, it shows that we have little gratitude for what the Lord has done for us.

BURDENSOME UNTO YOU

The phrase, *"And in all things I have kept myself from being burdensome unto you, and so will I keep myself,"* in effect says, *"I have not asked anything from you in the past, and I'm not asking anything now, at least as it regards material support."*

For Paul to go to the length of this much explanation, evidently points to accusations of some sort made by the false apostles, which had snared some of the Corinthians; consequently, the Apostle attempts to set the record straight.

As someone has ventured, and to which we have previously alluded, these detractors had evidently said that Paul had received nothing in the way of material support, because he was worth nothing. They could not claim he was there for money, considering that he received absolutely nothing in the way of material support, for the length of the 18 months he was there raising up the Church. Inasmuch as they could not accuse him of greed, they evidently attempted to turn against him his consecration.

Or quite possibly they did accuse him of greed, not knowing that he had not received any financial remuneration whatsoever, with him now reminding the Corinthians of that fact.

Irrespective, whatever accusation they made against him, was a lie. Still, some of the Corinthians evidently, had been taken in by these false accusations.

(10) "AS THE TRUTH OF CHRIST IS IN ME, NO MAN SHALL STOP ME OF THIS BOASTING IN THE REGIONS OF ACHAIA."

It was the fixed and settled purpose of his life never to be burdensome to any man. What a noble resolution! How fixed were the principles of his life! And what an instance of magnanimous self-denial and of elevated purpose! Every man, minister or otherwise, should adopt a similar resolution. He should resolve to receive nothing for which he has not rendered a fair equivalent; and resolve, if he has health, never to be a burden to his friends or to the Church of God.

In fact, no man need be burdensome to anyone; and all should resolve that by the Grace of God they never will be.

THE TRUTH OF CHRIST

The phrase, *"As the Truth of Christ is in me,"* in effect, states that he is declaring this in the Presence of Christ. He is saying, *"I am bound to declare the truth, as I must answer to Christ."* It is a solemn statement, equal to an oath.

The idea is, that if the *"Truth of Christ"* is in an individual, which it surely is if one is truly Born-Again, they are then bound to tell the truth in all things. There is no deceitfulness, deviousness, subterfuge, or trickery about such a one. Everything is open and above, with nothing hidden.

NOTES

How so much that modern Christians need to hear these words. How so much so, that we set the example that everything is 12 inches to the foot, 16 ounces to the pound, 5,280 feet to the mile. In other words, it is straight. Every Child of God is to function in this capacity. He pays his debts! He tells the truth! His word is his bond! You can depend on what he says, which he will do without fail, at least if it is possible. Otherwise, he will give a truthful, aboveboard, factual explanation. He will attend to his own business, therefore, not meddling in the business of others. He will not be a gossip, nor will he speak evil of others. His judgment will be with Mercy and Grace, because God has shown great Mercy and Grace to him, and because the *"Truth of Christ"* abides in him.

BOASTING

The phrase, *"No man shall stop me of this boasting in the regions of Achaia,"* actually means that no man can disprove what the Apostle is saying. When he speaks of *"Achaia,"* he is evidently speaking only of this particular part of Greece. For some reason, he felt he should not take any financial remuneration concerning this particular region.

This tells us that the Apostle was led by the Lord in all things, even as he always sought to be. He evidently listened attentively for the voice of the Holy Spirit in order that guidance may be given on a constant basis. This should be the norm for all Preachers, and actually for all Believers whether Preacher or not. We are to be led by the Spirit, guided by the Spirit, empowered by the Spirit, and upheld by the Spirit. In this fashion, our steps will be sure, and the Will of God will always be maintained.

A PERSONAL EXPERIENCE

On January 1 (if I remember correctly) 1969, I went on radio with our daily, 15 minute program, *"The Campmeeting Hour."* To be sure, its beginnings were very humble to say the least; however, the Lord wondrously blessed, and in a short time we were airing the Gospel over some 600 stations daily.

In 1975, according to instructions given by the Holy Spirit, we went on Television, which as well had a very humble beginning. Even so, the Lord blessed abundantly, until the Program soon covered this Nation, plus nearly 50 other countries in the world, even translated into several languages.

NOTES

From that time, January 1, 1969, considering all the funds and offerings we have received for the Cause of Christ, Frances and I have taken nothing for ourselves from this source. All of our income, such as it has been, has come from the sale of our products, such as Recordings, etc. Even then, compared to the whole, we have received very little, with all of that as well, minus what little we have received going to help take the Gospel to the world. In other words, my family, even though provided with a good living, has not enriched itself at the expense of this Ministry.

Even as Paul said, I thank the Lord that I can boast of this, even as he did, but at the same time, not even remotely placing ourselves up to his status.

But yet I will say even as he said, *"I am the least of the Apostles, that am not meet to be called an Apostle, because I persecuted* (failed) *the Church of God.*

"But by the Grace of God I am what I am: and His Grace which was bestowed upon me was not in vain; but I labored more abundantly than they all: yet not I, but the Grace of God which was with me" (I Cor. 15:9-10).

(11) "WHEREFORE? BECAUSE I LOVE YOU NOT? GOD KNOWETH."

The idea of this Verse has little or nothing to do with the Corinthians as such, but primarily because this is what the Lord has told him to do. In other words, his direction is based not foremost on people, for that would be political, but rather that of which the Holy Spirit directs.

WHEREFORE?

In effect, Paul is asking by this one word a question, as to the purpose and reason for his actions. In fact, he probably cannot tell the ultimate reason, which is the whole character and nature, and because he probably does not know all the answers himself, regarding the money situation at Corinth.

The Lord seldom tells us the reasons why. The direction given by the Spirit, has more to do with obedience than anything else. But of course, anything that the Lord requires that we do, is for purpose and reason, even though He may not reveal such to us in total detail, and sometimes little detail at all!

LOVE

The question, *"Because I love you not?"*, actually is meant to have the opposite meaning. In other words, I do what I do, because I love you.

What I do is not because I do not love you. It is not from pride, because I would not as willingly receive aid from you as from any other. It is not because I am more unwilling to be under obligation to you than to others. I have a deep and tender attachment to you. But it is because I can thus best promote the Gospel and advance the Kingdom of the Redeemer, at least in this area, and as the Lord directs me.

GOD KNOWS

The short phrase, *"God knoweth,"* refers to the fact that what he is saying is true, and above that, he is doing what he does according to the leading of the Lord.

Possibly it might have been thought that his unwillingness to receive aid from them was some proof of reserve towards them or want of affection, and this may have been urged against him. This, if in fact that's what it was, he solemnly denies.

It seems that some at Corinth may have been judging Paul, and as is usually the case, were judging him wrongly.

Irrespective as to what others think, irrespective as to what is said, the one sure foundation on which the Faith-filled Believer stands, is that *"God knows!"* As someone has well said, *"People say things about me, the Devil says things about me, and God says things about me. It is only what God says that matters."*

(12) "BUT WHAT I DO, THAT I WILL DO, THAT I MAY CUT OFF OCCASION FROM THEM WHICH DESIRE OCCASION; THAT WHEREIN THEY GLORY, THEY MAY BE FOUND EVEN AS WE."

The Holy Spirit through the Apostle is about to give some of the most detailed teaching concerning false apostles, in other words, deceivers, found in the entirety of the Word of God.

If it is to be noticed, this situation concerned money, at least in some degree as it always does. That's the reason why Paul would later write, *"The love of money is the root of all evil"* (I Tim. 6:10).

NOTES

THAT WHICH I DO

The phrase, *"But what I do, that I will do,"* in effect says, *"The course of life which I have been pursuing I will continue to pursue."* This was said and done for several reasons:

1. First of all, and as stated, what he was doing was not because of what the people wanted, but rather what the Lord had directed him to do.

2. Inasmuch as the Lord had directed him to do this, he would continue on this course until the Lord said otherwise. What people said, wanted, desired, or demanded, mattered not. It was what the Lord wanted that really mattered.

3. This shows that his purpose in life was not to please men but rather to please God.

OCCASION?

The phrase, *"That I may cut off occasion from them which desire occasion,"* in effect means that he would pull the teeth of the monster before it had the opportunity to bite.

Paul meant that what he was doing, was at the behest of the Lord, but as well, it was a course which gave his enemies little recourse. To be sure, they criticized just the same; nevertheless, their accusations were that made out of whole cloth, with no validity. In other words, they could not point a finger at Paul and accuse him truthfully of any negative thing. To be sure, they certainly desired occasion of accusation and labored diligently to find such, but the Apostle provided them nothing at all. As someone has said, these false apostles have embarked upon a hill which they cannot climb.

GLORY?

The phrase, *"That wherein they glory,"* is meant to point to a lie on their part.

In effect, Paul is saying, *"These new teachers boast to you how disinterested they are in your money. Well, then, I have proved myself to be equally disinterested."*

However, these words as used by Paul involve a most stinging sarcasm. For these teachers were *not* in reality disinterested, though they boasted of being so; on the contrary, they were exacting, insolent, and tyrannical, and did not preach without charge, even as the next phrase will say. The idea is, while they were openly boasting, they were secretly taking money and, therefore, were not *"even as we."*

EVEN AS WE

The phrase, *"They may be found even as we,"* in effect says, even as we have stated, that they are not telling the truth concerning money.

Of course, the money was only a part of their deception, with actually everything about them false. But as stated, according to the space devoted to the subject, money played a bigger part in all of this scenario than one would at first suspect.

(13) "FOR SUCH ARE FALSE APOSTLES, DECEITFUL WORKERS, TRANSFORMING THEMSELVES INTO THE APOSTLES OF CHRIST."

In Verses 13-15 Paul says that these Preachers of *"an ethical Gospel"* were sham apostles, deceitful workers, servants of the Devil and doomed to the lake of fire.

Such language shocks modern religious feelings; but the shock proves the existence of the immense gulf lying between the teaching of the Apostles and of some who profess to be their successors but actually aren't.

We learn from this, that one cannot be of God and at the same time, oppose that which is of God. The mere fact that these people opposed Paul, tells us that they were not serving the Lord, but were actually false despite their claims.

How far can this position be carried, in other words, that one is identified by what they accept or oppose?

DOCTRINE AND DECEPTION

When it comes to Doctrine, the situation is somewhat of a different complexion. For instance, there are millions who are genuinely saved and truly love the Lord; however, when it comes to the Baptism with the Holy Spirit, with the evidence of speaking with other tongues, it is opposed by many of these people. Even though their position is Scripturally wrong, and it will definitely stunt their spiritual growth, still, one cannot deny their Salvation, because of their trust in Christ. In other words, that is a different thing than the deception which we will momentarily address. While these may oppose that which is truly of the Lord, and at times even do so strongly, it doesn't mean they are false as Paul here describes. It just means they are not walking in all the light they have been shown, which of course, within itself is very serious. But that is different than being Satanic, as the Apostle here reveals.

Deception as it regards these false apostles, is something else altogether. It is not a matter of doctrine, even though it may certainly involve that, but moreso of claiming to be what they really aren't — Apostles of Christ.

Such type individuals, even though talking the talk and acting the part, have that in mind of which is not of the Lord. Their motives are entirely different. In fact, they have not been called of God, or if they truly have, they have long since departed from that which is right. These people preach *"another Jesus,"* have *"another spirit,"* and present *"another gospel."*

FALSE APOSTLES

The phrase, *"For such are false apostles,"* means they have no claim to the apostolic office. They are deceivers. They pretend to be apostles; but they have no Divine commission from the Redeemer.

Paul had thus far argued the case without giving them an explicit designation as deceivers. But here he says that men who had conducted themselves thus; who had attempted to impose upon the people; who had brought another gospel, whatever pretenses they might have — and he was not disposed to deny that there was much that was plausible, in fact which generally is — were really impostors, and the enemies of Christ. In fact, concerning these kinds, of which there are many in the Church, and in fact always have been, they generally preach some Truth, which only serves as the bait. In fact, this is the greatest danger to the modern Church, and actually, always has been. Let us be a little more specific.

According to the Book of Acts and the Epistles, God has designated the Office of Apostles as the leaders of the Church. In other words, the Holy Spirit deals with Apostles concerning direction, doctrine, and leading, which are to set the tone for the Church respecting direction. As well, the Holy Spirit doing such through Apostles, means that He does not do such through denominational heads, or self-appointed leaders, etc. Naturally, this is the area that Satan opposes the most, seeking to replace the God given designation, for that of man's devising. He generally carries out these devious efforts in two ways:

DENOMINATIONS

Denominationalism: Religious denominations can be of a great boon to the Work of God and totally Scriptural; however, in most cases they cool off spiritually, even if they begin correctly. The spiritual cooling generally results in an unscriptural form of Church Government. In other words, they generally bring the ways of the world over into the Church, which is a total departure from that outlined in the Book of Acts and the Epistles.

Even though the Leadership in these Denominations normally does not fall under the heading of *"false apostles,"* however, the general rule is, with some few exceptions, that they in fact do oppose those who are truly God-called Apostles.

SELF-APPOINTED

Certain individuals raise themselves up, making great claims of Apostleship, while at the same time opposing those who are truly of God. These people are generally very talented, sometimes very eloquent, or at any rate have some type of charisma that pulls in a following. However, their motives are the same as those at Corinth, they are not preaching and teaching the true Word of God, but actually hindering that which is of God and sometimes very greatly, with money generally finding its way in the mix, and if the truth be known, a great cause and reason for the deception.

They are generally successful, for the simple reason that they seek to accommodate the powers that be, and actually preach and teach some Truth. As a result, they sometimes gather to themselves a large following; however, the results will not be spiritual victory for these followers, but the very opposite. Many will lose their souls, and all who follow in this train if not totally lost, will be seriously hindered in a spiritual sense.

DECEITFUL WORKERS

The phrase, *"Deceitful workers,"* gives us the manner in which these *"false apostles"* operate. It is all by deception.

These individuals have no regard or concern for the spiritual welfare of their followers, only seeking to use these people, whomever they may be, for their own deceitful purposes. They are crafty, fraudulent, and hypocritical!

NOTES

Everything is done for a purpose, and the purpose has to do with their own agenda.

These individuals are generally very political. By that I mean, that they seek to do things which will please the most people, make them look good in the eyes of others, and to say what they think people want to hear.

They are very subtle in opposing that which is of God, doing so only when they think it's in their best interest. In other words, they will just as much attempt to ride the coattails of the true Apostle, as they are to oppose the true Apostle. It is according to what they think is best at the time.

So, those who are True Apostles have to be very careful, that those around them, are truly of God. Most of the time, even as we see with Paul, it is only those who are raised up under one's own Ministry, which can actually be referred to as true and faithful. As well, these *"false apostles"* will just as quickly turn on the True Apostle, if they think it's to their advantage to do so.

As we have stated, their only purpose is to use others for their own devious ends, which have absolutely nothing to do with their spiritual enrichment. *"Deception"* is their chief weapon, with every move tailored to that conclusion.

WHY ARE CHRISTIANS ATTRACTED TO THESE IMPOSTORS?

We can begin with those at Corinth, even though they certainly were not the first ones, with Adam and Eve fitting that description. Regrettably, the problem is pandemic.

If one in fact had the knowledge to attempt to explain the *"whys"* and *"wherefores,"* the volume of explanation would probably cause the true meaning to be lost. However, oversimplification sometimes leaves the problem unaddressed. Irrespective, we will be brief. Perhaps the following will give some clue:

1. As someone has said, a con artist cannot really con a truly honest man; likewise, a false apostle will have no attraction to those of true consecration to the Lord.

2. Self-will causes many to be attracted to that which is false, for the simple reason that appeal is made to that self-will.

3. Flattery is one of the biggest weapons of *"deceitful workers."* They flatter the individual for their own devious purposes, with the Believer then drawn in.

4. Most Believers regrettably, have a very weak relationship with the Lord. Consequently, the voice of the Holy Spirit is muted. So they fall for that which is offered up, little knowing any better, at least at the outset.

5. Almost all who are drawn into this vortex, have little knowledge of the Word of God. While they may know some part of the Bible quite extensively, they little have an overall grasp. In that case, most of the time, what that type of person actually knows is skewed and perverted. Consequently, they are grist for the Devil's mill.

6. As well, these people have very little prayer life, if any at all. In fact, most Christians pray not at all except in cases of emergency. Having no communion with the Lord, it is impossible to have any type of consecration. As a result, if it glitters, they're made to think that it is gold.

As we look at that list just given, and if we know anything about the Church as a whole, we realize that these particular points fit almost the entirety of those who claim Christ. Thank the Lord there are exceptions, although small! Nevertheless, almost the entirety of the Church fits into the category of the susceptible. Most Christians, sadly and regrettably, don't know the difference between the real and the unreal, the true and the false, the genuine and the fabricated, etc. As such, they are prey for devious means.

TRANSFORMING THEMSELVES . . .

The phrase, *"Transforming themselves into the Apostles of Christ,"* has reference to two things:

1. They work at appearing to be something they aren't.

2. They have called themselves to be Apostles of Christ, actually having no true Call of God.

Let's look at the word *"transformed"* or *"transfigured"* as it is sometimes used.

TRANSFIGURED SAINTS

We read in Matthew 17:2 that our Lord *"was transfigured before them: and His Face did shine as the Sun, and His raiment was white as the light."* The word *"transfigured"* is from a Greek word made up of two words, one word referring to the outward expression one gives to his inmost true nature, the other signifying a change of activity. We could translate, *"His mode of expression was changed before them."*

NOTES

Our Lord's usual mode of expression while on Earth in His humiliation was that of a servant. He came (Mk. 10:45) *"not to be ministered unto, but to minister, and to give His life a ransom for many."* But now, that usual mode of expression was changed.

Our Lord now gave expression to the glory of His Deity. The word *"transfigured"* here means that He changed His outward form of expression, namely, from that of a servant to that of Deity.

TRANSFORMED

We have in II Corinthians 11:13-15, the text of our discussion, another Greek word of the direct opposite meaning, namely, the act of changing the outward expression of that which inwardly remains the same, that outward expression not being representative of that person's inmost nature.

Satan, his false apostles and ministers assume an outward expression which does not correspond to their true natures. Before masquerading, and that is what the Greek word means, as an angel of light, Satan gave outward expression to his inmost nature.

But in order to mislead the human race and gain followers, he had to pose as an angel of light. He changed that outward expression which was expressive of his inmost nature, and assumed another, which did not correspond to it. Satan masquerades as an angel of light, whereas he is all the while an angel of darkness.

TRANSFIGURED AND TRANSFORMED

In Romans 12:2, we have both words used.

Paul exhorts the Saints not to be conformed to this world. Here he uses the word found in our Corinthian Passage. Christians must not change their outward expression from that of a true expression of their inmost nature, to an assumed expression not true of their new regenerated inmost being, an assumed expression patterned after the world.

He exhorts them instead to be transformed, and here we have the same Greek word which is used in the Matthew Passage and translated *"transfigured."* Saints are to change their outward expression from that which was true of them before Salvation, when they gave expression to what was in their indwelling sinful nature, to an expression of their inmost regenerated being. Then they would be transfigured Saints. In other words, what they're supposed to have on the inside, they are to allow it to radiate on the outside.

SHEEP IN WOLVES CLOTHING?

A short time back, a Preacher was over television promoting worldly rock music, claiming that this was the way to win the youth to Christ. In his words he said that he was a *"sheep in wolves clothing."* Unfortunately, even as here described, that is grossly unscriptural.

Paul exhorts the Saints not to assume as an outward expression the fashions, habits, speech expressions, and artificiality of this evil age, thus hiding their expression of theirselves which should come from what they are intrinsically as Children of God, or at least are supposed to be. How Saints sometimes like to have just a dash of the world about them so as not to appear too unworldly. How a coat of worldliness can cover up the Christ within!

But instead, Saints are to be transformed, that is, give expression of what they really are, partakers of the Divine Nature, indwelt by the Spirit. They are to do so by having their inward life renewed by the Holy Spirit so that the Lord Jesus may be seen. Thus, they will be transfigured Saints.

And as our Lord was seen by the Disciples, shining resplendent in the Glory of His Deity, so the Saints are to shine with a heavenly radiance pervading their thoughts, words, and deeds even on their earthly pilgrimage, lighting many a lost wanderer home amide the darkening shadows of this age (Wuest).

So, while there definitely are *"wolves in sheep's clothing"* (Mat. 7:15), there is no such thing as a *"sheep in wolves' clothing."*

In other words, it is not possible to win the youth to the Lord, or anyone else for that matter, by posing as the world. Anyone who has even a smattering of knowledge of the Scriptures, knows better than such foolishness. People are won to the Lord, youth included, by the Holy Spirit moving upon the preached or proclaimed Word of God.

(14) "AND NO MARVEL; FOR SATAN HIMSELF IS TRANSFORMED INTO AN ANGEL OF LIGHT."

NOTES

Satan inspires his ministers to imitate Christianity and even do miracles (Mat. 24:24; I Thess. 2:8-12; Rev. 13; 16:13-16; 19:20).

Where are his ministers who are transformed as ministers of righteousness? Would they be in the Churches or outside of them?

The answer is obvious!

NO MARVEL

The phrase, *"And no marvel,"* means that the True Believer should not be surprised at such.

Since Satan himself is capable of appearing to be an angel of light, it is not to be deemed strange that those who are in his service also should resemble him. Jesus plainly said, *"Beware of false prophets, which come to you in sheep's clothing, but inwardly they are ravening wolves."*

He then said, *"Ye shall know them by their fruits. Do men gather grapes of thorns, or figs of thistles? Even so every good tree bringeth forth good fruit; but a corrupt tree bringeth forth evil fruit"* (Mat. 7:15-17).

The *"fruit"* of the *"good tree"* will always be souls saved, lives changed, sick bodies truly healed, bondages broken, and Believers Baptized with the Holy Spirit.

Conversely, the *"corrupt tree"* can only bring forth the evil fruit of spiritual deception, which destroys lives, wrecks marriages, stops all spiritual growth, if not destroying the person altogether, and then on top of all that, relieves the people of their money.

In other words, no one is saved, no lives are changed, no one is delivered, and no one is Baptized with the Holy Spirit.

HOWEVER, IT IS NOT QUITE THAT SIMPLE . . .

False apostles have a way of disguising who they are, and through sham and manipulation, making people believe what is really not there.

In other words, it is quite common for these people to announce staggering numbers in whatever capacity that is desired. The *"Truth of Christ"* not being in them, they are free to make up any type of lie that will fit their purpose.

As well, these *"deceitful workers"* are so adept at their deceptive craft, that they can make the unwary think that God is doing great and mighty things, when all the time, very little, if anything, is actually being done — at least for the Lord.

I will say it again; the *"fruit"* is souls being saved, lives being changed, people being delivered by the Power of God, the sick truly being healed, with Believers being Baptized with the Holy Spirit. If those things are not truly present, the people are following a lie.

As well, it is quite common for such to announce great miracles, and even to get people to claim miracles, when in fact, nothing has actually happened. While we certainly want to give God all the Glory for any and everything He does, to be sure, He does not need false Glory, and in fact, will not accept such and for the obvious reasons.

ANGEL OF LIGHT

The phrase, *"For Satan himself is transformed into an angel of light,"* means that he pretends to be that which he is not. That's the reason the Lord said to Samuel, *"For the Lord seeth not as man seeth; for man looketh on the outward appearance, but the Lord looketh on the heart"* (I Sam. 16:7).

As we have said several times, Satan is a master at getting Believers to believe the opposite of that which is really true. He endeavors to get Christians to believe that that which is truly of God, isn't, and that which isn't of God, is!

Again, as he did in Verse 3, Paul brings out the connection of all false apostles with Satan. He uses the same verb. The present tense is important: Satan does this again and again, it is his practice, in other words he continues to do so, even unto this hour.

He makes people think that they are dealing with the true Spirit of God, when in fact they are dealing with the prince of darkness. How else can Satan get his deadly lies across except by presenting them as God's words that are being spoken by one of God's messengers.

When in the Bible, Angels appeared to men, they used a physical form and bright and shining garments that were visible to the human eye. Satan imitates this in the spiritual sense. In other words, he tries to look like the Lord, act like the Lord, speak like the Lord, and in every way appear to be the Lord, while all the time being the very opposite.

NOTES

To do this, he talks the talk. In other words, he quotes Scripture, he prays and praises, he preaches, he teaches. It all sounds so right, but in fact is so wrong!

MANY!

Let not the Reader think that this effort is in short supply. The Truth is, that for every true Apostle of the Lord, there are several if not many, who are the very opposite. In fact, this is Satan's greatest means of hindering the true Work of God. He uses deceivers and deception.

(15) "THEREFORE IT IS NO GREAT THING IF HIS MINISTERS ALSO BE TRANSFORMED AS THE MINISTERS OF RIGHTEOUSNESS; WHOSE END SHALL BE ACCORDING TO THEIR WORKS."

These Passages as should be obvious, hold amazing Truths.

Some may ask, *"Was Paul's judgment regarding these men just?"* Should we not hear also *"the other side"*? Some are very quick with this denunciation: *"of the devil!"*, even when their own passion plays a strong part.

Yes, Paul was just in his summary. Actually, he was led and guided by the Holy Spirit, which actually makes his judgment infallible, at least as it pertains to this particular situation.

SATAN'S MINISTERS

The phrase, *"Therefore it is no great thing if his ministers also be transformed as the ministers of Righteousness,"* in effect says that irrespective of the claims, these are *"Satan's ministers."* To be sure, that is quite an accusation, but yet quite the truth! It cuts through all the fluff, and says it just like it is, and if the Holy Spirit addresses such in this manner, so should we.

Whatever these Preachers may be called by the Church, the Holy Spirit rightly designates them as *"Satan's ministers."*

What exactly were these Preachers, these false apostles, doing, which brought about this designation as given by the Holy Spirit through Paul?

First of all we know from Verse 22 that they were Jews. This in no way spoke ill, for Paul himself was a Jew. However, it does tell us that the Law/Grace issue was involved. According to Verse 23 they claimed to be *"ministers of Christ,"* which meant that they had claimed to accept Jesus as their Saviour; however, they were also attempting to tag the Law of Moses onto Christ. In other words, to be saved, they were saying, one had to accept Christ and keep the Law of Moses. In effect, they were repudiating the great Covenant of Grace.

THE PERSON OF PAUL

To further their doctrine, they evidently felt that they had to denigrate Paul. They did so in many and varied ways, by attacking his person, his consecration, or whatever was handy. They felt they had to demean him, destroy the people's belief in him, and erode confidence in him, before their false gospel could be accepted.

It is one of Satan's age-old tactics, destroy the effectiveness of the Messenger, and then his Message is suspect. Thank the Lord, that Satan did not succeed at Corinth.

WHY DID THEY PICK PRIMARILY ON PAUL?

It was Paul who claimed to be the Apostle to the Gentiles, in fact, who claimed that the Lord had given him this great Covenant of Grace, which replaced the Covenant of Law (Gal. 1:6, 11-12).

As well, Paul was rapidly planting new Churches, which meant the Covenant of Grace was expanding rapidly.

We have little knowledge as to what the original Twelve were doing at this particular time, or if they were opposed by these Judaisers as well? However, it seems that whatever the opposition, that Paul was their main target, and for the obvious reasons.

He was strong indeed in his demands that the Law was finished, fulfilled in Christ, consequently, there being no more need of its services. The idea that it was done and finished, was anathema to them. Consequently, they felt they had to destroy Paul, if they were to weaken his Message.

As we have repeatedly stated, they were not content to raise up congregations of their own, for the simple reason that their false gospel could not bring anyone to Christ; consequently, they were forced to parasite off of others, namely Paul.

ARE ALL FALSE APOSTLES LOST?

A quick retort would be *"yes,"* especially considering that Paul has referred to them as *"Satan's ministers."* However, that may not necessarily be true in all cases.

During the Lord's Ministry, when Jesus mentioned His coming demise in Jerusalem, the Scripture says that *"Peter took Him, and began to rebuke Him, saying, be it far from Thee, Lord: this shall not be unto Thee."*

Then it says that Jesus *"turned, and said unto Peter, 'Get thee me behind Me, Satan: thou art an offense unto Me: for thou savourest not the things that be of God, but those that be of men'"* (Mat. 16:22-23).

At that moment, Peter was actually being used by Satan, but it didn't mean that Peter was at that time lost.

As well, at another time, even after Pentecost, Peter succumbed to the Law/Grace issue, with Paul saying to him, *"You are to be blamed,"* considering that he *"withdrew and separated himself, fearing them which were of the circumcision"* (Gal. 2:11-12). Even though Peter at that time was preaching that which was wrong, he was not lost.

In fact, the greatest danger of all, and the greatest help to Satan I think, is for a man who is truly saved, and who thinks he is truly right, in fact, preaching something that is wrong. In fact, untold numbers fall into this category, and to be sure, quite possibly, all Preachers have experienced this in one way or the other, at one time or the other.

However, that of which Paul speaks, goes much farther than that of which we have outlined regarding Simon Peter, who in fact, was one of the greatest men of God whoever lived.

WHILE PROFESSING LIGHT, THEY ARE MINISTERS OF DARKNESS

These of which Paul speaks, are those who have brushed aside the pleadings of the Holy Spirit time and time again, until they are now past feeling. In other words, they have chartered their own course. If the Lord once lived within their own hearts, He is no longer there. It is impossible to keep sinning against Light, without ultimately losing that Light. Consequently, the light they now profess is feigned light, therefore, *"transforming themselves into an angel of light."*

Even though it is the Lord Who draws the line and not man, still, I do not see how these who Paul mentions, or anyone like them even unto this present hour, could in fact know Christ, and at the same time be a minister of Satan. As

NOTES

stated, they have long since chartered their course, probably falling into the category of Hebrews 6:4-6 and 10:26-31.

Their modern counterparts fit the same bill! They claim to be *"ministers of Righteousness,"* but they aren't!

They are lost, at least these of whom Paul speaks, and their Disciples will fall into the same category if they maintain the same course. In fact, that is the purpose of Satan.

THEIR WORKS

The phrase, *"Whose end shall be according to their works,"* speaks of the final destiny. Their doom in eternity shall not be according to their fair professions and plausible pretenses, for they cannot deceive God; but shall be according to their real character and their works.

Their work is a work of deception, and they shall be judged according to that. What revelations there will be in the day of judgment, when all impostors shall be unmasked, and when all hypocrites and deceivers shall be seen in their true colors! And how desirable it is that there should be such a day to disclose all beings in their true character, and forever to remove imposture and delusion from the universe!

It is said by some that Paul ought to have told the Corinthians to sever themselves completely from these ministers of Satan, the moreso since they were still active, it seems, in Corinth. However, is there any stronger way of demanding separation than by pointing to men as being ministers of Satan? Should any other admonition be necessary?

To be frank, the statements of Paul, as urged upon him by the Holy Spirit, are so to the point that no one need misunderstand. In fact, the number of Preachers who would presently take the stand that Paul then took, is very small indeed! To be sure, such terminology as rendered by the Apostle in no way endeared him to those who were of the persuasion of the Law of Moses being tacked onto the Grace of God. Most Preachers simply aren't willing to face the opposition which will always be tendered upon such a stand. Consequently, they attempt to please all men, but in the process greatly displease God.

NEUTRALITY?

There is no such thing as neutrality when it comes to the Word of God or the Work of God. Jesus said, *"He that is not with Me is against Me; and he that gathereth not with Me scattereth abroad"* (Mat. 12:30).

This is the true test of discipleship. God and Satan cannot be reconciled and there is no possibility of loving and serving God and Satan at the same time (Mat. 6:24; Rom. 6:16-23).

Anyone who does not seek to help gather the flock only desires to scatter them that he might steal or destroy them for personal gain (Mat. 7:15-20; Acts 20:28-30; Rom. 16:17; Gal. 1:6-9; Phil. 1:14-18; 3:17-19; II Pet. Chpt. 2).

There are thousands of Pastors who know that the direction their Denomination is taking on certain issues is wrong, but they say or do nothing. By taking such a position in the matter, whatever the matter may be, they feel they are not culpable. However, they are culpable, which will result in a leanness to their souls and an absence of the Holy Spirit in their hearts, lives, and Ministries.

If something is unscriptural, the Preacher must not obey. If obeying God means disobeying religious heads, so be it. It would be far better to resign from a Denomination rather than disobey God. And again we emphasize, silence or acquiescence to something which is unscriptural does not provide neutrality, but rather disobedience to the Lord. To be frank, to obey God or men is that which faces a Preacher of the Gospel almost every day of his life. It applies to the Laity as well! (Acts 5:29).

Jesus made the situation very clear: if one is not with Him, and that means all the way, then one is *"against Him"* (Mat. 12:30).

(16) "I SAY AGAIN, LET NO MAN THINK ME A FOOL; IF OTHERWISE, YET AS A FOOL RECEIVE ME, THAT I MAY BOAST MYSELF A LITTLE."

Before describing the sufferings which prove his sincerity, Paul followed a line of argument which was suggested by his opponents. It is a form of ridicule but such as is genuine and legitimate.

His opponents were proud and carnal boasters who were always seeking to elevate themselves above Paul by recounting their own deeds and experiences. Paul turned the ridicule they had heaped upon him back upon them. He used their weapons.

If they had things to boast of, so did he. If they had a record to display, so did he. He not

NOTES

only matched them, but exceeded them and justified his claims by his performance.

A PROCLAMATION

The phrase, *"I say again,"* reverts back to the subject matter of Verse 1.

The sense is, *"I have said much respecting myself which may seem to be foolish. I admit that to boast in this manner of one's own self in general is folly. But circumstances compel me to it. And I entreat you to look at those circumstances, and not regard me as a fool for doing it"* (Barnes).

A FOOL?

The phrase, *"Let no man think me a fool,"* proclaims the embarrassment of the Apostle at having to deal with this issue, but yet being forced to do so.

Why?

Evidently these false teachers had presented letters of recommendation which may have been signed by someone of note, or at least thought to be of note (II Cor. 3:1). They had obviously regaled the Corinthians with their importance, their place and their position, whatever that may have been. Irrespective, it was all man-devised, with nothing which spoke of the Holy Spirit; nevertheless, it impressed greatly, it seems, the Corinthians.

Along with showing their supposed credentials, they as well began to denigrate Paul, knowing that the Apostle did not have much support, in fact if any at all, in Jerusalem. Once again, this does not speak of the original Twelve, who were probably scattered all over the world of that day preaching the Gospel. How it impacted James, who in fact was the senior Pastor (Bishop), of the Church in Jerusalem, is anyone's guess.

James was a great man of God, and of that there is no doubt; however, the Church in Jerusalem was so large, possibly containing as many as 50,000 members, that there may have been many things which transpired of which James was not fully aware. And yet, what little contact we have in the Scripture as it pertained to James and Paul, as far as I'm concerned, leaves something to be desired (Acts 21:18-24).

It is my feeling that James was being led by the Spirit when he gave instructions at the Council in Jerusalem, regarding the Gentiles and the Law of Moses (Acts 15:28-29). However, I personally think he did not carry the instructions far enough. In other words, he excluded the Jews from these instructions, with them continuing to attempt to keep the Law of Moses along with accepting Christ as Saviour. As a result, whether with Jews or Gentiles, it is an intolerable situation. Consequently, it ultimately destroyed the Jewish sector of the Church.

If Gentiles did not have to continue to keep the Law, then the same ruling should have been applied to the Jews. There is only one Salvation, and it is all in Christ. This we do know:

These false apostles who had come into the Church at Corinth and caused so much trouble, even bringing it to the brink of spiritual destruction, as well as most, if not all other Churches planted by Paul, in fact were Jews, no doubt from Jerusalem, and were attempting to pedal the Law of Moses, etc. So, the statements which Paul makes, by calling these people *"ministers of Satan,"* could not have set well at all in Jerusalem, but yet was a position which Paul had to take, that is if he was to obey God. Consequently, his strong statements have not ended.

HEAR WHAT I HAVE TO SAY

The phrase, *"If otherwise, yet a fool receive me,"* in essence says, *"Whatever you think of me, hear what I have to say, simply because it is very important."*

The Apostle is saying, consider how much I have been provoked to this; how necessary it is to my character; and do not reject and despise me because I am constrained to say that of myself which is usually regarded as foolish boasting.

BOAST MYSELF A LITTLE

The phrase, *"That I may boast myself a little,"* presents behind this apparent folly that there is something that is vastly other than folly. This cannot be said about other boasters.

But Paul's wish, as one Commentator put it, will perhaps not be granted; the Corinthians will perhaps take him to be the fool he is acting. *"Well then,"* Paul adds, *"take me so and grant me the indulgence you grant a fool, let me do a little boasting!"*

This Commentator went on to say that the translation from the Greek to the English, even

NOTES

though bringing over the sense of the statement, in no way brings over the exact manner in which Paul makes this statement, for the simple reason, that such cannot be said in that manner in English.

(17) "THAT WHICH I SPEAK, I SPEAK IT NOT AFTER THE LORD, BUT AS IT WERE FOOLISHLY, IN THIS CONFIDENCE OF BOASTING."

As we read the balance of this Chapter, we can well understand the reluctance of the Apostle.

This foolish boasting, which he feels he must do, will not follow the norm and principle of Jesus, for it will be done, not, indeed, *"in folly,"* yet *"as in folly."* In other words, it will look like folly.

It will thus stoop to a lower norm than Jesus used. If it were done in actual folly, it would, of course, be stooping to sin; since it is done only in apparent folly it is not sin but at the same time, is ethically on a lower plane than the one on which Jesus moved.

AFTER THE LORD?

The phrase, *"That which I speak, I speak it not after the Lord,"* means that the balance of this Chapter is not exactly after the example of the Lord. But yet, it was inspired, which means that the Holy Spirit desired that he say these things, irrespective of his normal reluctance.

Jesus was eminently modest, and never vaunted or boasted. And Paul probably means to say, *"I do not in this profess to follow the example of the Lord entirely. I admit that it is a departure from his pure example in this respect. But circumstances have compelled me; and much as I would prefer another strain of remark, and sensible as I am in general of the folly of boasting, yet a regard to my Apostolic Office and authority urges me to this course"* (Barnes).

We learn from this and many other statements made by Paul, that Jesus was always his example. Even though he very little referred directly to the Ministry of Christ, and I speak of His Miracles, etc., leaving that to the original Twelve; however, it is obvious that Paul knew the Life and Ministry of Christ in totality. The manner in which he learned it we are not told; nevertheless, we do know that his knowledge in this respect was in no way deficient.

NOTES

BOASTING

The phrase, *"But as it were foolishly, in this confidence of boasting,"* presents this on the level of that as was human, and not Divine. In other words, it was an earthly necessity, not a heavenly example; a sword of the giant Philistine which yet David may be forced to use.

The word *"confidence,"* means that what he says, will not be an exaggeration as boasting normally is, but is rather the truth on all counts.

The idea is, that many, if not most of the things said by his detractors were in fact exaggerations or outright fabrications, which generally is the case in *"boasting."* Paul, as should be obvious, engages none of this, but tells things exactly as they are, adding to or taking away, not at all.

(18) "SEEING THAT MANY GLORY AFTER THE FLESH, I WILL GLORY ALSO."

In this one short Verse of Scripture, we are given the dividing line for the Church. It pertains to the things of this world, i.e., *"approval of men, riches, place, position, ways of the world,"* and the things of God, i.e., *"the Moving and Operation of the Holy Spirit, the mighty Power of God in the Salvation of souls and deliverance from darkness, the things of God."* The Church cannot have both; consequently, it must be one or the other!

AFTER THE FLESH

The phrase, *"Seeing that many glory after the flesh,"* does not speak here of sin, as the word *"flesh"* is used, but rather that which is human, earthy, etc.

It speaks of what men refer to as *"success!"* Unfortunately, the Church has borrowed the ways of the world all too often.

Consequently, the Preacher who pastors a big Church, or the Layperson who is rich, is looked at as successful, having great Faith, etc., whereas God may not look at the situation in that manner at all, and probably doesn't.

There is certainly no harm in having a big Church, or in being rich for that matter, but the wrong comes in when we place undue emphasis on such, actually giving it the wrong definition. Unfortunately, this is where most of the modern Church is.

In some cases the one with the big Church or the riches may be looked at by God as successful, i.e., *"in the center of His Will"*; however, not often!

As an example, the Church of Jesus' day, would never have chosen Peter, James, and John, as well as the other Disciples to be the followers of the Messiah. But the Lord chose them!

Preachers all too often (as well as Laypersons) jockey for position to gain advantage, when all the time they are playing the *"flesh game."* In other words, it is all *"after the flesh,"* and that means, it is not of God.

Christians are too easily impressed by the *"flesh."* The Church has become very adept at Madison Avenue techniques of advertising. Everything is hype, because everything is *"flesh!"* Consequently, the advertisement becomes lies, with all too often, the reports being lies as well! All of these things have to be done to keep up appearances, so it is hyped.

So the Corinthians were greatly impressed, by the credentials of these false apostles, i.e., *"Satan's ministers!"*

ALSO?

The phrase, *"I will glory also,"* but yet, will be in an entirely different mode.

His endowments in the flesh, or what he had to boast of pertaining to the flesh, related not so much to birth and rank, though not inferior to them in these, but to what the flesh had endured — to stripes and imprisonments, and hunger and peril. This is an exceedingly delicate and happy turn given to the whole subject, which is the reason the Lord allowed him to do such (Barnes).

(19) "FOR YE SUFFER FOOLS GLADLY, SEEING YE YOURSELVES ARE WISE."

Paul is here using irony. People of intelligence cannot endure fools. But these Corinthians are so intelligent that they not only bear with them but bear with them gladly.

In other words he is saying, *"If you have put up with these fools as you have, even falling for their foolishness, surely you will bear with me a little while in my foolishness."*

TO SUFFER FOOLS GLADLY

The phrase, *"For ye suffer fools gladly,"* presents the Apostle now referring to these false apostles as *"fools."* As stated, I doubt very seriously this Letter was appreciated very much in Jerusalem, that is, if a copy was ultimately taken there.

NOTES

The Corinthians had accepted these false apostles whomever they may have been, been impressed by them, and had thusly come close to allowing themselves to be turned away from the True Gospel of Christ. And yet, the Holy Spirit refers to these false apostles as *"fools."*

How many in the modern Church are doing the same? Many are feeding their money to false apostles, lauding and praising them, claiming their great Godliness, when all the time, the Holy Spirit is referring to them as *"fools!"*

Tens of millions of dollars are poured into projects which claim to be of God, some promoted heavily over that which purports to be Christian Television, with Christians falling for the lure, actually believing it is of God, when the Holy Spirit is referring to them and it as *"fools"* and *"foolish!"*

If the Corinthians were supporting fools, did that make the Corinthians fools themselves?

If modern Believers are supporting that which is foolish, does that make the modern Believers fools?

It is a question that needs to be answered.

WISE?

The phrase, *"Seeing ye yourselves are wise,"* presents the highest of irony. In other words, he is saying the very opposite of what actually is.

If they were truly *"wise,"* they would not be supporting fools!

Bloomfield says, *"This is the most sarcastic sentence ever penned by the Apostle Paul."*

Its sense is, *"You profess to be wondrous wise. And yet you, who are so wise a people, freely tolerate those who are foolish in their boasting; who proclaim their own merits and attainments. You may allow me, therefore, to come in for my share, and boast also, and thus obtain your favor."*

How wise is the modern Church?

When one observes some of the *"stuff"* which passes for Christian Television, and one realizes that such is being supported to the tune of tens of millions of dollars, then one must conclude that many Believers are not very *"wise."*

Why did the Corinthians suffer these fools?

Why does the Church suffer these fools?

As we've already stated, it surely wasn't because Paul had failed to lay a good foundation respecting proper Teaching and Preaching. In fact, these Corinthians had the greatest foundation of all. So, the fault did not lay with Paul, but rather with the Corinthians.

In fact, the modern Church at least to a degree, falls into the same category. While it may or may not have a proper Scriptural foundation, it can have if it so desires. And that goes pretty much for the entirety of the Church all over the world. If they entertain foolishness, it is because that's what they desire to do. That is the reason Jesus said, *"Straight is the gate, and narrow is the way, which leadeth unto life, and few there be that find it"* (Mat. 7:14).

People support a *"Hollywood gospel"* because they want a *"Hollywood gospel!"* People support a *"feel-good gospel"* because they want a *"feel-good gospel."* People support a *"get-rich gospel"* because they want a *"get-rich gospel."*

Paul also said, *"For the time will come when they will not endure sound doctrine; but after their own lusts shall they heap to themselves teachers, having itching ears;*

"And they shall turn away their ears from the truth, and shall be turned unto fables" (II Tim. 4:3-4).

That time has already come!

(20) "FOR YE SUFFER, IF A MAN BRING YOU INTO BONDAGE, IF A MAN DEVOUR YOU, IF A MAN TAKE OF YOU, IF A MAN EXALT HIMSELF, IF A MAN SMITE YOU ON THE FACE."

All of these *"ifs"* used here by Paul denotes reality. All of them refer to past actualities that occurred in Corinth.

Not only have the Corinthians actually tolerated such treatment on the part of the false apostles, but the manner in which the original Greek states the case, implies that they are ready to have it repeated again and again. So *"smart"* are they? Smart fools!

Such fools are the false prophets, mighty smart ones! The irony is devastating, but it is the irony of the cold facts — that produces the devastation.

Irony is really of two kinds: one that aims only to wound and disregards facts, the other that lets the facts speak, to wound in order to help, which Paul here uses.

BONDAGE

The phrase, *"For ye suffer, if a man bring you into bondage,"* actually means *"to bring one into slavery."*

NOTES

The idea is, that these false teachers set up a lordship over the consciences of these Corinthians. It destroyed their freedom of opinion and made them subservient to their (false teachers') will. They really took away their Christian freedom as much as if they had been slaves. This is identical as well to much that is happening in the modern Church.

For instance, a young couple the other day took a vacation. When they arrived back in their Church, one of the Pastors asked them where they had been?

They replied that they had been on vacation.

He grew somewhat angry with them because they had not asked permission to go, stating that they should take the beginning discipleship class all over again, in order that they may know how to conduct themselves.

This is not a joke, it actually happened, and furthermore, it happens constantly in thousands of Churches all over this nation and other parts of the world. These people are slaves, for that is what Paul is addressing.

Such foolishness is not Bible Christianity, but rather the very opposite. Those who proclaim such are *"fools,"* and those who suffer such are *"foolish!"*

In fact, that which I have just related, is a form of the old *"shepherding cult"* which was quite prominent a few years ago. The people were taught to look to their *"Shepherd,"* i.e., *"Pastor,"* in effect, as God. They had to receive his permission, or permission from the ones he had appointed, for everything that was done. Where they were to live, if they could buy furniture, what type of car they were to drive, when they took vacations and where they took vacations, ad nauseam.

The word *"fools"* as used by Paul, adequately describes the whole thing.

DEVOUR YOU

The phrase, *"If a man devour you,"* actually refers to much of the modern prosperity gospel.

Under the guise of Faith, Christians are *"devoured,"* in other words, separated from their money, made to believe that they are going to receive great riches, etc.

Over Television a short time ago, and which no doubt continues, a so-called Preacher, stands before the Camera and says, *"The Lord has told me, that all who call in the next 30 minutes, will receive a hundredfold return on their gifts."*

This is worse than robbing a 7-Eleven with a 38 Revolver, for the simple reason that the robber does not bring the Lord into his crime, whereas this Preacher does. In other words, the Preacher makes the Lord a part of the lie that he is telling, which deceives the people, actually *"devouring them."*

Some may ask, *"Could not the Lord do such a thing?"*

No! The Lord will never appeal to greed or covetousness, which that so blatantly is.

In fact, millions of Christians are being *"devoured,"* but the sad fact is, it seems that most of them desire to be *"devoured."* The truth is, these practitioners of religious scams, are seeking the property of the people, not the souls of those to whom they minister.

Not satisfied with maintenance, they aim to obtain all, and their plans are formed to secure as much as possible of those to whom they minister.

It is all done under the guise of Faith, with the Name of the Lord freely used, but in reality, it is a *"lie"* pure and simple. Once again I'll go back to Paul's very words, *"For ye suffer fools gladly."*

TAKE OF YOU

The phrase, *"If a man take of you,"* means *"He takes of you to rob you, takes you captive, so that he has you where he wants to have you, to do with you what he pleases."*

How many are presently attending Churches, because they think the teaching there presented will help them to be rich? Say it any way you like, address it in any manner you so desire, that is the reason for them being there.

There is little interest in Holiness, Sanctification, or the great fundamentals of the Faith. And yet, the false message is presented so cleverly, that the people do not seem to realize what these false teachers are doing. Once again, the word *"fools"* applies!

The Gospel is meant to *"give,"* and not to *"take!"* However, the word *"take"* as given by the Holy Spirit to the Apostle, ruthlessly applies to this particular spirit. Even though the Preachers are claiming that all the people in the Church are going to become millionaires, the truth is, he is going to *"take"* what little they do have, with no return to them, because God cannot bless a lie.

NOTES

EXALT HIMSELF?

The phrase, *"If a man exalt himself,"* adequately describes much of the modern ministry. It is not exalting Christ, but rather *"self."* In effect, almost the entirety of tint and tone of this modern gospel, *"exalts self."* Self is the object, with self-esteem being the goal.

This is the age when many Preachers are exalting themselves as *"great teachers," "great preachers,"* and *"great etc."* As well, they are preaching messages that exalt people, i.e., *"self-help programs, motivational messages, King's kids,"* etc. Whatever, there's not much exalting of Christ.

In fact, many Churches are little more than giant *"motivational clinics."* Whatever it is, it is not the Gospel, and can be adequately described even as Paul said, *"fools and foolish!"*

SMITE YOU

The phrase, *"If a man smite you on the face,"* doesn't actually mean that it was literally done, but that the false teachers treated them with as little respect as if they smote them on the face. Let me give you an example:

I heard a message some time back on *"K-Mart Christians."* The idea was, that if anyone bought anything at K-Mart, that meant they had inferior Faith, etc.

I left half way of the message, taking about all of that drivel that I could take, and drivel it was!

Another Church, and actually there are many in this category, would not allow one of their bumper stickers to be placed on a particular car, because *"it was not a new enough model."* In other words, all the people who attended *that* Church, were successful, *"wealthy, winners, achievers,"* etc.

That is so far off-base Scripturally, that it would be difficult to find the proper terminology to explain such idiocy. In the words of Paul, the so-called Preachers in these particular Churches, are *"fools,"* and the people who attend those type of Churches fall into the same category, i.e., *"fools!"*

The amazing thing is, and which Paul so sarcastically reproves, is that the people put up with such foolishness. Why will people do that?

NOTES

WHY?

Why would people attend a Church, with the Pastor telling certain of them that their car was not *"good enough"*? Why would people attend a Church, where they had to ask permission to go on vacation?

Believe it or not, most people, even Believers, have a tendency to desire that someone else do their thinking for them. In some way, it makes them feel that they are absolved of all responsibility. Consequently, they continue to submit to such, even when they are *"smitten on the face."*

A friend of mine visited a lady in the hospital, or at least happened to pass by her room while he was there to pray for someone else, and went in. He knew her vaguely!

Inquiring as to her physical condition, and then offering to pray, she quickly remonstrated that it was of no use.

"Why?" he asked.

She went on to relate how she had left a particular Church, and now because she was no longer under the *"covering"* of that Church, she could expect manifold judgment, etc.

So she said, *"It's no use, I'm doomed!"*

She left the Church because she felt she had to. To be frank, I'm acquainted with that particular Church, and she would have been much better had she never even begun attending there; however, she had come to believe because of the error she was taught, that if she went to Church anywhere else, that she was inviting judgment. Consequently, there was no point in my Preacher friend praying for her.

Such doctrines do not set people free, but rather imprison them. In fact, this is the motif of false teachers. Once again *"fools"* adequately describes the entirety of the situation.

EXPLOITATION OR DEVELOPMENT

Many years ago when I first began on radio with our daily Program *"The Campmeeting Hour,"* and then a short time later on Television, the Lord quickly gave us a very large audience. However, He began to deal with me about something very important and this is what He said:

"If you ever exploit the people in any way, I will take My Anointing from you. You must always develop them in the Faith."

I have never forgotten that warning. It is so easy for a Preacher of the Gospel to exploit the people. It can be done in a hundred and one ways.

Whenever a Preacher says, *"God told me,"* and in fact the Lord has told him nothing, that is exploitation of the worst kind. Whenever Preachers dangle the bait of riches in front of the eyes of Saints, telling them they can get so much return for their Offerings, in other words, placing this entire Gift of God on a materialistic basis, that is exploitation pure and simple, and of the worst sort. Whenever Preachers instill fear in the hearts of people, not for God, but rather for their own foolish notions, such as I have just described regarding the woman, that is exploitation.

Preachers of the Gospel are supposed to be Shepherds, not wolves in sheep's clothing, not money managers, not motivational experts, not therapists, *"but Shepherds."*

(21) "I SPEAK AS CONCERNING REPROACH, AS THOUGH WE HAD BEEN WEAK. HOWBEIT WHEREINSOEVER ANY IS BOLD, (I SPEAK FOOLISHLY,) I AM BOLD ALSO."

What an astounding picture of the false apostles, the super-fine apostles, who had come to Corinth as high lords — and the Corinthians bowed in sweet submission!

But the worst cut of all follows in a sudden and wholly unexpected turn. The Reader thinks: *"What a disgrace for the Corinthians!"*, and would stop at that. Not Paul, not Paul by any means.

"I am speaking by way of disgrace," he says, *"I am using this category or norm"*; and now comes the sudden flash: *"that we on our part have been weak!"* What a disgrace for me and my assistants, poor, weak fellows who could not act the abusive lords like that so that you could submit to us with this gladness of yours! The disgrace is mine.

As is obvious, Paul continues to use irony!

REPROACH

The phrase, *"I speak as concerning reproach,"* now turns the attention from the Corinthians to himself. He had suffered terrible reproach at the hands of these detractors.

In II Corinthians 10:12 Paul has already admitted that he and his assistants are not in this class of high and mighty men and cannot even faintly be compared with them.

In II Corinthians 10:10 he says, *"My bodily presence is held to be so weak, and my word amounts to nothing.*

"These false apostles know how real Apostles ought to act so as to impress you with what real Apostles are; we — we do not even know how to act as Apostles, at least if lording it over you is actually the hallmark of a real Apostle."

Now I think we begin to get the drift of these things which were taking place at Corinth. It becomes clear at the reproach suffered by Paul.

Reproach is to be expected from the world. It is obvious as to its spirit; however, one does not, or at least should not expect reproach from the Church, but oftentimes that's where the greatest reproach of all comes from.

I remind the Reader, that it was not the drunks, harlots, and thieves who crucified Christ, but rather the *"Church!"*

However, the cut is even worse, when those who are involved in such reproach, were actually saved under the Ministry of the Apostle. In other words, had it not been for Paul, they would have never known the *"joys of sins forgiven, and the bliss the bloodwashed know."* And yet, they allowed these liars, these ministers of Satan, these deceitful workers, these *"fools,"* to denigrate, to sarcastically reproach, to low rate, to castigate, the greatest Apostle who has ever lived.

WEAKNESS?

The phrase, *"As though we had been weak,"* is in answer to the accusation that Paul was a *"weak sister,"* which he will answer in II Corinthians 12:9-10.

How in the world could anyone refer to the Apostle Paul as weak? At least as we think of weakness in the sense of lack of courage, etc.

Generally the accusations of detractors such as this against God's Anointed, falls into the category of the very opposite of that which is actually the truth. Unfortunately, there will always be Christians (most) who will believe what they hear. Considering that we are speaking here of Paul, and of the people who were saved under his Ministry, who in fact, would have almost certainly been eternally lost had it not been for him, we are made to realize just how lethal, how deadly is such a spirit. If it could turn these people against the greatest Apostle who ever lived, then we should be made to realize the power of such an effort by Satan. No wonder that Paul used the word *"fools!"*

If a Christian entertains such gossip, such slander, such whispering, such an attitude, even for a short period of time, the spirit which is behind such an attitude, will soon captivate those who lend their ears to such drivel. Consequently, it is just as much a sin to listen to such as it is to speak such.

BOLD!

The phrase, *"Howbeit whereinsoever any is bold, (I speak foolishly,) I am bold also,"* speaks of the Apostle meeting these detractors on their own ground, and now speaking of qualifications not inferior to theirs at all.

In effect, the Apostle is saying, of whatever they have to boast, he is prepared also to show that he is equal to them. Be it pertaining to birth, rank, education, labors, they will find that he does not shrink from this comparison.

He reminds the Corinthians, that he is speaking foolishly, and because he feels foolish at having to stoop to this level; however, it seems that some of the Corinthians, believing these impostors, had brought the Apostolic Office down to this level; therefore, Paul will meet them on their own ground, that is, if that's what they demand. To be sure, it will not turn out to be enjoyable for their claims.

TRUE SPIRITUAL LEADERSHIP

To properly understand as to why the Holy Spirit allowed Paul to defend himself and his Apostolic Office in this fashion, one must realize that this was an attack by Satan against true Spiritual Leadership, which is one of Satan's favorite tactics.

As the Reader surely should understand, for the world to disavow Paul would amount to little, and in fact is to be expected; however, for a great part of the Church, and especially those from Jerusalem to do such, presents a mighty blow. And yet, this is the tactic that Satan always uses. It is a struggle for Leadership in the Church.

Will it be man-appointed Leadership, or will it be God-appointed Leadership? This is the area of greatest contention. This is where Satan has his greatest success. It comes down to a *"work of the flesh"* in opposition to the *"Work of the Spirit."* It did not begin with Paul, actually beginning in the Garden of Eden.

Immediately following the Fall, Cain murdered Abel, over Leadership. God accepted Abel's Sacrifice, but would not accept that of Cain, because it was of his own hands, and, consequently, diametrically opposed to the Word of God (Gen. 4:1-10). Satan will fight God's appointed Leadership, moreso than he will fight anything else. And as stated, he uses the Church to do so, exactly as he did here with Paul.

If Satan had succeeded at Corinth, there is a good chance that all the Churches would have succumbed to this false teaching concerning the Law, generated by these false apostles. So, the stakes were very high, hence the reason, or at least one of the reasons, that the Holy Spirit allowed the Apostle to take this particular stand in this fashion.

(22) "ARE THEY HEBREWS? SO AM I. ARE THEY ISRAELITES? SO AM I. ARE THEY THE SEED OF ABRAHAM? SO AM I."

From this Verse we know that these false apostles were Jews. As well, they probably were from Jerusalem. And if so, the very name *"Jerusalem"* carried weight, as would be obvious. So they boasted of a proud lineage.

They gloried in their ancestry. Theirs was the aristocracy of birth. They were gloating over their Jewish privilege.

It was first as *"Hebrews,"* then as *"Israelites,"* and finally as *"the seed of Abraham."* The first was *"racial."* The second was *"national."* The third was *"religious."*

They were called Hebrews because they were those who had *"crossed over"* leaving Chaldea behind and forming the nucleus of a new race, so to speak. They were Israelites because of Jacob or Israel whose 12 sons became the national structure of their commonwealth.

They were the seed of Abraham because herein lay the spiritual significance of the Jews. It included the promise of a place, a people, and a purpose. Their great purpose in the world was a redemptive one. Consequently Judaism came into being and out of it grew Christianity.

In fact, it is still true that in these people all the families of the Earth will be blessed (Gen. 12:3) (Laurin).

HEBREWS

The question, *"Are they Hebrews? so am I,"* gives us a distinction which will prove to be of interest.

NOTES

Abraham (Gen. 14:13) and Joseph (Gen. 39:14) are the first persons in the Bible to be called Hebrews. The word appears in Babylonian and Egyptian texts, probably to identify immigrants or foreign contract workers.

When Potiphar's wife used this term in speaking of Joseph, it seems to have been a tern of racial contempt: *"This foreigner!"*

Only later did *"Hebrew"* develop as an ethnic term for the Jewish people. In fact, Paul calls himself *"a Hebrew of Hebrews"* (Phil. 3:5).

The name or title *"Hebrew,"* came to refer to those, whether dwelling in Israel or elsewhere, who had retained the sacred Hebrew tongue as their native language, irrespective as to where they may have lived, irrespective as to how many other languages they knew.

This distinction first appears in Acts 6:1, and is probably intended in the two other Passages where the word occurs (II Cor. 11:22; Phil. 3:5).

The idea is, that Jews who forsook the sacred Hebrew tongue in place of Greek, came to be called *"Hellenist."* Consequently, a person was a *"Hebrew,"* wherever domiciled, who retained the use of the language of his fathers.

Thus Paul, though settled in Tarsus, a Greek city in Asia Minor, describes himself as a *"Hebrew,"* and of *"Hebrew"* parents, *"a Hebrew of Hebrews."*

So, the Apostle is actually saying, that even though he lived in Tarsus, a city of the Roman Empire, and hundreds of miles away from Israel, still, his parents and, therefore, he, retained the ancient Hebrew tongue, not succumbing to the use of Greek even though they did know and use that language.

Even though we have no way of actually knowing all that was said at Corinth, most probably they were accusing Paul of not being a true Hebrew but rather a *"Hellenist,"* which he here disavows.

However, it should quickly be asked, what did this matter anyway? The truth is, it mattered not at all, but these detractors had made an issue of the situation, because they seemed to have thought that it gave them some type of spiritual status.

It is about the same presently as someone saying that they are a *"fifth generation Baptist,"* or a *"third generation Pentecostal,"* etc. It matters not at all, but yet, some people seem to think that it does.

NOTES

ISRAELITES

The question, *"Are they Israelites? so am I,"* presents the absolute name, that which expressed the whole dignity and glory of a member of the theocratic nation, of the people in peculiar Covenant with God, who were Israelites.

This name was for the Jew his special badge and title of honor. To be descendants of Abraham, this honor they must share with the Ishmaelites (Gen. 16:15); of Abraham and Isaac with the Edomites (Gen. 24:25); but none except themselves were the seed of Jacob, such as in this name of *"Israelite"* they were declared to be.

Nor was this all, but more gloriously still, their descent was herein traced up to him, not as he was Jacob, but as he was Israel, who as a Prince had power with God and with men, and prevailed (Gen. 32:28). That this title *"Israelites"* was accounted the noblest, we have ample proof.

We can see from Paul's answer, that these Teachers from Judaea, considered the fact of being an Israelite as something greatly spiritual, and, therefore, of note, which meant that they believed themselves to be far above the Gentiles. Consequently, this was at least a part of the reason for their domineering attitude as proclaimed by Paul in Verse 20 over the Corinthians. In other words, they were superior!

Consequently, they would not have been too very happy with the Second Chapter of Romans written by Paul a short time earlier.

THE SEED OF ABRAHAM

The question, *"Are they the seed of Abraham? so am I,"* had to do with the great Covenant of Abraham, which spawned the Jewish people, and above all, laid the groundwork for Salvation by Faith (Gen. 15:6).

However, Paul in Romans Chapter 4, reckoned the *"seed of Abraham"* as being by *"Faith"* and not nationality (Rom. 4:3, 11-16). This would have rankled them as well!

One can tell from these statements as given by the Apostle, that these false apostles, due to being Jews, and as stated, more than likely from Jerusalem, felt they were superior to the Gentiles, and conducted themselves accordingly. Paul placing Gentiles on the same level with the Jews, would have been to them an insult. So they evidently denigrated his Jewish ancestry, implying that he was not a true Jew.

Due to the fact that this constituted their claims, these poor Corinthians who had not so long been brought out of paganism, evidently forgot what Paul had taught them, and submitted to these braggarts.

(23) "ARE THEY MINISTERS OF CHRIST? (I SPEAK AS A FOOL) I AM MORE; IN LABOURS MORE ABUNDANT, IN STRIPES ABOVE MEASURE, IN PRISONS MORE FREQUENT, IN DEATHS OFT."

We are here given more information as to exactly who these people were, consequently, understanding somewhat their doctrine, which seems to fit squarely the Law/Grace issue.

MINISTERS OF CHRIST?

The question, *"Are they ministers of Christ?"*, proclaims the fact that they claimed to be; however, Paul had already said despite their claims, that they were in fact, *"ministers of Satan"* (11:15).

This question resembles the three that precede and is thus connected with them; but it is not intended as number four but is opening the new, astounding line which runs through Verse 31.

The three questions are concerned only with birth and outward descent, which was a minor issue with Paul, even though it was a great issue with these false apostles. But *"ministers of Christ"* is the supreme and in reality the *only* issue. In fact, all four designations are not terms chosen by Paul but terms that Paul caught up from these false boasters.

In effect, by Paul asking this question in the manner in which he did, is saying that they have applied the title *"ministers of Christ"* to themselves.

This clears up a number of questions. Paul cannot in any way admit that these false apostles are in any sense *"ministers of Christ."* He has already said what they actually are and, therefore, his statement is not to be misconstrued as comparing himself with them, which he in no way does. Paul opens all the batteries of the facts, all of which prove overwhelmingly that he is in fact more than these false boasters ever even dreamed of including in their false claims.

MINISTERS OF CHRIST PRESENTLY!

All Preachers and even Priests at least in some fashion, consider themselves to be *"ministers of Christ."* Is that true?

It is no more true presently than it was then.

Only those who preach the same Gospel that Paul preached, can be Scripturally concluded to be *"ministers of Christ."* He said, and emphatically so, and inspired by the Holy Spirit, *"I marvel that ye are so soon removed from Him that called you into the Grace of Christ unto another gospel:*

"Which is not another; but there be some that trouble you, and would pervert the Gospel of Christ.

"But though we, or an Angel from Heaven, preach any other Gospel unto you than that which we have preached unto you, let him be accursed.

"As we said before, so say I now again, If any man preach any other Gospel unto you than that ye have received, let him be accursed" (Gal. 1:6-9).

I don't know how much clearer it could be!

So what does that say?

It says that not a single Catholic Priest is a *"minister of Christ,"* for the simple reason, that they are not preaching and teaching the same Gospel as preached and taught by Paul.

The Gospel as preached by Paul, is *"Justification by Faith"* (Gal. 2:16).

That means that many Protestant Preachers are not true *"ministers of Christ,"* for the simple reason that they tag *"Water Baptism"* or *"The Lord's Supper,"* or even *"belonging to certain Churches,"* as necessary for Salvation. So, according to Paul, anyone who differs from his Gospel, is *"accursed,"* and certainly could not be considered as *"ministers of Christ."*

WHY IS PAUL THIS HARSH?

Serious situations, of which this certainly is one, calls for strong measures.

What we are discussing here is the single most important thing in the world and to each human being — the Salvation of the soul. As someone has said, there is nothing worse than a false way of Salvation, and to be sure, the efforts to tag the Law onto the great Gospel of Grace presents that which is serious indeed! In fact, most people who would attempt such, would lose their way.

Any error is constituted in the Word of God as leaven (I Cor. 5:6). As such, if it is not rooted out, it will ultimately corrupt the whole.

There are untold millions in Hell at this moment, who wish that someone would have been strong enough, bold enough, even as Paul, to have told them the truth. They lost their eternal souls because no one was willing to take the abuse that would necessarily come because of such a stand.

NOTES

As I have said many times, and will continue to say, what the people want to hear has no bearing whatsoever on what the Preacher is to preach. The Minister of Christ is to hear from the Lord, and then deliver what he has heard to the people, irrespective of what it is, or whether they agree or not. Their reaction is not the business of the Preacher, but rather his being faithful to the Word of the Lord. To be sure, as least as far as the whole is concerned, precious few are willing to take this God-ordained course. However, the few who do, have pleased the Lord, and that's all that matters.

The Lord said to the Prophet Ezekiel, which holds true for all other Preachers as well, *"Yet if thou warn the wicked, and he turn not from his wickedness, nor from his wicked way, he shall die in his iniquity; but thou hast delivered thy soul"* (Ezek. 3:19).

THE MESSAGE

Many have accused me of being harsh with our Catholic friends. No, I'm not harsh! The truth is, I love them enough to be honest with them. Catholic Doctrine is not Biblical. As such, if it is followed to its conclusion, it can only lead to Hell. I realize that is blunt, but it happens to be the truth. As well, the Lord has specifically told me to deliver a Message to them, the Message of Justification by Faith, and I dare not be disobedient to the heavenly vision (Acts 26:19). As well, the Lord has directed me to deal with the subject of the Holy Spirit as it concerns our Denominational friends. He has also instructed me regarding the lukewarmness of Pentecostals, plus the tremendous amount of error of many of the Charismatics. In fact, this is the reason and the reason alone, for the attitude of the Church as a whole toward my person and this Ministry.

Irrespective, that most of the Leadership of the Church world, which includes the Pastors, tells their people not to heed this Ministry, the truth remains that I am of God, and not only that, by His Grace and Mercy, I walk close to Him. As such, they will answer to my Message, whether they even take the time to listen or not. To be sure, that not only goes for me, but every God-called Apostle.

Refusing the Message, or even refusing to hear the Message, in other words ignoring it, in no way absolves the individual from responsibility to that Message, whatever it may be. Whatever is done, I have delivered my soul and by the Grace of God, irrespective of the opposition and the hatred, I have done my best to be faithful to that which He has called me to do. In fact, the next phrase, fits this unworthy Evangelist just as it did the Apostle Paul.

I AM MORE

The phrase, *"(I speak as a fool) I am more,"* proclaims the Apostle stooping to a level in which he is not comfortable.

The Truth is, Paul should not have had to defend himself in this measure. Neither should any other true man or woman of God. If the Word of God had been followed by the people, these false Apostles would have been rejected out of hand, and this situation would never have risen. It is the same presently:

If the Word of God is faithfully followed, it and it alone, charts the course, gives direction, and proclaims the way. The problem is, the Word of God most of the time is not followed. It is ignored in favor of made up rules or personal jealousy and bias.

Paul's frequent reminding them of this charge (how foolish he felt in having to stoop to this level) was eminently fitted to humble them that they had ever made this necessary, especially when they were reminded by an enumeration of his trials, etc.

The words *"I am more,"* are not merely the result of a wounded ego. The Truth is he had much higher claims to the Office of the Apostle than they had, with in fact, them having no legitimate claims at all. In fact, he had been called to this Office in a most remarkable manner, and he had shown, by his labors and trials, that he had more of the true spirit of a Minister of the Lord than they ever thought of having.

He, therefore, goes into detail, to show what he had endured in endeavoring to spread the knowledge of the Saviour — trials which he had borne, with these impostors in fact, undergoing no trials at all.

NOTES

TRIALS?

Satan does not oppress his ministers as should be obvious! He only oppresses, opposes, hinders, and in every way possible, the true Apostle. In fact, such opposition, even as Paul will very capably enumerate, is one of the sure signs of the Call of God and that one is in the very center of God's Will.

Consequently, in Verses 21-29, he challenges these false teachers to prove their fidelity to the Gospel and to suffering humanity, by a similar or a superior record of devotion, of affliction, and of national privilege. In other words, they claim this distinct privilege of being a Jew, so why not be a completed Jew in Christ.

LABOURS

The phrase, *"In labours more abundant,"* refers to the labor necessary in propagating the Gospel.

Jesus said as much when He made the statement, *"The harvest truly is great, but the laborers are few: Pray ye therefore the Lord of the harvest, that He would send forth laborers into His Harvest"* (Lk. 10:2).

The true Work of the Lord is in fact, the most difficult labor in the world, that is, if it is done right. It is a task as one might say, that fills 25 hours to the day and eight days to the week. In fact, if the Preacher of the Gospel is true to his Calling, he will have little time for anything else such as secular business dealings, or games of golf for that matter.

People have asked me many times as to what I do for a hobby. The truth is I don't have a hobby, I simply don't have the time. That which God has called me to do, requires all that I am and all that I have.

To be sure, this is not meant to be a diatribe against innocent activities such as golf, etc., it is rather a proclamation of the fact that the Lord does not call *"loafers"* into His Harvest, but rather *"laborers."* In fact, Paul lists four expressions respecting his life and Ministry. I wonder how much these four fit the modern variety. They are as follows:

1. Labors
2. Stripes
3. Prisons
4. Deaths

I think that one should notice these false apostles used prideful positions as a sign of their credentials, while Paul uses trials and difficulties as his credentials.

It is ironical, the modern so-called Faith Ministry, with thankfully some exceptions, fits the exact same pattern as these false teachers of Paul's day. They boast of their great Faith by making *"money"* and *"things"* the yardstick, while at the same time claiming that if one truly has Faith, one will not have any problems. It doesn't sound too much like Paul, does it?

STRIPES

The phrase, *"In stripes above measure,"* presents the Ministry, True Ministry that is, as one of the very few Callings — perhaps it stands alone in this — where it is proof of peculiar qualifications for Office that a man has been treated with all manner of insults, and has even been often publicly whipped. What other Office admits such a qualification as this?

The Truth is, and as I think by now should be overly obvious, that great opposition is going to always come against the true Child of God, and especially the true Preacher of the Gospel.

Some may claim that times have changed, and this is no longer the case; however, could it be possible that the lack of opposition signals the lack of the true preaching of the Word? The facts are, even now, if the Preacher of the Gospel ministers as he should, hears from the Lord and delivers his soul, the opposition will be little less now than then. The Devil is the same Devil, and his children are still his children, and to be sure, religious devils are the worst devils of all.

So, even though the law of the land, at least in most countries, may prevent the actual *"stripes,"* still, figuratively speaking, the *"stripes"* are no less now than then.

As well, the *"measure"* of these stripes, will at times be above what one thinks he is able to stand.

WHY WOULD THE LORD ALLOW SUCH?

In fact, Paul asked that same question, knowing that the Lord could easily prevent any and all hindrances and difficulties. To be sure, it was not a lack of Faith on the part of Paul. He will tell us why, when we get to Commentary on the Twelfth Chapter.

NOTES

PRISONS

The phrase, *"In prisons more frequent,"* no doubt speaks of this situation being of greater number than the account given in the Book of Acts. Luke, in the Book of Acts, mentions only one imprisonment of Paul before the time when this Epistle was written. This was at Philippi, with Silas (Acts 16:23).

But we are to remember that many things were omitted by Luke. He does not profess, in fact, to give an account of all that happened to Paul; and an omission is not a contradiction.

The Truth is, the word *"prisons"* can refer to more than a cell with bars.

Any time forgiveness is refused anyone, in effect, the person refusing to forgive, is placing the particular individual in question in a prison of sorts. To condemn another, in fact, does the same thing.

Entire Religious Denominations place individuals in prison figuratively speaking. In other words, they blacklist certain ones, and do so unscripturally, which figuratively speaking, constitutes a prison sentence.

A short time ago, a prominent Pastor in a large Pentecostal Denomination asked the General Superintendent of that particular Denomination, as to how long a certain thing was going to continue. He was speaking of an unscriptural (grossly unscriptural) position they had taken regarding a certain situation.

The answer was quite revealing, *"forever,"* the man said!

When asked for Scriptural foundation for such action, even though adamantly claiming it was Scriptural, when pressed, he had to admit that their position was not in the Word of God. It was a *"prison"* he had constructed himself, or rather his Denomination. The regrettable thing is, whether realizing it or not, they're following in the train of Catholicism.

Catholicism says that the Bible is what they say it is. In other words, the Church is the final authority and not the Word of God. This Pentecostal Leader was doing the same thing. The Word of God was not and is not the authority for what they do, but rather the *"Church."* As should be obvious, this is a very serious thing, in fact so serious, as to contain the seed of destruction for that particular Denomination. To be sure, it will do the same on a personal basis for anyone who forsakes the Word of God for the word of man.

DEATHS

The phrase, *"In deaths oft,"* actually means that he was exposed to death often, or suffering pain equal to death.

Once again, this is what Jesus meant when He said, *"He that findeth his life shall lose it: and he that loseth his life for My sake shall find it"* (Mat. 10:39).

(24) "OF THE JEWS FIVE TIMES RECEIVED I FORTY STRIPES SAVE ONE."

On this Verse and the following Verse it is of importance to make a few remarks preliminary to the explanation of the phrases.

It is admitted that all the particulars here referred to cannot be extracted out of the Acts of the Apostles. A few can be identified, but there are many more trials referred to here than are specified there.

This proves that the Book of Acts and this Epistle were not framed from the history, but that they are written independently of one another (Paley). Yet they are not inconsistent one with the other. For there is no article in the enumeration here which is contradicted by the history; and the history, thought silent with respect to some of these transactions, has left space enough to understand that they actually did occur. In other words, there is no contradiction between the accounts.

AN EXAMPLE

Where it is said by Paul that he was thrice beaten with rods, though in the Acts but one beating is mentioned, yet there is no contradiction. It is only the omission to record all that occurred to Paul. But had the history contained an account of four beatings with rods, while Paul mentions here but three, that would have been a contradiction. And yet, when he wrote this in II Corinthians, his life was not over, with many things yet to happen.

It is thought that the date of II Corinthians synchronizes with the beginning of the Twentieth Chapter of Acts. The part, therefore, which precedes the Twentieth Chapter is the only place in which can be found any notice of the things to which Paul here refers.

NOTES

It is evident from Acts that the author of that history was not with Paul until his departure from Troas, as related in Acts 16:10. From that time, Luke attended Paul in his travels, but even then not all the time (Acts 17:1).

From that period to the time when this Epistle was written, occupied but four Chapters of the history; and it is here, if anywhere, that we are to look for the minute account of the life of Paul. But here much may have occurred to Paul, which it no doubt did, which Luke did not record.

The period of time after the conversion of Paul to the time when Luke joined him at Troas is very succinctly given. That period embraced some 16 years, and is comprised in a few Chapters. Yet, in that time, Paul was constantly travelling.

He went to Arabia, and then some think he returned to Damascus, went to Jerusalem (which he may have), and then to Tarsus; and from Tarsus to Antioch, and thence to Cyprus, and then through Asia Minor, etc. During this time, he must have made many voyages, and been exposed to many perils. Yet all of this is comprised in a few Chapters, and a considerable portion of them is occupied with an account of public discourses.

In that period of 16 years, therefore, there was ample opportunity for all the occurrences which are here referred to by Paul. In fact, it is altogether probable that he had endured much more.

THE JEWS

The phrase, *"Of the Jews,"* is used in this manner, because public whippings were a Jewish mode of punishment. It was usual with them to inflict but 39 blows. The Gentiles were not limited by law concerning the number which they inflicted.

Deuteronomy 25:3 tells how this is to be done, if such is called for, which means extreme wickedness is found in someone. Of course, one would have to quickly ask as to what type of wickedness was found in Paul?

In fact, there was no wickedness, but rather the very opposite. It was his stand for Christ which caused the great animosity. As well, the Jews, in fact his fellow countrymen, would have hated him more than possibly any others. They considered him a traitor, a turncoat.

He had once been the great champion of the Pharisees, and the greatest opponent of Christ

(Acts Chpt. 9). But then he had the Damascus Road experience which changed him completely. Thereafter, he became the greatest proponent of Christ.

That glaringly obvious of him, and the fact that he was now Preaching that Christ was the end of the Law, in other words, the Law of Moses had no more purpose, only intensified their hatred.

As I am sure the Reader understands, the Jews who beat Paul were not the same type of Jews as these false apostles. This was the nation proper of Israel, actually those who hated Christ.

THE MANNER OF THESE BEATINGS

When Paul says he got 39 stripes five times, he means that he received all of them. To suggest that on a few occasions he got less because the scourging was stopped before the full count was reached, in cases where the victim was weak and had collapsed, contradicts what Paul says about his experiences. Five times he got the full 39; if he ever got a smaller count, it did not happen in these five instances. In fact, he names the scourgings with the full count because each one brought him to death's door.

As stated, Deuteronomy 25:3 fixes the extreme number of blows at 40. The Jewish Judge might decree a lesser number, but he might not go above 40. Beyond that lay the death penalty. So Paul says he got the penalty just below death five times from Jewish courts.

The victim was laid with his face on the ground, was held by his arms and his feet until the blows were administered before the eyes of the court itself. Originally, rods were used. But later, despite the fact that the Jews were so scrupulous about not exceeding the number 40, the rod was exchanged for a leather strap made of calf's hide.

The end of the strap was split into five stripes, which made the penalty much severer.

This type of beating states that the victim was bound to a pillar, the breast and the shoulders were bared, the body was bent, and 13 blows were administered upon the breast, and 26 upon the shoulders.

FIVE TIMES

The phrase, *"Five times received I forty stripes save one,"* probably refers to this grievous thing happening in the Jewish Synagogues (Acts 9:20; 13:5, 14-15; 14:1; 17:17; 18:4).

Considering this, one stands amazed at the courage of this Apostle who kept going back to the Synagogues in order to preach the Gospel, irrespective of the fact that it could result, and no doubt did, in severe beatings of this nature. Only love, the Love of God, could command such a thing and continue to carry it out in the face of such awful opposition.

The reason for the opposition is actually threefold:

1. There is a Divine Nature in the heart and life of every Born-Again person, which always attracts the enmity of the sinful nature.
2. Satan, of course, does everything he can to hinder the Work of God.
3. Self-will in the hearts and lives of Believers will always tender opposition toward the true Work of God, and will normally do such by attacking the Messenger.

(25) "THRICE WAS I BEATEN WITH RODS, ONCE WAS I STONED, THRICE I SUFFERED SHIPWRECK, A NIGHT AND A DAY I HAVE BEEN IN THE DEEP;"

Someone has said that these beatings received by Paul were so severe, that they effected his spine somewhat, causing his legs to be banded, which means they bowed outward somewhat, the very opposite of being bowlegged. It is also said that had he received another beating, he would not have survived, or at the least would no longer have been able to walk.

BEATEN WITH RODS

The phrase, *"Thrice was I beaten with rods,"* refers to that administered by Romans.

This indicates that this was a penalty which was decreed in Roman courts, and inflicted by lictors or, where a court was of lessor grade, by common court servants. Actually, Acts 16:22-23, gives us the account of one of these three scourgings mentioned.

The question naturally arises as to how Roman courts could scourge Paul since he was a Roman citizen, and heavy penalties forbade scourging of Roman citizens in the Empire. The account given in Acts is valuable for showing that this did happen in Philippi where the Judges lost their heads before the howling mob and Paul could not possibly assert his rights and thus, together with Silas, received we do not know how many blows. The trouble was that a tumult was generally raised, and no orderly trial took place. How serious the penalty was for scourging Roman citizens, we discover in Acts Chapter 16 where the Judges were badly frightened when they discovered whom they had allowed to be scourged. We see the same thing in Acts 22:24. Here Paul was able to assert his rights as a Roman, with the proposed scourging being halted.

STONED

The phrase, *"Once was I stoned,"* pertains to the usual mode of punishment among the Jews for that which they considered to be blasphemy. The instance referred to here occurred at Lystra (Acts 14:19). This action was so severe, that Paul was given up for dead.

SHIPWRECKED

The phrase, *"Thrice I suffered shipwreck,"* actually does not portray the shipwreck recorded which occurred when on his way to Rome, which happened after this Epistle was written, and should not be supposed to be one of the instances referred here (Acts 27). So, we have no record whatsoever of the three shipwrecks in question.

Paul made many voyages in going from Jerusalem to Tarsus, and to Antioch, and to various parts of Asia Minor, and to Cyprus; and shipwrecks in those seas were by no means such unusual occurrences as to render this account improbable.

THE DEEP

The phrase, *"A night and a day I have been in the deep,"* probably refers to one of those wrecks where the Apostle was very likely adrift on the open sea for a night and a day and was in constant danger of being drowned.

"In the deep" does not mean under the water, it simply refers to the high Seas, on a raft or clinging to wreckage. These are a few of the almost fatal experiences of Paul. They reveal of the strenuous life of this Apostle which is hidden from us.

(26) "IN JOURNEYINGS OFTEN, IN PERILS OF WATERS, IN PERILS OF ROBBERS, IN PERILS BY MINE OWN COUNTRYMEN, IN PERILS BY THE HEATHEN, IN PERILS IN THE CITY, IN PERILS IN THE WILDERNESS, IN PERILS IN THE SEA, IN PERILS AMONG FALSE BRETHREN;"

NOTES

This Verse catalogs the constant dangers respecting evangelism in those days, but which had to be done, that is if the Church was to be founded. The need automatically presupposes the obstacles. In other words, whatever the Lord says is to be done, it is to be immediately undertaken, trusting Him to take care of the problem areas. Even then, the situation can be perilous at times, even as Paul here reiterates.

JOURNEYINGS

The phrase, *"In journeyings often,"* proclaims the necessity of travel, that is if Churches were to be established in major cities and elsewhere in the Roman Empire. To be sure, travel was very hazardous in those days, with the means limited to horses, ships, and walking, with the latter two utilized mostly by Paul. As should be obvious, the accommodations were few and far between, and of course, I speak of the land and not the Sea. Paul no doubt, along with his associates, spent many nights out in the open, whether the weather was good or bad.

Due to the constant travel, this is probably one of the reasons that the Apostle never married.

PERILS OF WATERS

The phrase, *"In perils of waters,"* referred no doubt, to the Sea and the crossing of streams and rivers, which many times lacked bridges. In fact, few rivers had bridges in those days, with many fords being extremely dangerous, especially when the rivers had risen because of floods.

"Perils" in the Greek is *"kindunos,"* and means *"danger."*

ROBBERS

The phrase, *"In perils of robbers,"* portrays a serious problem. Robbers infested the wilds despite Roman rule. They waylaid travellers, robbed, and often killed them. Remember the Samaritan who rescued the man who had fallen among *"robbers."*

How many times had Paul and his party been held up on the long and the frequent journeys which he had to undertake? In fact, during all of his travels HE constantly took his life into his hands. Yet see how much he travelled despite this fact! Divine providence alone preserved him. Yet he had many distressing experiences.

COUNTRYMEN

The phrase, *"In perils by mine own countrymen,"* refers to the Jews who constantly tried to kill him. The hostile Jews ever wanted Paul's blood. As they murdered Jesus and Stephen, so murder was ever in their hearts — a lurid commentary on their morality.

As Acts shows, the Jews often stirred up the Gentiles, in fact, purposely endeavored to stir up the Gentiles to murderous hate. They drove Pilate to crucify Jesus against his will. Having turned their backs upon God, they became fertile territory for the Devil and his evil designs.

HEATHEN

The phrase, *"In perils by the heathen,"* no doubt refers to situations such as Philippi when he and Silas were beaten almost to death and then imprisoned (Acts Chpt. 16).

THE CITY

The phrase, *"In perils in the city,"* refers to Derbe, Lystra, Philippi, Jerusalem, Ephesus, etc. And yet, even though the perils existed in these cities, with the danger at times being acute, still, the Gospel brought to these places by the Apostle changed them for time and eternity. Even though only a small nucleus gave their hearts to Christ in each place, at least as it regards the whole, still, even this little bit of *"salt"* and *"light"* served as a preservative and illumination.

WILDERNESS

The phrase, *"In perils in the wilderness,"* refers to the desert or wherever, where he would be exposed to ambushes, or to wild beasts, or to hunger and want. Instances of this are not recorded in the Acts, but no one can doubt that they occurred.

The idea here is that he had met with constant danger wherever he was, whether in the busy haunts of men, or in the solitude and loneliness of the desert.

THE SEA

The phrase, *"In perils in the sea,"* concerns the storms which came up, which occasioned the shipwrecks of the previous Verse. Frail vessels as they were in those days, were little able to stand even the slightest inclement weather.

NOTES

FALSE BRETHREN

The phrase, *"In perils among false brethren,"* probably represents the crowning danger and trial to Paul, as it is to all others.

A man can better bear danger by land and water, among robbers and in deserts, than he can bear to be betrayed by those who claim to serve the same Lord, and in fact should be helping instead of hindering. Who these were he has not informed us.

Inasmuch as it is mentioned last, tells us that it is the chief trial to which he had been exposed. He had met those who pretended to be his friends, and who yet had sought every possible opportunity to expose and destroy him. No doubt, the *"false brethren"* mentioned in Galatians 2:4, are among this group.

This of which Paul mentions, I can well empathize. Of all the things the Apostle mentions, quite possibly my own personal experience in that particular area would be to even a greater extent than the great Apostle. And yet, I certainly say that with no joy, but rather with a broken heart.

As I have said already in this Volume, *"When one is defenseless, and anyone can do any negative thing to him they so desire, without any fear of censure but rather approval, then one quickly finds out what is in the hearts of men."* I pray that the Reader never has to find that out. You will find a few who truly have the Love of God in their hearts, and who those few will be may surprise you; however, one thing is certain, you will be shocked at how few that number actually is.

I heard Richard Nixon, the former President of the United States, say something once when asked how many friends he had *after* Watergate. His answer was revealing.

"Most of the time," he said, *"people are 'friends' because of what you can do <u>for</u> them, or <u>to</u> them!"* Of course, that means that those people, whomever they may be, are not actually friends at all. Regrettably, what he said is true.

(27) "IN WEARINESS AND PAINFULNESS, IN WATCHINGS OFTEN, IN HUNGER AND THIRST, IN FASTINGS OFTEN, IN COLD AND NAKEDNESS."

The description here brings out the strain and the effort of exertion which produced great fatigue.

Much of the modern Gospel would refer to Paul's statements as a *"bad confession,"* or else a *"lack of Faith."* However, the Holy Spirit did not place upon these words such a label, and neither must we. This is merely the Truth, and instead of little Faith, actually was an exhibition of Great Faith.

WEARINESS AND PAINFULNESS

The phrase, *"In weariness and painfulness,"* proclaims the results from exposure, labor, and want. It means toil and wearisome effort.

The Holy Spirit does not exempt the true Child of God from such situations, but as Paul will later say, He does give us Grace to bear what we must (12:9).

WATCHINGS

The phrase, *"In watchings often,"* had to do with being unable to sleep. This could be for many reasons.

Many times no doubt, while attempting to sleep out in the open, danger or inclement weather, with the latter bringing on plain misery, no doubt prevented sleep. And then I am positive that the care and concern of all the *"Churches,"* as he will say in the next Verse, contributed greatly to the difficulties.

HUNGER AND THIRST

The phrase, *"In hunger and thirst,"* simply refers to the fact that at times, the Apostle and his associates ran out of food and sometimes of water as well. This could have been because they were in places to where food was not available, and it could have been at times because they simply did not have any money with which they could purchase what they needed.

FASTINGS

The phrase, *"In fastings often,"* probably had little to do with going without food for spiritual purposes and reasons. That was a discipline which Paul certainly seldom needed, but which he no doubt engaged anyway.

However, these were probably fastings that were caused by the fact that one had no food at all, in other words, forced fastings.

NOTES

"Often," Paul writes for the fourth time. What information it would render if we could get the details which this adverb covers!

COLD AND NAKEDNESS

The phrase, *"In cold and nakedness,"* simply means a lack of sufficient clothes. Many a day is hot, but bitter cold is the night. When the road led over mountains, which it often did, cold nights were frequent. Paul camped wherever he could. In the Fall and the Spring, wet could be added to cold.

After reading this, how many volunteers do we now have?

What did Paul do about these sufferings? What was his reaction? Did he say that Christianity exacts too great a price? Did he lament his lot and say it was too hard? Did he rebel against God and blame Him for his adversities? Not at all.

He considered his adversities a privilege. He gloried instead of complained. He reviewed this long list of sufferings and said, *"If I must needs glory, I will glory of the things which concern mine infirmities."*

THE DIFFERENCE

Here was the essential difference between Paul and his opponents. They gloried in their triumphs. Paul gloried in his difficulties. They gloried in their pleasures. He gloried in his pain. They gloried in their opportunities. Paul gloried in his infirmities. They gloried in the things that made them strong. Paul gloried in his weaknesses. They gloried in outward appearances, in popularity, and applause. Paul gloried in the treasures of the soul, in honesty, sincerity, and the approval of God.

We are troubled with the problem of suffering without considering the purpose of suffering. The problem has no solution except we understand its purpose.

We prune our trees in order to improve them and to induce growth and fruit. If you wish a tree to grow on a certain side, you prune it there. Then, where one blossom came previously, two more will appear. Fruit will be abundant when pain has been apparent.

ATTITUDE

Much of the benefit of seemingly adverse experiences results from our attitude. If Paul's attitude had been less than it was, his blessing would not have been as much as it was. If he had complained instead of gloried, he would have felt the complainer's woe and grief. Instead, he took the utility attitude. Whether it was shipwreck, beating, prison, robbers, or weariness, it was to be for his ultimate good.

While Paul suffered, he was not overwhelmed. He came out at last as victor rather than victim. This cannot be said of Paul's enemies and the early tyrants and persecutors of Christianity. Those who sought to destroy these Christians came themselves to destruction. And what destruction it was!

TOUCH NOT THE LORD'S ANOINTED . . .

Nero was driven from his throne and perceiving his life in danger, became his own executioner; Domitian was killed by his own servant; Hadrian died of a distressing disease, which was accompanied by great mental agony; Severus never prospered in his affairs after he persecuted the Church, and was killed by the treachery of his son.

Maximinus reigned but three years, and died a violent death; Decius was drowned in a marsh, and his body never found; Valerian was taken prisoner by the Persians, and after enduring the horrors of captivity for several years, was flayed alive; Diocletian was compelled to resign his empire, and went insane; Maximanus Valerius was deprived of his government, and strangled himself; Maximanus Galerius was suddenly and awfully removed by death (Laurin).

(28) "BESIDE THOSE THINGS THAT ARE WITHOUT, THAT WHICH COMETH UPON ME DAILY, THE CARE OF ALL THE CHURCHES."

Paul was the *"Masterbuilder"* of the Church, meaning that the foundation of the Church was given to him in respect to the New Covenant (I Cor. 3:10). Others contributed, and some no doubt did so greatly; however, the manner, purpose, and direction of the Church were given to him. In brief, it consisted of the following:

DOCTRINE

1. Salvation by Faith and not by works, meaning Faith in what Jesus did at Calvary and the Resurrection (Eph. 2:8-9).

2. The Baptism with the Holy Spirit with the evidence of speaking with other tongues, which is an experience subsequent to Salvation (Acts 19:1-7).

3. A victorious, overcoming Christian life, made possible by what Jesus did at Calvary and the Resurrection, which benefits are to be appropriated on a continuing basis (Rom. Chpts. 6-8; I Cor. 2:2; Gal. 6:14; Phil. 3:10).

4. Divine healing according to Faith in Christ and by the Power of God (Acts 19: 11-12).

5. The Rapture of the Church (I Thess. 4:13-18).

6. The Second Coming of the Lord (II Thess. 2:8).

CHURCH GOVERNMENT

1. The Book of Acts and the Epistles, especially as it refers to the Apostle Paul gives us the pattern for Church Government, and is meant by the Holy Spirit to be followed.

2. Jesus Christ is the Head of the Church and to be sure, an active Head at that (Eph. 1:22).

3. The Lord has given to the Church, Apostles, Prophets, Evangelists, Pastors and Teachers, all *"for the perfecting of the Saints for the work of the Ministry, for the edifying of the Body of Christ"* (Eph. 4:11-12).

4. The Church is *"built upon the foundation of the Apostles and Prophets, Jesus Christ Himself being the Chief Cornerstone"* (Eph. 2:20).

Whereas Prophets were used by the Lord to guide Israel of old, the Holy Spirit now uses Apostles to lead and guide the Church, according to the Will of God.

5. The authority of the Local Church is not to be usurped or infringed upon by outside forces of any nature. In other words, the Local Church can be said to be the highest Spiritual Authority (Rom. 1:7; I Cor. 1:2; II Cor. 1:1; Gal. 1:2; Eph. 1:1, etc.).

This means there was no such thing as a Hierarchy in the Early Church and neither were there any Denominations. The Church was basically a fellowship of Churches of like doctrine and purpose.

6. Government respecting discipline was very simple. In the first place the Local Church attended to whatever problems were in that particular Church. If a member offended and failed, repentance was demanded. If the offending member refused, they were to be disfellowshipped (I Cor. Chpt. 5).

NOTES

If the offending member repented, they were to be instantly restored (II Cor. Chpt. 2; Gal. 6:1).

7. Entrance into the Church was by the Born-Again experience (Rom. 4:3; Eph. 2:8-9).

8. Deacons are to be a part of the Church. They are to aid and abet the Pastor or Pastors, in any manner possible. The Scripture does not tell us as to what the number of Deacons should be, that seemingly left up to the Local Church (I Tim. 3:8-13).

BESIDES THOSE THINGS

The phrase, *"Besides those things that are without,"* speaks of that listed in Verses 23-27. Apart from these things just mentioned, lies Paul's real burden. In fact, all of those things were undergone in order that the Church might be built and that it might grow. The main emphasis is always the Church.

DAILY

The phrase, *"That which cometh upon me daily,"* is said in the Greek with great force, and would probably be better translated, *"that which rushes upon me."* The idea here is, that these cares rushed upon him, or pressed upon him like a crowd of men or a mob that bore all before it. In fact, this is one of Paul's most energetic expressions, and denotes the incessant anxiety of mind to which he was subject (Barnes).

THE CHURCHES

The phrase, *"The care of all the Churches,"* of course refers to those he had planted under the guidance of the Holy Spirit. These Churches even as Corinth serves as an example, needed his constant supervision. They were young; many of them were feeble; many were made up of different types of people in fact, as any Church should be; many had a mixture of Jews and Gentiles, with conflicting prejudices, habits, preferences; many of them were composed of those who had been gathered from the lowest ranks of life; and questions would be constantly occurring, relating to their order and discipline, and which Paul would naturally feel a deep interest, and which oftentimes would be referred to him for a decision.

Besides this, these Churches had many trials. They were persecuted, as would be obvious. In their sufferings Paul would feel deep sympathy, and would declare, as far as possible, to afford them relief.

NOTES

In addition to the Churches which he had planted, he would feel an interest in all other Churches as well; and doubtless many cases would be referred to him, as an eminent Apostle, for counsel and advice. No wonder that all this came rushing on him like a tumultuous assembly ready to overpower him (Barnes).

(29) "WHO IS WEAK, AND I AM NOT WEAK? WHO IS OFFENDED, AND I BURN NOT?"

Here we see a true Pastor's heart. There is a constant concern over the progress of every Believer. It is the true Shepherd taking each lamb unto himself, giving it personal attention, at least as far as possible.

Paul was an Apostle as is obvious. However, the calling of the Apostle also includes all the other Offices: Prophet, Evangelist, Pastor, and Teacher. In other words, the true Apostle can function in any of these Offices, and is meant to do so. Consequently, Paul shows the Pastor's heart.

WEAK

The question, *"Who is weak, and I am not weak?"*, presents the Apostle carrying the burden of each and every member of these Churches, at least as far as he was acquainted with each of them. It was like he had to personally nourish them back to spiritual health.

In effect, the Apostle is saying, *"I sympathize with all. I feel where others feel, and their sorrows excite deep sympathetic emotions in my bosom. Like a tender and compassionate friend I am affected when I see others in circumstances of distress."*

The idea is, if they suffer, he suffers.

OFFENDED

The question, *"Who is offended, and I burn not?"*, concerns those who fail in times of temptation and trial. In all such cases, Paul deeply sympathized with them, and was prompt to aid them.

The word *"offended"* actually means *"to catch in a deathtrap."* The word denotes the crooked stick to which the bait is affixed so that to touch the bait is to spring the trap that kills the victim. The point of comparison is deadliness.

It does not mean as some have said, *"to be a stumblingblock,"* or *"to stumble,"* or even *"to be made to stumble."* The idea is always moral offense, offense that kills spiritually.

So real was his love for all his converts that he consciously felt their weakness, and burned with shame or indignation when anyone was injured spiritually or caused to sin (Williams).

The idea is, which is totally Christlike, whatever the situation, irrespective as to its terrible reproach, there was not a hint of recrimination or condemnation, but rather every effort toward Redemption. In other words, the Apostle grieving over the situation, feeling its pain, set about tirelessly to pick the person up, and aid in every way possible to restore the individual to spiritual health. What a Pastor! What a man of God! What a true Shepherd! What Christlikeness!

How so different from the judgmental attitudes of many in the Modern Church. How so different from the self-righteous fake piety of the present. How so different from those who would attempt to make everyone else second-class Christians, with the exception of themselves and their little circle.

With all, the Apostle sympathized; and the condition of all, whether in a state of feeble Faith, or feeble body, or falling into sin, excited the deepest emotions in his mind. The Truth taught here is that Paul felt a deep sympathy for all others who bore the Christian name, and this sympathy for others greatly increased the cares and toils of the Apostolic Office which he sustained. The general sense is, and it can be summed up in the fact that he sympathized, irrespective of the difficulty or problem, with all others.

(30) "IF I MUST NEEDS GLORY, I WILL GLORY OF THE THINGS WHICH CONCERN MINE INFIRMITIES."

What Preacher presently would advertise himself accordingly? These Corinthians wanted credentials from Paul and so he replies by enumerating his many *"infirmities."* Even though he referred to himself as *"boasting,"* I think all the time he knew he really wasn't boasting. No one would boast of these particular things. So, the word must have been used with some irony.

If this is boasting, it is the only boasting I have ever heard that is totally bereft of the flesh.

NOTES

It is the only boasting that does not appreciate self, but rather the opposite, depreciation. In no way could the enumeration of these things make the Apostle look good, big, or powerful in the eyes of the Corinthians or anyone else for that matter. Actually, it had the opposite effect, even as it was designed to have the opposite effect.

As Believers, are we going to allow this lesson to have its intended effect upon us, or will we continue on the modern path, which glorifies flesh?

GLORY

The phrase, *"If I must needs glory,"* refers to the fact that demands had been made upon him for such.

In effect, he is saying, *"It is unpleasant for me to boast, but circumstances have compelled me. But since I am compelled, I will not boast of my rank, or talents, but of that which is regarded by some as an infirmity."* Other men take pride in their personal strength and power. Paul's pride lies in the fact that he is weak, yea, nothing at all.

The very idea seems contradictory, paradoxical in the highest degree: boasting — weakness. But the greatest thing that Paul has come to see in himself is his weakness. He is himself astonished to see how great his weakness is. Men boast of the greatest things they have; well, Paul says, this is my greatest, so this shall ever be my boast when boast I must (Lenski).

INFIRMITIES

The phrase, *"I will glory of the things which concern mine infirmities,"* actually means, *"the things of my weakness."* The word used here is derived from the same word which is rendered *"weak"* in Verse 29.

Once again, we must ask the question as to how the Gospel of Paul fits in with the modern gospel of fame, strength, power, riches, and popularity?

I think not at all!

So where does that leave us presently?

It leaves us in serious need for Revival, which will take us back to the Cross, ever to the Cross, to where we will see Him as He actually is, which then will cause us to see ourselves as we actually are, *"wretched, miserable, poor, blind, and naked"* (Rev. 3:17). We will then be on the right track.

Even though we are that which Jesus said in Revelation Chapter 3, until we see ourselves in that fashion, nothing can actually be accomplished.

(31) "THE GOD AND FATHER OF OUR LORD JESUS CHRIST, WHICH IS BLESSED FOR EVERMORE, KNOWETH THAT I LIE NOT."

As stated, men boast of their strength but Paul boasted of his weakness; an appeal to God as to the Truthfulness of the statement.

GOD AND FATHER

The phrase, *"The God and Father of our Lord Jesus Christ,"* appeals to the highest authority of all, *"God the Father,"* and *"the Lord Jesus Christ."*

Paul was accustomed to make solemn appeals to God for the Truth of what he said, especially when it was likely to be called in question.

The solemn appeal which he makes here to God is made in view of what he has just said of his sufferings, not of what follows — for there was nothing in the occurrence at Damascus that demanded so solemn an appeal to God.

The reason of this appeal is, probably, that these things to which he had referred are known to but few, and perhaps not all of them to even his best friends; that his trials and calamities had been so numerous and extraordinary that his enemies would say that they were improbable, and that all this had been the mere fruit of exaggeration; and as he had no witnesses to appeal to for the truth of what he said, he makes a solemn appeal to the ever-blessed God. In fact, this appeal is made with great reverence. It is not rash, or bold, and is by no means irreverent or profane.

He appeals to God as the Father of the Redeemer Whom he so much venerated and loved, and as himself blessed for evermore.

BLESSED FOR EVERMORE

The phrase, *"Which is blessed for evermore, knoweth that I lie not,"* places his words at the very highest level. In effect, the Apostle is saying that if his detractors call him a liar, they at the same time, will be calling God a liar — that which no sane person should desire to do.

I think the idea is, the more of weakness there is, at least the more of weakness we recognize, for all are weak whether they admit such or not, the more room there is for pure Grace and all-sufficient Divine Power; the less there is at least regarding admittance of our own weakness, the less room is there for Divine Grace and Power. When we are reduced to nothing, God is allowed to be our everything.

The world cannot comprehend such an experience. It is utterly beyond the false ministers and apostles in Corinth. But it is literally true: our greatest asset, our highest cause for boasting if we must boast, is this our weakness and all the things in our lives that exhibit this weakness. Consequently, Paul writes more than a God's Truth, he writes a most instructive one.

CAUTION

Let us add the caution: this is not what is called *"sinful weakness."* Nor is the word used as it is in Romans 14:1, etc., regarding a *"weak"* brother, weak in regard to the Faith, weak in knowledge, grace, etc. Of this weakness one should be ashamed; he could never make it a boast.

To be wholly weak as Paul is here using the word, which means we are in absolute dependence on God's Grace, help, gifts, etc., *that* is the weakness which God works in us by His Spirit and also fills with His Power (Lenski).

(32) "IN DAMASCUS THE GOVERNOR UNDER ARETAS THE KING KEPT THE CITY OF THE DAMASCENES WITH A GARRISON, DESIROUS TO APPREHEND ME:"

Verses 32 and 33 seem at first glance to be out of place in this narrative; however, they are not out of place at all, at least when we get the big picture as to what Paul is saying.

One Commentator ventured that Paul had forgotten this Damascus experience, and now adds it at the last. No, he had not forgotten it, but in fact, had something else altogether different in mind.

APOSTOLIC AUTHORITY

Compelled by fidelity to the Gospel, and by affection for the Corinthians, to establish his Apostolic superiority to his opponents who had introduced themselves into the Church at Corinth, he contrasts his being let down in a basket (II Cor. 11:33) and his being lifted up in a vision (II Cor. 12:2).

The one happened to a man in the flesh; the other to *"a man in Christ."* Of the former man (II Cor. 11:30) he would boast — for how small

NOTES

and contemptible was great Saul of Tarsus crouching terror-stricken in a basket! Of the other man (II Cor. 12:5) he could boast, for he was *"a man in Christ"* having no conscious physical being, experiencing that which a man in the flesh could not boast, for it was an exertion of Divine Power in which man had no part. Self and everything that could exalt him as man were forgotten. He, as a man, had no share in a power which raptured him into Paradise. It was as stated, *"a man in Christ"* that was so raptured. Of such a man he could boast; but of himself he would not boast except in his infirmities (Williams).

DAMASCUS

The phrase, *"In Damascus the Governor under Aretas the king kept the city of Damascenes with a garrison,"* gives us a little more information than that related by Luke (Acts 9:24-25). Luke did not mention the name of the king, or that the Governor had kept the city with a garrison.

Luke informs us (Acts 9:23-24) that the Jews took counsel against Paul to kill him, and that they watched the gates night and day to effect their object. Paul having recently been converted, represented at least in their eyes, a turncoat or traitor. He had come with an important commission to Damascus, and had failed to execute it; he had become the open friend of those whom he came to destroy; and they doubtless claimed of the civil authorities of Damascus that he should be given up and taken to Jerusalem for trial.

The king mentioned here was the father-in-law of Herod Antipas. He made war with Herod, because he had repudiated his daughter, the wife of Herod. This he had done in order to marry his brother Philip's wife (Mat. 14:3).

On this account, Aretas made war with Herod; and in order to resist him, Herod applied to Tiberius the Roman Emperor for aid. Vitellius was sent by Tiberius to subdue Aretas, and to bring him dead or alive to Rome. But before Vitellius had embarked on this enterprise, Tiberius died, and thus Aretas was saved from ruin.

It is supposed that in this state of things, when thus waging war with Herod, he made an incursion to Syria and seized upon Damascus, where he was reigning when Paul went there; or if not reigning there personally, he had appointed a Governor, who administered the affairs of the city in his place.

NOTES

TO KILL PAUL

Luke says that they watched the gates day and night to kill him (Acts 9:24). This was probably the Jews. Meantime the Governor guarded the city, to prevent his escape. The Jews would have killed him at once; the Governor wished to apprehend him and bring him to trial. In either case, Paul had much to fear, and he, therefore, embraced the only way of escape.

Evidently Paul's conversion to Christ had aroused such a tumult that every effort was being made to apprehend him. A body of men was stationed in order to guard the city. The true idea is, that there were men who were appointed to guard the gates of the city, and to keep watch lest he should escape them. Damascus was surrounded, as all ancient cities were, with high walls, and it did not occur to them that he could escape any other way than by the gates.

ORDERS FOR THE ARREST OF PAUL

The phrase, *"Desirous to apprehend me,"* presents the opposition beginning immediately. Satan did not lose any time, marshalling both Jews and Gentiles to apprehend Paul.

Fortunately or unfortunately, according to the way one looks at the situation, this opposition would continue in this vein with his life in constant danger, for the entirety of his Ministry.

Time and time again, with what seems like opposition on every side, I have wondered why it must be regarding my own Ministry. And then I think of Paul, realizing that what few difficulties I face are comparatively insignificant when placed beside that of the great Apostle. I think at times I would have been overwhelmed, were it not for his example before me and all others. It tells me several things:

1. The more anointed the Ministry, the greater the opposition.
2. God will seldom lift the opposition, but will give one Grace to stand the test.
3. The opposition is meant for our good, even though Satan actually designs it for our harm, as would be obvious.
4. All of these things keep us on our face before the Lord, constantly seeking Him for

leading and guidance, constantly depending on Him, which is the intention of the Holy Spirit all along.

5. If I am to do the Will of God, I can very well expect all the hindrances of the Evil One.

6. In all of this, the intention of the Holy Spirit is that I recognize how weak I actually am, and that I, therefore, depend totally upon the Lord.

(33) "AND THROUGH A WINDOW IN A BASKET WAS I LET DOWN BY THE WALL, AND ESCAPED HIS HANDS."

Our Salvation has cost much suffering, not only pertaining to the most awful price paid by the Lord Jesus Christ, but as well of those such as the Apostle Paul, and in fact, untold others down through the many centuries. We have in this Chapter as has been obvious, a detail of extraordinary trials and sorrows in establishing this of which we enjoy so abundantly today. Perhaps we even have reason to be thankful, at least in some degree, that the enemies of Paul made it necessary for him to boast in this manner. Thus we have some most interesting details of facts of which otherwise we should have been ignorant; and we see that the life of Paul was a life of continual self-denial and toll. By Sea and Land; at home and abroad; among his own countrymen and strangers, he was subjected to continued privations and persecution. So it has been always in regard to the establishment of the Gospel.

It began its career as we have stated, in the sufferings of its great Author, and the foundation of the Church was laid in His Precious Blood. It progressed amidst suffering; for all the Apostles accept John, it is supposed were martyrs.

ADVANCEMENT

It continued to advance amidst sufferings — for fiery persecutions raged throughout the Roman Empire, and thousands died in consequence of their professed attachment to the Saviour.

Indeed, the Gospel has always been propagated in heathen lands by self-denials and Sacrifices.

All that we presently enjoy is the fruit of the sufferings, toils, and Sacrifices of others. We have not one Christian privilege or hope which has not cost the life of many a martyr. How thankful should we be to God that He was pleased to raise up men who would be willing thus to suffer, and that He sustained and kept them until their work was accomplished!

NOTES

SINCERITY

We may infer the insincerity of the men engaged in propagating the great Christian Message. What had Paul to gain in the sorrows which he endured? Why did he not remain in his own land, and reap the honors which were then fully within his grasp? The answer is an easy one.

It was because he believed that Christianity was true; and believing that, he believed that it was of importance to make it known to the world. Paul did not endure these sorrows, and encounter these perils, for the sake of pleasure, honor, or gain. No man who reads this Chapter can doubt that he was sincere, and that he was an honest man.

OUR PRESENT POSITION

We should be willing to suffer now. If Paul and the other Apostles were willing to endure so much, why should not we be? If they were willing to deny themselves so much in order that the Gospel should be spread among the nations, why should not we be? It is now just as important that it should be spread as it was then; and the Church should be just as willing to sacrifice its comforts to make the Gospel known as it was in the days of Paul.

We may add, also, that if there was the same devotedness to Christ evinced by all Christians now which is described in this Chapter; if there was the same zeal and self-denial, the time would not be far distant when the Gospel would be spread all around the world.

My prayer is, that the Lord will help us to have the same self-denial as Paul; and especially when all who enter the Ministry shall be willing to forsake country and home, and to encounter peril in the city and the wilderness, on the Sea and the land — to meet cold, and nakedness, hunger, thirst, persecution, and death in any way — in order that they may make known the name of the Saviour to a lost world!

(The thoughts of this Chapter just given, were derived from Albert Barnes.)

THROUGH A WINDOW

The phrase, *"And through a window in a basket was I let down by the wall,"* presents the very beginning of Paul's Ministry, actually just days after he was saved, if that. So, we have here the very Ministry of Paul beginning with weakness. He had to run away as a fugitive. (Some say that the basket incident took place about three years later, which may have been the case).

We say his Ministry began thus, for the work in Damascus was not really part of his Apostolic Ministry. What work among the Jews he did there was abruptly discontinued.

He tried a bit of work among the Jews in Jerusalem, but this too, was soon interrupted. Then there follows a long period in which Paul is lost to view as he lives in Tarsus, or wherever his Ministry at that time, a silent time to us, took him.

Barnabas brought him to Antioch. There Paul at last really began to work until after this preliminary training in Antioch, at least if one could refer to such in that manner, the Spirit sent him forth on his real work among the Gentiles in all lands.

The flight from Damascus was the beginning. Paul's Ministry began, like that of Moses, with flight and with a long period of waiting, waiting, nothing it seems, but waiting. This makes the flight from Damascus, so significant. It forced Paul into the long wait in which he fully learned that he was nothing, that his mightiest asset was utter weakness, weakness which enabled God to do everything with him and through him.

THAT WHICH WAS NECESSARY

What the Holy Spirit was doing, becomes moreso supported by the historical evidence which began the night when Paul fled from Damascus so that he might learn the long lesson of his utter weakness, on the complete learning of which his Apostolic success depended. For this reason the story is told here; for this reason a brief reference would not suffice. For this reason it is told at this most proper place.

The tremendous energy of Paul, which at one time made him the worst ravager of the Church, which after his conversion sought to make him the mighty disseminator of the Gospel, must first of all be humbled in utter weakness and then learn the only reliance which was at last learned by Moses: *"I will be with thee!"* (Ex. 3:12; Mat. 28:20). More may be said; let this suffice.

NOTES

THE BASKET

This is the story related, as stated, in Acts 9:23-25. But Paul and Luke related independently. Luke received his account from Paul. To make certain of capturing Paul, the Jews enlisted the aid of the Governor by denouncing Paul as a dangerous disturber. This official posted special guards at the city gates, and, lest Paul elude them in disguise, the Jews, who knew Paul, helped to watch. But Paul escaped at night as both he and Luke described this incident.

Along the city wall, where houses were built against it, one house was found which had a door that had been cut through the great wall high up from the ground; the door opened out from the upper story or from the roof of the house. This was *"a little door,"* and not a *"window"* as we think of such.

In a wall which served as a fortification houses that adjoined the wall would not have windows. This one little door was so exceptional that the hostile Jews and nobody else even thought about it even if they knew of its existence. It was, of course, always tightly barred.

Paul was seemingly to be caught until some friend informed the Disciples, and then Paul got safely away, and the soldiers and the Jews watched for an indefinite time at the gates, but of course, with no success.

DAMASCENES

There's an interesting aside as it relates to the previous Verse, in the fact that after Paul names Damascus he does not say *"guarded the city"* but *"the city of the Damascenes."*

This sounds as though the city belonged to its inhabitants, and as though the king's overlordship through his Governor was loosely exercised.

It is a point for the historians to discuss; it is apparently one of the incidental touches that point to the absolute reliability of the historicity of Paul. In fact, the Book of Acts is full of such little tests.

ESCAPED

The phrase, *"And escaped his hands,"* pictures him being let down by a *"basket."*

Alone, miserable, a fugitive is a man to be pitied. The flight from Damascus to Jerusalem, at least in those days, was a long journey.

Mighty Paul proposed to enter Damascus with a force of Levite police; he entered as a weak, stricken, blind man.

When he left, never to return, he fled under cover of night. Weakness, weakness to learn so thoroughly as to allow God at last to use His strength in Paul (Lenski).

There are some who interpret Paul's escape in another manner, claiming that he did not at that time go to Jerusalem, but instead into Arabia, where he spent some time, and went to Jerusalem later. This very well could have been the case. However, it is my contention, according to the Acts Chapter 9 account, that Paul did go on to Jerusalem when he left Damascus.

"Show me Faith, O Christ the Author
and the end of Faith Divine.
"Faith to live and Faith to labor, what a
legacy is mine.
"Faith to live and Faith to labor, what a
legacy is mine."

"Teach me Faith, O Jesus Master as I
look away to Thee,
"Faith to help me follow faster, Faith to
win the victory.
"Faith to help me follow faster, Faith to
win the victory."

"Give me Faith, O Lord and Saviour,
Faith to win the victory.
"Faith to order my behavior, Faith to
sing the triumph song.
"Faith to order my behavior, Faith to
sing the triumph song."

CHAPTER 12

(1) "IT IS NOT EXPEDIENT FOR ME DOUBTLESS TO GLORY. I WILL COME TO VISIONS AND REVELATIONS OF THE LORD."

Paul appeals to another evidence which proved the veracity of his Apostolic Office — an evidence to which none of his accusers could appeal — that he had been permitted to behold the glories of the heavenly world, even though they could deny the veracity of his claims.

In the previous Chapter he had mentioned his trials. Here he says, that as they had compelled him to boast, he would mention the Revelations which he had of the Lord. He details, therefore, the remarkable Vision which he had several years before, when he was caught up to Heaven, and permitted to behold certain wonders.

NOTES

So, it is with this in view that we begin this Chapter.

NOT EXPEDIENT

The phrase, *"It is not expedient for me doubtless to glory,"* in effect says, *"It is not profitable for me to boast, but since it is necessary to answer my enemies at Corinth, I will continue with the following descriptions concerning Visions and Revelations."*

Men lay great stress on experience, even as they should. It is considered an important recommendation. When, in fact, our experiences are of the right sort, they do provide us commendation and give us access unto certain privileges.

This of Paul was a remarkable and unusual experience. If there were any occasion to boast of glory, Paul was determined to relate such things as would prove the reality of his Christian experience and Apostolic Calling. He was not an impostor. Neither was he a place-seeker or an opportunist.

How unlike his opponents he proved to be something else entirely, as was shown in his previous statement, *"If I must needs glory, I will glory of the things which concern mine infirmities."* These were tangible and common things. They were related to the usual run of life. But, there were uncommon, unusual, and outstanding happenings in this which Paul will now relate.

That which he will now tell, related to his relationship with God. It was such an experience of which one scarcely dare speak and when Paul did, he spoke of it as though it had happened in the life of another. He humbly and timidly drew the veil aside to reveal one of the most sacred moments of his whole life (Laurin).

VISIONS AND REVELATIONS

The phrase, *"I will come to Visions and Revelations of the Lord,"* refers to presentations given to Paul by the Lord, which pertained to various things, and no doubt, included the giving to him of the New Covenant.

Visions most of the time occur while one is awake, while dreams occur while one is asleep.

And yet it is not necessarily so that all Visions take place while one is awake, but I do think that normally that this is the case.

All Visions serve in some manner for the purpose of Revelation, but Revelation can definitely occur, and most of the time does, without a Vision.

When Paul included the crucial qualifier *"of the Lord,"* he was probably hinting at the fact that it is possible to have ecstatic experiences that do not come from the Lord. These counterfeit experiences are part of Satan's attempts to delude people (II Cor. 11:14). Paul knew his experiences were from the Lord and was quick to say so.

Incidentally, both *"Visions* (Optasias)*"* and *"Revelations* (Apokalupseis)*"* are plural nouns, so he must have had several in mind (Rossier).

THOSE GIVEN IN THE WORD CONCERNING PAUL

The Book of Acts records several of Paul's extraordinary spiritual experiences:

1. The Revelation of Jesus to him while on the road to Damascus (Acts 9:3-7).
2. The Macedonian Call (Acts 16:9-10).
3. The Vision while in Corinth (Acts 18:9-10).
4. The trance while praying in the Temple at Jerusalem (Acts 22:17-21).
5. The appearance of an Angel while he was at Sea on his way to Rome (Acts 27:23-25).

We have no way of knowing how many similar experiences he may have had, but we can be sure there were others (Gal. 1:12).

Incidentally, *"Visions"* relate to something visual, while *"Revelations"* are a broader term including any kind of significant spiritual manifestation that is outside of the ordinary.

While *"Visions"* are rare, still, it is pretty well obvious as to what they are — the observing of something with wide-open eyes which is spiritual. As stated, it can be given by God or even by Satan. *"Revelations"* are another matter altogether, and due to their wide range of meaning, perhaps would warrant further investigation:

REVELATION

The very essence of Christianity is a revealed or *"Revelation"* experience. It rests on the confidence that God has acted to make Himself known to human beings and to make known information not available from any other source.

NOTES

Although the Bible Texts that use the words *"revealed"* or *"Revelation"* are relatively few, the Doctrine does not rest simply on the use of these terms in the Bible.

THE HEBREW WORDS

The Hebrew word translated *"reveal"* is *"galah."* One of its two main meanings is *"to uncover."*

The other prominent meaning of this word is that of openness and visibility. What is revealed is to be exposed for all. Thus, Deuteronomy 29:28 says, *"The secret things belong to the Lord our God, but the things revealed belong to us and to our Children for ever, that we may follow all the words of this Law."* The Prophet Amos adds, *"Surely the Sovereign Lord does nothing without revealing His Plan to His servants the Prophets"* (Amos 3:7).

The Hebrew word for *"Revelation,"* or any of its derivatives, is never used in the Old Testament as technical theological terms. But it is clear from their use that the content of Revelation includes true information.

Old Testament Saints believed that God revealed Himself to Abraham and Moses; and the Prophets tell of a coming day of magnificent self-revelation, when *"the Glory of the Lord will be revealed, and all mankind together will see it"* (Isa. 40:5).

THE GREEK WORDS

Two groups of words in the Greek New Testament are translated *"revealed"* or *"Revelation."* These words help us develop a New Testament concept of Revelation and are also important for our understanding of the Second Coming of Christ.

The first group of words is constructed on a stem that suggests bringing to light, or making manifest. Among the words in the group are *"phaneroo"* (*"to reveal, show, make known"*), *"epiphaino"* (*"to show or appear"*), *"epiphaneia"* (*"an appearance of Revelation"*), and *"phanerosis"* (*"a disclosure or Revelation"*).

In Greek culture these words had an ordinary meaning but also the spiritual meaning of intervention by, or the personal appearance of, a Deity. These words *"reveal"* or *"Revelation"* are found in a number of Passages (Lk. 2:26; Jn. 1:31; 2:11; 17:6; Rom. 10:20; 16:26; I Cor. 4:10-11; II Tim. 1:10; I Pet. 1:20; Rev. 15:4).

Other of these Greek words are found in the following Passages: Matthew 10:26; 11:25, 27; 16:17; Luke 2:35; 10:21-22; 12:2; 17:30; John 12:38; Romans 1:17, 18; 8:18; I Corinthians 2:10; 3:13; 14:30; Galatians 1:16; etc.

WHAT THESE WORDS MEAN

Five concepts of *"Revelation"* appear in the New Testament — four in the Epistles and one in the Gospels.

END TIME EVENTS

First, *"Revelation"* is a future visible unveiling at history's end. This will be a Revelation of Jesus, of God's Attributes and Plan, and of Believers as God's Children (Rom. 2:5; 8:18-19; I Cor. 1:7; 3:13; II Thess. 1:7; I Pet. 1:5, 7, 13; 4:13; 5:1; Rev. 1:1).

The word *"revealed"* is also used of the future appearance of the Antichrist (II Thess. 2:3, 6, 8).

CURRENT KNOWLEDGE

Second, *"Revelation"* is our current knowledge in Christ of God's Plans, previously hidden even to Old Testament Saints (Rom. 1:17-18; 16:26; I Cor. 2:10; 14:6; Gal. 1:12; 3:23; Eph. 3:3, 5).

The same term is used of historic knowledge of God unveiled by the Old Testament Prophets (I Pet. 1:12).

In these uses, the implication is that the new Revelation is written in the Scriptures. But *"Revelation"* is also used of fresh, contemporary insights provided to the Early Church by its own Apostles and Prophets (I Cor. 14:26, 30; II Cor. 12:1, 7; Gal. 2:2).

JESUS IN THE BELIEVER

Third, *"Revelation"* is also a term applied to Jesus' expression of Himself through the life of a Believer (Gal. 1:16).

TRUTH

Fourth, *"Revelation"* is the Holy Spirit's work of shaping the Believer's understanding and attitudes to bring them into harmony with Truth (Eph. 1:17).

INNER ENLIGHTENING

Finally, three times the Gospels refer to Jesus' revealing the Father or to Jesus Himself being revealed (Mat. 11:27; 16:17; Lk. 10:22).

NOTES

The sense in each instance is an inner enlightening rather than an objective confrontation.

GOD'S SELF-REVELATION

The Old Testament declares in many places that God partly showed Himself to human beings. The New Testament era began with God's Self-Revelation in Jesus.

As our Lord Himself said, *"Anyone who has seen Me has seen the Father"* (Jn. 14:9). But the Doctrine of God's Self-disclosure is not found in the New Testament by the use of the word *"Revelation* (apokalypsis and apokalypto)*."*

Rather, the New Testament emphasis in these words is on:

1. Disclosure of information from and about God.

2. The future visible disclosure in history of Jesus and of God's Plan.

3. The outward manifestation of God and Truth in the lives of Believers.

GOD'S REVELATION OF REALITY

A critical passage for understanding the first meaning of *"Revelation"* is I Corinthians Chapter 2. Human beings are limited, unable to penetrate by the senses the thought of God or the meaning of life on Earth. But the Holy Spirit knows the hidden things, and so God revealed them by His Spirit (I Cor. 2:10). This Revelation is in words given by the Spirit (I Cor. 2:13).

So, *"Revelation"* in the New Testament primarily applies to the giving and interpretation of information from God.

(2) "I KNEW A MAN IN CHRIST ABOVE FOURTEEN YEARS AGO, (WHETHER IN THE BODY, I CANNOT TELL; OR WHETHER OUT OF THE BODY, I CANNOT TELL: GOD KNOWETH;) SUCH AN ONE CAUGHT UP TO THE THIRD HEAVEN."

Paul selected one of his glorious experiences to illustrate his point. Notice that the emphasis of this Passage is not on the Revelation itself, but on the Grace of God. The fact that this particular event transpired 14 years earlier probably places it during the general period of time of about A.D. 46.

Some have tried to connect this experience with his stoning at Lystra (Acts 14:19-20). They claim that he actually died at this time and his spirit went to Heaven temporarily. Even though the time frame may fit, it contradicts Paul's statement that he did not know if he was *"in the body"* or *"outside of the body."* Certainly, the Believers who gathered around him at Lystra would have known whether or not his body was present; therefore, he must have been alone when his vision occurred. So, the situation at Lystra is not the occasion of this of which Paul speaks.

IN CHRIST

The phrase, *"I knew a man in Christ,"* is simply meant to indicate his personal relationship with the Lord, and as well, that what he is about to say is definitely of the Lord. Consequently, once again he is insinuating that many claims of experiences were being made by many people concerning all types of experiences of this nature, claiming it was from the Lord, when in reality it was from Satan or else simply a figment of their imagination. Such is no less true presently, and probably even more so.

Also, if one is to notice, Paul is speaking of himself in the third person, which is not exactly uncommon.

For instance, one of the Caesars spoke of himself in that fashion constantly. As well, John in his Gospel speaks of himself in the third person (Jn. 13:23-24; 19:26; 21:20). John did it on account of his modesty, because he would not appear to put himself forward, and because the mention of his own name, as connected with the friendship of the Saviour in the remarkable manner in which he enjoyed it, might have savored of pride.

For a similar reason Paul may have been unwilling to mention his own name here; and he may have abstained from referring to this occurrence elsewhere because it might savor of pride, and might also excite the envy or ill-will of others.

In fact, those who have been most favored with spiritual blessings of this nature will soon learn, except in certain circumstances, not to be the most ready to proclaim it.

THE MANNER IN WHICH PAUL REVEALED THIS

We can tell from the manner in which Paul described this experience, that he had not the remotest idea as to how this happened other than what he said. The thing itself, the Vision and Revelation, was unspeakably glorious. That this person was Paul and not another, of course, is immediately obvious. And yet, Paul shrinks from saying so. He tells about it as though it had happened to another man and not to himself. Consequently, the idea of Paul's boasting about himself is thus completely removed.

NOTES

THE WORLD OF THE OCCULT

Even though the Lord definitely reveals Himself at times through Visions and Revelations, exactly as Paul here describes, all such activity, even to which we have already alluded, is not of the Lord.

In fact, the occultism of our day is proof of an unseen world, but it is such a world as Paul described in Ephesians 6:12 where he spoke of it in terms of *"the darkness of this world"* and *"spiritual wickedness in high places."*

There is indeed an occult world which unregenerate men contact, but it is a Satan-dominated world. It is a world of darkness and spiritual wickedness.

Of course, Paul's experience had no connection with this occult world of Satan. His was the experience, as stated, of *"a man in Christ."* He touched the unseen world where the living Christ is present. It is a world of light and beauty.

No informed or rational person will deny that there is another world just beyond the reach of our senses, both good and bad, even as we are here discussing.

The following is that which occurs in the spirit world of darkness, in other words, that headed up by Satan, and is absolutely forbidden to the Child of God. It is as follows:

1. Enchantments — practice of magical arts (Ex. 7:11, 22; 8:7, 18; Lev. 19:26; Deut. 18:10; II Kings 17:17; 21:6; II Chron. 33:6; Isa. 47:9, 12; Jer. 27:9; Dan. 1:20).
2. Witchcraft — practice of dealing with evil spirits (Ex. 22:18; Deut. 18:10; I Sam. 15:23; II Kings 9:22; II Chron. 33:6; Micah 5:12; Nahum 3:4; Gal. 5:19-21).
3. Sorcery — same as witchcraft (Ex. 7:11; Isa. 47:9, 12; 57:3; Jer. 27:9; Dan. 2:2; Mal. 3:5; Acts 8:9-11; 13:6-8; Rev. 9:21; 18:23; 21:8; 22:15).
4. Soothsaying — same as witchcraft (Isa. 2:6; Dan. 2:27; 4:7; 5:7, 11; Micah 5:12).
5. Divination — the art of mystic insight or fortune-telling (Num. 22:7; 23:23; Deut. 18:10-14; I Sam. 6:2; II Kings 17:17; Jer. 14:14;

27:9; 29:8; Ezek. 12:24; 13:6-7, 23; 21:22-29; 22:28; Micah 3:7; Zech. 10:2; Acts 16:16).

6. Wizardry — same as witchcraft. A wizard is a male and a witch is a female who practices witchcraft. Both were to be destroyed in Israel (Ex. 22:18; Lev. 19:31; 20:6, 27; Deut. 18:11; I Sam. 28:3, 9; II Kings 21:6; 23:24; II Chron. 33:6; Isa. 19:3).

7. Necromancy — divination by means of pretended communication with the dead (Deut. 18:11; I Sam. Chpt. 28; I Chron. 10:13; Isa. 8:19).

8. Magic — any pretended supernatural art or practice (Gen. 41:8, 24; Ex. 7:11, 22; 8:7, 18-19; 9:11; Dan. 1:20; 2:2, 10, 27; 4:7, 9; 5:11; Acts 19:19).

9. Charm — to put a spell upon. Same as enchantment (Deut. 18:11; Isa. 19:3).

10. Prognostication — to foretell by indications, omens, signs, etc. (Isa. 47:13; Jer. 10:2; Dan. 1:20; 2:2, 10; 4:7; 5:7-15).

FAMILIAR SPIRITS

All the above practices were and still are carried on in connection with demons, called familiar spirits. All in Israel of old, who forsook God and sought help from these Demons were to be destroyed (Lev. 19:31; 20:6; Deut. 18:11; I Sam. Chpt. 28; II Kings 21:6; 23:24; I Chron. 10:13; II Chron. 33:6; Isa. 8:19; 19:3; 29:4; Mat. 24:24; II Thess. 2:8-12; I Tim. 4:1-8; Rev. Chpt. 13; 16:13-16; 19:20).

Old Testament times were somewhat different from the present, in that God had brought forth a nation, the nation of Israel for specific purposes. Consequently, certain actions were taken, such as putting witches to death, etc., which are not practiced now in Christianity, and for all the obvious reasons.

Irrespective, anyone who deals with the spirit world of darkness, will always in one form or the other suffer spiritual judgment, which will ultimately fall out to the loss of their eternal souls.

LED BY THE HOLY SPIRIT

The Believer is to be led exclusively by the Spirit of God (Jn. 16:7-15; I Cor. 2:9-16).

However, the very idea of all of this is, that there is a spirit world divided into two directions. I speak of that which is of God, which includes all the holy Angels, and all who truly serve Him. As well, the spirit world of darkness headed up by Satan and demon spirits, is very much a fact. Everyone who is not Born-Again, therefore, not a follower of Jesus Christ, belongs to that spirit world of darkness. There is no in-between. One is either of God or Satan.

In fact, Paul is going to relate to us in brief, that which happened to him regarding the spirit world of *"Light."*

FOURTEEN YEARS AGO

The phrase, *"Above fourteen years ago,"* takes us back, as stated, to about A.D. 46.

On what occasion, or where this occurred, or why he concealed this remarkable fact so long, and why there is no other allusion to it, is unknown; and conjecture is useless.

If this Epistle was written, as is commonly supposed, about the year 60, this vision was then several years after his conversion. So it did not happen at that time. Whenever it was given, this means that Paul had kept secret for fourteen years or more, this momentous happening.

I think the following Verses tell us why he had not mentioned it previously, at least of that which we have record. The *"pride"* factor was ever before Paul, as it is ever before all Believers; consequently, anything that would tend toward that subtle sin, must be avoided at all costs. Consequently, it is only when he is compelled to refer to this evidence of his Apostolic mission that he refers to it here; however, in no way does that mean that such (Visions and Revelations) are necessary to validate the Calling of the Apostle. In fact, many have such who are not Apostles!

Another person might shout: *"I, I have been in Paradise!"* And exalt himself above all his fellowmen. Another man might tell about it on every possible occasion. Paul kept it a secret for over fourteen years; it is now forced from him only by utter necessity.

Even under this compulsion he is able to tell about it only as though it had happened to another person. It seemed incredible to Paul that it should have been *he* who had been in Paradise through such an act of the Lord's.

Paul's humble character is here revealed; consequently, we have the rarest of all examples; a boastless boast. More than that, an extreme boast without a trace of common boasting.

NOTES

THE BODY

The phrase, *"Whether in the body, I cannot tell; or whether out of the body, I cannot tell,"* presents the Apostle removing a question that will occur to at least some of his Readers: *"Was this a bodily transfer into Paradise similar to that of Enoch and of Elijah although it endured only for a short period of time, or was it a transfer only of the soul like that of other Saints at death and temporarily, of course, in Paul's case?"*

Paul simply does not know. He does know that it was entirely miraculous. In fact, how could he, a mere human being, know? With the fact he was acquainted; but how it was brought about he did not know. In reality, how it was done is immaterial.

No one can doubt that God has power, if He so chooses, to transport the body to Heaven; or that He has power for a time to separate the soul from the body; or that He has power to do anything, for that matter!

GOD KNOWETH

The short phrase, *"God knoweth,"* actually means that with what mode in which it was done, God only could be acquainted. Paul did not attempt to explain that. Actually, that was to him of comparatively little consequence, and he did not waste his time in a vain attempt to explain it. In Truth, this is the dividing line of Christianity.

UNDERSTANDING GOD

It should be understood, that the creature can only vaguely understand the Creator, and even then, only as the Creator reveals Himself to us. The Lord does not explain everything to us, and for several reasons:

1. He wants *"Faith"* to be the underlying foundation of all that we know and do concerning Him, and not Science, etc. Many may object to that, but the Truth is, that this is the only manner (Faith) in which man can understand God to any degree. We must believe, even though at times we do not understand.

2. If God in fact, explained to us in detail exactly as to what is done and how it is done, I think I can venture to say, that in our finite state, the smartest of us, whomever that may be, simply would not understand still.

There will be a day when all Saints will fully understand the Mind and Workings of the Creator, but that will be only after *"this corruptible* (has) *put on incorruption, and this mortal* (has) *put on immortality"* (I Cor. 15:53). *"Then shall I know. . . ."* the Apostle continues to say (I Cor. 13:12).

Those who claim they will not accept anything they do not totally understand, simply don't know what they are talking about. All of us accept things everyday of which we have little knowledge. For instance, I don't know how electricity works, but I accept it. In Truth, there is not a single Biochemist, Biologist, or Botanist who knows or understands how a small seed germinates and produces a plant. They know it does, but they have no idea as to how it does what it does.

So, for those who claim they must have scientific proof for everything before acceptance, simply are not being honest. Even the most brilliant in this world little understands that in which they are supposed to be prolific. No, when it comes to God, these individuals, whomever they may be, are engaging in what is referred to as *"cop-out!"*

Vain speculation is of little consequence. To be frank, if Faith in God is excluded, such speculation becomes more and more ludicrous!

For instance, just the other day I heard over the news that Archaeologists had discovered the fossil remains of a type of bird. If I remember correctly, they claimed that it was about a hundred million years old. The astounding thing to them was that the fossil remains show that the bird was fully mature, in other words, not in a stage of evolution. They had previously taught that there were no fully developed specimens that far back.

How senseless!

First of all, their dating methods are all but useless. Second, there is no such thing as an evolutionary process. And last, whatever fossil remains there are, if honestly investigated, will always show the fully-developed specimen. In fact, it takes far more Faith to believe in evolution than it does in God. Evidences of God are abundantly everywhere, while there are no evidences of evolution.

THAT IS ENOUGH!

For anything of which we do not have understanding, the knowledge that *"God knows,"* is enough. Complete trust in Him is all that is

NOTES

necessary, and is actually here what Paul teaches, even though that is not basically the subject matter at hand.

CAUGHT UP

The phrase, *"Such an one caught up to the third heaven,"* is at least partly the same phraseology as used in I Thessalonians 4:16-17, as it refers to the Rapture (Resurrection) of the Church.

"Caught up" in the Greek is *"harpazo,"* and means *"to carry off; grasp hastily; snatch up; to seize and overpower."* From this we get our word *"Rapture,"* meaning the act of transporting. While Paul was definitely *"raptured"* at this particular time, he was not *"resurrected,"* meaning, to receive the Glorified Body. In fact, even though Paul is now with the Lord, even as are all other Saints who have gone on, he has not yet received his Glorified Body, and will not until the coming Resurrection (I Cor. 15:51-54).

THE THIRD HEAVEN

The first heaven is that of the clouds, the second that of the far firmament of the sky and the stars, the third is the actual abode of God, of the Angels, and of all departed Saints in Glory. Even the Old Testament speaks of the *"Heaven of heavens"* or the *"Highest Heaven"* (Deut. 10:14).

The Jews sometime speak of seven heavens, and Mohammed borrowed this idea from the Jews. But the Bible speaks of but three heavens, even as we have just related.

We must consider all this Jewish material as worthless, at least that which is not backed up totally by Scripture, and that would go for such material by anyone else as well. Are these Jews, who were never in Heaven, able to shed any light on Paul's experience, who actually did go to Heaven at that time?

To give a little more Scriptural foundation regarding the three heavens, please note the following:

1. The first heaven is the clouds and atmospheric heavens (Gen. 1:8; Ps. 77:17-18; 104:2-3).

2. The second heaven is the starry space (Gen. 15:5; 22:17; 26:4; Deut. 1:10; Isa. 13:10; 14:13).

3. The third heaven, is the planet Heaven, the abode of God (Gen. 1:1; Isa. 14:12-14; 66:1; Rev. 21:2, 10).

(3) "AND I KNOW SUCH A MAN, (WHETHER IN THE BODY, OR OUT OF THE BODY, I CANNOT TELL: GOD KNOWETH;)"

NOTES

As is obvious, Paul is repeating what he has just stated in the previous Verse. Why did he do that?

Obviously, we have no way of knowing positively, but perhaps it relates somehow to the claims made by his adversaries. They may as well have claimed some type of personal experiences such as this, but which in reality, were not genuine.

I KNOW

The phrase, *"And I know such a man,"* is so said in the Greek, that it designates an initial event followed by results that continued up until the time he penned these words. In other words, that which he was shown in this Vision of being taken to Heaven, contributed in some way to the things he was teaching.

In fact, why did the Lord give Paul this type of Vision?

Whatever the reason, of this we can be sure. It was of great value to Paul in many ways.

Not only did he see the wonder and splendor of Heaven, but as well, I personally believe that due to the fact that he mentioned the word *"Revelations,"* that he quite possibly received some or all of the New Covenant at that time. Of course, we have no way of knowing as to exactly what did happen, but we do know that the Vision was for purpose, and due to the fact that the results continued, there must have been some instruction involved.

I CANNOT TELL

The phrase, *"Whether in the body, or out of the body, I cannot tell,"* I think, refers to the fact that he did not know if he was at that time transported bodily to Heaven, or only saw such in a Vision. This we do know, the experience was so real, so powerful, that beyond the shadow of a doubt he knew it happened, but not exactly how.

Of course, the Lord could have easily transported him bodily to Heaven without any difficulty whatsoever. Or He could have shown Paul the entirety by Vision form. One would have been just as real as the other.

It is tragic, when men will spend almost all of their time in preparation as it regards this life, which in fact is very short and temporal, and almost no preparation at all for that which is coming, and which is eternal. This life is only a dress rehearsal for eternity. Consequently, everything we do, irrespective as to what it might be, must be passed under the scrutiny of the Word of God, doing all that we can to abide by the Word, to be led by the Holy Spirit, to be all we can be in Christ, making all preparations for the life that is to come. That's the reason Jesus told us to *"lay up treasures there, and not here"* (Mat. 6:19-20). Everything must be done in the light of the coming *"Judgment Seat of Christ."*

GOD KNOWETH

The short phrase, *"God knoweth,"* is repeated, and again for purpose.

Of course, and as stated, Paul is speaking of the situation at hand regarding the Vision; however, broadening out the subject, we know that God knows all things, past, present, and future. In other words, He has foreknowledge concerning all futuristic events. And yet, the foreknowledge He has, does not mean that He has predestinated all events. While He definitely has predestined some things, those things never tamper with man's free moral agency. So, foreknowledge does not necessarily mean that God has planned the situation in a certain way, and then uses His Power to bring it to pass, but it does mean that He has the ability to know what is going to happen in the future irrespective as to how it is brought to pass. *"God knoweth!"*

(4) "HOW THAT HE WAS CAUGHT UP INTO PARADISE, AND HEARD UNSPEAKABLE WORDS, WHICH IT IS NOT LAWFUL FOR A MAN TO UTTER."

As no other man, Paul settled many questions concerning spiritual things. I speak of the New Covenant which fleshed out many vague promises in the Old Testament. For instance, the *"Resurrection"* was spelled out in detail by Paul, which completed the shadowy Promises of the Old Covenant (I Cor. Chpt. 15). As well, the Apostle gives us the present abode of the Saints who have gone on, which is now Heaven instead of Abraham's Bosom of Luke Chapter 16. All of this was made possible by what Jesus did at Calvary and the Resurrection (Phil. 1:21-24).

PARADISE

The phrase, *"How that he was caught up into Paradise,"* presents this word being used by Paul in a general manner. The word actually means *"a garden."* However, the manner in which Paul now uses the word, refers to the place of God's abode, in other words, where His Throne is now located. It is also the residence of all the Holy Angels and all the Saints who have lived and died.

Jesus used this word *"Paradise"* when speaking to the thief on the Cross who begged for remembrance when Christ came into His Kingdom. This made the Kingdom and Paradise one and the same place. It is a descriptive reference to the unseen world beyond our physical sphere — an unseen world which is the abode of those who have gone on to be with the Lord.

As stated, the word means *"a garden,"* and, therefore, must be a place of beauty. It must also be a place of material reality.

As a result, it is not mere speculation to conclude that Believers are to inhabit spheres and worlds in that vast universe which are yet unknown to us. If we inhabit a planet called the Earth now, is it incredible that we should inhabit another sphere somewhere else? However, in the final phase, the Bible declares the renovation of our present planet for the habitation of God's Children, plus the transfer of God's Throne from planet Heaven to planet Earth — that is, if we are to refer to Heaven in such a manner (Rev. Chpts. 21-22).

WHAT TYPE OF PLACE IS HEAVEN?

We are not amiss in thinking that the unseen sphere called Paradise is of material reality. The Bible plainly states that it is. In fact, the spirit is just as real as the body. The body has cellular substance that has size and shape. The Spiritual Body will have another kind of substance suited to the new kind of life that is to be found beyond the veil of the senses.

Many people think about the other world in terms of ghostly vagueness, as if it were some kind of haven for mysterious spirits that flit and vanish in the air.

We have every Scriptural and reasonable right to believe it to be a world as tangible and as real as ours. In fact, it will be more so, for it will be a world liberated from the liabilities of this present one. It will be perfect and complete and in it we shall exist with the maximum contentment and joy.

If we were to attempt to explain the reason for the present debacle of civilization, many ideas would be expressed. Of course, any explanation would include more than one cause. There would be the common items of greed, dishonesty, politics, and religion. These are not all.

There are ramifications to our plight that few suspect. If we delved deeply enough, we would uncover a major contributing cause. It is our loss of Faith in the reality of immortality.

By immortality we do not mean what is commonly meant, but that indisputable fact that life never dies — the fact that each of us and all of us, regardless of our paganism or Christianity, our Faith or our unbelief, our good or our evil, will live in a state of life beyond death. Somewhere and sometime, we shall be answerable to a Supreme Being Whom the Bible reveals as God.

UNBELIEF

The collapse of our phase of civilization has been caused by materialism. Dictators run amuck in the world because, for them, God does not exist. If they believed themselves answerable for their crimes, they would abandon their course. So would all the evil little men — the criminals, the thieves and the kidnappers, etc. When the present moment and the immediate object is all that concerns us, then the emphasis is on what we can get now. We write off everything else but the gain and glory of today. We abandon conscience. Christ becomes a relic of the past. The Bible is referred to as a religious opiate. Hence, the tendency is to deny the claim of the future. Consequently, we become indifferent to tomorrow. We laugh at the idea of judgment and retribution. We conveniently idealize the future in terms of an empty vacuum. We construct a comfortable idea of God as a God of love without justice, that is, if we recognize Him at all.

In this oblivion of untruth we live as we choose, unwilling to listen when the Bible speaks, *"It is appointed unto man once to die, but after this the Judgment."* Or to heed when it says, *"Be sure your sin will find you out."*

AN UNDERSTANDING OF DEATH

We have taken an unnatural and wholly illogical attitude as it regards death. Naturally, there is no satisfactory understanding of death, except by the Christian meaning of life.

NOTES

A Columnist wrote: *"The mother of a friend of mine died the other day. My friend's 11-year-old daughter was sent away until after the funeral. She must be spared the knowledge of death.*

"Is this not characteristic of our society? We treat death as if it were an aberration. Age approaches, but beautician, masseur and gland specialists cooperate to keep alive the allusion that we are not really growing older. Anything that reminds us of the inescapable fact that we are to die seems morbid to us."

As for the Christian, death is not a conclusion — it is a transition. Even as far as this temporal house called the *"body"* is concerned, the grave is not permanent — it is temporary.

In this almost unspeakable experience of the Apostle Paul we notice his reference to being out of the body. Actually, he didn't know whether he was in the body or out of the body regarding the Vision, etc.

The point is, being unaware or lacking in knowledge regarding the body, did not detract from the experience itself. It proved one thing: namely, a person does not require a *"body"* to be conscious. Paul was conscious in this vision, but he was not conscious of having a body. Of course, he knew he had a body, but we further know that whatever happened to Paul, could have in fact, occurred outside of the body. In other words, what he is describing to us, is a spiritual experience rather than a physical experience. His body may have been transported into Paradise or it may not have been; irrespective, whether in or out of the body, such did not take away from that which he experienced.

A PREVIEW

This experience of Paul's is related for more reasons than merely to refute his opponents. Among other things, it was given as a preview of what happens after the death of Believers, i.e., *"those in Christ."* Death releases us from our body and places us in the Presence of Christ (Phil. 1:21-24). This release is immediate and instantaneous. Consequently, that means there is no punishment in Purgatory, for such does not even exist, nor unconsciousness in the grave, as some teach.

In Ephesians 3:15 Paul refers to *"the whole family in Heaven and Earth."* This family is God's family. It is the family of the twice-born.

You notice this family is either in Heaven or on Earth. It does not say that some of them are sleeping in the grave in unconsciousness. It is true that the bodies of those who have gone on are there (in the grave), but only their bodies. The person, actually the soul and the spirit, of which the person actually is, is in Heaven with Christ awaiting the Resurrection, when at that time a new body will be received (I Cor. 15:51-57).

All those who have died outside of Christ, are now in Hell (Lk. 16:19-31). These eternal souls, which include every person who has ever lived but did not accept Christ, will be released from this place only at the second resurrection of damnation, where they will be judged at the *"Great White Throne Judgment,"* and then cast into the Lake of Fire, where they will remain forever and forever (Rev. Chpt. 20).

PARADISE AND THE THIRD HEAVEN

Some have thought of Paradise as being that which was described by Jesus in Luke Chapter 16, and which is in the heart of the Earth. From Luke 23:43, that description is proper. However, that place is now empty, with Jesus having liberated all of these righteous souls at His Own Personal Resurrection (Eph. 4:8-10).

Righteous souls at death before Calvary, were taken down into Paradise (Lk. Chpt. 16), which Jesus referred to as *"Abraham's Bosom"* (Lk. 16:22). They were in effect held there as captives by Satan, even though he could not get them over into the burning side of Hell, where all unrighteous souls went at death. Before Calvary, Satan had a claim on all, even the Righteous, for the simple reason that the blood of bulls and goats (the Sacrifices), even though covering the sin, could not take it away (Heb. 10:4). However, when Jesus died on Calvary, satisfying the claims of heavenly justice, which paid the terrible sin debt, in effect removing all charges, at least for those who Believe, Satan's claim was ended, and Believers could then be taken to Heaven at death, and as well, Baptized with the Holy Spirit (Jn. 1:29; Acts 1:4-5).

Some have supposed that Paul here, by the word *"Paradise,"* means to describe a different place from that denoted by the phrase *"the third heaven"*; however, that is incorrect. They both mean the same thing. In fact, the word *"Paradise"* has always referred to the abode of the Saints who have passed on irrespective as to when.

NOTES

UNSPEAKABLE WORDS

The phrase, *"And heard unspeakable words,"* in effect, says *"inexpressible words."* In other words, it was not possible for the Apostle to properly put into words that which he saw and experienced regarding this Vision.

The utterances heard in Paradise were uttered there; Paul could otherwise not have heard them; but they were intended only for him and not as a Revelation to be communicated to men in general. For this reason Paul had never revealed this experience.

We may say that what Paul heard was for his personal encouragement, to be kept for himself alone lest it be used in a fanatical way by those who were not satisfied with what the Gospel reveals.

What Paul saw, was designed for the support of Paul himself, especially in view of the very remarkable trials which he was about to endure. God had called him to great toils and self-denials. He was to labor much alone; to go to foreign lands; to be persecuted, and ultimately put to death; consequently, it was the Lord's purpose no doubt, to qualify the Apostle for this work by some peculiar manifestation of His favor.

THE NEW COVENANT

Paul was given the New Covenant, of which many in the Early Church, especially of the Jewish sector, did not accept too readily. This definitely did not include the original Twelve, but it did include many of the Christian Jews.

Knowing that the task would be difficult, the Lord accordingly gave him such views of Heaven that he would be supported in his trials by a conviction of the undoubted Truth of what he taught, and by the prospect of certain glory when his labors should end. It was evidently one instance when God gave peculiar views to prepare for trials, as He often does to His people now, preparing them in a peculiar manner for peculiar trials.

I think it might be proper to say, that Paul underwent more trials, more difficulties, more opposition, more pain and suffering, than possibly any Believer who has ever named the Name of Christ. While it is admitted, that untold thousands gave their lives on the torture racks and elsewhere, it must be remembered that Paul suffered difficulties, from the limited to the extreme, for the entirety of his Ministry, with it finally ending by him being martyred.

JOHN THE BELOVED

On the other hand, John the Beloved was taken into Heaven (in the body or out of the body, we are not told), and was told to put in writing the things he saw, and then convey them to all. It is called *"The Book of Revelation"* (Rev. 1:11).

However, that which he saw, was so astounding, so miraculous, so glorious, so unexplainable, that Scholars have been debating his experience from then until now.

To be frank, most people in the world do not believe the things that John said, and to be frank, most would not have believed Paul either.

The Word of God is all that men need in order to be saved. That's what Abraham told the rich man in Hell, *"They have Moses and the Prophets; let them hear them"* (Lk. 16:29).

NOT LAWFUL?

The phrase, *"Which it is not lawful for a man to utter,"* actually means, *"It is not permitted."* Consequently, while the Apostle will allude to the fact of this experience, he will not say what he saw or heard. We are not told why.

In fact, there is no indication here that he was told by the Lord to keep silent, but rather infers that what he saw was so inexpressible, that any man if privileged to observe the same, would take the same position. Beyond that, we cannot say as to what Paul meant, for the simple reason that he gives no further explanation.

It is the same as when Jesus wrote on the ground, when the young woman was brought to Him taken in the act of adultery (Jn. 8:6). The Holy Spirit did not tell us what He wrote, and neither does He inform us as to what Paul heard and saw. Inasmuch as the Divine Spirit is the actual Author of these Words, we should know that what was done, was best for all.

(5) "OF SUCH AN ONE WILL I GLORY: YET OF MYSELF I WILL NOT GLORY, BUT IN MINE INFIRMITIES."

Notice now how the scene of Paul's experience changed. The next phase of his experience was with pain. The scene of experience changes from Heaven to Earth.

NOTES

So to speak, it was from the clouds to the clods. Paul was made conscious of the reality of his present existence. He might have had his head in the clouds, but he was walking with his feet on the Earth.

It was from the Throne to the thorn. No doubt he would have delighted to continue the Throne experience, but the thorn came lest he *"should be exalted above measure through the abundance of the Revelations."*

It was from praise to pain. Paul had just been speaking of an experience too wonderful for utterance or adequate expression. Now he has descended to suffering which, except for the Grace of God, was too great to bear.

One might say, that there is both the glory-side and the gory-side to our Christian experience. There is the mountaintop and the valley.

OF SUCH AN ONE

The phrase, *"Of such an one will I glory,"* should have been translated, *"Of such a thing will I glory."* This tremendous Vision to which he briefly alludes, was all of the Lord, and none of him, as should be obvious. Paul did not instigate such, had no idea of such until it instantly happened, wherever the place and whatever the time. So, while he could glory in the experience, which he does, it is in the experience only and the One Who gave it, Namely the Lord of Glory, and not himself.

To be frank, every person in the world who knows Christ, and who has been blessed by the Lord in any manner or way, which all of us have, should glory in those Blessings. In fact, as we've already stated, the Lord through Jeremiah said a long time ago:

"Thus saith the Lord, let not the wise man glory in his wisdom, neither let the mighty man glory in his might, let not the rich man glory in his riches:

"But let him that glorieth glory in this, that he understandeth and knoweth Me, that I am the Lord which exercise Lovingkindness, Judgment, and Righteousness, in the Earth: for in these things I delight, saith the Lord" (Jer. 9:23-24).

INFIRMITIES

The phrase, *"Yet of myself I will not glory, but in mine infirmities,"* proclaims that, which I think I can say without any fear of contradiction, is totally opposite of most of the modern-day gospel, which in reality is no gospel at all! *"Infirmities"* speak of weaknesses, trials, pains, sufferings, etc. Actually, those infirmities are listed in the previous Chapter.

This reemphasis concerning weaknesses and infirmities, helps point to the authentic humility of this man of God. Carnal people would never boast about their weaknesses. They obviously would want to amplify their strengths. Actually, this is probably what Paul's rivals were doing.

The modern Church has been inundated since the 1970's with the idea that if one truly had Faith in God, and understands the rudiments of proper confession, then all difficulties such as Paul mentions, can be eliminated. Some of these false teachers among the many thousands who teach this error, have even suggested that if Paul had had their Faith, thereby properly understanding how to confess his way out of such situations, he could have eliminated these dire problems.

To be frank, such piffle, and piffle it is, is hardly worth a response. The Truth is, that this which they propagate is no gospel at all, but rather the ramblings of man. But yet, it gains a wide audience, because it promises a life free of adversity, a life free of sickness, and a life filled with monetary riches. Consequently, those are heady promises, and pretty much attract a wide following wherever they are propagated.

In fact, there is some Truth in this error, which of course, serves as bait. The Lord does bless people abundantly so and in every capacity; however, He has not promised a life free of adversity, but as we soon shall see, He has promised His Grace regarding these things.

MISPLACED FAITH

What makes this which Paul called *"another gospel,"* so dangerous is, that Faith is such a powerful force, and one might even say such a powerful commodity, that if a Believer sets his sights on the things we have mentioned, which admittedly are very, very attractive, if he truly has Faith, these things can be brought about. Consequently, that makes it seem even more right. Let me explain:

ISRAEL

Israel in the wilderness and after becoming a nation, demanded some things of the Lord which were not in their best interest, and were not His Will, or else were premature in their demands. The Scripture plainly says, *"And He gave them their requests; but sent leanness into their soul"* (Ps. 106:15).

NOTES

The idea is, that if one wants to pervert their Faith that God has given them, making money, riches, things, etc., priority, they can in fact have these things, but such will fall out to their spiritual detriment. And that's where a great part of the modern Church is at present.

The Holy Spirit is treated like an errand boy, or a bellhop, or One Who brings room service, etc.; however, the Holy Spirit Who is God, is not in our hearts and lives to bring about our will, but rather the Will of God (Rom. 8:27).

The right way in which the Lord works all of this is, that we are to *"Seek first the Kingdom of God, and His Righteousness; and all these things shall be added unto you"* (Mat. 6:33).

The idea is, that we seek Holiness and Righteousness, which in effect means to make Jesus real within our hearts and lives, in other words *"All in all,"* and then these things, or that which the Lord wants us to have, will automatically come. The Lord wants to bless His people. In fact, He is a Blesser, and He blesses abundantly; however, these things are to be a result of our closeness to the Lord, instead of the primary objective. Jesus is always to be the end of our Faith and not things (Heb. 12:2).

WHY WOULD PAUL GLORY IN INFIRMITIES?

The questions of the inevitability and purpose of suffering in the life of Christians in general, and in the life of Paul as an Apostle in particular, are recurring themes of great significance throughout Paul's Epistles. In addition to the issues of death, his own imprisonment, and other specific instances of hardship and persecution, Paul speaks of affliction and suffering per se over 60 times. However, his most sustained treatment of the subject occurs in II Corinthians, the Epistle of our study, where he defends his Apostleship against those who maintained that his suffering called into question the legitimacy of his Apostleship (II Cor. 1:3-11; 2:14-17; 4:7-12; 6:3-10; 10:13).

NOTES

PAUL'S SUFFERING AS AN APOSTLE

According to Acts 9:15-16, Paul's Call was inextricably linked to the fact that he would suffer greatly *"for the sake of* (the Lord's) *Name."* The reality of this is attested throughout the Book of Acts and reflected in everyone of Paul's Letters.

Hence, rather than questioning the legitimacy of his Apostleship because of his suffering, Paul considered suffering to be a characteristic mark of his Apostolic Ministry (I Cor. 2:1-5; II Cor. 11:23-29; Gal. 6:17; Phil. 1:30; II Tim. 1:11-12; 2:9; etc.), and an aspect of his own mortal life concerning which he was content, in which he rejoiced and about which he could appropriately *"boast"* (II Cor. 11:30; 12:10; Phil. 1:19-26).

THE REASONS

Paul's reason for this evaluation of suffering, however, was not experiential but spiritual. Paul understood that as an essential part of his Calling to be an Apostle, God Himself was continually leading him into situations of suffering, like one sentenced to death in the Roman Arena or led to death in the Roman Triumphal Procession (I Cor. 4:9; II Cor. 1:9; 2:14; 4:11; II Tim. 1:11-12).

God's purpose in doing so was to reveal His Divine Power and to demonstrate the reality of the Cross and Resurrection of Christ in and through Paul's life (I Cor. 2:1-5; II Cor. 2:14; 4:11), while at the same time making it clear that the age to come had not yet arrived in all its fullness, which will do away at that time with all suffering (I Cor. 4:8-13).

Paul could thus interpret his suffering in terms of the Cross of Christ, while his ability to endure it or God's action of deliverance from it, were an expression of the same Divine Power revealed in Christ's Resurrection (I Cor. 4:8-13; II Cor. 1:3-10; 4:7-12; 6:4-10; Phil. 3:10-11; II Tim. 3:10-11).

The Wisdom and Power of God first made known through the Cross and Resurrection of Christ were, therefore, now being further manifested and revealed publicly through Paul's own suffering as an Apostle. In Galatians 3:1 Paul is thus referring to his own suffering as an embodiment of the Gospel and as the vehicle for displaying the Truth of the Cross when he reminds the Galatians that Jesus Christ was publicly portrayed as crucified before their very eyes.

THE CROSS?

Viewed from this same perspective, Paul's statement in Colossians 1:24 that his suffering *"completes what is lacking in Christ's afflictions"* does *not* refer to the concept of a certain amount of *"Messianic suffering"* or *"woes of the Messiah"* that must be fulfilled before the age can be consummated, as commonly interpreted (Dan. 12:1; Mat. 24:8; Mk. 13:8).

Nor does Paul view his suffering as having an atoning significance in II Corinthians 4:7-12. For Paul, Christ's suffering stands alone as unique and totally sufficient (Rom. 3:21-26; I Cor. 1:18-31; II Cor. 5:16-21; Gal. 1:4; Col. 2:13-14).

Rather, Paul completes what is *"lacking"* in Christ's afflictions on behalf of the Church in the sense that his Ministry *extends* the knowledge and reality of the Cross of Christ and the Power of the Holy Spirit to the Gentile world (Eph. 3:13; Col. 1:23).

Paul's suffering also functioned to make it clear, therefore, that the Power and Knowledge of the Gospel was God's and not his own, so that those who encountered Paul, or anyone like Paul, would place their Faith in the Power of God and not in the person of the Apostle (I Cor. 2:1-5; II Cor. 4:7; 12:9-10).

Whatever Paul's much debated *"thorn in the flesh"* actually was, it too functioned in this way by keeping him from boasting in the abundance of the Revelations that he had received, in other words, so that he would not be exalted above measure (II Cor. 12:7).

THE SUFFERING OF BELIEVERS

The fact that others not only accepted Paul as a genuine Apostle despite his sufferings, but were also willing to imitate him by joyfully continuing in Faith, Hope, and Love in the midst of their own afflictions, became a sign for Paul of the legitimacy of their standing in Christ, even as it was a sign of his own legitimacy as an Apostle (Gal. 4:12-15; Phil. 1:3-7; 4:14-15; I Thess. 1:6; 3:1-5; II Tim. 1:8).

In addition, Paul's willingness to suffer on behalf of the Churches also provided a model of Christian Love, so that Paul could call the Churches to follow his example of giving up their rights for others, even when this meant undue suffering and hardship (I Cor. 4:8-13; 6:7; 9:1-27; Chpts. 12-14).

Yet unlike the martyrdom theology of the later centuries, Paul stopped short of teaching that all Believers are called to suffer in the same way that he did as an Apostle. Rather, Paul recognizes that all Christians simply will suffer as a result of identifying themselves with Christ (Rom. 8:17; Phil. 1:29-30; II Tim. 3:12) and, to varying degrees, as a result of their distinct circumstances, since such suffering is inevitable in this evil age (I Cor. 7:28; 12:26; I Tim. 5:23).

THE REACTION OF CHRISTIANS TO SUFFERING

Nevertheless, for Paul, whenever Christians do suffer, they too must meet their suffering with joy, knowing that their affliction is not senseless but becomes the Divinely-orchestrated means by which God strengthens their faithful endurance and hope by pouring out His Own Love and Spirit to sustain or deliver them in their distress (Rom. 5:3-5; 8:12-39; II Cor. 1:6).

As a result, they too come to embody the Cross and Resurrection in their lives as a witness to others of the Truth of Christ, especially as this is seen in their ability to love others even when they are experiencing affliction (II Cor. 8:1-2; I Thess. 1:2-7; II Thess. 1:3-5).

Paul can, therefore, encourage his readers to be patient and to endure in the midst of adversity, which is the outworking of their Faith (Rom. 12:12; II Tim. 4:5), since He knows that only those who suffer with Christ in the endurance of Faith will also be Glorified with Christ (Rom. 8:17).

Finally, then, because of the Faith and Love made real in their lives through suffering, all Believers will join Paul in experiencing not only the Power of God made known in the Cross of Christ as God sustains them in the midst of their adversities, but also the Resurrection Power of God as He uses their suffering as the pathway to sharing in Christ's Glory (Rom. 8:35; II Cor. 4:14; II Thess. 1:7). It is this hope which keeps one persevering in Faith (Rom. 4:18-25; 8:18-25; I Cor. 15:20-34, 58; II Cor. 4:16-18).

As for those who do not share Christ's suffering by identifying with Him, but who persecute those who do, they will experience suffering on the Day of Judgment, to be sure (Rom. 2:9; II Thess. 1:6-10).

NOTES

THE MANNER OF SUFFERING

The Believer is living in a hostile environment. In other words, Satan is the god of this present world, and has been since the Fall (II Cor. 4:4). As such, he is not in sympathy, and neither are his children, with those who serve God.

As an example, I have personally suffered the efforts of certain segments of the News Media to destroy this Ministry, and me personally as well. I have had them to pointedly tell me such, and then use all their vast resources to attempt to bring it to pass. Those of that stripe have no regard for the Truth, but seek only to twist and pervert it to their own satisfaction. They are of their father the Devil, and the lusts of their father they will do (Jn. 8:44).

As it regards opposition and persecution from within one's own ranks, to be frank, this has always been the greatest source of opposition. For instance, when I preach against the *"Psychological Way,"* considering that most of the Leadership and Preachers of the major Pentecostal Denominations have accepted this Satanic way, they are not too happy with my Message, and will do anything they can to hinder that Message.

Whenever we speak of the *"Prosperity Gospel,"* which we feel according to the Scripture is error, those who accept that way, as well, are not too happy with such a Message or the Messenger. The same can be said for the *"Political Message"* and the bringing of Hollywood into the Church, etc.

The proponents of these particular belief systems, which in fact, make up the far greater majority of the modern Church, will greatly oppose anyone who addresses these things, as should be obvious. To be frank, and I do know what I am talking about, were it not for the Law of the Land, some would inflict the same type of punishment that Paul experienced, beatings, etc., even to silencing one by murder. I realize that most of the Laity of the Church do not understand such a thing, but please believe me, it is true.

SATAN AND PARAMETERS

Of course the author of all of this is Satan. But he uses as instruments those of whom we have mentioned.

It was the same in Paul's day, and from the same sources. The Devil hasn't changed, and neither has he gotten saved.

However, let no one think that Satan draws the boundaries and neither do those who follow him. The Lord draws these boundaries. He allows what He deems is necessary as it regards our Sanctification. Satan cannot go beyond the parameters drawn off by the Lord (Job Chpts. 1-2).

So, Paul did not so much glory in the *"infirmities,"* as he did in what they produced.

It is not that we desire these things, as it was not that Paul desired them. Actually, and we shall see, he asked the Lord for relief. So, we should do all within our power to avoid difficulties and problems as should be obvious; nevertheless, irrespective of how much Faith we have, or how close to the Lord we are, the Lord is going to allow certain things. For those He allows, the intention by the Holy Spirit is that we learn the lesson which these things teach. That lesson is the crucifixion of self, a ceasing of dependence on the flesh, and a total dependence on the Lord for leading, guidance, and direction. In fact, the Lord wants us to look to Him for everything.

Unfortunately, the self-will and pride factor, loom so large over the Believer, that it takes the *"infirmities"* to properly bring us to where we ought to be in Christ. It is not that the *"infirmities"* within themselves contain any saving grace or sanctifying power, for they don't. The idea is, that we realize how weak we actually are, which these *"infirmities"* bring out, thereby looking entirely to the Lord for all things.

As well, I wish it could be said that there is a place of graduation, to where *"infirmities"* are no longer necessary; regrettably, I think the balance of this Chapter tells us that such is not to be.

A BEAUTIFUL EXAMPLE

Jesus exemplified this in a beautiful way by the miraculous feeding of the thousands with five loaves and two fish. The following is the order in which this was done (Mat. Chpt. 14; Mk. Chpt. 6; Lk. Chpt. 9; Jn. Chpt. 6):

1. He took the five loaves: This pertains to the believing sinner coming to Christ and being saved by Faith. The Lord thankfully and wondrously (takes us).

NOTES

2. He blessed: Immediately after the person comes to Christ, at least with almost all, great Blessings follow. These Blessings cover almost every angle, be it domestic, physical, spiritual, and financial.

3. And break: After He blessed the bread, He then *"broke the bread."* This is the process of which Paul speaks, and is very painful. As well, it is a process that every Believer must go through, and as stated, continues to go through, if one is to be a blessing to lost humanity.

As someone has said, if we do not bleed we cannot bless.

4. And gave the loaves: We can only be given to a hurting world, if we have first been broken. Our problem is, we try to touch the world through the process of *"Blessing."* In other words, after He *"takes us,"* and then *"blesses us,"* we think surely, that we now have the answers to hurting humanity. Come to Jesus and be blessed, etc. However, that is not God's Way. And yet, this is the mode in which the modern Church mostly finds itself at present.

While it is true that we can get a lot of people who come for the Blessing, still, we find that they receive little if anything for their souls.

The *"broken way"* doesn't seem to be too appetizing; it doesn't seem to be a way that one would want; nevertheless, what gets people to the Lord is not our machinations, or talent, or ability, nor even the dangling of the carrot of *"Blessings"* before their eyes, but rather Christ. In other words, if we present only Blessings, which the modern Church is mostly doing, it is the wrong lure. While many may come, they are coming for the Blessings and not for the Giver of the Blessings, the Lord Jesus Christ.

Before one can receive that for which the heart craves, one must receive Christ. He Alone, and not Blessings, can satisfy the thirst of the soul. And, we can only properly present Christ, when we are broken, which as stated, is always a painful process and a continuing process (Mat. 14:19). Then the world will see Christ and not us.

If Jesus is properly presented, which must be done with a broken life, then *"they will all eat, and be filled"* (Mat. 14:20), and beside that, there will be plenty left over. In other words, it is impossible to exhaust Christ, while the Blessings can be exhausted quickly.

(6) "FOR THOUGH I WOULD DESIRE TO GLORY, I SHALL NOT BE A FOOL; FOR I

WILL SAY THE TRUTH: BUT NOW I FORBEAR, LEST ANY MAN SHOULD THINK OF ME ABOVE THAT WHICH HE SEETH ME TO BE, OR THAT HE HEARETH OF ME."

Many of us cling to the notion that life ought to be made to suit us. We feel that if adversity befalls us then unnatural evil has overtaken us. We may even think of life as an easy road for carefree wanderers of pleasure.

We must awaken to the fact that life is a struggle and its greatest victories arise out of that fact.

We must all continually remember that *"There hath no temptation taken you but such as is common to man."* It is also written that we are to *"Think it not strange concerning the fiery trial which is to try you, as though some strange thing happened unto you: but rejoice, inasmuch as ye are partakers of Christ's sufferings; that, when His Glory shall be revealed, ye may be glad also with exceeding joy"* (I Pet. 4:12-13).

To what purpose and what cause then shall we attribute these experiences of pain? There is a purpose in their cause and a blessing to be found in their effect (Laurin).

I SHALL NOT BE A FOOL

The phrase, *"For though I would desire to glory, I shall not be a fool,"* refers to the fact that all is done, whatever it is, before the Lord, i.e., *"in the Face of the Lord."* The idea is, that if we forget that, we are foolish indeed!

Boasting is done for the purpose of impressing other people. Consequently, most of the time it is filled with lies. Paul is saying, *"I would be a fool to do such, knowing that the Lord, Whom I serve, knows any and all things."*

Paul could not care less about impressing other people. He only engaged in this folly (II Cor. 11:1), as he referred to it, for the sake of the Believers in the Church at Corinth.

It is unfortunate, that some Christians seem to need such. This only shows one's immaturity. It's like a baby when given the choice of a one hundred dollar bill or a little toy rattle, will without fail take the toy. So, Paul hands them a *"toy!"*

THE TRUTH

The phrase, *"For I will say the Truth,"* at the same time, says these others are not telling the Truth.

NOTES

As we have stated, boasting almost always drifts into a *"lie."* In other words, the boasts become larger and larger, which in fact, is the spirit of such an attitude which glorifies the boaster. So, the Holy Spirit through Paul, chose two things of which to boast, of which no one would boast, at least if they are thinking straight.

Who would boast about *"infirmities"*? As well, who would hint at a Glorious Vision of Heaven, and then not give any details?

So, we can see that these things which the Holy Spirit allowed the Apostle to do, not at all glorified him, but in fact, did the very opposite. What he said did glorify the Grace of God, and as we shall see, that is the intended purpose.

I FORBEAR

The phrase, *"But now I forbear, lest any man should think of me above that which he seeth me to be, or that he heareth of me,"* in effect says, *"I will not relate more about this Vision, and for the obvious reasons."* He wanted the eyes of all Believers on Christ, and to remain on Christ, and not at any time upon him.

Regretfully, most Believers have a tendency to follow men to the extreme. In other words, once they settle upon a person (whether right or wrong) as being a man or woman of God, far too often, they then lift that person to rarified spiritual heights, in a sense, making a demigod out of the individual. However, if that individual disappoints them in any way, they will be just as quick to destroy him. So, the Holy Spirit has Paul to boast about his *"infirmities."*

Consequently, very few people would want that as an example. Very few would see any glory in that. So, the eyes of Believers will not be fastened onto Paul, but rather the Christ of Glory, which is the intention of the Holy Spirit, and for all the right reasons.

It is somewhat ironical. Many, if not most, Preachers are trying to find a way to get people to idolize them, while Paul was doing the very opposite. *"God's man of faith and power,"* is too often the advertisement, while Paul said, *"In labours more abundant, in stripes above measure, in prisons more frequent, in deaths oft"* (II Cor. 11:23).

What a difference!

(7) "AND LEST I SHOULD BE EXALTED ABOVE MEASURE THROUGH THE ABUNDANCE OF THE REVELATIONS, THERE

WAS GIVEN TO ME A THORN IN THE FLESH, THE MESSENGER OF SATAN TO BUFFET ME, LEST I SHOULD BE EXALTED ABOVE MEASURE."

Even though Paul was mightily used of God, he was still an earthen vessel, and nothing can amend the carnal nature — not even a rapture into Paradise. So to save him from falling he was impaled upon a stake.

The Holy Spirit has, I think, revealed what that stake was (II Cor. 11:23-27), but what is most necessary to learn is its moral purpose in saving the Apostle from destruction. To be in Paradise, in or out of the body, can minister to pride, and can be a subject of carnal boasting.

Paul could have been exalted in his own eyes, and could have boasted of the fact that he alone had had such an experience. And had he been taken up into even a deeper experience, that would only have increased the danger of a deeper fall. The presence of God Alone can silence the carnal nature. So soon as that presence is removed nature boasts of the experience enjoyed.

Therefore, corrupt nature must be bridled; and such was the ministry of the stake in the Apostle's flesh. He says it was *"given to him"* — given by God although it was *"a messenger of Satan."*

DIVINE INSTRUMENTS

Prevention and humiliation are both Divine instruments. Paul was saved from failing by prevention; Peter was permitted to fail in order to experience humiliation. There was no difference between them; they were both indwelt by a corrupt nature incapable of amendment, irrespective of man's efforts to the contrary. This is one of the most bitter and humbling lessons for the human heart.

It is painful but salutary for the Christian to have an experimental sense of the principle of evil which indwells him. But a Greater Power also inhabits the temple of his body, and its victorious warfare is a profitable exercise for the heart.

If the Apostle Paul needed so humbling and painful an experience of what the carnal nature is, it is evident that all Christians need it; and it is plain that whatever weakens, belittles, and humiliates that proud and willful nature should be regarded by the Believer as most worthful.

NOTES

CHRIST ALONE

The distinction between the sinless nature of Christ and the sinful nature of Paul is seen in that Christ needed no stake in His Flesh on descending from the Mount of Transfiguration. Facing Satan at the foot of the Mount He was the same Person Who shone in the Glory of God on the top of the Mount. The scenes were different, but He was alike perfect in both.

All was evenness in Him — the fine flour of the Meal-Offering. On such chords as Paul the Divine Hand can awaken exquisite music; but Christ is all the music itself.

(I am indebted to George Williams for the above thoughts regarding Paul's thorn in the flesh.)

EXALTATION

The phrase, *"And lest I should be exalted above measure,"* presents the reason for the *"thorn in the flesh."*

"Exalted" in the Greek is *"huperiaromai,"* and means *"to raise oneself over, to become haughty, to exalt self."*

It is used only here and of the Antichrist exalting himself above all that is called God (II Thess. 2:4). Actually, this is what caused Lucifer to fall (Isa. 14:12-14; Ezek. 28:11-17; I Tim. 3:6). So, we see here how absolutely dangerous this spirit is.

The idea is, if Paul was in danger of spiritual pride, who is not? If it was necessary for God to adopt some special measures to keep him humble, which He did, we are not to be surprised that the same thing should occur in other cases as well. There is no sin that is more subtle, insinuating, deceptive; none that lurks more constantly around the heart, and that finds a more ready entrance, than pride. He who has been characterized by pride before his conversion, even as was Paul, will be in special danger of it afterwards; he who has eminent gifts in prayer, or in conversation, or in preaching, will be in special danger of it; he who is eminently successful in any capacity will be in danger of it; and he who has any extraordinary spiritual comforts will be in danger of it as well.

Again, and strangely enough, of this sin he who lives nearest to God may be in most special danger.

If Satan cannot drag us into worldliness, he will attempt to take advantage of our consecration, and drag us into the terrible sin of pride. He succeeds much of the time! Consequently, if men wish to keep themselves from the danger of this sin, they should not be forward to speak even of the most favored moments of their communion with God.

PRIDE

The emphasis placed on pride, and its opposite which is humility, is a distinctive feature of Biblical Salvation, actually unparalleled in other religious or ethical systems. Rebellious pride, which refuses to depend on God and be subject to Him, but attributes to self the honor due to Him, figures as the very root and essence of sin.

We may say that pride was first revealed when Lucifer attempted to set his throne on high in proud independence of God (Isa. 14:12-14). This fallen angel (Lk. 10:18) instilled the craving to be as gods into Adam and Eve (Gen. 3:5), with the result that man's entire nature was infected with pride through the Fall (Rom. 1:21-23).

In fact, the *"condemnation of the Devil"* is associated with pride in I Timothy 3:6, *"The snare of the Devil"* in I Timothy 3:7; II Timothy 2:26; pride was his undoing and remains the prime means by which he brings about the undoing of men and women. Hence, we find a sustained condemnation of human arrogance throughout the Old Testament, especially in the Psalms and the Wisdom Books.

In Proverbs 8:13 both *"arrogance,"* and *"insolence,"* are hateful to the Divine Wisdom: their manifestation in the form of national pride in Moab (Isa. 16:6), Judah (Jer. 13:9), and Israel (Hos. 5:5) are especially denounced by the Prophets.

ITS MEANING

The notorious *"pride which goes before a fall"* is called *"swelling excellence,"* in Proverbs 16:18, and is rejected in favor of the *"lowly spirit"* (Mat. 11:28-30).

"Haughtiness," appears as a root cause of atheism in Psalms 10:4. It is the downfall of Nebuchadnezzar in Daniel 4:30, 37.

A milder word, *"presumption,"* is applied to David's youthful enthusiasm in I Samuel 17:28, but in Obadiah Verse 3 even this is regarded as a deceitful evil. Further warnings against pride occur in the later Wisdom Literature (Eccl. 10:6-26).

NOTES

THE GREEKS

Greek teaching during the four last centuries B.C. was at variance with Judaism in regarding pride as a virtue and humility as despicable. Aristotle's *"great-souled man"* had a profound regard for his own excellence; to underestimate it would have stamped him as meanspirited. Similarly, the Stoic sage asserted his own moral independence and equality with Zeus.

Insolence, however, is a deep source of moral evil in the Greek tragedy.

CHRISTIANITY

The Christian ethic consciously rejected Greek thought, and because the Word of God in the Old Testament was contrary to that thinking. Humility was accorded supreme excellence when Christ pronounced Himself *"gentle and lowly in heart"* (Mat. 11:29).

Conversely, pride was placed on a list of defiling vices proceeding from the evil heart of man (Mk. 7:22). In the words of Mary, the Mother of our Lord (Lk. 1:51) God is said to scatter the proud and exalt the meek. In both James 4:6 and I Peter 5:5, Proverbs 3:34 is quoted to emphasize the contrast between the meek whom God favors; and the proud, whom God resists. Paul couples the insolent and the boastful with the proud sinners in his sketch of depraved pagan society in Romans 1:30; and II Timothy 3:2.

Arrogant display or ostentation are disparaged in James 4:16 and I John 2:16. Love, in I Corinthians 13:4, is stated to be free from both the arrogance and the self-conceit which mar the heretical teachers of I Timothy 6:4.

PAUL

Paul saw pride (boasting in knowledge of the Law and in works/righteousness) as the characteristic spirit of Judaism, which incidentally had been so diluted by man's additions that it was little more now than an ethic, as a direct cause of Jewish unbelief. He insisted that the Gospel is designed to exclude boasting (Rom. 3:27) by teaching men that they are sinners, that self-righteousness is, therefore, out of the question, and that they must look to Christ for their Righteousness and take it as a free gift by Faith in Him.

Salvation is *"not because of works, lest any man should boast"*; it is all of Grace. No man, therefore, not even Abraham, may glory in the achievement of his own Salvation (Rom. 4:1-2; I Cor. 1:26-31; Eph. 2:9).

The Gospel Message of Righteousness through Christ sounds the death knell of self-righteousness in religion; that is why it was a stumbling-block to the proud Jews (Rom. 9:30-10:4).

(Bibliography: Arndt; Niebuhr, *"The Nature and Destiny of Man,"* Guting, C. Brown, G. Bertram.)

LACK OF FAITH OR ACTUALLY PRIDE?

We attribute most of our difficulties and adversities to unbelief as if lack of Faith were the cause of these things. More often the cause is stubbornness, which is a by-product of pride.

There is a spiritual stubbornness in which people refuse to yield their tenacious desires. They insist that certain prayers be answered. They insist on their desires being granted, and on their plans being completed. Stubbornness of this kind is always fatal to a happy, contented, and consistent Christian experience.

As we traverse the path of Paul's experience and go with him down into the valley of suffering, we do not look at Paul the great Apostle, or Paul the Christian warrior, or Paul the great man of Faith, or Paul the man of answered prayer. We rather see Paul the thorn-bearer and Paul the sufferer. In fact, by comparison with today's modern gospel, it seems very significant that suffering of a permanent character should seize such a man as Paul. He was God's chosen Apostle and if anyone deserved by right of merit and by reason of usefulness to be free from suffering, certainly Paul did. He was a man of Prayer and a man of Faith. Yet, with all these recommendations and all his ability and usefulness, Paul was a man of humility and suffering.

OPPOSITION

To begin with, we must remember that Paul was a much-maligned man. He had many enemies both inside and outside the Church. There were false teachers who were denying the Divine Apostleship of Paul. Perhaps one of the things cited to prove this was Paul's thorn.

They probably pointed the finger of scorn and said of Paul that if he were actually an Apostle sent from God, then God would remove the thorn.

However, that projected by the false apostles was not the Gospel then, and it is not the Gospel now. So, the modern Believer can settle *only* for what Christ can do, which will bring only leanness to the soul, or for Who Christ is, which will definitely bring difficulties and problems, but also will fill the aching void of the soul.

The idea of the phrase, *"And lest I should be exalted above measure,"* pertains to the fact that the Visions and Revelations within themselves were exaltation enough, with the individual, in this case Paul, not due any further exaltation. In fact, that is true in all cases such as this, irrespective as to whom the person may be.

As well, the Greek text concerning this phrase contains two notable facts:

1. This danger was something that existed continuously.
2. As well, it spoke of Paul personally.

REVELATIONS

The phrase, *"Through the abundance of the Revelations,"* indicates not only the incident spoken of when he was *"caught up to the third Heaven,"* but implies other Revelations thereafter and given in whatever capacity, seemingly in abundance.

"Abundance" in the Greek is *"huperbole,"* and means *"a throwing beyond others, super-eminence, far more exceeding, out of measure."* Paul as well was probably speaking of the New Covenant given to him, *"By the Revelation of Jesus Christ"* (Gal. 1:12).

The Apostle received an abundance of these Revelations, while most Preachers have received none at all. In fact, and regrettably so, I think I can say without fear of exaggeration, that most Preachers do not even believe that the Lord does such at this time. However, to be sure, He continues to speak to earnest, seeking hearts presently, just as much as He did in the past.

Concerning my own unworthy Ministry, the Lord, I believe, has related things to me which I do not feel free to share with others. In the first place, I doubt I would be believed, and in the second place, it would serve no purpose to relate that of which I speak.

Revelations consist of two things on the part of the Believer:

NOTES

First of all, the degree of Revelations would pertain to the particular Call of the person in question. Second, it would have to do with one's consecration and prayer life.

A THORN IN THE FLESH

The phrase, *"There was given to me a thorn in the flesh,"* would have to be looked at as a *"gift."* This means that even God's afflictions are meant for Gifts.

There is no problem identifying the meaning of the word *"thorn."* In the Greek, it is *"skolops,"* and means *"a splinter, stake, or thorn."* The problem comes from trying to pinpoint the word *"flesh."* Some people take it to mean the physical body of Paul. They conjecture all kinds of physical infirmities that God supposedly gave him to keep him humble.

Some, for example, use Galatians 4:13-15 as evidence that he labored with poor eyesight. Others claim he contracted malaria, and still others suggest migraine headaches, epilepsy, insomnia, etc.

While any of the above may have been possible, there is one fact that especially militates against the thorn being a physical malady.

The general impression from Acts and Paul's Epistles, especially II Corinthians, is that he was a remarkably strong physical specimen. How else could he have endured all that he faced? Consequently, it seems more plausible to consider the thorn spiritual in nature and to use the word *"flesh"* the way Paul himself normally used it — to refer to the fallen Adamic nature (Rossier).

WHAT THE HOLY SPIRIT IS TEACHING

I think the Holy Spirit did relate to us what this *"thorn in the flesh"* actually was. It was all the difficulties of II Corinthians 11:23-27.

However, if Paul had told us exactly what it was beyond doubt, then we would think that only that particular type of difficulty would constitute the proverbial *"thorn."* So, the Holy Spirit wanted us to understand that this *"thorn"* can take many directions.

The idea is that there was something which kept him humble. That was the intention of what God allowed, and that's exactly what happened.

The Holy Spirit is not desiring that we spend all our time and attention dissecting the *"thorn."* That is not the idea of the statement. His intention is that we understand the *reason* for the thorn. That is the lesson He is teaching.

NOTES

ON A PERSONAL BASIS

I know what it is to be adored by much of the world. I know what it is to be able to pick up the phone and speak to almost any world leader. I know what it is to have some of the largest crowds in history come to our meetings. Airing our Telecast in many countries of the world, and having one of, if not the largest, audience in any given country, at times even larger than the secular programs, constitutes tremendous power.

I also know what it is, proverbially speaking, to be stripped naked in public, and to be made the laughing stock of the world. I know what it is for humiliation to be so deep and so awful that death would be sweet. I know what it is to have almost every friend turn against you, and with almost all the Church world demanding that your Ministry cease.

The pain is all the worse, when you love the Lord with all of your heart, and are doing everything within your power to walk as close to Him as you know how, and despite all of that, failing anyway — but not knowing why! To be called a *"hypocrite,"* a *"scoundrel,"* an *"impostor,"* an *"insincere scam artist,"* etc., hurts so much, that there is no way that it could properly be defined.

And yet, looking back from this present time (October, 1998), I can say that the first position described, the one of fame, power, etc., is far more pleasurable to the flesh, but greatly harmful to the spirit. The second position, although greatly hurtful to the flesh, believe it or not, is greatly invigorating to the spirit.

As I have already stated, prevention and humiliation are both Divine instruments. Paul was saved from failing by prevention; Peter was permitted to fail in order to cause humiliation. There was no difference between them. This is one of the most bitter and humbling lessons for the human heart. And again, allow me to repeat myself.

If the Apostle Paul needed so humbling and painful an experience of what the carnal nature is, it is evident that all Christians need it; and it is plain that whatever weakens and belittles and humiliates that proud and wilful nature should be regarded by the Believer as most worthful.

No, the Lord receives no glory out of spiritual failure of any nature, but He does receive great glory out of victory over that failure or sin in any capacity.

Living for the Lord, and living for Him with all that is within me, and having the Holy Spirit to accomplish His Divine task within my heart and life, means more to me than anything in the world. Whatever it takes, and I mean that with all of my heart, that's what I want, if it will draw me closer to God. To know Him, to love Him, to be in the perfect center of His Will, is the greatest Blessing, the most wonderful fulfillment, the most ultimate Divine reality, which one could ever know. As Peter said, *"we rejoice with joy unspeakable and full of glory"* (I Pet. 1:8).

MESSENGER OF SATAN

The phrase, *"The Messenger of Satan,"* actually means *"an angel of Satan."* The Greek word *"Aggelos"* is translated *"Angel"* 179 times and *"Messenger"* seven times. It is never translated disease or physical infirmity, and never means any such thing.

An angel of Satan is one of the spirit beings which fell with him, and who the Lord allowed to follow Paul and buffet him, when he was tempted to become exalted. Paul lists in II Corinthians 11:23-27 some of the things that this angel caused him to go through, and there is not a disease in the whole list.

So, at least some of the things the *"thorn"* may have been are listed in II Corinthians 11:23-27, plus maybe some things not listed.

The idea is that Paul knew that this messenger of Satan would not be allowed this latitude if God had not desired such. Consequently, all the troubles, difficulties, and problems that Paul faced constantly, which were so humiliating and hurtful to the flesh, could have been stopped by the Lord with one word.

As an example, when Paul and Silas went to Philippi, which was the direct result of the Macedonian Call (Acts 16:9), they little expected what greeted them.

To make the story brief, Paul delivered a girl from Demon possession (Acts 16:16-19), which resulted in them being beaten almost to death (Acts 16:22-24).

NOTES

The Scripture says they were thrust *"into the inner prison, and their feet made fast in the stocks."*

It also says that the Lord at midnight sent a *"great earthquake,"* so that the *"foundations of the prison were shaken: and immediately all the doors were opened, and everyone's bands were loosed"* (Acts 16:25-26).

This resulted in the Jailer being saved, and as well the entirety of his household. However, the question remains as to why the Lord did not intervene and stop the beating which both Apostles experienced? A few hours later, the Lord sent an earthquake, so intervening previously would have been no difficulty whatsoever for Him.

But yet He did not do so. He allowed Paul and Silas to undergo that tremendous torture.

Now some may think the Lord cruel for allowing such, especially considering that He has the power to do anything desired. The following only deepens the mystery.

BUFFET ME

The phrase, *"To buffet me,"* actually means *"to smite with the hand"; "to maltreat in any way."* The meaning is that the effect and design of this was deeply to afflict him.

The general truth taught in this Verse is that God will take care that His people shall not be unduly exalted by the manifestations of His favor, and by the spiritual privileges which He bestows on them. He will take measures to humble them; and a large part of His dealings with us are designed to accomplish this.

Sometimes it will be done, as in the case of Paul, by constant problems, at other times by bodily infirmity, sometimes by great poverty, and sometimes by reducing us from a state of affluence, where we were in a danger of being exalted above measure. Sometimes He does so by suffering us to be slandered and calumniated, by suffering foes to rise up against us who seek to blacken our character, and in such a manner that we cannot defend ourselves. At other times, it is by other types of persecution, and sometimes by want of success in our enterprises. He can even allow us, and sometimes does, by suffering us to fall into sin, and thus greatly humbling us before the world.

As we have already stated, such was the case with David and with Peter; and God often permits us to see in this manner our own weakness, and to bring us to a sense of dependence and proper humility, by suffering us to perform some act that should be ever afterward *"a standing source"* of our humiliation; some act so base, so humiliating, so evincing that deep depravity of our hearts, as forever to make and keep us humble.

How could David be lifted up with pride after the murder of Uriah? How could Peter, after having denied his Lord with a horrid oath?

Thus, many a Christian is suffered to fall by the temptation of Satan, to show him his weakness and to keep him from pride; consequently, many a fall is made the occasion of the permanent benefit of the offender.

The idea is that we should be thankful for any calamity that will humble us; and we should remember that clear and elevated views of God and Heaven are, after all, more than a compensation for all the sufferings which it may be necessary to endure in order to make us humble (Barnes).

Yes, the Lord could have easily stopped the lictor's lash from hitting the backs of Paul and Silas, but He chose not to do so, and even though it hurt, it was for the good of the great Apostle and his associate.

HOW DOES SUCH AFFECT GOD?

Do we think that such does not hurt the heart of God? Do we think that He takes delight in allowing such, and to put it another way, to be forced to allow such? Did He take to Himself any pleasure in seeing the backs of the Apostles cut to ribbons? Or whatever it is that has happened to me and you?

Having studied the Word of God for over half a century, I know in my heart that such action which the Lord is forced to take for our benefit, hurts Him far more than it does us. He is, after all, our Heavenly Father. He loves us with an undying love, a love in fact which is so great, that He gave His Only Begotten Son Who died on Calvary, in order that we might be saved.

Knowing how awful and terrible that the sin nature actually is, what a terrible hold that sin can have on even the strongest of God's children, that even great Apostles such as Paul are not exempt, strong measures are needed and taken for the simple reason that there is no other way.

NOTES

ABOVE MEASURE

The phrase, *"Lest I should be exalted above measure,"* presents Paul concluding this sentence as it began. The Holy Spirit had him do this for purpose and reason.

This is the problem, this pride factor, this self-exaltation, this self-righteousness, this personal piety, this lack of humility! As well, this problem of the flesh, this clinging leech, this problem which is so often covered with Scriptures and made to seem so pious at times, is in reality the deadliest sin of all. It is so deadly, so powerful, that even the most choice of God, such as Paul, were plagued, and so are me and you. In fact, none are exempt!

Also, I think the Scripture teaches us that there is no way for this problem to be handled except through the avenue of *"suffering"* in some nature. I am sorry, but there is no Scripture in the Word of God that it tells us that hands can be laid on individuals, and this problem be handled. I believe in the laying on of hands and the anointing with oil, but there are no shortcuts to victory over this monster.

As well, I do not see anything in Scripture that tells us that we can pray our way out of this thing, or fast our way out of this thing, even as powerful and wonderful as these twin attributes are. One being mightily used of God does not exempt one, as by now certainly should be obvious. In fact, it seems that the more that one is used, the more that the favor of God is expended, the more His Power is lavished, only demands greater suffering, even as Paul here portrays. It seems that those who are greatly used of God face this danger even in a greater way than all, and, therefore, must be subject to the *"thorn."*

SPIRITUAL PRIDE

The most dangerous and destructive form of pride is spiritual pride. There is social pride, place pride, fashion pride, and class pride. There is talent pride, money pride, appearance pride, etc. Actually, the list is almost endless, but the deadliest is spiritual pride.

Paul's pain was a form of preventive suffering. The spiritual constitution of the greatest of Apostles and the greatest of Saints was apparently too weak to sustain the effect of the unspeakable Revelations he had experienced, and God permitted the thorn as a preventive against spiritual pride. This is what Paul meant when he wrote *"to buffet me, lest I should be exalted above measure."*

The words *"above measure"* is an expression which means *"too much."* It implies that there is a legitimate measure of exaltation for us to enjoy, actually, as stated, the fact of God using us. Christian experience is not a system of either physical or spiritual asceticism. It does not require the abuse of the flesh, as some of the eastern religions, for the development of the spirit. It is designed to give a proper expression of the emotions as well.

Exalted feelings have a safe limit but there is such a thing, and it can happen all too quickly, as being exalted *"above measure."* At this point, spiritual pleasure becomes spiritual pride (Laurin).

(8) "FOR THIS THING I BESOUGHT THE LORD THRICE, THAT IT MIGHT DEPART FROM ME."

Paul's desire was normal. It was the natural reaction to pain and suffering to desire its relief. Paul asked God for its removal. It was not a casual request.

Paul believed in prayer. He believed that prayer was as effective in the practical necessities of life as in any spiritual matter. In other words, prayer had an object as well as a subject.

In fact, much of our praying presently has only a subject. Its subject is words and phrases. What is its object? Is it directed to specific conditions and needs?

Men say, *"If God knows what we need, why ask Him for it?"* People pray as if God needed information or as if He needed to be coaxed into acquiescence.

The purpose of prayer is not to coax God into doing what we want, or to try to change His Will. Instead, it is to help us to find out what is God's Will for us.

HE ASKED IN FAITH

Faith is not something which forces God to do what we want. Instead, it is something which unites us with the Source of Divine Energy and Blessing.

As I have said many times, God gives us some great and mighty Promises in His Word; however, He will not allow us to use His Word against Himself. His Will always stands as a barrier relative to His Word.

NOTES

Many modern Christians have attempted to use Mark 11:24 or John 15:7, etc., in ways that the Lord never intended.

The idea is, exactly as Paul illustrates, is that we pray in the Will of God. We are to find out what His Will is, which He will readily give to us, and then seek accordingly. In fact, any Believer who does not seek earnestly the perfect Will of God is foolish indeed!

So, Paul asked in Faith, but in effect, the answer was *"No!"* One could say that his prayer was answered although his request was denied.

HE ASKED WITH PERSISTENCE

Paul said he *"besought the Lord thrice."* It was the perfect proportion of persistence. He was not weak in Faith so that he stopped after the first denial of his desire. Nor was he stubborn about it that he continued praying a purely selfish petition.

We notice that he prayed thrice and then stopped praying. He did not pray for years about this thing. Paul undoubtedly knew what God's Will was, at least after the third request.

As stated, in this respect his prayer was answered although his request was denied. If prayer's purpose is to discover God's Will, which it certainly should be, then that purpose was realized.

Because all these conditions — namely, prayer, Faith, and persistence — prevailed, we cannot say that the continuance of Paul's thorn was in the lack of Paul's spiritual experience. Neither need we assume the same thing in our own experience when these things are present. We must always consider God's higher purpose.

I BESOUGHT THE LORD

The phrase, *"For this thing I besought the Lord thrice,"* indicates the fact that Paul knew that God was permitting it, otherwise he would have rebuked the devil rather than pray to God three times. However, he did not understand, at least at the outset, why God was allowing Satan to harass him.

Some have said that the word *"thrice"* is a Hebraism, which means any number of times.

While that is possible, the structure of the Text indicates, that Paul actually took this thing to the Lord on three special occasions, earnestly praying for the removal of this calamity.

It should be recollected that the Lord Jesus prayed three times in the Garden of Gethsemane that the cup might be removed from Him (Mat. 26:44). After the third time, He ceased, and submitted to what was the Will of God.

Consequently, this proves that there should be a limit to some prayers. The Saviour prayed three times; and Paul limited himself to the same number of petitions, and then submitted to the Will of God. This does not prove that we should be limited to exactly this number in our petitions; but it proves that there can be a limit; when it is plain from any cause that the problem will not be removed, we should submit to it. The Saviour in the Garden knew that the cup would not be removed, and He acquiesced. Paul was told indirectly that his problem would not be removed, and he submitted. Prayer is unsuccessful when it contradicts God's plan. Consequently, no one can correctly say that this prayer was not answered because of insufficient Faith on the part of the Apostle.

DEPART FROM ME

The phrase, *"That it might depart from me,"* proclaims the Apostle being specific in his prayers, which is exactly what he should have been and what we should be.

Paul was quite clear about what he wanted, and to be sure it was not wrong to take this to the Lord, in fact, this is exactly what he should have done.

Even though the Lord did not give Paul that for which he asked, He did enlighten him as to the reason why, even as we shall see, which greatly benefitted the Apostle in tremendous ways, even greater than if the thorn had been removed.

This tells us that prayer offered in Faith, and in the Will of God, is never without great benefit. While we may not get exactly what we want, to be sure, if we will always follow the Will of the Lord, we will always receive something far better than what we want or desire. We must trust the Lord in this fashion. The idea is that we are to get our wants in line with His Will.

He has our good at heart. In fact, He is the Only One Who knows us as we really are, and, therefore, knows exactly what we need.

So, even though the Apostle did not get exactly that for which he asked, in fact, he received something far better. In that light, and especially considering that he wanted the Will of God, his prayer was answered, but not in the manner in which he first desired. Irrespective, he quickly brought his desires into line with that which the Lord desired, which should be a great lesson for us.

NOTES

(9) "AND HE SAID UNTO ME, MY GRACE IS SUFFICIENT FOR THEE: FOR MY STRENGTH IS MADE PERFECT IN WEAKNESS. MOST GLADLY THEREFORE WILL I RATHER GLORY IN MY INFIRMITIES, THAT THE POWER OF CHRIST MAY REST UPON ME."

In this Verse we have, I think, the greatest teaching in the entirety of the Word of God, regarding the Grace of God, personal weakness, infirmities, and the Power of Christ. So much is said in so few words.

HE SAID

The phrase, *"And He said unto me,"* refers to the Lord answering Paul's prayer in the way He (the Lord) wanted it answered.

The words *"He said,"* and as it refers to the Lord, carries the idea of an initial statement with continuing results. The idea is *"it stands said,"* meaning, that it has a definite finality. In other words, God was not going to change the situation.

God was more concerned about Paul than he was about Paul's Ministry, which all of this indicates. He knew if He could keep the Apostle straight, the Ministry would follow suit. It is a matter of *"being"* and *"doing."* The *"being"* must be first! (Rossier)

WHEN WAS THIS PRAYER ANSWERED?

It may have been in one of several ways.

The Lord may have answered Paul accordingly even after the first petition, with the Apostle going to Him two more times, attempting to change the situation; however, such is not likely with Paul.

As well, the Lord could have answered him immediately after the third petition.

Or maybe no answer came immediately after the third petition, with the Lord answering some days or even weeks, or possibly months later. In fact, I think one can say, that the Lord does this often.

Using Paul again as an example, I think it is obvious that Acts Chapter 16 portrays him seeking the Lord several times regarding direction, and not receiving the answer until some days, or even possibly weeks later, which resulted in the Macedonian Call (Acts 16:6-10).

A PERSONAL EXPERIENCE

If I think a bit, I'm sure that several illustrations from my own experience would come to me; however, one which took place in 1994, if I remember correctly the year, will suffice.

Frances and I both had gone to the Lord several times regarding a particular situation. The period of time involved must have been at least six months or maybe even more. No answer was forthcoming.

And then one Thursday night in prayer meeting, the Lord beautifully and wondrously spoke to my heart regarding the very thing I had been asking, even though at that moment it was not even on my mind. In fact, I had somewhat given up that we would receive any answer at all.

As I went to prayer that night, in a moment's time, the Lord brought my petition to mind. He said to me in my heart, *"You have asked Me as to why . . . ?"*

He then gave me the answer. He did it in the form of a particular Scripture found in Isaiah, to be sure, one in which I would not have thought of in one hundred years; however, it perfectly and beautifully answered my petition.

Why didn't the Lord answer the first time I made the request?

Why did He have me make the same petition several times, and then answer me some weeks after I had somewhat given up of obtaining an answer?

I do not have the answer to those questions. This I do know:

Every single thing that the Lord does for us, to us, with us, or about us, is always designed for our good, and is always meant to serve as a lesson from which we can learn.

HOW WAS PAUL'S PRAYER ANSWERED?

Inasmuch as he doesn't say, we of course, have no way of knowing.

Quite possibly the Lord spoke to his heart, revealing the information. It could be that the Lord gave him the answer in a dream. As well, the Lord could have even appeared to him, Personally divulging this extremely important

NOTES

information. Or maybe Paul was reading the Book of Job, and the Holy Spirit through that Patriarch of old divulged to him that which he sought, or any other part of the Old Testament for that matter. The idea is, whatever way He did speak to Paul, Paul believed that he would receive an answer and he did.

It should be obvious by now, that Paul sought the Lord constantly, and about everything he did. In other words, he was led by the Lord constantly, exactly as all Believers should be led.

The trouble is, most Believers little seek the Lord for anything, except in rare cases of emergency; however, if we wait until those particular times, it may be too late. As well, if we truly seek Him about everything, as we should, and which we are very foolish not to do, some of these so-called emergencies may never arise in the first place.

The Lord has the answer to any and all things. Also, He is available at all times. As well, He desires that we seek His Face, thereby deriving the leading which He Alone can give. So, I implore the Reader to earnestly make it a practice to seek the Lord constantly, laying everything before Him, seeking leading, guidance, and direction. He will be faithful to give such, and to be sure, that which He gives is always perfect, whereas that which man gives is seldom right.

GRACE

The phrase, *"My Grace is sufficient for thee,"* speaks of enabling Grace.

Every single thing the Believer receives from the Lord is by the vehicle of Grace, one might say. So, these things of which Paul mentions, only increases the Grace, which is the greatest thing that could ever happen to a Believer.

It is this blessed word *"Grace,"* which in the fullness of its meaning, refers to the Lord's undeserved favor toward one who as a sinner has deserved the very opposite, this boundless favor with all that it bestows, pardon and peace, support and deliverance, comfort, strength, assurance, hope, joy, and every gift for that matter.

This Grace cannot be insufficient; it cannot abandon Paul; it is mightier than *"the thorn,"* mightier than any *"messenger of Satan."* It will support him in every ordeal and shine the brighter as pure, undeserved Grace the more it is put to the test. What a sweeter reply from the Lord could Paul have designed!

It might quickly be added, that this Grace is not imparted to those who feel that they are strong, and who do not realize their need, and total need at that, of Divine aid. It is not so completely manifested to those who are vigorous and strong, or at least think they are, as to the feeble. It is when we are conscious that we are feeble, and when we feel our need of help, that the Redeemer manifests His power to uphold, and imparts His purest consolations.

HOW WAS THIS GRACE SUFFICIENT?

The idea is, that Grace was parceled out as was needed by the Apostle. It was sufficient to keep Paul standing every time that Satan struck a blow. That is: every time he received a buffet there was a sufficiency of Grace immediately given to meet the blow — not a moment too soon, not a moment too late, or not too little or not too much (Williams).

The Lord's answer to Paul was not the removing of the thorn so as to make it easy for Paul, but rather by giving sufficient Grace for the bearing of his thorn.

Why should this be? Why does not God remove my difficulty instead of giving me Grace? To those of us who know and believe God, it would be just as easy for Him to give one answer as the other. However, the reason at times, that He does not remove certain problems, is that we may learn discipline, trust, and dependence on Him.

The railroads use a device known as the derail. It lies on the track for the purpose of throwing off the wheels of the locomotive. It's intention is not to cause a wreck, but to protect other trains.

God, as well, has derailing devices. When we need the sidetrack for repairs or correction, yet willfully go against His caution and danger signals, and at times, even as Paul, not willfully in this manner, still, He has means of derailing us. These are the stops which are as necessary for our well-being as the starts.

PERSONAL EXPERIENCE

I look at my own situation presently, and what the Lord has taught me; consequently, I thank Him for all He has done, irrespective as to how hurtful it may have seemed at the moment.

NOTES

Even though I am certain that I still have much to learn, there are two things which stand out in my mind, as being the most rewarding of all.

I have learned through the Word of God, and as is obvious from bitter experience, that what Jesus Christ did at Calvary and the Resurrection is the answer for every problem of mankind. I realize that most Believers reading these words, would automatically think that most of the Church already knows that great Truth. I beg to disagree!

In fact, I think the Church as a whole little knows this of which I speak. I have learned that the mightiest of demon forces yield totally and completely, not to my great strength and Faith in hurling about the Name of Jesus, even though that Name is all potent, that is if we properly understand Scripturally its use, but rather my understanding of my being in Christ when He died at Calvary, in Christ when He was buried, and in Christ when He was raised from the dead, and likewise raised in *"newness of life"* (Rom. Chpt. 6).

I have learned that that which I could not do, despite all my efforts, He can do easily, and in fact, has already done. I have learned that I am not trying to gain the victory, but in fact in Christ, I am already victorious. I have learned that all my struggles to be an overcomer are fruitless, when in fact, in Christ, I'm already an overcomer. All of this is by Faith, which is the great commodity which pleases God, and on which He works; however, He cannot work in this capacity, irrespective as to how much He desires to do so, if we in fact, have an improper understanding of Calvary and the Resurrection, which in fact, most do. He has shown me in His Word, how to live in perpetual victory, and I personally do not know of anything that is greater than that, at least as it regards our daily living and walk before God.

Second, I have learned even as the Lord told Paul, that God's Grace truly is sufficient. We may think we cannot stand certain things, and in reality we are right, that is if we are trying to do it within our own strength and power; however, if we allow His enabling Grace to be properly dispensed to us, in other words, to realize our need for such, it will always be forthcoming, and will always be sufficient. I have lived it! I have proved it! I know it is true.

GRACE AS TAUGHT BY PAUL

Nearly two-thirds (108 of 162) of the New Testament occurrences of *"Charis"* normally translated *"Grace,"* are found in the Pauline Epistles. The term is found in all 14 of the traditional Pauline Letters, and is heavily clustered in Romans (23 times) and the Corinthian Letters (10 times in I Cor.; 18 times in II Cor.).

In Pauline usage the word *"Charis"* carries the basic sense of *"favor"* and *"loving kindness."* And when God or Christ is its subject, acting in Grace toward humankind, it is undeserved favor. This is especially apparent in the Texts referring to Salvation or Gifts of the Spirit.

With human subjects Grace sometimes refers to thanksgiving to God, to a collection or offering (recalling Divine Grace), or to gracious or encouraging speech directed toward others (II Cor. 8:1, 6-7, 9, 19; 9:8, 14).

THE GRACE OF GOD AND CHRIST

Paul refers numerous times to *"the Grace of God"* (or *"His Grace"*) and *"the Grace of Christ"* (or its lengthened version, *"the Grace of the Lord Jesus Christ"*). This last phrase adorns the conclusion of over half of Paul's Letters (Rom. 16:20; I Cor. 16:23; II Cor. 13:14). The Holy Spirit could well have desired that Paul do this, in order to link Grace to the full Divine-Messianic title *"the Lord Jesus Christ."* In II Thess. 1:12 the expression, *"the Grace of our God and the Lord Jesus Christ,"* indicates the inseparable bond between the Grace of God and Christ.

Fisher said, *"Paul understands Grace as God acting in accordance with His Own Character and Being,"* and that *"Grace means not merely a Divine attribute or attitude but God Himself."*

Whether or not Paul intended such an identification, we cannot be certain; however, neither can one disprove the summation given by Fisher, which I personally think is true.

So, in our efforts to define Grace, which men have been attempting to do from the time the New Testament was written, perhaps we can understand it better by saying that Grace is God and Christ. If that is the case, it is not a matter of God or Christ having Grace, but rather that They are Grace, which if correct, and I believe it is, paints an entirely different picture.

In Ephesians 1:7 we read that appreciation of *"the riches of His Grace"* in Christ should result in praise of *"the Glory of His Grace"* (Eph. 1:6). This *"Praise"* apparently entails a *"Blessing"* of *"the God and Father of our Lord Jesus Christ"* Who has greatly *"Blessed"* Believers in Christ (Eph. 1:3).

Consequently, essentially, to offer praise to His glorious Grace is to praise God.

STRENGTH AND WEAKNESS

The phrase, *"For My strength is made perfect in weakness,"* gives us God's manner.

What did the Lord mean by that statement?

The Truth is, when it comes to the flesh, all Believers are weak. It's not a case of some being weak and some not being weak, all are weak. The problem is, we refuse to recognize our weakness, and that's what this is all about.

When we realize that whatever needs to be done in our hearts and lives, that we cannot do it, we cannot bring it about, we cannot affect our own Sanctification, at least in our own strength, then we will depend totally and completely on the Lord, which is the intention of the Holy Spirit all along.

The idea is, that the strength which the Lord imparts to His people is more commonly and more completely manifested when His people feel they are weak, in fact, as they actually are.

The first phrase about Grace would have been enough, but the Lord added an explanation in regard to the very agony that had pressed these intense prayers from Paul's lips: *"For the power is brought to its finish in weakness."* The verb used here, is the very verb that is employed in John 19:28, 30 where Jesus cried: which our versions properly translate: *"It is finished!"* Literally, *"It has been and is now finished."* But in the case of our Passage our versions have translated the same verb with the present tense *"is made perfect."* It should have been translated, *"For My strength is finished in weakness."*

Consequently, the sense of our Passage is not, as our versions have it, the power *"is made perfect,"* or comes to perfection only in the midst of weakness. That is wrong!

THE TASK IS FINISHED

The Lord's power is certainly always mature, complete, and it cannot be made perfect, for it is already perfect, and in fact, has always been so. But this *"power"* works and does things in us. It has much to do.

NOTES

The idea is, when it has brought us to the point where we are utter weakness, and realize it, its task is finished. It has then shaped us into a perfect tool for itself.

As long as we Believers imagine that we still have some power we are unfit instruments for the Lord's hands; He still has to work on us before He can work properly through us. But when He has reduced us to utter nothingness, then the end is reached; with such a tool the Lord can do great deeds.

In fact, *"the power"* is generally identified with *"My Grace."* Strictly speaking, the Lord's Grace possesses power, and works and operates in and through us with this power.

This brief explanation showed Paul why the Lord gave him the thorn for the flesh. It was done lest he lift himself up unduly and thus become a tool that was unfit for the Lord. Actually, the structure of the Greek shows, and as we've already said, that the thorn was a gift to Paul, a blessing for him. It was the Lord's way of reducing Paul to total weakness so that he no more lifted himself up but lay prostrate and weak.

So, Paul became the wonderful instrument that we see him to be during all these past years, and the Lord worked great things through him.

GLORY IN INFIRMITIES?

The phrase, *"Most gladly therefore will I rather glory in my infirmities,"* presents the Apostle not only having been shown this by the Lord, but *"gladly"* even *"most gladly"* accepting it as God's way and benefitting thereby.

In fact, Paul discloses the deepest secret of his spiritual life as an Apostle. It was his weakness that made him so excellent a tool for the Lord. Nor is Paul an exception.

The way the Greek is structured, makes this proposition general. It is ever thus with the Lord's instruments although He uses various means to produce this weakness and its constant realization.

Since Paul had received this word from the Lord, which showed him the great value of all his weaknesses for the Lord's purpose, such now makes his heart *"very glad."* He now makes all his weaknesses his one and only boast. It includes the weakness of the thorn, which brought him down to the lowest point, and all the other weaknesses of which he has already spoken.

NOTES

"Infirmities" in the Greek is *"asthenia,"* and means *"strengthless, impotent, feebleness of body or mind, sickness."*

THE POWER OF CHRIST

The phrase, *"That the power of Christ may rest upon me,"* actually says, *"That the Power of Christ may spread its tent over me."*

The figure is beautiful. The Power of Christ spreads its tent over Paul and all his weaknesses, does so once for all and permanently. All Paul's weaknesses are covered and hidden away under that tent.

It cannot be spread over one whose boast is in his own strength.

As well, the way the Greek is structured does not mean that this is yet to be done, that Paul is still waiting for it after all these years, but rather that it is already done. The tent of power has been spread over him, and will definitely remain over him.

A Christian should rejoice that he may obtain what he does obtain in affliction, cost what it may. It is worth more than it cost; and when we come down to the end, whenever that will be, the things that we shall have most occasion to thank God for, will be our afflictions. And if they are the means of raising us to a higher seat in Heaven, and placing us nearer the Redeemer there, who will not rejoice in his trials?

(10) "THEREFORE I TAKE PLEASURE IN INFIRMITIES, IN REPROACHES, IN NECESSITIES, IN PERSECUTIONS, IN DISTRESSES FOR CHRIST'S SAKE: FOR WHEN I AM WEAK, THEN AM I STRONG."

Why did Paul take pleasure in adversity? Because he knew that this is what affected his weakness, which meant the more the Holy Spirit could work through him.

When he was boasting Paul spoke to others about all his great weaknesses, something incidentally in which few others would boast. But he took pleasure in them. They looked beautiful and lovely to him.

He adds a few phrases by letting his eye run over four groups of evidence that exhibit his weaknesses even to other people.

Any man is weak who has to submit to *"insulting, violent mistreatments"* instead of violently denouncing and bringing to justice such enemies; who cannot rise above *"necessities,"* wants, and difficulties like the strong men whom the world admire; who flees from *"persecutions"* instead of turning against his pursuers with devastating power and wrath; who is ever in *"distress,"* and tight places, where he can do nothing but suffer. What a statement to say that all such situations are one's pleasure and delight!

PLEASURE?

The phrase, *"Therefore I take pleasure in infirmities,"* presents one who has come to terms with what the Lord is doing in him, sees its great advantages, knows what it has brought about and is bringing about, which brings great *"pleasure"* to him.

If one is to notice, the modern gospel, at least for the most part, denies all of these things. It has no patience with infirmities, and does not know its value. Consequently, Paul's experiences here, which really enabled him to do all the great things he did, are considered by many at the present time to be a lack of Faith. How wrong! How foolish!

To these people, Jesus is not the Saviour and Instructor, but rather Santa Claus. Consequently, they seldom if ever, grow out of the infant stage.

God's answer to Paul's desire was not the subtraction of Paul's pain, but the addition of God's Grace.

Let not the Believer misunderstand and think that Paul was gloating over and glorying in difficulties and problems. That was really not the case at all.

He was glorying in the fact that the infirmity was, in God's purpose, to be the medium of something greater. This something greater was power, and more perfectly, it was the Power of Christ, and the fact that it rested upon him.

MISTAKE!

In the Second and Third Centuries, and even on into the Middle Ages, many in the Church erroneously thought that the suffering itself brought some type of Holiness or Sanctification. Consequently, they submitted themselves to all types of self-induced suffering, etc. Of course, that is error.

The Truth is, as I think Paul has amply proved, that we should ask the Lord to remove

NOTES

any and all difficulties which come our way; however, if He does not see fit to remove them, we should then understand He wants them there, at least for a period of time for our good. As stated, we are glad for the infirmities, only because of what they produce within our lives.

REPROACHES

The phrase, *"In reproaches,"* refers to the contempt and scorn which Paul constantly met as a follower of Christ. Regrettably, much of that scorn came from those inside the Church, even as we are studying in this Book of II Corinthians. In fact, that *"reproach"* or *"scorn"* hurts most of all!

NECESSITIES

The phrase, *"In necessities,"* refers to want or need. In other words, there were times that he had to do without.

In fact, that's the basic reason that he said, *"I can do all things through Christ which strengtheneth me"* (Phil. 4:13).

Most Christians read this Verse out of context. While it means exactly what it says regarding the plus side, Paul at the same time is saying that if he has to be *"hungry"* or *"suffer need,"* he can do that too, through the strength of Christ.

PERSECUTIONS

The phrase, *"In persecutions,"* pertains to that which actually never ended, in fact none of these things ever ended until Paul was finally taken home to Glory.

I realize that none of this seems very appetizing to most modern Believers, especially considering that most are basically taught the opposite; however, these things were necessary in the life of Paul, and to be sure, they are necessary in the lives of all who would name the name of Christ, at least in one form or the other. Perhaps it could be better said this way:

The lesson of Verses 1-10 is that the higher the Christian experience the sharper must be the *"thorn,"* i.e., the difficulties allowed to come our way, needed to guard the Believer from failing.

DISTRESSES

The phrase, *"In distresses,"* refers to difficulties.

As we've already stated, the Lord could easily lift these things at any time. He has the power to do such, as should be obvious.

However, what the Holy Spirit has been instructed to do with us, is of far greater magnitude than many have been led to believe. He is bringing us toward Christlikeness, which will insure Righteousness and Holiness. Accordingly, I think the Scripture teaches, which seems to me to be obvious, that one cannot get from point A to point B, that being the place the Holy Spirit is taking us, without the process of the *"thorn,"* i.e., *"infirmities,"* etc. As stated, the higher the calling, the sharper the thorn!

CHRIST'S SAKE

The phrase, *"For Christ's sake,"* refers to the fact that all of this is on account of Christ. As well, it puts an entirely different complexion on the entirety of the process.

In view of the fact that Christ has done so much for us, and at such great price, whatever He calls upon us to do, seems to be small by comparison.

If one is to notice, besides physical infirmities he named *"reproaches"* — this is mental; *"necessities"* — this is economic; *"persecutions"* — this is social; *"distresses"* — this is emotional. When his attitude to this was pleasure, then their effect was strength (Laurin).

WEAK — STRONG

The phrase, *"For when I am weak, then am I strong,"* presents the paradox. It is one of the most valuable lessons we can ever learn.

We have a mistaken idea of strength of character. The strongest are not necessarily they who can defend themselves against others. To be self-sufficient, which the world of course lauds, we assume we must avenge our wrongs, carry our point, demand justice; but to be Christ-sufficient we are strong when we are weak. True strength is the overpowering of Divine Love. Love is always strong. It dwells with Holiness, Righteousness, and Truth. It is strong enough to be meek.

Many have mistaken meekness for weakness, forgetting that it is a mark of superior strength to bear evil and refuse to retaliate. With strength is found quietness and calmness of spirit. He who has found the strength of the Lord can wait patiently while God works His Will.

NOTES

AN EXAMPLE

The story has been told of a man who made a clock and showed it to a friend who had never seen one of this design before.

The fashioner of the clock opened the back of it and then asked the man what he thought of its maker. The man saw some big wheels and other small ones, some wheels going one way and others the opposite way and some wheels going slowly and others fast.

Seeing this confusion he answered, *"I think the man who made that is insane."*

Then the maker took his friend to the front side of the clock and asked what he now thought of its maker.

The man looked at the two hands of the clock moving smoothly and regularly, each one in its appointed circle and both of them telling perfectly the time of day, and he replied, *"I think the man who made that is the wisest person who ever lived."*

This story gives us a glimpse of a profound truth. The fault of our thinking arises from the fact that we stand on Earth on the wrong side of God's Providences, and thus fail to see His perfect designing.

One day we shall stand on the right side and then we shall understand. In the meantime, God asks us to believe, even though we do not understand.

(11) "I AM BECOME A FOOL IN GLORYING; YE HAVE COMPELLED ME: FOR I OUGHT TO HAVE BEEN COMMENDED OF YOU: FOR IN NOTHING AM I BEHIND THE VERY CHIEFEST APOSTLES, THOUGH I BE NOTHING."

The idea of this Verse is, that Paul not for a minute, would allow anyone to gainsay his call to Ministry. He knew who he was in Christ, and he knew what he was in Christ. He was saved by the Blood of the Lamb, and he was called of God to perform a particular task. Anyone who said he wasn't, could expect an answer from him.

GLORYING

The phrase, *"I am become a fool in glorying,"* refers to the fact that he should not have had to defend himself at all, much less to the

Corinthians, who of all people knew who he was, or at least certainly should have known. Even so, this of which Paul has had to do, is extremely distasteful to him.

As such, if anyone, therefore, is disposed to imitate Paul in speaking of himself, and what he has done, let him do it only when he is in circumstances like Paul, and when the honor of the Ministry and his usefulness demand such.

COMPELLED

The phrase, *"Ye have compelled me,"* refers to the fact that the Corinthians had made it necessary for him to vindicate his character, and to state the evidence of his Divine commission as an Apostle.

In fact, this very well comes under the heading of the *"reproaches,"* he constantly suffered. What a reproach to have to defend himself and even prove himself to the very people who had been saved under his Ministry! To be frank, such could be looked at as no less than an insult. And yet the Apostle does it with Grace.

COMMENDED OF YOU

The phrase, *"For I ought to have been commended of you,"* in fact, is a gross understatement.

Instead of forcing Paul to boast like a fool about himself and thus making him reveal all his weaknesses as his boast, the Corinthians should have been commending him. Consequently, they are to blame.

Paul was not a spurious servant. His Apostleship was accompanied by genuineness. There was fruit in his Ministry. He justified his claims by presenting a record of many souls saved, and of signs, wonders, and mighty deeds. These were Apostolic signs.

So, there was no excuse on the part of these Corinthians.

We as Believers have the choice of making the load which our brother bears, either heavier or lighter. Which will it be?

Paul's task was difficult enough, his life distressful enough, the obstacles abundant enough, without fellow Believers making the task harder, and especially those who should have known better.

On a personal basis, I have suffered in this capacity enough, that whatever anyone else does to me, I want to do my very best, irrespective as to whom the person is, to make his load a little lighter, a little easier to bear, a little less chaffing. God forbid, that I be guilty of doing otherwise.

NOTES

CHIEFEST APOSTLES

The phrase, *"For in nothing am I behind the very chiefest Apostles,"* refers here to True Apostles, even the original Twelve, and not impostors. In fact, this of which he speaks presents one of the greatest problems of all.

It is almost certain, that many were jealous of Paul. In the minds of his detractors, how could he place himself on the same level with the Original Twelve, who had literally walked and talked with Jesus throughout His earthly Ministry? Above that, how could he claim to be the *"Masterbuilder"* of the Church, in fact to have been given the New Covenant, which in a sense made him the Moses of the New Testament? I think the Text bears it out, that this was whispered around constantly, with many even denying that he was an Apostle at all, much less in the category of Peter and others, etc. (I Cor. 3:10; Gal. 1:11-12).

Consequently, the Apostle does not back down in stating his position, even comparing himself on the same level with Peter, and any others who might be named for that matter.

In fact, I don't think he could even be considered here as boasting. What he is saying is the Truth, and to say otherwise, would have been a denial of what God had called him to do.

In fact, this is one of Satan's favorite tactics. He denies the Call of God on certain lives, and most of the time, if not all the time, uses fellow Believers to do so.

PLEASE ALLOW ME THIS LIBERTY

As well, if I did not say the following, I think the Lord would not be pleased.

God has called me for the task in which I am engaged, and I speak of World Evangelism among other things. That Call has not been lifted or diminished. If anything, the Anointing of the Holy Spirit for which we constantly seek, is I believe, greater than ever.

Some may not like what I preach, and, therefore, attempt to deny my Calling; however, I will say as Paul, and not flinch when I say these words, as it refers to the present time, *"In nothing am I behind the very chiefest Apostles, though I be nothing."*

NOTHING

The phrase, *"Though I be nothing,"* presents the humility of the Apostle, and at the same time stating that all he is, is what the Lord has made of him.

Consequently, the following should be noted:

1. The highest attainments in piety are not inconsistent with the deepest sense of our nothingness and unworthiness.

2. That the most distinguished favors bestowed on us by God are consistent with the lowest humility.

3. That those who are the most favored in the Christian life, and most honored by God, should not be unwilling to take a low place, and to regard and speak of themselves as nothing.

In fact, compared with the Lord, what are we? Nothing!

Let a man look over his past life, and for the most part, see how vile and unworthy it has been; let him look at God, and see how great and glorious He is; let him look at the vast universe, and see how immense it is; let him think of the Angels, and reflect how pure they are; let him think of what he might have been, and how much more he might have done for his Saviour; let him look at his body, and think how frail it is, and how soon it must return to dust; and no matter how elevated his rank among his fellow-worms, and no matter how much God has favored him as a Christian or a Minister, he will feel, that is if he feels right, that he is nothing.

The most elevated Saints are distinguished for the deepest humility; those who are nearest to God feel most their distance; they who are to occupy the highest place in Heaven feel most deeply that they are unworthy of even the lowest (Barnes).

(12) "TRULY THE SIGNS OF AN APOSTLE WERE WROUGHT AMONG YOU IN ALL PATIENCE, IN SIGNS, AND WONDERS, AND MIGHTY DEEDS."

In this statement given by Paul, we have what should be the criteria for Ministry, or at least pointing in that direction. The tragedy is, that the far greater majority of the modern Ministry, doesn't even believe in these things listed by Paul, much less having them operative in their efforts.

NOTES

So one would have to come to the conclusion, that most of that today which is referred to as *"Ministry,"* in fact, is not recognized by God as such at all. The major reason falls into two categories:

1. Preachers who do not believe in the Baptism with the Holy Spirit with the evidence of speaking with other tongues.

2. Those who claim to in fact believe in such, but little depend on Him for anything.

The Holy Spirit is the One Who performs these things, and if He is denied, or ignored, very little, if anything, is going to be done, at least for the Lord. In fact, Paul addressed this by saying, *"Having a form of godliness, but denying the power thereof: from such turn away"* (II Tim. 3:5).

SIGNS OF AN APOSTLE

The phrase, *"Truly the signs of an Apostle were wrought among you,"* presents that which should characterize every true Ministry, in one way or the other. It doesn't mean that all will be used on the same level as Paul, but it does mean that the earmarks will be there in some capacity. The idea is that our Faith be positive in that regard.

Luke has no account of the Miracles that were wrought by Paul during his stay in Corinth. Of course, I am speaking of the Book of Acts which was written by Luke. However, that accords with the object with which Acts was written, namely to show how the Gospel made its course outward from Jerusalem.

In fact, one could probably say that hundreds of Miracles, at least as to the fact of relating them, were omitted, and because only those that were pertinent to Luke's object are mentioned, with a few described. As well, this is the way the Holy Spirit wanted the Book of Acts written.

Even though Miracles are mentioned in Acts, they are mentioned even as here, not as the prime object, but as a by-product of the thrust of the Gospel. In other words, the Gospel of Jesus Christ if believed correctly, if preached correctly, will produce Miracles, among other things.

Not until now does Paul refer to Miracles, and even now he does so incidently not as pointing to the chief evidence of his Apostleship.

What Miracles attested the false apostles? Absolutely none. As far as the chief evidence goes, Paul has already presented that in the most effective manner in II Corinthians 3:2, etc.

The great monument to his Apostleship which Paul had erected in Corinth was the Corinthian Church itself, which was so great that every inhabitant and every visitor could see it and read its inscription.

PATIENCE

The phrase, *"In all patience,"* refers to trust in the Lord that He will perform what He has promised in His Word, which actually speaks of Faith.

I think it is impossible for one to truly have Faith and evidence Faith, if one is lacking in patience. The Lord does not always perform on cue. Neither does He perform the same way twice, at least most of the time. Some are healed, and some are not healed. Some are delivered, and some are not delivered (Heb. 11:32-40).

Many factors go into that which is done for God, and which we receive from God. On top of that, the Lord seldom explains to us what He is doing, or why He is doing what He is doing. So, as should be obvious, it takes *"patience"* in respect to all these things. In fact, James plainly says, *"Knowing this, that the trying of your Faith worketh patience"* (James 1:3). This is basically that of which Paul speaks.

SIGNS

The phrase, *"In signs,"* in essence speaks of pointers, much like traffic signs point to the authority behind them. In other words, the idea is that those who behold these *"signs,"* know that God is actually the One performing them, and that they always in one way or the other point to Jesus. In fact, Jesus told us what they were. He said:

"And these signs shall follow them that believe; in my name shall they cast out devils; they shall speak with new tongues; they shall take up (put away) *serpents* (demon spirits)*; and if they drink any deadly thing it shall not hurt them; they shall lay hands on the sick, and they shall recover"* (Mk. 16:17-18).

WONDERS

The phrase, *"And wonders,"* relates to miracles producing wonder or amazement. It pertains to something that is so out of the ordinary, that people know beyond a shadow of a doubt that it is God who has done such a thing. That of which Paul was speaking, is not obvious, for he did not explain exactly what he meant or give an illustration.

NOTES

MIGHTY DEEDS

The phrase, *"And mighty deeds,"* indicates that which can be accomplished only by Divine Power, which in fact, refers to all three. Actually, all three terms designate the major purpose for miracles — to point people to Jesus, the One Who can deliver from sin (Mk. 2:10).

In this, I think we are safe to say that Paul was speaking not only of miracles of healing, etc., but as well, miracles of deliverance, which in fact, are the greatest miracles of all.

These Corinthians who of course had been pagans before hearing the Gospel, were no doubt, at least many of them, bound by all types of immorality, alcohol, drugs, etc. The Gospel wondrously and gloriously, even miraculously set them free. As stated, there could be no greater miracle than that (I Cor. 6:9-11).

PERSONAL WITNESS

In ministering all over the world, the Lord has given us that which I consider miracles as it regards healings, etc.; however, the greatest display of the Power of God, at least in my own personal Ministry, has been in the realm of deliverance. We have seen untold thousands instantly set free from drugs, alcohol, nicotine, hate, religion, etc. Only the Power of God can do such a thing, and the Power of God will only express itself according to the purity of the Gospel preached. Also, the vessel, plays a big part in what is done, be it Paul, myself, or anyone else for that matter.

One does not have to be an Apostle to see these things happen, with Jesus making Faith alone the criteria. He plainly said, *"These signs shall follow them that believe"* (Mk. 16:17).

As well, these particular *"signs"* are not necessarily the fact that one is an Apostle; however, I think the evidence is clear that a true Apostle will definitely have this type of working of the Holy Spirit within his Ministry. The manner in which Paul uses the phrase *"signs of an Apostle,"* makes that crystal clear.

(13) "FOR WHAT IS IT WHEREIN YE WERE INFERIOR TO OTHER CHURCHES, EXCEPT IT BE THAT I MYSELF WAS NOT BURDENSOME TO YOU? FORGIVE ME THIS WRONG."

Even down to miracles the Corinthians have received everything from Paul that attested his being a true Apostle. What could they, then, complain about as treatment that was inferior to, or worse than, that which the rest of the Churches received, those that had been founded by the Twelve, Peter, John, etc.? Or even other Churches founded by Paul?

INFERIOR?

The beginning of the question, *"For what is it wherein ye were inferior to other Churches . . . ?"*, contains, actually in the entirety of the Verse, a striking mixture of sarcasm and irony. The sense is, *"I have given among you the most ample proofs of my Apostolic Commission. I have conferred on you the highest favors of the Apostolic Office."* This question arose because Paul's detractors claimed the Church at Corinth to be inferior because of Paul's inability, etc.

In fact, he may even be saying, that he had conferred upon them, or rather that the Lord had done so, such Blessings, that Corinth was superior to all other Churches.

Beginning with Verse 12, the Apostle once more returns — and for the last time — to the subject of his credentials as a true Apostle. They might esteem him to be *"nothing,"* but he was on the contrary, not at all behind the Great and True Apostles, much less these self-made apostles of whom it seems, these Corinthians were so proud.

BURDENSOME?

The completion of the question, *"Except it be that I myself was not burdensome to you?"*, refers to the fact that he did not take any financial support from the Corinthians, to which we have already addressed. That was the only difference in his situation with Corinth than other places.

Of course, this statement also verifies the fact that Paul did take support from other Churches.

It undoubtedly cost Paul a great deal to assume the role of a foolish boaster and to play it through to the end. No more stunning answer could he have given to the mean attempts to disparage him. He absolutely outdoes all his vilifiers.

NOTES

They made him out as amounting to nothing; Paul declares that exactly *is* his boast — I am nothing! I say it in utter truth (II Cor. 11:31), yea, the Lord Himself has reduced me to nothing (II Cor. 12:7, etc.), and this is my joy and my satisfaction.

But what have you Corinthians lost thereby? In my nothingness I did not ask even a penny for support. Pardon me for this great loss which you have thus suffered!

WRONG?

The phrase, *"Forgive me this wrong,"* drips with sarcasm, even as it should!

He had spared them any financial obligation mainly because he was concerned for them; however, it seems that some of the Corinthians criticized him for this action. As we saw earlier, he was most likely charged with demeaning the Ministry because he made tents to support himself during the period of time he ministered there.

I think by now, the Reader has come to the conclusion that it's no fun being an Apostle. To be sure, I greatly understate the case. No one in their right mind would truly want the task, unless God truly called them to such.

At the same time, at least as far as appearances are concerned, it's no problem whatsoever in being a false apostle. The Devil does not oppose such, and the Lord does not temper such, for the simple reason that He has not called them to start with.

However, these of which Paul mentions, could definitely lose their souls, which is possibly what happened. So, in the final alternative, to be sure, there will not be any fun in being a false apostle either.

(14) "BEHOLD, THE THIRD TIME I AM READY TO COME TO YOU; AND I WILL NOT BE BURDENSOME TO YOU: FOR I SEEK NOT YOURS BUT YOU: FOR THE CHILDREN OUGHT NOT TO LAY UP FOR THE PARENTS, BUT THE PARENTS FOR THE CHILDREN."

According to the Seventh Chapter of this Epistle, Corinth has experienced a great Moving of the Holy Spirit, in fact, a Revival. Consequently, they were now ready for Paul's visit, and were no doubt, looking forward to such with great anticipation.

I personally think that the Revival had accomplished the needed task; consequently, the warnings now given, would be heeded.

NOTES

THE THIRD TIME

The phrase, *"Behold, the third time I am ready to come to you,"* could possibly hark back to II Corinthians 2:1. There is some evidence that Paul had visited the Church at Corinth before he wrote I Corinthians. However, if that actually happened, we have no record of what took place at that time.

If in fact, the Apostle is actually speaking of a proposed third visit, he could well be speaking of the time he was there when the Church was founded, and the second visit of which we have just mentioned.

(There is some thought that Paul had not been back to Corinth since founding the Church, and his references here and in 2:1 are merely *"proposed visits."* In fact, that may be correct, but I think not.)

BURDENSOME TO YOU

The phrase, *"And I will not be burdensome to you,"* presents him saying the same thing again, but for reason. In effect, he is saying, *"I will not be a dead weight."*

As it regards Corinth, whatever objection had raised against this practice of Paul's, he will not alter his course. But what he now says on this subject is stated in view of his impending arrival. Paul wants it understood that he and his assistants, at least for their own support, will take nothing whatever from the Corinthians. The issue is to be considered as closed (Lenski).

NOT YOURS, BUT YOU

The phrase, *"For I seek not yours, but you,"* in effect says, *"I seek your Salvation, not your property. Furthermore, I will continue this policy."* In fact, this short sentence as uttered by the Apostle, should be a resolution formed by every Minister of the Gospel.

While a Minister of Christ has a claim to a competent support, his main purpose should not be to attain such a support. It should be the higher and nobler object of winning souls to the Redeemer.

The idea is, that false apostles could never feel or show such affection as this.

PARENTS FOR THE CHILDREN

The phrase, *"For the children ought not to lay up for the parents, but the parents for the children,"* presents the Apostle speaking to the Corinthians as a father to his children. His desire is to enrich them and to fill them with the spiritual treasures which He is able to provide for them and make their own.

Also, it is unwarranted to derive from Paul's statement, that if a parent becomes unable to provide for himself, that the children should not provide for him. Paul was still fully able to provide for himself. He is merely saying that parents, as should be obvious, should do all they can to provide for their children.

It is thought by some that Paul is overthrowing the very Law and Principle which he lays down at length regarding giving, in I Corinthians 9:6-14; however, that is incorrect. Paul himself distinguishes between the right that he had respecting the situation at Corinth, and his making use of that right. As we've already stated, there should be no doubt that the Holy Spirit directed Paul to do what he did respecting not taking financial support from the Corinthians, and for several reasons. This was an isolated case, however, within itself, and should not be taken as a standard of operation, with the exception of one being very susceptible to the leading of the Holy Spirit.

Paul is speaking here about the Spirit which animates him in the foregoing that's right, his readiness to act as parents do toward their children. As well, Paul uses this relation of parents to their children as an illustration and as no more.

(15) "AND I WILL VERY GLADLY SPEND AND BE SPENT FOR YOU; THOUGH THE MORE ABUNDANTLY I LOVE YOU, THE LESS I BE LOVED."

Here again, and in fact in all of these Verses, we see the true Pastor's heart. Actually it is meant to serve as an example for all who would follow.

We learn from this example that the Work of God is not a business, but rather a Calling. We also learn that money must not be a deciding factor in any situation regarding the Work of God. While money is needed of course, as should be obvious, the True Minister of the Gospel must never make that the primary objective in any case.

The Pastor must do all within his power to affect spiritual growth in the hearts and lives of those who sit under him. He must be concerned over each person over whom he has been placed, irrespective of their spiritual weakness or difficulties. He is to love, and to continue to love, and to ever love, and to never stop loving, irrespective of whether such love is returned or not. In other words, the response has nothing to do with the initial effort. The Pastor is to love each individual, in fact loving the ones who do not care for him, just as much as he does those who truly care for him.

BE SPENT FOR YOU

The phrase, *"And I will very gladly spend and be spent for you,"* means, *"I am willing to spend my strength, time, and life, and all that I have for your welfare, as a father cheerfully does for his children. Any expense which may be necessary to promote your Salvation, to that I am willing to submit."*

The labor of a father for his children is cheerful and pleasant. Such is his love for them that he delights in toil for their sake, and that he may make them happy. The toil of a Pastor for his flock should be in the same spirit.

He should be willing to engage in unremitted efforts for their welfare; and if he has any right feeling he will find a pleasure in that toil. He will not grudge the time demanded; he will not be grieved that it exhausts his strength, or his life, any more than a father will who toils for his family.

The phrase, *"And be spent for you,"* should have been translated, *"And be spent for your souls."* The sense is, that he was willing to become wholly exhausted if by it he might secure the Salvation of their souls.

LOVE

The phrase, *"Though the more abundantly I love you, the less I be loved,"* is actually designed as a gentle reproof. It refers to the fact that not withstanding the tender attachment which he had evinced for them, they had not, as is obvious, manifested the love in return which he had a right to expect. Consequently, the Doctrine here is, that we should be willing to labor and toil for the good of others, even when they evince great ingratitude. In fact, the proper end of laboring for their welfare is not to excite their gratitude, but to obey the Will of God; and no matter whether others are grateful or not; whether love us or not; whether we can promote our popularity with them or not, let us do them good always.

NOTES

In fact, it better shows the Love of God in our own hearts, when we endeavor to benefit others when they love us the less for all our attempts, than it does to attempt to do good on the swelling tide of popular favor (Barnes).

Love usually kindles love. And if it doesn't, one may be sure that spiritual adultery is involved. In other words, an alien power or force has stolen the love of the individual which should be reserved for God and those whom He has sent.

In this case, as it often is, impostors had stolen the love of some of the Corinthians. In such a case, whether it be then or now, it is impossible for that person's love to remain right with God or with those who are His. One cannot love unrighteousness and Righteousness at the same time. It is impossible for the Corinthians, or anyone for that matter, to love the impostors and at the same time love Paul. It is the same thing as an interloper stealing the love of a wife or husband from their rightful mate.

The person in question may claim that they continue to love Paul or those who follow in his train, but despite their claims, the Truth is otherwise. I have seen it happen over and over again, as has every Preacher of the Gospel.

THIS IS WHY SUCH A SITUATION IS SO EVIL

If the heart of the Believer is pulled aside at all toward that which is false, error, or anything which is not the Will of God, in effect, and as stated, that person is committing spiritual adultery. Their love, attention, and affections are divided, which will ultimately fall out if not corrected, to no love for God at all. This is the struggle that the Lord had with Israel constantly. They were over and over again forsaking the Lord, and running toward idols and other pursuits.

It is not possible to love the world and the Lord at the same time, at lest for any length of time. It is not possible to follow after that which is error and not have one's Love for God ultimately dissipated, if the problem is not corrected. Jesus plainly said, *"No man can serve two masters: for either he will hate the one and love the other; or else he will hold to the one, and despise the other. Ye cannot serve God and mammon"* (Mat. 6:24).

(16) "BUT BE IT SO, I DID NOT BURDEN YOU: NEVERTHELESS, BEING CRAFTY, I CAUGHT YOU WITH GUILE."

The heart of a person will ultimately show what that person is. So, the Lord allows many things to happen in order to portray what actually is in the heart.

The Corinthians did not fare too well. The false apostles brought to the fore in the lives of many of these Corinthians, the hidden recesses of the heart, which portrays evil. In other words, if the evil had not been there, they would not have fallen for the falseness and hypocrisy of these impostors. Thank the Lord it was corrected, but it should be a lesson to all of us.

I DID NOT BURDEN YOU

The phrase, *"But be it so, I did not burden you,"* presents the *"I"* as emphatic.

It is shocking to think that, even after Paul has so triumphantly cleared himself from the disgraceful charge of trying to make gain out of the Corinthians, he should still be obliged to meet the slanderous innuendo that, even if he had not personally tried to get anything out of them, still he had done so indirectly, they claimed, through the agency of Titus (Farrar).

Paul is actually saying these Corinthians said, *"We admit that you did not burden us. You did not exact a support for us. But all of this was a mere trick. You accomplished the same thing in another way. You professed when with us not to seek our property but our souls. But in various ways you contrived to get our money, and to secure your object. You made others the agents for doing this, and sent them among us under various pretexts (money for Jerusalem) to gain money from us."*

It is to be remembered that Paul had sent Titus among them to take up the collection for the situation in Jerusalem (II Cor. 8:6); and it is not at all improbable that some there had charged Paul with making use of this pretence only to obtain money for his own private use. To guard against this charge was one of the reasons why Paul was so anxious to have several of the men appointed by the Church to take charge of the contribution (Barnes).

A FALSE ACCUSATION

The phrase, *"Nevertheless, being crafty, I caught you with guile,"* should have been translated, *"Nevertheless, you say, being crafty, I caught you with guile."*

As I trust the separate translation has brought out, Paul is not saying here that he is *"crafty,"* or that he is using *"guile,"* but in reality that he was accused of being these things.

"Crafty" in the Greek is *"panourgos,"* and means *"unscrupulous, in order to take advantage of someone through deceitfulness."* The terminology here is the same that would be used in reference to trapping animals or catching fish (Rossier). As one can see, these are very serious slurs against his character, but they are typical of the kind of gossip that was being circulated by the people who were practicing the very *"guile"* they said he was using.

"Guile" in the Greek is *"dolo,"* and means, *"trick, bait, wile, deceit, subtlety."*

(17) "DID I MAKE A GAIN OF YOU BY ANY OF THEM WHOM I SENT UNTO YOU?"

One may wonder why Paul continues to address some of the error of the Corinthians, even after the great Move of God has taken place in that Church, as recorded in the Seventh Chapter. The answer is obvious.

Even though there was a great Move, with the Lord touching many hearts and lives, quite possibly some few did not yield to the pleading of the Holy Spirit, consequently, continuing to make some accusations. Whenever God moves in this fashion, as He obviously did at Corinth, it is not usual that every single person will repent. For the few who do not repent, to be sure, they continued to try to poison the minds of others, hence Paul continuing to address these subjects.

A GAIN OF YOU

The beginning of the question, *"Did I make a gain of you . . . ?"*, has to be answered with a firm *"no!"*

In refuting this slander, Paul appeals boldly to the facts, and to what they knew.

The phrase, *"Make a gain,"* means, properly, *"to have an advantage; to take advantage, to seek unlawful gain."*

Quite possibly the reason the Holy Spirit desired that Paul not receive anything during his 18 month stay at Corinth by the way of financial remuneration, is because He knew these problems would arise. What would have been said, if in fact, Paul had received some

NOTES

financial help, even as he should have? The Holy Spirit knew all of these things were coming, and to save Paul the great embarrassment, He had the Apostle to support himself by making or repairing tents, even though such brought in hardly enough to keep body and soul together. In fact, had it not been for some of the Churches in Macedonia which in fact did help Paul at this time, the situation would no doubt have been even worse (II Cor. 11:7-11).

THOSE SENT BY PAUL

The conclusion of the question, *"By any of them whom I sent unto you?"*, includes all of the men whom Paul had sent to Corinth since he had left the congregation. Even though he mentions two in the next Verse, quite possibly there had been others as well. That point is immaterial.

I Corinthians Chapter 16 makes it plain that none of Paul's assistants ever touched a penny with their own hands. Paul includes men whom he had sent before he asked that a collection be started.

Consequently, his question is this: *"Can any man in Corinth stand up and say that any person that had been sent by Paul in any way whatever, ask for a single penny for Paul, or, without asking, ever received a single penny?"*

Of course, the answer is *"no!"*

(18) "I DESIRED TITUS, AND WITH HIM I SENT A BROTHER. DID TITUS MAKE A GAIN OF YOU? WALKED WE NOT IN THE SAME SPIRIT? WALKED WE NOT IN THE SAME STEPS?"

As we can see here, money is the source of contention many times in Church work. And if the Truth be known, one would probably find that money is at the root of all unscriptural situations, even when such does not appear to be on the surface (I Tim. 6:10).

TITUS

The phrase, *"I desired Titus, and with him I sent a Brother,"* presents Paul providing things honest in the sight of all men by sending these two Brethren to receive the Offering at Corinth (II Cor. 8:6) (the offering for Jerusalem).

There is nothing that could be any more right than this, but yet, for those who are evil, they see only evil. As previously stated, this is the sin of *"malignity,"* which means *"a malignity of the mind, which leads its victim to put the worst construction on every action, even ascribing to the best deeds the worst motives."*

NOTES

A GAIN OF YOU?

The question, *"Did Titus make a gain of you?"*, of course would as well have to be answered with a firm *"no!"*

How very painful it must have been to a noble heart like that of Paul's to have been compelled to discuss the motives which govern the false and selfish hearts of unconverted men! But love must bear such things; it must think for others, though it cannot think with them (Williams).

THE SAME SPIRIT

The question, *"Walk we not in the same spirit?"*, presents the fact that negative answers even as those answers should have been, would not satisfy Paul. He would end his questioning with two that call for positive answers. He now includes also himself together with all his assistants and others whom he had sent to Corinth.

Incidentally, the word *"spirit"* as Paul uses the word here, does not directly refer to the Holy Spirit, although indirectly. The Scriptures never speak of the Holy Spirit as a means or a norm that are used by us. Consequently, by *"spirit"* Paul means the inner motivation and desire.

THE SAME STEPS

The question, *"Walked we not in the same steps?"*, in effect says, the same *"tracks."*

As stated, by *"spirit"* Paul refers to inner motivation, by *"tracks"* the outward, visible conduct. His double question is: *"Are we not all alike inwardly and outwardly?"*, as he refers to those who worked with him.

Objection is raised on the ground that Paul relies only on questions. In addition to that he is accused of arguing in a circle by proving himself by means of Titus and Titus by means of Paul. Because he is honest and unselfish, his messengers must be the same; then vice versa.

Paul does neither; either would be a farce. These questions are blanket questions that are addressed to the entire congregation and include every member. Their convincing power does not lie in argument, even as none is made; it lies in the fact that every Corinthian is challenged to point to a single instance where Paul or any messenger of his ever got a penny from any Corinthian member (Lenski).

(19) "AGAIN, THINK YE THAT WE EXCUSE OURSELVES UNTO YOU? WE SPEAK BEFORE GOD IN CHRIST: BUT WE DO ALL THINGS, DEARLY BELOVED FOR YOUR EDIFYING."

All of this is meant by the Holy Spirit to be an example to us, with the Spirit treating us as mature Believers, in effect, that we see all the particulars of what is here being done. As we have stated repeatedly, Paul is not merely defending himself against slander. The Holy Spirit is using the Apostle to address many things, always with a far larger picture in view.

I trust that by the help of the Lord we have brought some of these things to the fore.

EXCUSE OURSELVES?

The question, *"Again, think ye that we excuse ourselves unto you?"*, presents Paul correcting a wrong impression that is prevailing in the minds of some Corinthians. He surmises that they are thinking that he is merely defending himself and his assistants, in other words, that he is writing merely in his own interest.

Two things are wrong about this assumption:

1. There is no self-interest on the part of Paul and his associates.
2. Paul is not pleading his case before the forum of the Corinthians.

That is not his point at all (Lenski).

BEFORE GOD IN CHRIST

The phrase, *"We speak before God in Christ,"* presents the forum before which Paul and his associates do stand. In effect, he is saying, *"In the sight of God, with Him as the Judge we speak."*

Let the Corinthians not think that they are the judges; they face that Supreme Judge as well as Paul and his associates face Him. *"In God's sight in connection with Christ"* makes plain the entire situation. Christ, His Gospel, and His Church are involved in all that Paul is writing. Hence, Paul says, *"We speak."* The Greek structure, in effect says, *"We are not and cannot be silent."*

The right way in which the Corinthians are to think about this Epistle is that it is open speech before God Himself and involves Christ Who commissioned Paul and his associates for their work. How could they dare to be silent unless they intended to abandon that work!

PAUL IS NOT ON TRIAL

Paul and his associates are not on trial, and the Corinthians are not the judges. The Truth is, Paul and his associates are greatly concerned about the Corinthians, namely about their standing before God in Christ.

Getting off track Spiritually and Scripturally is not a matter to be taken lightly. The ramifications are always extremely negative. In fact, they cannot help but be so.

Were we speaking here about the price of wheat, or some other mundane thing, we could afford to take it lightly. But considering that we're speaking about the eternal souls of men, the single most important thing in the world, we had best understand the ramifications involved. And yet the Truth is, there are precious few Christians who are where they ought to be with God. Most know the Word of God so little, which is the same as saying, that an individual is going to take a perilous journey, and he has paid almost no attention whatsoever to a road map at his disposal.

YOUR EDIFICATION

The phrase, *"But we do all things, dearly beloved, for your edifying,"* pertains to the fact, that all of this is for the edification of the Corinthians, and for us as well I might quickly add.

This is *"edification"* in the Biblical sense, which includes rebuke, warning, castigation, etc.

The idea is not that Paul is placing an indictment against the Corinthians before God, that he is putting them on trial before the Supreme Judge. The Great Judge is looking down on all of them, on Paul and on his associates and on all the Corinthians. Paul is speaking in the Presence of the Lord so that all may know that this is no trifling matter. In fact, as the Corinthians read this Epistle they must realize that God's eyes are looking down on them, that all these things are connected with Christ and are said to them in connection with Him. If they understand that properly, they will then stop thinking that Paul is on trial before them in some type of self-defense. They will read this Epistle as they ought to read it. Consequently, he inserts the word *"beloved"* most effectively; it is expressive of his entire concern for the Corinthians.

CORRECTION

See how simply Paul does this correcting of all foolish thoughts on the part of the Corinthians. Two little sentences are enough, but they go to the heart of the matter.

But is Paul's Epistle not in part a self-defense before the Corinthians?

Yes, in a sense it is, but only in the fallout and not as a direct thrust. He is setting himself right in their eyes; he has even refuted charges and slanders made against him. But he has never done so in his own interest but only in the true spiritual interest of the Corinthians themselves.

He wrestles with them in order to make them what they ought to be *"in the sight of God in connection with Christ."*

There is no difficulty whatever on this score unless we ourselves read this Epistle with the wrong thoughts which Paul removes from the minds of the Corinthians.

(I am indebted to R. C. H. Lenski for the above thoughts concerning the disposition of Paul.)

(20) "FOR I FEAR, LEST WHEN I COME, I SHALL NOT FIND YOU SUCH AS I WOULD, AND THAT I SHALL BE FOUND UNTO YOU SUCH AS YE WOULD NOT: LEST THERE BE DEBATES, ENVYINGS, WRATHS, STRIFES, BACKBITINGS, WHISPERINGS, SWELLINGS, TUMULTS:"

In this Verse, Paul gives us a list of eight unholy things which threaten to destroy the Church at any and all times. You will notice that none of these sins is a flagrant vice. They are not the violent sins of the flesh, but those vicious sins of the carnal disposition. These sins are destructive to the peace of the Church. They cause dissensions that result in divisions.

Remember, this Scripture is talking about sin among Christians. Unless this is dealt with and corrected, there can be scant hope of effectively dealing with sin in the world.

These are the dispositional sins.

HOW WILL I FIND YOU?

The phrase, *"For I fear, lest, when I come, I shall not find you such as I would,"* proclaims the Apostle telling the Corinthians that they must address every single wrong. If not, and as we shall see, the results can be catastrophic.

NOTES

To which we have already briefly alluded, there had been a great Move of God at Corinth (Chapter 7), but evidently, some problems remained, or else Paul was taking this opportunity to warn these Believers of the danger of falling into these traps once again. He plainly says *"I fear,"* which fears to be sure, were completely justified. We must assume that the Holy Spirit is inspiring Paul to write these words; consequently, there was cause for the fear.

That the Assembly at Corinth could have been guilty of the 11 terrible faults and sins set out in Verses 20 and 21 is inconceivable. But all Scripture, both of the Old and the New Testaments, invariably testifies that man immediately corrupts whatever God commits to him (Williams).

THE AUTHORITY OF THE APOSTLE

The phrase, *"And that I shall be found unto you such as ye would not,"* refers to the Office of the Apostle, and the disciplinary measures which may have to be taken.

What do we mean by disciplinary measures?

The type of measures of which we speak are all in the spiritual realm, but can have devastating consequences, and because of the Office in which Paul stands. The Church is led and guided by the Holy Spirit, Who functions under Christ, the Head of the Church. However, the Apostle is the instrument in all of this, i.e., *"the one through whom Christ and the Spirit of God works."*

And yet, that doesn't mean that everything an Apostle says must be blindly followed. Nothing or no one must be followed if what is suggested or demanded, is in the slightest way unscriptural (Gal. 2:11-14). But yet, if what any Apostle is saying is Scriptural, which would of course include all that Paul has here said, it is to be followed and obeyed. If such is ignored, the results ultimately will be the Judgment of God in some form. In fact, it cannot be otherwise.

Whenever *"discipline"* is mentioned, many people have the idea of some type of personal confrontation, i.e., *"one person or group of persons punishing another."* However, even though that may exist, and in fact does exist among many Denominations and Churches, such is *never* Scriptural. No Believer has the moral right, to take it upon himself to administer punishment to another Believer. That goes for the leaders of Religious Denominations as well! Even as we've said several times, James addressed that very succinctly when he said, *"Who do you think you are, thinking you are qualified to judge another, God Alone is qualified to do such"* (James 4:12).

Whenever the God-called Apostle lays down spiritual direction, and considering that it is given by God, such is ignored at one's own peril. That should be obvious; however, Scriptural Church Government has been so diluted, skewed, and perverted, all by man's additions and deletions, that the modern Church has pretty much lost sight of the true Government of God. Consequently, they obey that which they should ignore, and ignore that which they should obey:

SINS OF THE CHURCH

The phrase, *"Lest there be debates, envyings, wraths, strifes, backbitings, whisperings, swellings, tumults,"* presents that which are the results of ignoring the Truth. In other words, this is what the Church will reap, if the Word of God is ignored:

1. Debates: The word means contention and discord, which are the result of an un-Christlike spirit. Such is always the result, when one is at cross-purposes with the Word of God.

2. Envyings: The envy referred to here, is that which arises from the superior advantages and endowments which some claimed or possessed over others. Envy everywhere is a fruitful cause of strife. Most contentions in the Church are somehow usually connected with envy.

Envying shows that a person is not fully trusting the Lord for leading and guidance, or looking to the Lord for sustenance. For the person who truly is following the Lord, seeking to be in the center of God's Will, what He gives you is what you want, and nothing else. So, in that frame of mind, the mind which is totally Christlike, there is no room for envy, and no position in which one can find him or herself, which would excite envy.

3. Wraths: This is anger or animosities between contending factions, the usual effect of forming parties.

NOTES

Once again, this speaks of an individual who is not fully trusting the Lord, because if so, there would be no occasion for such.

4. Strifes: This is contention and dispute. It is one striving for something, for which one should not have, or else because of self-will.

A person who is in the center of God's Will will not strive, for there is nothing to strive about.

5. Backbitings: This speaks of those who slander, or speak ill of those who are absent. Whisperers declare secretly, and with great reserve, the supposed faults of others. Backbiters proclaim publicly and avowedly.

6. Whisperings: This speaks of those who secretly, and in a sly manner by hints and innuendos, detract from others, or excite suspicion of them. It does not mean those who openly do such, but that more dangerous class who give hints of evil in others, who affect great knowledge, and communicate the evil report under the injunction of secrecy, knowing that it will be divulged.

This class of people abounds everywhere, and there is scarcely anyone more dangerous to the peace or happiness of society.

7. Swellings: This speaks of undue elation, being puffed up, such as would be produced by vain self-confidence.

8. Tumults: This is disorder and confusion arising from the existence of splinter groups or parties. Paul, deeply sensible of the evil of all this, had endeavored in this correspondence to suppress it, that all things might be pleasant when he should come among them.

SELF-WILL

Whenever these ugly sins of the flesh begin to be predominant in a Church or individuals, one could probably look to the cause as being that of self-will. The moment that Christ ceases to be the Supreme Person in one's life, at that moment self-will takes over, and the result is always this of which Paul mentions. As someone has said, it is an ugly list.

There are millions who call themselves *"Christians,"* but yet these ugly manifestations appear in their lives and every day walk. Why? How?

Most Christians, regrettably, have very little prayer life, if any at all. Consequently, there is very little communion with the Lord and, therefore, very little opportunity for the Holy Spirit to perform His Office Work. Without a daily prayer life and a daily study of the Word of God, one cannot hope to have victory; consequently, these things will abound.

The Holy Spirit Alone can subdue these passions of pride, and He can do so only as we understand the rudiments of Calvary and the Resurrection.

Yes, that's where the answer is to all of these problems, and any problem that may arise, the Cross, the Cross, the Cross!

(21) "AND LEST, WHEN I COME AGAIN, MY GOD WILL HUMBLE ME AMONG YOU, AND THAT I SHALL BEWAIL MANY WHICH HAVE SINNED ALREADY, AND HAVE NOT REPENTED OF THE UNCLEANNESS AND FORNICATION AND LASCIVIOUSNESS WHICH THEY HAVE COMMITTED."

Paul speaks lightly here, even though he is speaking about a very serious matter, so serious indeed, that it could destroy the Church, or at least certain Believers in the Church. He is speaking here of his Apostolic authority.

Having just alluded to this, due to the seriousness of its nature, please allow me to explain it a little further.

If the Biblical Admonitions are not heeded, the end result is always judgment; however, it is always Judgment tendered by God and not by man. The only thing that responsible, Spiritual Leadership can do, and I speak of the Leadership in a Local Church, is to disfellowship a recalcitrant Believer who refuses to repent (I Cor. Chpt. 5). Momentarily we will look at what true repentance actually is. Even then, such is to be done with every thought and idea of the person being redeemed, in other words, brought back and restored to a place of Service to the Lord (II Cor. Chpt. 2).

Some may claim that the Word of God, irrespective as to who delivers it, whether Apostle or not, must be obeyed in any case. They are exactly right; however, when an Apostle delivers the Word, whatever that Word may be, that is the last resort. If ignored or denied, Judgment is most sure to follow.

PAUL, AS AN EXAMPLE

While the fornicator at Corinth would ultimately have most certainly suffered the Judgment of God, had he continued in that lifestyle, still, when Paul the Apostle delivered the Word to him (I Cor. Chpt. 5), if repentance had not been forthcoming, Judgment would have been right around the corner.

It should be quickly said that it doesn't matter whether the Church recognizes the Apostle or not, or whether so-called Spiritual Leaders recognize such a one, the Church will still be responsible for the Word delivered by the Apostle. I am trying to say that such is ignored at one's peril.

As the Prophet was under the Old Covenant, so is the Apostle in the New Covenant. When the Prophets of old spoke, it didn't matter whether it was to Israel or to a heathen nation. It didn't matter what the heathen thought. They could claim they did not serve Jehovah and, consequently, were not subject to Him. Irrespective, what the Prophets of God said, came to pass.

Even though Prophets continue in their Office in the New Covenant, their role has changed in one respect. Leadership is now given into the hands of the Apostle who now stands in the same place that the Prophets of old once stood (Eph. 2:20-22). It is not in the hands of Denominational Leaders unless one or more of these Leaders is actually a God-called Apostle, which is possible but seldom the case. Apostles are not elected by popular ballot. That is not meant to say that the Word of God delivered by anyone is not important, for it certainly is. It is meant to say that this the manner in which God has chosen to establish Leadership.

WHAT TYPE OF JUDGMENT?

Whenever the word of the Apostle is denied or ignored, providing it is truly given by the Lord, the Spirit of God automatically lifts, at least as His role of Helper and Comforter are concerned (Gen. 6:3; I Sam. 16:14; Ps. 51:11; I Cor. 5:5; Eph. 4:30; I Thess. 5:19).

To be frank, and I think I exaggerate not, most of the Religious Denominations presently, function without the Spirit of God and because they have ignored the Apostolic Word. Of course, many of these Denominations do not even believe there is such a thing as Apostles presently. In fact, if the truth be known, many of them don't believe in much of anything. However, as the response of the heathen of old

NOTES

to the Prophets of God, such makes no difference. They are answering and they shall answer just the same.

Without the Spirit of God to lead and guide, the Church is like a blind giant, that stumbles from one side to the other with no clear direction in mind. And then God begins to send judgment of many and various kinds and in many and various ways. It may be a while in coming, but come it shall.

When Israel crucified Christ, they lumbered on for about thirty-seven years without seemingly being affected in the negative sense; however, in A.D. 70 the Roman General Titus completely destroyed Judea and Jerusalem. As someone has said, *"The mills of God grind slowly* (They take their time.)*, but they grind exceedingly fine* (They miss nothing.)*."*

A PROPOSED VISIT

The phrase, *"And lest, when I come again, my God will humble me among you,"* refers to the fact that such pronounced Judgment because of a lack of repentance will inflict great pain on Paul, just as much as on the guilty party. This is the attitude and feeling of the True Apostle, which are the opposite of the glee and delight registered by many false apostles presently.

The true Apostle knows what is involved. He has no bias nor prejudice toward the rebellious individual. In other words, irrespective as to what has been said about him or done to him, he has no ax to grind, or pound of flesh to obtain, symbolically speaking. When one delights in such a role, all others can be certain that particular one is not a true Apostle, irrespective of his claims.

HUMBLE ME?

Paul loved these people. In fact, either directly or indirectly, every single person in the Church at Corinth had been brought to Christ under the Ministry of this Apostle. Consequently, in a sense, they were his *"children."*

He loves them enough to tell them the Truth and to hurt greatly if they reject that Truth.

He had stood before these people and brought them the Gospel which had saved their souls. And now to stand before them again and be forced to deliver a *"repent or else"* Message, humbled him greatly. In this, we again see the heart of the True Apostle and not the heart of the dictatorial lord.

NOTES

For one to be humbled means they are brought low. In fact, this type of spirit which Paul registered means that he did not place himself in a *"holier than thou"* attitude, but rather the very opposite. This is so important that I hope the Reader can see and understand what the Spirit is here saying.

This is the very opposite of the *"stone throwing spirit"*; the very opposite of the *"self-righteous spirit."*

Paul puts it all in a striking way: Not that the Corinthians might suffer disgrace and humiliation, but that he, Paul, might be humbled by God before the Corinthians at the sight of their disgraceful condition, that he might be caused to mourn over many guilty ones. The Corinthians should feel that way, but would they? Well, Paul would!

"Lest my God shall humble me," the God whom I serve so earnestly in Christ, brings out the full poignancy of what Paul would feel — his own God bowing His Head in the dust. That would be a sad, sad dispensation of providence for Paul.

Jesus had labored in vain for Judas, as well as for many others who then turned from Him; that sorrow Paul, too, had often enough experienced. Would it then be his again in Corinth?

BEWAIL MANY?

The phrase, *"And that I shall bewail many which have sinned already,"* means if they have repented of their sin, he could still rejoice in them. If they continued in their sin, until he came, it would be to him a source of deep lamentation.

It is evident from the word *"many"* that disorders had prevailed very extensively in the Church at Corinth.

The word rendered *"have sinned already"* means *"who have sinned before"*; and the idea is that they were old offenders, in other words, had been committing this sin or sins for some time and that they had not yet repented.

REPENTANCE

The phrase, *"And have not repented of the uncleanness and fornication and lasciviousness which they have committed,"* refers to the old pagan vices into which some of the Corinthians had been drawn and were ever in danger of being drawn.

This final fear of Paul's so plainly reaches back into I Corinthians that it is useless to deny the fact. The fear is that Paul might have to mourn *"many of those who have been hitherto sinning and had not repented of their uncleanness,"* etc. Not repenting, they would, of course, be lost. In these passages he is not thinking of excommunication from the Church as he was in I Corinthians Chapter 5, but rather the loss of their souls, because of their refusing to repent.

The idea is that the sinning which started in the past is pictured as going on unchecked to the present, despite Paul's warnings of about a year previous. No decisive act of repentance at any time in the past, it seems, has been engaged. So, he is now speaking of the loss of their souls. In other words, that this ungodly activity must stop, or else!

THE LAST FOUR CHAPTERS OF II CORINTHIANS

Those who separate Chapters 10-13 from II Corinthians and call this *"The Four Chapter Letter,"* which they claim was written earlier or later than II Corinthians make much of the eleven evils listed in Verses 20 and 21, on the plea that the first Seven Chapters show that things were so far improved in Corinth that Paul could not have harbored these fears when he wrote those Seven Chapters of II Corinthians.

However, they fail to note that those Seven Chapters plainly show that enough trouble is still active in Corinth, that these further admonitions are needed. Even though a great move had taken place at Corinth, even as Chapter Seven records, still, it is obvious that all did not repent. At any rate, Paul is also warning those who did repent that this danger ever lurks, and they must always be watchful that they do not slip back.

WHAT IS BIBLICAL REPENTANCE?

1. The call for repentance on the part of man is a call for him to return to his creaturely (and Covenant) dependence on God. Such calls are particularly frequent in the Prophets of old.

Amos 4:6-11 makes it clear that the evil that God intends as a consequence of Israel's sin is not malicious or vindictive, but rather is intended to bring Israel to repentance. He who commits evil finds further evil willed by God. But he who repents of his evil, finds a God who repents of His intended evil or judgment.

2. Whoever repents, even at the eleventh hour, whoever turns again to God, finds a God of Mercy and Love, not of Judgment (Jer. 18:8; 26:3, 13, 19; Jonah 3:9).

By contrast, when man refuses to repent, and removes himself by his self-will from God's direction and care, he finds that the God-willed consequence of his evil is more evil (Gen. 6:6; I Sam. 15:11, 35; II Sam. 24:16; Jer. 18:10).

3. Repentance is not just a feeling sorry, or merely changing one's mind, but rather, a turning around, a complete alteration of the basic motivation and direction of one's life. An example is the Ministry of Jesus.

Jesus' call for repentance receives little explicit mention in Mk. 1:15; 6:12 and Mat. 4:17; 11:20; 12:21, but is emphasized by Lk. 5:32; 10:13; 11:32; 13:3, 5; 15:7, 10; 16:30; 17:3; 24:47.

Other sayings and incidents in all three Gospels, however, express very clearly the character of the repentance which Jesus' whole Ministry demanded. Its radical nature, as a complete turning round and return is emphasized by the parable of the Prodigal Son (Lk. 15:11-24).

4. Repentance means acknowledging that one has no possible claim upon God, and, therefore, submits himself without excuse or attempted justification to God's Mercy (Lk. 18:13).

5. Repentance is God's Gift and man's responsibility. Consequently, it is the responsibility of Christians to repent, at least when needed, just as much as it is for the sinner who desires Salvation (II Cor. 7:9; 12:21; James 5:19; I Jn. 1:5-2:2; Rev. 2:5, 16, 21; 3:3, 19).

UNCLEANNESS, FORNICATION, AND LASCIVIOUSNESS

The term *"uncleanness"* refers to all types of sexual perversions of men and women, but moreso to the sin of *"homosexuality"* (Rom. 1:24; 6:19; Gal. 5:19; Eph. 4:19; 5:3; Col. 3:5; II Pet. 2:10).

"Fornication" in the Bible means: repeated adultery with various partners of married or single people (Mat. 5:32; 19:9; I Cor. 7:2; 10:8; I Thess. 4:3; Rev. 9:21).

Incest (I Cor. 5:1; 10:8).

NOTES

Idolatry and adultery in honor of idol gods (II Chron. 21:11; Isa. 23:17; Ezek. 16:15, 26, 29; Acts 15:20, 29; 21:25; Rev. 2:14-21; 14:8; 17:2-4; 18:3-9; 19:2).

Natural harlotry (Jn. 1:41; I Cor. 6:13-18).

Spiritual harlotry (Ezek. 16:15, 26, 29; Rev. 17:2-4; 18:3-9; 19:2).

Sodomy and male prostitution (Rom. 1:24-29; I Cor. 6:9-11; II Cor. 12:21; Gal. 5:19; Eph. 5:3; Col. 3:5; Heb. 12:16; Jude vss. 6-7).

Some people claim that fornication applies to those who are unmarried while adultery applies to those who are married. That is incorrect.

Concerning the meaning of fornication, do all these Scriptures we have just given apply to single people only? If not, then fornication does not apply only to single people as some teach.

"Lasciviousness" is that which promotes or partakes of that which tends to produce lewd emotions. It is anything that tends to foster sex sins and lust. That is why many worldly pleasures have to be avoided by Christians — so that lasciviousness may not be committed.

These sins which Paul mentions in this Verse are the sins to which they were particularly exposed in Corinth, as these were the sins for which that corrupt city was noted. Hence, the frequent cautions in these Epistles against them; and hence, it is not to be wondered at, that some of those who have become professing Christians had fallen into them.

CORINTH

The principal heathen deity worshipped in the city of Corinth was Venus; as Diana was the principal worshipped at Ephesus, Minerva at Athens, etc.

Ancient cities were devoted, usually, to some particular god or goddess, and were supposed to be under their peculiar protection. Corinth was devoted, or dedicated, thus to the goddess of love or licentious passion; and the effect may be easily conceived.

The temple of Venus was erected on the north side or slope of the Acrocorinthus, a mountain about half a mile in height on the south of the city; and from the summit of which a magnificent prospect opened on the north to Parnassus and Helicon, to the eastward the island of Aegina and the Citadel of Athens, and to the west the rich and beautiful plains of Sicyon.

NOTES

VENUS

This mountain was covered with temples and splendid houses; but was especially devoted to Venus, and was the place of her worship. Her shrine appeared above those of the other gods; and it was enjoined by law, that 1,000 beautiful females should officiate as courtesans, or public prostitutes, before the altar of the goddess of love.

In a time of public calamity and imminent danger, these women attended at the sacrifices, and walked with the other citizens singing songs dedicated to Venus.

The effect of this on the morals of the city can be easily understood. It became the most dissipated, corrupt, and ultimately the most effeminate and feeble portion of Greece.

THE CHURCH AT CORINTH

It is necessary to make these statements because they go to show the exceeding Grace of God in collecting a Church in such a city; the Power of the Gospel in overcoming the strongest and most polluted passions of our nature: and because no small part of the irregularities which arose in the Church at Corinth, and which gave the Apostle occasion, at least in part, to write this Epistle, were produced by this prevailing licentiousness of the people; and by the fact, that gross and licentious passions had received the countenance of law and the patronage of public opinion.

The contrast between the first and last Verses of this Chapter is humbling and salutary: a man in the purity of paradise, and a man in the putridity of Corinth; and yet, Corinth claimed occasion with Paradise!

Yes, repentance was demanded at Corinth and for all the obvious reasons.

"Jesus my Lord will love me forever, from
Him no power can sever,
"He gave His Life to ransom my soul, now
I belong to Him."

"Once I was lost in sin's degradation, Jesus
came down to bring me Salvation,
"Lifted me up from sorrow and shame,
now I belong to Him."

"Joy floods my soul for Jesus has saved
me, freed me from sin that long had
enslaved me,

"His precious Blood He gave to redeem, now I belong to Him."

CHAPTER 13

(1) "THIS IS THE THIRD TIME I AM COMING TO YOU. IN THE MOUTH OF TWO OR THREE WITNESSES SHALL EVERY WORD BE ESTABLISHED."

There is a life that meets all foes with triumph. There is a life that faces disaster with conquest. There is a life that supplies us with the necessary elements of existence. There is a life that is indispensable. That life is the life of Christ.

The Christian Life is not merely an improvement on human life. The spiritual life is not an advanced step beyond the natural life. It is something unique and different. It begins in a moment and lasts through eternity. It requires a birth that begets a new creature. This very Epistle says, *"Therefore if any man be in Christ, he is a new creature: old things are passed away; behold all things are become new."*

THE NEW LIFE AND OLD PROBLEMS

This new life is immediately faced with old problems. It marches into the arena of human conflict where the age-old disputes, distresses, diseases, and disasters are thrown against it.

The Apostle, whose autobiographical account this letter is, ran the gamut of human experience. He met and mastered every kind of foe. He did it, not as Saul of Tarsus, but as Paul the Disciple and Apostle of Jesus Christ. He did it not as a Philosopher, Scientist, or Religionist, but as a Believer in, and a follower of, the Lord Jesus Christ.

Since this Epistle deals with so wide a variety of experience and since it shows us the applicability of Christianity to those experiences, it consequently shows the proximity of God and His Way, which is the Bible Way, to our problems.

If we could be persuaded that God is where the solution to our problems is, we would have the confidence that gives victorious living, but how few of us are confident of that fact. We think in vague religious terms instead of in terms of a Personal God. We think in terms of Church instead of Christ. We think in terms of liturgy instead of Life.

NOTES

A NEW FREEDOM

One day the telephone in the Office of the Rector of President Roosevelt's Washington Church rang, and an eager voice said, *"Tell me, do you expect the President to be in Church this Sunday?"*

"That," the Rector explained patiently, *"I cannot promise. But we expect God to be there, and we fancy that will be incentive enough for a reasonably large attendance."*

Yes, He will, but God will also be in your home. He is not restricted to a Church. Our bodies are temples of Divine residence and operation. We do not have to go to a Church Building for God's Blessing. If we are new creatures we have the new basis for life. This new basis for life means a life that endures under assault, pressure, disaster, and tribulation. It means a new freedom (Laurin).

THE THIRD TIME

The phrase, *"This is the third time I am coming to you,"* probably refers to the third visit the Apostle will make to Corinth. His first time was the planting of the Church, and of the second, we have little information, except what is given in the next Verse.

The repetition here is emphatic. In II Corinthians 12:20-21 and in II Corinthians 13:2 he also mentions his coming. All of these accumulated references to his coming, save II Corinthians 12:14, have a note of warning.

Some have claimed that these references only refer to Paul proposing to come, but never did, other than his first stay in Corinth, which pertained to the founding of the Church. However, the force of the Greek in this Verse actually says, *"I am going a third time."* So, it seems to me this seals the argument, that Paul had in fact, been to Corinth two other times, and was now coming the third time.

TWO OR THREE WITNESSES

The phrase, *"In the mouth of two or three witnesses shall every word be established,"* is derived from Deuteronomy 19:15.

This again states the Law of interpretation of Scripture. Every Doctrine must be proved by at least two or three Scriptures to be accepted as Truth and binding upon Christians.

As Paul uses this word here, he is referring back to the statements given in Verses 20 and 21 of the previous Chapter. In other words, when he gets to Corinth, if these problems have not been rectified totally and completely through repentance, he will deal with them.

IF NECESSARY, HOW WILL THE APOSTLE DEAL WITH SUCH SITUATIONS?

Paul would, of course, not take such cases into his own hands and out of the hands of the congregation, meaning that he would not act as judge supreme and dictate the verdict by virtue of his Apostolic authority. In I Corinthians 5:3-5 he did the very opposite; and, in II Corinthians 1:24 he declares the direct opposite. The congregation alone can expel. It hears the necessary witnesses, it passes every motion in every case.

What would be Paul's function? The same as that which he exercised in his letters: to advise and to guide the congregation in the true Spirit of Christ.

This is a far cry, as should be obvious, from most modern Denominational exercises regarding discipline at least as it pertains to Preachers. In their doing, it is taken completely out of the hands of the Local Church, where in fact, all matters of this nature should be handled, whether it regards members of the congregation or Preachers over the congregation, even including the Senior Pastor, etc. It should be obvious as to the rightness of this, due to the fact that the Local Church knows far more about the circumstances, whatever those circumstances are, than anyone outside its interest and location.

In fact, there is every evidence that the individual addressed in I Corinthians Chapter 5 who was guilty of gross immorality, actually was one of the Leaders or Pastors of that Church. In his case, as in all cases of this nature, the Holy Spirit through the Apostle demanded repentance, even as He did in the last Verse of the previous Chapter. That repentance not forthcoming, the individual was to be expelled from the Church. However, if repentance was forthcoming, exactly as the Second Chapter of this present Epistle proclaims, the individual was to be instantly restored.

Incidentally, the *"two or three witnesses"* referred to here by Paul, are not referring to his visits to that Church, as some have claimed, but rather *"two or three witnesses"* regarding accusations against certain individuals in the Church who may be guilty of the sins mentioned by Paul in Verse 21 of the previous Chapter.

So, the *"witnesses"* refer not only to the proving of particular Doctrines in the Word of God, but also witnesses against someone regarding wrongdoing, etc.

(2) "I TOLD YOU BEFORE, AND FORETELL YOU, AS IF I WERE PRESENT, THE SECOND TIME; AND BEING ABSENT NOW I WRITE TO THEM WHICH HERETOFORE HAVE SINNED, AND TO ALL OTHER, THAT, IF I COME AGAIN, I WILL NOT SPARE:"

This Verse proves I think, that Paul had been to Corinth a second time. The sense here is, *"I foretell to you as I did when I was present with you the second time. Being absent now I write what I said on my second visit."*

This is why he speaks of being ready to come to them a third time. The theory that his first visit was when he founded the Church and second and third visits were his two Epistles to them is not reasonable. He could not call his letters visits to them. Because there is no record of his second visit is not proof that he did not make it, anymore than no mention in history of all his sufferings of II Corinthians 11:23-28 is proof he did not go through them.

Since he repeatedly mentions coming to them a third time, that should be sufficient to prove there was a second visit.

THE SECOND TIME

The phrase, *"I told you before, and foretell you, as if I were present, the second time,"* in effect says, *"I told you these things on my second visit to you."*

In some way, Paul is equating his two previous times in Corinth, plus the third he proposes to make, and in fact did make (Acts Chpt. 20), with the *"two or three witnesses"* mentioned in the previous Verse. The idea does not so much pertain to his visits, for such within themselves cannot be classified as witnesses, but rather that he has given them the same warnings now some three times. In fact, his word, at least in this case, is the Gospel, therefore, serving as a proper witness, i.e., *"witnesses."*

NOTES

NOTES

DOES THE WORD OF OTHER APOSTLES, EVEN UNTO THIS HOUR, SERVE AS WELL, AS THE WORD OF GOD?

Even though a Word given by any True Apostle, that is if it is truly from the Lord, is definitely a Word of God; however, it is not in any way the same as the Holy Scriptures. In fact, what modern Apostles give, is already in the Word of God in the first place. The present Canon of Scripture which we refer to as *"the Bible,"* is finished. There will be nothing added to that, because it is not necessary to add anything to that, all having been given, which is obvious from reading the final Chapters of the Bible.

Actually, there were Letters written by Paul, although containing excellent advice, and no doubt blessed by the Lord, still, were not considered by the Holy Spirit to be the Word of God, in the sense of the Holy Scriptures. Only that which we have in our present Canon of Scripture regarding the Letters of Paul, are considered *"These Scriptures."* The same would go for all the other writers, be it Old or New Testaments.

Whenever the Holy Spirit presently uses Apostles to give leading to the Church, and in whatever capacity, whatever He gives through them, will always coincide with the Word of God. As well, there will be found somewhere in the Bible, two or three witnesses (two or three different Scriptures or Passages), to verify what is being said. If those *"witnesses"* aren't obvious, what is said should be ignored.

Paul is speaking here with Apostolic Authority, and it would be the same if Simon Peter were speaking accordingly or any of the other Apostles at that particular time. In their case, as is obvious, it was the Word of God.

TO THEM WHICH HAVE SINNED

The phrase, *"And being absent now I write to them which heretofore have sinned,"* proves by the words *"absent now,"* that the words *"second time"* actually pertain to a definite visit.

The idea of this statement, is to allow the sinners, whomever they may have been, time to repent and to amend, which also does not hurry the congregation in its discipline. Paul now forewarns all concerned that his delayed arrival, in fact when it does happen, will bring this period of Mercy and Grace to an end, at least as it refers to discipline.

The meaning of his statement is clear. If they repent, the matter is to be dropped and no action will be taken, and for all the obvious reasons. Consequently, he is pleading with them that this be done, in order that they may avoid discipline, i.e., *"Judgment."*

How beautiful and wonderful are the Grace of God! How merciful is our Lord! How longsuffering He is, not desiring that any should perish, but that all should come unto repentance (II Pet. 3:9).

WHY ISN'T REPENTANCE GOOD ENOUGH FOR THE MODERN CHURCH?

That's a good question!

The sadness is, repentance is not good enough for most of the modern Church. In fact, repentance, at least in most circles, is given no credibility at all. In the modern Church, any of the three mentioned in Verse 21 of the previous Chapter, if in fact guilty, would require extensive psychological counseling. In other words, the Word of God presently is given lip service only, if any service at all. Almost totally, the psychological way is demanded and demanded in totality. This means most modern religious Leaders have abandoned the Word of God, even though they would deny such.

The Truth is, that Jesus took care of these problems at Calvary and the Resurrection. In fact, He took care of *all* problems at that momentous event. So, either the modern Church does not believe that, which is the situation in most cases, or else it does not understand what Calvary and the Resurrection actually are. This is a tragedy of unparalleled proportions, for the simple reason, that no help whatsoever is forthcoming from the psychological way. In fact, not only is no help forthcoming, but actual harm will be the result, and in many ways.

First of all, such direction takes one completely away from the true answer of the Word of God. While I realize that so-called Christian Psychologists claim to meld the Word of God with psychological counseling, the Truth is, what they are advocating is actually a lie.

In effect they are saying, that the Word of God does not meet all the needs of humanity, especially modern man as they put it, and it needs help. The psychological way is that help, they claim! If thought through, that is blasphemy pure and simple.

DOES THE BIBLE HOLD ALL THE ANSWERS TO THE PROBLEMS OF LIFE?

Yes, and in totality!

Peter plainly said, *"According as His Divine Power hath given unto us all things that pertain unto Life and Godliness, through the knowledge of Him that hath called us to glory and virtue:"*

He then said, *"Whereby are given unto us exceeding great and precious Promises: that by these ye might be partakers of the Divine Nature, having escaped the corruption that is in the world through lust"* (II Pet. 1:3-4).

Now either that is true, or else the Holy Spirit through Peter lied about the situation.

One need not fear, it is true!

The knowledge of what I am saying, comes not only from belief in the Word of God, but as well from my own personal experience of having proved the Word of God. Not only have I seen untold thousands set free from the worst bondages of darkness, by the Power of Almighty God, but over and over again, and in every conceivable way, I have seen it work in my own life.

To be brief, all of this, the great victory given by Christ, the answer to all of life's problems and difficulties, can be found in what Jesus did at Calvary and the Resurrection. In fact, all the tens of millions of Sacrifices offered up in the Old Testament, were a symbolism of this coming great Sacrifice at Calvary. There, Jesus not only paid the terrible sin debt that hung like a sword of Damocles over all of humanity, but as well, He broke the grip of sin from the Believer's life. All of these great victories given by the Lord to any and all, come simply by Faith in what was done there that day, and at least, somewhat of an understanding of its principles.

When I say Calvary, and that the answer is found there, I am meaning for every problem irrespective as to what that problem may be.

That means that the answer to marriage problems is found in Calvary and the Resurrection. It means that the cure for all aberrations and perversions is found in what Jesus did at Calvary and the Resurrection. It is the cure for all depression, discouragement, fear, and suchlike infirmities. It is the cure for personality problems, unholy habits, anything in fact, which has a tendency to *"steal, kill and destroy"* (Jn. 10:10).

NOTES

CALVARY AND THE RESURRECTION ADDRESSED IT ALL

That's why Paul said, *"But God forbid that I should glory, save in the Cross of our Lord Jesus Christ, by Whom the world is crucified unto me, and I unto the world"* (Gal. 6:14).

Why in the world would anyone want to glory in the *"Cross,"* which was such an instrument of horror, suffering, and humiliation? The answer again is obvious!

It was there that Jesus destroyed Satan's claims on the human race. Those claims were made upon the basis of sin in the life of the sinner, in both the fact of sin and the acts of sin. When Jesus paid the sin debt, Satan's rightful claim was broken and that refers to all of humanity. However, the fruit and benefit of what Jesus did, come about only on the acceptance by the sinner of Jesus as Lord and Saviour. This is done by Faith (Jn. 3:16; Rom. 10:9-10, 13; Eph. 2:8-9).

The explanation of the victory of Salvation and the victory of Life, is found in totality in Romans Chapters 6, 7 and 8. I would strongly advise the Reader, at least if you have not already done so, to secure for yourself our Commentary on the great book of Romans, and minutely study the three Chapters in question.

I WILL NOT SPARE

The phrase, *"And to all other, that, if I come again, I will not spare,"* pertains to those of Verse 21 of the previous Chapter. Of course, it could refer to anyone, and to any type of sin.

The words *"I will not spare,"* contain strong meanings. Some of those meanings are as follows:

1. Some were denying the Apostleship of Paul. If his words are ignored, which in effect is the Word of the Lord, these individuals, whomever they may have been, will find out quickly as to the veracity of his Apostleship.

2. If his admonitions are ignored, Judgment will come. It may come soon or not so soon, but it will come, barring repentance. Let no one think the opposite. Because all do not fall dead immediately as Ananias and Sapphira as recorded in Acts Chapter 5, doesn't mean that Judgment is not coming. God must judge

NOTES

unrepentant sin, His Nature and Righteousness demand such.

3. As an Apostle, Paul had the right to state this case and make these demands. Consequently, a denial of what he says, is in fact, a denial of God. In fact, this (through Apostles) is the manner in which God governed His Church then, and the manner in which He does presently. Even though men have attempted to change this manner of Government, their changes are not recognized by God.

(3) "SINCE YE SEEK A PROOF OF CHRIST SPEAKING IN ME, WHICH TO YOU-WARD IS NOT WEAK, BUT IS MIGHTY IN YOU."

Christians who have tasted genuine miracles often succumb to the temptation to be able to control the occurrence and increase of God's power through methods, principles, and laws. Perhaps many who do this are not aware that they have thereby denied the true miraculous and have locked God in a box where He must respond in a predetermined manner to their positive possibility thinking, positive confession, visualizations, and affirmations. The fact that they may have stepped over the line into the occult without realizing it doesn't help either them or their followers to escape the consequences.

The false apostles of Paul's day were laying stress on miracles, signs, and wonders, which they evidently claimed were not prominent in Paul's Ministry. In fact, these things *were* priority in Paul's Ministry, but were not emphasized as the premier of Christ, but rather the development of Holiness and Righteousness within the hearts and lives of Believers.

The Truth was, there were no genuine signs and wonders among these false apostles, simply because the Holy Spirit will not work through error, which should be blatantly obvious. Nevertheless, the power of seduction is so strong, that the Believers at Corinth, or at least many of them, had been led to believe that these false apostles were performing miracles galore, when in reality there were none. Paul briefly refers to *"signs, and wonders, and mighty deeds,"* in 12:12, which the Corinthians seemed to have forgotten.

AT PRESENT

There are some modern Ministries which attempt to build themselves on the aura of *"miracles,"* which within itself is not Scriptural, that is if the Book of Acts is to be the criteria. While these things are somewhat prominent in that account, and should be presently as well, still, the major thrust always was the Salvation of souls, the Baptism with the Holy Spirit, and a victorious, overcoming Christian life, which can only be found in the Spirit. In other words, the Work of the Spirit is to make one ever more Christlike.

The amazing thing is, that those who build their ministries on the aura of *"miracles,"* in fact, have very little, if any, of that which they trumpet so loudly, despite their claims. Once again, if the major thrust, which should always be the Salvation of souls is held lightly, the Holy Spirit is hindered, because He will not honor wrong direction.

I want *"signs, and wonders, and mighty deeds,"* in my Ministry. I believe that the Bible teaches that such should always follow the true, Spirit directed Ministry (Mk. 16:15-18); however, I want those things to be in their proper place, in other words to *"follow them that believe,"* and not be the major emphasis, that being *"the Gospel"* (Mk. 16:15, 17).

PROOF?

The phrase, *"Since ye seek a proof of Christ speaking in me,"* means that some of the Corinthians, who in fact, had been saved under Paul's Ministry had become so deceived and deluded, that they now questioned the Apostleship of Paul. Actually, they were calling into question his Apostolic authority, which the false apostles had denigrated. In other words, they had made the Corinthians believe that they did not have to heed Paul's admonitions, in effect, obey what he said. To bring the Corinthians to this place, even as we have already said, they had to tear Paul down in their eyes. So, they denigrated him in many and varied ways.

THIS HAS ALWAYS BEEN THE PROBLEM

The matter is really very simple, but yet falls out to that which is very complex. This has always been Satan's method. The Lord gives His Word, and Satan attempts to pull the person away from that Word. In the Garden of Eden he used the serpent, but thereafter he used false prophets and false apostles.

The manner of his seduction is always very subtle, in other words, very careful. That's why Paul referred to him as *"an angel of light"* (II Cor. 11:14).

So, the people are presented the Word of God and they are presented the false word, but packaged very neatly and nicely, which deceives many (II Tim. 4:3-4). The Believer now has to make a choice, and what will that choice be?

THE TELLTALE SIGNS

What should the Believer look for respecting false directions? The following will hopefully provide some information:

1. False teachers, that is, those who are peddling a false gospel, do not attempt to get people saved. In fact, there is no point in doing so, for their gospel being error, cannot have any convicting power of the Holy Spirit; therefore, people cannot truly be saved. So, they parasite on the harvest of others, claiming their ministries lead people to *"deeper life,"* or *"greater enlightenment."* In fact, this is exactly what the false apostles of Paul's day were doing, and they continue unto this present hour.

While we know and understand that there are different types of Ministries, whether *"Evangelists"* or *"Teachers,"* with the former definitely seeing more people saved; still, the true Teacher will seek to develop Believers in Christlikeness. The next point will give more light on that statement.

2. False teachers always appeal in some manner, to the baser motives of the individual. In other words, it is not Christlikeness, but rather *"how to use the Word of God to get rich," "how to be a prophet"* and, therefore, to have a word for everybody, *"to bring in God's Kingdom by electing Christians to high office, which appeals to pride,"* etc. In fact, the list is almost endless. These so-called Teachers have little interest in Righteousness and Holiness, but have another agenda in mind altogether (II Cor. 13:5).

3. According to the Words of Jesus, there will be proper *"fruit,"* and not just baseless, wild claims (Mat. 7:15-20). In other words, the *"fruit"* will be *"Righteousness and Holiness,"* and not other things.

SUCCESS IN THE MODERN CHURCH

Almost all of the modern Church has bought into the *"success message,"* despite the fact that the Lord has not called any of us to be successful, but rather faithful. And yet, success is the name of the game today, not only in the world, but inside the Church as well. Humility is out and self-esteem is in, even though we are urged in Scripture, *"let each esteem others better than themselves"* (Phil. 2:3).

It used to be common knowledge that the besetting sin of the human race was pride. Now, however, we are being told that our problem is not that we think too highly of ourselves, but too lowly, that we all have a bad self-image, and that our greatest need is to build up our self-esteem.

Though Peter wrote, *"Humble yourselves, therefore, under the Mighty Hand of God, that He may exalt you at the proper time"* (I Pet. 5:6), we are being urged to *"visualize"* ourselves into success, which is but one of many so-called methods. Paul's inspired declaration that Christ *"emptied Himself, taking the form of a servant . . .* (and) *humbled Himself by becoming obedient to . . . death on a cross"* (Phil. 2:7-8) is now explained by Robert Schuller, in the context of today's success-oriented world, to mean:

"Jesus knew His worth" Schuller says, *"His success fed His self-esteem . . . He suffered the Cross to sanctify His self-esteem. And He bore the Cross to sanctify your self-esteem.*

"And the Cross will sanctify the ego trip" (emphasis in the original)!

To be frank, this is blasphemy!

He also said, *"I don't think anything has been done in the name of Christ and under the banner of Christianity that has proven more destructive to human personality and, hence, counterproductive to the evangelism enterprise, than the often crude, uncouth, and unchristian strategy of attempting to make people aware of their lost and sinful condition."*

According to Schuller, the Ministry of John the Baptist was *"crude, uncouth, and counterproductive to the evangelism enterprise"* (Mat. 3:7-12).

Christ Himself said that He came to call *"sinners to repentance"* (Lk. 5:32).

THE SUCCESS MESSAGE

If Moses lived today, it would not be said of him that he chose to *"suffer affliction with the people of God"* (Heb. 11:25), but that he chose to *"obtain wealth, success, and popularity with*

NOTES

NOTES

the people of God." In fact, Moses would have been greatly encouraged to have remained in the Egyptian Palace, for it is obvious, at least according to modern-day thinking, that he could have much more influence for God in that position, possibly even as the Pharaoh of Egypt, than he could otherwise. But that's not what the Holy Spirit said.

It once was said, *"All who desire to live Godly in Christ Jesus will be persecuted"* (II Tim. 3:12), but today it is said, *"Those who live Godly lives will be honored and successful in the world."*

Not just individual Christians, but Churches also now pursue success, and the larger the Church the more successful it is considered to be. In that vein, Paul Yonggi Cho teaches that *"positive thinking, positive speaking, and positive visualizing are the keys to success."* Anyone, he says, can literally *"incubate"* and give birth to physical reality by creating a vivid image in his or her mind and focusing upon it. In the foreword to Cho's book, *"The Fourth Dimension,"* Robert Schuller writes:

"I discovered the reality of that dynamic dimension in prayer that comes through visualizing. . . .

"Don't try to understand it, just start to enjoy it! It's true. It works. I tried it."

Christian Colleges, Seminaries, Missions, and relief organizations are also in the success game, and most of them look to the techniques of big business for running their own affairs. If it works for the University of California, why not for a Christian College?

This is no doubt true when it comes to certain things such as accounting and management. However, sorcery, and sorcery it is, which we have just mentioned, is rampant in the business world and enters the Church in the form of success/motivation techniques and the latest psychotherapy baptized with Christian terminology.

CONTENDING FOR THE FAITH

Jude wrote that we must *"contend earnestly for the Faith which was once for all delivered to the Saints"* (Jude vs. 3). It is impossible to always be *"positive"* while contending for Truth.

H. A. Ironside, longtime Pastor of Moody Memorial Church in Chicago, declared: *"The Faith means the whole body of revealed Truth, and to contend for all of God's Truth necessitates some negative teaching . . . Any error, or any Truth-and-error mixture, calls for definite exposure and repudiation. To condone such is to be unfaithful to God and His Word, and treacherous to imperiled souls for whom Christ died."*

THE POWER OF THE MIND

The power of the mind has been taken to its extremes by the Eastern Religions, such as Buddhism, etc. The teaching of Buddhism of course, is totally unscriptural and, therefore, invalid. So, for their techniques to be taken up by Christians, such as visualizing, etc., show a complete lack of knowledge respecting the Holy Spirit and how He works.

This false teaching claims that one's destiny is in the power of one's mind. *"Whatever you can conceive is yours,"* they say! *"Speak it into being. Create it by positive mind-set. Success, happiness, perfect health is all yours — if you will only use your mind creatively. Turn your dreams into reality by using mind power."*

Let it be known once and for all, God will not abdicate His Lordship to the power of our minds, negative or positive. We are to seek only the Mind of Christ, and His Mind is not materialistic; it is not focused on success or wealth. Christ's Mind is focused only on the Glory of God and obedience to His Word.

No other teaching so ignores the Cross and the corruption of the human mind. It bypasses the evil of our ruined Adamic nature, and it takes the Christian's eye off Christ's Gospel of eternal Redemption and focuses it on earthly gain (Wilkerson).

It is strange, some of the Corinthians were doubting the Apostleship of Paul. They were demanding proof! The Truth is, if he were false even as these impostors claimed, then that means he was preaching a false message, and it also means that these Corinthians are not saved. I wonder if they had thought of that? Their very Salvation proved his Apostleship. Once again, this shows us how easy it is for one to be deceived.

MIGHTY IN YOU

The phrase, *"Which to you-ward is not weak, but is mighty in you,"* proves what I've just said.

The Lord Jesus had saved these Corinthians, bringing them out of deep paganism and idol-worship, had gloriously changed their lives, which they now certainly could not deny, all, through the Gospel as preached by Paul.

In other words, the Corinthians already have the greatest proof of the Power of Christ as preached by Paul, in all that He has wrought in them. I'll say it again:

If Paul had been preaching a spurious Gospel, was not really what and who he said he was, such a Gospel would have had no power, and could not have lifted them out of sin. However, what he preached, did lift them out of sin, because it was all-powerful, i.e., *"The Word of the Lord."*

Inasmuch as that is true concerning the Word preached unto them which saved their souls, it is also true concerning the corrective word he has given, and in fact, must be true. Both stand or both fall! They cannot accept the Gospel he preached for Salvation and at the same time, reject the Gospel he preached of correction, i.e., *"Sanctification."*

What a glaring, obvious Truth this is, and yet a Truth they did not seem to see.

(4) "FOR THOUGH HE WAS CRUCIFIED THROUGH WEAKNESS, YET HE LIVETH BY THE POWER OF GOD. FOR WE ALSO ARE WEAK IN HIM, BUT WE SHALL LIVE WITH HIM BY THE POWER OF GOD TOWARD YOU."

The Bible contains many Promises of God's Blessing to His Own. Whether to Israel or Christians, however, and whether for healing or prosperity, these Promises are always conditioned upon God's Wisdom and Will in the particular situation and upon the obedience of His people.

However, it is our natural inclination to make the only condition, our ability to *"believe,"* which will then cause God to give us what we want. Those who try to develop a *"Faith"* that always gets one's interpretation of a *"Promise"* to work out according to our own desires, may in fact, not have the genuine Faith to trust God's Love and the true wisdom to let Him work all according to His Will and not ours. His answering *"exceeding abundantly above all that we ask or think"* (Eph. 3:20) may, therefore, not be what we *"confessed"* but something that would be even better for us in the end, though our limited view may not see it that way at the time (Hunt).

NOTES

CRUCIFIED THROUGH WEAKNESS

The phrase, *"For though he was crucified through weakness,"* refers to the manner in which He died. To men the Crucifixion appeared to be Christ's weakness and defeat. To them He seemed powerless to help it, but this very seeming defeat demonstrated His Power (I Cor. 1:18-24; Col. 2:14-17; I Pet. 2:24).

However, the Truth is, that which the world saw at Calvary was the *appearance* of weakness which He manifested. He did not choose to exert His Power. Consequently, He appeared to His enemies to be weak and feeble. In fact, they taunted Him, that if He actually was the Son of God, that He should come down from the Cross; consequently, His not coming down from the Cross, at least in their eyes, proved Him to be the opposite of what He said He was (Mk. 15:29-32).

The Truth is the Crucifixion transpired only because Jesus permitted it to happen (Jn. 10:18). On the Cross He seemed to be completely at the mercy of ungodly sinners; however, the *"weakness"* He manifested was a voluntary weakness. He had to lay aside the prerogatives of Deity in order to give Himself as the perfect Sacrifice for mankind (Rossier).

He appeared to His enemies to be weak and feeble. This idea would be an exact illustration of the point before the Apostle. He is illustrating his own conduct, and especially in the fact that He had not previously exerted His Apostolic authority among them respecting particular offenders. He uses the example of Christ, Who though abundantly able to have exerted His Power and to have rescued Himself from His enemies, yet was willing to appear weak, and to be crucified. The following, I think, makes it clear:

1. The Lord Jesus seemed to His enemies to be weak and incapable of resistance.

2. He did not put forth His Power to protect His Life. He in fact offered no resistance, as if He had no power.

3. He had a human nature that was peculiarly sensitive, and also sensitive to suffering; and that was borne down and crushed under the weight of mighty woes. From all these causes He seemed to be weak and feeble; and these

appear to be the principal ideas in the expression as used by Paul (Barnes).

AN ATTACK ON THE FUNDAMENTALS OF THE FAITH

The manner in which Paul uses the phrase concerning Christ being crucified in weakness, could very well allude to the fact, and no doubt did, that these false apostles were failing to accrue to Calvary all its potential. In other words, it seems they were possibly saying that while Calvary was necessary for Redemption, thereafter it plays little if any part at all in one's everyday walk before God. They would have admitted that Christ dying in this weakness was necessary regarding Redemption, but the significance of this event would have stopped and started, at least in their thinking, with that event. To be sure, the modern Church, at least for the most part, follows suit.

Paul was teaching, and rightly so, that not only does one's Salvation hinge on Calvary, in other words, Jesus died for sinners, and Faith in Him and what He did, affords Salvation (Jn. 3:16; Eph. 2:8-9). However, he as well taught (Rom. Chpt. 6), that Calvary and the Resurrection are the source of all victory and overcoming power respecting our everyday walk before God. In other words, everything, and he meant everything, harks back to Calvary.

This means, that the Sacrifice which brought one into Redemption, gives victory also in our everyday walk. Let us say it in another way:

That which Calvary and the Resurrection is to our *"Justification,"* it also is to our *"Sanctification."*

If the Believer has a temper problem, understanding what Jesus did at Calvary and the Resurrection, and the Believer's place and position in that great Sacrifice, guarantees one victory over this particular problem. The same could be said for any and every problem, irrespective as to what it might be. In other words, we don't need Marriage Seminars to solve the problems of married life, but rather a proper understanding of, and Faith in, what Jesus did at Calvary and the Resurrection.

IMPROPER UNDERSTANDING

Most all Believers understand Calvary as it refers to Salvation, but that's about as far as they go. Most do not understand, that Calvary and the Resurrection play just as much a part in our continued victory as it did our Salvation. Jesus not only *"paid the sin debt"* by His Death at Calvary, but as well, *"broke the grip of sin"* in the human heart and life. Let's say it another way:

There are millions of Christians around the world, and I exaggerate not, who are greatly troubled with sins of the flesh, such as alcohol, nicotine, gambling, drugs, lust, jealousy, uncontrollable temper, pride, etc., who are struggling with all their might to overcome these things, whatever they might be, and instead of obtaining victory, the situation is rather growing worse. Please believe me, this is not an isolated problem, but rather that which is pandemic.

As well, I'm not speaking of hypocrites, or those who want God and the world at the same time, but rather of people who love the Lord. In fact, they love Him with all of their heart, but they are failing, and failing miserably, despite all their efforts to the contrary.

Why?

The Truth is, the more they struggle, the worse the situation will get, and that's what's so heartbreaking about the thing. However, whether they think so or not, their struggle is in the flesh and not the Spirit. Consequently, they are bound to lose, because the flesh (personal effort and ability), no matter how much it is papered over with Scriptures, is no match for the Devil, and is not intended to be.

THE PARAMETERS OF THE HOLY SPIRIT

Even though all of our struggles in the flesh cannot bring about victory, in fact is impossible of victory, that which is so difficult, even impossible for us, is not difficult whatsoever to the Holy Spirit. He can easily do these things, and in fact, strongly desires to do them, actually has been sent to carry out all that is needed in our hearts and lives to make us what we ought to be (Jn. Chpt. 16). He is truly a *"Helper"* and *"Comforter"*; however, the Holy Spirit only works in the legal confines of Calvary and the Resurrection. I realize that the word *"legal"* throws some Christians, thinking that we are reverting back to Law. However, that's not the case.

When I use the word *"legal,"* I am referring to Romans 8:2, *"For the Law of the Spirit of*

NOTES

Life in Christ Jesus hath made me free from the Law of sin and death."

Even though these *"Laws"* mentioned by Paul are not a part of the Law of Moses, still, they are actual *"Laws."*

The definition of Law is, *"a rule of conduct or action prescribed or formally recognized as binding or enforced by a controlling authority."*

The reason that the Believer cannot overcome within his own strength, *"the Law of sin and death,"* is simply because such is far stronger than the flesh. However, it is not stronger than the Holy Spirit, Who is the *"Law of the Spirit of Life in Christ Jesus."*

The trouble is, almost all Believers think they are opposing these terrible sinful impulses by the Spirit of God, when in reality they are doing so by the flesh. Consequently, they are doomed to failure!

WHY DO THEY THINK IT'S OF THE HOLY SPIRIT, WHEN IT REALLY ISN'T?

In the first place, these people, and they are myriad, do not fully understand Calvary and the Resurrection as they should. Consequently, whenever the Evil One attacks, and in whatever capacity, they try to overcome him by their willpower, which is a hopeless task (Rom. 7:18). What makes it seem so holy, and the reason they think it is the Holy Spirit in Whom they are trusting, is because they paper their willpower with Scriptures, or any other spiritual thing they can think of.

I heard a Brother say just the other day, *"The answer to these problems is fasting."* No it isn't! Quoting Scriptures is excellent. Fasting is Scriptural as well, and in their proper place will do one great good. Likewise, having hands laid on one is excellent and Scriptural, and will help, but it will not solve these problems of which we speak. One can do all of these things, as good as they are in their rightful place, and still not receive victory. The reason is simple, if we needed these other things to overcome, that would mean that Jesus did not finish the work at Calvary, and He needs something added. We may not think in these terms, but that's exactly what we are saying and doing, whether we realize it or not.

Again I emphasize, that all of those things we have named are Scriptural, and as such, will be of great benefit in their proper place.

NOTES

However, when we attempt to drive nails with a handsaw, or to saw wood with a hammer, we are not going to be very successful. The problem is not in the tools, the problem is in not knowing how to properly use them.

CALVARY IS A FINISHED WORK

Let's see what we mean by that statement, *"Calvary is a finished work."*

It means, that what Jesus did at Calvary and the Resurrection, addressed every single thing about the sin question and sin problem, leaving absolutely nothing undone. That means to the believing sinner, not only is the sin debt paid, but as well, everything was afforded for me to be completely victorious over sin in every capacity. No, I am not teaching sinless perfection, but I am teaching victory over sin (Rom. 6:1-2).

Now the Believer must understand, that the Holy Spirit Who has been sent to help us, and He does His job well, will help us only in the legal limits provided by Calvary and the Resurrection. In other words, He will not break the *"Law,"* by giving us victory over sin by our attempts to find such in another way than that prescribed by the Cross. He works in the confines of those legalities, because that's what Jesus did, so, consequently, that's what He does.

As well, considering that the Work of Christ is a finished Work, meaning that everything was done that needs to be done, and nothing needs to be added, why should we desire Him to work otherwise.

What am I saying?

I am saying, that the Believer can fast until he is so thin they can pull him through a keyhole, and while the fasting will definitely do him good in other ways, it will not furnish any victory over sin. The same can be said for the *"laying on of hands,"* or any other Scriptural effort. Again, these things are great in their own way but we cannot use them to finish out the Work of Calvary, for the simple reason that such are not needed.

THE FOLLOWING IS WHAT THE BELIEVER MUST DO

1. The Believer must know and understand, that mankind has a double curse on him, the *"sin debt"* and the *"grip of sin,"* and that Jesus provided a double cure, *"the paying of the sin*

debt," and *"the breaking of sin's grip"* (Rom. 6:7-14).

2. The Believer must have explicit Faith in the Finished Work of Calvary. He must believe that Jesus did this and must not veer away in his Faith (Jn. 3:16; Heb. 11:6).

3. He must understand from Romans Chapter 6, that when Jesus died on Calvary, that we were *"buried with Him by Baptism into death"* (Rom. 6:4). This has nothing to do with Water Baptism, but rather into His Death. In other words, it was all done for us, and belief in Him, places us in this great event.

As well, we must believe that *"our old man is crucified with Him, that the body of sin might be destroyed, that henceforth we should not serve sin"* (Rom. 6:6). That means the old man with all of his former passions and pride was buried with Christ, meaning that it no longer has a hold on us.

Also, the Believer must understand, that we were actually Resurrected in Him *"in newness of life"* (Rom. 6:4). In other words, we are now a *"new creature: old things are passed away; behold, all things are become new"* (II Cor. 5:17).

4. Understanding this and having Faith in this, which means we are trusting totally in what Christ did at Calvary and the Resurrection, and not at all in ourselves, then allows the Holy Spirit the latitude to perform His Work within our lives, which He can easily do. The Scripture plainly says, *"There is therefore now no condemnation to them which are in Christ Jesus, who walk not after the flesh, but after the Spirit"* (Rom. 8:1).

To be sure, and irrespective as to whom we may be, or how much God is presently using us, if we walk after the flesh, we are going to fail every single time. However, we will never fail, if we continue to *"walk . . . after the Spirit."*

Your understanding of, and your Faith in, what Jesus did at the Cross, gives the Holy Spirit the latitude to do what is needed. To be sure, He can do it without any trouble. That which was so impossible to us (because the flesh is weak), is no problem to Him whatsoever. When He takes over, and as we have stated, He will only do so within the confines of the legalities of Calvary and the Resurrection, that which was such a struggle is now so easy.

That's what Jesus was speaking about, when He said, *"Come unto Me, all ye that labour and are heavy laden, and I will give you rest"* (Mat. 11:28).

NOTES

REST

What does He mean by *"rest"*?

He is speaking of *"rest"* from all of our struggles of trying to be what we ought to be, but never succeeding, because we are trying within ourselves. The tragedy is, most Believers think they are doing all of this in the Spirit, when as stated, they are actually in the flesh, and because of not properly understanding the great victory of the Cross.

HOW DOES THE SAINT KNOW WHETHER HIS IS IN THE FLESH OR THE SPIRIT?

If he is in the flesh, he doesn't have victory over the problem at hand. If he is walking after the Spirit (Holy Spirit), he has victory. It is that simple (Rom. 8:1).

The Cross of Christ, which certainly includes the Resurrection, is the only means of Salvation and the only means of Victory. This is the only parameter in which the Holy Spirit will work, and in that parameter, He does great and mighty things — making us into what we ought to be in Christ.

As we originally stated, even though Paul does not spell it out, quite possibly these false apostles were denigrating these great Truths of Calvary, even as many are doing so presently.

You can be what you ought to be, but you cannot be what you ought to be, unless the Holy Spirit does the work Himself. There is no way that the Believer, and irrespective of his Faith, can bring about this work himself. In fact, he is not intended to do so and for the simple reason, that he cannot do so. However, we think that just because we are a Believer, even a Spirit-filled Believer, that all these things automatically are ours.

In fact, they are! But only if we properly understand how they are ours! Even though the Cross was a one-time thing, and because that was totally sufficient, still, it has unending results.

(Please see our Commentary on Romans for an extended treatment on this very important subject.)

THE POWER OF GOD

The phrase, *"Yet He liveth by the Power of God,"* sets the example for us. Paul said, *"But if the Spirit of Him that raised up Jesus from the dead dwell in you, He that raised up Christ from the dead shall also quicken your mortal bodies by His Spirit that dwelleth in you"* (Rom. 8:11).

Isn't that wonderful!

Even though Jesus died in weakness, simply because that was required of Him, still, the Power of God raised Him up. As well, at least as far as the flesh is concerned, we are very weak. However, when we know that, thereby ceasing to trust in ourselves, but rather trusting totally in the Lord, the Holy Spirit will take over, and by His Power which is Almighty, He will guarantee the victory we need. In other words, the same power that raised Jesus from the dead, resides in us, and to be sure, can overcome Satan in any capacity.

Some of you reading these words, may think that the problem which affects you, whatever it may be, is so strong and so powerful, that you wonder if it is possible for one to have victory. Oh yes it is!

If the Holy Spirit could raise Jesus from the dead, even though He died in weakness, especially considering that every demon power of darkness was trying to keep Him dead, then I should think that we should know, that He is able to handle our little problem, whatever it may be. However, and I emphasize again, He will only do so within in the legal confines of Calvary and the Resurrection, and in no other manner.

Just as the Lord was raised from the dead by the Power of God, likewise, we live by the Power of God, which means, not by our own power, or the power of any other man or woman, etc. Inasmuch as that is the *only way* in which we can have and maintain victory in this Faith walk, we should, *"glory . . . in the Cross of our Lord Jesus Christ, by Whom the world is crucified unto me and I unto the world"* (Gal. 6:14).

It is a shame to have the *"Power of God"* at our disposal, and still resort to pitiful, human, failing efforts of the flesh, which we all have done. Admittedly, it has been done mostly in ignorance, but the end result is always the same, at least if it is done in that capacity — failure. However, when it is done by the *"Power of God,"* failure is not possible.

WEAK IN HIM?

The phrase, *"For we also are weak in Him,"* is true, irrespective as to how much we are being used by God.

NOTES

Before the sinner came to Christ, he was weak, unable to control his passions, consequently, the cause of all the problems in the world. However, when he came to Christ, he remains weak, but that is something that most Believers do not understand.

Instead, we are constantly boasting as to how strong we are in the Lord, how powerful we are, how great our Faith is, and in fact, all of that may be true, that is if we properly understand what we are saying, which most of the time we don't!

The Truth is, that all these wonderful things mentioned, are totally and absolutely of the Lord and, therefore, from the Lord; however, irrespective of these great things, we within ourselves, are still just as weak as we were before coming to Christ.

Poor sinners by the untold millions, are fighting at this very moment, to try to stop the drinking of alcohol. It has wrecked their lives, their families and everything they hold dear, but they are unable to stop. The same can be said for gambling, drugs, religion, etc. Others are overcome by fear and depression, and despite all of their efforts to improve themselves, they are none the better, but rather grow worse. In other words, against these powerful forces of Sin, Satan, and Darkness, man is helpless.

However, if the Believer and for whatever reason, finds himself under attack by Satan respecting any one of the vices we have mentioned, plus many we have not mentioned, and he attempts to overcome by his own strength, to which we have already addressed ourselves, he will have no more success attempting to find help in that manner, as he did before he came to Christ. That is a shock to most Christians, but it is the Truth.

Why is it the Truth?

It's the Truth, because the Holy Spirit, Who in fact is sent to help us, cannot help us, as long as we are depending on our own strength, which in fact is nonexistent. We are weak, and we need to admit this, in fact, what the Scripture plainly says.

It is not a matter of some few Christians being weak, and others strong. We all are weak, at least within ourselves. When are we going to understand this?

Christians look at the world, thinking how hopeless it is for the unsaved to attempt to solve their problems without Christ. Then we turn around, and do the same identical thing. Even though we are Believers and talking about Christ constantly, still, we attempt to obtain victory through the efforts of the flesh, and always fail as fail we must. The Songwriter said it, and he was right:

"I am weak, but Thou art strong."

LIVE WITH HIM

The phrase, *"But we shall live with Him by the Power of God toward you,"* does not refer to the Resurrection as some think, except in an indirect way, but for the most part to our everyday living. In other words, it is done by the *"Power of God."*

The words *"toward you"* lend a startling turn to the statement.

Most Commentators think that Paul is speaking here strictly of punishment for offenders. However, that is not the gist of his statement at all.

Even though his statement is brief, he is in fact addressing their false doctrine as well. He is telling the Corinthians, that despite what these impostors have said, the weakness of Calvary was actually His strength. As well, our weakness is our strength, if we properly understand what is being said.

The Apostle is saying to the Corinthians, that he delivered this great Message of the Cross to them, which has brought about tremendous victory within their lives, at least those who have believed. This Power of God is manifested in them as well, and in fact all Believers who properly understand the Cross.

The false apostles were claiming some type of superior knowledge, causing their followers to look at them as *"super apostles,"* or *"demigods."* However, Paul says that the same knowledge of the Scriptures which gave him victory, he has passed on to the Corinthians, and to all others for that matter, for this is the Way of the Lord.

True Christendom does not have lords many, who stand above the people claiming to contain some type of truth which is above the understanding and faith of those below. True Christianity has its Apostles to give all they have to the people, in fact, themselves trusting in the same thing.

Paul is saying, that the manner in which he learned this great Truth of Victory, he now gives to the Corinthians, and to all others who believe. Consequently, all are on the same level — weakness, but yet tremendous strength.

NOTES

Does anyone in Corinth seek proof of Christ speaking in Paul? He should be satisfied, more than satisfied, with God's Power which has been manifested within their lives, because of that which Paul taught them.

(5) "EXAMINE YOURSELVES, WHETHER YE BE IN THE FAITH; PROVE YOUR OWN SELVES. KNOW YE NOT YOUR OWN SELVES, HOW THAT JESUS CHRIST IS IN YOU, EXCEPT YE BE REPROBATES?"

In 1973 Jay Adams, Author of many books on Christian Counseling, gave a series of lectures at a leading Evangelical Seminary emphasizing the necessity to stick strictly to the Bible and avoid psychological influences. Adams told the students and faculty: *"I do not think I need to labor this point . . . I am sure that the reason why I was invited to deliver these lectures in the first place was because of our common conviction about this vital imperative."*

Adams has made his conviction crystal clear: *"In my opinion, advocating, allowing and practicing psychiatric and psychoanalytical dogmas within the Church is every bit as pagan and heretical (and therefore perilous) as propagating the teachings of some of the most bizarre cults. The only vital difference is that the cults are less dangerous because their errors are more identifiable."* He warned that group of future Pastors;

"Members of your congregation, Elders, Deacons, and fellow Ministers (not to speak of Christians who are Psychiatrists and Psychologists) may turn on the pressure and try to dissuade you from any resolute determination to make your counseling wholly Scriptural.

"They may insist that you cannot use the Bible as a textbook for counseling, try to shame you into thinking that the Holy Spirit has inadequately trained you for the work, tempt you to buy all sorts of shiny psychological wares to use as adjuncts to the Bible, and generally demand that you abandon what they may imply or openly state to be an arrogant, insular, and hopelessly inadequate basis for counseling.

"They may even warn and threaten, as they caricature the Biblical method: 'Think of the harm that you may do by simply handling out Bible Verses like prescriptions and pills.'"

However, since 1973, the Church almost as a whole, has embraced the pagan influences of Psychology. In doing so, they have forsaken the Word of God, for the two cannot coincide, being opposites.

We must do what Paul said, *"Examine ourselves."*

EXAMINATION

The phrase, *"Examine yourselves,"* was used by Paul, because there was occasion to fear that many of them had been deceived. Such had been the irregularities and disorders in the Church at Corinth, and partially because of the false apostles.

Consequently, such an examination, is never unimportant or useless for Christians; and an exhortation to do such is always in place. So important are the interests at stake, and so liable are the best to deceive themselves, that all Christians should be often induced to examine the foundation of their hope of eternal Salvation (Barnes). Incidently, he said, *"Examine yourselves,"* and not others.

TO SUBJECT TO A TEST

When the word *"examine"* is used in an evil sense, it means *"to tempt"*; however, here it is used in the good sense and has the meaning *"to try"* and is followed by the synonym *"to subject to a test"* as coins are tested to determine their genuineness and their full weight.

We would probably use terminology in the English as *"put to the proof,"* and if disproved, it is rejected, hence *"reprobate."* If approved, that means it is *"tested out and proved, thus accepted as genuine."*

TO FAIL OR PASS THE TEST

The word *"fail"* is used in the Old Testament in a number of ways: Individuals may fail to carry out God's Commands (Lev. 26:15; Num. 15:22). David's family will never fail to have a man for the Throne of Israel (I Ki. 2:4). One's flesh and heart may fail (Ps. 73:26).

The Hebrew language does not have any single or specific words for such failures or for failure in general. Instead, *"fail"* is an interpretation of words that signify one or more of the following concepts: To be at an end, to be cut off, to pass over, to sink or relax, to be at a distance, or to stumble.

NOTES

THE NEW TESTAMENT

There is no specific Greek word for *"fail"* either. In the statement *"Love never fails"* (I Cor. 13:8) the Greek word translated *"fails* (ekpipto)*"* means *"to become ineffective."*

The same word is used in Romans 9:6, where Paul points out that Israel's refusal to respond should not be interpreted *"as though God's Word had failed."* Human rejection of God's Message is a sign of failure in mankind, not in the efficacy of God's Word.

OUR TEXT

In II Corinthians 13:5-7 Paul says, *"Examine yourselves to see whether you are in the Faith; test yourselves. Do you not realize that Christ Jesus is in you — unless, of course, you fail the test? And I trust that you will discover that we have not failed the test . . . that people will see that we have stood the test and that you will do what is right even though we may seem to others to have failed."*

Here Paul uses the Greek word *"dokimazo* (to put something to the test in order to approve it)*"* and *"adokimos* (to be disqualified as not standing the test, and thus, to fail).*"*

Paul's authority had been challenged by many in Corinth. The dissidents had demanded proof that Christ did indeed speak through the Apostle, or in fact, if he was actually an Apostle. Paul's answer focuses attention on the indwelling Christ, Who is powerful within and among His people and will deal with those who reject one whom He sends.

So Paul calls the Corinthians to put themselves to the test of exploring this inner reality: *"Do you not realize that Christ Jesus is in you?"*

If Jesus was within them, He would bear inner witness to the validity of the Message Paul communicates (Richards).

THE FAITH

The phrase, *"Whether ye be in the Faith,"* refers to Faith in Jesus Christ, and the Promises of God through Him, which is the greatest distinguishing characteristic of a True Believer.

To try and test oneself is simple enough. A few honest questions honestly answered soon reveal where one stands. There is *"the Faith"* itself, which stands for the Gospel, actually the entire embodiment of that we refer to as

"Christianity." Do we believe it in total, receive it without change of any kind? Do I reject some or any part of it? Does my heart truly believe this Gospel of Christ? Do I trust it? Is my confidence full and strong?

WHAT IT MEANS

For Paul the great central Truth is that God has acted in Christ to bring about the Salvation of sinners. Salvation cannot be merited or earned; it must be received as a Gift of Grace. Sinners cannot merit Salvation, they can only trust God or, as Paul puts it, have Faith in God (in Christ). This brings out the Truth that Christians rest their Faith *"on"* Jesus and are brought *"into"* union with Him.

Romans 10:9 shows that believing in one's heart and *"acknowledgment of Jesus as Lord is intrinsic to Christian Faith along with acknowledgement of the miracle of His Resurrection."*

In other words, it is absolutely imperative that one believes that Jesus is the Lord of Glory, that as a Man, even though fully God, He died on Calvary in order to pay the terrible sin debt of humanity. One must believe as well, that He was raised from the dead.

MANY ASPECTS

Faith has many aspects. *"It is response to Revelation as contrasted with discovery of new knowledge."* It implies our recognition that we are sinners and thus unable of ourselves to forsake evil and to do good.

Socrates, the great Greek Philosopher, might hold that knowledge and virtue are much the same, so that to know what is right leads people to do what is right, but Paul would not have agreed. For him Faith implies both that we have come to see ourselves as sinful and also that we have come to recognize that God has provided for our forgiveness through what Christ's Death has done for us.

Faith means coupling the recognition of the impossibility of our achieving our Salvation, with the acceptance of the Truth that God has done all that is necessary in order for us to be saved. The *"Good News"* is *"The Power of God for Salvation to everyone who believes"* (Rom. 1:16).

And Faith means commitment. Those who believe have not only come to see their shortcomings, they have committed themselves to be Christ's people.

NOTES

FAITH AND THE CROSS

God's Saving Work is done in and through Christ. Paul constantly emphasizes the centrality of the *"Cross,"* sometimes by using just that word, sometimes by using some figure to bring out the truth. Thus, he speaks of God as effecting *"Redemption"* and *"Propitiation,"* and immediately adds, *"Through Faith"* and *"In His Blood"* (Rom. 3:24-25).

The latter expression makes it clear that the Apostle is referring to the Saviour's Atoning Death, and the former insists that this does not come to anyone automatically. Faith is the Divinely-appointed Way. Indeed there is *"One Lord, one Faith"* (Eph. 4:5); the two go together.

REDEMPTION

Redemption means the payment of a price to set people free, and we should not miss the importance of freedom in Paul's understanding of Faith.

He does not link freedom expressly with the *"Faith"* terminology, but such a Passage as Romans 5:16-21 assumes that the Believer enters a freedom impossible without Faith, which is the gateway to the new age of Salvation in Christ.

Paul sees what God has done in Christ as central, and he links Faith to Grace (Rom. 4:16). Indeed, he writes to the Ephesians, *"By Grace you have been saved through Faith"* (Eph. 2:8).

Grace is important in understanding Faith, for it emphasizes that Salvation is a free Gift, not a reward for human achievement of any sort, even as a reward for outstanding Faith. So, too, it is Faith that gives access to the Grace in which Believers stand and which leads to joy (Rom. 5:2).

Paul stresses *"That your Faith might rest not on human wisdom but on the Power of God"* (I Cor. 2:5).

When we use terms such as *"Paul sees,"* etc., we are *not* meaning that these are merely Paul's opinions, but rather that this is the manner in which the Holy Spirit gave these Truths to him, and, therefore, his expression by way of explanation.

PROVE YOUR OWN SELVES

The phrase, *"Prove your own selves,"* presents a very strong term.

The word used here is stronger than that used before, and rendered *"examine."* This word, *"prove,"* refers to assaying or trying metals by the powerful action of heat; and the idea here is, that they should make the most thorough trial of their profession, to see whether it would stand the test.

The proof of their piety was to be arrived at by a faithful examination of their own hearts and lives; by a diligent comparison of their views and feelings with the Word of God; and especially by making trial of it in life.

The best way to prove our Salvation is to subject it to actual trial in the various duties and responsibilities of life.

FOR INSTANCE . . .

A man who wishes to prove an ax, to see whether it is good or not, does not sit down and look at it, or read all the information which he can find on ax-making, or on the properties of iron and steal, valuable as such information would be; but he shoulders his ax, and goes into the woods, and puts it to the trial there. If it cuts well; if it does not break, if it is not soon made dull, he understands the quality of his ax better than he could in any other way.

So, if a man wishes to know what his Salvation is worth, let him try it in the places where Salvation is of any value.

Let him go into the world with it. Let him go and try to do good; to endure affliction in a proper manner; to combat the errors and follies of life; to admonish sinners of the error of their ways; to urge forward the great work of the conversion of the world; and, he will soon see there what his Salvation is worth — as easily as a man can test the qualities of an ax.

A PERSONAL EXPERIENCE

This Salvation of which I write about, of which I preach, I have proved. In other words, I have put it to the test. Does it work? I can assure one and all that it does work! I have felt the Powers of Darkness attempting to destroy my soul. I know what it is to try with all of one's strength and still fail; however, I also know what it is to cry to the Giver of my Salvation, asking Him to show me what is wrong, what I should do, how I was missing it regarding His Word.

He did exactly what I asked Him to do. He told me where I was believing wrong, how that I was not properly understanding the great Truths of Calvary and the Resurrection. He showed me where my defeat was and where my Victory could be found.

In our Commentary on Verse 4, I gave to you that which He gave to me, and I gave it with confidence because first of all, it is the Word of God, and second, I have proven that Word; I have tested that Word; with my life and even my soul at stake, I can tell one and all, that it works. As well, it more than works, doing everything and then some which is promised in the Word of God. So, this statement by Paul *"Prove your own selves,"* is very dear and very special to me, for I have done that. In fact, I had to do that, I had no choice.

REPROBATES

The question, *"Know ye not your own selves, how that Jesus Christ is in you, except ye be reprobates?"*, proclaims the total essential of Salvation, which is Jesus Christ, and better yet, that He lives within our heart. Such language is that derived from the close union which subsists between the Redeemer and His people.

The verdict is simple!

If Jesus Christ does not live within a person, one is then a *"reprobate."*

"Reprobate" in the Greek is *"adokimos,"* and means *"one rejected."*

The emphasis on this question is summed up in two words, *"Jesus Christ,"* and *"reprobates."* There is no middle ground here. Either one knows Christ and is, therefore, saved, or else he doesn't know Him, and in the Eyes of God, is a *"reprobate,"* i.e. *"rejected."*

The all-encompassing thrust of this Verse, however, is different than at first believed. While it certainly lends credence to the idea that Believers should *"examine themselves,"* still, the major thrust is Paul pointing out that if he were a reprobate Apostle, then were they reprobate Christians, for they were all his converts. Consequently, he challenged them to examine themselves as to whether they were really Christians or not, with two thoughts in mind.

First of all, to honestly examine themselves, and naturally, their reply would be that they were True Christians, and so their confidence about themselves would admit and establish Paul's claim to be a True Apostle (Williams).

NOTES

CHRIST

The universe of Paul's thought revolved around the Son of God, Jesus Christ. Actually, Paul's Christology illumined his thought in its entirety, sometimes shedding its light on aspects of his thought that one might have expected would have gone relatively untouched by Christology, i.e., *"Christ."*

For instance, who would have expected Paul, to tell his Corinthian listeners that the Rock that gave forth water to the Israelites during their period of wilderness wanderings was Christ (I Cor. 10:4)? However, the reason he did that, is because since his conversion he properly saw Jesus in the entirety of the Old Testament. In other words, the Old Testament came alive as he saw that all of its Types and Symbols pointed to the Lord Jesus Christ.

In fact, Paul's view of Christ was so broad, even as it should have been, that he could conceive of Him as being involved in God's dealings with His people long before He (Christ) was born and began His earthly Ministry. In other words, Christ was the Jehovah of the Old Testament.

IN CHRIST

When Paul speaks of Believers being *"in Christ,"* of course, he is speaking of Jesus as God. Such terminology could apply only to a Divine Being.

Our understanding of Paul's view of the Divinity of Christ is enhanced by comparing what Paul says about Christ in comparison to what he says about the Holy Spirit. It has been noted often how closely Paul identifies Christ and the Spirit in his Letters — indeed, at points they seem to be identical.

For instance, Paul can speak of the Spirit coming to Believers only because Christ is Risen, Ascended, and Exalted. In discussing Jesus' Resurrection Paul speaks of Jesus, the Last Adam, as a *"Life-giving Spirit"* (I Cor. 15:45). He is the One Who sends the Spirit and without His Resurrection and Exaltation the Spirit would not have come.

Romans 1:3-4 indicates that it was through the Power of the Spirit that Jesus was enabled to be the Son of God in Power. The Spirit empowered Him, and He sends that Power to Believers. It is Christ Who makes the eschatological (prophecies of the future) age possible, and that age focuses on Him.

Frequently in Paul's Teaching, the functions of Jesus and the Spirit are identified, so much so that being in Christ is simply another way of speaking of being in the Spirit.

The following are examples:

1. Believers are righteous in Christ (Phil. 3:8-9) but also in the Spirit (Rom. 14:17).
2. Believers have life in Christ (Col. 3:4) but also in the Holy Spirit (Rom. 8:11).
3. Believers have hope in Christ for life to come (I Cor. 15:19) and in the Power of the Spirit to give them Eternal Life (Gal. 6:8).
4. Believers rejoice and have joy in the Holy Spirit (Rom. 14:17) but also in the Lord (Phil. 4:4).
5. Believers have Truth in Christ (Rom. 9:1), and Truth is also spoken as in the Spirit (I Cor. 12:3-6).
6. Believers have fellowship in Christ (I Cor. 1:9) but also fellowship of the Spirit (II Cor. 13:14).
7. Believers are consecrated and sanctified in Christ (I Cor. 1:2) but also in the Spirit (Rom. 15:16).
8. Believers are sealed both in Christ (Eph. 1:13) and in the Spirit (Eph. 4:30).

THE REASON FOR PAUL'S TERMINOLOGY

This identification between Christ and the Holy Spirit is taken even further when Paul ascribes to Christ various features characterizing the Holy Spirit in the Old Testament. Thus, for instance, Psalms 104:29 states that it is the Spirit Who gives Life, but in I Corinthians 15:45 it is Christ Who gives Life. This seems to mean that at His Resurrection and Exaltation Jesus assumed the functions previously ascribed to the Holy Spirit.

However, Paul speaks in this manner, because it is Jesus Christ Who has made everything possible which the Holy Spirit does. This was true even in the Old Testament, inasmuch as in the Mind of God the work was already done, even though it was future. And yet, Christ was veiled somewhat in the Old Testament, portraying Himself in the various symbols of the Sacrifices and other particulars. Nevertheless, it was Christ Who was to make everything possible, even though it was spoken of as the Holy Spirit doing whatever was done, for instance in Psalms 104:29.

In fact, every single thing done on this Earth by the Godhead, is done through the Office, Ministry, and Person of the Holy Spirit. Romans Chapter 8 makes it abundantly clear that it is the Holy Spirit Who does all the things that the Believer needs, and irrespective as to its content; however, He does it only through the legal confines of Calvary and the Resurrection (Rom. 8:2).

Consequently, when one understands the functions of the Holy Spirit, His purpose to glorify Christ (Jn. 16:14), His carrying out the effect of what Christ did at Calvary, then everything becomes more clear. Only when Paul was brought to Christ, could he properly understand the Old Testament, which then formed the foundation of the New.

It is not hard at all to see, and rightly so, that with Paul everything was Jesus. In fact, if one does not properly understand that Jesus is the focal point of all things, then one cannot properly understand the Word of God, for it all points to Him as the Answer to the Promise given by God in the Garden of Eden immediately after the Fall (Gen. 3:15).

(6) "BUT I TRUST THAT YE SHALL KNOW THAT WE ARE NOT REPROBATES."

Once again, this lends credence to the idea of the Truth that Paul is proclaiming, that if he is false, as his opponents claim, then the Corinthians are false as well, i.e., *"not saved."* The argument is telling, to say the least!

I TRUST

The phrase, *"But I trust* (I hope) *that ye shall know,"* pertains to that which is extremely important. Spurious Christians, those who profess only but actually do not possess, would not be able to know, their judgment would be worth nothing. But Christians who are able to test themselves and to realize their own genuineness, one may hope, will know the genuineness also of Christ's True Ministers. The idea is, if they are able to detect the Presence of Jesus Christ in themselves, they should be able to recognize others in whom Christ's Power operates, especially those who helped to put Christ into their hearts. I would hope the Reader would

NOTES

read these words very carefully, thereby, understanding their significance.

If one does not recognize that which is truly of God, it is a strong sign that they really do not know the Lord themselves. Jesus plainly said, *"And when He putteth forth His Own sheep, He goeth before them, and the sheep follow Him: for they know His Voice. And a stranger will they not follow, but will flee from him: for they know not the voice of strangers"* (Jn. 10:4-5).

So, if the *"voice"* is truly that of the Lord, and if the person is truly of the Lord, that means they will know. If they don't know, that says they are not of the Lord.

Consequently, the Truth of this matter is, of the vast number who claim to be followers of Christ, only a few actually are!

WE ARE NOT REPROBATES

The phrase, *"That we are not reprobates,"* specifically swings the action to the one called of God, in this case, Paul.

One of the greatest problems in the Church presently is, professing Christians who do not know *what* is of the Lord and what is not of the Lord. In other words, they don't know *who* is of the Lord, and who isn't. Consequently, whatever direction they take, is because of popular opinion, what someone else has said, what most believe, etc. In other words, they have no convictions themselves, or else, their convictions are not based on the Bible, which means they are not only following that which is wrong, but most probably are not even themselves saved.

LET ME ASK THIS QUESTION

Does the Reader think that those who actually thought that Paul was a reprobate, were themselves saved? Let's ask it in another way.

Could anyone who truly knew the Lord, actually conclude Paul to be a reprobate? I think the answer to that is obvious.

While the Corinthians may have been confused for a short period of time, they in no way thought of Paul as a reprobate; however, I would dare say, that these interlopers who came in from Jerusalem (if in fact, that was their origination), were not saved, despite their great religious profession. How could one be saved and try to tear down what the Holy Spirit was doing through Paul? In fact, how could anyone

NOTES

be saved who would attempt to destroy that which the Lord is doing?

While a True Believer as stated, may be confused for a while and may actually oppose that which the Lord is doing, which has no doubt happened many times, the Holy Spirit, if allowed, will ultimately set that person straight. However, it must be quickly said, that if they continue to turn a deaf ear to the pleadings and direction of the Holy Spirit, that there can very well come a time, that He will leave altogether, which means that that particular person totally loses his way and will ultimately be lost.

The idea is, that we can follow the Lord or men, or even our own prejudices, but we cannot follow both. If the Divine nature is truly in one's heart, he will ultimately recognize the Divine nature which is in the heart of another, or the lack thereof.

(7) "NOW I PRAY TO GOD THAT YE DO NO EVIL; NOT THAT WE SHOULD APPEAR APPROVED, BUT THAT YE SHOULD DO THAT WHICH IS HONEST, THOUGH WE BE AS REPROBATES."

I'm sure the Reader can recognize the tremendous significance of the tremendous Truths which are being addressed by Paul. We should listen carefully to what the Apostle is saying, considering that the Holy Spirit is directing him.

DO NO EVIL

The phrase, *"Now I pray to God that ye do no evil,"* does *not* present the Apostle speaking in general about doing any kind of evil; he is speaking about the specific act of siding with the opponents who claimed him to be a reprobate. Consequently, this would be *"evil"* of unimagined proportions. In other words, if the Corinthians did such a thing, or anyone for that matter, they would in effect, be placing themselves in opposition against God. In fact, that is the great question of the ages.

Am I truly following the Lord and those who are truly His, or in fact, going in the opposite direction, while all the time thinking I am following the Lord? To oppose the Lord, while all the time thinking the opposite, is the paramount sin. It is deception of the highest order.

APPEAR APPROVED?

The phrase, *"Not that we should appear approved,"* in effect has the Apostle saying, that he is not that interested whether people approve of him or not, but that he be approved of Christ, which of course he was. How he and his associates may appear to the Corinthians, and all others for that matter, is a secondary matter.

This is a far cry from much of the modern ministry, which seeks the approval of men above all else. The Truth is, and to which we have already alluded, one can have the approval of God or one can have the approval of men. One can seldom have both.

HONEST

The phrase, *"But that ye should do that which is honest,"* speaks to the fact that in the self-denial and self-annihilation of Paul, that he was indifferent as to what others thought of him so long as they advanced in Christian character. Of course, the thought itself is incongruous. It was very near impossible for them to grow in the Lord, and have a wrong opinion or viewpoint of Paul. But of course, what the Apostle is saying, is that it did not really matter to him about himself, but rather the spiritual condition of the people.

THINK WHAT YOU WILL!

The phrase, *"Though we be as reprobates,"* in effect says, *"Irrespective that some may think we are reprobates."*

The idea is, let the false prophets say what they will, his concern is not about that, but rather about the Corinthians themselves.

To see the heart of the Apostle sets for us an example which should be warmly copied by all Preachers of the Gospel, and in fact, everyone for that matter. Few men were vilified as much as Paul, and few suffered as Paul and at the same time, few were as close to God as Paul, if any! While the Lord honored him in a way that He has honored few men in history, by giving him the New Covenant, which in effect, made him the Moses of the New Testament, still, even with that, the suffering and difficulties were awful.

I wonder how many presently, if they had to follow in the footsteps of Paul would prove as faithful?

(8) "FOR WE CAN DO NOTHING AGAINST THE TRUTH, BUT FOR THE TRUTH."

This great Salvation Message which we refer to as the Truth, was not designed for man's head, but for his needs. It was not intended to be a system of education, but regeneration. It was not made for man at his best, but at his worst. Therefore, it must be simple, elementary, and fundamental. Because of its simplicity it is wiser and more effective than all the philosophy and cultured reasoning of man. The simple Preaching and Teaching of Jesus have outlived the brilliant wisdom of the wise, because He in effect, was and is *"Truth."* If men know the Lord they have *"Truth,"* but that is different from Jesus, Who in fact, is Truth.

THE TRUTH

The phrase, *"For we can do nothing against the Truth,"* is not referring to the actual facts as they exist in Corinth, whatever those facts may be, but rather *"The Truth"* — the Blessed reality comprised in the Gospel. Paul and his associates are devoted wholly to this Truth. They have no selfish interest such as thinking that they must stand before the Corinthians as approved, as tried and true. Just as their interest is only that the Corinthians may make no mistake, may do only the right thing, so their one interest is in the Divine, Blessed Truth of the Gospel, i.e., *"The Lord Jesus Christ."*

FOR THE TRUTH

The phrase, *"But for the Truth,"* in essence proclaims, that everything that is done, every direction taken, every word said, every attitude and spirit, every Message preached, every thought of one's mind, all our actions toward others, must be in the realm of Truth, i.e., *"Gospel Truth,"* i.e., *"The Lord Jesus Christ."*

The idea of *"Truth"* in the manner in which Paul uses the word, is that everything, and I mean everything, must pass under the scrutiny of the Word of God. *"Is it Scriptural?"*, must be the sought after result, the ever intended goal, the criteria for all things. If it is not Scriptural, i.e., *"Truth,"* then we must pull back.

THE TRUTH OF GOD

On a number of occasions Paul refers too *"The Truth of God"* (God in His Self-revelation, Rom. 1:25; 3:7; 5:8) or *"The Truth of Christ"* (II Cor. 11:10); once he refers to *"speaking the Truth in Christ"* (Rom. 9:1).

The Judgment of God is *"according to Truth"* (Rom. 2:2); human judgments might be biased according to class or creed, but with God Truth is the only consideration. Paul speaks of the Preachers as commending themselves *"in the Word of Truth"* which he immediately follows with *"in the Power of God"* (II Cor. 6:7).

We should also consider here the Apostle's recognition of *"the form of the knowledge of the Truth in the Law"* (Rom. 2:20). He denounced those who proclaimed Salvation by way of the Law, but that did not prevent him from acknowledging the Divine Truth enshrined in the Law. Paul also finds Divine Truth (which people reject) in creation as well as in the Law (Rom. 1:18-20).

THE TRUTH IS JESUS

Paul has an unusual expression when he says *"As Truth is in Jesus"* (Eph. 4:21). However, if we're not careful, we will misunderstand what Paul is saying in this statement.

Paul is not saying that Truth is many-sided and that he is concerned with that aspect of Truth that we see in Jesus. Rather he is saying that real Truth, ultimate Truth, is to be found in Jesus and that we find it nowhere else. It is a claim that the Revelation of Truth in Jesus is utterly reliable.

Often Paul has the thought that people have not received the Truth. They suppress it in unrighteousness (Rom. 1:18), exchange it for *"the lie"* (Rom. 1:25). They refuse to obey it (Rom. 2:8; Gal. 5:7; II Thess. 2:12). They did not receive a love for it and so lost Salvation (II Thess. 2:10).

Sinners turn away from Truth (II Tim. 4:4; Tit. 1:14). They are bereft of the Truth (I Tim. 6:5). God has revealed the Truth, indeed has sent His Son to live it and to proclaim it, but sinful people have refused to listen.

THE GOSPEL OF JESUS CHRIST

Paul can speak of *"The Word of the Truth of the Gospel"* (Col. 1:5) and again of *"The Truth of the Gospel"* (Gal. 2:5). He refers to *"The Word of Truth, the Gospel of our Salvation"* (Eph. 1:13). The Truth that is so closely bound up with God finds its expression here on Earth in the Gospel, which sets out the ultimate Truth of the Love of God especially as shown in the Cross, the sinfulness of the human race, and the provision God has made for Salvation.

The Gospel of Jesus Christ and Truth can be said to be one and the same. Paul speaks of

NOTES

God's Will for people *"to be saved and come to the knowledge of the Truth"* (I Tim. 2:4).

REFUSAL OF TRUTH

But while there is this true Revelation of the Truth in this provision for sinners to be saved through the Truth of the Gospel, Paul regrettably sets forth the Truth that sinners often refuse to receive the Truth. They have missed it or turned from it (II Tim. 2:18).

They resist it like Jannes and Jambres of old (II Tim. 3:8). Paul himself was *"for the Truth"* and declared that he could not do anything against it, even the subject of our Text (II Cor. 13:8), but he had to recognize that the sinners to whom he preached did not always emulate him. The Truth of the Gospel is real, but in the conditions of this world it is always possible for people to decline to receive it.

TRUTH AND THE BELIEVER

English does not have a verb *"to truth,"* but Paul uses such a verb (aletheuo), when he urges the Ephesians that *"Truthing in Love"* they should grow in Christ in all things (Eph. 4:15).

We might understand this as *"speaking the Truth in Love,"* but more probably we should seek Truth as a quality of action as well as of speech. Paul warns his converts to live the Truth as well as to speak the Truth.

Paul says that he himself speaks the Truth (II Cor. 7:14; 12:6), and of course he looks for a similar practice in his converts. He calls on the Corinthians to keep the Feast (Passover) with the unleavened bread of Sincerity and Truth, which he contrasts with *"malice and evil"* (I Cor. 5:8).

Just as the Jews cleared out all leaven before their Passover, so Believers must be rid of malice and wickedness since Christ, their Passover has already been sacrificed. He points out that Love *"rejoices with the Truth"* (I Cor. 13:6); real Love can take no pleasure in falsehood and unrighteousness, but Truth and Love go together. *"The new self"* he says, *"is created in Righteousness and Holiness of Truth"* (Eph. 4:24).

The *"belt of Truth"* is part of the Christian's armor (Eph. 6:14). It protects against the attacks of evil (II Cor. 4:2).

When Paul asks the Galatians who has prevented them from *"obeying the Truth"* (Gal. 5:7), he is referring to the *"Truth of the Gospel"* (Gal. 2:5, 14) for which he has just argued (Gal. Chpts. 2-4).

NOTES

The Truth of the Gospel does not merely call for intellectual agreement. It is to be obeyed and to characterize the new Life in Christ.

(Bibliography: Barclay, *"Obeying the Truth."* O'Connor, *"Truth."*)

(9) "FOR WE ARE GLAD, WHEN WE ARE WEAK, AND YE ARE STRONG: AND THIS ALSO WE WISH, EVEN YOUR PERFECTION."

By men's standards, the Cross is a display of weakness. Jesus was born of peasants instead of the ruling class. He was an artisan (Carpenter) instead of an aristocrat. He spurned the usual methods of achieving success. He did not use force. He did not have an elaborate organization. He was not a politician. He did not cater to public favor. When the crisis of His Life came, He did not answer when falsely accused. He did not fight with the usual weapons of man.

However, He was not impotent. His apparent weakness was only His unwillingness to use unworthy weapons. Nevertheless, His weakness was His strength. He ruled by Love and not by Law. He conquered by Faith and not by force (Laurin).

GLADNESS, WEAKNESS AND STRENGTH

The phrase, *"For we are glad, when we are weak, and ye are strong,"* carries within it several nuances.

First of all, Paul uses the word *"glad,"* which places it in the position of most emphasis.

A gladness was produced in his heart because of certain things which were happening, which pertained to the Corinthians, but as well as it regarded himself.

Second, the *"weakness"* is the cause of the *"gladness,"* and has contributed toward the spiritual welfare of the Corinthians. Paul and those with him rejoiced when they were weak, for they knew then that they were strong (12:10), for God's Power works in their weakness. Hence, they are willing to appear totally weak. All that they desire is that the Corinthians may be powerful, i.e., that in their weakness, too, God's Power may show itself most effectively. For this also Paul and his associates are ever praying, namely for the complete fitting out of all that the Corinthians may need.

This whole business concerning *"weakness"* evidently had come up because of Paul being accused by his detractors of being weak. How in the world, anyone could think of Paul in this fashion, is beyond me; however, there is a possibility that his constant array of problems was looked at by others as *"weakness."*

Obviously, at least in the thinking of these detractors, if Paul was a genuine Apostle and had great Faith, he would not have to undergo all of these difficulties. So, the Holy Spirit counters this opposition against the Apostle, by giving Paul this great Teaching on the matter of true spiritual strength. In other words, and even as he has already said (II Cor. 12:9), when we realize and recognize our weakness, then we will learn to lean on the Lord, Who is our real Strength.

If in fact, Paul's detractors were judging him accordingly, what a lesson such should be to us of how wrong our judgment can be, and usually is. The great difficulties which Paul constantly faced, were not at all because of a lack of Faith. The situation was actually twofold, that which pertained to Paul personally, and the lesson that the Holy Spirit desired to teach the entirety of the Body of Christ. As we have previously stated, all of mankind is weak, even Believers. Of course, we are speaking of weakness in comparison to the Powers of Darkness. Within himself, man is no match for Satan and his cohorts.

OVERCOMING POWER

The Believer makes a grand mistake when he thinks he can use his Faith to overcome the Powers of Darkness. While Faith, of course is needed and used in all things, the fact is, many times our Faith is misplaced. Faith in God, must at the same time be aware of our personal inability. That is the weakness of which Paul speaks. If we attempt to exert Faith without such understanding, it simply will not work.

Consequently, when throughout weakness we totally trust in and depend upon the Lord, Victory is always ours. Such brings a tremendous joy.

A PERSONAL EXPERIENCE

I can attest to this of which Paul has said on a personal basis. It took me a long time to fully understand my weakness, but only when I came to that place, could the Power of God be brought to bear on whatever was needed. We must never forget, that the Lord will not work outside of the confines of His Word. He does not function according to our good intentions, our good motives, as necessary as these things may be. We must understand His Way, and then act accordingly.

NOTES

YOUR PERFECTION

The phrase, *"And this also we wish, even your perfection,"* pertains to the conclusion which the Apostle desired.

The word *"perfection"* as it is used here, occurs nowhere else in the New Testament, though the verb from which it is derived occurs often.

Regarding the meaning of the word, it pertains to *"equipping, improving, repairing, or restoring."* As is obvious, it is a process.

The idea is, that these great problems of the past be completely healed, put behind them, and now the Church marching in unison for the Glory of God, spiritually healthy, spiritually strong. That was the end result that the Apostle desired.

The word *"wish"* in essence means *"I desire."*

(10) "THEREFORE I WRITE THESE THINGS BEING ABSENT, LEST BEING PRESENT I SHOULD USE SHARPNESS, ACCORDING TO THE POWER WHICH THE LORD HATH GIVEN ME TO EDIFICATION, AND NOT TO DESTRUCTION."

In view of what the Apostle desires to see accomplished in these Corinthians, he encourages them, as we have already stated, to *"examine yourselves."* We are not obliged to examine others, only ourselves. We are not answerable to God for anyone but ourselves.

It is much more interesting and exceedingly more comfortable and easy to examine someone else.

Two boys went into a Dental Office. One said boldly, *"I have a tooth to be pulled. You need not give me any anesthetic, just yank it out."*

"All right, young man," said the Dentist, *"where's your tooth?"*

The boy turned to his companion and said, *"Willie, show him your tooth."*

Most of us are very brave about the solution of other people's problems and the examination of other people's Faith. We must be careful to note that the resultant knowledge of the test is the discovery of ourselves as either Christians or reprobates. Jesus Christ is in us or else the alternative is true.

There is another side to self-examination. It is not only to prove, but to improve. We can constantly improve ourselves (through the Holy Spirit) by discovering flaws and eliminating faults.

I WRITE THESE THINGS

The phrase, *"Therefore I write these things being absent,"* presents the Apostle desiring that these admonitions will cure the problem. When he does finally make the trip to Corinth, he doesn't want it to be a time of correction, but rather of rejoicing. You can feel this as a heartthrob in the things said by the Apostle. He is looking forward to a joyous meeting, and not otherwise.

I'm sure the Reader knows and understands, that Paul knows that what he is writing, is actually the Word of God. As such, it would have a powerful effect over and above what might be normally said. In fact, the Word of God is alive, meaning that it is impossible to exhaust its contents.

SHARPNESS?

The phrase, *"Lest being present I should use sharpness,"* in effect means that he will do so when he comes in person to Corinth if necessary, but in no way does he desire this avenue or approach.

If correction is needed, it is absolutely imperative that it be done, as distasteful as it may be. In fact, I think one could say without fear of exaggeration, that the majority of that written by Paul was in the form of correction. He was responding to false doctrine or false apostles, and in this climate, the Holy Spirit gave us most of the direction we have as it regards the New Covenant.

MINISTRY

Of course, the Lord gives different Ministries, even among the Fivefold Calling (Eph. 4:11). With some few, even with Paul as should be obvious, the Holy Spirit orders the capacity of *"correction,"* within the Message. To be sure, it is not a pleasant task, because those who are being corrected, are seldom happy with the correction. Consequently, very great animosity

NOTES

at times can be tendered toward the one doing the correcting.

For instance, I think when Paul said, *"For ye suffer fools gladly,"* and speaking of these false apostles at Corinth, that they would not have been too very happy about that particular statement. As well, those who denied the fact of the coming Resurrection, would not have been too pleased with Paul referring to them in the same manner, *"Thou fool"* (I Cor. 15:36). Of course, his referring to these individuals in that manner, had nothing to do with correction, but it did have to do with the reason the correction was needed.

THAT WHICH THE LORD SPOKE TO MY HEART

Back in 1982 (I believe it was) the Lord gave me explicit instructions regarding a Message I was to deliver to our Catholic friends. In fact, there was a Message as well, to the Denominational Church World, as well as the Pentecostals.

To make the story brief, I eventually consecrated to deliver my soul in respect to that which I believed the Lord told me to do. In those days, we had the largest Christian Television audience in the world; consequently, whatever we said was instantly noted.

The Lord spoke to my heart, and told me emphatically, *"Your own will turn against you."* Little did I know or realize, to the extent and the far-reaching effects the fulfillment of that prediction would have. However, it has come to pass exactly as the Lord said. Also, it has not been pleasant nor pretty.

Whenever the Preacher with a worldwide audience tells the Catholics who have truly come to Christ, that they are going to have to come out of the false doctrine, it does not set well with many people. In fact, it sets well almost with none, when it is considered that most of the preaching in those days was in the opposite direction — stay in that Church.

As well, when we took a strong stand against the encroachment of Humanistic Psychology in the Church, it was not met with endearment by most Pentecostal Leaders, who in fact, had opted in totality for the Psychological Way. The animosity accrued because of that, was so sharp, that it would be difficult to explain.

It would be easy to continue in this vein, but I feel that you the Reader know and understand that of which I speak. However, I will quickly add the following:

During the midst of all of this, literally tens of thousands of people were coming to a saving knowledge of Jesus Christ in our Crusades and through the Telecast, all over the world. As well, thousands were being Baptized with the Holy Spirit with the evidence of speaking with other tongues, as the Spirit of God gave the utterance. People were being delivered of every type of bondage of darkness that one could ever think. My contention is this:

If that which I was preaching, which definitely was contentious, but which only made up a part of the Message as a whole, was wrong, the Holy Spirit would not have been working so mightily to bring many thousands of souls to Christ. The Lord does not anoint sin or error, as should be obvious.

What we have suffered for that, is exactly what the Lord said we would suffer; however, the suffering is immaterial; the doing of God's Will is the only thing that matters, whatever the cost.

EDIFICATION AND NOT DESTRUCTION

The phrase, *"According to the power which the Lord hath given me to edification, and not to destruction,"* proclaims the fact, that the *"correction"* will not tend toward *"destruction,"* irrespective of the immediate fall-out, but ultimately to *"edification."* However, the getting from point A to point B, even as Corinth symbolizes, is a painful process.

Paul is actually speaking here of Apostolic authority. However, this is no Papistic, Legalistic, or Autocratic authority. The Lord never gave him anything of this kind. Paul defines it well: It is *"for upbuilding and not for wrecking."*

The false apostles did the reverse; they wrecked what had been built up. Regarding the wrecking which every Believer is obligated to do, see the grand Passage of II Corinthians 10:4-5.

The point to be noted here is that if after coming to Corinth Paul did not finally take strong measures by not using his Divinely given authority, he himself would be helping to wreck. To be guilty of anything such as that is impossible to him.

NOTES

WHAT DO WE MEAN BY THE USE OF APOSTOLIC AUTHORITY?

First of all, and as is plainly said, this Authority is not given for *"destruction,"* but rather for *"edification."* It is authority to build up, to construct, to edify, to strengthen, to lead to victory, to point to victory, etc.

As such, this authority is never used for punishment, for vengeance, to penalize, to forfeit, to force, to obstruct, to hinder, etc.

So, if Paul from a personal basis, could not use this Authority to bring judgment or punishment, exactly where do the negatives come in?

In fact, there is always judgment which follows the disobedience of God's Word. The idea is this, and as we have previously stated, when the Word is given by an Apostle, and it definitely is a True Word of the Lord, if it is disobeyed or opposed or ignored, judgment definitely will follow; however, it will be at the discretion of the Lord, and not Paul, or any other Apostle who has ever lived.

This means it is terribly unscriptural, for Denominational Heads to take it upon themselves to exact punishment on someone, irrespective as to what they have done. That is God's domain alone (Rom. 12:19-21).

The only thing that Church Leaders can do, at least if they desire to be Scriptural, and which applies only to local Church Leaders, is to demand repentance of one who is doing wrong (I Cor. Chpt. 5), and if they will not repent, they are to be disfellowshiped. But even that doesn't mean they are to be destroyed, in fact, every effort is to be made to bring the person to Redemption, as should be obvious. The Lord doesn't give up on anyone until they have died.

When it comes to punishment, if one desires to use that term, the only thing that Believers are allowed to do, and that goes for Apostles as well, that is if a person refuses to repent, is to *"deliver such an one unto Satan for the destruction of the flesh, that the spirit may be saved in the day of the Lord Jesus"* (I Cor. 5:5).

Getting back to the original thought, whatever doing is to be done respecting discipline, so-called Leaders outside of the local Church, have no authority whatsoever. It is only those in the local Church, where the problem resides, who are authorized Scripturally to take whatever action needs to be taken (I Cor. Chpt. 5; II Cor. Chpt. 2).

Of course, that flies in the face of accepted practice presently. Almost exclusively, problems in the local Church, wherever that particular Church may be, at least as it regards Preachers, are handled by those outside of that particular Church, which is unscriptural.

BACK TO EDIFICATION

The Holy Spirit is emphatic in this statement. Everything that we do, every decision made, every action taken, every idea presented, every course followed, must be for but one purpose as it regards the Cause of Christ, and irrespective of the problem, it is to ever be toward *"edification, and not toward destruction."*

As well, in this Godly effort, all opinions, prejudice, bias, wishes, or desires, are to be laid aside, with the Word of God followed strictly. As stated, it alone is to be the criteria. If what is suggested is not plainly Scriptural, it should be discarded! If any action proposed is not plainly Scriptural, it should be discarded! The problem with all of these things is men leaving the Word of God, instituting their own thoughts and desires, which in fact, always introduces leaven. If not rooted out, after a while, the leaven will corrupt the whole (I Cor. 5:6).

(11) "FINALLY, BRETHREN, FAREWELL. BE PERFECT, BE OF GOOD COMFORT, BE OF ONE MIND, LIVE IN PEACE, AND THE GOD OF LOVE AND PEACE SHALL BE WITH YOU."

The personal element which has been so pronounced and prominent in the writings of this document to the Corinthians is now revealed in its best form. The man who has been so zealous for the spiritual improvement of the Believers at Corinth has also been severe and brutally frank in his censure and judgment, but upon all this he has drawn the veil of kindness in the covering of charity.

He did not find life perfect among the Corinthians. It was polluted by sin and torn by strife, but despite this it was enduring. He found for himself a way of life that could look trouble and disaster in the face and say, *"I am victor."*

In these Chapters we have followed Paul through every conceivable situation. We have seen him in prison, in floggings, in labors, in shipwreck and in such a variety of experiences that we marvel at his fortitude and endurance.

For this man it was a life that endured. It was not endurance in the sense in which we sometimes speak — endurance by reason of miserable patience. Paul endured because of glorious perseverance. His endurance had the quality of an inner triumph; it was the success of a life within.

The life that endures is the life that is durable. It is the Life of Christ in the life of the Christian. It has come from the fountainhead which is Christ. It has been tested on the anvil of experience. It has been proved through the centuries of time. It is yours for the taking and living.

FINALLY

The phrase, *"Finally, Brethren, farewell,"* presents the last word, and, in many respects, the most important word. It must leave nothing in doubt or in a state of suspension. All that is to be said must be in the light of what has been said.

There is something sad about this *"finally."* It gives a feeling of regret that the Epistle is to close. It is filled with expressions of Truth which have grown out of the Apostle's experiences. They are not professional literary phrases coined by a clever mind. They are not sayings gleaned by a dictionary of wit and wisdom. They are living Truths forged out of the hot metal of experience.

However, much we may regret this *"Finally, Brethren,"* there is something about it that is satisfying as well as sad. We have been privileged to read in this autobiography eternal Truths which will enrich our lives and increase our responsibilities. That is so, not just because of the excellent manner in which it has been written, but because it is the Word of God (Laurin).

FAREWELL

The word here rendered *"farewell,"* means usually to joy and rejoice, or to be glad (Lk. 1:14; Jn. 16:20, 22) and it is often used in the sense of *"joy to you!" "hail!"* as a salutation (Mat. 26:49; 27:29). It is also used as a salutation at the beginning of an Epistle, in the sense of *"greeting"* (Acts 15:23; 23:26; James 1:1).

NOTES

It is generally agreed, however, that it is here to be understood in the sense of farewell, as a parting salutation, though it may be admitted that there is included in the word an expression of a wish for their happiness (Barnes).

His concluding words are marked by great gentleness, as though to heal the effects of the sharp rebuke and irony to which he has been compelled to have recourse (Farrar).

PERFECT

The phrase, *"Be perfect,"* is actually a wish that every disorder might be removed; that all that was out of joint might be restored; that everything might be in its proper place; and that they might be just what they ought to be.

A command to be perfect, however, does not prove that it has ever in fact been obeyed; and an earnest wish on the part of an Apostle that others might be perfect, does not demonstrate that they were; and this Passage should not be adduced to prove that any have been completely free from sin.

It may be concluded, however, to prove that an obligation rests on Christians to make every attempt to be perfect, in other words to always work toward that conclusion, and that there is in actuality, no natural obstacle to their becoming such, since God never does command us to do an impossibility. However, I think at the same time, we must say, that there has only been one perfect individual, and that has been the Lord Jesus Christ. So what are we saying?

We are saying, that the Doctrine of Sinless Perfection is not a Biblical Doctrine, at least as it refers to human beings other than Christ.

To properly understand what Paul is saying, suggests a continuous growth in Grace that will lead them on to increasing maturity. Paul did not pass a verbal wand of holiness over them to give them a negative perfection. He challenged them to Christian progress and maturity (Laurin).

COMFORT

The phrase, *"Be of good comfort,"* means to be consoled by the Promises and Supports of the Gospel. In other words, take comfort from the hopes which the Gospel imparts.

The word, at least as far as Paul uses it here, does not mean comfort for sorrow but rather good cheer and encouragement in the attainment of the previously mentioned perfection.

Or the word may possibly have a reciprocal sense, and mean, *"comfort one another."* In that capacity, it means that we are to stimulate one another. This shows a heart-interest in another's progress. It is the helpfulness of our encouragement instead of the hindrance of criticism.

Too many times we stifle instead of stimulate. We stifle another's sincere but halting efforts because we are too critical. It would add immeasurably to the efforts of others if we took a more charitable attitude and said, *"God bless you, my Friend."*

ONE MIND

The phrase, *"Be of one mind,"* addresses the different parties and factions which had taken place at Corinth. They are to lay aside these strifes, and to be united, and manifest the same spirit.

The sense is, that Paul desired that dissensions should cease, and that they should be united in Doctrine, opinion, and feeling as Christian Brethren. In fact, he addresses them in this manner, *"Brethren,"* in order to stimulate their oneness, or at least as they should be.

This is the unison of unbroken communion. We observe the Lord's people being divided and scattered. It is an ancient trouble for it appeared in very violent form at Corinth. They were quarrelsome and contentious. Their divisions were not over great issues, but were the result of personal preferences and prejudices that brought estrangement.

Christians have been likened unto burning coals. If they are scattered far apart, they are easily extinguished, but when they are burning close together the heat of one preserves the heat of the other.

Christians in Communion strengthen each other and add a collective glow and fire that brightens and blesses the world. When they fall out and separate there are usually casualties among them. Some will grow cold and their lives will cease to glow with usual warmth and spiritual fire (Laurin).

PEACE

The phrase, *"Live in peace,"* refers to the fact that they should be at peace with each other. Let contentions and strifes cease. Actually, to promote the restoration of peace had been the main design of these Epistles.

As well, it should be understood that the Holy Spirit would not command us to do something through the Apostle, if it were not possible for such to be done. The Truth is, that we can live in peace if we want to live in peace. We have the Holy Spirit to help us, we have His Power manifested within our lives, we are new creatures in Christ Jesus, the Divine Nature resides within us; consequently, there is no reason that these admonitions cannot be obeyed.

The *"Peace"* depends on the unity, comfort, and striving toward maturity. If any one of these fall down, the *"Peace"* is disturbed. As well, as we will see in the next phrase, the *"Peace of God"* is one of the most beneficial qualities and attributes that any individual could ever have. So, anything that disturbs that peace, should be addressed immediately.

However, *"Peace"* does not mean an absence of difficulties or problems, but rather an inner quality which one can have, which is only given by the Holy Spirit, irrespective of the exterior circumstances.

LOVE AND PEACE

The phrase, *"And the God of Love and Peace shall be with you,"* presents the One Who is all Love, and Who is the Author of all Peace. What a glorious appellation this is! There can be no more beautiful expression, and it is as true as it is beautiful, that God is a God of *"Love"* and of *"Peace."* In fact, He delights in exhibiting His Love; and He delights in the Love which His people evince for each other. At the same time He is the Author of Peace, and He delights in peace among men.

When Christians love each other, as we certainly should, we have every reason to expect that the God of Love will be with us; when we live in Peace, we may expect the God of Peace will take up His abode with us.

In contention and strife we have no reason to expect His Presence; and it is only when we are willing to lay aside all animosity that we may expect the God of Peace will fix His abode with us (Barnes).

(12) "GREET ONE ANOTHER WITH AN HOLY KISS."

When the Letter had been read in their hearing, they were, in sign of perfect unity and mutual forgiveness, to give one another the kiss of peace (Farrar).

NOTES

For men to kiss other men on the cheek was the custom in those days. Now the same thing is accomplished by the shaking of hands.

(13) "ALL THE SAINTS SALUTE YOU."

This Epistle was written from Macedonia, probably from Philippi. So, Paul is sending Greetings from these particular individuals, whomever they may have been.

As well, and as we have addressed previously, the moment a person accepts Christ, at that very moment, they are a *"Saint."*

The idea of men making someone a Saint after they are dead, which of course they cannot do, but which is practiced by the Catholic Church, is not Scriptural to say the least!

Thank God, due to the Gospel of the Lord Jesus Christ, and the burden of Paul and others like him, there were those who had once been pagans, but now could be referred to as *"Saints."* Then they sent greetings, now they are in the portals of Glory, and by the Grace of God we will meet them on that grand and glad Resurrection Morning.

(14) "THE GRACE OF THE LORD JESUS CHRIST, AND THE LOVE OF GOD, AND THE COMMUNION OF THE HOLY SPIRIT, BE WITH YOU ALL. AMEN."

Here ends this personal postscript. He had written what his heart governed by the Holy Spirit, impelled him to say. He had poured out the love and anxieties of that heart upon them, and now, he closes with these brief salutations and benediction (Williams).

GRACE

The phrase, *"The Grace of the Lord Jesus Christ,"* presents Paul closing with what has come to be called and with what is used as the New Testament Trinitarian Benediction, the counterpart to the Old Testament Trinitarian Benediction found in Numbers 6:22-27.

The order of the Divine Persons as well as the order of their Gifts are significant. We have *"The Lord Jesus Christ"* first, then *"God"*; we have *"The Love of God"* second and not first. This benediction is pronounced upon people who are already Christians.

The reason the Love of God is referred to second, is because it is that which embraces His Own and not the Love which reaches out to make men His Own. God's Love is able to bestow thousands of Gifts upon Believers which He could not possibly bestow upon people who are not yet Believers or who are unbelievers. Consequently, and as stated, *"The Love of God"* properly occupies the second place in this benediction.

The Blessings of God impart Grace. Who of us can live a satisfying Christian experience without Grace? It is that quality which covers our sins and compasses our weaknesses. It is as necessary to our existence as it is sufficient to our needs.

THE LOVE OF GOD

The phrase, *"And the Love of God,"* refers to that Love, as we already have stated, which comes to Believers.

This must refer peculiarly to the Father, as the Son and the Holy Spirit are mentioned elsewhere in this sentence.

The *"Love of God"* here referred to is the manifestation of His goodness and favor in the pardon of sin, in the communication of His Grace, in the comforts and consolations which He imparts to His people, in all that constitutes an expression of Love. The Love of God brings Salvation, imparts comfort, pardons sin; sanctifies the soul; fills the heart with joy and peace; and Paul here prays that all the Blessings which are the fruit of that Love may be with them (Barnes).

THE COMMUNION OF THE HOLY SPIRIT

The phrase, *"And the Communion of the Holy Spirit,"* presents the Holy Spirit making all of this possible to us — all the Grace and all the Love. That is the manner, in which this *"Communion"* is carried out. In fact, and as we have previously stated, everything done by God on Earth, whether the Father or the Son, is done through the Power, Agency, Person, and Office of the Holy Spirit.

The word *"Communion"* means, properly, *"participation, fellowship, or having anything in common"* (Acts 2:42; Rom. 15:26; I Cor. 1:9; 10:16; II Cor. 6:14; 8:4; 9:13; Gal. 2:9; Eph. 3:9; I Jn. 1:3).

WORSHIP OF THE HOLY SPIRIT?

Some have misconstrued this statement as given by Paul, as the right to pray to the Holy Spirit or even worship the Holy Spirit; however, the word *"Communion"* as it is used here, does not lend credence to that assumption. To be sure, there is *"Communion"* with the Holy Spirit constantly, for it is impossible for such Communion not to be, if a person is saved. As we have stated, any and all things which come from the Godhead, must come through the Office and the Person of the Holy Spirit. So, the Holy Spirit is constantly interchanging with the Believer, which constitutes *"Communion,"* in making real all the great qualities and attributes of God.

As it regards prayer, we are commanded to pray to the Father in the Name of Jesus; consequently, that's the manner in which all prayer should be made (Jn. 16:23).

GRACE-LOVE-COMMUNION

The Grace- the Love- the Communion are not conceived in the abstract but as including all Gifts and Blessings that emanate from them. Nor are Grace, Love, Communion conceived as being separate from each other. We see that Grace is only a form of Love, Love toward the undeserving. In II Corinthians 1:2 Grace emanates from both God and Christ. So both Grace and Love toward Believers also involve Communion with them, and Communion involves Grace and Love toward them.

In fact, Communion is the crowning form of Grace and Love. We should guard against intellectual distinctions. Those who would separate *"Communion"* from the other two, give evidence of the fact that they do not rightly understand what any of these three actually are.

Yet each concept is distinct in the union of the three, and each is in its proper place. It is pure, unmerited Grace on which every Believer depends until he draws his last breath. He is and remains one who constantly comes short of the Glory of God until his end. Consequently, the Blood of Christ's Grace must cleanse him daily, as it does (I Jn. 1:7). By Grace alone he enters Heaven at last.

"Grace" keeps its full connotation of guilt and sin, of unmerited pardon in II Corinthians 1:2 and here at the end. It is always *"The Grace of the Lord Jesus Christ."* To think that this disassociates it from the Father and from the Spirit is to think that it is disassociated from the Love and the Communion, neither of which

NOTES

is true or could be true. The Triune God is the Fount of Grace for us in Christ Jesus.

THE LORD JESUS CHRIST

"The Lord" — He Who has purchased and won us and to Whom we belong; *"Jesus"* — the Name He bore here on Earth when He came to save us with His Grace; *"Christ"* — this Person in His saving Office. Each part of His Name glows with Grace, and this form of His Name has become infinitely precious to the Church from the days of the Apostles onward.

GOD AND HIS LOVE

We have already shown how *"The Love of God"* follows. It is again the Love of full comprehension and corresponding purpose which in this benediction enfolds those who have been won by Christ's Grace. Since it is here ascribed to *"God,"* the infinitude of this Love is emphasized. And this includes the infinitude of its Blessedness for us.

If the sinner bows his head at the pierced feet of the Lord because he is overwhelmed by the Grace, shall he not be utterly lost in this ocean of the Love which is as great and as blessed as God Himself? Our little understanding staggers and falls, and only worship and adoration are left.

FELLOWSHIP

The third place in this Heavenly Trio belongs to the word *"Union with," "Communion"* or *"Fellowship."* The Holy Spirit stoops down to us and enfolds us in His Communion in which are found all the Grace and the Love. Not from afar are these extended to us but in a union which is beyond our comprehension.

The Personality of the Holy Spirit is often denied. However, only a person can establish Communion. The Holy Spirit is named here beside the other two Persons. So, as is obvious, He is a Person, i.e., *"God!"*

AMEN

The phrase, *"Be with you all,"* actually presents the great Communion and Fellowship enjoyed by all True Believers.

With the picture of the great Apostle spreading his hands over the Corinthians with this profound New Testament Benediction his voice sinks into silence. But the Benediction remains upon our hearts.

NOTES

(Throughout that of which we have written concerning II Corinthians, I wish to express my deepest appreciation to the scholarship of R. C. H. Lenski, who has provided not only excellent research in the form of Greek Scholarship, but as well a heart which has obviously been touched by the Holy Spirit. Even though he is now in Glory, I wish to express my deepest gratitude to his memory even though I never had the privilege of acquaintance except through his writings; however, the coming glorious Resurrection Morning will correct that. I will then personally thank him.)

THE TRINITY

This Scripture furnishes a proof of the Doctrine of the Trinity that has not yet been answered to the contrary, and, it is believed, cannot be. On the supposition that there are Three Persons in the adorable Trinity, united in essence, and yet distinct in some respects, all is plain and clear.

But on the supposition (as some claim) that the Lord Jesus is a mere Man, an Angel, or an Archangel, and that the Holy Spirit is an Attribute, or an influence from God, how unintelligible, confused, and strange does all this become! That Paul, in the solemn close of the Epistle, should at the same time invoke Blessings from a mere creature, and from God, and from an attribute, surpasses belief. But that he should invoke Blessings from Him Who was the equal with the Father, and from the Father Himself, and from the Sacred Spirit sustaining the same rank, and in like manner imparting important Blessings, is in accordance with all that we should expect, and makes all harmonious and appropriate.

IT IS PROPER

Nothing could be a more proper close of this Epistle; nothing is a more appropriate close of public worship, than such an invocation. It is a prayer to the ever-Blessed God, that all the rich influences, which He gives as Father, Son, and Holy Spirit, may be imparted; that all the benefits that God confers and the interesting relations in which He makes Himself known to us, may descend and bless us.

To be sure, may that Blessing pronounced by the great Apostle rest alike upon all of us, though we may be strangers in the flesh; and may those heavenly influences guide us alike to the same everlasting Kingdom of Glory! (Barnes).

Now we have finished. The Apostle has laid down his pen and we are about to conclude our reading. We do it with regret, but it is hoped, with purpose. Let it be the purpose of pursuit in which we will pursue with determined consecration the goal of Grace and the opportunities of experience that its Truth sets forth.

Bibliography: The First and Second Letters of Paul to the Corinthians, Cambridge: University Press; Kenneth S. Wuest, Wuest's Word Studies; II Corinthians, Dr. Roy L. Laurin; St. Paul's First and Second Epistles to the Corinthians, R. C. H. Lenski; Myer Pearlman, *"Knowing the Doctrines of the Bible,"* George Williams, *"The Student's Commentary on The Holy Scriptures;" "Dictionary of Paul and his Letters"*; Farrar; New Bible Dictionary; Vine's Expository of New Testament Words; Strong's Exhaustive Concordance of the Bible.

It is October 23, 1998, 4 p.m., as I conclude the notes on this Commentary. I pray that it will be as much blessing to those who would take the time to peruse and study its contents, as it has been to me in the writing and compiling of this material. I have been blessed beyond measure.

To know and understand just a little more about the great Apostle Paul, is worth any effort, any time spent, especially knowing and understanding that it is the Holy Spirit Who has instructed this information to be given respecting the Second Epistle to the Corinthians. What a wealth of information! What a privilege to study this which is the infallible, unchangeable Word of God.

To those of you, who have joined with me in the study of this material, if your hearts and lives have been enriched, even to a small degree, then our efforts have been well worth while. Above all, it has been our desire to glorify Christ. If this has been done, then you will have been blessed. My prayer is that that has been the case.

I will conclude as did one Greek Scholar, even though by no means can I even begin to claim such lofty status.

Soli Deo Gloria.

NOTES

INDEX

The index is listed according to subjects. The treatment may include a complete dissertation or no more than a paragraph. But hopefully it will provide some help.

As well, even though extended treatment of a subject may not be carried in this Commentary, one of the other Commentaries may well include the desired material.

For information concerning the *Jimmy Swaggart Bible Commentary,* please request a Gift Catalog.

You may inquire by using Books of the Bible.

- Genesis (656 pages) (11-201)
- Exodus (656 pages) (11-202)
- Leviticus (448 pages) (11-203)
- Numbers
  Deuteronomy (512 pages) (11-204)
- Joshua
  Judges
  Ruth (336 pages) (11-205)
- I Samuel
  II Samuel (528 pages) (11-206)
- I Kings
  II Kings (560 pages) (11-207)
- I Chronicles
  II Chronicles (528 pages) (11-226)
- Ezra
  Nehemiah
  Esther (288 pages) (11-208)
- Job (320 pages) (11-225)
- Psalms (688 pages) (11-216)
- Proverbs (320 pages) (11-227)
- Ecclesiastes
  Song Of Solomon (288 pages) (11-228)
- Isaiah (688 pages) (11-220)
- Jeremiah
  Lamentations (688 pages) (11-070)
- Ezekiel (528 pages) (11-223)
- Daniel (416 pages) (11-224)
- Hosea
  Joel
  Amos (496 pages) (11-229)
- Obadiah
  Jonah
  Micah
  Nahum
  Habakkuk
  Zephaniah (544 pages) (11-230)
- Haggai
  Zechariah
  Malachi (448 pages) (11-231)
- Matthew (888 pages) (11-073)
- Mark (24 pages) (11-074)
- Luke (736 pages) (11-075)
- John (736 pages) (11-076)
- Acts (832 pages) (11-077)
- Romans (704 pages) (11-078)
- I Corinthians (656 pages) (11-079)
- II Corinthians (608 pages) (11-080)
- Galatians (496 pages) (11-081)
- Ephesians (576 pages) (11-082)
- Philippians (496 pages) (11-083)
- Colossians (384 pages) (11-084)
- I Thessalonians
  II Thessalonians (512 pages) (11-085)
- I Timothy
  II Timothy
  Titus
  Philemon (704 pages) (11-086)
- Hebrews (848 pages) (11-087)
- James
  I Peter
  II Peter (736 pages) (11-088)
- I John
  II John
  III John
  Jude (384 pages) (11-089)
- Revelation (592 pages) (11-090)

For telephone orders you may call 1-800-288-8350 with bankcard information. All Baton Rouge residents please use (225) 768-7000.

For mail orders send to:
Jimmy Swaggart Ministries
P.O. Box 262550
Baton Rouge, LA 70826-2550

Visit our website: www.jsm.org

NOTES

NOTES

NOTES

NOTES

NOTES

NOTES

NOTES

NOTES